THE FORCED WAR
WHEN PEACEFUL REVISION FAILED

THE FORCED WAR
WHEN PEACEFUL REVISION FAILED

DAVID L. HOGGAN

INSTITUTE FOR HISTORICAL REVIEW
1989

THE FORCED WAR
When Peaceful Revision Failed
By David L. Hoggan

Copyright © 1989 by
Institute for Historical Review

First English language edition
Published February, 1989

Published by
Institute for Historical Review
1822½ Newport Bl., Suite 191
Costa Mesa, CA 92627

Manufactured in the
United States of America

ISBN 0-939484-28-5

INTRODUCTION

Shortly after midnight on July 4, 1984, the headquarters of the Institute for Historical Review was attacked by terrorists. They did their job almost to perfection: IHR's office were destroyed, and ninety per cent of its inventory of books and tapes wiped out. To this day the attackers have not been apprehended, and the authorities—local, state, and federal—have supplied little indication that they ever will be.

The destruction of IHR's offices and stocks meant a crippling blow for Historical Revisionism, the world-wide movement to bring history into accord with the facts in precisely those areas in which it has been distorted to serve the interests of a powerful international Establishment, an Establishment all the more insidious for its pious espousal of freedom of the press. That one of the few independent voices for truth in history on the planet was silenced by flames on America's Independence Day in the year made infamous by George Orwell must have brought a cynical smile to the face of more than one enemy of historical truth: the terrorists, whose national loyalties certainly lie elsewhere than in America, chose the date well. Had IHR succumbed to the arsonists, what a superb validation of the Orwellian dictum: "Who controls the past controls the future. Who controls the present controls the past."!

One of the chief casualties of the fire was the text of the book you now hold in your hands. Too badly charred to be reproduced for printing plates, over six hundred pages of *The Forced War* had to be laboriously reset, reproofed, and recorrected. That this has now been achieved, despite the enormous losses and extra costs imposed by the arson, despite the Institute's dislocation and its continued harassment, legal and otherwise, by the foes of historical truth, represents a great triumph for honest historiography, for *The Forced War*, more than a quarter century after it was written, remains the classic refutation of the thesis of Germany's "sole guilt" in the origins and outbreak of the Second World War.

By attacking one of the chief taboos of our supposedly irreverent and enlightened century, David Hoggan, author of *The Forced War*, unquestionably damaged his prospects as a professional academic. Trained as a diplomatic historian at Harvard under William Langer and Michael Karpovich, with rare linguistic qualifications, Hoggan never obtained tenure. Such are the rewards for independent thought, backed by thorough research, in the "land of the free."

The Forced War was published in West Germany in 1961 as *Der erzwungene Krieg* by the Verlag der Deutschen Hochschullehrer-Zeitung (now Grabert Verlag) in Tübingen. There it found an enthusiastic reception among Germans, academics and laymen, who had been oppressed by years of postwar propaganda, imposed by the victor nations and cultivated by the West German government, to the effect that the German leadership had criminally provoked an "aggressive" war in 1939. *Der erzwungene Krieg* has since gone through thirteen printings and sold over fifty thousand copies. The famous German writer and historian Armin Mohler declared that Hoggan had brought World War II Revisionism "out of the ghetto" in Germany.

While *Der erzwungene Krieg* was considered important enough to be reviewed in more than one hundred publications in the Bundesrepublik, West Germany's political and intellectual Establishment, for whom the unique and diabolical evil of Germany in the years 1933-1945 constitutes both foundation myth and dogma, was predictably hostile. A 1964 visit by Hoggan to West Germany was attacked by West Germany's Minister of the Interior, in much the same spirit as West Germany's President Richard von Weizsaecker attempted to decree an end to the so-called *Historikerstreit* (historians' debate) due to its Revisionist implications in 1988. More than one influential West German historian stooped to *ad hominem* attack on Hoggan's book, as the American was chided for everything from his excessive youth (Hoggan was nearly forty when the book appeared) to the alleged "paganism" of his German publisher.

The most substantive criticism of *The Forced War* was made by German historians Helmut Krausnick and Hermann Graml, who, in the August 1963 issue of *Geschichte in Wissenschaft und Unterricht* (History in Scholarship and Instruction), attacked the book on grounds of a number of instances of faulty documentation. A Revisionist historian, Professor Kurt Glaser, after examining *The Forced War* and its critics' arguments in *Der Zweite Weltkrieg und die Kriegsschuldfrage* (The Second World War and the Question of War Guilt), found, that while some criticisms had merit, "It is hardly necessary to repeat here that Hoggan was not attacked because he had erred here and there – albeit some of his errors are material – but because he had committed heresy against the creed of historical orthodoxy."

Meanwhile, in the United States, Hoggan and Harry Elmer Barnes, Hoggan's mentor and the most influential American Revisionist scholar and promoter, became embroiled in a dispute over Hoggan's failure to revise *The Forced War* in the face of the few warranted criticisms. Hoggan, proud and somewhat temperamental, refused to yield, despite a substantial grant arranged for him by Barnes. Barnes's death in 1968 and financial difficulties created an impasse with the original publisher which blocked publication until IHR obtained the rights; IHR's difficulties have been mentioned above. *Habent sua fata libelli.*

Whatever minor flaws in Hoggan's documentation, *The Forced War*, in the words of Harry Elmer Barnes, written in 1963, "In its present form, . . . not only constitutes the first thorough study of the responsibility for the causes of the Second World War in any language but is likely to remain the definitive Revisionist work on this subject for many years." Hoggan prophesied well: the following quarter century has produced no Revisionist study of the origins of the war to match *The Forced War*; as for the Establishment's histories regarding Hitler's foreign policy, to quote Professor H.W. Koch of the University of York, England, writing in 1985, ". . . such a major work is still lacking" (*Aspects of the Third Reich*, ed. H.W. Koch, St. Martin's Press, New York, p. 186). Thus its publication after so many years is a major, if belated, victory for Revisionism in the English-speaking world. If the publication of *The Forced War* can contribute to an increase in the vigilance of a new generation of Americans regarding the forced wars that America's interventionist Establishment may seek to impose in the future, the aims of the late David Hoggan, who passed away in August 1988, will have been, in part, realized.

IHR would like to acknowledge the assistance of Russell Granata and Tom Kerr in the publication of *The Forced War*; both these American Revisionists gave of their time so that a better knowledge of the past might produce a better future, for their children and ours.

—Theodore J. O'Keefe
January, 1989

TABLE OF CONTENTS

PREFACE

This book is an outgrowth of a research project in diplomatic history entitled *Breakdown of German-Polish Relations in 1939*. It was offered and accepted as a doctoral dissertation at Harvard University in 1948. It was prepared under the specific direction of Professors William L. Langer and Michael Karpovich who were recognized throughout the historical world as being leading authorities on modern European history, and especially in the field of diplomatic history.

During the execution of this investigation I also gained much from consultation with other experts in this field then at Harvard, such as Professor Sidney B. Fay, Professor Harry R. Rudin (who was guest professor at Harvard during the academic year, 1946-1947), and Professor David Owen, at that time the chairman of the Harvard History Department and one of the world's leading experts on modern British history.

It has been a source of gratification to me that the conclusions reached in the 1948 monograph have been confirmed and extended by the great mass of documentary and memoir material which has been made available since that time.

While working on this project, which is so closely and directly related to the causes of the second World War, I was deeply impressed with the urgent need for further research and writing on the dramatic and world-shaking events of 1939 and their historical background in the preceding decade.

It was astonishing to me that, nine years after the launching of the second World War in September 1939, there did not exist in any language a comprehensive and reliable book on this subject. The only one devoted specifically and solely to this topic was *Diplomatic Prelude* by Sir Lewis B. Namier, an able English-Jewish historian who was a leading authority on the history of eighteenth century Britain. He had no special training or capacity for dealing with contemporary diplomatic history. His book, published in 1946, was admittedly based on the closely censored documents which had appeared during the War and on the even more carefully screened and unreliable material produced against the National Socialist leaders at the Nuremberg Trials.

This lack of authentic material on the causes of the second World War presented a remarkable contrast to that which existed following the end of the first World War. Within less than two years after the Armistice of November 1918, Professor Sidney B. Fay had discredited for all time the allegation that Germany and her allies had been solely responsible for the outbreak of war in August 1914. This was a fantastic indictment. Yet, on it was based the notorious war-guilt clause (Article 239) of the Treaty of Versailles that did so much to bring on the explosive situation which, as will be shown in this book, Lord Halifax and other British leaders exploited to unleash the second World War almost exactly twenty years later.

By 1927, nine years after Versailles, there was an impressive library of worthy and substantial books by so-called revisionist scholars which had at least factually obliterated the Versailles war-guilt verdict. These books had appeared in many countries; the United States, Germany, England, France, Austria and Italy, among others. They were quickly translated, some even into Japanese. Only a year later there appeared Fay's *Origins of the World War*, which still remains, after more than thirty years, the standard book in the English language on 1914 and its background. Later materials, such as the Berchtold papers and the Austro-Hungarian diplomatic documents published in 1930, have undermined Fay's far too harsh verdict on the responsibility of the Austrians for the War. Fay himself has been planning for some time to bring out a new and revised edition of his important work.

This challenging contrast in the historical situation after the two World Wars convinced me that I could do no better than to devote my professional efforts to this very essential but seemingly almost studiously avoided area of contemporary history; the background of 1939. There were a number of obvious reasons for this dearth of sound published material dealing with this theme.

The majority of the historians in the victorious allied countries took it for granted that there was no war-guilt question whatever in regard to the second World War. They seemed to be agreed that no one could or ever would question the assumption that Hitler and the National Socialists were entirely responsible for the outbreak of war on September 1, 1939, despite the fact that, even in 1919, some able scholars had questioned the validity of the war-guilt clause of the Versailles Treaty. The attitude of the historical guild after the second World War was concisely stated by Professor Louis Gottschalk of the University of Chicago, a former President of the American Historical Association: "American historians seem to be generally agreed upon the war-guilt question of the second World War." In other words, there was no such question.

This agreement was not confined to American historians; it was equally true not only of those in Britain, France and Poland but also of the great majority of those in the defeated nations: Germany and Italy. No general revisionist movement like that following 1918 was stirring in any European country for years after V-J Day. Indeed, it is only faintly apparent among historians even today.

A second powerful reason for the virtual non-existence of revisionist historical writing on 1939 was the fact that it was—and still is—extremely precarious professionally for any historian anywhere to question the generally accepted dogma of the sole guilt of Germany for the outbreak of hostilities in 1939. To do so endangered the tenure and future prospects of any historian, as much in Germany or Italy as in the United States or Britain. Indeed, it was even more risky in West Germany. Laws passed by the Bonn Government made it possible to interpret such vigorous revisionist writing as that set forth after 1918 by such writers as Montgelas, von Wegerer, Stieve, and Lutz as a political crime. The whole occupation program and NATO political set-up, slowly fashioned after V-E Day, was held to depend on the validity of the assertion that Hitler and the National Socialists were solely responsible for the great calamity of 1939. This dogma was bluntly stated by a very influential German political scientist, Professor Theodor Eschenburg, Rector of the University of Tuebingen: "Whoever doubts the exclusive guilt of Germany for the second World War destroys the foundations of post-war politics."

After the first World War, a strong wave of disillusionment soon set in concerning the alleged aims and actual results of the War. There was a notable trend towards peace, disarmament sentiment, and isolation, especially in the United States. Such an atmosphere offered some intellectual and moral encouragement to historians who sought to tell the truth about the responsibility for 1914. To do so did not constitute any basis for professional alarm as to tenure, status, promotion and security, at least after an interval of two or three years following the Armistice.

There was no such period of emotional cooling-off, readjustment, and pacific trends after 1945. Before there had even been any opportunity for this, a Cold War between former allies was forecast by Churchill early in 1946 and was formally proclaimed by President Truman in March 1947. The main disilllusionment was that which existed between the United States and the Soviet Union, and this shaped up so as to intensify and prolong the legend of the exclusive guilt of the National Socialists for 1939. The Soviet Union was no more vehement in this attitude than the Bonn Government of Germany.

There were other reasons why there was still a dearth of substantial books on 1939 in 1948—a lacuna which exists to this day—but those mentioned above are the most notable. Countries whose post-war status, possessions and policies rested upon the assumption of exclusive German guilt were not likely to surrender their pretensions, claims, and gains in the interest of historical integrity. Minorities that had a special grudge against the National Socialists were only too happy to take advantage of the favorable world situation to continue and to intensify their program of hate and its supporting literature, however extreme the deviation from the historical facts.

All these handicaps, difficulties and apprehension in dealing with 1939 were quite apparent to me in 1948 and, for the most part, they have not abated notably since that time. The sheer scholarly and research opportunities and responsibilities were also far greater than in the years after 1918. Aside from the fact that the revolutionary governments in Germany, Austria and Russia quickly opened their archives on 1914 to scholars, the publication of documents on the responsibility for the first World War came very slowly, and in some cases required two decades or more.

After the second World War, however, there was soon available a veritable avalanche of documents that had to be read, digested and analyzed if one were to arrive at any certainty relative to the responsibility for 1939. Germany had seized the documents in the archives of the countries she conquered. When the Allies later overcame Germany they seized not only these, but those of Germany, Austria, Italy and several other countries. To be sure, Britain and the

United States have been slow in publishing their documents bearing on 1939 and 1941, and the Soviet leaders have kept all of their documentary material, other than that seized by Germany, very tightly closed to scholars except for Communists. The latter could be trusted not to reveal any facts reflecting blame on the Soviet Union or implying any semblance of innocence on the part of National Socialist Germany.

Despite all the obvious problems, pitfalls and perils involved in any effort actually to reconstruct the story of 1939 and its antecedents, the challenge, need and opportunities connected with this project appeared to me to outweigh any or all negative factors. Hence, I began my research and writing on this comprehensive topic, and have devoted all the time I could take from an often heavy teaching schedule to its prosecution.

In 1952, I was greatly encouraged when I read the book by Professor Charles C. Tansill, *Back Door to War*. Tansill's *America Goes to War* was, perhaps, the most learned and scholarly revisionist book published after the first World War, Henry Steele Commager declared that the book was "the most valuable contribution to the history of the pre-war years in our literature, and one of the notable achievements of historical scholarship of this generation." Allan Nevins called it "an admirable volume, and absolutely indispensable" as an account of American entry into the War, on which the "approaches finality." Although his *Back Door to War* was primarily designed to show how Roosevelt "lied the United States into war," it also contained a great deal of exciting new material on the European background which agreed with the conclusions that I had reached in my 1948 dissertation.

Three years that I spent as Scientific Assistant to the Rector and visiting Assistant Professor of History in the *Amerika Institut* at the University of Munich gave me the opportunity to look into many sources of information in German materials at first hand and to consult directly able German scholars and public figures who could reveal in personal conversation what they would not dare to put in print at the time. An earlier research trip to Europe sponsored by a Harvard scholarship grant, 1947-1948, had enabled me to do the same with leading Polish figures and to work on important Polish materials in a large number of European countries.

Three years spent later as an Assistant Professor of History at the University of California at Berkeley made it possible for me to make use of the extensive collection of documents there, as well as the far more voluminous materials at the Hoover Institution at Stanford, California, where I had done my first work in the archives while an under-graduate student at Stanford. Research grants thereafter permitted me to be free from teaching duties for several years and to devote myself solely to research and writing. Whatever defects and deficiencies my book may possess, they are not due to lack of application to cogent research in the best collections of documents for over nearly a decade and a half.

In various stages of the preparation of my book I gained much from the advice, counsel and assistance of Harry R. Rudin, Raymond J. Sontag, Charles C. Tansill, M.K. Dziewanowski, Zygmunt Gasiorowski, Edward J. Rozek, Otto zu Stolberg-Wernigerode, Vsevolod Panek, Ralph H. Lutz, Henry M. Adams, James J. Martin, Franklin C. Palm, Thomas H.D. Mahoney, Reginald F. Arragon, Richard H. Jones, and Ernest G. Trimble.

By 1957, I believed that I had proceeded far enough to have a manuscript worthy of publication and offered it to a prominent publisher. Before any decision could be reached, however, as to acceptance or rejection, I voluntarily withdrew the manuscript because of the recent availability of extensive and important new documentary materials, such as the Polish documentary collection, *Polska a Zagranica*, and the vast collection of microfilm reproductions based on the major portion of the German Foreign Office Archives from the 1936-1939 period, which had remained unpublished.

This process of drastic revision, made mandatory by newly available documentation, has been repeated four times since 1957. It is now my impression that no probable documentary revelations in any predictable future would justify further withholding of the material from publication. The results of my work during the last fifteen years in this field have recently been published in Germany (November, 1961) under the title *Der Erzwungene Krieg* (*The Forced War*). The German edition went through four printings within one year.

Neither this book nor the present English-language edition will exhaust this vast theme or preclude the publication of many other books in the same field. But it will not strain the truth to assert that my book constitutes by far the most complete treatment which has appeared on the subject in any language based on the existing and available documentation. Indeed, amazing as it seems, it is the only book limited to the subject in any language that has appeared since 1946, save for Professor A.J.P. Taylor's far briefer account which was not published until the spring of 1961, the still more brief account in Germany by Walther Hofer, the rather diffuse symposium published under the auspices of Professor Arnold J. Toynbee at London in 1958, and Frau Annelies von Ribbentrop's *Verschwoerung gegen den Frieden* (*Conspiracy Against Peace*, Leoni am Starnbergersee, 1962).

It represents, to the best of my ability, an accurate summation and assessment of the factors, forces and personalities that contributed to bring on war in September 1939, and to the entry of the Soviet Union, Japan, and the United States into the conflict later on. Valid criticism of the book in its present and first edition will be warmly welcomed. Such suggestions as appear to me to be validated by reliable documentation will be embodied in subsequently revised editions.

Although the conclusions reached in this book depart widely from the opinions that were set forth in allied war propaganda and have been continued almost unchanged in historical writing since 1945, they need not be attributed to either special ability or unusual perversity. They are simply those which one honest historian with considerable linguistic facility has arrived at by examining the documents and monographs with thoroughness, and by deriving the logical deductions from their content. No more has been required than professional integrity, adequate information, and reasonable intelligence. Such a revision of wartime propaganda dogmas and their still dominating vestiges in current historical writings in this field is inevitable, whatever the preconceived ideas held by any historian, if he is willing to base his conclusions on facts. This is well illustrated and confirmed by the example of the best known of contemporary British historians, Professor A.J.P. Taylor.

Taylor had written numerous books relating to German history, and his attitude had led to his being regarded as vigorously anti-German, if not literally a consistent Germanophobe. Admittedly in this same mood, he began a thorough study of the causes of the second World War from the sources, with the definite anticipation that he would emerge with an overwhelming indictment of Hitler as solely responsible for the causes and onset of that calamitous conflict. What other outcome could be expected when one was dealing with the allegedly most evil, bellicose, aggressive and unreasonable leader in all German history?

Taylor is, however, an honest historian and his study of the documents led him to the conclusion that Hitler was not even primarily responsible for 1939. Far from planning world conquest, Hitler did not even desire a war with Poland, much less any general European war. The war was, rather, the outcome of blunders on all sides, committed by all the nations involved, and the greatest of all these blunders took place before Hitler came to power in 1933. This was the Versailles Treaty of 1919 and the failure of the victorious Allies and the League of Nations to revise this nefarious document gradually and peacefully in the fifteen years preceding the Hitler era.

So far as the long-term responsibility for the second World War is concerned, my general conclusions agree entirely with those of Professor Taylor. When it comes to the critical months between September 1938, and September 1939, however, it is my carefully considered judgment that the primary responsibility was that of Poland and Great Britain. For the Polish-German War, the responsibility was that of Poland, Britain and Germany in this order of so-called guilt. For the onset of a European War, which later grew into a world war with the entry of the Soviet Union, Japan and the United States, the responsibility was primarily, indeed almost exclusively, that of Lord Halifax and Great Britain.

I have offered my reasons for these conclusions and have presented and analyzed the extensive documentary evidence to support them. It is my conviction that the evidence submitted cannot be factually discredited or overthrown. If it can be, I will be the first to concede the success of such an effort and to readjust my views accordingly. But any refutation must be based on facts and logic and cannot be accomplished by the prevailing arrogance, invective or innuendo. I await the examination of my material with confidence, but also with an open mind in response to all honest and constructive criticism.

While my primary concern in writing this book has been to bring the historical record into accord with the available documentation, it has also been my hope that it might have the same practical relevance that revisionist writing *could* have had after the first World War. Most of the prominent Revisionists after the first World War hoped that their results in scholarship might produce a comparable revolution in European politics and lead to the revision of the Versailles Treaty in time to discourage the rise of some authoritarian ruler to undertake this task. They failed to achieve this laudable objective and Europe was faced with the danger of a second World War.

Revisionist writing on the causes of the second World War should logically produce an even greater historical and political impact than it did after 1919. In a nuclear age, failure in this respect will be much more disastrous and devastating than the second World War. The indispensable nature of a reconsideration of the merits and possible services of Revisionism in this matter has been well

stated by Professor Denna F. Fleming, who has written by far the most complete
and learned book on the Cold War and its dangers, and a work which also gives
evidence of as extreme and unyielding a hostility to Germany as did the earlier
writings of A.J.P. Taylor: "The case of the Revisionists deserved to be heard . . .
They may help us avoid the 'one more war' after which there would be nothing
left worth arguing about."

Inasmuch as I find little in the documents which lead me to criticize seriously
the foreign policy of Hitler and the National Socialists, some critics of the
German edition of my book have charged that I entertain comparable views
about the domestic policy of Hitler and his regime. I believe, and have tried to
demonstrate, that the factual evidence proves that Hitler and his associates did
not wish to launch a European war in 1939, or in preceding years. This does not,
however, imply in any sense that I have sought to produce an apology for Hitler
and National Socialism in the domestic realm. It is no more true in my case than
in that of A.J.P. Taylor whose main thesis throughout his lucid and consistent
volume is that Hitler desired to accomplish the revision of the Treaty of
Versailles by peaceful methods, and had no wish or plan to provoke any general
war.

Having devoted as much time to an intensive study of this period of German
history as any other American historian, I am well aware that there were many
defects and shortcomings in the National Socialist system, as well as some
remarkable and substantial accomplishments in many fields. My book is a
treatise on diplomatic history. If I were to take the time and space to analyze in
detail the personal traits of all the political leaders of the 1930's and all aspects
of German, European and world history at the time that had any bearing
on the policies and actions that led to war in September 1939, it would require
several large volumes.

The only practical procedure is the one which I have followed, namely, to
hold resolutely to the field of diplomatic history, mentioning only those outstanding political, economic, social and psychological factors and situations
which bore directly and powerfully on diplomatic actions and policies during
these years. Even when closely restricted to this special field, the indispensable
materials have produced a very large book. If I have found Hitler relatively free
of any intent or desire to launch a European war in 1939, this surely does not
mean that any reasonable and informed person could regard him as blameless or
benign in all his policies and public conduct. Only a naive person could take any
such position. I deal with Hitler's domestic program only to refute the preposterous charge that he made Germany a military camp before 1939.

My personal political and economic ideology is related quite naturally to my
own environment as an American citizen. I have for years been a warm admirer
of the distinguished American statesman and reformer, the late Robert Marion
La Follette, Sr. I still regard him as the most admirable and courageous
American political leader of this century. Although I may be very much
mistaken in this judgment and appraisal, it is sincere and enduring. What it does
demonstrate is that I have no personal ideological affinity with German National
Socialism, whatever strength and merit it may have possessed for Germany in
some important respects. Nothing could be more presumptous and absurd, or
more remote from my purposes in this book, than an American attempt to

rehabilitate or vindicate Germany's Adolf Hitler in every phase of his public behavior. My aim here is solely to discover and describe the attitudes and responsibilities of Hitler and the other outstanding political leaders and groups of the 1930's which had a decisive bearing on the outbreak of war in 1939.

David Leslie Hoggan

Menlo Park, California

Chapter 1

THE NEW POLISH STATE

The Anti-Polish Vienna Congress

A tragedy such as World War I, with all its horrors, was destined by the very nature of its vast dimensions to produce occasional good results along with an infinitely greater number of disastrous situations. One of these good results was the restoration of the Polish state. The Polish people, the most numerous of the West Slavic tribes, have long possessed a highly developed culture, national self-consciousness, and historical tradition. In 1914 Poland was ripe for the restoration of her independence, and there can be no doubt that independence, when it came, enjoyed the unanimous support of the entire Polish nation. The restoration of Poland was also feasible from the standpoint of the other nations, although every historical event has its critics, and there were prominent individuals in foreign countries who did not welcome the recovery of Polish independence.[1]

The fact that Poland was not independent in 1914 was mainly the fault of the international congress which met at Vienna in 1814 and 1815. No serious effort was made by the Concert of Powers[2] to concern itself with Polish national aspirations, and the arrangements for autonomy in the part of Russian Poland known as the Congress Kingdom were the result of the influence of the Polish diplomat and statesman, Adam Czartoryski, on Tsar Alexander I. The Prussian delegation at Vienna would gladly have relinquished the Polish province of Posen in exchange for the recognition of Prussian aspirations in the German state of Saxony. Great Britain, France, and Austria combined against Prussia and Russia to frustrate Prussian policy in Saxony and to demand that Posen be assigned to Prussia. This typical disregard of Polish national interests sealed the fate of the Polish nation at that time.[3]

The indifference of the majority of the Powers, and especially Great Britain, toward Polish nationalism in 1815 is not surprising when one recalls that the aspirations of German, Italian, Belgian, and Norwegian nationalism were flouted with equal impunity. National self-determination was considered to be the privilege of only a few Powers in Western Europe.

The first Polish state was founded in the 10th century and finally destroyed in its entirety in 1795, during the European convulsions which accompanied the Great French Revolution. The primary reason for the destruction of Poland at that time must be assigned to Russian imperialism. The interference of the expanding Russian Empire in the affairs of Poland during the early 18th century became increasingly formidable, and by the mid-18th century Poland was virtually a Russian protectorate. The first partition of Poland by Russia, Prussia, and Austria in 1772 met with some feeble opposition from Austrian diplomacy. Prussia made a rather ineffective effort to protect Poland from further destruction by concluding an alliance with her shortly before the second partition of 1792. The most that can be said about Russia in these various situations is that she would have preferred to obtain the whole of Poland for herself rather than to share territory with the western and southern neighbors of Poland. The weakness of the Polish constitutional system is sometimes considered a cause for the disappearance of Polish independence, but Poland would probably have maintained her independence under this system had it not been for the hostile actions of neighboring Powers, and especially Russia.

Poland was restored as an independent state by Napoleon I within twelve years of the final partition of 1795. The new state was known as the Grand Duchy of Warsaw. It did not contain all of the Polish territories, but it received additional land from Napoleon in 1809, and, despite the lukewarm attitude of the French Emperor toward the Poles, it no doubt would have been further aggrandized had Napoleon's campaign against Russia in 1812 been successful. It can truthfully be said that the long eclipse of Polish independence during the 19th century was the responsibility of the European Concert of Powers at Vienna rather than the three partitioning Powers of the late 18th century.[5]

The 19th Century Polish Uprisings

The privileges of autonomy granted to Congress Poland by Russia in 1815 were withdrawn sixteen years later following the great Polish insurrection against the Russians in 1830-1831. Polish refugees of that uprising were received with enthusiasm wherever they went in Germany, because the Germans too were suffering from the oppressive post-war system established by the victors of 1815.[6] The Western Powers, Great Britain and France, were absorbed by their rivalry to control Belgium and Russia was allowed to deal with the Polish situation undisturbed. New Polish uprisings during the 1846-1848 period were as ineffective as the national revolutions of Germany and Italy at that time.[7] The last desperate Polish uprising before 1914 came in 1863, and it was on a much smaller scale than the insurrection of 1830-1831.

The British, French, and Austrians showed some interest in diplomatic intervention on behalf of the Poles, but Bismarck, the Minister-President of Prussia, sided with Russia because he believed that Russian support was necessary for the realization of German national unity. Bismarck's eloquent arguments in the Prussian Landtag (legislature) against the restoration of a Polish state in 1863 reflected this situation rather than permanent prejudice on his part against the idea of an independent Poland. It is unlikely that there would have been effective action on behalf of the Poles by the Powers at that time had Bismarck heeded the demand of the majority of the Prussian Landtag for a pro-Polish policy. Great Britain was less inclined in 1863 than she had been during the 1850's to intervene in foreign quarrels as the ally of Napoleon III. She was desengaging herself from Anglo-French intervention in Mexico, rejecting proposals for joint Anglo-French intervention in the American Civil War, and quarreling with France about the crisis in Schleswig-Holstein.[8]

The absence of new Polish uprisings in the 1863-1914 period reflected Polish recognition that such actions were futile rather than any diminution of the Polish desire for independence. The intellectuals of Poland were busily at work during this period devising new plans for the improvement of the Polish situation. A number of different trends emerged as a result of this activity. One of these was represented by Józef Pilsudski, and he and his disciples ultimately determined the fate of Poland in the period between the two World Wars. Pilsudski participated in the revolutionary movement in Russia before 1914 in the hope that this movement would shatter the Russian Empire and prepare the way for an independent Poland.[9]

The unification of Germany in 1871 meant that the Polish territories of Prussia became integral parts of the new German Empire. Relations between Russia, Germany, and Austria-Hungary, the three Powers ruling over Polish territories, were usually harmonious in the following twenty year period. This was possible, despite the traditional Austro-Russian rivalry in the Balkans, because of the diplomatic achievement of Bismarck.[10] The situation changed after the retirement of Bismarck in 1890, and especially after the conclusion of the Franco-Russian alliance in 1894.[11] There was constant tension among the three Powers during the following period. Russia was allied with France against Germany, and it was evident that an Eastern European, a Western European, or an Overseas imperial question might produce a war. This situation seemed more promising for Poland than when the three Powers ruling Polish territories were in harmony. It was natural that these changed conditions were reflected in Polish thought during these years.

Pro-German Polish Nationalism

Most of the Polish territory was ruled by Russia, and consequently it was quite logical for some Poles to advocate collaboration with Germany, the principal opponent of Russia, as the best means of promoting Polish interests. Wladyslaw Studnicki, a brilliant Polish scholar with contacts in many countries, was an exponent of this approach. He believed that Russia would always be the primary threat to Polish interests. His historical studies had convinced him that the finest conditions for Poland had existed during periods of peaceful relations and close contact with Germany.[12]

He noted that Poland, while enfeoffed to Germany during the Middle Ages, had received from the Germans her Christian religion, her improved agricultural economy, and her flourishing medieval development of crafts. German craft colonization had been the basis for the growth of Polish cities, and the close cultural relationship between the two countries was demonstrated by every fourth 20th century Polish word, which was of German origin. He recalled that relations between Germany and Poland were usually friendly during the Middle Ages, and also during the final years before the Polish partitions.

Studnicki believed that Poland's real future was in the East, where she might continue her own cultural mission, and also profit nationally. He asserted during World War I that Poles should cease opposing the continuation of German rule in the province of Posen, which had a Polish majority, and in the province of West Prussia, which had a German majority. Both of these regions had been Polish before the first partition of 1772. He favored a return to the traditional Polish eastern policy of federation with such neighboring nations as the Lithuanians and White Russians.[13]

Studnicki believed that collaboration with Germany would protect Poland from destruction by Russia without endangering the development of Poland or the realization of Polish interests. He advocated this policy throughout the period from World War I to World War II. After World War II, he wrote a moving account of the trials of Poland during wartime occupation, and of the manner in which recent events had made more difficult the German-Polish understanding which he still desired.[14]

Pro-Russian Polish Nationalism

The idea of permanent collaboration with Russia also enjoyed great prestige in Poland despite the fact that Russia was the major partitioning Power and that the last Polish insurrection had been directed exclusively against her rule. The most brilliant and popular of modern Polish political philosophers, Roman Dmowski, was an advocate of this idea. Dmowski's influence was very great, and his most bitter adversaries adopted many of his ideas. Dmowski refused to compromise with his opponents, or to support any program which differed from his own.[15]

Dmowski was the leader of a Polish political group within the Russian Empire before World War I known as the National Democrats. They advocated a constitution for the central Polish region of Congress Poland, which had been assigned to Russia for the first time at the Vienna Congress in 1815, but they did not oppose the further union of this region with Russia. They welcomed the Russian constitutional regime of 1906, and they took their seats in the legislative Duma rather than boycott it. Their motives in this respect were identical with those of the Polish Conservatives from the Polish Kresy;[16] the new constitution could bestow benefits on Poles as well as Russians. The Polish Kresy, which also served as a reservation for Jews in Russia, included all Polish territories taken by Russia except Congress Poland. The National Democrats and the Polish Conservatives believed that they could advance the Polish cause within Russia by legal means.[17]

Dmowski was a leading speaker in the Duma, and he was notorious for his clever attacks on the Germans and Jews. He confided to friends that he hoped to duplicate the career of Adam Czartoryski, who had been Foreign Secretary of

Russia one century earlier and was acknowledged to have been the most successful Polish collaborator with the Russians. Unwelcome restrictions were imposed
on the constitutional regime in the years after 1906 by Piotr Stolypin, the new
Russian strong man, but these failed to dampen Dmowski's ardor. He believed
that the combined factors of fundamental weakness in the Russian autocracy
and the rising tide of Polish nationalism would enable him to achieve a more
prominent role.

Dmowski was an advocate of modernity, which meant to him a pragmatic
approach to all problems without sentimentality or the dead weight of
outmoded tradition. In his book, *Myśli nowoczesnego Polaka* (Thoughts of a
Modern Pole), 1902, he advised that the past splendor of the old Polish
monarchy should be abandoned even as an ideal. He recognized that the Polish
nation needed modern leadership, and he proclaimed that "nations do not
produce governments, but governments do produce nations."[18] He continued to
envisage an autonomous Polish regime loyal to Russia until the latter part of
World War I. His system of thought was better suited to the completely independent Poland which emerged from the War. He demanded after 1918 that
Poland become a strictly national state in contrast to a nationalities state of the
old Polish or recent Habsburg pattern. Dmowski did not envisage an unexcep-
tional Poland for the Poles, but a state with strictly limited minorities in the
later style of Kemal in Turkey or Hitler in Germany. He believed that the inclusion of minorities in the new state should stop short of risking the total preponderance of the dominant nationality.[19]

Dmowski opposed eastward expansion at Russian expense, and he argued that
the old Lithuanian-Russian area, which once had been under Polish rule, could
not be assimilated. Above all, the Jews were very numerous in the region, and he
disliked having a Jewish minority in the new Polish state. In 1931 he declared
that "the question of the Jews is the greatest question concerning the civilization of the whole world."[20] He argued that a modern approach to the Jewish
question required the total expulsion of the Jews from Poland because assimilation was impossible. He rejected both the 18th century attempt to assimilate by
baptism and the 19th century effort at assimilation through common agreement
on liberal ideas. He insisted that experience had proved both these attempted
solutions were futile. He argued that it was not Jewish political influence which
posed the greatest threat, but Jewish economic and cultural activities. He did not
believe that Poland could become a respectable business nation until she had
eliminated her many Jews. He recognized the dominant Western trend in Polish
literature and art, but he did not see how Polish culture could survive what he
considered to be Jewish attempts to dominate and distort it. He firmly believed
that the anti-Jewish policy of the Tsarist regime in Russia had been beneficial.
His ideas on the Jewish question were popular in Poland, and they were either
shared from the start or adopted by most of his political opponents.[21]

Dmowski's basic program was defensive, and he was constantly seeking either
to protect the Poles from threats to their heritage, or from ambitious schemes
of expansion which might increase alien influences. There was only one notable
exception to this defensive pattern of his ideas. He favored an ambitious and
aggressive policy of westward expansion at the expense of Germany, and he used
his predilection for this scheme as an argument for collaboration with Russia.

He believed in the industrialization of Poland and in a dominant position for the industrial middle class. He argued that westward expansion would be vital in increasing Polish industrial resources.[22]

The influence of Dmowski's thought in Poland has remained important until the present day. His influence continued to grow despite the political failures of his followers after Józef Pilsudski's *coup d'état* in 1926. Dmowski deplored the influence of the Jews in Bolshevist Russia, but he always advocated Russo-Polish collaboration in foreign policy.

Pro-Habsburg Polish Nationalism

Every general analysis of 20th century Polish theory on foreign policy emphasizes the Kraków (Cracow) or Galician school, which was easily the most prolific, although the practical basis for its program was destroyed by World War I. The political leaders and university scholars of the Polish South thought of Austrian Galicia as a Polish Piedmont after the failure of the Polish insurrection against Russia in 1863. Michal Bobrzyński, the Governor of Galicia from 1907 to 1911, was the outstanding leader of this school. In his *Dzieje Polski w Zarysie* (Short History of Poland), he eulogized Polish decentralization under the pre-partition constitution, and he attacked the kings who had sought to increase the central power. In 1919 he advocated regionalism in place of a centralized national system. He also hoped that the Polish South would occupy the key position in Poland as a whole.[23]

The political activities of the Kraków group before the War of 1914 were directed against the National Democrats, with their pro-Russian orientation, and against the Ukrainians in Galicia, with their national aspirations. Bobrzyński envisaged the union of all Poland under the Habsburgs, and the development of a powerful federal system in the Habsburg Empire to be dominated by Austrian Germans, Hungarians, and Poles. He advocated a federal system after the collapse of the Habsburg Empire in 1918, and he supported the claims to the old thrones of the Habsburg pretender. He argued with increasing exasperation that Poland alone could never maintain herself against Russia and Germany without additional support from the South.[24]

Pilsudski's Polish Nationalism

A fouth major program for the advancement of Polish interests was that of Józef Pilsudski, who thought of Poland as a Great Power. His ideas on this vital point conflicted with the three programs previously mentioned. Studnicki, Dmowski, and Bobrzyński recognized that Poland was one of the smaller nations of modern Europe. It seemed inevitable to them that the future promotion of Polish interests would demand a close alignment with at least one of the three pre-1918 powerful neighboring Powers, Germany, Russia, or Austria-Hungary. It is not surprising that there were groups in Poland which favored collaboration with each of these Powers, but it is indeed both startling and instructive to note that the strongest of these groups advocated collaboration with Russia, the principal oppressor of the Poles.

Pilsudski opposed collaboration with any of the stronger neighbors of Poland. He expected Poland to lead nations weaker than herself and to maintain alliances or alignments with powerful but distant Powers not in a position to influence the conduct of Polish policy to any great extent. Above all, his system demanded a defiant attitude toward any neighboring state more powerful than Poland. His reasoning was that defiance of her stronger neighbors would aid Poland to regain the Great Power status which she enjoyed at the dawn of modern history. Dependence on a stronger neighbor would be tantamount to recognizing the secondary position of Poland in Central Eastern Europe. He hoped that a successful foreign policy after independence would eventually produce a situation in which none of her immediate neighbors would be appreciably stronger than Poland. He hoped that Poland in this way might eventually achieve national security without sacrificing her Great Power aspirations.[25]

This approach to a foreign policy for a small European nation was reckless, and its partisans said the same thing somewhat more ambiguously when they described it as heroic. Its radical nature is evident when it is compared to the three programs described above, which may be called conservative by contrast. Another radical policy in Poland was that of the extreme Marxists who hoped to convert the Polish nation into a proletarian dictatorship. These extreme Marxists were far less radical on the foreign policy issue than the Pilsudski group.

For a period of twenty-five years, from 1914 until the Polish collapse of 1939, Pilsudski's ideas had a decisive influence on the development of Poland. No Polish leader since Jan Sobieski in the 17th century had been so masterful. Poles often noted that Pilsudski's personality was not typically Polish, but was much modified by his Lithuanian background. He did not share the typical exaggerated Polish respect for everything which came from abroad. He was not unpunctual as were most Poles, and he had no trace of either typical Polish indolence or prodigality. Above all, although he possessed it in full measure, he rarely made a show of the great personal charm which is typical of nearly all educated Poles. He was usually taciturn, and he despised excessive wordiness.[26]

Pilsudski's prominence began with the outbreak of World War I. He was personally well prepared for this struggle. Pilsudski addressed a group of Polish university students at Paris in February 1914. His words contained a remarkable prophecy which did much to give him a reputation for uncanny insight. He predicted that a great war would break out which might produce the defeat of the three Powers ruling partitioned Poland. He guessed correctly that the Austrians and Germans might defeat the Russians before succumbing to the superior material reserves and resources of the Western Powers. He proposed to contribute to this by fighting the Russians until they were defeated and then turning against the Germans and Austrians.[27]

This strategy required temporary collaboration with two of the Powers holding Polish territories, but it was based on the recognition that in 1914, before Polish independence, it was inescapable that Poles would be fighting on both sides in the War. Pilsudski accepted this inevitable situation, but he sought to shape it to promote Polish interests to the maximum degree.

Pilsudski had matured in politics before World War I as a Polish Marxist revolutionary. He assimilated the ideas of German and Russian Marxism both at the university city of Kharkov in the Ukraine, and in Siberia, where hundreds of thousands of Poles had been exiled by Russian authorities since 1815. He approached socialism as an effective weapon against Tsarism, but he never became a sincere socialist. His followers referred to his early Marxist affiliation as *Konrad Wallenrod* socialism. Wallenrod, in the epic of Adam Mickiewicz, infiltrated the German Order of Knights and became one of its leaders only to undermine it. Pilsudski adhered to international socialism for many years, but he remained opposed to its final implications.[28]

Pilsudski was convinced that the Galician socialist leaders with whom he was closely associated would ultimately react in a nationalist direction. One example will suggest why he made this assumption. At the July 1910 international socialist congress in Kraków, Ignaz Daszynski, the Galician socialist leader, was reproached by Herman Lieberman, a strict Marxist, for encouraging the celebration by Polish socialists of the 500th anniversary of Grunwald. Grunwald was the Polish name for the victory of the Poles, Lithuanians and Tartars over the German Order of Knights at Tannenberg in 1410, and its celebration in Poland at this time was comparable to the July 4th independence holiday in the United States. Daszynski heaped ridicule and scorn on Lieberman. He observed sarcastically that it would inflict a tremendous injury on the workers to tolerate this national impudence. He added that it was positively criminal to refer to Wawel (the former residence of Polish kings in Kraków) because this might sully the red banners of socialism.[29] Pilsudski himself later made the cynical remark that those who cared about socialism might ride the socialist trolley to the end of the line, but he preferred to get off at independence station.[30]

Pilsudski was active with Poles from other political groups after 1909 in forming separate military units to collaborate with Austria-Hungary in wartime. This action was encouraged by Austrian authorities who hoped that Pilsudski would be able to attract volunteers from the Russian section. Pilsudski was allowed to command only one brigade of this force, but he emerged as the dominant leader. The Kraków school hoped to use his military zeal to build Polish power within the Habsburg Empire, and one of their leaders, Jaworski, remarked that he would exploit Pilsudski as Cavour had once exploited Garibaldi. Pilsudski, like Garibaldi, had his own plans, and events were to show that he was more successful in realizing them.[31]

Poland in World War I

World War I broke out in August 1914 after Russia, with the encouragement of Great Britain and France, ordered the general mobilization of her armed forces against Germany and Austria-Hungary. The Russians were determined to support Serbia against Austria-Hungary in the conflict which resulted from the assassination of the heir to the Austrian and Hungarian thrones and his wife by Serbian conspirators. Russian mobilization plans envisaged simultaneous military action against both the Germans and Austro-Hungarians. Poincaré and Viviani, the French leaders, welcomed the opportunity to engage Germany in a conflict, because they hoped to reconquer Alsace-Lorraine. Sir Edward Grey and the majority of the British leaders looked forward to the opportunity of winning the spoils of war from Germany, and of disposing of an allegedly dangerous rival. Austria-Hungary wished to maintain her security against Serbian provocations, and the German leaders envisaged war with great reluctance as a highly unwelcome development.[32]

Russia, as the ally of Great Britain and France, succeeded in keeping the Polish question out of Allied diplomacy until the Russian Revolution of 1917. A Russian proclamation of August 18, 1914, offered vague rewards to the Poles for their support in the war against Germany, but it contained no binding assurances. Dmowski went to London in November 1915 to improve his contacts with British and French leaders, but he was careful to work closely with Alexander Isvolsky, Russian Ambassador to France and the principal Russian diplomat abroad. Dmowski's program called for an enlarged autonomous Polish region within Russia. His activities were for the most part welcomed by Russia, but Isvolsky reported to foreign Minister Serge Sazonov in April 1916 that Dmowski went too far in discussing certain aspects of the Polish question.[33]

Pilsudski in the meantime had successfully resisted attempts by the Austrian War Department to deprive his cadres of their special status when it became obvious that they were no magnet to the Poles across the Russian frontier. Responsibility for maintaining the separate status of the forces was entrusted to a Polish Chief National Committee (Naczelnik Komitet Narodowy). The situation was precarious because many of the Galician Poles proved to be pro-Russian after war came, and they did not care to join Pilsudski. They expected Russia to win the war. They might be tolerated following a Russian victory as mere conscripts of Austria, but they would be persecuted for serving with Pilsudski. As a result, there were only a few thousand soldiers under Pilsudski and his friends during World War I. The overwhelming majority of all Polish veterans saw military service only with the Russians. Large numbers of Polish young men from Galicia fled to the Russians upon the outbreak of war to escape service with either the Austrians or with Pilusdski.[34] It was for this reason that the impact of Pilsudski on the outcome of the war against Russia was negligible. He nevertheless achieved a prominent position in Polish public opinion, whatever individual Poles might think of him, and he managed to retain it.

General von Beseler, the Governor of German-occupied Poland, proclaimed the restoration of Polish independence on November 5, 1916, following an earlier agreement between Germany and Austria-Hungary. His announcement was accompanied by a German Army band playing the gay and exuberant Polish anthem from the Napoleonic period, *Poland Still Is Not Lost!* (Jeszcze Polska nie Zginele!). Polish independence was rendered feasible by the German victories over Russia in 1915 which compelled the Russians to evacuate most of the Polish territories, including those which they had seized from Austria in the early months of the war. Pilsudski welcomed this step by Germany with good reason, although he continued to hope for the ultimate defeat of Germany in order to free Poland from any German influence and to aggrandize Poland at German expense.[35]

A Polish Council of State was established on December 6, 1916, and met for the first time on January 14, 1917. The position of the Council during wartime was advisory to the occupation authorities, and the prosecution of the war continued to take precedence over every other consideration. Nevertheless, important concessions were made to the Poles during the period from September 1917 until the end of the war. The Council was granted the administration of justice in Poland and control over the Polish school system, and eventually every phase of Polish life came under its influence. The Council was reorganized in the autumn of 1917, and on October 14, 1917, a Regency Council was appointed in the expectation that Poland would become an independent kingdom allied to the German and Austro-Hungarian monarchies.[36] The German independence policy was recognized by Poles everywhere as a great aid to the Polish cause, and Roman Dmowski, never a friend of Germany, was very explicit in stating this in his book, *Polityka Polska i Odbudowanie Państwa* (*Polish Policy and the Reconstruction of the State*), which described the events of this period.[37] Negotiators for the Western Allies, on the other hand, were willing to reverse the German independence policy as late as the summer of 1917 and to offer all of Poland to Austria-Hungary, if by doing so they could separate the Central Powers and secure a separate peace with the Habsburgs.[38]

The Germans for their part were able to assure President Wilson in January 1917, when the United States was still neutral in the War, that they had no territorial aims in the West and that they stood for the independence of Poland. President Wilson delivered a speech on January 22, 1917, in which he stressed the importance of obtaining access to the Sea for Poland, but James Gerard, the American Ambassador to Germany, assured German Chancellor Bethmann-Hollweg that Wilson did not wish to see any Baltic port of Germany detached from German rule. It is not surprising that in German minds both before and after the 1918 armistice the Wilson Program for Poland envisaged access to the Sea in terms of free port facilities and not in the carving of one or more corridors to the Sea through German territory.[39] There was no objection from Germany when the Polish Council of State in Warsaw sent a telegram to Wilson congratulating him for his speech of January 22, 1917, which had formulated Wilsonian Polish policy in terms later included as the 13th of the famous 14 Points.[40]

The Russian Provisional Government raised the question of Polish independence in a statement of March 29, 1917, but they stressed the necessity of a permanent Russo-Polish "alliance," with special "guarantees," as the *conditio sine qua non*. Arthur James Balfour, the Conservative leader in the British Coalition Government, endorsed the Russian proposition, although he knew that the Russians intended a merely autonomous Poland. Dmowski responded to the March 1917 Russian Revolution by advocating a completely independent Poland of 200,000 square miles, which was approximately equal to the area of the German Empire, and he attempted to counter the arguments raised against Polish independence in Great Britain and France.[41]

Pilsudski at this time was engaged in switching his policy from support of Germany to support of the Western Allies. He demanded a completely independent Polish national army before the end of the war, and the immediate severance of any ties which made Poland dependent on the Central Powers. He knew that there was virtually no chance for the fulfillment of these demands at the crucial stage which the war had reached by the summer of 1917. The slogan of his followers was a rejection of compromise: "Never a state without an army, never an army without Pilsudski." Pilsudski was indeed head of the military department of the Polish Council of State, but he resigned on July 2, 1917, when Germany and Austria-Hungary failed to accept his demands.[42]

Pilsudski deliberately provoked the Germans until they arrested him and placed him for the duration of the war in comfortable internment with his closest military colleague, Kazimierz Sosnkowski, at Magdeburg on the Elbe. It was Pilsudski's conviction that only in this way could he avoid compromising himself with the Germans before Polish public opinion. His arrest by Germany made it difficult for his antagonists in Poland to argue that he had been a mere tool of German policy. It was a matter of less concern that this accusation was made in the Western countries despite his arrest during the months and years which followed.[43]

A threat to Pilsudski's position in Poland was implicit in the organization of independent Polish forces in Russia after the Revolution under a National Polish Army Committee (Naczpol). These troops were under the influence of Roman Dmowski and his National Democrats. The conclusion of peace between Russia and Germany at Brest-Litovsk in March 1918 stifled this development, and the Polish forces soon began to surrender to the Germans. The Bolshevik triumph and peace with Germany dealt a severe blow to the doctrine of Polish collaboration with Russia. The surrender by Germany of the Cholm district of Congress Poland to the Ukraine at Brest-Litovsk in March 1918 dealt a fatal blow to the prestige of the Regency Council in Poland, and prepared the way for the establishment of an entirely new Government when Germany went down in revolution and defeat in November 1918.[44]

Polish Expansion After World War I

It was fortunate for Pilsudski that the other Poles were unable to achieve anything significant during his internment in Germany. He was released from Magdeburg during the German Revolution, and he returned speedily to Poland. On November 14, 1918, the Regency Council turned over its powers to Pilsudski, and the Poles, who were in the midst of great national rejoicing, despite the severe prevailing economic conditions, faced an entirely new situation. Pilsudski knew there would be an immediate struggle for power among the political parties. His first step was to consolidate the Polish Socialist Party (PPS) of Congress Poland, and the Polish Social-Democratic Party (PPSD) of Galicia under his own leadership.[45]

Pilsudski had an enormous tactical advantage which he exploited to the limit. He was a socialist, and he had fought for the Germans. His principal political opponents, the National Democrats, were popular with the Western Powers. Poland was not mentioned in the November 1918 armistice agreement with Germany, and soon after the armistice a protracted peace conference began. Pilsudski was *persona non grata* at Versailles. He gladly expressed his confidence in the Paris negotiation efforts of the National Democrats in the interest of obtaining a united Polish front. It was not his responsibility, but that of his opponents, to secure advantages for Poland at the peace conference. This effort was almost certain to discredit his opponents, because Polish demands were so exorbitant that they could scarcely be satisfied. Pilsudski was free to turn his own efforts toward the Polish domestic situation. He made good use of his time, and he never lost the political initiative gained during those days. His cause was aided by an agreement he made with the Germans as early as November 11, 1918, before the armistice in the West. According to this agreement, the occupation troops would leave with their arms which they would surrender at the frontier (German-Congress Poland frontier of 1914, which was confirmed at Brest-Litovsk, 1918). The operation was virtually completed by November 19, 1918, and the agreement was faithfully carried out by both sides.[46]

The Polish National Committee in Paris, which was dominated by Roman Dmowski and the National Democrats, faced a much less promising situation. The diplomats of Great Britian and France regarded the Poles with condescension, and Premier Clemenceau informed Paderewski, the principal collaborator of Dmowski in the peace negotiation, that in his view Poland owed her independence to the sacrifices of the Allies.[47] The Jewish question also plagued the Polish negotiators, and they were faced by demands from American Jewish groups which would virtually have created an independent Jewish state within Poland. President Wilson was sympathetic toward these demands, and he emphasized in the Council of Four (United States, Great Britain, France, Italy) on May 1, 1919, that "the Jews were somewhat inhospitably regarded in Poland." Paderewski explained the Polish attitude on the Jewish question in a memorandum of June 15, 1919, in which he observed that the Jews of Poland "on many occasions" had considered the Polish cause lost, and had sided with the enemies of Poland. Ultimately most of the Jewish demands were modified, but article 93 of the Versailles treaty forced Poland to accept a special pact for minorities which was highly unpopular.[48]

The Polish negotiators might have achieved their extreme demands against Germany had it not been for Lloyd George, because President Wilson and the French were originally inclined to give them all that they asked. Dmowski demanded the 1772 frontier in the West, plus the key German industrial area of Upper Silesia, the City of Danzig, and the southern sections of East Prussia. In addition, he demanded that the rest of East Prussia be constituted as a separate state under Polish control, and later he also requested part of Middle Silesia for Poland. Lloyd George soon began to attack the Polish position, and he concentrated his effort on influencing and modifying the attitude of Wilson. It was clear to him that Italy was indifferent, and that France would not be able to resist a common Anglo-American program.[49]

Lloyd George had reduced the Polish demands in many directions before the original draft of the treaty was submitted to the Germans on May 7, 1919. A plebiscite was scheduled for the southern districts of East Prussia, and the rest of that province was to remain with Germany regardless of the outcome. Important modifications of the frontier in favor of Germany were made in the region of Pomerania, and the city of Danzig was to be established as a protectorate under the League of Nations rather than as an integral part of Poland. Lloyd George concentrated on Upper Silesia after the Germans had replied with their objections to the treaty. Wilson's chief expert on Poland,

Professor Robert Lord of Harvard University, made every effort to maintain the provision calling for the surrender of this territory to Poland without a plebiscite. Lloyd George concentrated on securing a plebiscite, and ultimately he succeeded.[50]

The ultimate treaty terms gave Poland much more than she deserved, and much more than she should have requested. Most of West Prussia, which had a German majority at the last census, was surrendered to Poland without plebiscite, and later the richest industrial section of Upper Silesia was given to Poland despite the fact that the Poles lost the plebiscite there. The creation of a League protectorate for the national German community of Danzig was a disastrous move; a free harbor for Poland in a Danzig under German rule would have been far more equitable. The chief errors of the treaty included the creation of the Corridor, the creation of the so-called Free City of Danzig, and the cession of part of Upper Silesia to Poland. These errors were made for the benefit of Poland and to the disadvantage of Germany, but they were detrimental to both Germany and Poland. An enduring peace in the German-Polish borderlands was impossible to achieve within the context of these terms.[51] The settlement was also contrary to the 13th of Wilson's 14 Points, which, except for the exclusion of point 2, constituted a solemn Allied contractual agreement on peace terms negotiated with Germany when she was still free and under arms.[52] The violation of these terms when defenseless Germany was in the chains of the armistice amounted to a pinnacle of deceit on the part of the United States and the European Western Allies which could hardly be surpassed. The position of the United States in this unsavory situation was somewhat modified by the American failure to ratify the Treaty of Versailles in 1919 and 1920. The Polish negotiators remained discredited at home because they had failed to achieve their original demands, which had been widely publicized in Poland.

An aspect of this situation especially pleasing to Pilsudski was the confused condition of Russia which caused the Allied diplomats to postpone the discussion of the eastern frontiers of Poland. Pilsudski was more interested in eastward expansion than in the westward expansion favored by Dmowski. The absence of any decisions at Paris concerning the *status quo* in the East gave Pilsudski a welcome opportunity to pursue his own program in that area.

The left-wing radical tide was rising with Poland, but Pilsudski was not unduly worried by this situation. He allowed the sincere Marxist, Moraczewski, to form a government. The government proclaimed an electoral decree on November 28, 1918, which provided for proportional representation and universal suffrage. Pilsudski secretly undermined the Government in every direction, and he encouraged his friends in the army to oppose it. He also knew that the National Democrats hated socialism, and played them off against Moraczewski.[53]

On January 4, 1919, while Roman Dmowski was in Paris, the National Democrats recklessly attempted to upset Moraczewski by a poorly planned *coup d'etat*. Pilsudski defended the Government, and the National Democrats lost prestige when their revolt was crushed.[54] Pilsudski did not relish the barter of parliamentary politics, but Walery Slawek, his good friend and political expert, did most of this distasteful work for him. This enabled Pilsudski to concentrate at an

early date on the Polish Army and Polish foreign policy, which were his two real
interests. Pilsudski won over many prominent opponents; he had earlier won the
support of Edward Smigly-Rydz, who directed the capture of Lwów (Lemberg)
from the Ukrainians in Novermber 1918. Smigly-Rydz later succeeded Pilsudski
as Marshal of Poland.[55]

There was action in many directions on the military front. A Slask-Pomorze-
Poznań (Silesia-West Prussia-Posen) Congress was organized by the National
Democrats on December 6, 1918, and it attempted to seize control of the
German eastern provinces in the hope of presenting the peace conference at
Paris with a *fait accompli*. Ignaz Paderewski arrived in Poznań a few weeks later
on a journey from London to Warsaw, and a Polish uprising broke out while he
was in this city. Afterward the Poles, in a series of bitter battles, drove the local
German volunteer militia out of most of Posen province.[56] The Germans in
January 1919 evacuated the ancient Lithuanian capital of Wilna (Wilno), and
Polish forces moved in. When the Bolshevik Armies began their own drive
through the area, the Poles lost Wilna, but the Germans stopped the Red advance
at Grodno on the Niemen River. The National Democrats controlled the Polish
Western Front and Pilsudski dominated the East. The National Democrats were
primarily interested in military action against Germany. Pilsudski's principal
interest was in Polish eastward expansion and in federation under Polish control
with neighboring nations.[57] On April 19, 1919, when the Poles recaptured
Wilna, a proclamation was issued by Pilsudski. It was not addressed, as a
National Democratic proclamation would have been, to the local Polish
community, but "to the people of the Grand Duchy of Lithuania." It referred
graciously to the presence of Polish forces in "your country." Pilsudski also
issued an invitation to the Ukrainians and White Russians to align themselves
with Poland. He intended to push his federalist policy while Russia was weak,
and to reduce Russian power to the minimum degree.[58]

Pilsudski's growing prestige in the East was bitterly resented by the National
Democrats. They denounced him from their numerous press organs as an anti-
clerical radical under the influence of the Jews. They argued with justification
that the country was unprepared for an extensive eastern military adventure.
They complained that the further acquisition of minorities would weaken the
state, and they concluded that Pilsudski was a terrible menace to Poland.
Pilsudski cleverly appealed to the anti-German prejudice of the followers of his
enemies. He argued that Russia and Germany were in a gigantic conspiracy to
crush Poland, and that to retaliate by driving back the Russians was the only
salvation. He tried in every way to stir up the enthusiasm of the weary Polish
people for his eastern plans.[59]

Pilsudski also did what he could to stem the rising Lithuanian nationalism
which objected to every form of union with Poland. By July 17, 1919, Polish
forces had driven the Ukrainian nationalist forces out of every corner of the
former Austrian territory of East Galicia. It was comparatively easy afterward
for Pilsudski to arrive at an agreement with Semyon Petlura, the Ukrainian
socialist leader who was hard pressed by the Bolsheviks. Petlura agreed that the
entire territory of Galicia should remain with Poland, and Pilsudski encouraged
the organization of new Ukrainian armed units.[60]

Pilsudski believed that Petlura would be more successful than Skoropadski, the earlier Ukrainian dictator, in enlisting Ukrainian support. He deliberated constantly on delivering a crushing blow against the Bolsheviks, who were hard pressed by the White Russian forces of General Denikin during most of 1919. He negotiated with Denikin, but he did not strike during 1919 on the plea that the Polish forces were not yet ready. He dreaded far more than Bolshevism a victorious White Russian regime, which would revive Russian nationalist aspirations in the West at the expense of Poland. [61]

While Pilsudski was planning and postponing his blow against the Bolsheviks, his prejudice against the parliamentary form of government was augmented by the first Sejm which had been elected on January 26, 1919. Two coalition groups of the National Democrats sent 167 deputies.[62] The Polish Peasant Party, which endorsed the foreign policy of Dmowski and denounced Pilsudski, elected 85 deputies.[63] These three groups of Pilsudski opponents occupied 260 of the 415 seats of the Sejm. Many of the other deputies, who were divided among a large number of parties, were either Germans or Jews. These election results were no chance phenomenon, but they represented a trend in Polish opinion which had developed over a long period. It was evident that this situation could not be changed without severe manipulation of the election system. No politician of Pilsudski's ambitions could admire an election system which demonstrated his own unpopularity. His natural inclination toward the authoritarian system was greatly increased by his experience with parliamentary politics in his own country.[64]

Dissatisfaction with the terms of the Versailles treaty was uppermost in Polish public opinion by June 1919. The Poles were in consternation at the prospect of a plebiscite in Upper Silesia. They had claimed that most of the inhabitants favored Poland, but they were secretly aware that the vast majority would vote for Germany in a free election. The Poles were also furious at the Allied inclination to support the Czechs in their attempt to secure by force the mixed ethnic area and rich industrial district of Teschen.[65]

Adalbert Korfanty, a veteran National Democratic leader, set out to accomplish Poland's purpose in Upper Silesia by terror and intimidation. The French commander of the Allied occupation force. General Le Rond, collborated with invading Polish filibuster forces. The Italian occupation forces stationed in Upper Silesia were attacked by the Poles and suffered heavy casualties because they sought to obstruct the illegal Polish advance. It was widely assumed in Poland during 1919 and 1920 that the desperate campaign in Upper Silesia would be futile. The unexpected Polish reward there was not received until 1922.[66]

These reverses suffered by the Poles in the West added to the demand for effective action in the East. Interest gradually increased during the latter part of 1919 while Pilsudski continued his preparations. The high nobility from the eastern territories led much agitation, but support for the program also had become noticeable in all parts of the country. Pilsudski concluded a second pact with Petlura in October 1919 which provided that further Ukrainian territory east of the old frontier between Russia and Austrian Galicia would become Polish, and, in addition, an independent Ukrainian state in the East would remain in close union with Poland. The collapse of Denikin in December 1919 was a signal to the Bolsheviks that they might soon expect trouble with Poland on a much larger scale than in the preceding sporadic hostilities which had extended from Latvia to the Ukraine. The Bolsheviks on January 28, 1920, offered Pilsudski a favorable armistice line in the hope of trading territory for time. Pilsudski was not impressed, despite the fact that the Western Allies disapproved of his plans. Pilsudski categorically informed the Allies on March 13, 1920, that he would demand from the Bolsheviks the right to dispose of the territory west of the 1772 Polish-Russian frontier. This frontier was far to the East of the line proposed by the Bolsheviks, and it was evident that a decisive conflict would ensue.[67]

Pilsudski and Petlura launched their offensive to drive the Bolsheviks from the Ukraine on April 26, 1920. The Skulski cabinet, which had followed earlier governments of Moraczewski and Paderewski, did not dare to oppose Pilsudski's plans, and Foreign Minister Patek openly approved Pilsudski's eastern program. The Polish troops under the command of General Smigly-Rydz scored conspicuous successes, and on May 8th a Polish patrol on a streetcar rode into the center of Kiev, the Ukrainian capital. A huge celebration of the Kiev victory took place in the St. Alexander church in Warsaw on May 18, 1920. Pilsudski was presented with the old victory laurels of Stephen Bathory and Wladislaw IV.[68]

Russia was less prostrate than in the 17th century "time of troubles (Smetnoye Vremya)," and dreams of Polish imperialism were soon smashed under the hoofs of Budenny's Red Army horses. The Russian counter-offensive strategy of outflanking the Poles was completely successful. The military reversals in the east created a cabinet crisis and the Skulski Government was forced to resign. On June 24, 1920, Wladislaw Grabski, a National Democrat and an opponent of Pilsudski, formed a government. His first step was to go to Belgium to plead with the Western Allied Command for aid. The Russians had penetrated deeply into Poland from two directions when Grabski arrived at Spa on July 10th. One of their armies had broken across the old Niemen defense line, and the other was driving on Lwów.

The poorly disciplined Russians had become totally disorganized by the rapidity of their advance, and the major commanders failed to cooperate because of petty jealousies. Pilsudski had the expert advice of General Maxime Weygand and other French officers when he directed the Poles to victory in the battle of Warsaw on August 16, 1920. The famous expression in Poland, "the miracle of the Vistula (cudnad Wisla)," was coined by Professor Stanislaw Stronski, a National Democrat, to suggest that any Polish victory under Pilsudski's leadership was a miracle.[69]

The Vistula victory brought tremendous prestige to Pilsudski, and it solidified his position as the strongest man in Poland, but the opponents of Pilsudski remained in office and the popular dissatisfaction with the war increased. Pilsudski was willing to strike eastward again after the Russian retreat, and to launch a second expedition against Kiev, but he knew this was an impossibility because of public opinion in war-torn Poland. Jan Dabski, who was selected by the Government as chief delegate to negotiate with the Russians, was a bitter critic of Pilsudski's policy and was influenced by Dmowski. Dmowski opposed the idea of federating with the White Russians and the Ukrainians, but he believed that Poland could assimilate a fairly large proportion of the people from the regions which had been under Polish rule in the past. Consequently, at the Riga peace in early 1921, the White Russian and Ukrainian areas were partitioned between the Soviet Union and Poland, with the bulk of both areas going to the Soviet Union. Federalism had been abandoned as an immediate policy, and the followers of Pilsudski resorted to Dmowski's program of assimilating the minorities.[70]

The Polish people who had been influenced by the romanticist ideas of Henryk Sienkiewicz, the popular Polish author, denounced the Riga peace as an abandonment of their ancient eastern territories. Pilsudski himself shared this view, and in a lecture on August 24, 1923, he blamed "the lack of moral strength of the nation" for the Polish failure to conquer the Ukraine following the victory at Warsaw in 1920.[71]

The Dmowski disciples chafed at their failure to realize many of their aspirations against Germany in the West. It seemed that no one in Poland was satisfied with the territorial limits attained by the new state, although most foreign observers, whether friendly or hostile, believed that Poland had obtained far more territory than was good for her. It soon became evident that the post-war course of Polish expansion had closed with the Riga peace, and with the partition of Upper Silesia. Poland had reached the limits of her ability to exploit the confusion which had followed in the wake of World War I. Her choices were to accept her gains as sufficient and to seek to retain all or most of them, or to bide her time while awaiting a new opportunity to realize her unsatisfied ambitions. The nature of her future foreign policy depended on the outcome of the struggle for power within Poland.

The Czechs during the Russo-Polish war had consolidated their control over most of the rich Teschen industrial district, and the Lithuanians, with the conni-vance of the Bolsheviks, had recovered Wilna. The Czechs were extremely popu-lar with the Allies, and enjoyed strong support from France. The Czech leaders also had expressed their sympathy and friendship toward Bolshevik Russia in strong terms during the recent Russo-Polish war, and they had done what they could to prevent Allied war material from reaching Poland. The Poles were un-able to revenge themselves upon the Czechs immediately, but, when the League of Nations awarded Wilna to Lithuania on October 8, 1920, local Polish forces under General Zeligowski seized the ancient capital of Lithuania on orders from Pilsudski. The Lithuanians received no support from the League of Nations. They refused to recognize the Polish seizure, and they protested by withdrawing their diplomatic representatives from Poland and by closing their Polish frontier. The Soviet-Polish frontier also was virtually closed, and a long salient of Polish territory in the North-East extended as far as the Dvina River and Latvia without normal economic outlets. The Lithuanians revenged themselves upon the League of Nations, which had failed to support them, by seizing the German city of Memel, which had been placed under a League protectorate similar to the one established at Danzig in 1920. It was a sad reflection on the impotence of the German Reich that a tiny new-born nation could seize an ancient Prussian city, and it also indicated the problematical nature of Woodrow Wilson's cherished international organization, the League of Nations.[72]

The Pilsudski Dictatorship

Years of reconstruction followed in Poland, and for a considerable time there
was much talk of sweeping economic and social reforms. Poland in March 1921
adopted a democratic constitution, which lacked the approval of Pilsudski. The
constant shift of party coalitions always hostile to his policies irritated him, and
the assassination immediately after the election of 1922 of his friend, President
Gabriel Narutowicz, did not improve matters. Pilsudski, whose prestige remained
enormous, bided his time for several years, and he consolidated his control over
the army. Finally, in May 1926 he seized a pretext to overthrow the existing
regime. A recent shift in the party coalitions had brought his sworn enemy,
Wincenty Witos, back to the premiership, and the subsequent sudden dismissal
of Foreign Minister Alexander Skrzyński, in whom Pilsudski had publicly
declared his confidence, was considered a sufficient provocation. Pilsudski
grimly ordered his cohorts to attack the existing regime, and, after a brief civil
war, he was able to take control. Fortunately for Pilsudski, Dmowski was a great
thinker, but no man of action. The divided opponents of the new violence were
reduced to impotence.[73]

These events were too much even for the nationalists among the Polish socialists, and the break between Pilsudski and his former Party was soon complete.
This meant that Pilsudski had no broad basis of popular support in the country,
although he had obtained control of the army by gaining the confidence of its
officers. He was feared and respected, but not supported, by the political parties
of Poland. It seemed possible to attain the support of the Conservatives, but
they required the pledge that he would not attack their economic interests. This
pledge would be tantamount to the rejection of popular demands for economic
reform.

Pilsudski at an October 1926 conference in Nieswicz arrived at a far-reaching
agreement with the great Conservative landowners led by Prince Eustachy
Sapieha, Count Artur Potocki, and Prince Albrecht Radziwill. On this occasion,
Stanislaw Radziwill, a hero of the 1920 war from a famous family, was awarded
posthumously the *Virtuti Militari*, which was the highest decoration the new
state could bestow. Pilsudski declared himself to be neither a man of party nor
of social class, but the representative of the entire nation. His hosts in turn
graciously insisted that Pilsudski's family background placed him equal among
them, not only as a noble, but as a representative of the higher nobility.[74]

The effect of these negotiations was soon apparent. In December 1925 a land
reform law had been passed calling for the redistribution of up to five million
acres of land annually for a period of ten years. Most of the land subdivided by
the Government was taken from the Germans and distributed among the Poles.
This intensified minority grievances by depriving thousands of German
agricultural laborers of their customary employment with German landowners.
Nothing was done on the agricultural scene to cope with the pressing problem of
rural overpopulation in Poland. The Polish peasantry was increasing at a more
rapid rate than the urbanites, and the city communities, with their relatively
small population, could not absorb the increase. The backward Polish system of
agriculture, except on a few of the largest estates, and the absence of extensive
peasant land ownership in many areas, increased the inevitable hardship of the

two decades of reconstruction which followed World War I. The large number of holdings so small as to be totally inadequate was about the same in 1939 as it had been in 1921. The regime after 1926 increased the speed of the reallocation of the most poorly distributed small holdings, but the scope of this policy was minor in relation to the total farm problem. The Peasant Party leaders, who were soon persecuted by Pilsudski for their opposition to his regime, were regarded as martyrs in the Polish countryside, where the new system was denounced with hatred.[75]

The Polish socialists had sufficiently consolidated their influence over the urban workers by the time of Pilsudski's *coup d' état* to control most of the municipal elections. The socialist leaders turned against Pilsudski, and chronic industrial unemployment and scarce money embittered the Polish urban scene. The industrialization of Congress Poland had proceeded rapidly during the two generations before World War I, and progress in textiles was especially evident. The Russian market was lost as a result of the war, and Polish exports were slow to climb tariff barriers abroad, while low purchasing power restricted the home market. Profits in Polish industry were not sufficient to attract truly large foreign investments, although much of the existing industry was under foreign capitalistic control. Despite a 25% increase in the population of Poland between 1913 and 1938, the Polish volume of industrial products passed the 1913 level only in 1938, and the volume of real wages in Poland had still failed to do so. As a result of economic stagnation, the new regime was able to offer the Poles very little to distract them from their political discontent.[76]

These unfavorable conditions illustrate the situation of the Polish regime on the domestic front, and they offer a parallel to the unfavorable relations of Poland with most of her neighbors in the years immediately after 1926, and especially with the Soviet Union, Germany, Czechoslovakia, and Lithuania. The domestic and foreign scenes presented a perpetual crisis which accustomed the Polish leadership to maintain its composure, and to develop an astonishing complacency under adverse conditions. Roman Dmowski on the home front in December 1926 directly challenged Pilsudski's claim to represent the nation by establishing his own Camp of Great Poland. For nearly four years this organization dominated the ideological scene. It demanded the improvement of relations with Russia, the permanent renunciation of federalism, the intensification of nationalism, a program to assimilate the minorities, and a plan to expel the Jews.[77]

Pilsudski retaliated with great severity on September 10, 1930, by means of a purge organized by Walery Slawek. No one dared to silence Dmowski, but Pilsudski deprived him of many followers, and adopted many of his ideas. The arrest of opposition leaders, the use of the concentration camp system, and the adoption of terroristic tactics during elections intimidated the opposition at least temporarily. A new coalition of Government supporters was able to obtain 247 of 444 seats in the Sejm elected in November 1930. This was the first major election won by Pilsudski.[78]

There was much talk about a governing clique of colonels in Poland, and many of the principal advisers and key officials of the new regime held that rank. This situation reflected Pilsudski's policy of rewarding his military collaborators and disciples. These men were intensely loyal, and their admiration

for their chief, whom they regarded as infallible, knew no limits. They
energetically adopted Dmowski's campaign against the minorities, and they discussed many plans for a new constitution which would buttress the executive
power and reverse the democratic principles of the 1921 document. It was
claimed that the 1921 constitution had been constructed with a jealous eye on
Pilsudski, and that this explained its purpose in placing extraordinary limits on
the executive power, and in providing for a weak president on the French
model.[79]

The key to the 1935 document, of which Walery Slawek was the chief
author, was a presidency sufficiently powerful to "place the government in one
house," and to control all branches of the state, including the Sejm, the Senate,
the armed forces, the police, and the courts of justice. The president also was
given wide discretionary powers in determining his successor.[80]

The Polish Dictatorship After Pilsudski's Death

Pilsudski died of cancer in May 1935 at the comparatively early age of sixty-
eight. This raised the question of the succession in the same year that the new
constitution was promulgated, and Walery Slawek hoped to become the Polish
strong man. He was widely regarded as the most able of Pilsudski's collaborators,
and the conspiracy of the other disciples against him has often been regarded as
a major cause of the misfortunes which soon overtook Poland. A carefully organized coalition, which was originally based on an understanding between Ignaz
Mościcki, the Polish scientist in politics, and Edward Smigly-Rydz, the military
leader, succeeded in isolating Slawek and in eliminating his influence. The constitution of 1935 had been designed by Slawek for one powerful dictator, but
the new collective dictatorship was able to operate under it for the next few
years. Walery Slawek committed suicide in April 1939, when it seemed increasingly probable that the collective leadership would submerge the new Polish
state in disaster.[81]

There is an impressive analysis of the new Polish state by Colonel Ignacy
Matuszewski, one of Pilsudski's principal disciples. It was written shortly after
the death of the Marshal. It reads more like an obituary than a clarion call to a
system lasting and new, and its author is extraordinarily preoccupied with the
personality and actions of Pilsudski at the expense of current problems and the
road ahead. In this respect the book mirrored the trend of the era, because this
was indeed the state of mind of the *epigoni* who ruled Poland from 1935 to
1939.

Matuszewski was editor of the leading Government newspaper, *Gazeta
Polska*, from 1931 to 1936, and later he was president of the Bank of Warsaw,
the key financial organ of the regime. Originally he had been a disciple of
Dmowski and an officer in the Tsarist forces, but he gladly relinquished both for
the Pilsudski cause in 1917. He was one of the heroes in the 1920-1921 war
with Russia, and he remained with the Army until the *coup d' état* of 1926,
which he favored. He had an important part in Polish diplomacy both in Warsaw
and abroad during the years from 1926 to 1931.[82]

His book, *Próby Syntez* (*Trial Synthesis*), appeared in 1937. It defined the

Polish regime ideologically and explained its aims. The author's thought, like Roman Dmowski's, was influenced mainly by the political philosophy of Hegel.[83]

Matuszewski declared that it was the will of the Polish nation to secure and maintain its national freedom. He believed that only the condition of the Polish race would decide Poland's ability to exercise this will. He added that the extraordinary achievement of one man had simplified Polish endeavors. He listed 1905, 1914, 1918, 1920, and 1926 as the years in which Pilsudski raised Poland from oblivion. In 1905, during a major Russian revolution, Pilsudski led the Polish radical struggle against Russia. In 1914 he led the Polish military struggle against Russia. In 1918 he returned from Magdeburg to arrange for the evacuation of Poland by the Germans. In 1920 he led the Poles to victory over Communist Russia. In 1926 he crushed the conflicting elements at home and unified Poland.[84]

Matuszewski ominously warned his readers that the Polish national struggle of the 20th century had scarcely begun when Pilsudski died. He insisted that Poland had far-reaching problems to solve both at home and abroad. He described the 1926 *coup d' état* as an important step on the home front, and as a victory over anarchy. He declared that the first Sejm had shown that Poland could not afford to surrender the executive power to legislative authority. He extolled the 1935 constitution which invested the basic power in the presidency. He maintained that unless the government of Poland was kept in one building (i.e., unless central control was completely simplified), the country would have civil war instead of domestic peace.

Matuszewski argued, as did other advocates of authoritarian systems, that the Polish regime retained a truly democratic character. He praised the Government for an allegedly enlightened awareness of the traditional past, in contrast to the Dmowski group, and for an awareness of the traditional needs of Poland. He also argued that the fixed ideological dogmas of such other authoritarian regimes as Russia, Italy, and Germany deprived them of flexibility in responding to popular needs, and consequently gave them an "aristocratic character" which he claimed Poland lacked. he described the constitutional regime of 1935 as a "traditional synthesis" and not an arbitrary system.[85]

It was to his credit that Matuszewski did not claim a broad basis of popular support for the existing Polish system. He did assume from his theory of statism that it would eventually be possible to bridge the gulf between the wishes of the citizens and the policy of the state without sacrificing the essential principles of the system. Matuszewski regarded his book, his numerous articles, and his editorials as contributions to an educational process which would one day accomplish this.

Matuszewski denied any affinity between Poland and the other authoritarian states or Western liberal regimes. He proclaimed Polish originality in politics to be a precious heritage for all Poles who cared to appreciate it. It was not his purpose to cater to whims and fancies, but to reshape mistaken systems of values. The people would not be allowed to impose their will on the new Polish state, either in domestic affairs or foreign policy. Whatever happened would be the responsibility of the small clique governing the nation.[86]

Matuszewski neglected to mention that there were people in Poland not opposed to the regime who regarded the future with misgiving for quite another reason. They feared that the governing clique lacked the outstanding leadership necessary to promote the success of any system, whatever its theoretical foundations.

The new Polish state on the domestic front faced many grave problems arising from unfavorable economic conditions, the dissatisfaction of minorities, and the general unpopularity of the regime. The situation was precarious, but far from hopeless. Within the context of a cautious and conservative foreign policy, which was indispensable under the circumstances, the Polish state might have strengthened its position without outstanding leadership. It was indisputable that foreign policy was the most crucial issue facing Poland when Pilsudski died.

If Poland allowed herself, despite her awareness of past history, to become the instrument of the old and selfish balance of power system of distant Great Britain, if she rejected comprehensive understandings with her greater neighbors, and if she became involved in conflicts beyond her own strength, her future would bring terrible disappointments. The new Polish state could not possibly survive under these circumstances.

The issue can merely be suggested at this point. Later it will become clear how great were the opportunities, and how much was lost. The situation, despite its problems, held promise when Pilsudski died.

Chapter 2

THE ROOTS OF POLISH POLICY

Pilsudski's Inconclusive German Policy

The Polish Government was concerned on the home front from 1935 to 1939 with plans for the industrialization of Poland, and in doing what could be done to gain popular support for the regime. These endeavors were relatively simple compared to the conduct of Polish foreign policy during the same period. There was a mystery in Polish foreign policy: what was the real Polish attitude toward Germany? An answer is necessary in explaining all other aspects of Polish policy. This question does not apply to the early period of the new Polish state because there was no real chance for a Polish-German understanding during the 1919-1933 period of the German Weimar Republic. The weakness of the Weimar Republic would automatically have confined any understanding to the *status quo* established by the Treaty of Versailles, and Poland made several overtures to reach an agreement with Germany on this basis. These overtures were futile, because the leaders of the Weimar Republic considered that the *status quo* of 1919 was intolerable for Germany.[1]

The situation changed before Pilsudski died. Germany became stronger, and relations between Germany and Poland improved after a ten year non-aggression pact was concluded by the two countries on January 26, 1934. This non-aggression pact failed to include German recognition of the 1919 *status quo*, but the Polish leaders no longer expected Germany to recognize it. It was under-stood among Pilsudski's entourage that Hitler was more moderate about this question than his predecessors. It also was clear by 1935 that Hitler desired more than a mere truce with Poland. He recognized the key position of Poland in the East, and he was aiming at a policy of close collaboration. This had become one of his most important goals.[2]

It was current Polish policy when Pilsudski died in 1935 to place relations with Germany and the Soviet Union on an equal basis. This was not what Hitler had in mind. Polish policy seemed to remain unchanged during the following

years while Germany continued to recover her former strength. It was questionable if the Polish leaders would permit any change in policy toward Germany.

German foreign policy from 1933 to 1939 emphasized the need to cope with
the alleged danger to European civilization from Bolshevism. This was less vital
to Hitler than the recovery of German power, but the steps he took to revise the
Paris peace treaties of 1919 were explained as measures necessary to strengthen
Germany and Europe against Bolshevism.[3] The position of Poland between
Germany and the Soviet Union indicated that Hitler would require complete
clarity about Polish policy. Poland's unfortunate geographical position made an
ambiguous Polish policy the one thing which Hitler could not tolerate indefinitely. The Polish leaders recognized at an early date that Poland would be
compelled to choose between the roles of friendly neighbor or enemy of
Germany. The choice was not a foregone conclusion if Hitler was prepared to be
generous to Poland, and by 1939 the Polish diplomats were in disagreement
about this crucial issue. They wished to treat the problem as Pilsudski would
have done, but it was impossible to fulfill indefinitely the intentions of their
deceased leader. Conditions continued to change after his death.

An American parallel offers an illustration of this problem. President Roosevelt issued instructions for the use of atomic weapons while Germany was still
participating in World War II. He died before the end of war with Germany.
President Truman claimed to be following Roosevelt's policy when he ordered
the use of atomic weapons against Japan in August 1945, but neither he nor his
advisers knew whether Roosevelt would have permitted this atrocity after the
unconditional surrender of Germany. This is another example of the dilemma
presented to *epigoni* by changing circumstances.[4]

Pilsudski was renowned for his ability to adapt his policies to changing
circumstances. If he had died in 1932, his successors would never have known
whether or not he would have concluded the non-aggression pact of 1932 with
Germany. It was impressive when the followers of Pilsudski spoke of carrying
out the policies of the dead Marshal. In reality, they had to conduct their own
policies. It would be a disadvantage whenever they thought they were responding to the wishes of Pilsudski. Independent judgment is the most essential
attribute of foreign policy. Nothing is more fatal for it than the weight of a
dead man's hand.

The Career of Józef Beck

The leadership of Poland was collective after 1935, but primary responsibility
for the conduct of foreign policy rested with Colonel Józef Beck. He was
appointed foreign minister in 1932. He held this post until the Polish collapse
in 1939, and he considered no one in Poland to be his equal in the field of
foreign relations.[5]

Beck was descended from a Lower German family which had emigrated to
Poland several hundred years earlier. His affluent father had conspired against
the Russians and had been imprisoned by them. His mother came from a family
of land-owning gentry in the region of Cholm. Beck was born at Warsaw in 1894,
but he received his earliest impressions in the German cultural environment of

Riga, where his family moved shortly after his birth. The family soon decided to elude the persecutions of the Russians altogether, and in 1900 they moved to Austrian Galicia.

Beck went to school in Kraków and Lwów, and he improved his contact with the Germans by a period of study in Vienna. He was nineteen years of age when World War I came. He had no political affiliations, but he decided at once to join Pilsudski's Forces. He followed Pilsudski's line of opposing the Polish Council of State in 1917, and he was interned by the Germans. He was released when he offered to join a Hungarian regiment. His admiration for the Magyars was increased by military service with them. He became intimately acquainted during this period with the Carpatho-Ukrainian area, which acquired decisive importance for Poland in 1938. He returned to service in the Polish Army at the end of World War I, and he participated in the Russo-Polish War of 1920-1921. He achieved distinction in this war, and he was frequently in close personal contact with Pilsudski in the fighting along the Niemen River during the autumn of 1920. A military alliance was concluded between France and Poland shortly before the close of the Russo-Polish War, and Beck was selected to represent the Polish Army in France as military attaché.[6]

Beck was satisfied to remain with the Army, and he was on active service until after the *coup d' état* of 1926. Pilsudski then selected him as his principal assistant in conducting the business of the War Office, which was personally directed by the Marshal. Pilsudski was disconcerted in 1930 by the inclination of Foreign Minister Zaleski to take the League of Nations seriously. It was evident that a change was required. Pilsudski recognized the problematical character of League pretensions, although he admitted that they could sometimes be exploited for limited purposes. He decided that Beck should terminate his military career, and enter diplomacy. He knew that he could trust Beck to share his views. Beck was appointed Under-Secretary of State at the Polish Foreign Office in December 1930. He succeeded Zaleski as Foreign Minister in November 1932.[7]

Beck's ability to get on well with Pilsudski for many years reveals much about his personality. He had a sense of humor, and an ability to distinguish between pretentious sham and reality. His successful career also reveals personal bravery, a good education, and extensive administrative experience. He had personal charm and sharpness of intellect. He had never known reverses in his career, and he possessed a supreme degree of confidence in his own abilities. This success was a weakness, because it made Beck arrogant and disinclined to accept advice from others after Pilsudski's death. The relationship between Pilsudski and Beck was based on the prototypes of father and son, with Beck in the role of the gifted, but slightly spoiled son.

Pilsudski appointed Count Jan Szembek to succeed Beck as Under-secretary of State at the Polish Foreign Office. Szembek was the brother-in-law of an earlier Polish Foreign Minister, Count Skrzyński, who had been a favorite of the Marshal. Szembek had acquired valuable experience as a diplomat of Austria-Hungary, and after 1919 he had represented Poland at Budapest, Brussels, and Bucharest. Pilsudski relied on Szembek to exert a steadying influence on Beck. It was unfortunate that Beck usually ignored Szembek's advice during the difficult months prior to the outbreak of World War II.[8]

The Hostility between Weimar Germany and Poland

The improvement of German-Polish relations after 1934 contrasted with the enmity which had existed between the two nations during the preceding years.[9] A German-Polish trade war had begun in 1925 shortly before Pilsudski took power in Poland. This was an especially severe economic blow to Poland, because 43.2% of Polish exports had gone to Germany in 1924, and 34.5% of Polish imports had been received from the Germans. A trade treaty was finally signed by Germany and Poland in March 1930. It would have mitigated some of the hardship caused by five years of economic warfare, but it was rejected by the German Reichstag.[10]

The Locarno treaties of October 16, 1925, were considered to be a diplomatic defeat for Poland. They provided for the guarantee of the German borders with Belgium and France, and for the improvement of German relations with those two Powers. The Poles at Locarno raised the question of a German guarantee of the Polish frontiers without success. It was easy for German Foreign Minister Gustav Stresemann to convice the British and French that such a guarantee would be an impossibility for Germany. This event terminated the uniform treatment of all European frontiers under the Paris treaties, and it produced a distinction between favored western and second-class eastern frontiers. This distinction implied a victory for the doctrine of eastern territorial revision in favor of Germany.[11]

The 1926 Russo-German Treaty of Friendship followed Locarno, and if offered a basis for the coordination of Russian and German programs of territorial revision at Poland'a expense. The Russians had urged an anti-Polish understanding since the economic agreement of 1922 with the Germans at Rapallo. Stresemann gave the Russians an explicit assurance after Locarno that Germany planned to conduct her territorial revision at Poland's expense in close collaboration with the Soviet Union.[12]

The British considered themselves free of any obligation to defend the Poles against German or Russian revisionism. Sir Austen Chamberlain, the British Foreign Secretary at the time of Locarno, paraphrased Bismarck when he said that the eastern questions were not worth the bones of a single British grenadier. Poland had her 1921 military pact with France, but the Allied evacuation of the Rhineland in 1930 modified the earlier assumption that French military power was omnipresent in Europe. Pilsudski distrusted the French, and he resented their policy of favoring the Czechs over Poland. He was convinced that Czechoslovakia would not survive as an independent state.[13]

Relations between Russia and Poland appeared to improve somewhat after 1928 and the inauguration of the Soviet First Five Year Plan, which absorbed Russian energies in gigantic changes on the domestic front. An additional factor was Russian preoccupation with the Far East after the Russo-Chinese War of 1929 and the Japanese invasion of Manchuria in 1931.[14] This trend culminated in the 1932 Russo-Polish non-agression pact, and in the understanding that the Soviet Union would not aid Germany in a German-Polish conflict.[15] The Russians were not informed that the Polish-Rumanian alliance of 1921 was directed exclusively against the Soviet Union. They made no inquiries about the alliance when they signed their treaty with Poland. This was natural, because the initiative for the Russo-Polish treaty came from Russia.[16]

The policy of Poland toward Germany during the last years of the Weimar Republic was a combination of threats and an effort to keep Germany impotent. Polish Foreign Minister Zaleski told the President of the Danzig Senate in September 1930 that only a Polish army corps could solve the Danzig question.[17] The Bruening Government in Berlin frankly feared a Polish attack during 1931.[18] The general disarmament conference opened at Geneva in February 1932 after a twelve year delay. Poland opposed the disarmament of the Allied nations or the removal of restrictions on German arms contained in the Treaty of Versailles. It was feared at Geneva that Pilsudski's decision to send the warship *Wicher* to Danzig in June 1932 was a Polish plot to seize Danzig in the fashion of the earlier Lithuanian seizure of Memel. Pilsudski received many warnings against action of this kind. Pilsudski was merely intimidating the Germans. He would have liked to take Danzig, but he considered the step impossible while the West was conducting a policy of conciliation toward Germany.[19]

Pilsudski's Plans for Preventive War against Hitler

Adolf Hitler was appointed German Chancellor by President Paul von Hindenburg on January 30, 1933. Pilsudski regarded Hitler as less dangerous to Poland than his immediate predecessors, Papen and Schleicher, but the Polish policy of hostility toward Germany went further in 1933 than in 1932. This was because Pilsudski viewed the appointment of Hitler as an effective pretext for Allied action against Germany. Pilsudski's 1933 plans for preventive war against the Germans have been a controversial topic for many years, and there have been impressive efforts to refute the contention that Pilsudski did have such plans.[20] The question remained in doubt until 1958. Lord Vansittart, with the approval of the British Government, revealed the authenticity of the Pilsudski war proposals of 1933 twenty-five years after the event. He observed that Pilsudski's plans were "an idea, of which too little has been heard."[21] Vansittart believed that a war against Germany in 1933 might have been won with about 30,000 casualties. He added that in World War II Hitler was "removed at a cost of 30,000,000 lives."[22] Vansittart revealed that the opposition of the British Government to the plans in 1933 was the decisive factor in discouraging the French, and in prompting them to reject a preventive war.[23] It should be added that Pilsudski's willingness to throttle a weak Germany in 1933 provides no clue to the policy he might have pursued toward a strong Germany in 1939.

Hitler told a British correspondent on February 12, 1933, that the *status quo* in the Polish Corridor contained injustices for Germany which would have to be removed. The Conservative Government in Danzig several days later adopted a defiant attitude toward Poland in a dispute concerning the mixed Danzig-Polish Harbor Police Commission. News of these events reached Pilsudski at the vacation resort of Pikiliszi in Northern Poland. He decided to conduct a demonstration against the Germans at the worst possible moment for them, on the day following their national election of March 5, 1933. The Polish warship *Wilja* disembarked Polish troops at the Westerplatte arsenal in Danzig harbor during

the early morning of March 6, 1933. Kasimierz Papée, the Polish High Commissioner in Danzig, informed Helmer Rosting, the Danish League High Commissioner, that the Polish step countered recent allegedly threatening events in
Danzig. The Poles, it should be noted, were inclined to distort the demonstrations of the local National Socialist SA (Storm Units) as troop movements.
Pilsudski supported his first move several days later by concentrating Polish
troops in the Corridor. His immediate objective was to occupy East Prussia with
the approval and support of France.[24]

Hitler was not inclined to take the Polish threat seriously despite warnings
from Hans Adolf von Moltke, the German Minister at Warsaw. The German
generals were worried about possible aggressive Polish action, and they reported
to Defense Minister Werner von Blomberg that Germany had almost no chance
in a war against Poland. This would even be true if Poland attacked without
allies. The Danzig authorities enlisted British support against Poland at Geneva,
and Sir John Simon, the British Foreign Secretary, delivered a sharply critical
speech to Józef Beck in the League Council. The Danzig authorities promised to
conciliate Poland in the issues of current dispute, and Beck announced on March
14, 1933, that Poland would soon withdraw her reinforcements from Danzig.[25]

The internal situation in Germany was calm again at this juncture, and Hitler
turned his attention to relations with Poland. He launched efforts to conciliate
the Poles and to win their confidence, and these became permanent features of
his policy. He intervened directly in Danzig affairs to establish quiet, and he
endeavored to win the Poles by direct assurances. These efforts were temporarily
and unintentionally frustrated by Mussolini's Four Power Pact Plan of March
17, 1933, which envisaged revision for Germany at Polish expense in the hope of
diverting the Germans from their interest in Austria. Pilsudski responded by
resuming his plans for military action against Germany in April 1933. A series
of unfortunate incidents contributed to the tension. A wave of persecution
against the Germans living in Poland culminated in 'Black Palm Sunday' at Łódź
on April 9, 1933. German property was damaged, and local Germans suffered
beatings and humiliations.[26]

Hitler adopted a positive attitude toward the Four Power Pact Plan because
he admired Mussolini and desired to improve relations with his Western
neighbors, but he explained in a communiqué of May, 1933, that he did not
intend to exploit this project to obtain concessions from Poland. This announcement followed a conversation of Hitler and German Foreign Minister Konstantin
von Neurath with the Polish Minister at Berlin. The conversation convinced
Hitler that it might be possible to reach an understanding with Poland.

The Four Power Pact (Great Britain, France, Germany and Italy) was signed
on June 7, 1933, but French reservations rendered it useless. This did not
prevent the Poles from regarding the Pact as a continuation of Locarno
diplomacy at the expense of Poland. Józef Beck condemned the Four Power
Pact on June 8, 1933. Hitler's assurances in May 1933 had produced some effect
and Beck did not direct any special criticism toward Germany.[27]

The ultimate aims of German policy in Eastern Europe were never clearly defined, but Hitler was shaping a definite policy toward Poland. Hitler had said
little about Poland from 1930 to 1933 while the National Socialists were rapidly
increasing their influence in Germany prior to heading the Government. It was

widely assumed that Hitler was anti-Polish because his chief ideological spokes-man, Alfred Rosenberg, had written a book, *Die Zukunft einer deutschen Aussenpolitik (A Future German Foreign Policy,* Munich, 1927), which con-tained a number of sharply anti-Polish observations. Hitler in 1933 exper-ienced no difficulty in correcting the views of Rosenberg, a mild-mannered and devoted subordinate, and he began to combat the wishes of the German Army and German Foreign Office for an anti-Polish and pro-Soviet policy. Hitler began to envisage a full-scale alliance between Germany and Poland. He termin-ated the last military ties between Russia and Germany in the autumn of 1933, and military collaboration between the two countries became a thing of the past. The political situation within Danzig was clarified by the election of May 28, 1933. The National Socialists obtained the majority of votes, and they formed a Government. Hitler in the future could exert the decisive influence in that crucial and sensitive area.[28]

It gradually became apparent that Polish fears of an anti-Polish policy under Hitler were without foundation. King Gustav V of Sweden had predicted to the Poles that this would be the case. The Swedish monarch was aware of foreign policy statements made to prominent Swedes by Hermann Goering, the number 2 National Socialist leader of Germany. Goering had realized that Hitler was not inclined toward an anti-Polish policy long before this was evident to the world.[29]

On May 30, 1933, Pilsudski announced the appointment of Józef Lipski as Polish Minister to Berlin. Lipski was born in Germany of Polish parents in 1894. He was friendly toward Germany, and he favored German-Polish cooperation. His appointment was a hint that Pilsudski wished to support Hitler's efforts to improve relations with Poland. Under-Secretary Jan Szembek presented a favorable report on recent developments in Germany after a visit in August 1933, and discussions were held in Warsaw and Berlin to improve German-Polish trade relations.[30]

A last crisis in German-Polish relations in 1933 took place when Hitler with-drew Germany from the League of Nations. This step on October 19, 1933, was a response to the Simon disarmament plan of October 14th which denied Germany equality nearly twenty-one months after the opening of the disarma-ment conference. Pilsudski could not resist this opportunity of returning to his plans for military action while Germany was weak, and history would have taken a different course had the French supported his plans. Hitler was extremely worried by the possibility of retaliation against Germany. He urged the other German leaders to exercise extreme caution in their utterances on foreign affairs, and on every possible occasion he insisted that Germany was dedicated to policies of peace and international cooperation.

The 1934 German-Polish Non-Aggression Pact

An important meeting took place between Hitler and Lipski on November 15, 1933. The French had refused to support Pilsudski in a war against Germany. Hitler gave new assurances of his desire for friendship with Poland. A sensation was caused on the following day by a German-Polish communiqué which announced the intention of the two countries to conclude a non-aggression pact. The Czechs since May 1933 had enjoyed the prospect of an improvement in German-Polish relations which would exacerbate relations between Paris and Warsaw.[31] The Czech envoys in Berlin and Warsaw after November 16, 1933, confirmed these expectations which had first been expressed by Stephan Osusky, the Minister of Prague at Paris.[32]

Pilsudski hesitated once more in December 1933 before he gave his final order to conclude the Pact. His attitude toward the treaty at the time of signature was frankly cynical. He believed that the Pact might postpone a day of reckoning between Germany and Poland, but he doubted if it would endure for the ten year period specified in its terms. He believed it could be used to strengthen the diplomatic position of Poland. The Czechs were right about French resentment toward Poland, but they were wrong in their expectation that France would react by ignoring Polish interests. France cultivated closer relations with Poland after January 1934 in a manner which had been unknown in earlier years.[33]

Hitler regarded the Pact as a personal triumph over the German Foreign Office, the German Army, and the German Conservatives. The role of President von Hindenburg was important in questions of foreign policy until his death in August 1934, and Hindenburg was identified with the groups hostile toward Hitler. Hitler had succeeded in convincing the old President that an improvement in relations with Poland was a wise step. He promised him that no proposals for eventual German-Polish action against Russia had been made in connection with the Pact.[34]

Hitler knew that the non-aggression pact was merely a first step in his courtship of Poland. This fact received emphasis from Beck's visit to Moscow in February 1934. No other Polish visit of this kind took place during the period from World War I to World War II, and Beck's visit was a deliberate demonstration. The purpose of the visit was to show that Poland was maintaining impartiality in her own relations with Russia and Germany while Russo-German relations were deteriorating.[35]

A series of practical agreements were concluded between Germany and Poland after Beck returned from Russia. These concerned border traffic, radio broadcasts, activities of journalists in the respective countries, and the exchange of currency. The world was much impressed by the sensible pattern of German-Polish relations in contrast to the earlier period. The 1934 Pact doubtless increased the prestige of both Germany and Poland. It would be difficult to determine which country received the greater benefit. The Poles were not willing to attack Germany without French aid, which was not available. The Germans were powerless to revise the Versailles Treaty by force. A policy of German collaboration with the Russians might have hurt the Poles, and a policy of Polish collaboration with the Czechs might have injured Germany. These alternative policies were discussed in various quarters, but both would have been difficult to implement at the time. The Pact was an asset to both parties, and it brought approximately equal benefits to both.

Jan Szembek played in important role on behalf of the Pact on the Polish side with his conversations in Germany and the Western countries. A similar role was played on the German side by Joseph Goebbels, German Minister of Propaganda and Public Enlightenment.[36] Beck accepted an invitation to discuss current problems at Geneva with Goebbels and German Foreign Minister von Neurath in the autumn of 1933. Beck later observed that the motive "of knowing his adversaries" was sufficient to prompt his acceptance. Beck and Goebbels communicated without difficulty, and the Polish Foreign Minister was not offended when the German propaganda expert referred to the League as " a modern tower of Babel." Beck explained that Poland intended to remain in the League, but she had no objection to bilateral pacts which ignored the League. Goebbels assured Beck that Hitler was prepared to renounce war as an instrument of German policy toward Poland, and to recognize the importance to Poland of the Franco-Polish alliance. Beck agreed not to raise the question of a German guarantee of the Polish frontier. The clarification of these points was decisive for the conclusion of the Pact.[37]

Joseph Goebbels came to Warsaw in the summer of 1934, and his visit was a great success. Hermann Goering began a series of annual visits to Poland in the autumn of the same year. The exchange of views in 1934 between Goering and the Polish leaders on the Czech situation and the German and Polish minorities of Czechoslovakia was especially significant. Goering criticized the contrast between the liberal Czech facade, and the actual stern police policies directed against the Germans, Poles, Slovaks, Hungarians, and Ruthenians. Pilsudski assured Goering that the Czechs were neither respected nor loved in Poland. Goering advocated an alliance between Poland and Germany within a common anti-Soviet front, but Pilsudski displayed no inclination to coordinate Polish policy with German aims in the East. He evaded Goering's suggestion by observing that Poland was pursuing a policy of moderation toward Russia.[38]

Beck's Position Strengthened by Pilsudski

Beck attempted to follow up the 1934 Pact by securing Polish equality with the Great Powers. He insisted that Poland, "in all objectivity," was a Great Power, and he retaliated against all slights received by Polish leaders. He had visited Paris shortly after his own appointment as Polish Foreign Minister, but he had not been received at the railroad station by French Foreign Minister Joseph Paul Boncour. Louis Barthou, a later French Foreign Minister sincerely admired by Beck, visited Warsaw in April 1934. Beck refused to meet him at the station, and he evidently enjoyed this opportunity to settle accounts. It was not surprising that a sharp note of tension pervaded the Warsaw atmosphere during the Barthou visit.[39]

Beck had another reason for dissatisfaction at this time. He had tried in vain to secure an agreement from the League Council which would relieve Poland from unilateral servitudes in the treatment of minorities under article 93 of the Versailles Treaty. Beck was on the watch for some pretext to repudiate this part of the 1919 settlement. An opportunity arrived with the decision to admit the Soviet Union to the League of Nations in September 1934. Beck declared that it would be intolerable to permit a Communist state to intervene in Polish affairs. He added that it was necessary to abrogate article 93 before Russia attempted to exploit it as a League member. The abrogation took place on September 13,

1934, five days before the Soviet Union entered the League.[40]

Pilsudski held an important conference on foreign policy with Beck and other Polish leaders at Belvedere Palace after Barthou departed from Warsaw in April 1934. Pilsudski conceded that Poland enjoyed a favorable situation, but he predicted that it would not endure. He announced that plans existed for every wartime eventuality, but it would require great efforts to increase Polish strength to a point where these plans might be pursued with some prospect of success. He denounced anyone who suspected that attractive personalities among the German leaders had caused him to modify Polish foreign policy, and he insisted that no foreigners should be allowed to influence Polish policy. President Moscicki, who presided at the conference, confirmed the fact that he had inspected the Marshal's various war plans.[41]

Everyone was impressed when Pilsudski made a special gesture of expressing personal confidence in Beck and in his successful conduct of Polish foreign policy. This was exceptional treatment, because the taciturn Marshal rarely complimented one subordinate in the presence of others. It was his custom to bestow rare praise in strictly private audiences. Pilsudski was obviously seeking to inspire maximum confidence in Beck among the other Polish leaders. His gesture at the conference made the position of Beck virtually impregnable.[42]

Pilsudski addressed an important question to the Ministers which reflected his distrust of Germany after the 1934 Pact. He asked them whether danger to Poland from East or West was greater at the moment. The conference agreed that Russian imperialism had slowed down since Stalin had established his supremacy. They also recognized that both Germany and Russia were coping with important internal problems which were absorbing most of their energies at the moment. They failed to agree on a definitive answer to the Marshal's principal question.

Pilsudski appointed a special committee under General Fabrycy to study the question. The Foreign Office was directed to collaborate with the Army in preparing a series of fact-finding reports. Edward Smigly-Rydz did not like the new agency, because it produced an overlap of Army and Foreign Office jurisdiction, and he forced it to adjourn *sine die* after the death of Pilsudski. The committee concluded that Russia presented the greatest threat to Poland during the period of its deliberations in 1934 and 1935.[43]

Pilsudski customarily discussed the reports of this committee with Beck. He confided on one occasion that in 1933 he had been tempted to wage a preventive war against Germany without French support. He had decided to negotiate, because he was uncertain how the Western Powers would have reacted to a Polish campaign against Germany.[44]

Pilsudski conducted his last conference with a foreign statesman when Anthony Eden came to Warsaw in March 1935. The British diplomat intended to proceed to Moscow. Pilsudski asked if Eden had previously discussed questions of policy with Stalin. Eden replied in the affirmative, and Pilsudski exclaimed: "I congratulate you on having had a conversation with this bandit!." The Polish Marshal hoped to participate in conversations between Beck and Pierre Laval on May 10, 1935. He intended to warn the French leader, who was about to visit Moscow, not to conclude an alliance with the Soviet Union. It was too late when Laval arrived in Warsaw, because Pilsudski was dying of cancer. Beck entertained

the French Premier at a gala reception in Raczynski Palace. He hastened afterward in full dress and orders to report to the Marshal. Pilsudski greeted him with
a few personal remarks characteristic of their intimacy. He then asked with
customary bluntness if Beck was ever afraid. Beck replied that Poles whom
Pilsudski had honored with his confidence knew no fear. Pilsudski observed
that this was fortunate, because it meant Beck would have the courage to
conduct Polish policy. The two men discussed the French situation, and they expressed their mutual detestation of the proposed Franco-Russian alliance.[45]

The Marshal died on May 12, 1935. His last major decision on policy had
been to oppose attempts to frustrate Hitler's move to defy the Versailles Treaty
on March 16, 1935. The remilitarization of Germany was proclaimed, and the
Germans restored peacetime conscription. Pilsudski observed that it was no
longer possible to intimidate Germany.[46]

Beck's Plan for Preventive War in 1936

There were six weeks of official mourning in Warsaw after Piludski's death,
and then Beck visited Berlin. Beck met Hitler for the first time. The German
Chancellor proclaimed his desire to arrive at an understanding with England. He
also discussed his program to maintain permanently good relations with Poland.
He admitted that Germany's current policy toward Poland could be interpreted
as a tactical trick to gain time for some future day of reckoning, but he insisted
that it was in reality a permanent feature of his policy. Hitler conceded that his
policy toward Poland was not popular in Germany, but he assured Beck that he
could maintain it. He mentioned his success in persuading President von
Hindenburg to accept this policy in 1934.

Hitler warmly praised Pilsudski's acceptance of the non-aggression pact. Beck
observed that Pilsudski's attitude had been decisive on the Polish side. He added
that the general Polish attitude toward the treaty was one of distrust. Beck confided that he intended to base his own future policy on Pilsudski's instructions.
Hitler, who hoped that these instructions were favorable to Germany, made no
comment, but he probably considered Beck's remark to be extremely naive.
Beck added that Pilsudski had been profoundly convinced that the decision to
improve German-Polish relations was correct.

Beck concluded from this conversation that Hitler was alarmed by Pilsudski's
death, and feared that it might lead to the deterioration of German-Polish relations. Beck was also convinced that Hitler was sincere in his effort to obtain
German public approval for his policy of friendship toward Poland.

The major issues of European diplomacy at this time were the problems
arising from the wars in Spain and Ethiopia and the Franco-Russian alliance pact
of May 1935. The alliance pact remained unratified for more than nine months
after signature. The Locarno treaties of 1925 had recognized the existing alliance
system of France, but this did not include an alliance with the Communist East.
Hitler warned repeatedly after the signature of the pact that its ratification
would, in his opinion, release Germany from her limitations of sovereignty under
the Locarno treaties. The Franco-Russian pact was a direct threat to Germany,
and Hitler believed that a demilitarized Rhineland, as provided at Locarno and in

the Versailles Treaty, was a strategic luxury which Germany could not afford.[48] The French were constantly discussing steps to be taken if Germany reoccupied the Rhineland, but they were unable to obtain an assurance from London that Great Britain would consider such a move to be in 'flagrant violation' of the Locarno treaties.[49]

Józef Beck asked a group of his leading diplomats on February 4, 1936, to study possible Polish obligations to France in the event of a German move.[50] It was more than doubtful if Poland was obliged to support French action against Germany in this contingency. In reality, the principal Polish preoccupation was to discover whether or not France would act. Beck hoped for a war in alliance with France against Germany. He believed that the unpopular Polish regime would acquire tremendous prestige and advantages from a military victory over Germany. His attitude illustrates the deceptiveness of the friendship between Poland and Germany during these years, which on the Polish side was pure treachery beneath the facade. No such step against Germany after the signing of the 1934 Pact was contemplated while Pilsudski still lived. Pilsudski refused to sanction steps against Germany in 1935 when Hitler repudiated the military provisions of the Versailles Treaty.

Hitler announced at noon on March 7, 1936, that German troops were reoccupying demilitarized German territory in the West. Beck did not hesitate. He did not consider waiting for France to request military aid against Germany. He hoped to force the French hand by an offer of unlimited Polish assistance. Beck summoned French Ambassador Léon Noël on the afternoon of March 7th after a hasty telephone conversation with Edward Smigly-Rydz. Beck presented the French Ambassador with an unequivocal declaration. He said that Poland would attack Germany in the East if France would agree to invade Western Germany.[51]

Many volumes of documents explain French policy at this crucial juncture. The incumbent French Cabinet was weak, and the country was facing national elections under the unruly shadow of the emerging Popular Front. French Foreign Minister Pierre-Étienne Flandin was noted for his intimate contacts with Conservative circles in London, and he was considered to be much under British influence at this time.[52] The indiscretions of Sir Robert Vansittart in December 1935 had enabled unscrupulous journalists to expose the Hoare-Laval Plan to conciliate Italy, and the subsequent outcry in Great Britain had wrecked the plan. This led to the overthrow of the strong Government of Pierre Laval in January 1936, and it destroyed the Stresa Front for the enforcement by Great Britain, France, and Italy, of the key treaty provisions against Germany. British opinion was aroused against Italy, and inclined to tolerate anything Hitler did at this point. The British leaders continued to favor Germany as a bulwark against French and Russian influence.[53]

The French Military Counter-Intelligence, the famous 2nd Bureau, informed the Government that Germany had more divisions in the field than France, and that the outcome of a war between France and Germany would be doubtful in the event of French mobilization.[54] The French did not believe that Poland was capable of striking an effective blow against Germany, and no arrangements could be made to bring the more impressive forces of the Soviet Union into the picture. It was decided that the prospect of ultimate success would not be favorable without active British support against Germany. France did not care to take the risk alone, or merely in the company of one or two weak Eastern European allies. There was danger that Great Britain might support Hitler. The fact that Hitler sent only 30,000 troops in the first wave of Rhineland occupation was not of decisive importance. French counter-intelligence was less concerned about occupying the Left Bank of the Rhine than with prosecuting the war after that limited objective had been attained. French experts doubted if their armies would be able to cross the Rhine.[55]

Beck's effort to plunge most of Europe into war had failed. He was not entirely surprised by the French attitude, and he had taken the precaution of instructing the official *Iskra* Polish news agency to issue a pro-German statement about recent events on the morning of March 8th.[56] It is impossible to find any trace of Pilsudski in tactics of this sort.

Beck soon realized that his *démarche* with the French had produced no effect. He contemptuously described French Foreign Minister Flandin as a weakling, and as a "most sad personage." He hurriedly visited London in an attempt to influence the British attitude. The British were not prepared to take Beck seriously, and he suffered a rebuff. Discussions with King Edward VIII and the Conservative leaders produced no results.[57]

The Germans failed to understand what Beck was doing during the early phase of the Rhineland crisis. Beck assumed an aloof position when the League of Nations met at London in mid-March 1936 to investigate the Rhineland affair. Beck was dissatisfied with Polish Ambassador Chlapowski at Paris, and he appointed Juliusz Lukasiewicz to succeed him. Lukasiewicz had represented Poland at Moscow for several years, and Beck considered him to be the most able of Polish envoys. The March 1936 Rhineland crisis convinced Beck that it was indispensable to have his best man at the Paris post.[58]

Hitler's Effort to Promote German-Polish Friendship

Hitler was content to keep Germany in the background of European developments during the remainder of 1936 and throughout 1937. Goering visited Poland again in February 1937, and he presented a new plan for closer collaboration between Poland and Germany. He supported this project with great vigor in conversations with Marshal Smigly-Rydz. He conceded that Germany would eventually request a few advantages from Poland in exchange for German concessions. He promised that the price would not be high. Hitler had empowered him to assure the Polish Marshal that Germany would not request the return of the Corridor. He added that in his own opinion Germany did not require this region. He promised that Germany would continue to oppose collaboration with Soviet Russia. Smigly-Rydz was told that Goering had refused to discuss such projects with Marshal Tukachevsky, the Russian Army Commander, when the latter was in Berlin. Goering promised that collaboration between Germany and Poland would ban forever the Rapallo nightmare of a far-reaching agreement between the Soviet Union and Germany.[59]

Goering did an able job of clarifying the German position in his discussions with Polish leaders, but these meetings produced no immediate fruit. Beck at this time had no intention of placing Poland in the German-Japanese anti-

Comintern front. He was pursuing a policy of complete detachment toward both Russia and Germany. He did not assume that this policy would prevent friction between Poland and her neighbors, because this was not his aim. It was his purpose to advance the position of Poland at the expense of both Germany and Russia, and this precluded collaboration with either country. His policy became more unrealistic with each passing day as Germany recovered from the blows of World War I and from the treatment she had received under the subsequent peace treaties.

The Dangers of an Anti-German Policy

Historical changes always have suggested the need for parallel adaptations of policy. A warning to this effect was offered by Olgierd Górka, a Polish historian, on September 18, 1935, at the Polish historical conference held in Wilna. Górka pointed out that conditions for the existence of Poland were worse in 1935 than at the time of the first partition of Poland in 1772. The population ratio between Poland and the three partitioning Powers of 1772 had been 1:2, but the population ratio between Poland on the one hand, and Germany and the Soviet Union on the other, was 1:8 in 1935. A hostile Polish policy toward both Germany and Russia was like a canary seeking to devour two cats. Górka concluded that it was necessary for the Polish leaders to take account of these realities in the formulation of their policies.[60]

There were many attempts during this period to analyze the heritage of Pilsudski in the conduct of Polish foreign policy. The most comprehensive was *Miedzy Niemcami a Rosja* (Between Germany and Russia, Warsaw, 1937) by Adolf Bocheński. It is vital to emphasize at least one of these studies in order to illustrate the extraordinary complexity of current Polish speculation of foreign policy. It must be understood that it is impossible to measure with exactitude the political influences of such a book, but the importance of Bocheński was recognized throughout the Polish emigré press following his death in action near Ancona, Italy, in 1944. Indeed, W.A. Zbyszewski, in the distinguished London Polish newspaper *Wiadomosci*, on December 7, 1947, went so far as to describe Adolf Bocheński as the greatest Polish intellectual of the 20th century, thus placing him, at least in this respect, ahead of Roman Dmowski. Bocheński was a member of the Kraków school of historians, both the foreign policy pursued by Józef Beck during the following two years appeared to be in complete harmony with Bocheński's ideas.[61]

Bocheński, along with others of the Kraków group, was unwilling to accept the pro-Russian ideas of Dmowski and the National Democrats. He denounced Dmowski's thesis of the bad German and good Russian neighbor.[62]

A Pilsudski-type policy was more to Bocheński's liking, although, like Beck, he lacked Pilsudski's flexible approach. Bocheński argued against a policy of collaboration with either Germany or Russia under any circumstances. He regarded an eventual German attempt to recover both West Prussia and East Upper Silesia as inevitable, and he noted that Studnicki and his pro-German group were as much in fear of German territorial revision as other Poles.[63]

War with both Germany and Russia was regarded by Bocheński as inevitable.[64]

He predicted that there would be an understanding between Hitler and Stalin, and that the Soviet Union would seek to obtain territorial revision in the West at the expense of Poland.[65]

Bocheński's statement that it would be unendurable for his generation of Poles to be dependent on either Germany or Russia was more emotional than factual. It was inconsistent with his numerous attacks on the large numbers of pro-Russian Poles.[66]

The Soviet Union appeared more dangerous than Germany to Bocheński, because France constituted a greater allied weight for Poland against Germany than Rumania did against Russia, He predicted a new Russo-German war, but he was mistaken in expecting that such a conflict would ultimately guarantee "the great power status of Poland."[67] Had Bocheński proved, or at least made plausible, his claim that Poland could profit from such a war, he would have created an imposing theoretical basis for the reckless Polish foreign policy which he advocated. Instead, he merely returned to the familiar old story of how World War I was advantageous for Poland, and to the naive assumption that history would repeat itself in the course of a second major conflict of this sort.[68] He was on more solid ground in claiming that Soviet-German rivalry in the 1930's was responsible for the allegedly brilliant showing made by Beck on the European stage, but this fair-weather phenomenon was no basis for a Polish foreign policy.[69]

Bocheński admitted that Polish oppostion to both Germany and Russia would make inevitable the temporary collaboration of these two rivals against Poland. He claimed this was advantageous, because Poland was not a *status quo* state but a revisionist state, and conflict with Germany and Russia would justify later Polish claims against them both.[70]

Bocheński made it quite clear that Poland was not in a position to smash either Germany or Russia by her own efforts. Poland required a disastrous international situation to destroy or weaken both Germany and Russia. Bocheński was intoxicated by the vision of distant Powers, such as Great Britain and the United States, running amok in Germany and Russia. He considered the possibility of partitioning Germany into a number of small states, but he concluded that this was unfeasible because of the irresistible national self-consciousness of the German people. He decided that it was possible to inflict greater damage on Russia than on Germany, because the former contained a huge population of hostile minorities.[71]

Bocheński speculated that the dissolution of the Soviet Union would remove a strong potential ally of Germany, and would make it easier for Poland and France to control a defeated Germany. He admitted that "a small group" in Poland favored an alliance with Germany to smash Russia. Bocheński called Russia and Czechoslovakia the two sick men of Europe, because both states, in his opinion, contained minorities more numerous than the ruling nationality. There could be little objection in Bocheński's view to policies working toward the destruction of both states.[72]

Bocheński admitted that the creation of an independent Ukraine would create a problem for Poland, because such a state would always seek to obtain Volhynia and East Galicia, the Ukrainian territories controlled by Poland. He counted on a much greater conflict of interests between Russia and an independent Ukraine, and he observed that it did not matter with which of these states Poland collaborated.[73] The primary objective was to have two states in conflict where there was now one. An independent White Russian state would add to the confusion, and to the spread of Polish influence. He noted that there was a Ukrainian minority problem within Poland with or without an independent Ukraine. The ideal solution for Bocheński would be a federal imperium in which Poland persuaded the Ukraine and White Russia to associate with her.[74]

Bocheński believed that the destruction of Russia would improve Polish relations with France. He complained that France always had sacrificed Poland to any stronger Ally in the East, and that the French policy of seeking to bring Soviet troops into the heart of Europe was contrary to the interests of Poland. The dissolution of Russia would render Poland the permanent major ally of France in the East.[75]

Bocheński denounced the Czech state as a menace to Poland, and he ridiculed the Czechs for their allegedly fantastic claims to German territory at the close of World War I. He added that the pro-Soviet policy of the Czechs made it necessary for Poland to count them among her enemies. He recognized that Germany would inevitably profit most from the collapse of the Czech state, but he refused to accept this as an argument against an anti-Czech policy. He believed it would be calamitous for Polish interests if the Czechs succeeded in assimilating the Slovak area, and he noted that Andreas Hlinka, the popular Slovak leader, recognized this danger when he advised Slovak students to go to Budapest instead of Prague. Bocheński admitted that the Slovaks, in contrast to the Czechs, were friendly toward Germany, but he believed that Polish policy might eventually reap rewards in Slovakia.[76]

Bochenski insisted that the Little Entente (Czechoslovakia, Rumania, Yugoslavia) combination of France was virtually dead, and would not be of concern to Poland much longer. Poland was primarily interested in maintaining her own close relations with Rumania. He admitted that Rumania was pro-German because of the danger from Russia, but he noted that she was also pro-Polish. He hoped that it would be possible to reconcile Rumanian-Hungarian differences, and he advocated the assignment of Ruthenia to Hungary when the Czech state was dissolved. Bocheński believed that Poland needed to establish her influence over a number of weaker neighboring states (Ukraine, White Russia, Lithuania, Rumania, Hungary, Slovakia) and then proclaim her own Monroe Doctrine. He cited en passant the axiom that Poland could not afford to surrender one inch of the territory gained at Versailles or Riga. He added ominously that Poland, in the face of some irretrievable disaster, might meet the crushing fate of Hungary at Trianon in 1919.[77]

Bocheński concluded that defeats would be in store for Poland until radical changes were made in Europe.[78] He welcomed the allegedly inevitable future conflict between Poland and Germany.[79] He believed that the worst thing which could happen would be to have a Communist Russia in the East and a Communist German state to the West of Poland.[80] It is easy to see today that this is exactly what did happen as the result of the adoption and pursuit of the poicy advocated by Bocheński.

Allied propagandists in the period of World War I were in the habit of citing obscure German books, which scarcely anyone in Germany had ever read, to prove the alleged rapacity and baseness of Germany.[81] This type of propaganda has made every later attempt to cite an allegedly important book understandably suspect. Nevertheless, Bocheński's book contained the blueprint of Polish policy during the 1935-1939 period, and it was the most important book on foreign policy which appeared in Poland at that time. Its salient points were accompanied by several brilliant insights into the earlier epochs of European history.

Bocheński advocated a policy of blood and disasters. He decried any attempts to arrive at understandings with either Germany or Russia. He conceded that Polish enmity toward Germany and the Soviet Union would lead to collaboration between these two states. He pointed to an illusory rainbow in the sky, but this was scant consolation for the Poles who would fail to survive. He felt no compunction in desiring the ruin and destruction of the principal neighbors of Poland.

The salvation of Poland depended upon the repudiation of this policy. Bocheński declared that Poland would not give up one inch of territory obtained as a result of World War I and its aftermath. He insisted that Germany would eventually demand large stretches of former German territory. It remained to be seen what the Polish leaders would say when Hitler agreed to recognize the Polish Western frontier and to forego any German claim to the former German territories held by Poland. In 1937 it was still not too late for Poland. Conditions in Europe were changing, but Polish policy could reflect the change. The danger was that Great Britain would ultimately encourage Poland to challenge Germany and plunge the new Polish state into hopeless destruction. The roots of Polish policy were in the experiences of World War I. If the Polish leaders could be shown that the changes in Europe precluded the repetition of World War I, they might be expected to adapt their policy to new conditions. On the other hand, if Great Britain announced anew her intention to destroy Germany despite the absence of any conflict between British and German interests, the Poles, under these circumstances, could scarcely be blamed for failing to liberate themselves from their old World War I illusions. The key to Polish policy, once the reasonable German attitude toward Poland had been revealed, was in London. The undistinguished Polish leaders after 1935 could scarcely resist lavish and intoxicating offers of support from the British Empire. This would be true despite the fact that any Anglo-Polish alliance against Germany would be a disaster for the sorely-tried Polish people.[82]

Chapter 3

THE DANZIG PROBLEM

The Repudiation of Self-Determination at Danzig

The establishment of the so-called Free City of Danzig by the victorious Allied and Associated Powers in 1919 was the least defensible territorial provision of the Versailles Treaty. It was soon evident to observers in the Western World, and to the people of Germany, Poland, and Danzig, that this incredibly complicated international arrangement could never function satisfactorily.[1]

Danzig in 1919 was an ordinary provincial German city without any expectation or desire to occupy a central position on the stage of world politics. The Danzigers would have welcomed special Polish economic privileges in their city as a means of increasing the commerce of their port. They were horrified at the prospect of being detached from Germany and separately constituted in an anamolous position under the jurisdiction of an experimental League of Nations, which did not begin to exist until 1920.[2]

One might well ask what the attitude of the people of Portland, Oregon, would be if their city were suddenly detached from the United States and placed under the jurisdiction of the United Nations in the interest of guaranteeing special port facilities to Canada near the estuary of the Columbia River. It would be small consolation to recall that the area around Portland, before passing under the sovereignty of the United States in 1846, was settled by the British Hudson Bay Company. The traditionally friendly relations between Canadians and Portlanders would soon deteriorate under such exacerbating conditons.

It is not surprising that the National Socialists of Adolf Hitler won an electoral majority at Danzig before this was possible in Germany. The Danzigers hoped that perhaps Hitler could do something to change the intolerable conditions established during 1919 and the following years. It was easy in 1939 for Margarete Gaertner, the National Socialist propagandist, to compile extensive quotations from approximately one hundred leading Western experts who deplored the idiocy of the Danzig settlement of 1919. Her list was merely a sampling, but it was sufficient to substantiate the point that at Danzig a nasty blunder had been made.[3]

The issue exploited by Lord Halifax of Great Britain to destroy the friendship between Germany and Poland in March 1939 was the Danzig problem.[4] The final collapse of the Czech state in March 1939 produced less effect in neighboring Poland, where the leaders were inclined to welcome the event, than in the distant United States.[5] The Polish leaders had agreed that the return of Memel from Lithuania to Germany in March 1939 would not constitute an issue of conflict between Germany and Poland.[6] Hitler emphasized that Germany would not claim one inch of Polish territory, and that she was prepared to recognize the Versailles Polish frontier on a permanent basis.[7] Polish diplomats had suggested that a settlement of German requests for improved transit to German East Prussia would not present an insuperable problem.[8] The German leaders were disturbed by Polish discrimination against the Germans within Poland, but they were not inclined to recognize this problem as an issue which could produce a conflict between the two states.[9] It was primarily Danzig which made the breach. It was the discussion of Danzig between Germany and Poland which prompted the Polish leaders to warn Hitler that the pursuance of German aims in this area would produce a Polish-German war.[10]

Polish defiance of Hitler on the Danzig question did not occur until the British leaders had launched a vigorous encirclement policy designed to throttle the German Reich.[11] It is very unlikely that the Polish leaders would have defied Hitler had they not expected British support. The Polish leaders had received assurances ever since September 1938 that the British leaders would support them against Hitler at Danzig. Many of the Polish leaders said that they would have fought to frustrate German aims in Danzig had Poland been without an ally in the world. They were seeking to emphasize the importance which they attached to Danzig in discussing what they might have done in this hypothetical situation. This does not mean that they actually would have fought for Danzig in a real situation of this kind, and it is doubtful if Pilsudski would have fought for Danzig in 1939 even with British support. It is evident that Danzig was the issue selected by the Polish leaders to defy Hitler after the British had offered an alliance to Poland.[12]

It is easy to see to-day that the creation of the Free City of Danzig was the most foolish provision of the Versailles Treaty. A similar experiment at Trieste in 1947 was abandoned after a few years because it was recognized to be unworkable, and it is hoped that Europe in the future will be spared further experiments of this kind.[13] Danzig had a National Socialist regime after 1933, and Carl Burckhardt, the last League High Commissioner in Danzig, said in 1937 that the union between Danzig and the rest of Germany was inevitable.[14] The Polish leaders professed to believe that it was necessary to prevent Danzig from returning to the Reich. This is especially difficult to understand when it is recalled that the Poles after 1924 had their own thriving port city of Gdynia on the former German coast, and that otherwise the Poles had never had a port of their own throughout their entire recorded history. The Poles claimed that the Vistula was their river, and that they deserved to control its estuary. When Joseph Goebbels observed that it would be equally logical for Germany to demand Rotterdam and the mouth of the Rhine, the Poles answered with the complaint that the

Germans controlled the mouths of many of their rivers, such as the Weser, the Elbe, and the Oder, but for unfortunate Poland it was the Vistula or nothing.[15] The Germans might well have answered this complaint with one of their own to the effect that it was unfair of God to endow Poland with richer agricultural land than Germany possessed. The Poles were usually impervious to logic when Danzig was discussed. This in itself made a preposterous situation more difficult, although a compromise settlement on the basis of generous terms from Hitler might have been possible had it not been for British meddling.

The Establishment of the Free City Regime

Danzig was historically the key port at the mouth of the great Vistula River artery. The modern city of Danzig was founded in the early 14th century, and it was inhabited almost exclusively by Germans from the beginning. There had previously been a fishing village at Danzig inhabited by local non-Polish West Slavs which was mentioned in a church chronicle of the 10th century. The Germans first came to the Danzig region during the eastward colonization movement of the German people in the late Middle Ages.[16] Danzig was the capital of the Prussian province of West Prussia when the victors of World War I decided to separate this Baltic port from Germany. The city had been a provincial capital within the German Kingdom of Prussia prior to the establishment of the North German Federation in 1867 and of the German Second Empire in 1871.[17]

The Allied Powers in 1920 converted Danzig from a German provincial capital to a German city state in the style prevailing in the other Hanseatic cities of Bremen, Hamburg, and Luebeck. The latter three cities remained separate federal states within the German Empire created by Bismarck. The difference was that the victorious Powers insisted that Danzig should not join the other states of the German Union, or again become a part of Germany. They also decreed that Danzig should submit to numerous servitudes established for the benefit of Poland.[18]

The renunciation of Danzig by Germany and the creation of the Free City regime was stipulated by articles 100 to 108 of the Versailles Treaty. A League High Commissioner was to be the first instance of appeal in disputes between Poland and Danzig. The foreign relations of Danzig were delegated to Poland, and the Free City was to be assigned to the Polish customs area. The Poles were allowed unrestricted use of Danzig canals, docks, railroads, and roads for trading purposes and they were delegated control over river traffic, and over telegraph, telephone, and postal communications between Poland and Danzig harbor. The Poles had the privilege of improving, leasing, or selling transit facilities. The residents of Danzig forfeited German citizenship, although formal provision was made for adults to request German citizenship within a two year period. Double citizenship in Danzig and Germany was forbidden. The League of Nations, as the sovereign authority, was granted ownership over all possessions of the German and Prussian administrations on Danzig territory. The League was to stipulate what part of these possessions might be assigned to Poland or Danzig.[19]

The formal treaty which assigned specific property of Poland was ratified on May 3, 1923. The Poles received the Petershagen and Neufahrwasser barracks, naval supplies, oil tanks, all weapons and weapon tools from the dismantled Danzig arms factory, supply buildings, an apartment building, the state welfare building on Hansa square, the major railroad lines and their facilities, and ownership over most of the telegraph and telephone lines. Other facilities were assigned to the Free Harbor Commission supervised by the League of Nations in which the Poles participated. The Poles requested a munitions depot and base for a small Polish Army garrison. The Westerplatte peninsula close to the densely populated Neufahrwasser district was assigned to Poland on October 22, 1925. The Danzig Parliament protested in vain that this decision constituted " a new rape of Danzig." The Poles also received permission to station warships and naval personnel in the area. These various awards meant that by 1925 the Polish Government was the largest owner of property in the Free City area.[20]

The Danzig constitution was promulgated on June 14, 1922, after approval by Poland and the League of Nations. Provisions were enacted to guarantee the use of the Polish language by Poles in the Danzig courts, and a special law guaranteeing adequate educational facilities for the Polish minority was passed on December 20, 1921. The Danzig constitution was based on the concept of popular sovereignty despite the denial to Danzigers of the right of self-determination. The constitution stipulated that the construction of fortifications or manufacture of war material could not be undertaken without League approval.

The constitution provided for a *Volkstag* (assembly) of 120 members with four year terms. It was primarily a consultative body with the right to demand information about public policy, although the formal approval of the *Volkstag* for current legislation enacted by the Senate was required. The Senate with its 22 members was the seat of carefully circumscribed local autonomy. The President and the other seven major administrative officers, who were comparable to city commissioners, were elected for four years and received fixed salaries. The seven Senate administrative departments included justice and trade, public works, labor relations, interior (police), health and religion, science and education, and finance.[21] There was no separate executive authority.

The Danzig constitution of 1922 replaced the Weimar German constitution of August 11, 1919, which had been tolerated as the fundamental law of Danzig until that time. The election to the Weimar constitutional assembly in January 1919 had taken place throughout West Prussia, and it constituted a virtual plebiscite in favor of remaining with Germany. The Allies refused to permit them a plebiscite of their own which they knew would end in a defeat for Poland. The British Government played a more active role than any other Power, including Poland, in the organization of the Danzig regime. British policy was decisive in the regulation of early disputes between Danzig and Poland. The British at Danzig furnished the first three League High Commissioners, Sir Reginald Tower, General Sir Richard Haking, and Malcolm S. MacDonnell, and the last of the British High Commissioners, after an Italian and Danish interlude, was Sean Lester from Ulster, who held office from 1934 until late 1936. British interest was largely a reflection of British investment and trade, and much of the industrial enterprise of Danzig came under the control of British citizens during these years. The British also played a decisive role in securing the appointment of Carl Jacob Burckhardt, the Swiss historian who succeeded Lester and who held office until the liberation of Danzig by Germany on September 1, 1939.[22] The so-called liberation of Danzig by the Red Army on March 30, 1945, referred to in recent editions of the *Encyclopaedia Britanica*, was actually the annihilation of the city.[23]

The territory of the Free City had approximately 365,000 inhabitants in 1922. The Polish minority constituted less than 3% of the population at that time, but the continued influx of Poles raised the proportion to 4% by 1939. The introduction of proportional representation enabled the Poles to elect 5 of the 120 members of the second *Volkstag* following the promulgation of the unpopular 1922 constitution. The German vote was badly split among the usual assortment of Weimar German parties. The Conservatives (DNVP) elected 34 deputies and the Communists elected 11. The Social Democrat Marxists elected 30 and the Catholic Center 15. The remaining 25 deputies were elected by strictly local Danzig German parties. This disastrous fragmentation in the face of a crisis situation was changed after the National Socialists won the Danzig election of 1933. The divided Danzig Senate presided over by a Conservative president was followed by a united National Socialist Senate. This created a slightly more favorable situation for coping with the moves of the Polish Dictatorship at Danzig.[24]

It would not be correct to define Danzig's status as a Polish protectorate under the new system despite extensive Polish servitudes (i.e. privileges under international law). Danzig was a League of Nations protectorate. This was true despite the fact that the Allies, and not the League, created the confusing Free City regime, and despite the absence of a formal ceremony in which actual sovereignty was transferred to the League. The protectorate was administered by a League of Nations High Commissioner resident in Danzig, by the Security Council of the League of Nations in Geneva, and, after 1936, by a special committee of League member states. The capital of the political system which included Danzig was moved from Berlin to Geneva, and this was an extremely dubious move from the standpoint of the Danzigers. The League was in control at Danzig as it had been in Memel before Lithuania was permitted to seize that German city.

The Poles with varying success began an uninterrupted campaign in 1920 to push their rights at Danzig beyond the explicit terms of Versailles and the subsequent treaties. One of the earliest Polish aims was to establish the Polish Supreme Court as the final court of jurisdiction over Danzig law. This objective was never achieved because of opposition from the League High Commissioners, but Poland was eventually able to establish her Westerplatte garrison despite the early opposition of League High Commissioner General Sir Richard Haking. The Poles never abandoned these efforts, and everyone in Danzig knew that their ultimate objective was annexation of the Free City.[25]

The existing system was unsatisfactory for Poland, Germany, and Danzig. The Poles wished to usurp the role of the League, and both Germany and Danzig favored the return of the new state to the German Reich. There could be no talk of the change of system in Germany in 1933 alienating the Danzigers, because the National Socialists won their majority in Danzig before this had been accomplished in Germany. The change of system in Germany was matched by the unification of Danzig under National Socialist leadership.[26]

The Polish Effort to Acquire Danzig

Dmowski and Paderewski presented many arguments (at Versailles) to support their case for the Polish annexation of Danzig. It should occasion no surprise that Poland sought to achieve this program of annexation. The strategic and economic importance of Danzig at the mouth of the river on which the former and present capitals of Poland, Kraków and Warszawa (Warsaw), were located, was very great. The National Democratic leaders were not worried that they would create German hostility by making this "conquest." They argued at Versailles that Germany in any case would seek revenge from Poland because of the other treaty provisions. They claimed that the region on which Danzig was situated belonged to the Poles by right of prior settlement, and they spoke of the so-called recent German invasion of the territory some six hundred years earlier. The history of the Polish state, from the Viking regime imposed in the 10th century until the 18th century partitions, extended over eight hundred years, and the Poles were satisfied that their state was more ancient than Danzig.[27]

They were confident that they could contend with the German argument against their case on this point. The German argument was based on two principal facts. In the first place, Germanic tribes had occupied the Danzig area until the late phase of the "Wandering of the Peoples (*Voelkerwanderung*)" in the 4th century A.D. Secondly, the Poles had never settled the Danzig region before the Germans arrived to found their city in the late Middle Ages.

The Polish reply to this German argument was two-fold. They contended that the early German tribes in the Danzig area were representative of the entire Germanic civilization, which included, besides Germany, Scandinavia, England, Switzerland, and the Netherlands. They concluded that the Germans had no right to base claims on the early history of these tribes. Secondly, the small early West Slavic tribes, which were bordered by the West Slavic Poles, West Slavic Czechs, Borussians, and Germans on land, and on water by the Baltic Sea, had been largely assimilated by their neighbors. These tribes had settled the Danzig region between the "Wandering of the Peoples" and the founding of Danzig by the Germans. It was argued that these early West Slavic tribes, who had maintained a fishing village on the site of the later city of Danzig, were more intimately related to the Poles than to their other neighbors. It was this doctrine which provided the claim that Poland might legitimately consider herself the heir to the entire German territory between the Elbe and the Vistula. At one time or another this area had been occupied by West Slavic tribes.[28]

These were the principal so-called historical arguments of the Poles. They claimed along ecenomic lines that Danzig had grown rich on the Polish hinterland. This was undoubtedly true, although the local West Prussian hinterland, which had long been German, also contributed to Danzig's prosperity.

We have noted the Polish natural law argument that Danzig should belong to them because they controlled most of the Vistula River. They also raised the strategic argument that ownership of Danzig was necessary to defend Poland and to guarantee Polish access to the Sea. The second point, if one overlooks the feasibility of granting Poland port facilities in German harbors, had been met after 1924 by the construction of the neighboring port of Gdynia. The first point concerning defense does not merit lengthy examination. Danzig was distant from the bulk of Polish territory, and therefore it could contribute little to the defense of Poland. Ian D. Morrow, the principal British historian of the treaty settlement in the eastern borderlands, concluded that the problem of Polish claims to Danzig "constitutes as it were a permanent background to the history of the relations between the Free City of Danzig and the Republic of Poland."29

The German Order of Knights played an important role in the early history of Danzig. The Order had been commissioned by the Roman Catholic Popes and German Emperors to end the threat of heathen invasion in Eastern Europe. The Order established its control over West Prussia by 1308. Danzig was developed within this territory by German settlers, and the Order permitted her to join the Hanseatic League. Danzig grew rapidly for more than one hundred and fifty years under the protection of the Order, and at one time it was the leading shipbuilding city of the world. The first Poles appeared in the area, and the tax register at Danzig indicated that 2% of the new settlers in the period from 1364 to 1400 were Polish.30

Polish historians have emphasized that a trading settlement of Germans on the Danzig site had first received approval for an urban charter in 1235 from Swantopolk, a West Slavic chieftain. They therefore concluded that the first German trading settlement in the area was under Slavic sovereignty. They have regarded this as a sort of precedent to suggest that the Poles were requesting a return to the original state of affairs when they demanded Danzig. This is an impossible *mystique* for anyone questioning the allegedly close affinity between the early West Slavic tribes of the coastal area and the Poles.31

Polish historians see a great tragedy for Poland in the conquest of West Prussia by the German Order of Knights in 1308. The Knights were able, at least temporarily, to establish a common frontier between their conquests along the Baltic Sea and the rest of Germany. They also attained a frontier with the German Knights of the Sword farther to the North. This linked up the German eastern conquests of the Middle Ages in one contiguous system from Holstein to the Gulf of Finland. It meant that any belated Polish attempt to attain territorial access to the Baltic Sea would have to contend with a solid barrier of German territory between Poland and the coast. The various German Orders in their conquests had never seized any territory inhabited by the Poles. This meant that the Poles, if they attacked the Germans, would be unable to claim either to Pope or to Emperor that they were seeking to liberate Polish territories under German control.32

Confusion in the Papacy during the 15th century, and distractions in the German Empire, enabled the Poles to isolate the German Order of Knights, and to attack the Order with the aid of Tartar and Lithuanian allies. The relations between the Poles and the German Emperors, however, remained peaceful throughout this same period. There were no wars at all between the German Emperors and the Polish Kings from this time until the disappearance of Poland in the 18th century.33

The Poles began their victorious struggle against the Order in 1410. They never lost the initiative after their great field victory at Tannenberg (Grunwald) in the first year of the war. The struggle dragged on to the accompaniment of sporadic bursts of activity from the Poles, and the Germans defended themselves stubbornly in their cities. The ultimate outcome of the war was influenced by internal German struggles between the colonists and the celibate knights from all parts of Germany. The colonists in both town and countryside had begun to consider themselves the native Germans several generations after the first settlement, and they regarded the Knights, who had no family roots in these provinces, as foreigners. The internecine struggles which followed decisively weakened the Order. The territorial integrity of the Order state was shattered at the peace of Thorn in 1466.[34]

Some Polish historians regard the period of the Order in West Prussia as a mere episode in which Poland at last had begun to make good her claims to the heritage of the West Slavic tribes.[35] The Poles in 1466 annexed most of West Prussia and part of East Prussia. They reached the Baltic coast, but they failed to establish Polish maritime interests. Danzig seceded from the Order state, but she retained her status of German city within the Hanseatic League. Her position was unique. Unlike the other Hanseatic cities, she was neither a member of a German territorial state nor under the immediate jurisdiction of the Emperor. Danzig enjoyed the theoretical protection of the Polish Kings, but she was independent of them. She never compromised her independence by permitting a Polish army to control the city. King Stephen Bathory of Poland became impatient with the state of affairs in 1576. He threatened the Danzigers with war if they did not accept his demand for a Polish military occupation and a permanent Polish garrison. Danzig in reply did not hesitate to defy Stephen Bathory. The war which followed was a humiliation for the proud Polish state at the zenith of her power. The Polish forces were unable to capture Danzig.

Danzig in the 17th century declined rapidly in commercial importance along with the other cities of the Hanseatic League. There were many complex causes both economic and political, but the principal factor was the successful manner in which the Dutch and the Danes conspired to thwart Hanseatic interests. Danzig continued to maintain her freedom from Polish control despite her decline, and indeed, the Polish state itself experienced a period of uninterrupted decline after the great Ukrainian uprising against Poland in 1648. The situation of Danzig remained unchanged until she was annexed by Prussia in the 18th century.[36]

Prussia surrendered to Napoleon I at the Peace of Tilsit in 1807. Danzig was separated from Prussia and converted into a French protectorate with a permanent French garrison. By this time the city had become ardently Prussian, and this unnatural state of affairs, which was also inflicted on Bremen, Hamburg, and Luebeck, was violently resented by the Danzigers. The French regime at Danzig was threatened by Napoleon's debacle in Russia in 1812. This event enabled the Prussians to recover Danzig early in 1814 after a long siege. Danzig remained enthusiastically Prussian until the city was literally annihilated by Russian and Mongolian hordes in 1945.[37]

Danzig's Anguish at Separation from Germany

Danzig saw nothing of war or invasion from 1814 until the defeat of Germany in 1918. The Danzigers did not contemplate the possibility of annexation by the new Polish state until after the close of World War I. They were assured by German Chancellor Hertling in February 1918 that President Wilson's peace program with its 13th Point on Polish access to the Sea did not threaten their affiliation with Germany in any way. The President's Ambassador had assured the German Government that this was the case when the point about Polish access to the Sea was discussed before American entry into the war. The President's program was based on national self-determination, and Danzig was exclusively German.[38]

The Danzigers thought of port facilities for the Poles in German harbors along the lines subsequently granted to the Czechs at Hamburg and Stettin. This arrangement satisfied the Czech demand for access to the Sea. No one thought of Polish rule at Danzig until it became known that the Poles were demanding Danzig at the peace conference, and that President Wilson favored their case. The disillusioned Danzigers petitioned the German authorities at Weimar to reject any peace terms which envisaged the separation of Danzig from Germany. There was still some hope in April 1919, when the Allies refused to permit Polish troops in the West under General Haller to return to Poland by way of Danzig. German troops occupied Danzig at that time, and the Poles were required to return home by rail.[39]

The Danzigers were in despair after receiving the preliminary draft of the Versailles Treaty in May 1919. They discovered that some queer fate was conspiring to force them into the ludicrous and dubious situation of a separate state. Danzig discovered in May 1919 that the 14 Points and self-determination had been a trick, a *ruse de guerre à l'américaine*, and in June 1919, with the acceptance of the treaty by the Weimar Government, it was evident that Danzig must turn her back on her German Fatherland. The Allied spokesmen in Danzig urged her to hasten about it, and not be sentimental. The Germans had been tricked and outsmarted by the Allies. After all, Danzig had lost World War I.[40]

Poland's Desire for a Maritime Role

The distinguished Polish historian, Oskar Halecki, has declared that the demands of Dmowski at Versailles were "unanimously put forward by the whole nation."[41] Polish spokesmen have insisted that the entire Polish nation was longing for a free marine frontier in the North, and for a coastal position which would enable Poland to play an active maritime role. This was doubtless true after 1918, although for more than three hundred years, when Poland from the 15th to the 18th centuries held most of the West Prussian coastline, the Poles played no maritime role. It should be added that they also held coastal territory east of the Vistula with harbor facilities during those years. When struggles occurred during the 17th century between rival Swedish and Polish Vasa kings, the Poles chartered German ships and crews from East Prussian bases to defend their coasts from the Swedes rather than to undertake their own naval defense.

Poland made no effort to build a merchant marine or to acquire colonies, although the neighboring German principality of Brandenburg, with a less favorable 17th century geographic and maritime position, engaged in foreign trade and acquired colonies in Africa. These facts in no way diminished the Polish right to play a maritime role in the 20th century, but it was unwarranted for Polish spokesmen to mislead the Polish people about their past. An especially crass example of this was offered by Eugeniusz Kwiatkowski, Vice-Premier of Poland from 1935 to 1939, and from 1926 the leading Government figure in Polish commerce and industry. Kwiatkowski was a close personal friend of President Mościcki, and he was entrusted with the organization of the Central Industrial Region (COP) of Poland before World War II. He was an expert engineer who had studied in Kraków, Lwów, and Munich, and he had earned the proud title "creator of Gdynia" for his collaboration with Danish colleagues in the construction of Poland's principal port. Kwiatkowski, like some other scientists, was guilty of distorting history, and he went to absurd lengths to identify Poland with the nests of West Slavic pirates of the early Middle Ages who had operated from Ruegen Island off the coast of Pomerania. Kwiatkowski announced at a maritime celebration on July 31, 1932, that, if the heroes of Poland's great naval past could raise their voices once again, "one great, mighty, unending cry would resound along a stretch of hundreds of miles from the Oder to the Memel: 'Long live Poland!'."[42]

At Paris the Poles had argued that Danzig was indispensable for their future maritime position. Lloyd Geroge frustrated their plan to annex Danzig, but they were told by the Danes that the West Prussian coast north of Danzig presented the same physical characteristics as the north-eastern coast of Danish Zeeland. The Danes had built Copenhagen, and there was no reason why the Poles could not build their own port instead of seeking to confiscate a city built by another nation. The Poles were fascinated by this prospect, and they were soon busy with plans for the future port of Gdynia.[43]

The construction of Gdynia and Polish economic discrimination in favor of the new city after 1924 produced a catastrophic effect on the trade of the unfortunate Danzigers. The Polish maritime trade in 1929 was 1,620 million Zloty, of which 1,490 million Zloty still passed through Danzig. The total land and sea trade by 1938 had declined to 1,560 million Zloty, and only 375 million went by way of Danzig. The Danzig trade was confined mainly to bulk products such as coal and ore. Imports of rice, tobacco, citrus fruits, wool, jute, and leather, and exports of beet-sugar and eggs passed through Gydnia. Danzig was virtually limited to the role of port for the former German mining region of East Upper Silesia. The trade of Gdynia had become more than three times as valuable as that of Danzig. Trade between Danzig and Germany was discouraged by a heavy Polish protective tariff.[44]

Polish concern about Danzig might have diminished after the successful completion of the port of Gdynia had Polish ambitions been less insatiable. Unfortunately this was not the case, and the Poles remained as jealous as before of their position within the so-called Free City.

The Poles had originally insisted that Danzig was the one great port they needed to guarantee their maritime access. They soon began to speak of modern sea power, and it was easy to demonstrate that one port was a narrow foundation for a major naval power. They described Danzig as their second lung, which they needed to breathe properly. It was a matter of complete indifference to them that Danzig did not wish to be a Polish lung. They were equally unmoved by the fact that millions of their Ukrainian subjects did not care to live within the Polish state, and that nearly one million Germans had left Poland in despair during the eighteen years after the Treaty of Versailles. Life had been made sufficiently miserable for them to do otherwise. It could be expected that the Germans would also evacuate a Polish Danzig, and thus make room for a Polish Gdańsk. The Polish leaders were encouraged to hope for this result because of the manifestly ridiculous and humiliating situation created for Danzig by the Treaty of Versailles.[45]

The preoccupation of the Polish leaders with Danzig was quite extraordinary. This was indicated by the press and by the analytical surveys of the Polish Foreign Office, *Polska a Zagranica (Poland and Foreign Lands)*, which were sent to Polish diplomatic missions abroad. These secret reports were also distributed among Foreign Office officials, Cabinet members, and Army leaders.[46] They emphasized the consolidation of National Socialist rule at Danzig after the 1934 Pact,[47] the economic problems of Danzig,[48] and the constitutional conflict between the Danzig Senate and the League.[49] It was possible to conclude from these reports that Danzig was the cardinal problem of Polish foreign policy despite the conclusion of the 1934 Pact with Germany. The line taken by the Polish Foreign Office was simple and direct. It was noted that Polish public opinion was increasingly aroused about Danzig, and that the Government continued to maintain great interest in the unresolved Danzig problem. Above all, it was stressed that Danzig, although it did not belong to Poland, was no less important to Poland than Gdynia, which was Polish.[50] It would be impossible to convey Polish aspirations at Danzig in terms more eloquent.

It should be evident at this point that no serious person could expect a lasting agreement between Germany and Poland without a final settlement of the Danzig question. The Danzig *status quo* of Versailles was a source of constant friction between Germany and Poland. The Polish leaders after 1935 continued to believe that the ideal solution would have been the annexation of Danzig by Poland, and Pilsudski himself had favored this solution, under favorable conditions, such as the aftermath of a victorious preventive war against Germany.[51]

Pilsudski's preventive war plans dated from 1933, when Germany was weak. After the 1934 Pact, the Poles opened an intensive propaganda campaign against the Czechs, and the prospects for a Polish success at Teschen, in cooperation with Germany, were not entirely unfavorable.[52] It seemed by contrast that Poland had nothing more to seek at Danzig. Pilsudski had declared in March 1935 that no Power on earth could intimidate Germany any longer.[53]

Hitler talked with good sense and conviction of abandoning claims to many German territories in Europe which had been lost after World War I. These included territories held by Denmark in the North, France in the West, Italy in the South, and Poland in the East.[54] Hitler expected Poland to reciprocate by conceding the failure of her earlier effort to acquire Danzig. Hitler was not prepared to concede that Danzig was lost to Germany merely because she had been placed under the shadowy jurisdiction of the League. Danzig was a German

National Socialist community plagued with a Polish economic depression and prevented from pursuing policies of recovery to improve her position. Danzig wished to return to Germany. Hitler had no intention of perpetuating the humiliating *status quo* of surrendering this purely German territory to Poland. He was willing to recognize extensive Polish economic rights at Danzig.[55] It would have been wise for the Poles to concentrate upon obtaining favorable economic terms and otherwise to wash their hands of the problem.

Hitler's Effort to Prevent Friction at Danzig

The Poles were seeking to extend their privileges at Danzig when Hitler was appointed Chancellor in 1933. There had been chronic tension between Danzig and Poland throughout the period of the Weimar Republic in Germany. Indeed, the 1919 settlement at Danzig virtually precluded conditons of any other kind. The improvement of German-Polish relations shortly after the advent of Hitler was accompanied by a temporary relaxation of tension between Poland and Danzig, but it would have required a superhuman effort to maintain a lasting *détente* within the context of the Versailles *status quo*. Hermann Rauschning, the first National Socialist Danzig Senate leader, was known to be extremely hostile to Poland, but Hitler persuaded him to go to Warsaw for talks with the Polish leaders in July 1933. Rauschning was accompanied by Senator Artur Greiser, who was known for his moderate views on Poland.[56] A favorable development took place on August 5, 1933. Danzig and Poland agreed to settle important disputes by bilateral negotiation instead of carrying their complaints to the League of Nations. Either party was obliged to give three months' notice before appealing to the League if bilateral negotiations failed. The Poles also agreed to modify their policies of economic discrimination against Danzig, but they failed to keep this promise.[57]

The following year was relatively calm although there were many irritating minor incidents involving economic problems and the operations of Polish pressure groups on Danzig territory. Danzig and Poland concluded an economic pact on August 8, 1934, which contained mutual advantages on taxes and the marketing of Polish goods in Danzig territory.[58] The conciliatory trend at Danzig was strengthened when Greiser succeeded Rauschning as Senate President on November 23, 1934. The Poles had no complaints about Greiser, but they objected to Albert Forster, the National Socialist District Party Leader. Forster was an energetic and forceful Franconian with the *Sturheit* (stubbornness) characteristic of the men of his district. He was one of Hitler's best men, and his assignment at Danzig was a significant indication of the seriousness of Germany's intentions. Forster was less cosmopolitan than Greiser, but he was highly intelligent, and he fully understood the scope and significance of the Danzig problem despite his West German origin. He was a stubborn negotiator with both Poland and the League, but he loyally supported Hitler's plans for a lasting agreement with Poland. He also shared Hitler's enthusiasm for an understanding with England. Lord Vansittart described Forster in his memoirs as "a rogue [Forster was exceptionally handsome] who came to our house with glib professions and a loving mate [Forster's wife was exceptionally beautiful]."[59] This brief rejection of Forster by the leading British Germanophobe tallied closely with the negative attitude of the Poles.

The effort of Hitler to achieve greater harmony with Poland at Danzig did not achieve lasting results. Friction began to increase again early in 1935, and this trend continued until the outbreak of war in 1939.[60] Many of the new disputes were economic in nature. Danzig was experiencing a severe depression, and the local National Socialist regime wished to do more to help the people than had been done by the Conservative regime in the past. The lack of freedom made it impossible to emulate the increasing prosperity which existed in Germany. The deflationary monetary policies of Poland were anathema in Danzig, where the Danziger Gulden was tied to the scarce Zloty of the Poles. An attempt to free the Gulden from the Zloty, without leaving the Polish customs union, produced a crisis in May 1935. Danzig received much expert advice from Hjalmar Schacht, the President of the German Reichsbank. The Polish financial experts regarded this as unwarranted German interference in the affairs of German Danzig. The crisis reached a climax on July 18, 1935, when Poland put Danzig under a blockade, and commanded the shipment of all goods through Gdynia. Danzig responded by opening her economic border with East Prussia in defiance of Poland. This involved an attempt to circumvent the Polish customs inspectors and to ignore the Polish tariff requirements. Hitler intervened at this critical point and used his influence to obtain the agreement of August 8, 1935, which amounted to a total retreat for Danzig. This capitulation ended any hope that Danzig might be able to ameliorate the economic depression through her own efforts.[61]

A typical dispute of this drab period transpired in 1936 when the Poles abruptly issued regular Army uniforms to the Polish customs inspectors in the hope of accustoming the Danzig population to a regular Polish military occupation. The Danzig Government protested, but the Poles, as usual, refused to accept protests from Danzig. A dangerous atmosphere was maintained by the constant agitation of the Polish pressure groups. The Polish Marine and Colonial League demonstrated in Warsaw in July 1936 for the expansion of existing Polish privileges at Danzig, and its activities were accompanied by a new campaign against Danzig in the Polish press. Relations between Poland and Danzig were as bad as they had been during the Weimar Republic. Hitler had attempted to reduce friction on the basis of the *status quo*, but this effort had failed.[62]

The Chauvinism of Polish High Commissioner Chodacki

Jósef Beck, Poland's Foreign Minister, soon decided that renewed tension had made Danzig the most prominent front in the conduct of Polish diplomacy, except possible Paris. He decided to recall Kasimierz Papée, the Polish High Commissioner, and to replace him with a man who enjoyed his special confidence. The choice had fallen on Colonel Marjan Chodacki, who ranked second in Beck's estimation to Juliusz Lukasiewicz at Paris. Chodacki in 1936 was Poland's diplomatic representative at Prague. Beck invited his friend to return to Warsaw from Prague on December 1936 for three days of intensive discussions on the

Danzig situation before clearing the channels for his new appointment. Beck told Chodacki at Warsaw of his decision, and he requested him to take the Danzig post. Chodacki accepted with the slightest hesitation. Beck asked if Chodacki was not afraid to accept such a dangerous mission. Chodacki, instead of replying, asked Beck a question in return: " Are you not afraid to send me there?." Beck agreed with a smile that this question had a point. He knew that his friend was the most ardent and sensitive of Polish patriots.

Beck outlined the situation. He expected Chodacki to maintain Poland's position at Danzig by means short of war, but he intimated that events at Danzig might ultimately lead to war. Beck emphasized the importance of the British and French attitudes toward Polish policy at Danzig, and Chodacki realized that Beck wished to have the support of the Western Powers in any conflict with Germany. It was evident that Paris and London would be decisive in the determination of Polish policy at Danzig. Beck admitted that the two Western Powers seemed to be indifferent about Danzig in 1936, but he expected their attitudes to change later. He discussed the details of current disputes at Danzig, and it was evident that the two men were in complete agreement. Chodacki assumed the new post several days later.[63]

The Danzigers had been annoyed with League High Commissioner Sean Lester for several years. Lester was an Ulsterman who seemed to delight in conducting a one man crusade against National Socialism and all its works in Danzig. The officers of the German cruiser *Leipzig* ostentatiously refused to call on Lester when their ship visited Danzig harbor in June 1936. The Danzigers repeatedly urged the British to withdraw him, and at last this request was granted. Several replacements were considered, but the choice fell on Carl Jacob Burckhardt, a prominent Swiss historian who was an expert on Cardinal Richelieu and the traditions of European diplomacy. Burckhardt was acceptable to the Poles, and he received his appointment from the League Security Council on February 18, 1937. Burckhardt had been extraordinarily discreet in concealing his fundamental sympathy for Germany. He was later criticized by many League diplomats, but at the time he was universally regarded as an admirable choice.[64]

Chodacki had been sent to Danzig to maintain the claims and position of Poland, whereas Burckhardt was merely the caretaker of the dying League regime. Chodacki was instructed to insist on Polish terms at Danzig, and he was not expected to believe in the permanent preservation of peace. The emphasis of his mission was on stiffening the Polish line without risking a conflict until Poland had British and French support. The attitude he adopted at Danzig was provocative and belligerent. He delivered an important speech to a Polish audience at Gross-Trampken, Danzig territory, on Polish Independence Day, November 11, 1937. He made the following significant statement, which left no doubt about his position: "I remember very well the time I went into the Great War, hoping for Poland's resurrection. The Poles here in Danzig should likewise live and wait in the hope that very presently they may be living on Polish soil."[65]

This was holiday oratory, but it should have revealed to the last sceptic that neither Chodacki nor Beck had abandoned hope of annexing Danzig to Poland. A final solution would be required to end the unrest caused by rival German and

Polish aspirations at Danzig, and there could be no lasting understanding between Poland and Germany until such a solution was achieved. Self-determination for the inhabitants was the best means of resolving this issue in view of the conflicting German and Polish claims. It was no longer news to the Danzigers that many Poles hoped for the ultimate annexation of Danzig to Poland. They would not have been surprised to discover that Beck's High Commissioner entertained similar sentiments privately. It would be difficult to argue that Chodacki's publicly announced campaign of Polish *irredentism* was calculated to reduce the growing tension between Danzig and Poland. Beck had responded to the Danzig situation by sending a chauvinist to maintain the Polish position.

The Deterioration of the Danzig Situation after 1936

Issues of dispute between Danzig and Poland were markedly on the increase throughout 1937. Chodacki later declared that fifteen one thousand page volumes would be required to describe the Danzig-Polish disputes prior to World War II. There can be no doubt that the year 1937 contributed its share. Times remained hard in both Danzig and Poland, and the great majority of disputes were economic in nature. The Poles placed heavy excise taxes on imports from the huge Danzig margarine industry to protect Polish competitors. They rejected the contention of Danzig that this measure was a violation of the August 6, 1934, economic treaties to eliminate trade barriers between the two countries. This single dispute produced an endless series of reprisals and recriminations.[66]

Irresponsible fishing in troubled waters by foreigners also occasioned much bad feeling. A typical example was the circulation of rumors by the *Daily Telegraph*, an English newspaper. The *Daily Telegraph* reported on May 10, 1937, that Joseph Goebbels had announced Germany's intention to annex Danzig in the near future. It is easy to understand the effect produced on the excitable Poles in the Danzig area by such reporting, and it would have been a pleasant surprise if this particular newspaper of Kaiser-interview and Hoare-Laval Pact fame had not contributed to alarmism at Danzig. The statement attributed to Goebbels in this instance was purely an invention.[67] By 1938, tension had been built up to a point where incidents of violence played an increasingly prominent role. Meetings of protest, more frequently than otherwise about imaginary wrongs, were organized by pressure groups in surrounding Polish towns. They invariably ended with cries of: "We want to march on Danzig!," and with the murderous slogan: "Kill the Hitlerites!."[68]

Chodacki told Smigly-Rydz at Polish Army maneuvers in September 1937 that the National Socialist revolution in Danzig was virtually completed, and that the *"Gleichschaltung* (coordination)" of Danzig within the German system had been achieved.[69] The one exception was that Danzig still had her made-in-Poland depression, whereas Germany was swimming in plenty. The effective organization work of Albert Forster convinced the Poles that Danzig was at last slipping through their fingers. Awareness of this increased Polish exasperation. Chodacki claimed that in 1938 one of his speeches at Toruń or elsewhere in West Prussia would have been sufficient to set a crowd of tens of thousands marching against Danzig. He admitted that he was often tempted to deliver such a speech.

He felt goaded by fantastic attacks in the Kraków press that he was too conciliatory toward Danzig.[70]

The Need for a Solution

The Danzig problem by 1938 was a skein of conflicting interests between exasperated Poles and impatient Danzigers. The absurd regime established at Versailles was a failure. Hitler intervened repeatedly for moderation, but he was no less disgusted with the humiliating farce than the Danzigers, and he was weary of conciliation at Danzig's expense. Intelligent foreign observers expected this attitude. Lord Halifax, who had out-maneuvered Gandhi of India on many occasions, visited Hitler at Berchtesgaden on November 19,1937. He inquired whether Hitler planned to do something about Danzig. Hitler was understandably evasive in his reply, but Halifax made no secret of the fact that he expected German action to recover Danzig.[71]

The current mentality of the Polish leaders indicated that a solution would be difficult, and it is painful to recall that the entire problem would not have existed had Danzig not been placed in a fantastic situation by the peacemakers of 1919. The Danzig problem resulted from a wretched compromise between Lloyd George and Woodrow Wilson. It epitomized the comment of the American publicist, Porter Sargent: "The Anglo-Saxon peoples held the world in the palms of their hands, and what a mess they made of it",[72] There was nothing left but to try for a solution. It would be scant consolation in the event of failure to know that the blame would be shared by men of two generations. The cost of failure would be paid by untold generations.

Chapter 4

GERMANY, POLAND, AND THE CZECHS

The Bolshevik Threat to Germany and Poland

The failure of two neighboring nations with similar interests to cooperate against a mutual danger posing a threat to their existence is a sorrowful spectacle. The civilizations of ancient Greece and of Aztec America were overwhelmed by alien invaders because of internecine strife. In the 1930's, the authoritarian and nationalistic states of Germany and Poland were seeking to promote the development, livelihood, and culture of their national communities, but they faced a common threat from the Soviet Union. The ideology of the Soviet Union was based on the doctrines of class hatred and revolutionary internationalism of Karl Marx.[1]

The peoples of Russia were suffering on an unprecedented scale from their misfortune in falling prey to the merciless minority clique of Bolshevik revolutionaries, who seized power in the hour of Russian defeat in World War I. The Bolsheviks later wrought untold havoc on the peoples of Poland and Germany. The Communists by means of murder and terror have depopulated the entire eastern part of Germany, and they hold Central Germany, the heart of the country, in an iron grip.[2]

It is a sad commentary that millions of Germans and Poles are now collaborating under a system which has destroyed the freedom of their two nations. They were unable to unite in defense of their freedom. It is of course possible that the Soviet Union would have triumphed over Germany and Poland had the two nations been allies. It is more likely that a Polish-German alliance would have been the rock to break the Soviet tide. The present power of the Bolsheviks is so great that no one knows if it is possible to prevent their conquest of the world, and the failure of German-Polish cooperation is one of the supreme tragedies of world history.

The conflict between Warsaw and Berlin became the pretext in 1939 for the implementation of the antiquated English balance of power policy. This

produced a senseless war of destruction against Germany. As it turned out, each
Allied soldier of the West was fighting unwittingly for the expansion of
Bolshevism, and he was simultaneously undermining the security of every
Western nation. Never were so many sacrifices made for a cause so ignoble.

Neither Germany nor Poland desired to evangelize the world or to impose
alien systems of government of foreign nations throughout the globe. There was
a monumental difference between them and the Soviet Union on this point. The
elements of friction between Germany and Poland, despite the senseless provisions of the 1919 Versailles Treaty, were markedly reduced under the benign
influence of the treaty between Pilsudski and Hitler. A few concessions on both
sides, if only in the interest of establishing a common front against Bolshevism,
could have reduced this friction to insignificance. The two nations were natural
allies. They were new states seeking to overcome the uncertainty and fear
occasioned by the frustration of their healthy nationalist aspirations over many
centuries. The leaders of both nations hated the Bolshevist system and they
regarded it as the worst form of government devised by man. They realized that
the Soviet Union possessed natural resources and population which made the
combined resources and populations of Germany and Poland puny by comparison.

It is evident from a survey of the international situation sent to missions
abroad by the Polish Foreign Office in 1936 that the Soviet Union was regarded
as the greatest foreign threat to Poland. This report confirmed the impressions
of the diplomatic-military committee established by Pilsudski in 1934 to study
the German and Russian situations. Nevertheless, Poland rebuffed the suggestions of Hermann Goering after 1934 for German-Polish collaboration against
the Soviet Union. The great question was whether or not Poland intended
permanently to follow a policy of impartiality toward the Soviet Union and
Germany.[3]

Polish experts in Moscow were impressed by mid-1936 with the improved
living conditions in Russia under the 2nd Five Year Plan, which appeared to be
far less drastic and cruel than the 1st Five Year Plan. They conceded that the
Soviet system was consolidating its position. A new series of Soviet purges began
later the same year. They lasted nearly three years, and dwarfed the bloody
Cheka purges of 1918, or the purge in 1934 which followed the assassination of
Sergei Kirov, the Leningrad administrator. Foreign observers wondered whether
the new purges would strengthen or weaken the Soviet regime. Opinions were
divided on this crucial point, but it was evident that the new upheavals constituted a crisis for the regime.[4]

Hitler's Anti-Bolshevik Foreign Policy

Recent Soviet developments did not affect the tempo of Hitler's policy, which
was geared to speed, although actual German preparations for defense were
exceedingly lax because of monetary inflation fears. Hitler was striving to win
the friendship of Great Britain, and to foster Anglo-German collaboration in the
spirit and tradition of Bismarck, Cecil Rhodes, and Joseph Chamberlain. He was
aware of the traditional British balance of power policy. He realized that he

must complete his continental defensive preparations against Bolshevism before the British decided that he was "too strong," and moved to crush him as they had crushed Napoleon.[5]

Hitler hoped that the British would not intervene while he was securing Germany's position through understandings with Germany's principal neighbors, and by a limited and moderate program of territorial revision. British leaders had opposed the German customs union before 1848, and they had opposed the national unification of Germany during the following years. Nevertheless, Bismarck had outbluffed Palmerston at Schleswig-Holstein in 1864, and it was evident by 1871 that Tories and Liberals alike were willing to accept the results of Bismarck's unification policy despite his repeated use of force. Germany was conceded to be the strongest military power on the European continent after 1871. The balance of power was operating, but the British faced colonial conflicts with France and Russia, and the 1875 Franco-German "war scare" crisis showed that Germany could still be checked by a hostile combination. At that time, a momentary coalition of France, Great Britain, and Russia was formed against Germany within a few days.[6]

Hitler hoped that a German program of territorial revision and defense against Communism would be accepted by the British leaders, if it was carried through with sufficient speed. If the tempo was slow, the latent British hostility toward everything German could easily produce new flames. The traditional warlike ardor of the British upper classes was momentarily quiescent, but it could be aroused with relative ease. Hitler hoped that a refusal to pursue political aims overseas or in the West or South of Europe would convince the British leaders, once his position was secure, that his program was moderate. His strength would still be insufficient to overshadow the primary position of the British Empire in the world. He was willing to place Germany politically in a subservient position to Great Britain, and to accept a unilateral obligation to support British interest at any point. Hitler hoped that the British would appreciate the advantages of this situation. They could play off the United States against Germany. Germany would be useful in resisting American assaults against the sacred British doctrine of colonialism, and the United States could be used to counter any German claims for special privileges.[7]

Hitler's ideas were confirmed by a brilliant report of January 2, 1938, from Joachim von Ribbentrop, German Ambassador to Great Britain. Ribbentrop pointed out that there was no real possibility of an Anglo-German agreement while conditions were unsettled, but that perhaps a strong German policy and the consolidation of the German position would make such an agreement possible. The German Ambassador emphasized that an understanding with Great Britain had been the primary aim of his activity during his many months in London. He had reached his conslusions after personal conversations with the principal personalities of British public affairs. Ribbentrop's report was decisive in winning for him the position of German Foreign Minister in February 1938. No other German diplomat of the period had presented Hitler with a comparable analysis of British policy and of the British attitude toward Germany. The Ribbentrop report was comparable to the 1909 memorandum of Alfred Kiderlen-Waechter on Anglo-German and Russo-German relations. This memorandum had been requested by Chancellor Bethmann-Hollweg, and it brought

Kiderlen from the obscure Bucharest legation to the Wilhelmstrasse despite the fact that he was disliked by Kaiser Wilhelm II.[8]

The controversial question of whether or not the Russian regime was successfully consolidating its position could not be decisive for Hitler under these circumstances. The impulse for rapid moves and definitive results arose from Hitler's evaluation of the situation in London. Hitler's basic program, after the recovery of the Saar and the restoration of German defenses in the Rhineland, was to liberate the Germans of Austria, aid the Germans of Czechoslovakia, and place German relations with France, Italy, and Poland, his principal neighbors, on a solid basis. It would be possible afterward to talk to the British about a lasting agreement, when the prospects for success would be more favorable. Improved German-American relations would follow automatically from an Anglo-German understanding. Hitler also hoped to act as moderator between Japan and Nationalist China to restore peace in the Far East, and to close the door to Communist penetration which was always opened by war and revolution. If this moderate program could be achieved, the prospects for the final success of the Bolshevik world conspiracy in the forseeable future would be bleak.[9]

No nation occupied a more crucial position in the realization of Hitler's program than Poland, because Hitler recognized that the Poland of Pilsudski and his successors was a bulwark against Communism. The Polish leaders failed to recognize the importance of German support against the Soviet Union. Germany and Poland were conducting policies of defense against Bolshevism, but there were no plans for aggressive action against Russia, and the Polish leaders failed to see the need for any understanding with Germany to cope with the existing situation.[10]

Polish Hostility Toward the Czechs

The attitudes of the German and Polish leaders toward little Czechoslovakia were identical. The Czech problem, in contrast to the problem of Bolshevism, had moderate dimensions, and both countries were inclined to contemplate a solution of their grievances against the Czechs by some sort of aggressive action. The Polish press was many years ahead of the press of Germany in advocating the dissolution of Czechoslovakia. A Polish press campaign with this objective began in 1934, after the conclusion of the German-Polish pact. The German and Polish leaders in the same year discussed their mutual dislike of the Czechs in terms more concrete than the Poles were willing to employ toward the Soviet Union.[11]

There have been many attempts to solve the Czech problem during the past five generations. This problem arose with the spread of a hitherto unknown anti-German Czech nationalism during the 19th century. The problem did not exist in the 12th century when Bishop Otto of Freysing, a princely medieval chronicler, related the exploits of Czech shock troops fighting for Frederick I (Hohenstaufen) in his wars against the Lombard League. It did not exist in the 13th century when the proud new city of Koenigsberg (Royal Hill) on the Pregel River in East Prussia was named after Ottokar, a Bohemian king of the Premyslid line, who was noted for his brave deeds and for his loyalty to the Holy Roman Empire. It did not exist in the 14th century when Charles IV (Luxemburg-Premyslid) made Prague the most glorious capital city the Holy Roman Empire had ever known. It did not exist in the 15th century when John Hus, the martyr of the Czech religious reform movement, reported back to Bohemia, on his trip to the Council of Constance, that the audience which listened to him at Nuremberg was the most enthusiastic and grateful congregation he had ever encountered. It did not exist in the 16th century, when the Austrian duchies and the Bohemian kingdom were firmly welded under the Habsburg sceptre within the framework of the Holy Roman Empire, or in the 17th century, when Bohemian Germans and Czechs fought on both sides in the Thirty Years' War. All historians agree that the 18th century period of Habsburg rule was the most tranquil in Bohemian history.[12]

By 1848, the modern intellectual movement of Czech nationalism, which originated from the impact of the Slavophile teachings of Johann Gottfried Herder in the late 18th century, had begun to make considerable headway with the Czech masses. The Frankfurt Parliament in 1848 anticipated the dissolution of the Austrian Empire, and it quite naturally assumed that Bohemia and Moravia, which had been integral parts of the Holy Roman Empire of the German Nation, would find their future in a modern national German state. It came as a rude shock when the Czech historian and nationalist leader, Francis Palacky, addressed the Frankfurt Parliament with the announcement that his Czech faction hoped Austria would be preserved, and that they would oppose union with Germany if this effort failed. Only the continuation of the Austrian Empire stood as a buffer between the Czechs and Germany [after 1848]. Edvard Beneš, the 20th century Czech nationalist leader, advocated full autonomy for both Germans and Czechs of Bohemia in his Dijon dissertation of 1908. He envisaged a Habsburg Reich in which full equality would exist among Slavs, Germans, and Magyars. This seemed feasible, since the experiment of granting full equality to the Magyars in 1867 had proven successful.[13]

The Austro-Hungarian Empire held out with amazing vitality during the first four years of bitter conflict in World War I. The overwhelming majority of Czech deputies to the Austrian *Reichsrat* (parliament) were loyal to the Habsburg state during these four years. In the summer and autumn of 1918, during the fifth year of the war, unendurable famine and plague produced a demoralization of loyalty among the many nationalities of the Austrian part of the Empire. The Habsburg state was paralyzed. It had attempted to escape from the war by means of a separate peace, but it had failed. The problem of the Czechs and Germany could be postponed no longer. Arnold Toynbee, in his massive survey, *Nationality and the War*, had predicted in 1915 that Austria-Hungary would collapse, and he had advised that Bohemia and Moravia, the two mixed German-Czech regions, should be assigned to Germany in the coming peace treaty.[14]

The world was confronted in the meantime with one of the most bold conspiracies of history. Czech revolutionaries went abroad during World War I to organize a propaganda movement among the Allies for the creation of a veritable Czech empire. The Dual Monarchy of Austria-Hungary was condemned because the allegedly dominant German and Magyar nationalities constituted merely half the total population of the federated Habsburg states. The Czech revolutionaries

although constituting less than half the total population. The situation would
have been still worse had not some of their more extravagant schemes failed,
such as the creation of a Slavic corridor from Bohemia to Croatia. It was surely
the most brazen program of national aggrandizement to arise from World War I.
It was also the program least likely to succeed over a protracted period, unless
the subject peoples could be appeased, and unless good relations could be established with neighboring states. The Czech nationalist leaders, and their small
group of Slovak allies, who in contrast to the mass of the Slovak people had
fallen under Czech influence, made little progress in either direction during the
twenty years following World War I. It is for this reason that there was still a
Czech problem after World War II, which had now become a problem of Czech
imperialism. They might have pressed for Czech autonomy within an independent Austrian state, which later could have been united with Germany at one
stroke, while retaining guarantees for the Czechs. If this did not seem feasible
following the accomplishments of Czech revolutionaries at Prague after October
1918, there were still other alternatives. They might at least have contested the
spread of Czech rule over the traditional German parts of Bohemia and Moravia,
or over the indisputably Magyar regions from the Danube to Ruthenia. It would
have been easy for them to insist that the Czechs keep their promises of
autonomy to the Slovaks. These promises had been incorporated in the famous
Czech-Slovak declaration of Pittsburgh, Pennsylvania, in October 1918 (prior
to the Czech declaration of independence at Washington, D.C., on October 23,
1918). The first Czech president, Thomas Masaryk, had declared that his pledge
to the Slovaks, which he later violated, was solemn and binding.

The Allies might have contested the assignment of the distant region of
Ruthenia to Czech rule, or they might have insisted on binding minority guarantees for a Czech state which had promised to become another Switzerland, but
which developed a unitary state system and centralized administration in the
French style. The Allies did none of these things, and the Czech Government
was soon spending lavish sums subsidizing foreign writers to fill the foreign
press with deceptively optimistic reports about their regime.[16]

The Czechs had a solid economic position in the unravished principal
Austrian industrial regions, the industrial heart of a former Great Power, which
had fallen under their control. They also had a flourishing agricultural economy,
and conditions of relative prosperity existed in their richly endowed country
until the advent of the world depression in 1929. Czechoslovakia appeared to be
a wealthy and progressive country when compared to such backward states as
Yugoslavia or Rumania, and the Czech leaders were not reticent in taking full
credit for this phenomenon.[17]

A system of liberal politics prevailed among the principal Czech political
parties, and this was part of their heritage from Austrian parliamentary
experience. Czech propagandists exploited this fact to claim that their country
was a model democracy. A war-weary generation in the West was looking for a
few good results from the recent holocaust, and it is not surprising that
Philoczechism became a popular phenomenon. There was also something romantic about it, because relatively few people in Great Britain or
France had been aware of the existence of the Czechs prior to World War I.
There had been talk of Bohemians in the old days, and few seemed to be

certain whether this term included Slavs, Germans, or both.[18]

The Czech emigrés during World War I were more successful than the Poles in ingratiating themselves with the Western Allies. This was not fully evident until the period of peacemaking, when Czech and Polish interests clashed. In the early phase of World War I, Roman Dmowski and Thomas Masaryk, the leading Polish and Czech spokesmen in the West, vied with one another in being pro-Russian. Thomas Masaryk dreamed of a Czech kingdom under a Romanov prince, but his dream was shattered by the Russian Revolution. The Polish state which emerged from the war developed a policy contrary to the pro-Russian attitude of Dmowski, but in the Czech state the pro-Russian attitude and policy of Masaryk, and of Edvard Beneš, his principal disciple, prevailed after the war. The accidental conflict in 1918 between the Czech prisoners of war in Russia, and the Bolsheviks, was not permitted by Masaryk to destroy the fundamental pro-Russian orientation of Czech policy.[19]

There was conflict between Poles and Czechs in the rich Austrian industrial region of Teschen, which was under the control of the local Polish community when Austria-Hungary concluded an armistice with the Western Powers. The Teschen area consisted of the five principal districts of Friedeck, Freistadt, Bielitz, Teschen, and Jablonkau. The Polish deputies of the Austrian *Reichsrat* proposed to their Czech colleagues at the end of World War I that Friedeck, which had a distinct Czech majority, should go to the Czech state, and that the latter four districts should be assigned to Poland. The Czechs and Poles in the area agreed to a provisional compromise along these lines, and it was decided that 519 square kilometers should be Czech and 1,762 square kilometers Polish. The Poles did not realize that Edvard Beneš had persuaded French Foreign Minister Pichon in June 1918 to support a Czech claim for the entire area.[20]

The Poles concentrated on securing their claims against Germany during the weeks following the Austro-Hungarian and German armistice agreements of November 1918, and they regarded the Teschen area with complacency. This mood was shattered on the eve of the Polish national election of January 26, 1919, when the Czechs ordered a surprise attack against the Poles in the Teschen area. Czech action was based on the assumption that the Teschen question could be resolved by force, and that the district was well worth a local war, particularly since Western Allied support of the Czech positionagainst Poland was assured.

The Western Allied leaders intervened on February 1, 1919, after the Czechs had completed their military advance, and they ordered a cessation of military operations pending a final solution by the Peace Conference. A plebiscite was proposed in the following months, but the Czechs, with French support, concentrated first on delaying, and then on cancelling, this development. Their objective was achieved in 1920 during the Russo-Polish war. The Poles were told in good ultimative form at the Spa conference in July 1920 that they must relinquish their demand for a plebiscite, and submit to the arbitration of the Allied Powers. The greater part of the Teschen area was assigned to Czechoslovakia on July 28, 1920. The Czech objective had been achieved by an exceedingly adroit combination of force and diplomacy.[21]

The Poles were aware of the fact that the Czechs had used their influence to prevent the assignment of East Galicia to Poland, although this issue was ultimately decided in favor of Poland by the separate treaty between Russia and

Poland at Riga in 1921. The Poles were equally conscious that Czechoslovakia favored the Soviet Union during the 1920-1921 war. The French were increasingly inclined to regard the Czech pro-Russian policy as realistic, and hence to favor Czechoslovakia over Poland. It was evident after the Pilsudski *coup d'état* in 1926 that Czech political leaders were in close contact with many of the Polish politicians opposing the Warsaw dictatorship.[22]

Polish Grievances and Western Criticism

Experts on Central-Eastern Europe have criticized the insufficient cooperation among the so-called succession states after 1918. The Poles in particular have received a large share of this criticism. It has been said that Polish differences with the Czechs over Teschen, or over the Czech pro-Soviet orientation, were minor compared to the importance of Czechoslovakia as a bastion which protected the Polish southern flank against German expansion.[23] It has been argued that the Poles and Czechs both profited from World War I, and that they should have been prepared to cooperate in defending their positions against revisionist Powers.[24] Emphasis has been placed on the contention that they were sister Slavic nations with special ties of ethnography and culture.[25]

Winston Spencer Churchill had much to say on the subject of Czech-Polish relations. Churchill was the most articulate advocate of the British encirclement of Germany in the period before the Czech crisis of 1938. Churchill was noted for his belligerency, which was often regarded by his compatriots as a romantic love of adventure. He was noted for adopting the most uncompromising view of a situation and also the one most likely to produce a conflict. This had been true of his attitude in the Sudan, South Africa, and India, during the 1936 British abdication crisis, and toward many other problems in addition to Anglo-German relations. The same Churchill saw no reason why Poland should not turn her other cheek to the Czechs. When Polish leaders failed to look at matters the same way, Churchill invoked strong criticism: "The heroic characteristics of the Polish race must not blind us to their record of folly and ingratitude which over centuries had led them through measureless suffering."[26] The arguments of strategy, politics and race appeared to Churchill to dictate a Polish policy of friendship toward Czechoslovakia.

The three arguments which impressed Churchill carried little weight with the Polish leaders. They were not inclined after the death of Pilsudski in 1935 to modify the existing anti-Czech policy. This did not mean that they were unwilling under all circumstances to fight at the side of the Czechs in some war against Germany, and they made this clear to their French allies during the Czech crisis in 1938. If France supported the Czechs, if the Czechs were willing to fight, and if the Czechs disgorged the territory seized from Poland in 1919-1920, the Poles would cooperate with the Czechs. The Poles did not expect these conditions to be met for the simple reason that they did not believe the Czechs would dare to fight the Germans.[27]

The primary aim of Polish policy was to secure Polish claims against the Czechs by agreement, by threat of force, or by force. Foreign Minister Rickard Sandler of Sweden asked Beck before the 1938 Czech crisis why it was difficult to achieve an *entente* between Warsaw and Prague.[28] The Polish Foreign Minister replied that one factor was Poland's lack of enthusiasm about a Power whose claim to an independent existence was problematical. Czechoslovakia, in his opinion, was an artificial creation which violated the liberty of nations, and especially of Slovakia and Hungary. Beck's attitude was that of Mussolini, who publicly referred to the Czech state as Czecho-Germano-Polono-Magyaro-Rutheno-Rumano-Slovakia.[29] Beck emphasized that the Czechs were a minority in their own state, and that none of the other nationalities desired to remain under Czech rule. He also objected to Czech hypocrisy in stressing the allegedly liberal and democratic nature of their regime. They granted extensive rights on paper to all citizens of the state, but they exercised a brutal and arbitrary police power over the nationalities which constituted the majority of the population. Sandler was much impressed by Beck's remarks, and he observed that the Czechs obviously lacked the capacity to achieve good relations with their neighbors.[30]

Beck's attitude was not based primarily on these abstract considerations. Pilsudski's program had called for the federation (of the Lithuanians, White Russians, and Ukrainians) under Polish control. If this program had been achieved, the Poles would have been a sort of minority within a large federation, although the granting of actual autonomy to the other peoples would have been in contrast to the Czech system. Ideological differences were not decisive for Beck, who did not consider the democratic liberalism of France an insurmountable obstacle to Franco-Polish collaboration. He could not consistently boycott the same ideology at Prague.

The situation, quite apart from the specific dispute over Teschen, was determined by purely power political considerations. Poland and Czechoslovakia were bitter rivals for power and influence in the same Central-Eastern European area. Both were allied separately with Rumania, and Warsaw resented the fact that Bucharest usually appeared to be closer to Prague. The Czech alliances with both Yugoslavia and Rumania gave Prague a position of power in the general area equal to that of Warsaw. The Czechs also had an alliance with France, and they enjoyed better treatment from Paris than Warsaw received. They had ties with other allies of France in a general system directed against Germany and Hungary. The warm friendship between Prague and Moscow gave Czechoslovakia an extra trump, which the Poles could match only by establishing closer relations with Germany.

In the Polish mind, the advantage of eliminating a dangerous rival far outweighed the consideration that Germany would be in a position to secure a greater immediate gain than Poland at Czech expense. Loyalty toward the Versailles treaty and the other Paris treaties of 1919 was not a compelling motive, because the Poles were dissatisfied with the terms of these treaties.

The argument that the two nations were sister Slavic communities was anathema to the Poles. This reminded them of the indiscriminate Pan-Slavic vehicle of Russian domination over the lesser Slavic peoples. The Poles did not reject ties with sister Slavic communities, but they opposed to the Czech or Russian idea of Pan-Slavism their own more exclusive concept, which substituted themselves for the Russians as the dominant Slavic force. The Czechs were at least half-German in race, according to many Poles, and they were considered predominantly German in the cultural, political and social spheres. The Russians

also were placed at the outside border of Slavdom because of their enormous
Asiatic racial admixture. The same criterion was applied to the Serbs and the
Bulgars, who had experienced a strong oriental influx in their Balkan environ-
ment. The Slavic community recognized by the Poles included themselves, the
Ukrainians, the White Russians, the Slovaks, the Croatians, and the Slovenians.
According to Beck, the two foreign Slavic peoples most popular in Poland
because of close cultural ties with the Poles were the Slovaks and the Croats.[31]

Relations between Warsaw and Belgrade, also, were cool, although there were
no disputes between two countries separated so widely geographically. The
Polish attitude toward Yugoslavia was negative, because the Roman Catholic
Croats in Yugoslavia were oppressed by the semi-oriental Greek Orthodox Serbs,
who possessed the real power in the state. The Slovak people in Czechoslovakia
were conspicuously unhappy under the alien rule and oppressive economic
domination of the Czechs. In Poland the argument of cultural affinity could be a
great force in condemning rather than in supporting the idea of collaboration
with Prague.

It would provoke endless controversy to decide whether Churchill or the
Polish leaders had the more noble understanding of what Poland owed Czecho-
slovakia, or what would best serve Polish interests. It is more relevant to realize
that the Polish leaders had a definite Czech policy, and that it was an intelligible
policy whatever one may think of it. Beck never would have been at a loss in
replying to any arguments on this subject from Churchill. The Czechs had taken
the initiative in provoking the antagonism between Czechoslovakia and Poland.
It is true that the ultimate dissolution of Czechoslovakia made the Polish
military position more vulnerable on the German side, but this would not have
been serious had not Poland provoked a conflict with Germany instead of
accepting German friendship. The main military threat to Poland came from the
Soviet Union. In this respect the removal of Czechoslovakia was a gain, because
the Czechs had made it clear that they would support Russia in the event of a
conflict between Poland and Russia.

The Anti-German Policy of Benes

The critical attitude of Hitler toward Czechoslovakia is much easier to analyze
and to explain. He had realized since his boyhood days at Linz that the Germans
were confronted with a Czech problem, although at the time this problem was a
matter of concern only to those Germans who were subjects of the Austro-
Hungarian monarchy. He had never sympathized with Czech aspirations for
political independence, and he regarded it as a misfortune that in many respects,
and particularly in local government, the Czechs of Bohemia enjoyed more
privileges than the Bohemian Germans under Habsburg rule. Habsburg policy
was based on the assumption that the loyalty of the Bohemian Germans could
be taken for granted, but special privileges were required for the Czechs to
appease their nationalism. Hitler became a German nationalist at an early date,
and, as such, an opponent of the multi-national Habsburg system. He knew that
Bohemia, which had been traversed on foot by his musical idol, Richard Wagner,
had been an integral part of the One Thousand Year Reich of Charlemagne.

Hitler, contrary to popular superstition, never referred to his own regime as the One Thousand Year Reich. Nevertheless, like any other German conscious of them, he had a profound respect for the traditions of German history. If the role of Bohemia within Germany had worked well for more than one thousand years, one could be pardoned for scepticism toward the radical solution of placing that region within the confines of a Slavic state.[32]

It might have been possible for a larger number of people to accept this radical solution in time had conditions within Czechoslovakia been tolerable for the Germans living there, and had these local Germans become resigned to their fate. The Sudeten Germans were divided into four groups of Bavarian, Franconian, Saxon, and Silesian dialects and local cultures.They were far less aggressive politically than the Czechs, and they submitted without violence to the establishment of Czech rule in 1918 and 1919. It would have been easy to appease them, and it could have been done with a little local autonomy and with an impartial economic policy. The Czechs should have realized the importance of this for the future of their state, since the ratio of Germans to Czechs in the entire region of Bohemia-Moravia was approximately 1:2, and there were far more Germans than Czechs in Slovakia. The Czechs, instead, soon developed a contemptuous attitude toward the Germans, and they began to believe that the Germans could be handled more effectively as passive subjects than as active citizens.

The Germans were divided politically, but a new development appeared after conditions became increasingly worse for them and better for the Germans across the frontier. In the 1935 national Czechoslovak election, the Sudeten German Party (SdP), which was inspired by admiration for Adolf Hitler and his policies, captured the majority of the German vote, and it became the largest single party in Czechoslovakia. There were 800,000 unemployed workers in Czechoslovakia at that time, and 500,000 of these were Sudeten Germans. Marriages and births were few, and the death-rate was high. It is not surprising that conditions changed after the liberation of the Sudetenland in 1938. The Northern Sudetenland (the three districts of Eger, Aussig, and Troppau: the two southern sections were assigned to Bavaria and German Austria) led all regions of Germany in the number of marriages in 1939 (approximately 30% ahead of the national average). The birth-rate in 1940 was 60% greater than the birth-rate of 1937. The period of Czech rule was a bad time for the Bohemian Germans, and conditions prior to the Munich conference became steadily worse. These people were patient, but they were not cowards, and the ultimate reaction was inevitable.[33]

It is impossible under these circumstances to claim that Hitler created an artificial problem, either in the Sudetenland or in the Bohemian-Moravian region as a whole. This problem had been created in the first instance by the peacemakers of Paris, and in the second instance by Czech misrule. It was evident that the Sudeten problem would come to a head of its own momentum if Hitler succeeded in liberating the Germans of Austria from the Schuschnigg dictatorship. Hitler had no definite plans before May 1938 for dealing with this problem, but he was determined to alleviate conditions for the Germans in some way, and there can be no doubt that he [no less ardently than the Polish leaders] hoped for the total dissolution of Czechoslovakia. It is for these reasons that the German and Polish leaders found a basis for agreement whenever Czechoslovakia was discussed.[34]

This situation, and especially the inevitable German attitude toward Czechoslovakia, was no mystery to foreign statesmen before the year of the Czech crisis, 1938. Lord Halifax, who was British Foreign Secretary throughout most of 1938, told Hitler after a luncheon at Berchtesgaden on November 19, 1937, that Great Britain realized that the Paris treaties of 1919 contained mistakes which had to be rectified. Halifax assured Hitler that Great Britain did not believe in preserving the *status quo* at all costs. He mentioned the burning questions of Danzig, Austria, and Czechoslovakia quite on his own initiative, and without any prompting from Hitler. This was before Hitler had made any statement publicly that Germany was concerned either with the Czech or Danzig problems. Indeed, no such statement was necessary, since the situation was perfectly obvious.[35]

At one time it seemed that common antipathy toward Czechoslovakia might cement a virtual alliance between Germany and Poland. It was evident that this common bond would disappear after the Czech problem was solved, unless the Poles realized that antipathy toward the Soviet Union was a much more important issue in uniting the two countries. In the meantime, the points of friction between Germany and Poland would remain unless an understanding far more comprehensive than the 1934 Pact could be attained.

Neurath's Anti-Polish Policy Rejected by Hitler

It remained established German policy after 1934 to expect some revision of the Versailles Treaty along the German eastern frontier. An enduring German-Polish collaboration would depend upon a successful agreement on this issue. The German-Polish non-aggression pact of January 1934 was as silent as the Locarno treaties about German recognition of the eastern *status quo*. The Germans did not consider the Versailles treaty binding, because it violated the armistice agreement of 1918, and it was signed under duress. The Polish leaders were aware of this, and occasionally Beck sought to obtain new guarantees without concluding a comprehensive agreement with Germany.

Beck instructed Ambassador Lipski at Berlin to propose a German-Polish declaration on Danzig in September 1937. The Germans were requested to join in avowing that "it is imperative to maintain the statute which designates Danzig as the Free City." Foreign Minister Konstantin von Neurath of Germany was less friendly than Hitler toward Poland, and he peremptorily instructed Moltke in Warsaw "to tell Beck again" that Germany would not recognize the peace treaties of 1919.[36]

Neurath had been Foreign Minister since 1932. He served under several Chancellors of the Weimar Republic, and he was retained at his post by Hitler. He was not a particularly zealous Foreign Minister of the Third Reich, because he was an aristocrat who had little sympathy for Hitler's egalitarian measures. Hitler admired Neurath personally, but he recognized him as a weak link in the chain of German policy. Hitler was more intimate with Joachim von Ribbentrop, an ex-officer and merchant sincerely devoted to Hitler's policies.[37] Ribbentrop gradually replaced Alfred Rosenberg as the principal National Socialist Party expert on foreign affairs, and he developed an extensive Party bureaucratic organization to keep in touch with foreign countries. This organization was known as the Ribbentrop Office, and it foreign contacts were so extensive that it came to be looked upon as Germany's second and unofficial foreign service. Ribbentrop wished to retain control of this organization, and at the same time come to the top in the regular German Foreign Office. His ambition was recognized by the professional diplomats, and they did what they could to place obstacles in his way.

Neurath was pleased that he had persuaded Hitler to send Ribbentrop, and not Franz von Papen, as German Ambassador to London in 1936. Neurath believed that Ribbentrop would be unable to cope with the British situation, and that he would ruin his career at this difficult post. Papen, who had known Ribbentrop for many years, was more astute, and he feared that the London embassy would provide the non-professional diplomat with an opportunity to show Hitler what he could do. The event was to prove that Papen was right.[38]

Neurath rejected Beck's gesture in September 1937 without consulting Hitler, because he assumed that no other German response was possible. Hitler did not wish to bind Germany permanently to the Danzig *status quo*, but he had a more flexible conception of German foreign policy. He was counting on Polish friendship in dealing with the crises which were likely to arise in Austria and Czechoslovakia.[39]

Beck's attempt to regulate Danzig affairs exclusively with Germany conformed to a trend. Great Britain and France were represented with Sweden on a new League Commission of Three to supervise League responsibilities as the sovereign Power at Danzig. This was clearly a caretaker arrangement, and Foreign Minister Anthony Eden of Great Britain tacitly spoke for the Commission when he told the new League High Commissioner, Carl Jacob Burckhardt, on September 15, 1937, that "British policy had no special interest as such in the situation in Danzig." This position was consistent with British policy established by Prime Minister David Lloyd George in 1919 when he said that Great Britain would never fight for the Danzig *status quo*.[40]

Burckhardt had no illusions about the role of the League at Danzig. He told Adolf Hitler on September 18, 1937, that he hoped the role of the League was merely temporary, and that the ultimate fate of Danzig would be settled by a direct agreement between Germany and Poland. Hitler listened to Burckhardt's views without offering any plan for a solution. Burckhardt surmised that Hitler feared to raise the Danzig question, because it would affect the related questions of the Corridor, Czechoslovakia, and Austria. Hitler, after nearly five years in power, had pursued no questions of territorial revision, although responsibility for the ill-fated Austrian revolution of July 1934 had been falsely attributed to him.[41]

Józef Lipski, the Polish Ambassador in Berlin, knew that Hitler was a sincere advocate of an understanding with Poland.[42] Lipski was not inclined to accept the categorical statement on Danzig by Neurath. He hoped to obtain the declaration of Danzig which Beck had requested, and he was encouraged by conversations with Marshal Goering. The German Marshal had many duties connected with the German Air Force, the second German Four Year Plan, and the Prussian State Administration, but he was also intensely interested in foreign affairs. He was the Second Man in the Reich, and Hitler employed him as an Ambassador-at-large to Poland. He knew the Polish leaders, and he desired a lasting understanding with Poland. He was accustomed to discuss important matters of state with Polish representatives. He usually gave the German Foreign Office full information concerning these discussions, but it was sometimes necessary to inquire what he had said to foreign diplomats.[43]

Lipski approached Neurath several times for a Danzig declaration. Neurath on October 18, 1937, bluntly told Lipski that "some day there would have to be a basic settlement on the Danzig question between Poland and us, since it would otherwise permanently disturb German-Polish relations." Neurath added that the sole aim of such a discussion would be "the restoration of German Danzig to its natural connection with the Reich, in which case extensive consideration could be given to Poland's economic interests."[44]

Lipski was surprised, and he asked if the question would be broached soon, or perhaps immediately. Neurath evaded this inquiry, but he requested Lipski to inform Beck of his attitude. Lipski mentioned that Robert Ley, Chief of the German Labor Front, Artur Greiser, President of the Danzig Senate, and Albert Forster, District National Socialist Party Leader at Danzig, had declared publicly in recent days that Danzig must return to Germany. Neurath did not question or seek to excuse these statements. He replied that there was a need to solve the Danzig problem, and his conversation with Lipski ended in an *impasse*.[45]

There was also the problem of German access by land to East Prussia, which had been severed from the Reich. In May 1935, when Germany was engaged in her huge superhighway construction project, German Ambassador Hans Adolf von Moltke informed Beck at Warsaw that Germany wished to build a super-highway across the Polish Corridor to East Prussia. He inquired about the Polish attitude toward this plan, and Beck said that he would study the question. This was the beginning of protracted evasion by Beck. Repeated reminders from Moltke did not produce a definite statement about the Polish attitude toward the project. Fritz Todt, the National Inspector for Roads in Germany, discussed German plans with Julian Piasecki, the Polish Deputy Minister for Transportation. Moltke concluded after more than two years of fruitless inquiry that the attitude of the Polish Government was negative. The plan embodied a vital German national interest, and its acceptance by Poland would have improved prospects for a comprehensive German-Polish agreement. Moltke was unwilling to concede a final defeat in this matter.

Moltke presented a startling proposition to the German Foreign Office in October 1937. He suggested that Germany should build a superhighway up to the Corridor boundary from both Pomerania and East Prussia without waiting for Polish permission to link the route through the Corridor. Moltke failed to see that this would be a provocation which would stiffen Polish resistance to the German proposal. He believed that possible Polish objection to the construction of major military roads into the frontier area would be rendered pointless, and the Poles would find it expedient to conclude an agreement. He also had another factor in mind. The influx of tourists into Germany had greatly increased since the 1936 Olympic Games at Berlin, and Moltke believed that the complaints of foreigners, and especially tourists, who would be irritated by the break in the superhighway to historic old East Prussia, could be exploited to apply pressure on the Poles.[46]

The Poles knew that the Germans desired a superhighway across their Corridor, and Neurath's conversations with Lipski suggested the possibility that Germany was about to demand Danzig. Lipski was reticent when he conversed with Neurath again on October 23, 1937, and Neurath retained the false impression that the Poles were prepared to accept a German solution of the Danzig question. Neurath was also weighing favorably a suggestion from Albert Forster in Danzig that an offer to use Polish steel for the superhighway and a new Vistula bridge might influence the Poles to accept the highway project.[47]

The attitude of Neurath was fully shared by Czech Ambassador Slavik in Warsaw. The Czech diplomat regarded the recovery of Danzig by Germany as inevitable. He reported to Foreign Minister Kamil Krofta that in the opinion of León Noël, the French Ambassador to Poland, Danzig was lost to Poland. The conclusion of a provisional agreement on Danzig between Germany and Poland on November 5, 1937, did not change his opinion. He reported to Krofta on November 7, 1937, that League High Commissioner Burckhardt continued to insist that the union of Danzig with Germany could not be prevented. It was not surprising that the Czechs were complacent in their expectation that the German campaign of territorial revision would begin at Danzig in the vicinity of Poland. They were counting on Italy to prevent a German move into Austria, and they had nothing to fear from Germany as long as the Schuschnigg dictatorship was maintained. The fate of Danzig was a matter of complete indifference to Czechoslovakia.[48]

The German-Polish Minority Pact of 1937

The Germans had sought a treaty on minorities with Poland since 1934, when Beck exploited Russian entry into the League of Nations as a pretext to repudiate the existing treaties. The Germans of Poland were in a weak position, and they lacked the compact organization of the Germans in Czechoslovakia. The Polish treatment of the Germans after 1918 was harsh. Approximately 70% of the 1918 German population of Posen and West Prussia had emigrated to Germany before the Pilsudski *coup d'état* in 1926, and this comprised no less than 820,000 individuals from these two former German provinces. Polish propaganda often pretended that the Germans who remained were largely great landowners, but this was not so. It is true that 80% of the 325,000 Germans remaining in the two provinces by 1937 lived from agriculture, but they were mainly peasants. There were still 165,000 Germans by 1939 in East Upper Silesia, which had been detached from Germany despite the German victory in the 1921 plebiscite. There were also 364,000 Germans in Congress Poland in 1939, and there were 60,000 within the former Kresy territory of Volhynia. Germans were scattered through the Wilna area, and as late as 1939 there were over 900,000 Germans in the former German and Russian Polish territories. This did not include Austrian Galicia, where the Germans were mainly agricultural, although the industrial town of Bielitz had a German population of 62%. A critical study of the 1931 Polish census, which contained startling inaccuracies in several directions, showed that the given figure of 727,000 Germans was short

80 THE FORCED WAR

of the real figure by more than 400,000.[49]

Polish policy toward the Germans during the early years was more severe in the former German territories than in Galicia, Congress Poland, or the Kresy. More than one million acres of German-owned land were confiscated during the years from 1919-1929 in the provinces of Posen and West Prussia. German language schools throughout Poland were closed during the years before 1934. There were 21 German deputies in the Polish Sejm after the 1928 election, 5 German deputies after the election in autumn 1930, and no German deputies after 1935. Two Germans were allowed to sit in the less important Polish Senate at that time, but they were denied their seats many months before the outbreak of the German-Polish war in 1939.

The exceptionally miserable conditions in the former German provinces inevitably produced protests from the local German population. There was much enthusiasm among the younger Germans in 1933 when the Hitler Revolution triumphed in the Reich, and this further irritated and antagonized the Poles. The older Germans were aware of this, and many of them were concerned about it. The younger Germans were attracted to the *Young German Party for Poland* (JDP) which had been founded by Dr. Rudolf Wiesner at Bielitz in 1921. A number of more conservative German parties had opposed this group, and in 1934 Senator Hasbach attempted to unite the conservative opposition in the *Council of Germans in Poland* (RDP). The conservatives controlled most of the remaining German language press, and in 1937 there was a split in the *Young German* leadership, when a more radical faction under Wilhelm Schneider sought to obtain control. Wiesner won out after much difficulty, but it was a conspicuous fact that no outstanding leadership emerged in any of the German groups. The contrast between the German factions in Poland and the Sudeten German Party in Czechoslovakia under Konrad Henlein was very great.[50]

Both the conservative and radical groups were nominally pro-Hitler, but the latter had more ambitious ideas concerning the extent to which social reforms like those of the Reich could be of benefit in improving conditions for the Germans of Poland. Neither group indicated the slightest expectation that they would or could come under German rule. The *Office for Ethnic Germans* (*Volksdeutsche Mittelstelle*) in the Reich, which promoted cultural contracts between Germans abroad and Germany, did not interfere with the struggle between the German political factions in Poland. Both factions hoped that the *rapprochement* between Germany and Poland would improve their position, but there was no indication of this in the years after the conclusion of the 1934 pact. The Germans of Poland, with very few exceptions, remained strictly loyal to the Polish state, and later research by the Dutch expert, Louis de Jong, contradicted the popular Polish claim that there was a German 5th column in Poland. The agents of the German intelligence service in Poland were almost exclusively Jews and Poles. Thousands of young Germans of military age were serving with the Polish Army when war came in 1939. The prominent Germans of Poland remained in the country in September 1939 and experienced arrest, transportation into the interior, or death.[51]

An article in *Gazeta Polska*, the Government newspaper at Warsaw, stated on October 21, 1935, that moral solidarity and cultural ties were clearly within the rights of the Germans of Poland. This was all that the German minority sought.

The Germans of Poland failed to unite, but their morale improved after 1933. They took an active part in the 1935 Polish national election, although it was known that they would be allowed no seats in the Sejm. The National Democrats, a strictly Polish party, boycotted the same election. They provoked the authorities in a manner of which the Germans would never have dreamed. The Germans of Poland, when allowance is made for a few individual exceptions, were passive, and not trouble-makers. Hitler was understandably concerned about their unfair treatment, but he merely wished that they would receive decent treatment as Polish subjects.[52]

The Polish minority in Germany was more united and more ably organized. The *Union of Poles in Germany (Zwiazek Polaków w Niemczech)* was organized at Berlin in 1922. All members automatically received the newspaper, *Polak w Niemczech (The Pole in Germany)*. It had been true for generations that many people of Polish descent in Germany preferred to be considered German. The *Union of Poles* sought to combat this tendency, and it opposed the so-called "subjective census" introduced by the Weimar Republic and continued by Hitler. The old Hohenzollern bureaucracy had counted Poles on the basis of documentary evidence. The modern technique called for a subjective declaration of ethnic identity in addition to an identification of the mother tongue. This meant in Weimar days that a person could say his mother tongue was Polish, but that he was ethnically German. Many thousands of Poles had emigrated to work in West German industry as well as in the industries of France, and now the census permitted them to identify themselves as Germans. Under the conditions, only 14,000 claimed to be Poles in the census of 1939, although the Germans estimated that there must be at least 260,000 Poles in Germany by objective criteria, and the Polish Government claimed that there were 1,500,000. Economic conditions in Germany were good, there was no economic discrimination against the Poles, and the national feeling of the Polish minority was lax. The same trend had been displayed in elections to the Reichstag during the Weimar Republic, but under Hitler it became an avalanche.[53]

During the 1928 school year, only 6,600 children had attended Polish schools in Germany, and of these 4,172 were in the Berlin and Ruhr areas. On the other hand, the Poles maintained many cooperatives, which were less explicitly an indication of national identity. The Polish press in Germany welcomed the improved economic and social conditions under Hitler, and it recognized the National Socialist program to secure these conditions for the Polish minority. The German citizen law of September 15, 1935, was explicit in recognizing that the Polish minority enjoyed full citizen rights. In 1937, the Polish minority organization still maintained 58 grammar schools and 2 high schools (*gymnasia*), and these institutions provided ample space for Polish children wishing to attend Polish schools in the Reich. A general meeting of the Polish organization was held on March 6, 1938, in the *Strength through Joy* (KdF) theater in Berlin with Father Domanski and Secretary-General Czeslaw Kaczmarek presiding. Many proud speeches were made. A large organization was formally in evidence, but there was little behind it, as the May 1939 German census clearly revealed.[54]

A promising German-Polish pact on minorities was concluded at last on November 5, 1937. It was agreed that on the same day Hitler would speak to the leaders of the Polish minority and President Mościcki of Poland would address the German minority leaders. Hitler was extremely pleased with what he regarded as a concrete step in the direction of a comprehensive German-Polish understanding. He could not know that the Polish leaders would consider the new pact a dead letter. He agreed to amnesty a number of German citizens of Polish extraction, who had violated German criminal laws. He also granted Lipski's request for a compromise declaration on Danzig. It was agreed that the Danzig question would not be permitted to disturb German-Polish relations. Hitler displayed his Austrian charm when he received the delegation from the Polish minority in Germany. He emphasized to them that he was an Austrian, and that precisely for this reason he could understand their situation especially well. The Poles were extremely pleased by the warmly personal nature of Hitler's remarks. The reception given to the German minority leaders by President Mościcki at a vacation resort in the Beskiden mountains was more reserved.[55]

The Bogey of the Hossbach Memorandum

A mysterious event which took place on the same day as the German-Polish minority pact has furnished ideal subject matter for professional propagandists. Hitler addressed a conference attended by some of his advisers, but without the majority of his Cabinet. The narrow circle included Defense Minister Werner von Blomberg, Army Commander Werner von Fritsch, Navy Commander Erich Raeder, Air Force Commander Hermann Goering, and Foreign Minister Konstantin von Neurath. Colonel Hossbach, an officer of the German General Staff assigned by the General Staff for *liaison* work with Hitler, was also present. This man was in no sense Hitler's personal adjutant, although this idea has persisted in many accounts.[56]

The so-called Hossbach version of the conference, which is supposed to have become one of the most celebrated documents of all time, was written several days after the event, and it could carry no weight in a normal court of law, even if an actual copy of this memorandum was available. Hossbach had been an opponent of Hitler and his system since 1934, and he was not averse to the employment of illegal and revolutionary means in eliminating Hitler. He was an ardent admirer of General Ludwig Beck, the German Chief of Staff, whose life he had once helped to save on the occasion of a cavalry accident. Beck was a determined foe of Hitler, and he was engaged in organizing opposition against the German Chancellor. Hossbach was naturally on the alert to provide Beck with every possible kind of propaganda material. Hitler was popular in Germany, and only extreme methods might be effective in opposing him.[57]

It would be the duty of every historian to treat the so-called Hossbach memorandum with reserve, even if it could be shown that the version introduced at Nuremberg was an authentic copy of the memorandum which Hossbach began to write on November 10, 1937 (he failed to recall later when he completed his effort). The fact is, however, that no copies of this original version have been located since World War II. The version introduced by the American Prosecution at Nuremberg, the only one extant, was said to be a copy made from the original version in late 1943 or early 1944, but Hossbach declared in a notarized affidavit on June 18, 1946, that he could not remember whether or not the Nuremberg copy corresponded to the original which he had made nearly nine years earlier. In other words, the sensational document, which was the primary instrument used in securing the conviction and execution of a number of Germany's top leaders, has never been verified, and there is no reason to assume that it is authentic. Raeder explained that Hitler's views, as expressed on November 5, 1937, offered no basis to conclude that any change in German foreign policy was about to take place, but the judges at Nuremberg, with the dubious help of an unconfirmed record, decided that Hitler had revealed unmistakably his unalterable intention to wage a war of criminal aggression.

Fritsch and Blomberg were dead when this conference was investigated after World War II, but Neurath and Goering agreed with Raeder about the essential nature of Hitler's remarks. Hitler had discussed German aspirations in Central Europe and the danger of war, but this was certainly a very different thing than announcing an intention to pursue a reckless foreign policy or to seek a war. Even the alleged Hossbach memorandum introduced at Nuremberg, as A.J.P. Taylor has pointed out, does not anticipate any of the actual events which followed in Europe during 1938 and 1939. It does contain some offensive and belligerent ideas, but it outlines no specific actions, and it establishes no timetables. Hence, error had been added to error. It was false to assume that the document was authentic in the first place, and it was incorrect to assume that even the fraudulent document contained any damaging evidence against Hitler and the other German leaders. Unfortunately, most of the later historians in Germany and elsewhere have blindly followed the Nuremberg judgment and have arrived at the mistaken conclusion that Hitler's conference of November 5, 1937, was relevant to the effort of determining the responsibility for World War II.[58]

Hitler's November 1937 Danzig Declaration

The November 5, 1937, treaty on minorities would have resolved one of the two major points of friction between Germany and Poland had it been observed by the Poles. It guarded against assimilation by force, restrictions against the use of the mother tongue, suppression of associations, denial of schools, and the pursuit of policies of economic discrimination.[59]

The other principal point of friction was the Danzig-Corridor problem. Hitler hoped to reassure the Poles by his statement that he was contemplating peaceful negotiation to resolve this problem. Neurath was not content to leave Hitler's vague assurance unqualified, and he sought to interpret it as part of a *quid pro quo* bargain. According to Neurath, Hitler's promise to the Poles on Danzig would be a dead letter if they did not respect the treaty on minorities.[60]

The Poles attempted to interpret Hitler's statement as a disavowal that Germany intended to acquire Danzig. They were on weak ground in this effort, because the German failure to accord them a voluntary recognition of their frontiers meant that Germany was automatically claiming the territory assigned to Poland on the western side of the German 1914 eastern frontier. The Polish Foreign Office on November 9, 1937, protested against a speech by Albert Forster in Duesseldorf on November 6th. Forster had declared to a large audience that his aim was to achieve the reunion of Danzig with the Reich. This speech was merely one incident in a major campaign to acquaint the German population with the Danzig problem.[61]

It was decided at the German Foreign Office on November 23, 1937, that the recent Danzig meetings carried out by Forster in various German cities had been so successful that this program should be intensified. Plans were made to prepare one hundred additional meetings in the near future, and an additional fifty meetings before April 1938. Arrangements were made to provide the best possible speakers from Danzig. The Danzig Senate President, the Volkstag President (Danzig Lower House), the Danzig District Propaganda Leader, the Danzig Labor Front Leader, and many other prominent Danzigers were enrolled in addition to Forster. It was discovered that *Der Danziger Vorposten* (*The Danzig Sentinel*), the principal news organ of Danzig, was an excellent newspaper, and plans were made to increase its circulation in the Reich. *Das Deutsche Danzig* (*German Danzig*), a travelling Danzig exposition, was also planned, and it was scheduled to open at Muenster in Westphalia by the end of November 1937. The German Foreign Office had concluded that current knowledge and awareness of Danzig in the Reich was "proper" but "insufficient." This activity was an excellent indication of the German attitude toward Hitler's Danzig declaration. It was regarded as the hopeful beginning of a definite diplomatic campaign to recover Danzig.[62]

Austria as a Czech Buffer

The German Foreign Office assumption about Danzig was basically correct although somewhat premature. Hitler did not pursue the Danzig question during the winter of 1937-1938, and by February 1938 the Austrian question commanded his full attention. It was soon evident that an Austrian crisis was approaching its climax, and there could be no doubt that a solution of the Austrian problem would automatically raise the Czechoslovakian problem. The existence of 3,500,000 unhappy Sudeten Germans could be ignored neither by the Czechs, by Hitler, nor by the world if the Germans of Austria were united with Germany. A Czechoslovakian crisis in turn could provide the first major opportunity for Germany and Poland to cooperate in an international crisis, because the attitudes of both of these states toward the Czechs were hostile and fundamentally identical. If this cooperation proved successful, it might be possible to deal with the two principal points of friction between Germany and Poland with greater prospect of success.

The Czechs were well aware of the hostility of their principal neighbors. It was not surprising that on February 22, 1938, during the early phase of the Austrian crisis, Kamil Krofta, Czechoslovakia's Foreign Minister, prepared a memorandum which explained why he favored definite Czech action to prevent the reunion of Austria and Germany. The complacent assumption that Danzig was the primary objective of German expansion would be shattered unless the puppet dictatorship in Austria could be maintained as a buffer against the realization of Hitler's dream of Greater Germany. Palacky had supported an independent Austria against the Frankfurt Parliament in 1848, and Krofta hoped that it would be possible to support an independent Austria, although merely a fragmentary rump-Austria, against Hitler.[63]

In the foreground the Czechs were facing a surprise, and the Germans and the Poles were soon in a position to score their separate triumphs at Czech expense. In the background was the Soviet Union, the greatest single peril either Germans or Poles had ever had to face. It was desirable for Germany and Poland to unite against this danger, although perhaps no one, including the German and the Polish leaders, knew how great the peril really was.

Chapter 5

THE ROAD TO MUNICH

Hitler's Peaceful Revision Policy in 1938

The year 1938 retains a special place in the annals of Europe. It was the year of Adolf Hitler's greatest triumphs in foreign policy. A.J.P. Taylor, in his epochal book, *The Origins of the Second World War*, has proved beyond dispute that Hitler's principal moves in 1938 were nothing more than improvised responses to the actions of others. Yet, in 1938, Hitler liberated ten million Germans who had been denied self-determination by the peacemakers of 1919. Hitler gained for the German people the same rights enjoyed by the peoples of Great Britain, France, Italy, and Poland. He managed to achieve his victories without provoking an armed conflict. Nothing of the kind had happened in Europe before. There had been dynastic unions in which territories had been united without actual violence, but never had the leader of one nation triumphed over two hostile foreign Governments without shedding blood. Hitler proved something which the League of Nations claimed that it would prove but never did. Peaceful territorial revision in Europe was possible. No one could have said this with any assurance before 1938, because empirical evidence was lacking. We now have the empirical evidence. The threat of force was used by Hitler to achieve these results, but the shedding of blood in senseless wars was avoided. A cursory examination of these triumphs will be vital in explaining why the major successes of Hitler in 1938 were not duplicated on a smaller scale in September 1939.[1]

Perhaps no statesman has been more violently criticized than Hitler by his compatriots and by foreigners throughout the world. This is not surprising when one considers that Hitler failed to carry out his program after 1939, and that his failure was total because of the savagery of his opponents. Some critics condemn Hitler from the hour of his birth. At the other extreme are those who perhaps regard themselves as friendly or sympathetic toward him, but who say that Hitler did not know how to wait, or did not know when to stop. It is customary to condemn failure and to worship success. This tendency is part of the fundamental desire of mankind to simplify the world in which we live and to find a natural order and purpose in things. Nietzsche had this in mind when he wrote that a good war justifies every cause. No one can be immune from this desire, because it is "human-all-too-human," but momentary detachment, within the context of past events, is and should be possible. It will be evident later that the Munich conference was not the final solution to Germany's problems, and that the adoption by Hitler of a passive wait-and-see policy at that stage would have been merely a simple and dangerous panacea.[2]

Hitler had no idea of what was in store when 1938 opened. There had been no sequel to the November 5, 1937, conference with Foreign Minister Neurath and the military men. He had no specific plans and no timetable for the accomplishment of territorial revision. When he looked out the *Berghof* windows at Berchtesgaden into the mountains of Austria, he did not know that within a few weeks he would return to his Austrian homeland for the first time in more than a quarter of a century. The achievements of Hitler in 1938 were not the result of careful foresight and planning in the style of Bismarck, but of the rapid exploitation of fortuitous circumstances in the style of Frederick the Great during the early years of his reign.

The January 1938 Hitler-Beck Conference

Hitler discussed the European situation with Polish Foreign Minister Beck at Berlin on January 14, 1938. This conference was important. The development of German-Polish relations since the November 5, 1937, declaration on minorities had caused disappointment in both countries, and it was necessary to clear the atmosphere. Polish protests about statements in Germany concerning Danzig had produced much bad feeling, although Albert Forster had agreed at Hitler's suggestion to go to Warsaw to discuss the situation with Polish leaders. German efforts to persuade the Poles to accept periodic talks on mutual minority problems met with evasion in Warsaw. The Germans presented protests on current Polish economic discrimination against minority Germans in the East Upper Silesian industrial area, but these protests remained unanswered. German Ambassador Moltke bluntly told Beck on December 11, 1937, that Germany was disillusioned in her hopes for favorable results under the new treaty.[3]

The Germans were also concerned about the Polish annual agrarian reform law which was announced early each year. These laws were used to expropriate land owned by Germans in Poland, and especially in the former German provinces. There was a rumor that the 1938 law would be more drastic than those of previous years, which later proved to be the case. Neurath had arranged to meet Beck on January 13, 1938, and he had prepared a careful memorandum containing many grievances. He intended to emphasize the agrarian law, and the special de-Germanization measures of Polish frontier ordinances, which proclaimed the right of the Polish state to prevent others than ethnic Poles from owning property in the region of the frontier. He also intended to protest the bitterly anti-German policy of Governor Grazynski in Polish East Upper Silesia, and to complain about the Polish press which remained anti-German despite the latest agreement. He intended to deplore the absence of a "psychological breakthrough" to better relations between the two countries.[4]

Neurath was frustrated by an order from Hitler which forbade him to raise these controversial points. The Polish Foreign Office on January 12, 1938, denounced the plan for periodic meetings to discuss minority problems as a "dangerous road" which could lead to friction. Moltke wired Neurath on the same day that Beck intended to concentrate on the Danzig question in his conversation with the German Foreign Minister. Neurath had little enthusiasm for his conference with Beck under these circumstances, and he was evasive when the Polish Foreign Minister suggested that the League High Commissioner should be removed from Danzig. He finally agreed that Beck should sound out the mood at Geneva in order to consider the possibility of pursuing the question at an "appropriate time."[5]

Beck confided to Neurath that he was delighted with the new anti-Jewish Government of Octavian Goga in Rumania, and with the elimination, which was only temporary in this instance, of the Rumanian liberal regime. Beck finally made the significant statement that Polish relations with Czechoslovakia could not be worse, and he "could not imagine that they would ever change." He added pointedly that Poland had no political interest whatever in Austria. He indicated that Polish interests south of the Carpathians were limited to Poland's Rumanian ally, to Polish territorial aspirations in Czechoslovakia, and to the eastern and largely non-Czech part of the Prague domain.

Beck assured Neurath that combatting Bolshevism, with which the Czechs had formally allied themselves in June 1935, was a primary aim of Polish policy. Neurath immediately raised the question of Polish participation in the 1936 German-Japanese anti-Comintern pact, which Italy had joined a few weeks previously. Beck hastily replied that this arrangement was "impracticable for Poland." Beck was convinced that the great Soviet purges were undermining Russian strength, and he was determined to avoid a commitment with Germany which he considered unnecessary.[6]

Hitler met Beck the following day, and he made a statement which the Polish Foreign Minister should have considered very carefully. They discussed the current Civil War in Spain, and Hitler observed that he was vitally interested in the struggle against Bolshevism in Europe. He then added that his anti-Bolshevik policy would, nevertheless, have to take second place to his aim of strengthening and consolidating German power. The restoration of Germany was the primary mandate which he had received from the German people. It is important to bear this declaration in mind when examining the contention that Hitler reversed his entire foreign policy in seeking an accommodation with Russia in 1939. Actually, such a policy was conceivable at any moment when German interests were in serious jeopardy.[7]

Hitler also informed Beck with studied emphasis that he would never give his consent to cooperate with Poland in securing a revision of the Danzig statute, if the purpose of such a revision was to perpetuate the Free City regime. He hoped that Beck would realize that his attitude was unalterable on this point. The conversation turned to Austria, and it was evident to Beck that Hitler was preoccupied with conditions in that country. Hitler informed Beck that he would invade Austria immediately, if any attempt were made to restore the Habsburg dynasty. He confided that his current Austrian policy was based on peaceful relations with Vienna along the lines of the 1936 Austro-German treaty. This treaty had been negotiated by Franz von Papen, who had been German envoy in Austria since October 1934, and Austrian Foreign Minister Guido Schmidt. It constituted a truce between the two countries in the undeclared war which had existed since Hitler came to power in 1933. Austria, under the terms of this treaty, had obliged herself to conduct a foreign policy consistent with her character as a German state.[8]

Hitler mentioned that his policy toward Czechoslovakia was confined to improving the status of the German minority, but he confided his opinion that "the whole structure of the Czech state, however, was impossible." Neither Hitler nor Beck were aware of the role of Czech President Benes in bringing on the Russian army purge by advising Stalin of alleged pro-German treason in the Red Army. Nevertheless, they both recognized the danger of Bolshevist penetration in Czechoslovakia, and Beck "heartily agreed" with Hitler's remarks about the Czechs.[9]

Beck confided something to Hitler that he had never told the Russians. He revealed that Poland's alliance with Rumania was directed exclusively against the Soviet Union, and he added that Poland hoped to strengthen Rumania against Bolshevism. He also claimed that he wished to increase German-Polish friendship, and "to continue the policy initiated by Marshal Pilsudski."[10]

The January 14, 1938, conversation between Hitler and Beck was the last one for nearly a year, and it played an important role in improving cooperation between the two countries despite the local incidents of friction which continued to occur. The relations between the two men were on a more friendly basis than before, and State Secretary Weizaecker was not overstating the case when he informed Moltke that the meeting had been "satisfactory on both sides." This was possible because points of interest had been emphasized, and differences had been ignored.[11]

The Rise of Joachim von Ribbentrop

Two scandals involving Defense Minister Werner von Blomberg and Army Commander Werner von Fritsch occurred in Germany in January 1938. The latter was acquitted by a special military court in March 1938 of having engaged in the homosexual practices with which he had been charged. The Blomberg scandal was caused by the Blomberg-Erna Gruehn marriage at which Hitler had been a witness. The fact soon came to light that Erna Gruehn had a record as a registered prostitute in Berlin. No one, including Blomberg himself, believed that the Defense Minister could continue his duties under these circumstances. The dismissal of Fritsch as Army Commander, before the final verdict on his case, was an injustice based on mere suspicion, but it was perfectly legal, since Hitler had the constitutional power to dismiss him.[12]

These developments necessitated changes, and Hitler decided to extend them. Ribbentrop was at last appointed Foreign Minister to replace Neurath, and several other important changes were made in the diplomatic service. Hassell was withdrawn as German Ambassador at Rome and replace by Mackensen, who had been State Secretary at the Foreign Office. The withdrawal of Ulrich von Hassell was a logical step, since he opposed the idea of a German-Italian alliance. Ernst von Weizsaecker was selected to replace Hans Georg von Mackensen as State Secretary, with the approval of Ribbentrop, who believed that Weizsaecker could be trusted to execute his policy, and that Mackensen could not. In reality, both men were in fundamental opposition to Hitler, but Ribbentrop was not aware of this at the tiime.

Dirksen was transferred from Tokio and later sent to London to replace Ribbentrop, and Ott was sent to replace Dirksen at the Tokyo post. Papen was informed at Vienna on February 4, 1938, that he would be recalled as German Ambassador to Austria. It was evident that Hitler believed the limit had been reached with Franz von Papen's conciliatory Austrian policy. It is uncertain what Hitler would have done in the following days with the Austrian post, because Papen immediately took the initiative in determining the course of events in Austria. He was dismayed when he received word of his recall. He took leave of his family on February 5th, and proceeded to Berchtesgaden for an interview with Hitler. It was his impression that the German Chancellor was much preoccupied with the situation in Austria, but undecided about the future course of German policy toward that country.[13]

The Fall of Kurt von Schuschnigg

Papen had earlier suggested to Hitler that an interview with Austrian Dictator Kurt von Schuschnigg might be useful, and Hitler had granted him permission to arrange one; Schuschnigg was understandably reluctant, and Hitler appeared to have forgotten about the matter. When Papen called on Hitler on February 5th, he mentioned that Schuschnigg had at last expressed a desire for a conference and that it could be speedily arranged. Hitler was at once enthusiastic, and he told Papen to continue temporarily as German Ambassador to Austria. Papen was somewhat nettled by this procedure, since he had taken leave of the Austrian Government in his ambassadorial capacity, but he realized that Hitler was in the habit of cutting through conventional practices when the need for action arose.[14]

Papen arranged a conference between Hitler and Schuschnigg at Berchtesgaden for February 12th. Hitler instructed Papen to tell the Austrian Chancellor that German officers would be present that day, so Schuschnigg came to Berchgaden accompanied by Austrian military officers and by Foreign Minister Guido Schmidt. Hitler greeted Schuschnigg courteously, and then proceeded to subject him, as a German, to moral pressure. By 11:00 p.m. Schuschnigg had agreed to cease persecuting Austrian National Socialists, to admit the National Socialist Austrian leader, Seyss-Inquart, to the Cabinet as Minister of Interior, and to permit Hitler to broadcast a speech to Austria in return for a Schuschnigg speech to Germany. The Austrian Chancellor was later ashamed that he had accepted these conditions, and he claimed that Hitler had been violent in manner during the first two hours of conversation. Papen denied this, and he insisted that the meeting had ended in general satisfaction. Papen was accustomed to Hitler and familiar with his occasional passionate outbursts, and from this perspective the day appeared less stormy to him. Schuschnigg recalled that

Hitler thanked Papen in his presence at the end of the meeting and said that "through your (Papen's) assistance I was appointed Chancellor of Germany and thus the Reich was saved from the abyss of Communism."[15]

Hitler was exhilarated by this personal success. In a major speech on February 20, 1938, he drew the attention of the world to the ten million Germans in the two neighboring states of Austria and Czechoslovakia. He stressed that these Germans had shared the same Reich with their compatriots until 1866. Austria-Hungary was closely allied a few years later with the new German Reich of Bismarck, and in this way a form of union continued to link the Germans. They had shared the same common experience of World War I as soldiers for the Central Powers. The peacemakers of 1919 had frustrated their desire for union within a new Germany.[16]

Schuschnigg began to consider means of repudiating the Berchtesgaden agreement of February 12, 1938, shortly after he returned to Austria. He realized that he required the appearance of some moral mandate to achieve this aim. He knew that his regime could never win an honest election of the issues of continued separation from Germany, and of his own scarcely veiled project of restoring the Habsburgs in the tiny Austrian state. At last he decided to stage a fraudulent plebiscite. He announced at Innsbruck on March 9, 1938, that a plebiscite on the important issue of the future of Austria would be held within the short span of four days, on March 13, 1938. It had been determined in advance that the balloting would be subjected to official scrutiny, which would render impossible the anonymity of the voters' choice. Negative ballots would have to be supplied by the voters themselves, and it was required that for validity they should be of such an odd, fractional size that they could be readily disqualified. The vote-of-confidence question in Schuschnigg was to be phrased in terms as confusing and misleading as possible. Schuschnigg forced Hitler's hand in the Austrian question by means of this chicanery. Great Britain had been hastily seeking an agreement with Italy since January 1938 in the hope of using it to preserve the independence of the Austrian puppet state. The agreement was not concluded until April 1938, when it was too late to be of use. Mussolini had vainly advised Schuschnigg to abandon his risky plan for a plebiscite. Apparently Schuschnigg, and not Hitler, had become impatient and was determined to force the issue regardless of the consequences.

Schuschnigg was informed by Seyss-Inquart on March 11, 1938, at 10:00 a.m., that he must agree within one hour to revoke the fraudulent plebiscite, and agree to a fair and secret-ballot plebiscite within three to four weeks, on the question of whether Austria should remain independent or be reunited with the rest of Germany. Otherwise the German Army would occupy Austria. The failure of a reply within the specified time produced a new ultimatum demanding that Seyss-Inquart succeed Schuschnigg as Chancellor of Austria. The crisis had reached a climax, and there was no retreat for either side.[17]

The principal danger to Germany was that Italy, the only other European Great Power which bordered Austria, would intervene. France had no engagements toward Austria, no common frontier, and was in the midst of a Cabinet crisis. Lord Halifax, who had been appointed British Foreign Secretary the previous month to succeed Anthony Eden, did everything he could to incite Italian action against Germany. The British diplomatic representatives in Vienna favored Schuschnigg's desision for a plebiscite. Halifax warned Ribbentrop in London on March 10, 1938, that there would be "possible consequences" in terms of British intervention against Germany if Hitler used force in Central Europe. Ribbentrop was in London to take leave of his ambassadorial post, and Neurath was directing the German Foreign Office during this interval. Early on March 11, 1938, Halifax instructed British Ambassador Henderson in Berlin to see Hitler and to warn him against German interference in Austria. On the same day, Halifax was informed from Rome that Italian Foreign Minister Galeazzo Ciano refused to discuss the Austrian situation with British diplomatic representatives. The situation had developed so quickly that Germany had been unable to arrive at an agreement with Italy, but Mussolini decided to make no difficulties for Hitler when the crisis came. Ciano had anticipated this situation when he wrote in his diary on February 23, 1938, that an Italian war against Germany on behalf of Schuschnigg would be an impossibility. This did not change the fact that the Italian leaders were very unhappy about the Austrian situation. Hitler received word at 10:25p.m., on March 11, 1938, that Mussolini accepted the *Anschluss* (*union*, i.e. with Austria).[18]

It was evident by this time that there would be no resistance to German troops entering Austria, and Hitler was now convinced that there would be no overt foreign intervention. He left Hermann Goering in charge at Berlin, and he proceeded to his Austrian homeland. He was greeted with a joyously enthusiastic reception from the mass of the Austrian people. Hitler knew that his undisturbed Austrian triumph had been possible because Mussolini had sacrificed a former sphere of Italian influence, and on March 13, 1938, he wired Mussolini from Austria: "Mussolini, I shall never forget this of you!."[19]

When Halifax saw that France was immobilized by a domestic crisis and that Italy was disinclined to act, it was decided at London to adopt a friendly attitude toward the Austrian *Anschluss* situation. This was easy to do, because the German leaders during the next few days were so happy to see Germany score a major success for the first time in twenty years that they were prepared to embrace the entire world in the spirit of Beethoven's 9th Symphony (*Seid umschlungen, Ihr Millionen!: Be embraced, you millions of humanity!*). The recorded version of a telephone conversation between Ribbentrop in London and Goering in Berlin on March 13, 1938, offers an indication of this. Ribbentrop praised the British attitude and added: "I do think one knows pretty well over here what is going on." He told Goering that he had emphasized [to Halifax on March 12th] the importance of an Anglo-German understanding and Goering commented: "I was always in favor of a German-English understanding." Ribbentrop suggested: "Chamberlain also is very serious about an understanding," and Goering replied: " I am also convinced that Halifax is an absolutely reasonable man." Ribbentrop concluded this phase of the discussion with the comment: "I received the best impression of Halifax as well as of Chamberlain."[20]

The Double Game of Lord Halifax

It was easy for Halifax to praise the Germans to their faces, and to seek to undermine them secretly, but one must inquire after the purpose of this double game. The official British policy in Europe was conducted under the label of appeasement. This attractive term for a conciliatory policy had been popularized by French Foreign Minister Aristide Briand in the 1920's and revived by British Foreign Secretary Anthony Eden during the Rhineland crisis in 1936. Appeasement to Britain meant a sincere French policy of conciliation toward Germany. Later the Communist press, and the "liberal" (19th century liberalism would have been hostile to the Soviet Union) journalists allied with it, succeeded in convincing the broad, unsuspecting masses in the Western countries that this term had an odious connotation. The Communists at this time also invented the epithet "Cliveden set," following a week-end which Neville Chamberlain spent at the Astor estate of Cliveden-on-the-Thames from March 26-28, 1938. The fact that Anthony Eden, who was popular with the Communists at the time, spent more week-ends at Cliveden than Chamberlain made no difference to them, because they were no more inclined to be honest about Cliveden than about the Reichstag fire of 1933, which had been attributed to the National Socialists by the Communist agent at Paris, Willie Muensterberg. The mass of the people in the Western countries accepted the story about the Reichstag despite the absence of proof, and the Communists were correct in anticipating that they would believe the charge of a sinister "pro-Nazi conspiracy" at Cliveden. Communist propaganda victories were easy when the majority of Western "liberals" were working as their allies. President Roosevelt, in a speech at Chicago in 1937, included the Soviet Union among the so-called peace-loving nations of the world in contrast to the allegedly evil and aggressive Germans, Italians, and Japanese.[21]

There was no Cliveden set and no genuine British appeasement policy. The use of this term by Neville Chamberlain and Lord Halifax, and by their principal parliamentary advisers, Sir John Simon and Sir Samuel Hoare, was a facade to disguise the fact that the British leaders considered themselves to be somewhat behind in their military preparations. It was recognized in 1937 and 1938 that German rearmament was not especially formidable, and that it would be easy for Great Britain, despite her much smaller industrial capacity, to score relative gains on Germany in this field. British armament efforts in the early 1930's had been hampered by the effects of the world depression, by the opposition from the Labour Party, and by interference from the British peace movement, which enjoyed considerable popularity for a time. It was recognized that the two previous Prime Ministers, Ramsay MacDonald and Stanley Baldwin, had been somewhat lax about overcoming these difficulties, but a major British armament campaign was now in full swing under Neville Chamberlain. It would require another year, after early 1938, before the full effects of this program would be realized, and in the meantime the British leaders believed it wise to tread softly, beneath the guise of impartial justice, in coping with European problems. Events were to show that it was a great gain for the Soviet Union that the British leaders were not sincerely devoted to the program to which they professed to adhere.[22]

There was another important factor which made appeasement a clever label for British policy. The injustices inflicted on Germany in 1919 and the following years converted many thinking Englishmen to that sympathy toward the Germans which had been the traditional English attitude in the 19th century. Popular sympathy toward a country on which one is contemplating a military assault is a bad basis on which to build war sentiment. A nominal adherence to appeasement for several years might enable British leaders to convince their subjects that sympathy toward Germany had been frustrated by the wicked and insatiable appetite of that country. The problem had been explained by the English expert, Geoffrey Gorer, in his book, *Exploring English Character*: "War against a wicked enemy—and the enemy must clearly be shown to be wicked by the standards the conscience normally uses—is probably the only situation nowadays which will release the forces of righteous anger for the whole (or nearly the whole) population."[23]

Prime Minister Neville Chamberlain was sixty-eight years of age when he attained the highest British parliamentary office in April 1937. He was a strong man at the peak of his mental powers, and a stern Tory Party disciplinarian. He was born with the privileges of the British merchant-industrialist upper class, and his repeated elections as Lord Mayor of Birmingham after 1915 were considered little more than the rightful acceptance of a traditional sinecure. His father, Joseph Chamberlain, and his brother, Austen Chamberlain, had enjoyed strikingly successful careers in British public life, and they had been associated with important decisions on the principal national-economic, colonial, and diplomatic questions of their day. Neville Chamberlain received much credit for launching the British protective tariff system of imperial preferences, and for securing the agreement of the British Dominions to this system at the famous Ottawa conference in 1932.

It has sometimes been suggested that Chamberlain, prior to March 1939, placed a blind trust in Hitler and believed that a comprehensive Anglo-German understanding would be achieved. This is untrue, because Chamberlain never ceased thinking that Great Britain might go to war with Germany again instead of concluding an agreement with her. When Hitler reintroduced conscription in March 1935, Chamberlain wrote: "Hitler's Germany is the bully of Europe; yet I don't despair." This emotional comment scarcely suggested that Chamberlain was enamored either of Germany or of Hitler.[24]

On July 5, 1935, Chamberlain was considering the appeasement of Italy in the Ethiopian crisis as a means of preventing a *rapprochement* between Italy and Germany. He defined appeasement on this occasion as a possible combination of threats and concessions, and this definition reflected the ambivalent nature of Chamberlain's thinking whenever he conducted a so-called appeasement policy. At the time of the alienation of Italy in December 1935, due to the scandal caused by the premature revelation of the Hoare-Laval treaty, Chamberlain insisted that this would not have happened had he been Prime Minister. He would have seen to it that Italy was securely retained in the anti-German front. After he became Prime Minister in 1937, Chamberlain considered it a principal aim of his policy to separate Italy from Germany.[25]

Chamberlain wrote to a friend in the United States on January 16, 1938, that he favored agreements with both Germany and Italy provided that the Germans could be persuaded to refrain from the use of force. This raised the question of

what Chamberlain understood by the use of force, and whether force meant to
him the actual shedding of blood or the mere threat of force. This question was
clarified when Chamberlain said, after the Austro-German *Anschluss* on March
13, 1938: "It is perfectly evident . . . that force is the only argument Germany
understands." The same Chamberlain defined his own program by saying that
British armament was the basis for Empire defense and collective security. The
use of force in this sense was right in Chamberlain's mind when it was British,
and wrong when it was German. The British had defined their position of
Empire defense at the time of the Kellogg-Briand pact in 1928. They listed a
large number of countries bordering the British Empire in which they claimed a
right of permanent intervention, outside the terms of a pact designed to outlaw
war as an instrument of national policy.26

Chamberlain considered himself detached and objective in his evaluation of
Hitler, and he no doubt felt charitable when he wrote after their first meeting
in 1938: "I did not see any trace of insanity. . . ." It has been said that, after a
series of meetings with Hitler, Chamberlain felt himself coming irresistibly under
the spell of the magnetic German leader. This is doubtless true, and Chamberlain
has verified it himself. It was not difficult for him to dispel this momentary
influence and to return to his habitual way of thinking after a few days back in
England in his accustomed environment. After all, Hitler was merely the upstart
leader of a Power recently crushed almost beyond recognition, and Chamberlain
was the Prime Minister of a proud Empire with an allegedly uninterrupted series
of victories dating back to Queen Elizabeth I in the 16th century. It was unrealistic to describe this proud man as the dupe of Hitler.27

Chamberlain was a formidable figure, but he was soon overshadowed by at
least one of his ministers. Edward Frederick Lindley Wood, Earl of Halifax, has
been one of the most self-assured, ruthless, clever, and sanctimoniously self-
righteous diplomats the world has ever seen. It has been said that Halifax was
born great, achieved greatness, and had greatness thrust upon him. He was an
angular, tall, and rugged man. He was born with a withered left arm, and he
compensated for his physical defect by an avid pursuit of sport, and especially
hunting. By the age of nine, after the death of his older brothers, he was sole
heir to his father's title. He received a "first" in modern history at Oxford in
1903, and, after a tour of the Empire, he published a biography of the Anglican
church leader, John Keble. He entered the House of Commons as a Conservative
in January 1910. He emphatically denied that all men are created equal in his
maiden speech in Commons. He called on the English people to remain true to
their calling of a "superior race" within the British Empire. It was a "blood and
iron" speech in the full sense of the phrase.28

He had some doubt about personally entering the war in 1914, but he later
spent a period on the Western front and participated in some of the battles of
1916-1917. Halifax had no patience with dissenters in this epic struggle, and he
declared in Commons in December 1917: "I feel . . . absolutely no sympathy
with the real conscientious objector (i.e. to war)." In 1918 he was a principal
organizer and signatory of the Lowther petition to Lloyd George for a hard
peace with Germany.29

Halifax occupied important positions in the years after World War I. He was
Under-Secretary of State for Colonies, President of the Board of Education,

British Representative on the League Council, and Minister of Agriculture. He often held several important posts simultaneously. Halifax was appointed Viceroy of India in 1925, and he arrived in that country on April 1, 1926, with the avowed intention of outwitting Gandhi, who was seeking payment in the coin of freedom for the sacrifices of India in World War I. Halifax hoped to beguile the Indian following of Gandhi by offering eventual rather than immediate dominion status, and in this respect he appeared deceptively liberal compared to a man like Churchill, who wished to govern India permanently in the fashion of a British crown colony. Halifax did not like pacifists, but he remembered that he was a diplomat, and he was always equivocal and evasive when asked what he thought about Gandhi.[30]

Halifax was fifty years old when he returned in triumph from India in May 1931. He continued to concentrate on Indian affairs for several years, and he again held the post of President of the Board of Education. He was appointed Secretary of State for War in June 1935, and in this capacity he pushed hard for an intensive armament campaign. Halifax declared with complacency, at Plymouth in October 1935, that there was no one on the continent who would not sleep more happily if he knew that Britain had the power "to make the policy of peace prevail over the world."[31]

Halifax was the right hand man of Prime Minister Stanley Baldwin, and he was Leader of the House of Lords and Lord Privy Seal. Halifax had an important voice in the conduct of British diplomacy from January 1935 onward. On March 10, 1936, during the Rhineland crisis, he accompanied Foreign Minister Eden to Paris for crucial negotiations with the French leaders. He also played a key role in supporting the Archbishop of Canterbury against King Edward VII during the abdication crisis of 1936. The November 1937 Halifax visit to Hitler had been discussed for many months, and it caused a flurry of speculation in the British press when it was announced publicly on November 10, 1937. The Halifax visit was merely a fact-finding mission, and it produced no immediate results, although it aroused great hopes in Germany.[32]

Three months later Lord Halifax replaced Anthony Eden as British Foreign Secretary under acrimonious circumstances which accompanied an irreconcilable difference between Chamberlain and Eden on the advisability of appeasing Italy. Eden had previously been in conflict on this point with Sir Robert Vansittart, the Permanent Under-Secretary at the British Foreign Office. Vansittart was promoted upstairs on January 1, 1938, to be Chief Diplomatic Adviser to His Majesty's Government, which was a new post of unknown importance, and he was replaced as Permanent Under-Secretary by Sir Alexander Cadogan. This change was interpreted as a victory of Eden over Vansittart, until the fall of Eden some seven weeks later. It was no longer easy after the fall of Eden to interpret the changed status of Vansittart, who actually retained all of his former influence, and this became a subject of speculation for many years. Halifax was solidly behind Chamberlain in the conduct of foreign policy, and, during the first eight months that he was Foreign Secretary, he permitted Chamberlain to keep the initiative in this field. Afterward he asserted his own authority, and Great Britain approached the holocaust of World War II under the diplomatic leadership of Halifax rather than Chamberlain.[33]

Halifax never remotely understood or appreciated the German viewpoint or the problems which confronted Germany. A simple example will illustrate this point. Halifax told Ribbentrop in London on March 11, 1938, that a German action against Austria would be the same as a British action against Belgium. Halifax apparently considered this a fair statement, and a recognition of the fact that Austria was important to Germany and Belgium important to Great Britain. The fact that Austria had been part of Germany for more than one thousand years, and that the legislators of Austria had voted to join Germany after World War I, carried no weight with him. Consequently, he did not recognize the *Anschluss* as an act of liberation for the Austrian people from a hated puppet regime. No problem confronting Germany could have been more simple for anyone capable of understanding German problems. Sir Nevile Henderson, the British Ambassador in Berlin, was able to comprehend the situation without difficulty, and he never would have made the misleading comparison between Belgium and Austria.[34]

Halifax wrote memoirs nearly twenty years later which were candid in explaining his attitude toward the European situation at this time. He recognized that Hitler was an "undoubted phenomenon," and he was "ashamed to say" that he did not dislike Goebbels.[35] Unlike Chamberlain, Halifax was single-minded in 1937 and early 1938 about the inevitability of another war with Germany. Indeed, he went so far as to say that an Anglo-German war had been inevitable since March 1936, the moment Germany had recovered her freedom of action by reoccupying the Rhineland.[36] It is important to recall that in March 1936 Halifax played a leading role in discouraging a vigorous French response to the military reoccupation of the Rhineland by Germany. No doubt a war in 1936 would have been inconvenient to the current British conception of the balance of power, but one can also regret that Halifax did not have a more accurate evaluation in 1939 of the balance of power to which he professed to be so devoted. Halifax also wrote that the Munich conference of 1938 was a "horrible and wretched business," but it was extremely useful, because it convinced the gullible English people in the following year that everything possible had been done to avoid war. This might seem to imply that working for peace in 1938 justified working for war in 1939, but this was not so. It was not the right that mattered, but victory. It was not the truth which counted, but it was important to have the English people thinking along lines which were useful.[37]

Hoare and Simon were constant advisers of Chamberlain and Halifax in the conduct of British policy in 1938. Hoare had been dropped as British Foreign Secretary in December 1935 because of his tentative Ethiopian treaty prepared with Laval, (it was repudiated for violating collective security), but he returned to the British Cabinet in 1936 as Parliamentary First Lord of the Admiralty. He worked hard for a policy of pro-Franco neutrality during the Spanish Civil War, and he was sent to Spain as Ambassador during World War II to keep Spain pro-British. It was recognized in London that he had excellent contacts with the Spanish aristocracy. Hoare also had close contacts with the Czech leaders of 1938, and these dated from his military and diplomatic missions in World War I. Hoare became Home Secretary (minister of the interior) in June 1937, and he spent long hours with Chamberlain discussing the best means of separating Mussolini and Hitler. This British policy succeeded before the outbreak of World

War II, and it was cancelled solely by the unexpected collapse of France in 1940.[38]

Hoare advised Chamberlain on American affairs. He regarded "Anglo-American friendship as the very basis of our foreign policy," but he was correct in recognizing that President Roosevelt was in no position to take active steps to intervene in Europe in 1938 or 1939. He did not hesitate to advise Chamberlain to reject Roosevelt's suggestion for an international conference in January 1938, at a time when the British Prime Minister was concentrating on achieving a bilateral agreement with Italy. Hoare claimed there was never any difficulty in being loyal to both Chamberlain and Halifax in foreign policy because the two were always in agreement. He recognized that Halifax was a strong personality, who could never be dominated by Chamberlain.[39]

Simon was British Foreign Secretary from 1931 to 1935 in the MacDonald coalition Government, which was dominated by the Conservatives. He established intimate understandings with the permanent service experts, Sir Robert Vansittart and Sir Alexander Cadogan. Simon was unimpressed by revisionist historical writing on World War I, and he persisted in describing it as the "freedom war," or crusade for freedom. He was in close agreement with Chamberlain, Halifax, and Hoare in this respect. He was also for a heavy armament program throughout the 1930's, and he criticized the Liberals and the Labour leaders for impeding it. It is amusing that Simon regarded Ribbentrop as a "pretentious sham" and complained of the "hard shell" which surrounded his "self-sufficiency," since these were precisely the complaints directed at Simon by his English critics. The position of Simon in the 1930's was that "Britain could not act alone as the policeman of the world," and the implication was that she should police the world with the support of others. He described Chamberlain as a man of peace who would fight rather than see the world "dominated by force." Simon was for peace in 1938 because he believed that Great Britain required another twelve months to complete her preparations for a victorious war against Germany.[40]

The British ability to rationalize an essentially immoral foreign policy and to moralize about it has always been unlimited. In 1937, with the approval of Vansittart and Chamberlain, William Strang succeeded Ralph Wigram at the Central Department of the British Foreign Office, which comprised German affairs in relation to both Western and Eastern Europe. The British by this time were shifting their foreign policy because of the purges in Russia, and they were moving from primary opposition to Russia toward conflict with Germany. It was essential that this change in policy be accompanied by some moral explanation, and it was supplied by Strang in the following words: "In our generation, the cup of hatefulness has been filled to overflowing by the horrors of the Nazi and Soviet regimes, but yet perhaps not quite in equal measure. The Soviet system, cruel, evil and tyrannous as it shows itself to be in the pursuit by its self-appointed masters of absolute power both at home and abroad, springs, however remotely, from a moral idea, the idea namely that man shall not be exploited by man for his own personal profit; and there is thus at least a case to be made for it that is dangerously attractive to many minds; for Nazism, on the contrary, there was and is, it seems to me, nothing to be said."[41]

This was the judgment of the man who was allegedly the chief expert on

Germany in the British Foreign Office. Apparently it did not occur to Strang that the Marxist slogan about exploitation was not much different and certainly no more noble than the National Socialist motto; "Gemeinnutz vor Eigennutz (The profit of the community must come before the profit of the individual)." Furthermore, the National Socialists believed that this doctrine could be implemented without the fostering of permanent class hatred, or the expropriation of at least half of the community (Werner Sombart had shown that by no stretch of the imagination did the proletariat constitute more than half of the German population). It is instructive in this context to cite the recent book, *The Rise and Fall of Nazi Germany*, by the Jewish historian, T.L. Jarman. Jarman's volume contains much bitter criticism of Hitler and his system, but at least he is sufficiently objective to state that under National Socialism, terrorism, unlike in Russia, was kept in the background, and that "Germany in the years 1933-1939 was an open country in a sense which Soviet Russia has never been."[42]

Strang complained that the months before World War II were a "crushing" period for him, but that 1939 was less burdensome than 1938 because "war would almost certainly come." Apparently the possibility that Hitler in 1938 might find some means of avoiding a new Anglo-German war was irritating to Strang. Certainly no militarist could have sought war more avidly and Strang's attitude is not a flattering commentary on his qualifications for diplomacy. The fact that this man, at his key post, was perfectly satisfactory to Chamberlain and Halifax speaks for itself.[43]

The Secret War Aspirations of President Roosevelt

The attitude of President Roosevelt and his entourage was perhaps more extreme than that of the British leaders, but at least the American President was restrained by constitutional checks, public opinion, and Congressional legislation from inflicting his policy on Europe during the period before World War II. A petulant outburst from Assistant Secretary F.B. Sayre, of the American State Department, to British Ambassador Sir Ronald Lindsay on September 9, 1938, during difficult negotiations for an Anglo-American trade treaty, illustrated the psychosis which afflicted American leaders and diplomats. Sayre later recalled; "I went on to say that at such a time, when war was threatening and Germany was pounding at our gates, it seemed to me tragic that we had not been able to reach and sign an agreement." To imagine Germany pounding on the gates of the United States in 1938 is like confusing *Alice in Wonderland* with the Bible.[44]

Secretary of the Treasury Henry Morgenthau, Jr., telephoned Paris on March 14, 1938, to inform the French that the United States would support and cooperate with a Socialist measure of the Blum Popular Front Government to control, and, if necessary, to freeze foreign exchange in France. This would have been a drastic measure contrary to the international system of arbitrage and to the prevailing international financial policy of the United States. Morgenthau was eager to see Léon Blum retain the premiership in the hope that he would plunge France into conflict with Hitler. He had no compunctions about taking this step without informing either the United States Congress or American business leaders. Leon Blum, the Socialist, did not dare to go that far, and his

Government fell because of an inadequate fiscal policy.[45]

The German leaders correctly believed that the unrestrained anti-German press in the United States was profoundly influencing both public and private American attitudes toward Germany. Goebbels told United States Ambassador Hugh Wilson on March 22, 1938, that he expected criticism, and "indeed, it was inconceivable to him that writers in America should be sympathetic with present-day Germany because of the complete contrast of method by which the (German) Government was acting." On the other hand he objected to libel and slander and to the deliberate stirring up of hatred. Wilson confided that it was not the German form of government which was at issue, but that "the most crucial thing that stood between any betterment of our Press relationship was the Jewish question."[46] Ribbentrop was able to challenge Wilson on April 30, 1938, to find one single item in the German press which contained a personal criticism of President Roosevelt. He also intimated that the situation could be otherwise.[47]

In early 1938, Jewish doctors and dentists were still participating in the German state compulsory insurance program (*Ortskranken-kassen*), which guaranteed them a sufficient number of patients.[48] Wilson relayed information to Secretary of State Hull that, in 1938, 10% of the practicing lawyers in Germany were Jews, although the Jews constituted less than 1% of the population.[49] Nevertheless, the American State Department continued to bombard Germany with exaggerated protests on the Jewish question throughout 1938, although Wilson suggested to Hull on May 10, 1938, that these protests, which were not duplicated by other nations, did more harm than good.[50] The United States took exception to a German law of March 30, 1938, which removed the Jewish church from its position as one of the established churches of Germany. This meant that German public tax receipts would go no longer to the Jewish church, although German citizens would continue to pay taxes for the Protestant and Catholic churches. The situation established by this new law in Germany was in conformity with current English practice, where public tax revenue went to the Anglican Church, but the Jewish churches received nothing.[51]

On March 14, 1938, Under-Secretary of State Sumner Welles complained to Polish Ambassador Jerzy Potocki about the German treatment of the Jews and praised Poland for her "policy of tolerance." Potocki, who knew that current Polish measures against the Jews were more severe than those in Germany, replied with dignity that "the Jewish problem in Poland was a very real problem." It is evident that the Jewish question was primarily a pretext of American policy to disguise the fact that American leaders were spoiling for a dispute with Germany on any terms. In September 1938 President Roosevelt had a bad cold, and he complained that he "wanted to kill Hitler and amputate the nose."[52]

Perhaps frustration and knowledge of the domestic obstacles confronting his own policy increased President Roosevelt's fury. Jules Henry, the French Charge d'Affaires, reported to Paris on November 7, 1937, that President Roosevelt was interested in overthrowing Hitler, but that the majority of the American people did not share his views.[53] French Ambassador Saint-Quentin reported on June 11, 1938, that President Roosevelt suddenly blurted out during an interview that

" the Germans understand only force," and then clenched his fist like a boxer spoiling for a fight. He noted that the President was fond of saying that if "France went down, the United States would go down." Apparently this proposition was supposed to contain some self-evident legalistic-moralistic truth which required no demonstration.[54]

Ambassador Saint-Quentin noted that the relations between President Roosevelt and William C. Bullitt, were especially close. This was understandable, because Bullitt was a warmonger. Bullitt was currently serving as United States Ambassador to France, but he was Ambassador-at-large to all the countries of Europe, and he was accustomed to transmit orders from Roosevelt to American Ambassador Kennedy in London or American Ambassador Biddle in Warsaw. Bullitt had a profound knowledge of Europe. He was well aware that the British did not intend to fight in 1938, and that the French would not fight without British support. He improved his contacts and bided his time during the period of the Austrian and Czech crises. He prepared for his role in 1939 as the Roosevelt Ambassador *par excellence*. He could accomplish little in either year, because the whole world knew that the President he was serving did not have the backing of the American people for his foreign policy.[55]

The Peace Policy of Georges Bonnet

The situation in France took a dramatic turn when Édouard Daladier, who triumphed over the left-wing tendencies of Édouard Herriot in the Radical Socialist Party, became French Premier on April 10, 1938. Winston Churchill had combined his efforts with those of Henry Morgenthau to keep in power the Government of Daladier's predecessor, Léon Blum, but he had failed. Blum had hoped to head a Government including not only the usual Popular Front combination of Socialists and Radical-Socialists supported by the Communists, but also Paul Reynaud and some of the Moderate Republicans of the Right who favored a strong stand against Hitler. Pierre-Étienne Flandin, who had close contacts with Chamberlain and Halifax in London, took the lead in opposing this combination. Churchill was in Paris from March 26-28, 1938, in a vain effort to convert Flandin on behalf of Blum. Churchill knew that a Blum Government could exert effective pressure for action on the British leaders in the inevitable Czech crisis. Churchill hoped to use the French to overthrow the appeasement policy in London.[56]

Daladier was inclined to follow the lead of London in foreign policy, where the appeasement policy was currently in effect. At the same time, a moderate trend of opinion was gaining ground in France which held that there was no longer any point in seeking to frustrate Hitler's aspirations in Central Europe. Hitler had been allowed to rearm in 1935, and on June 18, 1935, the British had concluded with him a bilateral naval pact which was clearly contrary to the military provisions of the Versailles treaty. No doubt at the time this had appeared a useful step in securing British interests and in opposing Communism, but the fact remained that it also had been a blow at French military hegemony in Western and Central Europe. The British policy of restraining France from interfering with Hitler's military reoccupation of the Rhineland on March 7,

1936, had greatly reduced the possibility that France could render effective military aid to the members of the Little Entente or to other French allies in the East. French military strategy in the meantime had been based on the creation of a strong defensive position in France. Sensible Frenchmen were asking if it would not be wise to draw the necessary political conclusions from these events, and to modify French commitments in the East in the interest of preventing war.[57]

Joseph Paul-Boncour had succeeded Yvon Delbos as Foreign Minister after the fall of the Camille Chautemps Government at the time of the *Anschluss*. He opposed the moderate trend, and he favored a strong policy in support of the Czechs. Daladier had been inclined to retain him as Foreign Minister, but he turned to Georges Bonnet, when he discovered that Paul-Boncour was adamant about the Czechs. Bonnet was one of the leading exponents of the moderate trend, and he favored an interpretation of French commitments which would promote peace. Bonnet, in contrast to the British leaders, was a sincere and single-minded advocate of a permanent appeasement policy toward Germany in the earlier style of Aristide Briand. He remained as Foreign Minister from April 1938 until shortly after the outbreak of World War II. His appointment was one of the most significant events of the period, and it increased the chances for peace in Europe. Bonnet was not an isolated figure in his conduct of French foreign policy. He exerted great influence over Daladier, he enjoyed the support of a large number of colleagues in the French Cabinet, and he was encouraged by important interest groups throughout France.[58]

A special Parliamentary Committee of Inquiry was established in France in 1946 to investigate the causes and events of World War II. The Communist tide was running high in France at that time. Many prominent Frenchmen had been imprisoned for no apparent reason, and approximately 100,000 French citizens were liquidated in a Communist-inspired purge. Georges Bonnet had departed from France toward the end of World War II for Geneva, Switzerland, the ancestral seat of the Bonnet family. He wisely declined to return to France until he received adequate guarantees that he would not be unjustly imprisoned. Bonnet did not testify before the Committee until March 1951, approximately one year after his return to France.[59]

Bonnet explained that he was convinced the United States would play no active role in Europe in the immediate future, when he returned to France in 1937 after a period as Ambassador to the United States. He was aware that the British were not inclined to send large forces to Europe in the event of a new war because of their bitter experience with heavy losses in World War I. He knew that the Soviet Union would do everything possible to avert war with Germany, and to embroil France and Germany in war in the interest of weakening the so-called capitalist Powers. It seemed stupid to Bonnet not to do everything possible under these circumstances to avoid war with Germany.[60]

Bonnet complained that he was weary of being called a fanatical partisan of the Germans. He had not been in Germany since 1927, and he had always preferred the French system of liberal capitalism to German National Socialism. On the other hand, he had spent nearly three months in the Soviet Union in 1934, and this had been useful in equipping him to deal with Russian policy in 1938 and 1939.[61]

Bonnet could point to uninterruptedly friendly and confidential relations with Premier Daladier in 1938 and 1939. He and Daladier were convinced that Hitler was determined to carry through his program of eastern territorial revision on behalf of Germany. Bonnet, as Foreign Minister, never conducted so-called private diplomacy. It was his rule that all dispatches, including the most secret ones, be translated or decoded and prepared in four copies. These copies went automatically to President Lebrun, to Premier Daladier, to Alexis Léger, the Secretary-General of the Foreign Office, and to Bonnet. Bonnet considered himself a disciple of Aristide Briand in foreign policy. He was in the Painlevé Cabinet at the time of the signing of the Locarno treaties in 1925. Briand, who was Foreign Minister, told the Cabinet that the treaties would be applied solely within the context of the League of Nations, and with the support of the necessary combination of preponderant Powers. Bonnet concluded that France had no obligation to fulfill unilaterally the collective security treaties concluded after the signing of the Covenant of the League.

Bonnet reminded the Committee that Great Britain had never given France a pledge of armed support for an active French policy of intervention throughout the entire period of the Czech crisis in 1938. Bonnet discussed the situation with the British leaders on April 28-29, 1938, and he was told that Great Britain was not yet ready for a European war. When Halifax and Chamberlain suggested that Hitler might be bluffing, Bonnet predicted that Hitler would use force against the Czechs if peaceful revision failed. Bonnet had great respect for the military strength of the Soviet Union, and his opinion in this regard was not shaken by the current Soviet purges. He was equally convinced from his current diplomatic contracts that the Soviet Union would resist every effort in 1938 to persuade her to take the military initiative against Germany. Under these circumstances Bonnet had no compunctions, in 1938, in seeking to persuade the Czechs to arrive at a peaceful settlement with Germany at the expense of surrendering the German districts seized by the Czechs in 1918 and 1919.[62]

The clarity of Bonnet's thought, and his habit of retaining detailed notes to illustrate his points, threw refreshing light on many obscure events of the period, and his revealing record was important in prompting several countries to publish a number of otherwise secret documents. He published two very full volumes of memoirs prior to his testimony before the Parliamentary Committee, and he produced a disconcerting amount of additional material to cope with the questions raised by his interrogators. It was not surprising when this man delivered an effective reply to each point raised against him.

The memoirs of Bonnet abound with penetrating insights, and they ignore the many defamatory comments made about him by popular writers. He recognized that President Roosevelt employed a genial manner to hide his violent passions.[63] Bonnet agreed in June 1937 to return from the United States to France as Minister of Finance in the new Chautemps Government, after Joseph Caillaux in the French Senate had succeeded in overthrowing the first Blum Government. Bonnet admired Joseph Caillaux, who had fought in vain for peace in 1914 against the aggressive policies of Poincare and Viviani, and he was pleased by the overthrow of Blum. Bonnet insisted in a last audience with President Roosevelt that a new war in Europe would be a disaster for the entire world.[64]

Bonnet noted that Premier Chautemps and Foreign Minister Delbos were invited to London on November 29-30, 1937, immediately after the return of Halifax from Germany, and that the British leaders were mainly concerned about urging the French to increase their military preparations. Bonnet noted, after meeting Chamberlain in April 1938 for the first time in several years, that the British Prime Minister was obviously sceptical of reaching a lasting agreement with Hitler. This attitude contrasted with the opinion of Bonnet, who saw no reason why a lasting Anglo-German agreement could not be attained, if the British leaders sincerely desired one.[65] The idea that the British were playing for time was confirmed when Chamberlain told Bonnet that one should select a favorable hour to stop Hitler rather than to permit the German leader to pick both the time and the place for a conflict.[66] Hitler actually had no desire to pick either the time or place for a conflict with the British. Hugh Wilson, United States Ambassador to Germany, sent Hull an analysis by an expert of the American Embassy staff on February 1, 1938, which contained the following significant statement: "an English-German understanding is Hitler's first principle of diplomacy in 1938, just as it was in 1934, or in 1924 when he wrote *Mein Kampf.*"[67]

Litvinov's Hopes for a Franco-German War

The Russians planned to play a cautious role in the Czech crisis. Maxim Litvinov, the Soviet Commissar for Foreign Affairs, told United States Ambassador Joseph Davies on March 24, 1938, that the League of Nations was dead, that no arrangements existed between France and Russia to cope with a Czech crisis, and that Czechoslovakia might capitulate without a struggle to German pressure.[68]

It was evident that Russia had no obligations to Czechoslovakia, unless the Czechs resisted Germany with active French military support. The Soviet policy did not imply a desire on the part of the Russian rulers to see the so-called capitalist Powers of Western and Central Europe compose their differences. A French representative at Geneva in January 1938 was attacked by Maxim Litvinov when he suggested to a group of League spokesmen that a French *rapprochement* policy toward Germany might also be of benefit to Russia.[69]

The Russians hoped that they could stay temporarily in the background while the states which were their ideological rivals became embroiled. It was believed with good reason that the interests of Stalin would best be served by a conflict in the West. The official Soviet diplomatic history of the period later condemned Great Britain and France in strong terms for refusing to fight Germany over the Czech issue. Soviet diplomats in 1938 adopted the insincere line that Hitler was bluffing, and that a strong Anglo-French front on behalf of the Czechs would force him to retreat.[70]

The Reckless Diplomacy of Edvard Beneš

Hermann Goering in Berlin on March 12, 1938, assured the Czechs in response to specific inquiries that Germany contemplated no action against

Czechoslovakia.[71] The truth of this statement has since been revealed by the diplomatic documents, but common-sense should have suggested at the time that it was true, when one considers the speed with which the Austrian crisis reached a climax within a few days.[72] Although Hitler had linked the fate of Austrian and Sudeten Germans in his speech of February 20, 1938, he had always considered that Austria and Czechoslovakia constituted two entirely separate prob problems, and he scarcely had an opportunity to consider the second of these while the first was coming to a head with unexpected rapidity. The Germans promised that their troops in Austria would remain a considerable distance from the Czech frontier.

It was clear to the Czechs, from the immediate reactions of the Sudeten Germans to the *Anschluss*, that a crisis was inevitable in which Czechoslovakia would occupy the central role. Jan Masaryk, the Czech envoy in London, discussed the situation with the British leaders. He reported to Prague on March 16, 1938, that the British were inclined to regard an Anglo-German war as inevitable but that it was evident that they were not contemplating such a conflict in 1938.[73] Chamberlain restricted himself in the House of Commons on March 14, 1938, to the enigmatic statement that Great Britain was and always would be interested in the events of Central Europe because of her desire to maintain the peace of the world.[74] It was clear to Masaryk that a British pledge to the Czechs in 1938 would be difficult if not impossible to obtain.

The excitement among the Sudeten Germans after the *Anschluss* forced the Sudeten question to the center of the stage. The German legation in Prague reported on March 31, 1938, that Konrad Henlein, the leader of the Sudeten German Party (SdP), was pleading for the curtailment of all propaganda efforts to arouse the Sudeten people who were already too much aroused.[75] In Great Britain and Canada a number of officially inspired articles were appearing which criticized the injustices inflicted on the Sudeten Germans over many years. Henlein realized that he would have to announce a program which met the requirements of the new situation, and he collaborated closely with German Foreign Minister Ribbentrop and Ernst Eisenlohr, the German Minister to Czechoslovakia, in preparing the famous Karlsbad demands for conditions of autonomy in the Sudeten region. The demands were announced by Henlein in a speech on April 24, 1938.[76] It was evident that Hitler would support the Sudeten Germans in their bid for concessions, and Jan Masaryk was instructed by Czech Foreign Minister Krofta to make another specific request for British military support in defying the Germans. Masaryk reported on May 3, 1938, that British Foreign Secretary Halifax was pessimistic about the military prospects for Czechoslovakia in a conflict with Germany, and he refused to commit Great Britain to the Czech cause.[77]

The Czech leaders adopted the pattern of Schuschnigg, revealing that they were much more impatient than was Hitler to force the issue. The Czech Cabinet and military leaders decided on the afternoon of May 20, 1938, to order the partial mobilization of the Czech armed forces, and to base this provocative act on the false accusation that German troops were concentrating on the Czech frontiers. It was hoped that the resulting emotional confusion would commit the British and the French to the Czech position before a policy favoring concessions to the Sudeten Germans could be implemented. The plot failed although

Krofta on May 27th, and Beneš on June 1st, granted interviews in which they claimed that Czechoslovakia had scored a great victory over Germany. An inspired press campaign to create this impression had begun on May 21, 1938, and it reverberated around the world.

The War Bid of Benes Rejected by Halifax

Halifax was not inclined to permit President Beneš to conduct the foreign policy of the British Empire. He was careful to side-step the Czech trap, although he went far enough to increase the indigation of Hitler toward the Czechs. He instructed British Ambassador Sir Nevile Henderson in Berlin on May 21, 1938, to tell the Germans that the British "might" fight if the Germans moved on the Czechs. Henderson was to add that France might intervene and that "His Majesty's Government could not guarantee that they would not be forced by circumstances to become involved also." It was a warning to Hitler but it was not a specific declaration that Great Britain would wage war for the Czechs. Henderson reported a few days afterward that British military experts had scoured the German-Czech frontier and had found no evidence of German troop concentrations.[78]

The Czech gamble failed, and it was a costly gamble. Hitler was sufficiently shrewd to see that the British had avoided a commitment to the Czechs under the dramatic circumstances created by the bold Czech mobilization move. The Czechs had tipped their hand: it was evident that they held no trumps. Hitler decided to force the issue with the Czechs in 1938, and to secure the liberation of the Sudeten Germans and the dissolution of the "Czech Empire."

Hitler's Decision to Liberate the Sudetenland

Hitler had discussed with General Wilhelm Keitel on April 22, 1938, an existing routine operational plan of 1935 for possible conflict with the Czechs. Hitler issued a directive which excluded an unprovoked German attack on the Czechs. Keitel returned the revised draft to Hitler on May 20, 1938, and it contained the explicit statement that Germany had no intention to attack Czechoslovakia. The Czech war-scare crisis of May 21, 1938, intervened before Hitler again returned the plan to Keitel on May 30, 1938. Hitler changed the political protocol, and he added the following significant statement: "It is my unalterable decision to smash Czechoslovakia by military action in the near future." General Alfred Jodl recorded in his diary on the same day that Hitler's belief that the Czech question could be settled in 1938 had produced a serious conflict of opinion between Hitler and the Army General Staff.[79] This conflict was quickly exploited by a small but ambitious German underground movement in an effort to overthrow Hitler in 1938. Gerhard Ritter, the leading German expert on this question, later expressed doubt that the military *putsch* plan against Hitler in 1938 would have succeeded under any circumstances, and he added that it was rendered completely impossible by the current British policy of concessions to Hitler. He also recognized that there was no chance for a successful military *putsch* against

Hitler in the period from the Munich conference to the outbreak of World War II.[80]

The initiative was retained by Hitler during the four months from the revised military plan of May 30, 1938, until the Munich conference of September 29-30, 1938. The Sudeten German leaders followed directives from Berlin, and they held fast to demands which the Czechs were unwilling to grant in full measure. Italy gave full diplomatic support to Germany, and neither Soviet Russia on the one side nor Great Britain and France on the other displayed any enthusiasm for taking the initiative to attack Germany. The Czechs, despite the grandiose ambitions of some of their leaders, were an intensely practical people, and most of them realized that life would still be worth living if Germany returned to her traditional role as the dominant Power in Central Europe. The Czechs had no taste for an isolated war against Germany, and they were ripe for the Anglo-French efforts of September 1938 to persuade them to surrender the Sudetenland to Germany without a struggle.[81]

Lord Halifax informed the French leaders in Paris on July 20, 1938, that a special British fact-finding mission under Lord Runciman would be sent to Czechoslovakia. The mission was announced publicly on July 26, 1938, and President Beneš was disturbed by this news. It was a definite indication that the British did not intend to adopt an uncompromising policy toward Germany in the crisis. The mission completed its labors early in September 1938, and it reported that the main difficulty in the Sudeten area had been the disinclination of the Czechs to grant reforms. This development was accompanied by the final rupture of negotiations between the Sudeten German and Czech leaders. It was evident that the peak of the crisis was close at hand.[82]

President Beneš delivered a defiant speech on September 10, 1938, at the time of the opening of the annual National Socialist Congress at Nuremberg across the border in Germany. The Czech President placed a bold front on the precarious Czech position. He declared that he had always been an optimist, and that his optimism was stronger than ever at the present time. Initial replies to President Beneš were made by Joseph Goebbels and Hermann Goering. The principal reply came from Hitler in a major speech delivered at Nuremberg on September 12, 1938.[83] The German leader denounced the policies of Beneš since 1918 in scathing terms, and he made an appeal to the leaders of foreign states not to intervene when he settled accounts with the Czechs.[84] He reminded the French leaders that the permanent renunciation by Germany of Alsace-Lorraine, including the ancient German city of Strassburg, had been a major sacrifice which had been made willingly in the interest of Franco-German amity. He added that Germany was seeking to settle a limited number of problems in Europe, and that she had completely satisfactory borders "in many directions."

The Sportpalast Pledge of September 26, 1938

The entire diplomatic corps had been present at Nuremberg to hear Hitler. Polish Ambassador Lipski contacted State Secretary Weizsaecker on September 13, 1938, to complain that he had distinctly heard Hitler say that Germany had "perfectly satisfactory boundaries in all directions," and that the published version was incorrect in referring to "many directions." Lipski warned ominously that unfortunate consequences might result if this change in the version of Hitler's remarks was noticed in Poland. Weizsaecker was unable to discover anyone else who had heard the words of the version Lipski claimed Hitler had used. He requested the text which had been written before the speech was delivered, and he noted that it also contained the words "many directions."[85] This incident was brought to the attention of Hitler. Two weeks later, Hitler delivered a second major speech at the Sportpalast in Berlin, on September 26, 1938, when it seemed that Europe after all might be plunged into war over the Czech question. Hitler on that occasion made an explicit statement which was consistent with his policies, but which left him extremely vulnerable to the attacks and misrepresentations of hostile propagandists.

The Berlin speech of September 26th took place in a highly charged atmosphere dominated by the slogan of Goebbels: "Fuehrer befiehl, wir folgen! (Command us, Leader, and we will follow!)." Hitler, in explaining German policy, asserted, "we have no interest in suppressing other peoples." He reminded the world that Germany was strong again after fifteen terrible years (before 1933), but he insisted that she harbored no hatred toward other peoples. He emphasized the importance of a lasting German-Polish understanding in the realization of his program. He insisted that Czech rule should be terminated in the Sudeten German area, and he promised that his demand for German rule in the Sudetenland was "the last territorial demand which I have to make in Europe."[86]

The Poles and the Germans knew that Germany at this time was automatically claiming the entire territory which she had lost in the East in 1918, but the world as a whole had taken no notice of this. The precedent set by Stresemann at Locarno in 1925 in refusing to recognize any of the German territorial losses to Poland had not yet been modified. It was easy for propagandists to claim that the specific German request for the return of Danzig in the following month was a violation of Hitler's solemn promise. Later, when the Czech state was disrupted in March 1939, the same propagandists were quick to claim that the establishment of a German protectorate in Bohemia-Moravia was a violation of Hitler's promise of 1938. This was extremely effective propaganda, and it was widely believed in Germany itself. Nevertheless, it does not take full account of existing realities. Boris Celovsky, himself a Czech and the leading expert on the Czech crisis of 1938, has expressed the considered opinion that the 1918 Czech state was doomed when the Sudeten areas were amputated.

The other minorities, including the Slovaks, were opposed to the continuation of Czech rule, and the total overthrow of the Prague system was merely a question of time. Hitler worked for a specific solution in the interests of Germany during the March 1939 crisis, but he did not insist that his provisional solution, which was achieved in the heat of crisis, need be permanent. He made it clear to the British leaders that he was willing afterward to discuss the ultimate solution of the Czech question in the councils of international diplomacy. If Hitler's later move to Prague was a major British grievance, it could have been discussed through normal diplomatic channels. In reality, the British in the period from March to September 1939 refused to respond to the various efforts made to raise this issue. In the meantime, the propagandists were seeking to

whip people into a frenzy, and to represent Hitler, who ruled a tiny state in comparison to the great empires of Britain, Russia, and the United States, as a
would-be conqueror of the world.[87]

Hungarian Aspirations in Czechoslovakia

The Poles and the Hungarians refrained from major efforts to settle their own
claims against the Czechs until Chamberlain's visit to Hitler at Berchtesgaden on
September 15, 1938. Regent Horthy of Hungary was invited to Germany in
August 1938 to christen the German cruiser, *Prinz Eugen*, which was named
after the famous Habsburg military hero and statesman of the early 18th
century. Horthy was accompanied by Premier Bela Imredy and Foreign Minister
Kanya. The visit was a ticklish one, because the Hungarians had instructed their
special representatives to the Little Entente conference at Bled, Yugoslavia, to
promise that Hungary would not offer Germany military support in the event of
a German-Czech war. On the other hand, the Hungarians expected the Germans
to take great risks to return the Hungarian ethnic territory which the Czechs had
seized. This meant that friction was inevitable, and Horthy later complained that
Hitler was less pleasant to him than at the time of his previous visit in 1936.[88]

Horthy imagined that he could buy Hitler's support by offering to mediate
in securing a comprehensive understanding between Germany and Poland.
Horthy reminded Hitler that he enjoyed intimate relations with the Poles and he
made the startling proposition that he was prepared to ask Warsaw to hand over
the Polish Corridor to Germany. Hitler, who had no intention of asking for any
Polish territory, did not like this plan at all. He strongly urged Horthy not to say
anything about the Corridor in Warsaw.[89]

Hitler informed the Hungarian leaders in no uncertain terms that he would
not play their game with Czechoslovakia. He made it clear that Germany would
tolerate no further provocation from the Czechs, and that a new challenge from
Prague would be answered with a German invasion. He noted that both Hungary
and Poland had claims against the Czechs, and he added that he would welcome
their participation in a war involving Germany and Czechoslovakia. He insisted
that it was necessary for Hungary and Poland to shoulder the entire initiative in
pushing their claims. The Hungarians pleaded that a war would involve greater
risks for a small country like Hungary than for Germany. Hitler was not impressed with this argument, and he refused to modify his position.

The Hungarians approached the British on September 16, 1938, immediately
after Chamberlain returned from Berchtesgaden and his first meeting with Hitler.
They scented British complicity in a future partition of Czechoslovakia, and
they attempted to make good their rebuff in Germany by requesting British
support for Magyar aspirations in Czechoslovakia. They talked boldly in London
for several days of their determination to secure justice from the Czechs. One
week later the European situation took a turn for the worse, after the unsuccessful talks between Hitler and Chamberlain at their second meeting in Bad
Godesberg. The Hungarians responded by retreating rapidly to a more cautious
and conciliatory position.[90]

British Encouragement of Polish Defiance at Danzig

The Poles used their own method to deal with the Czechs and they maintained their initiative with an insistence and vigor foreign to Budapest. The Poles also established contact with London on September 16, 1938, on the question of territorial claims, but they limited their action to an informative *démarche*. Polish Ambassador Edward Raczynski, a young and wealthy aristocrat, was instructed to avoid protracted discussions about Polish claims, and merely to inform the British of these claims rather than to consult with them. The previous month an important conference had taken place at the Hela peninsula on the Polish coast, between Polish Foreign Minister Beck and Alfred Duff Cooper, the British Parliamentary First Lord of the Admiralty.[91] Beck made it clear that Poland desired closer ties with London and that she would appreciate an indication of eventual British support against Germany at Danzig. Halifax informed the Polish diplomats in London, after the return of Duff Cooper, that Great Britain would support Poland for a permanent position on the League Council, which would imply recognition of the status of Poland as a Great Power. He also promised that Great Britain would support Poland "as much as possible" at Danzig. This pledge was phrased cautiously and ambiguously, but the first step along the road toward the Anglo-Polish military alliance had been taken before the conference at Munich.[92]

The attitude of Halifax toward Danzig had passed through a remarkable evolution during recent months. On May 21, 1938, League High Commissioner Burckhardt informed the Germans that a few days earlier "Lord Halifax had termed Danzig and the Corridor an absurdity," and probably the most foolish provision of the Versailles settlement. Halifax had expressed the hope that a change in the *status quo* might be achieved by bilateral negotiations between Germany and Poland. He told Burckhardt that he did not regard Hitler's November 5, 1937, declaration as the final German word on Danzig, and he suggested that Great Britain would be willing to mediate between Germany and Poland if an *impasse* was reached in negotiation between the two countries. Halifax added that he would welcome a visit to England by Albert Forster, the District National Socialist Party leader of Danzig, who subsequently went to London in response to this invitation. Halifax had expressed an interest in coming to Danzig for deer hunting, and of course an invitation went to him immediately after Burckhardt relayed this information.[93]

The May 1938 crisis, which was precipitated by President Beneš, followed closely on the talks between Halifax and Burckhardt. The invitation from Danzig Senate President Greiser for deer hunting in the forests of the Danzig state was rejected by Halifax in June 1938. In July 1938 Halifax told Viktor Boettcher, the chief unofficial diplomatic agent of Danzig, that Great Britain favored the retention of the *status quo* at the so-called Free City. He showered Boettcher with specious arguments to the effect that Danzig could play a natural "role of mediator" between Germany and Poland, and he urged the Danzigers to be satisfied with existing conditions. Halifax came full circle the following month when he assured the Poles that Great Britain was interested in supporting them to prevent changes at Danzig. It was evident to the Poles that this *volte face* was an indication of British determination to organize a coalition against Germany at some date after the Czech crisis, and that, in the British mind, Poland would be very useful in forming such a front. It was natural under these circumstances for the Poles not to humble themselves in London when informing the British of their demands against the Czechs.[94]

Polish Pressure on the Czechs

Further information about Polish intentions reached London from Warsaw almost immediately. Sir Howard Kennard, the British Ambassador in Warsaw, was well-known for his enthusiastic espousal of Polish interests. Kennard's sympathy for the Polish cause was matched among the Western diplomats by that of William Bullitt, United States Ambassador to France, but certainly exceeded by no one else. Kennard reported to London on September 16, 1938, that the Polish Government was preparing a note which would demand self-determination for the Polish minority in Czechoslovakia.[95] The Poles had informed the Czechs in general terms in May 1938 that Poland would present demands if the Czechs made minority concessions to other Powers. The Czechs had made no concessions to other Powers but the Chamberlain visit to Berchtesgaden convinced Beck that they would soon do so. Poland began to move on September 16th and she did not stop until she received her share of the Czech spoils.[96]

President Beneš conformed to his usual style in dealing with the Poles. He launched a subtle attempt to appease Poland without surrendering anything tangible. On May 24, 1938, he replied to Beck's original demand for equal treatment with the bland assurance that Poland would receive it. He did not plan to surrender anything to Germany at that time, and his response did not imply that he intended to cede territory to the Poles.[97] French Foreign Minister Bonnet attempted to settle the differences between Poland and Czechoslovakia, and he later blamed Poland for the lack of close contact between Paris and Warsaw during the Czech crisis.[98] The British historian, Lewis Bernstein Namier, later claimed that Bonnet was at fault in failing to obtain Polish cooperation with the Czechs, but Bonnet effectively defended his position against his charge in the London *Times Literary Supplement*.[99] Poland throughout the Czech crisis insisted that nothing less than the surrender of territory by the Czechs to the Poles would make the discussion of Polish assistance feasible. This proposition, when suggested at Prague by the French, did not stimulate whatever Czech desire there was to fight the Germans. The bitter rivalry between Prague and Warsaw prompted many Czechs to prefer the surrender of everything to Germany rather than one village to Poland.[100]

Raczynski delivered a formal note in London on September 19, 1938, which described the Polish position against the Czechs. There was some speculation that Poland and Germany had a previous secret understanding in the Czech question, but this was not so. In reality, there was no contact at all between the Germans and the Poles in their respective efforts against the Czechs unless one regards as an understanding the fact that German and Polish leaders had told one another for years how much they detested Czechoslovakia.[101]

A Government-inspired Polish pressure group, the OZON (Camp of National

Unity created by Colonel Adam Koc, which would have replaced the existing Polish political parties had it been more successful) was stirring up anti-Czech feeling in Poland and its propaganda in this instance was conspicuously successful. Kennard was "obliged to concede" that Poland might intervene on the German side in the event of a German-Czech war.[102] The British responded by delivering identical notes to the Hungarians and Poles which warned them to remain aloof from the current crisis. The gesture had no effect on the Poles, who indignantly brushed aside the British warning.[103] The Hungarian leaders, who had returned at this moment from a second unsuccessful mission to Hitler, were further shaken in their confidence by the British stand.[104]

Kennard understood that the Poles were sensitive about their alleged Great Power status, and he was appalled by the tactlessness of Halifax in sending identical notes to Warsaw and Budapest. He expressed his displeasure in a report to the British Foreign Office on September 22, 1938, and he simultaneously attempted to present Polish policy in a more favorable light in London. Kennard suggested that anti-German feeling in Hungary was too weak to be useful to Great Britain, but he insisted that in Poland there was a great reservoir of hatred against the Germans. He argued that it was a vital British interest to augment this hatred rather than to diffuse it by carelessly insulting Warsaw as Halifax had done. Kennard also reported that the Poles were not bluffing and that they had pushed their military preparations against the Czechs to an advanced stage.[105]

Beck revenged himself on Halifax for the mere "carbon copy" of a note addressed to Hungary. He replied to Halifax haughtily on September 22, 1938, that he had no reason to discuss with the British any measures he might deem advisable in securing "legitimate Polish interests." Beck believed that he had an impregnable basis for this reply because Great Britain had no commitment toward Czechoslovakia.[106]

The Soviet Threat to Poland

Beck wished to remain abreast of Germany in dealing with the Czechs without getting ahead of her. He knew the next step was an ultimatum with a time limit, but he believed the Czechs might surrender to Germany in exchange for German support if they received a Polish ultimatum. The Poles in a few days had reached the same point as the Germans in a crisis which had lasted nearly five months. Beck decided to advance no further until the Germans made their next move. As a result, an extremely tense but stagnant period in the Czech-Polish crisis arrived. Great Britain had been excluded from further contact with Poland in the crisis by Beck's brusque retort to Halifax, but contact between Poland and France remained close. Bonnet decided to make a last effort to secure a *détente* and then a *rapprochement* between Warsaw and Prague. At the very moment he launched this delicate maneuver, a third French ally, the Soviet Union, sent a thundering warning to Warsaw on September 23, 1938. The Poles were told that intervention against the Czechs would cause Russia to repudiate the Russo-Polish non-aggression pact of 1932 and would lead to unforeseeable consequences. Beck's first reaction was to believe that the Russians were bluffing, and he replied defiantly to the Russian note.[107]

The Failure of Benes to Deceive Beck

The specific incident which prompted the Russian *démarche* was Beck's repudiation on September 21, 1938, of the 1925 Polish-Czech minorities treaty. This
had been accompanied by the announcement that Poland would take active
measures to secure the welfare of the Poles beyond the Czech frontier.[108]
Bonnet used this development as a point of departure in his final mediation
effort. His first step was to inquire in Warsaw whether Poland had concluded an
agreement with Germany concerning Czechoslovakia, and whether Polish claims
against the Czechs were limited to Teschen or also included other areas. Beck
and Miroslaw Arciszewski, a leading Polish diplomat who had returned from a
mission in Rumania to assist Beck during the crisis, drafted a note to the French
and forwarded it to Polish Ambassador Juliusz Lukasiewicz in Paris. The Polish
note was elaborate in assurances of good faith, but was evasive. It did not answer
the two questions of Bonnet.[109]

The Polish position was clarified verbally in Warsaw on September 24th by
Marshal Smigly-Rydz, who granted an audience to French Ambassador Léon
Noël with the approval of Beck. The Marshal assured Noel that Poland had no
agreement with Germany on Czechoslovakia, and he claimed that Polish aspirations were limited to the Teschen area. He declared that Czechoslovakia would
be attacked if Polish demands were not accepted, but he added that a Polish
invasion would be confined as closely as possible to the area Poland intended to
annex from the Czechs.[110]

The second move of Bonnet was to apply pressure on President Beneš to
make concessions to the Poles. Beneš responded promptly but in characteristic
fashion. He wrote a letter to Beck which was delivered in Warsaw on September
26, 1938. He "agreed in principle" to cede Teschen to Poland if the Poles
supported Czechoslovakia in a war against Germany.[111] Beck was not satisfied
with this offer, and he observed with indignation that an "agreement in principle" from Beneš was not worth the paper on which it was written. Nevertheless, he was in close contact with the French, and he decided to make an effort
to reach an agreement with the Czechs along the lines advocated by Bonnet.[112]

Beck informed the Czechs that the matter could be settled if they would turn
the Teschen territory over to Poland without delay. They could count on full
Polish assistance against Germany if they accepted this propostion, and if France
fulfilled her obligations to the Czechs. This left scant room for maneuver to
Benes, who was insincere in his offer to Poland. The Czech President replied
with the feeble excuse that the railway system in Teschen territory occupied an
important place in the Czech operational plan against Germany. He insisted that
it would not be possible to surrender Teschen to Poland until Germany had been
defeated in the approaching war. Beck promptly disrupted negotiations when he
received this revealing reply. This development took place at the peak of the
seven days' crisis in Europe, which followed the failure of the initial Bad
Godesberg talks between Chamberlain and Hitler on September 22, 1938.[113]

Bullitt was in close contact with Lukasiewicz at Paris during these trying
days. Lukasiewicz received Bullitt at the Polish Embassy on September 25,
1938, to inform him that the Polish Government had changed its attitude about
the current crisis. They had believed that there would be no war, but now they

believed that war would occur. Lukasiewicz insisted that a conflict would be a war of religion between Fascism and Bolshevism, with Beneš as the agent of Moscow. Lukasiewicz confided to the American Ambassador that Poland would invade Slovakia in addition to Teschen if Germany advanced against the Czechs. It would be a primary Polish aim to establish a common front with friendly Hungary. The Polish diplomat believed that a Russian attack on Poland would follow this move, but he claimed that Poland did not fear it. He predicted that in three months Russia would be routed by Germany and Poland and he insisted that the Soviet Union was a hell of warring factions.

Bullitt accused Poland of betraying France, but Lukasiewicz denied this charge. He said that Poland would not make war on France, but that, if France, Great Britain, and the United States supported the Czechs, the Western Powers would be the tools of Bolshevism. Lukasiewicz urged Bullitt, who was friendly to Poland, to seek the support of President Roosevelt for territorial revision in favor of Poland and Hungary. He also told Bullitt that he could repeat any or all of these remarks to the French Foreign Office. Bullitt concluded that Poland would inevitably attack Czechoslovakia when Germany did, unless territorial concessions were made to the Poles.[114]

Bullitt realized when he received a report from American Ambassador Kennedy in London on September 25, 1938, that the Poles were speaking the same language everywhere. Polish Ambassador Raczynski claimed to Kennedy that British and French attitudes in support of Czechoslovakia had caused Poland to become the "little cousin" of Hitler. Raczynski declared that Poland and Hungary believed that Hitler's position at Bad Godesberg had been correct and that the British were to blame for the *impasse* which had been reached, because they did not take account of the urgency of the situation and the importance of Polish and Hungarian claims. It was known that Hitler had chided Chamberlain at Bad Godesberg for failing to take these issues into account. Kennedy complained to Bullitt that Raczynski was seeking to propagandize him, which was doubtless true.[115]

A further conversation with Lukasiewicz on September 26, 1938, convinced Bullitt that the Polish position would not change. The Polish diplomat asserted that Germany, Poland, and Hungary would act in unison in imposing their will in Czechoslovakia. Bullitt also had received confirmation of the Polish attitude from Czech Ambassador Stephan Osusky. Bullitt was extremely excited, and he was indignant with Bonnet, who obviously believed that the destruction of Czechoslovakia was a feasible price to avoid war. Bullitt reported scornfully to Roosevelt that Bonnet was for "peace at any price," and he followed this up with a further dispatch containing a host of unkind comments about the French Foreign Minister.[116]

Bonnet's initiative to secure a Polish-Czech *rapprochement* had failed, but this was not because Poland had modified her original offer to collaborate with France and Czechoslovakia. Beck's stand was identical toward the Czechs and the French. The difficulty was that Benes agreed to surrender territory to Germany after the Chamberlain-Hitler Berchtesgaden conference, but he was unwilling to cede the Teschen area to Poland. It was evident that only a Polish ultimatum with a time limit would resolve the issue of whether or not there would be a Czech-Polish war in 1938.[117]

The failure of the Czechs to accept Polish demands in the interest of creating a common front against Germany caused astonishment in many quarters. German Ambassador Moltke in Warsaw observed to Jan Szembek on September 24, 1938, that Polish demands were modest and easy to satisfy compared to Germany's interest in the entire Sudetenland, and so it would seem, if one ignored the fact of bitter Czech-Polish rivalry.

The Munich Conference

Moltke was no less astonished when Mussolini launched a last-minute mediation effort on September 28, 1938, which banished the danger of war over the Sudeten question, and brought the German-Czech crisis to a close.[118] Sir Horace Wilson, who had served Prime Minister Chamberlain in various capacities over many years, had been sent to Berlin on a special mission on September 26, 1938, the day of Hitler's *Sportpalast* speech. Wilson's instructions were inadequate to permit him to resolve the Anglo-German differences which had been created at Bad Godesberg on September 22-24, 1938. Hitler resented the fact that Chamberlain wished to arrange the entire program of events in Czechoslovakia himself, and Chamberlain in turn was annoyed by Hitler's effort to impose several conditions in the matter. Although the last conversations between the two leaders in Bad Godesberg had been conciliatory, the realization of a definite agreement on the Czech crisis had not been attained.[119]

Wilson discussed the situation with Hitler a second time on September 27, 1938. The main gist of Wilson's remarks was that there would be an Anglo-German war unless Hitler retreated. Wilson did not say this very explicitly, but Hitler helped him by cutting through the niceties of "fulfilling treaty obligations" and the like. He said that what Wilson meant was that if France decided to attack Germany, Great Britain would also attack Germany. He informed Wilson that he understood the situation and that he would "take note of this communication." The Wilson mission had failed to break the *impasse*.[120]

Hitler and the British leaders were equally anxious to avoid a conflict despite the stubborn nature of their respective comments at this late stage of the crisis. Chamberlain appealed to Mussolini to do something at 11:30a.m. on September 28, 1938. The effect was magical, and Hitler did not hesitate. The British Ambassador was able to telephone London at 3:15p.m. on September 28, 1938, that Hitler wished to invite Chamberlain, Daladier, and Mussolini to Munich on the next day to discuss a peaceful solution of the Czech problem. The British Prime Minister received this news while delivering a tense speech to the House of Commons on the imminent danger of war. When he announced the news of Hitler's invitation and of his intention to accept, he received the greatest ovation in the history of the British Parliament.[121]

The Bavarian city of Munich was wild with enthusiasm for peace when the European leaders arrived to negotiate on September 29, 1938. There was no appreciable enthusiasm for war in any of the European countries after the terrible experience of World War I, and in the light of the horrors of modern conflict currently revealed by the Civil War in Spain. A number of factors produced the Munich meeting. There was the strenuous initiative of Chamberlain to persuade the Czechs to capitulate. There was the patience of Daladier in agreeing to accept whatever his British ally could achieve. There was the restraint of Hitler in modifying his demands, and in resisting the temptation to strike at a time most favorable to win a war. Hitler was convinced that war in Europe need not be regarded as inevitable: otherwise he would never have invited the foreign leaders to Munich. There was the mediation of Mussolini, and the conviction that the respective parties were too close to an agreement to ruin everything by an unnecessary war.[122]

Never was an agreement more clearly in the interest of all Powers concerned. Great Britain had won time to continue to gain on the German lead in aerial armament. France extricated herself from the danger of a desperate war after having abandoned her military hegemony in Europe in 1936. Italy was spared the danger of involvement in a war when she was woefully unprepared. Germany won a great bloodless victory in her program of peaceful territorial revision. By resisting the temptation to fight merely because she had the momentary military advantage, she increased her stature and prestige. As A.J.P. Taylor put it: "The demonstration had been given that Germany could attain by peaceful negotiation the position in Europe to which her resources entitled her."[123]

Czech representatives in Munich were informed of developments, but they were not allowed to participate in deliberations, and there were no Hungarian or Polish representatives present.[124] Winston Churchill later argued that French honor had been compromised at Munich because France had a formal obligation to defend the Czechs.[125] It has been seen that this was not the view of Bonnet, and it is necessary to add that France, despite the pressure she imposed, might have aided the Czechs had they gambled again and actually resisted Germany. This situation never arose in reality. The Czechs had a young state which had been created by the efforts of others rather than by some fierce struggle for independence. Their state had been launched into a turbulent world under the problematical leadership of Masaryk and Beneš. They had been associated politically for hundreds of years either with Germany or Austria. They were surrounded by enemies in 1938, and their defeat in a war was inevitable. Their surrender under these circumstances might not satisfy the honor requirements of arm-chair chauvinists, but it was a wise move. The Czechs might have emerged from World War II in excellent shape had the later diplomacy of Benes, Churchill, and Roosevelt not permitted the Communists to dominate the Czech people, and to incite them in 1945 to deeds of horror and violence against the masses of unarmed Slovaks, Hungarians, and Germans.[126]

The Polish Ultimatum to Czechoslovakia

The Poles were extremely irritated by the Munich conference, and that the revival of cooperation among the principal non-Communist Powers of Europe. Hitler, after achieving his own success, took an indulgent view at Munich toward Polish and Hungarian claims, but the idea of the Powers discussing an issue of Polish foreign policy in the absence of Poland was anathema to Beck. It violated Pilsudski's principal maxim on foreign policy: Nothing about us without us![127] Beck did not wait to learn the results of the Munich deliberations. On the evening of September 30, 1938, he submitted an ultimatum to Prague demanding the town of Teschen and its surrounding district by noon on Sunday, October 2nd. He also demanded the surrender [within ten days] of the remaining hinterland claimed by Poland. Beck warned that if a Czech note of compliance was not received by noon on October 1st, "Poland would not be responsible for the consequences." The ultimatum gave the Czechs merely a few hours to decide on their reply.[128]

The Czechs hastened to capitulate, and their reply was received in Warsaw ahead of the deadline. Beck's action worried Kennard, who feared that his beloved Poles were jeopardizing their reputation abroad. He lectured Beck on the dangers of military action, and he added that "if the Polish Government proceeded to direct action they would draw upon themselves the serious reprobation of the whole world, which had only just emerged from a crisis of a far greater nature." It is amusing to note that in British diplomatic language the attitude of the British Empire, which meant the small proportion of people who were the masters of that Empire together with the friends of Britain at the moment, was supposed to be equivalent to the attitude of the entire world. British diplomats modified this at times, and referred to the attitude of the entire "civilized" world. It is almost unnecessary to observe that Kennard's lecture produced not the slightest effect on Beck.[129]

Lord Halifax was annoyed. His instructions to Kennard at 10:00 p.m., on September 30th, indicated that he had taken no notice of Pilsudski's maxim of "nothing about us without us," although this maxim had been reiterated publicly by Beck on innumerable occasions. Halifax observed that the Munich conference had recognized the necessity of settling Hungarian and Polish claims, and that the Polish Government would be "very short-sighted and ill-advised to take the law into their own hands instead of basing their policy . . . on the four Powers." This ignored the fact that the Munich Powers also had taken the law into their own hands. Halifax complained that with an ultimatum threatening occupation by force the "Poles put themselves entirely in the wrong." In all fairness, it should be recalled that the Czechs had not obtained the region in the first place by sending bouquets to Warsaw. The Polish Government disagreed with Halifax and believed it would place itself in the wrong if it waited for the crumbs to be swept from the Munich conference table.[130]

German Support to Poland Against the Soviet Union

German claims had been settled at Munich, and Beck knew that he was vulnerable. Major incidents and even air battles had taken place on the Russo-Polish frontier in recent days. Beck had become less confident that the Russians were bluffing. His two main fears were that Russia would attack him in the rear, and that the Czechs would receive German support by some additional concessions to Germany, of which he believed them totally capable. Beck badly needed some assurance of foreign support. The British attitude was momentarily hostile, and it would be too much to expect the French to support him against their Czech ally. There remained only Germany, and Beck decided to act upon this fact. German-Polish cooperation under the 1934

Pact reached a new summit at this moment.

Beck summoned Moltke on the evening of September 30, 1938, and announced that he was delivering an ultimatum to the Czechs. He wished to know if Germany would maintain a benevolent attitude during a Polish-Czech war. He added that he also wanted German support in the event of an attack on Poland by the Soviet Union. Beck assured Moltke with warmth that he was grateful for "the loyal German attitude toward Poland" during the Munich conference and for the "sincerity of relations during the Czech conflict." Beck was frank in his evaluation of the German policy, but the "sincerity of relations" sounds ironical when one considers that a few days earlier Poland was discussing the conditions under which she would attack Germany.[131]

Hitler immediately gave Beck all the protection he desired. The French had led a *démarche* in Warsaw protesting the Polish ultimatum, and Italy had participated in this step. Ribbentrop responded by telephoning Italian Foreign Minister Ciano to inform him that Germany was in full sympathy with the Polish position. He told Ciano that the Poles had informed him of "terrible conditions in the Teschen territory," and he reminded him that 240,000 Germans had been expelled from the Sudetenland during the recent crisis. He concluded that Ciano would understand if Germany did not care to use the same language as Italy at Warsaw.[132]

Ribbentrop did everything possible to comfort the Poles. He told Lipski that he believed the Czechs would submit quickly. He promised that Germany would adopt a benevolent attitude if Poland had to invade Czechoslovakia to secure her claims. He had Hitler's consent to inform Lipski that Germany would adopt a benevolent attitude toward Poland in a Russo-Polish war. He made it clear that this "benevolent attitude" was tantamount to giving Poland everything she might require in such a conflict.[133] He added that a Russian invasion would create a new situation in which Germany would not be inhibited by the attitude of the other Munich Powers. German support to Poland was instant, unequivocal, and complete.[134]

Bullitt in Paris was no less dismayed by the Polish attitude than Kennard. He persuaded the British to intervene again in the Teschen question, before Czech willingness to comply with Polish demands had become generally known. He pleaded with British Ambassador Eric Phipps, in Paris on October 1st, that if he had more time he would propose intervention in Warsaw by President Roosevelt, but that Chamberlain was the only person who could act under existing circumstances.[135] The British Prime Minister responded to this suggestion. He was preparing a message to Beck when a confused report arrived from British Minister Newton in Prague that the Czechs had rejected the Polish ultimatum and would "resist force."[136] The prospect of this disaster stiffened Chamberlain's message to Beck. He warned the Poles not to use force if the Czechs rejected their ultimatum, and he added that it was "quite inadmissable" for Poland to insist on "taking matters into her own hands."[137]

Word arrived in London shortly after Chamberlain's message to Beck that the Czechs had capitulated. Newton was acutely embarrassed. He complained angrily that the speed of the surrender was a great surprise after the brave words which had been spoken in Prague. He observed contemptuously that "the Czech spirit seems indeed somewhat broken," and his disappointment that the Czechs would not fight Poland was obvious. Nevertheless, it seems understandable that the Czechs had little stomach for a hopeless contest against the Poles after having been denied support against Germany.[138]

The Czech crisis which culminated in the Munich conference passed the acute stage with the settlement of the Polish demand for Teschen. It was obvious that the Hungarians would not dare to act against the Czechs as Poland had done. Events had moved rapidly in a direction not at all to the liking of the Soviet Union. After a luncheon with Soviet Foreign Commissar Litvinov at the Paris Soviet Embassy on October 1, 1938, Bonnet speculated that the Soviet Union might denounce the Franco-Russian alliance. Litvinov was especially furious about Chamberlain. He complained that Chamberlain should not have been "allowed" to go to Berchtesgaden or Bad Godesberg, but that these two "mistakes" were as nothing compared to the "enormity" of Munich. Litvinov insisted passionately that Hitler had been bluffing, and that he could have been forced to retreat without serious danger of war. Bonnet held exactly the opposite view. He "gently pointed out" that France wished to be on decent terms with Germany, Italy, and Franco Spain. He was aware that these nations were objectionable to Russia, but they also were the immediate neighbors of France, and he would not permit the Soviet Union to dictate French policy. Litvinov did not have the satisfaction of seeing his French guest seriously perturbed by the outcome of the recent crisis. Bonnet was concentrating on developing a new policy to meet the new circumstances.[139]

Anglo-German Treaty Accepted by Hitler

There was a dramatic epilogue to the Munich conference in which Chamberlain and Hitler were the principal figures. Chamberlain proposed a private meeting at Hitler's Prinzregentenstrasse apartment in Munich on September 30, 1938, at which Hitler's interpreter, Paul Schmidt, was the only third party. The British Prime Minister and the German leader discussed the European situation at length. In Schmidt's record of the converstion, which was confirmed in its authenticity by Chamberlain, Hitler declared that "the most difficult problem of all had now been concluded and his own main task had been happily fulfilled." Chamberlain said that if the Czechs nevertheless resisted, he hoped there would be no air attacks on women and children. This was ironical when one considers that Chamberlain knew the British Air Force, in contrast to the German strategy of tactical air support to the ground forces, was basing its strategy on concentrated air attacks against civilian centers in a future war. Hitler was not aware of this, and he insisted emphatically that he was opposed in every event to such air attacks, which would never be employed by Germany except in retaliation. Chamberlain and Hitler discussed the problem of arms limitation, and they agreed that there might be some future prospect for this. Hitler emphasized that he was primarily worried about the Soviet Union and by the Communist ideology which the Russians were seeking to export to the entire world. He was concerned because Poland refused to define her position toward the Soviet Union, and he observed that "Poland intervenes geographically between Germany and Russia, but he had no very clear idea of her powers of resistance." The two leaders discussed trade relations, but they were far apart on this issue. Hitler deprecated the importance of international loans in stimulating trade, or the need for uniform tariff policies toward all nations. This attitude was questioned by Chamberlain.

When the conversation was ending, Chamberlain suddenly asked Hitler if he would sign a declaration of Anglo-German friendship. There is a legend that Hitler signed this document without having it translated, but it is entirely untrue. After Hitler had listened to the terms, he signed without hesitation the two copies of the treaty in the English language which Chamberlain presented to him. Chamberlain signed both copies and returned one to Hitler. The agreement contained the following terms:

> We, the German Fuehrer and Chancellor and the British Prime Minister, have had a further meeting to-day and are agreed in recognizing that the question of Anglo-German relations is of first importance for the two countries and for Europe.
>
> We regard the agreement signed last night and the Anglo-German Naval agreement as a symbolic of the desire of our two peoples never to go to war with one another again.
>
> We are resolved that the method of consultation shall be the method adopted to deal with any other questions that may concern our two countries, and we are determined to continue our efforts to remove possible sources of difference and thus to contribute to assure the peace of Europe.[140]

This important agreement might have become the cornerstone for the preservation of peace in Europe and for the defense of Europe against Communism. It was accepted by Hitler without reservations, and by Chamberlain with reservations which were certain to become more vigorous when he returned to English soil. Many prominent Englishmen entertained a variety of superstitions, both old and new, about Germany which were not conducive to the perservation of peace. It was Hitler's problem to cope with this situation while carrying out his program, and it will be evident later, in the evaluation of the British scene after Munich, that the odds for success were not favorable. The initiative for the agreement came from Chamberlain, who knew that it would be a trump to show his critics at home. This does not alter the fact that Chamberlain was ambivalent and Hitler single-minded about it.

Hitler's unique achievements in Austria and Czechoslovakia in 1938, which consisted of territorial revisions without force, would not have been possible had the British favored war that year. The greatest single misfortune in 1939 was the changed British attitude in favor of war.

Chapter 6

A GERMAN OFFER TO POLAND

Germany's Perilous Position After Munich

The victory of Hitler at Munich convinced the last sceptic that Germany had regained her traditional position as the dominant Power in Central Europe. This position had been occupied by France in the years after the German defeat in 1918. Hitler challenged French military hegemony in the area when he reoccupied the German Rhineland in 1936. The acquisition of ten million Germans in Austria and Czechoslovakia in 1938 greatly improved the German strategic position toward the East and the South. Germany established new common frontiers with Italy, Hungary, and Yugoslavia. The Italian sphere of influence in Central Europe north of the Brenner Pass was demolished, and the French and Soviet sphere of influence in Czechoslovakia was insignificant after the Czechs lost the strategic natural frontier of Bohemia with its elaborate fortifications.[1]

The German Reich after Munich had a population of 78 million Germans. The principal neighbors of Germany in Europe were France, Italy and Poland. The Germans were almost twice as numerous as the Italians, nearly twice as numerous as the French, and approximately four times as numerous as the Poles, when one discounts the Ukrainians and other eastern minorities of the Polish state, whose loyalty was extremely dubious.[2] Industrial capacity had become the decisive criterion in measuring a modern Power, and Germany was many times stronger in this respect than any of her immediate neighbors. The German people were noted for their energy, vigor, and martial valor. The fact that Germany was the leading Power in Central Europe was no less logical or natural than was the dominant role of the United States on the North American continent. The United States enjoyed her position for much the same reasons.[3]

Nevertheless, the situation of Germany after Munich was precarious to an extent which had been unknown in the United States for many generations. It is not surprising under these circumstances that it was difficult, if not impossible, for Americans in 1938 to understand the problems which confronted

Germany. The impressive and seemingly impregnable position of Germany, which had been created by Bismarck in 1871 following Prussian victories in three wars, had been shattered by the single defeat of 1918. The defeat of Germany had been exploited so thoroughly that it seemed unlikely for many years that the Germans would recover their former position. The leading role of the Germans in Central Europe had existed for many centuries before the defeat and emasculation of the Holy Roman Empire of the German Nation in 1648. More than two centuries elapsed before the new German state created by Bismarck in 1871 restored the traditional German position, although it is true that the Prussian state alone was sufficiently powerful to obtain recognition as a major European Power during the interim period. The Hohenzollern Empire lasted only from 1871 to 1918. It was clear that the ability of Germany to occupy her rightful place in Europe had become problematical for a number of reasons, some obscure.[4]

Although Germany after Munich could doubtless have coped with a combined attack from all of her immediate neighbors on land, she had to face the elementary possibility that she might be attacked by an overwhelming coalition of distant Powers, if she became involved in a conflict with any of her immediate neighbors. The Bagdad railway question, the last direct point of friction between Germany and the British Empire in the years before World War I, had been settled by peaceful negotiation in June 1914. This did not prevent Great Britain, the dominant Naval Power of the world, from attacking Germany a few weeks later, or from inflicting an unrestricted blockade on an industrial nation, which did not enjoy any degree of self-sufficiency. It did not prevent Japan from attacking Germany in 1914, although there was no direct point of conflict between Germany and Japan. It did not prevent the United States from holding Germany to strict accountability in the conduct of naval warfare, and from accepting gross violations of maritime international law when they were British. In 1917 the United States declared war on Germany on the specious plea that the Germans were violating the same freedom of the seas which the British failed to recognize. The British refused to conclude the armistice in 1918 until point 2 about freedom of the seas was dropped from President Wilson's program, and there were never any American protests about British unrestricted submarine warfare in the Baltic Sea during World War I. It was this coalition of distant Powers which made inevitable the defeat of Germany in World War I.[5]

There was no appreciable difference between the German situation of 1914 and 1938 except that Hitler had learned from experience. It was no longer possible to accept the facile proposition that Germany was secure, merely because she could cope with attacks from her immediate neighbors in the West or in the East. The Soviet Union was a gigantic unknown factor in the world power relationships of 1938. The attitude of the British Empire toward Germany was problematical. The British leaders warned Germany repeatedly in 1938 that they might not remain aloof from a conflict involving Germany and some third Power. The United States since 1900 was usually inclined to follow the British lead in foreign policy, and there could be no certain guarantee that the United States would remain aloof from a new Anglo-German war.[6]

Hitler correctly recognized the British attitude as the crux of the entire situation. Neither the United States nor the Soviet Union was likely to attack

Germany unless she became ensnared in a new conflict with Great Britain. Hitler knew that Germany had nothing to gain in a war with the British, but he feared the anti-Germanism of the British leaders. His sole ally in this situation was British public opinion. The British public would not be likely to support a war against Germany unless it was accompanied by some seemingly plausible pretext. But if Hitler became involved in some local European conflict, the British leaders might convince their public opinion that Germany had embarked on a program of unlimited conquest which threatened British security.[7]

The Inadequacy of German Armament

Winston Churchill and other British *bellicistes* circulated the greatest possible amount of nonsense about the current German armament program, and the British leaders in power were not averse to this exaggerated notion of German military strength. It was useful in gaining support for the current British armament program. But Burton Klein has pointed out that Hitler himself opposed large defense expenditures throughout the decade from 1933 to 1943, and that Germany, with her large industrial capacity, might easily have developed a much more adequate defense program. Many people in Great Britain were astonished to learn later that Great Britain and Germany were producing approximately the same number of military aircraft each month when World War II came in 1939. It was more surprising still that Great Britain was producing 50 more armored tanks each month than Germany: Great Britain and France greatly outnumbered Germany in this important category of mechanized armament when France fell in 1940.[8] German public finance before 1939 was conservative compared to the United States and Great Britain, and large-scale public borrowing was not undertaken in Germany. Public expenditure in Germany increased from 15 billion Marks (3.75 billion dollars) in 1933 to 39 billion Marks (9.75 billion dollars) in 1938, but more than 80% of this outlay was raised by current taxation. The value of German gross national production during the same period increased from 59 billion Marks (14.75 billion dollars) to 105 billion Marks (26.25 billion dollars). There was merely a slight rise in prices, and there was a higher level of German private consumption and investment in 1938 than in the peak year of 1929.[9]

Hitler declared in a speech on September 1, 1939, that 90 billion Marks (22.5 billion dollars) had been spent on defense by Germany since he had been appointed Chancellor on January 30, 1933. Hitler, in arriving at this figure, included items of public expenditure which had nothing to do with arms, and which would not have met the later official definition of the War Production Board in the United States. He was seeking to use intimidation to dissuade the British and French from attacking Germany. It is ironical that the League of Nations experts on armaments at Geneva were willing in this instance to accept Hitler's statement at face value, although they were sceptical about his remarks on every other occasion.[10] In reality, Germany spent 55 billion Marks (13.75 billion dollars) on military defense during the period of nearly seven years from January 1933 until the outbreak of World War II. It was said that Germany entered World War II with a "guns *and* butter philosophy."[11]

In the last peacetime year, 1938-1939, 16 billion Marks (4 billion dollars) or 15% of the German gross national product was spent on military preparation. The volume of arms expense in the United States during the last American peacetime year from December 1940 to December 1941 was much higher, although American critics claimed that the United States was woefully unprepared when Japan struck at Pearl Harbor. The Germans, on the other hand, had allegedly done everything humanly possible to prepare for war before the outbreak of World War II. In reality, Germany was spending a large proportion of public funds on municipal improvements and public buildings when war came. Hitler believed that Germany needed immediate military superiority over France and Great Britain to intimidate them for a short period from intervening against Germany while he completed his program of territorial revision, but he hoped to avoid war against a coalition of major Powers. Nearly one half of the total German expense on arms during the last year of peace went to the Air Force, but the British leaders were confident during the same period that they were gaining rapidly on Germany in the air.[12]

The Favorable Position of Great Britain

The British leaders had a problem of national security, but their situation was more favorable than that of Hitler. In 1938 Great Britain was at a temporary disadvantage toward Germany in the air, but the prospects for successful air defense against the Germans were extremely favorable in 1939. Germany had few submarines, and the British Navy was overwhelmingly powerful compared to the German Navy. The insular position of Great Britain offered an admirable defense against the employment of German land forces. In contrast to Germany, the British did not have to face the peril of an invasion from the Soviet Union in the event of a Western European war. They were backed by the tremendous resources of the British Empire and the United States. Had Hitler been determined to crush Great Britain, he would have had to recognize that the British strategic situation was superior to his own.[13]

Hitler had no intention to attack Great Britain. The British leaders could have remained neutral in any European conflict involving Germany without jeopardizing British security. The main danger in 1938 and 1939 was that Great Britain would attack Germany and seek to crush her completely. This would lead to involvement in a protracted war, which would exhaust British resources and expose the British Empire to the forces of disintegration. This is what later happened. The British strategic position was good in 1939, but it was sacrificed unnecessarily. The principal benefactor was the Soviet Union, the mortal enemy of the British Empire.[14]

This dread development was one which Hitler hoped to avoid. It seemed to him that German security would not be complete until Germany attained comprehensive understandings with her principal neighbors. He recognized that such understandings would demand a price. He was prepared to abandon the Germans south of the Brenner Pass to Italy: and to France he conceded the problematical Germans of Alsace-Lorraine, who seemed to long for Germany when they were French and for France when they were German. He hoped for an alliance with

Italy, and after the Munich conference he sought to attain a Franco-German declaration of friendship similar to the one which he had signed with Chamberlain at Munich.[15]

Hitler's Generous Attitude toward Poland

Poland was the third principal neighbor of Germany, and she was the sole neighboring Power with which Germany was in direct danger of conflict after the Munich conference. The problem of Danzig and the German-Polish frontier was more dangerous than that of Bosnia-Herzegovina before 1914. The position of Poland between Germany and her principal adversary, the Soviet Union, was one of paramount importance. It seemed to Hitler that the clarification of German-Polish relations was an absolute necessity. A policy of aimless drifting from one unexpected crisis to another had led to the ruin of Germany in World War I. Hitler believed that this vicious pattern had to be broken, and it is not surprising that he wished to establish German security on a rock-like foundation after the harrowing German experiences since 1900. Hitler's concern would have been intensified had he known of the secret Anglo-Polish negotiations of August 1938 to frustrate German aspirations at Danzig. He was greatly concerned as it was. He harbored no animosity toward Poland, and this is astonishing when one considers the bitter legacy of German-Polish relations from the 1918-1934 period, or the attitudes of the Polish leaders. He was prepared to pay a high price for Polish friendship, and, indeed, to pay a much higher price to the Poles than to either Italy or France. The renunciation of every piece of German territory lost to Poland since 1918 would have been unthinkable to Gustav Stresemann and the leaders of the Weimar Republic. Hitler was prepared to pay this price, and he believed that the favorable moment for a settlement had arrived after the close and unprecedented German-Polish cooperation in the latest phase of the Czech crisis. Hitler was inclined to be confident when he approached Poland with a comprehensive offer a few weeks after the Munich conference. He was warned in vague terms by Ambassador Moltke in Warsaw that a settlement would not be easy, but no one outside of Poland could have known that his generous proposals would actually be received with scorn.[16]

Further Polish Aspirations in Czecho-Slovakia

The further development of the Czech situation was a minor theme compared to the issue of a German-Polish settlement, but the Czech and Polish issues remained closely linked for many months, and it is impossible to consider one without the other. The hyphenated name "Czecho-Slovakia" was adopted by law at Prague, shortly after the Munich conference, as the official name to designate the Czech state. This was part of a series of half-hearted Czech appeasement measures to the Slovaks.[17] It was evident immediately after Poland's success in the Teschen question that Polish leaders were eager to realize other objectives in Czecho-Slovakia. These objectives were three in number, and not easily compatible. The Poles hoped to see Slovakia emerge immediately from Czech rule as an independent state. The prospect for this development was not good. The Slovakian nationalist movement had been ruthlessly suppressed by the Czechs after President Thomas Masaryk had betrayed the promises for Slovak autonomy contained in the Pittsburgh agreement of 1918. It was obvious that time would be required before the Slovak nationalist movement could successfully reassert itself.[18]

Josef Tiso and Karol Sidor, the two principal leaders of Slovak nationalism in 1938, were unable to command a single-minded following. Most Slovaks were opposed to the continuation of Czech rule, but they were divided into three conflicting groups. An influential group favored the return of Slovakia to Hungary, but the timidity of the Magyars was so great that no effective support could be expected from Budapest. Another group, of which Sidor was the principal spokesman, favored a close association between Slovakia and Poland and even a Polish protectorate. A third group, of which Tiso was the outstanding leader, favored a completely independent Slovakia, but they were doubtful if such a state could survive without strong protection from some neighboring Power. When one includes the Hlasist movement, which was pro-Czech, the Slovaks were divided into no less than four schools of thought on the fundamental question of their future existence.[19]

Slovakia was a backward agrarian country with a mixed ethnic population.[20] It was too much to expect Slovakia to declare her independence the moment Czech power was weakened. Polish disappointment was inevitable when the Slovaks failed to respond as expected. The Polish High Commissioner in Danzig, Marjan Chodacki, exclaimed to Jan Szembek at the Polish Foreign Office on October 11, 1938, that Slovakia and Ruthenia would become instruments of German eastward expansion unless they were quickly separated from Czech rule.[21] There was always the possibility of direct Polish intervention if the Slovaks failed to act for themselves, but the Polish military leaders expressed a negative attitude toward this project. The idea of a Poland eventually extending from the Danube River to the Dvina River was attractive to the military men, but they claimed that a conflict with Germany was likely, and they believed that a Polish protectorate in Slovakia would be bad strategy. The Carpathian Mountains, in their estimation, formed the most important natural frontier of Poland, and they argued that the Polish position would become over-extended if Polish troops were sent to occupy the land beyond the mountains.[22]

Many foreign observers were aware that a Slovakian crisis was likely in the near future. Truman Smith, the American military attaché in Berlin, sent a valuable report to President Roosevelt on October 5, 1938, concerning the strategic situation in Europe after the Munich conference. His report was accompanied by a prediction from Ambassador Hugh Wilson suggesting that Hitler in the near future might support Italy in some important question out of gratitude for Mussolini's mediation at Munich, because "the outstanding characteristic of Hitler in standing by his friends is well known." Smith explained to Roosevelt that "Hitler's hope and wish is to retain Italy's friendship while winning France and England's." He predicted that there would be trouble in Slovakia, and that Italy, Poland, and Hungary would support Slovakian independence aspirations. He said, "Hitler's diplomatic position at the moment is not an enviable one. He will require all of his diplomatic skill to avoid the many pitfalls which today confront him and hold to Italy while winning England and France." Smith declared that Germany desired peace, but that there was certain to be much trouble in Europe in the immediate future. He concluded his report with the ominous warning: "Lastly, watch the fate of Slovakia." He considered Slovakia to be the most important issue in Europe, and more so than Spain, where the Civil War was approaching its final phase.[23]

Polish Foreign Minister Beck was nettled by Hungarian timidity, and by the reluctance of Polish military men to extend their commitments to the South. Tiso wanted strong protection for an independent Slovakian state, and Germany was the only alternative if Hungary and Poland refused to accept this responsibility. Fulminations against the Czechs, and the promise that Poland would adopt a friendly policy toward an independent Slovakia, was all that Beck could offer the Slovaks for the moment. It was evident that he was extremely worried by this situation.

The second Polish objective in Czecho-Slovakia complicated the problem created by the first one. In the years before the first Polish partition of 1772, Joseph II, Kaiser of the Holy Roman Empire and King of Hungary, seized a region in the Carpathian mountains which had been in dispute between Poland and Hungary since the Middle Ages. He took this step with the reluctant consent of Maria Theresa, co-regent in the Habsburg dominions of her son Joseph's imperial domain. This region had been awarded to the favored Czechs by the Allied and Associated Powers at Paris in 1919. The circumstances of the allocation, for which the principal Powers were solely responsible, and the unimportant economic value of the region, made Polish reaction less intense than the passion aroused by Teschen. Nevertheless the Polish leaders had never forgotten their disappointment in failing to obtain the Zips-Orawy Carpathian area. The region was on the ethnic frontier with Slovakia, and it would have been prudent for them to play down Polish interest in territorial revision at Slovakian expense until the general situation of Slovakia had been clarified. Unfortunately they could not countenance the thought of losing their chance to acquire the disputed territory while general conditions remained favorably fluid. The temptation to exploit Czech weakness to achieve this second objective was too great. Polish impulsiveness ended by wrecking Polish-Slovakian relations, and Poland's primary objective of securing a favorable solution of the Slovakian question was sacrificed.[24]

The third objective of Polish policy in Czecho-Slovakia after the Teschen settlement was the elimination of Czech rule in Ruthenia. John Reshetar, the principal American historian of Ruthenian extraction, has pointed out that Ruthenia could be classified equally well as a Greater Russian or Ukrainian community. The geographic proximity of Ruthenia to the Ukraine presented the advocates of an independent or Soviet Ukraine with a distinct advantage in Ruthenian counsels.[25] It can be affirmed, with this consideration in mind, that the Ukraine in 1938 was divided among four partitioning Powers. The greatest number of Ukrainians were Soviet subjects, and they were twice as numerous as the entire Polish population of Poland. They inhabited the central and eastern Ukraine. Poland came second to Russia with her rule established over the eight or nine million Ukrainians of the Western Ukraine.[26] Rumania was third with her control over the Ukrainian section of the Bessarabian area between the Prut and Dniester Rivers north of the mouth of the Danube. Finally, the Czechs ruled over approximately one million Ruthenians south of the Carpathians, who were descended from the subjects of the Kievan Russian state of the Middle Ages. Czech rule in Ruthenia had been established at Paris in 1919, and it had always seemed fantastic to the Poles. The Rumanians, on the other hand, welcomed it because it provided direct Rumanian contact by land with the armament industry of Bohemia, and it deprived Hungary of a common frontier with Poland.

Polish thought on the Ruthenian question was simplicity itself. Ruthenia had belonged to Hungary for hundreds of years before 1919, and Ruthenia should return to Hungary. Hungary had suffered mutilation at the Paris peace conference in 1919, where they lost two-thirds of their population and three-fourths of their territory. They were understandably reluctant under these circumstances to take risks twenty years later. Poland was annoyed because the Hungarian leaders would not take matters into their own hands and march into Ruthenia. The Poles were no less determined because of this to see the territory return to Hungary, and they regarded a solution in this sense as absolutely essential.[27]

The Poles feared the emergence of an entirely independent Ruthenia. The Communists might succeed in gaining control of the area. This would enable them to exert pressure from both West and East on the restive and discontented Polish-Ukrainian population. No student of Polish history or literature forgot that the decline of Poland as a great Power in the early modern period began with a gigantic revolt in 1648 of the Ukrainians under Polish rule. This revolt had been successfully exploited by Russia.[28]

The Poles also feared that Hitler might return to the 1918 German policy in support of Ukrainian separatism. This program had been belatedly adopted by the Germans at the 1918 Brest-Litovsk conference, because of Trotsky's intransigence in refusing to conclude a peace settlement between Russia and Germany in World War I. The object now as then might be to strike a crippling blow at the Soviet Union. The treaty of Brest-Litovsk had been a favorite theme of Hitler's oratory in the early days of his political career. Hitler had defended the Brest-Litovsk treaty, because Germany had made no territorial annexations, but had extended self-determination to millions of Europeans, and had sought to protect them from the terrors of Bolshevik rule. Hitler considered Brest-Litovsk to have been a peace of justice when compared to Versailles, and he used a number of effective arguments to support this view. It seemed logical to the Polish leaders that Hitler might seek to follow this policy and attempt to push back the Bolshevik tide by liberating the Ukrainians. It was known that many Ukrainian refugees were allowed to conduct their propaganda activities from points within Germany. It was believed that Hitler could secure greater access for Germany to the valuable resources of Eastern Europe if he freed the Ukraine.[29]

A more effective Polish policy in Slovakia would have been useful in settling the Ruthenian question in a sense favorable to Poland. It would be impossible to maintain Czech rule in Ruthenia once Slovakia was independent. Polish thinking was so dominated by the idea of a war with Germany, and by strategic considerations for such a war, that an excellent opportunity to implement Pilsudski's policy of federation with neighboring nations was thrown away in Slovakia. The Poles and Slovaks were closely related in culture, temperament, and customs, and at this point a close association between the two countries was feasible as never before. The Poles did not stop to consider that concessions at Danzig, or in the superhighway question, would be a small price to pay for German support in acquiring Slovakia. The greatest foreign policy successes of Poland since the Riga treaty in 1921 consisted solely of the opening of the Polish-Lithuanian frontier after the Austro-German *Anschluss*, and of the acquisition of Teschen territory after the German success at Munich. Poland decided to proceed in the same manner by nibbling at the Carpathian mountains rather than by achieving a great success in establishing a Polish-Slovakian union. The policy of union had a much greater chance of success in Slovakia than in a non-Slavic country like Lithuania. The removal of Polish prejudice toward Germany at this point would have made the experiment feasible.

German Ambassador Moltke complained from Warsaw on October 6, 1938, that the Polish press did not hint that success at Teschen had been attained because Germany had cleared the path. The German diplomat had been wrong in his predictions about Polish policy throughout the Czech crisis, and a number of his remarks on October 6th about recent events betrayed considerable confusion. He was still insisting that the Poles were trying to collaborate with the Czechs against Germany when the news arrived that there would be a conference at Munich. This analysis undoubtedly increased his indignation when he reported that the officially inspired Polish press claimed unanimously that German success in the Sudeten question was possible because of Polish aid. The Polish press claimed that Germany would have failed had not Polish neutrality prevented Soviet Russian intervention. The wisdom of this propaganda line from the official Polish standpoint was questionable, since a recitation of alleged Polish aid to Germany was not calculated to appease anti-German public opinion in Poland.[30]

Moltke believed that the Munich conference had diminished the prestige of France in Poland, but he did not think that Poland would drop the French alliance merely to strengthen her relations with Germany. Moltke was wrong in assuming that Hitler intended to ask the Poles to drop their French alliance. He was right when he reminded the German Foreign Office that Polish policy in Ruthenia was directed primarily against the Soviet Union, but that "fears of German expansion also play a part." The principal theme in Moltke's report was that German-Polish cooperation in the Czech crisis did not guarantee the termination of a Polish policy hostile toward Germany.[31]

Continued Czech Hostility toward Poland and Germany

The Czech leaders knew that the chances for the continued existence of their state were not good, and they denounced the Polish leaders for seeking the total disruption of Czecho-Slovakia. Czech Foreign Minister Krofta informed the British on October 3, 1938, that events were proceeding smoothly in the Sudeten area where the Czechs were busily withdrawing, but he complained vehemently about the Poles. British Minister Newton reported that Krofta "displayed anxiety over the intrigues and propaganda which had been conducted by Poles in Slovakia." Krofta confided that Czech weakness might be exploited "to spread suggestions that Slovakia would be better off if associated with Poland." Krofta would not have entertained such fears had he not realized how deeply the Czechs were hated in Slovakia, and how much the Slovak people preferred almost any association to one with the Czechs. Krofta added that he "chiefly desired" French and British help against the Poles, but he also hoped that "Hitler would perhaps help in resisting such Polish ambitions."[32]

Hitler was irritated with the Czechs at this point, and scarcely in a mood to challenge Polish propaganda in Slovakia. There was vigorous disagreement between the Germans and Czechs on the delimitation of the non-plebiscite Sudeten regions to be assigned to Germany. The Munich agreement had provided that some areas were to be surrendered to Germany within ten days, and that other areas were to be occupied by an international police force pending a plebiscite. British Ambassador Nevile Henderson took an active interest in the regulation of the dispute. He was a sincere advocate of appeasement, and in this respect he was much closer to Bonnet, with whom he established close contact, than to Chamberlain and Halifax in London. He was considered the most promising of the younger British diplomats when he was sent to Berlin in 1937, but his devotion to those principles, which were professed without conviction by his masters in London, soon made his position in the British diplomatic service an isolated and unenviable one.[33]

Henderson believed that the Czechs were conducting a policy of hopeless obstruction when they made difficulties about the procedure which had been accepted by the Powers at Munich. It had been decided that the 1918 population figures would be used to delimit the non-plebiscite areas, and the 1910 Habsburg census was the last one taken before 1918. The Czechs suggested that their own (doctored) census returns from 1921 or even 1930 should serve as the criterion. At Munich it had been decided that areas assigned to Germany without plebiscite would be those which contained more than 50% German population. The Czechs insisted that 75% rather than 51% should be considered more than 50%. Hitler replied by threatening to send the German Army down to the Bad Godesberg line if the Czechs did not abide by the terms of the published British documents on Munich. At Bad Godesberg Hitler had demanded the immediate occupation of a much greater area than had been granted to Germany at Munich.[34]

Halifax favored a last minute game to modify the Munich agreement in favor of the Czechs, but he was opposed by the French and Italians, who insisted on the need "to respect the spirit of this Protocol."[35] Halifax consoled himself with the thought that something could be done for the Czechs in the plebiscite zone, but President Beneš decided that the last attempt to accomplish anything by opposing Germany had failed. He resigned in disgust on October 5, 1938. A Provisional Government was formed by General Jan Syrový, a Czech national hero who had helped to secure the withdrawal of former Czech prisoners-of-war from Russia in 1918.[36] The Milan Hodza Cabinet had been forced out by a demonstration directed by Klement Gottwald, the Communist Party leader, on September 22nd.[37] Syrový had succeeded Hodza as Premier and he became interim chief-of-state after the resignation of Beneš and pending the election of a new President. František Chvalkovský from the dominant Agrarian Party succeeded Krofta as Foreign Minister after the latter resigned from the Syrový

Cabinet on October 5th.[38] Chvalkovský had represented Czechoslovakia in both Rome and Berlin. He was a loyal Czech patriot but he did not share the fanatical hatred of his predecessor toward Fascism and National Socialism. It was too early to predict the ultimate policy of the new regime but the resignation of Benes produced an immediate relaxation of tension.[39]

The Czechs were seeking to stir up Great Britain against Poland, but Sir Howard Kennard in Warsaw was doing everything possible to restore Poland to favor in London. He argued that Polish resentment toward the Czechs was justified because of the Czech occupation of Teschen in 1919, which he described as "a short-sighted seizure, to use no stronger terms." He claimed that his own earlier evaluation of Poland's attitude toward a war of the Czechs, French, and British against the Germans had been incorrect. A new "appraisal" had convinced him that Poland would never have fought on the German side against the Western Powers. He insisted that Poland would have remained neutral a short time before entering the war on the side of the Allies "under the pressure of Polish public opinion." He claimed that President Roosevelt had taken a mysterious secret step during the Czech crisis, through American Ambassador Biddle, to modify the Polish attitude. This step had been overtaken by events, but Biddle had been favorably impressed with the Polish attitude. Kennard assured Halifax that he did not wish to appear naive by accepting either Polish or American claims, but he was convinced on his own account that there had been no German-Polish agreement on joint policy during the crisis. Kennard presented a series of additional reports to explain why Poland was seeking to exploit Czech weakness to secure a common frontier with Hungary. He declared that it was a principal feature of Polish policy to do this, and he regarded it as his most important task to explain and to justify this new policy to the British Foreign Office.[40]

The mysterious American step referred to by Kennard was little more than the information that President Roosevelt would not like to see Poland on the "wrong side" in a European war. Polish Foreign Minister Beck knew that Ambassador Biddle was friendly toward Poland and he had freely discussed the situation with him during the Czech crisis. Beck told Biddle on September 29, 1938, that Poland was extremely disappointed not to have been invited to the Munich conference.[41]

Kennard's efforts to elevate Poland and to deflate the Czechs in London were reinforced by the change in the Czech Government, which further dampened enthusiasm for Czechoslovakia among the Western Powers. Henderson predicted to Halifax on October 6, 1938, that "Czechoslovakia may be found within the German political and economic orbit much sooner than is generally expected."[42] The idea of sending Western troops into Bohemia to supervise the plebiscite and to secure everything possible for the Czechs began to lose its appeal. Roger Makins, a British Foreign Office expert on the Berlin International Commission to delimit the Czech frontier, announced on October 6th that he had joined with his Italian colleagues in opposing any plebiscite. He argued that the Czechs would gain nothing from a referendum.[43]

The Czechs themselves soon concluded that a popular vote would not advance their cause and that it might reveal some startling weaknesses. The Czech delegate to the International Commission informed the Germans on October 7th that his Government would prefer to forget the plebiscite. The

Germans were entitled to a plebiscite under the Munich terms and they reserved their decision for some time. Henderson confided to Halifax on October 11th that there was a strong swing toward Germany in Bohemia-Moravia, and that the Czechs might lose the Moravian capital of Bruenn (Brno) if a plebiscite was held. This possibility alarmed the Czechs because the loss of Bruenn would virtually cut them off from Slovakia. Kennard explained to Halifax that Poland favored the expulsion of the Czechs from Slovakia.[44]

The suspense was ended on October 13, 1938, when Hitler agreed to stop with the zone occupied by his troops on October 10th, and to abandon the plebiscite with the understanding that he was reserving minor additional German claims. The discussion of the plebiscite began with the suggestion of Halifax that it could be used as an instrument against the Germans. It ended with a sigh of relief in London when the Germans agreed to abandon the idea.

The Hungarians and Czechs began to negotiate on the settlement of Hungarian ethnic claims in Slovakia while the question of the German plebiscite was being regulated. Hungary was the least aggressive of Czecho-Slovakia's three enemies in the recent crisis, and it was no coincidence that she had obtained nothing from the Czechs. Beck feared that Hungary would conduct her negotiations without energy and settle for much less than Poland desired her to obtain.[45] Beck expressed the wish to discuss the matter with a special Hungarian envoy and Budapest responded by sending Count István Csáky, the new Hungarian Foreign Minister, on a special mission to Warsaw. Csáky arrived on October 7th to receive advice from Beck. Moltke informed Ribbentrop on October 8th that Hungarian alarm about Rumania was causing trouble for Beck. The Poles wanted Hungary to demand the entire province of Ruthenia, but Csáky was afraid that Rumania would attack Hungary if this was done. The Polish press had launched a vigorous campaign in favor of the annexation of Ruthenia by Hungary. Moltke noted that the Italian diplomats in Warsaw were jealous of Beck's exclusive policy in sponsoring Hungary, because Italy, although somewhat unrealistically, still considered Hungary an Italian sphere of influence. The Italians claimed that Poland was seeking to erect an independent bloc between the Axis Powers and the Soviet Union, and they were correct in this estimate. It was not clear to Moltke whether or not Beck was urging Hungary to seize Slovakia, but this was unlikely because the Hungarians were timid even about Ruthenia. The emphasis of the Polish press was entirely on an independent Slovakia.[46]

Polish Claims at Oderberg Protected by Hitler

Hitler had difficulty at this time in preventing a major German-Polish crisis because of the brutal treatment of Germans by the Polish occupation authorities in the Teschen district. Most of the German leaders believed that the Poles had claimed too much German ethnic territory in the vicinity of Teschen. Marshal Goering had advised State Secretary Weizsaecker that the territory beyond Teschen, along the southeastern German Silesian frontier, should not go to Poland unless Poland agreed to support the return of Danzig to Germany. He favored acquiring the territory for Germany or retaining it for Czecho-Slovakia, if the Poles refused.[47] The German Foreign Office experts were inclined to agree with Goering and it was decided to make an effort to keep the Poles out of the industrial center of Witkowitz, and out of poverty-stricken little Oderberg near the source of the Oder River. Goering was closely interrogated by Weizsaecker concerning all of his recent conversations with Polish representatives.[48]

Polish Ambassador Lipski was angry when he discovered the attitude of the German Foreign Office in the Oderberg question. He insisted to Ernst Woermann, the head of the Political Division in the German Foreign Office, that both Hitler and Goering had promised this strategic town to Poland. Woermann, who was familiar with Goering's attitude, refused to believe this and he reminded Lipski that Oderberg was preponderantly German. Lipski refused to be impressed. He warned Woermann that an official report on this conversation would complicate German-Polish relations, and he added that he would write Beck a private letter about it. Copies of official reports went to President Mościcki, and through him to other Polish leaders. The implication was clear. Poland was determined to make a stand on the Oderberg issue.[49]

The Lipski-Woermann conversation took place on October 4th. Hitler intervened the following day to demolish the recalcitrant position which had been adopted by Goering and the German Foreign Office. He insisted that he "had no interest in Oderberg whatever," and he added that he "was not going to haggle with the Poles about every single city, but would be generous toward those who were modest in their demands." After this rebuke the German Foreign Office had no choice but to retreat.[50]

This was merely the beginning of the problem, because the Poles began to wage a virtual undeclared war against the German inhabitants of the Teschen region. The resentment of the Germans across the border in the Reich was intense and news of the daily incidents began to appear in the German provincial press. Hitler moved swiftly to impose restraint while there was still time. He took strong measures to suppress publicity of the Teschen incidents, and he declared in a special directive that it was his policy "to release nothing unfavorable to Poland; this also applies to incidents involving the German minority."[51]

The German Foreign Office was alarmed anew when Polish propaganda maps began to appear with claims to Morava-Ostrava, the key North Moravian industrial city and railway center. Weizsaecker told Lipski on October 12th that Germany had given Poland a free hand at Oderberg, but that Morava-Ostrava was different. He added with sarcasm that he would support a Polish bid for a plebiscite at Morava-Ostrava, provided, of course, that the plebiscite was conducted under international control. Weizsaecker and Lipski knew that Poland could never win such a plebiscite, and the Polish Ambassador did not appreciate this unpleasant joke. He replied with dignity that Poland did not intend to take Morava-Ostrava from the Czechs. Weizsaecker did not believe him and rumors about new Polish demands in Moravia continued to circulate. Hitler decided to adopt an attitude of watchful waiting in the Morava-Ostrava question.[52]

The Failure of Czech-Hungarian Negotiations

A number of unfavorable new developments began to cloud the international scene while Hitler was coping with the aftermath of Polish claims in the Teschen area. The bilateral negotiations between Hungary and Czecho-Slovakia were disrupted on October 13, 1938, and it was evident that the two parties could not reach an agreement. This threw the question back to the Four Munich Powers. Hitler had delivered a speech at Saarbruecken on October 9, 1938, where he had gone to dedicate a new theatre. He took strong exception in this speech to the fact that prominent British Tories were heaping abuse on him in public speeches in and out of Parliament without receiving reprimands from the Conservative Party leaders. This seemed to Hitler a poor spirit in which to observe the Anglo-German declaration of friendship which had been signed a few days previously. Hitler's sole intention in making this speech was to remind the British leaders that international friendship had its price, but he was showered with terms of abuse from the British press for an alleged intervention in British domestic affairs. Anglo-German relations at this point had already become catastrophic rather than friendly.[53] The whole world knew that Great Britain was seeking a vast acceleration of her current armament campaign. The German press explained that it did not object to the British armament campaign. This was a British domestic affair. It did not object to the expansion of the British expeditionary force, because Great Britain was the ally of France, and it was her privilege to decide the extent of her obligations to that country. Unfortunately this was not the end of the matter, and the German press explained that "what is inexcusable is the fact that members of Mr. Chamberlain's Government should be making propaganda for rearmament once more on the ground of the German danger." Conditions were not favorable for a friendly meeting of the Munich Powers to settle the delicate problem of Hungarian claims against the Czechs.[54]

Italian Foreign Minister Ciano attempted to overcome the difficulty by ignoring the tension and by blandly proposing that the foreign ministers of the Munich Powers meet in Venice or Brioni without delay to settle the Hungarian-Czecho-Slovak problem. The Hungarians realized that the time was not propitious for this plan; they requested a renewal of bilateral negotiations with the Czechs, and the Czechs accepted.[55] There was no prospect of success, but a breathing spell was gained during which new methods of procedure could be explored.[56]

The Czech leaders presented the chief obstacle to the settlement of a question which did not directly concern the Czech people. It was the ethnic claims of Hungarians and of Slovaks, but not of Czechs, which were at stake. The situation in Slovakia was still confused. The pro-Czech Hlasist movement in Slovakia was virtually eliminated, and every political party had to stand at least for autonomy, if not for eventual independence, because of prevailing public opinion. A local Slovak Government had been formed on October 8, 1938, but it was soon evident that the divided Slovak parties were no match for the Czechs, who sought to circumscribe Slovak autonomy in every possible way. A consolidation movement was launched, and eventually the four principal Slovak parties joined into one Slovak Hlinka-Peoples' Party, the Party of Slovakian National Unity, but this was not achieved until November 11, 1938. The question of the

Slovak-Hungarian frontier had virtually been settled by that time without Slovakian participation. The formal constitutional amendment in Prague, which was known as the Slovak autonomy law, was not in effect until November 22, 1938. Its provisions were highly objectionable to all Slovak leaders, although the preamble contained belated recognition of the Pittsburgh agreement of 1918. Ferdinand Durčanský was the principal Slovak leader who attempted to make autonomy workable, but his complaints received little recognition in Prague. Adalbert Tuka, the veteran Slovak independence leader who had spent many years in Czech jails, warned Durčanský that lasting collaboration between Slovakia and Prague was impossible. Events in Slovakia were moving slowly, but the direction of public opinion was unmistakably toward independence, and the Czechs knew that they would receive the blame for the surrender of Slovak territory. The stubbornness of the Czechs and the indecison of the Hungarians were primarily responsible for the hopeless deadlock in bilateral negotiations.[57]

The Poles were not unhappy about the delay because they hoped that time would permit them to strengthen Hungarian demands. They concentrated primarily on Ruthenia, and on October 15, 1938, Jan Szembek accused Moltke in Warsaw of failing to admit that Germany was behind Ukrainian groups who hoped to use Ruthenia as the nucleus for an independent Ukrainian state. Lipski had returned from Berlin a few days earlier to report, and Beck and Szembek had decided that it was necessary to employ more energy with the Germans in seeking to settle the Ruthenian question.[58]

Moltke was upset by the accusation of Szembek concerning the Ukrainians. He feared that Szembek was right and that Hitler was flirting with the idea of playing the Ukrainian card. He complained to the German Foreign Office that the Poles were extremely sensitive about the Ukrainian question, and added, "I should therefore be grateful if I could be authorized to give Count Szembek a reassuring reply as soon as possible." The effect in Berlin was to convince Hitler that Ruthenia could be useful in obtaining concessions from Poland. He believed that Germany was prepared to offer Poland more than she asked from her, but every additional favor which he could offer Poland would be extra insurance for the success of his plan to reach a lasting agreement.[59]

There was considerable talk in Berlin about Hitler's projected offer to Poland, and President Greiser of the Danzig Senate was bewildered to encounter these rumors when he came to the German capital in mid-October. He feared that Hitler intended to shelve the Danzig question for an indefinite period and this impression had been reinforced by Hitler's *Sportpalast* speech of September 26, 1938. He visited the German Foreign Office to discover what was happening, but he encountered in State Secretary Weizsaecker a sphinx-like and impenetrable attitude. The Suabian diplomat confined himself to the comment that "Danzig's interests . . . should . . . be upheld with calm objectivity." Greiser heartily agreed, but this platitude did not satisfy his curiosity.[60]

When Greiser visited Berlin, the German Foreign Office was concerned with a request from Czech Foreign Minister Chvalkovský for the guarantee of the new Czech frontiers which had been promised at Munich. The German diplomats were astonished that Chvalkovský would request this guarantee before any of the Hungarian claims were settled, or before the Polish claims were settled in their entirety. They concluded that the Czech state was more wobbly, and more desperately in need of help, than they had supposed. Chvalkovský thought the matter over and he told German Minister Hencke in Prague on October 17th that his request for a guarantee had been premature.61

Germany's Intentions Probed by Halifax

British Ambassador Kennard in Warsaw speculated that Rumania would be an effective obstacle in postponing the realization of Polish aspirations in Slovakia and Ruthenia. He urged Halifax to adopt an indulgent view toward these Polish aspirations, and he proclaimed the alleged importance of a special "mission" to promote British influence in Eastern Europe "if European culture in the countries east and southeast of Germany is to be saved from the grip of totalitarianism." Kennard admitted that Poland was also a dictatorship, but he was favorably impressed by the Polish regime. He stressed Polish Catholicism and Polish individualism as virtuous influences which tempered the authoritarianism of the Polish state. He mentioned that Poland had recently accepted a loan from Germany, but he asserted: "It is improbable that Poland will willingly submit to complete German domination."

Kennard was not aware of the full content of the Hela peninsula and London talks on Danzig which had preceded the Munich conference. It still seemed to him "only a question of time before Danzig becomes wholly German." It had not occurred to Kennard any more than to Hitler that Poland might raise insurmountable obstacles to the peaceful acquisition of Danzig by Germany. Kennard predicted that Beck would accept the reunion of Danzig with Germany if Hitler placed the proposition on an attractive *quid pro quo* basis. He had discussed the matter with Beck who denied that "at present" a "deal" was in progress.

Kennard employed a patronizing tone toward Beck in his reports to Halifax. He was aware "of the less statesmanlike aspects of his character, including his personal ambition and vanity." It seemed that "as Polish history shows, there is always grave danger ahead if Polish statesmen cast their country for the role of a Great Power, when she has neither the political unity nor the military or economic strength necessary for such a part." This was a true statement, and it is unfortunate that he did not advise Beck in this sense with greater consistency. In reality, Kennard was thinking merely of Polish conduct during the recent Teschen crisis and of its adverse effect on official British opinion.62

Halifax was impressed by Kennard's comments on Polish aspirations in Slovakia and Ruthenia, and he concluded that the time had come to sound out the German attitude. He confided his assumption to Henderson, on October 15th, that German policy toward Slovakia and Ruthenia was "still in flux," but it seemed that "Germany is bound to have the deciding voice in the future of these territories." He mentioned that reports were reaching London of a deal in which Poland would seize Slovakia and Hungary would reoccupy Ruthenia. He requested Henderson to discover what the Germans knew about Polish aspirations in Slovakia and about the *impasse* in Czech-Magyar negotiations.63

Henderson responded by requesting Weizsaecker to explain Germany's position in relation to these two problems. Weizsaecker replied that current German policy toward Czecho-Slovakia was based on the application of self-determination. The Germans were assuming that future claims in Ruthenia or Slovakia would be made on that basis. Henderson received the impression that Germany was inclined to protect the Czechs against extreme Hungarian or Polish claims. After considering this idea further, he reported to Halifax that "if Germany feels that she can count upon the Czechs to adapt their foreign and economic policy to hers she would prefer to see Slovakia at any rate remain a component part of Czechoslovakia." This tentative formulation of the current German attitude was a remarkably shrewd guess.[64]

Hitler knew that the position of Czecho-Slovakia was extremely precarious after Munich, because Czech prestige had been reduced, and the Slovakian and Ruthenian minorities were extremely antagonistic toward the continuation of Czech rule. The new Czech leaders seemed to be inclined toward an effort to appease these minorities, but it was difficult to predict what the outcome would be because the Czech record in the field of appeasement was poor. The secret directive of Hitler to the German armed forces on October 21, 1938, indicates that he contemplated the possible collapse of the Czech state in the near future. The military leaders were instructed to be prepared to defend Germany from surprise attacks on the frontiers and from the air. The German forces were ordered to be prepared to occupy Memel, and there had been considerable concern, since the Polish-Lithuanian crisis of March 1938, about the fate of this former German city which had been seized by Lithuania. Lastly, the German armed forces were ordered to be prepared to occupy the region of Czecho-Slovakia. Hitler explained in a later directive of December 17, 1938, that a German move in the Czech area would not mean that there would be a major crisis, and he added that such a move would not require the mobilization of the German armed forces.[65]

Henderson had discussed the plan for a Four Power conference on the Czech-Magyar dispute with Weizsaecker. He had not indicated the British attitude, and he had no instuctions from Halifax on this subject. Weizsaecker noted that it would be unwise to call a Four Power conference as long as the Czechs and Magyars were willing to negotiate. The question of a guarantee to the Czech state was not discussed.[66] The Czech leaders claimed to British Minister Newton in Prague, on the following day, that Hitler had told Chvalkovský of German readiness to join the other Powers in guaranteeing the Czech state as soon as the Czech disputes with Poland and Hungary were settled. The Czechs were using every means to arouse British interest in the guarantee question. Events were to show that these efforts were fruitless and that Halifax was not interested in guaranteeing Czecho-Slovakia.[67]

Halifax was not satisfied with Weizsaecker's comment about the Czech-Magyar dispute. He instructed Henderson to discuss the matter again with the German State Secretary. Weizsaecker admitted in a second conversation that a Czech-Magyar settlement was unlikely unless the Four Munich Powers intervened. Henderson and Weizsaecker discussed the situation on the assumption that intervention would take place, and it was clear that Weizsaecker considered this to be the sole solution of bilateral negotiations failed.

It did not occur to Henderson that Halifax would object to the Four Power intervention plan arranged at Munich. He analyzed the problem for Halifax on the assumption that the British would participate in such a conference. He noted that the present Hungarian Prime Minister was "not specially friendly to Germany" and that it would be foolish for Great Britain to take a pro-Czech and anti-Hungarian stand. It seemed to him that the British should incline toward the Hungarians since Prague was moving into the German orbit.[68] Sir Basil Newton in Prague adopted a similar attitude. He observed that the Czech leaders were not disturbed by the fact that new hostility or intrigues within the country against Germany might mean the end of the current unstable regime. On the contrary, they asserted that they would be relieved to have a more definite solution of their problems, which would enable them to know just where they stood.[69]

Beck's Failure to Enlist Rumania Against Czecho-Slovakia

Poland had not attempted to maintain the close contact with Germany which had served her during the Teschen crisis. Beck realized that the policy of Germany might be decisive in the Ruthenian question, but his first reaction had merely been to warn the Germans not to encourage Ukrainian nationalist ambitions. He decided to revert to a more positive approach toward Germany, and he sent corresponding instructions to Lipski. The Polish diplomat called on State Secretary Weizsaecker on October 18, 1938, to discuss the Czech situation. Weizsaecker noted that the principal object of the visit was the announcement that Beck wished to "remain in friendly consultation with us in regard to the Hungarian-Slovak question." Weizsaecker confided to Lipski that Germany was exerting pressure on the Czechs and Hungarians to settle their differences, but that these efforts were producing no results. He attempted to sound out Lipski's attitude toward the possibility of Four Power intervention, and he received the impression that the Poles would like to participate in a settlement of the Slovakian and Ruthenian questions. Weizsaecker reported to Ribbentrop that concessions to Poland in settling these questions might be useful in attaining a comprehensive Polish-German understanding. Lipski had claimed that the Poles were "handling the Czechs with kid gloves" when Weizsaecker inquired about rumors of new Polish demands on the Czechs.[70]

The situation was ripe for comprehensive Polish proposals to the Germans about the settlement of these questions. Beck was reluctant to take this step, and he hoped that it would be possible to secure Polish interests in some other way. Csáky had claimed that the Rumanian attitude was an important factor in inhibiting Hungarian policy toward Ruthenia. Rumania was the ally of Poland and Beck hoped that a personal effort would enable him to influence policy. Beck left Warsaw for Galatz and a conference with King Carol of Rumania on October 18, 1938. He explained to his principal subordinates at the Polish Foreign Office before his departure that he hoped to persuade the Rumanian royal dictator to accept the elimination of Czech rule in Ruthenia.[71] There were fourteen thousand Rumanians in Ruthenia, and Beck hoped to tempt King Carol by offering him a share of the territory.[72] Count Lubienski was sent to Budapest on the same day to discuss this move with the Hungarians. Beck intended to tell King Carol frankly that he was working for the total dissolution of Czecho-Slovakia. He hoped to convince him that Slovak independence was inevitable, and that the disruption of Czech rule in Slovakia would destroy the King's direct line of communication through Czech territory to the Skoda works in any case. Beck hoped to bring about a *rapprochement* between Hungary and Rumania by persuading them to cooperate in a common cause. He told his subordinates that he hoped to acquire a position of strength from which he would request German neutrality toward Hungarian direct action, which would forestall the intervention of the Four Munich Powers. He was willing to tell the Germans that his plan was not prompted by anti-German considerations.[73]

After the departure of Beck the Polish Foreign Office admitted to foreign diplomats that the aim of his mission was to settle the Ruthenian question. It was explained that a common frontier with Hungary had become a "vital" Polish interest. Moltke reported on October 19th that the Poles were publicly referring to Ruthenia as a Ukrainian "Piedmont," which jeopardized Poland's control over the millions of Ukrainians under her rule. Moltke pointed out that emphasis on self-determination during the Czech crisis had stirred passions in Eastern Poland and had led to bloody rioting in Lwów for the first time since 1931. The German diplomat added that the Poles feared the spread of German influence, and that "the quick reversal of Czech policy in the direction of alignment with Germany has caused surprise here and made a strong impression."

Moltke noted that Polish leaders were disappointed in the Slovak failure to declare independence immediately after Munich. He predicted correctly that Beck's mission to Rumania, which had been accompanied with much fanfare, would end in total failure. He knew that Beck intended to offer territory to Rumania, but he did not believe that the Rumanians would join in the partition of an ally from the Little Entente.

The German Ambassador did not enjoy the prospect of Beck's failure with the Rumanians. He believed that the atmosphere would be improved if Beck succeeded in his Ruthenian policy. He warned that much of the Polish press was arguing that Germany would use her influence to oppose the establishment of a common Polish-Hungarian frontier. He concluded that if Polish policy failed "Germany will undoubtedly be held chiefly responsible."[74]

Beck's principal conversations during his Rumanian visit took place on the royal Hohenzollern yacht anchored in the Danube at the point where the Prut River flowed into the Danube from the North out of Poland. He had to face a barrage of criticism from Rumanian Foreign Minister Petrescu-Comnen whenever he thought he was making some progress in his effort to influence King Carol. The Rumanian diplomat displayed versatility in undermining Beck's plan to gain King Carol's support. Petrescu-Comnen solemnly accused Beck of seeking to involve Rumania in a war of aggression against the Czechs. He noted with satisfaction that the attitude of King Carol was serious and severe, and that Beck displayed a nervous tic. He taunted Beck with the claim that the Four Munich Powers, including Germany, had agreed to settle the Ruthenian question on the basis of self-determination. Petrescu-Comnen was especially hostile toward Hungary. He asked Beck with irony if the Hungarians would win the entire Ruthenian area by plebiscite, except for the few districts to be transferred to Poland and Rumania. Petrescu-Comnen reminded King Carol that Rumania had taken the trouble to fortify her existing 400 kilometer frontier with Hungary;

it was not in her interest to see this frontier extended. King Carol was persuaded by his Foreign Minister that Beck's plan to solve the Ruthenian question was reckless and contrary to Rumania's true interest.[75]

Beck challenged his adversary in vain to produce evidence of the prior decision of the Four Munich Powers. He explained that Rumania would be taking nothing from the Czechs, because the territory he was seeking to throw her way would otherwise go to Hungary. He insisted that two previous Czech capitulations proved that Czech resistance to his plan was out of the question. He did not take his ultimate rebuff from King Carol graciously, and he was full of scorn and contempt for Petrescu-Comnen, whom he described as "a perfect imbecile."[76]

Beck was especially irked because the Rumanians, in contrast to Poland, never challenged the arbitrary authority of the principal European Powers. He simply would have spat at the Rumanians and proceeded with his plan had it merely been a question of Polish action. The difficulty was that his plan called for Hungary, and not Poland, to occupy Ruthenia. Beck knew that the Hungarians would never budge without Rumanian consent, unless they had the support of one or more of the principal Powers.

Beck was convinced that the opposition of Rumania to his Ruthenian plan would carry with it the opposition of France. He concluded with reluctance that his sole chance of success was to appeal once again to Germany. The Czechs had the same idea, and they appealed to Germany for support against further Polish demands while Beck was in Rumania. Hitler replied through the German legation in Prague that it was not possible to comply with Czech requests to restrain Poland. The German diplomats in Prague were also told to avoid discussions about Poland with the Czechs.[77]

Beck's Request for German Support to Hungary

Moltke reported to Ribbentrop on October 22, 1938, that Beck was greatly disturbed after his trip to Rumania. It was bad enough that Rumania had refused to cooperate, and it was worse when she declared her intention to oppose Polish plans. Beck was telling anyone who cared to listen that he would use force if necessary to destroy Czech rule in Ruthenia, and to achieve a common frontier with Hungary. Beck also decided to present his demands for Slovakian territory at this time.[78]

The Polish press had been speculating for many days about forthcoming Polish demands in Slovakia, and the Slovakian press commenced to reply to the Poles with increasing hostility while Beck was in Rumania. The Slovaks refused to concede that Polish territorial demands were justifiable, and Slovak nationalists opposed concessions to Poland. Karol Sidor visited Warsaw while Beck was in Rumania. Jan Szembek had assured Sidor on October 19, 1938, that Poland had complete sympathy for Slovakian independence aspirations. Sidor frankly stated that he was seeking an independent Slovakia with such close military, political, and cultural ties with Poland that it would actually be "a sort of political and military Polish protectorate."[79]

Szembek was compelled to reply in the negative when Sidor asked if Poland would send troops to Slovakia and abandon her territorial demands in exchange for a close Polish-Slovakian alignment. Sidor continued his converstions with Szembek the following day, and it seemed at first that the Polish refusal to accept his original proposals had not shaken his confidence in Poland. Nevertheless, within forty-eight hours of his return to Bratislava, Sidor had changed his mind completely, and he announced publicly that his attempt to arrive at an understanding with Poland had failed. This was too much for Beck, who decided to press Polish claims against the Slovaks as soon as possible and to increase them for good measure.[80]

Beck moved rapidly to improve contact with Germany. Lipski called at the German Foreign Office on October 22, 1938, to present to the Germans a detailed list of Slovakian districts which Beck thought should be allocated to Hungary. Lipski added that Beck wished Germany to help Poland to secure the entire province of Ruthenia for Hungary. He requested that Germany keep Poland completely informed of her plans in the Hungarian frontier question. Lipski gave the Germans no indication of the territories Poland intended to take from Slovakia, because Beck did not feel that this matter was of direct concern to Germany.

Lipski confided that the Rumanian Foreign Minister had attempted to play Poland off against Germany during Beck's recent visit. Lipski mentioned the Rumanian assertion that Germany intended to apply self-determination to Hungarian claims, and he proceeded to contradict this without waiting for any comment from the Germans. He asserted that the Polish Government knew that Germany had no intention of partly smothering Hungarian claims under the cloak of self-determination.

The Germans were astonished by the audacity of this contention. Baron Ernst Woermann, the Chief of the Political Division of the German Foreign Office, recorded after the conversation that he contradicted Lipski at once: "I told the Ambassador on this point that we continued to stand for the right of self-determination for the (Carpatho-) Ukraine, whatever this might imply."[81] Lipski countered by feigning astonishment, and he exclaimed that the Ruthenian area was not Czech in population, and not suitable material for an independent state. He insisted that Prague could not maintain authority there, and that Poland feared the spread of Communist agitation in the area. These formidable arguments produced no apparent effect on the German Foreign Office leaders. They reiterated that Germany refused to exclude Ruthenia from the application of self-determination.

The Germans asked Lipski what Karol Sidor had been doing in Warsaw, but the Polish Ambassador replied stiffly that he was unable to give them any information on this point. Lipski hastened to report to Beck after this conversation that his attempt to secure the cooperation of the German Foreign Office in the Ruthenian question had failed. The Germans were evidently committed to a Ruthenian policy which ran counter to Poland's interests.[82]

Beck was not unduly alarmed by Lipski's report. It seemed that an old situation was merely repeating itself. Poland had encountered opposition from the German Foreign Office in the past, and she had responded by bringing the matter in question to the attention of Hitler. Beck instructed Lipski to pursue the issue, and the next step was a conversation between the Polish Ambassador and the German Foreign Minister.

Hitler's Suggestion for a Comprehensive Settlement

Hitler's attention had been called to an interview granted by Beck to the Hearst press on October 10, 1938. The Polish Foreign Minister had denounced rumors that Germany and Poland were negotiating about the return of Danzig to Germany. Beck claimed that the German people of Danzig had sufficient opportunity to express their German individuality under the existing constitution of the Free City. He added that lasting peace in Europe would be possible only when the nations reached a lasting understanding with Germany. This interview encouraged Hitler to raise the Danzig issue. He hoped that an understanding with Germany would be more important to Beck than the retention of the unsatisfactory *status quo* at Danzig.[83]

Hitler decided to act when he heard that Lipski had requested a meeting with Ribbentrop.[84] He instructed Ribbentrop to listen to whatever Lipski had to say before introducing German proposals for a comprehensive agreement, and for the settlement of the Danzig and superhighway questions. He advised Ribbentrop that German support for Polish plans would depend upon the degree of cooperation between the two countries.[85]

Ribbentrop met Lipski for lunch at Berchtesgaden on October 24, 1938. This date marked the beginning of Germany's attempt to acquire Danzig by means of a negotiated settlement between Germany and Poland. Polish failure to accept this idea, and the subsequent Polish challenge to Germany, led ultimately to a German-Polish war. This local war provided the pretext for the British attack on Germany which precipitated World War II.

Lipski had requested the meeting and he took the initiative in its early phase. He repeated his earlier arguments at the German Foreign Office about Ruthenia, and he added that there could be no stabilization in the entire Danubian area unless the Ruthenian question was settled. He emphasized that Yugoslavia, as one of the three Little Entente Powers, would offer no objection to the Polish plan for Hungarian rule in Ruthenia. He admitted that Rumania was opposed and he said that "Beck's trip to Rumania had been a disappointment to Poland." He remarked contemptuously that all Czecho-Slovakia had ever done for Ruthenia was to build "a few airports for Soviet Russian flyers." He denied that Poland's motivation for her Ruthenian policy was the desire to construct a bloc to oppose Germany.[86]

Ribbentrop's attention appeared to be thoroughly absorbed by Lipski's remarks. The German Foreign Minister began to reply by criticizing recent Hungarian policy. He confided to Lipski that Germany had discovered the secret Hungarian commitment to the Little Entente which dated from the Bled, Yugoslavia, conference of August 23, 1938. Hungary had "renounced recourse to force" during the Czech crisis in exchange for the arms equality offered to her by the Little Entente. This seemed to indicate a weak Hungarian policy. Hungary would have been unwilling to join Germany to secure her aims by force in the event of a showdown. Ribbentrop hoped that Lipski would understand the difficulty implicit in the abandonment of self-determination merely to acquire Ruthenia for Hungary. The German Foreign Minister was convinced that the Ruthenians would not vote for union with Hungary in a plebiscite.

Ribbentrop quickly added that he was not adopting a totally negative attitude toward the Polish plan. Lipski had introduced many new ideas which would have to be taken into account in a final evaluation of the situation. It was evident that the problem of Rumania's attitude also required further consideration. It was Ribbentrop's aim to remind the Poles that their plan was not a simple one which Germany could support without running risks. The attitude of Rumania, where Hitler hoped to improve German trade relations and to acquire more supplies of fats, cereals, and petroleum, was no negligible matter for Germany.

Ribbentrop proceeded to change the subject. He had "a large general problem" in mind which he had wished to discuss when he agreed to receive Lipski at Berchtesgaden. He emphasized that he was about to say something strictly confidential, and he intimated that it was to be a secret shared solely among Beck, Lipski, and himself. Lipski, who was a diplomat able to understand half a word, knew that Ribbentrop was suggesting that he alone and not Hitler was responsible for what was to follow. Ribbentrop made his point well, and Beck believed for several years after this conversation that the real initiative in the Danzig question stemmed from Ribbentrop and the German Foreign Office rather than from Hitler. The obvious motive for this maneuver was caution. Hitler, before discovering the Polish attitude, did not wish the Polish leaders to believe that he had adopted a rigid or unalterable position in a question where it might be difficult to attain an agreement.[87]

Ribbentrop requested Lipski to convey a cordial invitation to Beck to visit Germany again in November 1938. Lipski promised to do this, and the German Foreign Minister proceeded to outline Hitler's plan. Germany would request Poland to permit her to annex Danzig. She would ask permission to construct a superhighway and a railroad to East Prussia. Lipski was assured that these carefully circumscribed suggestions represented the total of German requests from Poland.

It was clear that there had to be a *quid pro quo* basis for negotiation and Germany was prepared to offer many concessions. Poland would be granted a permanent free port in Danzig and the right to build her own highway and railroad to the port. The entire Danzig area would be a permanent free market for Polish goods on which no German customs duties would be levied. Germany would take the unprecedented step of recognizing and guaranteeing the existing German-Polish frontier, including the 1922 boundary in Upper Silesia. Ribbentrop compared the German sacrifice in making this offer with concessions recently made to Italy in the Tirol question. He added that Germany hoped to make a similar agreement with France about the Franco-German frontier, since the Locarno treaties were no longer in effect.

Germany had many other ideas for further proposals which would be of advantage to Poland. Ribbentrop proposed a new formal treaty to include these provisions for a general settlement. It need not be an alliance pact, and a new non-aggression pact which might be extended to twenty-five years would suffice. He hoped that the new pact would contain a consultation clause to increase cooperation, and he thought it would be helpful if Poland would join the anti-Comintern front.

Hitler's offer contained generous terms for Poland. It included an enormous German renunciation in favor of Poland in the question of the frontiers. Besides,

Hitler's offer to guarantee Poland's frontiers carried with it a degree of security which could not have been matched by any of the other non-Communist Powers. This more than compensated for the return to Germany of Danzig, which had been under a National Socialist regime for several years. Polish prestige in agreeing to the change at Danzig would be protected by this fact. It would be easy for Polish propagandists to point out that Poland was securing great advantages in such a policy.

An Ambassador would normally have confined his response to a discussion of the individual points in such an offer with the aim of obtaining complete clarity prior to receiving new instructions. This was not Lipski's method. He replied at once that he "did not consider an *Anschluss* (Germany-Danzig) possible, however, if only—and principally—for reasons of domestic policy." He developed this theme with great intensity, and he insisted that Beck could never prevail upon the Polish people to accept the German annexation of Danzig. He added that in Poland the Free City of Danzig, unlike the Saar, was not regarded as a product of the Versailles Treaty, but of an older historical tradition.

Lipski was insincere in his presentation of these carefully prepared arguments. He knew perfectly well that the chief obstacle to the German annexation of Danzig was the determination of Beck that Germany should never recover this city. The Polish diplomat deliberately created the misleading impression that Beck was unable to decide about Danzig because of public opinion. It was astonishing that Lipski displayed no enthusiasm about German recognition of the Polish frontiers. He would have been enthusiastic had he been more optimistic about lasting good relations with Germany, but unfortunately this was not the attitude of the Polish Foreign Office under Beck's leadership.

Ribbentrop tried to conceal his impatience, but he was obviously irritated by the strange attitude of Lipski. He warned Lipski that recognition of the Polish Corridor was no easy matter for Hitler. Lipski's response was to change the subject and to return to the Czech question. He requested the abandonment of the Munich conference procedure in dealing with the Czech-Hungarian frontier. He suggested a new plan in which Poland, Germany , and Italy would settle the question. Lipski knew perfectly well that the Italians were supporting extreme Hungarian claims in the interest of maintaining their influence in Hungary, and he anticipated that Italy and Poland could outvote Germany, if necessary, at a conference. Ribbentrop replied that something might be done if Germany and Poland could reach an agreement about their own problems. Lipski merely promised to transmit the German proposals to Warsaw. Ribbentrop did not refer to new Polish demands on Lithuania, which had been made on October 20, 1938. Poland had insisted on the suppression of anti-Polish pressure groups in Lithuania and on the granting of new privileges to the Polish minority.[88]

Beck's Delay of the Polish Response

Reports about this confidential discussion spread rapidly through Europe. Kennard informed Halifax on October 25, 1938, "on fairly good authority," that Germany and Poland were negotiating on provisions for a general agreement in addition to a common Hungarian-Polish frontier. Kennard recapitulated the points raised by Ribbentrop the previous day with complete accuracy. He added that he had received this information from a number of different sources in Warsaw.[89]

Moltke was pessimistic about the chances for an understanding with Poland. He continued to worry about the activities of Ukrainian propagandists in Germany. He noted that the Poles mistrusted Germany and that "we frequently give grounds for this mistrust." He also had changed his earlier attitude about the advisability of suppressing news about the German minority in Poland in the German press. He contended that this made the Poles uneasy and that "a calm, factual presentation of these matters would not be seriously disturbing to the Poles at all."

Moltke also claimed that Germany had soft-pedalled the anti-Soviet line since the Munich conference, and that the Poles were worried about a possible German-Soviet deal. Of course, a German pro-Soviet policy would be incompatible with a Ukrainian *irredentist* policy, but Moltke was claiming that individual Poles were worried about both prospects. It was clear that he was himself worried about the unfavorable prospects for a German-Polish understanding, and he was not confident that generous concessions from Germany could overcome the obstacles.[90]

Beck was shrewd enough to realize, after October 24, 1938, that he would not receive German support in the Ruthenian question unless he adopted a positive attitude toward German proposals for an understanding. He knew that Great Britain wished to support Poland against Germany, but realized that the British leaders were playing for time. He was inclined to stake the future of Poland on a successful British preventive war against Germany rather than to reach an understanding with the Germans. His belief that Great Britain would oppose Germany discouraged serious consideration of the German offer. His realization that the British needed time to prepare their war prompted him to adopt elaborate delaying tactics in dealing with the Germans.

His first step was merely to delay a Polish response to the German proposals, and his second step was to withdraw from the policy of seeking German cooperation in Ruthenia. He adopted the attitude, in his conversations with Moltke, that the Ruthenian question after all was not so important to Poland. He observed that it had been foolish to give the territory to the Czechs in 1918, and he added that it would be better for Hungary to have it rather than see it "hanging completely in the air." Moltke was told that the Rumanians were idiotic not to support Hungarian claims in Ruthenia, since this might appease Hungary and deflect Magyar ambitions from Transylvania. He insisted that the Ruthenians were poor material for a Ukrainian *irredentist* movement because they "did not have the slightest sympathy for the Galician Ukrainians." Moltke confined himself to the observation that the acquisition of poverty-stricken Ruthenia would scarcely appease the Hungarian appetite for the rich lands of Transylvania, which had been ceded to Rumania in 1919.[91]

Beck lost no time informing Lipski in strict confidence what he really thought about Ribbentrop's proposals. He declared that the time would never come when Poland would accept the restoration of Danzig to Germany. He reminded Lipski on October 25, 1938, that Pilsudski had called Danzig the barometer of Polish-German relations, and this meant that Poland should seek to

retain the upper hand at Danzig. He confided that a German attempt to incor-
porate Danzing would produce a Polish attack on Germany. Beck did not say this
to the Germans until March 1939, when he knew that the British were prepared
to oppose Germany and to form an alliance with Poland. Nevertheless, he was
counting on the Birtish in October 1938 rather than merely contemplating an
isolated Polish war against Germany, and he shaped his tactics accordingly. Beck
might have adopted an entirely different attitude had the British not revealed
in September 1938 that it was their intention to oppose Germany when they
were ready.[92]

Beck Tempted by British Support Against Germany

The British attempt to foment a German-Polish conflict, which dated from the
Duff Cooper-Beck converstions of August 1938, was the worst possible influence
on the formation of Polish policy. The glamor of a prospective Anglo-Polish
alliance blinded the Polish leaders to the practical advantages of an understanding with the Germans. A British alliance would render inevitable the
hostility of both Germany and the Soviet Union toward Poland, without giving
Poland the slightest military advantage. An alliance with the British would be
equivalent to a death warrant for the new Polish state.

Polish diplomacy was floundering badly after the Teschen crisis. The
alienation of Slovakia was a colossal blunder, and the attempt to win Rumanian
support in the Ruthenian question was a farce. Poland had no chance of establishing cordial relations with the Soviet Union. Her sole hope of attaining
national security lay in an understanding with Germany, and Poland was lost
unless she awakened to the need for such an understanding.

The one positive element in the situation was the patient attitude of Hitler
toward the Poles. He was not inclined to apply pressure on Poland, and later
events suggest that he might have waited indefinitely for a favorable Polish
response to his offer had Beck not become impatient and forced Hitler's hand
just as Schuschnigg and Beneš had done. It is ironical that Hitler had been
denounced for impatience in the context of his territorial revision policy, where
in every instance it was the impatience of his adversaries which forced the issue.

An understanding with Germany would have given Poland a strong position
from which to face future problems with equanimity. The terms offered by
Ribbentrop were ideal for the realization of a lasting understanding. The
solution envisaged at Danzig would have clarified that perennial problem on
terms eminently satisfactory to both Germany and Poland. German willingness
to accept the 1919 Polish frontiers twenty years after the Versailles Treaty was
most conciliatory diplomacy. The 1919 settlement with Poland was far more
unjust to Germany than the 1871 settlement with Germany was to France.
Nevertheless, the voluntary recognition by the French leaders of the Franco-
German frontier would have been unthinkable in 1890. The mirage of effective
British support for the realization of their grandiose dreams blinded the Polish
leaders and prevented them from recognizing this simple fact. The Great Poland
of 1750 was a dangerous legacy which clouded their judgment. The British plot
to destroy Germany was the fatal item which undermined their judgment entirely.

Chapter 7

GERMAN-POLISH FRICTION IN 1938

The Obstacles to a German-Polish Understanding

It was a tragedy for Eurpoe that the Munich conference was limited to the Sudeten question and failed to include a settlement of German-Polish differences, although Mussolini was probably right in favoring a successful limited conference prior to any general conclave. It might have helped had Great Britain received a prize such as Helgoland at Munich. The acquisition of Cyprus at Berlin in 1878 had made palatable the statement of Disraeli that he returned bringing "peace with honour." The British were not accustomed to attend conferences involving transfers of territory without acquiring new territory themselves.[1]

There were four major obstacles to a German-Polish understanding after the Munich conference. The most important of these was the notion of Polish leaders that the defeat of Germany in a new war would serve the interests of Poland. The prevalence of this attitude after the death of Pilsudski was implicit in the Polish attempt to foment a war against Germany during the Rhineland crisis of March 1936. There were two primary reasons for this Polish attitude. There was the idea that Poland could not really attain the status of a European Great Power if she was overshadowed by any of her immediate neighbors. There was the dissatisfaction with the territorial provisions of the Versailles Treaty, and the hope of Polish leaders that future territorial expansion at German expense would be possible.[2] Neither of these reasons would have carried much weight after Munich had the British not reverted to a hostile policy toward Germany.[3]

The second hindrance was the failure of Polish leaders to recognize the danger to Poland from the Soviet Union. Soviet Foreign Commissar Maxim Litvinov and the American diplomat, William Bullitt, once travelled together on the train to Moscow, when Bullitt was Ambassador to the Soviet Union. They arrived at the town of Bialystok in Central Poland, and Litvinov commented that this was his native city. Bullitt observed that he had not realized the Soviet diplomat was of

Polish birth. Litvinov replied that he was not of Polish birth and that the city of Bialystok would not remain Polish. This incident occurred shortly after the admission of the Soviet Union to the League of Nations and at a time when Litvinov was the acknowledged leader of the League attempts to outlaw aggression.[4]

Bullitt repeated the incident to Polish Foreign Minister Beck. The Polish Foreign Minister had no illusions about the Soviet attitude toward the new Polish state, but he underestimated the industrial strength and military striking power of Russia. Georges Bonnet later said that he did not require a battle of Stalingrad to be convinced of Soviet strength, and this was doubtless true. The majority of European diplomats were prejudiced against Communism to the point of blindness, and they simply could not admit that the Communist system was capable of producing the most formidable military striking power in Europe until they were shown by irrevocable events. Anthony Eden declared after his visit to Moscow in March 1935 that the Soviet Union would be incapable of aggression for the next fifty years.[5]

The Polish Foreign Office on March 9, 1938, circulated a complacent survey of the Soviet scene among its missions abroad. The current Terror in Russia was seen to be the dominant factor on the Russian internal front, and the 1936 democratic Soviet constitution was correctly described as a fraud. The balance of the report was preoccupied with the alleged decline of Soviet power, and with the current Popular Front tactics of Communist parties abroad, which were described as a protective front to veil the weakness of the Soviet Union. There was no suggestion that the Soviet Union might emerge more ruthlessly and efficiently united than ever before when the current purges were completed. A realistic Polish appraisal of the Soviet danger might have been an effective force in promoting German-Polish cooperation. The contemptuous dismissal of Russian power prevented the Poles from perceiving their common interests with Germany. It also caused them to suspect some sinister motive in the repeated German attempts to form a common front with Poland against Bolshevism.[6]

The third problem resulted from feelings of German insecurity about two of the German communities in the East which were neither under German nor Polish rule. These communities were Danzig and Memel, with a total German population of more than 500,000. Many German communities in the East had been uprooted since 1918, and the thought was unbearable to many Germans that this might also happen to Danzig and Memel, after Germany was strong again. There could be no lasting confidence in German-Polish cooperation until these communities were restored to Germany.[7]

German concern about Memel was apparent during the March 1938 Polish-Lithuanian crisis. This occurred at the time of the *Anschluss* between Germany and Austria, when Beck was visiting in Italy. The Italian Foreign Minister, Count Galeazzo Ciano, who rarely seemed to have a good word about anyone, referred to Beck as not "particularly strong nor singularly intelligent." He noted with evident satisfaction in his diary that Mussolini was not the least impressed with him.[8] Beck, on the other hand, was an interested spectator of the humiliation of the Italian leaders when Hitler occupied Austria. After all, both Austria and Hungary had been within the Italian sphere of influence for many years, and this had been evident to the entire world following the Rome agreements with the two states in 1934. Mussolini made a tremendous effort to explain the situation in his speech to the Italian Parliament on March 16, 1938, but the loss of Italian prestige implicit in the *Anschluss* simply could not be denied.[9]

A Polish frontier guard was killed on Lithuanian territory on March 11, 1938. Polish Senator Kazimierz Fudakowski insisted, in a Senate interpellation on March 14th, that Lithuania should be forced to submit to extensive Polish demands.[10] It was evident that the Polish leaders were in a mood to score some success at Lithuanian expense, to parallel Hitler's triumph in Austria. Beck returned to Poland on March 16, 1938, by way of Vienna, where he received a brief glimpse of the excitement in the former Austrian capital.[11]

Beck discovered that many Polish leaders advocated demands on Lithuania which he considered to be exorbitant under the circumstances. He believed that Lithuania would gradually come within the Polish orbit if too much was not attempted all at once. There were demonstrations in Warsaw and Wilna favoring the acquisition of Memel by Poland, and the creation of a new Polish port on the Baltic Sea. The response in Germany was to order the immediate military occupation of Memel if Polish troops invaded Lithuania.[12] Ribbentrop requested information from Lipski about Polish intentions in Lithuania, but he received no satisfaction from the Polish Ambassador until March 18th. In the meantime there were several days of uncertainty.[13] Poland presented a forty-eight hour ultimatum to Lithuania on March 17th which demanded Lithuanian recognition of the *status quo*, including Polish possession of the ancient Lithuanian capital of Wilna. Beck also demanded the exchange of diplomatic representatives between the two countries, and the opening of the dead Lithuanian-Polish frontier to normal trade. The Lithuanian Government on March 19, 1938, decided to submit at the last minute. An attempt to solicit the support of the Soviet Union against Poland had failed, because the Russians had no intention of taking the initiative to promote a conflict at that time. The old Lithuanian policy of hostility toward Poland was abandoned under pressure, and relations between the two countries improved rapidly during the months which followed. Hitler did not object to the gradual transformation of Lithuania into a Polish sphere of influence, but he was convinced that German interests would remain insecure until Memel returned to the Reich.[14]

The fourth obstacle to a German-Polish understanding was the ruthless Polish treatment of minorities. This concerned primarily the Polish mistreatment of the Germans, but the Polish attempt to strand more than 50,000 of their Jewish nationals in the Reich, in 1938, also had a bad effect on German-Polish relations. The Polish policy in this maneuver to rid Poland of a large number of Polish Jews was both cruel and audacious. The step itself is not comprehensible unless one takes account of the rising tide of anti-Jewish feeling in Poland early in 1938.

The Polish Passport Crisis

Considerable attention was given to the problem of encouraging Jewish emigration from Germany in the years from 1933 to 1938, but far more Jews departed from Poland than from Germany during these years. An average

100,000 Jews were emigrating from Poland each year compared to 25-28,000 Jews leaving Germany annually. From September 1933 to November 1938 a special economic agreement (Havarah agreement) enabled German Jews to transfer their assets to Palestine, and the German authorities were far more liberal in this respect than Poland. There were also special arrangements for wealthy Jews in Germany to contribute to the emigration of others by capital transfers to various places. 170,000 Jews had left Germany by November 9, 1938, compared to approximately 575,000 who had departed from Poland during the same years. It was noted that thousands of Jews who left Germany in 1933 returned to the country after 1934, and that scarcely any of the Polish Jews returned to Poland during the same period.[15]

Polish Ambassador Jerzy Potocki made it clear to American Under-Secretary of State Sumner Welles in March 1938 that Poland wished to increase the emigration of Polish Jews, and Welles agreed to aid the settlement of Polish Jews in Latin America, and especially in the rich country of Venezuela. A special Polish mission under Major Michal Lepecki was sent to Madagascar in 1937 to study the possibilities for Jewish settlement in that rich, but sparsely populated, French possession. It was clear that the Poles were seeking to encourage the emigration of the greatest possible number of Jews at the least possible cost.[16]

American Ambassador Biddle reported from Warsaw on March 28, 1938, that many Polish Jews would welcome a new European war. The destruction of the new Polish state might improve the status of the Jews, and many of them believed that the Soviet Union was a veritable paradise compared to Poland. Biddle added that conditions for the Jews in Poland were becoming constantly more unfavorable, and, of course, this trend increased Jewish disloyalty toward Poland. Biddle declared that both Jewish and Polish leaders favored maximum Jewish emigration, although they did so for different reasons. The Jews had been accused of creating a financial panic during the March 1938 Polish-Lithuanian crisis, when there was a noticeable run on the savings banks. Distrust and dislike of the Jews in Poland extended right to the top. Prime Minister Stawoj-Sktadkowski claimed, in a conversation with League High Commissioner Burckhardt at Warsaw in 1937, that 60% of all Polish Jews were Communists and that 90% of the Polish Communists were Jews.

Biddle announced on March 29, 1938, that the Polish Sejm was passing a large number of new anti-Jewish laws. He explained that 53% of Polish lawyers were Jews, whereas the Jews accounted for merely 8% of the total Polish population. The aim of the new legislation would be to limit Jewish lawyers to a quota based on their proportion of the population. This type of law was sponsored by the Government, but there was always the danger that the situation would get out of hand. A bill passed the Sejm in March 1938 which made the eating of kosher meat illegal, although 2.5 million Jews in Poland ate only kosher meat. The Government naturally feared the effect on the Polish meat industry of such a forced conversion to vegetarianism, and steps were taken to prevent the implementation of this law. The extremity of the legislative measure provided a good indication of Polish hatred of the Jews.[17]

A law also passed the Sejm in March 1938, which permitted the Polish Government arbitrarily to withdraw Polish citizenship from nationals abroad.

The specific provisions stipulated that individuals could be declared stateless if they had been out of the country for five years. The implementation of the law was postponed until the Czech crisis had run its course. The law had been passed as part of the 1938 Polish anti-Jewish program, and its obvious purpose was to prevent the return to Poland of as many Jews as possible. Many of the Polish-Jewish citizens abroad were in Germany. Friction between Germany and Poland was inevitable when the Poles published an ordinance on October 15, 1938, to implement the March 1938 citizenship law.[18]

The Poles were well aware of the German attitude toward the Jewish question. Years had passed since Hitler had introduced his anti-Jewish policy in Germany, and his program had received legal sanction in the Nuremberg Reichstag laws of 1935. Hitler believed that the policy of granting full legal and political equality to the Jews, which had been adopted in Germany and Great Britain during the previous century, had been a great mistake for Germany. He believed that inter-marriage between Germans and Jews harmed the German people and should be discontinued. He shared the conviction of Roman Dmowski in Poland that the Jews were harmful in the economic and cultural spheres. He also believed that the Jewish influence on German politics had weakened Germany. Hitler worked for the day when there would be no more Jewish subjects in Germany, just as Abraham Lincoln in his last years had worked for an exodus of Negroes from America. Hitler's view on the Jewish question was intolerant, and this was perfectly clear to the Polish leaders when they implemented the law of March 1938.[19]

The Russian Government in 1885 had created difficulties for the Polish and Russian Jews who had sought to return to Poland from Germany. Chancellor Bismarck, at a time when Germany pursued no anti-Jewish policy, insisted that Polish and Russian Jews be deported in increasing numbers until the Russians abolished their restrictions. He argued that, unless he responded in this way, Germany would be tacitly recognizing the right of one nation to dump large numbers of unwanted citizens permanently in a neighboring country.[20]

Poland had learned nothing from this example, and she attempted to rid herself of part of her Jewish minority at German expense.[21] The Poles suspected that Hitler might not like this, but they were prepared to use methods to counter German retaliation which the Russian Empire had not dared to adopt. They decided to stop Polish-Jews, whom Germany might seek to deport, at the border, with the help of the bayonet. In this tactic they completely surprised the Germans, who never suspected that Poland would go this far.[22]

The German Foreign Office made several efforts to persuade the Poles to cancel their decree, but these efforts met with no success. Moltke made a last attempt on October 26, 1938. Time was growing short, because the Polish passports of the Jews would automatically become invalid after October 29, 1938, two weeks after publication of the decree. The Polish Consuls in Germany had been empowered to issue special stamps which would free the passports of certain individuals from the decree, but it was evident that these stamps were not granted to Polish citizens of Jewish extraction. It was apparent to Moltke that his last protest produced no effect on Jan Szembek at the Polish Foreign Office. He proceeded to give Szembek fair warning by confiding that the Germans would expel the Polish-Jews unless they received satisfaction from

Poland. This produced a reaction, and Szembek expressed his astonishment at the allegedly severe reprisal planned by Germany.[23] Moltke explained that the question could easily be settled if the Polish Government agreed that the decree would not apply to Reich territory, or if it promised that Polish citizens in Germany would be allowed to return to Poland without the special stamp.[24]

Beck's reply on October 27th to Moltke's *démarche* contained an interesting set of arguments in support of the Polish stand. He argued that Polish resident aliens of Jewish extraction in Germany had suffered from anti-Jewish legislation, despite the fact that they were not German citizens. He contended that this justified Poland in divesting herself of responsibility for this group. He admitted that Poland herself employed anti-Jewish measures, and that she did not desire the return of Polish-Jews abroad. He claimed that this was justifiable because German currency controls would prevent Polish Jews from bringing most of their wealth to Poland. This would mean that they would constitute a drain on the resources of the Polish state.[25]

Beck's language was unmistakably clear and it was apparent to the Germans that there was no point in pursuing the negotiation. The German authorities took great pains to act without guilt or blame. They organized the transport of Polish Jews with great care, and they made certain that the travellers had good facilities, including plenty of space and ample good food. The story told years later by the American journalist, William Shirer, about "Jews deported to Poland in boxcars" under brutal conditions, was clearly fictitious. The first trains passed the border to Polish stations before the Poles were prepared to stop them. After that, the unbelievable happened. Although the last day for issuance of the stamps was not until October 29th, and the new exclusion policy was not scheduled to take effect until October 30th, and Polish border police attempted to prevent the Jews from entering Poland. The Germans had made no preparation for this development, and soon thousands of Polish Jews were pouring into a few small border towns in Upper Silesia and elsewhere. W.K. Best, the German police official in charge of the operation, declared that "through the massing of thousands of Polish Jews in a few border towns on the Germman-Polish frontier, some very disagreeable conditions resulted." The German police decided to bring as many Jews as possible into Poland at night by means of the "green border," which meant by obscure paths in heavily wooded areas or across unguarded meadows. This was dangerous work. There was considerable small-arms fire from the Polish side, but no actual engagements occurred between the Germans and the Poles along the border.[26]

The Poles retaliated immediately by driving across the border into Germany small numbers of Jews from Western Poland, who had retained German citizenship since World War I. The Polish Government issued a decree on the afternoon of October 29, 1938, for the expulsion of enough ethnic Germans from Posen and West Prussia to make up for the discrepancy in numbers between the two Jewish groups. This Polish act of defiance brought the German action to a halt. It was feared that the Poles, with deliberate exaggeration, would organize vast transports of Germans, and exploit the occasion to empty the former Prussian provinces of their remaining German population. Furthermore, Hitler did not like the bitter nature of the affair, and he feared that German-Polish relations might be wrecked if the incident was not checked. Most of the Jews who had been successfully deported were sent across on the night of October 28/29. The Polish Jews who arrived at the border on the afternoon of October 29th were returned to their homes in Germany.[27]

The German authorities had not rushed the Polish-Jews out of their homes under the impression that they would never be permitted to return. They were explicit in promising them that they could return, when their passports were validated in Poland, and when the Poles gave them re-entry permits. Negotiations on this subject were conducted in Warsaw, since Lipski had deliberately left Germany and remained in Poland throughout this crisis. The negotiations were transferred to Berlin in late November 1938. Nothing like a conprehensive settlement was ever attained, but the Poles at last agreed that the Jews actually deported could return to Germany without forfeiting their right to return to Poland. The majority of the Polish-Jews in Germany had not participated in the deportation action, and they did not receive special entry stamps entitling them to return to Poland. They became stateless Jews, and many of them emigrated later from Germany to other countries. Most of the Polish-Jews resident in Germany at the time of the Polish decree preferred for economic reasons to stay there rather than to return to Poland. There is no doubt that more Polish-Jews returned to Poland because of the decree than otherwise would have been the case, but the Polish leaders had the satisfaction of reducing the actual number of Polish-Jews in Poland, at least on paper.[28]

The Polish decree and its repercussions produced an important impact on the current treatment of the Jews in Germany. Large numbers of Jews had been coming to Berlin from other areas after the *Anschluss* between Germany and Austria. The *Anschluss* increased the German-Jewish population by nearly 200,000, or more than the total number of Jews who had departed from Germany. American Ambassador Hugh Wilson reported on June 22, 1938, that an alleged 3,000 new Jews had entered Berlin during the past month, and on the week-end of June 18th there had been demonstations against Jewish stores in Berlin for the first time since 1933. The German Government in October 1938 was preparing a series of measures to restrict the participation of Jews in the legal profession, and it was evident that there might be other measures designed to restrict Jewish activities. There was obviously considerable disagreement among the German leaders about what, if anything, should be done, but the repercussions of the Polish passport crisis played into the hands of the more radical group, headed by German Minister of Propaganda and Enlightenment, Joseph Goebbels.[29]

The parents and sisters of Herschel Grynszpan, a syphilitic degenerate living in Paris, had been on one of the German transports. Grynszpan received a postcard from one of his sisters on November 3, 1938. This postcard described the journey to Poland, but it did not contain any special complaint. The German transports were carefully provided with comfortable facilities and adequate food. Grynszpan had been living with an uncle in Paris since 1936, but there was a French police order demanding his expulsion from France. Grynszpan had been thrown out of his uncle's house on the day before he assaulted the German diplomat, Ernst vom Rath. Grynszpan had decided to murder German Ambassador Welczeck, and he actually spoke to him without recognizing him in front of the German Embassy on the morning of November 7, 1938. Afterward he

entered the German Embassy, and he fired his revolver at vom Rath after he discovered that Welczeck was absent.

Grynszpan was still living in Paris after World War II, and the story of his trial
and imprisonment by the French, and of his imprisonment by the Germans, is
an interesting chapter in legal history. Dorothy Thompson in the United States
sponsored the collection of large sums for the legal defense of the allegedly
heroic young Jew, who actually belonged in an institution before the affair at
the German Embassy. Ironically, Ernst vom Rath had been a resolute opponent
of Hitler's anti-Jewish policy.[30]

The tragedy in Paris was exploited by Goebbels in an obvious effort to
increase the severity of the general German policy toward the unfortunate
German-Jews. At the time of a previous murder of a prominent German abroad
by a Jew, in 1936,[31] Goebbels had warned that the next incident of this type
would lead to severe measures against the Jews. When vom Rath died of his
wounds on November 9, 1938, Goebbels did what he could to carry out this
threat. He gave an anti-Jewish speech at Munich on November 9th which was
seized upon by German S.A. leaders as an excuse to attach Jewish property.
Some of the Jewish synagogues in Germany were destroyed by fires set by
organized groups on November 10, 1938, and much business property was
damaged. There were demonstrations against the Jews, but no pogroms, since no
Jews lost their lives. The mass of the Germans were horrified by the destruction
of Jewish property, which was contrary to their sense of decency and their
feeling for law and order. Goebbels welcomed this as a turning point which
would lead to the elimination of the last vestiges of Jewish influence in
Germany.[32]

American reaction to the events in Germany was more vigorous than elsewhere, and for the first time it appeared that conditons for Jewish life were
becoming worse in Germany than in any other country of Europe. Hull ordered
Ambassador Wilson on November 14th to leave Germany within a few days, and
he forbade him to sail on a German ship. Wilson relayed an assurance from
Goebbels on the following day that there would be no financial penalty or other
measures against foreign Jews in Germany. Wilson reported on November 16th
that the British diplomats in Berlin were rather complacent about he Jewish
question. They noted that German public opinion was not behind the recent
anti-Jewish measures and they wisely concluded that this sort of thing would not
be repeated. This was the last report which Wilson sent to Hull before leaving
the country.[33]

Hitler was persuaded by Goebbels, after the demonstrations, to levy a 1
billion Mark (250 million dollar) fine on the wealthy and moderately wealthy
Jews of Germany. Goebbels had argued that otherwise the Jews would be able
to pocket vast amounts of money from the German insurance companies,
because the assets damaged or destroyed on November 10, 1938, had been
heavily insured. The poorer Jews who had less than 5,000 Marks in immediate
cash assets were exempted. The German insurance companies were ordered to
pay the Jews promptly for all damages suffered to property on November 10th,
and it was permissible to use part of this money in paying the fine. The fine was
to be paid in four installments, on December 15, 1938, February 15, May 15,
and August 15, 1939. The Jews complained that their total capital in Germany

in November 1938 was only 8 billion Marks, and that the fine was tantamount to the confiscation of a large share of their assets. A German law was announced on November 26, 1938, that would eliminate Jewish retail stores, and its provisions were to go into effect on January 1, 1939. At the same time it was promised that welfare care and other state relief measures on behalf of the Jews would be continued.[34]

The Polish passport crisis and its repercussions had little effect on the official relations of Germany with foreign countries other than with the United States and Poland. German-American relations were catastrophically bad in any event because of the hostility of the American leaders toward Germany. The main effect in Poland was to stimulate more severe measures toward the German minority, and to produce an indefinite postponement of Beck's visit to Germany. It was obvious to the Germans, without knowing Beck's attitude on Danzig, that the prompt negotiation of a general settlement with Poland had met with serious delay.

Persecution of the German Minority in Poland

The entire year of 1938 was a bad period for the German minority in Poland because of the intensification of the official Polish anti-German measures. It seemed as if the Poles were suddenly in a great hurry to eliminate the German minority. The Polish leaders rationalized their policy of persecuting Germans with the specious argument that conditions facing the Polish minority in Germany were worse than ever before. Chairman Jan Walewski, of the Foreign Policy Committee of the Sejm, brought the attention of Polish public opinion to this issue in an important speech of April 23, 1938. Walewski charged that the November 1937 minority agreement was observed solely in the German Reich Chancellery and nowhere else in Germany. He claimed that conditions for the Germans in Poland were far better than the situation of the Poles in Germany. This speech had a disastrous effect on the attitude of the Polish masses toward the Germans in Poland, and the theme of the speech was constantly reiterated in the Polish popular press. The speech and the press campaign were inconvenient for Germany at a time when Hitler was seeking to improve conditions for the Sudeten Germans in Czechoslovakia. It was easy for the international press to claim that Germany deserved no sympathy because she mistreated her own minorities.[35]

Polish complaints reached a staccato peak when the results of the May 15, 1938, census were announced, and a mere 15,000 individuals in Germany claimed to be ethnically Polish. This result had been anticipated by the Polish leaders. Lipski had presented a first complaint against the methods of the German census as early as March 31, 1938. It was astonishing to note that the Poles hoped to dictate a return to the census methods of the Prussian monarchy before 1918.[36] 15,927 individuals had voted for union with Poland in the South-East West Prussian and Southern East Prussian plebiscite zone in 1920. This had been at a time when Germany was prostrate and defeated. In May 1938, only 212 individuals in this entire area claimed Polish ethnic origin.[37] This was too much for the Poles, and they invoked the clauses of the 1937 treaty which prohibited assimilation by force. The Union of Poles in Germany began a campaign on orders from Warsaw to demonstrate that the situation of the Polish minority was deteriorating. The Polish organization claimed that the activities of Poles were being restricted in many spheres.[38]

The Germans realized that the grievances of a minority are never entirely imaginary, and they hoped to appease the Poles in the interest of the much larger German minority in Poland. The German Ministry of the Interior promised to deal with Polish complaints after calling a conference of experts. They were under strong pressure from the German Foreign Office to do this, and they were advised that the Polish press was "drawing ugly parallels with the oppression of the Polish minority in Czechoslovakia." It was noted that "the war-mongering Jewish New York *Times*" had taken up the theme.[39]

The German Ministry of the Interior in a report on June 24, 1938, admitted that certain Polish grievances "correspond to some extent with the actual situation." Instances of discrimination against Polish students and of restrictions on the distribution of books by Polish cooperatives had been discovered. German Minister of the Interior Wilhelm Frick received the leaders of the Polish minority, and he promised them that Polish grievances would be remedied. The German Ministry of the Interior also insisted that "the position of the German minority in Poland offered far greater cause for complaint." The need for periodic conferences among representatives from the two nations was stressed, and the German Foreign Office was secretly informed that this was "the only effective means of alleviating the difficult position of the German minority in Poland."[40] The Ministry of Interior realized that unilateral concessions to the Poles in Germany would not solve the problem of the Germans in Poland. Coordination of German and Polish policies was demanded, but it was precisely this coordination that the Germans were never able to attain.

Frick's reception of the Polish minority leaders on June 24, 1938, was publicized in the Polish press. Nevertheless, the official *Gazeta Polska* argued in an editorial devoted to the question that coordination of policies by the two nations was unnecessary. The editors took the position that minority questions should be treated as a purely domestic concern by each Government. This declaration was tantamount to an abrogation of the November 1937 German-Polish minority pact, which stipulated official Polish interest in the Poles of Germany and official German interest in the Germans of Poland.[41]

The difficulty was that the German minority in Poland was more numerous and prominent than the Polish minority in Germany. It was easy for the Polish leaders to conclude that the elimination of the large German minority in Poland would more than compensate for any possible losses to the Poles in Germany were the Germans eventually goaded into retaliation. Indeed, a less tolerant German policy might have encouraged a revival of Polish nationalism among the Poles of Germany. Most of the Polish-speaking people of Germany were proud of German prosperity and efficiency, and they preferred to be considered German. The Polish leaders hoped that they would rediscover their Polish hearts if Germany adopted a less favorable policy or experienced another disaster as bad or worse than 1918. In the meantime they could take care of themselves. It was much as if Germany and Poland were nations at war. The Poles had a vast number of German hostages and the Germans had a considerably smaller number of Poles. The reciprocity which sometimes prompts belligerent nations to treat prisoners humanely, because many of their own People are in the hands of the enemy, was sadly lacking in this instance.[42]

There were signs that the German Foreign Office would not desist forever from according to the Polish mistreatment of the German minority the major emphasis which it deserved. Lipski appeared at the German Foreign Office on June 13, 1938, to protest about obstacles to the completion of a new Polish school for girls at Ratibor in West Upper Silesia. The local German authorities were exasperated about this new school. They claimed that it was being erected on the wrong side of the frontier, because most of the girls studying there would be from Poland. The incident seemed a minor one to State Secretary Weizsaecker, and he admitted to his colleagues that he was sorely tempted to challenge Lipski about current Polish measures against the Germans in Poland, but he had desisted because of the Czech crisis.[43] At last, on June 17, 1938, Foreign Minister Ribbentrop issued an order for German diplomats in Poland to assemble a list of grievances from the German minority in Poland.[44] It was evident that the Poles were going too far and that the German Foreign Office was reluctantly contemplating recourse to diplomatic protests on behalf of the Germans in Poland.

Senator Hasbach, the leader of the Conservative German faction in Poland, was appalled by this situation. He argued that the German Government should confine itself to requests for the coordination of minority policies. He was terrified by the increasing tension between Germans and Poles in Western Poland. There were rumors that the German press was about to retaliate against the anti-German Polish press campaign and Hasbach was convinced that this would be a disaster. He pleaded with German diplomats in Poland that press retaliation would whip the provincial Poles into a frenzy. They had been told by their local newspapers that the Germans never complained about conditions in another country unless they intended to conquer it. Hasbach predicted fearful consequences if the restrictions on the German press were removed.[45]

Moltke did not favor complete press silence about Polish treatment of the German minority, but he did agree with Hasbach that the question should be handled with great caution. Moltke was scornful about the complaints of the Polish minority in Germany, and he noted that they had admitted on June 2, 1938, that they had no complaint about discrimination in the economic sphere. Economic discrimination was the major issue for the Germans in Poland, although they also had to face much more cultural and educational discrimination than the Poles of Germany.[46]

Moltke reported with great indignation on July 7, 1938, that the Poles had discovered that Germany was planning a press campaign to expose Polish mistreatment of the Germans. The German newspapers had discovered that the Foreign Office was collecting material about Polish outrages, and the editors proceeded to do likewise. They had sent instructions to several correspondents by public telephone, and in Poland where the wires were tapped this was equivalent to broadcasting the news. Moltke strongly advised that the Polish Government should be given some assurances about this situation.[47]

The warning from Moltke suggested to the German Foreign Office that Lipski might raise the question in Berlin. A special memorandum was prepared on July

8, 1938, for use in possible conversations. It contained a few of the major grievances about the mistreatment of the Germans in Poland. The Polish 1938 annual land reform law was heavily biased against German interests. Most of the larger agricultural holdings in Posen and West Prussia belonged to Poles, and only these larger holdings were subject to confiscation and redistribution under the law. Nevertheless, the Germans in these two provinces were compelled to supply more than two thirds of the acreage for confiscation in 1938. The new Polish program of establishing a thirty kilometer border zone, in which the Germans could own no land, included all of East Upper Silesia and broad strips of Posen and West Prussia.

The memorandum accused the Polish authorities of tolerating and encouraging a private boycott of all industrial firms which employed Germans. Eighty percent of the German labor force in East Upper Silesia was unemployed, and it was apparent that an increasing number of desperate young Germans were abandoning their homes in that area. The German youth were denied the apprenticeships which would have enabled them to find employment in the many craft professions. The Poles had intensified their program of closing German schools. The memorandum, which sketched the existing situation in general terms, concluded with the suggestion that future concessions to the Poles of Germany should be dependent on the improvement of conditions in Poland.[48]

Moltke was instructed to tell Beck, on the same day, that the complaint of the Polish minority and the extensive treatment of this complaint in the Polish press had done "extremely great damage in many respects." The response of Beck was characteristic. He agreed to inform the Polish Ministry of Interior of Moltke's complaint, but he added pointedly that the question was not within his competence as Foreign Minister. This statement followed the line adopted by the *Gazeta Polska*, and it indicated that the Poles regarded the 1937 minority pact as a dead letter.[49]

It was feared in the German Foreign Office that Hitler would not raise a finger to prevent the doom of the German minority in Poland. In August 1938 the Political Division of the German Foreign Office prepared a memorandum on the question for Werner Lorenz, the chief of the Central Agency for Germans Abroad. This organization had maintained strict neutrality toward the feuds and conflicts of the German political groups in Poland. Hitler did not wish the Agency to pursue an active policy in Poland and he intervened to prevent the memorandum from reaching Lorenz. The text of the memorandum was in conflict with Hitler's policy. It suggested that no considerations of higher policy could justify the abandonment of the German minority in Poland. The situation of the Germans in the former Prussian, Austrian, and Russian sections of Poland was described, and the lack of initiative and unity among the German minority communities was deplored. It was noted that the principal Polish effort was directed against the German community in former Prussian teritory, and that the Poles had exploited the 1934 Pact with Germany to intensify their de-Germanization policies.

The memorandum contained the dangerous suggestion that the German authorities should take the initiative to secure greater unity among the Germans in Poland. This fact alone was sufficient to prompt Hitler to suppress it.[50]

Polish Demonstrations Against Germany

Moltke attempted to explain the increasingly unfavorable situation of the German minority in a report on September 2, 1938. He blamed much of the trouble on the OZON (Camp of National Unity) which had been founded by Colonel Adam Koc. This vast officially-sponsored pressure group was seeking to secure a broad basis of popular support for the policies of the Polish Government. Moltke charged that the Government Departments in Poland were under OZON influence, and that they were seeking to increase their popularity by exploiting and encouraging the rising anti-German sentiment. The Government was trying to be more anti-German than the people, rather than opposing popular superstition and prejudice about the Germans. This policy was incompatible with the spirit of the 1934 Pact.

The German Ambassador admitted that this development was stimulated by German successes. The *Anschluss* had produced a catastrophic effect, and the uneasiness and excitement had increased with the opening of the Sudeten crisis. The Poles knew that the militant Sudeten German minority in Czechoslovakia was the most powerful ally Hitler had in dealing with the Czechs, and they were determined that the Germans in Poland should remain intimidated. Moltke noted that an increasing number of Germans were being sentenced to prison by Polish courts for such alleged remarks as "the Fuehrer would have to straighten things out here," or "it would soon be Poland's turn." There was no way of knowing how many of these unfortunate individuals were entirely innocent of the remarks attributed to them.

The flames were fanned by Poles who returned from Germany with the claim that they had encountered German propaganda directed against Poland. It was said that propagandists were encouraging the Ukrainians to revolt against Poland, and that they were demanding the return of the Corridor to Germany. Moltke was especially annoyed by the apparent indifference of the Polish Government toward the increasing number of anti-German mass demonstrations. He was indignant that groups of Poles had recently appeared before German consulates, without official interference, to sing the provocative *Rota*, a popular anti-German song with many different versions. One central theme in 1938 was that God would reward Poles who hanged Germans. Moltke concluded his report with a list of prominent individuals in Poland who had recently adopted a more hostile attitude toward Germany. He remained completely deceived about Józef Beck, whom he continued to regard as pro-German. It was unfortunate for Hitler that Moltke was unable to penetrate Beck's attitude to some extent. Hitler might have been able to avoid the trap that Halifax was preparing for him had he realized that Beck was one of his enemies.[51]

The Outrages at Teschen

The situation at Teschen in October 1938 offered a vivid illustration of the problem created by Polish persecution of the Germans. Hitler had given Poland full support in her successful effort to acquire this district from the Czechs. The Poles, however, proceeded to treat the German and pro-German elements of the district as archenemies. De-Germanization measures began immediately after the Polish military occupation of the area. Every German school in the district was closed at once. The Germans were told that the schools would be re-opened later, but in the meantime the parents of the school children were threatened with unemployment if they did not send their children to Polish schools. Merely one tenth of the previous number of children reported, when it was announced that the schools would be re-opened, and only a fraction of these were subsequently allowed to attend German schools. The original staffs of German teachers had been dismissed. It was announced that Polsih was the sole official language, and the doctors and lawyers of the area were told that they would not be allowed to practice unless they learned Polish within three months. Bank assets were frozen for a considerable period, and pensions and state salaries to Germans were reduced. The mayors of both Teschen and Oderberg were removed. Mayor Kozdon of Teschen was the leader of the local Slonzak community, which was a small West Slavic group similar to the Kassubians of West Prussia, or the Lusatian Sorbs of Saxony. When Kozdon was disgraced and sent to prison in Poland, the local Slonzak community replied with the scornful slogan that they would rather be inmates of a German concentration camp than so-called citizens of Poland.[52]

The situation was aggravated when the local Slonzak population offered considerable resistance to the Poles. It seemed for a time that the Germans might also resist. The leaders of the German community, Dr. Harbich of Teschen, and Dr. Pfitzner of Oderberg, hastened to Berlin to appeal for German assistance. When the German Foreign Office ignored their pleas they threatened to appeal to France, Great Britain, Italy, and Japan, as signatories of the 1919 minority agreement on Teschen. They were coolly advised by the German diplomats to leave out the Japanese, because it was repugnant to envisage an Asiatic Power intervening in a European question. They were told that "for the German Government the question of Teschen was to be regarded as settled."

Harbich exclaimed in despair that he would return home to lead his community in battle against the Poles. Baron Woermann later recalled: "I tried to explain to them the renunciation of Oderberg in the context of general German policy, but apparently without success." This failure is not surprising when one considers that the homes and livelihood of these men were at stake.[53]

On October 3, 1938, after the occupation of the city of Teschen, the Polish armed forces pushed on to Trynetz, Lazy, and Karwin in the Teschen district ahead of the schedule agreed upon with the Czechs. The Polish excuse for the rapid advance was the hostility of the local population. The *Gazeta Polska* explained that it was necessary to anticipate the formation of "German shock troops" at Oderberg. It was added that the German authorities were not permitting these forces to receive arms from Germany.[54] In reality, the Poles were not fighting German shock troops, which did not exist, but a few desperate Slonzak workers and farmers. Polish placards posted during the day were torn down at night, and a pitched battle took place between the Polish soldiers and the Slonzaks at Trynetz. Governor Grazynski of East Upper Silesia, who was scheduled to administer the new district for Poland, concluded that the Slonzaks needed considerable re-education before they could become useful Polish citizens.[55]

A first major step in the Polonization program was to drive out as many Germans and Czechs as possible, and to bring in Polish specialists and industrial workers from East Upper Silesia. The effect of this policy is well illustrated by the following example. The Oderberg Wire Factory, which annually produced 90,000 tons of iron, steel, and copper wire, had 1,324 employees on October 10, 1938. There were also 126 engineers, merchants, and master craftsmen connected with the firm, and they comprised the group of specialists. The Germans furnished 758 factory workers and 52 specialists, the Czechs 547 factory workers and 73 specialists, the Poles 19 factory workers and 1 specialist. Approximately 20% of the Czechs had close Polish contacts and won acceptance in the Polish ethnic group after the Polish occupation. By May 10, 1939, there were 635 Polish factory workers and 82 specialists, 112 Czech factory workers and 11 specialists, and 324 German factory workers and 17 specialists. The Poles had become the dominant group, after the arbitrary dismissal of large numbers of German and Czech workers, and this pattern was repeated in other crucial industries.[56]

Approximately 20% of the total German population of the district fled within the first month of Polish occuaption, and it was necessary to house 5,000 of the refugees in emergency camps in West Upper Silesia.[57] Thousands of refugees received temporary quarters in private German homes. Governor Grazynski had raised feelings to a white heat among his followers with charges that the Teschen Germans were guilty of an insurrectionary conspiracy. Most of the refugees entered Germany without frontier passes from the Polish authorities, simply glad to be alive. Passes in any event were issued solely on the condition that those receiving them renounce their right to return. On October 15, 1938, the Germans began to present a series of careful formal protests which received no publicity. Conditions in Teschen were never rectified while the region was under Polish control.[58] A protest note containing a detailed list of grievances about Teschen was presented at Warsaw on November 26, 1938. Several weeks later Moltke was told that this protest should not have been made, because most of the Germans in the Teschen area were not German citizens. The Poles had promised to review the entire matter, but this was their sole response. Their stand was remarkably bold when one recalls that the German-Polish minority treaty of November 1937 applied to ethnic Poles in Germany and to ethnic Germans in Poland, and not merely to Polish and German citizens in the opposite countries.[59]

A series of anti-German measures accompanied the national election to the Polish Sejm in November 1938. The German minority leaders urged their people to vote, although candidates of German extraction were no longer allowed to stand for election.[60] Four of the remaining six German secondary schools in Posen province were deprived of their status as public schools at this time, and they forfeited both the special state protection extended to public institutions and their tax privileges. Governor Grazynski of East Upper Silesia considered an election a favorable time to agitate publicly against the Germans. He presided at a meeting which had the temerity to resolve that the Polish minority in West Upper Silesia should place its allegiance in Poland, rather than in Germany. He also intensified his campaign to secure the discharge of the remaining German workers in East Upper Silesian mining and industry.[61]

New Polish measures of school censorship were introduced in West Prussia. The index of forbidden Germanic books was expanded to include such works as the *Nibelungenlied* (the most highly prized early German heroic epic), Goethe's *Poetry and Truth*, Defoe's *Robinson Crusoe*, and Stanley's *Through Darkest Africa*. The leading German charity organization in the city of Grudziadz (Graudenz) was closed and its property was confiscated. The exclusively German private school in little Neustadt was told that it would be forbidden to hold its annual Christmas play in 1938. The anti-German and anti-Jewish pressure group, Association of Young Poland, planned a major boycott against all German firms in Polish West Prussia for January 1939, and at that time it was permitted to picket German firms without interference from Polish authorities. Indeed, the boycott would probably never have been attempted had the Polish authorities given the slightest indication that they would oppose it. The encouragement of anti-German measures was part of the formula with which the Polish leaders were seeking to promote the popularity of their regime.[62] It is incredible under these circumstances to read in a widely-accepted Polish source, outside of the Communist orbit and more than twenty years later, that the persecution of the Germans in Poland was entirely "imaginary."

It was evident that Hitler was willing to close one eye to a great amount of Polish mistreatment of the German minority. It was not clear at the end of 1938 how far the Poles would push this policy in the immediate future, or whether or not Hitler would be willing to tolerate whatever the Poles might decide to do. It would have meant a great deal had the Poles indicated a positive attitude toward a comprehensive settlement along the lines proposed by Germany on October 24, 1938. It is probable that Hitler in such circumstances and for reasons of higher policy would have ignored anything they chose to do to the Germans of Poland short of slaughtering them. The failure of the Poles to indicate a positive attitude contributed to the increasing German-Polish friction toward the end of 1938.

The Problem of German Communication with East Prussia

Ribbentrop, after his conversation with Lipski on October 24th, requested a special report from Fritz Todt, the Inspector for German Highways, about the problem of German transit over the Corridor. Todt discussed the matter with Hitler. Hitler and Todt were close personal friends. The German leader told Todt that a German guarantee of Polish possession of the Corridor was conditional on the acquistion of a German route to East Prussia. Hitler confided that he would like to have both a superhighway and a railway, but that he would be willing to settle for a superhighway. Todt was also inclined to favor the Poles, and he and Hitler found themselves in close agreement on this issue. Todt reported to Ribbentrop that "nothing could more effectively lend force to a guarantee of the Polish Corridor than the elimination, through such a corridor highway, of the economic disadvantage of the Corridor for Germany; namely, the interruption of traffic between East Prussia and the Reich."

Todt believed that there were two feasible possibilities for a transit route through the Corridor. A superhighway might be constructed from Buetow,

Pomerania, to Elbing, East Prussia, via Praust in Danzig territory. This route would run 75 kilometers through Danzig territory and only 40 kilometers through Polish territory. Nevertheless, Todt feared that the Poles might object to this route for strategic reasons. They would consider the road a German military asset, and they might claim that this route was too close to the coast and would place the entire coast under German control. The German Inspector was inclined to believe that the Poles would prefer a route from Schlochau, Pomerania, to Marienwerder, East Prussia, which would extend 85 kilometers through Polish territory. This route would avoid Danzig territory, but it would be close enough to connect Danzig with the highway by means of a feeder road on German territory. Todt believed that any route farther from Danzig would be distinctly disadvantageous for Germany, because Danzig was the largest metropolis within the German-populated region on the eastern side of the Corridor.

It was easy for Todt to supply a number of convincing arguments to justify the road scheme. German land traffic between Pomerania and East Prussia was hampered by current Polish control measures. The high Polish fees for the use of Polish roads involved the loss of much foreign exchange by Germany at a time when the balance of German trade was far from favorable. Todt calculated that the Poles were making 500% profit on road maintenance and on the servicing of rolling stock.

Todt mentioned a comparable road project which had been proposed at Prague. This plan for a superhighway connecting Breslau and Vienna, by way of Bruenn in Moravia, had been worked out in complete detail. He believed that it was easy to illustrate that this plan made full allowance for the protection of Czech interests, and that it contained economic features which would prove attractive to the Czechs. Todt concluded his report by requesting Ribbentrop to consult with him and to inform him at once if an agreement with Poland could be achieved.[63]

Tension at Danzig

On November 9, 1938, the very day that Baron vom Rath in Paris succumbed to the wounds inflicted by Grynszpan, the Germans received some disquieting information from League High Commissioner Burckhardt in Danzig. Burckhardt confided that there had been a "peculiar change" in Poland's attitude toward Danzig. The Poles had earlier indicated their desire to eliminate the League regime in the area, but recently they had switched their policy to support for the League regime. This was disappointing to Burckhardt, who had hoped that Poland and Germany were about to agree on the return of Danzig to Germany. Burckhardt mentioned that foreign diplomats were aware that "there was evidently some disharmony between Germany and Poland."[64]

The November 1938 Ribbentrop-Lipski Conference

Lipski returned to Warsaw shortly after his conversation with Ribbentrop on October 24, 1938, and he participated in a conference at the Polish Foreign Office on November 4, 1938, to discuss the Ruthenian problem. Ribbentrop's recent offer was also freely discussed at the conference. The Poles had not taken seriously the suggestion that Beck and Lipski were to share a secret with Ribbentrop, and the British had been aware of the content of the German offer since October 25th. Lipski predicted that the Germans would never retreat at Danzig, and that they would never drop their plan to recover the city from the League. He spoke of Ribbentrop in unfavorable terms as a "disagreeable partner" in negotiation. He added that Ribbentrop wasted much time in insisting that Danzig was a German city, and he claimed that the German Foreign Minister did not understand Danzig at all. Lipski exclaimed that Danzig had returned to the orbit of its Polish hinterland, and that it was therefore no longer German.[65]

Lipski returned to Berlin with instructions from Beck. The Polish Foreign Minister knew that the British wished to gain more time for their armament campaign before challenging Germany, and he chose to adopt delaying tactics in the interest of synchronizing Polish policy with British policy. Ribbentrop asked Lipski on November 19, 1938, if he had received instructions from Beck in response to the German offer. Lipski replied in the affirmative, and he blandly assured the German Foreign Minister that an agreement might be reached for a German superhighway and railway through the Corridor.

Lipski reminded Ribbentrop that Polish neutrality had been useful to Germany during the Czech crisis. He added the deceptive claim that "during those critical days, the Polish Government had turned a deaf ear to all siren songs emanating from certain quarters."[66] Ribbentrop accepted Lipski's statements at face value, and he expressed the hope that Poland recognized the importance of German friendship during the Teschen crisis.

Lipski proceeded to discuss the Danzig question. His two principal themes were that the maintenance of the Free City was essential to the vital interests of Poland, and that any Polish decision about Danzig would have to take account of the Polish domestic situation and Polish public opinion. He announced that Beck had instructed him to introduce counter-proposals. These included a very general statement about the importance of improving German-Polish relations, and a suggestion that Germany and Poland conclude a special Danzig treaty. The principal purpose of this treaty would be to recognize the permanent independence of the Free City of Danzig. Lipski seemingly favored the termination of League sovereignty despite the report from Burckhardt about the current Polish attitude in favor of the League regime.

Ribbentrop was disappointed. He replied that the proposed treaty indicated an attitude on the part of Beck which he deplored. He did not deny that the acquisition of Danzig by Germany would represent a sacrifice for Poland, but he failed to understand why the Poles did not realize that a guarantee of Polish rule in the Corridor would be a much greater sacrifice for Hitler. He said to Lipski, "the purpose underlying my suggestion was to establish German-Polish relations on a foundation as lasting as solid rock, and to do away with all possible points of friction." He complained that the Poles apparently thought that he was merely interested in engaging in a little diplomatic chat.

These remarks did not discourage Lipski from espousing Beck's proposal. He continued to discuss with intensity the alleged advantages of the Danzig treaty. It was evident that Ribbentrop wished to avoid the danger of disrupting negotiations. He finally replied that "the proposal did not seem very practicable," but that he would discuss it with Hitler.[67]

Ribbentrop passed briefly to a specific German grievance. He noted that the Polish postal authorities had recently issued Polish stamps for use in Danzig which represented Danzig as a Polish city. Lipski admitted at once that he could understand the negative reaction this had produced among the Germans. Ribbentrop reminded Lipski again that his offer was motivated by the desire to promote a German-Polish understanding. Lipski replied that it was clear to him that the German Foreign Minister was seeking to achieve a permanent understanding. This remark pleased Ribbentrop, and he told Lipski that anything as important as a permanent understanding could not be achieved in one day. He added that "if M. Beck would give our proposals his best thought, he might see his way to adopting a positive attitude." Lipski claimed that Beck was seeking to maintain complete secrecy, and he asserted that Beck had told an American correspondent of the Hearst press, in late October 1938, that no negotiations were being conducted between Germany and Poland. This was a lapse on Lipski's part, because the interview to which he referred had taken place on October 10, 1938, two weeks before the German offer.[68]

German Confusion about Polish Intentions

League High Commissioner Burckhardt was visiting Beck in Warsaw at the time of Lipski's conversation with Ribbentrop. He was pleased to discover that Beck seemed to be in a very friendly mood toward Germany. Beck told Burckhardt that he was willing to surrender the Polish right to represent Danzig diplomatically in foreign countries. He believed Danzig should receive permission to maintain her own diplomatic representatives in Germany, Poland, and elsewhere. He deprecated the role of the League at Danzig. Beck observed that Poland's interest in Danzig was mainly economic, and not political. Burckhardt was delighted with this remark, and he interpreted it as a confession that Poland was willing to have Germany acquire Danzig. He advised the Germans on November 21, 1938, that "only a German suggestion was necessary for discussions with Poland."[69]

The effect of this report on the Germans is easy to understand. They did not know where they stood with Poland. The discrepancy between the Burckhardt reports of November 9th and November 21st was obvious. They could not base their policy on the remarks which Beck made to a League representative. Burckhardt did not know that negotiations on Danzig had been in progress between Germany and Poland for four weeks. The adamant position which Lipski had taken on Danzig two days earlier did not permit the German diplomats to share the optimism of Burckhardt.

Hitler was considering every possible means of resolving the dilemma. He wondered if it might not be possible to gamble on Beck's willingness to accept a *fait accompli*. Negotiation of an agreement with Poland would be incomparably easier once Germany was established at Danzig. Hitler issued an order to the German armed forces on November 24, 1938, to prepare for the swift occupation of Danzig independently of an agreement with Poland. He placed special emphasis on the fact that he was not contemplating a war with Poland, but that he wished to be prepared for "a politically favorable situation." Hitler was considering a Danzig *coup* at the moment when relations with Poland were as cordial as possible and when Polish armed reprisals against Germany were least likely.[70] This did not mean that he was willing to take such a gamble on the day that he issued the order. The risk was too great because he knew very little about the real Polish attitude.

It was extremely significant that the German Foreign Office received permission on the same day to convey full information to the Danzig leaders about the current German-Polish negotiation. The Danzig leaders were to be kept abreast of all future developments. Hitler might not have taken this step had he believed that it would be a simple matter to reach a settlement with Poland at Danzig. He wished Forster and Greiser to be fully informed so that he could coordinate steps with them on the shortest possible notice.[71]

It was useful for the Danzig leaders to have accurate information directly from Hitler. Burckhardt had returned to Danzig on November 21, 1938, and his description of the Polish attitude in conversations with the Danzig leaders was entirely too favorable. He suggested that a Ruthenian solution favorable to Poland might be adequate compensation to Beck for the abandonment of Polish obstruction tactics at Danzig. Burckhardt had succeeded in creating the impression among his listeners that Poland was prepared to give way at Danzig. He seemed to think that Poland's improved diplomatic situation would prompt her to be generous. He observed that "Poland was no longer in the very difficult situation of four weeks ago, and that she could now again count much more on the support of England and France, particularly since Germany had injured herself politically, at least for the present, through her action against the Jews." Burckhardt told the Danzigers that he had accepted a hunting invitation from Goering, and that he planned to discuss the European situation with Goebbels before returning to Danzig. He obviously believed that an auspicious moment had arrived to settle the Danzig question.[72]

Burckhardt was disgusted by the attitude of the American Ambassador to Poland, Anthony Biddle, who predicted on December 2, 1938, that the Poles would fight Germany in the near future. Biddle declared that he would welcome this development. He reminded Burckhardt of the great hatred of Germany in the most influential American quarters, and he also predicted that Great Britain and France would intervene in a German-Polish war. Burckhardt summarized his conversation with Biddle in pithy fashion:"Fine perspectives! Calvin against the descendants of Luther, and Lenin as Calvin's ally."

Secret Official Polish Hostility toward Germany

Lipski returned to Poland on November 22, 1938, to discuss the Danzig situation. His assurance to Ribbentrop about the superhighway and the railway had been a mere ruse designed to appease the Germans. The Polish leaders agreed that no concessions would be made to Germany either at Danzig or in the Corridor transit question. The affable manner of Ribbentrop, despite the adamant Polish stand on Danzig, impressed the Polish leaders. Beck speculated that Danzig might not be the issue after all which would produce a conflict between Germany and Poland. He suggested that Hitler might be allowing Ribbentrop unusual liberty in the Danzig question to see what he could accomplish. Lipski's attitude was similar to Beck's. His latest conversation with Ribbentrop had caused him to modify his earlier opinion that Germany would never retreat at Danzig. He suggested that the injury done to German relations with the United States by the anti-Jewish policy might affect German policy toward Poland.

Lipski tended to exaggerate the effects on German foreign relations of the demonstrations against the Jews in Germany on November 10, 1938. He predicted that a Franco-German declaration of friendship, which had been discussed by Hitler and the French leaders since the preceding month, would never be signed because of the negative reaction to the anti-Jewish demonstrations. This prediction proved to be false, and Ribbentrop signed the declaration at Paris on December 6, 1938.[73]

Lipski and the other Polish diplomats were influenced in their judgment of this question at the moment by a report which had been telegraphed by Count Jerzy Potocki from Washington, D.C., on November 21, 1938. The Polish Ambassador was informed by William C. Bullitt, the American Ambassador to France who was visiting in the United States, that President Roosevelt was determined to bring America into the next European war. Bullitt explained to Potocki at great length that he enjoyed the special confidence of President Roosevelt. Bullitt predicted that a long war would soon break out in Europe, and "of Germany and her Chancellor, Adolf Hitler, he spoke with extreme vehemence and with bitter hatred." He suggested that the war might last six years, and he advocated that it should be fought to a point where Germany could never recover.

Potocki did not share the enthusiasm of Bullitt and Roosevelt for war and destruction. He asked how such a war might arise, since it seemed exceedingly unlikely that Germany would attack Great Britain or France. Bullitt suggested that a war might break out between Germany and some other Power, and that the Western Powers would intervene in such a war. Bullitt considered an eventual Soviet-German war inevitable, and he predicted that Germany, after an enervating war in Russia, would capitulate to the Western Powers. He assured Potocki that the United States would participate in this war, if Great Britain and France made the first move. Bullitt inquired about Polish policy, and Potocki replied that Poland would fight rather than permit Germany to tamper with her western frontier. Bullitt, who was strongly pro-Polish, declared it was his conviction that it would be possible to rely on Poland to stand firmly against Germany.[74]

Potocki incorrectly attributed the belligerent American attitude solely to

Jewish influence. He failed to realize that President Roosevelt and his entourage considered World War I to have been a great adventure, and that they were bitter about those Americans who continued to adopt a cynical attitude toward American militarism after President Roosevelt's quarantine speech in 1937. President Roosevelt had been one of the few advocating permanent peacetime military conscription in the United States during the complacent 1920's. Such factors were more than sufficient to prompt Roosevelt to adopt an aggressive attitude toward Germany. He had no strong pro-Jewish feelings; he jokingly said at the 1945 Yalta Conference that he would like to give the Arabian leader, Ibn Saud, five million American Jews. The Jewish issue was mainly a convenient pretext to justify official American hostility toward Germany, and to exploit the typical American sympathy for the under-dog in any situation.

Potocki overestimated the Jewish question because of his own intense prejudices against the Jews, which were shared by the entire Polish leadership. He was highly critical of the American Jews. He believed that Jewish influence on American culture and public opinion, which he regarded as unquestionably preponderant, was producing a rapid decline of intellectual standards in the United States. He reported to Warsaw again and again that American public opinion was merely the product of Jewish machinations.[75]

The Poles themselves had a grievance against Germany because of the recent anti-Jewish demonstrations, but it was not prompted by any sympathy for the Jews. They resented the fact that recent German measures against the Jews placed Germany in a better position to compete with Poland in disposing of her Jews abroad. The majority of the remaining German Jews were at last ready to believe that emigration was better for them than life in Germany, and most of them were in a far better financial position to contemplate emigration than the Polish Jews.

Moltke reported from Warsaw on November 22, 1938, that the Polish press had maintained reserve in describing "the reprisal action carried out in Germany against Jewry." The *Dziennik Narodowy* (*National Daily*) had complained that Germany was right in seeking to get rid of her Jews, but wrong in her methods. Only a few of the leading newspapers had given their unreserved approval to the recent German measures. *Czas* (*The Times*) claimed that the Germans had gone too far in some instances. Moltke noted that the Polish Government feared a Ukrainian insurrection, and that this consideration was prompting them to slow down the campaign against the Jews within Poland. At the same time, they were stepping up their diplomatic offensive to find new goals for the Polish-Jewish exodus, and they were convinced that the recent events in Germany would handicap them in these efforts.[76]

Lipski claimed at the Polish Foreign Office conference on November 22, 1938, that there was a bright side to this picture. He asserted that German public opinion had been alienated by the recent anti-Jewish measures, and that this had shaken the position of the Hitler regime. He suggested that a strong Polish stand on Danzig might threaten Ribbentrop's position and convince Hitler that Ribbentrop was not an able diplomat. Polish High Commissioner Marjan Chodacki, who had come to Warsaw for the conference, was quick to agree with Lipski. He suggested that Poland might influence the situation by adopting a more stern policy in dealing with the Danzig authorities.[77]

Beck did not seem particularly concerned about the deterioration of German-Polish relations after the Munich conference. He told Jan Szembek on December 7, 1938, that relations with Germany had reached an *impasse*. This was a simple statement of the situation which Beck was not inclined to remedy. He still hoped that Germany would support him in Ruthenia, and he did not believe for one moment that Hitler intended to use Ruthenia as a base for Ukrainian *irredentism*. He knew that Hitler was sincerely pro-Polish, and he complained to Szembek that it might have been possible to obtain more concessions from him had it not been for the opposition of the anti-Polish Junker aristocracy, and the members of the German Cabinet who had belonged to the former conservative German National People's Party.

Beck indulged in some wishful thinking when he claimed to Szembek that Hitler and Ribbentrop were not in close agreement, and that it was Neurath, and not Ribbentrop, "who understood and executed perfectly the projects and instructions of Hitler." Neurath was actually one of the anti-Polish diplomats whom Beck had condemned, and he was far less tolerant toward Poland than was Ribbentrop. The similarity between Beck's career and that of the German Foreign Minister stimulated Beck's dislike for his colleague in Berlin. Neither Beck nor Ribbentrop were actually career diplomats. Beck had pursued a military career for many years, and Ribbentrop had earned a fortune as a merchant after serving as a German army officer in World War I. It had been possible for both men to obtain top posts in the diplomatic services of their respective countries for the same reason. Beck had been intimate with Pilsudski for many years, and Ribbentrop had won the confidence of Hitler. The two men had established their supremacy over the career diplomats because they enjoyed the favor of their respective dictators.[78]

The Polish Foreign Minister decided that Lipski, for tactical reasons, should continue to take a positive attitude toward the German superhighway, but that he was not to involve Poland in any definite commitments, nor admit that there was any connection between the problems of Danzig and Corridor transit. Beck would continue to press for a bilateral treaty with the Germans to be based on a German renunciation of Danzig. Beck suspected that Hitler would insist on the annexation of Danzig, but he was not certain about it, and, above all, he did not know how long he could count on Hitler's patience.[79]

Beck had decided to direct his main attention toward Anglo-Polish relations, and his entire policy was based on the assumption that he would obtain British support against Germany. Beck was clever in his relations with the British. He wished to impress them with his independence and to tantalize them by the reserve with which he approached important problems. He permitted Count Raczynski in London to tell Halifax, at the time of the German offer on October 24, 1938, that Poland would stand firmly against any German demands, but he denied Raczynski permission to come to Warsaw to discuss the situation. It was nearly two months before the Polish Ambassador was allowed to appear in Warsaw to discuss Beck's plan for an understanding with the British. Beck agreed in December 1938 to come to London within a few months to discuss the coordination of Polish and British policies, but he balanced his agreement by arranging on his own initiative for a meeting with Hitler in January 1939. He wished the British to know that he could make a deal with the Germans if he desired it, and he assumed correctly that this would increase Polish prestige in London. He did not wish the British to regard Poland as a mere puppet state in the style of Austria or Czechoslovakia. Beck had learned a great deal since his hurried visit to England in March 1936, and his vain plea for British military intervention against Germany.[80]

A German-Polish Understanding Feared by Halifax

The British diplomat, Ogilvie-Forbes, reported from Berlin on November 9, 1938, that there were increasingly frequent rumors of an impending agreement between Germany and Poland. It seemed to him only a matter of time before "the ripe fruit" of Danzig fell into the German lap, but he predicted difficulties in the question of German transit through the Corridor. He speculated that the Germans might seek to offer Poland special compensation for a transit arrangement by supporting them against the Czechs, the Lithuanians, and even the Russians.

Ogilvie-Forbes had received the impression from Polish circles in Berlin that there was a genuine Polish desire to "compound with the Mammon of Iniquity." He correctly assumed that this quaint reference to Hitler would amuse and please Halifax. He was also watching out for his own interest, because he was considered in London to be pro-Hitler. He did not believe that German acquisition of Danzig would solve the problem of German-Polish friction. He concluded that "a speedy settlement of all German-Polish questions in a manner permanently acceptable to the national pride and the political and economic interests of both parties would seem to be a miracle of which not even Hitler is capable."[81]

William Strang, the chief of the Central Division of the British Foreign Office, predicted to Ambassador Kennard in Warsaw on the following day that there would be trouble between Germany and Poland. He instructed Kennard, "you will no doubt be interested to know that we have received reliable information to the effect that Hitler now holds the view that Poland has not yet consolidated her position as an independent state, and that he has plans for dealing with the Polish question. He expects to be able to do this without a European war." Strang invented this rumor in the hope that it would make Beck nervous when Kennard repeated it to him, and that it would discourage any temptation he might have to reach an agreement with Hitler.[82]

Kennard feared at this time that Beck would accept Hitler's proposals about Danzig and Corridor transit. Nevertheless, he hoped that German-Polish friction in the minority question would spoil an agreement on the other points. He saw no solution to the minority problem, concluding, "nor do I think that any arrangement for the exchange of populations is practicable." Kennard knew virtually nothing about the German minority in Poland. He claimed that the Poles in Germany were mainly laborers, which was correct, but he was mistaken when he described the Germans in Poland as mostly land-owners and shop-keepers who were "fairly well to do." The great majority of the Germans in Poland were agricultural and industrial laborers. This lack of accurate information is not surprising when one considers that Kennard was not interested in the conditions of the Germans except to minimize whatever complaints were made about their situation.

Kennard denied that the Poles were either nervous or in any hurry to settle their differences with Germany. He informed Halifax, at the time of the Burckhardt visit to Warsaw in November 1938, that the League High Commissioner shared his belief that the Poles would be willing to relinquish Danzig to Germany.[83] Kennard reminded Halifax that nothing had been done since the Teschen crisis to secure for Poland the permanent seat on the League Security Council which Great Britain had advocated, and he warned him that Beck would remain critical of the League of Nations until this point was settled.[84] Kennard had made no secret of his hatred for Germany when he discussed the situation with Burckhardt, and the Swiss diplomat in turn lost no time in supplying the Germans with full information about Kennard's attitude toward them. Hitler was interested to learn that the British Ambassador in Warsaw, who enjoyed the confidence of Halifax, was an enemy of appeasement.[85]

Burckhardt had complained to the Germans that Kennard had been "haughty at first," and Halifax was apparently worried about Burckhardt's attitude and the possibility that Kennard's arrogant manner may have alienated him. Halifax did not like to contemplate the possibility that the League High Commissioner might identify himself with the German position at Danzig. He explained to Kennard that Burckhardt had been told in 1937 that the main object of his mission was "to prevent . . . the establishment of a full National Socialist regime in the Free City." It is interesting that Halifax emphasized this in December 1938, when one recalls that he told Burckhardt in May 1938 that he hoped Danzig would return to Germany by means of a negotiated settlement. Halifax also reminded Kennard that Burckhardt possessed "exceptional diplomatic and political skill," and that he was not to be taken lightly. He confided that he would raise the Danzig question at the next meeting of the League Security Council, in January 1939, regardless of whether or not Beck or Burckhardt favored such a step.[86]

Halifax discussed the situation with Raczynski in London on December 14, 1938, in the hope of obtaining more information about the current Polish attitude toward a settlement with Germany. He began the conversation by complaining that the Poles had not been helpful about promoting League of Nations activities at Danzig. Raczynski replied that Poland recognized the importance of the League position and did not desire to see Burckhardt withdrawn. Halifax then asked the Polish Ambassador point blank if Hitler had recently raised the question of German claims to Danzig. The Polish Ambassador responded with an evasive answer. He declared that the main problem for Poland at the moment was to obtain international aid to rid the country of its Jewish population. He assured Halifax that the Jews constituted "a really big problem" in Poland.[87]

Raczynski emphasized that Poland favored an active British policy in Eastern Europe, although "it was perhaps not possible for His Majesty's Government to intervene directly in practical fashion in the event of trouble in Eastern Europe." It was clear to both Halifax and Raczynski that British soldiers could not be landed on the Polish coast in the event of war, but Raczynski hoped that the British would not disinterest themselves in the area. Halifax promised that he was prepared to give the question of British support to Poland careful consideration.[88]

Halifax was annoyed that Beck had not allowed Raczynski to give him tangible information about current German-Polish negotiations. The certainty of a German-Polish conflict was an essential element in the formulation of his plans. He instructed Kennard to use every means to discover Beck's real attitude. Kennard ingeniously suggested to Beck that it might be better to allow the Germans to take Danzig now, rather than permit them later to link Danzig with demands for the return of the entire Corridor. Beck "stated categorically that any question of concession in the Corridor would involve war." Kennard eagerly inquired if this would apply to a German request for transit facilities across the Corridor. Beck replied that any such German suggestion "could hardly be considered," although he had allowed Lipski to nourish the illusion among the Germans that Poland might accept this. Halifax was able to conclude that a German-Polish understanding was virtually impossible because of the chimera of British aid to Poland, and despite the fact that Beck was currently refusing to inform him about his negotiations with the Germans.[89]

Poland Endangered by Beck's Diplomacy

The tortuous diplomacy of Beck during this period had a double purpose. The British were prevented from taking for granted Polish opposition to Germany at a time when appeasement was the official British policy. It was evident that the British leaders would have to educate their public to hate and fear Germany before a shift in British policy could take place which would permit a British commitment to Poland. The Polish diplomat knew that he would not be treated as an equal by Great Britain unless he maintained a similar reserve in the conduct of his own policy. The Germans were deceived abut Polish policy in the interest of gaining time. Beck realized that Hitler would have more room to maneuver if he tipped his hand before the British leaders were ready to attack Germany. He knew that the patience of Hitler was his greatest asset, and he intended to challenge Germany when the time was ripe, rather than to receive an unexpected German challenge.[90]

This tortuous diplomacy would have been unnecessary had Beck perceived that the interests of Poland could best be served by joining Germany in a common front against Bolshevism. Hitler had offered reasonable and honorable terms which were highly advantageous to Poland. The friction caused by the minority question would have been a minor issue within the context of a German-Polish understanding. The Germans of Poland were far too disunited and intimidated to cause trouble if Hitler gained a success at Danzig, and a German guarantee of the existing German-Polish frontier would have convinced the few chauvinists among them that there was no point in hoping for union with the Reich. Poland could have played an important role as a bulwark of European defense against Bolshevism, and, with German support, she would have stood a good chance of surviving an attack from the Soviet Union.

The British had nothing to offer Poland. Their policy of hostility toward Germany, which was thinly veiled by appeasement while they prepared for war, placed the Soviet Union in the enviable role of *tertius gaudens*. A suicidal internecine struggle among the capitalist powers of Europe was the answer to a Soviet Marxist prayer. The geographical position of Poland was such that she would be the first victim of ultimate Soviet expansion toward the West. The British leaders did not intend to send a large army to Europe, as they had done in World War I, and the British Navy and British Air Force could offer no protection to Poland.

The dream of the Great Poland of 1750 was the fateful legacy which clouded the judgment of Beck. Pilsudski had shared this dream, but he was also a realist who would have been capable of making many major adjustments in Polish policy. It was the fate of Poland to find herself in the hands of the *epigoni* at the most crucial moment of her history. There was no sign that the Polish leaders were awake to the realities of the European situation when the year 1938 drew to a close.

Chapter 8

BRITISH HOSTILITY

TOWARD GERMANY AFTER MUNICH

Hitler's Bid for British Friendship

The Anglo-German relationship was the most important European issue after the Munich conference. An Anglo-German understanding could mean peace, prosperity, and security for Europe. A new Anglo-German war would bring destruction, ruin, and despair. The former condition would offer nothing to the doctrine of Bolshevism, which thrived on human misery. The latter situation would present a unique opportunity for expansion to the Bolshevist leaders. It is not to be wondered that the Bolshevist leaders hated the Munich conference which had prevented an Anglo-German war. They feared that from its aftermath a permanent Anglo-German understanding would emerge.[1]

The British attitude toward Germany was the crux of the problem. The attitude of Hitler toward Great Britain was favorable from the standpoint of establishing the permanent peace between the two nations which had been envisaged in the Anglo-German friendship declaration of September 30, 1938. Hitler hoped to avoid what he considered to have been the failures of Hohenzollern Germany. He condemned the idea of a large German navy, which had been brilliantly advocated before 1914 by Admiral von Tirpitz. He was unenthusiastic about the acquisition of German colonies overseas, and he regarded Germany's legal right to her former colonies as a mere bargaining counter. Hitler opposed trade rivalry between Germany and Great Britain. He wished the British to preserve their world commercial supremacy.[2]

The attitude of Hitler was familiar to the British leaders. The prominent Labour Party spokesman, George Lansbury, who had been the chief of the British Labour Party until 1935, had done what he could to inform the British Conservative leaders of Hitler's ideas. Lansbury met Hitler in Berlin on April 19, 1937. He was greatly impressed with the German leader, and he was convinced that he did not desire war. Lansbury discussed Hitler with Lord Halifax, and he rendered strong support to Chamberlain at the time of the

Munich conference. He emphasized that no important section of the British population opposed Chamberlain's trip to Munich.[3]

Arnold Toynbee, a leading English historian and an expert on international affairs, had visited Hitler in March 1936. He returned to England with a clear impression of Hitler's ideas. He informed Conservative Prime Minister Stanley Baldwin that Adolf Hitler was a sincere advocate of peace and close friendship between Great Britain and Germany.[4]

Thomas Jones, the closest friend of Lloyd George and Stanley Baldwin, had excellent connections with British statesmen. He was with Hitler in Munich on May 17, 1936. Jones was on close terms with Ribbentrop, and he was fully informed about Hitler's attitudes. Hitler had said that, if an Anglo-German understanding was achieved, "my biggest life's desire will be accomplished." Jones promised Hitler in Munich that Great Britain hoped "to get alongside Germany," and he praised Hitler's decision to give the English language priority after German, in the German schools, as a significant contribution to future contacts between the two nations.[5]

Leopold Amery, one of the principal Conservative statesmen, was in Germany on a vacation in August 1935. He was hostile toward Hitler's aspirations, and he had not intended visiting the German leader. Hitler was informed that Amery was in Germany and he immediately extended an invitation to him. He and Amery discussed recent developments in Germany and future German aims for several hours. Hitler assured Amery that Germany accepted the Polish Corridor settlement, and he hoped one day to be in a position to offer Poland a German guarantee of her western frontier. Amery reluctantly concluded that Hitler was "not unpleasantly boastful," and he was charmed by Hitler's statement that he "could not claim originality for any of his reforms."[6]

Viscount Rothermere was a prominent British newspaper publisher and a leader of the British armament campaign. He was with Hitler in Berchtesgaden in 1937 shortly before the Hitler-Halifax conversations. Rothermere believed that the Hitler with whom he spoke was "convinced that he had been called from his social obscurity to power not to make war, but to preserve peace and rebuild both spiritual and physical Germany." Rothermere and Hitler were also in correspondence. Hitler wrote to Rothermere that his ultimate objective was a comprehensive understanding among Germany, Great Britain, and the United States. Rothermere also remained in correspondence with Ribbentrop until a few weeks before the outbreak of World War II in 1939. Rothermere explained in a wartime book, which contained an introduction by Winston Churchill, that Ribbentrop had never been unfriendly toward Great Britain.[7]

David Lloyd George, the Prime Minister of the victorious British coalition Government of 1918, visited Hitler in September 1936. Hitler made no secret of the fact that he was tremendously impressed with the achievements of the British wartime leader, and it was evident that he was extensively informed about his career. Lloyd George replied that he "was deeply touched by the personal tribute of the Fuehrer and was proud to hear it paid to him by the greatest German of the age." Lloyd George returned to Great Britain convinced that Hitler had performed a herculean task in restoring prosperity and happiness to truncated Germany.[8]

The prominent British Conservative leader, Lord Londonderry, and the popular British journalist, Ward Price, both visited Hitler on numerous occasions. Each of these men published books in 1938 which favored an Anglo-German understanding, and which explained the aims and ideas of Hitler to their countrymen.[9]

Hitler tried repeatedly to arrange a meeting with British Prime Minister Stanley Baldwin in 1936, but neither he nor Ribbentrop were able to overcome Baldwin's anti-German prejudices. Baldwin remarked at the time of his retirement on April 20, 1937, that he "envied Lansbury the faith which enabled him to go and tackle Hitler." He might also have envied Hitler the faith which enabled him to seek out Baldwin and other British leaders in a vain effort to appease their distrust of Germany.[10]

Hitler knew that a personal visit to Great Britain, before an Anglo-German understanding had been achieved, would not be possible because of this anti-German prejudice. He had offered to meet Baldwin at sea in the vicinity of the British coast. Later he received three visits from Prime Minister Chamberlain, but these occurred during a crisis when conditions were not normal. Chamberlain noted that Hitler "seemed very shy" at their first meeting on September 15, 1938. Hitler confessed his fear that he would "be received with demonstrations of disapproval" if he visited England, and Chamberlain agreed that it would be wise to choose the right moment.[11]

Winston Churchill never met Hitler. He was in Munich for a few days in April 1932 and he expressed a desire to see Hitler. He claimed later, on the strength of an unlikely supposition, that Hitler refused to see him because Churchill had allegedly criticized Hitler's attitude toward the Jews. Ernst Hanfstaengl, who was commissioned by Hitler to entertain Churchill in Munich, explained that Hitler was in Nuremberg and that he was distracted by several important crises during a crucial phase of his struggle for power. Churchill made no effort to see Hitler after the latter was appointed Chancellor. There is no evidence that he had criticized Hitler's attitude toward the Jews prior to 1932. Churchill wrote in 1937: "If our country were defeated I hope we should find a champion as indomitable to restore our courage and lead us back to our place among the nations." The champion to whom he referred with such enthusiasm was Adolf Hitler.[12]

Anthony Eden met Hitler on several occasions. The first meeting took place in 1934; Eden noted that Hitler was "restrained and friendly" and "showed himself completely master of his subject (European armaments)." The second meeting occurred in March 1935 after the British Government had severely criticized Hitler for introducing peacetime military conscription a few days earlier. The personal relations between Eden and Hitler remained friendly at the second meeting.[13] But there was not much real communication, because Eden had little awareness of German problems. This fact was apparent at a discussion between Foreign Minister Eden and Nevile Henderson at Cliveden on October 24, 1937. Thomas Jones noted that the British Ambassador to Germany "has lived in the countries we talked about and Eden has not and this was apparent."[14]

Sir John Simon, one of the closest advisers to Chamberlain in 1938, accompanied Eden to Berlin in March 1935, and he afterward recorded his impressions of Hitler at that meeting. He noted that Hitler displayed no desire during their conversation to play the role of dicatator. He had no doubt that Hitler was sincere in his desire for a permanent understanding with the British. He was equally convinced that Hitler considered the moral rehabilitation of defeated Germany an urgent task. But Simon also remained convinced that it was a vital British interest to challenge Hitler at the favorable moment. It was this attitude, based on anti-German prejudice, which constituted the great obstacle to an understanding between Great Britain and Germany.[15]

Chamberlain's Failure to Criticize Duff Cooper

The first few days after the Munich conference provided a startling revelation of the depth of resentment toward Germany among British officials. It should be emphasized that it was the hostility within the British leadership which constituted the danger. The mass of the British people were obviously desirous of peace with Germany. The ovation which Chamberlain received in London on the rainy Friday afternoon of September 30, 1938, when he returned from Munich, was unprecedented. He was the hero of the hour among the common people because he had prevented war. The enthusiasm remained unbroken until the debates on the Munich conference opened in the British Parliament on Monday, October 3, 1938. King George VI departed for Balmoral castle in Scotland on October 2nd. He issued an announcement prior to his departure in which he expressed his confidence in Chamberlain and his hope that the peace of Europe would be preserved.[16]

The British war enthusiasts lost no time in launching their effort to spoil the celebration of peace. The first blow was a message to Chamberlain from Parliamentary First Lord of the Admiralty, Alfred Duff Cooper, on October 1, 1938. Duff Cooper announced that he distrusted the policy which had avoided war. He was resigning from the British Cabinet, and he intended to deliver a major speech in Parliament to explain this decision. Chamberlain replied in mild tones that he was aware of the fundamental disagreement which existed.[17]

Duff Cooper was an ideal ally of Churchill in the struggle against peace. He hated the Germans, and he had disliked the German language and German literature since his student days.[18] He was appointed Secretary of State for War in 1935, and by that time his principal concern was the "ever-growing German meance."[19] He agreed with Sir Robert Vansittart, the Permanent Under-Secretary at the Foreign Office, that everything possible should be done to prevent Italy from aligning with Germany. He was convinced that it was more important to oppose Hitler than to oppose Communism. He condemned the entire German nation as a "cruel people," and he criticized Englishmen who were inclined to forget the German "crimes" of World War I. He had been convinced since 1936, as had Lord Halifax, that an Anglo-German war was inevitable. Duff Cooper delivered numerous bellicose speeches in 1936 and 1937, and he doubted if Chamberlain, when he succeeded Baldwin in April 1937, would care to retain him in the Cabinet. He was retained, and he was promoted to the Admiralty. He was young and handsome, and he delighted in the flamboyant cruises to foreign places afforded by his new post. He joined Vansittart in supporing Chamberlain against Eden in the February 1938 British

Cabinet crisis, and his breach with Chamberlain did not occur until the Prime Minister returned from his first visit to Hitler in September 1938.[20]

The derogatory comments which Chamberlain made about Hitler after their first meeting failed to appease Duff Cooper. He wanted war with Germany, and he feared that the chance might be lost. He believed that he could do more to promote war if he joined the Churchill faction of Conservatives outside the Cabinet. Duff Cooper had informed Chamberlain on September 25, 1938, that he intended to resign, but had agreed to reserve his announcement until the termination of the Czech crisis.[21]

Duff Cooper was allowed to deliver the first speech of the debate in the House of Commons on October 3, 1938. He criticized the Government for not assuming a definite commitment during the Czech crisis. He asserted that Great Britain would not have been fighting for the Czechs, because this would have been an insufficient basis for war. He insisted that she would have been fighting for the balance of power, which was precious to some British hearts. He believed that it was his mission and that of his country to prevent Germany from achieving a dominant position on the continent.[22]

Chamberlain astonished his critics by refusing to reply to this condemnation of his policy by a former subordinate. He said instead, in the tones of mawkish sentimentality which he frequently employed, that he always was moved by the resignation speeches of Cabinet ministers. It was obvious that he cherished a deep affection for Duff Cooper, and the differences between them were those of tactics rather than basic principles. He praised Duff Cooper for doing a good job at the Admiralty, and he apologized for him by observing that many of the Cabinet ministers would carry the scars of the recent crisis for a long time to come.[23]

The British Tories in Fundamental Agreement

There was no disagreement between Chamberlain and Duff Cooper about the antiquated British policy of the balance of power. The theory had first been espoused in England in the 16th century by Thomas Cromwell, a disciple of Machiavelli, and a wealthy adventurer who had witnessed at first hand the late phase of balance of power diplomacy in Renaissance Italy. It was Thomas Cromwell who persuaded Cardinal Wolsey to conduct English policy along these lines. The policy had been employed to prevent a strong state, such as Milan, from gaining supremacy over the weaker Italian states. It was useless when outside Powers such as France and Spain appeared on the scene with overwhelming forces and crushed a divided Italy. The balance of power policy was effectively employed in Europe by England for several centuries to prevent any single Power from attaining the sort of supremacy over the divided continent which was enjoyed in North America by the United States after 1865. It meant the relentless curtailment of any seemingly preponderant continental state, regardless of the domestic institutions or foreign policy of such a state. The purpose of the policy was to give Great Britain a permanent position of control over the destinies of her neighbors. The policy was futile by the 1930's, when outside Powers such as the Soviet Union and the United States were in a position to appear upon the scene with overwhelming forces and to share dominion over a crushed and divided Europe.[24]

There were several occasions, after Thomas Cromwell and Henry VIII, when English policy rejected the balance of power. Oliver Cromwell, the Lord Protector of England during the 1650's, was scornful of the balance of power theory, which he regarded as a decadent basis for policy. He sometimes promoted alliances, such as the one he proposed to Holland and Sweden to promote the Protestant cause. His fundamental attitude was that England could provide her own defense, and that she need not fear an attack from a preponderant European Power. This attitude of Cromwell's was useful to Giulio Mazzarini in building up French supremacy in Europe. He persuaded Cromwell to join France in despoiling weaker Spain. Cromwell did not throw English resources and manpower into a futile struggle to support declining Spanish power merely because France was stronger than Spain.[25]

Louis XIV discovered in the War of Devolution in the 1660's that Holland was an irritating obstacle to the continuation of French supremacy. Dutch diplomacy had reduced French gains in that war. The English had waged two wars of aggression against the Dutch in recent years. It was comparatively easy for Louis XIV to cement Anglo-French relations in the treaty of Dover in 1670 with Charles II of England, and to prepare a combined Anglo-French war of aggression against the Dutch. The English were persuaded to attack the Dutch without warning in April 1672, and Louis XIV soon intervened to support the English. French plans to crush Holland were foiled, because the Dutch were able to defeat the combined Anglo-French fleets in one of the great military upsets of history (battle of Solebay). This was a second important instance in the 17th century when the English conducted their policy without consideration for the balance of power.[26]

The balance of power policy was revived by King William III of England in the 1690's in a remarkable series of speeches from the throne to Parliament. King William, the great-grandson of the German prince of Nassau-Orange, William the Silent, was flexible in his national loyalties. He built up English power at the expense of his native Holland because in England there was greater respect for the monarchical institutions which he cherished. William used French support of the Catholic Scotch-English Stuarts as the pretext for plunging England into the war of the League of Augsburg, but he explained after the war was well under way that the balance of power was his primary consideration.[27]

The balance of power was used to justify English participation in the next major European and Overseas struggle, the War of the Spanish Succession. England made great gains when she concluded a separate peace with France at Utrecht in 1713, and the balance of power received a new lease on life, once the horrors of the war had been forgotten. The English statesman, James Stanhope, led a brief attempt to organize a preponderant League of European States, but it collapsed in 1720 during a severe economic depression and a change in English leadership. England returned to the balance of power under Robert Walpole, and no subsequent English statesman was able to equal his skill in conducting English policy under this system. He kept England out of the European War of the Polish Succession in the 1730's because he realized that the balance of power was not threatened by the war. He was unable to prevent England's entry into an unnecessary war against Spain in 1739, and he was soon forced from power.[28]

England subordinated the balance of power, in the following period, to her effort to acquire the overseas colonies of France. There were four principal continental Powers of approximately equal military strength at that time. They were France, Prussia, Austria, and Russia, although France was by far the most wealthy. England had taken over most of the French colonies by 1763, but there had been a change of English leadership in 1761. Pitt's advocacy of a preventive war against Spain was used by Bute as a pretext to overthrow him, and this led to the ruin of English relations with the principal continental states. This unfavorable development resulted from the incredible arrogance and crudeness of English diplomacy under Bute.

England was the principal European Power when her American mainland colonies revolted in 1775. She was unable to crush the insurgent American colonies because of her inability to hire sufficient mercenary troops in Europe, but she defended her European position with the ease against an enemy coalition which included France, Spain, and Holland. The English leaders sought to frustrate the attempts of Russia, France, and Spain to expand during the decade between the end of the American war in 1783 and the outbreak of war between England and Republican France. No single Power offered an impressive challenge to the balance of power at that time.[29]

The balance of power received dramatic emphasis during the four wars of coalition waged against France under the first Republic, and after 1804 under the first Napoleonic Empire. The fourth coalition waged a second war against Napoleon when he returned from Elba in 1815. The balance of power was used on several occasions during this period to justify the continuation of English warfare against France, when the other enemies of France had left the field. Robert Castlereagh was conducting British foreign policy when France was crushed in 1815, and he hoped to abandon the balance of power policy. He repeated the performance of Stanhope in the preceding century by seeking to associate England permanently with a preponderant League of European States. His opponents at home demanded a return to the balance of power, and in 1822 Castlereagh abandoned his task and committed suicide.[30]

England followed the balance of power policy without interruption after 1822. This was true either when she was in "splendid isolation," or when she was a member of some alliance system. England supported Napoleon III against Russia in the Crimean War of the 1850's because she believed that Russia was stronger than France. She refused to protect Belgium from a possible German invasion in 1887, because she believed that a Franco-Russian combination was more powerful than Germany and her allies. Decisions were difficult during these years, because opposing forces were almost in perfect balance without England. This meant, on the positive side, that England could pursue her balance of power policy in "splendid isolation" without promoting a complicated system of alliances, although at one time she was closely associated with Bismarck's Triple Alliance.

There was a period of great confusion in English foreign policy during the 1890's. The five principal continental Powers were organized into two alliance systems. It was feared in London that the two systems might combine against England in one of the frequent colonial crises of these years. Joseph Chamberlain, the father of Neville, led a group who favored an English alliance policy. Prime Minister Salisbury opposed an alliance policy. He insisted that alliances were superfluous for England and would impair the flexibility of English policy. The military reverses suffered by England in the early phase of the Boer War helped to carry the day for Chamberlain and alliances. Salisbury was right when he insisted that the opposite conclusion should have been drawn, because the continental Powers did not intervene against England in this crisis when she was most vulnerable. [31]

The growth of German wealth and productive power during these years was phenomenal, and it seemed to more than compensate for the reverses currently suffered by Germany in diplomatic affairs. Many of the British leaders began to suspect that German growth was a challenge to the balance of power. The balance of power had its own morality. Any nation which seemed to challenge it should be treated as an enemy. It did not matter whether or not Germany planned to attack British interests, or whether or not she was in a position to strike a blow at England. The prospect that she might become stronger than any possible hostile continental combination suggested that it was time "to redress the balance of power." [32]

The situation was more complicated than it had been during earlier centuries. Great Britain launched her alliance policy by concluding an Anglo-Japanese alliance in 1902, but it was easy to see that the rising imperial power of Japan might become a real challenge to British interests in Asia. Both the United States and Germany surpassed Great Britain in industrial strength before 1914. British power since 1750 had been based more on industrial and naval supremacy than on diplomacy, and the loss of industrial supremacy made the British position more difficult. A challenge to Germany would play into the hands of the United States, just as a challenge to America, which almost occurred during the 1895-1896 Venezuelan crisis, would have played into the hands of Germany. Cecil Rhodes, the architect of British imperial expansion in Africa, recognized this dilemma, and this prompted him to advocate permanent peace and cooperation among Great Britain, Germany, and the United States. This would have meant the abandonment of the balance of power policy, but Cecil Rhodes was sufficiently shrewd to see that the policy was obsolete. The ruling British leaders did not see it that way, and Great Britain suffered an enormous loss of power and prestige in World War I despite her victory over Germany. [33]

The Soviet Union began to emerge as an industrial giant of incalculable power during the two decades after World War I. It was evident that there were at least four nations immediately or potentially far more powerful than Great Britain. These four nations were the United States, the Soviet Union, Germany, and Japan. This was different than in the old days when it had merely been a question of one preponderant Spain, or one preponderant France. The bankruptcy of the British balance of power policy should have been evident to everyone. It was as obsolete as Italian balance of power politics after the intervention, with overwhelming forces, of King Charles VIII of France in Italian affairs in 1494. The balance of power policy always had been an unhealthy and decadent basis from which to approach diplomatic relations. It substituted for a healthy pursuit of common interests among states the tortuous attempt to undermine or even destroy any state which attained a leading position. It took no regard of the attitude of such a state toward England. The policy was also extremely unstable. It demanded otherwise inexplicable shifts of position when it was evident that one state had been overestimated or another underestimated. It was particularly tragic when France abandoned an independent policy and became dependent on Great Britain. This meant that France was in danger, along with Great Britain, of contributing to the blunders of an obsolete British policy.[34]

It seemed momentarily that Great Britain might be returning to the policies of Stanhope and Castlereagh when she joined the League of Nations in 1919. Unfortunately this was not the case. France after 1919 was no longer as powerful as Great Britain, but she enjoyed continental preponderance for several years because of the treaty restrictions on Germany, the intrinsic feebleness of Italy, and the disappearance of Austria-Hungary. Revolutionary upheavals after the defeat in World War I temporarily reduced Russian power. The British responded by employing their balance of power policy against France. There had been notorious rivalry between the two nations in the Near East during World War I, because of oil and traditional prestige factors, and the British nearly succeeded in "biffing" the French out of their Syrian claims. The British and French took opposite sides in the post-war struggle between the Greeks and the Turks. The British continued to oppose French policies with increasing vigor when the Turks emerged victorious with French support.[35]

The climax came when Great Britain opposed the efforts of France and Belgium to collect reparations in the Ruhr in 1923-1924. The French were confidently pursuing a policy of independence under Poincaré's bold leadership, but the debacle suffered in the Ruhr was a stunning psychological blow to the French. Édouard Herriot, who took the reins of policy from Poincaré, concluded that nothing could succeed without British cooperation. There were later instances of friction between France and Great Britain, but the French leaders were always inclined to accept the British lead. It was apparent to everyone during the Czech crisis in 1938 that Anglo-French policy was conducted from London.[36]

The British occasionally pursued policies which seemed to strengthen French preponderance on the continent. They joined France and Italy in squelching the feeble attempt of Chancellor Bruening of Germany to conclude a customs union with Austria in 1931. It did not seem that the "Hunger Chancellor" was capable of removing the threat of Communism in Germany, which implied a new preponderant Russo-German combination, or of challenging the old preponderance of France.[37]

The situation changed with the arrival of Hitler in 1933. The new Chancellor dealt a few annihilating blows to German Communism, and challenged France by withdrawing Germany from the disarmament conference at Geneva, where German claims to equality received farcical treatment. The balance of power on the continent was restored when Hitler sent German troops into the Rhineland in 1936. The French might have challenged this move successfully had they received an assurance of British support. As it was, the French feared that action would mean an Anglo-German combination against them as in 1923.[38]

Duff Cooper and Chamberlain agreed in October 1938 that Great Britain should continue the balance of power policy. They agreed that everything possible should be done to prevent a permanent alignment of Italy with Germany. They both underestimated the Soviet Union and believed that she was much less powerful than Germany. They also agreed that the Czech cause as such was not worth British participation in a European war. The sole point where they disagreed was whether or not it would be wise for Great Britain to attack Germany in 1938. Duff Cooper believed that Great Britain was sufficiently strong in 1938 to attack Germany, but Chamberlain believed that it would be wiser to play for time. Neither Chamberlain nor Duff Cooper had any sympathy for Germany, the nation which Chamberlain called the bully of Europe as early as 1935. It is possible from this perspective to see that the differences within the British Conservative Party in October 1938 were not really very profound. Anti-German prejudice was the dominant attitude within the entire Conservative Party.[39]

Tory and Labour War Sentiment

The London *Times* seemed to incline toward the evaluation of Duff Cooper when it announced on October 3, 1938, that Germany was relieved to escape from a war "which, in the opinion of most sections of the population, it would almost certainly have lost." The *Times* predicted that "Mr. Chamberlain will find plenty of critics" in the current parliamentary debates. It is important to recall that Geoffrey Dawson, the editor of the *Times*, had provided valuable support for Halifax and Chamberlain during the Czech crisis. On the afternoon of September 6, 1938, he had revised the famous article which appeared in the *Times* on the following day, and advocated the cession of the Sudeten districts to Germany.[40]

Dawson was especially close to Halifax, whom he had met in South Africa in 1905. He published an article on October 30, 1925, which praised Halifax without stint or limit when it was announced in London that the latter had been appointed Viceroy of India. Halifax had given Dawson a detailed private analysis of his visit to Hitler in November 1937, and he had told Dawson that he was well-satisfied with the visit. Dawson noted that Halifax probably could have negotiated a lasting agreement with Germany at that time, had Great Britain agreed to remain aloof from possible complications between Germany and her eastern neighbors. Dawson also realized that Halifax was not willing to do this.[41]

It was significant that the London *Times*, which had been the principal journalistic organ of appeasement during the Czech crisis, began to adopt a more critical attitude toward Germany immediately after the Munich conference. It followed the policy of Halifax in this respect. The differences between the attitudes of the *Times* and of the *Daily Express* toward Germany became increasingly pronounced. This was because Lord Beaverbrook, the owner of the *Daily Express*, was a sincere advocate of appeasement as a permanent policy, whereas Geoffrey Dawson was not. The *Daily Express* continued to hope and to predict that there would be no war with Germany until within a few days of the outbreak of World War II in September 1939. This attitude reflected the wishes of wide sections of the British population in the autumn of 1938, and in

November 1938 the *Daily Express* noted that its circulation had increased to over 2½ million within a very short time, which gave it the largest circulation of any newspaper in British history. When Halifax at last launched a gigantic propaganda campaign in March 1939 to sell the British public on war with Germany, the editorial policy of the *Daily Express* gradually became a liability for circulation rather than an asset. It is not surprising that Beaverbrook finally made concessions to the warlike mood in order to preserve his newspaper. It became evident that a large-circulation British newspaper with consistent principles was an impossibility in the modern age.[42]

Chamberlain paid special tribute to Halifax in the British House of Commons on October 3, 1938. He claimed that Halifax felt a duty not only to England, but to all humanity. There was no point in wondering what prompted Chamberlain to make this sentimental statement, because it was consistent with his usual oratorical style. There is no record that Halifax ever recanted his maiden speech to Parliament, in which he denied that all men were equal and insisted that the British were the "superior race" within an Empire which comprised more than a quarter of the population of the world. Chamberlain leaned on the prestige of Halifax to protect his own position.[43]

Chamberlain reminded Commons that there was a very considerable difference between the terms of Munich and the proposals of Hitler at Bad Godesberg. The Munich agreement permitted the Czechs to withdraw important strategic materials from the areas about to be ceded, and the region which the Germans were permitted to occupy in five gradual stages was smaller than the area Hitler had requested. He reminded the members that the avoidance of a catastrophe at Munich was in the interest of the Four Munich Powers rather than merely a triumph for one of them. These cogent remarks of the Prime Minister were greeted with shouts of "Shame!, Shame!" from the Opposition benches. This was to be expected. The current Labour Party leaders had supported Chamberlain's trip to Munich, but they hoped to make political capital by denouncing his policy after he returned.[44]

The situation was explained later by Hugh Dalton, one of the top Labour Party leaders. Dalton, like many of his colleagues, was pro-Communist, and he referred to a visit to the Soviet Union in July 1932, during the greatest famine in Russian history, as an "inspiring experience." Dalton and the other Labour Party leaders actually had considerable confidence in Chamberlain's leadership. They knew that he would never permit the return of the German colonies, or make any tangible concession to Germany at British expense. They were angry that Charles Lindbergh had discouraged war in 1938 by emphasizing current German strength in the air. They agreed with Duff Cooper after Munich that 1938 would have been a favorable year to oppose Germany. They hoped that by contesting the results of the Munich conference they could either unseat Chamberlain or push him into an anti-German policy. They knew that the Labour Opposition was much too weak in Parliament to accomplish this result without important allies from the British Conservative Party. The Labour Party leaders professed to believe that cooperation with National Socialist Germany in foreign affairs would discourage necessary reforms at home.[45]

Chamberlain continued his speech by reading the text of the Anglo-German declaration of friendship of September 30, 1938. He mentioned that this agreement would not be effective unless there was good will on both sides. This left room to claim later that the British had to oppose Germany because Hitler did not show good will toward England. Chamberlain noted that Munich had merely provided a foundation for peace and that the structure was still lacking. He then turned to his favorite theme of British armament, and he reminded the House with pride that the pace of the British armament campaign was increasing daily. He promised that the British Empire would not relax her efforts unless the rest of the world disarmed. He concluded with the announcement that military power was the key to successful British diplomacy.

Clement Attlee, the new Labour Party leader, spoke of the Munich agreement as a huge victory for Hitler and "an annihilating defeat for democracy," which of course was meant to include so-called Soviet democracy. Eden gave a speech in which he criticized Chamberlain on detailed points, and expressed doubt that Great Britain would implement her promised guarantee to the Czech state. He drew on his old experience as special British representative to the League of Nations, and he denounced the idea of the Munich Powers deciding an important question without consulting the smaller states. He advised the House to regard the current situation as a mere pause before the next crisis. He claimed that the British armament campaign was still somewhat too slow.

Hoare concluded the debate in Commons on October 3, 1938, with a mild defense of Chamberlain's policy. He introduced an argument which was to be one of his favorites, except when applied to Poland. He suggested that a new World War would have been useless as an attempt to maintain the old Czech borders. The Germans and other minorities were saturated with Czech rule and would not accept it again. He added that the British Government would be willing to give the Czechs an effective guarantee at some future date, but only after the outstanding problems which afflicted the Czechs were settled.[46]

Halifax delivered an important speech in the British House of Lords on October 3, 1938. He shared the opinion of Hoare that Great Britain should never fight for a foreign state unless she was in a position to restore its old frontiers after a victorious war. This was an interesting idea, especially when one considers that Halifax refused to guarantee the Polish frontier with the Soviet Union when he concluded the Anglo-Polish alliance of August 25, 1939. It was obvious that this argument was largely sophistry to Halifax, and a sop to appease the Opposition. He revealed to the Lords that he had done what he could to improve British relations with the Soviet Union by placing the blame solely on Germany and Italy for refusing to invite the Soviets to Munich. He had given a formal declaration to this effect to Soviet Ambassador Maisky on October 1, 1938. Halifax regarded all this as a permanent trend in British foreign policy. Relations between Maisky and Halifax became more cordial in the months after Munich, and the Soviet Ambassador scored a great triumph on March 1, 1939, when Chamberlain and Halifax attended a reception at the Soviet embassy in London shortly before Stalin himself delivered a bitter speech denouncing the Western Powers. Halifax was obviously intent upon switching British appeasement from Germany to the Soviet Union.

The key to the Halifax speech of October 3rd was the statement that Great Britain would continue to prepare for a possible war against Germany despite the Anglo-German friendship declaration of September 30, 1938. Halifax, like

Chamberlain, devoted the latter part of his speech to a discussion of the British armament campaign. He emphasized that the need for more weapons was the principal British concern at the moment.[47]

Baldwin delivered a speech in Lords on the following day. He complained that it had been difficult to establish personal contact with the German and Italian dictators during the past five years. This was an astonishing statement when one recalls that Hitler had made repeated efforts to meet Baldwin at any time or place while the latter was Prime Minister. Baldwin dropped the mask completely when he claimed that Great Britain needed the spirit of 1914 to solve contemporary world problems. He was supposedly defending the peace settlement of Chamberlain, but in reality he was invoking the glory of the British attack on Germany in 1914. He mentioned that in the recent crisis he had been reminded of Sir Edward Grey, who looked like a man who had gone through hell when he pushed for war in 1914. Baldwin did not mention that the main reason for Grey's concern was the fear that the mountain of deceit on which he had built British foreign policy would be discovered by the British Parliament. The British Parliament did not realize in 1914 that Grey had given the French a commitment to fight Germany whether Belgium was invaded or not. The French had concentrated their navy in the Mediterranean, and had entrusted the defense of their northern coastline to the British, before there was the slightest sign of an impending German invasion of Belgium. This situation was explored and explained by historians of many nations after World War I, but Baldwin, like Halifax, preferred to evaluate Grey in terms of 1914 war propaganda.[48]

Arthur Greenwood and Herbert Morrison resumed the Labour attack on Chamberlain in Commons on October 4, 1938. They repeated many of the arguments which Clement Attlee and Hugh Dalton had made on the previous day. It was known that President Roosevelt in January 1938 had advocated a world conference on European problems, which was supposed to include both the United States and the Soviet Union. The Labour leaders adopted the world conference slogan and stressed the importance of the voice of the Soviet Union in the councils of Europe. Leslie Burgin, Minister of Transport, spoke on behalf of Chamberlain, and he repeated the argument that a war for the Czechs would have been immoral, unless it could have been shown that it was possible to restore the Czech state in its entirety after the war. It is astonishing that these same people accepted war on behalf of Poland without a murmur, when it was obvious after August 22, 1939, that the Soviet Union was hostile to Poland, and that Great Britain had no intention of opposing Russia. It should have been apparent to anyone that the defeat of Germany would not enable the British to restore the new Polish state. In reality, the British leaders were not truly concerned about either the Czechs or the Poles.[49] The same argument about not being able to restore the Czechs was repeated on October 4th by Sir Thomas Inskip, another British Cabinet member. In the following weeks the argument was repeated *ad nauseam*. It seems impossible that anyone could have forgotten it within the short span of one year. Nevertheless, the deluge of propaganda in England, after March 1939, was so great that it would have been easy to forget the Ten Commandments.[50]

Sir John Simon declared complacently in Commons on October 5, 1938, that history would have to decide whether or not the Munich agreement was the prelude to better times. The debate was entering the third day, and it had already surpassed all other parliamentary debates on British foreign policy since World War I. Simon admitted candidly that article 19 of the League covenant for peaceful territorial revision had always been a dead letter. Eden pursued the tactics of October 3rd, and he inquired of Simon if the Government in the future intended to participate in the settlement of European problems by means of Four Power diplomacy. Simon emphatically denied this, and he intimated that the British leaders hoped that the Soviet Union and the smaller Powers would have more to say in the future. Winston Churchill followed with his long awaited anti-German speech. The other English war enthusiasts hoped that he would make his speech as provocative as possible, and he did not disappoint them. He agreed with his close friend in America, Bernard Baruch, that Hitler should not be allowed to "get away with it."[51]

Churchill claimed that Hitler had extracted British concessions at pistol point, and he loved to use the image of Hitler as a highwayman or a gangster. He hoped to worry Hitler by intimating that he had contacts with an underground movement in Germany. He suggested that a common Anglo-Franco-Soviet front in support of the Czechs would have enabled an opposition movement within Germany to cause trouble for Hitler, and possibly to overthrow him. He used flowery rhetoric to describe the allegedly mournful Czechs slipping away into a darkness comparable to the Black Hole of Calcutta. The speech was couched in elegant phrases dear to the hearts of many of Churchill's countrymen. The simple and stark purpose of the speech was to foment a war of annihilation against Germany.

Churchill had been excluded from Conservative Governments in England for many years, but he had made countless speeches, and his personal influence remained tremendous. He had propagated the myth that Great Britain was disarmed in 1932, indeed, that she had wrongly practiced a policy of unilateral disarmament in response to the noble sentiment of the League Covenant. In reality, the British military establishment in 1932 was gigantic compared to that of Germany, and much larger than that of the United States. Great Britain had less than one million men in all of her ground forces throughout the Empire, but it had never been traditional British policy to maintain a large standing army. She had the largest navy in the world, despite the Washington conference of 1921-1922 which envisaged eventual British equality with the United States. The maintenance of a navy was no less expensive or militaristic than the upkeep of an army.[52]

Churchill had conducted an uninterrupted campaign of agitation against Germany since March 1933, and he was a veteran in the field. Some of his inaccurate statements about alleged German armaments in this period are contained in his 1948 volume, *The Gathering Storm*, and in his 1938 book of speeches, *While England Slept*. Churchill wanted to convince his countrymen that Germany was governed by an insatiable desire for world conquest. In his speech of October 5, 1938, he did more than anyone else to warn Hitler that Germany was in danger of being strangled by a British coalition in the style of 1914. Churchill does not bear direct responsibility for the attack on Germany in 1939, because he was not admitted to the British Cabinet until the die was cast. The crucial decisions on policy were made without his knowledge, and he was frankly amazed when Halifax suddenly shifted to a war policy in March 1939. Churchill was useful to Halifax in building up British prejudice against Germany, but he was a mere instrument, at the most, in the conduct of British policy in 1938 and 1939.[53]

The most convincing speech in defense of the Munich conference was delivered by Rab Butler, the Parliamentary Under-Secretary for Foreign Affairs. Butler held moderate views on international questions, and he admired the diplomacy which had produced the Munich conference. He declared on October 5th that a war to deny self-determination to the Sudeten Germans was unthinkable, and he defended Munich as the only possible solution of a difficult problem. He denied the proposition that Great Britain had departed from democratic principles in seeking an agreement with Germany.[54]

The debate was interrupted but not terminated when Chamberlain proposed a motion on the following day to adjourn until November 1, 1938. Churchill supported the Labour Opposition in opposing the motion, and he delivered a bitter personal attack against Chamberlain. He had refrained from doing this in his major speech on the previous day because he was concentrating his fire against the Germans. The adjournment motion was followed by a vote of confidence. Chamberlain carried the vote, but many of the prominent Conservatives refrained from voting, and of course Labour and the Liberals voted against him. The roster of Conservatives who refused to accept the Munich agreement or vote for Chamberlain is impressive. It included Churchill, Eden, Duff Cooper, Harold Macmillan, Duncan Sandys, Leopold Amery, Harold Nicolson, Roger Keyes, Sidney Herbert, and General Spears. These men comprised about half of the leading figures of the Conservative Party in 1938, and they were well-known to the British public. They were joined by a score of lesser figures in the House of Commons, and they were supported by such prominent peers as Lord Cranborne and Lord Wolmer in the House of Lords. It was recognized that many other members of Parliament refrained from joining them solely because they were concerned about Conservative Party discipline, particularly in case they were men of limited reputation. Chamberlain won the vote of confidence, but it was doubtful if he possessed the confidence of the British Conservative Party.[55]

Chamberlain produced his major rhetorical effort on behalf of Munich just before the vote of confidence on October 6th. He declared that his conscience was clear; he did not regret that Great Britain was not fighting Germany over the Czech issue. He stressed the horrors of modern war as the main justification for any peace policy. Chamberlain suggested that the Czech state might best survive in the future if it became permanently neutral in the Swiss style. He added proudly that new elections at this time would be an unfair advantage for the Government because of the sentiment of the country. Everyone listening knew that the current Conservative majority was unnaturally large because advantage had been taken of the sentiment aroused by the Ethiopian crisis in 1935. Baldwin had given the country the false impression that the Government was prepared to win a great victory for collective security at Ethiopia, and the stirring slogans which followed had rallied the voters.[56]

Chamberlain reverted to his previous tactic of painting the contemporary situation in somber rather than bright colors. He implied that Europe was gripped by a great crisis despite the Munich conference and the Anglo-German friendship declaration. He warned that elections might impair the unity of the nation at a crucial moment. He added that great efforts would be demanded from the nation in coming weeks because of the expanded armament campaign, and he claimed that it was important to keep differences of opinion about British policy to a minimum. He created the impression, which he had to do under the circumstances, that war was not inevitable. Hitler had accepted the Munich conference because he believed this. Chamberlain declared that war would be inevitable unless some sort of relations were maintained with the "totalitarian states." He said that there was no reason to suppose that a new war would end the European crisis more successfully than the last war had done. He rejected the idea of the world conference, proposed by Labour, with the argument that it had no prospect of success. He finished his speech by emphasizing Anglo-French unity and the need to increase the production of British arms. The Prime Minister was obviously not optimistic about the prospects for peace.[57]

Chamberlain went much further in this speech in stressing the need for war preparation than can be indicated in a brief summary. He nearly persuaded Anthony Eden and Leopold Amery, who denounced Munich and favored war, to vote for him. Amery and Eden would not have reacted in this manner had the dominant theme been an expression of faith in the continuation of peace.[58]

Control of British Policy by Halifax

One of the most dramatic incidents in England after Munich was the firm bid of Halifax to take the reins of British foreign policy into his own hands, or resign. Halifax permitted Chamberlain to have the lead during the Czech crisis, but he made it clear afterward that the time had come for a change. He wanted sole responsibility, and he did not wish Chamberlain to travel abroad to important conferences again without his Foreign Minister. This situation reached a climax before Chamberlain's speech on October 6th. Halifax was firmly in control after this date. Halifax, like Eden earlier, had rejected Chamberlain's policy, but, unlike Eden, Halifax put through his own policy. Chamberlain chose to conform, as illustrated by the following excerpt from his apologetic letter to Halifax of March 11, 1939: "Your rebuke . . . was fully merited . . . I was horrified at the result of my talk . . . I promise faithfully not to do it again, but to consult you beforehand."[59]

The roles of Chamberlain and Halifax were reversed. Halifax felt like a mere spectator of events during the Sudeten crisis, and Chamberlain felt the same way after October 6th.[60]

The change of tactics by Halifax, during the months of October and November 1938, offers striking evidence of this. American Ambassador Kennedy had tea with Halifax on October 12th, and he received a complacent picture of the European situation from the British Foreign Secretary. It was evident that Halifax did not wish to create the impression of an abrupt change of course. It should be noted that this tea occurred after the furor created by Hitler's Saarbruecken speech of October 9th, which had criticized Conservative warmongering tactics against Germany. Halifax admitted to Kennedy that everyone in a position of influence knew that Hitler did not desire war against England. Great Britain intended to increase her air strength, but this did not necessarily mean that she planned to interfere with Hitler on the continent. Halifax told Kennedy that he expected Hitler to make a bid for the annexation of both Danzig and Memel, and he suggested that Great Britain might not intervene if Hitler moved as far as Rumania. He added that Great Britain was seeking to prepare for all eventualities by improving her relations with the Soviet Union.[61]

Halifax discussed the same European situation with Kennedy again on October 28th. The only new development in the interim was the German offer to Poland, and Halifax himself had predicted on October 12th that Hitler would seek to acquire Danzig. Halifax painted a somber picture of Hitler's attitude toward Great Gritain in this second conversation, and he also gave Kennedy a great quantity of unreliable information about Hitler's alleged attitudes toward a number of current continental problems. A few weeks later he claimed to Kennedy that Hitler was consumed by passionate hatred of England, and that he had a plan to tear the Soviet Union to pieces in the Spring of 1939. The purpose of these deceptive tactics was obvious. Halifax was exercising his diplomatic talents in preparation for a British attack on Germany. He was also indulging in the easy task of adding fuel to the dislike of the American leaders for Germany. World War I had amply vindicated the efficacy of propaganda.[62]

Tory Alarmist Tactics

The speeches which Chamberlain delivered for public consumption during the debate on the Munich conference are important. They show that the British public was not receiving a cheerful picture of the European situation, and that the Anglo-German declaration of friendship received far less emphasis than the need to prepare for war against Germany. These speeches provided no clue to Chamberlain's real motives in going to Munich. The motive at one moment seemed to be a genuine desire to avert war permanently, and, at another, to postpone war until Great Britain was ready. It is necessary to consider what Chamberlain told his intimate advisers in private conversation. These men learned after Munich that the attempt to come to terms with the dictators was not the primary reason for Chamberlain's Munich policy. They were told by Chamberlain that two other factors were more important. The most weighty was momentary British unreadiness for a test of arms with Germany. The second consideration was French opposition to a military offensive on behalf of the Czechs. Chamberlain's attitude would have been different in 1938 if the French had possessed a brilliant offensive strategy to aid the Czechs, and were prepared to use it. It is probable that Chamberlain would have pushed Great Britain into war against Germany had British armaments reached the 1939 level, or had the French pursued a more aggressive policy.[63]

The Conservative leaders delivered two important speeches on British foreign policy between the adjournment of Parliament on October 6th and the reopening of Parliament on November 1, 1938. Sir Samuel Hoare spoke at

Clacton-on-Sea on October 20th. His speech explained an elementary fact of great importance. He pointed out that a war against Germany on behalf of the Czechs would have been a preventive war. He reminded his listeners that the verdict of history condemned the doctrine of preventive war. Hoare noted that preventive wars always were great mistakes, and that a nation had no right to appeal to arms except in defense of her own interests. It seems almost incredible, when one reads this speech, to anticipate that Hoare supported a policy of preventive war against Germany a few months later. Hoare reminded his listeners that Hitler had abided by the terms of the 1935 Anglo-German Naval Treaty. Hoare also lauded the British armament campaign, and he promised that no nation which favored peace need fear British arms. It was a promise which received little support from the British record. It was the expression of an ideal which Great Britain had not attained. It was an ideal totally incompatible with the policy of the balance of power.[64]

Halifax spoke at Edinburgh on October 24th. He explained to his listeners that the British leaders were not satisfied with the existing peace because it was an armed peace. He hoped that a peace of understanding could be attained, but it was too early to say how this might be achieved. He was seemingly conciliatory toward Germany, and he described the Anglo-German declaration as an important step toward obviating existing dangers. He then suggested that Czechoslovakia had been saved at Munich, because the Czech state would have been destroyed by war, regardless of the number of Powers participating in war against Germany. Halifax had begun to emphasize the salvation of Czechoslovakia as a principal justification for Munich. This was clever strategy at a time when competent observers were predicting that the Czech state was on the verge of collapse. Halifax was interested in discrediting Munich while appearing to defend it. This was not apparent to all of his listeners, and the speech was well-received in Scotland, where there was much less dissatisfaction with the Munich agreement than in England.[65]

The debate about Munich was resumed in Parliament on November 1, 1938, when Clement Attlee delivered another speech which described the Munich agreement as a tremendous British defeat. Chamberlain replied with a prepared speech. He added a few objections to Attlee's remarks, but he concentrated his principal fire on Lloyd George. The unpredictable Welshman, who later advocated peace with Germany after the defeat of Poland in 1939, had delivered an inflammatory speech against Chamberlain to the American radio audience on October 27, 1938. Chamberlain denounced this speech with great bitterness, and he accused Lloyd George of performing a disservice to the country by claiming that the British Empire was in a condition of decline under Chamberlain's leadership. The debate on Munich continued with sound and fury, and it was not terminated until the following day. Chamberlain at that time won an important parliamentary victory when the April 1938 Anglo-Italian agreement was ratified by an overwhelming vote.[66]

The furor about the Munich agreement might have subsided in the following months had not the Conservative leaders contrived by various means to keep the public in a state of alarm about Germany. A few of the more important instances will illustrate this problem. Earl De la Warr, Education Minister in the Chamberlain Cabinet, insisted in a speech at Bradford on December 4, 1938, that the feeling was prevalent in Great Britain that nothing could ever be done to satisfy Germany. This was a propaganda trick designed to create the very opinion which he claimed existed. It was tantamount to saying that the appeasement policy which culminated at Munich was a farce.[67] Prime Minister Chamberlain pointedly declared in the House of Commons on December 7th that he did not disagree with the inspired remarks of his Minister. On December 13th he delivered a speech stressing the importance of his coming visit to Italy, and praising the increased tempo of the armament campaign and the support which it enjoyed.[68]

Sir Auckland Geddes, the Administrator of the British National Service Act, predicted in a speech on January 17, 1939, that the British people would be in the front line of a coming war, and he explicitly urged them to hoard food supplies in anticipation of this eventuality. This horrendous suggestion produced great public alarm. Geddes added that the British Air Force would take a heavy toll of the invading bombers which he had conjured with frightening clarity, and he urged the British people to show the world that they did not fear war.[69]

The most provocative of these speeches was delivered on January 23, 1939, by Chamberlain himself. Chamberlain urged public support of the national service program, "which will make us ready for war." He denied that Great Britain ever would begin a war, but his next statement demolished whatever assurance one might have deduced from this announcement. He warned that Great Britain might participate in a war begun by others. This was a different situation than responding to an attack on Great Britain or on British interests. Chamberlain was embracing the doctrine of preventive war which had been denounced publicly by Hoare three months earlier. That the British leaders were not at all accurate in their estimates of the respective strength of such Powers as Germany or the Soviet Union illustrated the supremacy of the balance of power policy. It was an evil omen for the future.[70]

Tory Confidence in War Preparations

The alarmist public utterances of the British leaders, when Hitler had done nothing contrary to the Anglo-German declaration or the Munich agreement, were mild compared to statements made through the channels of secret diplomacy. The January 1939 visit of Halifax and Chamberlain to Rome offered eloquent testimony of hostile British intentions toward Germany. The British leaders were in excellent spirits because of the unexpected successes of the aerial armament campaign after the Munich conference. The production of British fighter aircraft was 25% beyond the figure which had been predicted at the time of Munich in the early autumn of 1938.[71]

The American expert Charles Lindbergh, who lived in England, made a considerable impression on the English leaders before Munich with his report on German air power. Lindbergh praised the quality of German aerial armament in the strongest terms which the facts would permit. He was glad to contribute what he could to pointing out the senselessness of a new European war, and he surmised correctly that the British attitude was the key factor in deciding whether or not there would be such a war. He was overjoyed by the news of

Munich, and he sincerely hoped that peace had been saved.[72]

Unfortunately, the British leaders realized that the German lead in the air was very narrow in 1938. They were not merely interested in defense against a possible German aerial offensive. They hoped that their own air power would be a decisive offensive instrument in a future war. British aerial strategy since 1936 had been based on the doctrine of mass attacks against objectives far behind the military front. Their strategy contrasted sharply with that of the Germans, who hoped that aerial bombardment would be restricted to frontline military action in the event of war. The difference in strategy was reflected in the types of aircraft produced by the two countries. Germany produced many light and medium bombers for tactical operations in support of ground troops, but the major British emphasis was on the construction of heavy bombers to attack civilian objectives far behind the front. The British Defence Requirements Committee decided as early as February 1934 that "the ultimate potential enemy" in any major war would be Germany.[73]

The British in the Spring of 1938 were hoping to build 8,000 military aircraft in the year beginning April 1939, and this goal was later achieved and surpassed. They had expected to build only 4,000 military aircraft in the year April 1938 to April 1939, but they were far ahead of schedule by January 1939, and their key secret defense weapon, the "radar project," had made gigantic strides since 1935. The British leaders and experts were concerned about their air defenses, but they had not lost sight of a possible aerial offensive against the civilian population of Germany. The ratio of fighters to bombers in the autumn of 1938 program of Air Minister Sir Kingsley Wood was 1:1.7. The constuction of medium bombers had been discontinued, and the emphasis was solely on heavy bombers capable of attacking distant objectives. The British leaders admitted that defensive preparation of British civilian centers to meet German retaliation bombing was "insufficient to dispel anxiety" during the final months before the outbreak of World War II. Nevertheless, they were convinced that they were reasonably secure against successful German retaliation, and hence the strategy for the bombardment of the German civilian masses was developed with single-minded energy.[74]

Mussolini Frightened by Halifax and Chamberlain

It is not surprising that the sudden and unexpected increase in military power made the British leaders more aggressive in attitude, and this was reflected in their conversations with the Italian leaders. It is interesting to compare the British and Italian records of these talks. Two of the principal conversations included Chamberlain, Halifax, Mussolini, and Ciano, one included Halifax and Ciano, and one included Chamberlain and Mussolini. The first conversation of the four leaders took place at Mussolini's office in the Palazzo Venezia in Rome on the afternoon of January 11, 1939. The British record noted that Mussolini pledged Italy to a policy of peace for internal reasons, and for the general stability of Europe. The Italian leader asserted that a new war could destroy civilization, and he deplored the failure of the Four Munich Powers to cooperate more closely to preserve peace. He reminded Chamberlain and Halifax that he had envisaged close cooperation when he proposed a Four Power Pact of consultation and friendship among Great Britain, France, Italy, and Germany in 1933. He favored the limitation of arms. The Jewish question was discussed, and Mussolini stated his personal opinion that the best solution would be for all Jews to come under the laws of a sovereign Jewish state, although they need not all live there. Mussolini was concerned about the British attitude toward Germany. Chamberlain declared that he had considered the possibility of conversations with the Germans toward the end of 1938, but that he had changed his mind. He claimed that he had reconsidered because he was disappointed in the German attitude.

A conversation took place between Halifax and Ciano on the morning of January 12, 1939, at the office of the Italian Foreign Minister in the Palazzo Chigi. This conversation was devoted entirely to problems connected with the Spanish Civil War. Ciano gave Halifax assurances that Italy intended to withdraw her volunteers from Spain, and that she did not intend to establish military bases in that country.

Mussolini, Ciano, Chamberlain, and Halifax met at the Palazzo Venezia again on the afternoon of January 12, 1939. Franco-Italian relations were on the agenda. The Italian leaders insisted that the mysterious recent demonstrations against France in the Italian Chamber of Deputies on November 30, 1938, were entirely spontaneous. They blamed the French for much of the recent tension between Italy and France, which had culminated in this incident. Chamberlain turned the discussion to Germany. He claimed to be impressed by rumors of sinister German intentions. He had heard that Germany was planning to establish an independent Ukraine, and to attack Great Britain, France, Poland, and the Soviet Union. Mussolini assured the British leaders that German armaments were defensive, and that Hitler had no plans for an independent Ukraine or for attacks on the various countries which Chamberlain had mentioned. He added that Germany desired peace. Chamberlain disagreed. He declared that German arms were more than sufficient to deal with attacks from countries immediately adjacent to Germany, and that hence the Germans must be harboring aggressive plans. He claimed that Great Britain, on the other hand, was merely concerned with defending herself from the German menace. He defended the extremists of the British Conservative Party, and he denied that anyone, including Churchill, advocated a British military offensive against Germany.

The British and Italian leaders agreed that it would be difficult to guarantee the Czechs, and the British mentioned a guarantee formula which the French had previously rejected. This formula stipulated no aid to the Czechs unless three of the Four Munich Powers agreed that aggression had taken place. Mussolini mentioned a series of requirements, including the need for stable conditions within the Czech state, which would have to be met before a guarantee could be considered. The conversation concluded with comments about the British General Election planned for the autumn of 1940 and the Rome International Exposition scheduled for 1942. Mussolini was much concerned about plans for the Rome Exposition, and Chamberlain made the obvious remark that the British would like to participate.

Chamberlain and Mussolini discussed the general situation, following a dinner at the British Embassy on the evening of Friday, January 13, 1939. Chamberlain told Mussolini that he distrusted Hitler, and that he remained unconvinced by Mussolini's arguments that the German armament program was defensive in scope. He hoped to make Mussolini uneasy by referring to a rumor that Germany had launched special military preparations in the region near the Italian frontier. He assured Mussolini categorically that Great Britain and France, in contrast to 1938, were now prepared to fight Germany.[75]

The Italian record of these conversations corresponded closely to the British record in the matter of topics, but there were decisive differences of emphasis and factual points. The Italians gave German Ambassador Mackensen a copy of their record of the January 11, 1939, conversation on January 12th, and Mackensen forwarded the information to Hitler at once. Mussolini told the British leaders that the Anglo-Italian pact of April 16, 1938, was an essential factor in the conduct of Italian policy. He said that Italy's association with Germany in the Axis was also important, but he emphasized that this association was not "of an exclusive nature (*di natura esclusiva*)." He added that Italy had no "direct ambitions (*ambizione diretta*)" in Spain. Chamberlain thanked Mussolini for his assurance that peace was essential for the consolidation of Italy, and he added that he and Halifax had never doubted the good will of Mussolini. He contrasted his attitudes toward Italy and toward Germany, and he complained that he had seen no signs of German friendship toward Great Britain since Munich.

Mussolini promised that he would make an effort to improve Franco-Italian relations. He hoped that this would be possible after the end of the Spanish war. Chamberlain complained of "feverish armament" in Germany, and alleged German offensive plans. Mussolini, in denying that such plans existed, placed primary emphasis on the point that German defensive requirements should be considered in relation to the Russian armament campaign. It is significant that there is no mention of this point in the British record.[76]

The Red Army had been vastly increased in recent months, and an attempt was underway to replace recently purged Red Army officers with officers from the reserves, and with officers from the training schools in the younger cadres. The incorporation of reserve units in the Red Army in late 1938 had increased the Russian peacetime army to two million men, which was nearly triple the number of peacetime German soldiers. A Supreme War Council directed by Stalin had been created in 1938 to supervise the War Council headed by People's Commissar of Defense Voroshilov. The Red Army and Red Air Force were under Voroshilov and the Red Fleet was under a separate command. The new Council under Stalin was intended to coordinate the commands in a program of preparation for war. The *Krasnaya Zvezda* (*Red Star*) on the morning of January 11, 1939, demanded the victory of Communism over the entire world. These were public facts available to everyone, but the British leaders preferred to believe that Stalin's arrest of 20,000 officers had banned the danger of Communism. Their prejudice against Communism prompted them to belittle Soviet power. The British considered Mussolini's comments about their own complacency toward the Russian threat too insignificant to be included in their record of the conversations at Rome.[77]

The British also neglected another major point made by Mussolini. The Italian leader could understand British concern about rumors suggesting an impending attack on their own country or on neighboring France. He could not appreciate their apparent concern about the welfare of the Soviet leadership. Mussolini denied that Hitler had plans for the dismemberment of Russia, but he could not refrain from commenting that the end of Communism in Russia would be a blessing for the Russian people. This remark did not impress the British leaders. Mussolini swore that he knew with absolute certainty that Hitler had no hostile plans against the West.

Mussolini also was surprised that Chamberlain was predicting trouble between Germany and Poland. He shared the optimism of Hitler that an understanding between Germany and Poland could be attained. Polish Foreign Minister Beck had recently visited Hitler, and the German Foreign Minister was scheduled to visit Beck at Warsaw in a few days. The Italian leader was unaware that Polish Ambassador Raczynski in London had requested British support against Germany in December 1938, or that Halifax had expressed a desire to support Poland at Danzig as early as September 1938. Mussolini warned Chamberlain not to be influenced by anti-National Socialist propaganda. Chamberlain stridently denied Mussolini's claims about German defensive needs, and he insisted that Russia did not have the strength to be a menace to anyone. One is reminded here of the statement of Anthony Eden in March 1935 that the Soviet Union would not be in a position to wage a war of aggression for fifty years. Mussolini was amazed by Chamberlain's remark, and he repeated that Germany had good reason to fear a hostile coalition of overwhelming strength.

The Italian leader used every possible argument to cope with Chamberlain's anti-German phobia. He cited the Siegfried line, along the German frontier with France and Belgium, as an indication of the defensive nature of German armament. Chamberlain insisted that German armament was far too impressive, and he suggested that Hitler should speak publicly of his desire for peace, if he was truly peaceful. This suggestion astonished Mussolini, and he inquired if Chamberlain was unaware of Hitler's New Year Declaration of January 1, 1939, in which the German leader had professed a fervent desire for the perpetuation of European peace. Mussolini repeated that the current scope of German armament was fully justified by the existing situation. He wished to be helpful in allaying Chamberlain's alleged fear of German intentions. He was willing to cooperate with Chamberlain in organizing a conference for qualitative disarmament as soon as the war in Spain had ended. Chamberlain displayed no interest in this proposal.

Mussolini referred to the inner instability of the Czech state, the failure of the Czechs to dissolve their ties with Russia or to adopt a policy of neutrality, and the fact that the new Czech borders in many directions had not received their final definition on the ground by international border commissions. The Italian record was emphatic in stating that Chamberlain agreed with Mussolini's remarks about the Czechs.[78]

The Italian record also shows that Mussolini was disappointed by Chamberlain's attitude. The visit was successful from the British perspective, but unsuccessful from the Italian standpoint. The British leaders had hoped to intimidate Mussolini, and to discourage him from supporting Hitler if and when war came. They were successful in this effort, although this diplomatic success was cancelled in 1940 because of the unexpected fall of France. The Italians, on the other hand, had hoped that their assurances would prompt the British to adopt a more tolerant attitude toward Germany and a more cooperative policy toward the settlement of current European problems. They were fully disappointed in this expectation. It was evident that British hostility toward Germany was implacable.

Mussolini discussed the situation with German Ambassador Mackensen at the British Embassy reception on the evening of January 13, 1939. He said that the results of the visit were meager, and he complained that the British had made him feel like a lawyer in one of their courts when he had attempted to explain German armaments and German foreign policy. He left no doubt in Mackensen's mind that the British leaders were ready to find Germany guilty of every crime.[79]

The Germans received further information about the Rome visit from Italian Ambassador Attolico in Berlin on January 17, 1939. This included an excellent condensed summary of the conversation of January 11, 1939. It was followed by a report from Mackensen, which contained an account of the conversation of Chamberlain, Halifax, Mussolini, and Ciano on January 12, 1939. The Germans learned that their armament program provided the main topic of discussion. Mackensen also discovered that Chamberlain had been clever in making table-talk propaganda with Mussolini. Chamberlain referred to Italy and Great Britain as imperial Powers, with colonies overseas, in contrast to Germany, a mere continental nation. This was satisfactory to Hitler, who had no desire to hoist the German flag in distant parts.[80]

It was evident to Mussolini that Germany was threatened by a possible British attack. The British leaders were in full motion against Germany many weeks before their public switch in policy after the German occupation of Prague in March 1939. It is for this reason that the Rome conversations stand out so sharply in the diplomatic history of 1939. Mussolini knew that war would be a disaster, and he hoped that Hitler would be able to avoid it. He made it clear to the Germans that his efforts to allay British prejudice against them had failed. He hoped to play a constructive role in helping to avoid an unnecessary war, but he recognized that his first obligation to his own people was to keep Italy out of a disastrous Anglo-German conflict. It was for this reason that he had been careful not to offend his British guests, and he explained this to the Germans. The suggestion of Churchill that Mussolini was contemptuous of British military strength at this time was inaccurate. Mussolini was sufficiently wise to fear British military power and to recognize the vulnerable position of his own country. Mussolini's decision for war against Great Britain in June 1940 does not alter this fact. He resisted pressure to enter the war during its early months despite a British blockade on Italian trade. The German victories over Great Britain in Norway and France in 1940 altered the situation, and Mussolini entered a war which he believed was nearly finished in order to give his country a voice at the peace conference. He never would have taken this action had it not been for the amazing German victories of 1940 over superior Allied Forces.[81]

Hitler's Continued Optimism

The tragedy which overtook Italy in World War II indicates that Mussolini's alarm at British hostility toward Germany in January 1939 was amply justified. There had been no German moves since Munich. Nevertheless, the same British Prime Minister who had persuaded Hitler to sign the declaration of Anglo-German friendship on September 30, 1938, was branding Germany an aggressor nation in January 1939. His assurance that Great Britain was ready for war with Germany indicated that he envisaged the likelihood of a conflict, and his defense of Churchill's attitude toward Germany was ominous.

Collin Brooks was one of the leading British writers of the 1930's who advocated huge British armaments. He explained in his persuasive book, *Can Chamberlain Save Britain? The Lesson of Munich*, which was written in October 1938, that "the Four Power Conference of Munich in September 1938 gave to the world either an uneasy postponement of conflict or the promise of a lasting peace." This was true, but the promise of lasting peace was undermined by the attitude of the British leaders toward Germany. Brooks was an alarmist. He claimed that Great Britain was in peril because the balance of power was threatened. He called on British youth to be equal to the British imperialistic tradition, and not to be further influenced in their attitudes by the unusually heavy losses suffered by Great Britain in World War I. He reminded his readers that Great Britain had spent 102 years fighting major wars during the past 236 years since 1702, and that she had fought many minor wars during the otherwise peaceful intervals. He recognized that Great Britain had a record of aggressive military action unequalled by any other Power in modern times. He wished British youth to recognize this obvious fact, and to prepare for the new struggle against Germany. He was one of the best examples of the militant England of 1938 which Maring Gilbert and Rich Gott were still seeking to justify with reckless abandon in their chronicle, *The Appeasers*, some twenty-five years later.[82]

Karl Heinz Pfeffer, a cosmopolitan German expert on British and American attitudes, attempted in a 1940 book, *England: Vormacht der buergerlichen Welt (England: Guardian of the bourgeois World)*, to explain British hostility toward Germany during this period. He noted that the alleged British disarmament between World War I and World War II was a myth, but that the British public had been deluged with the peace propaganda of private groups late in 1931, on the eve of the much-heralded general disarmament conference of February 1932. French obstruction wrecked the conference, and Great Britain began to search for justification for an increase in her already considerable armament. Propaganda was needed to overcome the popular longing for peace. The experience of World War I suggested the answer, and this partially explained the initial hate campaign against Germany in the period 1932-1938.

Pfeffer emphasized that German power did not grow at British expense during this period. He expressed the devout wish that the German people would never again accept British claims about the alleged sins of German leaders, and hoped that German experience in the recent *Pax Britannica* would discourage this tendency, which had undermined German morale in 1918. The German middle class had been ruined by inflation during the interwar British peace, the

German farmer class had been brought to the brink of destruction, and the German workers had been exposed to the threat of total unemployment.

Pfeffer wished that the German people would never forget that the contemporary British leaders did not have the correct answers to the problems of the world. Awareness of these facts contributed to the excellent morale which was maintained by the vast majority of the German population throughout World War II.[83]

Hitler had been warned by Mussolini. Ribbentrop's prediction of January 2, 1938, that it would be impossible for Germany to arrive at a lasting agreement with England, before Hitler had completed his program of peaceful revision, had received new confirmation. Hitler hoped that he could complete his program before the British were ready to attack Germany, and that he could persuade them afterward to accept the new situation. This had been the sole answer to the dilemma of British hostility in the age of Bismarck. It offered a fair prospect of success, but a policy of drift offered none at all.

Germany was the major Power in the European region between Great Britain in the West and the Soviet Union in the East. British hostility was reaching a crest, and the aternatives were peace or war. Hitler was in the middle of the stream. He was determined to reach the high bank. He wished to rescue Germany from the swampland of insecurity, decline, and despair. He wished Germany to have the national security and the opportunity for development which had been the heritage of Great Britain and the United States for many generations. He hoped to bring Germany out of danger, and to reach solid ground which was safe from any hostile British tide. He believed that this objective could be attained without harming Great Britain or the United States in any way.

Hitler looked forward to an era of Anglo-American-German cooperation. This would have been the best possible guarantee of stability and peace in the world. There was good reason to believe in January 1939 that this objective could be achieved, although the perils which faced Germany were very great. The worst of these was British hostility after Munich.

Chapter 9

FRANCO-GERMAN RELATIONS

AFTER MUNICH

France an Obstacle to British War Plans

The belligerent attitude of the British leaders by January 1939, and the unwillingness of the Poles to settle their differences with Germany, might seem to
imply that World War II was inevitable by that time. Many people in the Western
world accepted the contention of Halifax and other British leaders after World
War II that an Anglo-German war has been inevitable after the German military
reoccupation of the Rhineland in March 1936.[1] There were some who said that
Hitler's program might have been stopped without war as late as Munich in
September 1938, but that this was the last possible moment when the otherwise
inevitable catastrophe might have been avoided. These opinions were predicated
on the hypothesis that Hitler started World War II. They ignored the fact that
World War II resulted from the British attack on Germany in September 1939.
The British Defence Requirements Committee branded Germany "the ultimate
potential enemy" as early as November 14, 1933, because they considered it
likely that Great Britain would eventually intervene in some quarrel between
Germany and one of her continental neighbors. The British leaders themselves
did not believe that Hitler intended to attack their country.[2]

Hence, it might be concluded that British hostility toward Germany after
Munich, and German-Polish friction in 1938 and 1939, made World War II
inevitable. The British leaders were planning an attack on Germany, and a
German conflict with a continental neighbor such as Poland would provide the
pretext for such an attack. There was no indication that Hitler was about to
present more drastic demands to the Poles after they failed to respond to his
offer of October 1938, but it would be a simple matter for the British leaders
to advise the Poles to provoke Hitler, when British war preparations were
deemed sufficient. European history offered many examples of similar policies.
British Ambassador Buchanan at St. Petersburg in July 1914 urged the Russians
to provoke Germany by ordering a Russian general mobilization against her.

This step encouraged Great Britain to intervene against Germany in a continental war. Napoleon III advised Sardinian Premier Cavour at Plombieres in 1858 to foment a war against Austria, and this step enabled the French to attack the Austrians in the Italian peninsula in 1859. This style of diplomacy was familiar to the British leaders of 1939, and they were sufficiently imaginative and unscrupulous to resort to it in achieving their goal.[3]

The plain truth, however, is that the British had to work very hard until the evening of September 2, 1939, to achieve the outbreak of World War II. The issue was in no sense decided before that time, and there was no justification for the later fatalism which suggested that World War II was inevitable after 1936 or 1938. This fact should eliminate every element of anti-climax in the story of events which preceded September 1939. The fundamental issue of war or peace for Europe remained undecided until the last moment. This would not have been true had Poland been the sole factor in preparing the stage for the British assault. It was true because the British leaders had decided that the participation of France as their ally was the *conditio sine qua non* for the launching of British hositlities against Germany. The French leaders, unlike Halifax, were increasingly critical of the alleged wisdom of a preventive war against Germany. It became evident as time went on that they might call a halt to the British plan of aggression by refusing to support any such scheme. It became clear that the British would have to work hard to push France into war; and there was good reason to hope that this British effort would fail. The leaders of France were eventually regarded in both Italy and Germany as the principal hope for peace.[4]

These circumstances illuminate the key role of France in Europe after the Munich conference. There was a strange and ironical reversal of roles. The French leaders in the past had solicited British support for action in one situation or another, and they had usually been turned down. The British leaders began to press for action against Germany after the Munich conference, and the French, who were inclined to adopt a passive policy, occupied the former British position of deciding whether or not to grant support. The French had considered British support essential in the past, and now the British regarded French support as indispensable.[5]

The difficulty was that the French were habitually inclined to follow the British lead, and a tremendous effort of will was required to deny the importunity of British demands. Furthermore, the British situation was uniquely favorable compared to that of France. The United States and Germany were both intent on establishing intimate and friendly relations with Great Britain. The two countries were also friendly toward France after 1936, but it was obvious that Great Britain occupied the primary place in their consideration. This was not off-set by the French alliance with the Soviet Union, which desired to embroil France and Germany in a war. Lazar Kaganovich, the Soviet Politburo leader and brother-in-law of Stalin, announced in *Izvestia* (*The News*) on January 27, 1934, that a new Franco-German war would promote the interests of the Soviet Union.[6]

The strategy of encouraging a Franco-German war while the Soviet Union remained neutral continued to be the principal feature of Soviet foreign policy. The French leaders faced the combined threats of isolation and British resentment if they failed to do the bidding of Chamberlain and Halifax. It was evident that it would not be easy for France to pursue an independent policy while British pressure was exerted upon her. Nevertheless, the British recognized that Georges Bonnet, the French Foreign Minister after April 1938, was an extremely capable man. They could never assume that France would accept the role of puppet while he was at the Quai d'Orsay.[7]

The Popularity of the Munich Agreement in France

The reception of the Munich agreement in France was very different from that in Great Britain, apart from the initial demonstrations of popular enthusiasm for Daladier and Chamberlain when the two leaders returned from Munich by air to their respective countries.[8] The Munich agreement was received with enthusiasm by the French Parliament on October 4, 1938. The vote of approval for Munich in the French Chamber was an overwhelming 535-75. Premier Daladier delivered a moderate speech in which he stressed that there was hope for peace in Europe again, but that peace was not secure. The discussion of recent French diplomacy was extremely brief. A desire to spoil the atmosphere created at Munich by a protracted controversy, of the type which was raging in England, was conspicuously lacking. There were 73 Communists in the French Chamber of 1938, and 72 were present to vote against the Munich agreement. Only three deputies from other Parties joined the Communists in this vote, and Léon Blum, the leader of the Socialists, was not among them.[9] The triumph of Daladier was complete. It is ironical that Daladier was much more worried than Chamberlain about the reception he would receive at home. The event proved that Munich was politically far more popular in France than in England. Georges Bonnet correctly interpreted this situation as a mandate to conclude a friendship agreement with Germany, and he had the full support of the French Ambassador in Berlin, Francois-Poncet, who had great influence with French business and industry, in the negotiations which followed.[10]

The Popular Front Crisis a Lesson for France

It was fortunate for France that she had a stable Government at last. The Daladier Government, which was appointed in April 1938, had no difficulty in maintaining its position during the remaining months of peace in Europe before the outbreak of World War II. It seemed that the crisis which began with the Stavisky affair and the riots against the French Government in February 1934 was over at last. Furthermore, France began to make rapid strides after November 1938 to terminate the depression which had plagued the country throughout this period. It seemed that more than four years of instability and confusion had prepared the country to accept a greater amount of discipline. It also appeared that France was inclined to draw important conclusions about her foreign policy from the events of this period.[11]

France was the dominant continental Power when the 1934-1938 domestic crisis began. Nevertheless, her position was weakened by the depression and the instability of her Government. Unemployment had increased from 500,000 in 1931 to 1,300,000 at the end of 1933. This was a huge figure for France, which had a much smaller industrial population than Great Britain or Germany, and it did not include partial or seasonal unemployment. In the meantime, a dangerous attitude of complacency, which blocked reforms, was created by the fact that there was a deflation in which prices were falling faster than salaries. The Government had had a deficit budget since 1931, and several plans to increase production and employment by means of public works were defeated. The Government in November 1933 revived the National Lottery, an expedient of the old monarchy, in an endeavor to improve its financial position.

The Left Parties seized upon an old slogan of Joseph Caillaux, the father of the French income tax, that a point arrives where taxes devour taxes. This was true, but the Left used this as a pretext to oppose any increases in direct taxes to cope with the growing deficit. The Government responded by seeking to reduce public expenditure, but to no avail. The Cabinets of Joseph Paul-Boncour, Édouard Daladier, and Albert Sarraut were overthrown on this issue in 1933. Georges Bonnet was Finance Minister in the Sarraut Government, and he employed every possible tactic to gain the support which his predecessors had lacked. Nevertheless, the Chamber rejected his program in November 1933 by a vote of 321-247.[12]

Camille Chautemps formed a Government on November 26, 1933, but the repercussions of the Stavisky affair forced him to resign on short notice in January 1934. A number of paramilitary organizations reflected the dissatisfaction of France at this time. These included the dissatisfied peasants in the *Front Paysan* of Dorgères, the royalist *Camelots du Roi*, and the *Croix de Feu* veteran organization directed by the World War I hero, Colonel de la Rocque. There were also two tiny militant organizations, the *Solidarité française* of Jean Renaud, and the *Francisme* of Marcel Bucard, which believed that current German and Italian methods should be employed to end the crisis in France. The Communists exploited the existence of these groups to claim that France was in danger of a Fascist revolution. The Communist Party was growing rapidly at this time. The Socialist Party had split in May 1933 when young Marcel Déat and his friends rejected the leadership of Léon Blum and formed the Neo-socialists. The Communists gained from the confusion in Socialist ranks and won many converts from both the workers and the bourgeoisie. The prestige of Communism was served by the adherence of leading intellectuals, such as Ramon Fernandez and André Gide, and the growth of the movement created genuine alarm in other sections of the population. The atmosphere in France, and especially at Paris, was charged with tension. Many people were still complacent, but the Stavisky affair, which produced a major eruption of violence, shattered this complacency.[13]

Alexander Stavisky was a reckless criminal, currently conducting a fantastic embezzlement operation at the expense of the municipal credit systems of the cities of Orléans and Bayonne. At Bayonne alone he had seized 300,000,000 francs by the time his operation was exposed by M. de la Baume of the commercial section at the Quai d'Orsay in January 1934. The public was furious at the criminal temerity of yet another Jewish immigrant, not having forgotten the recent Oustric and Hanau scandals. Pressard, the brother-in-law of Premier Chautemps, had aided Stavisky in the issuance of fraudulent remissions, and the brother of the Premier was one of Stavisky's lawyers. Several leaders of the Radical Socialists, the party of Chautemps, were implicated, and one of them, Albert Dalimier, was obliged to resign from the Cabinet at once. Joseph Paul-Boncour was implicated because of his relations with Arlette Simon, the mistress of Stavisky. The public was denied the balm of a trial of the chief culprit. Stavisky fled eastward, and he was found dead near Chamonix with a bullet in his head. The veteran French statesman, André Tardieu, fanned the suspicion that Stavisky had been slain by the police, when he declared that he had at least been able to arrest Oustric and Hanau alive. This bitter jest of a statesman on the Right was echoed by Andre Botta from the Left. Botta explained to the readers of *Le Populaire*, the principal Socialist newspaper, that the police had neglected several opportunities to take Stavisky alive before he fled from Paris. This was no ordinary scandal, and it was evident that a crisis of major proportions was brewing.

It seemed that nearly everyone of importance in French public life had been involved with Stavisky in some way, although this did not necessarily imply a criminal association. Philippe Henriot, a Deputy of the Right, led a passionate attack against the Center Government and the contemporary parliamentary regime in the French Chamber. He received enthusiastic support from *Le Jour*, *La Victoire*, *La Liberté*, and *l'Action Francaise*, the principal newspapers of the Right. The Government responded by resigning on January 29, 1934, following a violent demonstration of 100,000 Parisians. There was a superficial shuffling of ministers, and Edouard Daladier replaced his friend Chautemps as Premier. The new Cabinet was appointed on January 30, 1934. One of its first steps was to retaliate against the Right by removing Chiappe, the Paris Chief Prefect of Police, and by transfering him to Morocco. Chiappe had known Stavisky and he was a leading figure of the Right. He held a key position at Paris. He had feared removal by a Center or Left Government since the election victory of the Left in 1932. He refused to accept the decision of the Daladier Government in 1934, and he had the support of the Paris municipal council. The Right had accepted the challenge of the Government, and the climax of the crisis had arrived.[14]

The Right staged a major demonstration against the Government and in support of Chiappe on February 6, 1934. The demonstrators intended nothing less than the occupation of the Palais-Bourbon where the Chamber met. It was believed that the dispersal of the deputies of the Left election victory of 1932 would clear the way for the appointment of a Government of the Right, which would conduct a major program of reforms. Everything depended on a successful demonstration at the Palais-Bourbon. Thousands of Parisians who had no political connection with the Right participated in the demonstration and shouted the slogan: "Down with the thieves!" The Paris municipal council marched at the head of the demonstration. The regular police organization was loyal to Chiappe, but the Government controlled important reserves. The main question was whether or not the Government would be willing to inflict heavy casualties on the demonstrators. Daladier was reluctant to make this decision, and he resigned on the following day. Edouard Herriot, another Radical Socialist leader, and French President Albert Lebrun did not hesitate. They persuaded Daladier to order the Paris Mobile Guard to protect the Chamber by attacking the demonstrators. The Chamber was in session and the demonstrators were at the portals when the Mobile Guard attack took place at 7:00 p.m. An attempt was made to keep fatalities at a minimum, and it was surprising in view of the scope of the attack that only twenty demonstrators were killed. Many hundreds of Parisians were severely wounded in the debacle. The Communist newspaper, *l'Humanite*, adopted the same line as the Right press on February 7, 1934, when it condemned the Government for attacking the people. This was merely part of the Communist campaign to discredit both the Government and the demonstrators. The defeat of the demonstration of February 6, 1934, played directly into the hands of the Communists. It marked an important turning point in French policy both at home and abroad.15

The 1934-1938 crisis in France was the crisis of the Popular Front. The Popular Front was made possible by the Stavisky affair. The Center and Right were discredited. The propaganda about fascism and insurrectionary plots became increasingly effective as time went on. The Communists were permitted by Stalin to adapt their tactics to this new situation. The Communists suddenly appeared in the guise of the Party of sweetness and light, which demanded nothing for itself and merely wished to align with other "democratic" groups to protect the existing order against the fascist wolves. The Socialist Party under the leadership of Léon Blum was not adverse to a close alliance with the Communists. It was believed that such an alliance would enable the Socialist Party to maintain its hold over its more radical following. Édouard Herriot, the Radical Socialist mayor of Lyons, had long relied on Communist support to maintain his hold over the metropolis of the Rhone. Blum, who preferred Herriot to Daladier, argued persuasively that the Radical Socialist Party, which held the proud reputation of providing most of the leaders of the Third Republic, could best recover its prestige and position by forming a coalition with Socialism and Communism. The desperate situation of the Radical Party promoted the majority of its leaders, by 1935, to accept this experiment, and Daladier was extremely clever in seizing the initiative in this movement from his rival, Herriot. The Popular Front Government under the leadership of Léon Blum did not achieve power until the overwhelming Left election victory of May 1936. Nevertheless, the Popular Front movement received its impetus from the events of February 1934, and it was the dominant trend in French public life from that time.16

Édouard Daladier and Édouard Herriot were the principal leaders of the Radical Socialist Party during this period. They had entirely different attitudes toward the Popular Front experiment. Herriot was sincerely pro-Communist, and he also favored the closest possible alliance between France and the Soviet Union. Daladier was much less enthusiastic about the Soviet Union, and he distrusted the French Communists and the Popular Front experiment, which he accepted for tactical reasons. Nevertheless, Herriot represented the Right within the Radical Socialist Party, and Daladier represented the Left. The Party was remarkably flexible in matters of dogma.17

The French Government press favored the Popular Front movement by claiming immediately after February 6, 1934, that it had been saved from a fascist revolution. Gaston Doumergue, a former French President who was in retirement at Toulouse, was called upon to form an emergency Government. Louis Barthou, whose policy gave the *coup de grace* to the international disarmament conference in April 1934, was appointed Foreign Minister. The new Government included Neo-socialists, but no Socialists, and it was opposed by both Socialists and Communists as an instrument of the "fascist revolutionaries" in countless demonstrations. Conditions in France remained chaotic. Eight persons were killed and three hundred were wounded in a Communist demonstrations on February 9, 1934. The first Popular Front gesture was a call for a general strike on February 12, 1934, by a committee which included the Communist, Jacques Doriot, the Radical Socialist, Gaston Bergery, and the Socialist, Georges Monnet. The action was disavowed, and Doriot and Bergery resigned from their respective Parties, but it was a portent of things to come.[18]

The Doumergue Government fell before the end of 1934, following the scandal which accompanied the assassinations of King Alexander of Yugoslavia and French Foreign Minister Barthou at Marseilles. The customary police protective measures, which ordinarily accompany the visit of a foreign chief of state, had been conspicuously lacking. The retirement of Albert Sarraut, Minister of Interior, and Henry Chéran, Minister of Justice, failed to appease the critics, and the Government was brought down. Louis Barthou died of his wounds on October 15, 1934, and Raymond Poincaré, the elder statesman who had been his closest friend, died on the following day. The Socialists were restrained in their mourning for the passing of the two statesmen of the Right. Léon Blum wrote an article which explained why Poincaré, despite his fame, had not been a great man.[19]

Louis Barthou had adopted a militantly hostile policy toward Germany during the short time that he was at the Quai d'Orsay. Barthou had been a member of the group of French *bellicistes* before 1914, who had silently and methodically prepared a war of revenge against Germany for 1870, and his attitude toward William II, Stresemann, and Hitler was the same. He claimed that he intended to frustrate the "congenital megalomania" of Germany. He advocated a series of "eastern Locarno" pacts with Italy, the Little Entente, and the Soviet Union, in an effort to keep the Germans pinned permanently within their existing frontiers. On April 20, 1934, he departed for Warsaw and a grand tour of the eastern capitals. He was particularly worried about Polish policy toward Germany and the Czechs, and he received scant solace in Warsaw. He knew that Foreign Minister Sir John Simon in Great Britain opposed his alliance policy. Barthou decided that the time had come to award the Soviet Union a more prominent place in European affairs.

The first step was to bring the Soviet Union into the League of Nations. The Swiss, Dutch, and Portuguese delegates at Geneva delivered valiant speeches against this step, but Barthou replied that the Soviet Union would rejuvenate the League of Nations. Barthou also sought to improve relations with Italy, and to tighten relations among Czechoslovakia, Rumania, and Yugoslavia. His major move was to prepare the foundation for the Franco-Soviet alliance which was concluded in 1935. A French commitment to conclude this pact was made by Barthou before his death at Marseilles.[20]

The 1935 Laval Policy Undermined by Vansittart

The year 1935 in France was dominated by the valiant effort of Pierre Laval to conduct a sensible French policy despite the rising threat of the Popular Front. He almost succeeded, but this did not reduce the repercussions when he failed. The failure of the Laval policy and the triumph of the Popular Front was disastrous for the position of France in Europe.

Pierre Laval was one of the most realistic French statesmen of all time. Like Briand and Caillaux, he advocated the Franco-German reconciliation embodied later in the policy of Charles de Gaulle and the French Fifth Republic. He was a man of courage, and his efforts to help France in the adverse circumstances following her military defeat in 1940 knew no limits. His execution in 1945, when the Communist tide was running high in France, was the worst of the many judicial crimes of that era. His influence on French politics from 1936 to 1940, following the overthrow of his Government in January 1936, was slight. Nevertheless, he used what influence he possessed in 1938 and 1939 to prevent France from joining Great Britain in an attack upon Germany. He had no dealings during those years with either official or private personages from Germany. Laval was especially important because of his influence on Georges Bonnet in the struggle to keep the peace.

Swarthy Pierre Laval came from Auvergne peasant stock, and he was said to have inherited Arab blood from his maternal line. He looked more like a Mongol, but he had the faculty to make a political asset of his distinctive and unusual appearance. He was not an eloquent speaker, but he was extremely intent upon being understood, and for this reason he became a master at communicating his ideas. He was never at a loss for a reply. He was a Socialist from 1903 to 1920, and afterward he was an independent. He was once asked during the early period whether he chose the red flag or the tricolor, and he replied, "I choose both." Auguste Blanqui, the great French independent theoretician of the 19th century, was the father of his socialism rather than Karl Marx or Léon Blum. When he was chided after 1920 for having no Party affiliation, Laval replied, "Isolation is a weakness, but independence is a force."[21]

Laval was held in high esteem by many of the leading Frenchmen of his day. He was the favorite of Aristide Briand, the eminent French diplomat who advocated a sincere policy of appeasement toward Germany until his death in 1932. He was especially close to Joseph Caillaux, the French financial genius, the leading figure in the French Senate and a courageous fighter for peace. During the 1930's, Laval also established close relations with André Tardieu, who, along with Caillaux, was one of the two principal French elder statesmen after the death of Poincaré. He failed to establish a close basis of cooperation with Pierre-Etienne Flandin despite a similarity of views, and this was a handicap in the political careers of both men.

Laval was eleven times a Cabinet Minister, and four times a Premier of France before the outbreak of World War II. He moved from the Chamber of Deputies to the Senate at the age of 41 in 1927. He was mayor of the Paris suburb of d'Aubervillers continuously for more than 20 years after 1923, and it was customary for him to be in the city hall office at least twice a week even when he was Premier. He earned up to 120,000 francs a year as a lawyer in the period from 1919-1927. He invested his money wisely in newspaper and radio stock, and he bought several valuable pieces of property. He was never immensely wealthy, and the Court which convicted him in 1945 was informed by financial experts of the perfect regularity and honesty of his financial operations.

Laval was appointed Foreign Minister in the Flandin Government of November 13, 1934, and he continued to conduct French foreign policy when he formed his own Government on June 7, 1935. He had an extremely clear conception of foreign policy. He recognized that either there would be a Franco-German *entente* or a catastrophe in Europe. He naturally wished France to negotiate an *entente* with Germany from a position of superior strength, but he did not fall into a rage and vow that the Germans should be destroyed, when France lost that position through no fault of his own. Laval recognized that Germany was intrinsically far more powerful than France, and that French supremacy depended upon the maintenance of an alliance system. Laval did not wish to alienate the Soviet Union by disavowing the alliance commitment which Barthou had made, but he hoped to keep the Soviet Union at a distance and to emasculate any Franco-Soviet alliance, just as Joseph Paul-Boncour had emasculated the Four Power Pact of Mussolini in 1933. Laval was mainly intent on consolidating French relations with Great Britain and Italy, and he recognized that a too close association with the Soviet Union might wreck that policy. He was also aware of the treacherous and disloyal foreign policy of the Soviet Union.[22]

Laval recognized the importance of the Italian position with perfect clarity. Italy was the one nation which could be relied upon to frustrate German aspirations in Austria. Laval recognized that the 1919 peace treaties contained many injustices toward Germany, but he was a conservative in foreign policy, and he feared that a successful German program of territorial revision would upset the European equilibrium and lead to disaster. Mussolini had delivered a speech at Milan on October 6, 1934, three days before the Croatian terrorists attacked Alexander and Barthou at Marseilles. The speech had been largely overlooked in the ensuing excitement, but Laval had not forgotten it. Mussolini had advocated the establishment of a Franco-Italian *entente*. Laval knew that Barthou had plans for the conclusion of an alliance with Italy. The *rapprochement* with Italy became the main feature of Laval's policy. It is easy to see in retrospect that Franco-Italian relations were the crucial European issue in 1935. The Popular Front in France hoped to frustrate Franco-Italian reconciliation.

The difference between the policies of Barthou and of Laval was mainly one of emphasis. They both desired alliances with Italy and the Soviet Union, but Barthou had placed primary emphasis on the Soviet Union, which was a mistake from the French standpoint, and Laval correctly placed major emphasis on the alliance with Italy. Barthou wished a preponderant French position form which to humiliate Germany. Laval wished to appease Germany. Barthou advocated a policy of hate, and Laval pursued a policy of peace.

The situation in Italy at this time was extremely favorable for France. Mussolini, like many Italians, had been greatly influenced by French thought, and he wrote that Sorel, Péguy, and Lagardelle were the main influences on his intellectual development. He had advocated Italian participation in World War I as the ally of France in 1914. He delivered a series of pronouncements from the autumn of 1932 until 1935 in favor of a definitive accord between Italy and France. He welcomed the appointment of Senator Henri de Jouvenel as French Ambassador to Rome in December 1932. The common Franco-Italian action against the German-Austrian customs union of 1931 had created a bond between the two countries. Mussolini dreamed of Latin cooperation in the Mediterranean region, and he did not begrudge France her military superiority. He declared without the slightest resentment in January 1935 that France had the finest army in the world.[23]

The French attitude toward Italy was complicated by several factors. The Little Entente of Rumania, Czechoslovakia, and Yugoslavia enjoyed great prestige with the permanent officials at the Quai d'Orsay, and these "succession states" resented the Italian policy of supporting truncated Austria and Hungary. They failed to realize that Austria and Hungary would come under German influence if Italian support was withdrawn, although King Alexander of Yugoslavia had said that he would rather see Italian macaroni than German sausage at Trieste. The French press was widely subsidized by the Czechs, who disbursed huge sums in France during this period. Many journals declared that every attempt to improve Franco-Italian relations was treason to the Little Entente.

Important sections of the press of the French Left believed that insulting Italy was a solemn duty, and they denounced attempts to improve Franco-Italian relations as ideological treason. The Italian press naturally retaliated, and it was difficult to terminate the press war which followed between the two countries. Jouvenel asked his superiors to take the usual measures to restrain the French press, but he received the trite answer that in this case such action would be contrary to "the free expression of opinion." When he protested the tone of the Italian press at the Palazzo Chigi, he received the obvious reply that the Italians were merely retaliating. The rising tide of the Popular Front in France made the situation more perilous than ever before.

Mussolini's attitude toward Germany was similar to Laval's. The Italian leader believed that for reasons of his own prestige he should not permit Hitler to triumph in Austria, but he hoped to establish friendly relations with Germany. He told Jan Szembek in 1933 that he would be willing to mediate between Germany and Poland for an agreement which would give Germany an extra-territorial transit connection with East Prussia, and he noted that Szembek did not seem hostile to the idea. He told Jouvenel that France should exert pressure on Poland, and that Italy should apply pressure on Germany in an attempt to promote a German-Polish agreement. Mussolini often employed a favorite aphorism: "One is not able to make Europe without Germany." Nevertheless, he hoped to establish closer relations with France than with Germany. Winston Churchill was impressed with Mussolini's enthusiasm for France, and he had declared as early as 1927 that "I would be a Fascist if I were an Italian."[24]

Laval visited Rome in January 1935. He actually made the visit which had been planned and scheduled by Barthou. A Franco-Italian accord was concluded at the Palazzo Farnese in Rome on January 6, 1935. The provisions concerning Ethiopia were crucial because of the crisis which had begun with the Ethiopian attack on the Italian post at Wal-Wal, Somaliland, in October 1934. Laval recognized that French acceptance of Italian expansion in East Africa would be valuable in retaining Italian support against Hitler's aspirations in Austria. The secret clauses of the general agreement provided that France was economically disinterested in Ethiopia, except for the Djibuti-Addis Ababa railroad which France controlled. A declaration of economic disinterest and a free hand had long been identical terms in the settlement of colonial revalry among the imperialist Powers. Mussolini took the initiative for a military *entente* with France on January 12, 1935, after the departure of Laval, and important conversations followed between General Gamelin and General Badoglio, the French and Italian military leaders. It seemed that Franco-Italian relations had been placed on a solid basis. The difficulty was that the Popular Front and the British leaders might seek to frustrate the realization of Italian aspirations in Ethiopia.[25]

The conversations between Anthony Eden and Mussolini at Rome on June 24-25, 1935, were a bad omen. Italian Foreign Minister Raffaele Guariglia claimed that Mussolini was patient with Eden, but the Italian leader objected to the conclusion of the Anglo-German naval pact of June 18, 1935. This pact was a violation of the Versailles Treaty, and the British had concluded it without consulting Italy and France. Eden was piqued, and he was tactless in his treatment of Mussolini. He had been offended by Mussolini's speech at Cagliari, Sardinia, on June 8, 1935. The Italian leader had declared that "we imitate to the letter those who gave us the lesson." The reference to British imperialism was not appreciated by Eden, and the Mussolini-Eden conversations ended on an unfriendly note.

The position of Laval was not enviable. He was caught between the fires of British prejudice toward Italy, and Popular Front hatred of Fascism. He received strong support from Sir Robert Vansittart, the Permanent Secretary at the British Foreign Office, who deplored Eden's prejudice against Mussolini. Nevertheless, it was the indiscretion of Vansittart at Paris in December 1935 which upset the situation altogether, and which produced the alienation of Italy from France despite the efforts of Laval. It is amusing to read in the *Autobiography of Lord Vansittart* that "the usual indiscretion occurred at the Quai d'Orsay." In this instance it was Vansittart, a British guest at the Quai d'Orsay, who committed the fatal indiscretion. It is ironical that Vansittart, who was obsessed by hatred of Germany, did more than anyone else to aid Hitler to win Italian friendship at a crucial moment. This friendship was the necessary foundation for Hitler's program of peaceful territorial revision.[26]

The indiscretion of Vansittart was made to Geneviève Tabouis. She detested Pierre Laval, whom she recognized as the disciple of Caillaux and Briand. She preached what she considered to be the correct foreign policy of France from the pages of *l'Oeuvre*, a newspaper of the Left for "intellectuals." She believed that Léon Blum and the Popular Front could provide the ideal leadership for the implementation of this policy. She blamed the assassinations of Barthou and King Alexander in October 1934 on a "Nazi plot," although she had not the slightest evidence other than Communist propaganda to support this charge. She borrowed her techniques in journalism from the Communists, and she favored the closest possible collaboration between France and the Soviet Union.

She exploited her position as a journalist in 1935 to accompany Laval on his various missions in the hope of compromising him in some way. She was with

Laval at Rome in January 1935, at London in February 1935, at Stresa in April 1935, and at Moscow in May 1935. She suspected at Geneva in September 1935 that there was some friction between Laval and British Foreign Secretary Sir Samuel Hoare about the handling of the Ethiopian question. She met Sir Robert Vansittart at an aristocratic Parisian salon on December 5, 1935. Vansittart told her that Hoare was coming to Paris to complete a plan for the conciliation of Italy at Ethiopian expense, at a time when Great Britain was supposedly leading the League of Nations in a collective security campaign against Italy. Vansittart added that he was working with colleagues at the Quai d'Orsay for the preparation of this plan. This was virtually all that Tabouis needed to know to frustrate the success of the project. Secrecy would be necessary for at least a few days until the consent of Italy and Ethiopia had been obtained for the plan. Vansittart had imagined in his boundless vanity that Tabouis would respect his confidence, but he was mistaken. He believed that she would be obedient to him, because he was the recognized dean of the school which preached the destruction of Germany, but the hatred of Tabouis for Laval was greater than her admiration of Vansittart.[27]

The last conversation between Hoare and Laval took place on December 8, 1935. Tabouis had hurried to London in the meantime to gain further information. Laval had issued an order at the Quai d'Orsay that there should be no public reference to his negotiation with Hoare, and Tabouis was merely guessing about certain details of the projected plan. She consulted with the French journalist, André Geraud (Pertinax), who equalled her in his enthusiasm for a Franco-German war. The alleged Hoare-Laval plan was published by Tabouis in *l'Oeuvre* and by Geraud in *l'Echo de Paris* in France on December 13, 1935, and Tabouis also had arranged for it to appear in the *Daily Telegraph* in London. The result was a storm of British public protest which prompted Prime Minister Baldwin, the master of expediency, to sacrifice both Hoare and the plan on December 18, 1935. The breach which resulted between Italy on the one hand and Great Britain and France on the other wrecked the projected *entente* between Italy and France. Mussolini proceeded to complete the conquest of Ethiopia in defiance of the Western Powers.[28]

Laval struggled hard to maintain his position, and for a time it seemed that he might succeed. Tabouis upbraided Édouard Herriot at a banquet held by Maurice de Rothschild on December 26, 1935, for continuing to support the Laval Cabinet. Herriot withdrew his support on January 23, 1936, and the six Radical Socialist members resigned from the Laval Cabinet. The Popular Front was truimphant, and an election campaign was launched which was destined to bring the Left an unprecedented political triumph in May 1936. The French Chamber approved the Franco-Soviet alliance pact on February 27, 1936, and Hitler reoccupied the Rhineland on March 7, 1936. Italy was lost, the Soviet Union was unreliable, and Great Britain failed to support France in the Rhineland crisis. Tabouis was triumphant, and the foreign policy of Laval was in ruins. French preponderance on the European continent was lost within a few weeks after the resignation of Laval.

The Preponderant Position of France Wrecked by Leon Blum

The attitude of Léon Blum, the Popular Front leader, toward a *rapprochement* between France and Italy had been clear throughout 1935. This attitude was the primary influence on the actions of Geneviève Tabouis and Édouard Herriot. Blum made the following statement at the time of the Laval visit to Rome in January 1935: "For the first time, a French minister is the guest of the assassin of Matteotti. For the first time, a representative of the French Republic recognizes in the tyrant of Italy a chief of state by the deferential initiative of his visit." The Communist method of smearing was clearly in evidence. There was not the slightest indication that Mussolini had had any advance knowledge of the fate of the Socialist leader, Matteotti, who had died from a heart attack during a beating he had received from local Fascist strongmen in 1926. This was an isolated incident in Italy, and it had taken place more than eight years earlier. The Soviet Union in the meantime had purged and killed hundreds of prominent Bolsheviks who were accused of opposition. Nevertheless, Blum did not raise the slightest objection to the visit of Laval to Stalin at Moscow in May 1935. Blum was much too ensnared by his own ideological prejudices to offer France effective leadership during this difficult period.[29]

The Albert Sarraut Government held office in France from January until June 1936. It was correctly described by the French press of the time as a mere caretaker regime which awaited the coming of Blum.[30] The Communists, in the elections of April and May 1936, increased their strength in the French Chamber from 10 to 73, and the Socialists came up from 97 to 146. The Radical Socialists agreed to participate in a coalition Government headed by Blum, and the Communists agreed to vote for it. The Popular Front was in the saddle at last, and the country was virtually paralyzed with 1,500,000 industrial workers on strike by June 1936. Mob violence was resumed, and five persons were killed and three hundred wounded in a demonstration at Clichy. The social security program of Blum produced a rapid decline of French production. The program was barely launched on January 13, 1937, when Blum announced in the face of overwhelming difficulties that the time had arrived for a "necessary pause." It was evident by the time the great Paris International Exposition opened on May 1, 1937, that the Popular Front experiment had failed in the economic, social, and political spheres.[31]

Léon Blum responded by requesting sweeping personal decree powers from the French Chamber on June 15, 1937, although he always had denounced others who had requested such powers. The Popular Front influence was sufficient to pass the measure in the Chamber by a vote of 346-247, but Joseph Caillaux succeeded in bringing down the Government with a vote of no-confidence in the Senate. Caillaux motivated his opposition with the explanation that the Blum decree would provoke the flight of capital from France to an unprecedented degree. The Blum Government resigned on June 21, 1937. Caillaux later explained that he had favored giving Blum every chance to prove himself, and that he had sought to advise him by referring him to the basic precepts of Jean Jaurès, the great French Socialist leader who had been assassinated by militarists in July 1914.[32] Blum blamed his failure on the fact that he was limited in his policies by his need to collaborate with the Radical Socialists, and he complained during World War II that bourgeois rule had remained uninterrupted in France since 1789. He also blamed the Communists for obstructing his program, and he argued that the ideal solution of European problems would have been to crush Germany by military action in 1933. The Popular Front in practice proved to be a fiasco in which coherent foreign and domestic policies were conspicuously lacking.[33]

The overthrow of Blum in June 1937 did not end the Popular Front era. Everyone knew that he would make another bid for power. The Socialist press advocated stripping the French Senate of its powers, and the Communists agreed to participate in a new Popular Front Cabinet. The Socialists accepted this offer, but the Radical Socialists refused. President Lebrun appointed Chautemps to form a Government, and Blum was included as Vice-Premier. No one was satisfied with the prevailing uncertain situation, and there was a clamor of voices asking for a new lease of life or a decent burial for the Popular Front. Chautemps failed to maintain his coalition with the Socialists and his Government resigned on January 14, 1938. He headed an interim Government of Radical Socialists for a few weeks until Blum was again appointed Premier. Blum won a vote of confidence before the Chamber on March 17, 1938, but he was soon overthrown again by the Senate. Blum was ready to quit, and the Popular Front era was over.[34]

The Radical Socialist Party, under the leadership of Daladier, Chautemps, and Bonnet, had recovered from the Stavisky affair André Tardieu, the French elder statesman, wrote a brilliant analysis of their position in 1938. They were the Party of Tradition, and Daniel Halévy had traced their origins to the reign of Louis Philippe. They were the Party of Inconsistency. They had overthrown Governments of the Right in 1923 and 1928, but they had entered Governments of the Right in 1926 and 1934. They had suffered lamentable reverses when they headed Governments in 1885, 1896, 1898, 1924, 1932, 1934, 1937, and early 1938, but they had amazing powers of recuperation. Anatole France had said: "They govern badly, but they defend themselves well."

Tardieu found that their Party doctrine was "infinitely vague." Their existing doctrine was the utilitarianism and materialism of 19th century liberalism. They simultaneously exalted both the individual and the state in the 20th century, and they claimed a monopoly of the revolutionary tradition of 1789. Their position on constitutional reform was clear. They refused to a) reduce the number of parliamentary deputies, b) reform the electoral system, c) permit dissolution and new elections when Cabinets were overthrown, and d) allow for the introduction of popular referendum or popular initiative. They defended the *status quo* with tenacity.

Tardieu recognized their complacency, which contrasted with his own attitude. He had been thrice Premier and eleven times a Minister, and he had decided in 1933 that the current regime was not tolerable for France. He complained that when he expressed these views to the Radical Socialists, they wondered if he had become an imbecile. Their complacency was their strength. They had shared in the disastrous Popular Front, but they now ignored Blum, although he still claimed to have a voice in their councils. The alternatives to their rule had been tried. A new Government of the Right or a Government headed by the Socialists was now unthinkable. There were no alternatives, and they were confident that they could maintain the support of the Senate and of the Chamber. The domestic situation was again in repose. The main concern of the Daladier Government in 1938 and 1939 was foreign policy. The French position in Europe had been transformed in the period between Laval in January 1936 and Daladier in April 1938.[35]

The Daladier Government and the Czech Crisis

The Daladier Government was immediately faced with the Czech crisis. The French press displayed a strange ambivalence toward the question of peace or war during the tense months which culminated in the Munich conference of September 1938. Three of the great French dailies had resolutely opposed war throughout the crisis. These were *Le Journal* of Pierre-Etienne Flandin, *Le Jour* of Léon Bailly, and *Le Matin* of Stephane Lauzanne. Genevieve Tabouis advocated war in *L'Oeuvre*, but Georges de la Foucherdière was permitted to dispute her theories, and to advocate peace, in the pages of the same newspaper. The Jewish editor of *Marianne*, Emmanuel Berl, fiercely denounced the pro-war Jewish Cabinet Minister, Georges Mandel. In the Socialist daily, *Le Populaire*, Louis Levy and Oriste Rosenfeld advocated war, but Paul Faure was given ample space in the same newspaper to oppose their views. Charles Maurras of *l'Action Française* came out strongly against war for the Czechs in 1938, as did Henri Beraud in *Gringoire*. This was refreshing news to many observers, because the newspapers of the Right had given strong support to the French system of eastern alliances in the past. It was evident that many people were revising their views. The Communist leader, Maurice Thorez, demanded a French war on behalf of the Czechs in the pages of *l'Humanité* on September 10, 1938, but this was a surprise to no one. The same newspaper condemned a French war in support of Poland the following year after the conclusion of the Russo-German Pact on August 23, 1939. *L'Ordre* of Pierre Lazareff and Georges Weisskopf was one of several non-Communist newspapers which were solidly for war, just as there were several newspapers which were solidly for peace. Nevertheless, a considerable number of newspapers featured the advocates of both policies, and this exposed most of the French public to extensive arguments on both sides of the issue.

It was evident that the Daladier Government was in an enviable free position as far as the conduct of foreign policy was concerned. There was no overwhelming body of public opinion which demanded the pursuit of either alternative. The public was confused by a situation which had changed so rapidly, and the public was prepared to accept whatever the Government chose to decide.[36]

The termination of the uncertainty, at Munich, was a relief to many minds. Pierre Gaxotte wrote in a spirit of exuberant triumph in *Je suis Partout* on September 30, 1938, that Czechoslovakia was "an imbecile and abject state" which had never deserved French military support. Very few of the French *bellicistes* raised their voices in protest against Munich. One of the exceptions was Paul Reynaud, who was counting on the ultimate triumph of Churchill in England. Reynaud, the chief of the small Republican Center Party, had astonished his cohorts of the French Right by defending the English repudiation of the Hoare-Laval pact in a Chamber speech on December 27, 1935. He had recently returned from one of his many trips to England, and he was promptly denounced as "the man of England." He declared that British opposition to Mussolini's Ethiopian venture was the most happy event since the American declaration of war against Germany in 1917. André Tardieu responded to this speech by announcing in a letter to *Le Temps* that he would have nothing more to do with Reynaud. [37]

Reynaud went to Germany in November 1937, and he returned to write a series of alarmist articles about alleged German designs against France. He advocated the closest possible military collaboration between France and the Soviet Union. Reynaud claimed in a Chamber speech on February 26, 1938, that Hitler was seeking the iron of Lorraine, the German minority of Alsace, and access to the Atlantic Ocean at French expense. Reynaud discussed future French policy with Churchill at Paris in March 1938 and with Halifax in England in May 1938. He advocated war during the Czech crisis, and he was delighted when Sir Robert Vansittart issued an unauthorized communique from the British Foreign Office on September 26, 1938, which stated that Great Britain, France, and the Soviet Union would declare war on Germany in the event of a German-Czech conflict. Reynaud was proud to be the only member of the French Cabinet who failed to meet Daladier at le Bourget airport after Munich. He knew that his talents as Minister of Justice, then as Minister of Finance, in the Daladier Government were highly prized. He would not follow the example of Duff Cooper in England and resign because of Munich. [38] It is also significant that Reynaud did not carry his utterances against Munich into the French Chamber. He enjoyed an appreciative audience, and he knew that it would have been useless to attempt to provoke a debate on Munich in the style of the British House of Commons. Nevertheless, Reynaud continued to follow the lead of Churchill after Munich. The case of Pierre-Étienne Flandin, who was known as the "man of the City" and the "man of Chamberlain," was entirely different. Flandin had become a sincere advocate of appeasement, and he refused to follow Chamberlain and Halifax in their later shift to a war policy. [39]

Reynaud was the most militantly anti-German figure of the French Right, but he was closely seconded by the publisher and journalist, Henri de Kerillis, who had led the aerial attack on the Easter 1916 childrens' parade at Karlsruhe. Kerillis did not share the enthusiasm of Reynaud for the Soviet Union, and he considered that Communism was a great threat to France. He deplored the failure of the Allies to destroy the Soviet Union after the end of World War I in 1918. Nevertheless, he considered that Germany was the principal threat to France. He admitted that the idea of a Franco-German *entente* was increasingly popular in France, but he claimed that Hitler could not be trusted when he promised that Germany had no territorial aspirations in the West. He also complained that France would be dwarfed by the Greater Germany of Hitler. Kerillis considered himself a prophet in the style of Alphonse Daudet, who had preached revenge against Germany after 1870. He accepted Munich at the time of the French Chamber vote of October 5, 1938, but he was soon proclaiming that France should block future German moves in the East. Kerillis declared that Hitler was not the disinterested Mahomet of a crusade against Communism, but merely a German imperialist.

The views of Kerillis were contested by the principal French historical expert on contemporary Germany, Jacques Benoist-Méchin, who had been severely wounded during the German bombardment of Paris in April 1918. Benoist-Méchin quoted Marshal Lyautey on the importance of reading *Mein Kampf*, and of becoming familiar with the theories of Hitler at first hand. Benoist-Méchin emphasized that Hitler had many grievances against France when he wrote *Mein Kampf*. These grievances had been settled with the German military reoccupation of the Rhineland in 1936. The fundamental fact was that the Hitler program in 1938 and 1939 was directed toward the East, and not against France.[40]

The position of Premier Édouard Daladier, the Marseilles Radical Socialist who had risen from the ranks to become a French officer in World War I, was crucial in the post-Munich situation. Daladier had shown great skill in out-maneuvering Herriot during the precarious Popular Front period. It was evident in 1938 that Georges Bonnet could rely on the support of Daladier for a policy of peace. Daladier knew that the military situation of France was utterly inadequate for an aggressive war against the Germans, and he continued to occupy the post of Minister of Defense in his own Government. Churchill was keenly aware of this situation. He had accepted an invitation from Reynaud to come to France on September 21, 1938. Churchill still hoped that the Czech crisis would lead to war at that time, and he suggested to Reynaud that negotiations with the Germans would be disrupted if Daladier could be overthrown, and if President Lebrun would appoint Édouard Herriot to succeed him. Reynaud was forced to explain that the influence of the anti-peace faction in the French Cabinet and Chamber was insufficient to bring down the Daladier Government.[41]

Daladier discussed the post-Munich situation with American Ambassador Bullitt at a luncheon on October 3, 1938. The French Premier made it clear to Bullitt that he had no illusions about the Munich conference, and he knew that Hitler had further demands to make in the realization of his program. He told Bullitt that Hermann Goering had been exceedingly friendly to him at Munich, and that the German Marshal had sought to flatter him and to praise France. The French Premier promised Bullitt that the military preparations of France would be accelerated in the months ahead, but he refused to give the slightest hint that France contemplated opposing future German moves in the East.[42]

Anatole de Monzie, the French Minister of Public Works, was a resolute champion of the project for a Franco-German *entente*. He noted during the Czech crisis that Premier Daladier and Vice-Premier Chautemps encouraged peace, but that they also sought to occupy the position of moderators between the two opposing groups in the French Cabinet. One group, which included Reynaud, Mandel, Champetier de Ribes, Rucart, and Zay, had favored war on behalf of the Czechs. A second group, which included Bonnet, Pomaret, Guy la Chambre, Marchandeau, and Monzie, had favored peace. The policy of Daladier and Chautemps, to throw their weight with the latter group, had decided the issue. The result would have been entirely different had Édouard Herriot headed the French Cabinet.[43]

Monzie also was grateful for the strong support [of Flandin and Caillaux]

which the Cabinet had received during the crisis. Flandin had denounced the
French pressure groups working for war, in the *Journal* on September 15, 1938.
Joseph Caillaux had returned to Paris from his retreat at Mamers in Normandy
to work for "good sense and peace." Monzie asked Daladier what he would do
if the principal Cabinet *bellicistes*, Reynaud, Mandel, and Champetier de Ribes,
offered to resign. Daladier replied that he would accept their resignations.
Monzie was with Bonnet in Paris on September 30, 1938, when Daladier was at
Munich. Bonnet gave lively expression to his legitimate joy that he had received
adequate support for his policy of peace. This did not mean that either Monzie
or Bonnet were complacent. Monzie was astonished to hear Otto Abetz, the
idealistic German champion of Franco-German amity, say, at this time, that the
foundation for future Franco-German collaboration had been achieved. Monzie
realized that the question was merely entering its crucial phase, and that extreme
watchfulness would be required in the days ahead.[44]

Monzie was aware that the Communists were spreading anti-Munich propaganda, and that Flandin had been criticized for his telegram of congratulations
to Hitler following Munich. Monzie recognized that it was necessary to launch
an active propaganda campaign in defense of Munich. He opened this campaign
with a brilliant and effective lecture to the French journalists at Toulouse on
October 12, 1938. Monzie rejoiced that the conduct of French foreign policy
was in the hands of Georges Bonnet, "with an intelligence as agile as his
face."[45]

The Franco-German Friendship Pact of December 1938

Franco-German relations were the bright spot on the European scene in October
1938. The French seemed much more advanced than their English neighbors in
adjusting to the new situation which had been created by the events of 1938.
Good relations with France increased Hitler's confidence that it would be
possible to arrive at a satisfactory settlement with Poland. The frontier tension
and minority problems which had plagued Franco-German relations during the
age of Bismarck were almost entirely lacking at this time. The most positive
element in the situation was the willingness of Germany to accept the loss of
Alsace-Lorraine.

Hitler granted a farewell audience to André Francois-Poncet on October 18,
1938. The French Ambassador had been the most popular foreign diplomat in
Berlin. He was eager to accept a mission to represent France to both Italy and
the Vatican, and to apply his charm to Mussolini. But the personalities of Hitler
and Mussolini were very different, and Francois-Poncet never succeeded in
establishing with Mussolini the friendly personal relations he had enjoyed with
Hitler.

The familiar atmosphere of cordiality between Hitler and the French
diplomat was much in evidence on the occasion of their farewell conversation.
Both men advocated a further improvement in Franco-German relations. Hitler
made a formal offer of a Franco-German declaration of friendship, which could
be used to settle points that had created anxiety in the relations between the
two nations following the abrogation of the Locarno treaties in 1936. The

French Government returned a favorable response to the German offer on October 21, 1938.[46]

The tentative provisions for a treaty were discussed in Paris by Bonnet and Count Welczeck, the German Ambassador to France. It was easy to agree on a formulation of Germany's willingness to guarantee the eastern border of France. The problem of German recognition of the Eastern European alliances of France was more difficult. Welczeck and Bonnet managed to reach an agreement on these points as early as October 25, 1938. It was assumed that France would proceed to invite Ribbentrop to Paris to conclude the formal treaty.[47]

An element of delay was produced by the Polish passport crisis, which culminated in the murder of Ernst vom Rath in Paris by Grynszpan, and in anti-Jewish measures and demonstrations in Germany. The French were worried by this situation, and the *Temps* predicted on November 17, 1938, that the anti-Jewish measures would produce a lasting bad effect on the relations of the Anglo-Saxon countries with Germany. Weizsaecker came to Paris to attend the funeral of vom Rath, and to discuss the general situation with Bonnet. The two men established good relations. Weizsaecker assured Bonnet that he shared Hitler's hope that there would be no third Franco-German war to blight the hopes of the present generation. It was evident that recent incidents and delays would not prevent the French and German leaders from proceeding with their plan to conclude the treaty.[48]

The Italian and English leaders proved to be extremely jealous in this situation. Italian Ambassador Attolico in Berlin had presented a message from Foreign Minister Ciano as early as November 8, 1938, containing a protest about the proposed provisions of the treaty, which had been communicated to the Italians by the Germans. Ciano complained that Mussolini had expected a "platonic" pact in the style of the Anglo-German declaration. He and Ciano objected to article three of the proposed draft, which provided for periodic consultation between Germany and France.[49]

The British leaders feared that France might shake off her dependence on Great Britain and arrive at an independent understanding with Germany. They realized that they had deprived France of many of her bulwarks against Germany by refusing to support French policy in the past, and that it would be a logical move for the French to retaliate. Halifax dealt with this theme at great length in instructions to Sir Eric Phipps, the British Ambassador to France. Halifax on November 1, 1938, claimed to reject the theory that "the French Government might be tempted by German intrigue to drift apart from His Majesty's Government." He recognized that Germany had attained a preponderant position in Central Europe, but he was not inclined to abandon the thought of possible future British intervention in Central and Eastern Europe. He observed wryly that he found no pleasure in the prospect of becoming entangled by Russia in a war against Germany, yet said, "I should hesitate to advise the French Government to denounce the Franco-Soviet pact." Tremendous changes had taken place in British policy since the time in 1935 when the British leaders had done what they could to prevent the conclusion of the pact.[50]

Halifax confided to Phipps that he would make a major effort to persuade Mussolini to be "less dependent on Hilter." This move would aid the conduct of

British balance of power policy against Germany. Halifax regarded it as axiomatic that Great Britain and France should remain preponderant in Western Europe, the Mediterranean, and the Near East, and that they should keep a "tight hold" on their colonial empires. He also emphasized the need of maintaining "the closest possible ties" with the United States.

The British Foreign Secretary admitted that this snug picture was disturbed by the prospect that France would leave the British system in order to achieve an independent understanding with Germany. He asserted that such a development would be a terrible blow to Great Britain, and he claimed that it might enable Germany "to hold us up to ransom" in the colonial question. Halifax was obviously worried, but he proclaimed again that he did not believe that France would "sign away her freedom."[51] Perhaps it would have been more truthful had he said that he did not believe France would attempt to regain her freedom.

Another wave of verbal assaults on Hitler by prominent Englishmen occurred at this time,[52] and new instructions from Halifax to Phipps on November 7, 1938, betrayed the fact that Halifax was increasingly worried by the Franco-German negotiations.[53] This was an old and familiar nervousness on the part of British leaders. It arose when it appeared that the leading continental nations might proceed to settle their differences independently of Great Britain. It was feared that this would destroy the British system of divide and rule by means of the balance of power. The British leaders believed that their position in the world depended upon the perpetuation of rivalries and divisions on the continent. The fears discussed by Halifax in 1938 were identical with those entertained by Sir Edward Grey in 1911, when Premier Joseph Caillaux of France and Chancellor Bethmann-Hollweg of Germany appeared to be approaching an understanding.[54]

The final text of the Franco-German declaration was approved by the French Cabinet on November 23, 1938. Much news of the pact leaked out to the public. The French press on November 24, 1938, was enthusiastic about the coming treaty, and it was called a milestone in world history. Chamberlain and Halifax had arrived in Paris on November 23rd for conferences with the French leaders on the following day. They hoped to obtain assurances which would diminish the importance of the Franco-German treaty. They were greeted with jeers and French booing (i.e. whistling) on the streets of Paris on November 23, 1938, in the first important anti-British manifestations in the French capital since the visit of King Edward VII to Paris in 1903. The announcement on the following day that Ribbentrop would soon visit Paris pushed their visit into the background of the public interest.[55]

The new French Ambassador to Germany, Robert Coulondre, had met Hitler for the first time on November 21, 1938. Cordial relations between Hitler and Coulondre were easily established, although the new ambassador could never replace Francois-Poncet in Hitler's estimation. Coulondre declared that his assignment to Germany was a mission of reconciliation. He was absolutely convinced that Hitler was sincere in his renunciation of Alsace-Lorraine. Hitler replied that he and Coulondre were both old front fighters, and they knew how to appreciate the value of peace. The final preparations for Ribbentrop's visit to Paris were concluded after this interview.[56]

The pact was completed several weeks before the departure of Ribbentrop and the German delegation for Paris. The Germans duplicated the French gesture of communicating the contents of the pact to the Poles, in advance of signature. Lipski expressed Beck's gratitude for this courtesy in Berlin on December 5, 1938. Beck replied to the French by giving the pact his blessing and by claiming that the Polish Government sincerely welcomed the Franco-German *rapprochement* outlined in the treaty. Beck instructed Lipski to inform the Germans confidentially that the Soviet Union did not look on the Franco-German declaration with the same unmixed feelings.[57]

The Germans arrived in Paris and concluded the treaty with the French on December 6, 1938. The pact was virtually the same as the Anglo-German declaration except for the provisions relating to the guarantee question, the French eastern alliances, and the consultation clause. The Germans agreed to recognize the pattern of the existing French alliances in the East, but this was widely regarded to be a mere formality. It was not known to what extent France herself would seek to maintain this alliance pattern in the future.

Phipps reported to Halifax on December 7th that the Germans had come with "a large team." He observed that some question had been raised about Bonnet's dinner for Ribbentrop on December 6th. The two Jews in the French Cabinet, Secretary for Colonies Georges Mandel, and Secretary for Education Jean Zay, had not been invited. Bonnet explained in a special interview that only a few guests from the French Government, and many non-governmental guests, had been invited. Both Mandel and Zay were invited to the festivities at the German Embassy on the following day.[58]

German Ambassador Welczeck had made many unflattering remarks to Bonnet about Ribbentrop, in the period before the visit. Bonnet had considered the source, and he desired to find out for himself.[59] Ribbentrop spoke excellent French, and he and Bonnet were able to engage in several intimate conversations without the presence of an interpreter. However, it seemed later that a serious misunderstanding about future French policy in Eastern Europe resulted from these talks, although it is also possible that later events, rather than the talks themselves, created the confusion. Ribbentrop received the impression that France intended to limit her commitments in Eastern Europe, and Bonnet later denied that he had intended to convey this. Polish Ambassador Juliusz Lukasiewicz was convinced from what he heard after Ribbentrop's visit that Bonnet had definitely made some remarks about reducing French commitments.[60]

Bonnet was concerned about a possible Italian *irredentist* program at French expense. Ciano had delivered a speech in the Italian Chamber on November 30, 1938. A group of Italian deputies had responded by raising the cry of Italian ethnic claims to Nice, Corsica, and Tunisia. Mussolini, who was a witness of the demonstration, had remained impassive. The Italians denied that the demonstration was officially inspired. Ribbentrop succeeded in reassuring Bonnet about this agitation. He was convinced that although there were many more Italians than Frenchmen in the regions which the deputies had named, Italy had no intention of presenting territorial demands to France. He assured Bonnet that such claims would not receive German support if they were made. Ribbentrop observed that Germany had no regrets in renouncing Alsace-Lorraine, and

he added that she would scarcely be willing to make war against France for
Italian claims to Djibouti or Corsica. The German Foreign Minister complained
about the British attitude toward Germany. He observed significantly that the
British leaders apparently regarded the Munich agreement as a mere expedient
to gain time in order to prepare for war.[61]

Bonnet was impressed by Ribbentrop's poise, and he later described him as an
imperturbable negotiator.[62] Ribbentrop laid a wreath on the tomb of the
French unknown soldier on December 7th, and that evening he engaged in
lengthy discussions with French political leaders. Monzie noted that Ribbentrop
was much at ease in the fashion of the *grand seigneur*. He spent much time with
Joseph Caillaux. The French elder statesman did most of the talking. He advised
Ribbentrop about dealing with future problems of German policy, but he did so
with tact. Monzie was moved by this serene and lengthy conversation between
these two handsome men, who he thought represented the best elements of their
respective nations.[63]

There were no hostile demonstrations in France during the visit of Ribbentrop. A group of French workers applauded Ribbentrop at the railway station as
he departed from Paris on December 8, 1938. There was a further friendly
demonstration for Ribbentrop when his train was forced to stop near Creil on
the return journey.[64] The Ribbentrop visit was a success, and the Franco-
German declaration contributed to the relaxation of tension in Europe. The
British were promptly informed by France that no secret agreements had been
made, but Halifax continued to be suspicious of French policy, and President
Roosevelt in the United States, and Joseph Stalin in the Soviet Union, expressed
their disapproval of the new treaty.[65]

The Flexible French Attitude After Munich

The Munich magazine *Simplicissimus* carried on the cover of its 1938 Christmas
issue a picture of Marianne and Michel, the symbols of France and Germany,
standing on the threshold of the front door to the House of Europe in perfect
amity. It was evident that France was inclined to follow the example of Italy in
seeking a *rapprochment* with Germany. The old attempt to form an Anglo-
Franco-Italian front against Germany had failed. The new situation called for
new measures. Hitler had made it clear that Germany intended to present no
demands to Italy or France, and it was evident that Italy and France had no
demands to make against Germany. The conditions for an understanding among
these three principal continental nations were extremely favorable. The ideal was
a solid Franco-Italo-German front for peace. It would be difficlut for the British
leaders to foment a war against Germany if the trend auspiciously launched in
December 1938 was continued. It would be impossible for them to do so if a
front among the Three Powers was actually created. The British were determined
to attack Germany, with France as an ally, but they would not do so alone. The
chances were favorable that they would become reconciled to the new situation
if France made a definite stand in favor of it. The prospects for peace in Europe
at the end of 1938 were still favorable despite British hostility toward Germany,
and German difficulties with Poland. The future of Europe depended upon the

prevention of another World War.

Bertrand de Jouvenel analyzed the problems of Europe in a thoughtful book, *Le Réveil de l'Europe* (*the Awakening of Europe*), which appeared in 1938. Jouvenel recognized that Europeans of the 20th century were no longer confident about progress. The experience of World War I and the problems which had emerged in the post-war era had destroyed this confidence. He deplored the decline of France in Europe, but he regretted much more the decline of Europe in the world. This trend could be reversed if the hates of the past were forgotten, and if Europe concentrated on peace and production instead of war and destruction. Sir John Maynard Keynes in Great Britain had exposed the idiocy of the Versailles Treaty. Keynes had reminded the so-called peacemakers that they wished to make the conquered pay, but in reality they ruined the conquerors. Henry Ford in the United States had pointed out the hope afforded by a higher standard of living for the masses. He had shown that a greater market for production was possible when the salaries of the workers were higher. The obstacles to the realization of the dream of productivity and reconciliation were to be found in the old obsolete prejudices, such as the British policy of the balance of power. Jouvenel believed that the purpose of history was to combat the presumption behind such dogmas: "L'étude de l'Histoire est bien faite pour abattre la présomption humaine (The study of history should be conducted to reduce human presumption)."[66]

Jouvenel sadly recalled that the Wilson propaganda slogan of 1918 had been a peace of justice. This sounded like some vague dream of perpetual peace. Jouvenel hoped that the time would come when mankind ceased waging perpetual war for perpetual peace. He was typical of the many Frenchmen who were making an honest effort to adjust to the new situation in Europe.[67]

Chapter 10

THE GERMAN DECISION TO

OCCUPY PRAGUE

The Czech Imperium Mortally Wounded at Munich

The Czech state lingered in a moribund condition for nearly six months after the cession of the Sudeten districts to Germany. Czech rule over numerous minorities for nearly twenty years after 1918 had been based on a policy of stern intimidation, and the assurance of military support from a preponderant France. One by one, the German, Polish, and Hungarian minorities had been separated from Czech rule. The Slovaks and Ruthenians were also eager to escape from Czech rule, and they received encouragement from Poland and Hungary.[1]

It seemed for a time that newly preponderant Germany might assume the old French role and protect the remnants of the Czech imperium. Hitler considered this possibility for about four months after Munich. He gradually came to the conclusion that the Czech cause was lost in Slovakia, and that Czech cooperation with Germany could not be relied upon. He decided, after receiving the news about the visit of the British leaders to Rome in January 1939, to transfer German support from the Czechs to the Slovaks.[2]

The success of the Slovak cause was assured, but the Slovak leaders wished to have the protection of German military units in Slovakia. This meant that German troops would have to occupy Prague, at least temporarily, in order to establish military communications with Slovakia. Hitler was able to legalize this development by special treaties with the Czech and Slovak leaders.[3] Czech President Emil Hacha did not believe that it would be wise to resist German plans. He received congratulations from Edvard Beneš when he was elected to the presidency in November 1938, but Beneš denounced him in March 1939 for cooperating with Germany.[4]

The Deceptive Czech Policy of Halifax

Hitler's decision to support the Slovaks and to occupy Prague had been based on the obvious disinterest of the British leaders in the Czech situation. There had been ample opportunities for them to encourage the Czechs in some way, but they had repeatedly refused to do so. The truth was that the British leaders did not care about the Czechs. They used Hitler's policy as a pretext to become indignant about the Germans.

Halifax resorted to trickery in a first major effort to sabotage the terms of the Munich agreement in October 1938. The Czech-Magyar dispute was on the agenda at that time. Polish Ambassador Lipski on October 24, 1938, had requested Polish participation in an international arbitration to settle the dispute. He had suggested that the arbitration team consist solely of Poles, Italians, and Germans. Ribbentrop was not enthusiastic about the proposal, but he agreed to sound out his Italian colleague. Ciano replied that the Polish proposition was unsatisfactory. Italy had worked for years to achieve a diplomatic concert among the Four Powers which had met at Munich, and Ciano did not favor abandoning this concert for the convenience of the Poles. It was evident that direct negotiation between the Czechs and Hungarians, which had been resumed on October 13th, was fruitless. Ciano invited Ribbentrop to discuss the problem at Rome, and the German Foreign Minister departed for the Italian capital on October 26, 1938.[5]

Ogilvie-Forbes, at the British Embassy in Berlin, discovered Italy's attitude toward the Polish proposal before Ribbentrop left for Rome. Ogilvie-Forbes contacted Halifax and informed him that everything seemed to point toward a Four Power arbitration effort. He was astonished when Halifax immediately replied that it would not be feasible to seek the agreement of the Four Munich Powers in the Czech-Magyar dispute. Halifax believed that Germany and Italy would disagree on the Czech-Hungarian dispute if Great Britain and France withdrew from the Munich program. Dissension in German-Italian relations would follow, and Great Britain might be able to exploit this situation in her effort to separate Italy from Germany. He confided to Ogilvie-Forbes that Italy "apparently was favoring the cession of Ruthenia to Hungary." He believed that Italy wished to keep Poland out of the arbitration effort in order to receive all the credit for the realization of Hungarian aims. He imagined that Italy was still intent upon preserving Hungary as a sphere of Italian influence, and that the Italians were jealous of the Poles, who were popular in Hungary. He hoped that Germany would oppose Italy in an arbitration effort by seeking to obtain a settlement in Ruthenia along the lines of self-determination.

Halifax suggested another motive for his refusal to permit Great Britain to assume her Munich conference obligations. Halifax wished to be spared the distasteful work of revising the territorial provisions of the 1919 peace treaties, which had remained unchallenged in Central Europe for nearly two decades before 1938. Halifax was also determined to maintain British supremacy in Rumania, and to prevent Rumania from forming closer relations with Germany. King Carol was planning to visit London on November 15, 1938, and Halifax did not wish to offend the Rumanian sovereign by appearing to support Hungarian claims. The Rumanians were bitterly opposed to Hungarian revisionism.

The British Foreign Secretary speculated that the Germans might be considering the possibility of supporting the national Ukrainian movement in the Ruthenian area. Halifax did not believe that Germany would succeed in maintaining self-determination in Ruthenia against the opposition of Italy, Poland and Hungary. He predicted that Germany would capitulate, and this would mean the end of self-determination in dealing with Czech problems. This consideration did not bother Halifax. He argued that the Ruthenian Jews would be better off under Hungary than under the Czechs. He hoped that a common Hungarian-Polish frontier would increase the opposition of both Poland and Hungary to Germany. It seemed to Halifax that Great Britain would be serving her own interests by withdrawing completely from Czecho-Slovakia.[6]

Halifax informed Budapest confidentially that arbitration excluding Great Britain and France could be safely proposed. He consulted the Czech and Hungarian diplomats in London, and requested them to approve British and French withdrawal from the Czech-Magyar dispute. Halifax wired Lord Perth, the British Ambassador in Rome, on the evening of October 26th, that his maneuver had been successful. The Czechs and Hungarians were prepared to accept Italo-German arbitration without the participation of the British and French support against Germany in the Czech-Hungarian dispute. He hoped to confront Ciano with a hasty *fait accompli*, and he instructed Perth to announce that "His Majesty's Government saw no objection to the settlement of the Czech-Hungarian question by means of arbitration by Germany and Italy." He sought to appease Ciano by declaring that the British were willing to participate in the discussions if both the Czechs and Hungarians insisted upon it. This was a clever gesture which cost Halifax nothing. Budapest and Prague had already agreed not to request British participation.[7]

Halifax reckoned with the possibility that this gesture might not fully satisfy Mussolini. He instructed Perth to appease Mussolini by asserting that Great Britain favored bilateral Anglo-Italian cooperation in the settlement of important European questions. Halifax was watching every factor when he instructed Perth: "You will, of course, appreciate that His Majesty's Government do not wish to give the impression of trying to profit by any Italo-German disagreement over the future of Ruthenia." A furious struggle over the future of Ruthenia was about to ensue in the imagination of the British Foreign Secretary. He pictured the Germans angrily and reluctantly submitting to combined pressure from Italy, Hungary, and Poland, and he rejoiced in the prospect. Great Britain would maintain an advantageous position on the sidelines. This was the culmination in the total abandonment of British responsibility toward the Czechs.[8] Józef Beck at Warsaw concluded that the British would elude their responsibility to guarantee Czecho-Slovakia after the settlement of Hungarian and Polish claims. His analysis proved to be correct.[9]

Halifax's anticipations were strengthened by another report from Ogilvie-Forbes on October 26th. Weizsaecker had told the British diplomats in Berlin that Germany would insist upon self-determination in both Slovakia and Ruthenia. Ogilvie-Forbes asked Weizsaecker if Ruthenia could be administered by the Czechs after the Magyar section was withdrawn. It appeared that the separation of the Magyar ethnic areas would disrupt Ruthenian communications. Weizsaecker "refused to be drawn and repeated that Ruthenia should have self-determination." The German State Secretary complained that the omission of Great Britain and France from the arbitration team was contrary to the provisions of the Munich agreement. He did not suspect Great Britain's responsibility for this situation, and he went to great lengths to explain that Germany was not responsible. The British diplomat did not enlighten Weizsaecker about the true state of affairs. He informed Halifax that the Italian diplomats in Berlin were convinced that Italy would insist on the return of Ruthenia to Hungary. It appeared that the Germans were about to walk into a trap which would produce friction with Italy, Hungary, and Poland.10

Józef Beck was doing what he could to facilitate matters for Hungary at this point. He offered to meet Rumanian objections on October 26th by guaranteeing Rumanian access to the Czechs through Poland. He told British Ambassador Kennard that Poland was using every possible argument with the Germans to prove that the return of Ruthenia to Hungary was the only sensible solution. He added that he would travel to Germany to discuss the matter personally with Hitler and Ribbentrop if Hungary did not receive satisfaction in Ruthenia.11

Beck made a last effort to bring Poland into the arbitration team. He exerted pressure for an invitation to Poland in both Prague and Budapest. The Czechs replied that they would admit the Poles to the negotiation if the Rumanians also were included. This reply irritated Beck. He had no desire to sit at the negotiation table on the Ruthenian issue with the Rumanians again, and he was compelled to drop the matter.12

Halifax failed in his effort to foment a conflict between Germany, on the hand, and Italy, Poland, and Hungary on the other. The effort itself, however, would never have appeared as an element in British foreign policy after the Munich conference had not Halifax been willing to countenance the abandonment of Czech interests by Great Britian, despite the promise of the British Government at Munich to protect those interests in exchange for Czech willingness to accept a negotiated settlement of the Sudeten-Czech crisis. One part of the British commitment was to take part in the arbitration of the Czech-Hungarian dispute in case bilateral negotiations between the Czechs and Hungarians failed. Halifax's refusal to fulfill this promise was tantamount to an abandonment of Czech interests by Great Britain, especially since Halifax hoped that Germany would fail to gain the more moderate solution for the Czechs which was actually achieved at Vienna.

The Vienna Award a Disappointment to Halifax

Ribbentrop discussed the Italo-German arbitration project with Mussolini and Ciano in Rome on October 28, 1938. He also told Mussolini that Hitler was worried about British hostility toward Germany. Hitler and Ribbentrop believed that an Italo-German alliance would discourage the war enthusiasts in England. There was no reference to Japan. This was embarrassing to Mussolini, because Japanese reluctance to sign an alliance pact with Germany and Italy had postponed the issue of an Italo-German alliance in the past. Mussolini was evasive about the proposed alliance, but he was conciliatory about Ruthenia. The settlement of Italo-German differences about Ruthenia was the main object of

Ribbentrop's visit, and his mission to Rome was a success. Ribbentrop also discussed German-Polish relations with the Italian leaders, and he assured them that Hitler intended to establish German-Polish friendship on a permanent basis.[13]

Halifax had been more optimistic than Beck about Hungary's chances to gain Ruthenia through Italo-German arbitration, and the British Foreign Secretary was destined to be disappointed. The main details were settled when Weizsaecker announced in Berlin on October 30, 1938, that Germany and Italy "have undertaken the arbitration of the new Czech-Hungarian frontier." The arbitration work was carried forward by Ciano and Ribbentrop at Vienna in a friendly atmosphere, and the two diplomats vied with one another in satirizing the reactionary Vienna Peace Congress of 1815.

The Czech and Hungarian missions arrived at Vienna on November 2, 1938, to receive the arbitration award. There were also delegations from Slovakia and Ruthenia. The Hungarians had been informed after the Ribbentrop visit to Rome that they must limit their claims to Magyar ethnic territory. The Hungarians had requested 14,000 square kilometers of territory from Slovakia and Ruthenia on this basis. Ciano and Ribbentrop granted them 10,000 square kilometers of territory.[14]

An agreement had been concluded on the basis of self-determination, which Great Britain was no longer willing to advocate in Czecho-Slovakia. Hungary received a very small part of Ruthenia, and Beck's dream of a common frontier between Hungary and Poland was not realized. The Czechs agreed to begin evacuation of the regions awarded to Hungary on November 5, 1938, and the Magyars were allowed to complete the occupation of the recovered territory by November 10th. The Germans had entered the negotiation with a free hand. Rumania had appealed to Germany on October 28th for a "sign of friendship," and a promise that Germany "would oppose a common Hungarian-Polish frontier." The German Government in reply had refused to make a promise to Rumania in a matter to be decided exclusively by Italy and Germany. The problem was simplified because Ciano never insisted on the surrender of the entire Ruthenian area to Hungary.[15]

New Polish Demands on the Czechs

The Polish Government exploited the Czech-Magyar dispute by presenting Prague with a new ultimatum on October 31, 1938. The Poles demanded six Carpathian border districts from Slovakia. They threatened to attack the Czechs if an affirmative answer was not received the same day. The Czechs capitulated to the latest Polish ultimatum at 5:00 p.m. on October 31st. They also tried to stir up the British against Poland. Newton was informed by Czech Foreign Minister Chvalkovský that there was reason to believe that this was only the beginning of a regular monthly series of Polish demands.[16]

Josef Tiso, who had become the leader of the Slovakian national coalition after the failure of the Sidor mission to Warsaw, was furious at the extent of the Polish demands. He appealed to Germany for protection for the first time. Tiso explained to German Consul-General Ernst vom Druffel at Bratislava on

October 31, 1938, that the Polish demands had no ethnic basis, and that they went far beyond the small frontier adjustment suggested earlier. Tiso charged that the Poles were interested in seizing important strategic regions and in obtaining control over the Cadca-Zwardon railway, which would enable them to control communications in a number of Slovakian areas. He complained that they could have no ethnic basis for claiming a number of the highest, and, of course, uninhabited, peaks of the Tatra range of the Carpathians. He insisted that an independent Slovakia would have rejected the Polish demands. The Czechs had accepted them in the name of Slovakia. Tiso developed his favorite theme that Slovakia required the protection of a powerful neighbor. He added that Slovakia in the future would welcome German support against the Poles. The Poles had completed the process of undermining their earlier popularity in Slovakia.[17]

The Czech authorities also were required to make new concessions to the Poles in Moravia. The Poles promised them that the final delimitation of the Polish-Moravian frontier would be completed by November 15th, and of the Polish-Slovakian frontier by December 1st. The Czechs informed the Germans that they had submitted to Poland because of the military threat. They claimed that Poland would undertake further steps against Czecho-Slovakia despite her promises to the contrary.[18]

Józef Beck was dissatisfied by the Vienna Award to Hungary of November 2, 1938, and he attempted several times to persuade the Germans to raise the Ruthenian question again. Ribbentrop responded by sending instructions to German Ambassador Moltke in Warsaw which illuminated the German strategy at Vienna. Moltke informed Beck on November 22, 1938, that Germany would offer no encouragement for a revision of the Ruthenian settlement unless an agreement was achieved between Germany and Poland. He added that Ribbentrop had warned the Hungarians not to challenge the recent Vienna Award "at the present time." This seemed a superfluous gesture to Beck, who had long since concluded that the Hungarians would take no military action to secure their further aspirations, such as the acquistion of the entire province of Ruthenia. He casually assured Moltke that he would not encourage them in any such endeavor. He vigorously requested that something be done by peaceful negotiation "to meet Hungarian interests." Moltke replied by emphasizing the need for a German-Polish agreement. He added a private assurance which he hoped would appease the Polish Foreign Minister. He informed Beck that Ribbentrop in Berlin had "told him only yesterday that he did not see why the Ukrainian problem should disturb German-Polish relations." Moltke assured Beck that Germany had no ambition to exploit Ukrainian nationalism.[19]

Beck responded to German obstruction of his Ruthenian program by improving Polish relations with the Soviet Union. Russo-Polish relations had been exceptionally unfriendly since the Russian threat on September 23, 1938, to repudiate the Russo-Polish Non-Aggression Pact of 1932. Beck hastened to accept a Russian initiative in November 1938 to improve relations. Soviet Foreign Commissar Litvinov and Polish Ambassador Grzybowski issued a joint declaration on November 26, 1938, which announced an increase in trade between the two nations and the reaffirmation of their Non-Aggression Pact. The heavily industrialized Teschen region had provided many exports for Russia while under Czech rule, and the Poles were willing to continue this trade. Moltke reported from Warsaw that Beck had conducted the negotiations as a reply to German obstruction in Ruthenia. German Ambassador Schulenburg in Moscow suggested that the Soviet Union considered the declaration to be an indirect protest to the forthcoming Franco-German declaration of friendship.[20]

Ribbentrop was dispeased by the secrecy of Beck's Russian policy. Lipski had given him no indication that Poland was negotiating with the Soviet Union. He discussed the question with Lipski on December 2, 1938. The Polish Ambassador said that the declaration was the consequence of a natural Polish desire to reduce tension along her eastern frontier. He described with intensity and color the series of border incidents and air battles with the Russians during the Teschen crisis. Ribbentrop assured him that Germany did not object to the Russo-Polish *détente*, but he was "surprised that Poland did not inform us beforehand."[21]

Schulenburg warned Ribbentrop from Moscow on December 3, 1938, that "the Russians have lost every interest in Czechoslovakia since the latter can no longer serve as a barrier against Germany." Schulenburg concluded that an alignment between the Soviet Union and Poland was no longer out of the question, since the Russians took no exception to Polish aims in Ruthenia. It was obviously in the interest of Russia to see any autonomous Ukrainian community suppressed. Ribbentrop concluded that the Soviet Union had joined the group of nations which favored, or were indifferent about, the further partition of Czecho-Slovakia.[22]

Czech-German Friction After the Vienna Award

There was considerable friction between the Czechs and Germans after the Vienna Award. The Czechs had by no means decided to throw in their lot with Germany despite the prognostications of Henderson at Berlin. They assured French diplomats at Prague that they had no intention of renouncing their alliance with the Soviet Union.[23] Foreign Minister Chvalkovský complained bitterly to Newton on November 5, 1938, that France was refusing economic aid to the Czechs, after the Munich conference, because she regarded the new Czech state as a German Satellite. The Czech Foreign Minister declared boldly that "it was too early to judge what Czechoslovakia's eventual position would be." He hinted that the situation would be clarified in three or six months, after the Czechs had coped with their immediate difficulties. Newton concluded that the Czechs had by no means abandoned the idea of participating in a front against Germany.[24]

Newton would have been impressed with these remarks had he believed in a future for the Czech state. He predicted to Halifax that Czecho-Slovakia would not survive much longer. Some expert local observers believed that both Slovakia and Ruthenia would be unable to avoid the conclusion that survival was impossible "without some form of association with Hungary." Chvalkovský insisted that the Czechs "would like to obtain the guarantee of the Four Munich Powers as soon as possible." Newton believed that a guarantee would be unwise. He discouraged the Czech Foreign Minister from approaching the British in this question. He assured Chvalkovský that Great Britain was the least interested of all the Munich Powers in such a guarantee.[25]

The Czechs complained loudly a few days later about the final delimitation of the Czech-German frontier. They were relieved in October 1938 when Hitler renounced a plebiscite, which undoubtedly would have separated from the Czechs large regions beyond the five zones originally assigned to Germany. It had been agreed that a compromise settlement on the remaining areas in dispute should be completed by November 24, 1938. It was understood that German claims in the final delimitation would be very limited, and in practice they were. This did not discourage the Czechs from using the issue to agitate against Germany. Their statistics on the minority balance between the two nations were a complete inversion of the German figures. It is odd that they feared a border plebiscite when they claimed that only 377,196 Germans remained in Czecho-Slovakia, compared to more than 700,000 Czechs in Germany. They issued a special communique on November 6, 1938, which charged that there were twice as many Czechs and Slovaks in Germany as Germans in Czecho-Slovakia.[26]

The Czechs hoped that this propaganda would prevent the Germans from making any gains in the final border delimitation. They were due for a surprise when they received the German note of November 14, 1938. The Germans suggested border changes which would surrender nearly 40,000 inhabitants of Czecho-Slovakia to Germany. The Germans warned that they would revert to the plebiscite envisaged at the Munich conference if the Czechs refused to be reasonable. The Poles exploited the situation to claim that the changes proposed by the Germans justified the official Polish attitude that the Vienna Award was not final. The tension in Czech-Polish relations was extremely great at this moment, because Poland had expelled a large number of Czechs from the Teschen region.[27]

The Czechs were powerless to retaliate against Polish expulsion of their nationals, but they could have appealed to the British, French, and Italian members of the International Commission for the delimitation of the Czech-German Border in Berlin. The Czechs instead decided to arrive at an agreement with Germany. The Germans contacted the International Commission and informed them about German policy and the Czech response. A German-Czech agreement was negotiated on November 21, 1938. It was obvious that British diplomats in Berlin were not pleased by the situation, and Ogilvie-Forbes reported to Halifax that "the whole affair is being rushed and I fully appreciate the indignation which may be aroused in the United Kingdom." In the upshot, this indignation was not very great.[28]

The Germans informed British diplomats in Berlin that arrangements had been completed with the Czechs for the Breslau-Vienna superhighway, for direct air service between Silesia and Austria, and for a canal to link the Oder and the Baltic Sea with the Danube and the Black Sea by way of the Moravian Corridor. Czech Minister Mastný at Berlin continued to complain to the British about Czech losses in the border delimitation. He emphasized that the Czechs were losing the winter sport area of Jilemnice, which was popular in Prague, and the historic monument commemorating the Hussite period at Taus, in the area where Jan Hus was born. The Czech envoy concluded with resignation that his Government had decided to sign the agreement with the Germans to avoid more unsatisfactory terms. The Czech Government communiqué of November 6, 1938, on minority figures, had also contained complaints about the cession of territory to Hungary on November 2nd. The sensitive Magyars were furious about the juggled Czech statistics. They published a communiqué on November 21, 1938, which denounced Czech statistics on minorities as a hoax. They offered their own statistics, which presented an entirely different picture.[29]

Sir Basil Newton inquired in Prague on November 22, 1938, if the Czech Government had raised the question of the territorial guarantee of Czecho-Slovakia in the recent negotiation with Germany. The Czechs replied that this point was not mentioned. The Czechs painted a lively picture of the German development-projects in the hope of alarming the British. They told Newton that German plans called for the completion of the superhighway to Vienna by 1940. The highway was to be fenced off, but the Czechs were free to use it without tolls on their own territory. The Czechs claimed the Germans had referred to plans for a superhighway system extending to Bagdad. They calculated at Prague that the British would be interested to learn of a scheme which was reminiscent of the Bagdad railway achievement of the previous German generation. The entire tone of the various Czech conversations with the British diplomats left no doubt that the Czechs still considered themselves to be the friends of the Soviet Union and the adversaries of Germany.[30]

The Poles continued to exert pressure on the Czechs. On November 26, 1938, Beck demanded the surrender of the remaining areas to be ceded to Poland on November 27th instead of December 1st. Kennard reported from Warsaw that Beck was furious with the Rumanians at this time. The Rumanian Government had answered Beck's communiqué on Ruthenia by warning Hungary to respect the provisions of the Vienna Award.[31]

The Czech Guarantee Sabotaged by Halifax

The British press in late November 1938 was flooded with rumors that Germany was "massing" her troops in preparation for an invasion of Czecho-Slovakia. These irresponsible alarmist rumors originated in London. The British diplomats in Prague informed London that there had been no speculation on such a development in the Czech capital, and Propaganda Minister Joseph Goebbels at Berlin complained about the irresponsibility of the British press. Current history consisted of wars and rumors of wars for the British journalists of the 1930's. The unfounded rumors in the British press attracted public attention to the question of the promised territorial guarantee of Czecho-Slovakia. This was a useful barometer, because the British Government did not share what little enthusiasm there was in England for a guarantee. Another rumor was circulated that the Soviet Union would join the guaranteeing Powers. Kennard responded to it from Warsaw with a report to Halifax which contained an interesting and valuable insight into the attitude of the Polish leaders toward the Soviet Union.

Halifax was informed that the Poles were opposed to a guarantee of Czecho-Slovakia, and that they would never respect any arrangement which included the Soviet Union as a guaranteeing Power. The Poles argued that the Russians could not execute a guarantee to the Czechs without crossing Polish territory.

Kennard warned Halifax that the Poles would never permit Russian troops to operate on their territory. Halifax did not contest the validity of this unequivocal declaration from Kennard. This did not prevent him from urging the Poles eight months later to permit the operation of Russian troops on their territory.[32]

Kennard explained to Halifax on November 30, 1938, that the Polish leaders regarded Russia as their hereditary enemy. They were convinced that Russia intended to create a Communist Poland. It seemed obvious to the Poles that the Russians intended to seize the Polish Eastern territories. These factors prompted them to reject categorically any plan which involved Russian military intervention in Central Europe. Kennard assured Halifax that there was "no hope of the Polish attitude changing." Furthermore, Kennard agreed that the Russian threat was "undeniably a position of real danger for them." Kennard admitted in this one instance that a German-Polish war would be disastrous for Poland. The hostile Soviet Union in the Polish rear deprived the Poles of any hope in such an encounter. Kennard was not yet aware that Poland would be assigned a crucial role in the campaign of Halifax to foment a major war against Germany. Kennard noted the concern of foreign diplomats at Warsaw "that the Poles may now drift into a clash with Germany," but he added that "in any case, even though the Poles are suffering from a swollen head at present, they are unlikely to provoke Germany beyond safe limits." Kennard did not define what he meant by Polish provocation within safe limits.[33]

Halifax sent several of Sir Howard Kennard's dispatches to Sir Basil Newton at Prague. Newton was less enthusiastic than Kennard about the Poles. He observed tartly in his subsequent report to Halifax that later events would decide whether the Polish anti-Czech policy was justifiable. He claimed that "nothing can be said in justification of their methods." Newton believed that Poland was incredibly foolish to incur the wrath of the Slovaks. He noted that "Poland could probably have had an influential position in Slovakia for the asking." Karol Sidor had been "notoriously pro-Polish up to a few weeks ago," but there were no longer any champions of Poland among the Slovak leaders. Newton noted that Slovakia was hostile toward both Poland and the Czechs, and that it was a natural consequence for the Slovaks to turn to Germany for assistance.

Newton condemned the Poles for "the utterly ruthless policy toward the Czech inhabitants" in the former Czech regions which had been obtained by Poland. He noted that not alone "were the Czechs the only sufferers, for the Germans too were often ill-treated." It was known in Czecho-Slovakia that at Teschen the local Germans and Czechs often made common cause against the Poles. Newton found it difficult to believe that Polish gains were "commensurate with the odium incurred." He noted that the Czech Government had recently promised to treat the remaining German minority within their territory more decently in the future. It may be wondered how Halifax could later accept the claims of Kennard that Polish treatment of the minorities within her jurisdiction was exemplary.[34]

Ogilvie-Forbes on December 6, 1938, reported to Halifax from Berlin on rumors that Hitler would abandon self-determination in dealing with the Czech problem if the conditions in the area remained unsatisfactory. Great Britain and France had taken no steps to implement the territorial guarantee promised to the Czechs at Munich. Halifax and Chamberlain had discussed the guarantee question when they visited the French leaders at Paris on November 24, 1938. Daladier and Bonnet was no reason why the guarantee could not be impemented if Germany and Italy had no objections. They told the British leaders that they assumed each guaranteeing Power would be individually responsible for the defense of the Czech *status quo*. The French were astonished to discover that Halifax did not share this view. He suggested a plan which seemed nothing more than a hoax to Bonnet. Halifax proposed that the guarantee would not be operative in the event of a German violation unless Mussolini agreed to support Great Britain and France against Germany. The French objected that this guarantee would be sterile and futile, and that it would be better to ignore the question than to propose it. Mussolini had refused to oppose the invasion of Austria by Germany, although Austria in early March 1938 was an Italian sphere of influence. It was unthinkable that Mussolini would oppose Hitler on behalf of the Czechs.[35]

These French objections left Halifax completely unmoved. He responded that there would be no guarantee at all unless the Powers accepted his formula. Halifax added that other states, such as Poland, could guarantee the Czech state if they wished to and on their own terms. He did believe that a Soviet Russian territorial guarantee to Czecho-Slovakia would be unwise, because it would provoke both Germany and Poland. The difficulty which was raised between the French and British leaders by the Halifax formula of November 24, 1938, was never resolved. The French and British took several perfunctory steps at Berlin in the guarantee question during the following months, but these steps were feeble and unconvincing, because there was no program behind them. Halifax never explained to the French leaders why he would not compromise in the guarantee question. The French naturally concluded that the British wished to avoid any guarantee to the Czechs. Newton inquired from Prague about the guarantee question on December 8, 1938, and Halifax admitted in reply that the French refused to accept the British formula.[36]

Newton was not displeased to learn that the Czechs would receive no guarantee. He predicted that the collapse of Czecho-Slovakia was inevitable with or without a guarantee. He knew "from several sources that the Czechs are to-day more worried by their internal than their external difficulties." He cited Slovakia as golden proof of the fact that "the Czechs for some reason lack the gift of making themselves popular." He found no sympathy whatever in Slovakia for the "woes" of the Czechs, and he noted that the German minority in Czecho-Slovakia continued to have many grievances. These valid points provided valuable support to Halifax in his policy of evading the British promises to the Czechs, which had been made at Munich.[37]

Czech Appeals Ignored by Halifax

The Czechs were annoyed and mystified by the *impasse* in the guarantee question. They did not know that Halifax at Paris had sabotaged the proposed guarantee on November 24, 1938. Czech Foreign Minister Chvalkovský complained to Newton on December 11th that the Czech Government had not been consulted at Munich, and that it had no basis to "express views to the four powers in regard to the fulfillment of their promises." Chvalkovský admitted that the Czechs were in a "delicate position" on the home front, and that they would be thankful for any kind of guarantee. He sensed that Great Britain and France were reluctant to take the initiative in the question, although he would have expected them to do so rather than Germany or Italy. The Czechs in the past had been more friendly to Great Britain and France than to the Axis Powers. He would not object if the natural order was reversed. He would accept separate guarantees from Germany and Italy, with the understanding that Great Britain and France would follow suit at some later date. Chvalkovský claimed that he was yearning for the "peace and neutrality" of Switzerland, which had been undisturbed since 1815. The Czech Foreign Minister may not have realized that there had been several instances in which Switzerland was in extreme peril from threatened French and Austrian invasions during the two generations after 1815. The Swiss security of 1938 had not been built in a day, despite the international guarantee of the Vienna Congress.[38]

Halifax was informed of Czech wishes, but nothing was done to meet them. The British Foreign Secretary interpreted Newton's report to mean that the Czechs did not expect the British to fulfill their guarantee obligation. Henderson and Coulondre announced in Berlin on December 22, 1938, that France and Great Britain would approve of a separate German guarantee to the Czechs. This proposal did not help the Czecho-Slovak cause. The Germans saw no reason why they should take the initiative in guaranteeing a state which recently had operated in a militant front against them, when France, the actual ally of the Czechs, displayed no willingness to do so. The Munich conference agreement had stipulated that identical action should be taken by the Four Powers.[39]

The Germans suspected that the British and French would soon pursue the question and offer some suggestion along the lines of the Munich agreement. Nothing of the sort happened. It seemed that the more interest the Czechs showed, the more negative the British attitude in the guarantee question became. The argument against the guarantee was eloquently expressed to Halifax by Ogilvie-Forbes on January 3, 1939. The British diplomats knew that Halifax opposed the guarantee, and they vied with one another in reinforcing his position. Ogilvie-Forbes contended that Great Britain could not "guarantee the status quo in Central and Eastern Europe," unless she was seeking a war.[40] This was a drastic statement, but it proved only too true when Great Britain guaranteed Poland three months later. The professional diplomats at the British Foreign Office were fully aware of the true nature of British policy toward the Czechs after Munich. Sir William Strang, the chief of the Central Office which dealt with Germany, declared that the guarantee which the British had promised the Czechs was merely "a sham."[41]

Hitler's Support of the Slovak Independence Movement

Hitler made no public pretense of having found a permanent policy in dealing with the Czechs during this period. He told anyone who cared to listen that he did not know what future developments would be in the Czech area. The Belgian legation at Berlin was elevated to an Embassy on November 21, 1938, and afterward Belgian Ambassador Vicomte Jacques Davignon attended a special reception held by Hitler at Berchtesgaden. The conversation between Hitler and Davignon turned to the Czech question. Hitler explained that German relations with Czecho-Slovakia were far from settled and he enumerated the difficulties which were unresolved. Davignon was impressed with the frankness of Hitler's remarks.[42]

The negotiations between Czech Foreign Minister Chvalkovský and the Germans in January 1939 were unsatisfactory. The Germans objected to the large Czech army, and to the continuation of the Czech-Soviet alliance. They were disturbed by the numerous higher officials in the Czech Government who expressed anti-German views, and by the tone of the Czech press. Chvalkovský came to Berlin on January 21, 1939, to discuss these problems. He adopted a defiant attitude, and he told the Germans that a reduction of the Czech army would depend on German willingness to take the initiative in granting a territorial guarantee to the Czechs. The Germans were annoyed by this defiance, and they were tired of the requests for unilateral German action in the guarantee question. The German-Czech communiqué of January 28, 1939, concluded the fruitless negotiation. It was limited to a few minor points about the exchange of railroad facilities and the treatment of minorities.[43]

Reports were reaching Berlin that opposition to Czech rule was increasing in Slovakia, and Edmund Veesenmayer, from the National Socialist Foreign Policy Office, was sent to Slovakia by Ribbentrop to investigate conditions. The Germans received abundant confirmation that the Slovaks wished to end Czech rule. A meeting was arranged on February 12, 1939, between Hitler and Adalbert Tuka, the veteran leader of the Slovak independence movement. Tuka told Hitler that his experience in Czech courts and Czech prisons gave him the right to speak for the Slovak nation. Tuka declared that the continuation of Slovak association with the Czechs had become impossible for both moral and economic reasons. The Czechs had broken their political promises to the Slovaks, and they had exploited and damaged the Slovakian economy. Tuka declared that he was determined to achieve independence for the Slovak nation in collaboration with the other Slovakian nationalist leaders. The remarks of Tuka were consistent with what he had been saying for several months. The important fact was that Hitler willingly invited him to Germany to hear him say it. It was evident that Chvalkovský had adopted an attitude of recalcitrance to provoke Hitler to choose a definite policy. The existing situation was one of complete uncertainty in which the Czechs received no support from abroad and constantly lost ground in their efforts to control their minorities at home. The response of Hitler was a definite decision against support to the Czecho-Slovak state, and a decision in favor of support to the Slovaks in their struggles against Prague. The result of this decision was soon apparent. The Czech position in Slovakia had been deteriorating before February 1939, but it collapsed altogether within a few weeks after Hitler received Tuka.[44]

President Roosevelt Propagandized by Halifax

Halifax continued to maintain a detached attitude toward the Czech problem, and he secretly circulated rumors both at home and abroad which presented the foreign policy of Hitler in the worst possible light. Hitler would have been condemned by Halifax for anything he did in Czechoslovakia. Had he decided to throw German weight behind the Czechs in an effort to maintain Czech rule over the Slovaks, he would have been denounced for converting the Czech state into a German puppet regime. His decision to support the Slovaks should be denounced as a sinister plot to disrupt the Czecho-Slovak state which the Munich Powers had failed to protect with their guarantee.

The situation is illustrated by the message which Halifax dispatched to President Roosevelt on January 24, 1939. Halifax claimed to have received "a large number of reports from various reliable sources which throw a most disquieting light on Hitler's mood and intentions." He repeated the tactic he had used with Kennedy about Hitler's allegedly fierce hatred of Great Britain. Halifax believed that Hitler had guessed that Great Britain was "the chief obstacle now to the fulfillment of his further ambitions." It was not really necessary for Hitler to do more than read the record of what Halifax and Chamberlain had said at Rome to recognize that Great Britain was the chief threat to Germany, but it was untrue to suggest that Hitler had modified his goal of Anglo-German cooperation in peace and friendship.

Halifax developed his theme with increasing warmth. He claimed that Hitler had recently planned to establish an independent Ukraine, and that he intended to destroy the Western Powers in a surprise attack before he moved into the East. Not only British intelligence but "highly placed Germans who are anxious to prevent this crime" had furnished evidence of this evil conspiracy. This was a lamentable distortion of what German opposition figures, such as Theo Kordt and Carl Goerdeler, had actually confided to the British during recent months. None of them had suggested that Hitler had the remotest intention of attacking either Great Britain or France.[45]

Roosevelt was informed by Halifax that Hitler might seek to push Italy into war in the Mediterranean to find an excuse to fight. This was the strategy which Halifax himself hoped to adopt by pushing Poland into war with Germany. Halifax added that Hitler planned to invade Holland, and to offer the Dutch East Indies to Japan. He suggested to Roosevelt that Hitler would present an ultimatum to Great Britain, if he could not use Italy as a pawn to provoke a war. Halifax added casually that the British leaders expected a surprise German attack from the air before the ultimatum arrived. He assured Roosevelt that this surprise attack might occur at any time. He claimed that the Germans were mobilizing for this effort at the very moment he was preparing this report.

The British Foreign Secretary reckoned that Roosevelt might have some doubt about these provocative and mendacious claims. He hastened to top one falsehood with another by claiming that an "economic and financial crisis was facing Germany" which would compel the allegedly bankrupt Germans to adopt these desperate measures. He added with false modesty that some of this "may sound fanciful and even fantastic and His Majesty's Government have no wish to be alarmist."

Halifax feared that he had not yet made his point. He returned to the charge and emphasized "Hitler's mental condition, his insensate rage against Great Britain and his megalomania." He warned Roosevelt that the German underground movement was impotent, and that there would be no revolt in Germany during the initial phase of World War II. He confided that Great Britain was greatly increasing her armament program, and he believed that it was his duty to enlighten Roosevelt about Hitler's alleged intentions and attitudes "in view of the relations of confidence which exist between our two Governments and the degree to which we have exchanged information hitherto." Halifax claimed that Chamberlain was contemplating a public warning to Germany prior to Hitler's annual Reichstag speech on January 30, 1939. This was untrue, but Halifax hoped to goad Roosevelt into making another alarmist and bellicose speech. He suggested that Roosevelt should address a public warning to Germany without delay.[46]

Anthony Eden had been sent to the United States by Halifax, in December 1938, to spread rumors about sinister German plans, and Roosevelt had responded with a provocative and insulting warning to Germany in his message to Congress on January 4, 1939.[47] Halifax hoped that a second performance of this kind would be useful in preparing the basis for the war propaganda with which he hoped to deluge the British public. He did not achieve the desired response to this specific proposal. Secretary of State Hull explained, in what a British diplomat at Washington, D.C., jokingly described as "his most oracular style," that the Administration was blocked in such efforts at the moment by hostile American public opinion. Halifax was comforted on January 27, 1939, when he was informed officially that "the United States Government had for some time been basing their policy upon the possiblity of just such a situation arising as was foreshadowed in your telegram." This was another way of saying that the New Deal, which had shot the bolt of its reforms in a futile effort to end the American depression, was counting on the outbreak of a European war.[48]

Halifax learned on January 30, 1939, that leading American "experts" disagreed with a few of the details of his analysis of the Dutch situation. They expected Hitler to mobilize his forces along the Dutch frontier and to demand the surrender of large portions of the Dutch East Indies without firing a shot. The ostensible purpose of this Rooseveltian fantasy would be to "humiliate Great Britain" and to "bribe Japan." This dispatch was not sent on April Fool's Day, and it was intended seriously. It enabled Halifax to see that he had pitched his message accurately to the political perspective of Roosevelt, Hull, and their advisers. Anyone in their entourage who did not declare that Hitler was hopelessly insane was virtually ostracized. Roosevelt hoped to have a long discussion with Joseph Stalin at Teheran in 1943 about the alleged insanity of Adolf Hitler. He was disappointed when Stalin abruptly ended this phase of the conversation with the blunt comment that Hitler was not insane. It was like telling the naked Emperor that he was wearing no clothes. It was evident to Stalin that Roosevelt was a clever and unscrupulous politician who lacked the qualities of the statesman.[49]

Halifax Warned of the Approaching Slovak Crisis

The British and French did not approach the Germans again on the Czech guarantee question until February 8, 1939. The Anglo-French disagreement about the guarantee remained, and their inquiry at Berlin was a casual one. Coulondre, the French Ambassador, merely said that he would welcome German suggestions about the guarantee. Ribbentrop discussed the matter with the Western Ambassadors, and he promised to study the current Czech situation before replying to them. The casual nature of the Anglo-French *démarche* encouraged Ribbentrop and Hitler to believe that the Western leaders were not vitally concerned about the problem.[50]

The Czech situation deteriorated rapidly during the weeks which followed. Ribbentrop discussed the guarantee question with Coulondre on March 2, 1939, and with Henderson on March 3rd. He told them that Germany had definitely decided against a German initiative in the guarantee question. He added that conditions in Czecho-Slovakia were exceedingly precarious and unstable. Ribbentrop believed that Czech internal conditions precluded a guarantee, and he dropped the pointed hint that a guarantee by the Western Powers might increase the existing difficulties. This was particularly significant, because Great Britain and France had shown no indication of taking any initiative.

The British and French Governments had received formal notes from Germany on February 28, 1939, which stated the German position against the guarantee. Ribbentrop noted in his conversations with the French and British Ambassadors several days later that no instructions had been sent to them which might have enabled them to contest the German position. The Germans had been frank in rejecting the guarantee, and the British and French Governments had failed to respond.

Czech-German friction was a dominant note during the period between the Anglo-French *démarche* of February 8, 1939, and the German reply of February 28th. The Czechs continued to reject the Sudeten Jews who had elected to remain Czech under the Munich terms. The Czechs simply insisted that they did not want the Jews. They complained to British diplomats in Prague that the Jews "had been even more active than Christian Germans in Germanising Bohemia in the old days." They further complained that 21,000 Czechs from the Sudetenland had elected Czech citizenship, but that very few of the Germans in Czecho-Slovakia had elected German citizenship. The Czechs attributed this state of affairs to a deliberate German plot to maintain a large minority in the Czech area.[51]

Halifax learned on February 18, 1939, that Germany was considering intervention in Czecho-Slovakia. Henderson reported one of his "usual frank talks" with Marshal Goering on the morning of February 18th. The German Marshal was in excellent spirits. He had taken off forty pounds of excess weight, and he was planning a pleasant vacation at San Remo early in March. The conversation soon turned to serious subjects of high policy. Goering knew that "the vast sums of money for British rearmament" were either for British defenses or for a British preventive war against Germany. Goering confided that the Germans had reduced their arms expenditure after Munich until British measures prompted them to increase their own military budget. Goering analyzed the current situation, and he claimed that German arms were costing less than British arms.[52]

Goering reminded Henderson that Hitler was more interested in peace than in war. Henderson reported to Halifax that in his opinion the German Marshal was absolutely sincere in this statement. Goering assured Henderson that there were no German plans for action on a large scale. He added that the British could expect to witness plenty of action on a relatively small scale in the immediate German neighborhood. He informed Henderson specifically ". . . that Memel will eventually and possibly sooner rather than later revert to Germany is a foregone conclusion and a settlement as regards Danzig equally so, Czecho-Slovakia may also be squeezed." This was a blunt and frank confession which ordinarily would have been made only between Allies. It was a clear warning that decisive developments could be expected on the Czech scene. Weizsaecker predicted to Henderson on the same day that none of the questions arising in 1939 would "lead to a serious risk in the relations between the two countries."[53]

Halifax's Decision to Ignore the Crisis

Halifax was aware that a crisis was approaching, and he responded in the manner best calculated to serve his own purposes. The newspapers close to the Government, such as the London *Times*, were advised to desist from spreading alarmist reports and to present an optimistic and complacent view of the contemporary scene. The leading spokesmen of the Government were encouraged to make optimistic and conciliatory statements. The alarmist campaign of the Government, which had begun to reach a climax after January 1939, was allowed to subside temporarily. Halifax hoped to convince the British public that Hitler was launching unexpected bolts from the blue when the inevitable climax of the Czech crisis arrived.[54]

Increasingly serious internal difficulties faced the Czech state. The Slovak ministers demanded of their Czech colleagues, at the mid-February joint-meeting of the Central, Slovakian, and Ruthenian ministries, to drop the anti-German men in the Central Cabinet from their posts. The demands were not met. The leaders of the German minority claimed that the Czechs were applying economic pressures to force them to elect German citizenship and move to German territory. Theodor Kundt, a German minority leader, delivered a sensational speech at the German House in Prague on February 17, 1939. He demanded a return to the treatment that the Germans had been accorded by the Bohemian kings, many of whom had been German princes, in the old days. The Slovaks were angered by the Czech refusal to permit the Slovak soldiers of the Czecho-Slovak army to garrison Slovakia. The Prague Government was determined to keep the Czech troops in Slovakia, and the Slovak units in Bohemia. It was evident that a final breach was approaching between the Czech and Slovak leaders.[55]

The Czech Government was desperately searching for added prestige with which to meet the domestic crisis, and to ward off the spreading conviction that the Czecho-Slovak experiment was doomed to failure. On February 22, 1939, the Czechs presented an *aide-mémoire* to the Four Munich Powers which contained an appeal for the territorial guarantee. The Czechs at last agreed to renounce their alliances and declare their neutrality in exchange for a guarantee.[56]

The Czech note aroused no enthusiasm in London. Sir Alexander Cadogan, the Permanent Under-Secretary at the British Foreign Office, complained that the Czechs had not made it clear whether or not they intended to declare their neutrality unilaterally in order to become eligible for the guarantee. The Swiss in the 19th century had declared their own neutrality before accepting the international guarantee of the Powers. This was an interesting point, but the British Government displayed no interest in obtaining clarification about it from the Czechs.[57]

Halifax conversed with German Ambassador Dirksen on the day the Czech note was received at London, but he did not mention the Czech problem. Dirksen was about to return to Germany on leave, and he reminded Halifax that Ribbentrop was more pro-British than ever in his attitude. Halifax responded by assuring Dirksen that England "would be glad to receive Ribbentrop on a visit."[58]

The Germans were very frank with the British at this time, and they had little reason to suspect that anything they might do in Czecho-Slovakia would compromise their relations with Great Britian. Dirksen spoke with Chamberlain on February 23, 1939, before departing for Germany. Chamberlain inquired if many Germans had fled from the Sudetenland to Prague, as political refugees from National Socialism. Dirksen conceded that 13,000 German opponents of Hitler had deserted the Sudetenland for the Bohemian interior, before German troops had completed the occupation of Sudeten territory.[59]

British diplomats in Prague reported on February 25, 1939, that the Czech Government had decided not to permit German and Jewish refugees from the Sudetenland to remain Czech citizens, and they continued to refuse entry permits to the Jews.[60] The Czechs were resolved to employ stern measures in dealing with the Slovaks. British diplomats in Bratislava, Slovakia, warned London on February 26, 1939, that Slovak dissatisfaction with the Czechs was approaching a climax, and that German influence in Slovakia was increasing. They further warned that the climax of the Slovak crisis could be expected in the immediate future. Halifax took this warning seriously, and he informed British Ambassador Lindsay in Washington, D.C., on February 27, 1939, that he had received information "pointing to the possibility of a military occupation of Czechoslovakia."[61]

Hilter served as host at his annual dinner for the Diplomatic Corps in Berlin on March 1, 1939, two days after the Halifax telegram to Lindsay. This was the last occasion on which he appeared in formal evening attire. He spoke to the accredited envoys individually. He declared fervently to Henderson, in the presence of the other envoys, that "he admired the British Empire." Hitler emphasized the absence of serious points of conflict in Anglo-German relations. He told Henderson that on this occasion he did not consider it necessary to invite the British Ambassador to call afterward for a special talk on the problems of Anglo-German relations. Henderson had no instructions to discuss the Czech question with Hitler.[62]

The Czech and Slovak leaders were deadlocked in important negotiations on financial questions throughout the first week of March 1939. The Czech Government moved to strengthen its military hold in Ruthenia on March 6, 1939, and the Ruthenian autonomous Government was summarily dismissed by the Prague authorities. Newton warned London again on that day that "relations between the Czechs and the Slovaks seem to be heading for a crisis."[63]

The Polish leaders discussed the Slovakian "movement for independence" with British diplomats at Warsaw. Kennard reported to Halifax on March 7, 1939, that a member of the Slovak Governement was due to arrive in Warsaw the same day on a special mission. The Poles were aware that Germany was becoming the dominant foreign force in Slovakia, and the Polish attitude toward Slovak independence was more reserved than in the past. Kennard learned that, nevertheless, the Poles intended to tell the Slovak emissary that "whatever they do Poland would still regard Slovakia with sympathy." The Poles were willing to give the Slovaks the encouraging assurance that Poland would guarantee the new frontier with independent Slovakia. The Slovaks were to be assured that the Polish leaders did not believe Hungary would object to Slovak independence.

Kennard believed that the continuing Polish policy of encouraging Slovak independence resulted from Polish impatience to settle the Ruthenian question. The Poles were still disappointed that Italy had failed them at Vienna, and they were complaining that Ciano "has clearly not the courage to do anything which might displease the Reich." Kennard concluded that the Poles remained opposed to the preservation of the Czecho-Slovak state.[64]

Chvalkovský asserted to British diplomats at Prague on March 8th that Hitler had used a clever formula to eliminate the possibility of further negotiation about a separate German territorial guarantee to Czecho-Slovakia. He recalled that the German Chancellor had said the Poles and Hungarians should be willing to accept the present territorial *status quo* as a condition for the guarantee. Chvalkovský complained bitterly that Poland and Hungary would never agree to this.[65]

The Climax of the Slovak Crisis

The climax of the Slovak crisis arrived on March 9, 1939, when the Prague Government dismissed the four principal Slovak ministers from the local Government at Bratislava.[66] Henderson reported from Berlin with conclusive evidence that Germany was supporting the Slovakian independence movement. The London *Times* responded by assuring its readers that the European situation was calm.[67] Geoffrey Dawson, the editor of the *Times*, noted in his private diary on March 12, 1939, that the Czechs and Slovaks were fighting in the streets of Bratislava. On the following day, the *Times* repeated that the European situation was calm, and it assured its readers that Germany had no demands upon her neighbors. Dawson wrote in his diary on the same day that Hitler was taking charge of the trouble in Slovakia "in his usual bullying way." This friend of Halifax had matched in journalism the duplicity which characterized the diplomacy of the British Foreign Secretary.[68]

246   THE FORCED WAR

Henderson was puzzled by the failure of the leading British newspapers to refer to the crisis in Slovakia. He reported to Halifax on March 11th that the German press was devoting much attention to the Czech-Slovak controversy, and that it was carrying the announcement that Tiso had appealed to the German Government for aid. Halifax learned from Warsaw on the same day that the Polish leaders expressed no concern about the future of Bohemia-Moravia, but they were bitter that Germany, and not Poland, was in a position to secure the dominant influence in Slovakia. The Polish leaders still hoped that some alternative to an independent Slovakia under German protection would emerge, but the prospects were distinctly unfavorable. The Poles were concentrating on their own campaign in support of the Hungarian acquisition of Ruthenia at Czech expense. Halifax was warned on March 12th that agitators in Bohemia-Moravia were blaming the Slovakian crisis on the Germans, and that fanatical groups of Czechs were marching through the streets of Bruenn singing *Hrom a Peklo* (Thunder and Hell, i.e. to the Germans).

Joseph Kirschbaum, at the time a prominent Slovak politician and later a professor at the University of Montreal in Canada, has refuted the claim of the American journalist, William Shirer, that the Germans intimidated the Slovaks and thus forced them to break once and for all with the Czechs. Karol Sidor had agreed on March 10th to head an interim administration in Slovakia. A mission of German notables from Vienna, including State Secretary Wilhelm Keppler, Austrian Governor Arthur Seyss-Inquart, and Gauleiter Joseph Buerckel, arrived in Bratislava late on the same day to discuss the situation with Sidor. There was a friendly exchange of views, and the German leaders departed with the satisfaction of knowing that Sidor had no intention of conducting a policy in opposition to Tiso and the other Slovakian leaders. Tiso continued to hold the initiative as the recognized leader in Slovakian politics, and all of his decisions during the crisis were made with the full approval of his principal confederates.

Hitler agreed on March 13, 1939, not to oppose a Hungarian invasion of Ruthenia, and he received a special message of thanks from Regent Horthy of Hungary on the same day. Josef Tiso, the Slovakian leader, arrived in Berlin by way of Vienna on March 13th, and he met Hitler in a hurried conference. Hitler explained that the German press had been criticizing Czech policies for several days because he had granted permission to do so. He had decided that Germany should not tolerate the permanent unrest and uncertainty which existed in Czecho-Slovakia. Hitler admitted that until recently he had been unaware of the strength of the independence movement in Slovakia. He promised Tiso that he would support Slovakia if she continued to demonstrate her will to independence. Tiso replied that Hitler could rely on Slovakia.[69]

Halifax prepared a curious analysis of this situation for Henderson in Berlin, which was obviously designed to occupy a prominent place in the future official record of events. This analysis culminated in the following statement: "During the last few weeks there had certainly been a negative improvement in the situation, in that rumors and scares have died down, and it is not plain that the German Government are planning mischief in any particular quarter. (I hope they may not be taking, even as I write, an unhealthy interest in the Slovak situation)."[70]

This is an extraordinary performance from the man who two weeks earlier predicted the likelihood of a German military occupation of Czecho-Slovakia in the immediate future. Fortunately, it is possible to compare this analysis with a memorandum written by F.N. Roberts and possibly dictated by Halifax on March 13, 1939. This memorandum, in contrast to the message to Henderson, contained a shrewd and accurate estimate of the Slovak crisis. It ended with the statement that "the position in Slovakia seems to have been thoroughly unsatisfactory since Munich," and that Hitler may "come off the fence, and march on Prague." The march on Prague was considered to be a logical move on the part of Hitler to meet the exigencies of the current crisis. One almost has the feeling that the author was saying that, if he were Hitler, he would march on Prague. It is important to note that the memorandum was prepared before there was the slightest indication of what Hitler would do beyond encouraging the Slovaks.[71]

German Ambassador Moltke at Warsaw, who had failed to interpret correctly the policy of Poland during the Czech crisis in 1938, was puzzled by the Polish attitude in March 1939. He wondered why Poland continued to advocate the dissolution of Czecho-Slovakia when it was obvious that Germany would benefit from this development far more than Poland. He knew that the Polish leaders were interested in Ruthenia, and that Slovakian independence would solve the Ukrainian problem by cutting off Ruthenia from Prague.

Moltke reported on March 13th that Poland was "quite obviously adverse" to an independent Slovakia under German influence, because this would increase the potential military danger from Germany. It seemed to Moltke that Poland would lose much more in Slovakia than she would gain by having Hungary in Ruthenia. Moltke concluded that the Poles might be playing a double game. There was a rumor in Warsaw that the Czechs had appealed for Polish help against the Slovaks, offering Ruthenia in exchange. Moltke considered it improbable that the Czechs had proposed this, but he believed that the Poles were capable of making this proposition to the Czechs.

Moltke did not deny that the Polish attitude toward Germany was currently friendly on the surface, but he argued that the stakes were high in Slovakia, and that Poland "has to fear that now the independence of Slovakia would only mean alignment with Germany." Moltke was again mistaken in his analysis of an important situation, and at Berlin the possibility of a Polish-Czech deal was ignored. The German diplomat had failed to weigh the factor of the Polish desire to witness the final elimination of their Czech rivals.[72]

The Hitler-Hacha Pact

Tiso had the support of Ferdinand Durčansky, who had formerly advocated the experiment of Slovak autonomy under Czech rule, in his bid for Slovak independence. Tiso and Durčanský together could count on the unanimous support of the Slovakian Diet. They decided at 3:00 a.m. on March 14th to convene the Diet later the same morning, and to request the Slovakian deputies to vote a declaration of independence. This strategy was successful, and March 14th became Slovakian independence day. When Hitler received word of the

Slovakian independence vote, he instructed Weizsaecker that Germany had decided to recognize Slovakia, and he ordered him to inform the foreign diplomats in Berlin of this fact. Weizsaecker discussed the situation with Henderson. The British Ambassador complained that the Vienna radio had encouraged the Slovakian independence bid. Weizsaecker replied by repeating what many foreign diplomats had reported during the months since the *Anschluss*. He commented to Henderson that in many respects "Austria was largely independent of Berlin."

Henderson had no instructions from Halifax to deal with the crisis, but he took a serious step on his own initiative. He contacted Czech Minister Mastny on March 14th and urged him to suggest that Chvalkovský should come to Berlin to discuss the situation with Hitler. The Czechs reponded favorably to Henderson's suggestion. Newton was working closely with Henderson, and he reported from Prague a few hours later that President Hacha and Chvalkovský had received permission from the Germans to come to Berlin. The Czech leaders left Prague by special train at 4:00 p.m. on March 14, 1939. The subsequent conference with the Germans proved to be a decisive event in Czech history. It began and ended on the early morning of March 15th. A Czech-German agreement was concluded which provided for an autonomous Bohemian-Moravian regime under German protection.[73]

The Czech President was correctly received at Berlin with the full military honors due to a visiting chief of state. Hitler met his train and presented flowers and chocolates to Hacha's daughter, who accompanied the Czech statesmen. Hacha's daughter denied to Allied investigators, after World War II, that her father had been subjected to any unusual pressure during his visit to Berlin. The meeting with the German leaders lasted from 1:15 a.m. to 2:15 a.m. on March 15th; Hacha described the full details to his daughter after returning to his hotel. Hitler, Hacha, Chvalkovský, Ribbentrop, Marshal Goering, and General Keitel had attended the meeting. Hacha made a plea for the continuation of full Czech independence, and he offered to reduce the Czech army. Hitler rejected this plea, and he announced that German troops would enter Bohemia-Moravia the same day. The Germans made it quite clear that they were prepared to crush any Czech resistance.

Hacha, who was bothered by heart trouble, had a mild heart attack during his session with the German leaders. He agreed to accept German medical assistance, and he quickly recovered. This was a great relief to everyone, for the Germans dreaded to think of what sensational foreign journalists might have reported had Hacha died in Berlin. Hacha and Chvalkovský agreed to telephone Prague to advise against resistance. The remaining time was devoted to the negotiation of an outline agreement, and some of the details were arranged between the Czechs and the Germans at Prague on March 15th and 16th. The main German advance into Bohemia-Moravia did not begin until after the conclusion of the Berlin meeting between the Czech and German leaders. An exception was made in one instance. The Germans and Czechs had been concerned since October 1938 lest the Poles seek to seize the key Moravian industrial center of Morava-Ostrava. Hitler had ordered special German units to enter the area late on March 14th to prevent this eventuality. The local Czech population understood the situation, and there was no violence.[74]

The Hungarian Government presented a twelve hour ultimatum to the Czechs on March 14, 1939. The Czechs submitted, and the Hungarian military occupation of Ruthenia began the same day.[75] Henderson had been informed of Germany's intention to occupy Bohemia-Moravia, before the arrival of Hacha and Chvalkovský at Berlin. The British Ambassador immediately informed Halifax of this German decision, but he received only ambiguous instructions in reply. Halifax empowered Henderson to say that Great Britain had no desire to interfere in matters where other countries were more directly concerned, but she "would deplore any action in Central Europe which would cause a setback to the growth of this general confidence on which all improvement in the economic situation depends and to which such improvement might in its turn contribute." This Sphinx-like pronouncement was not easily intelligible, and Henderson could do little more than assure the Germans that Great Britain would not interfere with their Czech policy.[76]

Halifax's Challenge to Hitler

Henderson hoped that the British reaction to the crisis would be mild. He wired Halifax that in this situation the best hope was "in the recognition of the fact that the guarantors of the Vienna Award (Germany and Italy) are the parties primarily interested." It would have been possible for Halifax to follow this sensible suggestion, and to exert a restraining influence on British public reaction to the hurried events of the crisis. Winston Churchill, who had expert knowledge of British public opinion and no knowledge of the current Halifax policy, did not expect the British leaders to change their course because of what had happened at Prague. He knew that it would have been possible for Chamberlain and Halifax to guide British public opinion along the lines of appeasement after March 1939, and he was amazed by the sudden switch in British policy a few days after Hitler arrived at Prague. It was evident that Halifax chose on his own volition to ignore the advice of Henderson, and not because he was responding to an imaginary pressure to do so.[77]

The story of the British reaction to Prague is the story of the British balance of power policy in 1939. Hitler's move to Prague was merely the signal for the British to drop the mask of their false appeasement policy. The British leaders had made extensive preparations for this step since the Munich conference, and they would not have been at a loss to find some other pretext to implement it, had the Czech crisis in 1939 taken a different course. The proof of their effort to place more emphasis on an imaginary crisis in Rumania in March 1939 than on the real crisis in Czecho-Slovakia will be analyzed later. British diplomacy in the Czech question since Munich had deprived them of any legitimate grievances relative to Hitler's solution of the Czech problem. Halifax had evaded British responsibilities in both the Czech-Magyar dispute and in the guarantee question, and he had been the first leading European statesman to advocate abandoning the application of self-determination to Czecho-Slovakia. He encouraged Germany to attempt a unilateral solution of the Czech problem by refraining from showing any interest in the Czech crisis during the final hectic weeks of the Czecho-Slovak regime.

It is astonishing that as late as 1960 William Shirer, who has received undeserved recognition for an allegedly definitive history of Germany under Hitler, failed completely to understand the Czech situation in March 1939. Shirer claimed no less than four times in his description of the situation that Great Britain and France at Munich "had solemnly guaranteed Czechoslovakia against aggression." Shirer's account throughout is characterized by his failure to consult most of the available documents dealing with the events which he describes. His work is a mere caricature of a genuine historical narrative. His scanty and infrequent use of British sources meant that it was impossible for him to understand any important phase of British policy in 1939.

Hitler recognized the British game immediately after Prague, but he hoped to out-maneuver his adversaries on the diplomatic board. He refused to admit that an Anglo-German war was inevitable, because he knew that the British, despite their momentary hostility toward Germany, would never dare to attack alone and unaided. The Anglo-German crisis was in the open after Prague, but war was not inevitable.

Stanley Baldwin, the former Conservative Prime Minister, had planned a series of lectures in January 1939 which he hoped to deliver at the University of Toronto in Canada the following April. The lectures were entitled: "England and the Balance of Power as illustrated in the fight against Philip of Spain, Louis XIV, and Napoleon, leading up to the fight against tyranny to-day." The conduct of Halifax in March 1939 in opening the public campaign for the destruction of Germany was so masterful that Baldwin decided any lectures he might give on foreign policy would be an anti-climax. He had been willing to give the original lectures in April as a patriotic duty in preparation for what Halifax had already accomplished in March 1939 without his help. Baldwin recognized that foreign policy had never been his strong point, and he realized that Halifax completely overshadowed him in that field. Baldwin decided in April 1939 to confine his Canadian speeches to the domestic affairs which he knew so well. The foreign policy of the British Empire was in the hands of Lord Halifax. The immediate issue was whether or not there would be another Anglo-German war. It was a contest between Halifax and Hitler, the British aristocrat and the German common man.[78]

Hitler's Generous Treatment of the Czechs after March 1939

Hitler believed that his decision to pursue this course was defensible. He attained results without bloodshed, and the danger of a war between the Czechs and the Slovaks was averted. He was willing to grant the Czechs the autonomy which they had persistently refused to give the Sudeten Germans. It was evident within a few weeks after the proclamation of the Protectorate of Bohemia-Moravia on March 16, 1939, that the new regime enjoyed considerable popularity among the Czechs. Baron Konstantin von Neurath, the former German Foreign Minister, was appointed chief representative of the German Government at Prague. The *Reichsprotektor* was noted for his pro-Czech views. Emil Hacha explained to journalists on March 22, 1939, that he had departed for Germany on March 14th on his own initiative in the hope of finding some solution for a hopeless crisis.

The German Minister in Prague never suggested this visit. The treaty which Hacha signed with the Germans on March 15, 1939, had been prepared after negotiation. No German document was presented in advance of the negotiation at Berlin.[70]

Bohemia-Moravia was constituted a separate customs area on March 24, 1939. It was announced on March 27, 1939, that Czech would continue to be the official language in Bohemia-Moravia. Minister Mastný, who had represented the Czechs at Berlin in the past, accepted a special decoration from Ribbentrop on April 2, 1939. The German military flag was lowered from the Hradschin Castle in Prague on April 16, 1939. The period of direct German military rule lasted only one month. The Commander of the German Army, General Walther von Brauchitsch, ordered that German garrisons should be concentrated in areas populated by the German minority so that friction between Czech civilians and German soldiers might be avoided.

President Hacha appointed a new Czech Government on April 27, 1939. The Beran Government had resigned on March 15, 1939. The new Premier, Alois Eliáš, also administered the Department of Interior. Chvalkovský succeeded Mastný as Czech Minister at Berlin. The new Czech administration retained the Departments of Transportation, Justice, Interior, Education, Agriculture, National Economy, Public Works, and Social Service. The Departments of Foreign Affairs and Defense were dissolved.[80]

Neurath was officially introduced to the new Czech Government a few days later. Premier Eliáš began and concluded his speech in Czech, but he also made a number of comments in German. This was courtesy rather than servility; the German language had been spoken and understood by educated Czechs for many centuries. Neurath replied with a few gracious remarks. He reminded the Czech leaders that Hitler had expressed his esteem for the Czech people in a speech before the German Reichstag on April 28, 1939.

Neurath presented a favorable report to Hitler on conditions in Bohemia-Moravia on June 1, 1939. Hitler replied on June 7, 1939, by declaring an amnesty for all Czechs held as prisoners for political reasons in both the Sudeten and Protectorate regions. The Czech Government at Prague was negotiating a series of trade treaties with delegations from foreign nations. A Norwegian-Czech trade pact was signed on June 23, 1939, and a Dutch-Czech trade pact was concluded on the following day.

The cooperative attitude of the Czech leaders and the Czech population prompted Hitler to make a further concession on July 31, 1939. An agreement was concluded which permitted the Czech Government to have a military force of 7,000 soldiers, which would include 280 officers. The officers were selected from the former Czech army, and it was provided that only persons of Czech nationality could serve in this force. A Czech Military General-Inspector and three subordinate Inspectors were appointed.[81]

Hitler allowed the British to know as early as April 1939 that the Protectorate Articles of March 16, 1939, were not necessarily the last word in the Czech question as far as he was concerned. Hitler was willing to negotiate about the Czech question and the Czech future through the channels of conventional diplomacy. He hoped that this attitude would be effective eventually in appeasing the British leaders, and he was willing to make concessions to support it.[82]

Hitler was pleased with the Czech response to his policy. Several regions of dangerous instability had been pacified without loss of life, and the strategic position of Germany was greatly improved. The German military frontier was shortened, and close collaboration between the Germans and the Slovaks was achieved. He was disappointed by the hostile British reaction to his policy, but he hoped that the British leaders were impressed by German strength and by his ability to deal with difficult problems without creating a conflict. His greatest disappointment, shortly after the German occupation of Prague, was the revelation of an Anglo-Polish plot to oppose Germany in Eastern Europe. Hitler had counted on German-Polish collaboration against the Soviet Union, and he deplored the decision of the Polish leaders to become the instruments of a British policy of encirclement.[83]

The Propaganda Against Hitler's Czech Policy

The policy of Hitler in Bohemia-Moravia was extremely vulnerable to the onslaught of hostile propaganda.[84] The argument was raised that German devotion to self-determination was a fraud because Hitler had reduced Czech independence to mere autonomy. This argument was unfair. Hitler had never proclaimed an intention to bring all of the Germans of Europe into the Reich. He recognized that strategic, geographic, political, and economic considerations had to be taken into account when self-determination was applied. There were more Germans living outside the German frontiers in Europe after March 1939 than there were alien peoples in Germany. Furthermore, these outside Germans (*Volksdeutsche*) at no place enjoyed the autonomy which the Czechs possessed.[85]

It was astonishing for the British leaders to claim that Germany had hoisted the pirate flag, when Hitler switched his support from the Czechs to the Slovaks in the crisis between the two neighboring Slavic peoples. The British were ruling over millions of alien peoples throughout the world on the strength of naked conquest. It was evident that the British leaders failed to appreciate Hitler's ability to solve difficult problems without bloodshed. Apparently they preferred their own methods. Halifax told German Ambassador Dirksen on March 15, 1939, that he could understand Hitler's taste for bloodless victories, but he promised the German diplomat that Hitler would be forced to shed blood the next time.[86]

It was astonishing to hear the British leaders claim that Hitler had broken promises by taking Prague. Chamberlain explained in the House of Commons on March 15, 1939, that Germany had no obligation to consult Great Britain in dealing with the Czech-Slovak crisis in the period March 14-15, 1939. The British Government had never fulfilled its promise to guarantee the Czech state after Munich, and the Slovak declaration of independence on March 14th had dissolved the state which had not received the guarantee. Chamberlain apparently believed that consistency was the virtue of small minds. He discussed the same situation at Birmingham two days later and he claimed that he would never be able to believe Hitler again. This was mere cant. Chamberlain relied upon British prestige and force rather than honor to hold foreign leaders to their commitments. He had said to his advisers at the time of the Munich conference that he did not actually trust Hitler. The German leader studied Chamberlain's remarks at Birmingham and remained cool. He knew that Great Britain would never strike a blow against Germany unless she considered that the moment was favorable. He correctly believed that there would be several opportunities ahead for him to deprive the British leaders of that favorable chance to attack Germany.[87]

Chapter 11

GERMANY AND POLAND IN EARLY 1939

The Need for a German-Polish Understanding

The collapse of the Czecho-Slovak state in March 1939 was preceded by crucial German-Polish negotiations in January 1939. The most significant diplomatic event in December 1938 had been the Franco-German declaration of friendship. This raised the possibility of a durable understanding between National Socialist Germany and the French Third Republic. The British leaders had replied with their visit to Rome in January 1939 and with intensification of their appeasement policy toward Italy. They hoped to make Rome dependent upon London in foreign affairs.

The British visit to Rome was very important, but it was overshadowed that same month by the visits of Beck to Berchtesgaden and Ribbentrop to Warsaw. The future of German-Polish relations had become a matter of supreme importance for the entire European situation. There would either be further progress toward a German-Polish understanding, which would strengthen the German bid for an understanding with France, or there would be a return to the chaotic situation of German-Polish relations before the Non-Aggression Pact of 1934. This could easily lead to war in Eastern Europe, which, at the very least, would undermine Franco-German relations and prompt the British leaders to intensify their efforts in Italy. The 1934 Pact was a useful basis for the improvement of German-Polish relations, but it was apparent that further steps were required to achieve a more fundamental understanding and to prevent the loss of the many gains which had been made. At the very most, a German failure in Poland might be exploited successfully by the British leaders to unleash another general European conflict like that of 1914. Hence, it would be difficult to exaggerate the importance of German-Polish negotiations in January 1939.[1]

The 1934 Pact between Germany and Poland was merely a nonaggression treaty in the style condoned by the League of Nations. The problems of Danzig and of Germany's undefined attitude toward the western border of Poland remained unresolved. Both Germany and Poland were opposed to the Soviet Union and its policies, but no attempt had been made to coordinate permanently the anti-Soviet orientation of the two states along the lines advocated by Goering during his many visits to Poland. The Poles had obtained a promise of German support against Russia during the 1938 Czech crisis, but the question of the more permanent German attitude, in the event of an attack on Poland by the Soviet Union during the months after Munich, had not been resolved. The Poles were concerned about the possibility of a Russian attack. They maintained a permanent military alliance with Rumania directed exclusively against Russia.[2]

There was nothing exaggerated in Ribbentrop's contention that no comprehensive settlement of differences between Germany and Poland had been achieved since the defeat of Germany in 1918. The German-Polish treaty of 1934 had merely avoided some very real problems inherited from the Versailles settlement of 1919. The situation would have been an entirely different one had the so-called peacemakers of 1919 established the territorial *status quo* between the two nations in conformance with point 13 of the 14 Point Peace Program of Woodrow Wilson.[3]

The tragedy of Europe in 1939, in the larger sense, resulted from the failure of the European states to solve short of war the problems created by the broken allied promises of 1918. The solemn contract concluded between Germany and the Allied and Associated Powers in the armistice agreement of November 1918 included Point 13 of the Wilson program. Germany agreed to accept the results of self-determination in the German-Polish borderlands, and Poland was to obtain access to the sea within this context of self-determination. The promise to Poland provided the basis for Czechoslovakia's successful campaign at the peace conference to obtain access to the sea by means of free harbor facilities at Hamburg and Stettin, and free harbors might easily have been granted to Poland at Danzig and Koenigsberg without violating self-determination. The unsatisfactory settlement in Danzig and the Corridor had remained unmodified for twenty years. A peaceful solution in 1939 would have been a major contribution to stability in Europe.[4]

The Generous German Offer to Poland

Ribbentrop and Hitler suggested a settlement in October 1938 which was far less favorable to Germany than Point 13 of the Wilson program had been. This proposed settlement would not enable Germany to regain the position she would have retained had the Allied Powers not violated the 1918 armistice contract. Poland received at Versailles large slices of territory in regions such as West Prussia and Western Posen which were overwhelmingly German. The census figures indicated that a Polish victory in a plebiscite for the province of West Prussia would have been impossible. Therefore the Allies refused to permit a plebiscite in the area. The bulk of West Prussia was turned over to Poland without further ado, and the protests of the defeated Germans were treated with contempt.

One might argue that the superhighway plan called for the return of at least some Polish territory to Germany. The Germans were aware, when proposing the plan, that they would have to tunnel under, or build over, all existing and future North-South Polish communications. The strip of territory involved in the plan would have been at most 5/8 of a mile wide and 53 1/8 miles in length. The applicable doctrines of international law indicated that the extraterritorial arrangement would constitute merely a servitude rather than an actual transfer of sovereignty. The Germans in this arrangement would receive a special privilege within an area under Polish sovereignty.[5]

The Hitler plan did not envisage the aggrandizement of Germany through the recovery of former German territory granted to Poland in 1919. His purpose was to encourage the renunciation by Germany of her claims to this territory in the interest of German-Polish cooperation. This concession of Hitler's was more than adequate to compensate for German requests in the Corridor and at Danzig. The October 1938 Hitler offer was the most modest proposal which Poland had received from Germany since 1918. Georges Bonnet had often reflected on the price in concessions which Bismarck had vainly paid France in an effort to obtain voluntary French recognition of the Franco-German border of 1871.[6] The Polish leaders would have recognized that German concessions were an adequate basis for an agreement had they placed any value on cooperation with Germany as a permanent policy. This would not have prevented them from seeking other commitments from Germany, such as a German agreement not to maintain German armed forces in Slovakia. The Poles preferred the unrealistic position that a German offer to guarantee their 1919 frontier was no concession to Poland.[7]

The German offer of October 24, 1938, was no mere feeler by Germany, to be withdrawn when the Poles failed to respond in October and November 1938. The Germans did not request larger concessions from Poland during the period of more than five months before the definitive Polish refusal of their offer, and it was the impatience of the Polish leaders, rather than of Hitler, which led to the rupture of negotiations in March 1939. The Polish diplomats themselves believed that the Germans were sincere in offering their proposals as the basis for a permanent agreement. Hitler was also willing to retreat somewhat from the original proposals and to abandon the German suggestion for a railway to accompany the superhighway to East Prussia. The issue of the definitive Polish response to the German offer remained in doubt after Ribbentrop's first conversations with Lipski. The Poles said nothing to indicate that there was no chance of reaching an agreement on the basis proposed.[8]

The Reasons for Polish Procrastination

The Poles had good reasons to wait more than five months, while the British increased their armaments, before categorically rejecting the German offer. They experienced little difficulty in keeping the negotiations open as long as they pleased and until they chose their own moment to disrupt them. They kept their own counsel, and they refused to confide the details of the negotiation to the French, who were their allies, and to the British, who were eager to support them. Beck maintained this attitude despite the fact that consultation on important questions was a basic feature of the Franco-Polish alliance. He also knew that the British were exhibiting great curiosity and impatience about the situation.[9] Beck treated the truly Great Powers of Europe with disdain during these months. He was aware of the importance of his own position while Great Britain and Germany were both courting Poland.[10]

The Poles were also secretive because they did not wish their problems with Germany to come before an international conference. They suspected, with good reason, that their French ally would conclude, in such an eventuality, that Germany had a more reasonable case. Poland was fundamentally hostile toward the mutual discussions which conference diplomacy implied. She preferred bilateral negotiation, and she did not care to have states which were not directly concerned pass judgment on Polish interests.[11]

Beck's tactics of secrecy and delay are easily intelligible under these circumstances. The situation would have been entirely different had Beck not counted upon the British intention to attack Germany. It cannot be said with certainty that the Poles would have settled their differences with the Germans had there been a friendly, or at least peaceable, British attitude toward Germany, but this was exceedingly likely. It is absolutely certain that the Poles would not have abruptly disrupted their negotiation with the Germans in March 1939 without an assurance of British support.

The recent experience of Czechoslovakia raised serious doubts in Polish minds about France. This was praticularly true of Józef Beck and Juliusz Lukasiewicz, the leading Polish experts on France. The Poles were gambling on the ability of Great Britain to dominate and decide French policy in a crisis.[12]

Beck knew that Great Britain was not ready to intervene against Germany, when Ribbentrop presented the German offer in October 1938. Beck had observed with disdain that Great Britian purchased peace in 1938 at Czech expense. He had British assurances dating from September 1938 that Poland would not be treated like Czechoslovakia. This encouraged Beck to take a bold stand, and to proclaim that the Poles, unlike the Czechs, were prepared to fight with or without assurances from other Powers. Beck was not bothered by the fact that the British would never be in a position to offer Poland immediately effective military support. He was less interested in preventing the momentary defeat of Poland than in promoting the ruin of both Germany and the Soviet Union.[13] Beck's foreign policy was based on the World War I *mystique*. A new defeat of Russia by Germany, and of Germany by the Western Powers, would permit the Great Poland of pre-partition days to arise from the ashes of a momentary new Polish defeat.

The Poles also attached great importance to the role of the United States. They knew that American intervention had been decisive in World War I. They knew that the American President, Franklin Roosevelt, was an ardent interventionist. Roosevelt differed markedly from his predecessor, Herbert Hoover, after whom many streets were named in Poland in gratitude for his post-World War I relief program. Hoover had been favorably impressed by a conversation with Adolf Hitler on March 8, 1938, and he was a leader in the struggle against current American interventionism. The Poles knew that Hoover, who was wrongly accused of being the father of the American economic depression, that began in 1929, had little influence on American policy in 1938. They knew that President Roosevelt was eager to involve the United States in the struggles of distant states in Europe and Asia. American opponents of Roosevelt who opposed his foreign policy were disdainfully labelled isolationists.

The Poles did not trouble themselves about the reasons for President Roosevelt's interventionism. They were too realistic to assume that he necessarily had any legitimate reasons. They were content to accept the convenient explanation of Count Jerzy Potocki, the Polish Ambassador to the United States. Potocki claimed that President Roosevelt's foreign policy was the product of Jewish influence. This was untrue, but there was little interest in Poland for an elaborate analysis of American policy. The surveys sent by the Polish Foreign Office to missions abroad rarely mentioned the American scene. The Poles recognized the importance of the American position, but they were content to leave the problem of promoting American intervention in Europe to their British friends.[14]

Hitler's Refusal to Exert Pressure on Poland

The friendly German attitude made it easy for Beck to defer his decision on the October 1938 offer without arousing German wrath. The German approach to Poland was very different from their earlier attitudes toward Austria or Czechoslovakia. Rump-Austria existed in 1938 merely because she had been refused the right to join Germany by self-determination in 1919. Hitler, as an Austrian German, could scarcely sympathize with Austrian leaders who hoped to establish an unpopular Habsburg monarchy in that tiny area. Hitler shared the attitude of Pilsudski toward Czechoslovakia. He believed that the nationalities state under Czech rule, which had been recognized at Versailles, was an unnatural phenomenon without any traditional position in the historical experience of Central Europe.[15]

There were some Germans who regarded the resurrection of Poland in the 20th century as a mistake, but Hitler did not share their views. He opposed the advocates of collaboration with Russia, who wished to cement Russo-German relations by partitioning Poland with the Soviet Union. Hitler recognized in *Mein Kampf* that a case could be made for an anti-Polish policy, and he observed that German policy in World War I had been unsuccessful in Poland because it was neither distinctly pro-Polish nor anti-Polish. Hitler believed that the issue had to be met squarely, and he had decided for a pro-Polish policy. It was for this reason that he was extremely patient in dealing with the Poles.[16]

There were many strong arguments in favor of a pro-Polish policy, once the attitude of Hitler was accepted that Germany should renounce the territories lost to Poland in World War I. France, Italy, and Poland were the three most important immediate neighbors of Germany in Europe. It was wiser from the standpoint of German defense and security to establish friendly ties with these three neighbors than to alienate any of them. The most valuable achievement of diplomatic statecraft is to achieve good relations with one's immediate neighbors. It was possible in terms of power politics to substitute Russia for Poland as a neighbor, but Hitler recognized that there was virtually no chance for permanent friendly relations with the Communist state under Stalin. The Soviet Union was pledged to the destruction of its capitalist neighbors.[17]

Beck's Deception Toward Germany

Beck deliberately misled the Germans about his intentions during the months after October 1938. He succeeded in convincing them that he favored a pro-German policy for Poland. He merely insisted that such a policy be consistent with vital Polish interests, and acceptable to Polish public opinion to some degree. Beck was so successful in this approach that most German experts concluded that he was acting almost against his will, and certainly against his preferences, when he finally came into the open with a vigorously anti-German policy.[18]

Beck used many devices to create the desired impression with the Germans. He constantly emphasized his alleged esteem for German-Polish cooperation. He was usually charming and attentive while discussing German proposals, and this was especially true of his conversations with Hitler, for whom he undoubtedly had a great personal liking. His opinion of the leading personalities in England and France was less favorable, but he shared Pilsudski's conviction that personalities should not be permitted to play a decisive role in Polish policy. Beck was adept at exploiting Polish public opinion, which undoubtedly was hostile to Germany, and in labelling it an important obstacle to a quick and easy settlement with the Germans. Beck, at the same time, was careful not to build up this public opinion factor to a point where the Germans might conclude that he was unable to cope with it. Beck was skillful at leaving the foor open, and at conveying hints that a settlement might eventually be achieved on approximately the terms offered by the Germans. Beck's game with the Germans is a fascinating episode in diplomatic history, but unfortunately it ended in tragedy.[19]

The Confiscation of German Property in Poland

The situation was complicated by the increasing harshness with which the Polish authorities handled the German minority. The important German-Polish conferences of January 1939 were held under the shadow of the approaching annual Polish agrarian reform decree, which was scheduled to be announced on February 15, 1939. Mieczlaw Zaleski, a prominent Polish spokesman, claimed in a speech at Katowice (Kattowitz) that the 1934 Pact with Germany was concluded solely for tactical reasons, because it was a convenient screen behind which the Polish Government could eliminate the German minority. The speaker declared that this Polish policy was necessary in "preparing the ground for a future conflict." The alleged purpose of the Polish Government was to rid itself of the German element in Poland before going to war with Germany.[20]

The German Government hoped to persuade the Poles to be more fair to the German landowners in 1939 than they had been in 1938. A larger area of German land had been expropriated in 1938 than in 1937, despite the conclusion of the November 1937 Minorities Pact with Poland. The current agrarian law dated from 1925, and 66% of the land expropriated under the law since that time in Polish West Prussia and Poznan (Posen) had been taken from the Germans. This was true despite the fact that a much larger proportion of the larger farms belonged to Poles rather than Germans in 1925. The principal German complaint was not so much against the breaking up of the large farms, but against the redistribution policy. Less than 1% of the confiscated German farm land was redistributed among the German minority. This was the primary reason for the flight of the German peasants from Poland to Germany. The total amount of land under cultivation in Polish West Prussia and Poznań had decreased during these years, whereas it had increased everywhere else in Poland.

The German Government resented the fact that the German owners of expropriated land received only 1/8 of the value of their holdings. It was difficult to sell the land in advance of expropriation, because the Polish public was aware of the German situation and desired to exploit it. Furthermore, the Frontier Zone Law forbade altogether the private sale of land by the Germans in a large area. The main aim of the Polish Government was to prevent private sale and to gain the land through public expropriation.

Beck assumed a nonchalant attitude when discussing this question with Moltke. He claimed that it was not important if the German holdings were confiscated first, because the Polish holding would be broken down under the law in just a few years. Moltke doubted that Minister of Agriculture Poniatowski, who pursued a generally conservative policy, intended to proceed vigorously against the Polish holdings. He was aware that organized pressure-group resistance would hinder in large measure the application of the law to the Poles. It seemed exceedingly unlikely to Moltke that the current Government would fully implement a reform law which had been passed before the Pilsudski *coup d'etat* in 1926. It was more likely that the law would merely serve as a convenient instrument to produce impoverishment among the Germans.[21]

Weizsaecker instructed Moltke to insist that the provision of the November 1937 Pact for equal treatment of German and Polish landowners be observed in 1939. Count Michal Lubienski, at the Polish Foreign Office, assured Moltke that current expropriation lists were being prepared with complete objectivity and without regard for the ethnic character of the landowners. Moltke was lulled into a sense of false security by this promise. He telephoned Berlin in a voice choked with indignation of February 15, 1939, to report the results of the new law. In Poznań 12,142 hectares of 20,275 hectares to be confiscated were German owned. In Polish West Prussia 12,538 hectares of 17,437 hectares were German owned. In East Upper Silesia all but 100 of the 7,438 hectares to be confiscated land was German. It virtually completed the elimination of German holdings under the law at a time when most of the larger Polish holdings were still intact. This was the Polish "complete objectivity" which had been promised by Lubienski.

Weizsaecker instructed Moltke on February 16, 1939, to present a sharp protest about this "incredible discrimination against German landowners" in Western Poland. He was to inform the Poles that their action was contrary to the November 1937 Pact, and to more recent assurances. The Polish Foreign Office responded on February 17th by disclaiming reponsibility for the situation. They appeared in the guise of seeking to protect German interests, and they claimed to have sought in vain a 50-50 ratio for the Germans in Poznan. They also used the remarkable argument that the rate of confiscation in the Western provinces had been influenced by factors in other Polish areas.

Their reaction was negative to Moltke's suggestion that there should be joint discussions between the two countries on minority questions. It was evident that nothing could be done to help the Germans in Poland by diplomatic means.[22]

The problem of the annual agrarian decree had been discussed for several months by the provincial press on the German side of the frontier. The German Government had decided to follow the advice of Moltke, and to take the first cautious step toward relaxing the complete censorship in Germany on the German minority grievances in Poland. A new censorship directive in December 1938 permitted the border area newspapers to report new excesses as they occurred, and to speculate on their consequences. It was forbidden to discuss earlier incidents, and the press in the German interior was ordered to continue with the complete suppression of German minority news. Ribbentrop had personally warned Lipski about the possible consequences of the intensified campaign against the German minority on December 15, 1938. He complained about Polish arrogance at Danzig, and he protested a recent series of Danzig stamps issued by the Poles which comemorated the Polish victories over the German knights in the Middle Ages. Lipski promised that the Polish Government would withdraw the offensive postal stamps.[23]

Kennard at Warsaw believed that tension increased between Germany and Poland in November and December 1938, and he was pleased by this development. This compensated for his worry about the attitude of France. French Ambassador Léon Noël returned from leave at Paris in late November 1938. He had warned Kennard that the French leaders were inclined to modify their alliance obligation to Poland. The French Ambassador confided that there was a strong movement in France to liquidate all French military obligations in Eastern Europe. The French had concluded a special subsidy agreement with Poland another 95 million francs according to the terms of the Rambouillet loan. It seemed to Noël that France made this payment with more than customary reluctance. These comments alarmed Kennard, who reported to Halifax that a marked relaxation of French interest in Poland might aid the Germans in arriving at a definitive German-Polish understanding.[24]

German-Polish Conversations at the End of 1938

Lipski and Ribbentrop had discussed the problem of a general settlement on December 15, 1938. The Polish Ambassador invited the German Foreign Minister to come to Warsaw to speak with the Polish leaders, and Ribbentrop accepted. Ribbentrop hinted that he hoped to complete the negotiation of an agreement with Poland at Warsaw. He said that the visit should constitute a serious effort to reach a "general settlement" rather than be a mere formality. Lipski at once agreed with this view, and he mentioned again that Poland was prepared to discuss a German superhighway and railway to East Prussia. He failed to mention Danzig.

Ribbentrop told Lipski that he hoped Poland would always follow a policy based on "the tradition of Pilsudski and his breadth of vision." He added that additional discussion of minorities was needed to remove current friction. He assured Lipski that his aim was cooperation between Germany and a strong

Poland against the Soviet Union.

Lipski mentioned the improvement of Polish relations with Lithuania, and he casually added that Poland was taking an increased interest in the maritime facilities at Memel. Ribbentrop replied that he hoped Polish interest in Memel was exclusively commercial and not political, "for Memel was entirely German and had always been so." Ribbentrop stated frankly that Germany stood for self-determination at Memel. Lipski raised no objection to Ribbentrop's comments, and he stated that Poland was interested in the city solely for economic reasons. Ribbentrop noted that German representations to the signatory Powers of the 1920 Memel statute always had been fruitless. He confided that Germany would not consult these Powers when she solved the Memel question.[25]

Moltke returned to Berlin from Warsaw to report, on December 16, 1938. Hans Frank, Hitler's ardently Catholic Minister of Justice, had been honorary guest the previous evening at a German Embassy dinner at Warsaw. Frank had discussed German-Polish relations with Józef Beck at the dinner. Beck claimed to place great value on the 1934 Pact with Germany, and he stressed his readiness to continue the policy of Pilsudski in German affairs. His German hosts interpreted this to mean that Beck was dedicated to an outspokenly pro-German policy. Beck complained that "a certain tension" now existed in German-Polish relations, but he described this as absurd. He believed that the attitude of the Polish public toward Germany had deteriorated, but he suggested that this was the result of the many crises in Europe during recent months.[26]

Moltke also discussed the situation with Beck. He insisted to Beck that the Polish policy in the Teschen area, and toward the German minority generally, was responsible for the unfavorable development in German-Polish relations. Moltke complained bitterly that affairs in Teschen were desperate, and that the local Germans had come to regard the twenty years under the Czechs as a paradise by comparison. Beck insisted in reply that this was merely a local phenomenon. He promised that the Polish Government at Warsaw desired to restrain the local East Upper Silesian authorities, and to provide "good living conditions" in Teschen. He said that the Polish Premier, General Slawoj-Sklad-kowski, had ordered the local authorities to improve their policy, and he promised that he would intervene personally whenever he was informed of incidents. Moltke was often inclined to believe the best about the intentions of the Polish leaders, and he was extremely pleased with the results of the dinner. He construed Beck's remarks to imply a standing invitation to discuss minority problems. This conclusion was altogether too optimistic. Moltke admitted to Ribbentrop that he had sought to contribute to the friendly atmosphere at the dinner by expressing his sympathy with the Polish viewpoint in the Ruthenian question.[27]

Moltke had a conversation with Beck on December 20, 1938, after his return to Warsaw. The Polish Foreign Minister was aware of Ribbentrop's plan to negotiate a general settlement at Warsaw. He knew that this negotiation would fail, and he wisely concluded that it would be expedient to ingratiate himself with Hitler before the visit took place. He informed Moltke that he intended to spend the Christmas and New Year holidays at Monte Carlo, and he suggested that his return trip to Poland would offer him an opportunity to stop off in

Berlin "or some other place." Moltke correctly interpreted "some other place" to mean Berchtesgaden, and another visit with Hitler.[28]

Beck said smoothly that he planned to leave Monte Carlo on January 5th or 6th, and that he would understand perfectly if this date was not agreeable. Moltke assumed charitably that Beck was trying to pave the way for Ribbentrop's visit to Warsaw later in January, but it was obvious that a Beck visit to Hitler would cause Ribbentrop's stay in Warsaw to appear as an anti-climax. In the upshot, Beck said that it would suffice for his plans if he were notified by January 1, 1939, either through the Polish embassy in Berlin, or through Moltke from Warsaw.[29]

The importance of Danzig in the approaching negotiations with Poland was emphasized for the Germans by a report of December 22, 1938, from Danzig Senate President Artur Greiser. He had discussed the future of Danzig with Polish High Commissioner Marjan Chodacki. The Polish High Commissioner called on Greiser, after a long interval, with the surprising announcement that "the fundamental Danzig-Poland question" had to be discussed. Chodacki charged bluntly that "a psychosis was being created in Danzig, the purpose of which was to convince the population of Danzig that the city would be returned to the German Reich within the forseeable future." The arrogant Polish High Commissioner made a number of insulting remarks, and he claimed contemptuously that it would be easy for Poland to protest current developments on the basis of "international law."

Chodacki threatened that the Polish Government might seek to crush the rising spirit of freedom in Danzig by means of punitive political and economic measures. He claimed that this would have been done earlier had he not advised the Polish Government against it. He said that future Polish concessions to Danzig would depend upon respect for the "Polish element" and for "vital Polish rights in Danzig." Greiser was seeking to interpret the storm of abuse which Chodacki had unleashed, and he observed casually that it was his impression that many discussions on Danzig had taken place recently between Warsaw and Berlin. He also knew that Chodacki had conferred with both Beck and Lipski while on sick leave recently in Warsaw. Greiser asked bluntly "whether in the opinion of the Polish Government the Danzig question was a national question for Poland, and whether to Poland a solution of the question in line with the wishes of the Danzig population would mean war." Anyone who knew Chodacki, and who was familiar with the nervous intensity of this temperment, could easily imagine how the Polish diplomat received this fundamental question. He drew a deep breath prior to confronting the mild-mannered Greiser with a reply which could leave no possible room for misunderstanding.

Chodacki instructed Greiser that Poland had only two national questions in the proper sense of the word. The first was the Polish Army and the second was the Baltic Sea. Chodacki extended his arm toward the South and described for Greiser in glowing terms the "natural protection" of the distant Carpathian mountains. He believed that other frontiers were still more formidable, and that "in the east and in the west there were two ideological walls (Soviet and National Socialist) with fixed boundaries which by treaty could not be altered." This could be interpreted as a Freudian slip which implied a suppressed Polish desire to expand in both directions. Chodacki then exclaimed triumphantly that "to the north was the open sea, toward which Poland and the entire Polish people were striving." He concluded that Danzig and her present unsatisfactory *status quo* were a necessary feature of this part of the Polish national question. Chodacki was satisfied that Greiser had understood his *non possumus* reply to German aspirations at Danzig. When he had finished making his point, he proceeded to discuss a lengthy series of specific Polish protests to recent enactments of the Danzig Senate.[30]

It might had made a difference had Beck been equally frank at this time and spoken his mind to Hitler about Danzig. Hitler would have known where he stood before he was confronted with a Polish mobilization and a British encirclement policy. He might have modified his Danzig policy before the British had a chance to intervene. The Ruthenian question was still unsettled at this time, and the Slovakian independence movement had not reached a climax. Hitler might have had more success had he forced the pace for a Danzig settlement immediately after the Munich conference. It is pointless to pursue this speculation at great length, because Beck was completely successful in deceiving Hitler about his policy. Hitler was counting on a friendly agreement with Poland. He never exerted pressure on the Poles until they disrupted the negotiations and confronted Germany with a number of hostile measures.

League High Commissioner Burckhardt had confided to the Germans that the outlook was favorable at Warsaw for a settlement of the Danzig question. Chodacki was merely the Polish High Commissioner at Danzig. He was noted in Berlin for his extreme chauvinism and eccentricity. The fact that he was an intimate friend of Beck was not generally known. This friendship, even had it been recognized by the Germans, would not have justified the conclusion that Chodacki was an authoritative spokesman in the highest sphere of Polish foreign policy. The Poles were noted for their extreme individualism, and they were accustomed to express themselves freely on the most controversial topics. Chodacki had actually expressed Beck's own ideas, but anyone who had preconceptions about Beck's policies would scarcely have accepted these remarks as a true formulation of Beck's position. Of course, Chodacki's remarks had some effect at Berlin. Ribbentrop could see that it was important to retain the moderate influence of Burckhardt at Danzig until a settlement was reached. Ribbentrop approved an appeal from Greiser to the League Committee of Three. This appeal suggested that Danzig was prepared to make further concessions, if Burckhardt was retained at his post. The German Foreign Minister could understand that the Danzigers did not care to be left alone with Chodacki.[31]

The Beck-Hitler Conference of January 5, 1939

It was announced publicly at Warsaw and Berlin before the end of December 1938 that Beck would visit Germany in a few days. The British hoped that Poland and Germany would fail to settle their differences, and they were eager to discover the significance of this visit. William Strang at the British Foreign Office made a determined but unsuccessful effort to obtain information from Polish Ambassador Raczynski on December 31, 1938. The Polish aristocrat parried Strang's questions with ease, and it was impossible to obtain any news at that source.[32]

The task of obtaining information was entrusted again to Kennard, but this time the British Ambassador was unable to turn up any leads. He attempted to compensate by reporting on such developments as he could from Warsaw. He wired Halifax on January 1, 1939, that to Burckhardt the Danzig situation was "paradoxical in that the Poles, the Danzigers and Germans all apparently wish him to remain at present." This was true, but it was no longer news in London.

Kennard also reported a fantastic claim from Chodacki that Albert Forster feared a new Danzig election because the German Catholics might vote the Polish ticket. The Polish High Commissioner was indulging in some typical wishful thinking, and, in any case, Danzig was overwhelmingly Protestant. The National Socialists emphasized earlier that both German Catholics and German Protestants abroad voted for them. The overwhelmingly Catholic Saar had voted for union with Germany in 1935, and Danzig had elected a National Socialist majority in 1933, before the National Socialists had been about to gain an absolute majority in a German election. The Danzig National Socialists were the uncontested representative of the Danzig community in 1939. Chodacki should have known that even in the days of the Hohenzollern Empire, when there was close cooperation between the Catholic Center Party and the Polish Fraction in the Reichstag, the German Catholic voters never voted the Polish ticket.[33]

Kennard admitted that he had nothing to report about Beck's visit to Hitler. He predicted that a successful negotiation between the Poles and the Germans would not take place, because "I feel M. Beck can hardly make any concession." No one in Warsaw was willing to tell Kennard how or why the mysterious project of Beck's sudden visit to Germany had been arranged. Kennard hoped that nothing would result from the visit, but he was uneasy about it.

The visit for Beck at Berchtesgaden took place on January 5, 1939. Hjalmar Schacht, the President of the German Reichsbank, received Montagu Norman, from the Bank of England, at Berlin on the same day. Schacht and Norman were close personal friends, and they were probing the possibility of reviving the declining trade between Great Britain and Germany. Hitler had delivered a public message to the German people on January 1, 1939, expressing his satisfaction with the events of 1938 and his confidence in the future. He emphasized the work of the National Socialist Party for the recovery and rehabilitation of Germany. He was optimistic about prospects for peace, and he expressed his gratitude that it had been possible to solve the principal foreign policy problems of Germany by peaceful means during the preceding twelve months. The new *Reichskanzlei* (chancellery building) at Berlin had just been completed. It was an imposing achievement of modern architectural construction and style. The official inauguration of the *Reichskanzlei* was scheduled for January 9, 1934. Hitler's New Year's message revealed that he was in high spirits, and his satisfaction was no doubt increased by the magnificent new architectural triumph in Berlin, and by the auspicious Schacht-Norman negotiations. This impression is confirmed by the tone of his personal negotiations with Beck.[34]

Beck was accompanied to Berchtesgaden by Count Michal Lubienski and Józef Lipski, although only Lipski was present with Beck at the decisive January 5th discussion with Hitler. Ribbentrop and Moltke were also present at the conference. The meeting took place in an atmosphere of cordiality, courtesy, and friendship.[35]

Beck began his remarks by deploring the deterioration of relations between Germany and Poland after the high point of cooperation which had been achieved during the Czech crisis in September 1938. He warned Hitler that Danzig was a question in which third parties might intervene. This was obviously an allusion to the possible support of Great Britain and France for the Polish position at Danzig. Beck emphasized that he was primarily interested at the moment in the further diminution of the Czech state and in the acquisition of Ruthenia by Hungary. He hoped that Hitler would not extend a guarantee to Czecho-Slovakia until the Ruthenian question was solved. He also doubted the wisdom of any guarantee for Czecho-Slovakia.

Hitler did not commit himself on the Czech question, but he went to considerable effort to convince Beck that Germany did not intend to slight Polish wishes on the Ruthenian question. Hitler denied emphatically that Germany was interested in Ukrainian nationalism, or that Germany had any interests beyond the Carpathians, where most of the Ukrainians lived. Hitler argued that German policy and the Vienna Award were the products of the Hungarian attitude during the September 1938 crisis. He repeated the remark of the Hungarian leaders that a war, even if lost, "would perhaps not be fatal to Germany, (but) it would definitely mean the end of Hungary." Hitler added that the Hungarians had refused to demand the entire Carpatho-Ukraine when Mussolini arranged for the inclusion of Polish and Hungarian claims at Munich.

The German Chancellor told Beck that the Czechs would probably have refused to surrender all of Ruthenia in November 1938. He was convinced that the Hungarians would have failed to take Ruthenia by force had they dared to attempt it. He predicted that the Czechs would have marched to Budapest in any war following a breakdown of Hungarian-Czech negotiations after Munich. He intimated that Germany would have been unwilling to do anything for Hungary under these circumstances. Hitler reminded Beck that Germany had greatly reduced her armed forces by November 1938, and he claimed that she would have been unprepared for the crisis which might have resulted had an attempt been made at Vienna to extend the Hungarian claims beyond ethnic limits. Hitler hoped to convince Beck with this elaborate and plausible explanation that Germany had not deliberately ignored Polish wishes at Vienna.

Hitler frankly admitted that the intervention of Chamberlain and Daladier had deflected him from his purely political solution of the Czech problem. This solution "would have been tantamount to a liquidation of Czechoslovakia." Hitler would have preferred a settlement in which only Poland, Germany, and Hungary had participated. This would have produced a solution different from the Munich agreement. Unfortunately, it gradually became evident in September 1938 that an attempt to exclude Great Britain, France, and Italy would have meant war. Hitler emphasized that he sympathized with the Polish attitude toward Czechoslovakia, but he refrained from encouraging the Poles to believe that he was prepared to support their Ruthenian policy. Beck concluded that Hitler was momentarily undecided about his future Czech policy.

Hitler told Beck that he favored a strong Poland under all circumstances. His attitude was not influenced solely by the Bolshevist threat and the system of

Government in Russia. The German Chancellor believed that each Polish division on the frontier against Russia was worth a German division. He declared with enthusiasm that Polish strength in the East would save Germany much military expenditure in the future. He conceded that Soviet Russia, because of her recent purges, might be weaker momentarily in the military sense than would be the case with some other Russian system. He also claimed that the Bolshevist regime easily compensated with effective propaganda for any momentary loss in the military sphere. He refused to agree with those who belittled the Soviet menace, and he believed that Europe would have to be strong and prosperous to cope with this danger. He painted a glowing picture of Poland as the prosperous economic partner of Germany. Hitler explained to Beck that Germany needed economic partners. The United States was not suitable in this respect, because the Americans produced the types of industrial products with which Germany herself paid for raw material and food imports. It seemed to Hitler that Germany and Poland were ideally suited for complementary economic relations. Hitler believed that heavier Polish exports to Germany would build Polish prosperity and enable the Poles to consume an increasing proportion of German goods.

Hitler stressed the great importance of achieving a general understanding between the two nations, and he complained that the 1934 German-Polish Pact was "a rather negative agreement." He insisted with enthusiasm that Poland and Germany required a positive understanding. He was glad to inform Beck confidentially that Germany would soon recover Memel from Lithuania, and he indicated that the attitude at Kaunas promised a peaceful negotiation without disagreeable incidents. Beck did not oppose Hitler's challenging remark that the political union of Danzig with Germany did not seem inconsistent with Polish interests, provided, of course, that the Polish economic position at Danzig was fully respected. Hitler told Beck that Danzig would return to Germany sooner or later. He was careful to add that he did not plan to confront Poland with a *fait accompli*, although Hitler had momentarily considered just such a plan in November 1938.

Hitler concentrated on the crucial Danzig issue. He devoted scant attention to the question of Corridor transit, because the Poles had conveyed the impression that they were prepared to accept a settlement on this point. The German Chancellor was obviously seeking to prepare the ground for successful negotiations between Ribbentrop and the Poles at Warsaw. He hoped to convince Beck that the concessions offered by Germany were adequate compensation for Danzig. He reminded Beck that no other German could both advocate and achieve a German guarantee of the Polish Corridor, and he hoped that Beck appreciated the importance of this fact. Hitler conceded that it might be difficult for anyone outside of Germany to understand the psychological problem involved in this renunciation. He asked Beck to believe him in this, and he added that heavy criticism of his Corridor policy in Germany was a certainty. He predicted that a German-Polish agreement would eventually cause this criticism to diminish and then disappear. He assured Beck that in the future one would hear as little about the Polish Corridor in Germany as one now heard about South Tirol and Alsace-Lorraine.

Hitler continued to stress the benefits to be gained from German-Polish cooperation. He anticipated greater Polish maritime activity, and he observed that it would be absurd for Germany to seek to deprive Poland of her access to the sea. Hitler discussed common German and Polish aims in the Jewish question, and he assured Beck that he "was firmly resolved to get the Jews out of Germany." He knew that Poland was worried by the allegedly insufficient speed of her own program to expel the Jews, and he hoped to interest Beck in a plan for German-Polish cooperation to solve this question. He suggested that it might be possible to establish a refuge for both German and Polish Jews within the area of the former German colonies in Africa.

Beck greeted Hitler's many suggestions with cordiality, but he also maintained considerable reserve. He reassured Hitler that Polish policy toward Russia was dependable. He had improved Polish relations with Russia in November 1938 in an effort to cope with the dangerously tense situation resulting from the Czech crisis. However, he promised that Poland would never, under any circumstances, accept a relationship of dependence on Russia. Beck emphasized repeatedly that he appreciated Germany's friendly attitude toward Poland. He displayed no awareness that he also appreciated the value of a comprehensive agreement on outstanding problems, and he went no further than to say that Poland would adhere to her old policy toward Germany. Beck insisted that the Danzig question was extraordinarily difficult, but he did not betray the defiance he felt when Hitler discussed the inevitable German annexation of Danzig. Beck stressed the problem of Polish opinion toward Danzig, and he emphasized that he meant the public opinion which counted, and not mere "coffee-house opinion." He intimated that the Polish public was unprepared for a German success at Danzig. He gave Hitler the misleading assurance that he was quite prepared to think about the matter, and to orient his thoughts toward a solution. He warned Hitler that "some day" he might intervene militarily in Ruthenia. He belittled Ukrainian aspirations for nationhood, and he claimed that the word "Ukraine," which was of obscure and controversial origin, meant "eastern march," and had been coined by the Poles. But he gave no indication that Poland intended to resume her march to the East.[36]

Hitler was perfectly satisfied about this conversation with Beck, and this is ample proof that he was in no great hurry to achieve his program at Danzig. The conversation had produced no positive result. Beck had nevertheless achieved his purpose of increasing Hitler's confidence in Polish foreign policy. Hitler had personally joined Ribbentrop in the negotiation on Danzig, and this had not prevented a friendly exchange of views. Hitler was willing to concede that Beck might require considerable time to prepare Polish public opinion for a Danzig agreement. The OZON (Camp of National Unity) forces, and hence the Polish Government, had suffered a reversal in the Polish municipal elections of December 1938. This did not represent a new trend, since many opposition voters had turned out to vote against the Government instead of boycotting the elections, but the result was impressive in a negative sense. Hitler was prepared to wait for the consummation of the agreement with Poland, but he hoped that Ribbentrop would obtain at least some confidential commitment from the Polish Government at Warsaw later in January 1939.[37]

Beck reacted quite differently. He had never entertained the idea of permitting Germany to have Danzig, and he was determined to oppose this development with every resource available. He had deliberately and successfully concealed this fact from Hitler for reasons of policy, and he had increased Hitler's confidence in Poland. This was no small achievement when one considers how strongly Beck felt about Danzig.

The discussion between Hitler and Beck at Berchtesgaden was an important event. Beck claimed that he was convinced from this conversation that a war between Germany and Poland was virtually inevitable in the immediate future. He hastened to inform President Mościcki and Marshal Smigly-Rydz, after his return to Poland, that it was necessary to assume that Poland could do nothing to avoid this eventuality. He claimed that if Poland made concessions in the issues at stake, questions "so secondary for them (i.e. the Germans) as those of Danzig and the superhighway," it would mean the loss of Polish independence and the demotion of Poland to a German vassal state. He did not explain why these questions were unimportant to the Germans and a matter of life and death to Poland. [38]

The Beck-Ribbentrop Conference of January 6, 1939

It is not surprising that Beck showed some signs of frayed nerves the next day in his conversation with Ribbentrop at Munich. It is significant that Beck had not even mentioned the earlier Polish counterproposal about Danzig in his conversation with Hitler.

Ribbentrop's objective in the conversation at Munich on January 6, 1939, was to elaborate on the German arguments on the Danzig question, and prepare the ground for his later negotiations at Warsaw. Beck was irritated by Ribbentrop's careful persistence, which made it difficult for the Polish Foreign Minister to conceal his true intentions as to Danzig. Beck warned Ribbentrop that the Danzig question might seriously disturb German-Polish relations. He urged that plans be completed for a provisional arrangement at Danzig in case the League of Nations withdrew the League High Commissioner. He expressed concern about new developments which might produce energetic Polish steps in the Danzig question. Beck described the Danzig problem as a dilemma in which "he had cudgelled his brains for a solution, but without result so far." He confided to Ribbentrop that his concern about Danzig made him pessimistic. He attempted to convince Ribbentrop that Polish public opinion toward Danzig was a primary factor, and he asserted that a great effort would be required to alter this opinion.

Ribbentrop endeavored to put Beck at ease by assuring him that Germany was not interested in a violent solution of the Danzig question. Ribbentrop hoped to negotiate on the question peaceably until the matter was settled. He urged Beck to give the German offer for an agreement further consideration. He advised Beck to keep Germany informed of any possible Polish steps in the Ruthenian question, because a sudden change in the Czech *status quo* might carry with it the risk of a conflict.

The German Foreign Minister announced that he had several blunt things to say about recent Danzig events, which he had not cared to mention in Hitler's presence. Ribbentrop then presented a number of specific grievances about recent Polish interference in Danzig's internal affairs. He stressed Germany's need to establish contact with East Prussia and to acquire Danzig to satisfy vital German interests, and to make Hitler's pro-Polish policy acceptable in Germany. Beck was told that Germany would support Poland's policy toward Ruthenia, and toward the Ukrainians generally, if Poland would adopt an increasingly anti-Soviet attitude. The Polish Foreign Minister replied that "at present" it would not be possible for Poland to adhere to the anti-Comintern pact. Ribbentrop then bluntly asked if the Poles still had aspirations beyond their present eastern frontier. Beck declared with feeling that the Poles had been in Kiev, and that "Pilsudski's aspirations were doubtless still alive to-day."

Ribbentrop's question reflected German preoccupation with the attitude of Poland toward the Soviet Union. Hermann Goering, who constantly stressed the importance of this aspect of Polish policy, had visisted Poland briefly for talks with Polish leaders in December 1938. Heinrich Himmler, the Chief of the German Secret State Police, had also visited Poland again the same month. These German leaders, on their visits to Poland, stressed the need of a German-Polish agreement as a bulwark against Communism, and they hoped to discover how the Polish leaders envisaged the role of Germany in relation to future Polish plans against the Soviet Union.[39] It was obvious on every occasion that important Polish spokesmen hoped for the dismemberment of the Soviet Union. Ribbentrop was informed by German diplomats in Warsaw, later in January 1939, that the Mayor of Warsaw, the editor of the official *Gazeta Polska*, and the Under-Secretary in charge of the Western Division at the Polish Foreign Office, favored the partition of the Soviet Union and the establishment of an independent Ukraine under Polish influence. These men made no secret of their views in conversations with German spokesmen.[40] Beck was not equally frank about this question in his conversation with Ribbentrop at Munich, but his attitude confirmed the general response. It was clear beyond every doubt that Poland was dissatisfied with the *status quo* in the East, and that she wished to change it at Russian expense. Kazimierz Smogorzewski, of the *Gazet Polska*, had the reputation with the Germans of reflecting accurately the secret views of the Polish Government. He emphasized more precisely the dynamic Polish eastern policy to which Beck alluded in generalities. It was evident that Polish policy toward the Soviet Union was more concretely hostile than the policy toward Russia of any other country, including Germany. Poland alone had a blueprint for the reduction of Russian power in the East.

The German Government, unlike Poland, did not advocate an independent Ukraine nor the use of Ukrainian nationalism to dismember Russia. They were less interested in Polish Ukrainian plans than in the obvious fact that the Polish policy toward the Soviet Union was aggressively hostile. The Germans could not imagine how the Poles, under these circumstances, could be indifferent about the opportunity of settling German-Polish differences and reaching a permanent agreement with Germany.

The German leaders knew that Poland would have no chance of survival in a conflict with the Soviet Union unless she had the support of a friendly Germany. Polish hostility toward Russia seemed to be the best possible inducement for a German-Polish agreement. Poland had nearly gone down under the Russian invasion of 1920 when the Soviet Union was weak. The Soviet

Union had experienced a gigantic growth of military power since 1920. Greater Germany could hope to match this growth to some extent, but it was an impossibility for Poland with her tiny industrial resources. An agreement with Germany was the sole means by which Poland could pursue her own dreams of expansion, or hope to establish her national security in the face of the Soviet policy of expansion toward the West. The Polish leaders were aware of Russian territorial aspirations, and in 1938 the Soviet leaders had begun to discuss the revision of the Russo-Finnish frontier with the leaders of Finland. The Polish leaders underestimated the Soviet Union, but it seemed inconceivable to the Germans, or to the British and French for that matter, that the Poles would simultaneously challenge both Russia and Germany. This would be the case of the canary seeking to devour the two cats.[41]

Ribbentrop was momentarily satisfied with Beck's assurances about the anti-Russian policy of Poland. He returned to the problem of the German minority in Poland, and he expressed his concern about this question. He told Beck that he hoped to negotiate with Lipski in Berlin on this problem, so that some progress might be made toward an easing of tension before his arrival in Warsaw later in January.[42]

Weizsaecker summarized the importance of Beck's visit in a circular addressed to German diplomatic missions abroad. He emphasized that the conversations had taken place in a friendly atmosphere. They had been motivated by Beck's desire to discuss the new European situation with Hitler. The 1934 Pact with Poland had proved its worth as far as Germany was concerned, and it was still the basis for German-Polish relations. The Danzig question had been discussed, but it "did not reach a practical stage." There had been no attempt to conclude agreements of any kind, and the next step in Germany's effort to achieve a comprehensive settlement with Poland would be the visit of Ribbentrop to Warsaw.[43]

German Optimism and Polish Pessimism

Beck discussed the European situation after his return to Warsaw with American Ambassador Anthony Biddle. Biddle reported to the American State Department on January 10, 1939, that Beck was not enthusiastic about his recent trip to Germany. The most he was willing to say about his conversation with Hitler was that it had been "fairly satisfactory," and that Hitler had promised him that there would be no "surprises." Beck confided to Biddle that Hitler was disappointed about President Roosevelt's address to Congress on January 4, 1939, which had been bitterly hostile toward Germany. Biddle noted that Beck was complacent about Anglo-French relations and concerned about current Polish relations with France. Biddle reported that "Beck emphasized that Poland and France must meet at an early date to clarify their joint and respective positions *vis-à-vis* Germany. They were now both in the same boat and must face realities." It was evident from the general nature of Beck's remarks that the official Polish attitude was incompatible with the successful negotiation of an agreement with Germany.[44]

The German attitude toward Poland was entirely different, and there was an official atmosphere of optimism about the future of German-Polish relations. Swedish Minister Richert discussed the European situation with Weizsaecker on January 13, 1939. He told Weizsaecker that he regarded the approaching Ribbentrop visit to Warsaw as a further indication of increasing intimacy in German-Polish relations. Weizsaecker confirmed this impression. He assured the Swedish diplomat that the Russo-Polish declaration of November 1938 was inconsequential and did not imply any new orientation of Polish policy. He declared to Richert that the fundamental basis of Polish policy was friendship with Germany.[45]

Ribbentrop conferred on the same day with Albert Forster, the Danzig Party Leaders. Forster was advised to take no major steps in Danzig domestic politics until after the return of Ribbentrop from Warsaw. The German Foreign Minister did not wish unexpected incidents at Danzig to trouble the atmosphere. Ribbentrop knew that Forster was planning to introduce the German salute and the displaying of German flags on official occasions, and to increase the local Danzig S.S. (security corps) unit. He told Forster that he would be willing to discuss these measures after his trip. He added that the negotiation of a general settlement with Poland at Warsaw would resolve all existing problems. It was obvious that Ribbentrop was optimistic about the prospects for a successful negotiation.[46]

Lipski had accompanied Beck to Warsaw for a series of policy conferences following the visit to Hitler. The Poles were evidently flattered by Hitler's comment that each Polish Army Division was worth one German Army Division. Hitler's statement that a strong Poland was "simply a necessity" had also pleased the Poles.[47] This did not prevent Beck from being "furious with the Germans and inclined to further consolidate our relations with England and France." The conferences attended by Lipski began on January 8th and lasted for several days. Beck reiterated on January 10th that Poland would not accept the restoration of Danzig to Germany. His subordinates were told that Ribbentrop had raised the subject of his approaching visit to Warsaw, and that "Beck did not reply nicely to him, because he was furious against the Germans." Beck discussed his impressions about Hitler's general attitudes. He claimed that Hitler seemed to have little resentment against the Jews, but "much bad feeling toward Roosevelt and America." The latter reaction was not surprising, on the day after Roosevelt's provocative speech of January 4, 1939. The Poles at home were interested in Hitler's alleged opinions. What Hitler had to say about the Jews sounded mild to Polish ears, which were accustomed to a strong local brand of anti-Jewish sentiment. Beck promised that he would do everything possible when he visited London to gain maximum support from the West.[48]

Kennard attempted to discover, after Beck returned to Warsaw, what had transpired in Germany. He informed Halifax on January 11, 1939, that Beck was regrettably evasive. The Polish Foreign Minister insisted that no detailed discussion had taken place, when Kennard pressed him hard for information about Danzig. Beck said that "a prolongation of the pact between Germany and Poland was possible, but he himself gave no indication that it was likely." Kennard concluded that Beck did not care to confide his problems to the British at this point.[49]

French Ambassador Léon Noël also sought to divine the consequences of

THE FORCED WAR

Beck's latest move. He reported to Bonnet on January 12th that Beck was reticent, and that he refused to reveal the true nature of his negotiations with Hitler. Noël complained that Beck attempted to pass off the visit as a routine clarification of views. The Danzig question came up for discussion at the League of Nations in Geneva a few days later. Burchkhardt was not called upon to resign, and the situation at Danzig remained unchanged.[50]

The Ribbentrop Visit to Warsaw

The first definite information from Polish sources, which the British received about Beck's visit to Germany, was provided by Raczynski in London on January 25, 1939, the date that Ribbentrop arrived in Warsaw. The Polish Ambassador was instructed by Beck to admit that Danzig had been the principal subject of discussion at Berchtesgaden. Raczynski promised Halifax that Beck had made no concession to Hitler on Danzig, and he emphasized that Hitler had promised there would be no German *fait accompli*. Halifax recognized the importance of the Danzig question, and he assured Raczynski that he was looking forward to personal conversations with Beck about this vital issue.[51]

German State Secretary Weizsaecker was increasingly pessimistic about the prospects for successful negotiation with Poland. He predicted in a memorandum of January 23, 1939, that Ribbentrop's proposals for a settlement would fall on barren ground at Warsaw. Weizsaecker took the liberty to differ with Hitler and Ribbentrop, and it seemed to him that "after the exhaustive discussions with Polish Foreign Minister Beck during the first days of January, any more fruitful discussion of certain questions with him will hardly be possible." Weizsaecker conceded that Beck did not constitute the entire Polish leadership, and that it might "be worth while to feel out their attitude on some of the more important questions." He believed that it would be necessary at Warsaw to cover the entire complex of problems discussed at Berchtesgaden, except for Memel and the Polish Jews. The former had been settled between Beck and Hitler, and it did not seem that any satisfaction could be obtained about the Polish Jews stranded in Germany. Weizsaecker believed that Hitler's final solution of the Jewish question, by means of establishing a Jewish haven in a former German colony, was still a remote possibility.[52]

Beck complained vehemently about the alleged misfortune of playing host to the "obstinate" German Foreign Minister at Warsaw. Ribbentrop was not worried about Beck's attitude, and he was eagerly anticipating conversations with the leading Polish military men. He hoped to make a favorable impression which would be useful to Beck in negotiating an agreement with Germany. He arrived in Warsaw on January 25th, and he proposed the following encouraging toast at a state banquet the same evening: "That Poland and Germany can look forward to the future with full confidence in the solid basis of their mutual relations!"[53]

Beck in reply delivered an elegant speech in Polish. He insisted that Frau von Ribbentrop, through the magic of her presence, increased the importance of this official visit. He noted that the visit occurred on the eve of the 5th anniversary of the "peace declaration" between Germany and Poland on January

26, 1934. Beck praised Hitler and Pilsudski in lavish terms. He said that their mutual courage, prophetic insight, and power of will had been necessary ingredients in the conclusion of the pact. Beck expressed the hope that the two nations would concentrate on creative work, and that they would not lose the value of the Pact in neighborly friction or misunderstandings. He ended his speech with a glowing toast to Adolf Hitler.[54] Frau von Ribbentrop later recalled that Beck had intended to deliver a similar speech on the following day, but that he cancelled it with the explanation that a freshly contracted cold prevented him from speaking at length.

Beck had instructed Lipski on January 24, 1939, to protest the appearance in the Berlin *Voelkischer Beobachter* (*People's Observer*) of a map which showed that the northern section of the Polish Corridor was traditionally ethnic German territory. Beck did not like this reminder that Hitler was generous in his offer to leave this region in Polish hands. Beck had granted an interview to the English *Daily Telegraph*, on the previous day, which was ominously negative on the subject of German-Polish relations. Beck insisted that he intended to maintain an absolutely impartial policy toward Germany and the Soviet Union. He declared that it was a major aim of Polish policy to acquire colonies overseas for settlement and raw materials, and that it was logical for Poland to cooperate with nations which had overseas colonies at their disposal. It was known in London that Poland hoped to inherit the colonies lost by Germany in 1918.[55]

The *Illustrowany Kurjer* (*Illustrated Courier*) at Kraków on January 25, 1939, did what it could to spoil the atmosphere for Ribbentrop's visit. It claimed to have reliable information that Germany and the Soviet Union were negotiating a comprehensive agreement on political and economic questions. The Germans were allegedly promising that they had no territorial ambitions in Russia, and they were reported to be asking for Russian neutrality in the event of a war with Poland or with some other third state. There was not the slightest truth in this report, but it was effective in arousing the indignation of the Polish public.[56]

Ribbentrop conducted his principal discussions with the Polish military leaders on January 26, 1939. He assured Marshal Smigly-Rydz that there were no differences between Germany and Poland which could not be settled between Beck and himself. Ribbentrop spoke optimistically of the future, and he predicted that the Soviet Union would continue to be weakened by military purges and internal upheaval. The Polish Marshal was attentive, but he spoke in vague generalities and carefully concealed the Polish attitude toward a settlement with Germany.[57]

Ribbentrop was soon aware that there would be no fruitful negotiations during his visit at Warsaw. He had lengthy talks with Beck on each of the three days of his visit, but the principal conversation took place on January 26th. Ribbentrop "reverted to the old subject of the German proposal concerning the reunion of Danzig with the Reich in return for a guarantee of Poland's economic interests there, and the building of an extra-territorial motor road and railway connection between Germany and her province of East Prussia." He urged Beck to give more thought to German moderation in renouncing the valuable eastern territories lost to Poland after World War I. The German public still regarded these cessions as a great injustice, and "ninety-nine out of a hundred Englishmen or Frenchmen would say at once, if asked, that at least the return of Danzig and the Corridor, was a natural demand on the part of Germany." Hitler responded to this situation by offering to guarantee permanent Polish possession of the entire Corridor. Beck at first "seemed impressed . . . (and) again pointed out that internal opposition was to be expected. Nevertheless, he would carefully consider our suggestion."[58]

Beck shifted to the superhighway question and proceeded to blast Ribbentrop's assumption that this problem had been virtually settled. Beck cast doubts on the possibility that the Polish leaders would accept the German superhighway. He made it difficult for Ribbentrop to argue the point in detail, because he carefully avoided giving the impression that either he or Lipski had the slightest objection to the superhighway plan. Beck returned to the Danzig question, and he requested a new assurance from Ribbentrop that there would be no German *fait accompli* at Danzig. He wished Ribbentrop to agree that Germany and Poland would cooperate to maintain the status of Danzig as Free City until a German-Polish agreement was reached, regardless of the position taken by the League of Nations. Ribbentrop gave Beck his personal assurance that Germany would adopt this policy.[59]

Ribbentrop discussed Polish adherence to the anti-Comintern Pact, but he made no progress. Beck "made no secret of the fact that Poland had aspirations directed toward the Soviet Ukraine and a connection with the Black Sea; but at the same time he called attention to the supposed dangers to Poland that in the Polish view would arise from a treaty with Germany directed against the Soviet Union." Ribbentrop asked Beck for a prognosis of future events in the Soviet Union. Beck predicted that the Soviet system "would either disintegrate as a result of internal decay, or, in order to avoid this fate, would first gather all its strength and then attack."

Ribbentrop was seeking to orient his arguments to Beck's assumptions about the Russian question. It seemed that the analysis he had just heard made all the more regrettable "the passivity of M. Beck's attitude." Ribbentrop urged the need to "take action against the Soviet Union by propaganda." It would be a major propaganda move for Poland to join the anti-Comintern pact and Poland "could only gain added security." This cogent argument fell on deaf ears. Beck merely promised to give the matter "further careful consideration."[60]

Ribbentrop made no pretence, at the German Embassy reception on the evening of January 26, 1939, of achieving important results at Warsaw. He told Kennard that "he was very satisfied with the results of his visit but that we need not expect anything sensational from it." Ribbentrop's only conspicuous success at Warsaw was with Polish high society. Noël reported to Paris that Ribbentrop was fashionable and poised, and that his clear and imperious mien greatly pleased the Polish ladies. The French Ambassador concluded that Ribbentrop had been exceedingly effective in conducting his mission. Unfortunately, Ribbentrop's mission was doomed to failure from the outset. The Poles were determined to resist German efforts to settle German-Polish differences.[61]

Hitler's Reichstag Speech of January 30, 1939

Poland issued an optimistic communiqué on January 28, 1939, which had been agreed upon with Ribbentrop before the German Foreign Minister departed from Warsaw. This announcement contained no hint of the actual nature of the German-Polish negotiation. Ribbentrop had sent a cheerful telegram to Beck when he arrived at the German frontier on January 27th: "I am convinced that the friendly relations between our two countries have been considerably improved by the conversations we have had in Warsaw." Hitler paid hearty tribute to successful German-Polish relations in his annual January 30th speech to the German Reichstag, although Ribbentrop's report indicated that the latest conversations with the Poles were far from satisfactory.

Hitler spoke to the 855 deputies of the new Reichstag elected in April 1938, which also included the Sudetenland deputies elected in December 1938. Marshal Goering, who had been the president of the German Reichstag since 1932, was re-elected. The enabling law of March 23, 1933, which gave Hitler special powers to deal with the crisis in German internal and foreign affairs, was extended for the second time. It was agreed that the emergency law was to remain in effect until May 10, 1943. It was this law which enabled Hitler to employ dictatorial powers without scrapping the traditional democratic Weimar constitution of 1919. The constitution of Hugo Preuss was not designed for the one Party state of Hitler, but the continuity provided by the constitution satisfied the popular demand for legality in German affairs.

Hitler reminded the Reichstag that he had scarcely more than 1/3 of the votes of Germany when he was appointed Chancellor on January 30, 1933. He noted that all of the other German political parties had been hostile toward National Socialism and its program. He regarded his appointment as a 12th hour decision to help Germany. He reviewed the foreign policy achievements of 1938, and he reminded his listeners that he was determined to unite the Austrian Germans with Germany in January 1938, but that he had no plan to accomplish this. He mentioned the Czech mobilization as the motive for his own military order of May 28, 1938, and for the decision to liberate the Sudeten Germans in 1938. He promised the world that Germany had not solved Central European problems in order to threaten outside Powers, but to secure her interests and to defend herself from outside intervention. He declared that everyone in Germany had been happy about the Munich agreement, and he praised Mussolini, Daladier, and Chamberlain for their efforts to secure a peaceful solution of the Czech crisis. He told the Reichstag that the assistance of Goering and Ribbentrop had been especially important in solving foreign policy problems. He contrasted the peaceful re-unification of the Germans in 1938 with the forceful methods employed by Bismarck to achieve the partial German unification of 1871.

Hitler was scornful about the prophecies in the foreign press of approaching German doom, which merely indicated that numerous foreign journalists desired the destruction of Germany. He admitted that Germany was a dictatorship, but he argued that the nation was essentially democratic because 99% of the people were behind the Government. There was much talk abroad about whether democracies and dictatorships could live together. This was not considered an international question in Germany, because the Germans were indifferent about the forms of government possessed by other nations. Hitler promised that Germany had neither a desire nor an interest in exporting National Socialism. He declared that rumors abut German aspirations in North or South America, in Australia or in China, or in Holland, merely because these nations had different governmental systems, were as fantastic as accusing Germany of seeking to annex the moon.

Hitler knew that the negative English attitude toward the trade of Germany before 1914 had been an important factor in poisoning the international atmosphere. He believed that Germany contributed to the outbreak of World War I because she misunderstood the requirements of alliance loyalty toward her Austro-Hungarian ally. He emphasized that no state had really profited from World War I, and he noted that the Englishmen who had imagined that the destruction of Germany would improve the English economic position were proved wrong. Hitler was aware that in recent months the old anti-German arguments had been revived by British political leaders and journalists. German naval power had been wrecked in World War I, but the United States and Japan had superseded the old German naval position. German trade had been destroyed, but this had harmed Great Britain as much as Germany. If the British fought World War I to spread democracy, it was evident that the earlier edition of this ideology was less prevalent than before. Hitler concluded that any possible advantage of World War I to Great Britain had long since disappeared.

Hitler noted that the British fought World War I to eliminate German foreign trade, but it would have been necessary for Germany to double her former world trade to meet the astronomical reparations demands of 1919 or 1920. It was no excuse to claim that popular feelings were too excited to permit a reasonable peace, because this would imply a sweeping condemnation of British democracy. Hitler denied the claims of Eden and other British politicians that Germany had been seeking to withdraw from the world economy through her Four Year plans. German competition in the foreign markets was reduced by the effort to satisfy more needs at home, but Hitler promised that Germany would always recognize the necessity of foreign trade. The German capacity to produce food was limited, and German trade competition in foreign markets would be further reduced if Germany had her former colonies, which were rich in food production. Hitler said he knew that the victors of 1918 did not favor the return of the German colonies, but he believed that it would be reasonable for them to recognize the German need of trade.

Hitler complained that his disarmament offers after 1933 had met with an "icy reception." He regretted that some of the increased German production to satisfy German needs had to find expression in the intrinsically unproductive form of armaments. It was recognized in Germany that present conditions required strong German defensive military forces to protect the German economy, and it was not necessary to secure this objective by instilling an artificial hatred toward foreign nations. Hitler concluded that it was apparently the prerogative of democracies to permit their political leaders to use distortions and inventions to create popular hatreds against peoples who had done nothing against them. Hitler considered that Duff Cooper, Eden, Churchill, and Ickes, the American Secretary of the Interior, were typical examples of war apostles. He was accused of interfering with the sacred rights of democracies when he replied to their accusations. He promised that he would not forbid Germans to reply to such attacks as long as Germany was a sovereign nation, and he added that "one single laugh" was an adequate answer to the charge that Germany intended to assault the United States.

Hitler regretted that it was necessary to reply to the English apostles of war, but the German people, who had no hatred for Great Britain, France, and the United States, would be psychologically unprepared if the war policy triumphed and if Germany was assaulted by the Western Powers. Hitler claimed that he could convince foreign peoples, in a debate with foreign critics, that Germany had no hostile intentions toward them. American soldiers came to Europe in World War I to help strangle Germany, and the Nye committee of the American Congress had proved in 1934 that American participation in World War I was unjustifiable. Hitler noted that there was a tremendous expression of sympathy abroad for the Jews, but that little was done to help them find an adequate place for settlement. He was determined to eliminate the Jewish influence from German life. Hitler did not wish to hear the foreign nations raise the question of humanitarianism in this connection, because he remembered that more than 800,000 German children died in the Allied Hunger Blockade of World War I, and that the 1919 peace treaty took one million dairy cows from Germany.

He charged that the Jews had monopolized the leading positions in German life, but he wanted his own people in those positions. He desired German civilization to remain German and not to become Jewish. Foreign spokesmen often claimed that Germany was driving away her most valuable cultural asset, and Hitler hoped that they were sufficiently grateful that Germany was making this asset available to them. He knew that there was ample room in the world for Jewish settlement, but he believed that it was time to discard the idea that the Jews had the right to exploit every other nation in the world. He urged the Jewish people to form a balanced community of their own, or to face an unpredictable crisis. He predicted that a new World War would not lead to the Bolshevization of the world and to the victory of the Jews, but that it would produce the destruction of the Jewish race in Europe. He based this prediction on the belief that the period of propaganda helplessness before Jewish influence over the non-Jewish peoples of Europe was at an end. He predicted that in a new World War, the same things would happen to the Jews in other European countries that had already happened to them in Germany.

Hitler heard foreign critics claim that Germany was hostile toward organized religion. This was a remarkable claim when one considered that no one in Germany was persecuted because of his religious affiliation. German public tax revenues to the Catholic and Protestant churches had increased from 130 million RM (42.5 million dollars) in 1934 to 500 million RM (125 million dollars) in 1938. These churches also received 92 million RM (23 million dollars) each year from units of local German Government. The churches were the largest property owners after the state, and their properties of 10 billion RM (2.5 billion dollars) produced an annual income of 300 million RM (75 million dollars). These figures of ecclesiastical wealth did not include the donations, collections, and tax exemptions. Hitler reminded his listeners that the National Socialist state had never closed a church nor prevented a religious service. He admitted that priests and pastors who committed moral crimes, or who tried to challenge and overthrow the state, were treated like any other citizens. Hitler also admitted that he had intervened in church affairs once, in 1933, in an effort to foster one united evangelical Protestant church. This effort had failed because of the resistance of certain bishops, and Hitler had recognized that it was not the function of the state to strengthen the church against its own will. Hitler wondered why democratic politicians intervened for certain punished priests or pastors in Germany, and were silent about the butchery of priests in Russia or Spain. Hitler noted that there had been no sympathy abroad in the old days for National Socialists who were punished by the Weimar German state.

Hitler admitted that he was worried about the many foreign dangers which threatened Germany, but he was pleased that Germany enjoyed the friendship of Italy and Japan. He declared that the purpose of Italo-German solidarity was salvation against Bolshevism, and he predicted that a collapse of Japan in the Far East would produce the triumph of Bolshevism in Asia. Hitler again praised Daladier and Chamberlain for their Munich policy in 1938. He noted that the atmosphere had changed since Munich, and that official British radio facilities were in use for propaganda broadcasts to Germany. Hitler promised that Germany would reply if the hostile broadcasts were continued. Hollywood was apparently interested in a big campaign of anti-German films, but Germany could reply by producing anti-Jewish films, and Hitler predicted that many states and peoples would be interested in seeing them. Hitler insisted that current tension would end quickly if this senseless agitation ceased.

Hitler expressed his conviction that there would be a long period of peace rather than another war. He could not imagine any concrete cause of conflict between Germany and Great Britain. He had often said that none of the German National Socialists wished to harm the British Empire in any way. He knew that confidence and collaboration between Germany and Great Britain would be a gain for the entire world, and the same would be true of cooperation between Germany and France. Hitler declared that there was no difference of opinion among the friends of peace about the value of the German-Polish Pact of 1934. He added that he was encouraged by the positive record of German-Polish friendship during the past year. Hitler welcomed a return to the old German friendship with Hungary. He stressed his admiration for Yugoslavia, the country of the brave Serbian soldiers of World War I. He counted Rumania, Bulgaria, Greece, and Turkey among the nations friendly to Germany, and he noted that German economic cooperation with these countries was increasing. He mentioned good German relations with the other smaller nations of Europe.

Hitler knew that German-American relations were suffering from the claims of American agitators that Germany was a threat to the independence of the United States. He was confident that the great majority of the American people did not believe that there was truth in this gigantic propaganda campaign. Hitler believed that German economic relations with Latin America were the private concern of Germany and the Latin American states. He ended his speech on an optimistic note, and he thanked God for allowing him to experience the completion of German unity.[62]

Hitler had stressed with unerring aim the importance of the British attitude toward Germany. His optimism about avoiding an Anglo-German war would have been justified to a greater extent had German-Polish relations been as solid and friendly as Hitler had indicated. Hitler was not aware of the extent to which Great Britain had fostered an anti-German policy in Poland, and he had been misled by the friendly attitude of Beck at Berchtesgaden. Hitler was disappointed by the failure of the Ribbentrop mission to Warsaw, but he remained confident that the Poles could be induced to cooperate, if they were handled with tact and patience. Hitler had made a formidable attempt to convince the foreign groups hostile toward Germany that another World War would be a disaster. It is surprising that it was necessary, after the experience of World War I, to expend so much eloquence to make such an obvious point, and it is depressing to note that the war enthusiasts of Great Britain were impervious to every such eloquent argument.

Hitler's speech of January 30, 1939, momentarily exerted a calming influence on Beck. The Polish Foreign Minister knew that the Ribbentrop mission had been a failure, and he was concerned lest the German leaders become impatient before Poland and Great Britain were prepared to challenge them. He wrote a highly colored report about his conversations with Ribbentrop shortly before Hitler addressed the Reichstag. He observed with satisfaction that Ribbentrop had at last discovered the impossibility of persuading Poland to join the anti-Comintern Pact. Beck noted that Ribbentrop had said Germany was painfully affected by the loss of Danzig after World War I. Beck claimed to have replied, "we also remembered that for hundreds of years Danzig was part of the Republic of Poland." Ribbentrop was well aware that Danzig had never been part of Poland. Beck would have enjoyed twisting the historical record to torment the German Foreign Minister, had he dared. He was correct in assuming that such a statement would have produced a great effect. His report was a pitiful example of a diplomat writing what consideration for high policy prevented him from saying in an actual situation.[63]

Beck was pleased by Hitler's plea for peace on January 30, 1939. Beck emphasized Hitler's sympathetic references to Poland at the Polish Foreign Office on February 1st. He concluded that this was "proof that this (Ribbentrop) visit had been a happy event." He declared proudly that Poland was showing the Germans that she did not intend to be treated like Czecho-Slovakia. Beck created some confusion at the Polish Foreign Office by incorrectly assuring Lipski, Szembek, and Lubienski that he had "categorically rejected" the super-highway plan. There was satisfaction among some of the Poles that Ribbentrop had been generous in praising the Polish Army to Marshal Smigly-Rydz.[64]

Polish Concern About French Policy

American Ambassador Bullitt in Paris reported on January 30, 1939, that he discussed recent German-Polish negotiations with Juliusz Lukasiewicz, the Polish Ambassador. Lukasiewicz admitted that Danzig and the Corridor transit problems had been discussed. He informed Bullitt that Beck had warned Hitler that Poland might act in Ruthenia. Bullitt also discussed general German policy with Lukasiewicz, French Foreign Minister Bonnet, and British Ambassador Sir Eric Phipps. The three men agreed that Hitler would not deliberately make war on any country in 1939. These views were an interesting contrast to the alarmist reports which Halifax had sent to President Roosevelt a few days earlier.[65]

American Charge' d'Affaires Gilbert reported from Berlin on February 3rd that Hitler's basic policy in the East was friendship with Poland. It seemed certain to Gilbert that Beck would be willing to allow the return of Danzig to Germany in exchange for a 25-year Pact, and for a German guarantee of the Polish Corridor. Gilbert noted that official German circles were quite open in announcing that the reunion of Memel with East Prussia was planned for the Spring of 1939. The Germans believed that the Lithuanians, British, and French would agree to this development without any ill-feeling.[66]

Beck told Kennard at the time of Ribbentrop's visit that he would be willing to come to London at any time after mid-March 1939. Kennard was still unable to give Halifax detailed information about the recent German-Polish negotiations.[67]

Kennard and Noël were instructed to discover what they could about the Ribbentrop-Beck discussions at Warsaw. Beck told Kennard on February 1, 1939, that a new agreement with Germany in the foreseeable future was unlikely. He was unwilling to reveal the details of the Warsaw talks, and he insisted that current German policy toward Poland was friendly. Beck was willing to confide more to Noël. He told the French Ambassador that he had adopted a negative attitude in the superhighway question, and that Poland would not allow "a corridor through the Corridor." Beck mentioned that Ribbentrop raised no difficulty about Polish engagements toward France. Beck obviously hoped to discourage the French tendency to reduce her commitments to Poland. The French Ambassador concluded that there was considerable friction between Poland and Germany.[68]

Polish Ambassador Lukasiewicz warned Beck, from Paris on February 1st, that the French attitude toward Poland had become increasingly negative since the Munich conference. He suggested that this trend would continue unless there was some new tension or crisis in Eastern Europe. He believed that a severe jolt would be required in the near future to prevent France from adopting an attitude of indifference toward Poland.[69]

Bonnet adopted an attitude of ironical surprise toward Polish attempts to conceal the differences between Germany and Poland. Lipski had endeavored to give Coulondre the most favorable impression possible about the Berchtesgaden conversations. Bonnet also noted the friendly public exchange of views between Germany and Poland at Warsaw. He believed that serious efforts by Beck to disguise the fact that Danzig was under discussion were doomed to failure. Bonnet, unlike Halifax, was uninterested in exploiting a German-Polish disagreement over Danzig for his own purposes. Bonnet was willing to concede that Poland had conformed to the letter of the Franco-Polish alliance during the 1938 Czech crisis. He was convinced that Polish policy had violated the spirit of the alliance. He intended to repay the Poles in kind in 1939. France would observe the letter of the Franco-Polish alliance, but Bonnet believed that she had ample justification to interpret its spirit according to her own interests. France was not obliged to support Poland in a Danzig conflict, and Bonnet did not intend that she should do so.[70]

Beck counted on the United States to help Great Britain prod the French into a conflict with Germany. Potocki claimed in a report of January 12, 1939, from Washington, D.C., that the New Deal was making progress in stirring up hatred toward Germany in the United States. He observed that "American propaganda is somewhat rough-shod, and paints Germany as black as possilbe — they certainly know how to exploit religious persecutions and concentration camps — yet, when bearing public ignorance in America in mind, their propaganda is so effective that people here have no real knowledge of the true state of affairs in Europe." Potocki noted that in America little attention was devoted to the terrible events taking place in Russia during the purges.[71]

Potocki emphasized that the United States was launching a gigantic armament program, and that the Munich pact, which created an exaggerated impression of German power in Europe, was a "great aid (wielka pomoca)" to this program. Potocki continued to exaggerate the importance of the Jews in American policy, and he ridiculed prominent American Jews, who claimed that they were "desirous of being representative of 'true Americanism'," but were, "in point of fact, linked with international Jewry by ties incapable of being torn asunder." He complained that the Jews hid their Jewish internationalism in a false nationalism, and "succeeded in dividing the world into two warlike camps."

Potocki reported on January 16, 1939, that Bullitt was returning to France from leave, on January 21st, with the avowed intention of encouraging French resistance to Germany, which he hoped to accomplish by distributing statistics on American preparation for war. Bullitt told Potocki that President Roosevelt had empowered him to tell the French leaders that the United States was abandoning isolationism, and placing her entire resources at the disposal of Great Britain and France. Bullitt praised the Polish policy of self-interest during the Czech crisis, but he predicted that the Western Powers would soon be prepared to resist German policies in Eastern Europe. Bullitt promised that this would mean the repudiation of "mere formal intervention."[72]

Kennard received confirmation at the Polish Foreign Office on February 6, 1939, of Beck's statement to Noël about the superhighway question. Kennard was flatly told "that of course there could never be any question of a corridor across the Corridor, or any extraterritorial arrangement." This stubborn Polish attitude was very pleasing to Kennard. He was told that Poland would be unwilling to modify any of the current restrictions placed on German traffic between Berlin and Koenigsberg.[73]

The German-Polish Pact Scare at London

Kennard noted with satisfaction that the exchange of German and Polish visits had produced no improvement in the situation of the German minority in Poland. Beck had merely made the token gesture of agreeing to send some experts to Berlin to discuss the problem. The Poles sent a team to Berlin on February 25, 1939, but nothing was accomplished. The Poles rejected a German suggestion for a public communiqué with the concluding statement: "The discussions will be continued as soon as possible." The Poles insisted on the formula: "The discussions will be resumed." They made it clear that they would not consider another meeting for at least four months.

Halifax was informed by Kennard that the Poles responded to German minority complaints by encouraging their own minority organizations in Germany to complain about conditions. Kennard admitted, "there can be little doubt that the Polish authorities are no less active than they ever have been in whittling away and undermining the position of the German minority." Kennard did not condemn the Poles for these tactics, and he speculated that Polish measures could always be justified by complaints about conditions in Germany. He noted coolly that this source of discord could easily become a major issue of dispute.[74]

Halifax was nervous about a misunderstanding which had occurred in a conversation with Polish Ambassador Raczynski in mid-February 1939. He hastily wired Kennard on February 15th that the Polish envoy had casually observed that "Beck wished to come to London, preferably after he had agreed with the German Government upon 'some solution for settling the Danzig problem for the time being'." Halifax was counting on Danzig as the pretext for an Anglo-German conflict, and he was upset by the possibility that the Poles and Germans might settle the Danzig issue. He was soon reassured that Raczynski's remark had no special significance, and that the Danzig question would not have been settled, when Beck came to London.[75]

The Germans were curious about Beck's projected trip to London. Moltke discussed the matter with Kennard on February 24, 1939. He confided that the German Government would never reduce its minimum offer of a settlement with Poland in exchange for Danzig and the superhighway, without the railway connection. Kennard replied with serene assurance that "the Poles would never agree to such proposals." This remark worried Moltke, but he replied that Germany had no intention of using force to obtain Polish compliance. Moltke was keenly inquisitive about Beck's visit to London, but Kennard refused to comment about it. He asked Moltke what Poland had thus far offered Germany. Moltke replied wryly that Poland had offered the current *status quo* at Danzig, to be guaranteed by Germany and Poland. It was obvious to Kennard, and, of course, to Halifax, when he read Kennard's report, that no progress had been made by the Germans in their efforts to reach a settlement with Poland.[76]

Anti-German Demonstrations During Ciano's Warsaw Visit

Beck, at the time of his own visit to Rome in March 1938, had invited Italian Foreign Minister Ciano to visit Poland. Ciano arrived at Warsaw on February 25, 1939, to find Poland in an uproar. The pretext for Polish excitement was a minor Danzig incident of January 29, 1939, which the Poles magnified to concoct an affair of honor. A fight had occurred between German and Polish students of the Danzig Institute of Technology at the Cafe Langfuhr. British Consul-General Shepherd investigated the incident, and he reported to Halifax that the Polish students were guilty of fomenting disorder in the restaurant. The proprietor feared new violence. He wrote a courteous letter to the *Bratnia Pomoc* (*Brothers in Aid*), a Polish student organization, and he requested that the Polish students avoid the restaurant in the future. The Polish students professed to be outraged by this alleged discrimination, and they organized a protest meeting for February 22, 1939. They passed an irrelevant resolution at this meeting that Poland alone had the right to control the mouth of the Vistula and the City of Danzig. They resolved to enter any Danzig establishment they pleased. The Polish students claimed that they returned afterward to Cafe Langfuhr and encountered the following sign: "No Admittance to Dogs and Poles." British Consul-General Shepherd investigated the new incident, and he reported to Halifax that the notice had not been posted by the proprietor. The most plausible hypothesis was that the sign was a deliberate Polish provocation. The expression prohibiting dogs and certain undesirables was common in Polish university towns, but it was unknown in Germany.[77]

A new meeting of protest was attended by Captain Krukierck, a Polish official at Danzig. It was charged at the meeting that German students had driven Polish students out of the Danzig Institute of Technology. Foreign journalists immediately seized upon this charge and repeated it abroad. The charge was wildly exaggerated, and the French radio at Strassburg claimed that 100 Polish students had been attacked in a lecture hall by German students and units of the Danzig S.S. British Consul-General Shepherd conducted an investigation, and he reported to Halifax that Polish claims were exaggerated. It seemed that German students, who had learned of the resolutions of the Polish student organization, had shouted for the Polish students to leave the lecture hall. The Polish students had responded to this suggestion, and there had been no violence of any kind.[78]

Polish High Commissioner Chodacki called on Greiser and demanded an immediate and formal apology. The Danzig Senate leader stood his ground, and he refused to accede to the Polish demand until the circumstances of the case had been clarified to the mutual satisfaction of both parties. The defiance of Greiser infuriated Chodacki. He threatened to resign, and he warned Greiser that he would have to face the consequences.

The Polish press went into action, and for two months the leading newspapers carried stories almost daily about the alleged mistreatment of Polish students at Danzig, under such captions as "Prosecution of the Struggle for Student Rights." Anti-German student meetings took place in the major towns of Poland. The German Embassy at Warsaw was warned that one more spark might suffice to produce Polish military action against Danzig. A demonstration against the Germans by students of the University of Poznań led to the destruction of German property and the injury of many Germans. There was a major demonstration before the German Embassy at Warsaw on February 24, 1939, which Moltke described as the worst since the conclusion of the 1934 Pact. Thousands of Poles chanted the horrible *Rota* song about receiving rewards from God for hanging Germans, and there were loud screams of "Down with Hitler!," "Down with the pro-German policy!," "Away with the German dogs!," and "Long live Polish Danzig!" The demonstration was not restricted to songs and slogans. The German Embassy was bombarded with stones. The place might have been stormed had not a police guard been placed before the entrance. This guard provided dubious protection, because it consisted solely of two Polish policemen.[79]

Many Poles were ashamed of these outrageous provocations. The Duke of Coburg, who represented the leading German veteran organizations, was in Kraków on February 24, 1939. He was accompanied by German veterans, and the group proceeded to Wawel Castle, where a wreath of honor was placed on the grave of Pilsudski. General Gorecki, the chief of the Polish federation of frontline veterans, gave a luncheon for Coburg and the German group. At this luncheon a number of comradely toasts were exchanged by the Polish and German veterans, and it was evident that the Polish group was ashamed of the excesses which were taking place throughout Poland.[80]

The presence of Foreign Minister Ciano in Warsaw did not prevent a second demonstration against the German Embassy on February 25, 1939. The Polish police were present in force, but the demonstration was allowed to proceed for fifteen minutes before they intervened. The Embassy was bombarded with heavy stones, and two large windows were broken. There were forty police present, and only three hundred demonstrators.

The scene was clearly illuminated, and Moltke and his assistants had an opportunity to make a careful survey of the demonstrators. Moltke reported that the German staff did not see any Jews, and that it was possible to identify the majority of the demonstrators as university students. Moltke suspected that these students represented rightist groups and organizations.[81]

The Danzig situation was the major topic of discussion when Ciano arrived at Warsaw. The English *Daily Herald* had carried a sensational story on February 24, 1939, that Albert Forster, the Danzig National Socialist leader, was planning to visit England in a desperate effort to prevent an Anglo-Polish agreement in defense of the *status quo* at Danzig. Forster was contacted by journalists at Danzig, and he vigorously denied the English rumors.

Ciano was met with a very hostile reception when he arrived at Warsaw. The crowd which gathered to welcome the Italian Foreign Minister shouted coarse anti-German slogans. The few cries of sympathy for Italy, a sister Catholic state for which the Poles had a traditional sentimental attachment, could scarcely be heard. The Poles were in a combative mood. The Polish band insisted on playing the *Marseillaise* instead of the Italian *Giovannezza* on one occasion during Ciano's visit. This discourteous gesture produced pandemonium, and a fight broke out between protesting Italian journalists and the Poles.[82]

The Germans did what they could to relieve Ciano of this embarrassment. They kept him directly informed from Berlin about the nature and scope of the anti-German demonstrations, and they agreed to publish nothing about the incidents in the German press during his visit. It was natural under these circumstances that the Germans were indignant when the Italian newspaper, *Popolo d'Italia* (*People of Italy*), published a pro-Polish and anti-German statement about the unpleasantness in Poland on February 27, 1939.[83]

Ciano's questions to Beck about the future of German-Polish relations were very pertinent. The Polish Foreign Minister said nonchalantly that it might be possible to continue the good neighbor policy with Germany, but that difficulties were being encountered. Beck discussed the Berchtesgaden conversation of the previous month, and Ciano noted: "Beck frequently emphasizes with satisfaction, though without conviction, the assurances given him by Hitler." The visit of Ciano to Poland was a lengthy one, and he did not leave the country until March 3, 1939. He spent the last few days on a hunting expedition in the lonely Bialowieza forest region of north-eastern Poland. He was pleased to exchange the hectic Polish urban scene for this pleasant diversion.[84]

Ciano discussed the situation with Moltke before he departed for Bialowieza. He said that it was perfectly obvious that the Poles did not really wish a close connection with the Axis Powers. He concluded that Polish action during the Czech crisis had merely served Polish policy, and that it was valueless as an indication of the future Polish official attitude. He had been unable to obtain any encouraging statements about Danzig from Beck. Ciano noted that the French press and radio had been extremely active in stirring up the anti-German mood in Poland during his visit. He concluded that this was a vindictive French effort to obtain revenge for the demonstrations in the Italian Chamber on November 30, 1938, on the eve of the Ribbentrop visit to Paris. The Germans could not help but note that they had to bear the brunt of this Franco-Italian feud.[85]

Ciano admitted that his own visit had produced no great enthusiasm in Poland. He modified his analysis about Polish policy somewhat, by concluding, after his return to Italy, that it would be foolish to imagine that Poland had been won over to the Axis, but perhaps too pessimistic to conclude that she was altogether hostile. Mussolini was disgusted with the Poles for their behavior during Ciano's visit. He admitted that the situation of Germany and Italy in Poland did not look favorable, but he concluded philosophically that Poland, after all, was merely an "empty nut."[86]

The demonstrations against the Germans died down after Ciano left Warsaw for the Polish forests. An attempt to organize a demonstration before the German Embassy on February 28, 1939, was quickly broken up by the Polish police. The official *Gazeta Polska* on the same day had called for the restoration of order and discipline in Poland. A boycott against German firms in Poland had been launched before this happened. The occasion had been a Polish annexationist meeting on February 27, 1939, which had been sanctioned by Polish Premier Slawoj-Skladkowski. The meeting was attended by the principal Polish military commanders. The principal speaker was Colonel Kazimierz Tomaszewski.

Tomaszewski deliberately misrepresented the German position by claiming that Germany was demanding territory from Poland. He exclaimed that Poland had no reason to return any territory to Germany, but that she had several territorial demands of her own. The audience responded to this cue, and lively shouts of "Polish Danzig!" and "Polish East Prussia!" filled the air. The speaker said grimly that Danzig was a festering sore on the body of Poland which had to be lanced. The crowd cheered this talk, and the meeting ended with a resolution for a boycott of Germans, and for the institution of a special "No-Germans Day" in Poland. The presence of official spokesmen indicated that the meeting was a deliberate provocation against Germany by the Polish Government.[87]

Beck's Announcement of His Visit to London

The action of the Polish Government in terminating excesses at Warsaw on February 28, 1939, was not effective immediately in the provinces. The German consulate in Poznán was damaged by a demonstration on March 1st. Ribbentrop and Moltke busily presented protests during these days, but they produced no effect. Moltke despairingly told Beck on March 8, 1939, that there were probably not more than six Poles in Poland who were sincerely interested in promoting cooperation and conciliation between Poland and Germany.

Beck on February 25, 1939, proposed to visit Halifax in England either during the last week of March or the first week of April. The British response to this suggestion was favorable, and Beck announced publicly on February 26th that this trip would take place around the end of March. Moltke was filled with foreboding by this prospect. It seemed obvious that Beck would seek to consolidate Polish relations with England. Moltke was aware of the deadly British enmity toward Germany. He deplored the fact that "in general, it is becoming increasingly apparent that Poland desires to get into closer touch with the Western democracies."

Moltke saw that the Danzig dispute was a link between Poland and the West. He speculated that Beck might visit Paris after London, despite his refusal to do so "in a rather unfriendly manner on the occasion of his Christmas sojourn on the Riviera."[88]

Ribbentrop adopted a more indulgent view toward the Polish situation. He assured Lipski in Berlin of his conviction that Beck regretted the excesses which were occurring in Poland. Ribbentrop blamed this agitation on the Polish press, and he warned that a serious situation would result if the German press was allowed the freedom to reply. He believed that a general settlement between Germany and Poland "could be rendered very difficult by such deplorable occurrences, and at the very least would be greatly delayed." He did not betray any impatience for a rapid conclusion of an agreement with Poland.[89]

League High Commissioner Burckhardt was under strong pressure to remain in Switzerland until a League investigation of Danzig conditions had been completed. He reported to the German consulate at Geneva on March 1, 1939, that he hoped to return to Danzig as soon as possible. He warned the Germans that the Poles had fomented recent incidents in Danzig to stir up trouble, and he suggested that it would be wise for the Danzig Government to remain calm despite Polish provocations. He offered to sound out Halifax about Danzig in London, and then to report to Ribbentrop at Berlin. Ribbentrop replied several days later that he was prepared to receive Burckhardt at any time. The Slovak crisis had reached a climax when Burckhardt arrived in Berlin on March 13th. He had been unable to arrange a meeting with Halifax. The Germans advised Burckhardt not to return to Danzig during the Slovak crisis. Burckhardt predicted that difficult days were coming for Danzig, and that the Poles would seek to misuse his authority, and to play him off against Germany. The visit of Burckhardt to Berlin produced the usual spate of fantastic rumors in the Western press. Weizsaecker wrote to Burckhardt at Geneva advising him to ignore these stories.[90]

The Germans received a report on Ciano's impressions of Poland on March 4, 1939. Ciano observed that "Poland is living under the dictatorship of a dead man." Everywhere the disciples of Pilsudski were the supreme authorities. Ciano found it difficult to interpret Polish policy, because "everyone regards himself as the appointed guardian of the Pilsudski heritage, but there is no one with really new ideas." Ciano misjudged the Poles when he predicted that in a general war they would delay their own decision and "then hurry to the aid of the victor." This was contrary to Polish strategy during the war between Denikin and the Russian Reds in 1920. The analysis of Ciano on this point would apply more aptly to Italy than to Poland.[91]

The Ciano visit revealed a contemptuous Polish attitude toward Italy. Kennard was told at the Polish Foreign Office that Ciano "clearly has not the courage to do anything which might displease the Reich." Kennard incorporated this in what he hoped was a clever report to Halifax. Grigorie Gafencu, the new Rumanian Foreign Minister, had recently been to Poland on a first brief visit. He had made a very favorable impression on Beck, who regarded him as a delightful contrast to his predecessor. Kennard summarized the recent state visits to Warsaw with the remark that "Ribbentrop was regarded with dislike, Ciano with contempt and Gafencu with distinct sympathy." It was perhaps natural for the exuberant and reckless Poles to have contempt for a cautious and experienced people like the Italians, but Poland could have profited from a closer study of Italian policy.[92]

German-Polish relations in March 1939 stood under the sign of Beck's approaching visit to London. Ribbentrop was complacent about this development, but Moltke continued to address solemn warnings to the German Foreign Office. It was announced on March 9, 1939, that Beck would arrive at London on April 3rd. Moltke reported on the same date that a top Polish military man had described recent excesses in Poland as "completely justified," and the provocative Polish press attacks against Germany showed no sign of abating.[93]

Moltke recalled three weeks of minor demonstrations in August 1938, because a Polish railway man on the Gdynia-Danzig run had lost his legs through his own carelessness. The demonstrations of August 1938 were mild compared to what he had experienced since January 1939. The Langfuhr incident was "the most incredible case of incitation that had ever come to my attention." He was suspicious about Beck's oft-repeated statement that the situation shoud not be regarded too pessimistically. Such an attitude was either completely unrealistic or deliberately evasive. It seemed too easy to claim that countries officially hostile to Germany, such as the United States, were responsible for much of the agitation. Equally unconvincing was Beck's argument that the trouble resulted from the failure to settle the Ruthenian question. Moltke noted that Polish agitators were spreading the impression "that with the problems of Austria and the Sudetenland solved, it was now Poland's turn." Beck, and not the Polish people, had received from Hitler "the very plain statements at Berchtesgaden." Beck was expending no effort to influence the attitude of the Polish people.[94]

Moltke discussed the situation with Beck on March 10, 1939, and he endeavored to discover why the Polish Foreign Minister was going to London. Beck truthfully asserted that the initiative for his visit came from England, but Moltke did not believe him. Beck observed casually that, in response to English initiative, he had requested an unofficial visit in order to have a maximum amount of time for political discussions. He claimed genially that he had no "special problems" in mind, but sought a "general *tour d'horizon.*" Beck admitted that "of course" he intended to discuss Danzig with the British, who were on the special Committee of Three to supervise League affairs in the Free City.

Beck hoped that the British Government would help "to prevent a vacuum" by maintaining the League position at Danzig until Germany and Poland arrived at some sort of agreement. He mentioned a report just received from Lipski, and noted to his "great joy" that Hitler did not intend to permit the Danzig question to disturb German-Polish relations. Beck was extraordinarily successful in reassuring Moltke with these pleasant generalities. The attitude of Moltke after this conversation was not dissimilar to that of Ribbentrop.[95]

Beck was not under the slightest pressure from Germany in March 1939 to negotiate a hasty settlement of German-Polish differences. The Germans were willing to accept at face value the claims of Beck that a settlement was difficult, and they displayed persistent serenity despite many Polish provocations. Nearly five months had passed since the launching of the German-Polish negotiation on October 24, 1938. There had not been one occasion during the ensuing period when the Germans had adopted a threatening attitude toward Poland. It was obvious that they placed a great value on cooperation with Poland, and that they hoped for an agreement on a basis of fairness and equality.

The Germans had much to offer Poland, including great economic advantages and real protection from any foreign invasion. The British were not inclined to offer Poland economic advantages, and they could not protect her by military means. They had condemned the role of Poland during the 1938 Czech crisis, and in 1939 they merely hoped to use the Poles as an instrument against Germany. It was ironical that Beck was about to embark for London to conclude a general settlement with England instead of with Germany.

Halifax had three great advantages over Hitler in this situation. Pilsudski was dead, and the Polish leadership was operating on his obsolete directives from 1934 and 1935. Great Britain was far away, and her immediate aspirations could not threaten Polish ambitions. Great Britain enjoyed a position of world influence in her Empire, in her dependent territories, and in France and the United States. The Poles were dazzled by the fame and grandeur of the British position. The British were about to present an open challenge to Germany, and Beck was aware of their intention. Beck planned to join the British in challenging Germany rather than to grasp the hand of friendship which Hitler had extended to him for such a long time. The policy of Beck in 1939 was incompatible with the survival of the new Polish state.

Chapter 12

THE REVERSAL OF BRITISH POLICY

Dropping the Veil of an Insincere Appeasement Policy

The German program in 1938 and 1939 to revise the territorial provisions of the Paris peace treaties was of direct concern to Austria, Czechoslovakia, Lithuania, and Poland. The Germans did not wish for changes at the expense of such neighbors as France, Italy, Yugoslavia, Hungary, Holland, Belgium, Denmark, Switzerland, and Luxemburg. Rump-Austria was absorbed by the German Reich in March 1938, and the Czecho-Slovak state disappeared in March 1939, with the establishment of the Bohemia-Moravia Protectorate and the independence of Slovakia. Lithuanian Foreign Minister Urbsys agreed at Berlin on March 20, 1939, to return Memel to Germany, and this decision was approved by the Lithuanian Cabinet on March 22nd.[1]

Germany did not ask for territory from Poland, but she had requested Polish approval for special German transit facilities through the Polish Corridor and the return of Danzig to the Reich. German objectives in Austria, Czechoslovakia, and Lithuania had been achieved without bloodshed, and Hitler hoped to negotiate a settlement with Poland. The Germans exerted no pressure and betrayed no impatience in discussing their proposals with the Poles. Hitler was willing to wait an indefinite period for a favorable Polish response. Germany had virtually completed her program of territorial revision, and she would soon enjoy a period of security which would enable her to consolidate her gains and to continue her program of internal reconstruction. Her security would be based on the strong foundation of satisfactory relations with all of her immediate neighbors. Italy was friendly to the German program, the Soviet Union was isolated from Central Europe by a hostile Poland, and France was not inclined to intervene in the Danzig question.[2]

The official British policy toward Germany, during the year from March 1938 to March 1939, while Hitler was realizing most of his objectives, was based on appeasement. The British had accepted the German annexation of both Austria and the Sudetenland. An Anglo-German declaration of friendship had been signed on September 30, 1938, at the special invitation of Prime Minister Chamberlain. The size of the German Navy was carefully restricted by the Anglo-German Naval Treaty of 1935, and the British public was assured by their Conservative leaders that Germany was scrupulously abiding by the terms of this agreement. Hitler had made it clear to the British leaders on numerous that he would never attempt to force the British to return the overseas colonies of Germany, which had been seized in the 1914-1919 period. British trade in overseas markets was gaining steadily at the expense of German trade during 1938-1939.[3]

The German program of territorial revision on the European continent was modest in its dimensions. Hitler had no intention of attempting to regain control over the remaining European territories which had been held by Germany and Austria in 1914. He had renounced Alsace-Lorraine, Eupen-Malmedy, North Schleswig, South Tirol, Austrian Slovenia, Poznań, East Upper Silesia, and Polish West Prussia. His program was based on a careful compromise between what the Germans of the Reich and allied Austria, excluding Hungary, had held in 1914, and what they had lost in 1919. His program was restricted to the return of approximately one-half of the lost German territories. Hitler, in *Mein Kampf*, had suggested for some distant future the importance of larger German aspirations in Eastern Europe at the expense of Bolshevism, but this program, which was in the interest of all enemies of Bolshevism, had found no official expression in German policy during the period 1933-1939. It was obvious in early 1939 that Hitler envisaged an Eastern European policy based exclusively on German-Polish cooperation.[4]

The British had no territorial commitments in Eastern Europe. The Czechs had been promised a territorial guarantee by the Four Munich Powers, but British Foreign Minister Halifax had carefully evaded the fulfillment of this promise. The assertion of Martin Gilbert and Richard Gott in their recent study, *The Appeasers*, that the Czech state had been guaranteed is manifestly untrue. Chamberlain explained to the British House of Commons on March 15, 1939, that the dissolution of the Czech state, which Great Britain had merely proposed to guarantee, put an end to this question. He added that Germany was under no obligation to consult with Great Britain during the final phase of the March 1939 Czech crisis. Geoffrey Dawson, the influential editor of the London *Times*, noted that the remarks of Chamberlain were "well-received" by the British Parliament. Furthermore, Gilbert and Gott are quite wrong in describing the Czech state of 1939 as "an old ally" of Britain. There had been no Anglo-Czech alliance.[5]

The British leaders had no unilateral obligation to intervene on behalf of Poland or any other state of Eastern Europe. The British leaders in March 1939 were much less concerned about the German rearmament campaign than had been the case at the time of the signing of the Anglo-German friendship declaration. The British leaders knew that they were gaining on Germany in the air, although nearly one half of the total German arms expenditure went to the German Air Force. It was evident that the German armament program was extremely limited to scope.[6]

The favorable outlook for European peace and prosperity in March 1939 was threatened by a British plan for preventive war. The British leaders took a series of steps which they hoped would make war inevitable. They worked for war against Germany despite the fact that there was no German challenge to British interests, and that the German leadership was entirely pro-British in both outlook and policy. The British leaders in March 1939 deliberately seized upon war as an instrument of national policy despite the British commitment to the Kellogg-Briand Peace Pact of 1928. The British policy was especially objectionable because it condoned an effort to draw as many nations as possible into the horrors of a new World War. Halifax and his colleagues were also determined to foist the entire blame for their conspiracy on Adolf Hitler.[7]

The British leaders recognized no strictures of conscience in seeking to achieve their objective of destroying Germany. They perpetrated a gigantic hoax about German designs on Rumania, which were purely imaginary, to incite a mininformed Anglo-Saxon public against Hitler. They begged the Soviet Union to sign an alliance against Germany, although this was a fateful and dangerous step which could lead to Bolshevist hegemony in Europe. They told the Poles that they would give them full military support if Poland refused to conclude an agreement with Germany, and they informed the entire world about this new diplomatic strategy in a series of public announcements. These steps, from an appeasement policy to a war policy, were taken in the short period of five days from March 15-March 20, 1939, and there was not the slightest effort during this period to negotiate about the situation with Germany. This British policy was without moral scruples, and, what was much worse from the viewpoint of successful statecraft, was based on a distorted appraisal of British interests. Adolf Hitler naturally deplored the apparent determination of the British leaders to undermine their own position in the world.[8]

It is instructive to consider the comments of the British leaders about what they believed was the opening of a righteous campaign to destroy Germany, and, in view of the British bombing strategy adopted in 1936, to destroy the German women and children. Alan Campbell Johnson, an enthusiastic admirer of Lord Halifax, referred to the "Halifax Diplomatic Revolution" of March 1939, "which culminated in the 'unprecedented' guarantees to Poland, Rumania and Greece." He believed that "the essence of his (Halifax's) achievement . . . was an attempt to revive Britain's historic and traditional role, the Balance of Power." Halifax rejoiced in what he considered a favorable opportunity to bring his inveterate hostility toward Germany into the open. He recalled an incident with a spokesman from a group of politically disaffected Italians at Rome in January 1939. Halifax was told that this group considered Germany to be "the only enemy we have got." Halifax replied "We also feel that." Halifax had to wait impatiently for another two months before it was opportune to announce this to the entire world. He was convinced in March 1939 that the British public could be persuaded that Hitler had an "evil mind." He was willing to tell anyone who cared to listen that Hitler was seeking "world domination."[9]

Sir John Simon believed that the speech which Halifax prepared for Chamberlain to deliver at Birmingham on March 17, 1939, was effective in uniting Great Britain for war. The theme of this speech was the insidious suggestion that Hitler was seeking to conquer the world. Simon observed with unparalleled cynicism that Chamberlain was an effective spokesman for this propaganda, because his Munich policy in 1938 had given him the reputation of being pro-German.[10]

Sir Samuel Hoare believed that the increase in British armament since the Munich conference justified the challenge to Germany in March 1939. He was convinced that the Danzig issue could be utilized to produce a conflict. He was quite candid about this situation after World War II, when he admitted that a military alliance with Poland was an absolute necessity in producing an Anglo-German war. Hoare was considering the British choice in concluding an immediate agreement with Poland rather than the Soviet Union. He conceded that the need to find a pretext to oppose Germany influenced this decision, rather than the mere military factor. This meant that Great Britain was more interested in fighting Germany than in accumulating a maximum amount of strength for the so-called defensive front.[11]

It is important to consider the attitude of Prime Minister Chamberlain, the fourth member of the British parliamentary group primarily concerned with the formulation of foreign policy. Chamberlain, unlike Halifax, was inhibited in his enthusiasm for a crusade against Germany by a "most profound distrust of Russia." This realistic alarm about playing Stalin's game in Europe emerged periodically in Chamberlain's thinking, but he did not contest Halifax's line of policy. He declared on March 19, 1939, that it was "impossible to deal with Hitler."[12]

The permanent staff at the British Foreign Office welcomed the shift in British policy in March 1939. The majority of the permanent staff had been strongly anti-German for many years. They considered that the denunciations of Germany by Halifax and Chamberlain in March 1939 were a belated recognition of their own anti-German attitudes. The two principal permanent officials were Sir Robert Vansittart, Diplomatic Adviser to His Majesty's Government, and Sir Alexander Cadogan, Permanent Under-Secretary at the British Foreign Office. These two men had been in close agreement for a long time. Cadogan took the lead in concerting British commitments in Eastern Europe with Halifax. The British military leaders were excluded from these deliberations, because Halifax and Cadogan did not welcome criticism about the weakness of their policy from a practical military standpoint.[13]

Sir Hughe Knatchbull-Hugessen, who had charge of the new Economic Warfare Department of the British Foreign Office during the months after the Munich agreement, believed that both the propaganda and practical military factors had received adequate attention before March 1939. He accepted the delay in the abandonment of appeasement until March 1939 as clever strategy which enabled Great Britain to hurry her war preparation. He agreed with Simon that the Munich conference strategy had enabled Chamberlain "to show the world beyond all possibility of contradiction the full measure of Nazi villainy."[14]

The anti-Munich war enthusiasts led by Winston Churchill were naturally delighted by the unexpected turn of events. Sir Arthur Salter declared that Halifax was worthy of his kinsman, Sir Edward Grey, who had led Great Britain into World War I. His attitude toward Chamberlain was softened by the new course of the Government, and he proclaimed that the Prime Minister was "more than usually resolute, authoritarian, and strong-willed." Leopold Amery was pleased that Chamberlain was "all for immediate action" after his Birmingham speech on March 17, 1939. Amery was inclined to conceal his misgivings about an unlimited British military commitment to the Poles, which he declared privately had "no conceivable military justification."[15]

Winston Churchill was not consulted by the British Government leaders in March 1939. He agreed with Geoffrey Dawson that Chamberlain's conciliatory remarks toward Germany in Parliament on March 15, 1939, after the German occupation of Prague, were well-received. He did not believe that Chamberlain was under strong public pressure to change his policy. Churchill expected Chamberlain to deliver another conciliatory speech at Birmingham on March 17, 1939, and he awaited the Prime Minister's remarks "with anticipatory contempt." He was not prepared for Chamberlain's bellicose speech, and he admitted that the "Prime Minister's reaction surprised me." It was evident that Chamberlian and Halifax were leading British public opinion rather than following it. There was nothing to force the British leaders, as Churchill put it, to do a "Right-about-turn."[16]

Thomas Jones, who was in close touch with the British leaders in March 1939, explained the situation in a letter to an American friend in New Jersey. He declared that Great Britiain "feels stronger and more united than it would have done had not Munich been tried as a gesture for peace and failed." He hoped that British preoccupation with distant Eastern Europe was intelligible. He explained that "we are busier on the eastern front of Germany so as to make her have to fight on two fronts." Jones agreed with Simon and Hoare that the Halifax strategy would make war inevitable.[17]

British Concern about France

The British were unable to unfold their strategy in Eastern Europe without considering the position of France. Pierre-Étienne Flandin had once been closer than any other political leader in France to Halifax and Chamberlain. Flandin had visited Germany in December 1937 shortly after the conversation at Berchtesgaden between Hitler and Halifax. He had received assurances from the German leaders that the Third Reich was dedicated to a permanent policy of collaboration with Great Britain, France, Italy, and Poland. Flandin was inclined to believe these assurances of the German leaders. He was sceptical about the possible survival of the Czecho-Slovak state after Munich, and he was scornful about the belligerent reaction of the British leaders to the events at Prague in March 1939. Flandin assured the German diplomats at Paris on March 20, 1939, that the events at Prague had not affected his attitude toward the need for lasting cooperation between Germany and France.[18]

The attitude of Flandin was a matter of great concern to Halifax. Flandin was close to Daladier and Bonnet, and it was clearly possible that the French Government might reject the British thesis that war was inevitable. A meeting of the French Supreme War Council had been held on March 13, 1939. General Maurice Gamelin, the Commander of the French Army, had based his remarks at the meeting on the assumption that the collapse of Czecho-Slovakia within two or three days was a certainty. Gamelin was aware that an effort might be made to involve France in war with Germany. He was inclined to be negative about such a war. He claimed that German defensive fortifications in the West were extremely formidable. He complained that the peace treaties of 1919 had virtually confined the Soviet Union to Asia, and that the attitude of Poland deprived the Franco-Soviet military alliance of appreciable value. He included Poland among the small states of Eastern Europe, which he said were in no position to play a major military role. He believed that the defensive position of France was stong, but he was negative toward any aggressive French military policy. His analysis of the military situation encouraged Georges Bonnet during the following days to adopt a sceptical attitude toward British plans for a military crusade.[19]

Premier Édouard Daladier was not inclined to be indignant about the Czech situation. His attitude toward the Czecho-Slovak state had always been negative, and he accepted the verdict of French Minister Lacroix at Prague that the Czech leaders had never been able to develop a true national sentiment among the nationalities of their country. He complained that Chamberlain on March 17, 1939, renounced the policy of mediating between Germany and France; he had returned to the policy of collective security and mutual assistance without consulting the French leaders.[20]

Foreign Minister Bonnet had hoped to head off a violent British reaction to the events at Prague by taking the initiative on March 16, 1939, for a mild Anglo-French formal protest to Germany. Bonnet believed that this step was necessary for the record, because Czecho-Slovakia had been formally the ally of France (not of Britain) when Hitler induced President Hacha to accept the German-Czech agreement of March 15, 1939. Bonnet had received a friendly personal letter from German Foreign Minister Ribbentrop on March 15, 1939. Ribbentrop justified German policy at Prague as a necessary step to preserve order and prevent bloodshed.[21]

Bonnet had anticipated a new European crisis in January 1939 after he discussed the European situation with Chamberlain and Halifax at Paris. The two British leaders had called on the French leaders before visiting Mussloini at Rome. Bonnet hoped to improve Franco-Italian relations in the interest of continental collaboration for peace. He was pleased when Premier Daladier took the initiative to send Paul Baudouin, the General-Director of the Bank of Indochina, on a special mission to Rome. Baudouin, who had enjoyed friendly contacts in Italy for many years, discussed the situation with Mussolini and Ciano, and he reported to Daladier and Bonnet on February 7, 1939. The mission had produced solid results. The Italian leaders agreed that special relations of confidence between France and Italy, based on periodic consultation, were necessary in the interest of European peace. The tension which had been produced by the annexationist demonstration in the Italian Chamber on November 30, 1938, was surmounted. Bonnet could anticipate with confidence that Mussolini would support France in any move for peace in a difficult situation. This new Franco-Italian cooperation, which was based on the concrete desire for peace in both countries, was a serious obstacle to the war policy of Halifax.[22]

William C. Bullitt, the leading American diplomat in Europe, was pleased by the reversal of British policy in March 1939. He knew that President Roosevelt would welcome any British pretext for a war in Europe. Ambassador Bullitt sent a jubilant report from Paris on March 17, 1939, in which he triumphantly concluded that there was no longer any possibility for a peaceful diplomatic settlement of European differences.[23]

Hitler Threatened by Halifax

Halifax did not await the speech of Chamberlain at Birmingham on March 17, 1939, before taking a strong stand on the Czech crisis. He admitted in the House of Lords on March 15, 1939, that the events at Prague did not oblige the British Government to take any action, but he dishonestly claimed that he had made a number of serious but unsuccessful efforts to persuade the other Munich Powers to join the British in guaranteeing the Czech state. He also claimed that Great Britain felt no less morally bound than if the guarantee had actually been made. He admitted that the events at Prague had taken place with the approval of the previous Czech Government, but he complained that the spirit of the Munich agreement had been violated.

Halifax was much more frank in expressing his views to German Ambassador Dirksen on March 15th. He claimed that Hitler had unmasked himself as a dishonest person. He insisted that German policy implied a rejection of good relations with Great Britain. He also insisted that Germany was "seeking to establish a position in which they could by force dominate Europe, and, if possible, the world."[24]

Halifax believed that he had been in good form during this conversation. He observed afterward that by comparison the German Ambassador had spoken "with little conviction" and with "considerable difficulty." The reports which Dirksen sent to Berlin during these days prove that he was considerably shaken by the violent British reaction to the latest Czech crisis. Dirksen was the heir of Lichnowsky, the last German Ambassador in London before the outbreak of war in 1914. Both men recognized the importance of an Anglo-German understanding, and they both became almost incoherent with grief, when confronted with the collapse of their respective diplomatic efforts. The entire German Embassy staff was dismayed by the events of March 1939.[25]

The British had done everything short of leaving their islands to create the impression that the future of Bohemia was a matter of complete indifference to them. They then turned about and declared that the events in Bohemia had convinced them that Hitler was seeking to conquer the world. It is small wonder that the German diplomats exposed to this London atmosphere were in despair.

Halifax's Dream of a Gigantic Alliance

The principal aim of Halifax after March 15, 1939, was an alliance combination which would fulfill the war requirements of British policy. He wished Great Britain to assume commitments in a dispute which could easily lead to war. He desired to command an alliance combination of preponderant power, which would guarantee victory, or at least make victory highly probable. Halifax believed that these requirements would be met in a combination including Great Britain, France, Poland, and Soviet Russia, provided, of course, that the United States could be relied upon to supply reserve power to cover any unexpected deficiency in the strength of the alliance. The difficulty with this plan was that an alliance combination including both Poland and the Soviet Union was a sheer impossibility.

Halifax was not fully aware of this fact despite the informative reports on the Polish attitude toward Soviet Russia which he had received from Kennard. Halifax regarded Poland as a minor Power, and it was customary for minor Powers to make concessions to the Great Powers which volunteered to protect their interests. He was never able to understand that the Polish leaders would not deviate from their policy toward the Soviet Union merely to please Great Britain. Halifax was compelled to choose between Poland and the Soviet Union, when Poland refused to join a combination which included Russia. He chose Poland, but he retained the mental reservation that he would be able to persuade the Poles to modify their attitude toward Russia. This enabled him to reason that his choice between Russia and Poland was temporary. He hoped to reconcile these two Powers, and to secure the services of both of them for the British balance of power program.[26]

David Lloyd George believed that Halifax was reckless in choosing Poland instead of Russia for his alliance combination. The point was brought out again and again in the British Parliament that Halifax had picked the weaker Eastern European Power for his encirclement front. It was shown that Great Britain was assuming commitments in Eastern Europe which could not conceivably be defended without the Soviet Union. This ignored the fact that Halifax had made the logical decision for his particular policy. There would have been no likelihood of a war for Danzig had Halifax appeased his critics by doing things the other way around. The Russians would not have fought for Poland when the Poles refused their aid, and France would have been inclined to follow the Russian lead. Halifax feared that the Poles might proceed to an agreement with Germany, if he slighted Poland in favor of Russia. This would have enabled Hitler to complete his program of territorial revision without war. The involvement of Germany in war was the cardinal feature of Halifax's foreign policy.[27]

Halifax welcomed the enthusiastic support for a change in British policy which he received from the American Government after March 15, 1939. The collapse of Czecho-Slovakia produced a greater immediate outburst of hostility toward Germany in Washington, D.C., than in any other capital of the world. German Charge' d'Affaires Thomsen reported to Berlin that a violent press campaign against Germany had been launched throughout the United States. There was much resentment in American New Deal circles when Sir John Simon delivered a speech in the British House of Commons on March 16, 1939, in support of Chamberlain's conciliatory message on the previous day. The Simon speech produced a vigorous American protest in London on March 17, 1939. Halifax replied by promising President Roosevelt that the British leaders were "going to start educating public opinion as best they can to the need of action." This is a different picture from the one presented by Gilbert and Gott to the effect that "for most men the answer was simple" after the events at Prague on March 15, 1939. Roosevelt warned Halifax that there would be "an increase of anti-British sentiment in the United States" unless Great Britain hastened to adopt an outspokenly anti-German policy.[28]

Roosevelt requested Halifax to withdraw the British Ambassador from Germany permanently. Halifax replied that he was not prepared to go quite that far. British opinion was less ignorant than American opinion about the requirements of diplomacy, and Halifax feared that a rude shock would be produced if the British copied the American practice of permanently withdrawing ambassadors for no adequate reasons. He promised that he would instruct Henderson to return to England for consultation, and he promised that he would prevent the return of the British ambassador to Germany for a considerable time. He also promised that Chamberlain would deliver a challenging speech in Birminghham on the evening of March 17, 1939, which would herald a complete change in British policy. He assured Roosevelt that Great Britain was prepared at last to intervene actively in the affairs of Central Europe.

Halifax requested President Roosevelt to join Great Britain in showing "the extent to which the moral sense of civilization was outraged by the present rulers of Germany." He knew that this lofty formulation of the issue would appeal to the American President. Roosevelt was satisfied with the response from Halifax. He promised the British Foreign Secretary that he would undermine the American neutrality legislation, which had been adopted by the American Congress, with New Deal approval, in response to pressure from American public opinion. Halifax also received the promise that American Secretary of the Treasury Morgenthau would take vigorous new steps in his policy of financial and economic discrimination against Germany. Halifax was greatly encouraged by the support he received from President Roosevlet for his war policy.[29]

The Tilea Hoax

Halifax had not waited for promptings from the American President before preparing his new policy. For several days, he had been organizing one of the most fantastic intrigues of modern diplomacy. The sole purpose of this activity was to ease the change in British policy by inventing a broader basis than the Czech crisis from which to justify it to the British public.

Halifax intended to claim that Germany was threatening Rumania. Germany had no common frontier with Rumania, but she did have diplomatic and economic relations with that country, and German territory extended to within about three hundred miles of the Rumanian frontier. Great Britain dominated Rumanian finances, and she had large holdings in Rumanian petroleum and other industries. The Rumanians were eager to receive shipments of arms from Great Britain, because their principal source of armament at the Skoda works in Bohemia was now in German hands. A German trade delegation was in Rumania to negotiate a commercial treaty, which was not signed until March 23, 1939. The main purpose of the German mission was to arrange for German aid in the modernization of Rumanian agriculture and to increase Rumanian agricultural exports to Germany. The presence of a German delegation at Bucharest was useful in claiming the existence of a German plot. The visit of King Carol to

London in November 1938 had enabled Halifax to confirm the fact that British influence was still dominant in Rumania. Virgil Tilea, the Rumanian Minister to Great Britain, was a pliable person and a willing accessory to the false charges which Halifax planned to present against the Germans. The British knew that Grigorie Gafencu, the new Rumanian Foreign Minister, was a man of honor who would not consent to participate in such a conspiracy, and they did not inform him of their scheme. They counted on British influence at Bucharest to prevent an effective protest to their action. Halifax intended to claim that the Germans were seeking to seize control of the entire Rumanian economy, and that they had presented an ultimatum at Bucharest which had terrified the Rumanian leaders.[30]

Tilea was carefully coached for his role by Sir Robert Vansittart, the vehemently anti-German Chief Diplomatic Adviser to His Majesty's Government. The British confided in Tilea, and they told him before the Germans went to Prague that Great Britain intended to oppose Germany. Tilea knew that King Carol had failed to obtain a British loan for arms in 1938, and he believed that his own prestige would be increased if he obtained such a loan. He had arrived in Great Britain as Rumanian Minister on January 9, 1939, with general instructions to do everything possible to bring the loan question to a successful issue, and he pursued these instructions with a single-mindedness devoid of any moral inhibitions.[31]

Tilea told Halifax on March 14, 1939, that he would welcome a hostile British reaction to the expected German occupation of Prague. He was pleased that the British had secretly decided before the culmination of the Czecho-Slovak crisis to abandon a projected mission for trade talks in Germany. He promised Halifax that a further increase of British influence in Rumania would be welcome. He suggested that the British could make an effective appeal to the vanity of King Carol if they elevated the British Legation in Bucharest to an Embassy. He believed that it would avoid suspicion and soothe easily ruffled Balkan feelings if they took the same step at Belgrade and Athens. Tilea made it clear that he was especially pleased by British interest in an armament loan which would be a source of personal profit for himself.[32]

The British assured Tilea that they were inclined to grant the loan and to elevate the British Legation at Bucharest, which of course meant that the Rumanian Legation in London would also become an Embassy. They were pleased that Tilea was prepared to pay the price by offering to cooperate unreservedly with their anti-German scheme. There were daily conferences between Tilea and British Foreign Office spokesmen during the interval between this personal agreement and the public hatching of the plot on March 17, 1939. Halifax was anxious to avoid the possibilities that Tilea might change his mind or misunderstand his role. Gilbert and Gott begin their effort to protect the reputation of Halifax in this unsavory situation by wrongly claiming that Bonnet expected a German move into Rumania, and that the first discussions with Tilea at the British Foreign Office did not take place until March 16, 1939, after the German occupation of Prague.

The crucial day arrived at last. Tilea issued a carefully prepared public statement on March 17th which charged that Germany had presented an ultimatum to Rumania. Sir Robert Vansittart hastened to release this "big story" to the

London *Times* and the *Daily Telegraph* before the Prime Minister spoke at Birmingham. Millions of British newspaper readers were aghast at the apparently unlimited appetite of Hitler and the alleged rapidity and rapacity of his various moves. The "big story" shook British complacency, and it produced bewilderment, anxiety, and outspoken hostility toward Germany. Chamberlain was presented by Halifax with the text of a speech on foreign policy, and he was persuaded to scrap his own speech on British domestic affairs. This development was explained with the quaint statement that Chamberlain had received "fuller knowledge" of recent events.[33]

The Tilea episode was crucial to the development of the Halifax policy, and the British Foreign Secretary was not bothered by the repercussions of the affair at Bucharest. The British Minister to Rumania, Reginald Hoare, appealed to Halifax on March 18, 1939, to stop British radio broadcasting of irresponsible statements from Tilea, and to desist from referring to them in official dispatches. This urgent appeal produced no effect at London. Hoare proceeded to explain in detail the ridiculous nature of Tilea's charges. He feared that what he regarded as London's astonishing credulity would seriously damage British prestige.[34]

Hoare considered it "so utterly improbable that the Minister of Foreign Affairs would not have informed me that an *immediate* (italics his) threatening situation had developed here that I called on him as soon as your telegrams to Warsaw and Moscow had been decyphered. He told me that he was being inundated with enquiries regarding the report of a German ultimatum which had appeared in 'The Times' and 'Daily Telegraph' today. There was not a word of truth in it." Hoare assured Halifax that he had been very inquisitive about Dr. Helmuth Wohlthat's German economic mission to Rumania, but Gafencu "expressed bewilderment," and maintained "under close cross-examination" that negotiations "on completely normal lines as between equals" were being conducted.[35]

Hoare naturally assumed that his detailed report would induce Halifax to disavow the Tilea hoax. Nothing of the sort occurred. Hoare had been surprised when Halifax accepted Tilea's story without consulting the British Legation in Bucharest. He was astonished when Halifax continued to express his faith in the authenticity of the story after its falsehood had been exposed.

Wilhelm Fabricius, the German Minister to Rumania, conducted an even more thorough investigation of the Rumanian attitude toward the Tilea hoax. He satisfied himself that King Carol had had no advance knowledge of the plot. He reported to Berlin on March 18, 1939, that Rumanian Foreign Minister Gafencu had presented to him a disavowal of the statements made at London by Tilea. Gafencu insisted that all charges concerning German demands on Rumania were entirely without foundation.[36]

American Minister Gunther reported from Bucharest on March 20, 1939, that "Tilea, the Anglophile Rumanian Minister," was guilty of "excessive zeal." Tilea had nonchalantly informed Gafencu that he was "merely trying to be helpful." Gafencu had assured the American diplomats in Rumania that economic negotiations with the Germans were proceeding on a normal basis. The Rumanian Foreign Minister complained that Tilea's false report "had been seized upon by the Jewish controlled sections of the western press." Gafencu was

furious with Tilea, but he did not dare withdraw him from London for fear
of offending Halifax.[37]

Poland Calm about Events at Prague

The British press was soon flooded with stories about the alleged German
mistreatment of the Czechs, and about the alleged German ultimatum to
Rumania. The attitude of the press in Poland, on the eve of Halifax's offer of
March 20, 1939, to conclude an alliance with the Poles, was entirely different.
There was virtually no comment on the Tilea hoax, and the Polish leaders had
made it known almost immediately that the alleged German ultimatum to
Rumania was a pure invention. The comments about events in Czecho-Slovakia
were restrained in contrast to those in the English or American press. The Polish
newspapers devoted much space to events in Slovakia after the crisis reached its
peak there on March 9, 1939. The press in Poland, with the exception of
Robotnik (*The Worker*) and the other Marxist newspapers, placed major
emphasis on Polish sympathy for the Slovakian independence movement. The
Marxist newspapers favored the Czechs because of their close ties with the Czech
Marxists. Józef Beck delivered a speech on March 12, 1939, which stressed
Polish sympathy for Slovakia, and his remarks were widely featured in the press.
Beck in his address also urged the foreign nations to aid Poland to get rid of her
Jewish population. He conveyed no anxiety about German intentions in
Slovakia.[38]

On March 14, 1939, after Germany had agreed to support the Slovak bid for
independence, the leading Polish newspapers blamed Czech difficulties on the
intimate relations between Prague and Moscow. The morning editions on March
15th carried the news that German troops had occupied Morava-Ostrava and that
Hungarian troops had entered Ruthenia. These reports showed great detachment
toward the German action, which seemed to be eliminating an old adversary of
Poland from the Central European scene.[39]

The Polish newspapers on March 16, 1939, carried the full story of recent
events. The feature headlines, such as *Swastika Standard on the Prague
Hradczyn*, were identical with the headlines in the German press. An official
Polish Government bulletin was cited, which stated that the Czechs were
principally the victims of their own political megalomania. It was hoped that
Slovakian independence would be a reality and not a mere fiction, and there
was some discussion about the need for Polish military strength in unsettled
times. There was little evidence of either the indignation or anxiety, not to
mention the hysteria, of much of the Western press. The official *Gazeta Polska*
explained on March 16, 1939, that Hitler's policy was based on a realistic
consideration of important factors, despite the fact that German power had been
extended beyond German ethnic limits. The echo of the howling wind of the
Western press was not apparent in the leading Polish newspapers until March 18,
1939, and then only faintly.[40]

The Polish press reaction was different from the British or the American
because Poland was not inclined to oppose German policy in such questions as
Bohemia-Moravia, which concerned the Poles. The Slovaks had escaped from

Czech rule, and the Hungarians had obtained Ruthenia.

The Poles were fully aware that the Czechs were prepared to accept their new relationship with Germany. Hitler had received a warm greeting from Czech Premier General Jan Syrovy' at Prague on March 15, 1939. A Czech National Committee had been formed at the Czech Parliament on the same day. It was based on a broad coalition of Czech patriotic organizations, Czech trade unions, farmer organizations, and Government officials. The Committee immediately issued "an appeal to the Czech nation recalling their historic association with the German people in the Holy Roman Empire." It was recalled that Prague had once been the capital of that Empire. It was evident that German-Czech collaboration could be established on a solid foundation without great difficulty. The Poles found it impossible under these circumstances to become hysterical about the events at Prague, and they did not have to contend with a conspiracy of their leaders to promote such hysteria by artificial means, as Halifax and Vansittart had done in London. The sovereign contempt of the British leaders toward their own public was manifest in the manner by which Halifax manipulated the events of these days.[41]

Beck Amazed by the Tilea Hoax

The British and French diplomatic representatives at Berlin had confined themselves to an informational *démarche* on March 15, 1939. They merely requested the German authorities to explain German policy in Czecho-Slovakia. Henderson on his own initiative formally recognized Germany's preponderant interests in Czecho-Slovak territory. No British protest was presented at Berlin before Chamberlain's Birmingham speech on March 17, 1939. Bonnet spoke to German Ambassador Welczeck at Paris on March 15, 1939. He mildly suggested that the Germans must have used at least the threat of force to persuade the Czechs to accept their new relationship with Germany. Coulondre had reported from Czech sources in Berlin that the Germans had made such a threat, and Bonnet felt sure of his ground. He noted that Welczeck was embarrassed by the entire affair.[42]

The first step taken by Halifax after the Tilea announcement on March 17, 1939, was to contact Kennard at Warsaw. This was a consistent move because Poland occupied the crucial position in Halifax's plans. Kennard was instructed to inform Beck that Halifax and Tilea were discussing the possibility of transforming the Polish-Rumanian anti-Soviet alliance into an anti-German alliance. Halifax wished to have Beck's reaction to this plan as soon as possible. Kennard was unable to discuss the matter with Beck until the morning of March 18th. In the meantime, a report about the Tilea statement in London had been sent to the British diplomats at Warsaw. This was fortunate for Kennard, because Beck was primarily interested in discussing the Tilea hoax.

Beck informed Kennard that he could not understand what Tilea was doing in London. Miroslaw Arciszewski, the Polish Minister to Rumania, had discussed the current situation with King Carol on the evening of March 17, 1939. The Rumanian monarch had not conveyed the slightest indication that Germany was threatening Rumania. Beck "could hardly believe" that the Rumanian diplomat

had made the remarks attributed to him in London, despite the fact that the
story had been released by the British Foreign Office. Kennard was somewhat
dismayed by Beck's version of the Rumanian situation, which differed markedly
from his own. He introduced Halifax's suggestion for a Polish-Rumanian alliance
against Germany, and he discovered that Beck did not like the proposition.[43]

Poland had guaranteed the Rumanian frontier along the Dniester River
against Soviet aggression. Beck believed that it would be nonsense for Poland
to guarantee the Rumanian western frontier against Germany. There was no
reason to assume that Germany and Rumania would ever have a common
frontier. Polish-Rumanian relations had been friendly for years and there was no
need to improve them. A Polish guarantee of the western border of Rumania
would alienate Hungary. The nations with territorial aspirations in Rumania
were the Soviet Union, Hungary, and Bulgaria. Beck did not mind guaranteeing
Rumania against the Soviet Union, but he would needlessly injure Polish
interests by doing so against Hungary. The Hungarians were interested in the
largest and most valuable section of disputed Rumanian territory.

Beck could not imagine what Halifax hoped to gain by a Polish-Rumanian
treaty against Germany. He did not regard the suggestion as a sensible idea. He
told Kennard that he refused to believe Rumania was under the slightest pressure
from Germany. Kennard, with unflagging persistence, asked Beck what he would
do in a hypothetical case of German pressure on Rumania. The Polish Foreign
Minister curtly replied that he was not in the habit of committing Poland in
hypothetical situations.[44]

Halifax appealed to the Soviet Union to help defend Rumania from "German
aggression," before Chamberlain spoke at Birmingham on March 17, 1939. This
appeal was the last thing that Bucharest wanted, because Rumania feared
Russian rather than German aggression. This consideration did not bother
Halifax, who had carefully avoided all contact with the Rumanian Government
since the Slovakian crisis. It is unnecessary to describe at length the reaction of
the Soviet Union to the German occupation of Prague. Kliment Voroshilov, the
Defense Commissar of the Soviet Union, had delivered a speech on March 13,
1939, which repeated the earlier claim of Stalin that Great Britain and France
were seeking to push Germany into war with the Soviet Union. The Russian
press responded to the Slovak crisis by condemning the Four Munich Powers for
undermining the Czecho-Slovak state.[45]

Halifax claimed to the Russians that the Germans were seeking control of
Rumania, and that their proposals at Bucharest were "in the nature of an ultimatum." The British Foreign Secretary was not worried about Russian scepticism
toward his claims. He could always contend that he had been misled by the
Rumanian Minister to London. His proposal for a Soviet guarantee of Rumania
was secondary to his main objective of proposing an Anglo-Soviet alliance. The
Tilea hoax met his requirements for a pretext to approach the Soviet Union.[46]

Halifax at last sent instructions to British Ambassador Henderson for a
protest about the German occupation of Prague. Henderson was informed in the
evening of March 17, 1939, that the Germans were guilty of "a complete
repudiation of Munich." Halifax charged that all changes were "effected in
Czecho-Slovakia by German military action," and that the new regimes at Prague
and Bratislava were "devoid of any basis of legality." He had consulted with

Bonnet, and the French were willing to submit a protest of their own in Berlin. Halifax avoided any reference to Rumania in his instructions to Henderson.[47]

Chamberlain's Birmingham Speech

The role assigned by Halifax to Prime Minister Chamberlain at Birmingham was one of outraged innocence. Chamberlain agreed to present himself as the victim of German duplicity, who had awakened at last in a great rage to admit that he had been duped. Chamberlain solemnly declared that he would never believe Hitler again. He claimed that Great Britain might have assumed her obligation to guarantee Czecho-Slovakia, but that this had been rendered impossible by the collapse of the Czecho-Slovak state.

Chamberlain warned his listeners at Birmingham that Hitler might be embarking on an attempt to conquer the world. He sought to create an impression of frankness by confiding that he was not absolutely certain this was the case. He then attempted to build up the impression in the minds of his listeners that any further developments in Hitler's program of territorial revision would be irrevocable proof that Hitler was attempting to conquer the world.

The speech of Halifax, which Chamberlain delivered on March 17, 1939, forced the British Prime Minister to present himself in the role of a naive person. The implication that he had blindly trusted Hitler, until the German occupation of Prague, was at variance with the facts. Chamberlain had never trusted Hitler, and he had always regarded appeasement toward Germany as a conditional policy in which the British could not afford to place their faith. He had always been unwilling to pursue appeasement to a point which, in his opinion, would seriously jeopardize the operation of the balance of power. Indeed, it may be stated as a certainty that Chamberlain never placed blind faith in any foreign leader. He placed his faith in British military power, and in the ability of the British leaders to maneuver successfully on the diplomatic scene. His willingness to appear in the role of dupe at the behest of Halifax was merely what he considered to be a patriotic duty best calculated to serve the aim of arousing the British public against Germany.

One might assume that the Chamberlain speech was too ambitious in attempting to achieve so much with the British public so soon, and that the excessive element of propaganda in the speech would create a dangerous revulsion in British public opinion. It is necessary to recall the historical context of the speech. The British public had received increasingly large doses of anti-German propaganda since the Munich conference, from the British radio, cinema industry, and newspaper press, and many highly respected figures in British public life had denounced both Hitler and Germany with great vehemence. Chamberlain had contributed to this process with his alarmist speech of January 23, 1939.[48]

There was some jolt to what remained of British public complacency when Hitler went to Prague, but the fraudulent news about Rumania on March 17, 1939, was especially useful in creating an atmosphere of nervousness and anxiety. Chamberlain was able to go surprisingly far in his remarks at Birmingham without seriously compromising the effectiveness of his speech. He assured his audience that Great Britain did not intend to wait until Hitler's next move, but that she was launching her own counter-measures against him at once.

The Anglo-French Protest at Berlin

Events moved rapidly in London after March 17, 1939, and there was no trace of the dilatory British attitude, which had been encountered by the Czechs during recent weeks when they had raised the question of the territorial guarantee. The British and French Ambassadors in Berlin lodged their formal protests about German policy toward Czecho-Slovakia on March 18, 1939. Halifax had carefully avoided accusing the Germans of not having consulted with Great Britain about their Czech policy. Rab Butler, the Parliamentary Under-Secretary for Foreign Affairs, had presented a detailed explanation to the British House of Commons that Germany was under no obligation to consult with Great Britain on her Czech policy. The consultation clause in the Anglo-German declaration of September 30, 1938, applied solely to questions of direct interest to both Great Britain and Germany. Butler explained that Great Britain had no direct interest in the Czech situation, because she had not guaranteed the Czecho-Slovak state.[49]

State Secretary Ernst von Weizsaecker, who received the British and French protests, showed no trace of the embarrassment displayed to Halifax by Dirksen at London, or to Bonnet by Welczeck at Paris. Weizsaecker had accurately explained to German diplomats abroad, on March 16, 1939, that the Munich agreement was superseded by the events of the Slovak crisis rather than violated by Germany. The success of the Slovak independence movement had rendered impossible the continuation of the Czecho-Slovak state, which at one time the Four Munich Powers had planned to guarantee. This interpretation was accepted by the Italian Government without hesitation. German Ambassador Mackensen at Rome forwarded the Italian statement of approval to Berlin on March 17, 1939.[50]

Weizsaecker had followed closely each step of the Slovakian crisis. He sympathized with Josef Tiso, the principal Slovakian leader, and he admired Adalbert Tuka, who had spent ten years in Czech prisons and had recently been threatened by the Czechs with new imprisonment. He was aware that the Germans had consulted with the Slovaks in Bratislava during the final phase of the crisis, and that Hitler had consistently encouraged the Slovaks since his meeting with Adalbert Tuka on February 12, 1939. He also knew that the movement for independence in Slovakia, since the Munich conference, had developed steadily with popular support, and of course he did not believe that the disruption of the Czecho-Slovak state was the artificial product of German machinations. These convictions of Weizsaecker were no mere rationalization, and they were steadfastly defended by him during and after World War II. He remained convinced that Hacha's agreement with Hitler on March 15, 1939, regardless of the motives which inspired it on the Czech side, gave to Germany an adequate legal basis for her Czech policy in March 1939.[51]

It is not surprising, therefore, that Henderson and Coulondre encountered a spirited defense of German policy at the Wilhelmstrasse. Indeed, Weizsaecker knew that British Ambassador Henderson privately agreed with his analysis of the Czecho-Slovak situation. It had been known in Berlin since March 17th that Halifax intended to recall Henderson to London for an indefinite period. Henderson had called on Weizsaecker on that date for a private discussion of recent events. He told the German State Secretary that he was eager to receive as many effective German arguments as possible to employ in discussions with the foes of appeasement at home.[52]

Weizsaecker informed Henderson and Coulondre on March 18, 1939, that he refused to accept their notes of protest. This refusal was consistent with the position of the German Government that the Munich agreement had been superseded by events. Weizsaecker told Coulondre that French Foreign Minister Bonnet had expressed the disinterest of France in the Czech question at the time of the Franco-German declaration of December 6, 1938. There was no way of proving what Bonnet had actually said in private conversation with Ribbentrop. It would have been perfectly consistent of Bonnet to make such a statement after the British leaders, on November 24, 1938, had effectively blocked the French plan for the implementation of the Czech guarantee. It was equally clear that Bonnet would not be inclined to admit publicly what he may have said privately. The strategy of Weizsaecker and Ribbentrop in making an issue of this point on March 18, 1939, was perfectly obvious. They hoped to demonstrate to France that the furor about the events at Prague was artificial, and that it was unworthy of France to be unduly indignant about these events merely because this was the reaction at Washington, D.C., or at London.[53]

Coulondre did not care to cope with this challenging blow, and he referred the matter to Bonnet. The French Foreign Minister elected not to be drawn into a complex discussion of the matter at this point. He merely claimed that Weizsaecker should not have received Coulondre in the first place, if the German State Secretary believed Ribbentrop's contention about the French assurance of December 1938 concerning the Czechs. The German State Secretary knew in advance that Coulondre intended to protest about the Czecho-Slavak crisis, and he was acknowledging the French right to deliver a protest by receiving him. Weizsaecker disagreed with this view. He recalled that the Four Munich Powers at one time had intended to assume a joint responsibility toward the Czechs, and he did not believe that an alleged unilateral statement from Bonnet altered this fact. He insisted that it was correct to receive the British and French Ambassadors, with the knowledge that they intended to deliver protests, and then to explain why Germany refused to accept their protest notes. Bonnet, on the other hand, believed that Weizsaecker had tacitly accepted the French right to protest when he received Coulondre.[54]

The Withdrawal of the British and French Ambassadors

Halifax announced publicly, after the presentation of the British protest, that Henderson would be withdrawn from Germany for lengthy consultation in England. This step was taken despite the fact that Henderson had returned to Germany from a long sick leave in England only a few weeks before. Bonnet agreed to take an identical step, and Coulondre was also withdrawn. The Western

Ambassadors departed from Germany on March 19, 1939, and they did not return for nearly six weeks. Beck noted the close synchronization of Anglo-French policy in this instance, and he concluded hopefully that the British leaders were still able to dictate French foreign policy. Polish Ambassador Lukasiewicz had warned Beck that France was reluctant to maintain old obligations or assume new commitments toward Poland. Beck hoped that by turning to London he could achieve whatever Poland required from France.[55]

The German Foreign Office hoped to persuade the British to modify their decision, by retaining Dirksen at London. The German Ambassador called on Halifax to inform him that he had permission to remain in London, if the British would agree to detain Henderson in England for only a short time. Halifax bluntly refused to indicate how long Henderson would remain in England, and Dirksen was forced to request Ribbentrop to recall him. The German Ambassador had come to Great Britain, from his previous post in Japan, in May 1938 with high hopes. He was reluctant to depart from London at a critical stage in the relations between Great Britain and Germany. He was forced to conclude, when he returned to Great Britain in May 1939, that Halifax had been completely successful in persuading the British public that a new Anglo-German war was inevitable.[56]

Polish Foreign Minister Beck received an assurance from Julius Lukasiewicz and William Bullitt on March 19, 1939, that President Roosevelt was prepared to do everything possible to promote a war between the Anglo-French front and Germany. Bullitt admitted that he was still suspicious about British intentions, and he feared that the British might be tempted to compose their differences with Germany at some later date. He promised that any such deviation from a British war policy would encounter energetic resistance from President Roosevelt. Bullitt had received word from Premier Daladier that the British were proposing an Anglo-French territorial guarantee to Rumania, and the American diplomat welcomed this plan.[57]

Bullitt informed the Poles that he knew Germany hoped to acquire Danzig, and that he was counting on Polish willingness to go to war over the Danzig question. He urged Lukasiewicz to present demands to the West for supplies and other military assistance. Lukasiewicz told Bullitt that Poland would need all the help the West could possibly offer in the event of war. Bullitt said that he hoped Poland could obtain military supplies from the Soviet Union, but Lukasiewicz displayed no enthusiasm for this possibility. He warned Bullitt that it was too early to predict what position Russia would take in a German-Polish dispute. Bullitt recognized from this remark that Lukasiewicz was assuming that Soviet policy toward Poland would be hostile. It was equally clear that Bullitt recognized the military hopelessness of the Polish position, if the Soviet Union did not aid Poland in a conflict with Germany.[58]

Halifax and Cadogan noted with satisfaction on March 19, 1939, that Tilea was tenaciously repeating his lie about the alleged German ultimatum to Rumania. They considered this a sufficient mandate to continue to base their policy on the Tilea hoax. They admitted privately that the disavowal of British Minister Hoare could not be entirely ignored. Cadogan cheerfully suggested that "in the circumstances it might be possible that there was some truth in both stories" with the "ultimatum having now disappeared as the basis of negotiation." Halifax was not troubled in the least by this arrant nonsense. Gilbert and Gott invoke "panic" to defend Halifax for ignoring the disavowal of Tilea: "Such news ought to have stopped the panic. It failed to do so. Tilea's timely indiscretion was allowed to determine British policy."[59]

The Halifax Alliance Offer to Poland and the Soviet Union

Halifax took a major step on March 20, 1939, to implement the new British effort to encircle Germany. He informed Paris, Moscow, and Warsaw that he wished to have an ironclad military pact of Great Britain, France, Russia, and Poland against Germany. He admitted that "doubts" had been raised about the reality of a German ultimatum to Rumania, but he insisted that German policy at Prague showed that the Germans were going beyond the "avowed aim of consolidation of the German race." It made no difference to Halifax that there were more Germans in Europe beyond the boundaries of Germany than foreign peoples in the Reich, or that Great Britain, France, and Russia ruled over hundreds of millions of foreign peoples. He was not disturbed by the fact that Poland was ruling over far more foreign peoples than Germany. He had created enough feeling against Germany in England to sustain the thesis before an uninformed public opinion that Germany was seeking world conquest.[60]

Halifax hoped that his plan for an alliance would produce a stunning British foreign policy victory over Germany within a few days. The ground had been carefully prepared, both in England and abroad. Halifax knew that Poland was not inclined to accept the German proposals for an agreement. He also knew that Poland would require an alliance of the type he proposed to prevent the defeat of Poland in a German-Polish war. He knew that Germany had failed to gain military alliances with the Italians or the Japanese, and he was counting on the continuation of a successful British policy to intimidate Italy. Germany would have no allies to aid her in coping with the gigantic combination which Halifax hoped to achieve. Halifax persuaded Chamberlain to write a letter to Mussolini on March 20, 1939, as part of the general plan to detach Italy from the informal Rome-Berlin Axis. The British Prime Minister claimed that his forebodings about Germany at Rome in January 1939 had since been confirmed by events. He also warned the Italian leader that the British policy of appeasement toward Germany had been permanently discarded.[61]

The Halifax alliance offer of March 20, 1939, marked the culmination of the five day shift in Great Britain from appeasement policy to war policy. The formal British alliance offer convinced the Poles that the British were ready for military action against Germany. It was no longer necessary for Beck to conceal his attitude toward Germany, and it was possible to assume in London that he would reveal the true Polish position in a very short time. Halifax had no problem as far as the Polish attitude toward Germany was concerned. He hoped that his bold initiative, in offering to conclude British alliance commitments in Eastern Europe, would be effective in dealing with some of the serious problems with which he still had to contend. The most difficult problem was created by the hostility between the Soviet Union and all of the western neighbors of Russia, which of course included Poland. There was also the problem of the

French attitude, and Halifax had good reason to fear that France would never consent to an adventure in Eastern Europe without Russian support. The attitude of President Roosevelt was not a very effective instrument to influence French policy, because Bonnet was keenly aware that the Rooseveltian war policy did not enjoy the support of the United States Congress or of American public opinion.

The problematical position of the Soviet Union in the plans of Halifax received eloquent emphasis in a communiqué released by the Soviet Foreign Office on March 21, 1939. The Russians emphatically denied that they had offered aid or assistance either to Poland or to Rumania. They also announced to the world that the British had been urging them to take steps along such lines since March 18, 1939. There was no comment about the British proposal of March 20, 1939, for the conclusion of an Anglo-Franco-Russo-Polish military alliance. The Soviet leaders merely indicated that they were receiving British proposals with interest. They specifically pointed out that the Soviet Union, unlike Britain, had thus far not offered to extend their existing commitments.[62]

There was no reason for Hitler or anyone else to conclude that the European war desired by Halifax and Roosevelt was inevitable. The British leaders would never attack Germany without the support of France, and it was unlikely that France would go to war without the support of the Soviet Union. Halifax was counting on Poland to provide the pretext for war, but the hostility between Poland and the Soviet Union rendered unlikely the participation of these two Powers in the same alliance combination. Halifax had taken a great risk in bringing the hostility of the British leaders toward Germany into the open at this stage. The situation had been entirely different when his kinsman, Sir Edward Grey, urged British participation in a comflict in 1914, after hostilities were in progress. There was no problem in sustaining war enthusiasm for a short period once it had been successfully aroused. It was a different matter when there was no war in progress, and it was uncertain if the conditions for successful British action would be fulfilled. It was evident that Halifax was merely gambling on his ability to sustain British enthusiasm for war and to create the conditions necessary for British participation in a conflict. The British response to the events at Prague created a major crisis. It was impossible to predict either the duration or the outcome of this crisis.

Chapter 13

THE POLISH DECISION

TO CHALLENGE GERMANY

The Impetuosity of Beck

The Poles threw down the gauntlet to the Germans during the week which followed the Halifax alliance offer of March 20, 1939. They mobilized hundreds of thousands of Polish Army reservists, and they warned Hitler that Poland would fight to prevent the return of Danzig to Germany. They were amazed to discover that the Germans were not inclined to take this challenge seriously. The Germans did not threaten Poland, and they took no precautionary military measures in response to the Polish partial mobilization. The situation was characterized by a conversation between State Secretary Weizsaecker and Italian Chargé d'Affaires Magistrati on March 30, 1939. Weizsaecker mentioned that Germany had been seeking to settle the differences between the two countries for many months. He remarked with good-natured humor that the Poles appeared to be a bit deaf, but he was convinced that in the future they would learn to hear better. He refused to admit that a dangerous situation existed, and that Germany and Poland might go to war.[1]

It was the impatience of Beck rather than of Hitler which produced the rupture of German-Polish negotiations in March 1939. The Germans hastened to conclude their agreement with Lithuania for the return of Memel, but the situation at the German port on the mouth of the Niemen River had been ripe for many months. Weizsaecker noted on March 22, 1939, after the Lithuanian Cabinet had consented to the return of Memel to Germany, that Lithuanian Foreign Minister Urbsys "seemed to be relieved and well content." The Germans continued their talks with the Poles after March 20, 1939, but they betrayed no impatience and gave no indication that the negotiation of an agreement was an urgent matter. Beck was eager to defy Germany as soon as he realized that British hostility toward the Germans was at last in the open, and he could not resist the temptation to do so. There is an obvious parallel between Beck's response and the rash acts of Schuschnigg on March 9, 1938, and of Beneš on May 20, 1938. Schuschnigg had challenged Germany with a fraudulent anti-German plebiscite scheme, and Hitler responded by intervening in Austria. Beneš challenged Germany with a Czech mobilization based on the false claim of German troop concentrations on the Czech frontier. Hitler responded with his decision to liberate the Sudetenland from Czech rule in 1938. Beck challenged Germany with a partial mobilization and a threat of war, and Hitler, who deeply desired friendship with Poland, refrained from responding at all. It was not until Beck joined the British encirclement front that Hitler took precautionary military measures against the Polish threat. It would have been incompatible with the security of Germany for him to refrain from doing so, after the formation of a hostile Anglo-Polish combination. The charge that Hitler did not know how to wait can be applied more appropriately to the Austrian, Czech, and Polish leaders than to Hitler.[2]

The Poles had informed the Germans earlier that they did not object to the return of Memel to Germany. This achievement restored the East Prussian frontier, in the Memel region, to the line confirmed by Napoleon and the Russians in their treaty at Tilsit-on-the-Niemen in 1807. This line in turn was recognized by the Congress of Vienna in 1815, and it was the identical boundary established at the Peace of Thorn in 1466 between Poland-Lithuania and the German Order of Knights. It was evident that the March 1939 Memel agreement was a conservative step rather than a radical innovation. The Allied victors at Paris in 1919 had detached Memel from East Prussia. They had seized a city which in the seven centuries of its history had never been separated from its East Prussian homeland.[3]

Beck's Rejection of the Halifax Pro-Soviet Alliance Offer

The Poles on March 20, 1939, were momentarily distracted from their challenge to Germany by the need to clarify misconceptions about their relations with the Soviet Union and Rumania. British Ambassador Kennard was informed at the Polish Foreign Office on March 21, 1939, that Poland refused to enter a military alliance which included the Soviet Union. Halifax was very displeased with this news, but it was vital for his plans to please the Poles and to include them in his alliance. They were the only nation likely to furnish a pretext for military intervention against Germany. British support to Rumania was unlikely to produce a conflict with Germany, and the same was true of British support to the Soviet Union, France, or any other European Power. The Poles were absolutely indispensable. Halifax had some time to consider his dilemma carefully, because Beck did not come forward immediately with a formal reply to the British alliance offer.[4]

The problem of Rumania had produced a quarrel between Polish Ambassador Lukasiewicz and Alexis Léger, the Secretary-General at the French Foreign Office. Lukasiewicz was exasperated by the attempts of Bullitt to convince him that Poland and Rumania should agree to permit Soviet troops to operate on their territory during a war against Germany. Lukasiewicz told Léger early on March 21, 1939, that Poland would definitely refuse to associate herself with a British declaration to oppose any or all attacks on Rumania. The Polish

Ambassador insisted that his country would continue to guarantee Rumania against the Soviet Union, but she would assume no additional commitment. Léger, who was critical of the policy of Bonnet, was seeking to promote as many new Anglo-French commitments as possible, and the independent attitude of the Polish envoy in the Rumanian question caused him to lose his temper. He produced a disgraceful scene, and Lukasiewicz denounced him to his face as a "malevolent" person. The Polish diplomat admitted afterward to Bullitt that a fist fight between Léger and himself had been narrowly averted. Bullitt hastened to call on Léger in a fruitless effort to mediate. He found Léger in a bitter mood, and more critical of Poland, if possible, than was Bonnet. Léger predicted that Poland would prove to be a very bad ally for Great Britain, as she had been for France.[5]

Halifax discussed his alliance project with American Ambassador Kennedy on March 22, 1939, and he complained at great length about the negative attitude of Beck toward an alliance front to include both Poland and the Soviet Union. He intimated that he was resolved to continue his anti-German policy, and that hostilities in Europe might be expected fairly soon. He was convinced that the British Navy was more than adequate to cope with German naval forces. He urged Kennedy to request President Roosevelt to concentrate the American fleet at Pearl Harbor, as an appropriate gesture to protect Australia and Singapore from a possible Japanese attack, after the outbreak of war in Europe. Halifax admitted at last that the story of a German threat to Rumania could not be substantiated, but he assured Kennedy that Tilea's statements at London had served a useful purpose.[6]

Józef Beck hoped that by this time he had clarified the attitude of Poland toward the Soviet Union and Rumania. He wanted to challenge the Germans before a specific Anglo-Polish agreement had been signed, because he wished to avoid the impression that Halifax had incited him to defy Germany. He loathed the prospect that he might be considered a mere puppet of the British Foreign Secretary. It is evident that he would not have contemplated this step but for the British policy of the past five days.[7]

Lipski Converted to a Pro-German Policy by Ribbentrop

Ribbentrop and Lipski met in Berlin at noon on March 21, 1939, to discuss the German proposals for a settlement with Poland. Ribbentrop apologized to Lipski for not having kept foreign diplomats fully informed during the hectic days of the recent Slovakian crisis. He declared that events had moved too quickly for him to meet ordinary requirements in this respect. He explained that he had recalled Moltke to Berlin at the time of the crisis for the express purpose of giving him detailed information to communicate to Beck. Ribbentrop then proceeded to recapitulate the events of the Slovakian crisis in painstaking detail.

Lipski indicated at the conclusion of Ribbentrop's remarks that Poland was primarily interested in the present situation of Slovakia. He hoped that German arrangements with the Slovaks would not include a German plan for the military occupation of the entire Slovakian area. He emphasized that recent events in Slovakia "had created a strong impression in Poland, for the man in the street could not help regarding such a step as one directed primarily against Poland. The Slovaks were a people linguistically related to the Poles. Polish interests in that area were also historically justified, and, from a purely realistic point of view, it had to be admitted that the proclamation of the Protectorate could be regarded only as a blow at Poland." Lipski's presentation of the matter conveyed an accurate impression of the seriousness with which the Poles regarded the Slovakian situation.[8]

Ribbentrop explained that the Slovak Government had appealed to Germany, and to Poland, for protection. He denied that the Slovak-German agreement was directed against Poland. He described it as the chance product of an immediate crisis rather than of a preconceived policy. Ribbentrop did not regard as permanent the present state of affairs in Slovakia, in which Germany enjoyed the principal foreign influence. He promised that Germany would be willing to discuss the means of establishing Poland's influence in Slovakia on a level at least equal with Germany's. He doubted that this discussion would be fruitful without first concluding a general German-Polish agreement.

It has been erroneously asserted that Beck would have preferred a more pro-German foreign policy, but that he was restrained by the Polish military men. If this had been true, the Slovakian situation would have presented Beck with a golden opportunity. He might have argued that it was necessary to negotiate and agreement with the Germans, at this point, to establish Polish influence in Slovakia and to remove the dangerous German striking arm from the South. Unfortunately, Beck had no such interest in negotiating a settlement of Polish differences with Germany.[9]

Ribbentrop proceeded to emphasize the need for an agreement between Germany and Poland. He deplored the failure of Poland to cooperate with Germany in coordinating the minority policies of the two countries. He expressed his regret for the commotion in Poland over the Langfuhr Cafe incident at Danzig, and he assured Lipski that Hitler believed the placard about 'Dogs and Poles' had been posted by the Polish students themselves. Lipski denied that the Polish students in Danzig had done anything wrong, or that they were in any way responsible for the trouble resulting from the incident.

Ribbentrop displayed his usual skill at avoiding an argument by carefully refraining from stating his own feelings in the matter. He attempted to focus Lipski's attention on the demonstrations which had followed in Poland. He assured Lipski that the temperature in official German-Polish relations would drop rapidly to the zero point, if the German press retaliated against the anti-German agitation in the Polish press. The German Foreign Minister confided to Lipski that his own visit to Warsaw had discouraged Hitler's hope for a settlement of German-Polish differences, because he had been unable to report any progress in Warsaw. He insisted that the existing situation was tense and dangerous, and that it would be advisable to plan a new effort to settle the matter by personal discussions. Ribbentrop extended an invitation for Foreign Minister Beck to visit Germany again in the near future.[10]

Ribbentrop offered a number of carefully prepared arguments in favor of a German-Polish agreement. He reminded Lipski that Germany's policy toward Poland during World War I had been characterized by the German decision of 1916 to recognize and help to establish an independent Polish state. Germany, but not Austria-Hungary or Russia, had taken the initiative in this question. The most disturbing factor in the subsequent relations between the two countries was that Poland owed much of her "present territorial expanse to Germany's greatest misfortune: namely, the fact that Germany had lost the World War."

Ribbentrop assured Lipski that it was beyond the shadow of doubt that the establishment of the Polish Corridor was the greatest single burden imposed upon Germany by the Treaty of Versailles. He asserted without fear of valid contradiction that "no former government could have dared to renounce German claims to revision without finding themselves swept away by the Reichstag within the space of forty-eight hours." Hitler thought otherwise about the Corridor problem, and he was prepared to place his entire prestige in Germany behind his idea for a solution. This called for German recognition of Polish possession of the Corridor within the exact limits established at Versailles. Ribbentrop reminded Lipski that Hitler sympathized with Poland's desire to play a greater maritime role, and that this was an important factor in his attitude. He concluded with pride that only Hitler, among all the German leaders, could venture to renounce German possession of the Corridor "once and for all."[11]

Lipski himself was convinced that only the Hitler dictatorship in Germany could propose a settlement with Poland on these terms. He argued later that Hitler was sincere in limiting his aims to Danzig and the superhighway in the interest of achieving German-Polish cooperation. He was sceptical, however, of the future should an agreement result from the terms proposed by Hitler. He doubted if Hitler could prevent the influential East German groups from insisting on further German demands against Poland, if Germany and Poland at some later date scored important successes against the Soviet Union. In other words, he accepted the sincerity of Hitler's attitude toward Poland, but he remained doubtful about the lasting value of a German-Polish agreement. This attitude was perfectly reasonable in itself, but it was unrealistic to allow such considerations to detract from the advantages of concluding an agreement. The prospect of a quarrel over some sort of Soviet booty was remote. The Germans for years had stressed the importance of a German-Polish front against Soviet Russia, but they had never suggested an actual plan to attack Russia, nor had they invited Poland to join them in a war against the Russians. A more important factor was the small price which Hitler was asking for an agreement. The remote possibility that such an agreement might fail did not justify the refusal to pay that price. This was self-evident, because Germany was willing to pay a much greater price. She was prepared to accept the territorial *status quo* of Poland.[12]

Ribbentrop repeated to Lipski the terms of the October 24, 1938, offer to Poland. He reminded the Polish diplomat that Germany had no desire to change the terms of that offer. He discussed the advantages of an agreement, and he repeated that Germany was requesting only the political union of National Socialist Danzig with National Socialist Germany, and the transit connection with East Prussia. He explained neatly that the Corridor problem required Polish acceptance of these two points because the situation as it stood "was a thorn in the flesh of the German people of which the sting could only be removed in this way."

Lipski promised to inform Beck of everything that Ribbentrop had said. Ribbentrop knew that he could rely on Lipski to do this. He realized with great satisfaction that in this conversation he had at last succeeded in making a strong impression on the Polish Ambassador. He sensed correctly that Lipski personally had been won over to the German plan, and that he would return to Warsaw as the advocate of the German-Polish agreement. He emphasized that it would be advantageous for Lipski to return to the Polish capital for a personal conversation with Beck. Ribbentrop repeated that the recent stress and strain in German-Polish relations was eloquent testimony of the need for an agreement on all outstanding problems. He confided that Hitler had been troubled by the attitude adopted by Poland on a number of specific questions. He warned Lipski that it would be unfortunate if Hitler were to "gain the impression that Poland simply did not want to reach a settlement."[13]

Ribbentrop had been informed of the Halifax offer to Poland of March 20, 1939, for Polish participation with the Soviet Union in an alliance directed exclusively against Germany. He warned the Polish Ambassador that Poland would expose herself to grave dangers if she became the ally of the Soviet Union. Lipski replied firmly and categorically that "no Polish patriot would allow himself to be drawn toward Bolshevism." Ribbentrop was convinced of the obvious sincerity of this statement, and the conversation between the two diplomats ended on a friendly note of mutual confidence. Ribbentrop hoped that German Ambassador Moltke at Warsaw might also be of some use in promoting a settlement at this stage. He wired Moltke on March 21st that Lipski was returning to Warsaw, and he instructed him to warn the Poles that Hitler might be inclined to withdraw his offer if no progress was made toward a settlement.[14]

Lipski's Failure to Convert Beck

The Polish Ambassador followed Ribbentrop's suggestion, and he returned to Warsaw immediately. He knew by this time that Kennard had presented to Beck the formal Halifax offer for an Anglo-Russo-Franco-Polish alliance. Lipski participated in the conferences at the Polish Foreign Office which began on March 22, 1939, and dealt with the British and German offers. He delivered a personal report in which he praised Ribbentrop for courtesy and consideration during the latest negotiation. He admitted to his listeners that he disagreed with Ribbentrop's interpretation of the German role in the restoration of Poland during World War I. He then proceeded to recapitulate the other points which Ribbentrop had made, and they culminated in the renewed German offer for an agreement with Poland.[15]

Beck's attitude toward the German offer remained hostile. Ribbentrop's invitation for a new visit to Germany was disposed of in short order. Even Lipski rejected it as "absolutely impossible." Germany was accused of encircling Poland, and Lipski conceded that the latest proposals of Ribbentrop might be the prelude to an ultimatum. Beck decided that Lipski would remain at Warsaw until a detailed reply to the Germans had been prepared. It was obvious that Lipski favored an agreement with Germany, and there was doubt about his reliability as a negotiator with the Germans. Beck resolved that Lipski should never be allowed again to participate in a discussion with Ribbentrop about an agreement.[16]

Count Michal Lubienski complained insultingly that Ribbentrop had succeeded in demoralizing Lipski. The Polish Ambassador knew that his plea for an agreement had been rejected, and that he no longer enjoyed the favor of confidence of Beck. It was not surprising that his foremost wish was to resign from his post.

The deliberations at the Polish Foreign Office were resumed with a discussion of the general situation of Poland. The usual charges were still heard in Poland that the country was committed to a pro-German foreign policy. Nevertheless, the country was quite calm, and there was no challenge to the free conduct of Polish diplomacy. It was emphatically decided that the pro-Soviet alliance proposed by Halifax was completely out of the question for Poland. Beck realized that he could reject this offer and conclude a bilateral alliance with Great Britain. The project of an Anglo-Polish alliance met with Beck's definite approval. The wording of the reply to Halifax on the pro-Soviet alliance plan was discussed. It was decided that it would be effective to claim that realization of the pro-Soviet alliance plan would provoke an immediate German attack on Poland. This claim simply ignored the fact that Germany was by no means prepared for such a venture. It was possible to do this because of the irresponsible propaganda which insisted that the Germans were prepared at all times to fight a major war.[17]

Beck's Decision for Polish Partial Mobilization

Beck was satisfied by March 23, 1939, that he had worked out the solutions for his immediate problems. The German offer and the pro-Soviet Halifax offer would be rejected categorically. The next steps toward Germany and Great Britain would present a complete contrast. Beck intended to create an atmosphere of crisis by following the May 1938 Czech precedent and persuading the Polish military leaders to declare the partial mobilization of the Polish armed forces against Germany. He did not believe that Poland could afford to maintain a full mobilization for an indefinite period. He intended to follow this step with an Anglo-Polish alliance, and with the coordination of Polish and British policy against Germany.

Beck conferred with the Polish military leaders on March 23, 1939. They agreed without hesitation to issue the necessary mobilization order the same day. The trained reservists born in the 1911-1914 period would be called to the colors, and additional reservists would be called from other years back to 1906. It was decided to mobilize the reserve officers of the technical troop units. The mobilization order immediately brought 334,000 additional soldiers into the ranks, and it more than doubled the strength of the standing Polish Army.[18]

The current Polish plan for fighting a war with Germany was distributed among the principal Army commands the same day. The Polish plan had been prepared by three of the principal Polish military leaders and their assistants. This group included Marshal Smigly-Rydz, the Commander-in-Chief of the

Army, General Kasprzycki, the Minister of War, and General Stachiewicz, the Chief of Staff. The plan had received strong criticism from Inspector-General Kazimierz Sosnkowski, the principal military collaborator of Józef Pilsudski in World War I. Sosnkowski, who was popular in Poland and affectionately known as the "gray general," condemned the plan on two counts. It called for a major military offensive against Germany, and for the simultaneous defense of all Polish territory. Sosnkowski argued that it was military nonsense to defend Polish West Prussia and the adjacent districts of Northwestern Poland from the Germans. An attempt to do so would needlessly extend the Polish military front by several hundred miles, and it would reduce available Polish strength for the defense of the vital areas. Sosnkowski doubted the wisdom of starting the war with a Polish drive on Berlin.

Sosnkowski was a close friend of Colonel Walery Slawek, the architect of the Polish 1935 Constitution. Both men were in the prime of life, and they possessed talents in the military and political spheres which were sorely needed by the new Polish state. They had been excluded from influential positions by Marshall Smigly-Rydz and his friends, and they were unable to decide the destiny of Poland during the turbulent days of March 1939. Sosnkowski remained an isolated figure after Walery Slawek committed suicide in April 1939. He was not given an active command in September 1939 until the battle of Poland was nearly over.[19]

The plan issued to the Polish armed forces on March 23, 1939, was never modified. The authors of the plan insisted that full mobilization of the Polish armed forces would have to be delayed until several days before the outbreak of a German-Polish war. They realized that it would be too great an economic drain on Poland to maintain this mobilization for a period of months without a conflict. It was decided that full mobilization would not be ordered unless war was considered inevitable in the immediate future. This was the reason why the later full mobilization of the Polish armed forces on August 30, 1939, was tantamount to a declaration of war against Germany. In the case of Poland in 1939, the old axiom of pre-1914 days that mobilization means war was still applicable. Beck was entrusted with the task of concocting the diplomatic justification for such a step.

The Poles planned to launch a drive against Berlin immediately upon the outbreak of hostilities. The Versailles Treaty had placed the Polish frontier within one hundred miles of the German capital. The Poles hoped to capture Berlin by surprise, as the Russians had done in 1760 in their operations against Frederick the Great. They intended to use horse cavalry in this operation, and the Polish Cavalry School at Bromberg trained young Polish officers to execute this plan. The Poles undoubtedly had the finest cavalry in Europe, but horse cavalry was no longer the effective instrument of war which it had been in the past.

The Polish failure to recognize that cavalry was obsolete is not so surprising when it is recalled that in World War I cavalry was extremely effective on the Eastern Front. The World War I operations in the East were different from those in the West. The distances in Eastern Europe are vast, and the mobile warfare in that theatre contrasted with the war of position in Belgium and France. Cavalry was an effective weapon against light-armed infantry and smaller artillery units. Cavalry also played a decisive role in the Russo-Polish War of 1920-1921. Poland's defeat in the Ukraine in 1920 was accomplished primarily by a successful Soviet cavalry operation. The Poles also knew that horse tranportation in 1939 continued to play a major role in both the Polish and German Armies. They knew that the Germans continued to maintain horse cavalry units. The Poles gave insufficient attention to the possible impact of German panzer units on a Polish horse cavalry offensive.

The Poles intended to defend their frontiers against possible German attacks at all points, but they reckoned with the possibility that these efforts might fail. They intended to withdraw the Polish armies to a line running approximately through the middle of Poland from North to South, if they lost the battles along the frontier. It was regarded as absolutely necessary to hold the Germans at the border in South-Eastern East Prussia to prevent the flanking of this line. It was decided to commit the Polish mechanized units to this sector. This later produced an ironical situation. The Germans ultimately decided to employ their horse cavalry in this sector. In the upshot, German horsemen in September 1939 fought Polish tanks while Polish horsemen were engaged by German tanks in the Western sectors.

The Poles decided to make their last stand on the line in Central Poland which followed the Narew, Vistula, and Dunajec rivers. It seemed pointless to plan operations for the eventuality that this line might also be smashed. The Polish military leaders were prepared to concede that the loss of this line would mean the total defeat of Poland.

In their recent sudy, *The Appeasers*, Martin Gilbert and Richard Gott offer an elaborate defense of Halifax's policy toward Poland during the weeks which followed the Polish partial mobilization of March 23, 1939. Their thesis depends entirely upon the unwarranted assumption that the British leaders were unaware of any friction in German-Polish relations during this period. The Polish partial mobilization, which was directed exclusively against Germany, to the knowledge of the entire world, refutes the interpretation of Gilbert and Gott. However, they do not permit themselves to be troubled by this obvious fact. In a special chronology of their own, which is not to be found elsewhere, they place this Polish partial mobilization five months later, on August 23, 1939. The result of this maneuver is to deprive their subsequent narrative of the element of historical reality.[20]

Hitler's Refusal to Take Military Measures

Hitler conferred with General Walther von Brauchitsch, the Commander-in-Chief of the German Army, after he learned of the surprising Polish partial mobiliaztion. He explained to Brauchitsch that important negotiations were in progress with Poland for a settlement of German-Polish differences. He emphatically declared that he had no desire to see Germany involved in a conflict with Poland. He emphasized that Germany was not interested in supporting Ukrainian nationalism, or in doing anything else which would be contrary to the interests of Poland. He told Brauchitsch that he had no intention of asking for the return of any of the former German West Prussian or Silesian territory held by Poland,

and he assured him that there were still favorable prospects for the settlement of German differences with Poland by peaceful negotiation. Hitler did not believe that the Polish partial mobilization was a formidable threat, and he did not request any special German military measures. He merely requested that normal precautions be taken in guarding Germany's eastern frontier.[21]

German Ambassador Moltke at Warsaw was much alarmed by the situation in Poland. He attached special significance to the arrest of the prominent Polish journalist, Stanislaw Mackiewicz, the editor of *Slowo* (*The Word*), Wilna's leading newspaper. Beck had insisted upon the arrest, because Mackiewicz for a long time had publicly advocated a German-Polish agreement. He had claimed that much valuable time and many good opportunities had been lost to achieve a profitable agreement with Germany. Moltke recognized the initiative of Beck in this outrageous arrest, but he continued to insist that Beck was modifying Polish foreign policy in response to pressure from the Polish military men. He failed to realize that the partial mobilization took place in response to Beck's initiative.

Moltke argued that Beck might adopt a more extreme course under pressure from Polish public opinion. He had been instructed to ascertain the Polish response to the pro-Soviet alliance offer of Halifax, but he was only able to report that Kennard had been calling repeatedly at the Polish Foreign Office. Moltke had been told at the Polish Foreign Office that Poland would be reluctant to serve the interests of other Powers, but he did not attach much significance to this statement. He was inclined to believe that Poland would accept the pro-Soviet alliance offer proposed by Halifax if it contained a possibility "of obtaining firm promises from Great Britain, which would augment her security."[22]

Moltke's report contained more than the usual element of confusion about the Polish position, and there can be no doubt that the German Ambassador was sincerely alarmed and distressed by the amazing Polish partial mobilization order. It was significant that Moltke, on this occasion, regarded it as futile to urge Ribbentrop to abandon his proposals for a settlement with Poland. The German diplomat obviously had concluded that the situation had deteriorated to a point where advice of this sort would no longer help matters.

The dramatic Polish partial mobilization was overshadowed in the West by speculation about the response to the Halifax pro-Soviet alliance plan. American Ambassador Kennedy reported from London on March 23, 1939, that the Soviet Union had made its acceptance of the Pact conditional on favorable responses from both France and Poland. Halifax had an assurance from Bonnet that France would accept the project, and the main attention of the Western diplomats was directed toward Poland. American Ambassador Biddle at Warsaw was unable to indicate Beck's intentions on March 23rd. He reported on the Polish response to the German annexation of Memel, which was visited by Hitler that same day. He claimed that the Memel agreement was a clever move by Hitler to discredit British and French diplomacy in Eastern Europe. Biddle's speculation was based on the fact that Hitler had solved a difficult Eastern European question without the participation of Great Britain or France.[23]

Beck decided to inform Halifax on March 24, 1939, of his refusal of the pro-Soviet alliance offer. Halifax was disappointed by Beck's response. He was unaffected by Beck's argument that an alliance with the Soviet Union would produce an immediate war. He knew that the Germans were not prepared for such a venture, and war was in any case the immediate objective of his policy. American Ambassador Kennedy reported the discouraging news to President Roosevelt at 8:00 p.m. on March 24, 1939. Poland would not consent to enter an alliance combination with the Soviet Union.[24]

Beck's War Threat to Hitler

Beck was mainly concerned on March 24th with the finishing touches on the reply he intended Lipski to give Ribbentrop. He insisted to Jan Szembek that decisive Polish interests dictated the *non possumus* reply he was about to hurl at Hitler. He described a Danzig politically dependent on Poland as the essential symbol of Polish power, and he claimed that it was "more reasonable to go forward to the enemy than wait for him to march on us." This was a reckless statement unsupported by any indication that Hitler intended to march on Poland. Beck was in a defiant mood, and he was completely under the exhilirating influence of the military measures which had been adopted by Poland. He now claimed that Hitler "seems to have lost all measure in thought and action." He cast aspersions on the submission of Schuschnigg and Beneš to Hitler, and he declared proudly that "our settlement of the political score with the Germans would not resemble the others."

Moltke called at the Polish Foreign Office on March 24, 1939, and his obvious nervousness excited a reaction of contempt among the Poles. Szembek noted that the German Ambassador seemed to be more interested in conveying his personal views than in representing his own Government. Moltke exclaimed in despair that he had always realized that Poland would never accept the German superhighway plan. This was an interesting statement in view of the fact that Moltke had been one of the principal originators of the same plan. Moltke explained that he disapproved of Albert Forster, the National Socialist District Leader at Danzig. He added that he regretted the establishment of the National Socialist regime at Danzig. Szembek noted that Moltke was contradictory in his remarks and that he talked at times as if Germany had never requested the return of Danzig. Moltke sought to emphasize the value to Poland of Hitler's offer to guarantee her western frontier, but Szembek observed that Poland had not requested either a German guarantee or German recognition. The deportment of Moltke in this interview was inadequate and he compromised his mission to Poland by this display of incompetence.[25]

Moltke attempted to conceal his fiasco by sending a soothing report to the German Foreign Office. He mentioned that the Poles had assured him on March 24th that Poland would not assume new obligations toward Rumania which could be directed against Germany. He added that the official Polish attitude toward the incorporation of Memel by Germany left nothing to be desired.

The German Foreign Office responded by ordering the unfortunate Ambassador to exert real pressure on the Poles for a settlement. He was advised to take the line that the time had come to discover whether Germany and Poland were to be friends or foes. Moltke was relieved when Hitler intervened to prevent him from attempting to take this brutal line with the Poles. Hitler was displeased with the instructions to Moltke as soon as he heard of them. He ordered Weizsaecker to cancel the instructions at once. The German State Secretary was forced to obey this command with alacrity. He apologized to Moltke for the confusion which resulted from his disagreement over policy with Hitler.[26]

The tendency of the German Foreign Office to "get tough" with Poland bothered Hitler, and he was worried about Italy. German Ambassador Mackensen reported from Rome on March 24, 1939, that there was much discontent beneath the surface in Italy because of the latest German success at Prague. Italian Ambassador Attolico, who had returned to Rome from Berlin to report, believed that the time had come for Italy to "get something" from the Axis. Italy had achieved her success in Ethiopia in the pre-Axis period, and she had also launched her policy to support the Conservatives in the Spanish Civil War before that time. It was unlikely that Italy would obtain concrete advantages from the Spanish Civil War. German support to the Spanish Conservatives had been on a very small scale, whereas Italy had expended a major effort to aid Franco. The Germans had scored a resounding series of successes since the beginning of the Axis in late 1936. Mackensen feared that the latest German success would shatter the current moderate Italian policy and cause Italy to do something foolish. He feared the possibility of new Italian pressure on France, and he believed that Germany should reinforce her previous declaration that she would not support Italian demands on France. It was evident to Hitler that the situation was dangerous, and he was uncertain to what extent he could exert a moderating influence on Italian policy.[27]

Hitler hoped that Lipski would return to Berlin with assurances which would improve German-Polish relations. When he heard that the Polish Ambassador was scheduled to return on Sunday, March 26th, Hitler declared that he would leave Berlin in order not disturb Ribbentrop in his conduct of negotiations with Lipski. Hitler believed that the German Foreign Minister had done an able job with the Poles, and he feared that his own presence in Berlin might complicate matters. He reckoned with the possibility that Beck might instruct Lipski to see him if he was in Berlin, and he believed that his own intervention in the negotiation at this point might do more harm than good. It would be impossible for him to talk to Lipski without protesting about the recent Polish partial mobilization. Hitler informed General von Brauchitsch on March 25, 1939, that he had no desire to threaten Poland, because this might drive the Poles into the outstretched arms of the British.

Hitler believed that the Danzig situation was the main problem which had to be solved, if the danger of an explosion was to be banished. He told Ribbentrop and Brauchitsch that it might be possible for the German armed forces to proceed to a lightning occupation of Danzig, if Lipski gave the desired hint that the Polish Government could not take the responsibility of voluntarily relinquishing Danzig to Germany. This would indicate that Beck would prefer to be relieved of the responsibility for a Danzig change by German *fait accompli*. Hitler emphasized that there could be no possibility of such a response unless the Polish reply conveyed by Lipski was friendly and accommodating. Hitler again refused to permit Brauchitsch to prepare military plans for a possible German-Polish war. He admitted that the outbreak of a war between Germany and Poland would nullify his proposals for a German-Polish settlement. Such an eventuality would raise anew the question of an "advanced frontier" from East Prussia to Upper Silesia, and also the questions of the huge Ukrainian minority of Poland and of German military relations with Slovakia.[28]

The moderate attitude of Hitler produced no effect on Beck on the eve of Lipski's return to Berlin. Beck told American Ambassador Biddle an outrageous flasehood about Hitler's policy toward Poland on March 25, 1939, which was a fitting prelude to his later public distortions about German policy. Beck claimed that Hitler had demanded the settlement of the Danzig question by Easter, which was only a few days away. In fact, Hitler had never set a time limit on the duration of his negotiation with Poland. Biddle reported with satisfaction on March 26, 1939, in a terse telegram: "Poland today on war footing having achieved same swiftly but quietly."[29]

The Germans received a great shock on March 26, 1939, when Lipski returned from Warsaw and categorically rejected Hitler's proposals for a settlement. The Poles refused to countenance any change of existing conditions. Their counter-proposals ignored the German request for the return of Danzig and a transit connection with East Prussia. The Poles also ignored the German offer to guarantee their frontiers. Lipski was instructed by Beck, before he boarded the train for Berlin on the night of March 25th, to remind the Germans that Pilsudski considered Danzig, as 'Free City,' to be the barometer or touchstone of German-Polish relations. The fact that the Marshal had been dead for nearly four years and might well have changed his mind was not taken into consideration. Lipski was ordered to inform Hitler, if the Chancellor was in Berlin, or otherwise to inform Ribbentrop, that Poland would fight to prevent the return of Danzig to Germany.[30]

Lipski requested to see Ribbentrop on March 26, 1939, when he discovered that Hitler had left Berlin. He was unenthusiastic about his instructions, and he hoped that he was performing his last act in Berlin as Polish Ambassador. He had come to Berlin in 1933 to facilitate conciliation between Poland and Germany, and he realized to his deep disappointment that his role had been played out. He naturally hoped to be recalled, and he would have been in greater distress had he realized that during the long months ahead Beck would restrict his authority without replacing him.

The Polish Ambassador submitted a written memorandum to Ribbentrop. The German Foreign Minister read the memorandum with astonishment. He made no attempt to conceal his surprise. He protested that the unwillingness of Poland to permit the German annexation of Danzig would destroy every chance of obtaining a German-Polish agreement. Lipski wasted no time. He quickly replied that "it was his painful duty to draw attention to the fact that any further pursuance of these German plans, especially where the return of Danzig to the Reich was concerned, meant war with Poland."[31]

The German Foreign Minister, despite his sensation of unpleasant surprise, immediately retorted that the statement he was about to make would be effective from the moment it was uttered. Germany intended to regard a Polish violation of the Danzig frontier in exactly the same light as a Polish violation of the German frontier. Lipski attempted to score another point by denying that Poland, in contrast to Germany, had any plan to annex Danzig.

Ribbentrop was unable to maintain his usual imperturbable composure on this historic occasion. He was unable to contain the feeling of despair which he experienced from this unpleasant interview. He vainly attempted to undo the consequences of the Polish note. He pleaded with Lipski, and he implored him to indicate that Poland might reconsider the entire question when the general situation was calmer. Germany was in no hurry to solve the Danzig problem. The Polish Ambassador replied by referring Ribbentrop to the written note of his Government. He then asked him if Germany, after all, would not reconsider, and agree for all time to renounce the German aspirations of Danzig. Lipski assured Ribbentrop that Beck would be glad to visit Berlin again in response to such a German concession.

Ribbentrop declared with sadness that a written Polish note really had not been necessary, since the Polish military measures of March 23rd appeared to be the true answer to the German proposals. The interview was over. Ribbentrop would have been inclined to abandon further efforts with the Poles had it not been for the stubborn conviction of Hitler that an agreement between Germany and Poland was worthy of every conceivable effort. Ribbentrop noted that Hitler remained quite calm when he read the Polish note of March 26, 1939.

Ribbentrop now had only the Polish note of categorical rejection to show for more than five months of difficult and patient negotiations. The first sentence of the note read as follows: "Today, as always, the Polish Government attach the greatest importance to the maintenance of neighborly relations with the German Reich for the longest possible period of time." It would have been shorter to substitute "permanent neighborly relations" for the last seven very enlightening words of this opening sentence. It would have been less accurate to do so. The sentence as it was phrased expressed Beck's conviction that there could be no such thing as permanent neighborly relations between Poland and the German Reich. It was this attitude which made Poland a natural object for the balance of power schemes of the British leaders.[32]

Poland Excited by Mobilization

Warlike enthusiasm momentarily gripped every section of Poland. The partial mobilization convinced the average Pole that his leaders contemplated war with Germany in the near future. The West Marches Society, an anti-German pressure group, held a public meeting on March 26, 1939, at Bydgoszcz (Bromberg), Polish West Prussia. The meeting was attended by thousands of Poles from the West Prussian area. Inflammatory speakers bitterly denounced the Germans, and the audience responded with passionate screams of "Down with Hitler!," "We want Danzig!," and "We want Koenigsberg!" Bands of Poles roamed the streets after the meeting and assaulted Germans whenever they encountered them. Subscriptions were pouring in from all parts of Poland for an internal Government loan to provide the Polish air force with one thousand additional combat airplanes within four months.[33]

Rumors spread throughout the country that war had broken out, and that German and Polish troops were fighting at Oderberg. The editors of *Polska Zbrojna* (*The Polish Army*) assured the public that Poland had every reason to be confident about the outcome of a German-Polish struggle. Polish readers were assured by the article, "We Are Prepared," that they had no reason to feel inferior before any of the powerful military nations of the world. It was asserted that Poland possessed many advantages which would guarantee military victory over Germany. It was claimed that Polish soldiers were superior to German soldiers, and that Polish military equipment was better. The readers were informed that the Polish heroic spirit was superior to anything which Germany had to offer. An assurance from General Gluchowski, the distinguished Polish Vice-Minister for War, was cited at length. The General explained that the armed forces of Germany were only a big bluff, and that the Germans were fatally deficient in trained reserves. The General was asked by the newspapermen if Poland was superior to Germany from an overall military standpoint. He replied: "Why, certainly!"[34]

The Polish Senate at a special session expressed its sympathy for the "arduous experiences" of Lithuania in ceding Memel to Germany. Count Jan Szembek, the Assistant Secretary for Foreign Affairs, was a prominent participant in this affair. He also joined in the prolonged ovation which greeted the Senate resolution.[35]

It was difficult for Ribbentrop to continue to seek a German-Polish agreement in this hectic atmosphere. He conferred with Lipski again on March 27, 1939. He complained about current Polish persecutions of the Germans at Bromberg and other places in Poland, and he observed that in Germany many people had the impression that the Polish Government could prevent such incidents if it cared to do so. He told Lipski that he frankly no longer knew what to make of the attitude and policy of the Polish Government. He did not threaten Poland, nor repeat his statement of the previous day about German policy toward a possible Polish violation of the Danzig frontier. Lipski also knew perfectly well that Ribbentrop's statement had been made solely in response to the Polish threat to use force in preventing the restoration of Danzig to Germany.[36]

Józef Beck received German Ambassador Moltke on the evening of March 28, 1939. The Polish Foreign Minister repeated the threat which Lipski had conveyed to Ribbentrop on March 26th. He said that a German attempt to obtain Danzig would produce Polish military action against Germany which would accordingly mean a German-Polish war. Beck added that he was still willing to consider friendly relations with Germany if the Germans would drop their plans to acquire Danzig. Beck added that in the future Germany would be held strictly accountable for any action taken by the Senate of the so-called Free City of Danzig. Moltke, who had just sent a report to Berlin describing the ceaseless official Polish provocations which accompanied the mobilization measures, exclaimed to Beck: "You want to negotiate at the point of the bayonet!" Beck replied coldly that the German Ambassador was absolutely right, but that Germany should not object to this procedure since "that is your own method."

It was difficult under these circumstances for Ribbentrop to maintain the impression that peaceful negotiations between Germany and Poland were in progress. The German Foreign Office was receiving a large number of reports from friendly foreign diplomats that the British were making all possible preparations for war against Germany, and if seemed certain at Berlin that Halifax would seek to exploit the bellicose Polish attitude. American Minister Joseph E. Davies reported to Washington, D.C., from Brussels on March 30, 1939, that in Belgium the Chamberlain speech at Birmingham was regarded as a disaster which had reversed the favorable prospects for peace in Europe.[37]

French Ambassador Léon Noël reported to Paris that he had attended a diplomatic dinner on the evening of March 27, 1939, at which Beck, Count Michal Lubienski, and the Polish Chief of Staff, General Stachiewicz, were present. Noël complained that the Polish leaders deliberately avoided any reference to the obviously unsatisfactory recent negotiations with Germany, and that they appeared to be distracted and preoccupied with private problems. Beck was also vague in his conversations with American Ambassador Anthony Biddle, but he told Biddle on the evening of March 28th that the Polish partial mobilization was "a firm answer to certain suggestions made by Berlin."[38]

Lukasiewicz informed Beck from Paris that he was continuing to collaborate closely with American Ambassador Bullitt. Lukasiewicz was repeatedly informed by Bullitt of the conversations between the British leaders and American Ambassador Kennedy at London. It was obvious to Lukasiewicz that Bullitt continued to distrust the British. The American Ambassador assured him that the United States would be able to exert sufficient pressure to produce a British mobilization at the peak of the next crisis. Lukasiewicz also suspected that part of this distrust reflected a childish desire on the part of Bullitt to exaggerate the importance of his own role on the European scene.[39]

Polish Ambassador Edward Raczynski reported on March 29, 1939, that the principal fear in Great Britain seemed to be that a German-Polish agreement would be reached despite the Polish partial mobilization. The British were arguing that such an agreement would be especially dangerous because it might lead to the rapid disintegration of Soviet Russia. The Polish Ambassador had learned that American Ambassador Kennedy was personally distressed by the war policy of the British leaders, and by the support for this policy which came from President Roosevelt. Raczynski warned Beck that Kennedy appeared to be privately somewhat out of step with Bullitt in Paris and Anthony Biddle in Warsaw, but that otherwise he was reluctantly carrying out his instructions from President Roosevelt to warn the British that their failure to act would produce dire consequences. Raczynski added that he received repeated requests from the British to reassure them that Poland would not accept the German annexation of Danzig. The Polish diplomat noted that it was difficult to convince the British that Poland was really willing to go to war over the Danzig issue.[40]

Hitler's Hopes for a Change in Polish Policy

The relations between Germany and Poland had reached a crucial stage by March 29, 1939. The Poles had challenged Germany with the threat of war and a partial mobilization, but Hitler stubbornly refused to regard these Polish acts as a challenge. He also refused to accept the effort of the Poles to rupture the negotiations between the two countries, although this rupture in point of fact had taken place with the categorical Polish rejection of the German offer on March 26, 1939. Hitler insisted that Ribbentrop should expend every effort to renew negotiations, and he continued to hope that Poland would refuse to conclude a military alliance with Great Britain. This hope appeared to have considerable foundation after the Poles rejected the British pro-Soviet alliance offer on March 24, 1939. Hitler also knew that Beck was refusing to play the British game in Rumania. It seemed, under these circumstances, that Anglo-Polish negotiations for an alliance might finally end in failure. Hitler hoped that it would be possible in the event of such a failure to renew negotiations with the Poles. He was prepared to assure them that Germany was in no hurry to achieve the realization of her program at Danzig.

Hitler's strategy in dealing with the Poles at this point was entirely the product of his own analysis and conviction. The German military leaders wondered why they were not allowed to prepare plans for a possible war with the Poles. It was extremely unusual that Germany possessed no plans of any kind for such a conflict. It was customary for European nations to have operational plans for a possible struggle against a neighbor with whom relations were on an insecure footing. For instance, Germany had plans for possible military operations against Austria-Hungary throughout the 1870's, and these were allowed to lapse only after the conclusion of the formal German-Austro-Hungarian alliance of 1879. The Germans maintained and repeatedly revised their plans for possible military operations against France and Russia from the 1870's down to 1914. The German military men, during the days of the German Weimar Republic, were constantly working on their plans for a possible conflict with Poland, and the Poles were engaged uninterruptedly in the same activity from 1919 to 1939. There never was a break in French planning itself, throughout the period from 1871 to 1939. It is only in this light that Hitler's stubborn refusal to permit military planning against Poland, throughout the period from the death of President von Hindenburg in August 1934, down to April 1939, can be understood. There was certainly no such restriction on military planning against the Czechs during the years after 1934. It adds up to only one conclusion, namely, that Hitler was determined to win Poland's friendship.

Ribbentrop loyally carried out Hitler's instructions to pursue negotiations with the Poles, but he was increasingly pessimistic. He could understand the desire of Weizsaecker and other officials at the German Foreign Office to take a more firm line with the Poles. Ribbentrop's wife recalled that her husband had been inclined to abandon the project of a German-Polish agreement after the futile negotiation at Warsaw in January 1939, but Hitler convinced Ribbentrop in February 1939 that it was necessary to persevere because an understanding was still possible. The German Foreign Minister had responded favorably, and the manner in which he convinced Lipski of the need for an agreement on March 21, 1939, was a brilliant achievement.[41]

It is important to note that none of the German leaders, including Goering, who shared Hitler's pro-Polish attitude, advocated the abandonment of the German claim to Danzig. Lipski had said that Beck might return to Germany on a visit if the Germans renounced Danzig. Hitler was not prepared to pay this one-sided price for an understanding, because he knew that an agreement on such a basis would be worthless. An understanding in which Germany made all the sacrifices and Poland made none would not produce a relationship of confidence between the two countries. It would foster Polish contempt for Germany and the unwarranted conviction that a smaller Power like Poland could intimidate the German Reich. It would encourage the Poles to continue their intrigues against Germany in the hope of achieving future gains at German expense.

The Roots of Hitler's Moderation Toward Poland

Countless Germans from the territories lost in 1919 complained with bitterness that Hitler was obsessed with the liberation of Danzig, but that he was indifferent about the fate of such former German cities as Kattowitz. They could not understand why Hitler was willing to renounce Kattowitz, which had not been in Poland any more than Danzig had been before the first Polish partition of 1772. Kattowitz, in contrast to Danzig, was little more than a village at that time, but the industrial revolution brought important changes, and the city had a population of 125,000 when it was assigned to Poland in 1922. The city of Kattowitz, despite French and Polish terror tactics, had voted overwhelmingly for Germany (82%) in the 1921 plebiscite. The Kattowitz region was one of the finest industrial areas in the world, and its coal deposits were far superior to those in any part of the Ruhr valley and much easier to exploit. The Kattowitz region had been part of Germany since the 12th century, and the exploitation of its industrial resources had been initiated by Frederick the Great. Steam engines for industrial purposes were first employed in 18th century Prussia in the Kattowitz region at Koenigshutte, which meant royal foundry of the King. The area was highly developed by the 20th century, and it would have been a far greater economic asset to Germany than Danzig and the super-highway to East Prussia combined.[42]

The claim that Hitler was indifferent about Kattowitz was unjust. He was sorely tempted to request the return of Kattowitz and the remainder of East Upper Silesia to Germany after the conclusion of the Russo-German Pact of August 1939, and he even discussed this temptation with British Ambassador Henderson. But he decided in this instance not to request the return of Kattowitz, because he feared that such an important additional claim by Germany would destroy the last chances of achieving a negotiated settlement with Poland.[43]

It was the political situation of Danzig, rather than its intrinsic importance, which decided Hitler's policy. The creation of the free-city regime after 1918 was a serious and lasting threat to peace. The citizens of Danzig demonstrated their unwavering loyalty to National Socialism and its principles, and they had elected a National Socialist parliamentary majority before this result had been achieved in the German Reich. The renunciation of Danzig would have been a repudiation of this loyalty and the spirit which inspired it. It would have been unthinkable to expect the Poles to renounce political control of Danzig had the population of the city consisted of loyal Poles who supported the Polish OZON (Camp of National Unity) regime. The Poles were never requested to make any sacrifice of this kind. The situation of the German minority in Poland was different from that of the German community at Danzig. The Germans of Poland had agreed to be loyal citizens of the Polish state, although they had never been accepted in Poland as equals. Many Germans were arrested in 1938 when they neglected to display the Polish national colors on the Polish national holiday in commemoration of November 11, 1918. This date was also the anniversary of the German defeat in World War I, but none of the ethnic Poles were arrested for failing to display national colors at that time. The Germans of Poland had nevertheless agreed to be Polish citizens. They had their own local political organizations, but, in contrast to the Danzigers, they were not National Socialists. Hitler was prepared to renounce them to Poland because of his desire for friendship with the Poles, and because of his wish to avoid the slaughter of an unnecessary war.[44]

It was known everywhere that Poland was constantly seeking to increase her control over Danzig. Hitler was not opposed to any of Poland's further economic aspirations at Danzig, but he was resolved never to permit the establishment of a Polish political regime at Danzig. Numerous Germans from the eastern provinces later asserted that they would have revolted against Hitler had he concluded an agreement with Poland on the basis of his offer of October 1938.[45] Such a revolt would have been improbable, and it would have been crushed ruthlessly had it occurred. The mass of Germans in the South and West were largely indifferent about the situation on the German eastern frontier. The situation of Danzig was an exception, and this was reflected in the extensive publicity it had received throughout Germany for many years. The larger question of German prestige would have commanded universal attention had Hitler passively witnessed the strangling of Danzig by his far weaker Polish neighbor. It was necessary to avoid this distinct possibility and to protect Danzig by bringing her back to the Reich. Hitler had never insisted that this had to be done immediately, but he was adamant in his determination never to renounce Danzig. He realized that the abandonment of Danzig would widen the breach between Germany and Poland rather than produce a relationship of friendship.

Hitler was willing to pay the price of abandoning the German territories lost to Poland before 1939 for reasons of high policy. He had always insisted that it would be childish to seek the recovery of every area which had been lost by Germany or by the Austrian Germans after World War I. His attitude in the Tirol question is one of the best illustrations of this policy. Hitler began his political career in Bavaria. The Bavarians and Austrians are the same branch of the German family. The entire Austrian area had been opened up by Bavarian poineers in the 8th and 9th centuries. The Bavarians were bitter about the repudiation of self-determination by the Allied Powers in the Tirol settlement of 1919. Hitler believed that the South Tirol territory should be renounced permanently in favor of Italy, and he frankly expressed this unpopular idea in his speeches throughout the 1920's. This unquestionably hindered the early growth of the National Socialist movement in Bavaria. The opponents of National Socialism charged untruthfully that Hitler was the paid agent of Mussolini, and this was widely believed. It was argued that otherwise a man who claimed to be a German nationalist would never abandon South Tirol. The South Tirol was the homeland of a solid bloc of vigorous and

independently-minded Germans, whose heroic historical tradition was familiar
to every German through the literature of Schiller.[46]

Hitler knew that an understanding with Italy would be impossible if the
Germans expected Mussolini to abandon the strategic Brenner frontier. He
knew that Italy would be the immediate neighbor of Germany if self-
determination was applied in Rump-Austria, and if the tiny Austrian Republic
joined the German Reich. He realized that cooperation with Italy would be an
important asset for any successful German foreign policy. There could be no
doubt of the fundamental wisdom of this attitude, but national sentiment has
often consititued a formidable obstacle to realistic policy. The situation was
complicated by German resentment toward Italy because of the Italian desertion
of the Triple Alliance during World War I in favor of war against Austria-
Hungary and Germany. Hitler knew that a pro-Italian policy would encounter
great obstacles in Germany. He did not waste time before seeking to educate the
German people to accept this policy, although he knew that it would cost him
votes to do so.[47]

Hitler's problem with South Tirol was not terminated by the formation of the
Rome-Berlin Axis. The Italians were no different from the Poles in their pursuit
of de-Germanization measures against the German minority. The Italian
diplomats at Berlin insisted in January 1939 that the entire German population
of South Tirol should be driven from their ancestral homes and forced to seek
refuge in the Reich. The South Tirol crisis was discussed in a special meeting
at the German Foreign Office on January 14, 1939. It is not surprising that
German resentment about the ruthless Italian demand was very great. Hitler
thought he could not afford the luxury of such feelings, and he instructed
Ribbentrop to inform Italy that Germany would agree to an expulsion program
if carried out slowly and gradually. It should be added that Hitler would have
been willing to cooperate in a similar program with the Poles had the relations
between Germany and Poland been established on a solid basis. Hitler agreed
to confer German citizenship on the South Tirol expellees before they left
their homeland for the trek to Germany.[48]

Hitler's agreement to the exodus in January 1939 merely represented one
stage in the handling of the problem. It was necessary for him to intervene again
and again to moderate the German response to a series of extreme Italian
provocations. The Italians knew that Alexander Bene, the German Consul-
General at Bozen, South Tirol, had opposed the exodus plan. Italian Foreign
Minister Ciano charged on May 3, 1939, that Bene had said the South Tirol
would one day be liberated by Hitler. German Ambassador Mackensen, who was
a close personal friend of Bene, knew that the charge was false. Bene had always
done everything possible to convince the Germans of South Tirol that their land
would remain irrevocably Italian. Mackensen knew that Ciano presented this
irresponsible accusation as a convenient pretext to eliminate Bene's influence
in the exodus question.[49]

It was impossible for Hitler to prevent the spread of Austrian National
Socialism before 1938 among the Austrian citizens resident in South Tirol. The
Italian Government arrested Rudolf Kauffmann, the local National Socialist
leader at Bozen, on June 16, 1939. The pretext for this action was that
Kauffmann had not secured the permission of the Italian authorities for an

all-day hike of a group of German gymnasts. The Italians claimed that this hike constituted a hostile demonstration against the Italian state. The situation was complicated by English propaganda agents in South Tirol, who were distributing inflammatory tracts published in bad German which denounced the Italians. Hitler realized that stern measures were necessary under these circumstances. The Italians released Kauffmann on June 18, 1939. Hitler ordered Weizsaecker to contact Rome on June 20, 1939, to arrange an exit visa to Berlin for Kauffmann. Hitler announced that he intended to punish Kauffmann for ignoring local Italian regulations. Kauffmann was placed in a German concentration camp for ten weeks, and he was not released until early September 1939. Ciano told Mackensen on June 23, 1939, that he was pleased to learn that Kauffmann had been imprisoned by Hitler. He claimed that this would be a good example in teaching the people of South Tirol that it was dangerous to defy Italy.[50]

The point in all this was that Hitler possessed the necessary authority to maintain friendly relations with such neighboring states as Italy and Poland despite the existence of serious points of friction. This was not sufficiently appreciated by the Poles, and the fears of Lipski that German internal pressures might compel Hitler to modify his policy toward Poland illustrate the problem. These fears did not take account of the ruthless will of Hitler, or the loyalty which characterized his attitude toward friendly foreign Governments.

It was for these reasons that Hitler remained calm in the face of Polish provocations during the week following the Polish partial mobilization of March 23, 1939. He learned of an interesting luncheon conversation at Berlin on March 24, 1939, between Count Dembinski and Baron von Stengl. Dembinski was a wealthy Pole residing in Berlin, and a close friend of Józef Lipski. Dembinski told his friend Stengl that the Polish partial mobilization had convinced him that war between Germany and Poland was inevitable. He had sent his wife and children to Poland, and he asked Stengl to care for his house and furniture when he too had to leave. Dembinski believed that the attitude of the Polish leadership was determined by the fact that the "world" was momentarily very anti-German. He told Stengl that the Poles were confident they could rely on Western support against Germany. He warned his German friend that the Poles might seek to take advantage of this situation very soon by provoking a conflict at Danzig.[51]

It would have been understandable had Hitler reacted to the many reports of this kind by concluding that a German-Polish understanding was impossible. This was not Hitler's way. He had been told after the fiasco of his unsuccessful conversations with Mussolini at Venice in June 1934 that there was no hope for a German-Italian understanding, but he refused to believe it. He remained patient, and later he succeeded in winning the friendship of Mussolini. He believed that it was necessary to remain patient with Beck and the other Polish leaders, because Polish friendship was an important objective. He was equally determined to remain patient with Great Britain and the United States, in the hope that one day German relations with these two Powers would be placed on a solid and satisfactory basis. One might have expected that the encirclement policy launched by Halifax on March 20, 1939, would have disabused Hitler of his remaining hopes for a lasting agreement between Great Britain and Germany, but this was by no means the case. He knew that important objectives were not easily achieved, and he refused to take a tragic view of the situation. Hitler hoped that Halifax and Beck would fail to reach an agreement. This would provide Germany with new opportunities to improve relations with both Powers. The Polish challenge of March 23-26, 1939, had failed to prompt Hitler to reconsider his Polish policy.

Chapter 14

THE BRITISH BLANK CHECK TO POLAND

Anglo-French Differences

Polish Foreign Minister Józef Beck on March 24, 1939, rejected the British plan for an alliance front to include the Soviet Union. Halifax responded one week later by extending a unilateral British guarantee to the Poles. The British Empire agreed to go to war as the ally of Poland if the Poles decided that war was necessary. The British public was astonished by this move. It is understandable that Hitler was also surprised. Sir Alexander Cadogan admitted to American Ambassador Kennedy on March 31, 1939, that Great Britain for the first time in her history had left the decision as to whether or not to fight outside her own country to another Power. Professor F.J.C. Hearnshaw, an ardent supporter of Halifax and his policies, hoped that the British public would believe that exceptional circumstances justified this step. His article, *The Only Way to Safety*, claimed that "never since the close of the Middle Ages have the peace of the world, the reign of law and the very existence of human freedom been so formidably menaced as they are at the present moment." This was undoubtedly true, but Hearnshaw failed to see that the actual menace was Halifax and his policy, which was needlessly exposing Europe to the latent threat from the Soviet Union. He hoped that the unconventional conduct of British foreign policy would be excused by his reference to the Middle Ages and the period before the reign of Queen Elizabeth I. It was the determination for war which Halifax had deliberately aroused, rather than such specious arguments, which caused the British ruling classes and the British public to accept whatever steps Halifax chose to take.[1]

The move of Halifax in guaranteeing Poland was a serious threat to Anglo-French unity. Franco-Polish relations were bad. French Foreign Minister Bonnet had agreed on March 23, 1939, to cooperate in the formation of an alliance front to include the Soviet Union, because he believed that such an achievement might produce a preponderant league of states to preserve the peace. It was not because he desired war that he cooperated in this plan. It was evident that the unilateral British guarantee to Poland jeopardized the prospect of including Soviet Russia in an alliance front and vastly increased the danger of war. Bonnet refused to emulate the British by extending a French blank check to Poland. He had no taste for an Anglo-Franco-Polish war against Hitler.[2]

Lukasiewicz had informed Bonnet before the Polish partial mobilization of March 23, 1939, that Beck was hostile toward Halifax's pro-Soviet alliance project. Bonnet did not sympathize with this attitude, and he told Lukasiewicz that he favored the Halifax plan. He reminded the Polish Ambassador that France had sought for years to reconcile Great Britain toward her own alliance policy with the Soviet Union. Bonnet claimed that the speech of Halifax in the British House of Lords on March 20, 1939, was more important from the diplomatic viewpoint than anything Chamberlain had said at Birmingham. Halifax in this speech had defined and explained the British alliance offer.[3]

Bonnet's Visit to London

Bonnet accompanied French President Albert Lebrun on a visit to England on March 22, 1939. The purpose of the visit was to discuss the French attitude toward the British encirclement policy. Rumanian Minister Tatarescu had explained at Paris on March 18, 1939, that the charges made by Tilea in London about German demands were without foundation, and Bonnet had subsequently received confirmation of the Tilea hoax from the French diplomats in Rumania. This did not prevent Daladier and Bonnet from agreeing to take a positive attitude toward the British plan to guarantee Rumania. They hoped that Rumania would serve as a bridge between Great Britain and the Soviet Union.

President Lebrun and Bonnet attended a banquet at the Guildhall in London on the evening of March 22, 1939. Bonnet was amazed to discover that Chamberlain was still insisting on the authenticity of the Tilea story, and of the existence of an immediate German threat to Rumania. He was surprised by the degree of excitement which Halifax had created in British high society. The wife of an important British functionary told Bonnet with passion that she had many children and that she loved them dearly, but she would prefer to see all of them die rather than to permit Hitler to dominate Europe. Bonnet had no doubt that the warlike spirit, for which the English upper classes had been famous for centuries, had been kindled successfully once again.

Important conferences took place between the French and British leaders at Windsor on March 23, 1939. Bonnet confirmed Halifax's fear that the Poles were not likely to accept his pro-Soviet alliance plan. Halifax discussed the possibility of separate Anglo-French guarantees to Rumania and Poland in case Beck formally decided to refuse the alliance offer. Bonnet was congenial in discussing these problems, and he was careful not to offend his English hosts. He knew that the English leaders of the past had attempted to overthrow French Governments which did not please them in crisis situations by means of back-stairs intrigue, and he hoped that it would be possible for Daladier and himself to avoid this problem. The English leaders were satisfied with Bonnet's attitude at Windsor, and they assured President Lebrun that they desired to see Daladier and Bonnet retained in office in France. Bonnet left the conferences with the conviction that British progress in the manufacture of war airplanes was the key explanation of the recent change in British foreign policy.[4]

Franco-Polish Differences

Lukasiewicz called on Daladier at Paris on March 23, 1939, to discuss the general situation. The Polish Ambassador complained that Beck had no enthusiasm for the deflection of the Anglo-French intervention policy to Rumania. He did not see why it was important to guarantee Rumania when that country had no problems with Germany. He bluntly told Daladier that the interest of France in Rumania caused him to doubt the sincerity of their policy in Eastern Europe. Lukasiewicz had received the misleading impression that Rumania would not accept a territorial guarantee without the participation of Poland, and he told Daladier that Poland would never extend a territorial guarantee to Rumania. The Rumanians had profited enormously from the 1919 treaties of peace. They had large minorities of Hungarians, Bulgarians, Ukrainians, Germans, Serbs, and Turks. They were not inclined to make a guarantee conditional on Polish acceptance. They were prepared to accept a guarantee of the territorial integrity of their country from any quarter except the Soviet Union.

Daladier claimed to Lukasiewicz that he understood the Polish position perfectly, but that he doubted if the Poles understood the position of Great Britain and France. He informed Lukasiewicz that Halifax was seeking to put a complete fence around Germany. He was attempting to block German expansion everywhere, and not merely in the direction of Poland. He hoped to anticipate possible German moves regardless of how remote some of them might seem.

Lukasiewicz was unimpressed by Daladier's explanation of the Halifax policy, and it seemed to him that the remarks of the French Premier lacked conviction. He told Daladier that the Halifax offer to Rumania betrayed a lack of common sense. Lukasiewicz feared that the Western Powers would be unable to resist the temptation of making agreements at the expense of Poland. He declared that Halifax's proposition for an alliance with the Soviet Union deserved condemnation and would be condemned by Poland. Lukasiewicz reminded Daladier that France had no commitment to support Poland at Danzig; nevertheless he believed that he had influenced Daladier to favor French support to Poland in that quarter. The French Premier, on the other hand, was very displeased by the attitude of the Polish Ambassador.[5]

American Ambassador Bullitt did what he could to support the Polish position at Paris. Lukasiewicz informed Bullitt on March 24, 1939, that Poland would reject the pro-Soviet alliance plan and press for a bilateral alliance with Great Britain. Bullitt assured Lukasiewicz that the British would agree to such an alliance. The Polish Ambassador admitted that he did not trust the British, and he asserted that the cynical English leaders were quite capable of leading Poland into an untenable position and deserting her. He knew that Bullitt shared this attitude to some extent. Lukasiewicz reminded Bullitt of British participation in the partition of Czechoslovakia in 1938. He feared that Great Britain would offer to support Poland, and then insist on Polish concessions to Germany.

He knew that until recently the British leaders had favored Polish concessions to Germany, and he was not certain that there had been a complete change in their attitude.

Bullitt used many arguments to reassure the Polish Ambassador. He declared that he was in complete agreement with every aspect of Beck's stand in the alliance question, and he regarded the creation of a solid Anglo-Franco-Polish front without the Soviet Union as the best thing which could possibly happen. He claimed that Halifax was not very serious about his Four Power Pact offer, and that it was mainly a gesture to increase British prestige and to appease the French. He said that the British leaders hoped that there would be a war between Germany and Russia, but that they were not eager to make commitments to the Soviet Union.[6]

Bullitt told Lukasiewicz on March 25, 1939, that he had instructed American Ambassador Kennedy at London to tell Chamberlain that the United States was in full sympathy with the Polish position in the alliance question. Bullitt contacted Kennedy again on March 26th. Kennedy was instructed to tell Chamberlain that the United States hoped that Great Britain would go to war with Germany if the Danzig dispute produced an explosion between Germany and Poland. Bullitt told the Polish Ambassador that he was confident that the British response to these suggestions would be favorable. Halifax, of course, was not displeased to know that he had unconditional official American support for his war policy. Lukasiewicz told Bullitt on March 26, 1939, that Lipski would reject the German proposals at Berlin the same day. He praised Bullitt as "an industrious friend who at many complicated points resolved our situation intensively and profitably."[7]

Beck's Offer to England

Polish Ambassador Raczynski was tactful in his approach to Halifax on March 24, 1939. He was "afraid that the communication he had to make . . . would rather complicate an already complicated situation," but he was instructed to reject the quadruple alliance offer, and to say that, in the Polish view, a pact with the Soviet Union might "provoke a catastrophe." He developed Beck's argument that the inclusion of the Soviet Union in an alliance would unduly threaten the peace. He added that he possessed plenipotentiary authority to propose an Anglo-Polish alliance. Halifax knew from previous conversations with the Poles that Poland wanted British military aid if "the Danzig question should develop into a threat to Poland's independence."[8]

Halifax admitted at once that he was interested in the Polish proposition. He also claimed with boundless hypocrisy that he would not object if Poland and Germany could negotiate successfully on the Danzig question. The fact that Halifax found it necessary to make this last point demonstrates his tactical skill as a diplomat. He had no desire to give the Poles the impression that he was pushing them into war.

Kennard submitted a jubilant report from Warsaw on March 25, 1939. He declared with considerable exaggeration that 750,000 Polish soldiers were already under arms. He admitted that many foreign diplomats in Warsaw believed that Poland was seeking to provoke a war. Kennard hoped that it would be possible to label Germany the aggressor in a coming war, and he assured Halifax that he did not believe that "the Polish Government intends to force an issue with Germany." He did not deny that the Polish partial mobilization had created an atmosphere of serious crisis. It is ironical, in view of this report, to discover Gilbert and Gott claiming that British policy was resting "on the assumption that Poland was in no danger."[9]

Halifax was studying his response to the Polish alliance offer, when the Poles, on March 26, 1939, threatened the Germans with war if their Danzig proposal was not abandoned. Beck was not directly informing either England or France of his steps with the Germans, but it should occasion no surprise that Halifax learned of the Polish refusal of the German offer almost immediately. The details were confirmed in reports from sources which ranged from Paris to Danzig. The French Embassy in Berlin was informed that Polish circles which favored the surrender of Danzig to Germany were disappointed in Beck's diplomacy. The story of the meeting between Lipski and Ribbentrop received extensive treatment in the Western press as early as March 27, 1939, and the emphasis was on the refusal of Poland to accept the German terms. Halifax received no official information from Beck, while deciding about the Polish alliance offer, but he knew perfectly well that Beck had thrown down the gauntlet to Hitler.[10]

French Ambassador Noël at Warsaw was impressed by the enthusiastic display of Polish patriotism following the partial mobilization, but he feared that support from the West would add to the proverbial Polish recklessness. He was aghast at the fantastic optimism of the Polish military men. He believed that it was the responsibility of France to urge the Poles to be prudent rather than to excite them. He did not display much confidence that French restraint would be very successful. He believed the Poles should be informed that France was unprepared for a struggle with Germany. He also believed that the French military men should talk sensibly with the Polish military men, and he hoped that France would have an opportunity to aid Poland in overcoming her obvious military deficiency.[11]

Halifax's Decision

Halifax came forward to his diplomats on March 27, 1939, with the definite decision to place Poland before Russia. He knew that the Russians on March 22, 1939, had insisted on Polish acceptance as a condition for the participation of the Soviet Union in an alliance front. The Poles had refused on March 24, 1939, and the British alliance offer of March 20, 1939, was dead as far as Halifax was concerned. He wired Kennard on March 27th that the Poles had won their point in the Russian question. He informed Kennard that the Poles had refused to collaborate with the Soviet Union "for reasons which I appreciate." Halifax concluded that it would be possible to approach the Soviet Union later with a new alliance proposal.[12]

Halifax had made an epochal decision, and he was impatient to bring his new policy into the open. He decided not to wait until the arrival of Beck in

London on April 3, 1939, before assuming a public British commitment to Poland. He wired Kennard on March 30, 1939, that a guarantee to Poland would be announced in the British Parliament on the following day. He added that this guarantee would be binding without commitments from the Polish side. He attempted to place the responsibility for his extraordinary impatience on President Roosevelt. He informed Kennard with a touch of ironical humor that the American Embassy had bombarded him with assertions that Ribbentrop was urging Hitler to invade Poland before the British assumed any commitment. This was a transparent pretext to rationalize a rash policy. It was true that Bullitt at Paris was for immediate British action, but the American diplomats at Berlin hoped that Great Britain would adopt a policy of caution and restraint. American Chargé d'Affaires Geist suggested from Berlin that it would be wise for Great Britain to avoid placing obstructions before German eastward expansion. No one could have been more emphatic in deploring a hasty British guarantee to Poland.13

Halifax carefully avoided giving the impression that he believed the alleged story about Ribbentrop's aggressive intentions. He did repeat the old argument that President Roosevelt and the United States of America would become hostile to Great Britain if she did not go to war against Germany. The constant reiteration of this theme by Bullitt at Paris was undoubtedly useful to Halifax. It also enabled him to shift part of the responsibility for his various moves to the United States, although in reality President Roosevelt was unable to play an active role in Europe at this stage. The official position of the United States was governed by neutrality legislation from the 1935-1937 period, and it is impossible, regardless of the attitude of Roosevelt, to saddle the United States with the responsibility for the moves which Halifax made. The decision of Halifax to confer an advance guarantee wiped out the hopes of Hitler that personal negotiations between Halifax and Beck would end in disagreement. The friction between the two men was a very real thing when Beck came to London, and it is possible that their negotiation would have ended in failure had it not been for the previous British guarantee.14

Halifax informed Kennard that he had decided not to restrict his pledge to Poland to mere cases of unprovoked aggression. He argued that German policy was "so varied" and "so insidious" that Great Britain might have to come to Poland's aid under different circumstances. He told Kennard that he had decided to ignore the question of the aggressor. He did not want Great Britain to remain neutral if the Poles forced Germany into war.15

Kennard met French Ambassador Noël on March 30, 1939, at the Bruehl Palace, which housed the Polish Foreign Office. The British Ambassador was holding the historic telegram which had arrived the same day, and which announced that a unilateral British guarantee would be extended to Poland. Kennard informed Noël that the British leaders had contacted President Mościcki and Marshal Smigly-Rydz by telephone to tell them of this step. The Polish leaders had given their consent. Kennard conferred with Beck, who also agreed to accept the British guarantee. Beck and Kennard agreed that a public announcement would be issued on the following day to inform the world of the great change in Europe. Noël correctly believed that he had witnessed one of the great events of history, and he greeted it with the classic sentence: "The die is cast."16

Beck's Acceptance of the British Guarantee

The Polish decision to accept the guarantee was the natural outgrowth of the Anglo-Polish negotiations, which had begun with the conference between Alfred Duff Cooper and Beck at the Hela peninsula in August 1938. These negotiations ante-dated the German-Polish negotiations by more than two months, and ultimately they completely overshadowed them. Beck preferred a war alliance with Great Britain to a peaceful understanding with Germany. Waclaw Jedrzejewicz, an ardent follower of Beck, and a brother of a former Polish Premier, sought to place the Polish decision on the highest possible moral plane. He declared that "when she made her choice between entering the German orbit or remaining loyal to the Western group, Poland certainly was not moved by cold calculation but by the historical tradition of many centuries and the feeling of close spititual kinship with the West." This Polish choice actually resulted in placing Poland securely and permanently in the Eastern orbit of the Soviet Union.

Jedrzejewicz explained that "the time is past when the peninsulas of Europe could hold back a flood from the Eurasian continent. Following this theory, a balance of power on the European continent cannot be obtained by permitting either Germany or Russia to get control of the gateway between the Baltic Sea and the Black Sea. Command of these areas not only leads to temptation but to ultimate domination of Europe and the world." Poland, by refusing to permit the return of Danzig to Germany, and by accepting the temptation to play the game of British policy, made a choice which contributed to placing this entire so-called gateway firmly under the control of the Soviet Union.[17]

Jedrzejewicz's curious compendium of the ideas of Polish geopolitics and of Chamberlain's Birmingham speech is of little value in explaining the true motivation of Polish policy. It did reflect the ideas which Beck and the other Polish leaders presented to the Polish people to justify their policy in March 1939 and afterward. It is instructive to note the absurd allegation repeated by the Poles throughout this period that Germany, like Russia, was fundamentally not a European nation. This would be equivalent to arguing that the United States, unlike Canada or Mexico, was fundamentally not an American nation. Jedrzejewicz suggested that Germany was an area containing Eurasian forces which could flood Europe. This description is applicable to the Soviet Union, but senseless when applied to Germany. There is also the suggestion that the vast land mass between the Baltic Sea and the Black Sea is some sort of gateway. If this were true, it might have been less difficult to prevent the later Bolshevik conquest of most of Europe. It is 750 miles by direct air line at the narrowest point of this land mass, from the Baltic Sea to the Black Sea, and this waswhy countries like Poland to the West of the Soviet Union were especially vulnerable to Russian invasion. One can but wonder at fantasy in politics when Polish views on this subject are considered. Henryk Baginski, an advocate of the Pilsudski federation program and the leading Polish geopolitician, asserted that "Poland forms an isthmus between the Baltic and Black Sea." It was for statements of this kind that Baginski rated a special photograph in the Polish *Who's Who* (*Czy Wiesz Kto to Jest?*) of this period.[18]

Polish territory extended to the Baltic Sea in 1939 through much traditionally non-Polish ethnic territory. The Polish point nearest to the Black Sea was deep in Ukrainian ethnic territory and more than 250 miles from the seashore. Beck had admitted to Ribbentrop that Poland hoped to return to Kiev and to reach the Black Sea. It was also obvious that there was much sentiment in Poland favoring expansion along the Baltic Sea at German expense. Poland welcomed British support against Germany as part of a grandiose and aggressive Polish plan of expansion at the expense of both Germany and Russia. This program was presented as a benefit to European civilization because it would allegedly improve the operation of the balance of power. The *Democratic Review*, in the United States, had rejected the balance of power as a suitable doctrine for the Western hemisphere as early as 1844. The Polish program unintentionally served the interests of Bolshevik expansion rather than the balance of power, but its value to Europe was extremely doubtful in any case. The achievement of the Polish program required the shedding of oceans of blood and the sacrifice of trillions of dollars of wealth. One might well wonder how such a program could be justified.

The Approval of the Guarantee by the British Parties

Halifax encountered little difficulty in persuading the British Conservative, Liberal, and Labour parties to accept the unilateral guarantee of Poland which was announced in Parliament on March 31, 1939. His friend Geoffrey Dawson, the editor of the London *Times*, described the guarantee as "a very careful document." The Labour Party people were jubilant because Halifax was pursuing a war policy, and they were caught off balance by the unexpected plan of a guarantee to Poland. The Labour Party leaders, after the Birmingham speech of March 17, 1939, congratulated Chamberlain for accepting the collective security policy which Labour had advocated in September 1938. Chamberlain continued to defend his earlier policy, but they accepted this with good-natured humor. He satisfied their hatred of Hitler by referring to the German leader as a "mad dog."[19]

The Labour leaders were mainly interested in an Anglo-Russian alliance because they sincerely wished to aid the program of the Soviet Union. The Halifax pro-Soviet alliance offer of March 20, 1939, convinced them that the British leaders were seeking such an alliance. They were not informed of the Polish refusal of the alliance on March 24, 1939, and Polish Ambassador Raczynksi cleverly misled them into assuming that Poland would accept it. The executive committee of the Labour Party did not learn the true facts until within a few hours of the announcement of the guarantee in the British Parliament. They were much concerned by the absence of the Soviet Union from this arrangement, but they were allowed no time to think about the matter or to concert an opposing strategy. They presented a number of objections of a general nature to the plan, but Chamberlain proceeded to announce it in the House of Commons at 3:00 p.m. on March 31st.

The Labour leaders were not informed that the guarantee was already in effect on March 30, 1939, before they heard about it. They did know that Soviet Ambassador Maisky had said that the Soviet Union did not approve of the guarantee plan, and the Russian diplomat also complained that no time had been allowed for him to confer with his Government before the announcement of the guarantee. In the upshot, the British Labour leaders had grave misgivings about the Halifax policy, but they agreed to support it in the Commons debates on April 3, 1939. Halifax had used the element of surprise with telling effect in dealing with the Labour leaders. Their later complaints about his policy toward the Soviet Union were met with the rejoinder that they themselves, and also the Liberals, had approved of the unilateral guarantee to Poland. Halifax experienced no difficulty at all in securing the agreement of the British Conservative Party for the guarantee, although the folly of the move was privately deplored by several prominent Tories.[20]

The officials at the British Foreign Office knew that it was impossible to explain the guarantee to Poland by rules of strict logic. William Strang, the chief of the Central Office which dealt with Germany, admitted that the general arguments against war in 1938 were no less valid in 1939. He believed that it was impossible to claim that Poland was more worthy of a European war on her behalf than Czechoslovakia. He rationalized the situation with the observation that in 1939 good arguments either way would not have carried weight because "our people had made up their minds." This rationalization confused cause and effect. The British public had welcomed the preservation of peace at Munich in 1938, and they were not at all in a bellicose mood on March 15, 1939, although their resistance to a war policy had been subtly undermined by a constant stream of war propaganda during the past five months.[21]

The decisive factor, which caused some of the British people to think that they had made up their own minds, was the strategy of Halifax in deceiving them. He had lied to them about British policy toward Czecho-Slovakia after Munich, and he had lied to them about Rumania. It was only by means of these palpable falsehoods that the British public had been whipped into a warlike mood. It was by these means that Halifax persuaded them to accept a policy which was dangerous and seriously devoid of logic. Thomas Jones was speaking the truth when he declared that "the declaration on Poland has given almost universal satisfaction." This was a sad commentray on the ease with which a modern people can be deceived by their leaders.[22]

The Statement by Chamberlain

Sir Samuel Hoare later expended much energy in a vain attempt to argue that Great Britain had not surrendered her initiative in foreign policy to Poland. He admitted that the Poles had the right to interpret what they considered a threat to their independence, but he claimed that they would permit the British to aid them in defining this threat. This was an unrealistic expectation, and subsequent events were to show that the Polish leaders resented interference from the British in this matter. They were certainly under no obligation to accept it. The following statement, which defined the guarantee, was made in the House of Commons by Prime Minister Chamberlain on March 31, 1939:

"In order to make perfectly clear the position of His Majesty's Government in the meantime before these consultations [with other governments] are

concluded, I now have to inform the House that during that period, in the event
of any action which clearly threatened Polish independence, and which the
Polish Government accordingly considered it vital to resist with their national
forces, His Majesty's Government would feel themselves bound at once to lend
the Polish Government all support in their power. They have given the Polish
Government an assurance to this effect."23

The text of the Chamberlain speech was broadcast to the continent by the
London short-wave radio at 3:58 p.m. on March 31, 1939. When the Belgian
Minister to Germany, Vicomte Jacques Davignon, received the text of the British
commitment to Poland, he exclaimed that "blank check" was the only possible
description of the British pledge. Davignon was extremely alarmed, and he
feared that the British move would produce a war in a very short time. He called
at the German Foreign Office and discussed the situation with State Secretary
Weizsaecker. Weizsaecker attempted to reassure Davignon by claiming that the
situation between Germany and Poland was not tragic. The Belgian diplomat did
not believe that this statement offered much consolation in view of the
proverbial recklessness of the Poles.24

The Challenge Accepted by Hitler

Hitler's attitude toward the proposed settlement with Poland was seriously
affected by the news that Poland had received unlimited British military support
for a policy of defiance against Germany. Józef Beck allegedly told American
Ambassador Kennedy, when he reached London, that he knew Hitler must have
been "roaring mad" when he learned that Poland was "tying up" with Great
Britain. These American colloquialisms, with their quaint frontier tinge, were
obviously not the exact words Beck used, but they indicate that the Polish
Foreign Minister knew that the Polish acceptance of the British guarantee was
a challenge which Hitler could not possibly ignore.25

Hitler proceeded without delay to order the preparation of plans "for the
gradual, seemingly unavoidable conflict with Poland, in such manner that these
can be executed in the late summer of 1939." He also gave Ribbentrop the
welcome order to abandon his efforts to persuade the Poles to resume negotiations for a settlement. The Poles had long believed that war between Poland and
Germany was necessary, and this view began to make rapid headway at Berlin.
Chamberlain admitted in Parliament on April 3, 1939, that he was attempting
to achieve the encirclement of Germany, but he claimed that this encirclement
was a defensive move, and not aggression. It must be recalled that Poland on
several occasions had offered to attack Germany if France would do the same,
and these instances were familiar to the British leaders. A British blank check
to Poland under these circumstances was not a reassuring element in an allegedly
defensive policy.26

The first "Operation White" order (military code name of preparations for a
possible German-Polish war) was issued by General Wilhelm Keitel, the German
Army Chief of the High Command, to the top German Army commanders on
April 3, 1939. The order called for the beginning of German planning and
preparation for a possible Polish campaign. It was hoped that the initial

timetable could be completed by May 1, 1939, and that total preparations for a possible conflict could be made within five months. Hitler by April 3rd had modified his initial sharp reaction that war with Poland was "seemingly inevitable," and he was careful to limit the prospect of such a conflict to the realm of possibility. The commanders were told that German relations with Poland were continuing on the basis of seeking to avoid any quarrels. He added that "a final settlement (i.e. a war) might become necessary, notwithstanding the pact in effect with Poland."

The Danzig question was settled by the statement that the Free City remained an object of German concern, and that it would be annexed immediately in the event of a German-Polish war. The commanders were assured that, if war did become inevitable, all efforts would be made to avoid a conflict until the isolation of Poland was assured. This meant that Hitler was unwilling to accept the prospect of a war between Germany and England. Hitler continued to trust in the refusal of Poland to cooperate with the Soviet Union. He noted that Germany probably would not have to contend with Russian aid to Poland in the event of war since "intervention by Russia . . . cannot be expected to be of any use for Poland, because this would imply Poland's destruction by Bolshevism."[27]

Hitler was scheduled to deliver a speech at Wilhelmshaven on April 1, 1939, on the occasion of the launching of the German battleship *Tirpitz*. The Polish acceptance of the British guarantee prompted him to devote extra attention to this major address. He hoped to convey two principal themes to his audience and to the world. He wished everyone to know that Great Britain could not intimidate Germany, but he also wished to make it clear that Germany continued to favor a peaceful solution of European problems. Hitler was remarkably successful in conveying these two ideas without creating the impression that they were mutually exclusive. He denounced the pre-1914 British encirclement policy, and he made the point that the German Government of that time had been mistaken in allowing British encirclement plans to ripen without taking effective counter-measures. He congratulated the community of Wilhelmshaven on its recovery from the misery and poverty of the economic depression during Weimar Republic days. He blamed lies and propaganda for the demoralization of Germany in 1918 and the following years. It seemed hypocritical of the British leaders to take exception to the German program of peaceful territorial revision, and Hitler reminded his listeners that the British had seized vast stretches of territory by force less than twenty years earlier. He recalled that Germany did not have the power to prevent them from changing the map in 1919. Hitler repeated his desire for peace in Europe, and he announced his decision to call the September 1939 National Socialist Party Day the Party Day of Peace.[28]

Beck's Visit to London

Beck departed from Warsaw by train on April 2, 1939, on his trip to London. He was accompanied by Józef Lipski and Colonel Szymunski, his military adviser. A protocol chief from the German Foreign Office appeared at the Silesian Station in Berlin on the morning of April 3, 1939, to welcome Beck during the few minutes that his salon coach was in the German capital. Halem asked Beck if he had any wishes, and the Polish Foreign Minister replied that he had none. A brief conversation of courtesy ensued. Beck claimed in the course of his remarks that it had been a great pleasure to receive Ribbentrop when the latter came to Warsaw on an official visit in January 1939. It was obvious that Beck, despite the events of recent days, was disappointed that Ribbentrop had not come to the station to exchange a few words with him. This would have been an impressive incident to relate in London. The Polish attitude toward Germany had long been secretly hostile, and hence it was not much different in April 1939 from what it had been in January. The German attitude toward Poland had changed.[29]

The Hungarians were especially distressed by this situation. They feared the consequences of a new European war for Hungary, which was easily understandable in view of the frightful treatment they had received from the Allies in 1919. The fact that their leaders had opposed war with Serbia in 1914 had brought them no mercy. Hungarian Ambassador Sztójay, who was later Premier of Hungary, had informed Weizsaecker on March 29, 1939, that Hungary desired to mediate between Germany and Poland. The Hungarians had never been at war with Poland in their entire history, and they were the traditional friends and allies of Germany. Weizsaecker learned that Hungarian Foreign Minister Csáky was prepared to urge the Poles to make concessions to Germany. Csáky believed that the intransigent Polish attitude was suicidal for both Poland and European peace. Weizsaecker replied that he did not believe that a Hungarian initiative would produce any impression on the Poles. He assured the Hungarian diplomat that Germany was anxious to avoid a conflict with Poland. He told the Danzig leaders on the same day to be exceptionally careful not to provoke the Poles during the current period of great tension.[30]

The Germans were more interested in the mission which had been proposed by Grigorie Gafencu, the Rumanian Foreign Minister. German Minister Wilhelm Fabricius informed the German Foreign Office on March 31, 1939 that Gafencu planned to visit Germany early in April as part of a *tour d'horizon* of the principal foreign capitals. He hoped that he could be useful in mediating between Germany and Great Britain, and the German leaders welcomed this prospect. Helmuth Wohlthat, the Commissioner of the German Four Year Plan, had returned to Berlin from his trade mission to Rumania. He noted that Tilea had been ordered to return to Bucharest from London for consultation. Wohlthat hoped that he would be recalled permanently, despite the fact that he was *persona grata* in Great Britain. The German diplomats, on the other hand, recognized that Gafencu could not afford to take this step.[31]

The news of the projected Gafencu mission prompted Ribbentrop and Weizsaecker to adopt a more optimistic attitude toward the current European scene. The German Foreign Office addressed a special circular to the German missions abroad on April 3, 1939. The German diplomats abroad were told that the British guarantee to Poland was merely a provisional arrangement, and that it might be possible to induce the British to adopt a more flexible policy toward the Poles.[32]

Józef Beck arrived at London in the late evening of April 3, 1939. The first formal conversations between Beck and the English leaders took place on the morning of April 4th. Beck greeted Halifax warmly and assured him that the British promise to support Poland was welcome to the Polish Government. He promised that Poland in return would fight Germany in the event of a direct conflict between Great Britain and Germany. Beck knew that such an eventuality was extremely unlikely, but his formal offer placed Poland on an equal footing with Great Britain in the matter of the guarantee. Halifax assured Beck that he would accept this offer, but he added that it was insufficient for his requirements. He desired to have far more extensive commitments from Poland. Beck received this news with some surprise, and he inquired what the British Foreign Secretary had in mind. Halifax said quietly that he wanted Poland to agree to go to war if Germany attacked Holland, Belgium, Switzerland, or Denmark. Beck was amazed by the sweeping nature of this request, which reflected a style and scope of permanent intervention with which he was unfamiliar. He replied that he would require some time to think it over.

Then the subject was turned to Beck's refusal of Halifax's pro-Soviet alliance offer of March 20, 1939. The British Foreign Secretary indicated that he required a personal explanation from Beck on the motives behind the Polish refusal. Beck carefully avoided a detailed discussion of this important question. He restricted his remarks to the previous argument presented by Raczynski, that a pact between Poland and the Soviet Union would provoke Germany. Halifax replied with sharpness. He asked if Beck was not at least aware that an Anglo-Polish pact would also have a provocative effect on Berlin. Beck was perfectly well aware of this, but he did not wish to admit if for the sake of his argument about Russia. He merely said that he felt under no obligation to give a definitive answer to this question. He was willing to discuss it in general terms and to make a few relevant observations. He asked Halifax to recall that Hitler had not objected to the old Franco-Polish alliance when he concluded the 1934 Pact with Poland. He argued that Hitler did not have the hostile feelings for Great Britain which he entertained toward the Soviet Union. This enabled Beck to imagine that Hitler might conceivably reconcile himself to an Anglo-Polish alliance. Halifax promptly dismissed this as a weak argument, which did not sound very convincing. He made it very clear to Beck that he was extremely disappointed by the Polish rejection of his March 20, 1939, alliance plan.

Beck informed Halifax that he was willing to "improve" Polish relations with the Soviet Union, but he would never consent to "extend" them. He declined to motivate this statement of policy. He requested the British leaders to accept it as one of the irrevocable facts in the situation. He repeated that "it was important not to provoke a conflict, though it was, of course, difficult to say whether, indeed, a conflict was unavoidable." Halifax responded by asking Beck to take notice of the fact that he intended to engage in further negotiations with the Russians. He reminded Beck that he had the support of the French leaders for this policy. Beck merely responded with a gesture of helpless resignation. He said the decision was entirely up to them, since he was powerless to prevent them from negotiating with the Russians. He believed the British Foreign Secretary should know that Poland would never under any circumstances assume any "liability" toward the Soviet Union. He reminded Halifax that he had always opposed the Franco-Russian alliance, which had been ratified in 1936. He regarded it as a "bad bargain," and he predicted that future agreements with the Bolsheviks would be of the same quality.

Halifax was unimpressed with Beck's opinion that a Polish "liability" toward the Soviet Union would be dangerous or even fatal for Poland. This was natural, because he was indifferent about the future of Poland. The new Polish state was merely a pawn in his game, and he hoped to use both Poland and the Soviet Union in achieving his aim. He asked Beck for an estimate of the military strength of the Soviet Union. Beck declined to go into this question. He merely remarked that his Government "had not a very high opinion of Soviet Russia."

Halifax changed his tactics and said sarcastically "that some members of the Labour party believed that, if Great Britain and the Soviet Union could join hands, the world would be safe for ever more." Beck was aware of the pro-Communist orientation of the British Labour Party, and he was pleased by Halifax's sarcasm about it. The Polish Foreign Minister replied with amusement that "he doubted the validity of this theory."[33]

The second meeting between Beck and the British leaders took place on the afternoon of April 4, 1939. Hitler had returned to Hamburg at noon on the same day from a two day cruise to Helgoland with 1,000 German workers and their families on the maiden trip of the new *Strength through Joy* (*Kraft durch Freude*) pleasure ship, *Robert Ley*. He would have been interested to know that Beck was worried about the determination of the British leaders to compromise Poland with Russia, and by the British attempt to gain a Polish pledge to guarantee such countries as Denmark and Switzerland against the alleged danger of German attacks. This would have confirmed his impression that the British were willing to expose Poland to the risk of domination by the Soviet Union, but that they were unable to offer her suitable protection against threats from any quarter.[34]

Beck defended his own policy on April 4th by telling the British leaders that everything Hitler had done until October 1938 was justifiable, but that "recent events were indefensible." He referred to "conversations" about Danzig with the German leaders over a long period, but he refused to concede that these discussions had amounted to formal negotiations. Beck distorted history somewhat when he said that "Danzig had lived upon the Polish hinterland for the last eight centuries." The Baltic city had not existed for that length of time. His remark was intended to convey the impression that Poland should control Danzig by natural right, but it was no more convincing than it would be to say that Rotterdam, which had lived on the German hinterland for many centuries, should belong to Germany. This did not bother the British leaders, because they were quite willing, while supporting Poland, to ignore the injustice of Polish claims. Halifax asked Beck what settlement at Danzig would be acceptable to Poland. He was pleased when the Polish Foreign Minister answered at once that he expected Germany to renounce her aspirations, and to guarantee the permanence of the Polish position there. Chamberlain asked Beck how he would react to the proposition of a German superhighway across the Polish Corridor. The Polish Foreign Minister replied that his country would never tolerate such a project. Chamberlain inquired if the Germans had ever asked for such a superhighway. Beck replied they had certainly asked for it orally, but never in writing.[35]

The last formal discussion between Beck and the British leaders took place in Chamberlain's office at the House of Commons on the afternoon of April 5, 1939. The Prime Minister observed that the proposed Anglo-Polish bilateral pact was not what the British public expected. There was much more public interest in an Anglo-Russian pact, and many people in Great Britain were inclined to consider that Poland was a reactionary country and unworthy of a British guarantee.[36] Halifax noted that certain questions had to be settled before such a pact could be concluded. He reminded Beck that he would expect him to guarantee Holland, Belgium, Switzerland, and Denmark against a German attack, and that otherwise the treaty would not be acceptable. Beck announced with finality that he could not make commitments about these states without consulting his Government. This ended the possibility that an Anglo-Polish alliance would be concluded during his visit. He refused to consider merely consulting with his colleagues on the telephone. He made it clear that his own attitude toward the Halifax terms was negative, and he was careful to avoid giving the impression that the ultimate reaction from Warsaw would be favorable.

The British leaders made another futile attempt to persuade Beck to transform the Polish-Rumanian alliance from an anti-Soviet pact into an anti-German pact. Beck replied that he opposed this plan. He reminded his hosts that Hungary was Poland's most friendly neighbor, and that she was also a revisionist state. He rejected the proposed transformation of the Polish-Rumanian alliance, as a measure which would deprive Rumania of protection against the Soviet Union and require an impossible Polish guarantee of the Rumanian frontier against Hungary.

The British leaders did not like Beck's response. They wished him to think exclusively in terms of destroying Germany, and to forget other considerations. In other words, they wished his thinking to be more similar to that of President Roosevelt in the United States. They began to employ the same propaganda methods on Beck which they used with Roosevelt. They began to suggest a number of hypothetical situations with their usual formula of saying "this may sound fantastic, but" what would you do in such and such a case. Beck put a stop to this by declaring bluntly that "it was against the tradition of the Polish Government to express definite opinions about third countries without directly consulting them."

Chamberlain switched from hypothetical fantasies to rumors, and he declared that he had heard Germany was planning a sudden invasion of Hungary. Beck did not like this English style of rumor-mongering. He was convinced that this assertion of alleged German designs against Hungary was entirely false. He wished that the British leaders would desist from their efforts to alarm him in this way. He assured the British leaders with studied emphasis that he was entirely convinced Germany was not planning any political action outside her present frontiers except at Danzig. This was an effective method of reminding them that Poland was indispensable to their plan of launching a British preventive war against Germany.

Beck reminded the British leaders that Germany had refrained from undertaking the full military occupation of Slovakia, and that "in Slovakia German action had been extremely cautious and hesitating." Chamberlain and Halifax soon concluded that the tactics which were effective with President Roosevelt could produce no effect on Beck. This was true because Beck was much better informed about European affairs than President Roosevelt and his advisers.

Chamberlain unintentionally touched a sore point with Beck when he asked to what extent Poland had been dependent on Czecho-Slovakia for munitions. The suggestion that Poland might have depended upon the hated Czechs for her military strength was galling to Beck. He was somewhat carried away in his response, and he made some incautious remarks to Chamberlain for which he was bitterly criticized later when England refused to send military supplies to Poland. Beck replied to the immediate question with an emphatic: "Not at all!" This was correct, but the Polish Foreign Minister proceeded to inform his hosts with pride that Poland produced 80% of her own arms, and also exported large quantities of war materials to Great Britain and to other foreign countries. These remarks were later remembered in London when Poland pleaded in vain for a large British loan to pay for the importation of expensive foreign war materials.

Chamberlain proceeded with his survey of European countries, and he inquired what Beck thought about Yugoslavia. Beck had no reason to be friendly toward the anti-Catholic Serbian regime of that extremely backward Balkan country. He replied neatly that Yugoslavia would probably cooperate with Italy in peacetime, and with Germany in wartime.

Chamberlain and Halifax were preoccupied with the Balkan area because of reliable reports that Italy intended to consolidate her position in Albania. This was a logical Italian move, and the Germans were relieved to learn that Mussolini was content to take this step instead of formulating more ambitious projects. An Italian protectorate in Albania would not be a major change. The Albanian state which had been carved from Turkish territory in 1912 had never succeeded in achieving much stability. Nearly one-half the Albanian population lived beyond the frontiers of the tiny state, in Yugoslavia or Greece. Albania had been a sphere of Italian influence since World War I, and the Albanian troops were mostly commanded by Italian officers. The proclamation of a formal Italian protectorate would merely be the "dot" on the "i." It was obvious that the Italians could consolidate their position in Albania with ease.

Hitler learned from German Ambassador Mackensen on April 4, 1939, that the Italians were negotiating with the Albanians for a protectorate. They were dissatisfied with King Zog, whom they claimed was conducting himself in the adventurous style of King Nikita of Montenegro. The Montenegrin king had caused much trouble in the Balkans on the eve of World War I, and the Italians complained that King Zog in 1939 was seeking to extend the Albanian frontier to the Vardar River in Macedonia. Ciano confided to Mackensen that King Zog had requested Italian troops on March 23, 1939, but Italy had refused, because she did not trust the Albanian king.

The Germans knew that King Zog had very little support in his own country. Albanian Foreign Minister Ekrem Bey Libohova complained to German diplomats at Tirana that the Italians were seeking to destroy Albanian independence against the wishes of the Albanian Government. There were threats that Albania would resist the arrival of unsolicited Italian troops. But Hitler was confident that Mussolini and Ciano could deal with the situation. He gave the German Foreign Office advance permission to support any Italian move in

Albania. Italian Ambassador Attolico telephoned Weizsaecker on the evening of April 6, 1939, that Italian troops would enter Albania at 4:30 a.m. on Good Friday, April 7, 1939. Weizsaecker was able to inform him immediately that the Italian move would receive German diplomatic and press support. Attolico was pleased with this prompt and helpful response. He told Weizsaecker that Ciano believed the Italian move would have specific and stabilizing consequences in the Balkan area.[37]

Beck was unimpressed with the British contention that an Italian move in Albania would produce a serious crisis. He admitted that an Italian occupation of Albania might place some strain on Italo-Yugoslav relations, but he did not think that this would be serious or that it would prompt the Yugoslavs to change their policy.[38]

The conversation was completed after several hours, when it was evident that nothing further could be accomplished. There was no Anglo-Polish alliance, but the advance guarantee to Poland of March 31, 1939, included all the conceivable alliance obligations for Great Britain, except for concrete promises concerning the wartime employment of the British armed forces. Beck was not impressed with Chamberlain and Halifax, and they did not regard him with much favor. But the British and Polish leaders were convinced that they needed one another, whatever their personal feelings, to achieve their respective goals.

A joint Anglo-Polish communiqué was issued on April 6, 1939, which stressed the alleged solidarity between the two countries. The public was informed that Poland had extended a pledge of military support to Great Britain. A fourth formal meeting was held on the same day, and the ground covered in the converstions was summarized and discussed for the last time. Beck never saw Chamberlain or Halifax again. He was satisfied that he could have his way on every point despite the unsatisfactory discussions, because he had the British guarantee of March 31, 1939, in his pocket. He had ample reason to be satisfied with his mission.[39]

Beck naturally did not restrict his contacts to the intensive formal conversations with his English hosts. He conversed with Winston Churchill, the prominent Tory Opposition leader, on April 4th. Churchill had been especially notorious for his lively imagination and his preoccupation with imaginary assassins and kidnapers.[40] He asked with naive seriousness if Beck thought he would get back to Poland safely by returning on the train through Germany. Beck found this very amusing, and he replied with gentle irony: "I think we shall have time for that."

Beck was repelled by Churchill's attitude toward general European questions, and he was not attracted to the personality of the adventurous Tory. He regarded Churchill as an unbalanced man, and he knew that he was obsessed by "total animosity" toward Germany. Both Churchill and his younger Tory disciple, Anthony Eden, sought to persuade Beck to enter an alliance with the Soviet Union. Beck in his own thoughts dismissed Eden contemptuously as a typical product of Oxford University and the League of Nations at Geneva. Beck knew that neither Churchill nor Eden understood the Russian problem.[41]

Theo Kordt of the German Embassy in London was able to telegraph information to Berlin on April 5, 1939, about the principal topics which had been discussed between Beck and the British leaders. Chamberlain admitted in the House of Commons on the following day that there had been no attempt to limit what might constitute a threat to Polish independence. The final word on this matter was left entirely to the Poles. Beck admitted to American Ambassador Kennedy before he left London that the British leaders had complained about the allegedly uncooperative Polish attitude. He also claimed that he had been able to diminish this dissatisfaction somewhat in the last conversations. Beck referred cleverly to his "old friend America" and his "new friend Britain." He confided to Kennedy that he was "more than happy" to have the British blank check. He assured the American Ambassador that he did "not want to be the direct cause of plunging the world into war." This was encouraging, but Beck deprived the statement of any real meaning by admitting that he had no concrete plan to preserve the peace. Indeed, it may be safely assumed that Beck's statement to Kennedy was entirely for the record.[42]

Kennedy talked with Halifax on April 6th. The British Foreign Secretary admitted that Beck was definitely opposed to a Russo-Polish understanding. Halifax believed that he deserved a vacation after the work of the past three weeks. He told Kennedy that Chamberlain was leaving for Scotland on the evening of April 6th, and that he was going home to Yorkshire the following morning. The Poles had their blank check, and a separate British approach to Russia would be the next step. The general European situation was discussed, and Halifax privately admitted to Kennedy that neither Hitler nor Mussolini wanted war.[43]

Count Michal Lubienski at the Polish Foreign Office received instructions from Beck to call at the German Embassy on April 6, 1939, to discuss the conversations at London. Lubienski was required to emphasize that Poland had rejected the British pro-Soviet alliance offer of March 20, 1939, and that she had only accepted the March 31, 1939, guarantee in order to block German aspirations at Danzig. A further attempt was made to mislead Hitler about Beck's attitude, and to create possible discord among the Germans. Lubienski flatly asserted to Moltke that Beck would have been forced to resign had he advocated Polish acceptance of German claims to Danzig. He conceded that the Anglo-Polish combination had produced a new encirclement of Germany. He also claimed that the Germans had encircled Poland by extending their own influence throughout Bohemia-Moravia and into Slovakia.[44]

Weizsaecker responded to this conversation by inviting Lipski at Berlin to discuss the situation on April 6, 1939, at the German Foreign Office. The Polish Ambassador insisted that Poland did not desire any change in German-Polish relations, and that she wished to abide by the terms of the German-Polish non-aggression pact of 1934. Lipski argued that Germany was willing to accept Polish obligations to France when she concluded the Pact, and that it would be logical for her to make another gesture of the same kind by accepting the British guarantee of March 31, 1939. Weizsaecker pointed out the elementary fact that the situations were entirely different, because the Franco-Polish alliance of 1921 had ante-dated the 1934 Pact and had not been concluded after the signing of the Pact. He "loftily and indifferently refuted Lipski's statements," and he "received these remarks of Lipski's with a smile." He told Lipski that Polish policy had become "altogether incomprehensible to him." He told Lipski that one fact was more important than all this sophistry, namely, that Germany was still anxious to arrive at an accommodation with Poland. He assured Lipski that it would still be possible to discuss questions of interest between Germany and Poland, despite the obvious Polish violation of the 1934 Pact. He added specifically that Germany was quite prepared to discuss the situation of Slovakia with the Poles, and to take Polish interests into account. He hoped that Lipski would realize from this statement that talk of Germany seeking to encircle Poland in Slovakia was idle falsehood.[45]

Hitler came to Berlin on April 6, 1939, to discuss plans for the German Army parade scheduled for his birthday on April 20th. American Chargé d'Affaires Geist reported that he was cheerful and in good spirits. The American diplomat also noted that the peaceful atmosphere of the German capital presented a stark contrast to Paris and London, where rumors of war and talk of war were the dominant themes. There was general confidence in Berlin that it would be possible to keep the peace in 1939.[46]

Sir Alexander Cadogan and Sir Maurice Hankey accompanied Beck to the railway station on April 6th. The Polish Foreign Minister was scheduled to arrive at Boulogne on the morning of April 7, 1939, for an important conference with his principal collaborator, Juliusz Lukasiewicz, the Polish Ambassador to France. Beck had given Lukasiewicz permission to bring American Ambassador Bullitt to Boulogne. It was agreed that Bullitt could accompany Beck and Lukasiewicz from Boulogne to Lille, but that the two Poles would travel alone and undisturbed from Lille to the Belgian capital. Beck made it clear to Lukasiewicz that he had no desire to visit Paris, or to discuss the current situation with Daladier and Bonnet.[47]

Beck's Satisfaction

Bullitt was delighted at the opportunity to greet Beck on his return from England to the continent. He knew that this privilege resulted from the fact that he "was a strong admirer of the policy of Minister Beck" and enjoyed "friendly relations" with him. Bullitt discussed Roosevelt's policy with Beck at some length. He claimed that he and Roosevelt were much dissatisfied with both English and American public opinion at this point. Beck expressed mild suprise at this remark as far as England was concerned, and he indicated that he was satisfied with the atmosphere which he had encountered in England. He was quite unperturbed that a formal Anglo-Polish alliance had not been negotiated, and he observed with satisfied irony that it would require much delicacy and discretion on the part of Chamberlain to handle the guarantee agreement other than by the standards of a normal alliance. Beck did not believe that the British Prime Minister possessed either delicacy or discretion. Beck observed, with a knowing smile to his listeners, that Chamberlain had said he was glad Poland had come instantly to an agreement with England. This amused Beck, because Poland had been waiting over a considerable period for the English offer of an agreement.[48]

Beck admitted that Halifax had sought to entangle him with obligations to Holland, Belgium, Denmark, and Switzerland, but he did not attach serious importance to this fact. He was more interested in speculating about the German response to his visit to England and to his acceptance of the British guarantee. He declared that the alliance with England (*sojusz z Anglia*) had dealt a real blow to Hitler's plans for a German-Polish agreement. He believed that British approval of Polish aspirations at Danzig had buttressed the Polish cause there as never before. A main topic of speculation was whether Hitler would respond to the British guarantee by denouncing the 1934 Pact with Poland.[49]

Bullitt took his leave from Beck at Lille and returned to Paris. He sent an exuberant report to Washington, D.C., at 11:00 p.m. on April 7, 1939. He informed Roosevelt and Hull that Beck was immensely pleased by recent developments in England, and that the degree of understanding which had been achieved was quite adequate to fill Polish needs. Beck had said that he knew that Hitler would be furious. Bullitt also added with obvious satisfaction that Beck had described Ribbentrop as a "dangerous imbecile."[50]

The principal topic of conversation between Beck and Lukasiewicz, during the trip to Brussels, was Polish diplomatic strategy toward France. The main purpose of this strategy was to persuade the French to follow the British lead by expanding their commitments to Poland. Lukasiewicz was instructed to contact Bonnet immediately upon his return to Paris in order to expedite matters. Beck was unjustifiably optimistic in expecting the French leaders to emulate the British policy of granting a blank check to Poland. Bonnet tenaciously refused to commit France, during the following months, to a war over Danzig on behalf of Poland.

Hitler waited for three weeks before responding to the diplomacy of Beck and Halifax in his speech to the German Reichstag on April 28, 1939. The principal organs of the German press were restrained from criticizing Poland during these weeks. The main fire of German press criticism was directed against England. Great Britain was presented to the German public as an impertinent governess who presumed to dictate standards of policy and morality to the nations of the world. This campaign reached its climax in a cartoon of April 25, 1939, which appeared in the official National Socialist Party organ, the *Voelkischer Beobachter* (*People's Observer*). The cartoon was entitled: *The moral umpire of the world*. It showed John Bull in a union jack vest which was dripping with blood from the latest British repressive measures against the Arabs of Palestine. He was pushing a placard on a hand cart. The placard carried the picture of a maiden aunt governess who claimed to be concerned about the welfare of humanity. Her comment about the recent events in Europe consisted of the one brief word so typical of English cant: "Shocking!" The point of the cartoon was that it was typical of the governess to profess shock at any action so long as it was not English brutality. Her back was turned on the British Empire and on the excesses practiced under English rule. This cartoon did not reflect any animus of Hitler toward the British Empire or toward the methods of English rule. It did reflect the point which Hitler had made in his speech of January 30, 1939, on the need to educate the German public about English policy.[51]

Hitler recognized that the British blank check to Poland on March 31, 1939, was the concrete expression of the alarmist statements which had been made in Great Britain about Germany since the Munich agreement. Hitler hoped that there would never be another Anglo-German war, although he knew that the danger of such a war existed, and he wished the German people to be morally prepared to face this eventuality. Hitler wished the German public to know that the English leaders were seeking to prevent the return of National Socialist Danzig to the German Reich. Hitler hoped to avoid war with Great Britain, but he was not prepared to do so at the price of an ignominious retreat before the pretensions of Poland.[52]

The danger of an Anglo-German conflict resulted exclusively from the decision of the British leaders to place themselves unreservedly at the side of Poland. The British pledge to Poland was issued after the British leaders realized that the Poles had challenged Germany with a threat of war at Danzig and with the partial mobilization of the Polish armed forces. It was the most provocative move which Halifax could have made under the circumstances, and it was the step most likely to produce another European war. It was the move which Halifax refused to make on behalf of President Beneš of Czechoslovakia on May 21, 1938. It did not make a European war inevitable, but it vastly increased the danger of war. It was the supreme challenge to the advocates of peace in Europe, and to the continental leaders who realized that the Soviet Union would be the principal benefactor from another European war.

Chapter 15

THE DETERIORATION

OF GERMAN-POLISH RELATIONS

Beck's Inflexible Attitude

The increased tension in German-Polish relations after March 31, 1939, was a consequence of the Polish decision to occupy the foremost place in Halifax's encirclement front. Beck knew perfectly well that Halifax hoped to encompass the destruction of Germany. The British Foreign Minister had considered an Anglo-German war inevitable since 1936, and he came into the open with his anti-German policy on March 17, 1939. Beck knew that Hitler would regard Polish acceptance of the British guarantee as a stinging blow. Beck had taken his decision against Germany with a full understanding of the consequences. There might have been some improvement in German-Polish relations after his return from London to the continent on April 7, 1939, but he precluded this possibility by pursuing a rigidly hostile policy toward Germany. This development reached an early climax in Beck's speech to the Polish Sejm on May 5, 1939. The Polish Foreign Minister distorted the record of recent events in this speech. He ignored the German suggestions for further negotiation made by Weizsaecker to Lipski on April 6, 1939, and by Hitler publicly in his speech to the German Reichstag on April 28, 1939.[1]

There was no further negotiation for a German-Polish agreement after the British guarantee to Poland for the simple reason that Beck refused to negotiate. It is significant that after the British guarantee Halifax never exerted any genuine pressure on Poland to negotiate with Germany. A German-Polish understanding would have been a great disappointment to Halifax. He was counting on Poland to provide the pretext for the British preventive war against Germany.[2]

Rumanian Foreign Minister Gafencu told German Minister Fabricius at Bucharest on April 7, 1939, that Beck intended to force the British to recognize Poland as an equal partner in their aggressive plans. Beck had informed Gafencu that the Anglo-Polish agreement would be equivalent to the recognition of Poland as one of the Great Powers. He assured his Rumanian colleague that

Poland would refuse to do business with Great Britain on any other basis.[3]

The Tilea hoax continued to embarrass the Rumanian Foreign Minister. He admitted to Fabricius that he did not trust either Tilea or the British. He had considered recalling Tilea, but he did not dare to do so for fear of British retaliation. He decided to solve the problem by sending Secretary-General Cretzianu of the Rumanian Foreign Office on a special mission to London. This was a clever move which enabled him to act through a man he trusted, in dealing with the British on important questions. Gafencu was furious with a Bucharest newspaper which had audaciously charged that King Carol was involved in Tilea's intrigue at London. Gafencu assured Fabricius on April 14, 1939, that there was not the slightest truth in this charge.[4]

The Poles were quick to take advantage of their new relationship with Great Britain after Beck's visit to London. Polish Ambassador Raczynski came to Halifax on the evening of April 6, 1939, to lodge a protest about the allegedly anti-Polish treatment of Danzig and the Corridor in large sections of the British press. It seemed that Great Britain was now receiving most of Poland's friendly protests previously directed to Berlin. Halifax was not particularly concerned about this situation, because he possessed great skill in evading friendly protests. He was delighted to learn from British Ambassador Kennard at Warsaw a few days later that the German Ambassador to Poland was demoralized by the recent events in Europe. Moltke confessed to Kennard that he was literally sickened by the complete wreckage of German-Polish relations, which had been built carefully and laboriously after 1933. He admitted that he was totally pessimistic about the future, and that he believed a German-Polish understanding had become a sheer impossibility.[5]

The unwarranted indiscretion of Moltke to Kennard offers a further proof of the shortcomings of the German Ambassador to Poland. Moltke was despised by the British and the Poles because he was an incompetent diplomat, and because he constantly excused himself from responsibility for the official acts of the Government which he continued to serve. The situation was no different with Schulenburg at Moscow, Welczeck at Paris, Mackensen at Rome, or Dirksen at London. The result was a severe handicap on the conduct of German foreign policy during a difficult period.[6]

Moltke spoke to Kennard about his fears on April 7, 1939. This would have been an appropriate date to summarize the impact of recent developments in a confidential report. Many things had taken place between March 9th, when the Slovak crisis became acute, and April 6th, when Beck departed from London. German-Polish disagreement about a general settlement was evident to the entire world. The Poles had rejected the German proposals and undertaken emergency military measures directed exclusively against Germany. Poland had obtained an unrestricted British blank check against the Germans. Beck was momentarily successful in excluding the hated Russians from the British coalition. The Germans in Poland were subjected to increasing doses of violence from the dominant Poles. The old courtesy had begun to fade entirely from the official intercourse between the Polish and German Governments. Things were far worse than at any time during the period of the Weimar Republic, because of the British intervention policy. The British blank check outweighed, in

Polish minds, the fact that Germany in the meantime had become a colossus of strength compared to Poland.[7]

Hitler's Cautious Policy

The British Guarantee did not mean that a German-Polish war was inevitable. Hitler was exceedingly reluctant to take military action against Poland despite the Polish challenge and the rejection of German friendship. This was not altered by the fact that he knew Germany could win an easy military victory over the Poles. World War I, despite Germany's military defeat, had proved that German soldiers in both defensive and offensive operations could cope successfully with equal numbers of enemy troops from any country in the world. Although the German program of military preparation was less intensive than that of Great Britain, in proportion to the industrial capacity of the two countries, her activities in this sphere far outstripped the feeble efforts of the Poles. The ratio of fighter aircraft between Germany and Poland in 1939 was 10:1, and the ratio in armored vehicles was 12:1.[8]

Poland had more trained soldiers in reserve than Germany, but the Germans were superior in the decisive infantry-age bracket of trained young men from twenty to twenty-two years of age. The superior Polish cavalry was more than outweighed by German mechanized strength. Germany and Poland were both easy countries to invade, but this had become a German advantage. The Poles were ahead in the important sphere of military planning, because they had never ceased to prepare for a German-Polish war, but their plans were faulty. The Germans were rapidly devising an effective offensive campaign strategy against Poland.

The reasonable certainty of victory over Poland did not persuade Hitler that a German-Polish war was a good idea. He regarded such a conflict as a highly unwelcome alternative to a German-Polish understanding. Hitler at first assumed that the Soviet Union would not aid the Poles in the event of a German-Polish war, but he soon concluded that it would be militarily irresponsible for Germany to trust in his political intuition, He had been wrong about the Polish attitude toward Germany, and he might be wrong about their attitude toward Russia. He issued an order to General Keitel on April 11, 1939, to draw up Polish war plans with the possible immediate intervention of Great Britain, France, and the Soviet Union clearly in mind. Keitel was advised that in this situation the first objective would be a lightning victory over Poland, while employing strictly defensive tactics against the three Great Powers. It was obvious that this was not an adventure to be embarked upon lightly, particularly since Germany had not placed herself in readiness for any major war.[9]

It was likely that the Poles would seek to provoke Germany into attacking them. Unlike Germany, they could not expect to achieve any of their objectives in a major war through their own efforts. Their hope of ultimate victory rested with distant foreign Powers. The Polish leaders were far more enthusiastic about a German-Polish war than Hitler ever was, but considerations of high policy suggested the wisdom of a role which was at least passive in appearance.

Poland was counting on the support of Halifax for the realization of her program at the expense of both Germany and Russia. It was conceivable that Halifax could lead Great Britain into a war which began with a surprise Polish invasion of Germany, but the Polish leaders knew that France and the United States were also of decisive importance to British policy. The Poles knew that Halifax would never support Poland unless he could drag France into war. This policy was dictated by the simple fact that Halifax did not believe Great Britain could win a war against Germany without the participation of France. The Poles also knew that it would be difficult for President Roosevelt to arouse the American people against Germany unless it was possible to maintain that Poland was the innocent victim of German aggression.

Polish provocation of Germany after March 31, 1939, was frequent and extreme, and Hitler soon had more than a sufficient justification to go to war with Poland on the basis of traditional practices among the nations.Nevertheless, Hitler could not justify German action, unless he believed that he was prepared to meet the consequences. He hoped to avoid war with Great Britain, and he knew that he would run a grave risk of an Anglo-German war if he invaded Poland. It was for this reason that German-Polish relations became progressively worse over a long period before they produced a conflict. Hitler, who was usually very prompt and decisive in conducting German policy, showed considerable indecision before he finally decided to act, and to face the consequences. He did not abandon his hope for a negotiated settlement with Poland until he realized that the outlook for such a settlement was completely hopeless.

Bonnet's Coolness toward Poland

The first major Polish diplomatic move, after the return of Beck from London, was an attempt to improve Polish relations with France. Polish Ambassador Lukasiewicz called on Bonnet on April 8, 1939, after his return from Brussels and his conferences with Beck. The French Foreign Minister, who had strongly supported the original Halifax proposal for a Four Power pact, admitted with obvious reluctance that Beck had been able to have his own way at London. Lukasiewicz insisted on immediate negotiations to augment Franco-Polish collaboration. Bonnet seemed to agree, and he conveyed the fatalistic attitude that he had no real choice in the matter.[10]

Bonnet had no intention of permitting negotiations with the Poles to occupy the crucial place in his program. He had received a report from French Ambassador Noël which indicated that Marshal Smigly-Rydz was delighted with the new situation created by the British guarantee. The Poles expected the French to match the British blank check without hesitation, but Bonnet was far more interested in bringing the British and Russians together. He decided to relegate Franco-Polish negotiations to Warsaw, rather than conduct them personally at Paris. This was contrary to the intention of Beck, who hoped that Lukasiewicz would be able to negotiate a new Franco-Polish agreement with Bonnet. Beck detested the French Ambassador at Warsaw, who had previously been a police official in Paris. He regarded him as an altogether unsavory individual. He would have insisted on the recall of Noël had he realized that the

French Ambassador had sought to overthrow him in 1936. Noël had attempted to make a French loan to Poland conditional on the dismissal of Beck. His motive was the alleged pro-German attitude of the Polish Foreign Minister. His plan failed because the French Government refused to accept it.

Bonnet's own attitude toward Noël was scarcely less unfavorable than that of Beck. The fact that he was retained at Warsaw is eloquent testimony of Bonnet's attitude toward Poland. The situation was especially crass when one considers that Polish Ambassador Lukasiewicz at Paris was Beck's best diplomat. Ultimately Noël turned author, and he wrote a book which contained a number of bitter and unjustifiable charges against Bonnet, who had ample opportunity to regret his decision to retain Noël at the Warsaw post.[11]

The disagreement between Bonnet and Beck about the suitable place for Franco-Polish negotiations produced a delay which was welcomed by the French Foreign Minister. Daladier and Bonnet were soon preoccupied with the Russian question, and with Anglo-French diplomacy in the Balkans. Lukasiewicz concluded with disgust that France was more interested in promoting her special Balkan interests than in collaborating with Poland.[12]

Daladier and Bonnet were not unmindful of the fact that the Polish population in the northern French industrial area had increased to almost 200,000 in recent times. The economic depression in Poland continued unabated, and Polish laborers emigrated in increasing numbers to foreign industrial areas. There was some concern in France lest the Polish Government request the return of Polish reservists for military service in Poland. Bonnet instructed Noël to discuss this question at Warsaw. He hoped that a special Polish corps might be organized in France for service in the Maginot line under French leadership. This idea also appealed to the Polish leaders. It meant that a separate Polish military force would remain in action against the Germans after a possible defeat of Poland, provided, of course, that France ultimately agreed to go to war on behalf of the Poles.[13]

The report of Noël about the elation of Marshal Smigly-Rydz over the new situation created by the British guarantee was accurate. The Marshal was gratified to receive a telegram from Beck on April 6th announcing that the *entente* with England had been solidified. Smigly-Rydz told the Polish diplomats at the Bruehl Palace that the Germans were in "a trance" and that an immediate war was quite possible. He assured them with satisfaction that such a war would mean the end of Germany. He did not deny that Germany might defeat Poland initially, but he emphasized to the diplomats that the Germans were unprepared for a general war.

Lukasiewicz was less sanguine than Smigly-Rydz about the position of the Western Powers following the British guarantee. He discussed the situation with American Ambassador Bullitt on April 9, 1939. He said that he hoped France would attack Germany from Belgium in the event of war, but he was pessimistic about the future course of French policy. Bullitt and Lukasiewicz also discussed their recent meeting with Beck. The American Ambassador told Lukasiewicz that he had given President Roosevelt extensive information about Beck's analysis of the situation. Beck had claimed that basically Hitler was a timid Austrian who might be expected to avoid a war against determined and strong opponents. He said that "it should be obvious now to Hitler that threats to

Poland would get Germany nowhere." These exuberant remarks seemed less convincing to Lukasiewicz after his conversation on the previous day with Bonnet.[14]

Bullitt was dissatisfied with the attitude of the French leaders, and he was inclined to blame what he considered the unwarranted complacency of American public opinion. He complained to President Roosevelt in a report on April 10, 1939, that the American public was not aware of the alleged direct threat to the United States from Germany, Italy, and Japan. He hoped that Roosevelt could do something to arouse the American people. His complaint was the decisive factor in persuading President Roosevelt to deliver sensational and insulting public notes to Mussolini and Hitler on April 15, 1939, after the Anglo-French guarantees to Rumania and Greece. Bullitt complained that Daladier was unresponsive to the attempt of Lukasiewicz to secure the same blank check from France which had been presented to Poland by England. Kennedy reported to Roosevelt from London on April 11, 1939, that Halifax was still pretending to entertain an idealistic hope for peace. Kennedy naturally supposed that it might be worthwhile for the British Foreign Secretary to announce to the world that peace was still possible, but Halifax claimed that to do so would convince everyone that he was "burying his head in the sand." These remarks illustrate the method by which Halifax sought to convince people that he was merely the prisoner of larger events.[15]

Beck's Displeasure at Anglo-French Balkan Diplomacy

The Italian occupation of Albania on April 7, 1939, furnished the pretext for the Anglo-French Balkan diplomatic activity which was highly unwelcome to the Poles. Bullitt had the impression that Beck was basically more friendly toward Italy than toward France. The Polish leaders were convinced that the Italian move in Albania threatened neither Great Britian nor France, and they suspected that the British and French leaders were well aware of this fact. The reaction to the Italian move was very pronounced in such distant places as Washington, D.C., London, Moscow, and Paris. Winston Churchill impulsively suggested on April 9, 1939, that the British should retaliate against the Italians by occupying the Greek island of Corfu. Corfu was directly adjacent to the Albanian coast at the entrance of the Adriatic Sea.

The suggestion of Churchill, which was rejected by the British Government, had an odd sequel. The London News Chronicle claimed on April 12, 1939, that the German Government planned an immediate invasion of Holland if British forces landed at Corfu. The British press had taken the lead of Halifax in suggesting that Germany had sinister designs against Holland. It was hoped that these rumors would be useful in arousing the American public. The Dutch had an extensive colonial empire in the East Indies, and the American leaders professed to fear that these islands would fall under Japanese control if Hitler occupied the Dutch homeland. The German press indignantly denounced the latest irresponsible British rumors.[16]

President Roosevelt was doing everything in his power to increase alarmist sentiment in the United States. He announced at Warm Springs, Georgia, on

April 9th that he might not return for his annual autumn health cure, because it was quite possible that the United States and the European countries would be involved with the problems of a major European war by that time. Fortunately, much of the reaction to this statement in the United States was extremely hostile, and many foreign observers concluded that this was merely an expression of wishful thinking on the part of the American president.[17]

The blustering of Churchill, the rumor-mongering of the British press, and the alarmist statements of Roosevelt were welcome to Halifax, who was seeking to extend the British encirclement of Germany. He believed that British commitments in the Mediterranean might be useful in intimidating Mussolini. He had discovered that the Rumanians objected to the transformation of the anti-Soviet Polish-Rumanian alliance into an anti-German alliance, but that they welcomed the prospect of an Anglo-French guarantee. Halifax hoped that this might be useful in postponing revisionist actions of the Russians, Hungarians, and Bulgarians against Rumania. Relations between Italy and Greece had been unfavorable for many years, and serious disputes between the two countries antedated World War I. The recent Italian move into Albania gave the two countries a common land frontier, and the Greek Government was quite willing to accept support in the form of a gurarantee from Great Britain and France. Yugoslavia preferred to rely on direct assurances from Italy, and Halifax was unable to persuade the Yugoslav leaders to accept an Anglo-French guarantee. This was evident by April 13, 1939, when the Western Powers proclaimed their guarantees of Rumania and Greece. The Albanian Constituent Assembly had presented the crown of the Albanian kingdom to King Victor Emmanuel III of Italy on the pervious day.[18]

The Germans were extremely pleased by the refusal of the Yugoslav Government to accept a guarantee from the Western Powers. The Germans offered to issue an official statement stressing the importance of a strong Yugoslavia for the maintenance of peace and stability in the Balkans. Yugoslav Foreign Minister Cincar Marković expressed his gratitude on April 14, 1939, for Germany's offer, but he asked Germany to refrain from openly taking this step. He argued that favorable official publicity for Yugoslavia in Germany would weaken the position of the Cvetković Ministry in Yugoslav domestic politics. It was exceedingly important at the moment for Yugoslav politicians to appear to be independent of foreign influences. Prince Regent Paul was seeking to pursue a policy of complete neutrality toward the Axis and the British encirclement front.[19]

Anglo-French diplomacy in the Balkans was ostensibly an answer to Italy's action in Albania, but it affected the interests of the Soviet Union and Poland. The guarantee to Rumania seemed to imply Anglo-French support for Rumanian rule in the former Russian territory of Bessarabia. The Soviet Union had announced as early as March 22, 1939, that the British desired them to guarantee Rumania and Poland. Polish Ambassador Lukasiewicz at Paris discovered, at the time of the Anglo-French guarantee to Rumania, that the Western Powers were asking the Russians to follow their example. The Poles hoped that the Rumanians would refuse to request or accept a Russian guarantee.[20]

An important conference on Polish policy toward Russia had taken place at the Bruehl Palace in Warsaw on April 12, 1939. Polish Ambassador Grzybowski had returned to Warsaw from Moscow to plead for limited collaboration between Poland and the Soviet Union. Beck was shocked to learn that Grzybowski advocated a Polish-Soviet understanding at the expense of the Baltic states. The Polish Ambassador argued that a new age of imperialism was replacing the Wilsonian era of self-determination. He recalled that the Baltic states, during the greater part of the 18th century, were divided between Poland and Russia, after Peter the Great of Russia succeeded in winning a window on the Baltic Sea at Swedish expense. Grzybowski believed that the Soviet Union would accept a new partition plan. Russia would seize Estonia, Poland could take Lithuania, and Lativa might be partitioned between the Poles and the Russians. Grzybowski argued that this plan would exclude Germany from any role in the region of the Baltic states.

Beck denounced this proposition. The plan of joining with the Soviet Union to carve up the anti-Bolshevik Baltic states was anathema to him. Grzybowski was advised to place no trust in any assurances from Soviet Foreign Commissar Litvinov. He was instructed to watch for indications that the Soviet Union was seeking to conclude a deal with Germany. Beck was convinced that any British attempt to win an alliance with the Soviet Union would be futile.[21]

The Beck-Gafencu Conference

Beck wished to confer with Rumanian Foreign Minister Gafencu to obtain a new assurance that there would be no collaboration between Rumania and the Soviet Union. He knew that Gafencu was about to depart on a peace mission to Berlin, Rome, Paris, and London. Gafencu, who was planning to go to Berlin by train, did not care to pass through Hungarian territory, because of the prevailing bitterness in Rumanian-Hungarian relations. His route would lead from Bucharest to the Polish frontier to Germany by way of Moldavia and the Bukovina, and from the Polish frontier by way of Lwow and Krakow. Beck suggested attaching his private salon-car to the Orient Express train on the evening of April 16th, after it crossed the Polish frontier. This would enable the two diplomats to discuss their problems during the night while they traversed the poverty-stricken southern Polish countryside. The transit meeting suggested by Beck was reminiscent of the famous conference between the Serbian and Bulgarian Premiers on the train from Belgrade to Nish before the outbreak of the 1912 Balkan War.[22]

Gafencu welcomed the conference because he wished to talk to Beck about Germany. He was convinced that the policy of Beck toward Germany was the principal threat to peace in Europe, and he hoped to exert a moderating influence on the Polish Foreign Minister. The two diplomats met on the evening of April 16th with a cordial exchange of greetings, but it seemed to Gafencu that Beck was nervous and under great strain. He assumed that this was the natural result of the events of the past few weeks and of the uncertainty about Poland's future. Gafencu asked Beck to discuss Polish policy toward Germany, before turning to Rumanian affairs. Beck responded by declaring that Hitler's proposal for the return of Danzig was at the bottom of the trouble between

Poland and Germany. He assured Gafencu that he would frustrate Hitler's Danzig aspirations. He confided that for many months he had led Hitler to believe that he would accept the German annexation of Danzig. He added, "if he counted on me to give it to him, he was mistaken. I am the last person who would abandon Danzig."23

Beck claimed that his English policy was an effective answer to Hitler's plans. The British guarantee meant that the so-called Free City was in a state of protective surety, regardless of what happened there at any given moment. Beck claimed that Poland would have been content to remain at peace with Germany had Hitler refrained from asking for any Polish concessions. He denied that he welcomed the idea of war with Germany for its own sake.

Gafencu was unable to believe this last assertion. He noted a strongly combative element in Beck's personality, which nullified the normal human conciliatory tendencies. Gafencu was astonished to learn that Beck had counted on Hitler to rupture diplomatic relations with Poland permanently when he learned of the British guarantee. This would have seemed the logical German move to Beck. The continued German interest in an understanding with Poland suggested the possibility to Beck of a German retreat. It seemed possible that Hitler would guarantee the existing German-Polish frontier without receiving Polish concessions in the Danzig and superhighway questions. Gafencu, on the other hand, doubted that there was even a remote possibility of this.24

Beck was soon aware that Gafencu did not sympathize with his policy toward Germany. He realized that Gafencu was seeking to influence him. Beck had received a challenge on his German policy from Polish Ambassador Lipski at the railway station in Berlin on his trip home from London. Lipski had carried out instructions with the Germans by insisting that the British guarantee was not contrary to the 1934 Polish-German Pact, but he confided to Beck that he did not believe this himself. The 1934 Pact was clear in stating that the recognition of existing alliance obligations did not imply the recognition of future alliances. A declaration of Russian support to Germany would have been quite unacceptable under the Pact. Beck's entire conversation with Lipski at Berlin was consumed by an inconclusive argument over this point.25

Beck hoped to convert Gafencu into acceptance of his policy toward Germany. He resented the suggestion that there were still many alternatives in dealing with the German situation. He responded with a lengthy analysis of the fundamental features of Polish foreign policy, and he claimed repeatedly that his major moves were based on instructions from Pilsudski in 1934 and 1935. Gafencu waited until Pilsudski's equilibrium theory was discussed before he interrupted Beck. The equilibrium theory called for Polish liberty of action based on identical relations of aloof detachment with the Germans and with the Russians.

Gafencu doubted if this so-called perfect equilibrium had existed in practice after 1934. Everyone knew that Poland had been far more friendly with Germany than with Russia. Beck denied this, and he claimed that it was a question of appearance or reality. He noted that the Polish attitude toward Germany had always been extremely reserved under the surface. Beck added that his own Polish patriotism had never been tarnished by Germanophilia, and he claimed that his Soviet policy was based on concrete facts, namely, animus against the Soviet system, rather than Russophobia. He denied that he was hostile toward the Russian people, "but I know Russia and I do not allow myself to be guided in this connection by the illusions of the west."

Gafencu refused to accept Beck's exposition. He suspected that Beck was strongly attracted to the Germans, repelled by the Russians, and not detached in his attitude toward either people. He considered that the recent moves by Beck on the diplomatic chessboard were incompatible with the basic attitude of the Polish Foreign Minister. Gafencu was certain that Beck was not outspokenly and violently anti-German, in the sense of the National Democrat disciples of Dmowski. He was positive that Beck had great personal admiration for Hitler.

Beck failed to convince Gafencu that his German policy was justifiable, and he changed the subject. He condemned Western policy toward the Soviet Union, and he described it as a degeneration from the realistic *cordon sanitaire* (containment of Russia), to the fantastic policy of mutual assistance, which encouraged Russian intervention in every direction. Beck argued that it was unnecessary to join the anti-Comintern front to oppose the spread of Bolshevism. He preferred to combat the Third International unofficially by denying its very existence. Beck admitted that he favored the *cordon sanitaire* and the exclusion of Russia from European affairs. Beck believed that the frontier of Europe was situated wherever the eastern Polish frontier happened to be at the moment. The Russo-Polish non-aggression pact was consistent with this policy, because such pacts stopped at the frontiers. They were treaties of delimitation rather than cooperation. He discussed the Russian problem at great length with Gafencu, and he was relieved to receive the positive assurance that Rumania would refuse to participate in a mutual assistance front with the Soviet Union.

Polish-Rumanian solidarity against Russia was extremely important to Beck. He did not object when the conversation drifted back to Germany, after having obtained the important assurance about Russia from Gafencu. Beck complained that Hitler had allowed nearly five years to elapse after the 1934 Pact before introducing his proposals for a general settlement in October 1938. He claimed that the Poles would have been justified in expecting him never to raise the Danzig issue had he waited much longer. Beck again admitted that he had pretended to favor the project of a general settlement between Germany and Poland without making any of the concessions expected from him.[26]

It was early morning by this time, and the Polish farmers of the surrounding countryside were about to begin their daily toil. Nevertheless, Gafencu had no desire to end the conversation. He had visited Warsaw six weeks earlier, and he had established friendly relations with Beck. Rumania and Poland had been allies for years, and they were close neighbors, with a common Eastern European perspective. Beck occupied the key position in a crisis of the greatest importance for the entire European continent. Gafencu hoped to exert a moderating influence on Beck which might be useful in avoiding a new disaster for Europe. He feared that Europe was drifiing into war, and he regarded it his most important diplomatic task to oppose this development.

Beck and Gafencu discussed their previous meeting, before the British guarantee to Poland. Gafencu recalled that Beck had said that "all explanations given me by Hitler since 1935 (death of Pilsudski) have been just and true, and have never been contradicted by the facts. I have spoken with him man to man, and as soldier to soldier; he has always held to the engagements he has taken, and he has never broken one with me even to this day."[27]

Beck had shared Hitler's attitude toward Rumania's Czecho-Slovak ally, and had said that "Czechoslovakia has always seemed to me to be a caricature of the Austria of the Habsburgs. Everything in this state was improper and provisional." Gafencu reminded Beck that he had also been critical of many aspects of British policy.[28]

Gafencu informed Beck of reports he had received from Rumanian Ambassador Franassovici at Warsaw after the Polish rejection of the German proposals. The Rumanian envoy had studied a map of the Baltic region with German Ambassador Moltke. The two diplomats had speculated about how they might describe the Danzig problem to some complete outsider. The territory of Germany on the map was shown in yellow, and that of the Free City in blue. Moltke suggested that Hitler was prepared to recognize all existing Polish rights at Danzig, and that therefore it was an affair of colors. Would Danzig remain blue on the map, or would Hitler be permitted to paint it yellow? Franassovici suggested that the Danzig problem was a combination of colors and subtle nuances.

Beck was not amused by the attempt of Gafencu to present the Danzig problem in a lighter vain. He exclaimed: "If they touch Danzig, there will be war!" Gafencu countered boldly by asking if the sudden change in Polish policy had caused Beck to consider resigning his post. Beck replied that he would never resign, because no other man in Poland knew enough about Polish policy to take his place. He claimed that Hitler would be unable to rid himself easily of the belief that a strong Poland was an asset to Germany, and this would be especially true if Beck remained at his post. Beck contended that Hitler could not be single-minded about retaliating against Poland, because he did not wish to open the gates of Europe to the expansion of the Soviet Union. Beck added that Hitler, unlike the Weimar Republic leaders, was fully aware of the danger from Bolshevism. Gafencu suspected that the argument of Beck was insincere and false, but he was unable to think of an effective reply.[29]

Beck insisted that he was still willing to give one assurance to Hitler: Poland would never accept an alliance with the Soviet Union. The Rumanian Foreign Minister knew that Beck was sincere in this statement. It seemed a tragedy to him that Beck's intransigence prevented an understanding between the anti-Bolshevik regimes of Germany and Poland. He knew that his own effort to influence the attitude of Beck had failed. Beck, on the other hand, was satisfied with the transit conference. He had received a new assurance that Rumania would never accept a Russian guarantee. He was pleased when Russian Foreign Commissar Maxim Litvinov repeated on April 19, 1939, that the Soviet Union would not guarantee Rumania and Poland.[30]

The Roosevelt Telegrams to Hitler and Mussolini

The British expected some lively developments at Danzig after their guarantee to the Poles. They did not realize that Hitler had ordered the Danzig authorities to go to extreme lengths in seeking to conciliate the Poles. British Ambassador

Kennard heard on April 12, 1939, that Lipski had returned to Warsaw from Berlin. He suspected that this might indicate some new development of major importance in the Danzig question. He asked Beck for the latest news about Danzig, but he was told that nothing had changed.[31]

The quiet at Danzig began to annoy Kennard. He called at the Polish Foreign Office ten days later to insist that Great Britain was "entitled" to receive information about any new steps at Danzig. He noted that the Germans were blaming Great Britain for the deadlock at Danzig, and he claimed that the British were "somewhat anxious" about the situation. Kennard was told once again that there was nothing to report. The Germans had requested the return of Danzig and a transit corridor to East Prussia. The Polish diplomats believed that the Germans expected Lipski to appear some day with "proposals of a detailed nature." Kennard was not told whether or not such proposals would actually be presented to the Germans by Poland.

The evasive vagueness at the Polish Foreign Office irritated Kennard. He complained to Halifax, and he noted with malicious satisfaction that there were objections to Beck in Polish financial circles. It was known in Poland that Beck had said nothing about British economic assistance during his visit to London. He had proudly emphasized Poland's alleged preparedness and strength. The Polish financiers regarded this as an unpardonable and expensive blunder.[32]

Beck was waiting impatiently for Hitler's response to Polish acceptance of the British guarantee. He wondered if Hitler would abrogate the 1934 Pact, which Poland had violated by accepting the guarantee. He did not realize that Hitler had no intention of increasing Poland's sense of self-importance by devoting a special public message to this matter. Hitler knew that the repudiation of the Pact would be a step of major importance which could scarcely be confined to an official communiqué and a few reports in the newspapers. This problem was unexpectedly resolved for Hitler by President Roosevelt. The American President responded to Bullitt's suggestion for an important move to influence American public opinion by committing a colossal diplomatic blunder, which played directly into Hitler's hands.

Roosevelt disclosed to the American public on April 14, 1939, the contents of telegrams to Mussolini and Hitler which were received in Rome and Berlin on the following day. Roosevelt sought to create the impression that Germany and Italy were exclusively responsible for every threat to European peace. He presented himself as an unselfish peacemaker, who had expended much thought and energy to devise a plan to remove the danger of war. This peace plan required Germany and Italy to declare that they would abstain from war under any and all circumstances for ten to twenty-five years, and to conclude non-aggression pacts with a large number of states, of which several had no independent existence other than in the imagination of the American President.[33]

The Roosevelt message met with a vigorous response in the German press. The German journalists wondered if the United States would agree not to attack Haiti or Santo Domingo within the next twenty-five years.[34] Joseph Goebbels addressed three questions to the American public on April 17, 1939. He wondered if they recognized that Roosevelt was similar to Woodrow Wilson in his desire to promote a permanent policy to American intervention throughout the world. He asked if the American people recognized that Roosevelt's recent message was a new maneuver to destroy the American neutrality laws, rather than to promote world peace. He inquired if they realized that Roosevelt had advocated a common American front with Bolshevism since his Chicago Quarantine speech in October 1937. The German press announced on April 17th that Hitler would answer President Roosevelt for the German people in a speech to the German Reichstag on April 28, 1939. This step had been agreed upon by Hitler and Ribbentrop in a special conference on the previous day.[35]

Hitler was presented with an opportunity to deal with the Poles as a secondary factor in a general situation. He planned to devote the greater part of his message on the Pact with Poland to a careful criticism of the American President and to a criticism of English policy. He also intended to abrogate the 1935 Anglo-German naval treaty. Hitler ordered the German press to abstain from criticizing the Poles during the period before he delivered his speech.

Marshal Goering was on a visit to Italy from April 14th until April 16, 1939. He had instructions from Hitler to discuss the total context of Italo-German relations. Ribbentrop was somewhat uneasy about the Goering official mission at this crucial stage when he was seeking to promote an Italo-German alliance. He was relieved to learn later that the Goering mission was completely successful.[36]

Goering discussed the Roosevelt telegrams with Mussolini and Ciano on April 16, 1939. He told Mussolini that it was difficult to avoid the impression that the American President was mentally ill. Mussolini criticized the factual text of the telegrams. It was ridiculous to request Germany and Italy to conclude non-aggression pacts with Palestine and Syria, which were British and French mandates rather than independent states. Mussolini was interested in improving Anglo-Italian relations, and he elected to react publicly to the American challenge in a minor key. A brief initial expression of indignation was followed by Mussolini's speech at Rome on April 29, 1939. The Italian leader merely denounced the alarmists who sought to disturb international relations, and he emphasized that Italy was peacefully preparing for the International Exposition in Rome scheduled for 1942. The privilege of delivering a detailed reply to the American President was left entirely to Hitler.[37]

The difficult situation between Germany and Poland was a touchy subject in the conversations between Goering and the Italian leaders. Goering did not attempt to minimize the seriousness of the situation, and he complained that "England had deviated from her old line . . . (and) now obliged herself in advance to render support (to Poland, Rumania, and Greece), and that under conditions which could be determined by the other partner." Mussolini declared that in the existing dangerous situation it was important for the Axis Powers to revert to passive policies for an indefinite period. This seemed to be the only way to cope with the warlike attitude of the British Government. Goering hoped that it would be possible to settle German differences with Poland by peaceful negotiation, and he predicted that Roosevelt would have little chance for re-election in 1940 if the basic European situation remained unchanged. He admitted that an increase in provocative Polish measures against Germany might force German action against Poland. It was evident that the problem of Poland had become the problem of Europe at this hour.[38]

Ribbentrop was encouraged by the Goering visit to press for a separate

Italo-German alliance. The first official discussion of such an alliance took place
in May 1938, when Hitler visited Italy. The original plan was to extend the anti-
Comintern Pact into an alliance by including the Japanese. It became
increasingly evident as time went on that the Japanese were unwilling to proceed
this far. The Japanese feared that such an alliance might involve them in
difficulties with Great Britain at a time when they were seriously committed
in China. The German and Italian attempts to mediate between Japan and
Nationalist China in 1938 were unsuccessful. Ribbentrop telephoned a last
special appeal to the Japanese for an alliance on April 26, 1939, by way of
German Ambassador Ott in Tokyo. The reply to this appeal was negative as
expected, and Ribbentrop proceeded to concentrate his efforts on a separate
Pact with the Italians. He knew that this was a difficult project, because many
Italians doubted the wisdom of an alliance connection with Germany. He also
knew that the Italian leaders might seek to impose reservations which would
deprive the alliance of its full effect.[39]

The Roosevelt message of April 15, 1939, was helpful to Ribbentrop in
improving German contacts with a number of countries. Ribbentrop also had the
satisfaction of knowing that the British were not pleased by the crudeness of the
Roosevelt telegrams. Sir George Ogilvie-Forbes, the British Chargé d'Affaires in
Berlin, declared quite candidly at the German Foreign Office on April 17, 1939,
that the British regarded Roosevelt's messages as "a clumsy piece of diplomacy."
Bullitt at Paris attempted to appease Roosevelt by placing the unsavory situation
in a positive light. He claimed that Daladier had been "encouraged" by the
latest move of the American President.[40]

Ribbentrop dispatched instructions on April 17, 1939, to the German envoys
in the countries named by President Roosevelt, with the exceptions of Great
Britain and France and their possessions, and Poland and Russia. The envoys
were to inquire if these countries believed themselves threatened, and if their
Governments had authorized President Roosevelt's plan. The German Government knew that they would receive negative answers to both questions, but in
coping with Roosevelt they required explicit confirmation of these
assumptions.

The British were actively pursuing their policy against Germany in the period
of the Roosevelt messages. Polish Ambassador Potworowski reported to Beck
from Stockholm on April 15, 1939, that the British were putting pressure on
Sweden to join them in blockading Germany during a future war. The Swedes
resented the British attempt to dictate their policy, but it was evident to Beck
that England was preparing her future blockade of Germany with single-minded
energy. Halifax was employing sphinx-like silence as a weapon against his critics
in the British House of Commons. He ignored charges that Poland and Rumania
would never permit Soviet troops to operate on their territory, and that the
guarantees extended to those countries rendered impossible a treaty with Russia.
Parliamentary Under-Secretary for Foreign Affairs Rab Butler refused to reply
to a direct question on April 18, 1939, about the role of Danzig in the British
guarantee to Poland. Only one speaker in the House of Commons contended
that Poland and Rumania alone had sufficient troops to cope successfully with
the Germans. The House as a whole found it quite impossible to accept such a
contention.[41]

Hitler's Assurances Accepted by Gafencu

Rumanian Foreign Minister Gafencu met Ribbentrop and Goering at Berlin on April 18, 1939. He was much impressed with the skill and ease of Ribbentrop in discussing difficult problems. The German Foreign Minister reminded Gafencu that he was in charge of the recent negotiation with Poland, and he attached decisive importance to the correction of existing abuses at Danzig and in the Polish Corridor. Goering was particularly concerned about the British attitude toward Germany. The Rumanian Foreign Minister agreed with him that the encirclement policy had definitely gained the upper hand in Great Britain. Gafencu hoped to modify this situation by revealing Hitler's willingness to discuss new arrangements on the Czech question with the British. Gafencu admitted to both Ribbentrop and Goering that he was unable to bring any encouraging news about the Polish attitude after his meeting with Beck.[42]

Gafencu met Hitler on April 19, 1939, and he was much impressed with the German Chancellor. He noted that Hitler's manner of speaking man-to-man immediately inspired his confidence, although Hitler made no attempt to convey an unusual impression. He found a magnetism in Hitler's words which conveyed moral inspiration and the aspirations of the mass of the German people. Gafencu was happy to speak with Hitler as a friend rather than an opponent, because "one does not speak with a man but with a million men." Gafencu opened the discussion with a lengthy recapitulation of his recent meeting with Beck. He tried to slant his remarks to create the impression with Hitler that Poland's intentions toward the Reich were still pacific in nature.

Hitler in reply greeted Gafencu as a representative from one of the succession states of the Habsburg Empire. The collapse of Austria-Hungary had brought large numbers of Rumanians beyond the old frontier under the rule of Bucharest. Hitler asserted that he would have intervened vigorously in the Habsburg-Serbian negotiations, which followed the murder of Franz Ferdinand and his wife by Serbian conspirators, had he been head of the German state in 1914. He added that he would have proposed the partition of the Dual Monarchy as the best means of avoiding a general war. He told Gafencu that Polish hopes for independence, and Serbian and Rumanian territorial aspirations, would have received unexpected support from Germany in 1914 had he determined German policy. Hitler's animosity toward the earlier Habsburg nationalities state had existed since his early youth, and there was no reason to suspect that he was insincere in making these statements.

Hitler asked if there was any truth in the charge that Rumania feared his intentions toward her were hostile. Gafencu replied that no Rumanian had any reason to believe that this was the case. Hitler criticized Beck for accepting the English guarantee, and he complained that he would "never be able to understand the change which has intervened in the attitude of Poland." He admitted that he intended to denounce Poland's policy toward Great Britain as an intolerable violation of the 1934 Pact. He said that he "would never have signed the accord under these conditions, (and) therefore I attach no more importance to this accord. I have shown the best intentions toward the Poland of Pilsudski. I have respected its frontiers and all the absurd arrangements of Versailles. I have prevented the press from protesting against the scandalous fashion in which the

German minority is treated." He contrasted the attacks against Germany in Polish journals with German restraint, and he produced for the Rumanian diplomat a bundle of Polish newspapers and magazines containing such attacks.[43]

Hitler admitted that he intended to make public the German proposals to Poland of October 24, 1938. He predicted that historians one day would recognize these proposals as "an act of unbelievable generosity," and not a one-sided proposition detrimental to Poland. He spoke of his fundamental policy of securing Anglo-German cooperation, and he insisted that frightful consequences would follow from any Anglo-German war. He noted with prophetic insight that "we would all, in the end, conquerors and conquered, lie under the same ruins; and the only one who would profit would be Moscow." Hitler noted that he was sometimes accused in Germany of being an impenitent admirer of the British Empire, and he admitted that this was true. He complained that only an inhuman fate would compel him to envisage a conflict with the British. Hitler added that he had been "a great Anglo-phile from his earliest youth."[44]

Gafencu received much inspiration from Hitler for his talks with the British, but he feared that things looked bad for Poland. He was convinced that no amount of Polish defiance would compel Hitler to abandon the German National Socialist community of Danzig. He hoped that at London he would find some sign of a willingness on the part of the British to revert to a moderate and helpful policy. This was unfortunately impossible with Halifax at the helm. The British Foreign Secretary was receiving with satisfaction a number of reports which indicated that Poland was increasing her war preparedness, and that the German people were not enthusiastic about Hitler's foreign policy.

Kennard reported from Warsaw on April 23, 1939, that the Poles were planning further mobilization measures, and Beck was requesting British financial assistance. This Polish *démarche* followed a conference at the Polish Foreign Office on April 21, 1939. Lipski, who was still in Warsaw, predicted that Hitler would disclose the points of the German offer to Poland in his speech to the German Reichstag. He believed that Hitler would place the chief emphasis of his remarks on Polish acceptance of the British guarantee. Lipski believed that it would be wise for Polish propaganda to anticipate this move, and to insist that Poland had desired to negotiate and had submitted counter-proposals.

Beck merely had contempt for the suggestion of his Ambassador. He argued that this would be equivalent to taking a defensive position, and that it would create the worst possible impression in Great Britain. He intended to do just the opposite. He would avoid words about the earlier negotiations with the Germans, and seek instead to increase the tempo of Polish military preparation. Jan Szembek was inclined to share the moderate views of Lipski. He mentioned that Hermann Goering had shown exceptional courtesy to his wife, Countess Isabelle Szembek, at San Remo in Italy a few days earlier. This courtesy amounted to a demonstration, because Goering at the time was accompanied by a group of the highest Italian military officers. Beck refused to attach any particular importance to such minor points of courtesy.[45]

Beck asserted to Kennard on April 23, 1939, that Ribbentrop was seeking to persuade Hitler to stiffen the German attitude toward Danzig, and that

EDWARD FREDERICK LINDLEY WOOD
Earl of Halifax
1881-1959

British Foreign Secretary 1938-1940;
Ambassador to the U.S. 1940-1946

NEVILE MEYRICK HENDERSON
1882-1942

British diplomat since 1905;
1935-1937 Ambassador to Argentina;
1937-1939 Ambassador to Germany.

SIR HOWARD WILLIAM KENNARD
1878-1953

British diplomat since 1901,
Ambassador to Poland 1935-1939
and to the Polish government-in-exile in Paris
and London 1939-1941

WILLIAM STRANG

Head of the German section of the
Foreign Office from 1937;
in favor of a British alliance with the
Soviet Union and the destruction of Germany;
in June 1939 unsuccessful negotiations
with Molotov in Moscow.

WILLIAM BULLITT
1891-1968

First American Ambassador to Moscow;
1936-1941 Ambassador to France and
Roosevelt's "Ambassador at large" in Europe

JOSEPH P. KENNEDY
1888-1969

One of Roosevelt's closest advisors after 1930;
1937-1940 U.S. Ambassador to Great Britain;
Father of President John F. Kennedy

COLONEL JOSEPH BECK (right)
1894-1944

Polish Foreign Minister 1932-1939; fled to Rumania
after Poland's defeat, where he was interned
and died of tuberculosis

JOSEPH LIPSKI (left)

Polish emissary and Ambassador to Berlin (1933-1939)

EDWARD RYDZ-SMIGLY
1886-1941

Polish Marshal and Pilsudski's closest collaborator;
1939 Commander-in-Chief of the Polish Army

Count Jan Szembek

Undersecretary of State, at Pilsudski's wish, in the Polish Foreign Ministry, yet without the moderating influence on Polish Foreign Minister Beck desired by Pilsudski.

COUNT JERZY POTOCKI

Polish Ambassador to Washington until 1939;
advocated an understanding with Germany

CARL JACOB BURCKHARDT

Professor of History in Geneva from 1932 on;
1937-1939 League of Nations High Commissioner in Danzig;
President of International Red Cross from 1939;
Ambassador to Paris 1945-1949

ROBERT COULONDRE

1936-1938 French ambassador to Moscow;
Ambassador to Germany from October 1938
to September 1939

ERNST BARON VON WEIZSAECKER
1882-1951

1938-1943 State Secretary in the Foreign Office;
member of the resistance against Hitler from 1933;
close cooperation with Italian Ambassador to
Germany Attolico

BERNARDO ATTOLICO
1880-1942

Italian Ambassador to Germany 1935-1940;
close cooperation with State Secretary
Baron V. Weizsaecker;
opposed to German-Italian cooperation

The Rumanian Ambassador in London, Virgil Tilea (left), in conversation with British Foreign Secretary Halifax. On March 17, 1939 Tilea, after an understanding with Halifax, deceitfully accused Germany of presenting an ultimatum to Rumania.

JOACHIM VON RIBBENTROP
1893-1946

1936-1938 Ambassador to Britain;
1938-1945 German Foreign Minister;
August 23, 1939 he signed the German-Soviet
Non-Aggression Pact in Moscow;
on October 16, 1946 hanged at Nuremberg

additional Polish military measures were therefore necessary. He wanted British financial support. He confided to Kennard that Hitler's offer to Poland was basically not unattractive, and that the British were fortunate that Poland had resisted German blandishments. He suspected that it was Germany's fundamental aim to enlist Poland in a crusade against the Soviet Union, and he noted that this might have separated Poland completely from the Western Powers. He failed to contemplate the possibility that British policy would lead to the creation of a Communist Poland which would have no friendly contacts with either Great Britain or France.

British Chargé d'Affaires Ogilvie-Forbes reported on the same day that the Germans were apathetic in the face of the latest crisis; they were saturated with crises and desired to be left in peace. He noted that there had been no unusual public enthusiasm on the occasion of Hitler's fiftieth birthday on April 20, 1939. This was true despite the fact that the largest troop parade in the history of Berlin had taken place on that day.[46]

Gafencu's Visit to London

Halifax was encouraged by the recent reports from Warsaw and Berlin, and he was looking forward to the arrival of Gafencu at London on April 24, 1939. He hoped to out-maneuver Beck by persuading the Rumanian diplomat to apply to the Soviet Union for protection against Germany. He had made it clear in advance that the Tilea hoax would not be accepted as a subject for discussion. Halifax had heard that Gafencu was a pleasant and attractive person with whom it was easy to negotiate.

The British Foreign Secretary experienced a series of unpleasant surprises. Gafencu refused to wear his harness in the Russian question, and he took the initiative in proposing a plan of his own for the solution of current European differences. Gafencu was touring Europe in April 1939 in the interest of conciliation rather than war. He believed that the chief obstacles to a settlement of European differences lay in Great Britain and Poland. He was receiving much encouragement and support from Germany for his peace plan, and he was prepared to present it in Great Britain with energy and vigor.

The British at the first conference on April 24, 1939, immediately raised the question of the extension of the Rumanian-Polish alliance against Germany. Gafencu expressed astonishment that the British adhered to this plan. Beck had made perfectly clear that it was unacceptable to Poland. He added for good measure that Rumania saw no reason to support this British plan. He informed the British that their plan conflicted with his own foreign policy, which included a program to improve Rumanian relations with Germany. He explained that this was especially necessary, since the elimination of Rumania's Czecho-Slovak ally had produced a bad effect on Rumanian public opinion, and it was undeniable that Germany had played an important role in Czech developments. He informed the British that he had placed special emphasis on this point in conversation with Goering at Berlin.

The Rumanian diplomat began to describe his discussion with Hitler. He spoke enthusiastically of the German Chancellor, and declared that he was "like a force of nature." Gafencu told the British that Hitler was also "very human." He pointed out that Hitler had not forgotten for a moment that his Rumanian guest was proceeding on to England. The German leader had said nearly everything with a British audience in mind. Above all, Hitler had successfully conveyed the impression to Gafencu that he was "incensed against Poland." Gafencu observed casually that he had criticized adversely a number of Hitler's remarks, but that the German Chancellor had invariably accepted this in good spirit. Gafencu confided to Halifax that he was now convinced the German-Polish situation was absolutely hopeless. He warned that Beck would order Poland to fight if the Germans touched Danzig. On the other hand, Hitler was understandably angry at the British for their Eastern European intervention, despite the Munich accord. This situation was dangerous for the peace of Europe, and it was necessary to arrange a solution of differences with all possible speed. Gafencu said that he had developed a plan which would meet the requirements of this ticklish situation.

The Rumanian Foreign Minister announced triumphantly that the German leaders were in complete agreement with his plan. This included a new Bohemian settlement, which could be devised in such a way as to reduce tension in other questions. It would pave the way for a general settlement. Gafencu then declared bluntly that the British should introduce negotiations by telling the Germans that all future concessions to them depended upon their willingness to make concessions at Prague.

Needless to say, Gafencu's British hosts did not like this proposition at all. The events at Prague in March 1939 had been one of the pretexts used by Halifax to make difficulties for Germany. He did not favor a new settlement at Prague which would extricate them from these difficulties. Halifax at once inquired "whether, as a matter of practical politics, M. Gafencu thought that it was likely the Germans would restore Prague." Gafencu replied that it was indeed likely, since he had the support of the German leaders for his peace plan. He made it painstakingly clear that he was not envisaging the overthrow of Slovakia, but he asserted that the Germans might be expected to permit the establishment of a different regime in Bohemia-Moravia. Sir Alexander Cadogan remarked acidly that "the restoration of Prague would hardly be a compensation to Poland." Gafencu assured Cadogan mildly that he was under no illusions himself on that score. On the other hand, it seemed to him that the Germans, at least as far as the Western Powers were concerned, would be entitled to consideration in Danzig and the Corridor if they made concessions in Bohemia. Gafencu hoped to anticipate further objections by adding that only the argument that Hitler was seeking a war could be raised against his plan.

Gafencu expressed his rejection of this argument in eloquent terms. He concluded by stating flatly to his hosts that "Hitler did not want war." Cadogan did not dispute this, but he made the banal comment that "men who must have successes were very dangerous." Gafencu responded with a further vigorous defense of his plan. He insisted that the world wished for some alternative to a hopeless deadlock. He believed that this desire could be met if the Germans were at least offered some proposition on which they could negotiate. Gafencu concluded, after this conversation, that he had failed to impress his British hosts with the need for keeping the peace.[47]

A further conversation took place the same afternoon at the Prime Minister's office in the House of Commons. Gafencu again presented Hitler's views. He mentioned that the German Chancellor had discussed the immediate origins of World War I, and that he had been very critical of German policy. Hitler had explained that he did not object to the Anglo-French guarantee of Rumania, provided, of course, that the Russians were not permitted to participate in it. Germany and Rumania were not immediate territorial neighbors, and there were no problems in German-Rumanian relations. Hitler had said that Great Britain, France, and Germany had a common interest in saving Europe, and that the Soviet Union was a great menace to Europe.

Chamberlain was not pleased by these remarks. He told Gafencu that Great Britain was determined to secure an alliance with the Soviet Union, and he argued that this move was necessary for the realization of genuine collective security. Gafencu retorted that the Soviet Union could not be a reliable member of a collective security front. The disagreement between Gafencu and the British leaders was profound, and the Rumanian Foreign Minister failed to influence Chamberlain and Halifax. A third and final meeting between Gafencu and the British leaders on April 25, 1939, failed to modify this situation. Halifax carefully refrained from confiding any detailed information about his next moves to his Rumanian guests.[48]

Hitler's Friendship with Yugoslavia

Yugoslav Foreign Minister Aleksander Cincar-Marković, Gafencu's Little Entente colleague, arrived in Berlin on April 25, 1939, at a very important time for the Yugoslavs, who were seeking German assurances of support against possible Italian pressure. This was a delicate matter from the standpoint of Italo-German relations, and Weizsaecker was annoyed that Belgrade had created the impression that German initiative was responsible for the visit. The initiative had actually come from Yugoslavia. The German capital was familiar territory to the Yugoslav diplomat. He had been Yugoslav Minister to Germany from 1935 to February 1939, when Prince Regent Paul had forced the resignation of the Stojadinović Government. Cincar-Marković was recalled to Belgrade to take the portfolio for foreign affairs in the new Government of Dragiša Cvetković. Cvetković was decidedly a lesser figure than Stojadinović, but the change did not indicate a new departure in Yugoslav foreign policy. Regent Paul emerged as the leading figure in the Yugoslav Government. Both Stojadinović and Regent Paul had favored a friendly policy toward Germany, and Cvetković and Cincar-Marković agreed to continue this policy.

Cincar-Marković explained to Ribbentrop on April 25, 1939, that Regent Paul had decided on a policy of close friendship with Germany at the time of the conclusion of the anti-Comintern Pact and the ideas which inspired it. But they feared that it would not be possible for the Yugoslav Government to adhere to the Pact in the immediate future because of public opinion in Yugoslavia.[40]

Hungarian territorial revisionism was one of the principal topics in the discussion between Cincar-Marković and Hitler on April 26, 1939. Hitler made no secret of the fact that he was dissatisfied with Hungary. Hitler was disgusted with the claim that Hungarian Premier Bela Imredy, who had advocated close cooperation with Germany, had been forced to resign on February 15, 1939, because it had been discovered that his ancestry was partly Jewish. Hitler assured Cincar-Marković that the real reason was that the big landowners in Hungary feared Imredy's reform program. It seemed to Hitler that almost any country in Europe was more progressive than Hungary. He claimed that the Germans of the Banat, which had been Hungarian territory before 1919, would rather remain in Yugoslavia than come under Hungarian rule again. He added that his interest in the German minorities had been a principal reason why he had protected Slovakia against Hungary. He told Cincar-Marković that the current arrangement for a German protectorate in Bohemia-Moravia was no necessity from the German standpoint. It was a provisional solution resulting from the recent crisis in that area. Hitler told the Yugoslav diplomat that there were no problems for Germany to settle in the West, South, South-East, or in any quarter other than Danzig and the Polish Corridor. He promised that Germany would oppose Hungarian expansion at Yugoslav expense, and that Italy would support Germany in this policy. Hitler referred contemptuously to the British policy of peddling territorial guarantees in South-Eastern Europe. He compared the British leaders to brush salesmen. The Yugoslav Foreign Minister was pleased with the assurances which he received from Hitler, and his visit was regarded at Belgrade as a great diplomatic success.[50]

Hitler's Reply to Roosevelt of April 28, 1939

British Ambassador Henderson appeared rather pessimistic when he called at the German Foreign Office on April 27, 1939. He had returned to Berlin the previous day, after having been compelled to remain forty days in England at the insistence of Halifax, who had waited until April 20, 1939, before announcing in the House of Lords that Henderson would soon return to Germany. Henderson admitted to Weizsaecker that he had suffered a great loss of prestige at the British Foreign Office. The reaction there toward the reports he had sent home before the March 1939 Czech crisis was distinctly negative. He complained that the task of defending recent German policy had been rendered difficult by Hitler's various earlier statements that he did not intend to seize purely Czech-populated territory. This situation was not changed by Hitler's willingness to negotiate about the current situation at Prague, because the British Government was unwilling to do so. Weizsaecker complained about the British guarantee to Poland, and he declared that it was "the means most calculated to encourage Polish subordinate authorities in their oppression of Germans there. Consequently it did not prevent, but on the contrary, provoked incidents in that country." Henderson submitted a formal statement about the British announcement of April 26, 1939, that peacetime military conscription had been established in Great Britain. The French leaders had requested the British to take this step as early as April 1938, and the German leaders had recognized for some time that the British were planning to introduce formal conscription to supplement the 1938 National Service Act. Weizsaecker told Henderson that the British note would receive formal acknowledgement, but that nothing would be done before Hitler's speech on the following day. He told Henderson that the text of Hitler's speech had gone to press. The printed text of the speech was delivered to the Diplomatic Corps in Berlin before Hitler addressed the Reichstag.[51]

Hitler had received considerable American advice for the preparation of his speech. Some of this had reached him by way of the American press, and the rest by means of private communication to the German Embassy in Washington, D.C. The German Government was especially grateful for the suggestion of General Hugh Johnson, who had administered the National Recovery Act for President Roosevelt. Hitler had received through Hans Thomsen, the German Charge d'Affaires in Washington, D.C., the detailed suggestions of General Johnson on April 24, 1939. Hans Dieckhoff, the last German Ambassador to the United States, had also made a number of suggestions. Dieckhoff worked at the German Foreign Office in Berlin after his permanent return from the United States in November 1938. He made no secret, in his conversations with the Diplomatic Corps at Berlin, about his fear of American intervention in the event of a new European war, and he expressed this concern in his suggestions to Hitler on April 25, 1939. He was convinced that President Roosevelt intended to invade Europe with powerful American forces in the course of any future war, and he added: "I do not believe that there are elements in the USA which have courage enough or are strong enough to prevent this." Hitler was impressed by this warning, but he continued to hope for American neutrality in any possible future European conflict.[52]

The German Foreign Office on April 27, 1939, completed the preparation of notes to be delivered at noon on April 28th in London and Warsaw. The notes announced German abrogation of the 1934 non-aggression Pact with Poland and of the 1935 Anglo-German Naval Pact. The note to the Poles, which contained a review of recent German-Polish difficulties, was more than twice the length of the note to London.[53]

Kennard surveyed the Polish scene for Halifax on April 26, 1939. He claimed that Poland might have fought Germany without British support, but he assured Halifax that the Poles after they received the British guarantee believed it was "absolutely fundamental" to fight Germany. The German note announcing the abrogation of the 1934 Pact with Poland was delivered at Warsaw early on the morning of April 28, 1939. Beck's immediate reaction was one of unbridled scorn. He noted that the Germans still envisaged the possibility of negotiation with Poland. He declared to his subordinates that Hitler was seeking to solve his problems by diplomacy, and he vowed that he would not permit Poland to be imposed upon in this way. Beck had anticipated Hitler's address on April 28th by persuading the Polish military authorities to declare a state of alert and danger of war for the Polish Navy based at Gdynia.[54]

French Ambassador Coulondre at Berlin discussed the situation with Lipski. The French Ambassador complained that the European scene was very confused, and that this was due in no small measure to the fact that the British in their diplomacy rushed abruptly from one extreme to another. Lipski described in detail the German offer for a settlement which Poland had rejected. Coulondre and Lipski agreed that the German offer was remarkably generous. Coulondre hoped to discover the true motive for Polish policy, but the Polish Ambassador merely mentioned that it was the avowed purpose of the Polish leaders never to be dependent on either Moscow or Berlin.[55]

The day of Hitler's greatest oratorical performance had arrived. The German Reichstag assembled on the morning of April 28, 1939, under the presidency of Marshal Hermann Goering. It received a good-humored speech from Hitler, which American Chargé d'Affaires Geist described as his "lighter vein of oratory." The Reichstag reciprocated this mood, and Geist noted that many of Hitler's remarks were received with "malicious laughter." The laughter seemed malicious to Geist because it was at the expense of the American President.[56]

Hitler carefully left the door of negotiation open toward both Great Britain and Poland. He made it clear that he intended to remain moderate in his future negotiations with these two states. He began his remarks by referring briefly to Roosevelt's telegram. He explained the German disillusionment in council diplomacy, which was the inevitable heritage of the deceitful mistreatment of Germany at Versailles. He had a formula which enabled Germany to participate in all negotiations with renewed confidence. This formula was a healthy determination to protect German national security. Hitler admitted that he did not believe Germany ever should negotiate again when she was helpless.

He analyzed and explained many of his principal domestic and foreign policies from 1933 until the German occupation of Prague in March 1939. He treated the prelude to the occupation of Prague at great length. He pointed out that deviations from the Munich conference program began at an early date. The Czechs and Hungarians in October 1938 appealed solely to Germany and Italy to mediate in their dispute although at Munich it had been decided that mediation was the obligation of the Four Powers.

Hitler placed special emphasis in the latter part of his speech on the failure of the United States to emerge from the world economic depression under Rooseveltian leadership. He announced that Germany was responding to Roosevelt's initiative of April 15, 1939, by proceeding to conclude non-aggression pacts with a number of neighboring states. But he ridiculed the idea of non-aggression pacts with states on different continents, or with so-called states which actually did not enjoy independence. Ridicule was Hitler's chief weapon, next to facts and statistics, in his reply to Roosevelt. He had been genuinely amused by Roosevelt's telegram, and he succeeded in avoiding the impression that he was personally angry with the American President. Hitler made it appear that Roosevelt's constant efforts to provoke him had been mere slaps at the water of the vast Atlantic ocean which separated the two countries.[57]

The German Chancellor paid glowing compliments to the British Empire, and he stressed his desire for permanent Anglo-German friendship. He revealed that he had decided with reluctance to abrogate the Anglo-German Naval Pact. He suggested that British resentment toward recent German foreign policy successes might have prompted the British leaders to select Poland as an obstacle to place against Germany.

Hitler devoted less than a tenth of his speech to Poland. He explained that he respected Polish maritime interests, and that this had prompted him to proceed with extreme moderation in the Corridor question. He praised Marshal Pilsudski for his desire to improve German-Polish relations. Hitler explained that in 1934 the two states had renounced war as an instrument of national policy in their relations. This was in accord with the terms of the Kellogg-Briand Pact of 1928. The pact had recognized one significant exception to this declaration on behalf of Poland. The Poles were allowed to maintain military obligations to France which were directed exclusively against Germany.

Hitler mentioned the many important questions which had not been settled either by the 1934 Pact or by his own efforts for a more comprehensive German-Polish agreement. He described in detail all the points of his offer for a general settlement with Poland. He declared that the Polish counter-proposals offered no basis for an agreement. They envisaged no change in the existing unsatis-factory situation with the exception of the suggestion to replace League authority at Danzig with a German-Polish guarantee. The German Chancellor regretted Poland's decision to call up troops against Germany, and to reject the German offer. He deplored Polish acceptance of the British guarantee. He announced that Germany was no longer willing to offer her October 1938 proposals as the basis for a settlement of differences with Poland. He explained that he was abrogating the 1934 Pact with Poland, which he had offered to extend for twenty-five years, because the Poles had violated it by accepting the British guarantee. He remarked that no non-aggression pact could survive a unilateral departure from its provisions by one of the contracting parties.

Hitler declared that the abrogation of the Pact did not mean that Germany would refuse to assume new contractual obligations toward Poland. He insisted that, on the contrary, "I can but welcome such an idea, provided, of course, that these arrangements are based on an absolutely clear obligation binding both parties in equal measure." Hitler avoided treating the Polish issue as the climax of his remarks. The principal theme throughout the speech was his reply to President Roosevelt, which he sub-divided into twenty-one principal points. He created the impression that such momentous decisions as the repudiation of important pacts with Great Britain and Poland were an anti-climax compared to his debate with the American President.

The immediate reaction to Hitler's speech in Poland was hostile, although French Ambassador Noël observed that Hitler was pressing for negotiations rather than closing the door.[58] The Polish Government announced that Beck soon would reply to Hitler in the Polish Sejm. *Polski Zbrojna* (*The Polish Army*) described Hitler's abrogation of the 1934 Pact as a tactical blunder. One Polish editor claimed that Hitler's speech gave the Polish press a moral basis to attack Germany without restraint. Wild rumors accompanied Hitler's announcement of his proposals to Poland. It was claimed in Warsaw that the Germans had demanded a superhighway corridor through Polish West Prussia over fifteen miles in width instead of the actual 5/8 mile. The *Gazeta Polska* claimed that Poland would have to go further in Danzig than she had done in the past. One million Polish soldiers under arms by the beginning of summer was considered a minimum necessity. The *Dziennik Narodowy* (National Daily), a National Democratic paper, asked whether or not Danzig really wished to return to the Reich. It was suggested that possibly a handful of Nazis in the Free City were making all the noise. A rumor circulated that Poland had decided to establish a protectorate in Danzig based on the model of Bohemia-Moravia. The *Kurjer Warszawski* (Warsaw Courier) expressed the general sentiment that Hitler would not ask anything of Poland if he were really a generous person.[59]

This time the German press retaliated. Joseph Goebbels had received permission to unshackle the press after the Reichstag speech. It was hoped that the German press, and an aroused German public opinion, would be effective weapons in inducing the Poles to negotiate under the less friendly circumstances which prevailed after the British guarantee. Goebbels himself began the campaign in *Der Angriff (The Assault)* with a commentary on the Polish press, entitled: "Do they know what they are doing?" The article was studded with citations, and its main thesis was that irresponsible Polish journalists were violating the precepts of Pilsudski. Hans Fritzsche, who was one of Goebbels' chief assistants in the newspaper compaign, later recalled that "each larger German newspaper had for quite some time an abundance of material on complaints of the Germans in Poland without the editors having had a chance to use this material." When the restrictions were removed, "their material now came forth with a bound."[60]

American Ambassador Bullitt at Paris refrained from reporting the reactions of Daladier and Bonnet to Hitler's speech, but he claimed that Secretary-General Alexis Léger at the French Foreign Office had denounced Hitler's oratory in sharp terms. The German Embassy in Paris reported on April 29, 1939, that the moderate tone of Hitler's speech had produced a reassuring effect on the French leaders. Chargé d'Affaires Theo Kordt also reported from London that Hitler's speech had produced a conciliatory effect in England. American Ambassador Biddle at Warsaw submitted a report to Washington, D.C., on April 28, 1939, which contained a tortuous attempt to square the circle in the face of Hitler's logic, and to support the Polish stand against Germany. German Chargé d'Affaires Thomsen reported the American press reaction to Hitler's speech on April 29, 1939. He expressed his personal fear that the Western countries would make an irresistible effort to produce a new World War out of the Danzig-Corridor problem. President Roosevelt read the English translation of Hitler's speech on April 28, 1939. Hitler's ridicule threw Roosevelt into a violent rage and produced undying hatred of Hitler personally. This personal factor was added to the other motives which prompted Roosevelt to desire the destruction of Germany. Roosevelt had been doing everything possible to promote war in Europe before Hitler's speech. Now his personal hatred of Hitler might cause him to make some mistake even more foolish than the telegrams of April 15, 1939, to Hitler and Mussolini. He did not have the support of the American public for his war policy, and it was possible that a few more blunders might lead to the total failure of his policy.[61]

Hitler's Peaceful Intentions Welcomed by Hungary

Hungarian Minister-President Paul Teleki and Hungarian Foreign Minister Istaván Csáky arrived in Berlin for a four day visit with the German leaders on April 29, 1939. Ribbentrop conferred with the Hungarian guests on the afternoon of April 29th. The German Foreign Minister was uncertain about the preservation of European peace, but he assured them that peace was desired by Germany, and that it was at least probable that a peaceful settlement of European difficulties could be achieved. He assumed that the Hungarians would stand with Germany and Italy in the event of a European conflict, and he was told by the Hungarian leaders that this assumption was correct. Ribbentrop sought to deprecate the possible role of the United States in a European conflict. The participants in the discussion knew that American military intervention had been the decisive factor in World War I, and that this had been disastrous for both Germany and Hungary. Ribbentrop predicted that the United States would refuse to send her soldiers into a new European war.

The German Foreign Minister emphasized the insignificance of Polish military strength, and he noted that Germany could win a quick victory over Poland in any conflict. Ribbentrop did not wish the Hungarians to believe that he considered their program of territorial revision as necessarily completed, but he suggested that they required time to consolidate their gains from Czechoslovakia. He urged Hungary to adopt conciliatory policies toward Yugoslavia and Rumania, but he was forced to conclude that Foreign Minister Csáky remained hostile toward both countries. It was evident that constant vigilance would be required to prevent the outbreak of a local conflict in the Balkans.[62]

The discussion had proceeded for more than an hour when the group was joined by Hitler, Hungarian Ambassador Doeme Sztójay, and German State Secretary Otto Meissner. Hitler jokingly told his guests that Germany and Hungary had come one step nearer to paradise in 1939. He was referring to the territories which the two countries had acquired in March 1939. Hitler hoped that it would be possible to solve the dispute with Poland peaceably. He observed that it was the honor of the soldier to serve by shedding his blood, but the glory of the politician to settle a dispute without recourse to bloodshed. "One must be prepared," Hitler said, "but the greatest merit in the eyes of history was to achieve success without having to resort to the last expedient."

Hitler discussed the importance of the United States and Russia in world affairs. He knew that the Hungarian leaders, who had experienced Communism in their own country, greatly feared the Soviet Union, and he hoped to reassure them. He spoke of "the colossal power of Russia in 1914 as compared with a weak Russia today." Hitler was convinced that the gigantic recent purges had reduced the strength of the Soviet colossus. Hitler spoke moderately about Poland, and he insisted that uninterrupted access to the sea was a vital and legitimate Polish requirement. He said that Europe needed a breathing space and a quiet period. He welcomed a period of protracted peace, and he was convinced that time was on the side of Germany and Italy. It was evident to his guests that he hoped to solve the Danzig dispute by diplomatic methods.

Beck's Chauvinistic Speech of May 5, 1939

Italian Ambassador Attolico informed Weizsaecker at the German Foreign Office on April 29, 1939, that Italy was willing to exert pressure on Poland for a reasonable settlement of German-Polish differences. The German State Secretary acknowledged this offer with gratitude, but he feared that an Italian *démarche* at Warsaw would be pointless. The Ciano visit of February 1939 had revealed that Italian prestige in Poland was very low. Beck was inclined to dismiss Italy contemptuously as a vassal state of Germany. The Hungarian leaders on May 1, 1939, repeated their earlier offer to mediate between Germany and Poland. Marshal Goering advocated the acceptance of this offer, but Ribbentrop favored its rejection. He noted that Gafencu had failed to influence the attitude of Beck in April 1939, and he did not believe that the Hungarians would be more successful.

The German Foreign Office was embarrassed a few days later by the *démarche* of Lithuanian Minister Skirpa. The Lithuanian diplomatic intervention was in a direction opposite to the Italian and Hungarian steps. Skirpa frankly stated that he regarded a German-Polish war as inevitable, and that he was instructed by his Government to request German support for the recovery of the ancient Lithuanian capital of Wilna from the Poles. He was told that friendly relations with Lithuania were of great importance to Germany, but that the German Reich was in no position to assume a commitment to Lithuania at Wilna.[63]

German Ambassador Moltke remained at Berlin during the first days of May 1939, but he returned to Warsaw on May 4th. Beck was scheduled to reply to Hitler's speech of April 28th on the following day. Józef Lipski, the Polish Ambassador to Germany, did not care to return to Berlin. He hoped that Hitler's abrogation of the 1934 Pact and the current press war between the two countries would motivate Beck to accept his resignation, which he had formally submitted on May 1, 1939. Lipski informed Beck that it was impossible for him to remain at Berlin under existing circumstances. Beck responding by ordering the unfortunate Polish diplomat to return to Berlin.

Beck was displeased by a visit of Professor Jan Kucharzewski to the Polish Foreign Office at this time. He knew that Kucharzewski, who had collaborated with Germany as a member of the Polish Regency Council in World War I, favored a German-Polish agreement. Kucharzewski was keenly aware of the Bolshevist threat to Poland, and he feared that a conflict with Germany would be permanently fatal to Poland. Kucharzewski claimed that British support to Poland was unreliable, and he solemnly announced that British Ambassador Kennard had informed him that it would be difficult to bring England into a German-Polish war over Danzig. Beck refused to accept this statement. Kennard was contacted and confronted with the exact day and hour of the alleged remark. The British Ambassador insisted that Professor Kucharzewski had presented a distorted version of his remarks. The attempt of Kucharzewski to moderate the response of Beck to Hitler was unsuccessful.[64]

The Poles received word on May 3, 1939, that Vyacheslav Molotov had succeeded Maxim Litvinov as Soviet Commissar for Foreign Affairs. Beck was not inclined to deduce important implications from this change. The initial reaction at the Polish Foreign Office was one of pleasure that the Polish-Jew Litvinov had been driven from his post. Neither Molotov nor Stalin was a Jew, although they were both married to Jewesses. It was known at Warsaw that Molotov was very close to Stalin, but the Poles had long since concluded that Joseph Stalin was the dominant force in the conduct of Soviet foreign policy.[65]

The Polish Foreign Office prepared for the Beck speech of May 5, 1939, by instructing its diplomatic missions throughout the world to criticize the Hitler speech of April 28, 1939. The diplomats were permitted to present the false claim that Hitler had attempted to enlist Poland for an invasion of the Soviet Union. The actual fact that Germany had invited Poland to join the anti-Comintern Pact was to be presented as a mild indication of the true scope of the German offer for collaboration against Russia. Beck wished to counteract repeated German references to the policy of Pilsudski. The Polish diplomats were empowered to inform foreign Governments that Pilsudski had always regarded an ultimate Polish-German war as inevitable. The emphasis on this Pilsudski prognosis from earlier days ignored the extraordinary flexibility which had characterized the policy of the deceased Marshal. Pilsudski had been dead for four years, and it was manifestly impossible to say what he would have done in the current situation.[66]

Beck had one central purpose in delivering his speech before the Polish Sejm on May 5, 1939. He wished to convince the Polish public and the world that he was able and willing to challenge Hitler. Beck knew that he was inaccurately accused of having been pro-German in his conduct of Polish policy. There was considerable excitement in Poland, and there was a danger that he might be assassinated by some hot-headed fanatic if he failed to produce the desired impression of unlimited defiance of Germany. He knew that Halifax had succeeded in creating a warlike atmosphere in Great Britain, and that it was completely unnecessary for him to take a moderate line toward Germany in the interest of appeasing British opinion. He could safely assume that he could go as far as he pleased without displeasing London. Beck wished to take an uncompromising attitude which would effectively close the door on further negotiations with Germany.

Beck prepared his speech with great care, and he was completely successful in creating the effect which he desired. The diplomatic loge was occupied to the last seat, press representatives were present from the entire world, and Premier Slawoj-Skladkowski and the entire Polish leadership were in attendance. Loudspeakers were placed throughout the streets of Warsaw for the first time, and thousands of ordinary Polish citizens were gathered about them to hear Beck's address.

The Polish Foreign Minister began his remarks with the observation that it had been many weeks (i.e. since March 12, 1939) since he had publicly discussed the foreign policy of Poland. He had withheld a declaration until the major problems had assumed their true shape and significance. He believed it safe to say that affairs had at last reached a decisive point. He wished to analyze the situation in relation to certain fundamental concepts of Polish policy. His Government favored contacts between states which were simple and direct. He personally favored bilateral pacts over multilateral treaties, and he welcomed this trend in the policies of states everywhere. He cited the Anglo-Polish agreement on British support to Poland as a successful example of this type of pact. Great Britain had agreed to fight for Poland, and Poland would support Great Britain in any conflict. He wished "Polish public opinion to know that I found, on the part of the British statesmen, not only a profound knowledge of the general political problems of Europe, but also an attitude towards our country such as permitted me to discuss all vital problems with frankness and confidence and without any reservations or doubts." He did not confide to the Sejm that he regarded the British proposal for an anti-German Polish-Rumanian alliance as a foolish plan. He did not admit that he had failed to convince the British leaders that Poland was justified in refusing the pro-Soviet alliance plan of Halifax. He did not confess his own misgivings over the British demand for Polish commitments to a number of lesser states. He did not concede that Poland was worried by British reluctance to provide extensive military supplies. In the upshot, he presented the Sejm with a distorted picture of current Anglo-Polish relations.[67]

Beck claimed that common Anglo-Polish interests rested on the solid foundation of a complete lack of aggressive intentions by either Power. This was an inversion of the facts, because Beck knew that the British were seeking a pretext to launch an assault on Germany, and that Poland welcomed the prospect of an Anglo-German war. He argued that the British guarantee to Poland had been used by Hitler without justification as a pretext to scrap the 1934 Pact. He alleged that the motive of Hitler was that the 1934 Pact had outlived its usefulness for Germany. This was another inversion. The fact was that Hitler placed great value on German-Polish cooperation and wished to improve the understanding begun by the Pact, whereas the Pact was no longer useful to Beck because the British were prepared at last to attack Germany. Beck failed to indicate why Hitler supposedly believed that the Pact was no longer useful. He claimed instead that Hitler had wantonly destroyed one of the pillars of European peace.

Beck declared sanctimoniously that it had been justifiable to conclude the Pact in 1934 because "an endeavor to oppose evil is always the best expression of political activity." This was unlimited hypocrisy. Beck was the willing accomplice of the British war policy, and war was undoubtedly the greatest evil of the modern age. Beck made the astonishing claim that Hitler had only press reports as the source of his knowledge about the British guarantee. This ignored the statements by the British leaders in Parliament, the official Anglo-Polish communiqué of April 6, 1939, and the conversations between German and Polish diplomats at Warsaw and Berlin on the same date. Beck claimed that Hitler's failure to consult with Great Britain and Poland about the motivation for their policy indicated insincerity and bad faith on the part of Hitler. This arrant nonsense was received with enthusiasm by the Sejm.

Beck mentioned that Poland had submitted a formal note in reply to Hitler's abrogation of the 1934 Pact. This note was presented to the German Foreign Office a few minutes before Beck began his speech. It claimed that Poland for years had sought to clarify Danzig difficulties caused by the role of the League of Nations. It claimed that Germany had evaded these efforts. The note contained a quotation from Hitler's speech of February 20, 1938, to the effect that Poland respected the German character of Danzig and Germany respected Polish economic rights at Danzig. Hitler had also claimed that cooperation between Germany and Poland had removed the poison from the atmosphere of German-Polish relations. The note added that Germany had first raised the Danzig question after the Munich conference. It was claimed that Germany had sought to impose a time limit on German-Polish negotiations about Danzig on March 21, 1939. This untrue charge was followed by the assertion that the British guarantee to Poland was compatible with the 1934 Pact. The Germans were warned that they would be held responsible for a violation of the 1928

Kellogg-Briand Pact if Anglo-German and Polish-German conflicts resulted from the dispute at Danzig.[68]

Beck made the astonishing claim that there was nothing extraordinary about the British guarantee to Poland. He described it as a normal step in the pursuit of friendly relations with a neighboring Power. This was in sharp contrast to the statement of Sir Alexander Cadogan to Joseph Kennedy, that the British guarantee was without precedent in the entire history of British foreign policy.

Beck spoke about Danzig with great feeling. He claimed that the Versailles treaty had restored normal conditions in the Baltic area by creating the Free City regime. He claimed that Polish supremacy at Danzig was the fulfillment of an ancient historical tradition. Beck considered that the 1919 peace treaty arrangements for Germany in the East were fair and just, and that Hitler had no justification to propose any changes. He intimated that Hitler's proposals were an artificial and sinister cover for different German aspirations. He found it necessary to ask the question: "What is the aim of it all?"

Beck made the false assertion that Danzig was free, and therefore not a legitimate object of German concern. He suggested that the prestige factor was involved, and that Germany was deliberately seeking to humiliate Poland. Beck claimed that Hitler was actually seeking to exclude Poland from the Baltic "from which Poland will not let herself be barred!" This remark was a deliberate falsehood. Beck knew perfectly well that Hitler respected and encouraged Polish maritime aspirations.

Beck declared proudly that he would talk about Pomorze (region by the sea, i.e. Polish West Prussia). He refused to use the word 'Corridor', because it "is an artificial invention, for it is an ancient Polish land, with an insignificant percentage of German colonists." One can only wonder at the temerity and disregard for historical accuracy of this remark. Polish West Prussia was colonized by Germans when it belonged to non-Polish West Slavic tribes and heathen Bo-russians, and there had never been a Polish settlement within the region before the coming of the Germans. The majority of the province was still German at the last pre-World War I census in 1910, although there had been a considerable infiltration by Polish settlers in recent years. The percentage of Poles in West Prussia in 1910 was considerably less than 35% and the Polish majority of 1939 was obtained by the ruthless expulsion of the German element, and by the arbitrary confiscation of German land. Hitler's generosity in agreeing to recognize permanent Polish rule over this ancient German territory received no recognition whatever from Beck. The Allied victors in 1919 naturally refused to allow a plebiscite in the region, because a German victory in such a plebiscite would have been inevitable. Beck made the ridiculous claim that the Polish Government had been amply generous in allowing for German facilities of transportation and communication through this area. He saw no necessity for concessions which would have provided adequate German transit facilities to East Prussia.

Beck claimed that Germany had not offered one real concession to Poland, but had merely presented demands. This was another inversion, because Hitler's October 1938 offer for a settlement was actually heavily slanted in favor of Poland. Polish Ambassador Lipski had conceded that only Hitler could have made such a generous offer. Beck denied these facts, and he proceeded to raise the crucial question of his speech: "Where is the reciprocity?" Beck claimed that various points of the October 1938 offer mentioned by Hitler on April 28, 1939, had never been made, and were merely irresponsible inventions of the German Chancellor. He was calling Hitler a liar for a speech in which there was not one single distortion of fact, whereas his own address was studded with impudent lies from beginning to end. Beck admitted that Hitler had offered to recognize the existing frontier of Poland, but he adopted a position unprecedented in European diplomatic annals by claiming that such guarantees were absolutely worthless.

Beck insisted ominously that Hitler had assaulted the fundamental honor of Poland with his proposals. This statement depended entirely on his distorted version of the actual facts. He explained that agreements between sovereign states had to be based on exchange. This was true, but Beck was wrong in arguing that Hitler had ignored this basic fact. Beck claimed that Hitler was seeking to degrade Poland into a mere vassal of Germany. He declared that defiance of Hitler was the minimum requirement of Polish honor. He added that "the motive for concluding such an agreement would be the word 'peace', which the Chancellor emphasized in his speech." Beck conceded that some people might prefer peace to national honor. He wished the Polish nation to know that "peace is a valuable and desirable thing. Our genereation, which has shed its blood in several wars, surely deserves a period of peace. But peace, like almost everything in this world, has its price, high but definable. We in Poland do not recognize the conception of 'peace at any price.' There is only one thing in the life of men, nations and States which is without price, and this is honor."[69]

The stirring climax of Beck's speech produced wild excitement in the Polish Sejm. Someone screamed hoarsely: "We do not need peace!," and pandemonium followed. Beck received a tremendous ovation when he finally descended from the tribune. He had made many Poles feel completely single-minded in their desire to fight Hitler. This feeling resulted from the ignorance which made it impossible for them to critize the countless flaws and falsehoods in Beck's oratory. The Polish Foreign Minister himself believed that he had successfully closed the door against further negotiation with the Germans.

Beck's contemptuous attitude toward his sudden personal popularity created some confusion in the evaluation of his true position.[70] The French and German diplomats at Warsaw discovered that Beck angrily tossed an entire sheaf of congratulatory telegrams into the wastebasket on May 6, 1939. This was supposed to prove that Beck was acting against his own will in defying Hitler. The opposite is true, because the Sejm speech by Beck was a triumph of the will. Beck personally was strongly attracted to the Germany of Hitler, and he never changed his attitude. He challenged Germany because he was obsessed with the fantastic notion that the destruction of Germany and Russia would be in the interest of Poland. Beck's speech was a victory of mind over heart, and it was a tragedy that Beck's thinking was distorted by illusions and false axioms. This did not change Beck's indignation toward the herd of Dmowski disciples and fanatics who had no feeling toward the Germans except blind hatred and rage. These were the people most emotional and enthusiastic about the Sejm speech, and Beck knew this perfectly well.[71]

There was a tremendous contrast between the speeches of Hitler and Beck.

The German Chancellor avoided giving the impression that Germany had been insulted by Poland, and there was no fanatical declaration about German honor having been compromised by Poland's rejection of the German offer. Hitler avoided any deviation from the facts in presenting his case. He knew that he could stand squarely on the record in presenting the German position. Hitler made it clear that he favored new negotiations with Poland. Beck used the national honor theme to preclude the possibility of a negotiated settlement.

Hitler received a critical analysis of the Beck speech from the German News Agency (DNB) on the evening of May 5, 1939. This report contained several important points. It was false of Beck to claim he did not know the full details of the German offer. Beck had concealed the friendly and peaceful nature of the German approach, and that the threat of war was introduced by Poland when she rejected the German plan. Beck failed to point out that the exception made for the Franco-Polish alliance in the 1934 Pact was limited and specific. It offered no justification for Polish acceptance of the British guarantee. It was inaccurate of Beck to claim that German diplomats were not available for discussions at any time after Beck returned from London. Beck himself had claimed that Polish interest in Danzig was exclusively economic in nature, and he had failed to explain that these considerations received full weight in Hitler's October 1938 offer. Beck admitted that Hitler offered to guarantee the Polish frontier, and this precluded a German attempt to exclude Poland from the Baltic. Hitler had offered to conclude a new Pact with Poland in his speech to the Reichstag. Beck claimed that this offer was not concrete, but this was not true, and Germany was prepared to discuss it with Poland at any time.[72]

Stanislaw Strzetelski, the Polish Conservative leader, later complained that the Polish nation was in a trance after Beck's claim that he was defending Polish national honor against Hitler. Strzetelski himself had sent one of the congratulatory telegrams to Beck, in an initial outburst of enthusiasm. He noted that the Polish nation, with the exception of a few individuals, had decided that it would be an excellent thing to fight the Germans. Strzetelski concluded after some reflection that this attitude was unrealistic, because Poland had not the slightest chance of victory in such a war.[73]

The Beck speech was a serious blow to the prospects for peace in Europe, and it was widely recognized as such. King Carol of Rumania concluded that the Beck speech had made war inevitable. He told German Minister Fabricius on May 6, 1939, that Rumania would remain neutral in the German-Polish war which he expected in the near future. He promised Fabricius that an event such as the ill-fated Rumanian military intervention against Austria-Hungary in 1916 would never be repeated.[74]

Weizsaecker attempted to discourage an alarmist attitude in his circular to the German diplomats abroad on May 6, 1939. He dismissed the Beck speech as an "insignificant pronouncement by a weak Government." He noted that Beck had displayed deplorable lapses of memory about German-Polish relations, and he admitted that the speech offered no help for an understanding. He conceded that it contained no echo whatever of Hitler's April 28, 1939, offer for an agreement with Poland.[75]

French Ambassador Noël at Warsaw hated Beck, and he misconstrued the import of Beck's speech. He claimed to Bonnet that the speech marked the collapse of Beck's earlier foreign policy. He mistakenly believed that Beck had delivered his speech with great reluctance under pressure from the other Polish leaders. British Ambassador Kennard had predicted that Beck would make a sharp speech, and he noted to Halifax after it was over that it would be interesting to evaluate its repercussions. The Polish press of all shades of opinion was proud of the performance of the Polish Foreign Minister. The Conservative *Czas (The Times)* presented an unconsciously ironical editorial on May 6, 1939, entitled "Contrast." It compared "the calm and reasonable speech" of Beck with the allegedly extremist and excitable speech of Hitler on April 28, 1939.[76]

Polish Intransigence Approved by Halifax

The situation between Germany and Poland had deteriorated rapidly during the brief span of six weeks from the Polish partial mobilization of March 23, 1939, to the Beck speech of May 5, 1939. American Ambassador Kennedy reported from London that the British were aware that Polish intransigence had increased since the British guarantee. He did not indicate that they expected or wished to combat this trend in any way. The Poles were inclined to dismiss people who were moderate toward Hitler as cowards. Polish Ambassador Raczynski went on a visit to Paris from London after the departure of Rumanian Foreign Minister Gafencu from the British capital. Raczynski told American Ambassador Bullitt that Gafencu had worked for a peaceful settlement at London merely because he was frightened of Hitler. Fear was considered to be the only motive which prompted certain diplomats to work for peace. Bullitt agreed with Raczynski and Lukasiewicz that Bonnet was the leader of the fight for peace in France, and he promised to do what he could to discredit the French Foreign Minister with Premier Daladier. He reported with satisfaction to President Roosevelt on May 6, 1939, that Daladier was allegedly increasingly distrustful of Bonnet. Bullitt hoped that Daladier would replace Bonnet with Champetier de Ribes, who advocated war. There was no chance that this would happen, but the report of Bullitt illustrates the optimism of the warmongers after the Beck speech.[77]

The German-Polish crisis had entered an acute phase. The Polish chauvinism incited by Beck produced numerous incidents which were an immediate menace to peace. The British leaders knew that Beck would not have adopted a position of provocative and uncompromising defiance without their blank check to Poland, but they refused to admit that they had any obligation to exert a moderating influence on Polish policy. They were inclined to encourage Polish intransigence in the hope that they would soon have the conflict which they required for their planned assault on Germany. Beck was their accomplice. They were displeased with his attitude toward the Soviet Union, but they applauded the tenacity with which he opposed Hitler's efforts to resume negotiations with the Poles. They had reason to be confident after May 5, 1939, that Poland would never negotiate with Germany again. They still had many problems to face in promoting war, but the Polish attitude toward Germany was not among them.

Chapter 16

BRITISH POLICY AND

POLISH ANTI-GERMAN INCIDENTS

Halifax's Threat to Destroy Germany

Germany was the deadly enemy of Poland according to the Beck speech of May 5, 1939. The Polish public received the impression that the German attitude precluded a peaceful settlement of German-Polish differences, and that war with Germany was inevitable. There were still more than one million citizens of German extraction in Poland at that time, and these people were the principal crisis victims during the following weeks. The British public was told again and again that the grievances of the German minority in Poland were largely imaginary. The average British citizen was completely unaware of the terror and fear of death which stalked these miserable people. Ultimately, many thousands of them paid for the crisis with their lives. They were among the first victims of the Halifax war policy.[1]

Halifax responded to the Beck speech by warning Germany officially that the British Empire would fight with the aim of destroying the third Reich whenever Hitler made an attempt to rescue Danzig from the clutches of Poland. British Ambassador Henderson delivered this threat at Berlin on May 15, 1939. The German Government had been aware for several days that this step was coming. The instructions to Henderson had been used previously by Halifax to intimidate Italy. The Italians informed German Ambassador Mackensen at Rome of the exact content of these instructions several days before the Henderson *démarche* at Berlin. This ominous British threat to destroy National Socialist Germany on behalf of the Poles reinforced a commitment which President Beneš had vainly attempted to secure for Czechoslovakia the previous year.[2]

The Terrified Germans of Poland

The leaders of the German minority in Poland repeatedly appealed to the Polish Government for mercy during this period. Senator Hasbach, the leader of the conservative German minority faction, made two public appeals for Polish moderation in March 1939. He argued that Poland would strengthen her political position and her cultural mission in the East with a better minority policy.[3] Dr. Rudolf Wiesner, the leader of the rival Young German Party, addressed an appeal to Premier Slawoj-Skladkowski from Bielitz, East Upper Silesia, on May 25, 1939. He complained about the current wave of mass arrests of the members of his organization, and he submitted a long list of individuals who had been arrested for no apparent reason. He informed the Premier that he was asking for protection on the basis of the loyal attitude of his group.[4]

The Central Office for the German Ethnic Community explained to Ribbentrop at Berlin on June 30, 1939, that most of the arrests were based on alleged insults to the Polish state. They cited a few typical examples. Georg Walter was sentenced to imprisonment for seven months at Toruń (Thorn) for having allegedly greeted a friend with "Heil Hitler!" The farmer, Kasimir Behrend, was sentenced at Konitz to imprisonment for six months because it was claimed that he had said Hitler should receive Danzig and West Prussia without war. The laborer, Erich Schiewe, was sentenced to imprisonment for six months at Czarnikau because allegedly he had criticized the economic depression in Poland. Heinrich Mroczkowski was severely beaten at Neustadt because he had been heard speaking German at a public place. The situation was such that no German could feel safe from possible denunciation and arrest. These measures might have found some excuse against a recalcitrant minority, but they were senseless when applied against the docile and thoroughly intimidated German minority in Poland.[5]

Polish Premier Slawoj-Skladkowski presided over the Department of Interior. The immediate responsibility for alleged security measures against the German minority rested with Interior Department Ministerial Director Waclaw Zyborski. He consented to discuss the situation on June 23, 1939, with Walther Kohnert, one of the leaders of the German minority at Bromberg. Zyborski admitted that the Germans of Poland found themselves in an unenviable situation. He claimed that Adolf Hitler was to blame for their plight, and that he had further damaged their prospects by abrogating the 1934 Pact with Poland. He criticized Hitler for his Danzig and East Prussian transit proposals, which were allegedly "demands without any foundation."

Zyborski claimed that the Poles in Germany were badly treated, and that the Germans in Poland were disloyal. Kohnert vigorously denied both charges. He suspected a fact, later confirmed, that German espionage agents in Poland were almost exclusively Jews and people of Polish stock. He pointed out that none of the persons mentioned as spies in the Polish press were of German ethnic origin. He hoped that the Poles in the Reich also were also largely excluded from Polish espionage operations. He knew that the situation of the Poles in Germany was favorable, and that reference to their lot was a poor excuse for the merciless persecution of Germans in Poland.

Zyborski flatly charged that Kohnert and his friends were under the influence of German National Socialism, and he argued that "you know as well as I do that National Socialism is no *Weltanschauung* (philosophical viewpoint), but a state concept." He cited a Polish proverb in accusing the German minority group of "lighting a candle for God (i.e. Poland), but also lighting a candle for the devil (i.e. Germany)." This was another way of saying that their loyalty to Poland was merely a pose. Zyborski added that the struggle which had been coming for a long time had arrived, and that he liked a struggle. He ended the lengthy conversation by stating frankly that his policy required a severe treatment of the German minority. He made it clear that there was no way in which the Germans of Poland could alleviate their hard fate. They were the helpless hostages of the Polish community and the Polish state.[6]

Rudolf Wiesner made another futile appeal to Premier Slawoj-Skladkowski on July 6, 1939. He referred to the waves of public violence against the Germans at Tomaszow near Lódz, May 13-15th, at Konstantynow, May 21-22nd, and at Pabianice, June 22-23, 1939. He protested the confiscation of the German Turnverein (sport club) hall at Pabianice on June 23rd. A Polish mob had attacked the building on the previous evening and destroyed many of its furnishings. The Polish flag was hoisted from the roof, and local Polish officials gave patriotic speeches to the mob within the building. The police confiscated the library of the club. An attack against the Pabianice German Gymnasium (secondary school) had resulted in property damage and the destruction of books. The local Young German Party Office had been attacked and destroyed. Similar attacks had taken place against the local Church Choir Club, the Baptist Church Hostel, and the Christian Trade Union. The Keil Bookshop had been attacked, and its stock of German books was completely destroyed. Wiesner noted that this was the third major outrage of its kind within the Lódz district in a matter of weeks, and he had waited in vain for disciplinary action against the offenders. Wiesner was directing his report on the affair at Pabianice to the highest Polish authority in the hope that he would receive an assurance about disciplinary action against future similar outrages. This hope was in vain, and the appeal of Wiesner produced no result. The leaders of the German political groups were forced to recognize that they possessed no influence with the Polish authorities despite their loyal attitudes toward Poland. It was "open season" on the Germans of Poland with the approval of the Polish state.[7]

The Polish authorities at this time were closing German business enterprises in Polish cities and confiscating a large number of community buildings owned by the Germans. It is for this reason that the property factor often came to the fore in the diplomatic exchanges, which consisted of Polish rejections of futile German protests. This did not change the fact that human suffering was the main feature of the situation. One need only imagine the scene at Pabianice on June 22, 1939, when the Bibles and old hymn books of the United Brethren fundamentalists were destroyed by a Polish mob. There was no way in which Germany could retaliate. Mob action against the Polish minority was impossible because of the impeccable atmosphere of public law and order in Germany. The single demonstration against the Jews in German cities on November 10, 1938, had been denounced throughout Germany, and it was obvious that nothing of this kind would ever be repeated. It was said that a Polish girl of sixteen could walk the streets of any German border city after midnight in complete safety, but a German woman of eighty-five was not safe on the streets of a Polish city at 2:00 in the afternoon.

The atmosphere of terror for the Germans in Poland continued unabated after the excesses in May 1939. Throughout the country the Germans were told: "If war comes you will all be hanged." Unfortunately, this prophecy was later fulfilled in many cases. The famous bloody Sunday in Toruń on September 3, 1939, was accompanied by similar massacres elsewhere which brought a tragic end to a long martyrdom for many people. This catastrophe was anticipated by many Germans during the long months before the outbreak of war. The Germans of Poland loved their native districts, but a point is reached when the most fanatical devotion to a particular landscape is overcome. This situation was reflected by the flight, or attempted escape, of increasing numbers of Germans. The feelings of these Germans were revealed by a desperate slogan: "Away from this hell, and back to the Reich!"[8]

Polish Dreams of Expansion

The outrages against the German minority were accompanied by a public campaign for the annexation of German territory to Poland. *Polska Zbrojna* (*The Polish Army*) on May 6, 1939, celebrated the rebirth of the Polish spirit of westward expansion from the 11th and 12th centuries. The *Illustrowany Kurjer* at Kraków claimed that an alleged 900,000 Poles in West Upper Silesia were suffering from German oppression. The Polish population expert, Józef Kisielewski, claimed that there were nearly two million Poles in France, and 870,000 Poles in the Soviet Union. The *Gazeta Polska* asserted on May 10, 1939, that East Prussia was becoming Polish in character because the Germans in the area were migrating to the West while the Polish population remained and multiplied. It was regarded as a misfortune for East Prussia that the area was still part of the German Reich. The *Kurjer Warszawski* on May 17, 1939, published a map which claimed that large stretches of German territory had sizable Polish minority populations. *Polska Zbrojna* suggested on May 27, 1939, that the outcome of the plebiscite in South East Prussia would have been different in 1920 had it not been for the Russo-Polish war in progress at that time, and for alleged German terror tactics. The *Kurjer Poznanski* claimed on June 11, 1939, that Jan Sobieski would have seized East Prussia as early as 1688 had he not been frustrated by the Polish nobility and by foreign policy difficulties. The *Illustrowany Kurjer* on June 29, 1939, criticized Lloyd George for the 1919 borders which were allegedly unfair to Poland, and it was suggested that future opportunities would permit the improvement of the Polish western frontier. It was evident that the Polish leaders had more attractive motives for war with Germany than the mere frustration of German aspirations at Danzig.[9]

Polish annexationist maps were posted along major thoroughfares in Polish cities. These maps were marked with Polish flags on German cities as far westward as Stettin. They often announced; "We are not looking for war! But, if war is forced on us, we shall take back the ancient Polish territory inhabited by Poles." Crowds would assemble around these large map placards to discuss "the new prospects thus opened up for Poland." The idea of expansion was not unwelcome to many citizens of a state which contained largely undeveloped national resources and millions of dissatisfied Ukrainians and White Russians.[10]

The Lódź Riots

The wave of riots in the Lódź area, which furnished the basis for the appeal of Wiesner to Premier Slawoj-Skladkowski, began on May 13, 1939. Tomaszow-Mazowiecki, the central point of the first riots, was a city of forty-two thousand inhabitants with a minority of three thousand Germans. Many Germans were injured and one woman was killed in two-day riots which damaged or destroyed most of the German property in the area. The Polish factory owners were compelled to discharge their German employees. A series of violent incidents took place during the same period in Poznań province and in East Upper Silesia.

Weizsaecker vainly appealed to Henderson and Coulondre at Berlin for the Western Powers to exert pressure on Poland to prevent the repetition of these outrages. Coulondre merely said that France was willing to advise the Poles in general terms to be cautious. Henderson admitted that he personally had no sympathy for Polish policy, but he warned Weizsaecker that German intervention in Poland would lead to the military defeat of Germany by Great Britain and France. Weizsaecker exclaimed scornfully that "the British guarantee to Poland was like offering sugar to an untrained child before it had learned to listen to reason!"

It was noted in Berlin that the German language press in Poland was not permitted to report incidents agsinst the German minority. The movements of German journalists in Poland were restricted after the opening of the press campaign in Germany against Polish excesses. The German Foreign Office concluded that their own consular representatives were the sole reliable source of news about the many anti-German incidents in Poland. The Poles were also aware of this situation, and an increasing number of German consular representatives was arrested during the following months. The German Foreign Office discussed anew the possibility of retaliating against the Polish minority in Germany, but it was decided on May 15, 1939, that this possibility should be rejected as harmful, futile, and unwise.[11]

The Germans were forced to conclude that attempts to arouse sympathy for the German minority in the West or to exert indirect pressure on Poland were ineffective. The only aternatives were direct intervention or passive acquiescence in the final elimination of the German minority. There were many indications that hostility toward Germany was increasing simultaneously in Great Britain and the United States. Chargé d'Affaires Thomsen sent word from Washington, D.C., on May 17, 1939, that President Roosevelt had told the Senate Military Affairs Committee that it would be a very good thing if both Hitler and Mussolini were assassinated. The situation in France was less unpromising. Ambassador Welczeck reported on May 20th that French Foreign Minister Bonnet had assured him on the previous day that he maintained his firm belief in the advantages of Franco-German cooperation. Bonnet declared that he was not folding his hands in his lap, and that he was working actively on a plan to preserve the peace. Official circles in the United States and Great Britain were more or less in step with Polish fanaticism, whereas France was obviously reluctant to go along with it.[12]

The Kalthof Murder

The Polish anti-German incidents of this period were not confined to the German minority in Poland. A crucial incident occurred at Kalthof on the territory of the Free City of Danzig near the East Prussian frontier on May 21, 1939. The arrogant behavior of the Polish customs inspectors at Kalthof had aroused the indignation of the local German inhabitants, who staged a protest demonstration on May 20th. The Polish customs authorities at Kalthof reported to the Polish High Commissioner's Office at 5:00 p.m. on May 20th that they feared an attack on Polish installations. Polish High Commissioner Chodacki was attending a social affair in Gdynia when this report arrived. Counselor Perkowski, the president of the Polish railroad company in Danzig, had been left in charge of affairs at the Polish High Commissioner's Office. He requested the Danzig police to intervene, and they agreed to deal with the trouble.

Perkowski decided later to conduct a personal investigation. He set out for Kalthof with an assistant, and with his chauffeur, Zygmunt Morawski, a former Polish soldier. The group discovered that the scene was quiet when they arrived at Kalthof, and that the Polish customs officials had gone to their homes.

Perkowski had ordered Zygmunt Morawski to remain in their automobile, which was parked several hundred yards from the customs house. The Polish driver left the bright lights on in the parked car. A Danzig car returning from East Prussia soon approached from the oppostie direction. The driver, Gruebnau, stopped to request the Polish car to turn down its lights. Morawski responded by killing Gruebnau with a shot from his pistol.

The incident itself would not have been so unusual had it not been for the incredible conduct of Polish High Commissioner Chodacki. He had been contacted at Gdynia and had returned to Danzig. A telephone call from Perkowski reported the murder of Gruebnau shortly after his arrival. Chodacki ordered the Poles to proceed to Tscew (Dirschau) on Polish territory, and to remain there until he gave them permission to return. Morawski had hurried to the Polish frontier on foot without waiting for these instructions. Perkowski and his assistant went to the railway station, which was near the customs house, and boarded a train for Poland. The murder of Gruebnau had taken place at 12:50 on the morning of May 21, 1939.

Chodacki presented a note to Danzig Senate President Greiser on May 21, 1939, in which he protested the German demonstration at Kalthof. He referred to the murder of Gruebnau without offering an apology. He demanded compensation for minor damages suffered by Polish installations. He claimed that the Danzig police were tardy in proceeding against the demonstrators, and that the Polish officials had received insufficient police protection. Greiser reminded Chodacki that the League of Nations, and not Poland, was the sovereign Power at Danzig, and he demanded that Perkowski, his assistant, and the Polish chauffeur return to Danzig for trial. Chodacki haughtily declined, and he was sustained in this action by Beck. It was obvious that the Poles in Danzig considered themselves above the law, and that they treated with contempt the effort of the Danzig authorities to exercise jurisdiction in the territory.[13]

Hitler was incensed by this incident in which an innocent German was killed on Danzig territory without Polish apologies of any kind. He sent a personal wreath to Gruebnau's funeral. Marshal Goering warned British Ambassador Henderson that Germany would soon intervene effectively in Danzig despite Polish and British opposition. Henderson replied sadly that the Poles would regard German intervention in Danzig as a threat to their independence, and that Great Britain would come to the immediate support of Poland with her entire armed forces. The Kalthof incident was discussed in the British Parliament on May 24, 1939. Chamberlain restricted his comment to the observation that a Danzig citizen had been killed, and that the League Committee of Three was investigating the affair. He did not claim that the League would undertake actual measures to deal with the incident.

The Danzigers responded to the Kalthof affair and other incidents by organizing small units of unofficial militia, reminiscent of the *Freikorps* (volunteer corps) German formations of the Napoleonic and Weimar Republic periods in Germany. Kennard claimed that nearly four thousand Danzigers were participating in this activity by the end of June 1939. Chodacki received support from Beck on June 5, 1939, to increase the number of Polish inspectors in military uniform at Danzig. He claimed that neither the League of Nations nor any other authority could limit Poland's freedom of action in this question.[14]

German Ambassador Moltke on May 23, 1939, responded to the increased tension between Germany and Poland by advocating the abandonment of the Danzigers by Germany. He claimed to have assurances that Józef Beck would renew conversations with the Germans if Hitler would permanently renounce Danzig. Moltke argued that Germany had made many other sacrifices of former German territory, and that Danzig was not worth a war. He was convinced that Great Britain would favor a German-Polish understanding following a definitive German retreat at Danzig.[15]

Moltke believed that peaceful relations with Poland were impossible unless Germany made all the concessions and recognized that Poland would make none. Hitler was convinced that friendly relations with Poland on this one-sided basis were an impossibility. It would be the same the other way around if Germany demanded the restoration of the 1914 frontier as the basis for an understanding with Poland. He refused to contemplate the possibility of abandoning the Danzig community. A Polish state which refused to contemplate the realization of legitimate German aspirations at Danzig could never be relied upon as a friendly neighbor. This view was shared by Pierre-Étienne Flandin, the former Premier of France. He told German Ambassador Welczeck on May 23, 1939, that a rigid Anglo-French policy in support of Poland at Danzig would be fatal for peace, and he complained that Germany and Italy were much more in favor of peace than the British leaders.[16]

League High Commissioner Burckhardt informed the Germans that Halifax had said at Geneva on May 21, 1939, that the British would fight for Poland in any German-Polish war regardless of the origins of the conflict. Burckhardt contradicted the position of Moltke by confiding to Ribbentrop at Berlin on June 1, 1939, that Józef Beck did not favor further diplomatic talks with

Germany. He had said, when pressed by Burckhardt, that he might be willing to consider new talks when conditions became more calm. It seemed obvious that this was a safe way of avoiding talks by confusing cause and effect.[17]

The Disastrous Kasprzycki Mission

Collaboration between the Anglo-French combination and the Poles remained surprisingly sterile during this period of excitement in Poland and at Danzig. Great Britain and France could have done many things for Poland in both the military and economic spheres had they really desired to do so. The Poles made every effort to secure effective cooperation with their Western Allies. They discovered that this was neither as easy nor as rewarding as had been their earlier dealings with the Germans.

Beck persuaded Bonnet in early May 1939 to negotiate with a special Polish mission at Paris. Lukasiewicz told Bonnet that Poland desired a new political protocol for the Franco-Polish alliance, which would tighten the French commitment to Poland. Beck wired Lukasiewicz on May 12, 1939, that the Polish Council of Ministers desired immediate action on a proposed 2 billion franc French loan to Poland. He added that General Tadeusz Kasprzycki would arrive in Paris on May 14th or 15th as the personal delegate of Marshal Smigly-Rydz for negotiations with the French military men. He wanted Bonnet to know that Poland wished to secure maximum coordination with France in her military effort against Germany. Beck informed Lukasiewicz that a French commitment to go to war on the Danzig issue was an absolute necessity. The French were under no obligation to do this, and Bonnet was opposed to assuming the commitment.

Lukasiewicz learned on May 13, 1939, that France was not prepared to advance Poland more than the 135 million francs provided by the Franco-Polish subsidy agreement of 1936. Daladier suggested that France might be willing to do more for Poland in 1940, but the Polish Ambassador, who expected war with Germany in 1939, did not believe that the French Premier was sincere in this offer. Lukasiewicz warned Daladier with some bitterness that the Germans in Paris were closely following this negotiation.

General Kasprzycki arrived at Paris on May 14, 1939. He explained to Lukasiewicz that he wished France to agree to a major offensive against Germany, with or without Italian participation in the war as the ally of Germany. He was instructed to confide that Poland was weak in artillery, and needed immediate French aid. Kasprzycki discovered with surprise and considerable suspicion, during the following few days, that the French military men promised him everything asked except the artillery. General Vuillemin, the French Air Force Commander, promised that French aircraft would operate from Polish bases in the event of war. General Gamelin, the French Army Commander-in-Chief, promised that France would concentrate her major military effort against Germany under all circumstances. The French military men promised on the second day of conferences that a heavy offensive to smash the German Siegfried line would be launched on the seventeenth day after

French mobilization. The French promised to employ nearly three quarters of the entire French Army in this operation.[19]

Bonnet was raising difficulties on the political sector by May 17, 1939. He claimed that Lujasiewicz was wrong in asserting that the British blank check to Poland contained a specific assurance that the British would fight for Poland at Danzig. The British had informed him that they had engaged in no political discussions with the Poles since the Beck visit, and that they had assumed no specific commitment at Danzig. This ignored the fact that the British had accepted repeated declarations by Beck that any German move at Danzig would constitute a threat to Polish independence. Bonnet claimed, without any real justification, that the Poles had said earlier that collaboration with the Soviet Union would be necessary after the outbreak of war, and he insisted on Poland assuming an immediate commitment to the Soviet Union in the interest of preventing. war. Bonnet hoped to make Beck's position of refusing to collaborate with the Russians appear preposterous.[20]

Daladier, Bonnet, Gamelin, Kasprzycki, and Lukasiewicz were among the prominent members of the special conference on May 17, 1939. The main problem was the question of the Danzig commitment. The French Cabinet had approved a formula on May 12, 1939, which excluded Danzig. Bonnet was obviously reluctant to accept the new protocol with the Danzig commitment, but the Poles hoped that he would eventually change his mind. They were not clearly informed that the French would refuse to regard military commitments as binding without the new political protocol. This protocol was never accepted by Bonnet in the period before the outbreak of World War II.[21]

The Poles admitted on May 17, 1939, that they did not have the necessary military supplies to resist the Germans successfully. They required immediate military aid from France and Great Britain. Daladier evaded the problem by claiming that the Soviet Union would be the most advantageous source of military supplies for Poland. Lukasiewicz and Kasprzycki warned the French that they never expected to receive aid in the form of war material from the Soviet Union. The new conditional French military commitment to Poland was forwarded to Warsaw on May 18, 1939, and approved the following day at both Warsaw and Paris. It provided that France would mobilize instantly upon the outbreak of war between Poland and Germany, and it stipulated that the major offensive against Germany could come on the fifteenth day of mobilization, which was two days earlier than the original French offer. The refusal of Bonnet to sign the political protocol with the Danzig commitment meant that France had not yet actually assumed new military obligations to Poland. The Poles elected to ignore this fact, and they continued to base their military planning on the disastrous and false assumption that there would be a major French offensive against Germany.[22]

Halifax's Refusal to Supply Poland

Colonel Adam Koc arrived in England at the head of an economic mission early in June 1939. Koc had founded the Polish OZON (Camp of National Unity), but his efforts on behalf of the new State Political Party were largely unsuccessful. General Stanislaw Skwarczynski succeeded to the leadership of OZON shortly after an unsuccessful attempt had been made to assassinate Colonel Koc. Koc was selected to lead the mission to England because of his expert knowledge of commerce and banking. He was known as an energetic and determined negotiator. He requested an immediate British grant of 60 million pounds for the   purchase of war material by Poland in foreign markets. The British suggested that they might grant Poland 8 million pounds provided that purchases were made exclusively on the British market.[23]

Koc sent Jan Wszelaki, the commercial counsellor at the Polish Embassy, to American Ambassador Kennedy with the request that the United States exert pressure on the British. Kennedy appeared to be well-informed about the situation, but he offered no encouragement. He promised to intercede with Halifax and Chamberlain, but he confided that the British and French were not inclined to share their war material with Poland. The Poles were discouraged by the apparent inability of the United States to use her influence in securing tangible advantages for them. This situation contrasted with the lavish promises of Bullitt to Lukasiewicz at Paris in the past. The conversation between Kennedy and Wszelaki took place on June 16, 1939. President Roosevelt boasted to French Minister of Education Jean Zay, on the same day, that he would have made trouble for Hitler at the Munich conference in 1938 had he been present at the head of an American delegation.[24]

Sir John Simon was in charge of British economic negotiations with the Poles, and Koc complained to Warsaw that he was unable to make any impression on him. Koc was stunned when Simon revealed that he intended to persuade the French to supply 40% of the niggardly 8 million pounds. Negotiations dragged throughout the summer, and Koc journeyed back and forth between Poland and England. Simon stubbornly refused to allow Poland to use any part of the British share of the credit for the purchase of other than British war material. In the up-shot, Poland received no war material on British credit before the out-break of war with Germany. Koc complained that the British were coldly indifferent to the desperate military plight of Poland.

The negotiations between the Poles and the Anglo-French combination were a complete failure from the standpoint of tangible results. The three Govern-ments were careful to conceal this fact from the public. The arrival of General Sir Edmund Ironside at Warsaw on July 17, 1939, received much publicity which was calculated to convince the public that military collaboration between Poland and the Western Powers was fruitful and successful. General Ironside was the Inspector-General of the British Army. Marshal Smigly-Rydz gave a rare special interview to the Warsaw correspondent of the English *News Chronicle* on the day Ironside arrived in Poland. The Polish Marshal declared that his country was prepared to fight even without allies if Germany touched Danzig. He added with special emphasis that Poland woud be fighting for her independence if she fought for her position at Danzig. He declared that every Polish man and woman of whatever age would be a soldier in the event of war.[25]

Ironside asked Beck on July 19, 1939, at a conference attended by Smigly-Rydz and Kennard, what Poland would do if Danzig proclaimed an *Anschluss* with Germany. Beck was evasive in his response to this hypothetical question. He stressed the need for Three Power unity in responding to the Germans, and he gave Ironside the impression that Poland would demand an explanation for any German action at Danzig before attacking Germany.

The Poles exhibited their bravery with reckless abandon at Polish Army maneuvers attended by General Ironside. The British Commander later noted with satisfaction that he "had seen a divisional attack-exercise under a live barrage, not without casualties." The British General privately disagreed with British policy in the question of credits to Poland, and he would have preferred to see the Poles receive effective and substantial aid. He agreed to describe the military preparedness of the Poles in glowing terms to the English public after his return to England. He claimed that the Polish Army was in fine condition, and that its morale was excellent. He did not stress the deplorable lack of modern military equipment which he had discovered in Poland.[26]

It was apparent behind the scenes that Great Britain and France had concluded that Poland was expendable, although General Gamelin hoped that the Poles in the event of war would be able to resist the Germans for several months and thus render impossible major German offensive against France in 1939. Sir William Strang visited Poland in May and June 1939 accompanied by Gladwyn Jebb, private secretary to Sir Alexander Cadogan. Strang, the chief of the Central Division of the British Foreign Office, had little sympathy for Poland. He believed that the Czech cause in 1938 was more worthy of support than the Polish cause in 1939. His critical attitude toward the Polish frontiers was more severe than that of Hitler, and he considered that these frontiers were "over-extended."

Strang personally believed that a close alliance between Great Britain and the Soviet Union would be worthwhile even if it was concluded at the expense of Poland. He was inclined to subordinate every other consideration to the destruction of Germany. He believed that "Europe had to expel the foul infection of Nazism from her system," and that war was the best means to accomplish this objective. The purpose of his mission was to confirm the hope that Poland would be willing to foment this allegedly necessary conflict with the Germans. He was quite content to envisage the prospect that Poland herself, despite her sacrifices, would emerge from such a conflict with diminished territory.[27]

Halifax's Contempt for the Pact of Steel

Halifax continued to pursue the objective of isolating Germany and obtaining the greatest possible number of allies for Great Britain. A British alliance with the Soviet Union was his principal objective after the guarantee to Poland, but he did not lose sight of the position of Italy. Halifax refused to be discouraged by the conclusion of a formal alliance between Germany and Italy at Berlin on May 22, 1939. He regarded Mussolini's step in concluding the alliance as a logical reply to the Britsh guarantees to Rumania and Greece, but he had reason to believe that the Italian commitment to Germany was conditional on the preservation of peace, and that it would be possible to separate Italy and Germany in the event of war. The Pact of Steel, as the new Italo-German alliance was called, demanded publicly that the two nations stand together whenever one of them, despite peaceful intentions, became involved in a conflict.[28]

Halifax knew that the Germans and Italians had exchanged assurances, prior to the signing of the Pact, that they would seek to avoid every conflict. Ciano and Ribbentrop had carefully arranged the details of the treaty in conferences at Milan on May 6-7, 1939. It was agreed that neither Germany nor Italy was prepared for a major war, and that it was in the interest of the two Powers to avoid a conflict. The Germans promised the Italians that they had no ambitions in the Mediterranean area. Mussolini approved the text of the treaty on May 17, 1939. Halifax was aware, when the Pact was signed in Berlin, that this fair-weather alliance need not imply that Great Britain would have to contend with Italian participation in an Anglo-German war. Halifax knew that Mussolini hoped to repeat, in 1939, his successful performance as mediator in 1938 between the contending factions. The role of Mussolini as mediator worried Halifax more than the possibility that Italy would become involved in war.[29]

The Germans received an important assurance on June 7, 1939, that they had no reason to worry about the policy of Turkey, the old ally of Germany in World War I. The British and Turks had concluded a mutual aid Pact for the Eastern Mediterranean on May 12, 1939, which was reminiscent of the British-Triple Alliance Mediterranean *status quo* agreement of 1887. The Germans were worried about an ominous article in the Pact which provided that Great Britain and Turkey were to be allies in any disputes in which either of them became involved. German Ambassador Papen was instructed to obtain clarification about the Turkish attitude. He was able to report on June 7, 1939, that Turkey would not intervene against Germany if the British attacked Germany in response to a German-Polish conflict. He had received this categorical assurance from President Inönü. The Turkish President added that his policy of alignment with the British was directed solely against Italy. It did not apply to Germany.[30]

Wohlthat's Futile London Conversations

There was unfounded speculation during the early summer of 1939 that Great Britain and Germany might settle their differences despite the conflict of interests between Germany and Poland. The German Foreign Office sent Adam von Trott zu Solz, a former German Rhodes scholar, on a special fact-finding mission to England from June 1-8, 1939. Trott spent a week-end at Cliveden as the only German among thirty guests, including Halifax and Philip Kerr, Lord Lothian. It was known at this time that Lothian, who had undertaken an important propaganda mission to the United States early in 1939, was scheduled to succeed Sir Ronald Lindsay as British Ambassador at Washington, D.C. Trott discovered that Lothian and Halifax were not in complete agreement, and that Lothian still hoped for peace. Trott discussed Anglo-German relations with Halifax for three hours, and he concluded that Halifax, in contrast to Lothian, accepted the inevitability of an Anglo-German war. The British Foreign Secretary assurd Trott with pride that the British public had arrived at an "emotional readiness for war." He obviously derived special satisfaction from this claim. He declared that "British confidence in German sincerity" had lessened "after Munich." He did not follow the official British propaganda line that German policy during the March 1939 Slovak crisis had been the decisive factor in creating the alleged official British distrust of Hitler. Trott noted tha that Lord Astor, who declared frankly that Hitler was a truly great man, was saddened by the apparently hopeless situation produced by the Halifax policy.

Trott conferred with Prime Minister Chamberlain on June 8, 1939. He noted that Chamberlain, in addition to Lothian and Astor, was more moderate about Germany than Halifax, but he was unable to conclude that this fact held out any hope for the future. Chamberlain confided that the extension of the British guarantee to Poland on March 31, 1939, had been personally displeasing to him, although he blamed Hitler for this British move. He gave the impression that Halifax was completely in charge of British policy, and that his own attitude was one of fatalism and resignation.[31]

The Trott mission to England did not receive newspaper publicity, but there was wild speculation about the visit of Helmuth Wohlthat to England the following month. Dr. Wohlthat, who had conducted the German trade mission to Rumania in March 1939, was known to be a close friend of Hjalmar Schacht, who maintained important contacts with British financial and official circles. Newspapers in Great Britain, France, and the United States claimed that Wohlthat, in his capacity as Commissioner of the German Four Year Plan, hoped to conclude a gigantic financial deal with Great Britain. It was asserted that Wohlthat's presence in England, as a delegate to the London international whaling conference, was a mere blind to conceal the true purpose of his mission. It was not surprising that these rumors produced a strong impact on the Poles, at a time when British financial recalcitrance blocked substantial foreign aid to Poland. Halifax noted with cool detachment on July 17, 1939, that Polish Ambassador Raczynski "Was distressed to the point of incoherence."[32]

Wohlthat signed the 1939 international whaling agreement for Germany on July 21, 1939. The *Daily Telegraph* and the *News Chronicle* continued to assert during his visit that Great Britain had offered a substantial loan to Germany. The climax came on July 23, 1939, when the *Sunday Times* (an entirely different newspaper from the London *Times*) asserted that Wohlthat had rejected a sensational British proposal for an Anglo-German understanding. Chamberlain issued an official *dementi* in Parliament on July 24, 1939, but speculation continued unabated about the alleged major importance of the Wohlthat visit.[33]

There were conversations between Wohlthat and the British leaders, and German Ambassador Dirksen hoped that the British would make an acceptable proposal for a settlement of Anglo-German differences.[34] This hope was destroyed by the recalcitrant British attitude. The conciliatory attitude of Sir Horace Wilson, the personal assistant of Prime Minister Chamberlain, aroused false hopes. Wohlthat and Wilson engaged in a rather meaningless general conversation at the British Foreign Office on July 18, 1939. The principal English spokesman in these negotiations at London was Secretary Sir Robert Hudson of the British Department of Overseas Trade. Hudson declared flatly on July 20, 1939, that Great Britain would never return any of the former German colonies to the Reich. Wohlthat was startled by this categorical statement because Hitler had no intention of pressing for the return of the former German colonies. He asked Hudson why the British "were forming an allied front in the East."

Hudson replied that "we expected to win if war broke out but we were anxious to secure that result as speedily and as certainly as possible." Hudson noted that Wohlthat "made rather a face at this."

Wohlthat asked Hudson why Great Britain was opposed to a strong Germany. Hudson responded with the usual explanation "that it had always been this country's policy never to allow any continental power to secure military preponderance in Europe." Hudson agreed that Anglo-German economic cooperation would result in mutual prosperity, but he insisted that Great Britain would not cooperate unless Hitler abandoned German aspirations at Danzig.[35]

Wohlthat submitted his report to the German Foreign Office on July 24, 1939, after his return to Germany. He pointed out that his meetings with Hudson and Wilson were promoted by German Ambassador Dirksen, and that the formal initiative for the meetings was taken by his British hosts. Wohlthat emphasized that he was fully aware of the rapid deterioration of Anglo-German relations. He noted that Chamberlain had stated publicly on July 10, 1939, (actually July 1st) that the *status quo* at Danzig was just and fair, and that German aspirations there were unjustifiable. Wohlthat knew that this position was contrary to the bulk of articulate comment on the Danzig question in Great Britain during recent years. He also knew that Halifax was using the balance of power theory to justify British hostility toward Germany.

Wohlthat believed that his conversations at London had thrown new light on British attitudes. There were those who believed that war was inevitable, but there were men like Horace Wilson who hoped that Halifax's pursuit of the balance of power policy would not necessarily lead to war. The tragedy of this situation was that ultimate decisions rested with Halifax. Wilson in the meantime rationalized his own attitude by claiming that Halifax would do everything humanly possible to keep the peace. This faith in Halifax led men who ostensibly opposed war to justify the war that might occur rather than to oppose its outbreak.

Wilson admitted that the British had attended the Munich conference merely because they were not prepared for war at that time. He added that the British now considered themselves ready for war. This meant that chances for conciliation were reduced rather than increased by British military preparations. Wilson boasted that British readiness for war was much greater than was realized either by Germany or the British public.

Wilson conceded that Hitler hoped to avoid a World War over Danzig. He hoped that Hitler would draw the logical conclusion that he could not simultaneously hope to have Danzig and to avoid such a war. The only solution was Hitler's abandonment of Danzig. Wilson professed to believe that an Anglo-German understanding could be achieved if Hitler renounced further foreign policy objectives and accepted the *status quo* at every point. Wilson believed that bilateral negotiations between Great Britain and Germany would be more successful than Four Power negotiations which included Italy and France. He wished Hitler to pledge himself to a policy of non-aggression toward all nations of the world. He believed that the question of the former German colonies should be evaded. He hoped that it would be possible to reduce armaments, and to conclude a profitable trade agreement. He wished Germany to collaborate with Great Britain in financial questions, and to abandon her barter trade policy.

Wohlthat noted that Hudson was more explicit than Wilson about the colonial question. The British Trade Secretary confided that the British Government did not wish Germany to recover any colonial territory. He spoke vaguely of a possible "colonial condominium" which would enable the British to keep watch over any German activities permitted overseas.

Wohlthat reported that Sir Joseph Ball, the Director of the Research Department of the Conservative Party, suggested that Chamberlain might call national elections for November 14, 1939, if Hitler retreated at Danzig. The British leaders made it clear on every occasion that they would not consider an understanding with Germany unless Hitler conceded an Anglo-Polish diplomatic triumph at Danzig. Hitler and Ribbentrop believed that such a retreat would be a disaster for Germany, and would fail to resolve the conflict in German-Polish relations. The British might be expected to support Poland against Germany in the resulting hopeless situation. Hitler suspected that the British were aware that he could not possibly accept their terms, and that the entire negotiation was an elaborate British attempt to split and confuse the German diplomats. Ribbentrop was particularly disgusted with Dirksen, and he believed that the German Ambassador had become the unwitting dupe of British policy.

This impression was confirmed for Ribbentrop by a report from Dirksen on July 24, 1939. Dirksen claimed that a responsible minority of British leaders continued to favor a peaceful settlement with Germany. He did not know if the British were sincere about an agreement during the recent negotiation, but he believed that Hitler's willingness to abandon Danzig might force their hand. He suggested that this step might enable the British Government "to feel strong enough" to acquaint the British public with Germany's desire to reach an agreement. This statement conveyed an almost pathetic acceptance of Halifax's clever propaganda argument that he was the mere prisoner of larger events. Dirksen believed that the British leaders might cooperate in reducing German-Polish tension if Hitler accepted the Polish position at Danzig and in the Corridor transit question. He plaintively concluded that an agreement with the British was a far more worthwhile objective than a new war. This statement reveals the full extent to which he had become the prisoner of British propaganda. He was suggesting that the failure of Hitler to accept the British terms would mean that war was the actual objective of Hitler's policy.[36]

It was obvious to Ribbentrop that Dirksen's usefulness at London was nearly over. The German Ambassador was no longer a reliable representative of German interests. Ribbentrop had suggested as early as July 14, 1939, that he would like to discuss the current situation with Dirksen when the latter came home in August on leave. The Wohlthat episode caused him to wonder if this would be worthwhile. He was especially annoyed because Dirksen failed to submit a detailed report about the conversations between Wohlthat and the British leaders. Wohlthat admitted that he had gone over each conversation with Dirksen at London. Wohlthat was not a diplomat, and his report lacked the analytical substance which one could expect from a German Ambassador at London. Ribbentrop on July 31, 1939, finally demanded a detailed report from Dirksen, and the German Ambassador complied the same day.

The Dirksen report of July 31, 1939, contained the odd assertion that the talks between Wohlthat and the British leaders were not primarily political in nature. This was directly contrary to the substance of Wohlthat's report. Dirksen claimed that Wohlthat had adopted a "purely receptive" attitude during the conversations. He had refused an offer from Wilson to have the British proposals confirmed by Chamberlain, because this would not be "within his province" as German delegate to a whaling convention. Ribbentrop could not fail to note that this was an odd place to draw the line after Wohlthat and Dirksen had agreed to the talks in the first instance. Dirksen failed to offer the careful recapitulation of the talks which Ribbentrop had requested.[37]

Weizsaecker informed Dirksen on July 31, 1939, that Marshal Goering had read the Wohlthat report before Ribbentrop received it. It was understandable that Ribbentrop was annoyed, that as German Foreign Minister he was not the first person to learn of important political conversations at London. Weizsaecker complained to Dirksen that Wohlthat had apparently failed to ask the obvious question about the connection between the British proposals to Germany and the current British negotiations at Moscow. The Wohlthat report did not indicate what effect, if any, successful Anglo-German negotiations would have on British efforts to enlist the Soviet Union in an encirclement front against Germany. Weizsaecker insisted that Dirksen should send Ribbentrop a detailed report on these matters as quickly as possible.

Dirksen submitted a second disappointing report on August 1, 1939. He claimed that a question from Wohlthat about the British encirclement policy would not have been consistent with the purely receptive attitude he had advised Wohlthat to assume. This raised the question of whether or not conversations in the proper sense of dyadic communication had actually taken place. Dirksen had the "impression" that the British had sought to be constructive in their contacts with Wohlthat. He referred vaguely to the desirability of a solution of the Danzig question, but he failed to analyze the implications of a German retreat at Danzig. He expressed no firm opinion about the actual possibilities for an agreement with the British. He claimed that the private report of General Ironside about the military situation of Poland might encourage a British desire for an understanding, because the report had been "not too favorable." He failed to note that a confidential report about Poland by a British general familiar with modern warfare could scarcely have been "extremely favorable." The value of the Dirksen reports about the Wohlthat conversations was merely negative. It confirmed the impression that the British had offered no terms for a settlement short of the abandonment of Danzig by Hitler. This was the decisive point, because Hitler had no intention of retreating at Danzig.[38]

Polish Provocations at Danzig

The absence of fruitful negotiations between Great Britain and Germany was matched by the relative unimportance of the treaties concluded by the two countries during these months. There was no noticeable change in the existing balance of forces, and nothing was done by Great Britain and France to remedy the military unpreparedness of the Poles. The new wave of Polish excesses against the German minority in Poland, after the Beck speech, infuriated

Germany without impressing the British leaders, who were aware of them, or the British public, which was uninformed. The failure of the Poles to allow new negotiations produced a dreary diplomatic deadlock which was accepted with the utmost complacency by Halifax. The monotony was broken only by the sufferings of the Germans in Poland and the perpetual excitement at Danzig after the arrogant Polish behavior in response to the Kalthof affair. The Danzigers were convinced that Poland would show them no mercy if she were permitted to obtain the upper hand.

Tension mounted without halt at Danzig after the Kalthof incident. Senate President Greiser presented two notes of protest to the Poles on June 3, 1939. One concerned Polish refusal to permit judicial proceedings against the Kalthof murderer, and the other dealt with the increase in the number of Polish customs inspectors on Danzig territory. Polish High Commissioner Chodacki ignored both protests.[39]

League High Commissioner Burckhardt told Greiser on June 6, 1939, that Ribbentrop had made the German position at Danzig very clear in conversations at Berlin a few days earlier. Ribbentrop admitted that Germany would accept the risk of war to secure the liberation of Danzig. He also told Burckhardt that Germany continued to hope for a negotiated settlement with Poland. Greiser assured Burckhardt that the people of Danzig would prefer a peaceful solution. Burckhardt was about to return to Basel to receive an honorary degree, and Greiser urged him to come back to Danzig afterward with his wife and family as a personal gesture, which would indicate that he was confident peace would be preserved. The currently ambiguous position of Russia was discussed, and Burckhardt wisely predicted that the Soviet Union would avoid entangling alliances with either side in the Danzig dispute. Burckhardt was convinced that the Russians were delighted with the prospect of a suicidal internecine conflict in Western Europe.

The Polish authorities at Danzig announced on June 11, 1939, that further complaints from Danzig authorities about the conduct of their customs inspectors woud be inadmissable. They warned the Danzigers that they were planning a further increase in the number of inspectors, on the grounds that the crisis situation made it impossible for the existing force to carry out its tasks. Weizsaecker discussed the Danzig crisis with British Ambassador Henderson at Berlin on June 13, 1939. Henderson announced that the official Halifax line about the alleged need to encircle Germany remained unchanged. He added confidentially that he personally disagreed with the policy of Halifax. He considered that the British blank check to Poland was a great evil, and he opposed the conclusion of a military alliance between Great Britain and the Soviet Union. Henderson knew that he was exceeding his authority in making this statement to the German State Secretary, but he could not tolerate the thought that the Germans might suspect him of agreeing with Halifax's war policy. It was evident that he was not the man to represent Halifax at Berlin. He was incapable of accepting or of executing the neat rationalizations of such men as Sir Horace Wilson, Sir John Simon, and Sir Samuel Hoare.[40]

Joseph Goebbels challenged Polish intransigence at Danzig by delivering a defiant speech at the Danzig civic theatre on June 17, 1939. He was attending the Danzig Cultural Exposition, which commemorated the historical role of the

Baltic port. He announced in his speech that Danzig would return to the Reich, and he added, "the Reich takes no declarations of Polish chauvinists seriously." Chodacki retaliated on the following day. The Free City authorities had recently ordered the demolition of a Polish dwelling on Danzig territory which was in dangerous disrepair and violated local housing ordinances. The Polish authorities, in neighboring Tscew (Dirschau), had retaliated by ordering a local German mill owner to tear down his house. When Greiser expressed his indignation at this incident, they ordered the mill owner to demolish his mill. It had been assumed that this was an arbitrary action of local Polish authorities. Chodacki intervened on June 18, 1939, with the approval of Beck, and officially informed Danzig that "every official action undertaken by Danzig authorities against Polish property or Polish citizens will be followed by an official Polish announcement that a Czech legion to fight the Germans was being organized on Polish territory under General Lev Prchala, who had moved from Prague to Warsaw. Prchala announced in turn that he favored a federation of Czechs and Poles under Polish leadership. The Germans knew that there were very few Czechs willing to fight for Poland on these terms, but they were interested to learn that Polish federation ambitions now extended westward into the Czech area. It was obvious that the Poles would require the annexation of German Silesia to improve their contact with the Czechs.[41]

The *Gazeta Polska* replied to the speech of Goebbels on June 20, 1939. The public was assured that it was a well-known fact throughout the world that Poland would not retreat before German pressure at Danzig. The arguments of Goebbels in favor of the reunion of Danzig with Germany were rejected, and it was considered deplorable that German rule at Tilsit and Memel in East Prussia enabled Hitler to control the mouth of the "Polish-Lithuanian Niemen River." The Polish leaders were determined that Germany should never again control Danzig and the mouth of the Vistula River.[42]

German Ambassador Welczeck at Paris reported that he had discussed the latest Danzig incidents with French Foreign Minister Bonnet. He told Bonnet that Ribbentrop believed that German differences with Poland had to be resolved in 1939, and he was basing this statement on conversations with Ribbentrop at Berlin the previous month. The German Foreign Minister was intensely displeased with this report, and he denied that he ever had conveyed the impression of a time limit on the settlement of German-Polish differences. He ordered Welczeck on June 21, 1939, to refrain from discussing German policy with Bonnet until he received exact instructions from Berlin.[43]

Ribbentrop sent detailed instructions to Welczeck on June 30, 1939. He admitted that Germany had been seeking to apply pressure to Poland since the Hitler Reichstag speech of April 28, 1939. He insisted that Hitler's purpose was to persuade the Poles to adopt a reasonable attitude, and not to apply an ultimatum with a time limit or to give the impression that German terms for a settlement were unchangeable. Ribbentrop continued to hope that Beck would align himself with the moderate group of Poles who were willing to come to terms with Germany. He added that it was not clear whether the more moderate group or the extremists would dominate the situation. He instructed Welczeck to tell Bonnet that the sole danger to European peace was a possible Polish "Harakiri-policy," which would force Germany to act. He admitted that it would be difficult to postpone a Polish-German settlement indefinitely because of the tension involved.

Weizsaecker added a memorandum to the instructions of Ribbentrop, which was designed to modify the impression created by the German Foreign Minister. Weizsaecker claimed that it would be wrong for Welczeck to deny explicitly that a settlement with Poland was necessary in 1939. He also implied that he accepted the right of Welczeck to have made his previous statement to Bonnet. He merely told him to create the impression that his previous statement was no longer entirely *au courant*.

The incident illustrates the liberty frequently taken by Weizsaecker in modifying instructions from Ribbentrop to German diplomatic envoys abroad. Weizsaecker knew that Welczeck disliked Ribbentrop for his loyalty to the National Socialist system, and he knew that the German Ambassador at Paris would take full advantage of the opportunity given him to avoid retraction of his previous statement to Bonnet. The German ship-of-state had many would-be captains in 1939.[44]

The Danzig authorities continued to refuse total submission to Poland in the question of the customs inspectors. Two of the Polish inspectors were arrested in June 1939 on charges of illegal military activities. The Poles hoped to break Danzig resistance by an effective policy of retaliation. They terminated contacts between Danzigers and the German minority in Poland. They announced that the Germans of Poland would be denied permission to attend the Vistula Singing Festival at Danzig or the International Rowing Regatta. This was a severe reprisal against the many minority Germans who lived within a few miles of Danzig, and it was injurious to the business interests of the Danzigers.[45]

The small Polish population at Danzig enjoyed complete freedom of movement during this same period. The Polish Festival of the Sea was held at Gdynia from June 25-July 2, 1939. Budzynski, the Polish minority leader in the Danzig Volkstag, delivered a sensational speech at the festival. He assured his fellow Danzig Poles that the union of Danzig with Poland would be achieved by the Polish Army. The actual Day of the Sea in Poland, which was an annual holiday, came on June 29th. President Mościcki delivered a radio speech which was broadcast over all Polish stations. He stressed the economic importance of both Gdynia and Danzig to the Polish national economy, and he repeated the performance of Beck by ignoring the fact that Hitler always had promised full protection to Polish economic rights at Danzig. President Mościcki poetically described the Polish coast, which had formerly belonged to Germany, as the sun and the air of Polish national life. General Kwasniewski, the chairman of the Polish Naval and Colonial League, also delivered a speech. He claimed that Hitler, in seeking Danzig, was attempting to reduce Poland's position on the Baltic Sea. He ignored the network of railways which connected Gdynia with the Polish hinterland and claimed that the mouth of the Vistula River was Poland's natural access to the Baltic Sea. His speech contained a number of obvious hints that he favored Polish annexation of the so-called Free City.[46]

The Poles were furious with the defiance of Danzig in organizing her own militia for home defense. They blamed Hitler for this situation, which reminded them of the conflicts between the impromptu Sudeten volunteer corps and the Czechs in September 1938. The Polish Government protested to German

Ambassador Moltke on July 1, 1939, about the current military defense measures of the Danzig Government. They persuaded League High Commissioner Burckhardt to send a memorandum to Berlin on July 1st expressing concern about these measures. Burckhardt personally was not seriously alarmed by this situation, and he considered the Danzig defense measures understandable under the circumstances. On July 8, 1939, he told Viktor Boettcher, the chairman of the Danzig Senate Foreign Relations Committee, that the world was becoming tired of hearing about Danzig. He added that irresponsible rumors about alleged German action at Danzig were becoming less frequent.[47]

Senate President Greiser, who held a reserve commission in the German Navy, was absent from Danzig for several weeks in July on a training cruise. Danzig District Party Leader Albert Forster was in sole charge of Danzig policy in the interim period. He had visisted England the previous summer, and he was much impressed with British military power. He feared that a Danzig conflict would involve Germany in war with Great Britain, and he continued to hope for a peaceful settlement which would permit the return of Danzig to the Reich. He concentrated his principal efforts during the absence of Greiser on a stiff Danzig press campaign against Polish restrictions and provocations. He continued to hope that it would be possible to arouse sympathy abroad, and especially in England, in favor of Danzig's aspiration for self-determination.

Beck told French Ambassador Noël on July 6, 1939, that the Polish Government had decided that additional measures were necessary to meet the alleged threat from Danzig. Noël requested Beck to agree to consult with the Western Powers before taking drastic measures in the Free City. Beck refused to accept this commitment. He argued that he was not opposed to consultation in principle, but that the pressure of events might not permit him to consult with the Allies of Poland.[48]

Potocki's Effort to Change Polish Policy

Beck was faced at this time with several pleas from Polish diplomats for an understanding with Germany. Polish Ambassador Jerzy Potocki, who was on leave from the United States, discussed the situation with Beck at the Polish Foreign Office on July 6, 1939. He told Beck that he had returned to Poland with the express purpose of proposing a change in Polish policy. He complained that the United States and England were suffering from a severe war psychosis. There had been wild rumors on the ship which brought him to Europe that the Germans had occupied Danzig. He insisted that the Jews, the leading capitalists, and the armament manufacturers of the West were united in a solid front for war. They were delighted to find their pretext in the Danzig issue and in Poland's defiant attitude. Potocki added that the most repulsive factor was their complete and cold indifference to the destruction of Poland.

Potocki insisted that the Poles were merely negro slaves in the opinion of the Western profiteers. They were expected to work without receiving anything in return. He sought to appeal to Beck's vanity by claiming that the Polish Foreign Minister was the only man they feared in Poland. He argued that the United States, despite Roosevelt's fever for intervention in Europe, were actually concentrating their own imperialist drive on Latin America. He assured Beck that it would be sheer illusion to expect the United States to intervene in Europe on behalf of Poland. Potocki was forced to conclude that his eloquent arguments produced no effect on the Polish Foreign Minister.[49]

Polish Ambassador Sokolnicki at Ankara supported Potocki in this effort. He was a close friend of Jan Szembek, and it was evident to Potocki and Sokolnicki that Szembek would accept their position if he were Polish Foreign Minister. It seemed likely, too, that Pilsudski would have rejected the Beck policy had he been alive. Sokolnicki confided to German Ambassador Papen at Ankara on July 14, 1939, that he would like to see a negotiated settlement between Germany and Poland before the Jews and the Free Masons had convinced the world that a catastrophic conflict was inevitable. The Polish diplomat added that he would be pleased to see the Anglo-Soviet alliance negotiations end in failure as soon as possible.[50]

Forster's Attempted Danzig Détente

The American diplomats in Europe continued to oppose peace and urge war. Bullitt was disgusted with the failure of Bonnet to encourage Poland with a blank check at Danzig. He continued to warn Roosevelt that the French Foreign Minister was working for peace. Bullitt was delighted at times to find that Bonnet was pessimistic about the chances for peace. He reported with satisfaction on June 28, 1939, that Bonnet could see no way out for Hitler other than war. Biddle at Warsaw gave uncritical support to Polish policy at Danzig. He claimed in a report on July 12, 1939, that Viktor Boettcher, the unofficial Danzig foreign minister and a close personal friend of Burckhardt, had become openly aggressive and was no longer a "repressed imperialist." Biddle failed to explain why a man who desired the reunion of his native city with his native country, according to the wishes of the vast majority of both parties, was an imperilist.[51]

Senate President Greiser returned to Danzig on July 16, 1939, and conferred with Burckhardt the following morning. Burckhardt admitted that he preferred to deal with Greiser rather than Forster. Burckhardt told Greiser that he continued to hope that Halifax did not desire war for its own sake. He predicted again that the British would fail in their effort to conclude an alliance with the Soviet Union. He hoped that this failure would persuade the British to adopt a more reasonable attitude.

Greiser joined Burckhardt at a luncheon on July 17, 1939, with Chodacki and Smogorzewski, a prominent Polish journalist. Kasimierz Smogorzewski had directed Polish propaganda against German revisionist aspirations in the Corridor area for many years. Burckhardt arranged the luncheon to enable Greiser to gauge the current Polish attitude. Greiser noted afterward that he permitted Chodacki as usual to do most of the talking. He differed in this respect from Forster, who insisted on his own share of speech in any conversation with Chodacki. The Polish High Commissioner explained to Greiser that Poland knew exactly how many men and guns were available in Danzig for use against Poland. He said that Poland would know how to make proper use of this information at the appropriate time. Chodacki added contemptuously that he had not responded to the recent wishes of Forster to discuss certain matters, because he was not certain that the latter had the permission of Hitler for such discussions. Chodacki said that he was always surprised by Forster's dependence on Hitler, and he knew that everyone present realized that Danzig was under no political obligation to Germany. Greiser received the impression at the luncheon that it was virtually impossible to discuss the current situation with the Poles.[52]

Forster approached Burckhardt on July 18, 1939, with instructions to explain the attitude of Hitler toward the Danzig problem. Forster emphasized that German plans for a negotiated settlement with Poland were virtually the same as they had been earlier in the year. He added that it might be possible to postpone a settlement of the Danzig question until 1940 or 1941 if some relaxation of tension could be achieved. He declared that Germany was prepared to negotiate through League channels at Danzig to achieve this objective.

The Forster démarche created the impression that Hitler was contemplating the possibility of a German retreat at Danzig. Halifax was curious to know what the attitude of Poland would be in such a situation. He instructed Kennard to ask Beck if he would be willing to restrain the Polish press in the event of a German retreat, and to prevent unnecessary gloating over any weakening in the attitude of the German Government. Beck rejected this hypothetical question on July 25, 1939. He claimed that the Germans were simulating a détente in an effort to separate Great Britain from Poland. He insisted that tension between Germany and Poland was increasing rather than slackening. He confided that he was contemplating vigorous steps at Danzig in the near future which might require French and British support. It was evident to Halifax that Beck would not encourage a German retreat or press for an understanding with Germany on that basis.[53]

The Polish press throughout July delighted in taking the position that German policy was weak. The Illustrowany Kurjer declared contemptuously that the German bluff was not fooling anyone. In replying to the question of whether or not war might soon break out, they declared: "Yes, but only through an error. Germany is the master of bluff. All her policies can be summed up in the single word: bluff!"

The same newspaper shifted its attention to the British attitude toward Germany after the Halifax inquiry at Warsaw. The editors observed on July 27, 1939, that things were very quiet in Germany, but that this was understandable because Hitler had "sick nerves." This largest circulating Polish newspaper was not an official organ, but the articles which it printed were passed by the Polish censors. The extensive activity of these censors is indicated by the large number of blank spaces which appeared continuously in the private Polish press, instead of articles censored and suppressed by the authorities at the last minute.[54]

The anti-German campaign gained momentum in the official Polish press too, during July 1939. The Gazeta Polska offered the amazing suggestion on July 31, 1939, that the best soldiers in the German Army of World War I had been Poles. It claimed that this conclusion followed from an objective analysis of the question. This was an incidental feature of a propaganda campaign conducted for many weeks to prove that Germany was afraid to accept the

Polish challenge. The German press accused the Poles of ingratitude for the German role in the liberation of Poland in World War I, but it never claimed that the Polish soldiers or their leaders were cowards.[55]

Forster took another step at Danzig toward a *détente* on July 25, 1939. This followed a disagreeable incident on Sunday, July 23rd, in which Forster had been incorrectly informed that Poland intended to create an armed railway guard for use on the Danzig railways. The Forster *démarche* of July 25th took place immediately after this incident had been clarified. Forster informed Burckhardt that the Danzig militia could be disbanded by mid-September if there was a relaxation of tension between Germany and Poland. Burckhardt reported this statement to the British, and British Ambassador Kennard inquired about the Polish attitude toward it at the Polish Foreign Office. He was told that the step by Forster was an empty gesture devoid of significance. Beck was preparing a decisive step to terminate these gestures by Forster. Ambassador Bullitt received advance information at Paris that a Polish ultimatum to Danzig would soon be forthcoming, and he hastened to report this news to President Roosevelt.[56]

The Axis Peace Plan of Mussolini

The Italian leaders were worried by the increasing tension between Germany and Poland. Italian Ambassador Attolico discussed the situation with Ribbentrop at Castle Fuschl near Salzburg on July 25, 1939. Mussolini was considering the advisability of a conference with Hitler at the Brenner Pass, and a diplomatic conference of the European Powers which would not necessarily require the presence of Hitler and Mussolini. Attolico informed Ribbentrop that Mussolini had decided that a German-Polish war would not remain localized, and he was convinced that neither Germany nor Italy could face a major war.

Ribbentrop expressed his personal view that a German retreat in the Polish crisis would not be advantageous for either Germany or Italy. He hoped that Mussolini would do everything possible to create the impression that Italy would fight at the side of Germany in the event of a showdown. He believed that a determined Italo-German attitude in the present crisis was the best guarantee of peace. He knew that Hitler agreed with Mussolini that an actual war at the present time would be disadvantageous for Germany as well as for Italy, and he added that the German leader hoped to avoid a conflict with Great Britain and France if war broke out between Germany and Poland.

Ribbentrop warned Attolico that the Poles could easily provoke a war by an attack on Danzig or a series of intolerable provocations against Germany. He feared that the proposal for a conference would be interpreted as a sign of weakness which would make war more likely. This could be the decisive factor in producing Anglo-French intervention in any war which might arise between Germany and Poland. He doubted that the Poles would agree to attend a conference proposed by Germany and Italy. Ribbentrop admitted that Halifax could probably produce a general war if he was seeking one at any price. He doubted if British military preparations were sufficiently advanced to warrant such a policy. He hoped that Germany would still find time to complete her

410 THE FORCED WAR

program of territorial revision before the British were ready for war. He was inclined to evaluate some of the comments made by Chamberlain and Halifax at Rome in January 1939 as mere bluff.

Ribbentrop believed that a meeting at this time between Hitler and Mussolini at the Brenner frontier railway station would be a theatrical gesture with nothing behind it. It would be more normal for Hitler to go to Florence with its art treasures, or to attend Italian Army maneuvers. Ribbentrop suspected that Count Massimo Magistrati, the counsellor of the Italian Embassy at Berlin, was the real author of the plans which Attolico presented. It was known that Magistrati was eager to reduce the Italian commitment to Germany. The text of the proposed Hitler-Mussolini communiqué for the Brenner meeting offers ample indication as to why Ribbentrop was suspicious:

"The Fuehrer and the Duce, who have met on the Brenner Pass, after a lengthy examination of the situation, have, in face of the policy of encirclement of the Axis which is being pursued by the great Democracies, reaffirmed their desire for peace, and have agreed on the view that a conference between the interested Powers, if prepared through the normal diplomatic channels in a suitable manner, could lead to a solution of the main problems which are disturbing Europe and inaugurate a period of peace and prosperity for the peoples."

The sentiments of the proposed communiqué reflected the admirable devotion of Mussolini to the preservation of peace, but they lacked every indication of firmness in the face of Polish provocations and unlimited British support to Poland.[57]

Attolico discussed the situation with Weizsaecker at Berlin on July 29, 1939. He insisted that Mussolini continued to favor the proposed communiqué for a Brenner meeting not later than August 4, 1939. Ciano was also urging the immediate preparation of a general diplomatic conference. The Italian Foreign Minister believed that it would be better to have the conference then than to wait for the pressure of events a month hence to force it on everyone. Attolico suggested that separate Italian and German statements along the lines of the proposed Brenner communiqué might be an adequate substitute for a Brenner meeting. The important point, according to Attolico, was the issuance of public declarations by Italy and Germany that the preservation of peace was necessary under all circumstances. The failure of the Germans to accept this view produced the initiative for the Ciano visit to Germany two weeks later. The disagreement between Germany and Italy was profound, and it was decided that personal conversations would be required before joint steps could be contemplated by the two allied Powers.[58]

The Peace Campaign of Otto Abetz

French Foreign Minister Bonnet wrote a revealing letter to Ribbentrop on July 25, 1939. It contained a belated denial of the German contention in response to the French protest of March 18, 1939, about the occupation of Prague. According to the Germans, Bonnet had promised Ribbentrop that France would reduce her military commitments in Eastern Europe. Bonnet reminded

Ribbentrop that the Franco-Polish alliance of 1921 had always remained a specific indication of French commitments in the East. Bonnet concluded his letter, which was made available to the public, with the comment that he could not "permit it to be said that our country would be in any way responsible for war because it had honored its signature." The German Foreign Minister suspected that this letter was a gesture designed to convince the Russians that France was sincere in her willingness to oppose Germany.

German relations with France at this time were complicated by the Abetz case. Two French journalists were arrested in June 1939 for allegedly accepting German funds, and the outcry was raised in the French press that Otto Abetz, who worked for the *Comité France-Allemagne*, was responsible for the spread of defeatism in France. The specific charge was that Abetz had said that the German cause at Danzig was just, and that Germany would regain possession of her lost city. Daladier informed the German diplomats at Paris on June 30, 1939, that he had ordered the expulsion of Abetz from France. Bonnet had previously advised Abetz to leave voluntarily in order to avoid an unpleasant expulsion incident, and Abetz departed from Paris on the morning of June 30th. The *Temps* on July 1, 1939, denounced Abetz as a German propagandist.

Welczeck discussed the situation with Daladier on July 11, 1939, and he stressed the fact that Abetz was a close personal friend of Ribbentrop. Daladier agreed to re-investigate the case, and Welczeck advised him to consult Senator Henry-Haye, the Mayor of Versailles, who was a close friend of Abetz. Welczeck, who denied that it was fair to classify Abetz as a propagandist, complained that much of the French press had regarded the expulsion order as proof that Abetz was guilty of "spy activity." He added that no one had claimed the slightest connection between Abetz and the French journalists, Aubin and Poirier, who were accused of accepting foreign funds. Daladier responded by issuing a special communiqué on July 15, 1939, that Abetz was not guilty of espionage activity. It was announced that Abetz had left the country voluntarily and that consequently no formal expulsion order had actually been issued against him.[50]

The situation was complicated by ruthless attacks against Abetz by Henri de Kerillis, after the former had departed from France. The veteran French *belliciste* claimed in *l'Époque* that Abetz was guilty of inciting Frenchmen to treason. Abetz knew that it would be impossible to sustain this monstrous charge before a French court, and he repeatedly requested Ribbentrop for permission to return to France. He argued that he had every right to do so in the absence of the threatened formal expulsion order. Ribbentrop at last consented on August 2, 1939, but Abetz was detained by the French authorities at Belfort and forced to return to Germany. Welczeck was instructed not to come to Germany on leave in August 1939 until he had done everything possible to enable Abetz to return to France, where he intended to launch a lawsuit against Kerillis. The issue was of major importance because of the large number of friends Abetz had made among Frenchmen through his selfless work over the years for a Franco-German understanding. The French Government decided that it was impossible to retreat in this question, and Abetz was compelled to remain in Germany.[60]

The Polish Ultimatum to Danzig

A dangerous new incident took place in Danzig at the time of Forster's *démarche* with Burckhardt on July 25, 1939. A Polish soldier, Budziewicz, was slain in mysterious circumstances on Danzig territory by Stein, a Danzig customs official. Stein swore that he had acted in self-defense, but he was immediately arrested on a charge of manslaughter. The Danzig authorities made a full apology to Chodacki, and promised to pay an indemnity. The contrast between the conduct of Danzig in the Budziewicz murder and Polish conduct in the Gruebnau murder at Kalthof was painfully obvious. This contrast was concealed from the Polish public. The Polish press claimed that Polish personnel in Danzig were being indiscriminately assaulted by Danzigers, and that Budziewicz had been murdered without provocation on Polish territory.[61]

The Danzig Government presented two protest notes to the Poles on July 29, 1939, concerning illegal activities of Polish customs inspectors and frontier officials. The Danzig Government objected to hostile Polish economic measures, and threatened to undertake reprisals. The Polish Government ignored this warning, and on August 1, 1939, it terminated the export of duty-free herring and margarine from Danzig to Poland, although the sale of these items to Poland constituted 10% of the total trade of the Free City. The local French representatives at Danzig noted with amusement that the *Amada Unida* company, which enjoyed a monopoly in the production of Danzig margarine, was financed by English and Dutch capital. *Danziger Vorposten* (*The Danzig Sentinel*) suggested that reprisals should be taken against Polish customs inspectors. It was pointed out that the number of Polish customs inspectors, before the recent increase, was 400% above the 1929 level, although the trade of Danzig remained much smaller in 1939 than it had been ten years earlier. The cost of the increased number of inspectors was carried exclusively by the impoverished Danzig community.

Chodacki used the irresponsible suggestion of the *Vorposten* editorial as a pretext to humiliate Danzig. He received permission from Beck to present an outrageous ultimatum to Greiser on August 4, 1939. Lukasiewicz confided to Bullittt on August 3rd that Poland intended to take this step at Danzig. Senate President Greiser received official notification in the early hours of August 5, 1939, that the frontiers of Danzig would be closed to the importation of all foreign food products unless the Danzig Government promised by 6:00 p.m. the same day, never to interfere with the activities of Polish customs inspectors. The threat was formidable, because Danzig produced a relatively small proportion of her own food. Greiser was informed that every Polish customs inspector would bear arms while performing his duty after August 5, 1939. League High Commissioner Burckhardt was not consulted by the Poles, and he did not receive official notification of the Polish step until August 6th. Burckhardt, in his detailed memoirs of his Danzig mission, recorded more than twenty years later, described the Polish ultimatum of August 4th as a major mistake which produced only adverse effects. It was obvious that the Poles intended to replace the League as the sovereign Power at Danzig. Chodacki concluded many years later that the Polish ultimatum of August 4th (dated August 4th, presented August 5th) was a serious tactical mistake. It was not based on any specific incident or hostile act of the Danzig Government. The fact remains that the ultimatum was approved by Beck, who continued to place his full confidence in Chodacki.[62]

Danzig's Capitulation Advised by Hitler

Hitler concluded that Poland was seeking to provoke an immediate conflict with Germany. He advised Greiser to capitulate at once, because he feared that the Poles might proclaim a blockade of Danzig before the expiration of the Polish note. Greiser contacted Chodacki on the morning of August 5th to inform him that Danzig submitted to the Polish ultimatum.

Greiser addressed a lengthy note to Chodacki on August 7, 1939, after the first phase of the crisis had passed. He reminded the Polish High Commissioner that no order for interference with the Polish customs inspectors had been issued by the Danzig Government. He expressed astonishment that Chodacki had threatened to starve Danzig for no apparent reason, and he protested against the new Polish directive which provided for the total militarization of the Polish customs inspectors in Danzig. This note was dispatched with the approval of the German Government. Hitler believed that it was necessary to encourage Danzig, after the humiliation of her capitulation to Poland, bu intervening directly in this question. Weizsaecker invited Polish Chargé d'Affaires Prince Lubomirski to call at the German Foreign Office on August 9, 1939. He read the contents of a German *note verbale*, which contained the significant warning that Germany renounced all reponsibility for the consequences of further Polish persecution of the Danzigers. The note stated that Germany vigorously protested against ultimata to Danzig based on non-existent measures. Lubomirski requested a written copy of the note. Weizsaecker explained that he had no authority to present a written note, but he granted Lubomirski permission to make his own copy from the German original.[63]

Beck had explained to Kennard late on August 4, 1939, and shortly before Chodacki presented the Polish ultimatum to Danzig, that the Polish Government was prepared to take military measures against Danzig if the Danzigers failed to accept the Polish terms. He later professed to believe that the German *note verbale* of August 9th was insulting to Poland. He instructed one of his subordinates on August 10th to summon German Chargé d'Affaires Baron Wuehlisch. The contents of a Polish *note verbale* much longer than the German note of the previous day were read to the German diplomat in the Polish language. The German Government was warned that Poland would consider further German intervention against Polish interests at Danzig an act of aggression. The Polish Government disclaimed responsibility for the consequences which would ensue if the German Government persisted in its efforts to protect Danzig. Baron Wuehlisch was told that the German step of the previous day allegedly constituted a legal violation. Poland, the League of Nations, and the Danzig Government had certain legal rights in Danzig territory, but Germany had no rights in that area. The German Government was informed that Poland did not consider that Danzig was a legitimate subject of German concern, and the Polish diplomats professed to be surprised that Germany had dared to intervene on the previous day.

The German Government was further informed that Polish willingness to discuss Danzig with Germany in the past had been a voluntary gesture of good will on the part of Poland, which the Polish Government was no longer willing to permit. Wuehlisch was told that the Polish ultimatum at Danzig of August 4th was delivered with the advance approval of the British and French Governments. This allegation was untrue. Beck had deliberately avoided consulting with the Western Powers in order to demonstrate his readiness to exercise an independent initiative at Danzig in the question of peace or war. He had informed Kennard that the Polish Government was prepared to take military action at Danzig, but he had not consulted with the British Government. The Danzigers, on their part, were fully convinced that Poland would have proceeded to execute a full military occupation of Danzig had Greiser rejected the Polish ultimatum.

Wuehlisch was informed on August 10th that it would be necessary for him to copy the text of the Polish note from the Polish language version if he wished to have it in writing. The German diplomat immediately expressed his willingness to do so. The exchange of German and Polish notes was interpreted in the various European capitals as a new indication that Poland refused to renew negotiations with Germany and that she insisted upon a unilateral Polish solution at Danzig.[64]

American Ambassador Bullitt at Paris informed President Roosevelt on August 3, 1939, that Beck was predicting that an intense and decisive phase of the crisis between Germany and Poland might occur before August 15, 1939. President Roosevelt knew that Poland was obviously to blame for the crisis which began at Danzig on August 4th, and he was alarmed at the prospect that the American public might learn the truth about the situation. This could be a decisive factor in discouraging his program for American military intervention in Europe. He instructed Under-Secretary Sumner Welles on August 11, 1939, to order American Ambassador Biddle to advise the Poles about this problem. President Roosevelt urged the Poles to be more clever in making it appear that German moves were responsible for any inevitable explosion at Danzig.

The response of Beck to American intervention was not encouraging. Biddle reported to President Roosevelt, at midnight on August 11th, that the Polish Government had decided that there could be absolutely no concessions to Germany. Beck was obviously unwilling to engage in a series of elaborate but empty maneuvers which might have been useful in deceiving the American public. Beck wished the American President to know that he was content at the moment to have full British support for his policy. Beck showed Biddle a report from Polish Ambassador Raczynski at London on August 13, 1939. The report contained the explicit approval of Halifax for recent Polish measures at Danzig.[65]

The Polish ultimatum of August 4, 1939, which was based on the most flimsy of pretexts, had effectively destroyed the efforts of Hitler and Forster to secure a *détente* in German-Polish relations at Danzig. The Polish Government had ignored the suggestion of Forster that it might be possible to disband the Danzig militia if the situation at Danzig became more calm. It was manifestly impossible for Forster to persist in his conciliatory efforts in the atmosphere created by the Polish ultimatum. It was apparent to the German Government that the British and French were either unable or unwilling to restrain the Polish Government from arbitrary steps which could produce an explosion. The Poles had extended their position at Danzig on August 5, 1939, by forcing the consent of the Danzig Government for the total militarization of the Polish customs service at Danzig. The Danzig Government had forfeited the right to intervene against Polish customs inspectors who violated the local ordinances of the Free City. There was reason to fear that the Polish Government might present a new ultimatum, without interference or restraint from Great Britain or France, demanding the final abdication of the National Socialist regime at Danzig. The alternatives in this situation would be the abandonment of German aspirations at Danzig or war.

League High Commissioner Burckhardt believed that Poland was utterly wrong in her claim that the Danzig Government had no right to restrict the activities of the Polish customs inspectors to specific areas based upon the existing agreements. He had received detailed information from Forster on August 3, 1939, about Hitler's instructions for an effort to end the friction with Poland at Danzig. Burckhardt discussed the question of the customs inspectors with Chodacki, but he admitted to Forster that he had received " a very unfriendly reception." He added that the Polish High Commissioner was not interested in the attempt of Hitler to exert a moderating influence on Danzig. Hitler consulted with Forster at the Obersalzberg from August 7-9, 1939. He did not give Forster permission to challenge Poland in the question of the Polish customs inspectors, but he indicated that there was obviously no point in further efforts by the local Danzig leaders to achieve a *détente* with Poland. Forster was told on August 9th that he would have to decide on the spot at Danzig whether or not anything could be gained from further discussions with the Poles about the customs inspectors. Forster returned to Danzig the same day with the impression that there was nothing to do but wait for further developments on the larger European scene.[66]

German Military Preparations

Germany's plans for a possible war with Poland were complete by this time. The various conferences between Hitler and his military leaders, after the operational planning order of April 11, 1939, have been the subject of speculation, but there are no official records available for any of these conferences. Colonel Rudolf Schmundt, who was Hitler's military adjutant, was the alleged author of two unofficial records, compiled after the event, of an important military conference on May 23, 1939. Schmundt died of wounds received in the assassination attempt against Hitler on July 20, 1944, and the question of his alleged authorship has remained unresolved.[67]

Several of Hitler's biographers have warned that it would be dangerous to attach much importance to the dubious records attributed to Schmundt. Ribbentrop recalled after World War II that Hitler "repeatedly told me that one had to talk with military men as if war was about to break out here or there on the next day." This is an obvious fact to every analyst of the relations between political and military leaders, but it does not seem to apply to this particular conference. General Wilhelm Keitel, who recalled the specific details of this meeting with great clarity after World War II, noted that he left the conference of May 23rd with the firm belief that there would be no war in 1939.[68]

The so-called Schmundt notes suggest that Hitler was envisaging the possibility of conflict with both Poland and the Western Powers, but that he hoped to prevent the intervention of the Western Powers by diplomatic means if there was war between Germany and Poland. This phase of the record is consistent with various declarations by Hitler, and it corresponds to the version of Keitel. The detailed comments in the notes, such as the alleged statement by Hitler that Germany was "at present in a state of patriotic fervor" are of doubtful validity.[69]

The actual German military plan had been worked out in most of its details before the conference of May 23, 1939. The Germans intended to rely heavily on airpower in the event of war with Poland, but it was stipulated that only military objectives would be bombed. The principal offensive operations of the ground forces were to be launched from East Prussia and Pomerania in the North, and from West Upper Silesia and Western Slovakia in the South. The preliminary deployment of German troops for possible operations was in process at the time of the Polish ulitmatum to Danzig of August 4, 1939, and it was completed on August 20th. The Slovakian Government had agreed to extend full cooperation to Germany in the event of war, although there was no German request for the deployment of the Slovak armed forces against Poland. German Ambassador Moltke at Warsaw was informed of this agreement on August 4, 1939. The German consulate at Lwów predicted on August 7, 1939, that the Ukrainian minority of Poland would stage an insurrection against the Poles in the event of a German-Polish war.[70]

Hungarian Peace Efforts

Hitler was considerably annoyed at this time by a needless *démarche* of the Hungarian Government. He received Hungarian Foreign Minister István Csáky at Berchtesgaden on August 8, 1939, to discuss the contents of a letter of July 24th from Hungarian Premier Paul Teleki to Hitler. Teleki had announced that moral considerations would prevent Hungary from joining Germany in war against Poland in the event of a German-Polish conflict. Hitler told Csáky that he was shocked by this letter. He had never expected Hungary to participate in such a war, and he added that Hungarian intervention in the event of a conflict would be unwelcome. Hitler conceded that Danzig had capitulated to the Polish ultimatum of August 4th, but he promised that a new Polish ultimatum would be answered by appropriate action from Germany. He predicted that Hungary would lose her recent territorial acquisitions if a major war took place in which Germany suffered a new defeat. Hitler admitted that Slovakia had achieved an important position in current German strategic plans for possible war with Poland, but he promised that Germany had no desire to retain the preponderant foreign influence in that country. He warned Csáky that a Bolshevist type of Pan-Slavism would triumph with terrible results for the

Germans and Hungarians if Germany lost another war.

Csáky replied that Hungary was fully aware of the validity of what Hitler had said. He added that Lord Vansittart, the Diplomatic Adviser to His Britannic Majesty's Government, had clarified this point by adopting a threatening attitude toward Hungary. Csáky was well aware of the vindictive British policy toward Hungary at the Paris peace conference in 1919. The Hungarian Premier had merely wished to make his position clear in the special situation concerning Poland. Csáky emphasized the traditional friendship between Hungary and Poland, and added that national honor would preclude Hungarian action against Poland.

Hitler replied that it was unpleasant to hear Csáky praising the Poles at a time when the Germans in Poland were suffering bestial treatment at Polish hands. Hitler discussed the current excesses in Poland at considerable length. He confided that he had forbidden publicity about Polish atrocities which involved the physical mutilation and torture of individual Germans. Csáky countered with a diatribe against the Rumanians and their alleged mistreatment of the Hungarian minority. He was irritated by the increasing friendliness in German-Rumanian relations, and he tried without success to obtain some indication that Germany favored Hungarian territorial revision against Rumania.

Hitler emphasized in a second conversation later in the day that the unsolicited letter from Teleki was a most unnecessary affront. He explained the insulting implications of the letter from the Hungarian leader in trenchant terms, and he produced a strong impression on Csáky. The Hungarian diplomat was unable to deny that Hitler had never offered the slightest hint that he wished Hungary to fight Poland. Csáky accepted Hitler's analysis of the situation, and he asserted that he would resign if Premier Teleki did not agree to disavow the letter. He returned to Budapest and persuaded Premier Teleki to apologize to Hitler. The Teleki letter and the Csáky visit were demonstrations calculated to influence German policy toward Poland, but they were staged without any concrete basis, and for this reason they inevitably failed to produce an effect. The unhappy Hungarians would have been delighted to mediate between Germany and Poland, but they knew that Beck opposed concessions to the Germans. Hungary confronted the tragedy of a conflict between the two nations which were traditionally her closest friends, and her leaders knew that a major war resulting from this local conflict might lead to the destruction of Hungary.[71]

James Farley, the American Democratic Party Campaign Manager and Postmaster-General, was visiting Berlin at this time. President Roosevelt feared that Farley might discover the facts about the hopeless dilemma which the provocative policy of Poland created for Germany. He instructed the American Embassy at Berlin to prevent unsupervised contacts between Farley and the German leaders. The German Foreign Office concluded on August 10, 1939, that it was not possible to penetrate the wall of censorship around Farley. They realized that President Roosevelt was determined to prevent them from freely communicating with visiting American leaders.[72]

The Day of the Legions in Poland

The Polish ultimatum to Danzig on August 5, 1939, had effectively undermined the conciliatory efforts of Hitler and Burckhardt in the Free City. Beck permitted the Polish radio on August 4th to begin Czech language broadcasts urging an insurrection against the Germans in Bohemia-Moravia. He considered that these steps were a fitting prelude to the great national holiday of the Polish regime on August 6, 1939. This was the day of the Pilsudski Legions in Poland. It had been twenty-five years since the small cadres of Polish auxiliary soldiers had gone into action against the forces of Tsarist Russia in the opening phase of World War I. These Polish soldiers had contributed to the German campaigns which forced the Russian troops to evacuate Poland. The mammoth three day celebration of this anniversary in August 1939 was centered at Kraków. Pilsudski's widow traveled from Warsaw to Kraków by automobile. She was the symbolic representative of the great Marshal who had died in 1935. It was a time of strong emotions. Alexandra Pilsudska willingly told everyone in August 1939 that her husband always had said that a war with Germany would be inevitable sooner or later. She also said that her husband had regarded war as the greatest school for mankind. She claimed that he had doubted if it ever would be possible to find an adequate substitute for war.[73]

A torch was lit over the heart of Pilsudski at Rossa cemetery in Wilna. A relay of Polish runners carried the torch 488 miles to Kraków. A total of 12,000 runners also carried similar torches from other outlying towns. At Kraków there were dedication cermonies for every Polish military group of the 20th century. There was a roll of drums for each man of the Pilsudski Legions who had been killed in battle. Everywhere the official slogan of the celebration was on display: "We are not Austria or Czechoslovakia! We are different!" The Government hoped to inspire a spirit of exultation in the allegedly glorious conflict with Germany. No one was permitted to question the assumption that war with Germany was inevitable.

Marshal Smigly-Rydz presented the keynote address on August 6, 1939. He assured his listeners that Poland was prepared to cope with any moves from the other side in the Danzig dispute. The audience responded with an enthusiastic cry: "We want Danzig!" The Marshal reminded his listeners that each Polish individual was bound by a sacred oath to defend the country and its cause. He exclaimed that the personal life of every citizen would be infamous if a stain was permitted to appear on the escutcheon of Polish honor. The Marshal claimed that Poland respected peace, "but there is no force that could convince us that the word 'peace' means 'take' for some people and 'give' for others." He followed the line of Beck's speech on May 5, 1939, by deceiving his audience about the true nature of Hitler's offer to Poland. He concealed the fact that Hitler had offered vital and extensive concessions to Poland in exchange for lesser German requests. The Marshal insisted that Poland would retaliate against any German move at Danzig. He described the Free City, which did not belong to Poland, as a vital lung of the Polish national organism.[74]

Moltke reported to Berlin on August 8, 1939, that the speech of Smigly-Rydz was more moderate than those of the other Legion leaders. The German Ambassador shared the opinion of Dirksen that Germany should abandon her effort to recover Danzig. He claimed that Smigly-Rydz was thinking exclusively in economic terms when he described Danzig as a Polish lung. He suggested that the speech of the Marhsal indicated that new negotiations with the Polish leaders were still possible. He failed to define the reasons which prompted him to arrive at this conclusion, and he presented no specific proposals for opening negotiations. He admitted that the tone of the Polish press was lacking in moderation.[75]

A startling presentation appeared in the Polish press on August 7, 1939. The Polish censors permitted the *Illustrowany Kurjer* at Kraków to feature an article of unprecedented recklessness. It was claimed that Polish units were constantly crossing the German frontier to destroy German military installations and to carry confiscated German military equipment into Poland. It was noted with satisfaction that these endeavors were stimulated by a keen spirit of competition. The Polish Government failed to prevent the newspaper, with the largest circulation in Poland, from advertising to the world that Germany was experiencing a series of violations of her frontier with Poland. The situation was trenchantly summarized by Polish Ambassador Jerzy Potocki after he returned to the United States in August 1939 from his unsuccessful mission to persuade Beck to seek an agreement with the Germans. Potocki explained that "Poland prefers Danzig to peace."[76]

The Day of the Legions was the last great national celebration to occur in the Poland of Pilsudski. It proved impossible for the Polish state, which Pilsudski had created, to survive the consequences of the foreign policy pursued by Józef Beck. The Polish state was heading for a war which was entirely unnecessary. Beck was deliberately gambling on the unlikely possibility that the inevitable defeat of Poland, in the early phase of the war, would be temporary because the Halifax war policy would provide for the destruction of both Germany and the Soviet Union. His prediction that there could never be lasting harmony between Great Britain and the Soviet Union was sound, but he overestimated the British and underestimated the Russians. He ignored the fact that Halifax and the other British leaders were coldly indifferent about the future of Poland, and that they would not fail to sacrifice Polish interests whenever it was considered expedient to do so. Poland was useful to Halifax in fomenting a war against Germany, but that was all. Beck might well have pondered the famous quotation from Schiller: "The Moor has done his duty; the Moor can go." The British Government willingly gave *ex post facto* approval to the Polish ultimatum of August 4, 1939. This was solely because Halifax wanted war. The British Government under normal circumstances would have denounced the diplomacy of Beck in scathing terms. Beck would have received the warning that further steps of this kind meant the end of British obligations to Poland, had the British Government favored peace.

The Peaceful Inclination of the Polish People

It would have been possible after August 6, 1939, for Beck to modify his policy and to retrieve his earlier position. He claimed to be a master of the equilibrium policy which required a careful balance between two rival neighboring Powers.

Beck was applying this policy in his relations with Germany and the Soviet Union. It would have been more profitable for him to do so, during August 1939, in his relations with Great Britain and Germany. It was not too late for him to arrive at a settlement with Hitler on terms highly advantageous for Poland. It was Beck, and not Hitler, who had discouraged further negotiations.

It was true that the Polish Government had succeeded in creating enthusiasm for war and excitement against the German minority in Poland. It would be a grave error to assume that the Polish population in August 1939 would have been deaf to a peace policy had the facts about German-Polish relations been presented with greater objectivity. It was noted by careful observers in Poland, in the Summer of 1939, that the morale among the common people was far from what the Polish press claimed. A long period of uncertainty had followed the exciting days of the partial mobilization in March 1939, and this had produced a depressing effect. Many men had been called into service, and the small businesses of the country were suffering from a new economic slump. Many rumors were circulating that the British had been extremely niggardly in their offers of financial support, and these rumors were all too true. It was often said that there would long since have been a settlement of the crisis had it not been for the acceptance of the British guarantee. The prolonged duration of the crisis increased the likelihood that the Polish public would welcome a peaceful solution.[77]

Poland had a unique and valuable mission to perform for Europe as a bulwark against Bolshevism. Her commitment to the war policy of Lord Halifax was the main obstacle to the successful performance of this mission in 1939.

Chapter 17

THE BELATED ANGLO-FRENCH

COURTSHIP OF RUSSIA

Soviet Russia as Tertius Gaudens

Halifax failed to draw the Soviet Union into a conflict with Germany after the British guarantee to Poland. The Soviet leaders hoped for a conflict between Germany and the Western Powers which would exhaust the capitalist states and create conditions favorable for the expansion of Bolshevism. The Soviet leaders had feared that Great Britain, France, and the United States would frustrate this hope by doing everything possible to promote an isolated war between Germany and the Soviet Union. This would have seemed the logical policy from the standpoint of nations allegedly opposed to both Communism and Fascism. The Soviet leaders were delighted by the apparent determination of Halifax, after March 1939, to foment an Anglo-German War with or without the participation of the Soviet Union. This was the greatest contribution he could possibly make to the realization of Communist goals.[1]

The Soviet Union in April 1939 was under no obligation to participate in an Anglo-French conflict against Germany on behalf of Poland. French Foreign Minister Bonnet was fully aware of this fact. The Soviet leaders had agreed to support France in the event of a German attack, but they had not consented to support a French attack against Germany in a conflict between Germany and some third country. This situation produced a sharp disagreement between Bonnet and Halifax. Bonnet did not relish the prospect of Stalin witnessing a European War with folded arms in Epicurean detachment. Bonnet was decidedly unsympathetic with Halifax's desire to go to war with Germany under these circumstances.[2]

Premier Daladier of France was inclined to believe that Soviet participation in a mutual assistance front against Germany would prevent the outbreak of a new European War. It is important to note that this attitude was not shared by the British Government, for very obvious reasons. Daladier was thinking in terms of a flexible policy toward Germany, largely reminiscent of the earlier

Chamberlain appeasement policy, in which the threat of force would be tempered by a certain amount of conciliation. The British were intent upon pursuing an uncompromising policy which would force Germany into war. It was for these reasons that the British Foreign Office emphatically denied that a treaty with Russia was the magic formula which would avoid a new European War. Indeed, they would not have been inclined to work for a treaty to prevent the outbreak of a new war.[3]

It is extremely doubtful that Russia would have concluded an alliance with Great Britain, had Halifax ignored Poland and pressed for an alliance with Russia after the Polish refusal of the pro-Soviet alliance offer on March 24, 1939. The Soviet reply of March 21, 1939, to the Four Power alliance plan appeared to be favorable, but it was carefully hedged by the qualification that the Soviet Union would expect Poland to agree to the treaty. Stalin and Litvinov were fully aware of the hostile Polish attitude toward their country, and they knew that Polish participation in an alliance front with Russia was exceedingly unlikely. Stalin had explained in his speech to the 18th Congress of the Communist Party on March 10, 1939, that he hoped to avoid a conflict with Germany.[4]

Russian Detachment Encouraged by the Polish Guarantee

The guarantee to Poland of March 31, 1939, further diminished whatever chances there might have been for an Anglo-Franco-Soviet alliance front. It was obvious after the guarantee that Great Britain, and not Russia, was in immediate danger of involvement in war with Germany. The different situations of the two Powers reduced the chances for an agreement. France and the Soviet Union had concluded their alliance in 1935 under more favorable conditions. British proposals to Russia in 1939 were reminiscent of the vain appeal of George III to Catherine II of Russia in 1776 for Cossack troops to use against the American colonists. The Tsarina had no desire to involve Russia needlessly in a British war.[5]

The guarantee to Poland in terms of power politics was equivalent to a major diminution of British power. Poland was a feeble country both militarily and economically. The ordinary motive for alliances is to obtain an important increment of power in exchange for assuming the liability of danger points in the foreign relations of any new partner. The British agreement with Poland carried with it a maximum of danger and a minimum of power. The Russians knew that Great Britain had weakened both her political and military position in Europe by extending the guarantee to Poland.[6]

The Soviet Union as a Revisionist Power

The attempt of Halifax to secure an alliance with Russia was further complicated by the fact that the Soviet Union was a revisionist Power. The Soviet Union was seeking to establish the Communist system throughout the world, and they also desired to annex important European territories to Russia. Soviet diplomats had begun to discuss their territorial aspirations in Finland, with Finnish Foreign Minister Rudolf Holsti, as early as April 14, 1938. There were Soviet requests for close military collaboration between Russia and Finland. The negative attitude of the Finnish Government toward these proposals led to the launching of a Soviet press campaign against Finland in August 1938. The Finns rejected a proposal from Soviet Foreign Commissar Litvinov on March 5, 1939, for Soviet bases in Finland. The Finnish leaders knew that the Soviet Union was determined to renew Russian domination over Finland, and they were no less alarmed than the Poles, Rumanians, and Baltic nations by the alliance negotiations between the Western Powers and Russia. It was obvious to everyone that Russian armies might penetrate into the heart of Europe in the event of an Anglo-Franco-Soviet war against Germany.[7]

American Ambassador Bullitt at Paris was not enthusiastic about the Anglo-French attempt to conclude an alliance with the Soviet Union. He was inclined to agree with the hostile Polish attitude toward Russia. Bullitt had been American Ambassador at Moscow from 1933 to 1936, and he had few illusions about the Soviet Union. He suggested in his final report from Moscow on April 20, 1936, that the Russian standard of living was possibly lower than that of any other country in the world. He reported that the Bulgarian Comintern leader, Dimitrov, had admitted that Soviet popular front and collective security tactics were aimed at undermining the foreign capitalist systems. He insisted that relations of sincere friendship between the Soviet Union and the United States were an impossibility. He admitted that a conflict between Germany and France would expose Europe to the danger of Communist domination. He believed that it was worth taking this risk in order to destroy Germany, but he was fully aware of the danger involved.[8]

President Roosevelt was aware that economic and social conditions in Germany were far superior to those in the Soviet Union. Ambassador Joseph E. Davies, who succeeded Bullitt at Moscow, reported to Roosevelt on April 1, 1938, that the terror in Russia was "a horrifying fact." Davies also complained about the gigantic Soviet expenditures on armaments, and he reported that about 25% of the total Soviet national income in 1937 was spent on defense, compared to 10% in Germany. Davies reported that Stalin, in a letter to *Pravda* on February 14, 1938, had confirmed his intention to spread the Communist system throughout the world. Stalin promised that the Soviet Government would work with foreign Communists to achieve this goal. He concluded his letter by stating: "I wish very much . . . that there were no longer on earth such unpleasant things as a capitalistic environment, the danger of a military attack, the danger of the restoration of capitalism, and so on." Davies mentioned that General Ernst Koestring, the veteran German military attache in the Soviet Union, continued to hold a high opinion of the Red Army despite the gigantic purges of 1937 in the Russian military services. Davies concluded that the Soviet Union could best be described as "a terrible tyranny." The presentation of these reports did not prompt President Roosevelt to withdraw the statement he had made in his major address at Chicago on October 6, 1937, that the Soviet Union was one of the peace-loving nations of the world. Roosevelt was fully aware of the danger from Communism, but he believed that this consideration was unimportant compared to his preferred objective of destroying Naional Socialist Germany.[9]

American Chargé d'Affaires Alexander Kirk reported on February 22, 1939, that there was much talk in the Soviet Union about a change in foreign policy. He noted that above all there seemed to be an almost universal desire to improve Soviet relations with Germany. He gave no reasons for this development, but the obvious deduction was that reports were reaching the Soviet Union that Great Britain was about to challenge Germany. This was undoubtedly a potent factor in diminishing the need to maintain the fiction of collective security and general pacts of mutual assistance. These devices had been useful in involving Great Britain and France in disputes with Germany and Italy, but there was no longer any need for them. Kirk noted that Anastas Mikoyan, the brilliant Commissar for Trade, was encroaching on Litvinov in the conduct of Soviet foreign policy. Mikoyan, who had fought the British on the barricades at Baku after World War I, was known as a staunch advocate of momentarily normal and peaceful relations with Germany. He was increasingly useful to Stalin at a time when the Soviet Union was seeking to distance herself from the disputes between Germany and the Western Powers. Kirk reported rumors that Litvinov, the apostle of collective security, would soon be retired.[10]

It was very late for a British approach to the Soviet Union when the 18th Communist Party Congress opened on March 10, 1939. Stalin claimed in his keynote speech that the capitalist countries throughout the world were becoming weaker. He predicted the outbreak of a new imperialist war between Fascism and an Anglo-Franco-American combination. He declared that Great Britain and France had good reason to fear revolution in the event of war. Stalin claimed that the British and French leaders were seeking for this reason to involve Germany and the Soviet Union in an isolated war, and he accused the press in the United States, Great Britain, and France of attempting to poison Russo-German relations after the Munich conference. These claims of Stalin were dutifully repeated by subsequent speakers at the Congress. Soviet Defense Commissar Kliment Voroshilov boasted on March 13, 1939, that the Red Army had been more than doubled during the past five years. He claimed that Russian victories, at Lake Khasan and Chenkufeng, over Japanese troops in July and August 1938 had given the lie to the alleged weakening of the Red Army in the recent purges. Voroshilov added that the Red Army had received 34,000 political commissars for the improvement of the morale of the troops. He denounced British and French diplomacy designed to promote a Russo-German war.

The Dismissal of Litvinov

German Ambassador Friedrich Werner Count von der Schulenburg, who had represented Germany at Moscow since 1934, reported to Berlin on March 13, 1939, that the speech by Stalin marked a new departure in Soviet foreign policy. He announced that the principal animus of Stalin was now directed against Great Britain. Schulenburg noted that Stalin for the first time had ridiculed the allegation that the German Reich had aspirations in the Soviet Ukraine.

Ribbentrop had earlier called Hitler's attention to the implications of the Stalin speech.[11]

The German Foreign Office learned on March 24, 1939, that Poland had rejected Halifax's pro-Soviet alliance offer of March 20th. State Secretary Weizsaecker predicted to Schulenburg that the British would respond by dropping Poland and by seeking to conclude a tripartite Anglo-Franco-Soviet pact. Weizsaecker was convinced that "the wooing of Moscow" would now constitute the principal feature of British policy, and he was surprised by the decision of Halifax on March 31, 1939, to place the Poles first and the Russians second. This act by Halifax, in combination with the earlier Stalin speech, gave a tremendous boost to German hopes for an improvement in Russo-German relations.

Prime Minister Chamberlain in the British House of Commons on April 3, 1939, refused to make a statement about the prospects for close Anglo-Russian military collaboration. It was generally understood that the British Government expected that much time would be required to clarify the Russian attitude toward an agreement. It was clear that France would play the central role in the negotiations because of existing French ties with both Great Britain and the Soviet Union. Bonnet began the formal negotiation for a tripartite pact with Soviet Ambassador Suritz at Paris on April 9, 1939. It was his task to ascertain the Russian views, and to seek to persuade the British to make proposals which the Soviet Union might be inclined to accept.[12]

The first formal British proposal to Russia was made on April 15, 1939. Halifax suggested that the Soviet Union should accept a pledge to aid any neighbor of Russia which was attacked, provided that the neighbor requested Soviet aid. Bonnet knew that this proposal would be unacceptable to Russia, because it failed to provide any Russian rights or privileges in exchange for the virtually unlimited obligations which the Russians were asked to assume. The Soviet Union ignored the British terms and submitted a Russian plan on April 18, 1939. This provided for the conclusion of a 5-10 year pact of mutual assistance by the Soviet Union, Great Britain, and France. The basic Soviet position provided that the three Powers should agree to aid the countries along the western frontier of the Soviet Union, and that the conclusion of an agreement should be dependent upon satisfactory military staff talks among the three Powers. The Soviet Union did not come into the open immediately with the demand that they should have the right to intervene militarily in these countries with or without their consent.[13]

The British were extremely dilatory about replying to the Soviet note, and their reply of May 9, 1939, was virtually a return to the unsatisfactory terms of their proposal on April 15th. The Soviet Union was requested to accept a pledge to aid Great Britain and France at any point in Eastern Europe where these countries became involved in a conflict with Germany. Stalin proceeded to dismiss Soviet Foreign Commissar Litvinov during the long interim before the British reply to the Soviet proposals. The removal of Litvinov created a great sensation of surprise in the Soviet Union despite the fact that there had been rumors earlier that he would be dismissed. It was known that Litvinov was engaged in important negotiations with Great Britain and France, and it was not expected that Stalin would replace the Soviet Foreign Commissar while

negotiations were in progress. Litvinov was dismissed on May 3, 1939. Two
days earlier he had occupied an honorary position on the tribune platform at
the great Red Army parade in Moscow, commemorating the May 1st proletarian
international holiday. American Chargé d'Affaires Kirk, on May 4th, reported
the dismissal of Litvinov and the appointment of Vyacheslav Molotov as Soviet
Foreign Commissar. He suggested that the replacement might mean a definite
decision on the part of Stalin to improve relations with Germany.[14]

A significant conversation had taken place at Berlin on April 17, 1939,
between Weizsaecker and Soviet Ambassador Alexei Merekalov. The Soviet
diplomat called on Weizsaecker two days after the original unsatisfactory British
offer. He wished to discuss the delivery of war materials to the Soviet Union
from the Bohemian Skoda works, according to the terms of the original Soviet-
Czech contracts. The conversation soon moved to general topics, and the two
diplomats agreed that normal and friendly relations should replace the
traditional hostility between National Socialist Germany and the Soviet
Union.[15]

German Ambassador Schulenburg was travelling in Persia on May 3, 1939,
when the appointment of Molotov was announced. Chargé d'Affaires Werner
von Tippelskirch was cautious in his analysis of the implications of the latest
change. He restricted himself to the comment that it was obvious that Stalin
was taking the direction of Soviet foreign policy into his own hands at a time
when the Russians were facing important foreign policy decisions.

Molotov, who had been chairman of the Soviet Council of Commissars
since 1930, had now embarked upon his ten year tenure as Soviet Commissar
for Foreign Affairs. He also retained the chairmanship of the Council of
Commissars, which included the sixty-one principal departmental chiefs of the
Soviet administration. He was one of the "old Bolsheviks" who had played an
important role in Russian affairs since 1917. He did not, in contrast to Litvinov,
speak any foreign languages. He was a taciturn and reserved man, whereas
Litvinov had always made a point of being affable. Sir William Strang, who
was sent on a special mission to Russia in June 1939, complained that he missed
"the comfortable Jewish appearance" of Litvinov, when confronted by Molotov,
who was of Russian ethnic stock.[16]

Molotov's Overtures Rejected by Beck

The first impression that Molotov made after his appointment was that he was
willing to proceed further than Litvinov in cultivating relations with Poland.
Molotov extended warm congratulations to Beck for his provocative speech to
the Polish Sejm on May 5, 1939. He sent Soviet Vice-Commissar for Foreign
Affairs Potemkin, who had recently toured the Balkan capitals, on a special
mission to Warsaw on May 10, 1939. Vladimir Potemkin offered Beck an
unequivocal assurance that the Soviet Union was prepared to favor Poland in
a struggle with Germany. He confided that he had leaned from Gafencu that the
Polish-Rumanian alliance was directed exclusively against the Soviet Union.
Potemkin suggested that it would be helpful to revise this treaty. He did not
press the question when Beck proved to be uncommunicative about it.[17]

Molotov continued to raise the question of the Polish-Rumanian alliance after Potemkin returned to Moscow. He suggested to Polish Ambassador Grzybowski that it would be a good idea for Poland and Rumania to direct their alliance exclusively against Germany. He added that this step would facilitate the conclusion of a Soviet-Polish-Rumanian pact of mutual assistance. Beck responded to this request with a categorical statement. He instructed Grzybowski to inform Molotov on May 17, 1939, that "Poland does not consider it possible to conclude a pact of mutual assistance with the USSR." He added that Poland would continue to refuse any changes in her other treaty obligations. Beck had slammed the door on Molotov. He believed that it would no longer be possible for the Soviet Union to mistake the implications of the Polish refusal of the Halifax pro-Soviet alliance offer on March 24, 1939. Beck hoped for an eventual war between Great Britain and the Soviet Union, and he wished to do everything possible to disrupt their current negotiations.[18]

The Russians in the meantime had rejected the unsatisfactory British offer of May 9, 1939. Strang admitted that the dilatory and half-hearted British approach to Russia was influenced by an underestimation of Soviet military power, which "had a powerful effect on policy." Indeed, the faulty British evaluation of the relative military power of Germany and the Soviet Union was the actual basis for the fatally unrealistic war policy of Halifax. There were questions in the British Parliament about the fate of the states which bordered Russia in the event of an Anglo-Russian agreement. Under-Secretary Rab Butler explained, in response to a query on May 15, 1939, in the House of Commons, that Great Britain had no special obligations to Finland, Estonia, Latvia, and Lithuania beyond the context of the League of Nations. The League was virtually defunct at this time, and it was possible to assume that the British Government considered it had a free hand toward these countries. Chamberlain admitted on May 19th that the British offer to Russia of May 9th was virtually the same as the original unsatisfactory offer of April 15th. He added that British proposals had not been extended beyond a request for unilateral Russian commitments in areas guaranteed by Great Britain and France. This produced a scornful shout from Gallacher, the Communist member of Parliament: "They are not children!" The Liberal leader, Sir Archibald Sinclair, demanded that Chamberlain proceed to offer tangible proposals to the Russians which would provide for mutual obligations to cover any eventuality.[19]

It was known in Commons that special Anglo-Franco-Russian talks would take place at Geneva on May 21, 1939. Halifax, Bonnet, and Ivan Maisky, the Soviet Ambassador to Great Britain, were scheduled to conduct the negotiations. Maisky had actively criticized in influential circles at London the British conduct of negotiations with Russia. Winston Churchill delivered a speech on May 19th which he hoped would be useful to Maisky in the approaching negotiations. Churchill addressed a stern warning to the Poles: "The Government will contradict me if they feel it necessary to do so, but I cannot believe that the Polish Governemnt will consider it any part of their duty to place a barrier between France, England and Russia for their own mutual security." Churchill unknowingly returned to the Grzybowski proposal which Beck had rejected, when he claimed that Poland and Russia should recognize a common policy in thwarting German interests in the Baltic states. Butler sagely replied to Churchill that it was necessary for Great Britain to avoid careless assumptions in these questions. He claimed that it was important to keep the British approach to Russia "more in harmony with the views of the other Governments most nearly concerned and less calculated to raise doubts and difficulties in their minds." Butler in this statement deliberately reaffirmed the original decision of Halifax to place Poland before Russia.[20]

Bonnet was momentarily optimistic about the prospects for a tripartite alliance after the conversations at Geneva on May 21, 1939. Maisky did not seem to regard the negative attitude of Poland toward Russia as a decisive obstacle to an agreement with Great Britain and France. The Baltic states were discussed, but Maisky gave Bonnet the misleading impression that the Soviet Union would not seek to extend guarantees to these states against their express wishes.

Bonnet hoped that the official reserve of the British could be surmounted by persuading Molotov to conclude a tripartite Pact which failed to stipulate identical policies of the Three Powers toward Poland and her neighbors. These hopes were blasted by a major Molotov address on foreign policy on May 31, 1939. The Soviet Foreign Commissar spoke approvingly of a possible Russo-German trade treaty. He insisted that a mutual guarantee by Russia, Great Britain, and France, for all states bordering Russia in Europe, was a necessary condition for a tripartite pact. He emphasized that the Soviet Union and the Anglo-French combination were in basic disagreement on this important question. Molotov completely ignored the rebuff he had received from Poland, but he strongly criticized the policy of Finland. The Molotov speech offered little encouragement either to Hitler or Halifax, but the Soviet diplomat praised the Roosevelt telegram to Hitler of April 15, 1939, as a "proposal imbued with the spirit of peacefulness." He criticized Hitler for abrogating the Polish and British treaties on April 28, 1939.[21]

A Russo-German Understanding Favored by Mussolini

The Russian draft for an agreement on June 2, 1939, introduced the favorite Communist proposal for protection against so-called indirect aggression. This was a clever formula justifying Soviet intervention against states which did not believe themselves threatened whenever Russia insisted they were in jeopardy. It included internal developments which Russia considered threatening to such states. It was a device to permit an unlimited Russian campaign of aggression against her neighbors. The Soviet Union was prepared to extend such guarantees to Belgium, Greece, Turkey, Rumania, Poland, Latvia, Estonia, and Finland. The British suggestion that guarantees be granted to Holland and Switzerland if those nations requested them was rejected. Holland and Switzerland had opposed Russian entry into the League of Nations, and they did not maintain diplomatic relations with the Soviet Union.[22]

The Germans were informed by Moltke at Warsaw on May 16, 1939, that Beck remained resolutely opposed to an agreement with the Soviet Union. This meant that an Anglo-French agreement with the Russians about Poland was extremely unlikely. Ribbentrop instructed Schulenburg to discuss the European situation with Molotov at Moscow. He hoped to ascertain the current Russian attitude toward Germany. Schulenburg reported on May 20th that he had called on Molotov but had failed to penetrate the reserve of the Soviet Foreign Commissar. Weizsaecker attempted to encourage Schulenburg in another attempt by warning him on May 27th that an Anglo-Russian combination would not be easy to prevent. Weizsaecker was actually much more optimistic about the Russian situation. He noted in a memorandum on May 30th that the lack of *rapport* between Molotov and the German Ambassador probably resulted from Molotov's personal distrust of Schulenburg, rather than from the basic trend of Soviet policy.[23]

Schulenburg repoted on June 5th that he had failed to win the confidence of Vice-Commissar Potemkin in recent talks. The Russians, who were aware that most of the German aristocrats were opposed to Hitler, were not taking chances with the German Ambassador. They knew that Schulenburg was critical of Hitler, and there was always the possibility in their minds that he was a British spy. Stalin and Molotov did not wish Halifax to receive confidential information about their conversations with Germany. Their suspicions were entirely without foundation, but Schulenburg was later convicted for revolutionary activities against the German Government in wartime.

Bulgarian Minister Parván Draganov at Berlin was a better source of information about Soviet attitudes. He informed the German Foreign Office on June 15, 1939, that Russian policy was undecided, but asserted that the Soviet Union preferred peaceful relations with Germany to an alliance with Great Britain. He intimated that it would be necessary for the Soviet Union to obtain some important assurances from Germany before this policy could definitely be considered. Draganov made no secret of the fact that the Russians were employing him to convey the general Russian attitude at Berlin.[24]

It was evident to the German leaders that it would be necessary to conclude a specific agreement with the Soviet Union to obtain Russian neutrality in the event of a German-Polish war. Hitler temporized for several weeks before he allowed Ribbentrop to take concrete steps in a decisive effort to come to terms with Stalin. The prospect of an agreement which might permit the expansion of the Soviet Union was distasteful to Hitler, but he decided in July 1939 that such an agreement might be the determining factor in preventing the outbreak of a major European war. Hitler had told Beck at Berchtesgaden in January 1939 that opposition to the schemes of the Soviet Union was a principal feature of German foreign policy. He added that even this important factor was secondary to his duty toward his people in promoting the interests of Germany and in revising the provisions of the Treaty of Versailles. Hitler knew that any attempt by Poland to come to terms with Russia was very unlikely. A Russo-Polish agreement was impossible unless Beck permitted the Red Army to operate on Polish territory. Beck and Hitler both knew that this would be followed by a Russian attempt to seize part or all of Poland. The Soviet leaders had demanded control over all the European territory of the Tsarist Empire at the Brest-Litovsk peace conference with Germany in 1918. The Germans told Joffe and Trotsky, the principal Russian negotiators, that the Poles, for instance, had no desire to come under Bolshevik rule. The Bolshevik response to this German argument was characteristic of Russian policy from 1918 onward.

The Germans were told that the Polish population would soon be converted to Bolshevik rule if Russian troops were allowed to occupy Poland.[25]

The German Government was convinced that the Soviet Union would seek to settle their own account with Poland in the event of a German-Polish war. It was evident that Stalin had never shared Hitler's inclination to respect the existing Polish frontiers. There could be no doubt that the Soviet Union entertained extensive territorial ambitions in many other directions. The Russian Communist Party newspaper *Pravda* declared on June 13, 1939, that the current European situation required special measures for the "protection" of Finland and the two Baltic states of Estonia and Latvia. It was known in both Berlin and London that none of these states desired any so-called protection from Russia, and this was fully understood in Moscow. Russian insistence, notwithstanding, on the protection of these states was a clear indication that the Soviet Union was determined to intervene in these countries as well as in Poland and also possibly in Rumania and Turkey. The Soviet leaders would have been unable to pursue these gigantic ambitions had it not been for the disastrous war policy of Halifax.

The danger of an agreement between the Soviet Union and the Western Powers made it imperative for the German Government to consider the possibility of appeasing Russia. Mussolini knew that Hitler was not enthusiastic about this situation. Hence, he urged German Ambassador Mackensen on June 14, 1939, to inform Hitler that the Italian Government favored a determined German effort to arrive at an understanding with Russia. Mussolini attempted to encourage Hitler to adopt this attitude. He told Mackensen on June 16, 1939, that important assurances from the Italian Embassy at Moscow indicated that the Soviet Union desired to avoid a military conflict with Germany.[26]

Strang's Mission to Moscow

Sir William Strang, the Chief of the Central Division of the British Foreign Office, arrived at Moscow on June 14, 1939. He was instructed to assist British Ambassador Sir William Seeds in what was hoped would be the final phase of negotiations with the Russians. Hitler was interested to learn that British policy toward Russia was causing deep concern to Virgil Tilea, the Rumanian Ambassador at London, who had cooperated with Halifax in perpetrating the hoax of an alleged German ultimatum to Rumania in March 1939. Tilea expressed his concern about the situation to a number of people, and the German Embassy at London received a full record of one of his conversations. The Rumanian diplomat was convinced that Great Britain was prepared to sacrifice both Poland and Rumania to Russia despite the British guarantees to these states in the Spring of 1939. Tilea began to see the potentially tragic consequences of his earlier devious connivance with Halifax and Vansittart, and he deplored what he called the soft attitude of the British Government toward Russian demands.[27]

Strang discovered upon his arrival at Moscow that French Ambassador Paul-Emile Naggiar was eager to conclude an agreement with Soviet Foreign Commissar Molotov on almost any terms. Strang was indignant when Naggiar inquired if the British Government was actually sincere in its efforts to reach an agreement with Russia. Strang assured Naggiar that he would not be in Moscow if this were not the case. Strang admitted that British and French recognition of the Russian formula of indirect aggression would be a pledge to support Russian intervention in Rumania, the Baltic states, or Poland. Naggiar received the same impression as Tilea about British willingness to consider the possibility of acceding to Russian wishes in this important matter.

Molotov conducted negotiations with the British and French representatives in an imperious manner. He sat before a desk on a platform; the Western negotiators were required to sit in a semi-circle without tables at a lower level. The new Russian attitude of lofty and contemptuous arrogance was the inevitable consequence of the British guarantee to Poland. Molotov knew that the Soviet Union now occupied an incomparably stronger position in the negotiations than the British Government. The British were seeking to persuade the Soviet Union to participate in the war they intended to launch against Germany. Molotov made it clear that he was not prepared to consider such an undertaking unless the British indicated that they were prepared to pay an exceedingly high price for Russian support.[28]

Molotov revealed on June 17, 1939, that he was not satisfied with the attitude of the British Government. He insisted that his formula of indirect aggression be applied to Poland, Rumania, Latvia, Estonia, and Finland. This sanctioned military intervention in reponse to strictly domestic changes within any of these states. Molotov demanded in subsequent conversations that indirect aggression permit Soviet intervention in any of these states "without threat of force" against them from some other quarter. This meant that Russia might intervene to "protect" Finland in the absence of a threat to Finland from any other foreign Power. Strang objected that the threat of force from some other Power should be the necessary condition for intervention. He proclaimed it to be obvious that President Emil Hacha of Czecho-Slovakia had submitted to a threat of force when he concluded the Czech-German agreement of March 15, 1939. Molotov denied this, and he also reminded Strang that President Hacha himself had denied it. The position of Russia remained unchanged during the following weeks, and Halifax repeatedly instructed Strang to move closer to the Russian position in the decisive questions. Strang complained to Halifax on July 20, 1939, about these "humiliating negotiations." It was decided by both parties on July 23, 1939, that there was virtual agreement on political terms which would meet Russian requirements. Molotov suggested that a final political agreement should await the outcome of military staff talks, and this proposal was accepted by the British and French representatives.[29]

Hitler's Decision for a Pact with Russia

The Germans continued to sound out the Russian position while Strang and Seeds were negotiating unhappily at Moscow. German Ambassador Schulenburg discussed Russo-German relations with Molotov on June 29, 1939. This step was taken in reponse to a *Pravda* article on the same day which claimed that the British and French Governments did not really desire a treaty of equality with the Soviet Union. The purpose of the article was to soften the Anglo-French attitude by stimulating criticism at home. Schulenburg failed to obtain any definite indication of Russian policy from Molotov. He was merely able to report in general terms that the attutide of Molotov was "encouraging but cynical."

Schulenburg attempted during these days to make an impression on Molotov by arguing that the 1926 Russo-German treaty of friendship was still in effect because it had never been expressly abrogated. Molotov doubted the validity of this assumption, and he added sharply that the recent experience of Poland seemed to indicate that nonaggression pacts with Germany were not of much value. The German Ambassador responded with a half-hearted defense of German policy in Poland which did not impress Molotov.

Molotov repeatedly provoked Schulenburg into further elaborate arguments, during the following month, about the 1926 German treaty with Russia and the 1934 Pact with Poland. These discussions were of no value in improving Russo-German relations, but this worried Schulenburg rather than Molotov. It was easy for Molotov to stimulate further German interest in a possible understanding by dropping occasional hints at Berlin. Schulenburg sought to attach great importance to a letter he received on July 4, 1939, from Rudolf Nadolny, his predecessor at Moscow. Nadolny insisted that the formal validity of the 1926 Russo-German Pact could not be denied.[30]

The Soviet Union announced on June 29, 1939, that the annual maneuvers of the Red Army would take place in the Leningrad district near the Finnish frontier. This news created great anxiety in Finland. The Finns shared the fears of the Rumanians, that rival British and German diplomatic efforts in the Soviet Union would lead to offers from both sides at the expense of the smaller nations. The Finns attempted to sound out the Germans by claiming to German Minister Wuepert von Bluecher that current rumors suggested German willingness to tolerate Soviet expansion in the Balitc area. The German Foreign Office instructed Bluecher on July 27, 1939, that the German Government had not offered to acquiesce in the Soviet conquest of Finland and the Baltic states. The fears of the Finns were not allayed, because the German Government did not offer to oppose Russian aspirations in the area.[31]

The German failure to encourage Finnish hopes was not surprising. Hitler had decided at last to push hard for an agreement with Russia, and he was encouraged by the willingness of Molotov to permit negotiations at Berlin for an important Russo-German trade pact. These negotiations were in progress when Hitler instructed Weizsaecker to inform Schulenburg on July 29, 1939, that the German Government would be inclined to tolerate Russian aspirations in the Baltic area in exchange for Russian neutrality in a possible German-Polish war. Weizsaecker added that Hitler still hoped to arrive at a peaceful settlement with Poland, but it was necessary to provide for every eventuality. The Russian diplomats in Berlin recognized that the ultimate return of Danzig to Germany was inevitable.[32]

Ribbentrop informed Schulenburg on August 3, 1939, that he had told Russian Chargé d'Affaires Astakhov that Germany desired to achieve a settlement of all outstanding questions with Russia. Schulenburg was instructed to repeat this assurance to Molotov. The German Ambassador conferred with the Soviet Commissar for Foreign Affairs on the following day. Molotov took delight in overwhelming the startled German with accusations. He claimed that Russian difficulties with Japan were mainly the result of the anti-Comintern Pact of 1936 between Germany and Japan. Hitler was accused of encouraging Japanese aggressiveness, and of rendering crucial support to Italy in the recent struggle against Communism in Spain. Molotov was amused when Schulenburg claimed that Germany desired to keep the peace with Poland. He suggested that Germany could have peace on Polish terms, and that no one was compelling Germany to go to war with the Poles. He ignored Schulenburg's assurance that Russian interests in Poland would be respected in the event of war. He disregarded the accusations of Schulenburg about British intervention in Poland.

The German Ambassador, who took all of these remarks very seriously, was reduced to despair. He reported to Berlin that "the Soviet Government is at present determined to sign with England and France if they fulfill all Soviet wishes." Schulenburg had no basis for this dogmatic assertion, and he failed to realize that his own diplomatic ineptitude encouraged Molotov to take liberties in their conversations. Schulenburg was unable to defend the German position against Molotov's arguments, and he was incapable of countering with critical comments about the conduct of Soviet policy.

The German Foreign Office virtually ignored Schulenburg's pessimistic report. Ribbentrop was receiving separate reports from the other German diplomats at Moscow which presented an entirely different picture. He was told that Molotov was very amiable in his conversations with most of the Germans at Moscow, and that his attitude was encouraging to German prospects for a pact with Russia.[33]

The British and French Military Missions

The British and French military missions arrived at Leningrad by water on August 10, 1939, after a slow journey which had required nearly a week. The reception of the missions at both Leningrad and Moscow was extremely modest, according to usual Russian standards, and this was widely interpreted as a deliberate insult to the Western Powers. The Russo-German trade pact at Berlin was virtually ready for signature by this time, and the Russian delegation was profuse with assurances that the Soviet Union desired better political relations with Germany. The Germans inquired about the significance of the British and French military missions. They were told that contact with Germany had modified the Russian attitude toward Great Britain and France, but that negotiations with the West were allowed to continue because they could not be disrupted without giving any reason. The Germans received the impression that the British and French were meeting Russian requirements at every point, but that the Russians were disinclined to conclude any treaty with them. It was obvious that Halifax had made no impression on the Russians.[34]

The first discussion between the British and French military teams and the Russian military delegation headed by Marshal Voroshilov took place on August 12, 1939. The Russians immediately concentrated the fire of their criticism on the tiny military commitment which the British leaders intended to make on the European continent in the event of war. They knew that their arguments would encourage suspicion and distrust between the British and French. Voroshilov was indignant that the British expected Russia and France to bear the brunt of the war which Halifax was seeking to provoke with Germany. Voroshilov also insisted on specific pledges of support from the British and French military men for possible Red Army operations in Estonia, Latvia, and Lithuania.

The Russians introduced the fundamental question of military operations in Poland and Rumania on August 14, 1939. Voroshilov claimed that both these countries would be defeated by Germany in short order if they did not accept military collaboration with the Soviet Union. This was a preposterous assertion when one considers that there was not even a remote prospect of a conflict between Germany and Rumania. Voroshilov added that Russia could not retaliate against a possible German attack on France unless agreements had been reached for a Russian offensive against Germany through both Polish and Rumanian territory. General Doumenc, the leader of the French military delegation, admitted that the Poles had failed to agree to Russian military operations on their territory. Doumenc attempted unsuccessfully to avoid this crucial issue by suggesting that the Poles would automatically request Soviet aid in the event that Poland was invaded by Germany. Voroshilov replied that Polish agreement on this point was essential, and he insisted on the passage of Russian troops through Poland.[35]

British Ambassador Sir William Seeds reported to Halifax on August 15, 1939, that "the Russians have now raised the fundamental problem on which the military talks will succeed or fail." Great Britain and France were willing to see Russian troops occupy Poland, but the problem was to obtain Polish consent. Seeds suggested that the French General Staff should put pressure on the Polish General Staff for an agreement along Russian lines. Seeds seemed to think that Beck and the military men could be made to consider a secret commitment, "to which the Poles would meanwhile turn a blind eye." General Musse, the French military attache at Warsaw, had been instructed by Premier Daladier to discuss military collaboration between Poland and Russia before General Doumenc departed for Moscow, but his conversations with Marshal Smigly-Rydz had produced no results.[36]

Seeds believed that the Russians were justified in expecting Anglo-French pressure for collaboration on the western neighbors of Russia. He had advised the French to send General Valin from their Moscow mission to Warsaw to demand Polish consent. The independent initiative of Ambassador Seeds in this important question was approved and supported by Halifax. The British Foreign Secretary was unmoved by the fact that the Poles feared the Soviet Union more than Germany.

The French considered the proposal from Seeds, but they decided that there was no point in sending General Valin to Warsaw at the present time. Seeds wired Halifax a few hours later that "Voroshilov stated categorically today (August 15th) that a definite answer to his question, as soon as possible, was of cardinal importance." Halifax was encouraged by a misleading report from Paris on August 16, 1939, that the initial Polish reaction to the proposed Russian military operations on their territory was "not unfavorable." He learned that the French leaders were prepared to make a final effort to persuade the Poles to submit to Russian demands.[37]

Bonnet shared the opinion of Daladier that a pact with the Russians might give France a position of strength from which to conduct a policy of conciliation toward Germany in the earlier style of Laval. Bonnet had profited from a visit of Sir Nevile Henderson to Paris in July 1939. The British Ambassador to Germany had analyzed the policy of Halifax for Bonnet. Henderson and Bonnet were in complete agreement in condemning the war policy of Halifax. Bonnet believed that an Anglo-French war against Germany was quite unnecessary, and he told Daladier that he would prefer to resign rather than to have any part in the launching of such a disastrous conflict. Daladier assured Bonnet that he sympathized with his attitude, and he urged him to remain at his post and to continue the fight for peace. Bonnet finally decided that he would concentrate on three policies to preserve the peace. He would continue to work for the conclusion of a tripartite pact with the British and Russians in order to guarantee France a position of strength. His next step would be pressure at Warsaw to secure Polish concessions to Germany. This would permit a settlement of the German-Polish dispute. He would also continue the promotion of close Franco-Italian relations, and he would encourage Mussolini's program for a general European conference which might enable the diplomats to erase the existing danger spots from the map of Europe.[38]

The Anglo-French Offer at the Expense of Poland

Bonnet was indignant with the Poles and he believed that the military talks with the Russians were breaking up because of Polish intransigence. He did not realize that the Russians had decided to conclude an agreement with Germany before they raised the question of military operations on Polish territory on August 14, 1939. It was not clear to him that the Polish issue was merely the pretext which the Russians had selected to disrupt the military negotiations with the Western Powers. League High Commissioner Burckhardt had discussed the situation with Hitler on August 11, 1939, and he had informed Bonnet that a German-Polish war was inevitable unless there was some change in Polish policy. Hitler had predicted that Poland would be defeated within three weeks, and Bonnet was inclined to suspect that he was right. He believed Burckhardt's assurance that Hitler did not desire war, and that it would be possible to settle the existing dispute by negotiation. Hitler had assured Burckhardt that he knew the Polish military plans, and that they were infantile compared to those of the Czechs the previous year. Burckhardt had asked Hitler if it would be safe for him to allow his children to remain at Danzig, and Hitler had advised him to send them to Switzerland. Bonnet had received this information on August 14, 1939, and he believed that the final crisis was close at hand.[39]

Voroshilov's question about the role of England and France in securing the consent of Poland and Rumania for the Russian forces to operate on their territory was received by Bonnet at 5:00 a.m. on August 15th. Bonnet immediately contacted Lukasiewicz, who was enjoying a splendid vacation at a beach resort in Brittany. Lukasiewicz arrived at the French Foreign Office the same afternoon. Bonnet was overworked and under great strain. He noted with some aversion that the handsome Polish Ambassador was tanned by the sun and very much at ease. Bonnet informed Lukasiewicz that there were now only two alternatives which the Russians were prepared to consider. They would either receive permission to operate militarily on the territory of their western neighbors and proceed to conclude a military pact with Great Britain and France, or they would conclude a pact with the Germans. Bonnet stated categorically to the Polish Ambassador that he expected the Poles to accept immediately the Russian terms for an agreement. Lukasiewicz coolly replied that Beck would not permit Russian forces to operate on Polish territory. He also put the following question to Bonnet: "What would you say if we requested you to allow the Germans to protect Alsace-Lorraine?"

Bonnet refused to admit that the query of Lukasiewicz was in any way relevant to the existing situation. He reminded the Polish Ambassador that the French and Polish situations were different. France had a common frontier with Germany, but, unlike Poland, she had the Atlantic Ocean instead of a revisionist Russia on her opposite flank. He did not believe that France needed to request the Germans to guard Alsace-Lorraine. He added that four days earlier Hitler had predicted that Germany could defeat Poland within three weeks. Lukasiewicz was furious when Bonnet candidly admitted that he shared this opinion with Hitler. The Polish Ambassador declared with indignation that "on the contrary, it is the Polish Army which will invade Germany from the first day."[40]

The French Foreign Minister was shocked by this revelation of an obviously hopeless delusion. He realized at once that it was impossible to influence Lukasiewicz with arguments of a military nature, although it was precisely these considerations which should have been uppermost in the minds of the Poles. He sought a different approach. He confided to Lukasiewicz that the question of war or peace might depend on the outcome of the present Anglo-French negotiation in Russia. He was horrified to discover that Lukasiewicz was completely indifferent about this consideration.

The ensuing strenuous debate between these two men with different aims and values produced no important result. Bonnet represented the French nation which desired peace, was inclined to tolerate the recovery of Germany as a major Power, and willingly accepted the *status quo*. Lukasiewicz represented a clique of Polish opportunists who chafed at the weakness of Poland under existing European conditions, desired a gigantic upheaval which would destroy both Germany and Russia, and wished for a new World War to accomplish this. Lukasiewicz merely agreed to relay to Warsaw the request of Bonnet for Russo-Polish military collaboration. He warned Bonnet that Beck would respond by rejecting this proposition.

Bonnet was unable to place any confidence in the promise of Lukasiewicz to relay his request to Warsaw. He prepared two lengthy and painstakingly detailed dispatches to guide French Ambassador Noël in personal negotiations with Beck. He repeated every argument in these dispatches which he had presented to Lukasiewicz, except Hitler's calculation about the rapid defeat of Poland. Noël responded by engaging Beck in several lengthy debates on the merit of the French position. He was obliged to report on August 18, 1939, that Bonnet's elaborate arguments had not produced the slightest impression on the Polish Foreign Minister. Bonnet replied by accusing Beck of the same duplicity with France which the Poles had employed against Hitler. Beck for many months had concealed from Hitler his unalterable opposition to the generous German offer to Poland of October 24, 1938. Bonnet claimed that for many years Beck had concealed from France his determination to prevent Russian aid to Poland under any circumstances, including a major war. Bonnet believed that France was entitled to go over the head of Poland and to support Russian operations in Poland without Polish consent. He managed to obtain the full support of Daladier for this policy by August 21, 1939.[41]

Beck at Warsaw noted with considerable amusement that the approaches of Noël and Kennard were entirely different in the question of Polish military collaboration with Russia. Noël, as the representative of a continental Power which might have to bear the brunt of any war with Germany, argued for Russo-Polish collaboration with great passion and insistence. Kennard approached the question with cool detachment and virtual indifference as a mere matter of form. Kennard considered his *démarche* a gesture merely designed to maintain Anglo-French solidarity. Beck told the Polish Council of Ministers that he did not intend to retreat before British and French demands in the Russian question. He was delighted that none of the Polish ministers raised any objections to his policy. The Polish Foreign Minister realized that his position at home was secure. He proceeded to reject the appeals of the French and British diplomats with great disdain.[42]

Bonnet hoped for maximum British cooperation in his effort to win the Poles for collaboration with Russia. He informed Halifax on August 16, 1939, that he had told Lukasiewicz that it would be "unthinkable if the Poles were not willing to accept Russian help." He added that the French military mission in Moscow agreed unanimously with the Russian attitude. Russia's right to intervene in Poland and Rumania was considered the *sine qua non* for Russian participation in any general war which was to be launched after the outbreak of a German-Polish conflict. The French mission noted that the Russians allegedly were willing to restrict the area of their military operations in Poland. They believed that an express Russian willingness to avoid the occupation of certain Polish districts would be a sufficient concession to the Poles.[43]

Halifax professed to be impressed with the arguments of Bonnet. He suggested to the French Foreign Minister that a Rumanian representative should join the Poles and the French in military talks at Warsaw. It was nonetheless evident behind the scenes that the British were not single-minded about the French position, and that Halifax, in contrast to Bonnet, was mainly interested in maintaining Anglo-French solidarity, and was seemingly indifferent about Polish concessions to Russia. The British military delegation at Moscow did not share the enthusiasm of the French team for the Russian attitude. Admiral Drax, who headed the British delegation, was very hostile toward the Russians. He wrote on August 16, 1939, to his personal friend and colleague, Admiral Lord Chatfield, that no agreement had been reached after five days of discussion on a variety of subjects. He noted repeated Russian insults to the British and French teams. The Russians enjoyed referring to the British and French as the yielding or surrendering Powers. They adopted the attitude of a victorious Power humiliating beaten enemies. They regarded British policy in Poland as a major defeat for British interests, and they were reasonably confident that their own policy would produce gigantic gains for Russia at minimum cost.

Drax privately ridiculed the Russian suggestion that an Anglo-French naval force should operate in the Baltic Sea in the event of war. He described this to Chatfield as a sheer impossibility. The Russians knew, on the other hand, that British submarines had been surprisingly effective in sinking German and neutral shipping in the Baltic Sea during World War I. The attitude of Drax toward all the Russian military proposals was extremely reserved. He confided to Chatfield that he hoped to sign a military pact which would contain as few advantages as possible for the Soviet Union.[44]

Drax noted with considerable cynicism, on August 17, 1939, that banquets and vodka were gradually warming up personal relations between the Russians and the military missions. This was not likely to produce important results, because Voroshilov was suggesting that the talks should be adjourned until favorable replies for military collaboration had been received from Poland and Rumania. The Russians had proposed a preliminary adjournment of the talks from Thursday, August 17th, until Monday, August 21st. Drax informed Chatfield with angry sarcasm that the Russians had developed a "new theory of war." They intended to limit the number of their forces in a general war to the number employed by the Western Powers, and Drax described this as "quite childish." It seemed that the halcyon days were ending when the continental Powers were willing to see their young men slaughtered in unlimited numbers in the interest of British balance of power policy, while the British restricted themselves to a mere token participation. The Russians were well aware of the British intention to make a much smaller commitment in the war which they were seeking to promote in 1939 than had been the case in World War I. Drax was angry because the Russians dared to adopt a realistic and critical attitude toward this policy.

Drax noted that Voroshilov was constantly assuming the inevitability of war between the Western Powers and Germany. This was a realistic awareness of the determination of Halifax to promote a general war at all costs. Drax feared that this insight might contribute to the failure of negotiations with Russia. He complained that the Russians would be content to remain neutral, "while the rest of us cut one another's throats." Drax was irritable because the weather in Russia was extremely hot, and he had been burdened with additional Anglo-French meetings after the four hours of daily conferences with the Russians. He regarded his mission to Moscow as a great personal sacrifice, and he was anxiously waiting to return to England. He suggested that a British cruiser should be sent for the seventeen officers of the two missions if a pact was achieved. He admitted that the slow naval voyage to Russia in the first instance had made the French officers restless, and that it was quite possible some of them would prefer to return by train. Drax hoped that after his uncomfortable stay in Russia he would at least receive the satisfaction of personally gloating over the discomfited Germans. He proposed, in the event of a pact, that his cruiser sail continuously within sight of the German coast on its return voyage.[45]

Halifax had instructed Kennard on August 17, 1939, to chide the Poles for their unwillingness to cooperate with Russia. The Poles were to be told that military considerations required the full use of Polish and Rumanian territory by Soviet forces. Kennard was instructed that an alliance with the Russians might not prevent the outbreak of war, but it would offer the best means of guaranteeing victory. Halifax was unwilling to accept the view that the Soviet Union was a greater threat to Poland than Germany. Halifax stated his position categorically: "If, in the event of war, Poland and Rumania find themselves with their backs to the wall, we cannot believe that they will not be glad of support, from no matter what quarter." Halifax insisted that a neutral Russia would constitute the "chief menace" in the world if her strength remained undiminished by the ravages of a new war. He failed to draw the obvious deduction that a new war with or without Russian participation could lead to this result. He was confident that he could cope with everyone, including Stalin, in his own misguided effort to strengthen British world supremacy. It was a tragedy for the British nation that by 1939 his ruthlessness had exceeded his sagacity. He failed to see that his policy was promoting the growth of Communism rather than British imperialism.[46]

Kennard knew that Halifax had never bothered to understand the Polish attitude toward the Soviet Union. He knew that the faulty arguments of Halifax would not make the slightest impression on the Poles. He confided to Halifax on August 18, 1939, that he was reluctant to ask Beck to admit the Russians. He argued that the efforts of French Ambassador Noël to influence the Poles had merely produced Polish resentment, and he saw no reason to draw this resentment from Noël to himself. He reported that Beck was employing a huge arsenal of arguments against the latest pro-Soviet plan. Beck was scornful of the French claim that an alliance with the Soviet Union might help keep the peace. He replied that Polish acceptance of the Russian terms would produce an immediate German attack against Poland.

Kennard claimed that to pursue the question with Beck was hopeless. General Stachiewicz, the Polish Chief-of-Staff, had informed General Musse, the French military attache at Warsaw, that Poland officially rejected the proposal for Russian military transit through Poland. Kennard admitted that he shared the attitude of Beck in this important question. He introduced arguments of his own against the plan, and he claimed that the British would jeopardize their special relations with the United States if they joined the French in applying pressure to Poland.[47]

Premier Daladier of France would have been furious had he known that Kennard was sabotaging British pressure on Poland with the argument that American sensibilities had to be taken into account. He told American Ambassador Bullitt at Paris on August 18th that he was shocked and angered by the "violence" with which Lukasiewicz and Beck had rejected Soviet aid to Poland. Daladier claimed that it would be easy to internationalize Soviet aid to the Poles by sending two French and one British divisions to Poland by way of Russia. Daladier repeated to Bullitt three times with increasing emphasis that he would not send a single French peasant to give his life for Poland if the Poles rejected Russian aid.[48]

Bullitt was alarmed by this revelation of what he considered a violently anti-Polish reaction on the part of Daladier. He had applied pressure for months on Daladier and Alexis Leger, the Secretary-General at the French Foreign Office, in the hope that they would distance themselves from the peace policy of Georges Bonnet and repudiate that policy. He had visited London in May

1939 to coordinate his strategy with the efforts of Sir Robert Vansittart. The Diplomatic Adviser to His Majesty's Government considered relations with France to be his own special province, and he hoped to support the Halifax war policy by securing French participation in any war against Germany. Vansittart assured Bullitt that Alexis Léger was his "intimate friend," and that Léger could be relied upon to support the efforts of Halifax and Roosevelt to involve France in war with Germany.

Bullitt, Vansittart, and Léger feared that Sir Eric Phipps, the British Ambassador to France and brother-in-law of Vansittart, shared the negative attitude of Prime Minister Chamberlain toward an alliance between the Western Powers and Russia. Bullitt had begun to dislike Bonnet, and he reported to President Roosevelt without any regard for accuracy: "in point of fact both Bonnet and Sir Eric Phipps were opposed to bringing the Soviet Union into close cooperation with France and England." Bullitt also feared that Prime Minister Chamberlain might attempt to challenge the policy of Halifax and restore his own control over the conduct of British policy. American Ambassador Kennedy had reported from London on July 20, 1939, that Chamberlain was "sick and disgusted with the Russians." The British Prime Minister believed that Hitler would welcome any tangible opportunity for a peaceful settlement. Chamberlain knew that Hitler was not bluffing and that he might gamble on a war, but he told Kennedy that Hitler "is highly intelligent and therefore would not be prepared to wage a world war."49

President Roosevelt had intervened directly in the negotiations between the Soviet Union and the Western Powers on August 4, 1939. Lawrence Steinhardt, who had succeeded Davies as American Ambassador to Russia, was instructed by confidential letter to tell Molotov that the interests of the United States and the Soviet Union were identical in promoting the defeat of Italy and Germany in a European war. President Roosevelt urged the Soviet Union to conclude a military alliance with Great Britain and France, and he intimated that the United States would ultimately join this coalition of Powers. The American Ambassador was informed that President Roosevelt had told Soviet Ambassador Konstantin Umansky, before the latter departed for Russia on leave, that the United States hoped to achieve a position of solidarity with the Soviet Union against Germany and Italy.50

The Russians were pleased with the Roosevelt message because it strengthened their position in negotiations with both the Western Powers and Germany, and the support of Roosevelt made it easier for them to gain consent for their ambitious program of expansion in Finland, Poland, Rumania, Lithuania, Latvia and Estonia. The Russians had no desire to conceal from the foreign Powers the contents of the confidential Roosevelt message. The news of the message appeared in the *Voelkischer Beobachter* at Berlin on August 11, 1939, and its contents were published by the *Ilustrowany Kurjer* at Kraków on August 13, 1939. Steinhardt knew that Umansky had been informed of the contents of the Roosevelt message before leaving the United States. The letter with the message was sent by way of Bullitt at Paris, and Steinhardt did not receive it until August 15, 1939. He concluded that Molotov had instructed Umansky to reveal the contents of the letter before it reached Russia, and that Molotov had proceeded to permit the news of the letter to reach the foreign Powers before he had actually received it himself.

Steinhardt presented the Roosevelt letter to Molotov on August 16, 1939, and the two diplomats proceeded to discuss its contents. Roosevelt, in writing the letter, had hoped to influence Russian policy in favor of the Western Powers, but it is not surprising that he failed completely in this effort, and that Molotov used the message for his own purposes. Molotov told Steinhardt that the British and French military missions had come to Russia to discuss military collaboration in terms which the Soviet Foreign Commissar characterized as "vague generalities." Molotov added that these missions were unable to contend with the specific points which Russia had raised.

Steinhardt reported to President Roosevelt on August 16th that he was personally convinced that the Soviet Union would seek to avoid participation in the early phase of a European conflict. This annoyed President Roosevelt, who seemingly would have led the United States into a European conflict on the first day of war had American public opinion and the American Congress permitted such a policy. The American President was perturbed to learn, a few days later, that Alexis Léger at the French Foreign Office was not the unconditional advocate of war-at-any-price which Bullitt had claimed. Léger revealed his opinion that it would be exceedingly unwise for Great Britain and France to attack Germany without military support from the Soviet Union. This seemed to indicate that there would be virtually no support for a war policy in France if the negotiations at Moscow failed. Roosevelt also learned that Premier Daladier was continuing to denounce the "criminal folly" of the Poles. President Roosevelt knew that Halifax would abandon his project for war against Germany if he was unable to gain the military support of either the Soviet Union or France. The possibility that the peace might be saved was perturbing to the American President who hoped to utilize a European war to achieve his dream for the perpetuation of his tenure and the increase of his personal prestige and glory.[51]

Halifax had an important advantage in this difficult situation. He had been receiving detailed information, throughout August 1939, of the conversations between the Germans and Russians from Theo Kordt, the German Chargé d' Affaires at London. Theo Kordt and his brother, Erich Kordt, who occupied the key position in Ribbentrop's personnel office at Berlin, were members of a small conspiratorial group which recognized no such thing as treason in their efforts to defeat the diplomacy of Hitler. Halifax knew that the Russians were considering a pact with Germany, and that the Anglo-French negotiations with Russia might end in failure at any time. This enabled him to prepare a strategy designed to drag France into war against Germany without Russian support. It cushioned him against the psychological shock of a Russo-German agreement. Halifax did not receive a warning from American sources, that Russia and Germany might conclude a pact, until August 18, 1939, when rumors of this possibility were forwarded by American Under-Secretary of State Sumner Welles. This was no longer news to Halifax by that time.[52]

The British Foreign Secretary continued to adopt a dilatory policy toward the Poles in the Anglo-Polish alliance negotiation. Polish Ambassador Raczynski was deeply disappointed by the niggardly British attitude toward the possibility of financial aid to Poland. He received no encouragement when he proposed to Halifax that a permanent Polish military mission should be stationed at London. Raczynski in July 1939 had begun to urge Halifax to complete the negotiation of an actual Anglo-Polish alliance, before the conclusion of the Western negotiations at Moscow. Halifax professed to be willing to do this, but he did nothing to encourage the negotiations before the middle of August 1939. He at last granted the Poles permission to send Legal Counsellor Kulski, from the Polish Foreign Office at Warsaw, to London. Discussions for the conclusion of an alliance, which had been interrupted in April, were resumed on August 17, 1939, between Sir Alexander Cadogan and the Polish diplomats.[53]

The Poles on August 18th again rejected the British proposition that Poland should guarantee Rumania against a possible German attack. The Poles insisted that the definitive agreement should state that the alliance was not directed against Germany's possible allies or confederates. The British were content to accept this formulation, because an alliance directed exclusively against Germany meant that Great Britain would not be obliged to protect Poland against the Soviet Union. The principal friction in the negotiation resulted from renewed British attempts to commit Poland against Germany at every point on the compass. The negotiation was interrupted for a short time on Saturday, August 19th, and Polish Ambassador Raczynski departed from London to spend a few days at the English seashore. It had not been possible to settle the terms of the alliance in three days of protracted negotiations.[54]

French Ambassador Noël made another attempt at Warsaw on August 19th to press for Polish concessions to Russia. He received in reply what Beck described as a final statement: "It is for us a question of principle; we do not have a military accord with the Soviet Union and we do not wish to have one." General Stachiewicz also issued a final statement to the French. He declared that Poland was unwilling to acquiesce in the penetration of any foreign troops on her territory.

Captain Beauffre was despatched to Warsaw from the French mission in Moscow on August 19, 1939. He requested an immediate audience with Marshal Smigly-Rydz. The Polish Marshal had been officially designated by a law of May 6, 1936, as the chief personage in the Polish state after President Mościcki, who fulfilled titular functions in the style of the French president. The request of Beauffre for an audience was granted, but the Polish Marshal did not permit the French envoy to present lengthy arguments. Marshal Smigly-Rydz declared that everyone in Poland knew that Russian transit meant the Russian military occupation of the country. He then exclaimed: "With the Germans, we risk the loss of our liberty, with the Russians we would lose our soul!"[55]

The statement of Marshal Smigly-Rydz was a categorical assertion that Poland considered the Soviet Union, and not Germany, to be her principal enemy. This announcement was scarcely a surprise to the French leaders. General Gauché, the chief of French counter-intelligence, had informed Premier Daladier and Foreign Minister Bonnet of this fact on numerous occasions. They knew as well as Halifax that the betrayal of Poland to the Soviet Union would be a worse crime in Polish eyes than the abandonment of the Poles in a conflict between Germany and Poland.

The arrogance of the Poles had long been a source of irritation to General Gauché. He was tired of Polish criticism about the Franco-Russian alliance, and about the defensive strategy employed by the French Army in their military planning. He was displeased by empty Polish boastfulness about the offensive spirit of their own army, and their alleged readiness to capture Berlin. He was weary of hearing their claims that Poland and Hungary could defend Eastern Europe from Germany and the Soviet Union. He was angered by their contention that the Czechs had received the fate they deserved, and that they never should have been allowed to form an independent state.

General Gauché firmly believed that France should allow Hitler to settle accounts with Poland if the Moscow negotiations failed, and he presented this opinion to Daladier, Bonnet, and the French military leaders. He argued that France would be entitled to ignore earlier obligations to Poland on any one of three counts. He claimed that the conclusion of the 1934 Pact with Germany without consulting France violated the spirit and purpose of the Franco-Polish alliance. He interpreted the Polish ultimatum to the Czecho-Slovak ally of France in October 1938 as a direct attack on French interests. He claimed that the Poles had violated the purpose and spirit of their alliance with France when they hastened to recognize the establishment of the German protectorate in Bohemia-Moravia in March 1939 without consulting the French leaders. General Gauché condemned the Halifax war policy, and he complained that complete rigidity in Anglo-French policy in 1939 had replaced the flexibility which characterized the policy of the two Powers in 1938. He denounced the obvious disinclination of Great Britain to assume a major commitment in land operations on the European continent. The British had called up their first conscription class in June 1939, and the class included only 200,000 men. Whatever doubts there may have been, about the British attitude toward the war which Halifax was seeking to promote, were dispelled in July 1939 when the British called up a mere 34,000 additional men. General Gauché assured Daladier and Bonnet that Hitler was not bluffing. Hitler did not desire war, but he would risk a war rather than capitulate before the extravagant pretensions of the Poles. It seemed obvious to the French counter-intelligence chief that his country should abandon any plans for war in 1939, if the Russians refused to join the Anglo-French front. This viewpoint was acceptable to Bonnet, and he proposed to conduct French policy accordingly.[56]

One of the principal complaints of General Gauché was that Poland insisted upon being treated as a Great Power, although she was obviously a Power of the second or third rank. This was the key to the British and French treatment of the Poles in August 1939. It seemed inconceivable that a minor Power would persistently defy and ignore the advice and threats of two allied Great Powers. The Poles had made it abundantly clear by August 20, 1939, that they refused to be treated as a satellite of either Great Britain or France, or to accept a proposition for so-called Bolshevik protection, which neither of these countries would have accepted under similar circumstances. The Poles were determined never to consent to the presence of Bolshevik forces on Polish soil, regardless of whether or not this was inevitable. ' Their attitude was later explained by Professor Umiastowski, the leading Polish expert on Russo-Polish relations, when he wrote that "it was impossible to visualize any Great Power willing, when the Second Great World War was over, to challenge the Soviets to withdraw from the occupied countries which they had first entered *with the consent of the governments of those same countries.*"[57]

The verdict was clear as far as Poland was concerned, but the British and French leaders were no more willing to accept this verdict than they were to defend Poland against the Soviet Union. The attitude of Halifax in this question should dispel any illusion that he was genuinely concerned about protecting the Poles, or that Poland was more to him than a pawn in promoting the struggle against Germany. Halifax agreed to support the French decision to violate the confidence of the Poles by pledging themselves to Russian military intervention in Poland without Polish consent. His decision to do so did not destroy the Russian pretext that Polish refusal of Russian terms made it impractical for the Soviet Union to conclude an alliance agreement with the two Western Powers.

General Doumenc, the head of the French mission in Moscow, and Paul-Émile Naggiar, the French Ambassador to Russia, advised Bonnet on August 19th to conclude an agreement with the Russians at once, over the head of Foreign Minister Beck. Bonnet decided to make one last effort with the Poles before following this advice. Naggiar and General Doumenc were correct in anticipating that the Beauffre mission to Warsaw, which had been agreed to previously, would fail, but Bonnet decided to secure greater British support than had been received in the past, for a new step by French Ambassador Noël. He informed Halifax of this plan, and he argued that it was "almost an impossible position" for Great Britain and France to defend Poland if she refused to accept Russian help. He informed Halifax that "he understood the Polish reluctance but in a case like this they could only choose the lesser of the two evils." Bonnet knew that the Poles regarded the Russians as a greater menace than the Germans, but he claimed that the immediate threat was directed at Poland from Germany. Bonnet warned Halifax that the Poles were committing a new series of blunders in their treatment of the German minority, and that they were guilty of further provocations at Danzig.[58]

Kennard was not inclined to support a new step by Noël at Warsaw. He wired Halifax the full details of the rejection statements by Beck and Stachiewicz shortly after 2:00 a.m. on August 20th. He added that Beck had told him that the Polish Government objected to the passage of Russian troops as strongly as they would object to any German invasion. Kennard insisted that this attitude was justifiable, and he assured Halifax that "no Pole would ever expect to recover any territory occupied by Soviet troops." The last statement was a considerable exaggeration of the true Polish attitude, and Polish policy would have been different had the Polish leaders not expected the ultimate collapse of the Soviet Union whether in a war against Germany or against the Western Powers. It is a sufficient indication of his attitude that Kennard used strong terms in presenting the Polish case against an Anglo-French agreement with Russia at the expense of Poland.[59]

Kennard was displeased with the reply of Halifax to this report. The British Foreign Secretary condemned Beck in no uncertain terms, and he observed contemptuously that the Polish diplomat was deluding himself if he thought he could avoid war by refusing Soviet aid. He added that Beck would be "giving away his own case" if he was thinking of possible Russian support after the war had begun. Halifax had no justification to assume that Beck was contemplating anything of the kind, and this was another indication that he had never bothered to understand the policy pursued by Beck since the death of Marshal Pilsudski in 1935.

Kennard replied that General Stachiewicz had now agreed to repeat his rejection of the Russian transit plan to anyone who cared to hear it. Kennard did not indicate that he was prepared to join Noël in a new effort to influence the Poles. This burden rested exclusively on the French representatives in Poland. General Gamelin had decided to send General Faurice to Poland in a last attempt to argue the French position. Faurice had directed the Polish War College at Warsaw for many years, and he had numerous friends among the Polish military men. His mission was exceptionally delicate, because he was instructed to advise the Poles that France had never agreed to support Polish military action against Germany in the event of a German annexation of Danzig. Needless to say, this mission for France did not increase the popularity of the French general in Poland.[60]

Daladier and Bonnet decided on August 21, 1939, to go over the heads of the Poles without further hesitation. Sir William Strang, who had returned from Moscow to London early in August, was informed by the French diplomats at London on August 21st that the French Government had decided to permit their military authorities to act as the "guarantor" of Poland, in the staff talks at Moscow which had been resumed earlier the same day. The French planned to give "an affirmative answer in principle" to the demand for Russian military operations in Poland. The sole condition which they intended to impose was that Russian troops refrain from entering Poland until the outbreak of hostilities between Poland and Germany. General Doumenc would receive plenipotentiary powers to accept any agreement which would include French approval of the Russian request.

Strang discussed the French *démarche* with Sir Alexander Cadogan. The two diplomats agreed that France was acting without formally consulting Great Britain, in the expectation of receiving *ex post facto* British support. This was a reasonable assumption, because Halifax had repeatedly encouraged Bonnet in the opinion that it was necessary to grant Russia permission to conduct military operations in Poland. Strang concluded that "it may well be that their judgment of the Polish attitude is the right one (and they should know by now, after all these years, what the Polish mind is like), and that while the Poles refuse their assent, they really mean to indicate that we are at liberty to go ahead with the Russians provided we say nothing to the Poles about it." This was an astonishing rationalization of an unpleasant situation, but it was typical of British diplomacy and of the official British mind. Both Strang and Cadogan believed that the British Government should support the French move.[61]

Premier Daladier spoke with Lukasiewicz at Paris on August 21, 1939, without offering the slightest hint that France had decided to offer the Russians permission to enter Poland. Daladier later claimed that, as a saving gesture to French conscience, he had threatened to break the French alliance with Poland in retaliation against Polish refusal to cooperate with the Russians. Lukasiewicz emphatically denied this. The Polish diplomat recalled that he was primarily impressed in this conversation by the fact that Daladier had very little to say.[62]

The last meeting between the Anglo-French military men and the Russians, before the Soviet press announced that the Soviet Union would conclude a separate treaty with Germany, took place on the afternoon of August 21, 1939. Marshal Voroshilov peremptorily announced that he was responsible for Red Army autumn "maneuvers," and that he would soon ask for the permanent adjournment of military talks with the West, so that he could better devote himself to this task. General Doumenc did not receive his commission of authority to propose a separate Anglo-Franco-Russian agreement on Poland until after this meeting. Marshal Voroshilov lectured the British and French military men about Poland. He declared that it had always been axiomatic that Russia should have the same right to operate in Poland and Rumania that the United States and Great Britain had possessed in France during World War I. He expressed astonishment that the Western missions had arrived in Russia without a clear commitment on this important question. The British and French military men received the news of the intended Russo-German non-aggression pact from the Russian newspaper press immediately after the close of the session.[63]

The British discovered afterward that Stalin had decided to conclude a pact with Germany as early as August 11th, on the second day that the British and French military missions were on Russian soil, and before the first preliminary conversations between the missions and the Russian military leaders. It was later evident that Stalin had deliberately protracted his negotiations with both the Germans and the Allied military missions. The British and French would never have made the final decision to offer an agreement to Russia at the expense of Poland had the Soviet Dictator shown his hand at an earlier date. The fact that the general public learned the true nature of Soviet policy before the military missions received any hint of this policy was typical of Soviet diplomacy, and it was a deliberate affront to both Great Britian and France. The British and French would not have exposed themselves to this needless insult had it not been for the reckless policy of Halifax in seeking to provoke war with Germany at all costs. The policy of Halifax was the greatest possible aid which Great Britain could render to the realization of Communist objectives, but this did not prompt Stalin and the other Russian leaders to display any gratitude. They knew that Halifax's policy was a series of blunders selfishly conceived, and of course not a deliberate attempt to advance the Communist world conspiracy.[64]

British Ambassador Henderson at Berlin expressed the indignation of many of his countrymen when he wired to Halifax early on August 22nd, "the treacherous cynicism of Stalin and Co., with our military missions sitting and negotiating at Moscow, is beyond belief." Henderson recognized at once that the circumstances of the Russian surprise were calculated to inflict the maximum injury to British prestige. He always had opposed an alliance pact with the Soviet Union, but he was saddened by the spectacle of the additional humiliation which his country was forced to endure.[65]

The Ineptitude of Halifax's Russian Diplomacy

The belated approach to Russia by Halifax was an abortive and sordid affair. Halifax had virtually ignored the Soviet Union throughout 1938. He launched his sudden and unexpected courtship of the Russians with an appeal for their help in Rumania, although this appeal was based on the hoax which he had fabricated with Tilea, and it ignored the fact that Rumania did not desire Communist protection. He followed this with his Four Power alliance pact proposition of March 20, 1939, which was torpedoed by Beck four days later. He then proceeded on March 31, 1939, to extend a unilateral guarantee to Poland without consulting Russia. He permitted Bonnet to inform the Russians that Great Britain continued to desire an alliance with the Soviet Union before producing his hopelessly onesided offer of April 15, 1939. Halifax allowed Strang to proceed to Russia two months later without having altered to any appreciable extent the unsatisfactory British terms. He instructed Strang during June and July 1939 to retreat one step at a time toward a position allegedly more acceptable to Russia, although this style of diplomacy inevitably produced Russian contempt. The British military mission was dispatched to Moscow in August 1939 by the slow means of naval transit without adequate instructions. This placed the British military men in an inferior position before their Russian counterparts. It was soon evident that the Polish question was at the root of the Russian criticism of the British position. Halifax permitted Kennard to avoid decisive steps in support of France at Warsaw which might have made some impression on the Poles. The Poles refused to modify their position, and Halifax, without having duplicated the strong French protests to Poland, acquiesced in the proposal of the French leaders to conclude a separate agreement with Russia at Polish expense. Halifax adopted this policy despite the fact that Kennard had repeatedly reminded him that the Soviet Union was the principal enemy of Poland.

Halifax's conduct of British relations with Russia and Poland during this period fully revealed the miserable reality behind the noble facade of his policy. It is impossible to avoid the conclusion that Soviet support in a war against Germany was less important to Halifax than the war itself. The unprecedented arrogance of the Communists in their treatment of the British military mission is beyond dispute, but it is difficult to deny that Halifax fully deserved this treatment.

The attempt of Halifax to conclude an alliance with the Russians had been the most publicized feature of European diplomacy for more than five months. For this reason the prestige factor involved was extremely great. When the effort ended in failure the humiliation was all the greater. The suitor had been found wanting, and he was rejected. The Franco-Russian alliance of 1935 had been deprived, in the process, of whatever significance it had once possessed. It is a general rule that friction arises between partners in defeat, and a considerable amount of French resentment against Great Britain after the debacle in Russia was inevitable. The disaster in Russia did not persuade Halifax for one moment to question the wisdom of a preventive war against Germany, but this war remained conditional in his mind on the participation of France. Halifax had courted Russia for a short period, but he was engaged in a perpetual courtship of France, and the policy of France had become the decisive element in the European situation.

Hitler hoped that the reversal in Russia would modify Anglo-French policy, and he intended to contribute to this development by diplomatic means. Hitler

THE FORCED WAR

was prepared to approach both Great Britain and France with new diplomatic proposals, but his Anglophilia prompted him to concentrate his major effort on Great Britain. He would have reversed this priority had he fully realized the contrast between the reasonable French attitude and Halifax's unshakeable desire for war. This fact remained concealed from Hitler in August 1939, and he would not have believed the truth about Halifax unless it had been presented to him with documentary confirmation. Hitler continued to entertain the natural, but utterly mistaken, assumption that Halifax would prefer a peaceful settlement of Anglo-German differences to an Anglo-German war. He failed to realize that Halifax, despite his diplomatic defeat in Russia, still preferred the destruction of Germany to peace.

Chapter 18

THE RUSSIAN DECISION

FOR A PACT WITH GERMANY

The Russian Invitation of August 12, 1939

The policy of Stalin and Molotov toward Germany in August 1939 was consistent with the foreign program outlined by the Soviet leaders at the 18th Congress of the Communist Party in March 1939, before the German occupation of Prague. The Russian leaders at that time had predicted that the Soviet Union would succeed in remaining neutral during the early phase of the conflict which they expected to occur in the near future between Germany and the Western Powers. The French believed that an alliance between the Western Powers and the Soviet Union might be a useful prelude to a policy of conciliation toward Germany which would prevent the outbreak of World War II. The British leaders hoped for Soviet assistance in the war against Germany which they considered inevitable. It is unlikely that the French leaders could have influenced the British to adopt a moderate policy even after an agreement with the Soviet Union had been achieved. It is extremely doubtful that a military pact with the Soviet Union would have been useful in preventing the outbreak of World War II. It has been argued that Russian neutrality was the real cause of the outbreak of World War II, but this paradoxical viewpoint has never been presented in a convincing manner. The contention has been made that the adherence of the Soviet Union to the coalition of Halifax would have created preponderant power sufficient to guarantee the peace. This does not take account of the fact that Halifax, unlike the French leaders, desired not peace but war, and that the British diplomats themselves did not believe that an alliance with the Soviet Union would preserve the peace.[1]

The German leaders received a definite indication on August 12, 1939, that the Soviet Union had decided to arrive at an understanding with Germany and to reject the Anglo-French alliance offer. Russian Chargé d'Affaires Georgi Astakhov called at the German Foreign Office and announced that Stalin wished to reach an understanding with Germany about Poland and about Russo-German political relations. Astakhov suggested that negotiations could be advanced "by degrees," and that Moscow would be a suitable place for final talks. He had no suggestion to make about the selection of negotiators by Germany. His *démarche* did not mean that a Russo-German pact had become a certainty, but it was evident that successful negotiations were probable if desired by Germany.

The Russians were not offering to conclude a pact which would ban the danger of war. They were hoping that Halifax would succeed in launching a major European war, without Russian participation. The Russians considered it worthwhile to gamble on this eventuality, because it would create the most favorable conditions for the expansion of Bolshevism in Europe. Hitler hoped that a Russo-German pact would be a decisive factor in preventing the outbreak of a new European war. He thought there was good reason to believe that the Western Powers would change their minds about war with Germany after the defection of the Soviet Union. It seemed less likely that there would be a new European war if the Soviet Union signed a neutrality pact with Germany instead of an alliance with the Western Powers. This was true despite the fact that many irresponsible Western journalists favoring war claimed that this step by Russia, which they disliked, made war more probable. They knew that arguing in this manner would increase the chances for war.[2]

The Private Polish Peace Plan of Colonel Kava

The Russian *démarche* of August 12, 1939, came when it was most needed at Berlin. There were new indications during these days that the situation with Poland was utterly hopeless. The Poles had followed up the success of their outrageous August 4th ultimatum at Danzig with an intensified reign of terror over the German minority in Poland. Rumanian Minister Radu Crutzescu asked Weizsaecker at the German Foreign Office on August 11th if the current situation between Germany and Poland involved the immediate threat of war. Weizsaecker replied that it would be more profitable for the Rumanian Government to direct this inquiry to Warsaw. The German Ambassador to Poland, who was awaiting new instructions at Berlin, expressed his concern to Weizsaecker about the German minority in Poland. Weizsaecker promised Moltke that he would discuss the situation with Ribbentrop in an effort to discover if anything could be done to improve the situation.

The German Foreign Office on August 12th received word of a bitter and discouraging conversation between Senator Hasbach and Waclaw Zyborski, of the Polish Ministry of the Interior, which had taken place that day. Zyborski astonished Hasbach by claiming that he had seen an official German map which illustrated a plan to divide Poland between Germany and the Soviet Union. Zyborski insisted that Germany planned to annex Galicia, which constituted the entire South of Poland, and to permit most of Congress Poland and the Polish part of the Kresy region to return to Russia. Zyborski also contended that the Russians had been persuaded to re-settle the entire population of ethnic Poles, which came to a total of twenty millions, in Siberia. It was obvious to Hasbach that this fraudulent plan could be used to justify savage treatment of the

German minority in Poland. He told Zyborski that the plan was too fantastic to be credible, but his pleas were rudely ignored. Zyborski said with brutal bluntness that a situation had arisen in which none of the desires or pleas of the German ethnic group in Poland would be discussed.[3]

Many of the lesser Polish officials were alarmed and distressed by this impossible situation, but they knew that it was futile to attempt the modification of the harsh policy of Polish Premier Slawoj-Skladkowski toward the Germans. The Polish Consul-General at Berlin, Colonel Kava, urged Robert Boening, the National Socialist Secretary of the German-Polish Society, to go to Warsaw on August 13th in an attempt to make the Polish leaders listen to reason. He insisted that the most important obligation of the Society and its Foundation was to augment the earlier understanding between Germany and Poland, and that a special effort was required from Boening at a moment when it appeared that German-Polish friendship would be irretrievably lost. Kava was aware that Germany would never abdicate in the Danzig and Corridor transit questions, and he personally believed that the settlement of these questions was the necessary basis for a lasting understanding between the two countries. He promised to precede Boening to Warsaw, and to prepare the way with his friends at the Polish Foreign Office, who chafed under Beck's leadership.

Kava hoped for fruitful contacts with Polish Under-State Secretary Arciszewski, Deputy Director of the Western Department Kunicki, and Count Michal Lubienski, Beck's *Chef de Cabinet*. Boening assured Colonel Kava that he knew these three men, and that it would be possible to have sensible talks with them about current problems. He was grateful to Colonel Kava both for his general attitude and for his helpful suggestion, but he believed that the efforts of a private German individual such as himself would be useless. He promised to discuss the matter at the German Foreign Office, and to request an official commission for a journey to Warsaw. He also intended that Ribbentrop should recieve the new information which Colonel Kava had given him about the sincere and conscientious Polish officials who continued to favor peace with Germany despite the policy of Halifax and Beck. It was tragic that these Poles were unable to exert a decisive influence on the conduct of Polish policy. The difficulty was that Hitler and Ribbentrop feared that an isolated efffort of Boening, with men who were not in control over Polish policy, would persuade Halifax that Germany was retreating under Polish pressure.

Italian Ambassador Bernardo Attolico, who had been stationed at Danzig by the League of Nations in the 1920's, revealed at the German Foreign Office on August 14, 1939, a compromise plan from private Polish sources friendly to Germany. Germany would receive the city of Danzig and slightly more than half of its territory, with the Mottlau tributary of the Vistula as the dividing line. The territory assigned to Germany would connect Danzig with East Prussia, whereas the Poles would receive territory in the direction of Gdynia, and the "sort of island," actually a peninsula, on which was situated the Polish Westerplatte arsenal in Danzig harbor. These private Polish circles were hopeful that Hitler would accept this solution, which would at least bring 300,000 Germans back to the Reich. They were less confident about the official Polish attitude, but they thought that it would be worthwile to try a plan which offered a considerable German retreat from the October 24, 1939, offer, but which

stopped short of a total capitulation to Poland. The plan was gratefully received
by the German Foreign Office, and it was filed for future reference. More might
have been heard about it later had Poland agreed to resume negotiations with
Germany.[4]

The Polish Terror in East Upper Silesia

The Polish authorities in East Upper Silesia launched a campaign of mass arrests
against the German minority on August 14, 1939, and they proceeded to close
and confiscate the remaining German businesses, clubs, and welfare installations.
The Poles were furious because Viktor Szwagiel, one of their police officials,
was shot and wounded by a Young German Party member during the first
phase of the arrests. The arrested Germans were not interned in the area, but
were forced to march toward the interior of Poland in prisoner columns.
Thousands of Germans were seeking to escape arrest by crossing the border into
Germany. Their efforts were sometimes aided by so-called smugglers, who led
them across the "green border" (away from main thoroughfares and control
stations) for prices ranging from to 10 to 600 Zloty. The refugees noted that in
some cases the smugglers worked in connivance with the border control officials,
who sympathized with the plight of the Germans. Senator Rudolf Wiesner,
the leader of the Young German Party, was arrested by the Polish authorities
at 11:50 p.m. on August 16, 1939. The German Foreign Office learned the same
day that official Polish policy was not encouraging for any Danzig compromise
plan. August Papée, the Polish representative to the Vatican, gave a negative
reply to the suggestion of Cardinal Secretary of State Luigi Maglione on August
16th that Poland contribute to the preservation of peace by permitting Germany
to recover Danzig. Papée replied that Poland would invade Germany with or
without British and French support if Hitler attempted to secure the return
of the Danzig to the Reich.[5]

The various German groups in Poland were frantic by this time, and they
feared that the Poles might attempt the total extermination of the German
minority in the event of war. German Chargé d'Affaires Baron Wuehlisch at
Warsaw received a desperate and highly compromising secret appeal from the
German minority spokesmen on August 15th. The German Government was
requested to command the German Air Force, in the event of war, to drop
leaflets in Poland threatening reprisals against the Poles for further atrocities
against the German minority. The German press denounced the Polish policy of
mass arrests, and the Poles were warned not to regard the German minority as
helpless hostages who could be butchered with impunity.[6]

Ciano's Mission to Germany

The desperate situation in Poland prompted Hitler to welcome the Soviet initiative for a pact of neutrality at a time when it was impossible to deny the
likelihood of a German-Polish war. It also influenced his attitude in
with Italy. Hitler feared that the policy of retreat advocated by Mussolini would

convince the Western Powers that the Axis was weakening, and that this attitude would increase the danger of a general European war. He had rejected the proposal of Mussolini for a Brenner meeting because the joint communique proposed by the Italians conveyed the impression of an Axis retreat. The divergence of views between Hitler and Mussolini had produced a serious disagreement on the conduct of high policy, and it was recognized by both parties that personal conferences were necessary if this disagreement was to be overcome. The German Government agreed to invite Italian Foreign Minister Count Galeazzo Ciano to Germany for conversations with Hitler and Ribbentrop. Ciano was received in Salzburg by Ribbentrop, Mackensen, and Attolico on August 11, 1939. He was scheduled to confer with Hitler at the nearby Obersalzberg on the afternoon of the following day. The German leader was conferring with League High Commissioner Burckhardt when Ciano arrived, and it was decided that Ciano and Ribbentrop should engage in preliminary talks on the morning of August 12th.[7]

Hitler took the same line in his conversation with Burckhardt on August 11th that he intended to employ with Ciano on the following day. Hitler told Burckhardt that further patience with the Poles was becoming an impossibility, and that grave danger existed of a German-Polish war. He predicted that Germany would defeat Poland in about three weeks if war came. He requested Burckhardt to inform the French and British of this situation, and to remind them that Germany did not desire a conflict with the Western Powers under any circumstances. Burckhardt agreed to undertake this mission.

Beck was nervous about this meeting, because he feared that Burckhardt would make a formidable effort to persuade the British and French not to attack Germany. He told Szembek that he was furious with Burckhardt for accepting an interview with Hitler at this juncture. The Burckhardt mission made an impression on Bonnet, but none whatever on Halifax. The British Foreign Secretary, who sent Roger Makins to Basel as his personal representative to ascertain Hitler's views, received some plain language from Burckhardt about the atrocious mistreatment of the German minority by the Poles. Halifax responded by instructing Kennard that the Poles would have to improve their tactics if they hoped to avoid giving any impression that they were guilty of provoking the approaching war. Halifax also advised the Poles to cease their provocations at Danzig and to restrain their press. Kennard responded with a purely formal *démarche* which could not possible worry Beck. The Polish Foreign Minister was relieved to note that the Burckhardt mission had failed to modify British policy. He claimed to Kennard that there was no point in discussing the situation of the German minority with the British, and he also made the astonishing claim that the Germans, and not the Poles, had started the so-called press war. He added that it was always the Germans, and not the Poles, who provoked incidents at Danzig. It was evident that Beck was not inclined to engage Kennard in a serious discussion of these problems.[8]

Ribbentrop discussed the Polish situation with Ciano at great length on the morning of August 12th. He described some of the worst recent atrocities against the German minority in Poland, including the mutilation of several Germans. Ciano later reported to Mussolini that Ribbentrop was very grave, and that he feared war between Germany and Poland might soon be inevitable.

Ribbentrop admitted that Great Britain and France might attack Germany, despite the fact that they could offer no effective help to the Poles. The German Foreign Minister continued to hope that it would be possible to localize a German-Polish conflict by diplomatic action.

Ciano was surprised to discover that Ribbentrop was relying on Russian neutrality in the event of a German-Polish war, and that he believed Great Britain and France would fail in their efforts to conclude an alliance at Moscow. Ribbentrop hoped that this development would be decisive in discouraging the British and French interventionists, and that it would banish the danger of an Anglo-French assault on Germany.

Ciano had been instructed by Mussolini to convince the Germans that any risk whatever of a major war should be avoided, because such a conflict would be catastrophic for both Germany and Italy. Ciano accordingly took a strong stand against Ribbentrop's analysis of the European situation. He did not deny that Germany had ample justification under the existing provisions of international law to chastise the Poles. He argued instead that action by Germany against Poland would be inexpedient, because, in the opinion of both Mussolini and Ciano, the British and French would seize this as a pretext for military operations against Germany. Ribbentrop was surprised by Ciano's tenacity in arguing for this interpretation, and he was startled to note that his own analysis of Russian policy did not modify this opinion. The two diplomats debated the issue at great length, but nothing was said about the role of Italy in the event of war.[9]

Ciano and Ribbentrop met with Hitler on the Obersalzberg in the afternoon for an intensive conference of more than three hours. Ciano insisted that a war with Poland should be avoided at any price, and he suggested that the Axis should issue an appeal for an international conference. The Italian Foreign Minister presented his arguments with energy and single-mindedness throughout this conference, and he succeeded in making a great impression on Hitler. The Chancellor agreed to consider the Italian viewpoint at length before discussing the matter again on the following day. The German Foreign Office was impressed by the ability of Ciano to present his views and to counter the arguments offered by Hitler. Weizsaecker was convinced that Ciano would repeat this performance with still greater effect on the following day. He failed to realize that Ciano had also been influenced by Hitler during this lengthy discussion. He was astonished to note on August 13th that Ciano reversed his position, and declared that Hitler was probably correct in calculating that Great Britain and France would not attack Germany if the German-Polish crisis culminated in a local war.[10]

Hitler's reply to Ciano's arguments on August 12th is important because it reveals the thoughts which were deciding the course of German policy at this point. Hitler claimed that a few fanatics in Warsaw and Kraków were responsible for the tragedy in Poland because they had succeeded in stirring an otherwise indifferent Polish population into a frenzy of hatred against Germany. He stressed the obvious weaknesses of the Polish state with its large Ukrainian, Jewish, and German minorities. He assured Ciano that Germany was prepared to deal with Poland, and he illustrated this with confidential information that the Germans now had more than 130,000 soldiers in East Prussia alone. He predicted that German defenses in the West would prove themselves impregnable against a possible Anglo-French offensive. Hitler discussed German defense problems with Ciano at length with the aid of a detailed map.[11]

Hitler inquired what Ciano would do if Trieste were in Yugoslav hands, and if a large Italian minority were subjected to persecution on Yugoslav soil. The German Chancellor thought that the danger of a general war in such a situation might discourage decisive action, but he added that it was his definite conviction that Great Britain and France, whatever their threats now, would not precipitate a general war. The German Chancellor showed Ciano two telegrams which he had recently received. The first one was from Tokyo, and it contained new confirmation that Japan would not conclude an alliance with Germany and Italy. The second telegram from Berlin confirmed the fact that Russia was prepared to discuss relevant political questions, including the Polish question. The Soviet diplomat, Georgi Astakhov, had personally informed the German Foreign Office that this was the case. Hitler pointed out that Germany, under these circumstances, would lose nothing in Japan by concluding an agreement with the Russians. He claimed that the British and French military missions in Russia were merely a blind to cover the failure of the Halifax effort to secure an alliance with Soviet Union.[12]

Ciano argued that Great Britain and France would attack Germany despite a Russo-German agreement. He claimed that a war at this moment would be highly advantageous for the Western Powers. Great Britain and France had made great progress with their military preparations, and a temporary *union sacrée* (consecrated unity above considerations of everyday politics) had been achieved in the Western countries. These alleged advantages, according to Ciano, would prompt Great Britain and France to intervene against Germany on the slightest pretext. He predicted that a war in 1939 would deal a catastrophic blow to German and Italian relations with the United States, because it would enable President Roosevelt to obtain a third presidential term of office.

Ciano predicted that Roosevelt would lose his political game of exploiting foreign crises to advance his position at home if war could be averted at least until after the American presidential election in November 1940. Ciano was convinced that the temporary unity of opinion in Great Britain and France would gradually disintegrate if there were no war. He argued that the true friends of Germany were not in good condition at the moment. Japan might succeed in extricating herself from the Chinese imbroglio. Spain would have an opportunity to consolidate under her new regime. Above all, Italy would increase her own military forces. Ciano stressed that Italy was totally unprepared for a major war in 1939.[13]

Ciano reported to Mussolini that Hitler had recognized the validity of each point in support of the Italian position, provided one could assume that a general war would ensue. The doubtful policy of the Western Powers was the crux of the problem. Hitler insisted again and again that Great Britain and France would not attack Germany. Mussolini was also informed that Ciano told Ribbentrop, after the conference with Hitler on August 12th, that Italy would not enter the war if Germany was attacked by Great Britain and France. Ciano did not wish his disagreement with the German leaders to receive publicity. He had no objection on August 12th to a German protocol drawn up in French, which announced publicly that complete harmony was resulting from the Italo-German exchange of views.[14]

Ciano later reported to Mussolini that his conference with Hitler on August 13th, in contrast to the meetings on the previous day, had been exceptionally cordial. Hitler announced that he had thought the matter over and had decided to reject Ciano's argument. He offered three principal reasons for arriving at this conclusion. In the first place, the Russians were apparently willing to cooperate with Germany, because they expected a German-Polish war which would enable them to acquire Eastern Poland. They would have no motive to support Germany at an international conference dealing with the Danzig question. Such support might be useful in solving Hitler's problems, but it would not gain the Polish eastern provinces for the Soviet Union. The Russians would also oppose a solution of the Danzig crisis for fear it might lead to a lasting Anglo-German agreement. This would be anathema to the Russians. Hitler could regard it as an absolute certainty that the Soviet Union would oppose German wishes at a Danzig conference. Germany and Italy might persuade Great Britain and France to admit Spain to a parley, but even in this case, provided that Spain actually did support the German position, Germany, Italy, and Spain would be a minority against an Anglo-Franco-Russo-Polish majority. Germany could not hope to obtain satisfaction from such a conference, particularly because of the Soviet influence.[15]

Hitler believed that a dangerous reaction of over-confidence among the Poles would follow a German retreat at Danzig. He suspected that the Poles would seek to provoke a war by seizing Danzig during the rainy season. A victory for Poland at an international conference would encourage such a move, and the German minority in Poland would be required to pay a heavy price for any new Polish prestige. Germany would continue to confront an intolerable situation. War with Poland would probably come in 1939 anyway, and, if held off until the rainy season, the sea of Polish mud and the unpaved Polish roads might force such delays that a second front might be opened, and Germany be faced with a protracted two-front conflict.[16]

Hitler was convinced that Ciano had failed to appreciate the impact of a Russo-German agreement on Great Britain and France. This was the third consideration which prompted him to differ with the analysis of the Italian Foreign Minister. Hitler was principally concerned lest the effect of the Russian pact be diminished by Italy's avowed intention, which Ciano had announced to Ribbentrop, not to come to Germany's support if Great Britain and France attacked her. This decision would soon be discovered by the British and French, because Italy, in the event of a crisis, would decline to take the necessary measures of military preparation.

Hitler made an eloquent plea on August 13th for a reconsideration of the Italian position. The defection of Italy from Germany would greatly increase the danger of war. Hitler was convinced that a solid Italo-German front, in combination with a Russo-German pact, would break that very unity of opinion in Great Britain and France which Ciano had emphasized. This development would outweigh whatever other advantages the Western Powers believed they possessed for an eventual war.

The German Chancellor was pleased to discover on August 13th that no elaborate statements were required to gain Ciano's support. Hitler stated his position very briefly, but he received no arguments whatever from Ciano. The Italian Foreign Minister assured Hitler instead that the German leader had often been right in his analysis of difficult situations in the past, and that his evaluation on this occasion was probably more accurate than the Italian one. A German observer later explained that Ciano folded up like a pocket knife. Ciano promised Hitler that Italy would maintain a common front with Germany. Italy had little to lose if Great Britain and France did not attack Germany. Everything was settled quickly, and the second conference between Hitler and Ciano, which terminated a basic disagreement of several weeks duration between Germany and Italy, was over in thirty minutes.[17]

The Reversal of Italian Policy

Ciano had given Hitler his personal word that Italo-German solidarity would be maintained, but Italian Ambassador Attolico refused to accept this situation. He believed that Italy should separate from Germany if the Germans refused to retreat before Polish pretensions. He was irritated by the reports in the German press on August 15, 1939, which confirmed the Italo-German solidarity pledged by Ciano. He wished that Ciano had not made this pledge, and he decided to do everything possible to reverse the course of Italian policy.

Attolico requested and received permission to come to Rome on August 15, 1939, to present his case. He had prepared a careful report at Berlin on the Salzburg and Obersalzberg meetings. He criticized the foreign policy decisions of Hitler, Ribbentrop, and Ciano, and he argued that Italy should not come to the support of Germany in the event of a general Euopean war. He turned over his Embassy at Berlin to Count Massimo Magistrate, the Italian Chargé d'Affaires, with whom he enjoyed relations of close confidence. Magistrati reported to Rome, immediately after the departure of Attolico, that the Germans had informed him of the likelihood of a pact with Russia in the very near future. The purpose of this report was to convince Mussolini that the final crisis was close at hand, and that he had a last opportunity to reconsider the Italian commitment.[18]

Attolico was delighted to discover at Rome on August 16th that Ciano regretted the commitment he had made to Hitler. Mussolini and Ciano agreed with Attolico that Italian support to Germany in a major war would be inadvisable. Mussolini expressed his hope that a negotiated settlement of the German-Polish dispute would relieve Italy of the distasteful prospect of cancelling the pledge Ciano had made to Hitler. The Germans were alarmed by the mission of Attolico to Italy immediately after the conversations between Hitler and Ciano at Berchtesgaden. The negative attitude of Attolico toward the Italo-German alliance was well known at Berlin, and it was easy to deduce the purpose of his mission. He would not have left Germany had he been satisfied with the Ciano pledge at Berchtesgaden. Weizsaecker telephoned German Ambassador Mackensen on August 17th to inquire if he had seen Attolico, and if the Italian diplomat had departed again for Germany. Mackensen replied that Attolico had left Rome for Salzburg on the afternoon train the same day. He had failed to see the Italian diplomat, who was "detained at the Ministry" in seemingly continous conferences. Weizsaecker replied with great concern that he would take the morning train to Salzburg to confer with Ribbentrop and possibly with Attolico.[19]

A crucial telegram from Mackensen arrived in Berlin at 2:30 a.m. on August 18th before Weizsaecker departed for Salzburg. Ciano had informed the German Ambassador shortly before midnight on August 17th that Mussolini rejected the Berchtesgaden analysis of Hitler, Ribbentrop, and Ciano that a German-Polish war could remain localized. Mussolini insisted that a local war in Poland would be followed by an Anglo-French attack against Germany. He repeated the statement, agreed to by Hitler, that such a struggle would be exceedingly unfavorable for the Axis. Mussolini expressed his keen disappointment at the failure of Germany to respond favorably to the proposed Brenner meeting of the previous month, and to the Italian plan for a general diplomatic conference. He complained that such treatment from Germany deprived him of further inspiration for new creative suggestions. Ciano claimed that Mussolini was insisting that the decision for further steps "now lay solely with Berlin." Mackensen noted suspiciously that Ciano had a still later appointment the same night with the British Ambassador. The German diplomat was curious to know how much Ciano would choose to divulge to Sir Percy Loraine about the Italian position.

The German leaders were exceedingly disturbed by the revelation of Mussolini's attitude. Weizsaecker knew that Attolico had gone to Rome with the express purpose of converting Mussolini to a different interpretation of the crisis from the one which had been agreed upon between Hitler and Ciano at the Obersalzberg. Mackensen did not deny the obvious purpose of Attolico's mission, but he argued that the Italian Ambassador had insufficient influence at Rome to accomplish this. It seemed to Weizsaecker that Ciano was revealing excessive weakness in this dispute, and the German State Secretary concluded that Ciano had failed to speak with *franchise brutale* on August 13th, although he had sought to convey this impression. Weizsaecker concluded that Mackensen was wrong about Attolico's influence. The Italian Ambassador had adopted a strong and consistent position, which contrasted with the vacillation of Ciano. Weizsaecker guessed correctly that this factor was decisive in influencing Mussolini.[20]

Italy's Secret Pledge to Halifax

Ciano received Sir Percy Loraine a few minutes after midnight on August 18, 1939. He offered to discuss the conversations with Ribbentrop and Hitler on August 12th and 13th. Ciano reminded Loraine that the Poles were violating the German frontier with great recklessness, and that he was receiving extensive information about this situation from exclusively Italian sources in Poland. Ciano explained that the German attitude in the Polish question was naturally very stiff under these circumstances. The Italian Foreign Minister pleaded with Loraine that peace could not be preserved indefinitely unless at least the Danzig problem was solved in the German sense. Loraine replied that it was a fixed

British policy to apply no pressure on Poland to settle her differences with Germany. Ciano conducted himself correctly throughout this conversation, and Loraine hastily reported to Halifax that Italy had decided to stand solidly with Germany.

It was unfortunate that Italian fear of a possible British military attack prompted Ciano and Mussolini to abandon their attitude of loyalty toward Germany. Loraine joyfully reported later on August 18th that a new discussion with Ciano permitted him to draw the opposite conclusion about Italian policy. Ciano had claimed that Italy "has not agreed" to support Germany in the event of war, and he intimated to Loraine that she had no intention of doing so. Ciano also confided that he was in serious disagreement with Ribbentrop about the Polish crisis. Loraine reported irresponsible rumors that Hungarian Foreign Minister István Csáky was in Rome on a pro-Polish and anti-German mission. Loraine hoped that this was true, because it would magnify the great differences which separated the Axis allies. The rumor about the Csáky visit originated from a Russian source, and it apparently did not occur to Loraine that the Russians were encouraging the British to persist in their disastrous policy of challenging Germany.[21]

Ciano's indiscretion produced an electric effect in London, and it greatly weakened the impact Hitler desired to produce with his surprise Russian agreement. The influence on France was still more decisive. Indeed, it is reasonably certain that France, and consequently Great Britain, would not have attacked Germany had it not been for the disloyal indiscretion of Ciano to Loraine on August 18, 1939. The French military leaders asserted later that they would never have advised the French Government to gamble on a Franco-German war had it not been for the advance pledge of Italian neutrality in such a conflict. It would have been a simple matter for Bonnet to continue his peace policy had the Grench military men declared that a war with Germany was not feasible. A firm Italian stand in support of Germany, as advised by Hitler, and accepted by Ciano on August 13, 1939, would have done much more for European peace and for the interests of Italy than the prostration of Italy on August 18, 1939, before the British military threat.[22]

The Germans at this time had no idea whether or not Italy would support them. They were suspicious about the conferences between Ciano and Loraine, but they did not know that the British Government was receiving a promise that Italy would remain neutral if Great Britain attacked Germany. The message from Mussolini which Attolico presented to Ribbentrop at Salzburg on August 18, 1939, offered no indication of the true Italian position. Mussolini observed that a conflict between Germany and Poland would be difficult to localize, but he did not say that, in his opinion, this would be impossible. He mentioned that conditions did not appear favorable for Italian participation in a war of long duration, but he did not indicate that Italy would refuse to support Germany. It was natural for the Germans under these circumstances to conclude that Ciano had exaggerated the negative attitude of Mussolini in his conversation with Mackensen on August 17, 1939.

Ribbentrop explained to Attolico that the localization of a German-Polish war would probably depend upon the maintenance of a solid Italo-German front. The German Foreign Minister did not realize that this common front had been smashed by Ciano as the result of the initiative of the Italian diplomat to whom he was addressing his remarks. Ribbentrop explained that no prolonged war under modern conditions could be a "successful war" for any European Power, and he pointed out that Great Britain and France, after the conclusion of a Russo-German pact, could not hope for a quick success in a war against Germany. He had given much thought to Ciano's point about the re-election of President Roosevelt in the event of war. He and Hitler hoped that opposition to Roosevelt in the United States was sufficiently strong to hold the American President in check. Attolico declared that he was less optimistic about all these points, and he complained that the shortage or raw materials in Italy was a serious problem. Ribbentrop suggested that Attolico's analysis was not sufficiently imaginative. Russian raw materials would be available to Italy after the conclusion of a Russo-German trade agreement. Polish ore products from former German East Upper Silesia would be helpful to Italy in the event of war with Poland. Ribbentrop was satisfied with the outcome of this conference, because he received the delusive impression from Attolico that his remarks had allayed Italian fears.[23]

Mussolini was encouraged on August 18th by a misleading report from Italian Ambassador Arone at Warsaw. The Italian diplomat was informed by the American journalist, John Gunther, that Beck was perfectly willing to negotiate with Germany for a peaceful settlement. The false report of Gunther was widely circulated, and it contributed to serious misunderstandings about Polish policy at a time when Beck was resolutely opposed to further negotiation with Germany.

Soviet Hopes for a Western European War

The indiscretion of Ciano to Loraine was very helpful to the Soviet Union in the last few days before the conclusion of the pact with Germany. The Russians hoped that their refusal of an alliance with the Western Powers would not check the effort of Halifax to plunge Great Britain, France, and Poland into war against Germany. The Soviet Union would be unable to expand at the expense of her six western neighbors if peace was inadvertently preserved by the Russian neutrality policy toward Germany. It was even more important that a favorable occasion when the major capitalist Powers might damage or destroy themselves through their own actions would be lost.

Halifax hastened to inform British diplomatic missions abroad that Italian defection from the alliance with Germany was a certainty, and he was correct in assuming that this news would create an impression on the British diplomats. British Ambassador Henderson at Berlin was a formidable and consistent critic of the Halifax war policy, but he was much impressed by the news about Italy. He suggested that Hitler might be forced to retreat before the Poles after all, although he could not refrain from suspecting that Loraine's analysis of the situation in Rome was incorrect. It seemed incredible to Henderson that Ciano was capable of making such a gigantic diplomatic blunder.[24]

Ciano hoped to atone partially for his treacherous disloyalty to Germany by preparing the way for a peaceful settlement of the Danzig dispute. He seemed to think that Italian prestige as a mediating Power would be increased if Italy remained "on the fence," but this was no longer true after he had indicated that Italy would not support Germany under any circumstances. The situation would have been different had Ciano at least maintained some suspense about Italian policy. Ciano discussed with Loraine on August 19, 1939, the idea of a conference of the Powers to settle the Polish question. He was disappointed to note that the British Ambassador replied evasively to his various questions, and displayed no enthusiasm for a conference.

Halifax approved Loraine's "handling of the Italian scene" on the night of August 19th. There was no place on the Halifax program for a peaceful settlement of the Danzig dispute. He informed Loraine that Great Britain hoped to evade responsibility for closing the door on the Italian proposition. He hoped that the Germans and Italians would fail to agree on the program for a conference. He believed that Loraine should display a vaguely positive attitude toward Italian efforts if Italo-German disagreement was evident. Loraine should indirectly discourage Ciano by insisting that both the Soviet Union and Poland would have to participate on an equal basis with the other Powers in the proposed conclave. This was, of course, before Halifax had received word of the coming Russo-German pact. The British Foreign Secretary was not astute enough to foresee that the Russians could later be relied upon to oppose German aims at such a conference.25

Halifax was prompted by the news from Italy to discuss the general European situation with Sir Robert Vansittart, and to write a letter to Chamberlain, who was enjoying several weeks of vacation and virtual retirement during this month of severe crisis. Halifax was convinced that Hitler did not expect British participation in a German-Polish war. Halifax assured Chamberlain that Hitler could still have peace if he abandoned German claims at Danzig, but neither of the two men expected that Hitler would do this. Halifax concluded, after writing to Chamberlain, that it would be prudent to reinforce the reversal of Italian policy by frightening the Italians. He dispatched a message to Rome, which Loraine delivered to Ciano on the following day. Italy was warned on August 20, 1939, that Great Britain would attack her immediately with most of her armed forces if she joined Germany as an ally in any future war.26

This threat from Halifax produced a great effect at Rome. Mussolini concluded that a successful conference was necessary for Italian security and survival. The Germans were not informed of this British ultimatum to Italy. The Italians feared that they would be attacked without making any move unless they announced repeatedly that they would not support Germany. On August 20th Mussolini developed a tentative agenda for his proposed conference. The experience of the Munich conference had convinced him that a new conference would not be effective unless it was comprehensive in scope. He advocated the following main topics for the agenda: 1) German-Polish settlement, 2) Franco-Italian settlement (i.e. of Italian charges of French discrimination against Italy in colonial questions, of the mistreatment of the Italian minority in the French colonies, of French fears of Italian *irredentism*), 3) German colonies (a definitive agreement one way or the other on the possible restoration of the German colonies), 4) Economic problems (i.e. elimination of trade barriers), and 5) Limitation of armaments (an effort to scuttle the arms race and return to a

462 THE FORCED WAR

normal basis). Mussolini gave much thought to including all the major problems. It was easy to see that there were fewer problems in 1939, after many of the mistakes of the Paris peace treaties of 1919 had been rectified, than had been the case in earlier years. The urgency of such a conference was underlined by a report from Ambassador Arone at Warsaw, on the following day, that conditions in Danzig and along the German-Polish frontier were terrible, and that the general atmosphere in Poland was perilously tense.[27]

The Crisis at Danzig

Chodacki returned to Warsaw by airplane from Danzig on August 16, 1939, to discuss the situation with Beck. An unrewarding and lengthy conversation between Chodacki and Senate President Greiser that morning had failed to modify the deadlock between Danzig and Poland. Chodacki told Greiser that the Polish economic boycott against Danzig products would continue until Danzig recognized the unlimited right of the Polish inspectors to perform their functions anywhere on Danzig territory. The Polish diplomat claimed that Danzig would capitulate in this question were it not for her interest in secretly unloading German arms and ammunition in the Free City. League High Commissioner always told him that a meeting with Greiser had "gone right" when in fact nothing had "gone right." Burckhardt was also furious with the *Danziger Vorposten* (*The Danzig Sentinel*) for the indiscreet printing of news about his supposedly secret meeting with Hitler on August 11th. Burckhardt had intended that the meeting should be known to the German, British, French and Danzig leaders, but concealed from the Poles. He complained that his relations with the Poles were sufficiently unfavorable without the charge that he was conducting important European diplomatic missions for Hitler.[28]

German Chargé d'Affaires Wuehlisch at Warsaw warned the German Foreign Office on August 18, 1939, that the Poles were about to launch a campaign of mass arrests against the German minority in the areas of Posen, West Prussia, and Central Poland, in addition to East Upper Silesia. The Poles justified the mass arrests in Upper Silesia by charging that "the arrests in Upper Silesia are obviously to be attributed to the organization of diversionary groups which is done from various centers in the Reich." The Poles now charged that similar groups existed in the other districts. The events in Upper Silesia had been a prelude for a general compaign of terror throughout Poland.

Polish High Commissioner Chodacki returned from Warsaw on August 18th with new instructions for conversations with Greiser at Danzig. He told the Senate President that he had a blank check to remove the Polish economic embargo of Danzig if the local authorities granted the right of unrestricted operation in the Free City for both custom inspectors and Polish frontier guards. Greiser complained that this demand was equivalent to a total Polish military occupation of Danzig. Greiser promised to release two inspectors arrested on August 14th for illegal activities, but he refused to accede to the general Polish demand which had no foundation in the existing treaty relationship between Danzig and Poland. Chodacki turned the subject to the German-Polish crisis, and he observed with biting sarcasm that the basis for an agreement between the two countries had to be narrow, because Beck had assured him that Poland was not prepared to make any concessions. Chodacki declared that Poland would not launch military operations against Germany unless Germany attacked Polish interests, but he warned Greiser that the Polish nation would stand together as a nation of soldiers in any war.[29]

National Socialist District Party Leader Forster concluded after this conversation that the Polish position prevented a solution of the embargo crisis. He advised Edmund Veesenmayer, an assistant of Ribbentrop visiting at Danzig, that the local authorities would be more successful with the Poles if they adopted a more vigorous position. Veesenmayer disagreed with this view, and he argued that the Danzig Government should continue to exercise restraint and to permit the Poles to shoulder the responsibility for whatever happened at Danzig. Forster was scornful to discover that three Germans were arrested in West Prussia as agents of the Danzig Government. The Poles were treating the so-called Free City as a separate hostile Power.

A sensation was created at Danzig on August 21st when Senator Rudolf Wiesner arrived on the territory of the Free City after escaping from Poland. He had been arrested by the Poles on August 16th on suspicion of conducting espionage for Germany in Poland. Wiesner, who was the most prominent of the German minority leaders in Poland, discussed the current situation with representatives of the German Reich at Danzig on August 22nd. He complained that the German national group had sought to establish loyal relations with the Polish state, but that this effort had failed. He had vainly hoped that German ethnic consciousness would not be incompatible with loyal citizenship in Poland. Wiesner spoke of a disaster "of inconceivable magnitude" since the early months of 1939. He claimed that the last Germans had been dismissed from jobs without benefit of unemployment relief, and that hunger and privation were stamped on the faces of the Germans in Poland. German welfare agencies, cooperatives, and trade associations had been destroyed. The exceptional martial law conditions of the earlier frontier zone had been extended to include more than one third of the territory of the Polish state. The mass arrests, deportations, mutilations, and beatings of the past few weeks surpassed anything which had happened before. The tragedy was that this punishment was undeserved. Wiesner insisted that the German minority leaders continued to hope for a peaceful solution between Germany and Poland. They were not seeking a return to the German Reich. They merely desired the restoration of peace, the banishment of the specter of war, and the right to live and work in peace.[30]

The German diplomats and Danzig authorities discussed the possibility that the publication of the Wiesner statements might alleviate the wretched conditions of the German minority. Albert Forster, the local National Socialist Party chief, did not believe that this would be the case. He argued that such protestations of good faith, after the bestial persecutions which had been endured, would debase the Germans without changing the attitude of the Poles. He was relieved to discover that Werner Lorenz, Chief of the Office for Ethnic Germans in the Reich, agreed with his analysis in a report on the Wiesner material on the evening of August 22, 1939.[31]

The Wiesner episode aroused Forster to an unprecedented degree. The news of the approaching Russo-German pact was made public in Danzig at this time, and Forster urged that the time had come for Danzig to change her own policy to coincide with the implications of this treaty. He advocated a firm policy which would restrict the activities of Polish customs inspectors and frontier guards to the areas stipulated by the treaties. He proposed a policy of meeting force with force if the Poles reacted violently to this firm attitude.

These discussions were relayed to Hitler, who supported Forster. The German Chancellor believed that the Danzig Government should make an effective gesture in support of the inauguration of this new policy. He advised the Danzig Senate leaders to proclaim the appointment of Forster as Chief-of-State in Danzig. This would make Forster the formal titular chief at Danzig, and Greiser would continue as *de facto* Premier in his capacity as President of the Danzig Senate. The suggestion of Hitler was approved by the Danzig leaders, and it was decided to proclaim Forster head of state at noon on August 23, 1939. The days of acquiescence in Polish encroachments at Danzig were nearly over, or at least until March 30, 1945, when the German forces at Danzig surrendered to the Red Army after the city itself had disappeared in rubble and ashes under the bombardment of Soviet artillery and aerial attacks. German Danzig by that time existed solely in the hearts of her surviving citizens. The ruined shell of the city was provisionally inherited by Poles who were the involuntary slaves of their tiny Communist minority, and of the powerful Soviet Union. The Polish refusal to permit the return of Danzig to Germany ended in indescribable tragedy for both Poland and Germany.[32]

Russian Dilatory Tactics

The fratricidal strife between Germany and Poland was profitable to the Soviet masters of Russia from the first hour. The Russians were not encouraging a neutrality pact with Germany because they were more friendly toward the Germans than toward the British and French. These ordinary human distinctions did not exist in Soviet diplomacy, for the Soviet leaders desired the destruction of all the countries involved in the European crisis. The Russian leaders preferred to expand peaceably with the consent of Germany rather than of Great Britain and France, because this would enable them to avoid losses in warfare while Poland and the Western Powers engaged in a desperate struggle against Germany.

The *démarche* of Astakhov at Berlin on August 12th prompted Ribbentrop to dispatch important instructions to Schulenburg shortly after the departure of Ciano from Germany. Schulenburg was ordered to seek an appointment with Molotov for August 15th. This was arranged on August 14th, and the German Ambassador received his detailed instructions at 4:40, the following morning. Ribbentrop emphasized the traditional German political line which had been advocated by Bismarck in the 1850's in the conduct of relations between Prussia and Bonapartist France. This policy required that ideological differences should not necessarily be an obstacle to friendship between states. The employment of this policy was dictated by consideration for German interests. The German Reich in August 1939 was threatened with the formation of an overwhelming hostile coalition. The German leaders would prefer to cope with this situation by arriving at lasting understandings with Great Britian and France, but there were no specific indications that this was possible.

Schulenburg was instructed to inform Molotov that the living spaces of Germany and Russia might one day touch again at certain points, but they need not overlap. Ribbentrop added that possibly conflicting interests in the area between the Baltic Sea and the Black Sea could be settled by negotiation, and he believed that no one would deny that the two nations were complementary in the economic sphere. History taught that things had gone well for both nations when they cooperated, and badly for both when on opposite sides in war. Ribbentrop suggested that the "natural sympathy" of the Germans for Russia had never disappeared, and he argued that the current policies of the Western Powers were incompatible with the interests of both Germany and the Soviet Union. Ribbentrop considered a western alliance policy dangerous for Russia, because in World War I "the Russian regime collapsed as a result of this policy." Schulenburg, who apparently identified the Bolsheviks with the Tsars, considered that this formulation was tactless, and he modified it to read: "In 1914 this policy had serious consequences for Russia." The instructions concluded with the warning that an explosion might occur before the outstanding problems were settled unless negotiations were hastened. Ribbentrop expressed his willingness to come to Moscow provided that Stalin would agree to a personal meeting. The exact content of these instructions from Ribbentrop were to be presented to Molotov as a *note verbale*.[33]

Schulenburg explained his personal views in a lengthy report to Weizsaecker on August 14th before the arrival of the instructions from Ribbentrop. The German Ambassador opposed "hasty measures" with Russia, because he apparently believed that German eagerness might spoil the chances for an agreement. He warned that the Russians were blaming Germany in advance for any conflict which might arise with Poland. He was convinced that it would be necessary to pay an enormous price for an agreement. He approved the suggestion of an American diplomat in Moscow that the abandonment of close relations with Japan and the sending of a new military mission to Nationalist China might help to win Russian approval. Schulenburg seemed to think that the British and French military missions would conduct protracted negotiations in Moscow over a very long period. The German Ambassador, who hated National Socialism, asked to be excused from attending the Nuremberg Rally for Peace in September 1939. He claimed that he should remain in Moscow as the man "who can best and most easily carry on conversations with M. Molotov." The views of Schulenburg obviously conflicted with the instructions he was about to recieve from Ribbentrop.

The meeting with Molotov on August 15, 1939, compelled the German Ambassador to conclude that he had been mistaken in his own analysis of the situation. Molotov agreed with Ribbentrop that speed in the negotiations was necessary because of the existing situation, and he agreed that Germany and the Soviet Union should clarify their relations by means of a non-aggression pact and the delimitation of spheres of interst. Molotov added that adequate preparations were a necessary prelude to an understanding. He obviously favored a settlement on the important points before conducting personal negotiations with one of the German leaders.

Schulenburg was instructed on August 16th to arrange a new interview with Molotov for the following day. The detailed instructions for the interview arrived at Moscow at 1:00 a.m. on August 17th. Ribbentrop announced that the German Government also favored a non-aggression pact, and that he was prepared to fly to Moscow at any time after August 18th. The Russians were urged to agree that the trip should not be later than Monday, August 21st. Ribbentrop hoped to convince the Russians that further preliminaries were unnecessary, and that it would be possible to settle all outstanding points in personal negotiations.[34]

Molotov had made the fantastic claim to Schulenburg on the evening of August 15th that the Soviet Union had always favored friendly relations with Germany, and that he was pleased that "Germany suddenly reciprocated." The persistent efforts of Litvinov to achieve the encirclement of Germany by an overwhelming coalition under the guise of collective security were conveniently ignored. Schulenburg was astonished to learn that Ciano had informed Russian Chargé d'Affaires Leon Helfand, as early as June 1939, of the alleged German desire at that time to conclude a treaty with Russia. Actually, Hitler had not then made up his mind, although the Italians were urging Germany to conclude such a pact. Schulenburg replied haughtily that the statements of Ciano were probably based on irresponsible rumors from Italian diplomatic sources in Moscow. This attitude amused Molotov, who inquired if the German Ambassador was suggesting that the Foreign Minister of Germany's Ally was guilty of inventing information. Schulenburg replied lamely that Ciano's information was apparently only partly correct.

Schulenburg was not able to see Molotov again until 8 o'clock on the evening of Thursday, August 17th. He was empowered to inform Molotov that Ribbentrop was prepared to discuss Russian aspirations in the Baltic states, and to exert whatever modifying influence he could on Japanese policy toward the Soviet Union. Molotov was to be warned that Germany would be unable to endure Polish provocation indefinitely. On August 14, 1939, Hitler had secretly cancelled plans to hold the August 1939 commemoration ceremonies of the 1914 German victory over Russia at Tannenberg, and the September 1939 Nuremberg Party Rally. The mass attendance customary on such occasions would deprive the Germany Army of necessary railroad facilities in the event of a sudden emergency.[35]

The Russians were not quite prepared to disrupt their negotiations with the British and French military misssions when Schulenburg called on Molotov on August 17th. The Soviet Foreign Commissar replied to the German *note verbale* of August 15th with a vigorous and extensive criticism of earlier German policy. He announced that Russia expected the conclusion of a Russo-German trade pact to precede personal negotiations on a non-aggression treaty. The trade pact was actually ready for signature at Berlin the following day, but the Russian delegation deliberately delayed matters by insisting on referring the final draft to Moscow for further consideration. It was agreed that the trade delegations would meet again on Monday, August 21st, at 10:00 a.m., but there was no indication that the Russians would actually sign the treaty at that time. Molotov assured Schulenburg on August 17th that he was honored by the offer of a visit from Ribbentrop, although he added maliciously that such a visit would be a bit spectacular. He explained that he wished both parties to submit separate drafts of the proposed treaty prior to personal negotiations.[36]

Schulenburg received new detailed instructions from Ribbentrop at 5:45 a.m. on August 19th. Ribbentrop emphasized that incidents with the Poles were increasing at a spectacular rate, and that war between the two countries might break out any day. Molotov was to be reminded that both the Soviet Union and Germany had ample experience in drawing up non-aggression pacts, and that it would be a simple matter to accomplish this without delay in this instance. Hitler had declared that it was necessary to know the Russian position at once, and he had noted that Molotov had not accepted the proposed flight of Ribbentrop to Russia. Molotov was not informed that Hitler had rejected the proposal of Ribbentrop that Goering should be sent on the special mission to the Soviet Union. Schulenburg was ordered to do everything possible to avoid delay in arranging a new meeting with Molotov.[37]

The Russian dilatory tactics did not actually reflect any indecision on the part of the Soviet leadership. Stalin announced to a secret session of the Politburo on August 19th that the Soviet Union would definitely conclude a non-aggression pact with Germany. This was followed by an announcement in *Pravda* on the same day that important differences existed in the military pact negotiations between the British and French military missions and the Soviet Union. Nevertheless, Schulenburg failed to obtain a definite date from Molotov, on the afternoon of August 19th, for the Ribbentrop visit to Russia. The Soviet Foreign Commissar objected to the German draft for a non-aggression pact, although the substitute draft which he proposed differed only in minor details. Molotov suggested that it might be possible to receive Ribbentrop one week after the public announcement of the trade treaty, and that it might be possible after all to sign the trade pact by Sunday, August 20th. This was actually achieved in a special session of the trade delegations at Berlin on the following day, and Schulenburg was left with the vague impression that the Russians would consider a Ribbentrop visit after August 26th or 27th.[38]

The Personal Intervention of Hitler

Hitler personally took charge of the German negotiation efforts on August 20th. Schulenburg was instructed to present himself to Molotov at once and to hand him a telegram from Hitler to Stalin. Schulenburg managed to contact Molotov at 3:00 p.m. on August 21st to present the telegram. Hitler informed Stalin that Germany accepted the Russian draft for a non-aggression pact, and that "the tension between Germany and Poland had become intolerable. Polish demeanor toward a Great Power is such that a crisis may arise any day. In the face of this presumption, Germany is determined in any case from now on to look after the interests of the Reich with all the means at its disposal." Hitler proposed that Ribbentrop fly to Moscow on August 22nd, but he added that the 23rd would be acceptable. He informed Stalin that the tense international situation would prevent Ribbentrop from remaining in Russia more than one or two days. He concluded, "I should be glad to receive your early answer."[39]

Stalin did not consider it worthwhile to protract the suspense by evading Hitler's direct proposition. The Soviet leader responded cordially to Hitler on August 21st. He invited Ribbentrop to come to Moscow on August 23, 1939, and he requested that a special communique be issued on August 22nd to announce the approaching pact. The Russian press on the evening of August 21st announced the conclusion of the trade pact with Germany, and the Soviet decision to conclude a political agreement with the Germans. Molotov informed Schulenburg that the Russians favored a formal joint communique announcing the pact for the morning of August 22, 1939. The die had been cast, and Ribbentrop organized an impressive staff of thirty advisers to accompany him to Moscow. The assault on German interests by Halifax had prompted Hitler, in the interest of preventing war and defending Germany, to deprive a number of the smaller states of Eastern Europe, including Poland, of German protection against Bolshevist expansion. It was obvious that Great Britain and France would do nothing to protect Eastern Europe against Bolshevism.[40]

Italy had been the first of the outside Powers to learn that Germany and the Soviet Union were about to conclude a treaty, and Ribbentrop was disappointed to note that this news failed to produce a decisive impact on the attitude of the Italians toward the current crisis. It was hoped at Berlin that news of the approaching treaty would produce a moderating effect on the Polish attitude, and Weizsaecker claimed optimistically in a circular to German missions abroad on August 22nd that the Poles were suffering from severe shock as a result of the announcement of the forthcoming treaty. Weizsaecker had based his prognosis on reasonable supposition rather than concrete fact. The Polish leaders were actually relieved to learn of the treaty because, in their opinion, it rendered more likely an ultimate conflict between the Western Powers and the Soviet Union. It also seemed to remove the serious threat to Polish relations with Great Britain and France which had been posed by the prospect of Western collaboration with Russia.

The military implications of the treaty did not affect the Polish attitude, because Beck did not believe in any case that Poland had the slightest chance of victory in a war against Germany. The basic situation could not be changed by Russian intervention, because Poland in one war could be defeated only once. Polish military prospects were hopeless, because Poland refused to countenance the equally suicidal course of collaboration with the Soviet Union. The Sultan of Turkey in 1833 had claimed that he had accepted Russian help against the Arabs because a drowning man will clutch at a serpent. Beck in 1939 believed that any fate was preferable to the assistance of the Bolshevik serpent. Beck was wise in refusing to collaborate with the Soviet Union, but he was wrong in goading Hitler into war on the false assumption that the Western Powers would proceed to destroy both Germany and the Soviet Union.[41]

The Complacency of Beck

Beck was not worried by the prospect that Great Britain and France might desert Poland until several days after the announcement of the approaching Russo-German treaty. Kennard was amazed to discover at 1:30 a.m. on August 22nd that Beck was utterly complacent about the situation. Beck explained that the pact made no difference to Poland, because, in contrast to Great Britain and France, she had not been counting on Soviet aid. He added that the understandable disappointment in Great Britain and France was the price these countries paid for having placed false hopes in the Soviet Union.[42]

Beck warned his subordinates at the Polish Foreign Office on August 23, 1939, that war with Germany would break out at any time, and he claimed without any foundation that the Germans were assigning nine-tenths of their military forces to ultimate operations in Poland. He confided that he would advise the Polish military leaders on the same day to mobilize the final twenty-one divisions of Polish reserve troops. This decision would be justified by his analysis that war in the immediate future was inevitable. It was decided at the Polish Foreign Office to inform Polish missions abroad that the approaching non-aggression pact exerted no effect on the fundamental situation other than to bring the inevitable war one step closer.[43]

It was soon evident that the approaching pact exerted a greater influence on France than on Italy, Poland, or Great Britain. This is not surprising when it is recalled that the Russian move effectively undermined the existing Franco-Russian alliance. Paul-Émile Naggiar, the French Ambassador to Russia, complained bitterly to American Ambassador Lawrence Steinhardt on August 23rd that the Poles were exclusively to blame for the failure of Western negotiations with Russia. It was obvious to Steinhardt that Naggiar favored French abandonment of the Poles. American Ambassador Kennedy at London obtained an entirely different reaction from the British Foreign Secretary. Kennedy suggested that it would be logical to respond to the situation in Russia by seeking a peaceful settlement with Germany, but Halifax replied stiffly that "my reason shows me no way out but war." This was because Halifax favored war with Germany at any price, and it was evident to Kennedy that he was impervious to reasonable proposals for peaceful negotiations.

Kennedy discussed the situation on the same day with Chamberlain, who had returned to London from his vacation. It was evident that Chamberlain was fatalistic and unprepared to exert a moderating influence on Halifax. Chamberlain admitted that Poland would not be encouraged to make any concessions to Germany. Kennedy personally hoped that Poland would finally agree to resume negotiations with Germany, and he was disappointed to discover that neither Halifax nor Chamberlain was prepared to urge the Poles to adopt this course. He was convinced that Warsaw rather than Berlin constituted the chief menace to peace. He suggested to the American State Department that if President Roosevelt "is contemplating any action for peace, it seems to me the place to work is on Beck in Poland and to make this effective it must happen quickly. I see no other possibility."[44]

Ribbentrop's Mission to Moscow

Ribbentrop flew to Moscow on August 23rd in a large German Condor transport airplane with a staff of thirty-two experts. He had received plenipotentiary powers from Hitler before departing for Moscow. The German team was received at Moscow wirh great cordiality, and their Russian hosts proved to be extraordinarily communicative. Various important European issues, such as intimate Turkish diplomatic relations with the British, or the intrinsic value of French military power, were discussed with apparent frankness. The hospitable Russians did everything possible to encourage the Germans to feel comfortable and at ease.

The Russians placed a request early in the evening of August 23rd for German toleration of their plans to establish military bases in Estonia and Latvia. The Russians insisted on a free hand in Finland, and on German neutrality in the conflict Russia intended to provoke with Rumania to recover Bessarabia. Ribbentrop, despite his plenipotentiary powers, telephoned Berlin to receive the consent of Hitler for German acquiescence in these aggressive Russian plans. He knew that the attitude toward Russia of the peoples of the former Russian Baltic provinces contrasted with the desire for union with Germany of the Germans of Austria, Sudetenland, Memel, and Danzig. The Baltic peoples did not desire the revisionist program implied by the Russian demand for bases in their countries. They were the tragic victims of the situation produced by the Anglo-German conflict of interests.

Ribbentrop had contacted Berlin at 8:05 p.m. on August 23rd, and the affirmative response of Hitler was received in Moscow at 11:00 p.m. The German Reich would not resist the westward advance of Communism. Germany was not actually surrendering nations to Russia, because she had no contractual obligations, other than promises not to attack them herself, toward any of the countries involved. Nevertheless, the policy of Hitler and Ribbentrop in August 1939 received much criticism within Germany during the months ahead. The National Socialist Party press replied to this criticism by pointing out that none of these countries had displayed any sympathy toward Germany during the period of Germany's greatest humiliation from 1918 to 1933. Above all, in contrast to Great Britain and France, the German leaders had never attempted to conclude an alliance with the Soviet Union. The Russo-German agreement of August 23/24, 1939, concerned the delimitation of interests rather than active collaboration between the two countries. These facts were ignored in the West by irresponsible propagandists who insisted without the slightest foundation that an alliance had been concluded between Germany and the Soviet Union.[45]

The Russo-German non-aggression pact contained a secret protocol which recognized a Russian sphere of interest in Eastern Europe. German recognition was contingent upon the outbreak of war between Germany and Poland. Hitler and Ribbentrop made it clear that Germany would not consider herself obliged to recognize these aspirations in the event of a diplomatic settlement of the German-Polish dispute. In the event of war, the northern frontier of Lithuania was to be the limit of the Russian sphere in the Baltic area, and it was stipulated that Lithuania was to recover Wilna from Poland. Russia announced her intention of intervening against Poland in the event of war, and the Narew-Vistula-San line was to constitute the frontier of the German and Russian zones of military occupation in Poland. This line corresponded closely to the front for a last defense against Germany in the secret Polish military plans, but it was obvious that it would be of little use to the Poles with the Russian forces approaching from their rear. This never became a tangible problem, because the Germans outflanked the last-ditch Polish line within the first few days after the outbreak of hostilities, and nearly two weeks before the military intervention of the Soviet Union.

The Soviet leaders also prefaced their intervention against Poland in September 1939 with a demand for Lithuania, and the proposal to establish an occupation zone line somewhat farther to the East in Poland. They wished the occupation line to correspond closely to the new permanent frontier between the Soviet Union and Poland. This was a clever move which could be exploited for propaganda purposes, and the Germans, who were engaged in war with the West by that time, were compelled to accept this virtual ultimatum from the Soviet Union.[46]

Ribbentrop was sincere when he informed the Russians on August 23rd that Germany had made no irrevocable decision to respond to Polish provocations with a military campaign in Poland. Hitler's first secret announcement that there definitely would be war with Poland came on August 25, 1939, and even this was subsequently contradicted by a new order from the German Chancellor. Nevertheless, both the German and Russian negotiators were reckoning with the likelihood of immediate war between Germany and Poland. Ribbentrop also issued a statement on August 24th, after the signing of the pact, that Germany would take concrete steps to encourage a relaxation of tension between the Soviet Union and Japan.[47]

Ribbentrop devoted August 24th in Moscow to the establishment of personal contacts with the Russian leaders. He told Stalin that the proverbial wit of the Berliners was quick to respond to any given situation. He had heard a story before he left for Moscow which carried the theme of Stalin's imaginary decision to join the anti-Comintern pact. Ribbentrop personally hoped for lasting peace between Germany and the Soviet Union, and he knew that the chances for peace would be improved if some means were found to modify the existing anti-Comintern pact, which was directed against international Communism. He hoped in vain that it might be possible eventually to persuade Stalin to abandon his plans for world revolution, and to concentrate on the realization of strictly national Russian interests. His joke about the anti-Comintern pact was an obvious but futile move to prepare the ground in this direction.

Molotov declared in one of his toasts that the Stalin speech of March 1939 had produced a reversal in political relations between Russia and Germany. This was an interesting suggestion, because it implied that the earlier attitude of Russia, rather than of Germany, had been the chief obstacle to an improvement in relations. The general theme of the celebration toasts exchanged by the Germans and Russians was that an era of friendship and mutual appreciation had replaced an era of hostility. This concealed the fact that Russian protestations of friendship were based upon the expectation that Germany was heading straight into a hopeless stalemate war with Great Britain and France. Stalin openly expressed his belief to Ribbentrop that the French Army would offer an enormous obstacle to Germany in the event of war. This pronouncement dispelled the illusion that the Soviet leaders were more accurate than the Western leaders in predicting the shape of things to come. The application of so-called scientific Marxism offered no magic formula for predicting future events.[48]

Hitler received the German military leaders at the Obersalzberg on August 22, 1939. He discussed the situation with them in morning and afternoon conferences, and he ordered the plans for possible military operations against Poland to be completed by August 26th. He refrained from issuing a final attack order. Hitler described German negotiations with Russia at great length, and he expressed the opinion that the Russo-German pact would discourage Great Britain and France from intervening against Germany in the event of a German-Polish war.[49]

One version of these conferences was presented by Louis P. Lochner of the American Associated Press to British diplomats at Berlin on August 25, 1939. This material was later cited by a number of historians as a valid record of the conferences, and it consciously or unconsciously influenced the thinking of British diplomats at the time. Otherwise, it would have been dismissed as something too ridiculous to receive serious consideration. The crass propaganda in the material would have been immediately discarded had people been permitted to think normally about important issues. Unfortunately, a furious and uninterrupted war propaganda campaign had been carried on in the West for more than five months, and nearly everyone, regardless of his mental caliber, had been seriously affected.

Why would anyone believe that Marshal Goering danced on the table and shrieked like a savage before a group of austere German Generals? Why would Hitler blandly announce to his Generals that "Goering had demonstrated to us that his Four-Year Plan is a failure and that we are at the end of our strength, if we do not achieve victory in a coming war?" This sounded more like a leaf from the book of President Roosevelt, who, unlike Hitler, was still facing a catastrophic depression. The statement would be sheer nonsense when applied to war with poverty-stricken Poland. Every informed person, including Lord Halifax, knew that Goering was the last person in Germany who would deliver arguments in favor of a general war at this time.[50]

The memorandum stated that Hitler told his Generals he planned to kill the Polish women and children. This would have been proper material for an American "comic book," and also for Hitler, if his purpose had been to goad his Generals into an immediate revolt against the German regime. The memorandum claimed that Germany could not hold out in a long war, but added in the same paragraph that "Poland will be depopulated and settled with Germans." The memorandum also claimed that Stalin was very sick, and that Germany would dismember Russia after his death.

Succinct and reliable references to the meetings of August 22, 1939, are available from the actual participants. The traditions of popular journalism cannot excuse people, from any country, who seek to precipitate wars by spreading lies when feeling is running high.[51]

Henderson's Efforts for Peace

Henderson, whose distasteful duty it was to relay the propaganda material from Lochner to Halifax, had been hard at work during the crucial phase of the Western and German negotiations with Russia to persuade Halifax to arrive at an accommodation with Germany before it was too late. He had been urging Polish Ambassador Lipski on his own initiative, ever since August 15th, to seek instructions from his Government for negotiations with the Germans. Henderson admitted to Halifax that Weizsaecker had been pessimistic about the Danzig situation since the Polish ultimatum of August 4th, but he drew encouragement from the fact that the German State Secretary was "more detached, calm and confident" than had been the case during the September 1938 crisis.

Henderson hoped that the Italians would produce proposals for a peaceful diplomatic settlement, and he had been assured by Italian Ambassador Attolico that this effort would be made. He urged Halifax to advise the Polish Government to instruct Lipski to make a *démarche* in Berlin. He pointed out that Polish mistreatment of the Germans "is not a Hitler grievance but a German grievance." He warned Halifax that "it may be bluff, but I feel bound to say that my belief is that, if driven into a corner, Hitler will choose war."[52]

Henderson was particularly irritated by repeated claims in the British press that Hitler had been intimidated by the firm support other Powers were giving to the Poles. He predicted that "history will judge the Press generally to have been the principal cause of the war." The press, with its vile and irresponsible tactics during this period, was undoubtedly an important factor, but Henderson failed to note that the worst phase of the press campaign in Great Britain followed inevitably from the distorted and dishonest official British version of the events at Prague in March 1939, and from the fantastic Tilea hoax, which had been deliberately perpetrated by Halifax and Vansittart to arouse the British public. The British Ambassador was confusing cause and effect when he assigned the principal blame for the current crisis to the Western press.

Henderson pointed out that an Anglo-German agreement was necessary for German security, and he reminded Halifax that he was quite convinced Hitler sincerely desired such an agreement. It seemed obvious to Henderson that a few resolute steps by Halifax could produce a satisfactory settlement, because "of all Germans, believe it or not, Hitler is the most moderate so far as Danzig and the Corridor are concerned." He charged that the British Embassy in Warsaw deliberately refused to recognize the actual desperate situation of the German minority in Poland. He observed with keen insight that "Warsaw with its civilized and intelligent, not to say astute clique with which one consorts there, is one thing. Outside in the country the Poles are an utterly uncivilized lot. 'Calm and restraint.' Yes, doubtless, at the top and if words mean anything. But elsewhere, no. I have heard too many tales from well-disposed neutrals to believe a word of it."[53]

Henderson urged Halifax to consider again the earlier Gafencu plan for a settlement. Hitler had recently told the British Ambassador that the protectorate in Bohemia-Moravia had been a necessity "for the moment," but that, as far as he was concerned, the area in the future could become anything, provided it was not a bastion against Germany. Henderson recognized this as indisputable proof that successful negotiations might be based on the Prague question.

Henderson explained to a friend at the British Foreign Office that it was no favor to Poland to support her in a war, since, in his opinion, the Poles had much to lose and nothing to gain by going to war. The British Ambassador added in pithy language: "I only pray that we shall not regret leading them up the garden path for the satisfaction of kicking Hitler and his Nazi gangsters in the pants." Halifax was informed by Henderson on August 22nd that Hitler was acquiring great prestige in Germany by concluding a pact with Russia. He described the news of the pact as a "satisfactory surprise to German public opinion." The German man-in-the-street now believed that Hitler had turned the trick again, and that there would be no war.

Halifax responded by informing Henderson that British determination to support Poland could not be influenced by Hitler's diplomacy. He reiterated his favorite theme that he was doing everything to avoid war simply by making the British position clear. This was a clever ruse, based on the fact that British failure to do this in 1914 had provided one of the principal criticisms of British policy at that time. Halifax ignored the fact that the British blank check to Poland was far broader in scope than the one the Germans had given to Austria-Hungary in 1914 in the crisis over the assassination of Franz Ferdinand. Germany was also accused of sharing responsibility for World War I, and the Allied victors at Paris had insisted that Germany and her allies were solely responsible for the war, but no one had ever suggested that this was because Germany had failed to make her position clear. Halifax was working single-mindedly for war in 1939, and the fact that he was avoiding one of the many mistakes made by the British in 1914 did not in any way reduce his guilt in choosing war as the principal instrument of British national policy.[54]

Halifax responded to the announcement of the coming Russo-German pact by continuing to push the negotiations for an Anglo-French alliance agreement with the Russians. He received passive encouragement in this policy from Bonnet. The French Foreign Minister, despite his actual pessimism, observed philosophically that the pact might prove to be meaningless if restricted to general principles in the style of the Franco-German pact of December 1938. Halifax informed Kennard on August 22nd that Western negotiations in Moscow were proceeding, and the British were more determined than ever to support the French in the question of Russian military operations in Poland.[55]

General Doumenc informed Marshal Voroshilov early on August 22nd that he had been empowered to support Russian plans for military operations in Poland. He added that he had plenipotentiary powers from Daladier to sign without any reservation a pact which included the other Russian interests and wishes. The French and British were prepared to go further than Ribbentrop in promoting the westward expansion of the Bolshevists, but they demanded the price of Russian willingness to participate at the outset in a war against Germany. Marshal Voroshilov replied that the Polish ally of France was a sovereign Power, and that plans could not be concluded for Russian military operations on her territory without her consent. He added that the Poles would have insisted on being present on this occasion had they agreed to give an affirmative answer to the Russian proposal. The Russian military leader lectured the French and British on their alleged betrayal of Czechoslovakia in 1938, and he denounced the failure of the Western Powers to arrive at an agreement with Russia at an earlier date.[56]

British Ambassador Sir William Seeds accused Molotov on the evening of August 22nd of "bad faith" during the Western negotiations. Molotov blandly replied that the "insincerity" of the British leaders deprived them of any valid basis from which to present such a charge. Nevertheless, Seeds wired Halifax on August 23rd that it was important for the allied missions to remain in Russia "in case the Soviet and Ribbentrop fall out." Halifax made one last attempt with the Russians shortly before the signing of the Russo-German pact on the evening of August 23rd. He instructed Seeds to assure the Russians that he fully shared their opinion about the indispensability of Russian military operations in Poland, and that he was prepared to offer them full support in such operations. This was tantamount to a British pledge to support a Russian invasion of Poland at the very time they were insisting on going to war with Germany over Danzig, which did not belong to Poland. The Russians had elected to conduct their invasion of Poland independently of the proffered British support, which they regarded as an unnecessary liability.[57]

Bonnet's Effort to Separate France from Poland

French Foreign Minister Bonnet was aware that an entirely new European situation had been created by the Russo-German pact. The Soviet Union, the principal eastern ally of France, was willing to conclude a separate agreement with the Germans, and he saw no reason why France should not do the same. He decided on August 23, 1939, to make a determined effort to liberate French foreign policy from British tutelage. This attempt would have succeeded, but for the unrealistic attitude of the French military men and the reversal of Italian policy. Bonnet knew that General Gamelin had been discussing the possible French response to a Russo-German pact with his principal collaborators since August 19th. He requested Premier Daladier to call an emergency meeting of the French Defense Council, which included the military chiefs and several of the key French Cabinet members. He knew that a similar step had been taken by Premier Rouvier in 1905 at the time of the first Moroccan crisis, by Joseph Caillaux in 1911 during the second Moroccan crisis, and by Léon Blum in March 1938 at the time of the German occupation of Austria.

Bonnet hoped to exert on the Poles the same pressure for peace that he had applied to the Czechs the previous year. He realized that the 1921 Franco-Polish alliance would be lost if the attempt was unsuccessful, but he was fully prepared to accept this eventuality. It was his plan to obtain from the military men a clear statement that French prospects in a war with Germany were dubious without the support of the Soviet Union. He knew that the British would quickly abandon their opposition to Hitler if they were deprived of French support.[58]

Bonnet was troubled about the attitude of General Gamelin, of whom he had no high opinion, although the scholarly French Commander-in-Chief was a favored protégé of the great French military leader, Marshal Henri Pétain. General Décamps had recently complained to Bonnet that Gamelin would never take a position either way in a question of major importance. Bonnet hoped that the conference of August 23, 1939, would prove a notable exception.

The conference met at 6:00 p.m. It was attended by Premier Daladier, Navy Secretary Campinchi, Air Secretary Guy La Chambre, Army Commander-in-Chief General Gamelin, Navy Commander Admiral Darlan, and Air Force Commander General Vuillemin. The Minister for Colonies customarily attended the meetings of the Defense Council, but Bonnet was successful in preventing the attendance of Colonial Minister Georges Mandel, who was a notorious *belliciste*, on the grounds that the issue did not concern the French colonies. Bonnet knew that Mandel would seek to thwart any major peace effort.[59]

The meeting took place in Daladier's office, and the chairs of the members of the Defense Council were arranged in a semi-circle around the Premier's desk. Bonnet opened the meeting with a discussion of the current European situation. He claimed that the Poles were responsible for the Anglo-French failure to secure an alliance with the Soviet Union. Bonnet announced that France could easily choose between two alternatives concerning Poland. She might offer the Poles unlimited and blind support, or she might force them to compromise on their differences with Germany. Bonnet suggested that the military outlook for France in a war over Danzig should be the primary consideration in determining this choice.

It was soon evident to Bonnet that Ciano's unfortunate assurance of Italian neutrality on August 18th carried great weight in the conference. Gamelin and Darlan both stressed the fact that Italy would almost certainly remain neutral in a general European war. Bonnet was annoyed by the excessive weight attached by the military men to the Italian attitude. He impatiently asked General Gamelin how long he thought the Poles would be able to hold out against the Germans. Gamelin solemnly replied that the Germans would be unable to encompass the defeat of Poland before the rainy season, and he predicted that fighting in Poland would still be in progress as late as Spring 1940. Bonnet was stunned when Gamelin claimed that French preparations for a war against Germany were already adequate. His suggestion that France should change her policy toward Poland because of her dangerous military situation was completely undermined by the military men.

Bonnet was furious with General Gamelin. He suddenly realized that Gamelin regarded the conclave, which threatened to expose French military unpreparedness, as a personal intrigue directed against the French Army Command. This accounted for the obvious insincerity and lack of realism of his assertions. He did not want to be made a scapegoat by Bonnet, and he did not want British wrath to be directed primarily against himself if France abandoned Poland. Gamelin had taken a sufficiently negative view of French military prospects at the French Defense Council meeting on March 13, 1939, but that was before British policy had changed. Neither Gamelin nor Bonnet wished to intervene for Poland, but they both feared British wrath, and neither of them wished to assume the primary responsibility in defying the Halifax war policy.

Bonnet recalled the details of the French Defense Council meeting called by Premier Caillaux in 1911. Caillaux had reminded the members that Napoleon once had said that a military venture was an unwarranted risk without at least a 70% chance of victory. General Joffre, not suspecting some intrigue when he was being asked to comment on French chances in a war, answered frankly that France did not have the odds ordinarily insisted upon by Napoleon.[60]

Gamelin himself later contended that, when he said the French Army was prepared on August 23, 1939, he actually meant prepared for an ordinary mobilization rather than for victory in a war against Germany. He added that his prediction about Polish resistance was based on the assumption of Russian neutrality. The ultimate Russian intervention was a poor excuse for Gamelin's faulty prediction about Poland, because the Polish Armies had been utterly routed by September 17th when the Russians intervened. It was unrealistic to assume that Russia would remain neutral in a German-Polish war after the conclusion of the Russo-German Pact. The claim that France was ready for war against Germany because she could mobilize her forces was childish. One might have used this criterion to conclude that Liechtenstein was prepared for war against Germany. General Gamelin did not suggest any plan for the defeat of Germany in the event of war. He told the conference that France would not honor her military engagement of May 1939 to Poland for a French offensive in the West, but would remain strictly on the defensive against the Germans. He failed to explain what France would do to defeat Germany after the expected defeat of Poland.[61]

Bonnet was fully justified in feeling that General Gamelin had evaded his responsibility as Commander-in-Chief at the fateful conference of August 23, 1939. Bonnet continued to work for peace, but he did not command the unanimous support of the French Government, which would have been his had the military men presented an honest evaluation of the French position. Bonnet was under strong pressure from London by August 24th to agree on the exact terms of a joint ultimatum to Germany, if a German-Polish struggle broke out over Danzig. The outcome of the August 23rd conference might have been entirely different had Ciano not made his fatal indiscretion to Loraine on August 18th. The combination of Ciano's duplicity and Gamelin's weakness struck a dangerous blow at Hitler's careful calculation that a Russo-German pact would prevent Anglo-French intervention against Germany during a German-Polish war. Hitler had done everything possible to convince Ciano that a revelation of Italian weakness would increase the chances of war. It was unfortunate that Attolico undermined the work of Hitler with Ciano. The Italian Ambassador at Berlin was exclusively concerned about obtaining Italian neutrality, and he ignored the need of an Italian effort to prevent a European war after Hitler refused to accept Mussolini's terms for a Brenner meeting.

The British Cabinet assembled briefly on August 22nd. A suggestion from Halifax that Great Britain should warn the Germans that the British would intervene in a German-Polish war was approved. It was agreed that Chamberlain should write a letter to Hitler emphasizing British determination, and that Halifax should rush to completion the British negotiations with the Poles for a formal alliance. Halifax was empowered to change the British terms for a pact to meet current Polish objections. It was noted that the Poles were not asking for a British pledge to defend them against the Soviet Union. It was decided that Henderson should deliver Chanberlain's letter in person, and should reinforce verbally, and with great energy, the arguments which this letter would contain. This step was decided upon without recognizing that it would present Hitler with an excellent opportunity to renew official negotiations with the British for a peaceful settlement.

Halifax informed British Ambassador Loraine at Rome of the decision of the British Government. Loraine replied that he was confident the new development in Russia would not alter Italy's decision to desert Germany in the event of war.[62]

478   THE FORCED WAR

The Stiffening of Polish Anti-German Measures

The Poles responded to the announcement of the Russo-German pact by inten-
sifying their propaganda campaign against Germany. Mistreatment of the
German minority was encouraged by reckless charges that hundreds of acts of
violence were occurring against the Polish minority in the Reich. A conflict of
opinion between Forster and Greiser resulted at Danzig on August 24th when
several Polish customs inspectors were arrested for disturbing the peace.
Chodacki demanded that the men be released at once without preferment of
charges. Greiser insisted to Forster that the Danzig Government capitulate. He
had not favored action against the offending Poles in the first place, and he
regarded any attempt to enforce the law in Danzig, when this was displeasing
to the Poles, as completely futile.[63]

The major topic of discussion in Poland was the Russo-German pact. The
more Beck considered this development, the greater his satisfaction became. He
declared with amusement to Nöel that "it is now Ribbentrop who is proving the
bad faith of the Soviets." The official *Gazeta Polska* alleged on August 24th that
the pact was an unsuccessful bluff, because it had produced no effect on the
nerves of Poles, Frenchmen, or Englishmen. The conservative *Czas* called the
pact a bluff which had been produced by "the new comedy in Berlin." The
Ilustrowany Kurjer claimed that the Hungarian leaders had denounced Hitler's
willingness to compromise with the Bolshevik peril. One Polish journalist assured
the New York *Times* that the new pact was of no military value to Germany.
The *Kurjer Warszawski* announced triumphantly that the new agreement furnished conclusive proof of the weakness of both its partners.[64]

The Poles took notice of the fact that the old restored German battleship and
training ship, *Schleswig-Holstein,* was scheduled to visit Danzig on August 24th
during a trip which had been announced much earlier. The Polish authorities
had expressed no objection to the proposed visit, and it was concluded that the
ship was too weak to present a military threat to Poland. The Danzig Government had selected Albert Forster to head the Free City administration, and the
Poles were informed that he would take his oath of office on August 30, 1939.
The Polish Government refused to approve this arrangement. Chodacki submitted an ominous protest note to Danzig on August 24th which declared that
full responsibility for all ensuing measures taken by the Polish Government
would fall on the Danzig Senate. Bonnet was alarmed by this development, and
he instructed Nöel to advise Beck to refrain from all military action in the
event of a Danzig Senate proclamation on the return of the Free City to the
Reich. Beck rejected this advice, and he declared that Poland would respond
with military force to any German attempt to annex Danzig. He indicated that
he was not opposed in principle to consultation with the French and British,
but if action was initiated by the Danzig authorities, the Poles might be compelled by the pressure of circumstances to act unilaterally without consulting
the Western Powers.[65]

Beck's Danzig declaration was formulated as an official Polish verbal note on
the following day, and Szembek presented it to Nöel. German Chargé d'Affaires
Wuehlisch reported from Warsaw that Polish confidence in assistance from Great

Britain and France remained unshaken by the conclusion of the Russo-German pact. It was evident that the Pact had not prompted the Poles to adopt a more moderate policy toward Germany or the German minority in Poland. The German Foreign Office took stock of its huge file of specific reports of excesses against national and ethnic Germans in Poland. More than ten detailed reports were arriving each day, and more than 1500 documented reports had been received since March 1939. They presented a staggering picture of brutality and human misery. Albert Forster had discussed the fate of the Germans in West Prussia and Posen with Edmund Veesenmayer, the special representative of Ribbentrop, on the afternoon of August 23, 1939. It was difficult to decide what advice if any should be given to these unfortunate people in the event of war. It seemed to Forster that they should either be told to stay where they were and defend themselves when attacked, or they should be advised to conceal themselves. Neither prospect was promising, because they had no means by which to resist and little possibility of successful concealment.[66]

The German Government repeated its earlier pledge to the Slovak Government at Bratislava on August 23rd that the Slovak armed forces would not be required in the event of war or requested to operate outside their own territory. Germany was prepared in case of war to facilitate the return of territories to Slovakia which had been seized by Poland in 1938. The German Government announced that it was willing to guarantee the 1938 Slovakian frontier against Hungary.

The Polish Government on August 25th dealt with a German protest that three German civilian airplanes carrying passengers and flying over the Baltic Sea had been fired upon by Polish batteries on the Hela peninsula. The Poles admitted firing on only one German airplane on August 24th, and they claimed that it had been sighted flying over Polish territory prior to the Polish attack.[67]

The German press devoted increasing space to detailed accounts of incidents against the Germans in Poland. The *Voelkischer Beobachter* announced that more than 80,000 German refugees had succeeded in reaching German territory by August 20, 1939, and that some of them had come from distant Volhynia near the Russian frontier. The Western diplomats in Berlin were aware that Poland was now making sweeping charges of German mistreatment of the Polish minority, but it was noted that specific individual incidents, which were common in the German press, were conspicuously lacking. The Polish diplomats in Berlin were asked confidentially why they did not make an effort to assemble exact and detailed information about alleged incidents in Germany. The Poles confided that such incidents were far and few between and hard to find. They claimed that this was not because of German magnanimity, but because Germany desired to preserve the Polish minority as a hostage for the German minority in Poland. This was a ridiculous charge, because the German authorities had concluded, and had made no secret of their opinion, that decent treatment of the Poles in Germany failed to produce the slightest effect on Polish mistreatment of the German minority.[68]

The Decline of German Opposition to Hitler

There was considerable conspiratorial activity against Hitler in Germany at the
time of the signing of the Russo-German pact, but this activity was less extensive
than during the Czech crisis in 1938. Several small conspiratorial groups continued to hope that the anti-Hitler conservatives, who held most of the commanding positions in the German Army, could be prevailed upon to arrest Hitler
during this crisis. It was argued that the Germany of Hitler was interested in
recruiting a new officer corps with National Socialist political indoctrination,
and that the last of the special privileges of the traditional military caste would
be destroyed if the Hitler regime survived. The misgivings of the great majority
of the military men approached were not sufficient for them to accept such
plans, and this was especially true after the conclusion of the treaty with Russia
on August 23, 1939.

The open opposition to Hitler's policy was more frequent and less dangerous.
General Thomas of the War Economy Office prepared a series of memoranda in
August 1939 which charged that the pursuit of Hitler's program at Danzig
would lead to a general war. General Keitel, who recognized the importance of
this issue, personally presented these memoranda to Hitler for careful consideration. General Ludwig Beck, who had resigned as Chief of the General Staff,
wrote a number of letters to his German military colleagues stressing the danger
of war. Hjalmar Schacht, who had resigned his presidency of the *Reichsbank*
early in 1939, reassured the German military men that German economic
prospects were excellent, and that Germany was the last country in the world
to require excessive military preparations or war to solve her economic
problems. The evidence was overwhelming that the prominent Germans
recognized the need of keeping the peace, and this opinion was also shared by
Hitler. The differences of opinion concerned the means of achieving this end.
Hitler remained free to make whatever decisions he chose. He was able, like
Beck in Poland, to pursue his elected policies without serious disturbance or
resistance.[69]

Hitler's Desire for a Negotiated Settlement

Hitler hoped to recover the diplomatic initiative through his Kremlin pact of
August 23, 1939. The effort launched by Halifax on March 17, 1939, to build
a formidable British alliance front in Eastern Europe had failed. Hitler also
hoped that Great Britain and France would react to this situation by withdrawing their support from Poland. He knew that his pact with Russia placed him in
a strong position to resume negotiations with the Western Powers. His recent
success was too sensational to permit new negotiation efforts to be readily confused with weakness. The British Government gave Hitler an excellent opening
for his new diplomatic campaign by commissioning Chamberlain to write to him.
The British leaders, of course, did not intend to embark on major negotiations,
but Hitler had other plans. The presentation of the Chamberlain letter by
Henderson on August 23, 1939, was the signal for a major German diplomatic
offensive in Great Britain.

The situation would have been relatively simple for Hitler by August 23, 1939, had it not been for the unpardonable indiscretion of Ciano and the incredible conduct of General Gamelin. The statement of Ciano on August 18th that Italy would not support Germany cushioned Halifax from the impact of the German treaty with Russia, and it gave General Gamelin an excuse to rationalize the unfavorable French military situation, which had been created by the Russian agreement with Germany. The action of Ciano was especially unwarranted because the Italian Foreign Minister knew that Hitler hoped to create the maximum effect of surprise with his Russian pact. Ciano knew that his own pledge to the British would greatly reduce the impact of Hitler's diplomacy. It was easy to argue in London that the position of Hitler would be insecure if the Italians refused to be loyal to their engagements with him. Italian loyalty to Hitler and a clear decision from France against war on behalf of the Poles would surely have pulled the teeth from the Halifax campaign to launch a preventive war against Germany. The absence of these contingencies made it exceedingly difficult for Hitler to capitalize on his Russian success in negotiations with the British leaders. He was not fully aware of this situation on August 23rd. He knew nothing of the Italian pledge to the British on August 18th, or of the crucial debate in the meeting of the French Defense Council. He failed to appreciate the adamant determination of Halifax for war. He knew that British Ambassador Henderson was opposed to war, and he hoped that the views of the British diplomat at Berlin were shared to some extent by his master at London. Hitler was more optimistic than the facts warranted, but this was mainly because he was not fully aware of the existing situation.

The Russians too were unduly optimistic about their prospects on August 23, 1939. They overestimated the military power of France, and they expected a hopeless military stalemate on the Franco-German front reminiscent of World War I. Stalin hoped to expand his position in Eastern Europe, and to intervene militarily against Germany in the latter phase of a European war, when both Germany and the Western Powers were exhausted. There was one notably great difference in the attitudes of Stalin and Hitler. The Soviet Dictator, like Halifax and Roosevelt, was hoping for the outbreak of a general European war. Hitler considered that a European war would be a great evil, and he was anxious to prevent it. It is ironical to anticipate that the leaders of the Soviet Union, Great Britain, and the United States ultimately joined together in true Orwellian fashion, at Nuremberg in 1945-1946, to condemn the German leaders for deliberately seeking, as "aggressors," to destroy the peace of the world.[70]

Chapter 19

GERMAN PROPOSALS

FOR AN ANGLO-GERMAN UNDERSTANDING

Chamberlain's Letter an Opening for Hitler

The signing of the Russo-German pact on August 23, 1939, clarified the situation in Eastern Europe. None of the immediate neighbors of Poland were prepared to aid her in an eventual conflict with Germany. Great Britain and France were far away. They had failed to support Poland with extensive credits or military supplies during the months after the Polish partial mobilization of March 1939. The Soviet Union had adopted a hostile attitude toward the Poles. The Polish military situation, regardless of any action taken by Great Britain and France, was hopeless in a war with Germany. Halifax encouraged the Poles to challenge Germany, but he failed to offer them effective support. Hitler hoped that Halifax would draw the logical conclusion from this situation and seek a compromise which would spare Poland from an otherwise inevitable military debacle.[1]

Henderson went up to the Obersalzberg on August 23, 1939, with a personal letter from Chamberlain to Hitler. He was instructed to convince Hitler of British determination to intervene in any German-Polish war. He was determined to do his official duty regardless of the difference between his instructions and his personal opinions. The German Chancellor he encountered was equally resolved to convince the British that he was not bluffing, and that he was determined to achieve the German program at Danzig. Every prerequisite existed for a stormy argument in which two strong wills clashed. Henderson telephoned in deep gloom to the British Embassy at Berlin at 3:00 p.m. that his first conversation with Hitler had been "unsatisfactory."[2]

Chamberlain warned Hitler in his letter that Great Britain would support Poland with military force regardless of the Russo-German pact. He announced that Great Britain was about to take additional military measures. The British Prime Minister asserted that "it would be a dangerous illusion to think that, if war once starts, it will come to an early end even if a success on any one of the several fronts on which it will be engaged should have been secured." Chamberlain conceded in unmistakable language that Germany could defeat Poland, but he warned Hitler that Great Britain would continue to work for the defeat of Germany after the defeat of Poland.3

Hitler received Henderson again after he had read the letter from Chamberlain. His first comment concerned Chamberlain's threat of additional military measures. He said: "Should I hear of further measures of this kind being put into effect on the part of Britain, today or tomorrow, I shall order immediate general mobilization in Germany." Henderson exclaimed that war would then be unavoidable, but Hitler repeated his challenge. The British Ambassador attempted at great length to prove the alleged fairness of recent British foreign policy. Henderson sought to deny, with the aid of considerable sophistry, that British policy had any connection with the Polish refusal of Hitler's October 1938 proposals for a German-Polish understanding. He noted that the Polish refusal preceded the formal British guarantee of March 31, 1939, by several days. Hitler was unimpressed. He remarked succinctly that the British position was perfectly clear at the time of the Polish refusal, and that "the British press had then stated that the liberty of both Poland and Rumania was being threatened."4

Henderson was somewhat taken aback when he noted that Hitler blamed the British exclusively for his difficulties with Poland. The British Ambassador impulsively made a personal statement which had no connection with his instructions. He declared with feeling that he had written recently to a prominent German friend that the Fuehrer had required ten years to win Germany, and that therefore he should give Britain more time before concluding that she could not be won. He added that he had personally never desired to see the conclusion of an Anglo-Franco-Russian pact against Germany, and that he would rather see Germany conclude a treaty with Russia than have Great Britain do so.

Hitler seized this opportunity to stress the great advantage to Germany of the new pact, and he concluded: "Make no mistake. It will be a treaty lasting for many years." Henderson feared that his initiative in the conversation was rapidly slipping away. He sought to place Great Britain's obligation to Poland on the solemn basis of national honor. The British Ambassador observed: "Throughout the centuries of history we had never, so far as I knew, broken our word. We could not do so now and remain Britain." Hitler's response was to scrutinize the British Ambassador closely to make certain that he really was awake, and not speaking in a trance. He concluded the second conversation by observing that he would reply to Chamberlain's letter within a few hours.

Henderson proceeded to report to Halifax. His two main purposes, aside from indicating that he had carried out instructions, were to emphasize German determination to settle the Danzig question and Hitler's desire to settle Anglo-German differences. Henderson in the latter connection returned to the question of Prague. He emphasized a new remark from Hitler that it had not been a necessity from the German point of view to establish the protectorate in Bohemia-Moravia, and that this regime was the chance product of a specific crisis situation. Hitler suggested that the Czechs might still be independent today had Great Britain co-operated with Germany in carrying out the provisions of the Munich conference. Henderson wished to remind Halifax of the Gafencu plan of April 1939 for a diplomatic settlement of the existing disputes based on German concessions at Prague.

Henderson was somewhat uneasy about his positive assurance to Hitler that the British had never broken their engagements. Halifax was informed that Hitler had been assured this was the case, "so far as I knew." Henderson had at least made the gesture of parrying Hitler's complaint about the German minority in Poland by charging, although without personal conviction, that Hitler was persecuting the Poles in Germany. Henderson was not actually convinced that there was any truth in this charge. Halifax was informed that Hitler would not retreat, and that he enjoyed far greater support in Germany for his policy than had been the case during the Czech crisis of September 1938.[5]

Hitler's Reply to Chamberlain

Hitler's letter to Chamberlain on August 23, 1939, placed principal emphasis on the intensity of suffering among the Germans of Poland. He hoped that the British would regard this situation from the standpoint of humanity rather than from abstract considerations of policy. He reminded Chamberlain that many prominent Englishmen within the past few years had recognized the gravity of the Danzig-Corridor problem. Hitler accused Chamberlain pointblank of creating the alarmist atmosphere which destroyed the willingness of the Poles to negotiate with Germany. He also accused Chamberlain of encouraging war between Poland and Germany by presenting the Poles with a blank check for British support in any conflict, regardless of its origin. Hitler asked Chamberlain to recognize two facts which were at the root of the trouble between Great Britain and Germany. Germany had informed Poland that the Danzig-Corridor question would have to be resolved with or without Polish cooperation. Great Britain had encouraged Polish intransigence by stating that she would support Poland in any conflict against Germany. Hitler concluded that this situation would destroy his life-long ambition to promote Anglo-German friendship and understanding.[6]

Hitler, who continued to hope that the British would reconsider their position, was far less pessimistic about Anglo-German relations than was suggested by his carefully prepared diplomatic letter to Chamberlain. He declared at a conference with the principal German leaders at the Berghof, on the evening of August 23, 1939, that he was more than ever convinced that Great Britain in a final showdown would not attack Germany. He attributed a far more rational basis to British policy than the facts warranted when he argued that Great Britain "had no need to wage war and consequently would not wage war." Marshal Goering was unable to share the optimism of Hitler. He had carefully studied a report received from German Ambassador Mackensen at Rome on the previous day. Italian Foreign Minister Ciano had assured Mackensen that Mussolini did not question the complete sincerity of Hitler. Mussolini recognized that Hitler had a mystical faith that wisdom would prompt the British leaders to avoid the tragedy of a new Anglo-German conflict. Mussolini wished it to be clearly understood in Germany that he did not share this faith despite the recent success of German policy in Russia. The Italian leader, who was mindful of the secret Italian neutrality pledge to the British on August 18th, had more reason than Hitler to believe that the Russo-German pact would fail to discourage the British from attacking Germany.[7]

The Mission of Birger Dahlerus

Marshal Goering had received permission from Hitler many weeks earlier to launch a private program calculated to improve German contacts with the British. Goering had approached Hitler with this suggestion in early July 1939 after Birger Dahlerus, a prominent Swedish engineer with many contacts in both Great Britain and Germany,   had called on Goering to offer his services to Germany as an unofficial negotiator. Dahlerus was motivated by his recognition that Hitler, in contrast to Halifax, sincerely desired to arrive at an Anglo-German understanding. Dahlerus knew that a new Anglo-German war would be an unparalleled disaster for every country on the European continent except the Soviet Union. He informed Goering that the British leaders in July 1939 were determined to attack Germany. Goering said at the time that he doubted the truth of this assertion, but he recognized that the situation was serious. Dahlerus proposed to organize an unofficial conference between important representatives from British Conservative Party groups, and the Germans.

Goering was delighted by the proposal of Dahlerus, and he promised to obtain the consent of Hitler for the plan. The German Chancellor accepted the proposition with alacrity, and Dahlerus was instructed to proceed with his mission on July 8, 1939. Dahlerus decided to go one step further. He received German consent for an ambitious plan to organize an official conference with representatives from the British and German diplomatic services. Dahlerus was disappointed when Halifax rejected this proposal, but he was successful in achieving his original objective. The British Foreign Secretary promised that no steps would be taken by the British authorities to prevent an unofficial conference on German territory.

The meeting ultimately took place on August 7, 1939 at Soenke Nissen Koog, in the Frisian area just inside the German border with Denmark. The German delegation was headed by Marshal Goering and General Bodenschatz, Goering's immediate subordinate in the German Air Force command. The British delegation consisted exclusively of loyal supporters of the Chamberlain Government appearing in a private capacity. The agenda of the conference was restricted to a preliminary exchange of views, but it was soon evident to both sides that the risk of an Anglo-German war was very great. The Germans agreed to a British proposal for a new conference which would also be attended by French and Ialian delegates. This conference had not been held when the Russo-German pact was signed. Goering was deeply disappointed to learn that the British responded to the Russian Pact by withdrawing from the project.[8]

The abortive Soenke Nissen Koog conference was followed by additional private contacts between the British and the Germans. Goering was worried by the implications of a report to the German Foreign Office on August 16, 1939, from Alfred Rosenberg, the chief of the Foreign Policy Office of the National Socialist Party. Rosenberg also forwarded a copy of his report directly to Hitler. The source of Rosenberg's information was Baron William S. von Ropp, who was born in the Baltic provinces of Tsarist Russia and later became a British citizen. Ropp, like many of the Baltic Germans from families who had served the Tsarist bureaucracy, was not particularly friendly toward Germany, and he was a devoted supporter of Halifax. He presented the startling suggestion that a British declaration of war against Germany might not preclude an Anglo-German settlement after the defeat of Poland.

Ropp, who had been selected to head the British Air Ministry intelligence service division for Germany in wartime, claimed that there was lively opposition to war with Germany in the British Air Ministry. He claimed that it was obvious to the British Air Force leaders that the Soviet Union would be the principal beneficiary of an Anglo-German war, and that Germany would not desire the destruction of Great Britain and France after her inevitable victory in Poland. Ropp predicted that Great Britain and France would declare war on Germany in the event of a German-Polish war, but he suggested that such a war need not be taken seriously, because it would be possible to conclude peace after the completion of the Polish phase of hostilities.

It was Goering, rather than Rosenberg, who feared the effect of this report on Hitler's attitude. It was possible that Halifax might be deliberately encouraging the Germans to gamble in Poland in order to involve them in a general war which might result in the destruction of Germany. Rosenberg was inclined to accept the information from his fellow Balt at face value. He concluded that the Poles were engaged in a desperate gamble to provoke war with Germany because they hoped to force the British hand without being at all certain that the British would actually support Poland. The illusory British attitude described by Ropp conformed closely to the wishful thinking of Hitler about the intentions of the British leaders. The Ropp disclosures were a clever propaganda achievement. The situation described by Ropp was ironical in the light of the feverish preparations of British air force leaders for an assault of unprecedented and prolonged ferocity against the unfortunate civilian population of Germany.[9]

The German Foreign Office also received a confidential report on August 16, 1939, from Paul Legrenier, a French journalist who was sincerely friendly toward Germany. Legrenier insisted that Great Britain and France would not go to war against Germany in a conflict between Germany and Poland arising from trouble at Danzig. He was basing his report on the determination of French Foreign Minister Bonnet not to fight for Polish interests at Danzig, and on the obvious fact that Great Britain would not attack Germany without French support. Joseph Barnes, the Berlin correspondent of the New York *Herald Tribune*, estimated to the German diplomats on the same day that there was still at least a 50-50 chance that Great Britain and France would not attack Germany. Barnes added that he was basing his estimate on the assumption that Germany would make a great effort to avoid needless provocation of Great Britain and France. The reports of Ropp, Legrenier, and Barnes were received by Hitler on August 16, 1939, before the announcement of the Russo-German Pact. Hitler was convinced that the conclusion of the Pact with Russia would increase the chances for peace. It is not astonishing under these circumstances that he was more optimistic than Goering or Mussolini about the possibilities of avoiding an Anglo-German war.[10]

The German Foreign Office was under no illusion about the official policy of President Roosevelt in the current crisis. They knew that his policy was based on the twin assumptions that there should and would be a general European war. There was also reason to believe that some of the American diplomats in Berlin did not share this attitude. British Ambassador Henderson informed the Germans that American Chargé d'Affaires Kirk was constantly prodding him to insist that Great Britain would fight rather than retreat, but there was ample evidence that Kirk hoped a show of British firmness would prompt Hitler to make new proposals for a settlement. The Germans also knew that Kirk had severely reprimanded Louis P. Lochner, the American journalist, for questioning the determination of Germany to go to war. Lochner was following the tactics of the Polish journalists by claiming that Hitler was bluffing, because he knew that these tactics would encourage German defiance and make war more likely. It was obvious that Kirk would not have intervened with Lochner on his own initiative had he personally favored war, and the German diplomats were pleased to learn that Kirk had denounced his warmongering.[11]

Charles Buxton's Advice to Hitler

The Germans had received many rumors about friction between Halifax and Rab Butler, the British Parliamentary Under-Secretary for Foreign Affairs. It was known at Berlin that Butler was opposed to war with Germany. Charles Roden Buxton, the Labour Party foreign policy expert and Quaker leader, arrived at Berlin on a visit on August 15, 1939. Butler and Buxton were close personal friends. Buxton was accompanied to Berlin by the British social worker, T.C.P. Catchpool, who was popular with the Germans because of the relief work he had undertaken in the Sudetenland during the period of Czech rule. Buxton announced that he was in Berlin to discuss an amicable settlement of Anglo-German friction. He had written to Dr. Hetzler, who was Ribbentrop's personal adviser on British affairs at Berlin, advocating a comprehensive settlement dealing with all points of difference between Great Britain and Germany. Buxton motivated his mission by informing Dr. Hetzler that "I am a good European."

The personal plan which Buxton presented contained everything which Hitler desired and much more than he would have requested in a settlement with Halifax. It began with the crucial point that the British Empire should disinterest itself in Eastern Europe after recognizing that the German Reich had special interests in that area. Buxton advocated the return of the German colonies held by Great Britain and France, and the convening of an international colonial conference on the basis of the Berlin conference of 1885 for a rational redistribution of colonial territory among the leading colonial Powers. This did not mean that any particular Power would necessarily receive a net increase of colonial territory, but it was hoped that an exchange of territories in specific areas would reduce future points of friction. Buxton also advocated the liquidation of British economic imperialism in Eastern Europe, for instance in Rumania, where Great Britain exerted pressure on the local authorities for unfair concessions at the expense of normal trade. He believed that it would be necessary for Great Britain to disavow her guarantees to Poland, Rumania, and Greece as the only means of terminating unwarranted British intervention in Eastern Europe. Buxton believed that the British Government should atone for their harmful influence in Poland by offering to mediate in the dispute between Poland and Germany. He advocated a program of mutual confidence which would include a new Anglo-German naval treaty, the reduction of armaments, and mutual inspection of the national military establishments in Great Britain and Germany.

The Germans were asked to recognize that the existing territory of the British Empire was the living space of the British nation. They were to agree on a diplomatic conference among Germany, Great Britain, France, Italy, Poland, and Spain for the settlement of European issues. The Germans were to withdraw any alliance commitment they might have with the new Spanish regime on the grounds that any such alliance would threaten either Great Britain or France with encirclement. This point, although Buxton did not know it, involved no actual concession from Germany, because there were no alliance commitments of any kind between Germany and Spain. Buxton did not ask for Spanish withdrawal from the anti-Comintern front, because he recognized that this constituted international ideological solidarity against Communism rather than national alliances.

Buxton expected Hitler to declare to the world that the system of temporary autonomy for the Czechs in the Bohemia-Moravia Protectorate would become and remain firmly established as a permanent autonomy. He was convinced that the implementation of this declaration would be an adequate response to British grievances about earlier German policy at Prague. It was obvious to the German diplomats that Buxton was presenting a very real and vital plan for the settlement of Anglo-German tension, and there were no German objections whatever to the points which he proposed. It was equally clear that the British Government would have accepted this program were Butler rather than Halifax responsible for the conduct of British foreign policy. The Buxton plan would have afforded a marvellous platform for a negotiated settlement had it been presented officially by the British Government. Hitler was aware that Buxton intended him to use these proposals in negotiations with the British Government, and he did not hesitate to do so after the conclusion of the Russo-German Pact.[12]

The Confusion of Herbert von Dirksen

The conversations between Buxton and the German diplomats were completed when German Ambassador Dirksen arrived at Berlin from London on August 18, 1939. Dirksen later claimed that he had been anxious to discuss the British situation with Ribbentrop, who was in the Salzburg area at the time. This alleged enthusiasm for a meeting with the German Foreign Minister was not reflected by the Ambassador's actions. He spent only a few hours in Berlin before departing for his home at Groeditzberg, Silesia. It would have been more logical for him to remain at least a few days in Berlin in an effort to see Ribbentrop. Dirksen, from his home in Silesia, addressed an extensive memorandum to Weizsaecker on Anglo-German relations. He displayed no interest in a personal meeting with Ribbentrop in his accompanying letter. He merely suggested that Weizsaecker should forward his memorandum to the German Foreign Minister.

The Dirksen memorandum contained the suggestion that a study of British motives in extending the guarantee of March 31, 1939, to Poland was essential to any analysis of current British policy in the Polish question. Dirksen recognized that the British guarantee was the product of abstract calculations based on the traditional British balance of power policy. He noted that Poland was the cornerstone of the British encirclement front against Germany. Dirksen believed that it would be necessary for Germany to persuade the British to abandon the encirclement policy as such before there could be any hope of British neutrality in the specific German-Polish conflict.

Dirksen followed this impressive introduction with the astonishing claim that Great Britain was seeking to "overcome her own inferiority complex." He pointed out that British prestige had suffered from a long series of diplomatic defeats from Japanese, Italian, and German policies during the past few years in Asia, Africa, and Europe. The virtual collapse of the League of Nations was recognized to be a blow to British prestige because Great Britain had occupied the commanding position in that organization. Dirksen failed to note that the attitudes of Chamberlain, Halifax, Simon, and Hoare toward the League of Nations had always been cynical, and that they had never scrupled to undermine the position of the League for their own purposes. He also failed to show why diplomatic reversals, which resulted from excessive British intervention in the problems of other Powers, were sufficient to undermine the notorious superiority complex, unrecognized by Dirksen, of the British leadership. Halifax was encountering no difficulty in intimidating Italy. He was confident that he could dictate French foreign policy, and he knew that President Roosevelt of the United States was eager to respond favorably to any bellicose suggestion he cared to offer. He also knew that Hitler and the other German leaders were intensely pro-British and single-mindedly desirous of promoting Anglo-German cooperation. The share of British trade in the world markets was increasing throughout 1939, and the enormous British Empire had suffered no losses of territory during the ten years which had followed the advent of the world economic depression in 1929. Dirksen gave away his case completely when he concluded that Great Britain had "pulled herself together morally" after the events at Prague in March 1939. He accepted the position of Halifax by declaring that the public adoption of a war policy by Great Britain was an act of moral rehabilitation. Dirksen was the hopeless prisoner of British propaganda.

Dirksen claimed that Chamberlain and the British public were staring at the Danzig situation with hypnotic intensity despite the fact that they were largely ignorant of affairs in that part of Europe. He noted that German publicity about the fate of the Germans in Poland was received with studied scepticism in Great Britain. It was easy to recall that Germany had not complained on this score during the 1934-1939 period when censorship in Germany prevented the German newspapers from exploiting incidents in Poland. The British leaders chose to ignore the fact that Hitler had suppressed unfavorable news about Poland in the interest of achieveing a lasting understanding with the Poles.

Dirksen was convinced that Polish military action at Danzig would be followed by British military action against Germany. He insisted that the British would support Poland even if the Poles started military action without any provocation from Germany. He concluded that British armed intervention was inevitable if Germany, for any reason whatever, launched a full military campaign against Poland. Dirksen believed that a German retreat before Polish pretensions might ulitmately cause the British to modify their policy toward Poland.

Weizsaecker studied the Dirksen memorandum and forwarded it to Ribbentrop. The German Foreign Minister was annoyed by Dirksen's inability to resist British propaganda, but he was impressed by the unequivocal warning that Great Britain would intervene in a possible German-Polish war. He was preoccupied, on his flight home from Russia on August 24, 1939, with thoughts about what he hoped would be a last minute diplomatic solution of the German-Polish dispute. He found it difficult to avoid the conclusion that a general diplomatic conference would be the sole possible means of accomplishing this objective. His thoughts returned to the Italian proposals for a conference, despite the objections which Hitler had voiced against the practicability of this plan. He knew that Dr. Fritz Hesse, the German Press Counsellor at London, shared the conviction of Dirksen that Great Britain would attack Germany unless there was a peaceful settlement of the Polish dispute. Ribbentrop knew that Hesse, who had been stationed at London for many more years than Dirksen, was a more astute observer of the British scene than the German Ambassador. He decided on August 24th to recall Hesse to Berlin for personal talks. Ribbentrop also instructed Hesse to prepare a special report for Hitler on the latest developments in England.[13]

The German Foreign Office recieved additional misleading information from Italian Ambassador Attolico on August 23rd, before Ribbentrop returned from Moscow. Attolico claimed that British Ambassador Loraine had agreed at Rome on August 20th that his Government would participate in an international conference under favorable conditions. This was a gross distortion of Loraine's chilly response to Ciano's conference plan, and Attolico concealed the important fact that Great Britain on the same day had threatened Italy, by announcing that the major British offensive would be conducted against the Italians if Germany received Italian military support in the event of war. The *demarche* of Attolico gave the German diplomats false hopes that Great Britain might be considering a peaceful settlement with Germany.

Hitler's Appeal to the British Foreign Office

The German Foreign Office was visited on August 23rd by William Cotton, a British Conservative who supported the Buxton plan for an agreement with Germany. The purpose of the Cotton mission was to persuade the Germans to send Marshal Goering on an *incognito* trip to England to negotiate with Halifax. The British Foreign Secretary was not enthusiastic about the plan, but he had given Cotton a written statement couched in cool terms which conceded that he was "willing to see Goering." The absence of positive encouragement from Halifax for the proposed Goering mission caused the German diplomats to fear that an attempt to settle differences in this manner would be abortive and produce a fiasco. Cotton was told that Hitler and Henderson were discussing the problems of Anglo-German relations, and that it was hoped that these renewed negotiations would produce concrete results. A decision on the proposed Goering mission was temporarily deferred, but both Hitler and Goering accepted the statement from Halifax as a commitment which might later be of use in maintaining contact between the two countries.[14]

Goering received permission from Hitler to follow up the Cotton mission by dispatching Birger Dahlerus on a new mission to England. Dahlerus was in Paris on the evening of August 23rd when he received a telephone call from Goering, who instructed him to return to Berlin at once. The Swedish engineer arrived at the German capital on the following morning. He assured Goering that he was prepared to devote his full time and energy toward achieving an Anglo-German settlement. He would not desist from this effort unless or until it was demonstrated that such a settlement was an impossibility.

Goering responded by instructing Dahlerus to fly to London as soon as possible. He was to convey an important private pledge from Hitler to the British leaders. Hitler hoped to create confidence by pledging Germany's word that the negotiations begun with Henderson the previous day would be continued as far as this was within his power, and that they would never be disrupted by any hostile action against Great Britain by Germany. Hitler did not wish the British attitude in the negotiations to be influenced by the existence of any alleged threat of a German surprise attack against Great Britain.

Goering permitted Dahlerus to assure Halifax that the German Marshal, who was responsible for all commands to the German Air Force, would also exert every influence to avert any German overt action against Great Britain while negotiations were in progress. Dahlerus contacted the British diplomats in Berlin after his conversation with Goering. He telephoned the British Foreign Office from the British Embassy in Berlin on the evening of August 24th, and he received permission to fly to London. Dahlerus confided on the telephone that Goering feared Chamberlain might make a declaration to Parliament that further Anglo-German talks would not be tolerated, and he requested that no such decision be made before his arrival in London. Dahlerus departed for London on the morning of August 25th, where he proceeded to play an important role in Anglo-German negotiations. His mission did not come to an end until more than a week later when his services as a negotiator were abruptly rejected by the British leaders. Dahlerus made numerous trips between Great Britain and Germany which extended the contacts between the British and German leaders. Halifax later admitted to the Joint Allied Tribunal which condemned Goering to death at Nuremberg in 1946 that the German Marshal, who employed Dahlerus with the knowledge and approval of Hitler, had done everything possible to preserve the peace during the final crisis which preceded the outbreak of World War II.[15]

Mackensen at Rome recognized the importance of the Italian position in the conduct of negotiations between Germany and Great Britain. He continued to hope that Ciano had not revealed recent Italo-German disagreements to the British. Mackensen reported on August 23, 1939, that the Russo-German pact might persuade the Italians to return to a policy of close support to Germany. He had at last received definite information at Rome that Attolico had done everything possible to prevent Italy from supporting Germany in the crisis, and he was now inclined to agree with Weizsaecker about the decisive importance of Attolico in producing the recent change of attitude at Rome. Italian sources now explained that Ciano had "succumbed" to the influence of Hitler at the Obersalzberg, but that Attolico had been successful in changing his mind again. The Italians now emphasized that Germany in May 1939 had promised to do everything possible to avoid war in the years ahead. They wished to concentrate on their program of public works in Albania, Ethiopia, and Sicily, and to prepare for the international exposition at Rome in 1942. It was insisted that the Italian Navy, with only two battleships, was not prepared for a struggle. The Italians also appeared to be positive that Italy would bear the brunt of an Anglo-French attack were she to enter a war. This attitude was not surprising after the secret British threat of August 20th.

Mussolini, unlike Bonnet, doubted that Poland could be defeated within a few weeks. He suspected that the United States might intervene directly in a general war before the elimination of Poland. The Italians favored a truce between Germany and Poland regardless of the terms which Germany might have to accept. It was obvious to Weizsaecker after reading the full details of this report that Mackensen was not really optimistic about the influence of the Russian pact on the Italian position. He also received a report from German Finance Minister, Schwerin-Krosigk, who was visiting in Rome, that Ciano did not believe that the Russian pact would have the slightest effect on the determination of Great Britain to attack Germany. It was unfortunate that British Ambassador Loraine had been more effective than Ciano during recent conversations in producing an impression of determination.[16]

Polish-Danzig Talks Terminated by Beck

Government offices in France by August 24, 1939, were receiving visits from prominant Frenchmen who urged decisive pressure on Poland in the interest of peace. Bonnet was able to tell them that Polish Foreign Minister Beck had at last agreed, with some irritation, to permit Polish Ambassador Lipski to request a general exchange of views with Weizsaecker at the German Foreign Office.

Lipski called on Marshal Goering on August 24th after he discovered that the German State Secretary had departed from Berlin for the day. The conversation between Lipski and Goering took place immediately after the meeting between Goering and Dahlerus. Goering did everything possible to calm the Polish Ambassador, who betrayed considerable excitement and frayed nerves. Lipski's condition is understandable when it is recalled that he had tried in vain for many months to persuade Beck to permit him to return permanently to Poland. Goering asserted flatly to Lipski that the danger of war between Germany and

Poland was being greatly exaggerated in many quarters. He confided that Hitler, as a keen diplomat, was easily able to create the impression of going a great deal further than he actually intended to go. Goering reminded Lipski that the principal cause for the deterioration of German-Polish relations was not the Polish refusal of the October 1938 German offer, but Beck's acceptance of the British guarantee of March 31, 1939. Goering was confident that German-Polish relations could be straightened out if the problem of the existing entangling alliances was solved by negotiation between Great Britain and Germany. Goering hoped that his remarks to Lipski would contribute to the relaxation of tension in Poland, but Beck concluded that the German Marshal was seeking to lull Poland into a false sense of security.[17]

The tension at Danzig mounted after Chodacki warned the Danzig authorities on the early morning of August 24th that Poland might retaliate against the appointment of Albert Forster as Danzig Chief-of-State. The Danzig authorities had informed Burckhardt of their decision regarding Forster, but the League High Commissioner suggested that it would also have been wise to inform the League of Nations Committee of Three, Senate President Greiser told Burckhardt shortly before noon on August 24th that no reaction from the Committee of Three could have any effect on the Danzig decision about Forster, and he added that this decision was final. The Danzig Government would refuse to surrender to the Polish threat on this occasion. Burckhardt warned Greiser that the situation was dangerous, and he complained that the attitude of the British had become more stiff and warlike after the visit of Henderson to the Obersalzberg the previous day. Burckhardt's personal reaction was to send his children from Danzig to Switzerland, although his wife insisted upon remaining in the so-called Free City. The League High Commissioner exclaimed to Greiser that he would ask for his own recall. He was convinced that political developments had run their course and that Danzig would make a final effort to return to Germany within a few days. Greiser and Burckhardt exchanged friendly remarks and agreed to meet later in Germany or Switzerland.

Inconclusive talks with Poland about the customs inspectors had been initiated by Greiser on August 9th after Forster's return from Berchtesgaden, but these negotiations were terminated by the Poles on the morning of August 24th. Hitler had told Forster that he had no objection to such talks if the Danzig authorities considered that they might be useful, but they had produced no results. The Polish Government decided to end conversations when they received new requests for the reduction of the number of customs inspectors and for the withdrawal of the Polish frontier guards from Danzig territory. The Poles terminated negotiations without considering these proposals. They presented a note of protest which charged that the Danzig authorities interfered with the operations of Polish railway employees and customs inspectors on Danzig territory.

The German Government advised Danzig on August 24th that no arms should be given to any Germans in Poland. The German Government insisted that under no circumstances should the Germans in Poland be advised to resist Polish attacks in the event of a German-Polish war. It was argued that resistance to such attacks at one place would be disastrous to the minority Germans elsewhere in Poland. Forster appealed to Hitler on August 24th for permission to take a strong line with the Poles after the rupture in negotiations on the customs inspectors. Forster contemplated a policy of arrests and of the confiscation of Polish arms in Danzig. Hitler refused to approve these measures because he feared they would produce an immediate conflict.[18]

The German Government was annoyed when Hungary announced on August 24th that troops would be called up to the Rumanian frontier in response to an alleged military threat to Hungary from Rumania. It was obvious at Berlin that this was a maneuver designed to divert attention from the situation in Poland. Rumanian Foreign Minister Gafencu responded the same day by offering to conclude a non-aggression pact with Hungary. The Hungarians had no intention of accepting this offer, but it compelled them, when combined with German pressure, to tone down their military preparations against Rumania. Regent Horthy of Hungary was convinced that Hitler preferred friendly relations with Poland to war, and he continued to hope that there would be no German-Polish war. He was equally determined to do everything possible in the event of war to secure Hungarian territorial revision at Rumanian expense.

Confusion in the British Parliament on August 24th

Hitler on August 24th was especially interested to receive news about the impact on foreign countries of his treaty with Russia. The neighboring Slovak Government was pleased to receive the German offer to restore the Slovakian territory seized by Poland in 1938 in the event of war between Poland and Germany. The conclusion of the Russo-German pact momentarily convinced the Slovaks that there would be no war. The Tiso Government responded to this situation by requesting Germany on August 24th to support the recovery of the territory taken from Slovakia by diplomatic means. The Slovak leaders predicted that the German dispute with Poland would be settled by an international diplomatic conference, and they hoped that their own claims would be placed on the conference agenda.[19]

German diplomats at Paris reported that extremists who were most opposed to Germany, such as Henri de Kerillis, the Right-wing journalist, and Léon Blum, the Socialist leader, were profoundly discouraged by the conclusion of the Russo-German pact. German Chargé d'Affaires Thomsen reported from Washington, D.C., that the pact had decidedly strengthened the hand of the so-called isolationists, who opposed the plans of President Roosevelt for American military intervention in Europe. Thomsen added, however, that the Pact had failed to discourage the efforts of President Roosevelt to prod Great Britain and France into war with Germany.

German Ambassador Franz von Papen reported from Ankara on August 24th that the Turks were tremendously impressed by the news of the Russo-German pact. He added that Turkish Foreign Minister Saracoglu had expressed his regret that the Turks were on the wrong side, from the standpoint of their own security, in the European diplomatic conflict. Saracoglu was "taken aback" by the new situation, and Papen reported with considerable satisfaction that new progress in important economic negotiations between Germany and Turkey had been achieved. The German Ambassador predicted that Turco-German

THE FORCED WAR

relations would improve steadily in the months ahead. Hitler was pleased with
a statement by Belgian Minister Vicomte Jacques Davignon to the Belgian press
at noon on August 24, 1939. The Belgian diplomat insisted that an Anglo-
German war would be a disaster which could not bring advantages to either side.

Pierre-Etienne Flandin, the former Premier of France, believed that new
German proposals for a settlement with Poland might save the peace of Europe.
He saw no reason why Germany should not demand the return of the entire
Corridor, and he believed that Warsaw might submit to this arrangement under
pressure. Flandin referred to the Russians as "born traitors," and he complained
that the British were suffering from a prestige complex because of the German
diplomatic success in Russia. He assured German diplomats at Paris that Bonnet
was prepared to be more logical, and to draw the necessary conclusions from the
Russo-German pact. There was no point in waging war to defend Poland after
the military defense of the Polish state had become an impossibility.[20]

German Chargé d'Affaires Kordt reported from London at 1:15 P.M. on
August 24th that the British Government had issued final orders to prepare the
British Air Force for immediate action against Germany. Prime Minister
Chamberlain spoke to a special session of the British House of Commons at
3:00 o'clock on the same afternoon. Chamberlain contended that the European
situation had become progressively worse since his previous statement to the
House on July 31, 1939. He warned the Members that they were facing the
danger of immediate war with Germany. Chamberlain admitted that he was
in no position to judge the accuracy of claims about the mistreatment of the
Germans in Poland. He defended the Poles at great length in general terms, but
he appeared to be on the defensive himself. He claimed that Great Britain had
reaffirmed her obligations to Poland on August 23rd, the date that the Russo-
German pact was signed. Chamberlain proceeded to declare that "in Berlin, the
announcement (of the pact) was hailed with extraordinary cynicism, as a great
diplomatic victory which removed any danger of war since we and France would
no longer be likely to fulfill our obligations to Poland. We felt it our first duty to
remove any such dangerous illusion."[21]

Chamberlain pleaded that "nothing that we have done or propose to do
menaces the legitimate interests of Germany. It is not an act of menace to
prepare to help friends to defend themselves against force." This statement
ignored the fact that Great Britain had offered to surrender Poland to the Soviet
Union, and that she would never consent to defend the Poles against Bolshevism.
It also overlooked the fact that the British had cultivated so-called special
relations of friendship with Poland solely because they regarded the Poles as
a useful instrument in furnishing the pretext for a British assault on Germany.
Chamberlain might equally well have argued that the British plan to destroy
Germany did not threaten legitimate German interests. The legitimate interests
of foreign nations in the opinion of Chamberlain were those which enjoyed the
special support and approval of the British Government. It was legitimate for
the Poles to torture their German minority and to provoke incidents at Danzig
because this course of action enjoyed British approval.

Chamberlain spoiled the effect of a speech intended to create an impression
of unlimited British defiance by declaring that he had explained to Hitler that
Great Britain had no interests of her own in Eastern Europe. He claimed that

the primary motive of British foreign policy was to prevent the unnecessary shedding of blood in foreign lands. This was pure cant, but Hitler concluded from these statements that the British might reconsider their decision to attack Germany.

The various Parliamentary factions displayed considerable confusion on August 24th. The Liberal leader, Sir Archibald Sinclair, suggested that a possible attack against the British Empire should be the primary consideration of Chamberlain rather than the defense of Poland. The Communist member, Gallacher, continued to insist that Great Britain should do nothing without a pact of mutual assistance with the Soviet Union. The statement of Ernest Bevin, who spoke for the British Labour Party, was particularly interesting. Bevin insisted that a British guarantee of Poland without support from the Soviet Union was a much too formidable undertaking. He suggested that the time had arrived for a solution of the Polish crisis by further negotiation.[22]

Hitler concluded, after analyzing the British Parliamentary debate on August 24th, that the united front of the Western Powers against Germany would begin to crack on the following day. He was seeking to strengthen the German position by obtaining a new declaration of support from Italy. Ribbentrop, who had just returned from Moscow, where the Allied military missions were still vainly seeking to negotiate, telephoned Ciano on the night of August 24th. He was instructed by Hitler to request a definite and conclusive statement of Italy's position. Ciano replied that Germany would receive a statement from Italy on the following day. He carefully refrained from indicating that the Italian response would be negative.[23]

The Roosevelt Messages to Germany and Poland

President Roosevelt sent insincere peace messages to Germany and Poland at 9:00 p.m. on August 24, 1939. He ignored in his message to Germany the rebuff he had received from Hitler's speech to the Reichstag on April 28th by claiming that "to the message which I sent you last April I have received no reply." He proposed a settlement between Germany and Poland by direct negotiation, arbitration, or mediation. He was treading on difficult ground, because Poland, whom he favored, rather than Germany, whom he opposed, blocked the resumption of negotiations. The messages from President Roosevelt forced President Mościcki of Poland to pay lip service to negotiation, although the Polish Government did not desire to resume contact with the Germans. The reply of President Mościcki was a definite pledge to President Roosevelt that Poland would negotiate, although the Poles actually had no intention of doing so.

President Roosevelt informed Hitler that "it is understood, of course, that upon resort to any one of the alternatives I suggest, each nation will agree to accord complete respect to the independence and territorial integrity of the other." President Roosevelt imagined that this arrangement would preclude in advance any tangible Polish concessions to Germany, but its terms were entirely consistent with the Hitler offer of October 1938 which the Poles had rejected. The original German proposals were actually based upon the respect of the independence and territorial integrity of Poland. This had not prevented the

Poles from rejecting them and from ordering the partial mobilization of the Polish armed forces against Germany. Hitler had revealed to the world the inaccuracies and fallacies in the Roosevelt proposals of April 15, 1939, to Germany and Italy, but President Roosevelt rarely accepted criticism. He blandly concluded his message to Hitler with the statement that the United States was prepared to contribute to peace "in the form set forth in my message of April 14 (advance release of the messages to the American press on that date)." The Roosevelt messages to Germany and Poland were made public at Washington, D.C., at 10:00 p.m. on August 24, 1939. The message to Hitler was not submitted to the German Foreign Office by American Chargé d'Affaires Kirk until 9:00 a.m. on August 25th. Hitler decided to defer his reply to President Roosevelt for several days. He was intent, because of the importance of German-American relations, upon preparing a carefully cogent and courteous exposition of the German position for the benefit of the American President.[24]

German Ambassador Mackensen had a satisfactory conversation with Mussolini about the Russo-German treaty early on August 25, 1939. The Italian leader warmly assured Mackensen that he approved of this Pact, and he recalled that he had suggested this himself the previous Spring. Mussolini told Mackensen that he was whole-heartedly in accord with Germany's position in the Polish question. The Italian leader described the worsening of German-Polish relations as "so acute that an armed conflict can no longer be avoided." He was convinced that the Polish mentality was "no longer responsive to reasonable suggestions, no matter from which side they might come."

Mackensen was immensely impressed by the attitude displayed by Mussolini in the absence of Ciano or Attolico. Mussolini claimed that the Poles should have responded to Hitler's original offer by accepting the German annexation of Danzig as an indication that they were sincere in their desire to come to a general agreement with Germany. Mussolini was convinced that "a general conference might have followed" which would have "assured European peace for fifteen to twenty years, as is desired by all." The attitude of the Italian leader on the morning of August 25th was everything which Hitler could have desired, and the German leader concluded that it would be possible to rely on Mussolini's full support. He expected a favorable statement from Italy later in the day in response to the earlier initiative of Ribbentrop.

Mussolini and Ciano had renewed their discussion about a general peace conference with Sir Percy Loraine after the announcement of the Russo-German pact. Loraine reported to Halifax on August 23rd that Mussolini wanted peace, and that he would like to mediate in the German-Polish dispute. Mussolini assured Loraine that Hitler would not accept the terms of a general settlement unless they included the German annexation of Danzig. Loraine reported that the Italians were concentrating on an attempt to gain a British concession on this one decisive point. Loraine informed Halifax that both Mussolini and Ciano were convinced that a successful diplomatic conference was the only hope for a solution of the current difficulties.[25]

American Ambassador William C. Bullitt was advising both Halifax and the French leaders to maintain their military missions in Moscow, and to continue their efforts to detach Italy from Germany. Halifax recognized that the situation in Russia was untenable by this time. The Anglo-French teams had no choice other than to leave Russia empty-handed. Molotov granted an audience to French Ambassador Naggiar on August 25th, immediately after the British and French military men departed from the Russian capital. The Soviet Commissar for Foreign Affairs took pleasure in announcing to the West that the Poles were exclusively responsible for the failure of Anglo-French negotiations with the Russians for a mutual assistance pact. This announcement confirmed suspicions which French Foreign Minister Bonnet had entertained for many days, and he was inclined for this reason to accept the Russian explanation at face value. Bonnet continued to be furious with the Poles. They had allowed Lipski to engage in an inconclusive conversation with Marshal Goering the previous day, but they had haughtily rejected his suggestion for Franco-Polish consultation on Danzig. The French Foreign Minister was resolved to retaliate by seizing the first opportunity of releasing France from her military obligations to Poland.[26]

Halifax was no longer concerned about Russia, and he did not share the desire of Bonnet to repress Polish excesses at Danzig. He was primarily interested in creating the impression everywhere in the world that the Russo-German pact had not caused him to reconsider his policy toward Germany. Halifax dispatched uniform instructions to British diplomatic missions in all countries on August 24th. He urged them to accept the superhuman task of correcting the impression that the pact had been a blow to the "peace front" headed by England and France. He also claimed that the pact "had produced no effect" on the British Cabinet. He exhorted his diplomats that the British course was straight ahead under the slogan of "preventing the domination of Europe by Germany." Halifax did not explain how a revived German nation of eighty million German citizens could fail to be the leading continental Power. After all, it had been said after 1871 that the Germany of Bismarck, with her forty million inhabitants, dominated Europe. The policy of Halifax was calculated to destroy Germany rather than to permit that normal growth and development which for centuries had been considered the natural right of every nation. It was a policy which led to the destruction of a friendly Germany and to the domination of Europe by a hostile Union pledged to overthrow the capitalist system in Great Britain.[27]

Percy Loraine in Rome exposed himself to ridicule in an effort to meet the diplomatic requirements of Halifax. He informed Ciano on August 24th that the Russo-German pact had given him "the first hearty laugh he had had for some weeks." The same man had previously informed the Italian leaders that a pact of mutual assistance with Russia was a necessary feature of the British program. The Italians could be pardoned for suspecting that his "hearty laugh" closely resembled an hysterical scream, because they had never heard him laugh. Loraine soon learned that Halifax was under heavy pressure at home on August 24th to modify the uncompromising British stand at Danzig. The British Foreign Secretary confided to Loraine, despite his circular instructions, that Great Britain might ultimately consider the return of Danzig to Germany as part of an international settlement. Loraine was bewildered by this information, and he wondered if Halifax intended after all to encourage Mussolini to take the initiative for a conference, which again might resolve British difficulties. There had been no similar suggestion from Halifax during the entire period from the British guarantee to Poland of March 31st to the conclusion of the Russo-German pact.

Unfortunately, the momentary weakening of Halifax's rigid stand at Danzig was
of short duration, and he soon concluded that he could maintain his original
position against the mounting opposition at home. Gilbert and Gott, in *The
Appeasers,* attempt to present this incident as a sustained effort on the part of
Halifax to come to terms with Germany at Danzig. Unfortunately, this was not
the case.[28]

The German Case Presented by Henderson

Henderson at Berlin was concentrating on obtaining recognition from Halifax
of the cruel fate of the German minority in Poland. He was especially contemptuous of the glowing reports about Polish restraint which poured into
London from Sir Howard Kennard at Warsaw. Henderson solemnly warned
Halifax on August 24th that German complaints about the treatment of the
minority in Poland were fully supported by the facts. Kennard received perfunctory advice from Halifax on the same day to caution the Poles. Kennard
refused to do this. He insisted to Halifax that there was no reason to warn the
Poles to exercise restraint. He dismissed in cavalier fashion all German complaints about incidents in Poland as "gross distortion," and he claimed that the
Germans were creating an atmosphere of panic by urging their nationals to leave
Poland. He implied that the shoe was actually on the other foot by praising
Beck for ostensibly restraining the Polish press from exploiting "atrocities"
committed against the Poles in Germany. He ignored information from Henderson
that there were no atrocities committed against the Polish minority in Germany.
    Henderson was asking Halifax to face the fact that war between Poland and
Germany was inevitable unless negotiations were resumed between the two
countries. Henderson knew that the Germans were prepared to negotiate. He
again insisted that the Poles should instruct their Ambassador at Berlin to
request an interview with Hitler. He pleaded with Halifax that it would be
contrary to Polish interests to attempt a full military occupation of Danzig in
response to the Danzig attempt to exercise self-determination and return to
Germany. Henderson was prompted by knowledge about Polish aims at Danzig,
and he knew that the Russo-German pact was beginning to arouse the Danzigers
from their mortal fear of the Poles. Hans Frank, the German Minister of Justice,
was visiting Danzig, and Henderson concluded that he was advising the Danzigers
on their political strategy. Henderson noted that Albert Forster was predicting
that Danzig would return to Germany within a few days.[29]
    Henderson wished Halifax to know that Hitler had accused England on
August 23, 1939, of seeking Germany's destruction. The German leader had
insisted that he was opposed to war, but he added philosophically that he
preferred to face a war crisis at the age of fifty rather than at fifty-five or sixty.
Halifax was informed that the remarks of the German Chancellor were the
opposite of bluff, and that he would never capitulate. Henderson desired Halifax
to learn exactly how he felt about the conversations with Hitler on August 23rd:
"It was heartbreaking since, as you know, I have held from the beginning that
the Poles were utterly foolish and unwise. But there it is and perhaps Providence
regards war as necessary to teach us not to do it again. With Russia in his pocket

I cannot see Hitler climbing down. If Poland prefers destruction to yielding, I am afraid she will suffer. And so will we. Personally I see no way out."[30]

Henderson in reality was a mere shade less pessimistic than his report indicated. His remarks were primarily calculated for their effect on Halifax, and possibly on Chamberlain. Henderson continued to fear that Halifax believed Hitler was bluffing, and he added for good measure that "intimidation will not deter him." The British Ambassador would have been unable to carry on had he faced the fact that Halifax was pursuing war for its own sake as an instrument of policy. No Ambassador had ever stated the position at a foreign capital more accurately, and Henderson had also added a scathingly effective denunciation of Polish policy. His most striking comment was the suggestion that still another conflict, despite the recent experience of World War I, might be necessaary to demonstrate the futility of Anglo-German wars to the British leadership. It would be valid to conclude under these circumstances that there was no reason to hope that the British leaders were capable of learning this obvious lesson. It would be pointless to learn it after the decline and fall of Great Britain and the other Western European nations.

Kennard at Warsaw Active for War

Kennard deliberately invited a reprimand from Halifax for his irresponsible conduct at the Polish capital. The British Ambassador created the impression on August 24th that he was feeling contrition for once, although it was actually an unrepentant feeling of insecurity at having gone too far in identifying himself with the Polish position. Kennard feared that the British Foreign Office might believe he had let them down on crucial issues of policy by supporting Polish opposition to Russian troop transit and negotiations with Germany. The issue about the Russian troops had become past history, but the question of possible German-Polish negotiations was vital, and the role of the British Ambassador at Warsaw might easily prove decisive. Halifax deliberately declined to reprimand Kennard because he was also opposed to German-Polish negotiations. The British Ambassador was allowed to conclude that the Foreign Office approved of his support to Polish intransigence in all directions, and he proceeded on the same bellicose course. As Gilbert and Gott have pointed out, he was supported in this cause at all times by Clifford Norton, of the Warsaw British Embassy staff, and by Frank Savery, the British Consul-General at Warsaw.

Halifax knew that President Roosevelt, despite his formal message to Poland, agreed that the British should exert no actual pressure on the Poles to negotiate. The main purpose of the Roosevelt messages was to make Germany appear guilty in a dispute which the American President hoped would lead to war. American Ambassador Bullitt informed British Ambassador Sir Eric Phipps at Paris that President Roosevelt was prepared to adopt any proposals which Halifax cared to make for the conduct of American policy. Halifax welcomed this assurance, but he was intensely displeased by the tactlessness and crudeness of Roosevelt's diplomacy. President Roosevelt had also prepared peace appeals to Italy and the Western Powers on August 24th. He had deliberately insulted Mussolini by addressing his Italian appeal exclusively to King Victor Emmanuel

III, apparently unaware that it was one of the main objectives of Halifax to separate Mussolini from Hitler. Halifax wired Loraine that he had no idea Roosevelt would take the initiative in this manner, and, above all, grossly insult Mussolini. Halifax added that Great Britain wished to distance herself as far as possible from tactless American peace gestures.[31]

Mussolini had presented a new appeal for a diplomatic settlement to Loraine on August 24th. Loraine replied that, according to information from Kennard, Beck was "in urgent consultation" with Lipski on the possibilities of new German-Polish conversations. This was an unpardonable exaggeration. Kennard had merely referred to Beck's grudging acceptance of Bonnet's plea to permit Lipski to talk to the Germans. Lipski was allowed to engage in a single conversation, which consisted primarily of a German attempt to reassure the Poles. Loraine flattered the Italians by assuring them that they were receiving from him the full text of Hitler's private reply to Chamberlain, whereas the French would obtain only a cursory summary. Loraine refrained from mentioning Halifax's instructions about a possible British concession at Danzig. He insisted that the British were not opposed to successful Italian mediation or a conference, but that they could not take the initiative in urging the Poles to sacrifice their rights to the Reich, or to recognize the right of Danzig to return to Germany. Loraine knew that the British alone were in a position to apply effective pressure on Poland.[32]

Loraine was seriously troubled by Halifax's suggestion about Danzig, which was inconsistent with the general line of British policy. Loraine wired to Halifax on August 25th to inquire if he really had understood the British Foreign Secretary. He asked bluntly if the British position now called for self-determination at Danzig in exchange for an international guarantee to Poland in which Hitler would participate. Loraine had repeated to the Italians on the previous day that Great Britain refused to urge Poland to accept such a solution. The previous year the British leaders had urged the Czechs to accept the cession of the Sudetenland. Loraine wished to know whether Germany, in the British view, was entitled to Danzig under certain circumstances, or whether she was not. If she was, Great Britain might logically be expected to present this position to all parties concerned, including Poland. It seemed to Loraine that the British stand at the moment did not make much sense.

Loraine was assuming, along with the other British diplomats, that war might break out at any moment. He addressed an urgent warning to London on the morning of August 25th that Italy was not preparing for war, and that it would be a grave mistake for the French to attack her without warning in an opening campaign. Halifax knew that Bonnet would not permit a French attack against Italy, but he was very much concerned about the French attitude toward a possible war with Germany. He had received a message from Bonnet that it would be necessary for the French Chamber of Deputies to approve of any steps leading toward war. Halifax was intensely displeased with this position of the French Foreign Minister. He feared that Bonnet would exploit the opposition to war in France in an effort to avoid French obligations to Poland.

Halifax was annoyed with the Dahlerus mission from the start, because the Swedish engineer repeated the tactics of Henderson in stressing Polish guilt for the excesses against the German minority in Poland. Dahlerus had telephoned the British Foreign Office again on the early morning of August 25th shortly before flying to London. He mentioned Goering's inconclusive conversation with Lipski, and he added that the German Marshal was alarmed by the impact of fresh incidents involving the Germans in Poland. Dahlerus added candidly that "Beck is a good man but they do not obey him and are getting wild."[33]

Kennard at Warsaw continued to oppose the idea that the mistreatment of the Germans in Poland constituted a serious problem. He disliked Henderson's suggestion that Lipski should discuss the possibilities for a settlement with Hitler. Kennard insisted that it would be a mistake for Lipski to see Hitler at all. He offered an odd explanation for this attitude. Kennard feared that Hitler, at the last minute, would make some attractive new proposal to Poland, which might, after all, separate Poland from the Western Allies. This is an excellent illustration of the preverse attitude of the British envoy in Warsaw. He did not propose means to avoid the unparalleled catastrophe of a new World War. He was merely concerned that at the last minute England might be deprived of some useful ally in the great struggle.

The response of Halifax to Kennard was exceedingly limited in scope. He merely warned that the Poles should take care not to commit acts which would reveal them as the aggressive party. He advised that they should accept the formality of registering a favorable response to President Roosevelt's peace appeal to Poland of August 24th. Kennard stubbornly refused to notice the deportation treks of brutally mistreated Germans into the Polish interior, and he would not admit that untoward events were taking place in the German minority areas. He claimed to Halifax that he was taking one adequate step which would prevent the occurrence of incidents. He was instructing General Carton de Wiart, chief of the British military mission in Poland, to inform Beck that it was necessary to avoid incidents. General de Wiart, who later commanded the ill-fated British military expedition to Norway, has recorded that he was in no position to influence Polish policy toward the German minority.[34]

The August 25th Goering Message to London

Dahlerus submitted a careful memorandum at the British Foreign Office on August 25th about Goering's remarks on the previous day. He reminded his British hosts that their seven countrymen at the Soenke-Nissen-Koog conference earlier in the month were unanimously convinced of the sincerity of the German Marshal. They all agreed that Goering "personally would support any attempt to arrive at a settlement." Goering had insisted that this evaluation should also apply to Hitler. He denied that there were any differences whatever between his position and that of the German Chancellor. Goering was working along lines decided upon by Hitler. Hitler wished for a peaceful settlement which would not sacrifice the national dignity of Germany recently regained after so great an effort. Goering had one main point to offer. If the British would reconcile themselves to a strong Germany on the European continent, Germany, in return, would aid, rather than oppose, the British Empire. Above all, Goering believed it was important that neither Power should intervene in the internal affairs of its neighbor. Goering was convinced that two commercial spheres of respective economic concentration could be defined by the two trading nations. He proposed British priority in the Far East and German priority in the Near East as a tentative suggestion. Goering was careful to stress that it would still be possible to renew the 1938 German proposals to Poland.

Dahlerus wished to confirm Goering's assertion that all ultimate decisions in German foreign policy rested with Hitler. Dahlerus and Goering hoped that a British special representative could come to Germany to negotiate, because they "felt that the Fuehrer could not possibly leave Germany, and such a discussion must therefore take place in Germany." It was not difficult for the British to accept the general validity of this point. Chamberlain himself had assured Hitler at Munich the previous year that it would not be opportune for Hitler to visit Great Britain within the near future because of the hostile reception he would receive. Chamberlain recognized that Hitler strongly desired to visit Great Britain when conditions were more favorable. It was obvious at the same time that the atmosphere in Great Britain was even less favorable for a Hitler visit in 1939 than had been the case in 1938. It was unnecessary for Dahlerus to elaborate on this point.

Dahlerus insisted warmly that it was evident to him from his intimate knowledge of Germany "that the German nation as such certainly does not want a war, but desire to build up their own country and endeavour to establish a higher standard of living for the whole nation." He could imagine that some radical persons in Germany, as in every country, might welcome war, but he assured his British hosts that the opposite was true of Goering. He could not personally speak for Hitler, because he had deliberately avoided meeting him in order "not to be persuaded or influenced by his strong personality." He knew from what he had heard that Hitler was strongly individualistic and "extremely sensitive," and that it was necessary to handle him with tact. Dahlerus concluded his first meeting with the British diplomats by reminding them of Goering's promise that Hitler would come very far to meet any offer from Great Britain.[35]

Hitler Disturbed about Italian Policy

A serious and almost fatal situation began to develop at Berlin during the afternoon of August 25, 1939. Hitler, who was anxiously awaiting news about the British situation, was also much concerned about the Italians. He had good reason to be. There had been no further confirmation from Rome of Ciano's pledge to Germany on August 13, 1939. Bernardo Attolico, who feared that Mussolini might throw caution to the winds at the last minute and remain loyal to Hitler in the real sense of the word, fired a final bolt of warning at the Italian leaders at 11:15 p.m. on August 24th, after Ciano's ambiguous telephone conversation with Ribbentrop. His warning formed the basis of the consultation between Mussolini and Ciano on the morning of August 25th, between Mussolini's conversation with Mackensen and the official Italian reply to Ribbentrop's appeal. Attolico claimed with deliberate exaggeration that Henderson was completely negative about his last conversations with Hitler. He asserted it was a virtual certainty that the Germans would address an ultimatum to the Poles on the evening of the following day; otherwise they would not have requested a final clarification of the Italian position. Attolico claimed that Ribbentrop was frustrated by his Moscow mission, and that he was doubtful about the pact concluded with Russia. This was completely untrue, but the Italian Ambassador was not interested in giving Mussolini an accurate report on German conditions. His sole interest was to prevent Italy from rendering support to Germany according to the terms of the May 1939 Pact of Steel.

Attolico's effort was completely successful. Mussolini was actually inclined to give Germany full support at the time of his conversation with Mackensen. He had drawn up a lengthy memorandum which demanded immediate Italian intervention if Great Britain and France attacked the Reich. The Italian leader recoiled when he received Attolico's warning, which indicated, without any actual basis, that the Germans would force the issue with the Poles on the following day. Attolico's comments about Henderson and Russia were especially important. The former suggested that British intervention was a certainty, and the latter indicated that Mussolini might not receive indirect economic aid from Russia in the event of war.[36]

The prospect of an open repudiation of the German alliance was intolerable to Mussolini. Ciano was at hand to suggest a means by which Mussolini might square the circle. He wrote a letter in which he formally offered to support Germany, but he stipulated conditions for German aid which the German Reich could not possibly meet. Ribbentrop later commented that Germany did not possess the transport equipment to convey goods and strategic raw materials to Italy within the time schedule indicated, even provided that such materials were actually available in Germany, which was by no means the case. Hitler received the Mussolini letter by telegraph in two parts. He realized when he had received the complete message that the Italian leader was deserting him at this crucial moment. He could see at a glance that the Italian move might be the decisive factor in the situation. Hitler's primary interest in Italian support was not that they should help him to wage war, but to discourage the British and French from attacking him. Hitler hoped that the Italians had at least informed him of their decision prior to communicating this information to the British and French. Concern about Italy and Great Britain prompted Hitler to make a momentous decision. He suddenly decided that it would be necessary to settle his account with the Poles without delay, before the British recovered from their surprise at the Soviet-German Pact or became aware of the true Italian position. He was convinced that delay might make a general war inevitable.[37]

Hitler's Alliance Offer to Great Britain

Hitler had earlier requested British Ambassador Henderson to call at 1:30 p.m. to receive formal German proposals for an Anglo-German agreement. He received Henderson on schedule and informed him that the Danzig question would be settled, and that his pact with Russia precluded the danger of a Russo-German war. He reminded Henderson that he had no aspirations in Western Europe, and that he wished the British Empire to remain prosperous and strong. He added that the colonial problem could be relegated to the far-distant future, and he asserted that it would be unwise in any event to discuss such problems until Great Britain and Germany had reached an agreement for the reduction of armaments.

The German leader reminded the British Ambassador that his purpose in arranging the meeting was to present a formal offer for an Anglo-German agreement. Germany wished to follow up her treaty with Russia by concluding a treaty of friendship with Great Britain. Hitler wished to criticize remarks made on the previous day by Chamberlain and Halifax in the British Parliament. He denied the charges of the British leaders that Germany entertained plans of world conquest. Hitler reminded Henderson that the integral parts of the British Empire comprised 40 million square kilometers of land. Germany occupied a modest area of less than 600,000 square kilometers. Many nations occupied formidable places between the top British position on the list of large Powers, and the German position farther down the list. For instance, the Soviet Union contained 19 million square kilometers, and the United States of America 9½ million square kilometers. Hitler refused to concede that any German plans to conquer the world could be feasible.

Hitler told Henderson that this did not change the fact that Germany faced an acute problem in her own immediate neighborhood. He was determined to regulate conditions in a part of the area lost by Germany twenty years earlier, and this meant Danzig and the Corridor. The only possible result Hitler could see from the Prime Minister's speech of the previous day was a bloody and incalculable war. He was prepared to take every possible step to avert this catastrophe, and he was now presenting terms for the comprehensive agreement with Great Britain which he had always desired. His offer was predicated on the assumption that Great Britain would be willing to recognize German obligations to Italy just as Germany accepted British obligations to France.

Hitler hoped the British would be prepared to declare in principle that they did not oppose the eventual consideration of German colonial claims. He was prepared to proceed along the lines of the Buxton plan, and to assume the greatest and most complex commitment on behalf of Great Britain that had ever been offered by any foreign political leader. This commitment was no less than his willingness to place the entire power of the Reich at the disposal of the British for the defense of the British Empire at any point and any time. The British leaders themselves, of course, would be free to decide in any threatening situation when and if they needed this aid. Hitler believed that an arrangement of Anglo-German differences would create conditions of complete security for both Powers, and it was obvious that a drastic reduction of armaments would be immediately feasible. He was willing to sign a guarantee at once that Germany desired no change in the *status quo* throughout Western Europe. Hitler added delicately that, if his proposals failed and war ensued, Great Britain would not emerge as a stronger Power, whatever the outcome. He declared that the vital interests of Germany required him to make his entire offer conditional on a settlement of the German-Polish dispute along lines acceptable to Germany.[38]

Henderson desired an Anglo-German agreement, and he was deeply moved by his meeting with Hitler on August 25, 1939. The British Ambassador offered a number of personal observations when he relayed Hitler's remarkable offer to

Halifax and Chamberlain. He noted that Ribbentrop was present during his entire conversation with Hitler, but that the German Foreign Minister remained raptly attentive without offering any comments. Henderson assured Halifax that he did not take the liberty to discuss the individual points of Hitler's offer without instructions from London. The British Ambassador had centered his remarks on the German-Polish dispute, which had become the crucial point in Anglo-German relations. He admitted that he had taken a personal step on his own initiative. He had warmly recommended that Hitler and Beck meet once again to settle their difference and to avoid war. The British Ambassador noticed that the German leader became silent and contemplative at the mention of this remote prospect. Hitler then suddenly exclaimed that if his differences with the Poles could be settled, he would be able to end his life as an artist rather than as an alleged warmonger. He added fervently that the very last thing he could possibly desire would be to turn Germany into nothing better than a military barracks. Henderson warmly recommended to Halifax that Hitler should be given an opportunity to demonstrate his good intentions.[39]

Hitler's Order for Operations in Poland on August 26th

Hitler believed that he had no moment to lose after this conversation. He wished to settle with the Poles while the impact of his agreement offer was still fresh, and before the British and French discovered that Italy did not intend to support him. He was convinced that his only real chance to settle the Polish dispute by isolated military action in a local war had arrived, and that hesitation at that moment would cost Germany great suffering in the time ahead. Hitler telephoned General Walther von Brauchitsch, the Commander-in-Chief of the German Armed Forces, immediately after the departure of Henderson. He ordered formal and full-scale military operations against the Poles for the following morning at dawn. General Wilhelm Keitel, the Chief-of-Staff, distributed orders by 3:05 p.m. on August 25th for the launching of "Operation White." The commands were received by the individual German Army commanders on the various sectors in the East, and by the commanders of the Siegfried Line in the West, where the relevant defensive preparations were soon underway. Polish telephone communications through Germany were interrupted by order of the German military authorities shortly before 3:00 p.m. on August 25th. Polish Foreign Minister Beck was worried by this development, but he concluded that it might be part of the war-of-nerves rather than an indication of a coming attack. The Poles did not order the mobilization of their last reserve units. An attack on August 26th would have found the Poles much less prepared than was the case when the German-Polish war actually broke out nearly a week later.[40]

Polish Ambassador Lipski called at the German Foreign Office twice on the afternoon of August 25th to present complaints about recent German border violations. He announced that the Polish border guard, Edmund Piatkowski, had been shot and killed from ambush at the Donnersmarck Park along the Upper Silesian frontier. He also announced that a German Corporal named Kapenhagen was shot and killed inside the Polish frontier in the Bialystok district. Lipski complained that Kapenhagen had penetrated Polish territory with a patrol of ten German soldiers. The Germans complained about two Polish air attacks over Danzig Bay against a German pontoon airplane from Pillau, East Prussia. They also objected to Polish violations of the German frontier. These incidents were a commonplace indication of the chaotic conditions resulting from the German-Polish crisis.[41]

The Announcement of the Formal Anglo-Polish Alliance

Hitler contacted Otto Dietrich, his personal press chief, and inquired if news of any important policy changes had been received from Great Britain and France. Dietrich was obliged to concede that he had no important developments of any sort to report. A break in the tense and anxious waiting came at last at 5:00 p.m. when the German News Bureau announced that a formal Anglo-Polish alliance pact was about to be concluded at London. The negotiations between the British and the Poles on the previous Saturday, August 19th, had ended on an inconclusive note. It had been agreed to resume discussions on Tuesday, August 22nd, but British Legal Counsellor Fitzmaurice cancelled the talks because the British Cabinet was considering a change of policy in response to the announcement of the Russo-German Pact. Halifax broadcast a short talk to Poland on the evening of August 22nd which stressed Anglo-Polish solidarity, but he refused to discuss the terms of a possible Anglo-Polish alliance with Polish Ambassador Raczynski on August 23rd. The British Cabinet decided to accept the Polish alliance terms and to abandon their own previous reservations, but the Poles were not informed of this decision until the morning of August 25, 1939. Raczynski obtained permission from Beck at Warsaw to complete the negotiation and to sign the treaty.

The Anglo-Polish alliance treaty of August 25, 1939, contained a secret protocol which provided that the treaty would be applied exclusively against Germany. The London *Times* carried a story on the morning of August 25th from their Berlin correspondent to the effect that a German-Polish war would inevitably produce the annexation of extensive Polish territories by the Soviet Union. The first official revelation that the British Government was not obliged to defend Poland against the Soviet Union was made by Rab Butler in the House of Commons on October 19, 1939, more than one month after the invasion of Poland by the Soviet Union. By that time the British were fully embarked on their campaign against Germany inspired by their alleged desire to defend the territorial integrity of Poland. The British merely agreed to consult with the Poles in the event of aggression against Poland by the Soviet Union. It was stipulated that Great Britain would not recognize the annexation of Polish territory by any third Power without obtaining the consent of the Polish leaders. This provision led to tremendous British pressure on the Poles during World War II to accept the annexation of Eastern Poland by the Soviet Union.[42]

The public terms of the alliance were not received at Berlin from the German diplomats in London until 4:00 a.m. on August 26th, but the announcements at London in the early evening of August 25th contained the gist of the treaty. The two Powers offered full support to each other against German acts of aggression. They agreed on full military support against "any action by an

European Power (i.e. Germany) which clearly threatened directly or indirectly the independence of one of the contracting parties and was of such a nature that the party in question considered it vital to resist it with its armed forces." The British in this article subscribed to the same doctrine of indirect aggression which had justifiably occasioned such extensive criticism when it was proposed by the Soviet Union. The Russians had favored the doctrine of so-called indirect aggression because they desired a blank check to intervene against neighboring Powers. The British were renewing their unconditional blank check to Poland by promising to support her in similar circumstances.

It was further stipulated that aggression in the first article would include threats to the independence or neutrality of other European states when such threats would allegedly constitute a danger to either contracting party. The third article stipulated that so-called economic penetration by Germany could be interpreted as aggression. The fourth and fifth articles provided for military consultation and the exchange of information. The sixth article provided that new understanding with other Powers would not limit existing obligations. The seventh article required that the two Powers would not conclude a separate peace in the event of war, and the final article announced that the pact would come into effect when it was signed for a period of five years.[43]

The London radio broadcast a false report a few minutes after the initial announcement of the treaty with Poland. It was stated that three German bombers had been forced down over Polish territory by Polish anti-aircraft batteries and pursuit airplanes. The actual signing of the treaty with Poland took place at 5:35 p.m.[44]

Military Operations Cancelled by Hitler

Hitler had at last received decisive news about British policy on August 25th, but for him it was a step in the wrong direction. The news of the Anglo-Polish Pact persuaded Hitler that the British might attack Germany despite the German treaty with Russia. He was faced with a terrible dilemma. If he retreated, the Germans of the East, including Danzig, would be abandoned to the cruelty and arrogance of a hostile Poland. If he took effective action against the Poles, the British might unleash another general European War.

Halifax received two urgent appeals from Henderson shortly before the Polish treaty was signed. The British Ambassador stated frankly in his first message that he favored the acceptance of Hitler's offer for an agreement. He urged Halifax to give the German proposals serious consideration. The second message reported a major atrocity against the Germans in Poland which had taken place on the same day. Henderson never relied on official German information concerning these incidents, and he was basing his report on confirmation which he had received from neutral sources. The latest atrocity had taken place at Bielitz, East Upper Silesia. The Poles were forcibly deporting the Germans of that area, and compelling them to march into the interior. Eight Germans were murdered and many more were injured during one of these actions on August 25, 1939. Henderson feared that the Bielitz atrocity would be the final straw to prompt Hitler to invade Poland. He made no secret of the fact that he deplored the failure of the British Government to exercise restraint over the Polish authorities.[45]

Hitler had invited French Ambassador Robert Coulondre to call on him at 5:30 p.m. on August 25th. Hitler met the French Ambassador on schedule and described the latest incidents against the Germans in Poland. He informed Coulondre that war between Germany and Poland could be expected at any time. The German Chancellor added that under these circumstances there was little point in discussing further German relations with Poland. He believed that it was much more important to discuss what the future might hold in store for France and Germany.

Hitler assured Coulondre that he wished to avoid war with France. Nevertheless, he exclaimed: "I will not attack France, but if she joins in the conflict, I will see it through to the bitter end." He emphasized the importance of the Russo-German Pact. After some time he added: "I believe I shall win, and you believe you will win: what is certain is that above all French and German blood will flow, the blood of two equally courageous peoples. I say again, it is painful to me to think we might come to that." Hitler requested Coulondre to convey these sentiments to Premier Daladier.[46]

Coulondre replied vigorously to Hitler. He gave his "word of honor as a soldier that he had no doubt whatever that in the event of Poland's being attacked, France would assist her with all the forces at her command." He also gave Hitler his word of honor that France would now do everything within her power to compel the Poles to moderate their policies. Hitler replied: "I believe you; I even believe that men like M. Beck are moderate, but they are no longer in control of the situation." Coulondre commented that Hitler was quite right in believing the French Ambassador was personally convinced France would emerge victorious in a coming war. The French envoy wished to add that, in a profound and fundamental sense, he feared that the only real victor would be Leon Trotsky, who was momentarily living in exile in Mexico, but whose disciples could be found in every country of the world. Coulondre noted that this reference to the fiery Russian-Jew, whose stormy and destructive career was well-known to Hitler, produced an electric effect. He did not know that he was talking to Hitler in the very hours of decision. Keitel's orders to the commanders had gone out at 3:05 p.m. It would not be even theoretically possible, after 9:30 p.m., for Hitler to halt the German war machine, which was already in motion toward Poland.[47]

There was a long pause before Hitler pensively asked Coulondre: "Why, then, did you give Poland a blank check?" The French Ambassador did his best to answer this difficult question. He discussed the events of March 1939 in great detail from the French angle. Hitler listened silently to this exposition for a long time. Coulondre finally finished his remarks. There were a few brief personal exchanges, and the interview was over.

Hitler immediately requested a conference with Ribbentrop, who was patiently waiting close at hand. The two men briefly discussed the situation, and Hitler complained that he had received two very bad pieces of news on this one difficult day. One was the defection of Italy, and the other was the conclusion of the Anglo-Polish Pact. Hitler was astonished that these two developments occurred in the wake of his treaty with the Soviet Union. He was sufficiently flexible to agree with Ribbentrop that his analysis of the Anglo-French position was probably wrong. Hitler required more than ordinary courage to meet this situation. If his evaluation of the Anglo-French position was incorrect, then his order for operations against Poland was a great blunder. This order was issued strictly on the assumption that local operations against the Poles would not plunge Europe into a general war. Fortunately, Hitler possessed courage in full measure. The German forces had still not invaded Poland. Halifax still did not have his war for the balance of power.

Hitler requested a conference with General Keitel, who was near at hand, at 6:30 p.m. on August 25th. The German Chancellor ordered the German operations against Poland to be suspended as soon as practicable for an indefinite period. Hitler knew this was feasible, because it was one of the many hypothetical situations he had discussed earlier with General von Brauchitsch. Of course, Hitler had been assured that there were a million chances that something would go wrong, that communications somewhere would break down, or even that orders would become confused or be disobeyed. The Bulgarians had stumbled into the Second Balkan War under similar circumstances in 1913, and they had suffered a crushing defeat. Hitler preferred to take the one million chances rather than be guilty of blundering into a general war in the style of the European leaders of 1914. Keitel contacted General von Brauchitsch and relayed Hitler's order that "the already started 'Operation White' will be stopped at 20:30 hours (8:30 p.m.) because of changed political conditions." When Colonel Hans Oster, one of the German Counter-Intelligence chiefs and a member of a small conspiratorial group against Hitler, heard this news, he exulted: "The Fuehrer is done for!"[48]

Oster was convinced that Hitler's act of courage would lead directly to disaster, but he was wrong. Despite Colonel Oster and his fellow-conspirators, the German military machine in 1939 was more efficient than the small Bulgarian Army of 1913. A few serious slips and subsequent grave incidents did in fact occur, but they passed almost unnoticed in the general chaos along the German-Polish frontier. The attempt to halt operations against Poland was successful.

Hitler had still not lost the game. He was faced with a terrible dilemma, but he saw it more clearly than before. Perhaps some third alternative to a general war, or to submission to Polish atrocities, could still be found. It was up to Hitler as diplomat and not as soldier to explore and test these possibilities. Hitler was especially mindful of his recent offer to the British for an Anglo-German agreement. He hoped that German concessions to Great Britain might prompt the British leaders to persuade the Poles to resume negotiations for a diplomatic settlement of the German-Polish dispute. Hitler was willing to follow up his proposals to Great Britain with new proposals to the Poles. His principal motive in doing so would be to avoid the tragedy of a new Anglo-German war.[49]

Chapter 20

THE NEW GERMAN OFFER TO POLAND

Halifax Opposed to Polish Negotiations with Germany

The new German offer to Poland on August 29, 1939, was the most important development during the several days after Hitler's decision of August 25, 1939, for a last diplomatic campaign to settle the German-Polish dispute. The terms of a new German plan for a settlement, the so-called Marienwerder proposals, were not disclosed to the Poles until August 31, 1939, and they were less important than the offer to negotiate as such. The terms of the Marienwerder proposals were essentially nothing more than a tentative German plan for a possible settlement. These elaborate terms would have required nearly a year to carry out had the Poles accepted them, and in this sense they revealed a German intention to substitute negotiation for force once and for all in German-Polish relations. The German Government insisted again and again that these terms were formulated to offer a basis for unimpeded negotiations between equals rather than to constitute a series of demands which the Poles would be required to accept. There was nothing to prevent the Poles from offering as a substitute the private Polish plan for the partition of the Danzig territory, or, for that matter, from presenting an entirely new set of proposals of their own.[1]

The Germans, in offering to negotiate with Poland, were announcing to the world that they favored a diplomatic settlement over war with Poland. The Poles, in refusing to negotiate, were announcing that they favored war. The refusal of Halifax to encourage the Poles to negotiate indicated that the British Foreign Secretary also favored war. He chose to ignore Hitler's offer to accept the British guarantee of Poland once the Danzig dispute was settled by negotiation. The important thing would have been for the Poles to resume negotiations, and to permit the opening of the door which Beck had closed without any adequate reason in his speech of May 5, 1939. The willingness of the Poles to negotiate would not have implied their readiness to recognize the German annexation of Danzig, nor would it in any way have implied a Polish retreat.

The Poles could have motivated their acceptance with the announcement that Germany, and not Poland, had found it necessary to request new negotiations.[2]

Beck undoubtedly would have adopted a different attitude toward the situation had Halifax insisted that he agree to compromise with Germany. The greatest worry at the Polish Foreign Office for several days after August 25, 1939, was that the British would change their minds about attacking Germany, and decide at the last moment not to honor their obligations to Poland. It was natural for Beck to conclude under these circumstances that it would be wise to provoke a conflict with Germany as soon as possible, and before the British leaders changed their minds. It was unrealistic to expect Beck to compromise with Germany unless and until there was pressure from Great Britain for him to do so. Indeed, Hitler did not presume to suggest negotiations until he had received a promise from the British that the Poles would accept them. Unfortunately, the British had no satisfactory basis for making this promise on August 28, 1939, and they did nothing to redeem it after it was made. Gilbert and Gott greatly exaggerate when they insist that on August 28, 1939, "British pressure on Poland to accept direct negotiations with the Germans had been successful." In reality, no serious British effort was ever made to compel them to do so.[3]

The British never received more than a perfunctory assurance from Beck that Poland would negotiate with Germany. The sole indication that the Polish leaders might negotiate was Beck's confirmation on the afternoon of August 28th of the public reply of President Mościcki to President Roosevelt on August 25, 1939. The Polish President accepted Roosevelt's suggestion for direct negotiations because the Poles had "always considered (them) the most appropriate method." The Polish President added that he would not accept arbitration, because he did not believe that foreign statesmen understood the vital interests of Poland. The Polish Government for this reason was not prepared to accept the results of arbitration. The British realized that Beck's confirmation of the statement of the Polish President about direct negotiations was merely for the record, and they never made a genuine effort to obtain concrete information about the alleged Polish willingness to engage in direct negotiations with Germany.

The Polish Pledge to President Roosevelt

President Roosevelt received the text of President Mościcki's message on August 25, 1939, and forwarded it to Hitler. Roosevelt emphasized to Hitler that he had a binding promise from Mościcki that Poland would engage in direct negotiations with Germany. The American President added that "all the world prays that Germany, too, will accept." Hitler knew that the message from President Roosevelt was merely a propaganda gesture to discredit Germany, and he was sufficiently shrewd to recognize that a promise made by Poland to the United States was not worth the paper on which it was written. The Poles knew that Roosevelt would support any Polish move to increase the prospect of conflict with Germany and that the American President would not react unfavorably if they refused to honor a pledge to negotiate with Germany. Hitler also knew this, and hence he concentrated on his effort to convince the British that the Poles should negotiate rather than seek to exploit the meaningless Polish response to President Roosevelt.[4]

Beck assured American Ambassador Biddle shortly before midnight on August 25, 1939, that war between Germany and Poland was inevitable. He claimed that Poland had an adequate legal basis for a declaration of war against Germany, in case the Germans failed to take the initiative against Poland within the next few days. Beck denied that there was any truth in the Bielitz massacre, which had been confirmed by neutral sources. He claimed instead that a Polish soldier had been killed by the Germans on August 16, 1939, and that the Germans had proceeded to cut open the stomach of the corpse and to conceal in it the skull of a baby. This story was widely repeated by Polish spokesmen in the days and years which followed, although no attempt was ever made to document the incident. They failed to realize that this type of savagery was based upon certain primitive voodoo-like superstitions in Eastern Europe which were not shared by the Germans. It would have been an unique historical event had modern Poland elected to base a declaration of war on this fantastic charge. American Ambassador Biddle was much impressed by the aggressive attitude of Beck. He predicted to President Roosevelt that Poland would present a series of *ultimata* to Germany if Hitler backed down in the Danzig dispute.

Beck was impressed by a public German announcement on August 25, 1939, that the Tannenberg and Nuremberg conclaves had been cancelled. The cancellation announcement, and the impressive number of incidents between the Germans and Poles on the following day, convinced the Polish Foreign Minister that a German attack would come at any moment. He did not conclude until August 27th that Hitler, after all, had taken no decisive military measures. French Ambassador Nöel claimed that Beck was a very sick man at this time. The French diplomat charged that he was suffering from aggravated fatigue, tuberculosis, and an excessive addiction to stimulants. The Polish Foreign Minister ultimately died of tuberculosis in Rumania in 1944, after the British authorities had denied him permission to come to England. The French Ambassador, who detested Beck, delighted in conveying the impression that the Polish Foreign Minister was both morally and physically decadent.[5]

German troops at the Slovak-Polish frontier had begun their advance on the morning of August 26, 1939, before countermanding orders reached them, and they crossed into Poland at Jablonka Pass. Fortunately, the Poles were not holding a position there, and an engagement was avoided when the Germans speedily retreated a considerable distance across the frontier and into Slovakia. The Poles engaged German patrols in nearly a dozen skirmishes in the Dzialdowo region directly north of Warsaw and across the East Prussian frontier. The engagements ended when the German units were suddenly withdrawn. It was significant that these serious incidents occurred on two of the most crucial sectors of the German operational plan. A massacre of minority Germans in the Lódź area and constant violations of the German frontier from the Polish side tended to deflect attention from these incidents. A Polish warship on August 26, 1939, fired at a German civilian transport airplane on which State Secretary Wilhelm Stuckart of the Ministry of Interior was returning from Danzig. Stuckart and the Danzig leaders had discussed the legal problems involved.

in the projected return of Danzig to the Reich.

Hitler's reversal of military orders naturally created perplexity in the German Army. One of the German Generals was dispatched to the Wilhelmstrasse on the night of August 25, 1939, to inquire indignantly why the soldiers had been sent out if it was intended to settle differences with Poland by diplomatic means. The German Foreign Office had no ready answer with which to meet this embarrassing question.[6]

Hitler's Failure to Recover Italian Support

Hitler was primarily concerned about improving his contacts with the British leaders, but he also hoped to persuade the Italians to renew a loyal relationship with Germany. He had hastily dictated a preliminary reply to Mussolini's message before receiving Henderson on the afternoon of August 25th. He complained to Mussolini that the situation in Poland was intolerable, and he requested the Italian leader to be mindful of the diplomatic gains which resulted from his pact with Russia. He assured Mussolini that he would have complete understanding for Italy in a similar situation, and that the Italians would be able to rely on his support.

Attolico delivered a second message from Mussolini to Hitler at 6:00 p.m. on August 25th. Mussolini reminded Hitler that he favored the treaty with Russia, and that he could see it was producing favorable diplomatic effects in such countries as Rumania and Turkey. He promised Hitler that Italy would offer political and economic assistance to Germany in a localized German-Polish war, but he insisted that intervention in a general war would not be "opportune" without the vast quantities of German material which Italy would require for such an effort.[7]

Hitler telephoned German Ambassador Mackensen in Rome at 7:40 p.m. on August 25th. He wished the Italians to be more specific in formulating their requirements for weapons and materials, and to include nothing which was not considered absolutely indispensable. He promised to give careful consideration to Italian requirements. Mackensen reported at 11:30 p.m. that Mussolini would forward an exact list of Italian needs to Berlin on August 26th. Mussolini declared that he remained anti-Communist despite his support of the Russian treaty for tactical reasons, and the German Ambassador assured the Italian leader on the basis of instructions from Berlin that his country would also remain unswervingly anti-Communist in her policies.

The exact list of Italian requirements was received in Berlin at 12:10 p.m. on August 26th. It included 6 million tons of coal, 2 million tons of steel, 7 million tons of petroleum, 1 million tons of timber, and many tons of copper, sodium nitrate, potassium salts, colophony, rubber, turpentine, lead, tin, nickel, molybdenum, tungsten, zirconium, and titanium, including 400 tons of the latter. The Italians requested 150 anti-aircraft batteries and ammunition for the Turin-Genoa-Milan-Savona industrial quadrilateral. There was also a separate list of German machinery required by the Italians. The Germans were informed that the lists would not have been necessary had Italy had adequate time for her own preparations.[8]

Hitler replied to Mussolini a few hours later. He declared that Germany could furnish the coal and steel, but that it would be impossible to supply the petroleum. He reminded Mussolini that Germany herself was required to use substitute materials for copper, because adequate supplies were not available. He believed that it would be impossible for Germany to deliver the entire supply of 150 major anti-aircraft batteries before the conclusion of hostilities in Poland, if war were to break out there within the next few days. He reminded Mussolini that Attolico had insisted that the entire material would have to arrive before hostilities were Italy to support Germany. Hitler concluded that it was impossible to meet the Italian terms. He requested suitable military demonstrations and active propaganda support from the Italian leader. He did not realize that the Italians had given assurances to the British which would render any demonstrations pointless. He concluded with the warning that Germany might have to solve the eastern question "even at the risk of complications in the West."

Mussolini attempted to modify the terms by informing Hitler at 6:42 p.m. on August 26th that Attolico, in his zeal to prevent an Italian commitment to Germany, had misunderstood his instructions. It was necessary to have the anti-aircraft batteries at once, but it would have been satisfactory to extend the other deliveries over a period of twelve months. Mussolini hastened to note that Hitler had conceded it would be impossible to supply certain strategic materials indicated on the Italian lists, and that therefore "it is impossible for you to assist me materially in filling the large gaps which the wars in Ethiopia and Spain have made in Italian armaments." Mussolini also insisted that a peaceful solution of the current dispute was essential for the peoples of both Italy and Germany. It was evident to Hitler that there was no point in further efforts to persuade Mussolini to renew full Italian support to Germany in the current crisis.[9]

Halifax Hopeful for War

There was considerable expectation in London and Paris during these days that war between Germany and Poland would break out without further important diplomatic developments. Bonnet complained that several prominent Frenchmen advocated the fantastic idea of attacking Italy in revenge for an inevitable defeat of the Poles by Germany. Léon Blum, the French Socialist leader, declared to British Ambassador Sir Eric Phipps that war was almost certain, although he added, with a careful eye on responsibilities, that he hoped Hitler was not "so demented" as to attack Poland.[10]

Halifax informed Kennard on the night of August 25th that Count Raczynski was "very firm" at the signing of the Anglo-Polish pact. Raczynski had expressed indignation over an alleged "kind of freikorps" in German Silesia, which ostensibly was raiding Poland. It was obvious that this was a feeble and misleading attempt on the part of the Polish Ambassador to distract attention from the massacre of the German minority at Bielitz. Halifax, who was ever mindful of Mussolini's conference plan, carefully tested Raczynski's reaction to the proposition of surrendering Danzig, which did not belong to Poland, in exchange for an international guarantee of Poland's frontiers. He informed Kennard with satisfaction that Raczynski had rejected this idea with scorn, and had insisted that the Allied nations concentrate exclusively on maintaining a "stiff attitude" toward the Germans. Kennard replied to Halifax that Beck would not accept an obligation to consult with Great Britain before taking decisive action at Danzig. The British Ambassador was pleased with Beck's attitude on this important point.[11]

Phipps reported from Paris that Bullitt had received new instructions from President Roosevelt designed to facilitate a closer coordination of British and American policy against Germany. The American President suggested that everything possible should be done by propaganda to bring down the German regime in revolutionary chaos. Roosevelt believed that wireless propaganda should be broadcast to Germany around the clock. He expected that it would produce a great effect to argue in advance that Hitler would be solely responsible for any war. He hoped that the pacific desires of the German people might be exploited to undermine the loyalty of Germans toward their Government after the outbreak of war.

Henderson continued to do what he could at Berlin to preserve peace. He contacted Polish Ambassador Lipski again on August 25th and urged him to discuss the problem of the German minority in Poland with the German Government. Henderson reported to Halifax that Italian Ambassador Attolico was horrified at the prospect of war. Attolico had declared with indignation that warmongers such as Anthony Eden should be hanged. Henderson avoided criticizing Attolico's statement about Eden in any way. Eden, to be sure, had worked with Churchill to sabotage appeasement, but the chief role in the scuttling of the appeasement policy had been played by Halifax, the man to whom Henderson addressed his report.[12]

Sir Ronald Lindsay, the British Ambassador to the United States, addressed a series of final reports to Halifax prior to his return to England and his replacement by Lord Lothian. Lindsay indicated that Roosevelt was delighted at the prospect of a new World War. The American President had damaged his prospects in May 1939 with his unsuccessful attempt to pull the teeth from the American neutrality laws, but he assured Lindsay that he would succeed in emasculating this legislation after the outbreak of war. He admitted that he would be forced to delay a new effort to do so "until war broke out." The American President also promised that he would not actually abide by the neutrality laws if he was compelled to invoke them. He would frustrate the purpose of the laws by delaying a proclamation of neutrality for at least five days after the outbreak of war. He would see that war material in the interim was rushed to the British in Canada in enormous quantities. Lindsay reported with his usual excessive moderation that there "was every indication in his language that the American authorities would be anxious to cheat in favor of His Majesty's Government."

Roosevelt also promised Lindsay that he would delay German ships under false pretenses in a feigned search for arms, so that they could be easily seized by the British under circumstances which would be arranged with exactitude between the American and British authorities. The British Ambassador was personally perturbed that the President of one of the important countries could be gay and joyful about a tragedy which seemed so destructive of the hopes of all mankind. He reported that Roosevelt "spoke in a tone of almost impish glee and though I may be wrong the whole business gave me the impression of resembling a school-boy prank." It was an American and world tragedy to have at this important juncture a President whose emotions and ideas could be rated by a friendly Ambassador as childish.

Halifax was inclined to regard the attitude of the American President as a product of one of the most successful British efforts in colonial propaganda. The American President, who was an enthusiastic militarist, had accepted the idea of World War II as his best escape from the hopelessly unsuccessful policies with which he had failed to cope with the economic depression in the United States. The British Foreign Secretary had studied the fantastic Lochner report about the alleged remarks of Hitler to his military men on the Obersalzberg on August 22nd. He wired Loraine in Rome on August 26th that recent information from Berlin indicated that Hitler had some kind of Polish partition in mind. His purpose was to convey to Mussolini the idea that the German leader was too extreme in his plans, at the expense of the Poles, to be amenable to a reasonable settlement of German-Polish difficulties. Halifax hoped in this way to discourage Mussolini's ideas for a diplomatic conference.13

The British Foreign Secretary was extremely pleased by the solidarity with which the British nation appeared to support his policy after the first shock caused by the Russo-German pact. George Lansbury, the former British Labour Party leader, and James Maxton, the Independent Labour MP from Scotland, were the only men who had spoken for non-intervention in a possible German-Polish war, in the Commons debate of August 25, 1939. Halifax was also satisfied with the attitude of the London and provincial press, and he was pleased that a threatened railway strike had been called off because of the diplomatic crisis.14

Halifax suggested to Kennard early on August 26th that the Polish leaders might be wise to seek the approval of the German Government for the expulsion of the entire German minority in Poland. The British Foreign Secretary believed that the return of these people to Germany would deprive Hitler of his complaints about the Polish mistreatment of the German minority. He noted that Hitler had been willing to conclude a similar agreement with Italy concerning the Germans of South Tirol in January 1939. Halifax ignored the fact that Hitler had concluded the January 1939 agreement with a Power not fundamentally opposed to collaboration with Germany. The Poles were unwilling to consider this proposition because they feared it might entail the departure of the Polish minority in Germany from regions which they later hoped to annex to Poland.15

Henderson sent a last report to Halifax warning that Germany was in a state of disguised partial mobilization, before departing for London on the morning of August 26th. He also wrote a personal letter to Ribbentrop from the British Embassy in Berlin at 7:30 on the same morning. He informed Ribbentrop that he was leaving for London to explain the "big proposition" for an Anglo-German agreement which Hitler had made on the previous day. He urged Ribbentrop that a peaceful settlement of the Polish question would be the best possible basis for such an agreement. Henderson mindfully remarked to Ribbentrop, "for four months Herr Hitler has shown great strength in his patience." He believed that Hitler should hold out a bit longer because of the tremendous stakes involved. He asked Ribbentrop to tell Hitler that it would be an unworthy delay on the part of the British Ambassador were he not to return to Berlin later that day or the next. Actually, Henderson was not allowed to return to Berlin until the evening of August 28, 1939. He begged Hitler to believe in his good faith, and he concluded his letter to Ribbentrop with the statement that another Anglo-German war would be the greatest possible catastrophe which could happen to the world. It was tragic that Halifax persisted in regarding this undoubted catastrophe in another way.16

British Concern About France

The British were intent on holding France in line after Hitler lost the support of Mussolini in the Polish question. American Ambassador Bullitt reported to Roosevelt that Daladier refused to be deceived by the claim that Hitler would abandon Danzig and retreat before Anglo-French pressure. British Ambassador Phipps admitted that Daladier was increasingly doubtful about supporting Poland, but the British diplomat claimed that his own energetic intervention had thus far restrained the French Premier from publicly announcing his disgust with the Poles. Phipps conceded that his own influence over Daladier was secondary to that of Bonnet, who favored serious Anglo-French consideration of a lasting agreement with the Germans. Sir Eric Phipps was also concentrating his attentions on Vice-Premier Camille Chautemps in the hope that he might counteract the influence of Bonnet on Daladier. Phipps was compelled to admit that Chautemps was one of the many members of the French Cabinet "less inclined to support Poland by force of arms."17

Phipps announced that he hoped to convert Chautemps to a policy of permanent French cooperation with Great Britain in peace and war. He wished Halifax to believe that he was doing everything humanly possible to support his policy in France. He believed that Halifax under these circumstances would permit him to express his own personal disagreement with the unconditional war policy pursued at London. The British Ambassador admitted that he personally favored an abiding Anglo-German agreement rather than another Anglo-German war, and he humbly requested Halifax to devote serious consideration to the latest proposals from Hitler. The earlier fears of American Ambassador Bullitt were confirmed. Phipps, the influential former British Ambassador to Germany and brother-in-law of Sir Robert Vansittart, favored peace rather than war. The majority of British leaders with expert knowledge on Anglo-German relations continued to favor peace rather than war despite the policy of Lord Halifax. This group included Prime Minister Neville Chamberlain, George Lansbury, Lord Lothian, Lord Astor, Lord Londonderry, Viscount Rothermere, Sir Horace Wilson, Parliamentary Under-Secretary for Foreign Affairs, Rab Butler, Ambassador Sir Eric Phipps, and Ambassador Sir Nevile Henderson.

Chamberlain complained to American Ambassador Kennedy after the outbreak of World War II "that America and the world Jews had forced England into the war." Kennedy himself was convinced that "neither the French nor the

British would have made Poland a cause of war if it had not been for the constant needling from Washington." Kennedy in 1939 was subjected to constant pressure from the American Ambassador at Paris, and he placed primary emphasis on "Bullitt's urging on Roosevelt in the Summer of 1939 that the Germans must be faced down about Poland." Kennedy was instructed by President Roosevelt on the telephone "to put some iron up Chamberlain's backside," a gratuitous instruction because Chamberlain had abdicated control over British policy to Lord Halifax in October 1938. Kennedy, Bullitt, and Roosevelt never succeeded in understanding this situation. They were neither well-informed, nor astute about discovering facts for themselves, and Halifax never chose to confide in them. The subsequent sting of conscience which caused Chamberlain to complain to Kennedy about America and the Jews was an attempt to shift the blame rather than a full confession. He was merely saying in different words that he and his friends might have found the courage to challenge Halifax had not the latter enjoyed the support of President Roosevelt. This was undoubtedly a defensive rationalization, because none of them ever displayed the slightest inclination to oppose Halifax. Furthermore, Halifax had decided upon a policy of war with Germany long before the German occupation of Prague, and before Roosevelt attempted to exert any considerable bellicose pressure on the British leaders. Halifax had stirred Roosevelt against the Germans before Hitler went to Prague, rather than the other way around. Roosevelt was a novice in international affairs compared to Halifax, and it was inconceivable that he could exert a decisive influence on the British Foreign Secretary.

Halifax had considered an Anglo-German war inevitable ever since 1936, and he never wavered in his campaign to destroy Germany, from October 1938, when he assumed personal control over British policy, to the outbreak of World War II in September 1939. He was more than a match for Chamberlain, the Unitarian business leader from the Midlands, or for any of his soft-spoken friends. He had refrained from wresting control over foreign policy from Chamberlain until the British leader returned from Munich to face the hostile critics within his own Conservative Party. He had never seriously criticized Chamberlain's conduct of policy until he was in a position to dominate it himself. Halifax would have been amused to hear Winston Churchill telling his friends in August 1939 that he feared the British Government "would run out over Poland." This was the wrong way to put it. Halifax was primarily worried by the possibility that France would run out over Poland. This was the only event which would prompt him to abandon his own policy of war against Germany.[18]

General Edward Spears of the British Expeditionary Force accompanied Winston Churchill on a tour of the Maginot Line in August 1939. He remained in France on a special mission to prepare for the arrival of British troops. General Spears, who enjoyed many contacts with prominent people in France, complained that "I could sense hostility amongst people I had known quite well, and it was very unpleasant." He noted that these people believed France was merely an instrument of an unreasoning British campaign to destroy Germany. The attitude of the French people in August 1939 was not essentially different from what the attitude of the English people had been before Halifax initiated his public campaign to destroy Germany on March 17, 1939. A.P. Scotland, a leading British military intelligence expert, noted that there was much pro-German and pro-Hitler sentiment among the ordinary business people of London in March 1939. This attitude was modified in the subsequent months by an unprecedented propaganda campaign.[19]

The Hitler-Daladier Correspondence

Hitler had written a personal letter to Daladier on the evening of August 25, 1939, during the hours of uncertainty about his attempt to cancel military operations against Poland. Hitler greeted Daladier as a statesman who had experienced the futility of World War I during four long years in the trenches of the Western Front. Hitler hoped that he and Daladier deplored in equal measure the prospect of a new conflict between France and Germany.

French Ambassador Coulondre delivered a lengthy reply from the French Premier on August 26th. Daladier informed Hitler that France found it necessary to offer her support to Poland, but he assured the German Chancellor that the people of France desired to live at peace with Germany. He promised that France and her Allies would follow a policy of good will rather than seek to exploit German difficulties for unworthy purposes.[20]

Daladier had expressed similar sentiments in a radio address to the French nation on the previous day. His speech was a vain attempt to restore the unity of France which had been torn asunder by the Russo-German pact. The French Government had suppressed the principal Communist newspapers, L'Humanité and Ce Soir. Most of the French press on August 25th and 26th expressed the hope that there would be some possibility for a peaceful solution. Charles Maurras charged in L'Action Française on August 25th that the existence of the Siegfried Line rendered futile any French attempt to aid Poland. He claimed that "it would be just as though one man were to run his head against a stone wall, to help another who was being murdered on the other side." L'Excelsior carried a sensational story which it claimed had originated with Polish diplomatic sources in Paris. It suggested that the Polish Government in new negotiations might permit Germany to have Danzig and a road to East Prussia, provided that the road was constructed by Polish engineers. It was further claimed that the Poles would be willing to remove their High Commissioner from Danzig, and that they would request the League to do the same, provided that the Germans renewed their offer to respect existing Polish economic rights at Danzig. This feature story raised hopes in France that it would be possible to settle the current dispute through bilateral negotiations between Germany and Poland.[21]

Coulondre made a vigorous appeal for peace after Hitler had read the letter from Daladier. The French Ambassador insisted that a war fought with modern arms would above all be a great tragedy for the women and children of Europe. Coulondre noted that these carefully calculated words produced a great effect on Hitler. There was a long pause, after which the German Chancellor observed pensively: "Yes, I have often thought of the women and children." The French

Ambassador noted that Ribbentrop, who was also present, refrained from joining in the conversation.22

Hitler wrote a careful reply to Daladier, which Ribbentrop personally delivered to the French Ambassador on the following day. The French Ambassador was filled with new hope that there would be no war after his conversation with Hitler on August 26th. Hitler recapitulated his requirements for a settlement of the Danzig issue in his letter to Daladier on August 27th. The German Chancellor reminded Daladier that he was not seeking a quarrel with France, and that he had gladly renounced Alsace-Lorraine. He asked Daladier what his feelings would be if Marseilles, a French port city more than twice the size of Danzig, were converted to a Free City, and were forced to accept constant lawless acts and usurpations from a smaller neighboring Power.

Hitler assured Daladier that a German-Polish war would be catastrophic, because the entire Polish state, as it was now constituted, would be lost. Hitler added with sadness that he was forced to conclude that the French would act as Germany was acting in a similar situation; Germany could not reverse her position, and react as the French in defending such an unsatisfactory Free City-Corridor aggravation. Hitler's letter ended abruptly on a sharply pessimistic note: "Unfortunately, as stated earlier in my letter, I see no possibility open to us of influencing Poland to take a saner attitude and thus to remedy a situation which is unbearable for both the German people and the German Reich."23

Hitler actually hoped that pressure from the French and British would prompt the Poles to accept a compromise. He hoped that his pessimistic letter would persuade Daladier to take energetic steps with the Poles. The Germans requested the French not to release the Hitler-Daladier correspondence to the public, but this suggestion was ignored by the French leaders, and the correspondence received full publicity in the French press. The German diplomats at Paris reported that Hitler's comment about Marseilles, in the native region of the French Premier, was especially effective.

Hitler requested Ribbentrop to extend a pledge to Coulondre, in response to the remark about the European women and children made by the French diplomat the previous day. Hitler promised not to take the initiative, in the event of hostilities, in the waging of war against enemy civilians. This pledge was later strictly observed. It was rendered inoperative by the indiscriminate British bombing campaign over Germany which had been planned as early as 1936. Hitler was also facing the possibility that he might soon be at war with Poland, and Great Britain and France. He wrote to Mussolini on August 27th that "should, as mentioned, the big war start, the situation in the East will be solved, before the two Western Powers can achieve any success."24

State Secretary Weizsaecker had invited American Chargé d'Affaires Kirk to call at the German Foreign Office on the evening of August 26th. Weizsaecker conveyed Hitler's acknowledgment of the two recent messages from President Roosevelt, and Kirk expressed his pleasure at this act of courtesy. Weizsaecker advised Kirk that it would be more timely to present warnings in Warsaw than at Berlin. German Chargé d'Affaires Thomsen reminded Hitler on August 28th that Roosevelt would do everything he could to encompass the downfall of Germany. He predicted that Roosevelt would employ ruthless tactics to force active American participation in a European war despite opposition from

American public opinion. Thomsen was convinced that American raw materials and machines would be made available to Great Britain and France immediately after the outbreak of war, and that this measure would be popular because it would aid in overcoming the extensive unemployment. Thomsen concluded that the existing American neutrality legislation would be either abrogated or circumvented.[25]

The German Foreign Office was interested in a report from German Minister Wilhelm Fabricius at Bucharest which arrived in Berlin at 7:45 a.m. on the 27th of August. The report conveyed information from General Tenestu, the Rumanian Chief-of-Staff, who Germans knew had close contacts with the French military leaders. He predicted that Poland would refuse a diplomatic settlement, and that war would follow between Germany and Poland. He was convinced that Great Britain and France at the last moment would decline to intervene in a German-Polish war. The prognosis of General Tenestu was based on information from French military sources. It was a great encouragement to Hitler after Italy's defection, and the conclusion of the Anglo-Polish alliance treaty.

Hitler feared that he could not afford to forfeit the favorable season for operations against the Poles in case they refused to negotiate. The almost exclusively dirt roads of Poland were a proverbial sea of mud during the autumn rainy season. He ordered the German armed forces to be prepared for possible operations against Poland at dawn on August 31st. This was not a repetition of his final attack order of August 25th, but rather a return to previous operational orders which had required the completion of preparations for a possible campaign against Poland by August 20, 1939.[26]

Hitler was informed by the German diplomats in Dublin on August 26th that Ireland would remain neutral in the event of an Anglo-German war. The Irish Government wished Hitler to make a statement, in the event of war, favoring the reunion of Ulster with the rest of Ireland. The German Government opposed this proposition because it would be construed as German interference in the affairs of the United Kingdom. The German Government sympathized with the sufferings of partitioned Ireland, but they did not relish the prospect of protracting possible hostilities with the British by raising the Irish question.

Hitler's Desire for Peace Conveyed at London by Dahlerus

Birger Dahlerus, who was conducting an unofficial mission for Germany, had conferred in London with Halifax on August 25th and 26th. The British Foreign Secretary was careful not to insist openly that an understanding between Great Britain and Germany was impossible. Halifax was unable to deny that Hitler's response to Chamberlain's letter of August 23, 1939, had reopened the official channels of negotiation. Dahlerus had much difficulty placing a call to Germany on August 25th. This is not surprising when one considers that he was attempting to call shortly after Hitler's cancellation of military operations. He at last succeeded in contacting Marshal Goering at 8:00 p.m. Dahlerus relayed the result of his first discussion with Halifax, and he noted that the German Marshal was obviously much excited by developments in Berlin, which were unknown to his Swedish friend. Goering emphasized that the situation was extremely serious, and that an Anglo-German conference was very much to be desired. He added that it would be an asset of incalculable importance if the British decided to return a favorable response to the agreement offer which Hitler had given to Henderson that same afternoon.[27]

The Swedish engineer conferred with Halifax on the morning of August 26th, after the arrival of Henderson in London. He informed Halifax of his conversation with Goering on the telephone the previous evening. Halifax presented Dahlerus with a personal letter to Goering, which recommended direct German negotiations with the Poles. Dahlerus requested the German diplomats at London to inform the German Foreign Office that he would return to Berlin at 5:30 p.m. on the same day. The Swedish envoy arrived at Berlin on schedule, and he delivered the letter from Halifax to Goering. He conferred with Hitler for the first time on the night of August 26th. He engaged in further conversations with Goering after his interview with Hitler and before flying back to London for what the German leaders hoped would be conferences of decisive importance with the British. Above all, he was scheduled to receive information about the British reply to Hitler's offer of August 25th.

Dahlerus was in London on August 27th conferring with the British when Hitler received a message from Mussolini which produced a marked effect on Hitler's subsequent treatment of Italy in the Anglo-German negotiation. The Italian leader requested that everything possible be done in Berlin to prevent the outbreak of war with the Poles for at least three or four years. Hitler, who believed that there would either be a diplomatic settlement with the Poles or war in the very near future, was annoyed with this suggestion, which seemed to indicate an unrealistic attitude toward the crisis he was facing.[28]

The British leaders assured Dahlerus on August 27th that a formal reply to Hitler's offer would soon be made, and that, in the meantime, they were willing to convey informally the substance of their response. The essence of the British reply was that an agreement for collaboration with Germany was acceptable in principle, but that the British would continue to support the position taken by Poland in the Danzig dispute. This meant that Great Britain and Germany were faced with an immediate conflict over the Danzig issue. Halifax was prepared to assure Hitler that Great Britain would welcome any new attempt by Germany to settle her differences with Poland by direct negotiation. Dahlerus conferred with Chamberlain and a number of officials at the British Foreign Office before returning to Berlin for a new conference with Hitler.

The German Chancellor was extremely pleased with the results of the Dahlerus visit to London on August 27th. His most pressing question at this point was whether or not Halifax was willing to consider an eventual Anglo-German alliance. Hitler assured Dahlerus that he would be willing to accept the British commitment to Poland once Germany had settled her own differences with the Poles. He believed that the British would recognize that he had made an important concession when he ceased to regard their guarantee to Poland as an obstacle to an Anglo-German understanding. Hitler then raised the crucial point. He insisted that it was necessary for the British to persuade the Poles to negotiate with Germany. Otherwise nothing would be accomplished, war would be inevitable, and a favorable opportunity for an Anglo-German understanding would be lost.

Dahlerus immediately contacted the British diplomats in Berlin to inform them that he strongly endorsed Hitler's response to Halifax's suggestions. He promised the British that the position of the Poles in any negotiation would be incomparably stronger than that of the Czechs at the time of the collapse of Czecho-Slovakia. Dahlerus also informed the British diplomats that Hitler was prepared to accept an international guarantee of Poland as part of any settlement. The Swedish engineer confided that Hitler was much impressed with what he regarded as British sincerity in seeking to compose Anglo-German differences.

Dahlerus telephoned a further report to the British diplomats at Berlin from the German military base at Oranienburg, not far from the German capital. He informed Sir George Ogilvie-Forbes, the British Chargé d'Affaires, that Hitler was now prepared to deny support against Great Britain to any third Power, including Italy, Japan, and Russia. Hitler believed that he was justified in offering this pledge, because Italy, his only ally, was refusing to support Germany against attacks from Great Britain and France. Hitler was convinced that this pledge would add strength to his earlier offer of support to the British Empire.

Dahlerus noted in a special report to the British that Goering had made a very realistic suggestion on August 26th. The German Marshal insisted that Germany wanted only the facts from both Dahlerus and the British, and that no concern should be given to avoid the wounding of German feelings. Goering believed that this frankness was necessary if the serious obstacles to an Anglo-German understanding were to be cleared away successfully. Dahlerus assured Halifax that personal contact with Hitler had convinced him that the German Chancellor did not desire war. Nevertheless, both Hitler and Goering had warned him that there would be war if a settlement was not achieved soon, and that Poland, in this unhappy event, would be divided into two occupation zones by Germany and the Soviet Union. Dahlerus was convinced that neither Hitler nor Goering favored this development over a negotiated solution. Dahlerus believed that he had done everything possible to prompt the British to make constructive suggestions in their reply to Hitler. There was nothing further to do but wait for the test of the official British note.[29]

Kennard Opposed to German-Polish Talks

Ribbentrop telephoned the German Embassy at Rome several times on August 27th to urge the Italians not to disclose to the British and French their neutral position in the current crisis. Ciano claimed to Mackensen that the true Italian position was known only to a very narrow circle in Italy, and Mussolini assured the German Ambassador that he would seek to meet German wishes *"cento per cento* (100%)." The Italians also promised to strengthen their forces somewhat along the French frontier and in Libya. Mussolini wired Hitler at 4:30 p.m. on August 27th that the "world does not and will not know before the outbreak of hostilities what the attitude of Italy is." The course of European history would probably have been very different had the Italians actually maintained this attitude during the previous ten days instead of hastening to disclose their neutrality to the British Government. The Germans remained suspicious about Italian policy, but they were totally unaware of the true state of affairs.

The Poles were in a state of feverish excitement over the renewal of diplomatic activity between Berlin and London. Raczynski protested to Halifax that the London *Times* on August 26th had stressed Henderson's dedication to peace in describing his talks with Hitler on August 25th. The Poles, who wished for the outbreak of war as soon as possible, were alarmed whenever the word 'peace' was mentioned. Raczynski claimed that the article in the *Times* could be interpreted as an attempt to separate Great Britain from Poland. The Polish Ambassador flatly denied that any negotiation plan from Hitler could offer a reasonable compromise, although he failed to explain to what extent, if any, the Poles would consider a compromise solution of the crisis. He claimed that Hitler was seeking to complete the encirclement of Poland and to divide the Allies. Halifax asked Raczynski if he did not believe that Germany might attack Poland at any moment. The Polish Ambassador replied evasively that the Germans might not dare to attack. He predicted that their next step would be a maneuver to separate Rumania from Poland. The Polish diplomat was apparently not aware that Hitler was not confronted with this task in Rumania. Rumanian Foreign Minister Gafencu on that same date, August 27th, had presented Germany with a formal pledge of Rumanian neutrality in any German-Polish war. King Carol of Rumania had also expressed his conviction that Great Britain and France would not attack Germany. The Rumanian sovereign had recently returned from a visit to Turkey, and he was impressed by the fact that the British were behind schedule on their deliveries of war material to the Turks.[30]

British Ambassador Kennard at Warsaw in his report to London vigorously denounced the possibility of renewed negotiations between the Germans and the Poles. He reminded Sir Alexander Cadogan that he had earlier denounced Henderson's proposal for Lipski to seek an interview with Hitler. Kennard was thinking exclusively in terms of an inevitable war, and he feared that Hitler's interest in negotiating with the Poles was a "German maneuver to break up our front." He was scornful about earlier British policy, and he warned that neutral observers inspecting minority conditions in Poland should not constitute a new "Runciman mission." He deplored the constant talk about avoiding incidents, and he claimed that the Poles had the right to "react" to German provocations. Kennard also emphasized that the Polish Government would refuse to negotiate on a possible exchange of minorities with the Germans.

Kennard had received five detailed documents from the British Foreign Office which contained confidential accounts about the mistreatment of the German minority in Poland. Kennard's mendacious reply to this material was nothing if not succinct: "So far as I can judge German allegations of mass ill-treatment of the German minority by Polish authorities are gross exaggerations if not complete falsifications." Kennard added testily that the various exceptions to this statement were the result of German "provocation" since March 1939. Kennard proceeded to give a new twist to his instructions about warning Beck against excesses. He would impress on Beck the need of "proving [that] Hitler's allegations about the German minority are false." The British Ambassador hoped that it would be possible to force the facts into the pattern of his preconceived notions.

One might wonder how Kennard would have reacted toward the fate of his own relatives in Brighton, or elsewhere in England, under a foreign rule which permitted daily atrocities. Kennard complacently accepted a threatening Polish attitude which also involved the immediate safety of his own countrymen. The Poles hoped to stifle a possible Anglo-German *rapprochement*. They demanded immediate information concerning any British reply to proposals from Hitler. They warned that, although their mobilization was virtually complete, they would immediately take additional military measures in the event that they considered any British reply unsatisfactory. They insisted that the sole purpose of Hitler's maneuvers was to destroy the "peace front." Kennard added that Beck refused to discuss minorities, and that he did not wish neutral observers to witness conditions in Poland. Kennard indicated that he was personally pleased with the stand the Polish Foreign Minister was taking in these important questions.[31]

Count Ciano followed up his misleading assurances to the Germans on August 27th with a personal telephone call to Lord Halifax. The Italian Foreign Minister informed Halifax that, on the basis of the friendly relations existing between Great Britain and Italy, he wished to urge the British Government to grant serious consideration to Hitler's offer for an Anglo-German agreement. He urged Halifax to encourage the Poles to negotiate with Germany. His telephone call occurred at a time when the British Foreign Office was preparing a very complacent analysis of the current situation. According to this analysis, the "fact that Herr Hitler regards the Secretary of State's message to Field-Marshal Goering as satisfactory and is quite content to hold his hand shows that the German Government are wobbling. This was confirmed yesterday by a member of the German Embassy, who said that the signature of the Polish Pact had fallen as a bombshell."[32]

The Pact had truly been a bombshell, although the German diplomat who confessed this fact to the British was known to them as a man of doubtful patriotism. Indeed, German Charge d'Affaires Theo Kordt at London was passing along more information at this juncture to the British Government than to the German Foreign Office at Berlin. This did not mean that Great Britain, regardless of the situation in Poland, was in a position to intimidate Hitler indefinitely. Hitler's hesitation, unlike that of Mussolini, was not produced by any fear of British military power, which in itself could never defeat Germany, but by a sincere friendship for the British Empire. The conclusion at the British Foreign Office on August 27th that it would be wise to be "conciliatory in form," but "be absolutely firm in substance," was not an adequate formula for the preservation of peace. The absolute firmness the British diplomats had in mind was a rigidity of policy which precluded pressure on Poland for a diplomatic settlement with Germany.

The most serious delusion at the British Foreign Office on August 27th concerned the allegedly favorable military position of Great Britain. It seemed to the British diplomats that the "latest news from Turkey and Italy was highly satisfactory. If war were to break out and Italy did not march, the moral effect on the German people would be tremendous and they would not feel compensated by dubious Russian assistance." The German people were unenthusiastic about a new war, but it was exaggerated to assume that anything Italy might do could seriously impair their morale. The man-in-the-street in

Germany, not to mention responsible military figures, placed a little value at this time on the military importance of Italy. It would be easy for Hitler to convince the people that it was in the best interest of Germany for Italy to stay out of trouble. The British analysis of the military situation concluded on the sorry note that the "latest indications are that we have an unexpectedly strong hand."[33]

Hitler delivered a private speech to the other German leaders on August 27th in which he stressed his hope for an agreement with Great Britain. The British case was so weak in reality that Hitler was convincing himself anew, with each further analysis of the situation, that it could not possible be either their intent or their interest to go to war for Poland. Unfortunately, the desire of Halifax and the British Foreign Office staff to lead a coalition into war against Germany permitted them to rationalize the existing situation in a reckless and superficial manner.

Karl von Wiegand, a well-informed American journalist from the International News Service of William Randolph Hearst, discussed the situation with British diplomats in Berlin on August 27th. He was able to inform the German diplomats later in the day that Sir Nevile Henderson personally favored a solution of the current crisis in the German sense. Nevertheless, Henderson had been sceptical about the results of his latest mission when he departed for London on the previous day. He had told his staff at Berlin that he doubted if the British Cabinet would support his efforts for a peaceful solution. Henderson knew that peace could not be maintained unless there was a compromise. He was prepared to advocate at London the return of Danzig to Germany and adequate German transit facilities to East Prussia. The British Ambassador was convinced that the original German offer to Poland was the best possible basis for a compromise settlement of German-Polish differences.[34]

The Russians were arguing day after day that the British had only themselves to blame for their weak position. Marshal Voroshilov, the chief Russian negotiator in the recent military talks with the West, explained in a special interview with *Izvestia* (*The News*) on August 26th that it was naive of London to argue that Russian negotiations with Great Britain and France had been broken because of the pact with Germany. Voroshilov pointed out that, on the contrary, the pact with Germany had been signed because of the deadlock in the Western negotiations, and that this deadlock, in turn, rested on the British guarantee to Poland and on Polish intransigence. Voroshilov was actually exploiting the pretext he had used to disrupt the negotiations with the West rather than revealing the true nature of Soviet policy, which had been based for many months on the hope of Russian neutrality in the early phase of a destructive Anglo-German war. His statements were a clever and plausible justification of Russian policy, calculated to create the maximum discontent about Polish policy in Great Britain and France. This did not mean that the Russians were playing the German diplomatic game. They had promised Ribbentrop to send a new Ambassador to Berlin to succeed Merekalov, who had been recalled, but they failed to do so during the week following the return of Ribbentrop from Moscow. They were also extremely dilatory in responding to a German request to deny the widely circulated rumors that Russian troops were actually being withdrawn from the vicinity of the Polish frontier. At last, on August 28th, Molotov issued a laconic *démenti* which explained that the reported Soviet troop withdrawals had no factual basis. Ribbentrop was not satisfied with this statement. He believed that an announcement of a Russian troop concentration against Poland might encourage the Poles to negotiate. He telephoned Moscow on August 28th to request Molotov to take this step. Molotov refused to comply, and German Ambassador Schulenburg reported on August 29th that the Soviet Foreign Commissar continued to neglect the appointment of a new Russian Ambassador to Germany. The Soviet Union, in defending their own policies, had no desire to aid Hitler in achieving a peaceful settlement of the German-Polish dispute.[35]

The Deceptive British Note of August 28th

The British had decided to delay their formal reply to Hitler's offer of August 25th until the evening of August 28th, and Henderson was compelled to remain in London in order to convey it personally to Hitler. The British Ambassador, who had expected to return to Germany with the British reply on August 26th or 27th, considered the delay at London irresponsible and inexcusable. Hitler was far less concerned about the situation, because, being uninformed as to the facts, he continued to hope that the British were taking energetic steps at Warsaw to persuade the Poles to compromise.

Dahlerus continued to supply the British with vital information for successful negotiations with Germany. He advised the British not to refer to Roosevelt's messages in their formal reply. This advice was unnecessary, because the British had avoided any public connection with the measures of Roosevelt. Dahlerus realized that President Roosevelt's messages had prompted the Polish Government on August 25th to issue a formal platonic statement favoring negotiations with Germany, which was entirely contrary to their real intention. Dahlerus stressed Hitler's hope that Poland would offer a meaningful pledge to Great Britain concerning her willingness to negotiate. Hitler feared, after his previous experiences, that the Poles would seek to avoid negotiations. The British themselves had stressed the possibility of German-Polish negotiations, and Hitler believed that they should make an effort to persuade the Poles to comply with this plan.[36]

Dahlerus renewed this argument in his conversations with the British leaders on August 28, 1939. Halifax had not made the slightest effort up to this point to sound out the Poles about negotiations. Halifax did not desire a settlement of German-Polish differences, but it is difficult to explain, from the purely tactical viewpoint, why he was so dilatory about going through the motion of at least sounding out the Poles. It was evident to him from the recent reports of Kennard and from conversations with Raczynski that Polish intransigence was sufficiently great to withstand peace efforts of a casual nature. His own position might have appeared superficially more favorable on the record had he made some earlier effort to convey the impression that he took seriously his own suggestion about German-Polish negotiations.

Halifax might never have reacted to this situation at all had it not been for the constant prodding of Dahlerus. At last, on August 28th, at 2:00 p.m.,

Halifax wired Kennard that the Polish reply to Roosevelt indicated that the Poles were willing to negotiate directly with Germany. He informed Kennard that Great Britain naturally expected Poland to conduct herself accordingly. Kennard, who was opposed to further German-Polish talks, decided to head off possible British pressure on Poland by replying nonchalantly the same afternoon, that Beck was quite prepared to enter into direct negotiations with the Germans at once. The absence of any details about specific proposals for a settlement made it obvious to Halifax that no really serious British *démarche* had been taken at Warsaw. Halifax's irresponsible treatment of Kennard's report produced endless confusion. The Polish Government had made no important declaration of policy on August 28th, and Beck noted afterward that the first direct appeal he received to renew negotiations with the Germans came much later from Lipski at Berlin. Halifax made not the slightest effort to persuade Kennard to undertake a genuine *demarche* in behalf of negotiations at Warsaw. The confusion was compounded because Halifax informed the other British diplomatic missions of his latest exchange with Kennard. The German Embassy at Budapest reported to Berlin at 3:10 p.m. on the following day that the British Government had exerted pressure on the Poles to negotiate with Germany on the basis of the Hitler speech to the German Reichstag on April 28, 1939. Hitler had announced in this speech that he was withdrawing his earlier offer to Poland, but that he would welcome negotiations with the Poles on some new basis. Beck was actually telling Kennard that the original October 1938 German offer remained entirely unacceptable in all of its points. There had actually been no British pressure whatever on Poland when the report from Budapest was received at Berlin at 6:40 p.m. on August 29, 1939.[37]

It was significant that Halifax did not instruct Sir Eric Phipps to inform Bonnet of what was taking place at Warsaw. The British Foreign Secretary undoubtedly feared that if he did Bonnet would insist upon exerting genuine pressure on the Poles. French Ambassador Noel did not receive instructions to urge the Poles to negotiate until early on August 30, 1939, after Bonnet had discovered from Berlin that Hitler was preparing a specific plan for a German-Polish settlement. The French then proceeded with alacrity to exert pressure on the Poles, but it was very late, and they received no support whatever in this effort from the British side. Halifax and Kennard had deliberately made a complete mess of Hitler's suggestion for Anglo-French diplomatic pressure in favor of a peaceful settlement at Warsaw.

Kennard never relaxed in his persistent efforts to encourage Halifax to disregard the fate of the German minority in Poland. Kennard, in a special report on the afternoon of August 28th, played upon the frontier incidents which had occurred early on August 26th during the German effort to cancel military operations against Poland. He was jubilant because he had discovered inaccuracies in the detailed German descriptions of two incidents among the thousands which had been described and reported. Two cases of mistaken identification of the instigators of incidents were used with utter sophistry by Kennard to suggest that all of the incidents must be *ipso facto* untrue. The partisanship of the British Ambassador was too intense to permit fairness, honesty, or objectivity. Kennard ignored every other consideration in his single-minded effort to aid Halifax in plunging Poland, Great Britain, and France into a disastrous war against Germany.[38]

Dahlerus urged the British at London on August 28th that time was of the essence in avoiding war. The British did not need this reminder. They had learned from their own contacts among the Germans about the perilous incident of the German attack order of August 25th and its last minute successful cancellation. Dahlerus was permitted by the German leaders to inform Halifax that the German Army would be in final position to strike a devastating blow at Poland on the night of August 30/31. Goering was allowed by Hitler to convey as much information as possible about the new proposals to Poland which were being prepared and discussed in Germany. Dahlerus informed the British on the afternoon of August 28th about the essential substance of the offer later known as the Marienwerder proposals. Goering realized that it would be an important assistance to successful negotiations if the British realized in advance that the German position remained moderate despite the uninterrupted crisis since March 1939.

Goering anticipated that the Poles might be reluctant to conduct important negotiations on German soil. He instructed Dahlerus to inform the British that the luxurious yacht of the well-disposed Swedish industrialist, Wenner-Gren, the chairman of the Electrolux corporation, would be an ideal location for a Baltic Sea conference off the Polish coast. The British had been informed of the military plans of the German Army, the important terms of a negotiation offer not yet arranged in paragraphs, and a convenient neutral location for negotiations between Germany and Poland. Goering naturally expected that all of this important information would be relayed to Warsaw, but the only item Halifax selected for Kennard was the revelation of the German military plans. Halifax knew that emphasis on German military preparations, without mention of the German desire to negotiate with Poland, would be the greatest possible encouragement for drastic new Polish measures to increase the danger of war and reduce the chances for a negotiated settlement.[39]

Henderson was prepared to fly from London at 5:00 p.m. on August 28th with the official British reply to Hitler's offer for an Anglo-German understanding. The British Ambassador wired ahead to Berlin that he wished to meet the German Chancellor as soon as possible, but that there would be some delay after his arrival, until the British Embassy staff at Berlin translated the official British text into German. The reply which Henderson carried to Germany was a most interesting document. The British Government took notice of the fact that Hitler had made his offer conditional on the settlement of the German-Polish dispute. The British would insist that any settlement of the controversy with Poland be subject to an international guarantee by a number of Powers including Poland and Germany. Halifax wished Hitler to know that the Polish Government had declared its willingness to negotiate directly with the German Government. It is surely an understatement to observe at this point that Halifax had displayed surprisingly small concern about verifying an allegedly sincere Polish declaration of such obvious importance. No doubt Halifax would have shown more care and energy in this matter had he actually desired a negotiated settlement of German-Polish differences.

Hitler was reminded in the British note that an Anglo-German conflict resulting from failure to reach a settlement "might well plunge the whole world into war. Such an outcome would be a calamity without parallel in history."

Halifax's intention was to warn Hitler that the British would again seek to plunge the rest of the world into conflict with Germany in the event of war. It was, of course, a tragedy that Halifax did not for one moment believe his own statement that an Anglo-German war would be a supreme calamity, despite the fact that it contained more truth than anything else he had ever written. Halifax would have ceased working for war and would have joined the leaders of France, Germany, and Italy in the search for peace had he believed his own words. This development alone would have been quite sufficient to save the entire situation.[40]

Birger Dahlerus returned to Germany on August 28th. He discussed the London situation with the German leaders before Henderson called on Hitler at 10:30 p.m. with the formal British reply. The Swedish engineer announced that Halifax refused to accept the Buxton proposal for German defense of the British Empire, which had been featured by Hitler in his offer to Great Britain. Halifax, in contrast to Buxton, seemed to regard this suggestion as an affront to the British nation implying that the British were unable to defend their world-wide possessions. It was difficult to understand Halifax's attitude on this point, because the Anglo-Japanese alliance of 1902-1922 had provided for Japanese defense of British possessions in East Asia. The British leaders had abandoned their earlier policy of 'splendid isolation' as early as 1902 when they concluded this alliance with the Japanese. Dahlerus believed that Halifax was pleased with Hitler's suggestion that colonial claims would not be discussed until disarmament had been achieved. Halifax was prepared to insist that the Soviet Union should participate in an international guarantee of the Polish frontiers. The Germans doubted if the Russians would accept this proposal, but they had no objection to an effort in this direction. Goering feared, from what Dahlerus had said about the German offer to defend the British Empire, that the official British response to Hitler's offer would not be favorable. Hitler was optimistic, because he was counting on the British to persuade the Poles to negotiate. He had not expected Halifax to accept at once the full text of his proposals for an Anglo-German agreement. Hitler believed that a settlement would be in sight if the formal British reply corresponded to the indications he had received from Dahlerus.[41]

The meeting between Hitler and Henderson on the night of August 28/29 took place in a very friendly atmosphere. Hitler was favorably impressed with the formal British reply, and he hoped that the British genuinely dreaded the prospect of another futile and disastrous Anglo-German war. There was heated conversation again on the Polish question, but this did not destroy the fundamental harmony of the meeting. Hitler began to discuss the new proposals he was planning to offer Poland, and he knew that the British leaders had previously received considerable information about them from Dahlerus. Hitler admitted that he was sorely tempted to request revisions of the confusing Upper Silesian border, which ran through kitchens, bathrooms, barnyards and mines. Polish rule in Upper Silesia had been exceptionally harsh, and the Allied and Associated Powers had been particularly dishonest about their choice of methods to transfer this territory to Poland in the first place. Hitler said that he would not tempt fate by raising this issue, because he knew that any change in the *status quo* of the area now would seriously affect vital Polish economic interests.

Hitler briefly interrupted his discussion with Henderson to arrange a conference between Ribbentrop and Goering on the proposed terms of a new German offer to the Poles. Henderson inquired when the German proposals would be completed for submission to the Poles. Hitler suggested that the work might be completed by the time Germany presented her reply to the British note of August 28th. Midnight had struck, and it was early August 29th. Hitler assured Henderson that at least the note to Great Britain would be ready the same day. Henderson feared that he had created the impression that Hitler was expected to reply in what might be considered undue haste. He wished to assure Hitler that this was not the case: "It took us two days to draw up the note. I am in no hurry." Hitler replied with great seriousness: "But I am!"⁴²

The German leader was in the unenviable position of seeking a diplomatic settlement without exposing Germany to a protracted two-front war. The German military planners had warned him that the success of "Operation White" was conditional on launching operations not later than September 1st. The British had wasted much time in replying to Hitler's offer of August 25th, and the German leader was determined to do everything possible to increase the speed of the negotiations.

Henderson hoped to encourage Hitler by recalling the traditional Anglo-German amity of the good old days. He cited a familiar schoolbook quotation from Prussian General Bluecher to his troops on the eve of the battle of Waterloo in 1815: "Forward, my children, I have given my word to my brother Wellington, and you cannot wish me to break it." Hitler, with a combined feeling of amusement and sadness, remarked that "things were different 125 years ago." Henderson replied stoutly: "Not so far as England was concerned." The German Chancellor refrained from further comment, and, after all, Henderson was right. The British were pursuing the same archaic balance of power theory in 1939 that had prompted their unrelenting wars against France from 1793 until the final defeat of Napoleon in 1815. It was merely an incidental feature that now Germany, and not France, suffered from the single-minded hostility of Great Britain. This was merely because Germany, in the course of an evolution determined primarily by natural causes, had replaced France as the leading Power in the European continental region west of Russia. This was the main reason for the change. Little else, including the threat from the Soviet Union, seemed to matter. The uncompromising rigidity of British foreign policy in a rapidly changing world has prompted much admiration. This does not change the fact that the policy which promoted British strength in 1815 was the fatal instrument of the British decline that began in 1939.⁴³

Henderson, in any lengthy conference with Hitler, could not resist throwing his instructions to the winds and putting everything on a personal basis. The British Ambassador suggested to Hitler on this occasion that he could solve his problems by renewing his October 1938 proposals to Poland. This undoubtedly would have produced a speedy solution had Henderson, Butler, or Lothian been conducting British foreign policy, but it was scarcely a very promising suggestion with Halifax unreservedly supporting the Polish position at Danzig. The British Ambassador eagerly assured Hitler that in this way he "could at a stroke change in his favour the whole of public opinion not only in England but in the world."

The current crisis would have ended on a very satisfactory basis had this actually been the case.

Hitler's Hope for a Peaceful Settlement

There was a brief interlude of very great optimism in Hitler's immediate circle following the conversation with Henderson on the night of August 28/29 and the reception of the British note of August 28th. This optimism seemed fully justified by the unequivocal but utterly false British assurance that the Poles had been induced to agree to renewed direct negotiations. It may be argued that Hitler and his entourage were extremely naive to believe any assurance which came from London. This was undoubtedly true, but it was simply not apparent to Hitler that the British had anything to gain by misrepresenting the Polish position.

Hitler, in his enthusiasm for the British Empire, was inclined to give the British leaders more credit for intelligence and integrity than they actually deserved. Halifax was quite prepared to play along with this feeling in Berlin, to a certain extent. He believed that this would be useful in maintaining British influence in Italy. He telephoned Ciano on August 29th that the response to the British formal reply, and the discussion in Berlin the previous evening, gave reason "to hope for" a settlement, and, with double caution, Halifax added that at least he "hoped so." He wished to convince the Italians that he was genuinely desirous of a peaceful settlement, and that the last British move had left the situation in excellent shape. It was now Hitler's move. The Italians were expected to blame the man in Berlin if things suddenly became worse again. The British Foreign Secretary offered the platonic gesture of assuring Ciano that he hoped Mussolini would persevere in his search for peace.[44]

Hitler's mood of optimism at Berlin was shared by Bonnet at Paris. France, like Poland, had virtually completed her mobilization by this time. Bonnet reminded Sir Eric Phipps of the old military and diplomatic axiom that mobilization means war. He declared that he could not cease wondering at the fact that France could call up 2,700,000 fighting men without any German warnings or threatening military measures. Bonnet confided that the military authorities would call up at the most another half million men in the event of a formal mobilization order. Phipps noted that Bonnet discussed these serious problems with apparent lightness of heart. The French Foreign Minister was again optimistic about the chances for preserving peace.[45]

Italian Ambassador Attolico had assured Weizsaecker on the evening of August 27th that Mussolini had a special plan for an international diplomatic conference in case the Poles refused to accept bilateral negotiations with Germany. Mussolini was prepared to insist that Danzig return to Germany, as part of any settlement. The Italian Ambassador telephoned the German Foreign Office on the evening of August 28th to request a copy of Hitler's latest letter to Chamberlain. He had received misleading reports about the mission of Dahlerus to England, and his impression that Hitler had written to Chamberlain again was incorrect. Weizsaecker assured Attolico that Hitler had never intended to write to Chamberlain before receiving the official British reply to the German offer of August 25th. He attempted to convince the suspicious Italian Ambassador that Germany would keep Italy fully informed of important developments in the Anglo-German negotiation.

Ribbentrop invited Attolico to call at the German Foreign Office on August 29th to discuss latest developments. He told Attolico that he hoped for a peaceful settlement after the latest conversation between Hitler and Henderson. Attolico wished to know the nature of the German reply to the British note of August 28th, but Ribbentrop indicated that the German answer was not yet ready. He gave the Italian diplomat some hint about German intentions when he confided that he had been advised by Henderson to invite the Poles to negotiate at Berlin.

Ribbentrop admitted that Hitler was sceptical about the success of new negotiations with Poland. Attolico agreed with this opinion, and he insisted that a diplomatic conference of the principal Powers offered greater promise for a settlement. Ribbentrop did not deny this, but he insisted that Hitler was wise to follow British advice and to seek direct contact with the Poles. It seemed obvious to Ribbentrop that the Poles, rather than Germany, would be blamed for any failure to establish contact. Attolico wished to offer Ribbentrop some encouragement. He told the German Foreign Minister that Papal Nuncio Orsenigo believed that there had recently been an improvement in the Polish attitude. Ribbentrop was inclined to attribute this to British influence. He would have been shocked to learn that the British Ambassador at Warsaw, Sir Howard Kennard, had not made the slightest effort to induce the Poles to accept talks with Germany. Ribbentrop was warned by German Chargé d'Affaires Wuehlisch at Warsaw on August 29th that the great majority of informed Poles considered that war with Germany was inevitable, but he continued to hope that Beck would respond to British pressure, which did not exist.[46]

The optimism at Paris and Berlin was shared at Rome after the telephone conversation between Ciano and Halifax. Mussolini claimed in a message to Hitler at 4:40 p.m. on August 29th that the British note to Germany of the previous day offered an adequate basis for a satisfactory settlement. Mussolini also made the revealing comment that his relations with Paris were cool, but that he was now in a position to intervene diplomatically at London. He did not admit that his relations with the British had been improved by the devious Italian promise not to intervene militarily if Great Britain attacked Germany. He concluded optimistically that a peaceful solution was assured, and "the rhythm of your splendid achievements will not be disturbed."[47]

Dahlerus had telephoned the British Foreign Office from Berlin at 7:00 a.m. on August 29th to inform Halifax that Hitler was optimistic about a peaceful settlement. Halifax received an angry warning from Beck shortly afterward that the Polish Government was contemplating new measures against Danzig. Beck complained that the Danzigers were displaying increasing reluctance to expedite the normal shipments of Polish goods from the Free City harbor into Poland. He was completely unaware that Halifax had assured Hitler that Poland was prepared to negotiate for a definitive settlement of the Danzig issue with Germany.[48]

Henderson wired additional information to Halifax shortly after noon on August 29th about Germany's forthcoming reply to Great Britain, and about her new proposals to the Poles. The British Ambassador announced that Hitler had decided not to raise the dangerous Upper Silesian question, and that he would restrict his proposals to Danzig and the Corridor region. Henderson added that Goering was anxious to receive some indication about the attitude of the Poles toward new negotiations. The Germans had decided to request the British Government to serve as intermediary in approaching the Poles. Henderson warned London that Goering feared the Poles would be stubborn and "try to ruin Germany by being so obstructive that war would be inevitable." Henderson emphasized again that Hitler was prepared to participate immediately in an international guarantee of any satisfactory results achieved in a new Polish-German negotiation.

Henderson was more anxious about the situation than Goering, because he had received no indication that the British Government had actually advised the Poles to negotiate. He knew that a terrible fiasco would result if Halifax failed to take steps at Warsaw. He wired Halifax again on the afternoon of August 29th to plead for a British step in Poland insisting that the Poles at least agree to negotiate with the Germans. He rejected the argument often used by the Poles to the effect that Germany's sole interest in negotiation was to split the Anglo-Polish front. Henderson flatly denied that Hitler believed such an objective was feasible. The British diplomat argued that Hitler knew he would have an Anglo-German war on his hands unless he could arrive at a German-Polish diplomatic settlement acceptable to the British. He emphasized to the British Foreign Secretary that Hitler preferred a negotiated settlement to any war, including a local war. Above all, Hitler had admired the Poles too long to desire their destruction.

Henderson followed these elaborate arguments a few minutes later with a new appeal. The British Ambassador urged that the French should be encouraged to join with Great Britain in applying strong pressure at Warsaw. The British Ambassador correctly suspected that Halifax had made no effort whatever to obtain French support for moderation at Warsaw. Henderson insisted that "the question of exaggerated prestige and *amour propre* on the part of Poland must not be allowed to stand in the way of a fairly negotiated settlement based on an international guarantee."[49]

New Military Measures Planned by Poland

Within minutes of Henderson's latest appeals on the 29th, which were ignored by Halifax, a telegraph arrived at London from Kennard. He wished to inform Halifax that the Polish Government had decided upon general mobilization. The Polish military plans stipulated that general mobilization would be ordered only in the event of a Polish decision for war. Halifax was primarily to blame for this rash Polish decision which made a German-Polish war virtually inevitable. He had failed to inform the Poles of Germany's peaceful intentions, but he had informed them that the German forces would be in their final positions for operations against Poland by the night of August 30/31. It was difficult to criticize the Poles for reacting as they did to Halifax's one-sided version of Goering's disclosures. Evil memories of 1914 were awakened by the news from Kennard. Historians of all nations had attributed great importance to the sequence in which the various nations had mobilized at the outbreak of World War I. The fact that the Russians and the French had declared general mobilization before the Germans in 1914 was rightly considered a matter of very great importance. Halifax should have been able to foresee the inevitable consequences of his deceitful policy at Warsaw, yet he was irritated by the Polish decision. He knew that Germany would defeat Poland in a war, and he knew that the calling up of another half-dozen Polish divisions could not avert the debacle. The Poles would merely incur greater responsibility for starting war without preventing the ruin which would inevitably befall them in the event of war. Halifax had decided, with cool and deliberate calculation, to exert pressure on the Poles to delay their mobilization.

Kennard had no advance instructions from which to deal with the announcement by Beck. He decided on the spur of the moment to advise general mobilization, but to discourage publicity about it. This ignored the fact that the Poles had no plans for a so-called secret mobilization in the German style. The Germans, without any publicity, had reached a stage of partial mobilization equivalent to that of the Poles and the French. With great reluctance, Kennard carried out the later instructions from Halifax, and he advised the Poles to delay mobilization. Nevertheless, he capitalized on the fact that Halifax had not stipulated how long the mobilization should be delayed. He wired Halifax at 6:45 p.m. that the Poles had agreed to delay the posting of their mobilization notices for a few hours. This was really no concession at all. The Poles intended the first day of mobilization to follow the day of the announcement. It would have created confusion had the Polish authorities posted announcements late on August 29th for a mustering of reserves at dawn on the following day. Beck had not made his original disclosure to Kennard about Polish intentions to complete their mobilization until the afternoon of August 29th. The Poles, in deciding to post their announcements before noon on Wednesday, August 30th, were tacitly rejecting the advice of Halifax for them to delay this decisive step.[50]

The prospect of Polish general mobilization was overshadowed by the news which Halifax received from Kennard a few minutes later. Beck had received vague rumors that Poland might seriously be requested to resume negotiations with Germany, and he decided to head off any such step by disclosing in advance that the Poles would refuse to do so. Beck declared flatly to Kennard that he was unprepared to grant any concessions to the Germans, and therefore he saw no point in negotiations. He explained that he would not accept any part of the proposals which he had rejected earlier in March 1939. Halifax received this statement with evident satisfaction, and he deliberately neglected to address any further communications to Warsaw for a lengthy period. He knew that Kennard would stoutly support Beck's fanatical intransigence. After all, if the Germans inquired why Halifax had stated that the Poles were prepared to negotiate, it would be simple to point to the meaningless Polish pledge in response to Roosevelt's message of August 24, 1939.

These facts were unknown at Paris, Berlin, and Rome, where an atmosphere of increasing optimism prevailed. Halifax was also optimistic, but for the opposite reasons. The French, German, and Italian leaders hoped for peace.

Halifax was reasonably certain that there would be war. He did not want war for its own sake, but he believed that the destruction of Germany, which could be accomplished only by war, would be a brilliant achievement. He had worked for war unceasingly during the past ten months, and he sensed that his triumph was close at hand. He failed to realize that his success would produce the eclipse of his own country. He ignored still another urgent telegram from Henderson that it would be in the vital interest of Poland to accept promptly a German invitation to negotiate. Halifax knew that the Poles would be doomed in the event of war, but he cared nothing for the fate of Poland.[51]

The German Note of August 29th

Hitler by this time had approved the finishing touches on the German reply to Great Britain. He agreed that the German-Polish dispute had become a crucial factor in Anglo-German relations. He confirmed his desire for a peaceful settlement and his willingness to negotiate with the Poles. Hitler wished the British Government to advise Poland to send an emissary to Berlin on the following day, Wednesday, August 30th. He emphasized that urgency was required by the pressure of events, and he wished the British to know that Germany expected the arrival of a representative from Poland not later than midnight on August 30th. Henderson was received by Hitler on the evening of August 29th, and the official German note was presented to him at 7:15 p.m.

Dahlerus telephoned the British Foreign Office from Berlin a few minutes after Henderson had been received by Hitler. He wished Halifax to know that Hitler and Goering were very pleased by the British attitude toward Germany revealed in the British note of August 28, 1939. Dahlerus assured the British that the German reply would reach London the same evening. It was noted at London that the Swedish engineer was "very cheerful and exuberant." He obviously believed that his labors were nearing a successful conclusion. Woermann at the German Foreign Office, on the evening of August 29th, told the Swiss, Lithuanian, and Slovak Ministers that prospects were favorable for a diplomatic solution of the Polish crisis as a result of Anglo-German talks.[52]

Halifax received a further communication from Kennard a few minutes after the call from Dahlerus. The British Ambassador confirmed the Polish decision to post general mobilization notices the following morning, and added that he had received the tart reminder that such notices could not be kept secret. Kennard had approved the Polish measure, despite the fact that Bonnet had instructed French Ambassador Noel to protest vigorously against general mobilization. Kennard minced no words in defending the Poles against possible criticism from Halifax. He bluntly accused Halifax of prompting the Polish move by passing on the information from Goering about German Army plans. Kennard concluded that the Poles "would hardly be justified in refraining from every possible measure of defense."

Beck requested Kennard to inform Halifax that there was only one development which could prevent the Polish general mobilization scheduled for 8:00 o'clock, on the following morning. This would be an explicit statement from Hitler that Germany had abandoned Danzig once and for all, and that she would never again seek to improve her transit communications to East Prussia through the Polish Corridor. Beck announced that he was prepared to receive and study the full text of Hitler's reply to Great Britain at any hour. Poland would proceed with her military measures unless Hitler retreated. Beck had previously made it perfectly clear that he would not negotiate with Germany.[53]

Hitler engaged in a lengthy discussion with Henderson about the German note to Great Britain of August 29th. Hitler emphasized that he would not object to the British guarantee of Poland if he could settle German differences with the Poles. The British had guaranteed Poland's vital interests and independence, and the German proposals of October 1938 had conveyed no intention of attacking one or the other. Hitler explained that the German draft of new proposals to the Poles was not yet complete, but that it would be finished very soon. He denied that his urgent request for a Polish emissary, which was addressed to the British rather than the Poles, constituted an ultimatum to Poland. Hitler, who noticed that Henderson was concerned about the time factor in the German plan, did his best to establish sound reasons for immediate negotiations, because he had no intention of sacrificing once more for no good purpose the carefully prepared operational plans of the German Army. Hitler defended his urgent request for a prompt Polish response at great length, and he succeeded at last in reassuring Henderson.[54]

Henderson departed from his conference with Hitler with the conviction that it would be possible to prevent a war between Germany and Poland. He contacted London at once, and he warmly recommended that the British Government make every effort to persuade the Poles to accept the German offer to negotiate on the exact terms laid down by Hitler. The British Foreign Office received the summary text of Hitler's reply at 9:15 p.m. on August 29th. There was ample time for the British Government to contact Warsaw, and for the Poles to send an emissary to Berlin at any time on the following day. Henderson indicated that Hitler had agreed to consult with the Soviet Union about an international guarantee to Poland. Ribbentrop actually informed Soviet Chargé d'Affaires Ivanov before midnight on August 29th that Germany favored the participation of the Soviet Union in any international arrangement concerning Poland. Henderson did not attempt to deny that the German note had the flavor of an ultimatum, but he repeated Hitler's arguments for the launching of negotiations with the greatest possible speed.[55]

The German Request for Negotiation with Poland

The Poles, of course, were completely free in their choice of a man for the mission to Berlin. There were ample men in Poland who could be trusted not to accept proposals merely because they were German. The Poles had in the past been brilliant in leading Hitler on without conceding anything, and they were presented with an excellent opportunity to repeat the performance. Beck elected not to modify in any degree his unconditional challenge to Germany of March 26, 1939. He believed that Poland would be defeated by Germany no matter what time of year operations started, but he feared that he might lose British and French support if the conflict was delayed. A decisive warning from the

British that he definitely would lose their support unless he negotiated would have prompted him to negotiate, but Halifax, who did not desire peace, had no motive to issue such a warning. Bonnet urged Beck to accept Hitler's offer as soon as he heard about it, but he was unable to achieve anything at Warsaw without British support.

Hitler was optimistic because he was completely out of touch with the actual British position represented by Halifax and Kennard despite the efforts of Henderson and Dahlerus. Henderson emphasized to Halifax on the night of August 29th that he had inquired if Germany would negotiate with Poland on a basis of full equality. Hitler had replied promptly and with unmistakable emphasis: "Of course!" Hitler added that he would inform the British Government of his suggestions for a settlement with Poland either shortly before or after the arrival of a Polish emissary. Henderson assured Halifax that these terms would be moderate.[56]

Henderson admitted that his interview with Hitler had been "stormy," and that the German Chancellor was indignant about the latest atrocity and mob-action bulletins from Poland. Henderson also knew, however, that Attolico, who had called on Hitler immediately afterward, had found the German Chancellor quite calm. Henderson was quite willing to attribute Hitler's earlier excitement to the importance of the issue involved in the Anglo-German negotiation. The British Ambassador had realized at once that a tangible basis for a settlement had been achieved, and he proceeded to support Hitler's initiative with all the energy he could command.

Henderson's first and obvious step was to contact Coulondre. The British Ambassador knew from his conversations with Bonnet in July 1939 that the French Foreign Minister would welcome Hitler's proposals for a solution of German-Polish difficulties. Henderson was able to convince Coulondre without much effort that the Hitler plan deserved full support. The French Ambassador had the full details of Hitler's cancelled operational order of August 25th, and he accepted this as indicative that a German-Polish war could be avoided. Coulondre, who was called the Huguenot diplomat because of his staunch Calvinism, presented the argument for the Hitler plan at Paris with great force. Above all, the French Ambassador insisted that strong pressure should be applied at Warsaw to bring a Polish emissary to Berlin on time. On the other hand, he saw no merit in Henderson's suggestion that the Polish Government be advised to send Beck to Berlin, and he did not recommend this at Paris.[57]

Henderson displayed his usual independence by approaching the Poles in Berlin without waiting for instructions from London. He urged Lipski before midnight on August 29th that Poland could and should send a special envoy to Berlin the following day. Lipski naturally informed Beck of this new development without delay, and the Polish Foreign Minister responded shortly after midnight by calling in Kennard. The British Ambassador was poorly equipped to discuss the situation, because he had received virtually no information from Halifax about the German reply to the British note of August 28th. Beck postponed his discussion with Kennard pending the arrival of adequate information from London.

Halifax had merely informed Kennard that Hitler's reply "does not appear to close every door." He might have added that Hitler was trying to open doors rather than to close them, and, above all, he was seeking to open the door slammed by Beck on May 5, 1939. There was a curious air of leisurely detachment in Halifax's reaction to Hitler's important offer. Halifax appeared to be more concerned in conveying his unreserved approval of Kennard's arguments in support of the Polish general mobilization. Halifax made the cynical statement that Great Britain "could not take the responsibility of advising the Polish Government against any action which they consider necessary for their security." This was really carrying the blank check policy to extremes. It obviously included acceptance of the Polish position that negotiations with the Germans also presented a threat to the security of Poland.58

Halifax persisted in adding that the Poles should do everything possible "to avoid advertising" their general mobilization, although Kennard had previously explained that they would advertise it to the greatest possible extent on the following morning. He repeated the time-worn admonition, which had for months been made ridiculous by the conditions in Poland, that the Poles should take care not to provoke the Germans. Halifax made the significant admission to Kennard that he was entirely depending on him for the conduct of British policy in Poland. He complained that Raczynski at London seemed to be out of touch with his Government. He virtually gave Kennard a free hand to conduct British policy at Warsaw as he saw fit. He knew that Kennard would do nothing to encourage the preservation of peace.

Halifax passed on to Kennard the full text of the German reply of August 29th shortly after midnight. He restricted himself to the vague comment that the German reply appeared to be not unpromising. Needless to say, this very restrained favorable comment failed to influence the British Ambassador at Warsaw, who had opposed Henderson's earlier suggestion that Lipski discuss the general situation with Hitler.

Kennard decided to advise Beck to reject Hitler's offer for negotiations. He argued in a subsequent report to Halifax on the morning of Augst 30th that it would "be impossible to induce the Polish Government to send Colonel Beck or any other representative immediately to Berlin to discuss a settlement on the basis proposed by Herr Hitler." He concluded melodramatically that Poland would sooner fight and perish than submit to such humiliation. The fact that Hitler was willing to negotiate in the face of countless provocations from Poland made no impression on Kennard.59

The situation at Warsaw was really quite incredible. Kennard knew that his Government had dishonestly assured Germany on August 28th that Poland was prepared to negotiate seriously with Hitler. Yet, it was unethical of Kennard even under these circumstances to advise Poland not to negotiate. This did not trouble either Halifax or Kennard. Halifax replied to Kennard later on August 30th that the Poles should desist from firing on the German minority, and should make some effort to restrain their reckless radio propaganda, which had been called to his attention at London. He expressed no disapproval of Kennard's decision to urge Beck not to negotiate with Germany.60

Kennard had a decisive advantage over Henderson in the Polish crisis. The British Ambassador at Warsaw had been in perfect step with Halifax's diplomacy since October 1938, whereas Henderson, who had been sent to Berlin by

Chamberlain to carry out the policy of appeasement, was sadly out of step. The situation was not changed by the fact that Henderson was more popular at Berlin than Kennard at Warsaw. Kennard's hatred of the Germans was so irrationally intense that the Poles concluded, as they did about Churchill, that he was somewhat unbalanced. They also did not care for his pedantic and dogmatic manner. Henderson was highly respected at Berlin, where good-humored anecdotes were told about his scrupulously correct manners and impeccable sartorial elegance. Hitler referred to him affectionately in his absence as "the man with the flower," because Henderson always wore a boutonniere. The reserved manner of the British Ambassador prohibited the joviality which had characterized the relations between Hitler and Francois-Poncet, but there was universal agreement among the German diplomats that Henderson was a credit to his craft. Henderson performed his finest work during the hectic days of the Polish crisis, but it was a largely wasted effort because Halifax did not desire the peaceful settlement which was supposed to be the objective of all constructive diplomacy.

Henderson supplied Halifax with voluminous information about his recent conversations with Hitler, and he added many personal touches to his accounts. He confided that on August 28th he had gone to meet Hitler "fortified by half a bottle of champagne." There was no doubt that he wished to make the best possible showing, and he hoped that the champagne would mellow his habitual reserve. He hastened to offer proof to Halifax that his head had remained clear on that occasion. Upon confronting Ribbentrop as well as Hitler, he made certain that the Foreign Minister, with his linguistic accomplishment, received the English original text of the British note, and that Hitler received the German translation. Henderson did not bother to emphasize that he was on a sufficiently informal footing with the German leaders to justify this procedure. A strict regard for formal protocol would have required him to present both copies to the Chief-of-State, and to allow him to make his own disposition of the documents.

Henderson communicated information of an extremely important nature to Halifax on the morning of August 30, 1939. He told Halifax that Birger Dahlerus, who was prepared to fly to England at any time, had been instructed to tell the British leaders that midnight August 30th was not an unconditional deadline for the arrival of a Polish emissary, and that Berlin was not an unconditional location for a German-Polish conference. The Germans were prepared to consider any alternative suggestions. Henderson reminded Halifax that a meeting on the Swedish yacht near the Polish coast remained open as an adequate alternative. He repeated to Halifax the gist of the terms the Germans were about to offer the Poles. They planned to suggest a plebiscite in the northern tip of the Corridor, with the losing party to receive a transit route over the Corridor. Gdynia, which was indisputably Polish, was not to be included in the plebiscite proposition, because the Germans had no desire to deprive Poland of her base on the Baltic coast. Henderson repeated that there would be no reference to East Upper Silesia in the German proposals.[61]

Henderson carefully described his meeting with Lipski on the night of August 29th. He had read to the Polish Ambassador the full text of Hitler's reply to Great Britain before the German note had reached London. The British

Ambassador warned Halifax that Lipski "expressed himself as quite hopeless," and that he was convinced that his Government at the most would permit him "to see Herr Hitler" without allowing him to negotiate. Lipski did not expect the Polish Government to send a special emissary to Berlin. Henderson believed that vigorous British diplomatic steps at Warsaw would modify this recalcitrant Polish attitude. Henderson emphasized that Hitler did not want war, but he would be unable to avoid war unless some last chance was offered to him.[62]

There was complete clarity at London, Paris, and Warsaw by the morning of August 30th about the latest German offer to Poland. The German Chancellor recognized that a diplomatic solution of the German-Polish dispute would produce a favorable atmosphere for an Anglo-German understanding along the lines of his offer to Halifax on August 25, 1939. He had appealed to the British to advise the Poles to accept direct negotiations with Germany. The British had responded by informing Germany on August 28th that Poland was prepared to negotiate. Hitler informed Henderson on the following day that he was preparing tentative proposals for a settlement with Poland, and that he wished the British Government to invite Poland to send a special emissary to Berlin on August 30th. Because of the urgency of the crisis situation existing between August 30th because of the urgency of the crisis situation existing between Germany and Poland. The British received an additional assurance shortly afterward that Germany would accept the arrival of a Polish envoy somewhat later than midnight August 30th, and that Berlin had merely been suggested for negotiations. It would be perfectly satisfactory to negotiate at some other place. The many and definite conciliatory steps taken by the German Government to avoid war with Poland during these days actually left very little to be desired.

The Germans on the early morning of August 30th were completely unaware of the situations at London and Warsaw. They did not realize that the August 28th British assurance of Polish readiness to negotiate was an inexcusable hoax. Halifax had neither requested nor received any indication from Poland that the Poles were willing to negotiate on a serious basis. The Germans did not realize that the Polish authorities at Warsaw on August 29th had decided to declare general mobilization on the following day, and that this step had been expressly approved by Halifax. They did not know that the British Ambassador at Warsaw had responded to the German offer to Poland of August 29, 1939, by advising the Poles not to negotiate with Germany. Indeed, Hitler did not suspect that Halifax was doing everything possible to promote war and nothing to prevent it. The German Chancellor would have abandoned his latest hope for a settlement with Poland much earlier had he been aware of the actual situation. It was completely hopeless to invite the Polish Government to negotiate when the British Government was urging them not to do so. British diplomacy at Warsaw on August 29th and 30th was a dishonorable and mendacious violation of the assurance to Germany in the British note of August 28th. The British Government for several days had fostered the false impression that they favored direct negotiations between Poland and Germany. Their advice to the Poles not to negotiate was an act of braxen duplicity unhappily characteristic of the British diplomatic tradition, which was based on cynical ruthlessness toward friend and foe alike. The excellent opportunity for a peaceful settlement between Germany and Poland was destroyed by Halifax's diplomacy, and the doom of Poland was assured.

Chapter 21

POLISH GENERAL MOBILIZATION
AND GERMAN-POLISH WAR

Hitler Unaware of British Policy in Poland

The German leaders assumed during the last few days of intense crisis before the outbreak of the German-Polish war that Great Britain had exerted pressure at Warsaw for Polish negotiations with Germany. The British Government allowed this impression to persist unchallenged at Berlin. This was inconsistent with the earlier claims of Halifax and Chamberlain in 1939 that they were seeking to avoid war by making their position crystal clear. Halifax was no less guilty, in this case, of failing to make the position of the British Government clear than his kinsman Sir Edward Grey during the last phase of the pre-World War I crisis in 1914. Hitler's attitude during the last days of the 1939 crisis might have been different had he realized that the British Government, despite their assurance to Germany on August 28th, had never seriously advised Poland to negotiate. Halifax left Hitler entirely in the dark about this most important item. Hitler naturally assumed that Poland was defying Great Britain by refusing to negotiate, and that Polish defiance would be construed at London as a breach of the Anglo-Polish alliance. He naturally assumed that Poland had broken her engagements to Great Britain by refusing to negotiate with Germany after having first promised to do so. In reality, the contention in the British note of August 28, 1939, that Poland had assured the British Government of her readiness to negotiate was, as we have seen, a deliberate deception. The iniquity of this deception was afterward compounded when the British Government refused to advise Poland to accept negotiations with Germany.[1]

General Mobilization Construed as Polish Defiance of Halifax

The general mobilization notices were posted throughout Poland by the afternoon of August 30, 1939. The news of this latest Polish challenge to Germany was officially confirmed in a report to Berlin from the German Embassy at

Warsaw. Woermann at the German Foreign Office explained to Hungarian Minister Sztójay on August 30th that the news of the Polish general mobilization was a great blow to the prospects for peace. He reminded the Magyar diplomat that there had been high hopes in recent days for a renewal of negotiations between Poland and Germany which would lead to a diplomatic settlement of the crisis between the two neighboring nations. These hopes were now destroyed. The Polish mobilization move was construed by the officials of the German Foreign Office as a definitive answer to the latest German offer to Poland, although Hitler, Goering, and Ribbentrop continued to hope until the evening of the following day that the Poles would change their minds and agree to send an emissary to Berlin. Poland's own General Kazimierz Sosnkowski, who had formerly been the chief military collaborator of Pilsudski, told allied journalists four years later that it was the Polish general mobilization order which rendered inevitable the German-Polish war. In retrospect, Sosnkowski insisted that Hitler could do nothing further to avert the war after this event.[2]

The Polish press on August 30, 1939, announced the decision for general mobilization, and it carried an official communiqué from the Polish Government motivating this decision. Foreign Minister Beck, who drafted the communiqué, audaciously insisted to the world that Poland had supported all efforts for peace by Allies or neutrals, but that these efforts had produced no reaction from Germany. The Polish Foreign Office on the morning of August 30th had received a report on the latest developments from Lipski, but Beck did not permit the slightest hint that the Polish Government was actually sabotaging the latest German peace effort by announcing general mobilization. The public statement by Beck contained allegations which were exactly the reverse of the actual situation. Beck claimed that Polish policy since August 25, 1939, conformed to the assurance given to President Roosevelt by President Mościcki. In reality, the Polish Government was violating the pledge to the American President by continuing to disapprove of direct negotiations with the Germans. The military motivation for the Polish step sounded somewhat more plausible to informed persons. The Polish military authorities pointed out that German troop moves in West Slovakia, where German troops had been stationed since March 1939, suggested that Germany was preparing a major front on the Polish left flank. It was allegedly necessary for Poland to call up additional troops in order to cover her extended front with Germany. The explanation of this military factor impressed Hitler, and it prompted him to hope that the mobilization order did not mean that Poland would not negotiate with Germany.[3]

The latest Polish reservists to be called to the colors were frequently told by their officers that Poland had presented a three hour ultimatum to Germany on August 29th. The purpose of this entirely fanciful ultimatum was supposedly for Germany to change her policy immediately and to renounce aspirations at Danzig. The recruits were told that Hitler had requested 24 hours to consider this ultimatum, and that the Polish Government had generously granted time to him. This caused the imaginary Polish ultimatum to expire on August 30th instead of August 29th. The recruits were told that their Government might have ordered general mobilization one day earlier, on August 29th, had it not been for Hitler's clever ruse in gaining time for his own preparations. The legend that Poland had postponed her final mobilization measures for one reason or another was extremely convenient. It enabled the Poles to argue later that their poor military showing against Germany resulted exclusively from their devotion to peace, which had prevented their leaders from taking the necessary precautionary military measures in time.[4]

The Polish press on August 31st offered a wide variety of reasons for general mobilization. The argument about the alleged threatening situation in Slovakia received major emphasis, but there was comment about a new crisis at Danzig which supposedly had influenced the decision of the Government. The other factors mentioned were the need to answer German propaganda, recent border incidents, German troop concentrations in the North, and the alleged refusal of Germany to negotiate with Poland.

Birger Dahlerus arrived at London on the morning of August 30th, shortly before Halifax received confirmation from Kennard that Poland was actually carrying out general mobilization. The Swedish envoy explained recent developments at Berlin to Chamberlain and Halifax in painstaking detail. No Government had ever been informed more promptly or fully of events in a foreign capital during a major crisis. Halifax forwarded the full text of the German reply of August 29th to Secretary of State Hull in Washington, D.C., shortly after listening to Dahlerus.[5]

Hitler's Offer of August 30th to Send Proposals to Warsaw

Dahlerus and Goering conversed on the telephone at 12:30 p.m. on August 30th following the conversation of the Swedish envoy with Chamberlain and Halifax. Goering repeated that he was almost certain that Hitler would include the proposition for a plebiscite in the tip of the Corridor in his new proposals to Poland. Dahlerus at the moment was not interested in the details of the tentative German plan. He pointed out that the British were arguing that Hitler was exerting too much pressure on the Poles in seeking to persuade them to consider his negotiation plan. Dahlerus asked Goering if it might not be possible to arrange for Lipski to receive the proposals on August 30th and relay them to Warsaw for further consideration.

Goering personally favored this idea, but he was unable to extend a German commitment without consulting Hitler. It was agreed to resume the telephone conversation after Goering had discussed the situation with the German Chancellor. Goering contacted Dahlerus again at 1:15 p.m. after talking to Hitler. The German Marshal first referred to the German proposals, which were now completed. He assured Dahlerus that they were "fabulous (*fabelhaft*)." He wished to add that there was no intention at Berlin to submit the terms to the Poles for unconditional acceptance, because these proposals were merely intended as a basis for discussion. He told the Swedish envoy that Hitler had decided to reject the suggestion for Lipski to relay the proposals to Warsaw, because this would not permit any indication that Poland was prepared to negotiate. Hitler was willing to permit a special representative from Poland to "fetch" the proposals and carry them to Warsaw. Hitler believed that this concession would meet any British objections about undue pressure without denying the Poles an opportunity to demonstrate their willingness to negotiate for a peaceful solution.

Hitler's thoughtful suggestion was both reasonable and extremely practical, and Goering was pleased with this latest development. He believed that this would remove the last British objection to the specific program for negotiations which had been suggested by Hitler. He was amazed when Dahlerus telephoned at 3:00 p.m. that the British did not like Hitler's new plan, and were insisting that the Germans agree to allow Lipski to go home with the proposals. Hitler's cogent point that the Poles should also display at least some concrete readiness to negotiate was ignored. Goering was incensed. He declared that he would not discuss this question with Hitler again, and he insisted that a Polish representative must come to Berlin. Goering had been quite proud of the fact that Hitler was willing to go so far in sacrificing the German operational plan and in risking a protracted two-front war in the cause of saving the peace. The British refusal to consider this vitally important concession came to Goering as an unexpected and discouraging blow. At one stroke, Berlin's optimism was challenged by new doubts and fears. The news about the Polish general mobilization arrived shortly afterward.[6]

Goering feared that the favorable position of Germany in Europe would be lost by involvement in another senseless war. He had persuaded Hitler to adopt an extraordinarily flexible position toward negotiations with the Poles, and Halifax was aware of this situation. The British Foreign Secretary responded by vaguely suggesting, in instructions to Kennard on the afternoon of August 30th, that Beck should agree in principle to eventual direct negotiations with the Germans, because "no opportunity should be given them for placing the blame for a conflict on Poland." These instructions indicated that Halifax was unwilling to contemplate a peaceful settlement of the crisis, and that he was merely interested in shifting the blame for a war to Germany. It was simple for Kennard to explain to Beck that Halifax wished for a vague platonic statement rather than an actual Polish commitment to negotiate with Germany.[7]

Hitler's Sincerity Conceded by Chamberlain

British Ambassador Henderson at Berlin hoped to forestall a hopeless fiasco by warning the Germans that it might be necessary to wait a little longer for a favorable response to the German negotiation plan. He telephoned Weizsaecker on the morning of August 30th that it was not certain whether or not the British Government could procure a Polish emissary the same day. He attempted to create the impression that everything possible was being done by the British diplomats to prevail on the Poles to negotiate. Henderson was able to inform Ribbentrop at 5:30 p.m. on August 30th that he had received a message for Hitler from Chamberlain. The British Prime Minister wished the German Chancellor to know that the official British reply to the German note of August 29th would reach Berlin before midnight on August 30th. The British Prime Minister recognized that the exchange of views between the German and British Governments during the week since August 23rd indicated that Hitler was genuinely desirous of achieving an Anglo-German understanding. Indeed, this desire on the part of Hitler had been evident to the British leaders for the past six years.[8]

American Ambassador Kennedy reported from London on August 30th that Chamberlain stubbornly refused to concede that Great Britain could advise the Poles to make concessions to Germany. There was no apparent reason why this should be the case, and, in any event, the main point was not whether the Poles should make concessions, but whether or not they should negotiate at all with Germany. The British Ambassador at Warsaw had advised the Poles not to negotiate with Germany. Otherwise there was nothing in European diplomatic experience which suggested that one ally could not advise another to make concessions. The Russians had not hesitated to advise the French to make concessions to Germany during the Second Moroccan Crisis in 1911, and Pilsudski had advised the French not to retaliate when the Germans revived their system of military conscription in March 1935. Chamberlain admitted to Kennedy that it was the Poles, and not the Germans, who were unreasonable. Kennedy informed President Roosevelt: "frankly he (Chamberlain) is more worried about getting the Poles to be reasonable than the Germans." It was especially tragic under these circumstances that the British Prime Minister was unwilling to make any effort to influence the Poles.[9]

Henderson's Peace Arguments Rejected by Halifax

Soviet Foreign Commissar Molotov was informed by Schulenburg on the morning of August 30th that Germany had requested a Polish emissary, and that it was intended to present reasonable proposals at Berlin for a settlement. The Russians feared that the latest diplomatic effort by Hitler might be successful, and that war between Germany and Poland, and with it very favorable Soviet prospects for westward expansion, might be averted. Stalin decided to reverse his earlier policy of assumed indifference toward the situation in Poland. The Tass news agency, the entire Russian press, and the Russian radio suddenly announced on the afternoon of August 30th that the Soviet Union was massing her armed forces along the Polish frontier. The Russian move was an obvious effort to encourage the Germans to take a stronger line with the Poles. It was announced before word of the general mobilization in Poland was received in Moscow. The Russians also promised to send a military mission, consisting of three Red Army officers and their secretaries, to Berlin on the morning of August 31st. The Germans had earlier waited in vain for some indication about the arrival of the promised military team. The Russian mission, despite the latest Soviet promise, did not actually arrive at Berlin before the outbreak of the German-Polish war.[10]

Henderson made a number of futile attempts on August 30th to persuade Halifax that a Polish emissary should be sent to Berlin. He reminded Halifax that a Polish diplomat could fly to Berlin from Warsaw in 1½ hours. The British Foreign Secretary refrained from comment, but he informed Henderson that Dahlerus would fly from London to Berlin on the evening of August 30th. He added that the presistent Swede intended to arrive at the British Embassy before 10:30 p.m. with information about the British response to Hitler's note of the previous day. Halifax carefully avoided giving any impression that the message would contain hopeful news.[11]

Henderson responsed by warning Halifax that outrages against the Germans in Poland were rapidly increasing in number, and that they constituted the most dangerous factor in the existing precarious situation. The British Ambassador suggested that Pope Pius XII would be willing to employ special nuncios in an effort to protect the minority by introducing at least some element of neutral intercession on their behalf. Halifax ignored this suggestion, but he informed Kennard at Warsaw that Great Britain wished to "deprive" Hitler of the excuse of outrages against the German minority as a "pretext" for employing force against Poland. Halifax added that the Polish leader should be urged to maintain "discipline." This was wasted effort, because Kennard was manifestly unwilling to exert pressure at Warsaw for more decent treatment of the Germans.

Henderson knew that Halifax was not responding effectively to his warnings about the consequences of Polish misconduct against the Germans. The British Ambassador decided to employ an elaborate argument in an effort to influence Halifax. He argued that Hitler's power thrived on the willingness of the outside world to tolerate and ignore the injustices inflicted on the Germans. He wished Halifax to recognize that Hitler's position in Germany was being strengthened because of the failure to protect the German minority in Poland. He claimed that it would be in the interest of Great Britain to intervene energetically on behalf of the minority, and to promote the settlement of the Corridor problem and the return of Danzig to Germany. Henderson suspected that Halifax sympathized with the suggestion of President Roosevelt "to get the German army and nation to revolt against the intolerable government of Herr Hitler." Henderson advised Halifax that ideological warfare against Hitler would always remain ineffective unless Great Britain was at last willing to demonstrate that she favored fair and reasonable conditions for the German people.

Henderson hoped to influence Halifax by reassuring him that he entertained no animosity toward Poland. He sought to excuse the intransigence of the Poles, which had been much in evidence since the first Polish ultimatum to Czechoslovakia in October 1938. The British Ambassador suggested that perhaps the Poles had rejected the German proposals in March 1939 because they had been alarmed by the pro-German course of Slovakia or the German success at Memel, rather than because they failed to recognize the intrinsic merit of the German offer. Henderson hoped to be absolved from the possible charge that he was one-sided in his approach, or failed to sympathize with the Poles. His various arguments failed to produce any effect, because Halifax was not interested in the attitude of Henderson toward Poland, and he was definitely hostile toward the project of restricting his campaign against Germany to mere ideological warfare. Halifax wished to discredit Hitler by forcing him to shed German blood in a disastrous war which would end in the defeat and ruination of Germany. Halifax believed that the sole effective method of opposing Hitler was to kill as many Germans as possible. He had employed clever propaganda to convert the majority of his countrymen to the same opinion.[12]

A Peaceful Settlement Favored in France

The situation in France was entirely different. The French press on August 30, 1939, revealed a far greater interest in preserving peace than in killing Germans. Marcel Pays, the editor of *L'Escelsior*, pointed out that there would be a good chance for an agreement between Germany and Poland if the British could be prevailed upon to secure the consent of Poland to negotiations. Lucien Bourgues complained in *Le Petit Parisien* that the issue of peace or war was in doubt because the British were not going far enough in urging a peaceful settlement. *Le Jour* and *L'Echo de Paris* agreed that no chance for peace should be missed, no extended hand should be rejected, and no effort should be made to humiliate Germany. Yves Morvan reported for *Le Journal* from London that Hitler had been moderate and reasonable in his recent talks with the British and French envoys at Berlin. *Le Figaro* insisted that Hitler's hesitation during the past six days was "an example of reason" rather than mere "caution, fear, or weakness." Edith Bricon of *La République* deplored the fatalism about war in England and Poland, and she insisted upon the need to repeat to everyone concerned that possibilities for a peaceful solution of the German-Polish problem still existed. Rene Gounin reminded the readers of *La Justice* that France was as ready as ever to negotiate with Germany. Genevieve Tabouis, who had advocated intransigence or even war in many previous crises, predicted that Mussolini would resolve the current crisis by presenting a successful conference plan at the last minute.[13]

French Foreign Minister Bonnet was shocked to learn that the Poles had proceeded to order general mobilization despite his efforts to restrain them. He continued to insist that the Poles send an envoy to Berlin. He requested Halifax to consider a plan to reduce tension by suggesting the withdrawal of German and Polish troops from the positions which both sides were occupying at the frontier. Bonnet failed to enlist the support of Halifax for this proposition, and he discovered that his various measures to influence the Poles were not effective without British support. He could not fail to note the contrast between his own efforts to improve the situation, and the almost complete inaction of Halifax.[14]

French Ambassador Coulondre made a further effort at Berlin on August 30th to impress Lipski with the seriousness of the situation. The French diplomat informed his Polish colleague of the full details about the narrow margin by which Hitler had succeeded in cancelling German military operations against Poland on August 25th and 26th. He insisted to Lipski that there was great internal opposition in Germany to war against France and Great Britain, and that a small amount of conciliation from the Polish side might make it possible to exploit this situation in order to avoid war. Coulondre suggested that the situation might still be saved if Lipski, in his capacity as Ambassador, would request the German proposals for relay to Warsaw. The French diplomat admitted that the Germans were insisting on a special Polish envoy, but he argued that the internal opposition to war was so great that Hitler might well decide to make the best of the situation, and to give the proposals to Lipski. Coulondre added that there would be no hope at all unless something was done from the Polish side in response to Hitler's offer. The foreign diplomats at Berlin were in agreement that there was tremendous opposition to war in Germany. American Chargé d'Affaires Alexander C. Kirk flatly asserted in a report to President Roosevelt at 1:00 p.m. on the following day that the German people, like the American people, were opposed to war.[15]

The Unfavorable British Note of August 30th

Halifax sent fateful instructions to Henderson at 6:50 p.m. on August 30, 1939, which virtually destroyed the last chance of avoiding a German-Polish war. These instructions contained the British reply to the German note of August 29th. The British leaders categorically rejected Hitler's proposal that they advise the Poles to send a representative to Berlin for direct German-Polish negotiations. Halifax, who had not consulted Warsaw in this important matter, condemned the German proposal, "which is wholly unreasonable." It was the unpleasant duty of Henderson to tell Hitler, when the hour of midnight struck, that Great Britain flatly refused to advise the Polish Government to comply with the German plan. Lipski later recalled that the Polish diplomats correctly concluded after this British decision that Kennard at Warsaw occupied a far stronger position in influencing British policy than did Henderson at Berlin.[16]

Halifax advised Kennard in the vaguest of terms that the Poles should be encouraged to contemplate eventual negotiations with the Germans. He explicitly informed him that Great Britain would never request Beck to formulate actual proposals for an agreement with the Germans. The British had applied pressure on the Poles to accept the penetration of Poland by Soviet troops ten days earlier, but they refused to exert pressure on Poland to resume direct negotiations with Germany. This appears especially grotesque when one recalls that the Poles considered the Soviet Union to be their principal enemy, and that Halifax had taken the lead in assuring Germany that Poland was prepared to resume negotiations.

Goering had sent Dahlerus to London on August 30th to explain carefully point by point Hitler's reply of August 29th. The German Marshal, after the shock produced by his unsatisfactory telephone conversation with London at 3:00 p.m., received additional advance information that the British response of August 30th would be unfavorable. Dahlerus reported on the early evening of August 30th, after discussing the situation with the British leaders, that "it was obvious that by that time the British Government had become highly mistrustful, and rather inclined to assume that whatever efforts they might make, nothing would now prevent Hitler from declaring war on Poland." It was difficult to understand their mistrust, because they had received an uninterrupted series of encouraging statements about Hitler's attitude from Henderson and Dahlerus. It was perfectly obvious from the German note of August 29th that Hitler preferred a peaceful settlement with Poland rather than war. The British leaders, in taking this position with Dahlerus, were claiming that they should sit with their hands in their laps and do nothing. There was not the slightest justification for this attitude. They quickly recovered their capacity for action when it became a question of extending a local German-Polish war into a general European war. It appeared that British diplomacy in 1939 was exclusively preoccupied with preparing and promoting war, and that it immediately ceased to function when confronted with the task of protecting the peace.[17]

Halifax had considered and rejected an alternative proposition prior to despatching his unpromising instructions to Henderson at 6:50 p.m. on August 30th. The plan which Halifax rejected consisted of advice to the Germans to forward their proposals to the German Embassy at Warsaw in order to seek contact for negotiations at that point. Halifax concluded that this suggestion would be too great a concession to the Germans. He merely instructed Henderson to inform Hitler that Warsaw was exercising restraint and that Poland was calm. Henderson knew only too well that this assertion reflected unrealistic reports from Kennard rather than information from reliable neutral sources, but it was his duty to present it to Hitler as the official attitude of His Britannic Majesty's Government.

Halifax professed to fear that Hitler's recent proposals for an Anglo-German understanding would have unfavorable repercussions for Great Britain. He wired Henderson that an Anglo-German alliance was not a feasible subject for practical politics, and he warned him not to mention it as a remote possibility. Halifax was aware of the earlier remark Henderson had made to Hitler about the need for patience in the effort to win Great Britain for an alliance, and he knew that his latest instructions denying the remote possibility of such an alliance would be a distinct disappointment to the British Ambassador. Halifax explained that reference to a possible alliance might "create the worst possible impression in the United States and all friendly countries." It was evident that Halifax was no longer including Germany among the friendly countries, although he knew that there was no war between Germany and Poland, and that Hitler was seeking an understanding with Great Britain. Halifax merely informed Henderson that in principle the British were willing to conclude ordinary treaties with Germany, and that this would remain the attitude of the British Government as long as there was no actual Anglo-German war.

The British Embassy in Berlin was inundated at this time by Germans of all descriptions and from all walks of life. Henderson was swamped with assurances that the German people did not want war. The British Ambassador was told that there was fear and confusion in German military circles at the prospect of a general war. Other people assured him that they would continue to sympathize with Great Britain no matter what happened as a result of the present British stand. These people did not suspect that the man to whom they were confessing their anxiety no longer had the slightest influence over British policy. Henderson would have helped them by negotiating an understanding with Germany had he been in a position to do so, but he had realized for several days that he was powerless.[18]

No one in the position of the British Ambassador could be blamed for desisting from further efforts to prevent war, but Henderson never stopped trying. It is this fact, combined with his unquestionable British patriotism and his determination to stand by his own country through thick and thin, regardless of the dreadful blunders of the British leaders, that make his mission to Berlin a study in courage. He tried every possible tactic to persuade Chamberlain to express his own views, and to encourage the British Prime Minister to resume leadership at the British Foreign Office before it was too late. He made a special effort to convince the British leaders that he had always been firm with Hitler, and he recalled that he had bombarded Hitler with arguments and answers in the conversation of August 28th, which had apparently turned out very favorably for Great Britain.

Halifax continued to advise Chamberlain to ignore the complaints of Henderson and others about the attitude and policies of Poland. He received a very useful letter from Count Raczynski on August 30th. The Polish Government in this letter solemnly swore that no persecution of the German minority was taking place in Poland. The American journalist, W.L. White, later recalled that there was no doubt among well-informed persons by this time that horrible atrocities were being inficted every day on the Germans of Poland. The pledge from Raczynski had about as much validity as the civil liberties guaranteed by the 1936 constitution of the Soviet Union.[19]

It was clever of Halifax to claim that further intimate Anglo-German conversations would displease President Roosevelt. Chamberlain had been severely criticized for failing to respond favorably to an impractical proposal from Roosevelt, in January 1938, for a grandiose diplomatic conference, which would not only have failed to commit the United States to the British imperialistic program, but undoubtedly would have weakened the effort of Chamberlain to increase British influence in Italy. Lord Lothian had succeeded Sir Ronald Lindsay as British Ambassador to the United States. Lothian, like Henderson at Berlin, favored a peaceful understanding with Germany, but he was a disciplined diplomat who subordinated his own personal views to the requirements of Halifax's war policy. The new British Ambassador was destined to play a more active role behind the scenes of American politics than any previous British diplomat. Lothian confirmed Lindsay's judgment that there was "nothing neutral" about Roosevelt's attitude. The American President insisted that "the most serious danger from the standpoint of American public opinion would be if it formed the conclusion that Herr Hitler was entangling the British Government in negotiations leading to pressure on Poland by England and France to abandon vital interests." It was obvious to Lothian that Roosevelt wanted war in Europe.[20]

The American President knew that a diplomatic settlement of the European crisis would extinguish his own plans for American military aggression in Europe. Lord Lothian assured Halifax that the partisanship of Roosevelt extended to the minute details. Roosevelt intended to urge the belligerents at the outbreak of the expected war not to bombard civilians, because he hoped in this way to protect Warsaw, one of the Allied capitals. Lothian knew that Roosevelt would never object to a later effort by Great Britain to massacre the civilian population of Germany by means of mass bombing attacks. Roosevelt confided to Lothian that his primary objective at the moment was to evade American neutrality legislation after the outbreak of war. He was intent on renewing the struggle in the American Congress to remove the legal embargo on war material. He promised that he would refuse to admit from the very start of hostilities that aluminum sheets for airplanes were "aeroplane parts" or that airplane engine blocks had anything to do with airplanes.

Lothian confirmed the report of his predecessor that Roosevelt was delighted at the prospect of a new World War. This warlike attitude of Roosevelt was exploited by Halifax in adducing artificial arguments for closing the door on further negotiations with Hitler. There was actually no reason to fear that President Roosevelt would be in a position to cause trouble for Great Britain in the event of a negotiated settlement in Europe. The American President did not have the support of Congress or public opinion for his aggressive foreign policy, and he was nearing the end of his final presidential term, final according to the sacrosanct political tradition established by George Washington and Thomas Jefferson. It was obvious that he would need a crisis of the greatest dimensions, such as a big war in Europe to campaign successfully for further terms of office. It would have been easy for the British Government to improve relations with a more conciliatory successor had war been averted and had Roosevelt been defeated in the American election of 1940.[21]

The Absence of Trade Rivalry as a Factor for War

Halifax hoped that the British reply to Germany on August 30, 1939, would end the current negotiations for an Anglo-German agreement and for a diplomatic settlement of the Polish dispute. Halifax was clearly intent upon closing the door, because he believed that the British balance of power policy required the destruction of Germany. The issue was not confused as it had been in 1914 by the further consideration that the expansion of German trade was a threat to the British economy, although the British undoubtedly did fear that the example of the successful social and domestic economic policies of Germany would create discontent among their own underprivileged masses. This was no different from previous concern about the impact of the American standard of living on the British masses. The German successes at home were achieved despite the fact that there was a very serious decline in German foreign trade during 1938 and 1939.

German trade with Italy declined sharply in 1938 because of a deliberate attempt by the Italian Government to reduce imports from Germany. German exports to Italy were 35 million RM (Reichsmarks) short of expectations, although 32,000 Italian agricultural workers and 20,000 Italian industrial workers found employment in Germany during this period. The combined exports of Austria and the rest of Germany to Hungary were 20 million RM less in 1938 than in 1937. Germany was unable to attain the trade level with Spain in 1938 and 1939 which she had enjoyed before the Spanish Civil War in 1936. German trade with Great Britain and India declined rapidly in 1938 and early 1939. Trade with the United States was made difficult by an unfavorable balance and by annual German payments on public and private loans from the Weimar period, although interest payments on the Dawes loan were reduced from 7 to 5% and on the Young loan from 5½ to 4½%. Total German exports to the United States in 1938 were only 150 million RM, and German trade with Latin America declined by 4% during the same year. German trade with Switzerland, a nation of four million people, was greater than with the entire United States, but German trade with the Swiss declined in 1938. French importation of German coal was sharply reduced in 1938, although Germany continued to import the same amount of French iron ore, despite the burden on German currency reserves. German trade with Belgium was about twice as great as with France, but the volume of the Belgian trade also declined in the latter part of 1938. Holland took about 8.3% of total German exports in 1938, but increasing Dutch protectionism produced a decline in trade toward the end of the year.

Great Britain was the principal trading partner of both Denmark and Norway, and there was a slight decline in the German share of Scandinavian trade in 1938. The Germans gained in trade with Finland, where the British also enjoyed the first place, but they were subjected to increasing pressure from British and American competition in Sweden. The Germans in 1938 managed to maintain their earlier level of trade with Turkey and Iran, but there was a decline of German trade with Japan. The total German trade in 1938 declined 10% from the 1937 level. There was also a major reduction of total world trade, caused primarily by the decline in American trade and production following the American recession of 1937, but British trade gained substantially at the expense of German trade in the world markets. The German economists were not seriously worried by this development because of the continuing expansion of the rich German internal market during the same period. Nevertheless, it was impossible for the British to claim with any honesty that German trade competition was forcing them out of the markets of the world.[22]

The German trade deficit with Italy and Hungary increased in 1939. German trade with the Balkan area remained roughly stationary, although there was an increase in German-Rumanian trade after the conclusion of the March 1939 trade pact. This resulted partly from the fact that Germany purchased Rumanian wheat above the world market price. German exports to the United States were subjected to a new 25% tariff penalty after April 23, 1939, on the ground that they were subsidized, which they had to be to meet previous tariff penalties. British and American competition against Germany in Latin America was especially effective, and German trade with the area declined an additional 30% during the early months of 1939. German efforts to negotiate improved trading agreements with Great Britain and France were rejected by the latter countries in March 1939. German exports to France had declined 32% below the 1938 level by April 1, 1939, and this trend continued despite the French economic boom which began in November 1938. The Dutch Government on March 1, 1939, increased tariff duties on German imports by more than 50%. The level of trade with Scandinavia remained roughly stationary in 1939, with a light increase of trade with Sweden and a decline in the Finnish trade. German imports from Poland increased throughout this period, but exports to Poland declined. There was also a major decline in German trade with Egypt, and a continuing decline of trade with Japan.

The Poles on April 15, 1939, announced that Polish agricultural laborers would not be permitted to go to Germany for the harvest, although 70,000 Polish migrant workers had helped to bring in the German sugar beets and potatoes in 1938. The continuing decline of German foreign trade convinced the German economists that it was necessary to reduce the importation of foreign raw materials to Germany. They were not particularly worried by this development because the exploitation of previously untapped natural resources within Germany, and the production of German factories for substitute raw materials, made it possible at home to provide for many of the raw material needs which had previously been met from abroad. The principal worry of the Germans was the domestic labor shortage. The Germans had planned to expand the export of German domestic sugar in 1939, but this scheme was frustrated by the increasing consumer demand on the home market.

The German economists noted that the British share of total world trade continued to increase in 1939. They knew that there was no basis for British resentment of German trade competition in 1938 and 1939, and they had made it clear at London before March 1939 that Germany was prepared to discuss compromise agreements on questions pertaining to currency and international financial practices. It was obvious, therefore, in 1939, in sharp contrast to 1914, that economic factors were not an important consideration in explaining British hostility toward Germany.[23]

The Tentative German Marienwerder Proposals

Hitler placed high hopes in the news that the British Government intended to reply to his note of the previous day, before midnight on August 30th. He had ordered the German military commanders to be prepared for possible operations against Poland by dawn on August 31st, but he declined to issue a new order for actual military operations against Poland. Hitler explained to General Walther von Brauchitsch and General Wilhelm Keitel, at the new Chancellery, on the evening of August 30th, that under no circumstances would he permit operations against the Poles before September 1st, the final deadline for military action under the "Operation White" plan. He expressed the hope that a Polish emissary would be sent to Berlin, and that there would be no need at all to go to war against the Poles.[24]

Henderson was received by Ribbentrop at midnight on August 30th. The fatal British note which Ribbentrop read at once began as follows: "His Majesty's Government repeat that they reciprocate the German Government's desire for improved relations, but it will be recognized that they could not sacrifice the interests of other friends in order to obtain that improvement." The British note displayed no interest whatever in persuading the Poles to negotiate with Germany. The German Foreign Minister studied the British reply with dismay. He informed Henderson after reading the text that the German Government had prepared proposals for a diplomatic settlement with Poland, but that there could be no basis for these proposals without the presence of a Polish emissary at Berlin. Germany had received no indication from either Great Britain or Poland that the leaders at Warsaw intended to negotiate, although Hitler had requested the Poles to send an emissary to Berlin on August 30th. Ribbentrop repeated that this suggestion was not an ultimatum, and that its urgency had been dictated by the prevailing circumstances.

The German Foreign Minister proceeded to read slowly and clearly the sixteen points of the German proposals to Poland, and to explain each one of them in detail. The fallacy of the wartime legend about proposals read

THE FORCED WAR

indistinctly at top speed was exposed after 1945. The German points were comprehensive and formulated with great care. They called for the return of Danzig to the Reich on the basis of self-determination, and for a plebiscite to be held in the Corridor region north of a line running westward from Marien-werder in East Prussia to Schoenlanke in Pomerania. The Germans suggested a plebiscite in this area after an interim of twelve months following the hoped-for agreement with Poland. Option would be extended to all Germans, Cassubians, and Poles who had been living in the area on January 1, 1918, or who had been born there before that time. The proposals derived their name from Marienwerder, the eastern point on the suggested plebiscite line.

The Cassubians were a West Slavic people who felt proudly independent of the Poles. They were a remnant from the old Slavic tribes who had occupied the territory between the Poles and the Baltic Sea during the centuries following the westward migrations of the early German tribes. They were mainly farmers, and they were divided into seventy-six small dialect groups. Their proverb during the period of Polish rule, that even the rain was better in German days, is eloquent testimony of their individuality. The Cassubians in the proposed plebiscite region were far less numerous in 1918 than the Germans or the Poles, but they could be counted upon to swell the German vote in any plebiscite.[25]

The plebiscite region in the interim was to be occupied by Russian, British, French, and Italian troops. All taxes raised in the area during this period would be divided between local needs and support for the international occupation. If the Germans lost the plebiscite, which was to be decided by a simple majority, they would be granted an extra-territorial connection with East Prussia along the lines of their October 1938 proposal. This would entail an extra-territorial corridor over the Corridor 5/8 of a mile in width. The holding of this plebiscite would rectify the injustice of the Treaty of Versailles in permitting the transfer of this territory to Poland in the first place without consulting the local inhabitants.

If the Poles lost the plebiscite, they would be granted an identical connection with Gdynia. The hinterland of Gdynia would be decided by an international commission, and it would be excluded from the plebiscite area as inalienable Polish territory. The Germans requested the demilitarization, except for naval craft, of Danzig, Gdynia, and the Hela peninsula. They requested a mutual Polish-German agreement to protect the rights of the respective minorities. An international tribunal would be established to guarantee the efficacy of this scheme. It would have final jurisdiction in the consideration of appeals. The sixteenth point suggested that Poland and Germany should examine additional means of securing friendly cooperation. The total extent of the area involved in the German proposals, including the Free City of Danzig and the plebiscite zone, amounted to only one-tenth of the region that Germany had surrendered in the East to Poland and the League of Nations after World War I.[26]

Ribbentrop read the proposals to Henderson in German, because the British Ambassador had earlier requested that the German Foreign Minister speak German rather than English in their various discussions. The excellent German interpreter, Dr. Paul Schmidt, was present to clear up possible linguistic misunderstandings. Schmidt was startled when Henderson asked if he might be permitted to have a copy of the proposals, after Ribbentrop had read the points and had completed his commentary. The interpreter had assumed that the text would be presented to Henderson as a matter of course. He was forgetting that the proposals were addressed to the Poles, and that the British were refusing to cooperate in establishing contact between Germany and Poland. Henderson was quite correct in placing a formal request for the text.

Schmidt noted to his further surprise that Ribbentrop was acutely embarrassed. The German Foreign Minister replied with a faint smile, "No, I can't give you these proposals." Henderson repeated his request and received the same answer. Ribbentrop had been instructed by Hitler to give the proposals to Henderson if the British offered some indication that the Poles would negotiate, but there had been no such indication. The point was a technical one, but Ribbentrop did not wish to displease Hitler by exceeding his instructions in this important matter. Schmidt hoped that Henderson would ask him to repeat the proposals in English translation. It would have been simple to proceed from this point to draft an English copy of the terms. He tried to catch the attention of the British Ambassador without actively intervening in the discussion. This was a ticklish business, and Schmidt was unsuccessful. He realized that it would be a gross violation of his position as interpreter were he to interrupt the two diplomats by making some remark. Henderson was unable to divine the purpose of the subtle facial gestures made by the interpreter.[27]

It was virtually impossible for Henderson to comprehend all the points of the detailed German plan from one reading and commentary. This was not because the British diplomat was deficient in the German language. The German plan was a long one, and there had been a heated discussion. Henderson wondered if Ribbentrop would consider the possibility that some of the violence against the Germans in Poland had actually resulted from German acts of espionage or even sabotage. Ribbentrop had deplored this unnecessary quibbling, and he had earnestly exclaimed that the situation was "damnably serious." Henderson had the temerity to retort excitedly that such language was not fitting for a statesman on such a serious occasion. Ribbentrop in turn was far from pleased by this puritanical remark. The situation was tragic, because both diplomats sincerely desired a diplomatic settlement, and they were equally frustrated by the inexplicably negative British reply to the German note of August 29th.

Schmidt was briefly alarmed that Ribbentrop might reject the puritanical comment of the British Ambassador about language by forcibly ejecting him from the room. Schmidt had never encountered any acts of violence during his long association with Ribbentrop, and his momentary sensation of fear indicates the pitch of excitement which prevailed furing this conference. Schmidt realized that Henderson was more nervous and ill at ease than he had ever seen him before. It was not surprising that the conference between the two men ended on an unsatisfactory note.[28]

Goering was much alarmed by the outcome of this conference, and he obtained immediate permission from Hitler for Henderson to receive the full text of the German proposals. Dahlerus slowly read the text over the telephone to Ogilvie-Forbes at the British Embassy shortly after 1:00 a.m. on August 31st. Henderson hastened to visit Lipski. He urged the Polish Ambassador to request the German Government to give him the proposals for relay to Warsaw. Lipski pointed out that he was not in favor at Warsaw, and that he had no instructions from Beck to do this. He flatly refused to exercise an independent initiative, which, without doubt, would have brought him into a Polish concentration camp when he returned to Warsaw.[29]

Henderson wired Halifax at 9:15 a.m. on August 31st that he had received information from the best possible authority that if nothing happened within the next few hours, Germany would declare war against Poland. This desperate warning was followed by a telegram from Kennard, who expressed his satisfaction that Great Britain had refused to exert pressure at Warsaw and had entered into no commitments with Germany. Beck had announced that he would consult the Polish Government to discover if, in their opinion, there was any point at all in merely agreeing in principle to direct negotiations with the Germans. The Poles, were they to make this gesture, would merely reiterate the statement made by President Mościcki in his reply to President Roosevelt on August 25, 1939. Events had amply indicated that this statement was devoid of any real meaning. Beck advised Kennard that he would be prepared to make some sort of statement to the British Government by noon on August 31st. Kennard assured Halifax that Beck would do nothing to reach an understanding with the Germans.[30]

Dahlerus accompanied Henderson and Ogilvie-Forbes to the Polish Embassy in Berlin at 10:00 a.m. on August 31st. Dahlerus carried his copy of the German proposals, and he read them to Lipski in German. The Swedish engineer received the impression that the Polish Ambassador did not grasp their import, and he left the room to dictate a copy of the note to a Polish secretary. Henderson in the meantime telephoned Weizsaecker at the German Foreign Office that he was advising the Polish Ambassador to negotiate with Germany, and he called this his personal *démarche* at Warsaw. He proceeded to explain to Lipski that the German proposals offered an excellent basis for a settlement between Germany and Poland. He added that it might still be possible to save the situation if Lipski would agree to receive them.[31]

The Polish diplomat by this time was in despair. He had ceased to have any influence in Warsaw since Ribbentrop had convinced him in March 1939 that his Government should negotiate on the basis of the October 1938 proposals. He had not been able to persuade Beck to withdraw him from Berlin despite months of effort to arrange his own recall. Finally, Lipski exclaimed to Henderson in great agitation that he "had no reason to negotiate with the German Government. If it came to war between Poland and Germany, he knew—since he had lived 5½ years in Germany—that a revolution would break out in Germany, and that they would march on Berlin." Henderson shook his head sadly. He knew that there was no longer any point in discussing the current situation with the Polish Ambassador.[32]

Attolico called on Weizsaecker at 11:30 a.m. on August 31st to deliver a message to the German leaders from Mussolini. The Italian Government was advising London the same morning that Poland should demonstrate her good will by agreeing to permit Danzig to return to Germany. The Italian leader believed that the remainder of the problem could be solved through bilateral negotiations between Poland and Germany. Mussolini, who was not adequately informed about the existing situation, had received the impression from London that Poland had agreed to negotiations. He was soon informed by Mackensen that conditions were entirely different that he had supposed. The Marienwerder proposals were sent to Mackensen in Rome at 10:53 a.m. on August 31st, shortly before the visit of Attolico at the German Foreign Office. Mussolini was impressed with the German plan for a settlement, and he instructed Attolico to advise the German leaders to receive Lipski as a last means of establishing contact. Ribbentrop and Attolico discussed the message on the afternoon of August 31st. The German Foreign Minister assured Attolico that the German leaders were as eager to receive the Polish Ambassador on August 31st as they had been on the previous day.[33]

Kennard informed Halifax on the afternoon of August 31st that Beck had formally expressed his gratitude for the British decision not to respond in any way to the German proposals. French Foreign Minister Bonnet found the dilatory tactics of the Poles unjustifiable and inexplicable. He insisted to Halifax that a joint step should be taken by Great Britain and France to demand that the Poles do something to help save the peace of Europe. The British Foreign Secretary had no desire to save European peace, but he was worried about the French attitude. He calculated that he could make a gesture toward cooperating with the French without running any great risk that the Poles would do something favorable. He instructed Kennard to join Noël in requesting that the Poles notify the Germans of their willingness to accept direct negotiations. Kennard and Noël accordingly called on Beck in the early afternnon of August 31st and requested that Lipski be authorized to receive the German proposals officially and to relay them to Warsaw for consideration. Kennard was pleased to note that Beck replied evasively that he was not prepared to respond to this request.[34]

Beck had actually dispatched instructions to Lipski shortly before noon to accept no proposals and to enter into no negotiations with the German Government. This telegram had been intercepted and immediately decoded by Goering's special investigation office. Goering realized at once that the situation was hopeless unless something could be done to change the Polish attitude. He wished the British to know about the Beck telegram because he believed that they might respond by exerting pressure at Warsaw. Goering willingly gave away the fact that Germany possessed Poland's diplomatic code when he showed the text of this Polish telegram to Dahlerus. The Swedish engineer was shocked by the intransigence of Beck, and he noted that the Germans in turn were extremely agitated by Beck's communication to Lipski.[35]

Hitler's Order for Operations in Poland on September 1st

The German response to the Polish refusal to negotiate was swift and decisive. Hitler, despite his many worries about the future, could act with a clear conscience. He had offered to negotiate a moderate settlement with the Poles despite months of Polish provocations and savage persecution of the Germans in Poland. It was impossible to deny that he had turned the other cheek to Poland. The Polish refusal to discuss a settlement with Germany on any terms was insulting. The offer to negotiate was actually an offer for an armistice, because there had been no real peace between the two countries for many months. Hitler had waited as long as possible without jeopardizing permanently the German operational plan, but he had told his Generals that he would continue to wait if there was at least some favorable gesture from Poland. There was no point in sacrificing the plan when it became evident that a negotiated settlement was clearly impossible without the employment of military sanctions to chastise the Poles.

Hitler did not desire war with Poland, but it was impossible for one nation to keep the peace by means of her own efforts alone. He issued the final attack order at forty minutes past noon, on August 31st. The operations could not conceivably be cancelled again later than 9:30 p.m. on the same day, because the beginning of operations was set for dawn on September 1st. Hitler introduced his order with the following statement: "Now that all the political possibilities of disposing by peaceful means of a situation on the Eastern Frontier which is intolerable for Germany are exhausted, I have determined on a solution by force." Hitler was deeply concerned about the attitude of the Western Powers. He hoped that Polish intransigence would prompt them to reconsider their own policies, but it was impossible to assume that this would actually be the case. He advised the military men: "It is important that the responsibility for the opening of hostilities (in the West) should rest unequivocally with England and France. At first purely local action should be taken against insignificant frontier violations. The neutrality assured by us to Holland, Belgium, Luxemburg, and Switzerland should be scrupulously observed." Hitler added, "if England and France open hostilities against Germany, the task of those sections of the Armed Forces which are operating in the West is to uphold . . . those conditions necessary for the successful conclusion of operations against Poland."[36]

Beck's Argument with Pope Pius XII

Beck was not disturbed by the Anglo-French *démarche* on August 31st. He recognized that the British were participating in the French step as a mere matter of form. He was experiencing formidable difficulties with Papal Nuncio Cortesi in Warsaw. Poland and her people were staunchly Catholic, and the Poles had long enjoyed special favor at the Vatican. Pope Pius XII was intent upon saving the Polish people from the fatal policies of their leaders. The Pope had been elected by the College of Cardinals in March 1939 primarily because of his great diplomatic experience, and because it was hoped that he could exert a major influence for peace in European diplomatic relations. The Pope had been stationed as a Vatican diplomatic representative in Munich at the time of the Communist atrocities and Communist dictatorship there in 1919. He feared with good reason that any new European war would lead to the growth of Communism throughout Europe, and he had not the slightest doubt that Poland would be defeated in a war against Germany.[37]

The Pope had launched a major peace effort in May 1939, and he had rejected with indignation an appeal from the Archbishop of Canterbury to earn the alleged gratitude of the Anglican, Protestant, and Greek Orthodox Christians by condemning the policies of Hitler. Instead, the Pope ostentatiously welcomed the victory of General Franco in Spain in May 1939. The Pope recognized as early as May 1939 that Poland was the primary threat to peace, because the British could not attack Germany unless the Poles were willing to serve as a pawn. Beck at that time flatly rejected the tentative proposal of the Pope for an international conference by declaring that "Poland could not accept as binding for her the opinion of other powers regarding the questions which had arisen between Poland and Germany."[38]

The Pope persuaded Admiral Nicholas Horthy, the Protestant Regent of Hungary, to deliver a speech on June 14, 1939, urging that the Powers accept papal good offices in settling the German-Polish dispute. This maneuver was aimed primarily at Poland, because of the intimate relations between Poland and Hungary. Pius XII appealed to the world on August 24, 1939, not to go to war over Danzig. He requested the envoys of Great Britain, France, Italy, Poland, and Germany to appear for an audience at the Vatican Palace on August 31, 1939. Dr. Kazimierz Papee, the Polish envoy at the Vatican, was unable to assure the Pope that Poland would negotiate with Germany. The Pope had feared that this would be the case. He responded by instructing Cortesi in Warsaw to urge Beck to accept negotiations with the Germans on the basis of the Marienwerder proposals, with which the Pope already was familiar. A furious scene followed between Beck and Cortesi, which surpassed the verbal duel between Ribbentrop and Henderson on the previous night. Beck angrily charged that the papal nuncio was working for the Germans. He complained that Pope Pius XII was ordering him to surrender to Germany. Cortesi was unable to calm the excited Polish diplomat. Beck later recalled that no single development during the final phase of the crisis caused him so much irritation as the persistent but unsuccessful effort of Pope Pius XII to persuade him to negotiate with the Germans and to accept the Marienwerder proposals. It was supremely tragic that there was a complete absence of similar activity from the British side. One need only imagine the situation had Henderson been at Warsaw with the support and confidence of Chamberlain.[39]

Italian Mediation Favored by Bonnet

The promising atmosphere created by the German acceptance of the British note of August 28th was entirely destroyed by the afternoon of August 31st. The spell of promise in Hitler's attempt to negotiate with the Poles was fading, and the Italians were responding by returning to their earlier project for an international conference. The British Ambassador at Rome had transmitted the British reply of August 30th to Ciano at 2:45 A.M. on August 31st. Attolico reported shortly afterward that Henderson had received the text of the German sixteen points almost immediately after his midnight conference with Ribbentrop. The situation was not entirely clear to Ciano, but he received a warning at Rome from Attolico at 9:04 A.M. on August 31st that war would come within a few hours unless some new step was taken.[40]

Ciano telephoned Halifax in London at 11:00 A.M. on August 31st that Attolico had reported on the gravity of the situation. Ciano did not realize that there was no longer much hope for direct German-Polish negotiations, and he urged the British to exert pressure on the Poles to negotiate. He promised that Mussolini would use his influence to encourage Hitler to maintain patience with Poland. Halifax neglected to inform Ciano that Great Britain was unwilling to exert pressure at Warsaw.[41]

French Ambassador Francois-Poncet reported to Bonnet from Rome at noon on August 31st that Mussolini was still convinced peace might be saved if the Poles would not object to the return of Danzig to Germany. The report from Rome encouraged Bonnet, who was inclined to place his last hope for peace on a successful Italian mediation effort. Raffaele Guariglia, the Italian Ambassador in Paris, reported to Ciano a short time later that France could be relied upon to provide strong support for an Italian mediation effort. He confided that there was a widespread impression in French official circles that British prestige was more at stake in the Danzig crisis than the prestige of France. He added that discontent with British policy was increasing rapidly in France. He believed that it would be possible to exploit this sentiment with great success, if the Italian Government was able to introduce some new positive factor into the situation at this point. Ciano knew that his Ambassador at Paris enjoyed excellent relations with Bonnet.[42]

Guariglia was a distinguished career diplomat who had entered the Italian diplomatic service in 1909, many years before Mussolini was appointed Premier of Italy in 1922. He received a favorable treatment in much of the French press when he arrived at Paris as Italian Ambassador in November 1938. *L'Ordre*, on November 28, 1938, and *Europe Nouvelle*, on December 3, 1938, claimed that the appointment of Guariglia was proof that Mussolini regarded France as the focal point of European diplomacy. Guariglia was a shrewd observer, and he was particularly concerned about counteracting the warmongering activities of American Ambassador Bullitt. He regarded this task as his special province. The Italian diplomat was convinced that the campaign of Roosevelt and Bullitt to promote a European was was exclusively in the interest of the Soviet Union. He believed that Halifax was equally blind to the true interests of Great Britain in his far more dangerous role of actually leading a formidable movement to destroy Germany.

Guariglia knew that the sudden popularity of Beck in Poland after March 1939 rested exclusively on the British guarantee, although the British were in no position to offer actual military assistance to Poland. He deplored the fact that Polish illusions about their future greatness were not affected by the Russo-German pact of August 23, 1939. Guariglia believed that France was having difficulty escaping from the British encirclement front because she was in "a sad stupor." General Gamelin told Guariglia on August 26, 1939, that he was placing his hopes in a successful Italian mediation effort, but the same French military leader had failed to support Bonnet's initiative to modify French obligations to Poland three days earlier. Guariglia was convinced that the French position was the key to war or peace in Europe. He hoped that Ciano would adopt a strong line in encouraging the French leaders to return to a foreign policy independent of British tutelage.[43]

The Marienwerder Proposals Defended by Henderson

Henderson continued to advise Halifax throughout the afternoon of August 31st that the German proposals to Poland were moderate, and that they offered an excellent basis for negotiation. The British Foreign Secretary was not impressed by the many appeals for peace which he was receiving from Paris, Rome, and Berlin. As a matter of fact, the British Foreign Office was becoming highly indignant at the tenacity with which the men on the continent, except in Poland, were struggling to preserve the peace. It was the unfortunate experience of Dahlerus to encounter the full impact of this resentment. He departed from the conference with Lipski at the Polish Embassy in a spirit of great indignation. It seemed to him incredible that the Poles should be allowed to sabotage a carefully prepared settlement after much good will had been displayed in other quarters. He now believed that the British would reconsider their decision to support Poland if they were told the truth about the actual situation. After all, the British themselves had first suggested that Germany submit proposals to Poland. They would surely desist from granting unconditional support to the Poles when they learned that the Polish Government was unwilling to consider the proposals.[44]

Henderson encouraged Dahlerus to telephone London from the British Embassy in Berlin. The Swedish engineer contacted Sir Horace Wilson at the British Foreign Office at 12:30 p.m. on August 31st. He began to describe the situation in detail, and to complain about the Polish attitude. Wilson, like Chamberlain, had capitulated to the war policy of Halifax. He protested that he did not like the tone of Dahlerus's remarks. He finally claimed that the Swedish engineer had no right to discuss the situation in this way, because the Germans might be listening on the line. This seemed a curious observation to Dahlerus. He saw no reason why the Germans should not hear his remarks, and the British had never before objected to telephone conversations with him over the Embassy line. Wilson began to shout repeatedly to the bewildered Swede: "Shut up!" Wilson concluded his report to Halifax on this incident with the following statement: "I again told Dahlerus to shut up, but as he did not do so I put down the receiver."[45]

The irritation of the British Foreign Office was no temporary mood, and the wrath of Halifax soon descended upon Henderson. The British Ambassador received several reprimands in very strong language for permitting Dahlerus to use the telephone. These reprimands were unjust, because Henderson had received instructions from London to extend the use of Embassy facilities to Dahlerus, and no instructions to the contrary had been received at the time of the unpleasant incident at 12:30 p.m. on August 31st.

Halifax at 1:00 o'clock that same afternoon disavowed the step of Henderson at the Polish Embassy in Berlin. He informed Henderson that he rejected the view that the German proposals offered a basis for German-Polish negotiation, and he disagreed with both Henderson and Dahlerus "as to the obstructive attitude of the Polish Government." He regretted that he had instructed

Kennard to join Noël in requesting that Lipski receive the German proposals. It is difficult to understand how he could feel so strongly about this insignificant gesture, especially since Beck understood perfectly well from Kennard that the British Government did not really wish Poland to negotiate with Germany. Kennard reported at 3:20 p.m. that the Polish Government was taking steps to contact the German Government, but "will not agree to accept a document containing a demand until methods of procedure have been agreed to." The Polish Government might as well have announced that it intended to contact the moon. The British and Poles had conspired to make a complete farce of the negotiation plan supported by Germany, Italy, France, and Pope Pius XII.[46]

Kennard had assured Beck privately after the Anglo-French *démarche* that the British Government did not actually wish Lipski to receive the German proposals, and that the formal step at Warsaw had been a gesture of appeasement to France. Kennard explained to Halifax that the British Government should not "insist" that the Polish Ambassador at Berlin accept any German document because of "the ultimatum danger." Kennard believed that inevitable war was a lesser evil than relaying proposals to Warsaw which might tempt the Polish leaders to resume negotiations with Germany. He asked Halifax if he should inform Beck "what we know" of the contents of the proposals, but he was obviously reluctant to do so. Kennard was not aware that Beck had received the text of the German proposals from Lipski many hours earlier. His only fear was that there might be a last minute peaceful solution instead of the war which he and Halifax desired.

The Lipski-Ribbentrop Meeting

Lipski informed Weizsaecker in the early afternoon of August 31st that he wished to call on Ribbentrop in his capacity as Ambassador. He made it clear that he had an announcement to make to the German Government, but that he did not intend to negotiate or to receive proposals for negotiation. Weizsaecker promised Lipski that he would report to Ribbentrop. The German Foreign Minister had received a copy of Beck's instructions to Lipski from Goering, and he knew that they contained no contribution toward a peaceful solution. He attempted to delay his meeting with Lipski as long as possible in the hope that the British, the French, and the Pope would prevail on Beck to send new instructions to the Polish Ambassador. Ribbentrop knew that it might still be possible to cancel German military operations if Beck empowered Lipski to relay the German proposals to Warsaw. Ribbentrop received word in the early evening that nothing was happening at Warsaw, and he was compelled to admit that further delay was futile. He had dispatched a telegram to Washington, D.C., while awaiting further word from Warsaw. He conveyed again the thanks of Hitler to President Roosevelt for the American messages of August 24th and August 25th. German Chargé d'Affaires Thomsen called on Secretary of State Hull on the night of August 31st to express Hitler's appreciation.[47]

Ribbentrop received Lipski at 6:30 p.m. on August 31st. The Polish Ambassador read the contents of a note from Beck. The note stated that Poland had just now received word about the recent talks between Great Britain and Germany which had started on August 23rd. The attitude of the Polish Government toward eventual talks between Poland and Germany had not been decided, but it was favorable in principle, and the German Government was informed that the Polish Government would soon indicate to the British Government its attitude toward such talks. Beck was not prepared to give the Germans an assurance that Poland was actually willing to renew negotiations with Germany.

Ribbentrop listened sadly to the senseless double-talk of the Polish note, which Beck undoubtedly considered sufficiently clever and misleading to confuse the Germans. It was obvious beneath the verbiage that Poland had not moved one step beyond her meaningless assurance to President Roosevelt on August 25th, and that Beck had remained unalterably opposed to negotiations. Ribbentrop told Lipski that he had hoped until the last minute that he would be empowered to negotiate. Lipski explained that he had been instructed merely to call on Ribbentrop and to present the Polish note. He was not allowed to give any personal assurances, or to make any statements. It is not surprising under these circumstances that the interview was a short one. Ribbentrop concluded the interview by asking if Lipski personally believed that his Government might reconsider its decision and permit him to negotiate. The Polish diplomat evaded this question by repeating that he had not received plenary powers.[48]

Kennard informed Halifax at 6:15 p.m. that Lipski had been instructed to seek an interview with Ribbentrop, but forbidden to engage in any conversations. Above all, he had been forbidden to receive any proposals from Germany. The note he was to present failed to contain an assurance that Poland would negotiate with Germany. Kennard observed with cynicism that Beck had met Halifax's requirements by establishing contact with the Germans. This had been done in such a way that the contact was disrupted again as quickly as it was made. Kennard added that Beck said the situation in Danzig was serious, which was scarcely news. The British Ambassador concluded with satisfaction that Beck had promised that he would never go to Berlin again.[49]

This dispatch was followed by the formal Polish reply to the earlier British statement that Poland was prepared to negotiate with Germany. The Polish Government announced that it accepted in principle the statements contained in the British note of August 28th, but that it refused to commit itself to negotiate until the proposed international guarantee to Poland was explained. This meant in plain language that the Polish Government still had not agreed at London to negotiate with the Germans despite the pledge of President Mościcki to President Roosevelt on August 25th. It is not surprising under these circumstances that the visit of Lipski to Ribbentrop on the evening of August 31st is one of the most sterile events in the long annals of diplomacy.

Hitler discussed the situation with Italian Ambassador Attolico at 7:00 o'clock, on the evening of August 31st. He gave Attolico a copy of the German proposals to Poland, which had earlier been forwarded to Rome. The German Chancellor continued in good faith to believe that the British Government had earnestly attempted to mediate between Germany and Poland. He told Attolico that the British mediation effort had failed. The Italian Ambassador suggested the unpromising possibility of Italian mediation between Germany and Poland. Hitler declared that the Poles had refused to listen to Chamberlain and Halifax, and he did not believe that they would listen to Mussolini. Actually, Chamberlain and Halifax had not given the Poles anything to "listen to" about negotiating with Germany. The Italian Ambassador asked if the German effort to negotiate with Poland was at an end. The German Chancellor replied that this was indeed the case.[50]

Soviet Foreign Commissar Molotov delivered a speech to the Supreme Soviet on the afternoon of August 31st in which he sharply criticized Poland and Western diplomacy. The speech was a fitting prelude to the later statement of Molotov that it was necessary for the Soviet Union to attack Poland in order to "extricate the Polish people from the ill-fated war into which they have been led by their unwise leaders." Hitler received information about the Molotov speech immediately after his conversation with Attolico. A report by telephone from Moscow was received in Berlin at 7:20 p.m. German Ambassador Schulenburg, who now made no secret of his intensely pro-Soviet attitude, concluded his remarks by exclaiming with enthusiasm that the Molotov speech was "brilliant."[51]

The Germans Denounced by Poland as Huns

The German radio broadcast to the world at 9:00 p.m. on August 31st the Marienwerder proposals which Poland had refused to consider. Weizsaecker also presented the Marienwerder terms to the British, French, Japanese, American, and Russian diplomatic representatives at Berlin between 9:00 and 10:00 p.m. on August 31st. The terms were accompanied in each instance by a diplomatic note which explained recent German policy. The main emphasis was on the fact that Hitler had waited in vain for two days to receive an indication that Poland would negotiate with Germany, although the British on August 28th had assured him that Poland was prepared to negotiate. Japanese Ambassador Oshima assured Weizsaecker that in his personal opinion a German victory in Poland would be in the interest of Japan.[52]

The German radio pointed out that the Poles had refused to receive the Marienwerder proposals for consideration at Warsaw, and this was correctly interpreted as definitive proof that the Polish leaders were resolutely opposed to negotiation with Germany. The Polish radio broadcast a distorted version of the German offer two hours later. It offered the world a glimpse of the mentality which was being encountered by the helpless German minority in Poland. The Polish broadcaster argued that the Germans in their proposals had revealed their aggressive intentions, and he concluded with the following statement: "Words can now no longer veil the aggressive plans of the new Huns. Germany is aiming at the domination of Europe and is cancelling the rights of nations with as yet unprecedented cynicism. This impudent proposal shows clearly how necessary were the military orders (general mobilization) given by the Polish Government."[53]

Hitler replied shortly before midnight to a recent telegram from the Duke of Windsor at Antibes, France. The Duke, who knew that Hitler had privately sympathized with his struggle in 1936 to marry the American woman of his choice and to hold the British throne, had expressed the hope that the German Chancellor would find some way of avoiding the pitfall of another senseless Anglo-German war. Hitler replied in ringing terms that "you may rest assured that my attitude toward Britain and my desire to avoid another war between our peoples remain unchanged." The German Chancellor continued to hope for an Anglo-German understanding despite the failure of his latest attempt to reach an agreement with Poland.[54]

Ribbentrop conceded at the Wilhelmstrasse, after the Polish radio broadcast, that full-scale war between Germany and Poland was now inevitable, and that there would be no new cancellation of German operations. Shortly afterward, Hitler and Ribbentrop discussed the irrevocable decision to settle the score with the Poles. Ribbentrop said to Hitler with great simplicity: "I wish you good luck." He was referring to the military campaign in Poland and to the further efforts to prevent the military intervention of Great Britain and France against Germany. The breakdown in relations was complete so far as Germany and Poland were concerned. Hitler had failed in his effort to win Poland as a stalwart Slavic ally against Bolshevism, and this in itself was a catastrophe of the greatest magnitude. German military operations commenced five hours later. Polish resistance began to crumble within a few days under the well-aimed German blows.[55]

The local German-Polish war need not have disturbed the peace of Europe for more than a few weeks. It would have been far easier for foreign Powers to intervene effectively to ameliorate the lot of the Poles, at least within the German area of occupation, had the war remained limited. The restoration of peace in Poland would have been an immediate concern, rather than some distant eventuality. Poland twenty years later is a Communist satellite of the Soviet Union. It would be impossible to imagine a result more distateful to the Polish leaders who recklessly plunged Poland into a hopeless war against Germany in 1939. Their grandiose hopes and dreams of a new Great Poland remained unrealized, and their people were subjected to the worst possible fate. To repeat the prophetic comment of Marshal Smigly-Rydz to Captain Beauffre on August 20, 1939: "With the Germans, we risk the loss of our liberty, with the Russians we would lose our soul!" The Poles need not have risked their liberty in a conflict with Germany nor have lost the soul of their country to Russia had they not been the victims of the fantastic delusion of their leaders that little Poland could become one of the Great Powers. Halifax did everything possible to encourage the desperate Polish challenge to Germany which resulted in the permanent domination of Poland by the Soviet Union.[56]

Chapter 22

BRITISH REJECTION

OF THE ITALIAN CONFERENCE PLAN

AND THE OUTBREAK OF WORLD WAR II

The German-Polish War

The outbreak of the local war between Germany and Poland on September 1, 1939, brought the European crisis to a climax. The military defeat of Poland by Germany was inevitable unless an armistice was speedily arranged. Hitler hoped that the British would not attack Germany in the light of the fact that Beck had refused to negotiate despite the British pledge of August 28th that he would do so. Hitler did not realize that the British Government had advised Poland not to negotiate with Germany. Halifax had actually done everything possible to create the war between Germany and Poland. He was indifferent about Poland, but he desired the destruction of Germany. He was the most deadly enemy of the German state and people.[1]

Italian Defection Accepted by Hitler

The issue of whether or not Great Britain would attack Germany was undecided on September 1st despite the attitude of Halifax, who had become the master of British policy. The British Foreign Secretary believed that the participation of France was the indispensable condition for the planned British assault. Halifax was convinced that it would be impossible for a British coalition to defeat Germany if France remained neutral. He saw no point in war unless it resulted in the destruction of Germany. The French, Italian, and German Governments, along with the smaller European states, favored the localization of the war in

Poland. The French leaders hoped for an armistice in Poland and a diplomatic conference which would avert the outbreak of World War II. French Ambassador François-Poncet informed Italian Foreign Minister Ciano at Rome on September 1st that the French Government believed a general war could be averted, despite the outbreak of war in Poland. France was prepared to join with Italy in arranging a compromise settlement which would prevent World War II.[2]

The Italians hoped to take the lead in arranging a settlement as they had done at Munich in 1938. Ciano reminded German Ambassador Mackensen on September 1st that the Italian diplomatic initiative had been decisive in averting war the previous year. The major Italian move for a diplomatic settlement in 1939 was not made until September 2nd. The first concern of the Italian leaders on September 1st was the safety of Italy. Great Britain on August 20th had threatened to launch her major effort against Italy, and many Frenchmen advocated swift military action against the Italians in the event of war.

The Italian Government, on the morning of September 1st, secretly promised Great Britain and France that Italy would not fight except in self-defense. Hitler assured Mussolini the same morning that he would not require Italian military support in the event of a general war. He sent another message in the early afternoon which courteously explained that he had not accepted Mussolini's offer to mediate between Germany and Poland because he knew this would be futile after what he supposed had been the British effort to influence the Poles. Mussolini and Ciano were encouraged by the conciliatory attitutde of Hitler to proceed from private pledges to a public announcement of Italian intentions. Mussolini called a session of the Italian Cabinet at 3:00, on the afternoon of September 1st. The Italian Government at 4:30 p.m. issued a public promise that it would undertake no military initiative in support of Germany. Ribbentrop sent a circular to German diplomatic missions abroad which warned them not to criticize Italian policy in conversations with foreigners. The close harmony in Italo-German relations had survived the failure of Italy to offer military support to Germany under the terms of the 1939 alliance.[3]

Polish Intransigence Deplored by Henderson and Attolico

British Ambassador Henderson at Berlin hoped that an Italian mediation effort would be successful. He had maintained a steady barrage of the British Foreign Office at the time of the outbreak of war between Germany and Poland. He hoped that he might still be able to influence British policy. He responded to the German public broadcast of the Marienwerder proposals by insisting to Halifax that they offered an adequate basis for negotiation. He declared that Beck had committed a great blunder in not negotiating, and that "from the long point of view, the Poles will miss their market, if they do not discuss." Henderson observed with sarcasm that the Marienwerder proposals were identical with the October 1938 proposals, from the Polish point of view. The Poles would expect to win the proposed plebiscite because they had asserted that "the corridor was 90% Polish since the beginning of the world."[4]

Henderson reminded Sir Alexander Cadogan in a later message that "Hitler intended to go off the deep end on August 25th, then changed his mind and sent for me." Henderson would have found it quite understandable had the Germans launched their operations on August 26th, and he believed that Hitler deserved recognition for postponing the decision under exceedingly difficult conditions and for trying again to reach a settlement by negotiation. The British Ambassador could not see that Poland had shown any interest in preserving the peace. He declared that "the Poles must put themselves in the right by making a gesture of some kind, or else we must all fight. Possibly, the second would be the best but the responsibility is too great for me to encourage the idea." It was tragic that the same responsibility did not seem too great to Halifax.

Henderson on September 1st struck out against the propagandists who sought to justify military measures on ideological grounds. He believed that the issue had been confused by the many people who sought to condone war against Germany with the argument about the allegedly immoral National Socialist regime. Henderson believed that an ideological crusade against Germany in a world threatened by Communism was ridiculous. He knew that war was "completely unjustifiable" when the ideological argument was deservedly placed in the background. He did not refer explicitly to the balance of power as the primary factor for war, but it was obvious from his many dispatches that he rejected the balance of power argument.[5]

Polish intransigence was the despair of Italian Ambassador Attolico at Berlin. Attolico complained to Ciano a few hours before the outbreak of the German-Polish war that it was unthinkable for Lipski not to have requested or discussed the German proposals for a settlement. The Ambassador shared the illusion of Hitler that the British were showing their good will and urging negotiations, but that Poland was not responding. His knowledge of the British attitude was limited to Henderson and his staff. He exclaimed despairingly: "Germany is not able to tolerate all this (*La Germania non puo tollerare tutto questo*)!" He concluded that Hitler had no choice other than to believe that the illusory English initiative with Poland had definitely failed.[6]

Attolico wired Ciano shortly afterward that, in his opinion, the German proposals were moderate and reasonable. He confided that until the last moment Goering had hoped that he might be able to save the situation by persuading Marshal Smigly-Rydz to meet him for a conference at the Polish frontier. Attolico wired Rome after the outbreak of war that it was positively criminal for the Poles not to have responded "to such a reasonable offer as the sixteen points."[7]

Hitler's Reichstag Speech of September 1, 1939

Hitler spoke to the German Reichstag at 10:10, on the morning of September 1st. He reminded his deputies that Danzig "was and is German." He made the same comment about the Corridor, which he had been willing to renounce to Poland, as he had renounced Alsace-Lorraine to France and South Tirol to Italy, in the interest of peace and cooperation. Hitler emphasized that he had attempted to solve all German problems by "peaceful revision (*friedlicher Revision*)." He confessed the failure of this attempt, and he deplored the fact that many of the practices of modern warfare were in evident contradiction to the provisions of international law. Danzig and the Corridor were problems which had to be solved. Hitler conceded that it might be a matter of indifference to the West when this was to be, but this was not true for Germany. Above all, time was no matter of indifference to the hundreds of thousands of people suffering from the absence of a settlement. Poland had rejected proposals which no German leader other than Hitler had dared to offer. The Polish partial mobilization of March 23, 1939, was the beginning of a series of countermeasures against Danzig and the German minority in Poland. Hitler reminded his listeners that Germany, unlike Poland, had faithfully carried out the provisions of the minority treaty of November 1937.

Hitler had announced his position in this dispute to the German Reichstag on April 28, 1939. He was prepared to resume negotiations for a settlement of differences with both Great Britain and Poland. He had waited four months in vain for some response from the Polish side. He knew that no Great Power in the world could tolerate such conditions indefinitely. The British advised him on August 28th that Poland was prepared to resume negotiations. He informed the British Government on the following day that Germany was prepared to negotiate. He waited in vain another two days for a response from Poland. The Polish Ambassador at last announced on August 31st that the Warsaw Government was considering whether or not it would negotiate with Germany. Lipski indicated that they would inform England, and not Germany, of their eventual decision. This meant that the Polish attitude on August 31st was actually far short of what the British had indicated it to be on August 28th.

Hitler would regret it if the statesmen in the West insisted that the German dispute with Poland affected their vital interests. Hitler promised that he n' ver had asked and never would ask anything from Great Britain and France. He ardently desired an understanding with England, "but love cannot be provided from one side if it is not received from the other (*aber Liebe kann nicht nur von einer Seite geboten werden, sie muss von der anderen ihre Erwiderung finden*)." This was an amazing declaration to the leaders of a nation which had attacked Germany in 1914, had starved to death hundreds of thousands of German children and old people, and was threatening to attack Germany twenty-give years later in a dispute which did not affect British interests. Indeed, the dispute in 1939 concerned what Winston Churchill and other prominent Englishmen had insisted for years was the most objectionable part of the 1919 settlement. Sir Austen Chamberlain, the brother of the Prime Minister, had promised in 1925 that no British grenadier would be required to die for Danzig or the Polish Corridor.

Hitler tactfully observed that the Italian leaders were aware that Germany did not care to request foreign help in solving her own problems. Hitler said that his understanding with the Russians was based on the expectation that they would no longer seek to export their doctrine of Communism to Germany. He endorsed the speech of Molotov on August 31, 1939, and he added that on th's occasion he could agree with every word of the Soviet Commissar for Foreign Affairs.

The German Chancellor announced his war aims in Poland. He intended to solve the Danzig and Corridor questions, and to bring about a change in German-Polish relations. He would fight until the present Polish Government agreed to peaceful co-existence or until another Polish Government was prepared to accept this. He was pursuing limited objectives in Poland, and he was not insisting on the annihilation of the Polish armed forces or the overthrow of the Polish state. He was prepared to insist that Germany should enjoy the same peaceful conditions on her eastern border which existed on her other frontiers as a matter of course. Hitler announced that he had ordered the German Air Force to restrict its operations to military objectives, because he did not wish to wage war against the defenseless women and children of Poland.

Hitler deliberately juggled financial statistics when he claimed that the German Reich had expended 90 billion RM (Reichsmarks) for defense purposes during the past six years. Much of this sum had been used for public works which had no direct connection with armament. He hoped that by doubling the figures for actual military expenditures he would discourage Great Britain and France from waging war against Germany. He claimed that Germany had the best military defenses in the world, and that the German war machine was better than in 1914. He himself intended either to be a soldier until victory, or not to survive the war. He dramatized the dangerous life of the German leaders in a world of secret conspiracies and assassination plots. Goering would succeed if anything happened to him, and Hess would follow in the event of the elimination of Goering. Hitler announced that a special assembly of National Socialist deputies would select a new German Chancellor in case Goering, Hess, and himself were eliminated. Hitler admitted that he had failed to learn the meaning of the word "capitulation." There was no room for traitors in Germany, and there would never be another November 1918. Hitler concluded his speech with the following statement: "It is unimportant if we live, but it is necessary for Germany to live." The Reichstag deputies rose from their seats and swore an oath of loyalty to Hitler. Minister of Interior Wilhelm Frick introduced a law for the annexation of Danzig to Germany. It was accepted unanimously.[8]

The Italian Ambassador reported to Ciano that most of the diplomatic corps was present to hear Hitler. American Chargé d'Affaires Kirk was forbidden by Roosevelt to attend the Reichstag session. Kirk informed the German Foreign Office before Hitler spoke that he would not be present, but he promised to send a special representative. He also offered to represent in Germany the interests of Great Britain and France if the latter entered the war. The British Ambassador was represented by a consul at the Reichstag meeting, and the French Ambassador by an embassy secretary. Attolico found it rather amusing that the name of each prospective successor to the chief executive power in Germany was greeted with a long ovation. This type of gesture seemed to give the Reichstag meeting something of the atmosphere of an American political convention. Apparently Attolico believed that these demonstrations of solidarity were ostentatious and unnecessary, although there was certainly no lack of the theatrical element in Italian conclaves of major importance. He seemed to ignore the fact that Hess, and especially Goering, enjoyed tremendous personal popularity in Germany. Attolico was self-conscious in his own position as a neutral Ambassador, having done more than anyone else to separate Italy from

Germany in the first major crisis after the conclusion of their alliance.[9]

German Chargé d'Affaires Theo Kordt, who was secretly working with Halifax, reported from London at 11:45 A.M. that the British Foreign Secretary requested him to call shortly after the beginning of Hitler's speech. Kordt left the group of German diplomats, who were listening to the speech on the radio, and visited Halifax. Kordt naturally denied in his official report that he gave Halifax any information. Halifax told him that he intended to send all further communications to Germany directly to Berlin. He added that the British Cabinet was about to meet. Kordt was careful to mention that Halifax shook hands with him when he was leaving. He did not indicate whether he received this handshake in his capacity of underground agent or German diplomat. Hitler naturally assumed that the latter was the case.[10]

Negotiations Requested by Henderson and Dahlerus

Halifax had telephoned Ciano a few hours before the outbreak of the German-Polish war that Great Britain would never advise Poland to permit self-determination at Danzig. The British Foreign Secretary added complacently that he would not object if the Poles themselves agreed to it. He knew that there was no chance that they would do so without British advice and pressure. Halifax admitted to Kennard shortly afterward that he was worried about the Polish refusal to receive the German proposals, because he recognized that this might be "misunderstood [i.e. understood] by world opinion." Halifax was pleased that the Poles had obstructed a settlement, but he feared that his propaganda might be unsuccessful in concealing the actual situation.[11]

German Consul-General Janson telephoned Berlin from Danzig at 9:35 A.M. to announce that League High Commissioner Burckhardt had departed for East Prussia. Polish High Commissioner Chodacki was still in the city. Janson announced heavy fighting in Danzig at several points. The Poles were defending the Polish Post Office and the Westerplatte arsenal in the vicinity of the densely populated Neufahrwasser district. The fighting inside Danzig was destined to continue for more than a week, but the complete liberation of the city was inevitable.[12]

The indefatigable Birger Dahlerus launched a new mediation effort on the morning of September 1st despite the severe rebuff he had received from London on the previous day. His avowed aim was to persuade Great Britain not to join the war in support of Poland. He telephoned the British Foreign Office at 9:50 A.M. saying, "the Poles are sabotaging everything," and he added flatly that they simply did not wish to negotiate. He announced that he desired to return to England. He promised to bring evidence, and especially Beck's August 31st instructions to Lipski, which proved that the Poles "have never meant to attempt to negotiate with Germany and that has been a proof to Germany that nothing can be done."

Dahlerus, like the French leaders, believed that a further attempt should be made to bring the Poles to the negotiation table despite the outbreak of war.

He knew that the German leaders were still in favor of negotiations with Poland. Goering suggested that General Ironside, who was admired in Poland, should join with Ogilvie-Forbes and some French personality in supervising negotiations between the Germans and the Poles. He insisted that it would not be necessary for the Polish diplomatic team to come into direct contact with the Germans. The Poles could operate from their Embassy in Berlin by discussing matters with the British and French, who in turn could transmit proposals to the Germans. Dahlerus added, "it will be a catastrophe if we cannot arrange it that way." He admitted that Henderson had allowed him to use the British Embassy telephone, despite the reprimands from London, and he advised the British official on the other end of the line to call back to the British Embassy in Berlin.13

Henderson followed this step by wiring Halifax that Goering had spoken with him for nearly two hours the previous evening about Hitler's desire for peace and friendship with Great Britain. The British Ambassador knew that Hitler and Goering were absolutely sincere about their feelings toward the British. Henderson added that Goering had discussed some of the last minute incidents which had preceded the outbreak of the German-Polish war.

Goering did not mention the mysterious Gleiwitz incident, which had received extensive treatment in the German press. An unsuccessful attempt was made at the 1945-1946 Nuremberg Trial, against the principal surviving German leaders, to prove that the Gleiwitz incident was the result of a fantastic German plot to dress prisoners in Polish uniforms and compel them to raid the municipal radio station, while a picked stooge delivered an incendiary broadcast in Polish.14

The Polish *Bank Ludowy* (People's Bank) maintained a lavish but seldom-frequented branch bank in Gleiwitz with the permission of the German authorities. The personnel of this bank hoped to organize an insurrection among the Polish minority in West Upper Silesia on the misguided assumption that the Polish armed forces would soon enter the area. Gleiwitz was only one mile from the Polish frontier, and the *Bank Ludowy* people disappeared into Poland about the time of the incident. The Gleiwitzers naturally assumed that the bank people perpetrated the momentary seizure of the radio station, but the mystery shrouding the actual deed has remained one of the numerous unexplained events of this period.15

Henderson informed Halifax of several of the verified Polish violations prior to hostilities. The Poles blew up the Dirschau (Tczew) bridge across the Vistula River on August 31, 1939, although the eastern approach to the bridge was on German territory. The Poles based at the Westerplatte occupied a number of Danzig installations and engaged in fighting with the Danzigers on the same day. Henderson informed Halifax of these events, because he knew that Kennard would never report them from Warsaw. Henderson received confirmation from Goering that Hitler was not insisting on the total military defeat of Poland. He was prepared to terminate hostilities if the Poles indicated that they were willing to negotiate a satisfactory settlement.16

Dahlerus had a further personal conversation with Hitler while awaiting a reply to his request to visit England. The attitude of Hitler immediately after the Reichstag speech was extremely encouraging. The absence of a reply from

London prompted Henderson to advise Dahlerus to telephone the British Foreign Office again. Dahlerus contacted Sir Alexander Cadogan at 12:20 P.M. on September 1st, and a sharp conversation ensued. Cadogan urged Dahlerus to desist from further mediation attempts, but the Swedish engineer stubbornly refused. Dahlerus insisted on discussing the factors which had produced the war in Poland. Cadogan professed to be indignant because the Swede "seemed to imply that it had been started by the Poles." Cadogan considered it an effrontery to criticize the conduct of an ally of Great Britain. Dahlerus shouted that Hitler had promised fifteen minutes earlier to renew negotiations with the Poles at any time. Hitler had announced that his principal objective was to avert a new World War. Above all, he desired new discussions with the British.

Cadogan coldly inquired what Hitler wished to discuss. The Swedish engineer replied that he wished to obtain the mediation of Great Britain for an armistice and compromise settlement with Poland. Cadogan could see no basis for a discussion, nor imagine anything to discuss. Dahlerus requested permission to fly to England, and he added that Ogilvie-Forbes wished to accompany him to present the German case. Cadogan said he could see no purpose in this flight, but Dahlerus continued with great insistence to plead for permission. At last Cadogan said that he would submit the question to the British Government. The Swedish engineer agreed to telephone the Foreign Office again at 1:15 P.M.

It was 1:25 P.M. when Dahlerus succeeded in contacting Cadogan again. This time he received a crushingly negative reply. The Permanent Under-Secretary for Foreign Affairs insisted that nothing could be done while Germany was invading Poland. The British Government would not agree to support negotiations unless German troops withdrew from Poland and Danzig. This conversation dealt a crippling blow to the mediation mission of Dahlerus. It remained to be seen what the Italians could do.[17]

Hitler Denounced by Chamberlain and Halifax

The British afternoon press on September 1st was ablaze with news about the war in Poland. The *Daily Telegraph* praised the Poles for not accepting the German offer to negotiate at Berlin. The return of Danzig to Germany was denounced as intolerable, and the Marienwerder proposals were described as excessive. The British readers were asked to pay their respects to the "wisdom of Poland" in refusing to negotiate for a settlement. The *News Chronicle* asserted that the British Government had guaranteed Poland in the first place because the Poles were not prepared to tolerate the return of Danzig to Germany. Self-determination was denounced as a convenient cover for the worst of crimes. It was obvious that most of the British Empire would be lost if the inhabitants were allowed to determine their own allegiance. The *Daily Mail* claimed that the moderate Marienwerder proposals were merely a trick to entice the Poles to come to Berlin.[18]

Prime Minister Chamberlain broadcast to Germany on the British short-wave radio at 6:05 P.M. on September 1st. He claimed that "the responsibility for this terrible catastrophe (war in Poland) lies on the shoulders of one man, the

German Chancellor." This Foreign Office speech delivered by the British leader was crass propaganda. He claimed that Hitler had ordered the Poles to come to Berlin with the unconditional obligation of accepting without discussion the exact German terms. He flatly denied that Germany had invited the Poles to engage in normal negotiations. Both of these statements were unvarnished lies, but the Polish case was so weak that it was impossible to defend it with the truth.

Chamberlain was on more solid ground when he claimed that the British military situation was superior to that of 1914. The British hoped to keep their own casualties to a minimum in 1939 by reducing their commitment of forces to the continent, and by seeking to pulverize Germany from the air. They were indifferent to the fact that this strategy left France in a much weaker position than in 1914. Chamberlain praised Mussolini's efforts for peace, but he dismissed them as a thing of the past by claiming that the Italian leader "had done his best." He revived the old British propaganda slogan of World War I by claiming that he had no quarrel with the German people, but only with the National Socialists. There had been similar talk about Kaiser Wilhelm II in World War I, but the overthrow of the Imperial Government had not softened the Allied treatment of the German people. Most of the German people recognized in 1939 that British hostility was directed against themselves as much as against Hitler.[19]

Halifax was in his best oratorical form when he delivered his cleverly hypocritical speech to the British House of Lords on the evening of September 1st. His remarks were pitched perfectly for the mentality of his audience. He knew that his listeners hoped to feel like knights of the holy grail in a great crusade against evil. He exploited to the uttermost the insincere British appeasement policy of 1938 when seeking to justify British policy in 1939. He did not admit that Great Britain refrained from attacking Germany in 1938 for purely tactical reasons while she completed her military preparations. He claimed that the best proof of the British will to peace was to have Chamberlain, the great appeasement leader, carry the nation into war. The paradoxical nature of this remark would have been recognized instantly under normal circumstances, but it was accepted as impressively profound wisdom on September 1, 1939. Halifax concealed the fact that he had taken over the direction of British policy from Chamberlain in October 1938, and that the British nation would probably not be moving into war had this not happened. Halifax assured the Peers that Hitler, before the bar of history, would have to assume responsibility for everything. He added with pride that, in looking back, he did not wish to change a thing as far as British policy was concerned. He insisted that the English conscience was pure.[20]

Anglo-French Ultimata Rejected by Bonnet

Bonnet at Paris was extremely indignant to learn of the meaningless instructions Lipski received from Beck on the afternoon of August 31st. Bonnet had persuaded Lukasiewicz to wire Beck that France insisted upon direct negotiations between Poland and Germany, but this step, without British support, did not produce the slightest effect. The French Foreign Minister concluded that a general conference would be more promising than German-Polish talks, but he was worried about British intransigence. French Ambassador Corbin warned Bonnet from London that the British were prepared to emasculate any proposal for a conference by presenting an impossible demand for prior German demobilization. Corbin's warning came a few hours before the outbreak of the German-Polish war. The British afterward aimed to produce the same effect by demanding the abandonment of Danzig by Germany. It is important to note that they were opposed to a conference with or without the outbreak of hostilities in Poland.[21]

Bonnet refused to be intimidated by the warning from Corbin. He recommended to Daladier that France should support any conference which would include Poland and at which general European problems would also be discussed. He argued that it would be easy to adjourn the conference if Hitler demanded too much. Daladier was prepared to accept this proposal. The approval of the majority of French Cabinet ministers was obtained without difficulty. Bonnet agreed with a suggestion from Daladier that the conference plan would not preclude direct negotiations between Poland and Germany. The personal attempt of Chamberlain, shortly before the French Cabinet meeting, to persuade the French Premier to reject further negotiations with the Germans was unsuccessful.

Bonnet now enjoyed the solid support of the French Government for his negotiation plans. He telephoned Corbin in London, and he instructed him to inform the British Foreign Office of the latest decision by France. Bonnet wished to know the British position at once. Corbin replied a short time later that the British diplomats were unwilling to state their position at the present time. This was the last news Bonnet received from London before learning of the outbreak of the German-Polish war.

The British responded to the outbreak of war in Poland by demanding an immediate Anglo-French ultimatum to Germany. Bonnet hoped that there would never be such an ultimatum, and he borrowed the customary British dilatory tactics in evading the question. He replied that it would be impossible to consider such action until after the convening of the French Parliament on September 2nd. The British would have gone to war with Germany on September 1, 1939, had they received French support for this plan. The French Cabinet met again at 10:30 A.M. on September 1st, and Bonnet received a new vote of support for his negotiation plans. Francois-Poncet at Rome had been unable to report if Italy still intended to undertake the initiative for a conference, but Bonnet was empowered to inform the Italians that France would support such a plan.[22]

Notes of Protest Drafted by Bonnet

The Poles knew that their challenge to Germany was a gamble which they would lose if the French, and consequently the British, refused to support Poland. They were anxious to end the suspense and to receive a decision one way or another. The Germans succeeded in destroying almost the entire Polish Air Force within the first thirty-six hours of military operations; hence it was not surprising that Beck demanded aerial protection from Great Britain on the first day of the war. Kennard wired Halifax at 2:00 P.M. on September 1st that Beck hoped for a British aerial offensive the same afternoon. Halifax had learned by this time that Bonnet refused to consider an Anglo-French ultimatum to Germany on the first day of the war in Poland. The French declared general mobilization on September 1st, but this did not necessarily mean that France intended to enter the war. There had also been a French general mobilization in September 1938. It had been arranged in advance that the remainder of the French reserves would be called up automatically in the event of the outbreak of war in Poland.[23]

President Roosevelt presented his hypocritical appeal against aerial bombardment of civilians to Germany and Poland on September 1, 1939. Lord Lothian had explained from Washington, D.C., several days earlier that the American President intended to take this step on behalf of the Poles. President Roosevelt declared that the bombardment of civilians in recent wars "has sickened the hearts of every civilized man and woman." Hitler replied to President Roosevelt on the same day. He declared that the Roosevelt message coincided with his own views, and that he favored a public declaration by belligerent Governments in any war condeming aerial attacks on civilians. The High Command of the German Armed Forces also issued a special communiqué on this subject on the evening of September 1st. Statements appearing in foreign newspapers about alleged German attacks on open cities were indignantly denied. The German military men insisted that their aerial attacks were directed exclusively against military targets. This statement was given scant publicity in the Western press where pictures of murdered minority Germans were presented as pictures of innocent Polish victims of German aerial warfare.[24]

Halifax had failed to persuade Bonnet to go to war with Germany on September 1st, but he decided to do what he could on that day to discourage an eventual Italian mediation effort. The British Foreign Secretary realized that an Italian diplomatic effort supported by France was the principal threat to his plans for war. Halifax instructed Sir Percy Loraine that Great Britain was grateful for previous Italian diplomatic efforts, but he insisted that the outbreak of war in Poland rendered inevitable the military intervention of Great Britain against Germany. The British Ambassador was ordered to convey this British viewpoint to Mussolini with great vigor.[25]

The British Foreign Secretary was pleased to learn on September 1st that Birger Dahlerus had apparently withdrawn from the diplomatic scene. The persistent Swede telephoned the British Foreign Office that afternoon to bid farewell, and to announce that he would return to Stockholm. He declared that he would gladly come to London again, if the British changed their minds and agreed to support diplomatic efforts for peace. He presented Goering's promise that the Germans would never bomb open cities if the British agreed to abstain from this practice. Halifax knew that the bombardment of open cities in Germany was the key British formula for victory, and that it would be employed after the outbreak of any Anglo-German war. Halifax was much irritated to

582   THE FORCED WAR

learn somewhat later that Goering had persuaded Dahlerus to continue with his mediation efforts.[26]

Halifax decided to make another effort to persuade France to enter war against Germany on September 1st. He telephoned Bonnet at 5:00 p.m. to recommend that the British and French Ambassadors in Berlin ask for their passports the same day. He suggested that it would be most effective if Great Britain and France went to war against Germany on the very day that the German-Polish war had begun. Above all, this would create the illusion that the German-Polish war and the Anglo-French war against Germany were a single war. The French Foreign Minister flatly refused to be plunged into war against Germany in this hasty fashion. Halifax insisted that Great Britain and France should respond at once to the war in Poland. Bonnet, after much argument, persuaded Halifax to accept a step at Berlin which would resemble an Anglo-French ultimatum to Germany, but which would have no definitive character, because it would lack a time limit. This entire sequence of events is distorted by Gilbert and Gott in *The Appeasers,* because they ignore entirely the conflict between Halifax and Bonnet over the nature of the Anglo-French notes to Germany of September 1st in their effort to create an imaginary Halifax still devoted to appeasement.

This strange step, which Halifax accepted in desperation, illustrates the diplomatic agility of Bonnet. Halifax dispatched instructions to Henderson at 5:45 p.m. for the proposed Anglo-French *demarché.* The British and French Ambassadors were to warn Germany that the pledges of their countries to Poland would be implemented unless they received satisfactory assurances about the suspension of "all aggressive action against Poland." This was carefully phrased by Bonnet to omit the requirement that the Germans need actually withdraw from Poland. The absence of any time limit left France a completely free hand in her dealings with the Germans. French Ambassador Coulondre later noted with restrained understatement that this note was widely criticized by those who desired an immediate war with Germany, but it was the only joint Anglo-French step which Halifax could produce at this time, and he decided that it was probably better than nothing. It should occasion no surprise that Hitler was exceedingly puzzled by the Anglo-French step. He did not know whether or not he had received *ultimata* from the Western Powers.[27]

Henderson called on Ribbentrop to present the British note at 9:00 p.m. on September 1st. Ribbentrop denied that German military operations against Poland constituted "aggressive action." He insisted that Germany had attempted to arrive at a peaceful understanding with Poland, and that war had resulted from Polish intransigence. The British Ambassador, who privately agreed with Ribbentrop, did not attempt to argue this point. He merely requested the German Foreign Minister to convey the British note to Hitler, and to inform him that London would like to receive a reply to it as soon as possible. Ribbentrop agreed to this. Henderson then confided to Ribbentrop that Halifax was seeking to make an important point out of the failure of the German Foreign Minister to give Henderson a copy of the Marienwerder proposals on August 30th. Both men knew that this had resulted from Ribbentrop's uncertainty about Hitler's instructions, and that it had been remedied shortly afterward when Goering conveyed the German proposals to Henderson. Nevertheless, Ribbentrop was quite willing to give Henderson an elaborate explanation.

The British Ambassador reported to Halifax after this lengthy conversation that the explanation of Ribbentrop had been comprehensive and satisfactory, and that the German diplomat had been "courteous and polite." Henderson was determined to explode the legend that His Majesty's Ambassador had been treated with discourtesy at Berlin. Henderson feared: "Hitler's answer (to the British note) will be an attempt to avoid war with Great Britain and France, but not likely to be one which we can accept." The British Ambassador had no idea that Hitler would agree on the following day to cancel further German military operations in Poland if the British would attend a diplomatic conference. Henderson added that Goering had persuaded Dahlerus to remain in Germany in the hope that he would soon be able to resume his mediation efforts. Halifax was not impressed with the report from Henderson. He had informed Raczynski at 10:00 A.M. on the same day that there was no longer the slightest doubt that Great Britain would go to war in support of Poland.[28]

Kennard at Warsaw had made short work of Halifax's suggestion late on August 31st that it might be wise for propaganda purposes to advise Beck to instruct Lipski to receive the German proposals. The British Ambassador to Poland confessed that he had neglected to mention this idea to Beck during the last hours of peace between Poland and Germany. He offered an exceedingly unusual explanation of his independent conduct. He argued that Lipski had called on Ribbentrop before the suggestion of Halifax reached Warsaw, and that it was pointless for this reason to discuss the matter with Beck. This was fantastic, because Halifax knew of Lipski's senseless visit to Ribbentrop when he sent his instructions to Kennard. Nevertheless, the British Foreign Secretary was content to accept this explanation from Kennard.[29]

Ribbentrop received French Ambassador Coulondre at 10:00 P.M. on September 1st. The French and British notes of protest about the war in Poland were identical, and Ribbentrop again "rejected the version alleging German aggression against Poland." He wired Budapest immediately after his conversation with Coulondre that he did not expect Hungary to offer armed assistance to Germany against Poland, but he hoped that they would refrain from issuing an express declaration of neutrality. He knew that there was no chance that Poland would attack Hungary, and he wished to create the impression that the Hungarians were on the German side in the dispute with the Poles.

The viewpoint of Ribbentrop was acceptable to Hungarian Foreign Minister Csaky. The Hungarians had hoped until the last moment that there would be no war between Germany and Poland. This did not prevent them from recognizing that Germany had a better case in the dispute than Poland, especially since the Hungarians had vainly advised the Poles on numerous occasions to permit the return of Danzig to Germany. Csaky informed Ribbentrop that the Hungarian press was stressing Polish responsibility for the outbreak of the German-Polish war. The Hungarian Government also sent a special note to Germany promising loyal Hungarian friendship. Ribbentrop was pleased to receive an assurance from Dictator Antonio de Oliveira Salazar that Portugal would remain neutral in the event of an Anglo-German war despite the ancient alliance between Great Britain and Portugal, which had prompted the Lisbon Government to attack Germany in World War I. Ribbentrop knew that Spain had exerted heavy pressure on Portugal for the observation of neutrality by both Iberian countries.[30]

The Italian Mediation Effort

Italian Ambassador Arone wired Ciano in great distress from Warsaw on September 1st that his Embassy was besieged by Polish police. He had appealed to the Polish Foreign Office for relief from this outrage, but he received the response that their "protective measures" were prompted by doubts about the Italian attitude toward the conflict between Germany and Poland. Ciano instructed Arone to assure the Poles that Italy did not intend to intervene in the conflict, but the Poles remained sceptical. Considerable effort was required to secure the release of the Italian Ambassador from his involuntary confinement.[31]

Ciano continued to fear a surprise British military offensive against Italy and he went to extreme lengths to discourage this dreaded prospect. He told Loraine on September 1st that the earlier ties between Germany and Italy had been greatly loosened. He claimed to be personally indignant that Germany had concluded a pact with the Communists, although Mussolini since May 1939 had repeatedly urged Hitler to take this step. Ciano added without the slightest justification that he had now become "Reich public enemy number one," because of the allegedly firm stand he had taken against Hitler at Berchtesgaden in August 1939. This claim was utterly ridiculous in the light of the fact that Ciano had expressed his complete agreement with Hitler at that time. Ciano's statements revealed that Italy's fear of Great Britain was very great. Ciano was aware that the British in the past had frequently launched surprise attacks against neutral nations.[32]

Ciano was gradually reassured that the Western Powers accepted Italian neutrality, and this prompted him in turn to revive Mussolini's mediation plans. The Italian Foreign Minister had vital information still unknown to Hitler. This information indicated that there was much hope for a successful mediation venture. Guariglia had reported from Paris at 1:00 P.M. on September 1st that Bonnet wished to support a diplomatic solution of the German-Polish conflict. The Italian Ambassador at 3:00 o'clock that same afternoon was able to forward a request from Daladier to Mussolini for diplomatic action to arrange a conference. It was obvious that the French leaders were sincere in their own efforts to avoid war in support of Poland, and there was a vast difference between French and British attitudes toward the crisis. It was evident that skillful Italian diplomatic action could exploit this difference in order to bring pressure to bear on England for a compromise settlement.[33]

The French Foreign Minister was extremely worried by the morning of September 2, 1939. He was under heavy pressure from the British and the Poles to go to war, and he had received no further indication from Ciano that Italy actually intended to organize a diplomatic conference. Lukasiewicz called on French Foreign Minister Bonnet at 9:00 A.M. on September 2nd to demand that France enter the war. Bonnet successfully evaded a commitment, but he complained afterward that the Polish Ambassador had been excessively "impatient" during this conversation.

Hitler's Acceptance of an Armistice and a Conference

Ciano and Mussolini had decided that it would be wise to secure full German support for a conference before approaching the British and French again. Ciano at last sent a highly important secret message to Germany at 10:00 A.M. on September 2nd. This message contained the important revelation that the French leaders were soliciting Italian action on behalf of a diplomatic conference. Ciano and Mussolini believed that the last minute consent of Great Britain and Poland for adequate terms of peace might still be obtained. Italy would propose an armistice which provided for the halting of the German and Polish Armies at the positions momentarily occupied. Arrangements would be made for a peace conference to convene within two or three days. The primary purpose of the conference would be to resolve the German-Polish dispute on a compromise basis in which both German and Polish interests received recognition.[34]

Attolico wired Rome at 10:40 A.M. that Ribbentrop feared the British and Poles would not cooperate with Italy, Germany, and France. The Italian Ambassador suggested to Weizsaecker that the substance of the mediation plan should be telephoned directly to Hitler at once. This advice was approved by Ribbentrop and Weizsaecker, and Hitler was informed of the contents of the Ciano message. Hitler was enthusiastic, and he ordered the German Foreign Office to sound out Henderson. This was done, but the British Ambassador admitted with reluctance that the British leaders would probably not accept a solution without the previous retirement of the German troops to the frontier. Attolico reported to Ciano that Henderson's response had discouraged the Germans.

Ribbentrop explained to Attolico at 12:30 P.M. that Germany was about to return negative replies to the British and French notes of the previous day when the message from Ciano arrived. Ribbentrop admitted that he was unable to decide whether or not the British and French notes were *ultimata*. Attolico believed that they were *ultimata,* but he claimed that the notes were superseded by the message from Rome, which contained an important assurance from France. Ribbentrop retorted that in this case it would be wise to inquire of the French and British Governments if their notes of the previous day were of an ultimate character. The matter was referred to Hitler. Attolico reported to Ciano at 3:15 P.M. that Hitler had decided it would be impossible to continue with plans for a conference until the British and French had defined their ambiguous notes of the previous day.[35]

Bonnet had still heard nothing from Ciano by this time, and he was beginning to lose hope that peace would be retrieved. Then Ciano contacted Bonnet by telephone, and the French Foreign Minister was overjoyed to learn that an effective mediation effort had been launched by the Italians. The Italian Foreign Minister noted from the sound of Bonnet's voice that his mediation effort was warmly supported by his colleague at Paris. Ciano told Bonnet that it was essential to receive an assurance that the French and British notes of the previous day were not *ultimata.* François-Poncet had been unable to give this important assurance at Rome. Bonnet was the actual author of both notes, and

he said at once that he could give Ciano his complete assurance that the notes
definitely were not *ultimata*. Knowing that the British would be compelled to
accept his judgment on this point, Bonnet added that he would take the precaution of consulting Daladier and Halifax to obtain a uniform response.[36]

The British were highly displeased that the notes of September 1st were
not considered *ultimata*. However, Sir Percy Loraine at Rome was therefore in
a position to inform Ciano that the British Government had not yet addressed
an ultimatum to Germany. The entire action at Rome had required by a few
minutes, and Ciano was soon able to assure Attolico that an Anglo-French
disavowal that *ultimata* had been delivered to Germany had been received.
Hitler responded by promising to give favorable consideration to the Italian
mediation plan, including the suspension of German military operations in
Poland. The Italian diplomats at Berlin were pleased by Hitler's conciliatory
attitude. Massimo Magistrati, a persistently hostile critic of the Pact of Steel,
and Attolico's principal diplomatic assistant at Berlin, noted that Hitler was
positively eager to terminate German operations in Poland, and he concluded
that "Germany has already achieved her military and moral satisfaction and
would be extremely happy to avoid a general conflict (*la Germania aveva gia
avuto la sua saddisfazione militare e morale ed ora arebbe stata bon lieta di
evitare una conflagrazione generale*)." Attolico was able to wire Chiano at
4:00 p.m. on September 2nd that Germany favored the Italian proposal for a
conference. Ribbentrop had urged Attolico to prepare the Italian leaders for an
important German announcement not later than noon on Sunday, September
3rd, concerning the plan to end the war in Poland. Ciano had managed within
six hours to score a victory in Germany for Mussolini's mediation plan.[37]

The Peace Conference Favored by Bonnet

The Italian mediation effort reached a crucial stage when Germany accepted
the conference plan. The time had come to exercise the utmost skill in exploiting the disagreement between Great Britain and France about going to war for
Poland. Hitler was optimistic about the chances for a last-minute settlement,
but he would have been less hopeful had he heard the telephone conversation
between Bonnet and Halifax shortly after 4:00 p.m. on September 2nd. Bonnet
received the frightening impression that the British Foreign Secretary was
determined to destroy the conference plan before it was presented to the Poles.
Halifax insisted that the Germans should complete the withdrawal of their
forces from Poland and Danzig before Great Britain and France agreed to consider the conference plan. Bonnet knew that no Great Power would accept such
treatment. He protested that the attitude of Halifax was unreasonable and
unrealistic. He considered that the Germans would be making an adequate concession if they agreed to discontinue their advance, but Halifax refused to accept
this view. Bonnet recalled the heroic efforts in July 1914 of Jean Jaurès, the
Socialist leader, who had attempted to prevent France from going to war for
Serbia. Jaurès was murdered by fanatics because of these efforts, and Bonnet
sought to derive inspiration from his heroism. He was resolved to continue

the fight for peace despite the obstructive tactics of Halifax.[38]

Bonnet required all the resolution he could command, because he was under tremendous pressure from the British to lead France into war. Sir Alexander Cadogan telephoned Bonnet at the Quai d'Orsay at 5:00 p.m. on September 2, 1939, Cadogan observed with irritating self-assurance that the British demand for a German troop withdrawal confined the plan for a diplomatic conference to the realm of remote possibilities. He insisted that it was time to get on with the war. He announced that Halifax was demanding an immediate joint Anglo-French ultimatum to the Germans which would expire at midnight on September 2, 1939. Bonnet replied that he intended to await further word from Italy about the conference plan.

Bonnet launched a unilateral effort to persuade the Poles to accept a conference. Kennard reported with great indignation to Halifax from Warsaw that French Ambassador Noel had been instructed not to reveal the contents of his latest instructions from Bonnet. It was a simple matter for Kennard to obtain confirmation of these French instructions from Beck. The Polish Foreign Minister told Kennard that France was requesting Polish agreement for a five-Power conference to include Great Britain, France, Germany, Italy, and Poland. Hitler was no longer bothered by the thought that Germany and Italy would have but two votes, because he realized at last that he could count on strong support from France for a settlement. Kennard advised Beck to reject the French proposal. Kennard admitted to Halifax that Beck refused to define his attitude toward the conference plan, but the British Ambassador believed that the Polish reply to France would probably be negative.[39]

The Polish Sejm met in special session on September 2, 1939. The Sejm President announced in a keynote speech that Pilsudski had taught Poland not only how to fight to attain independence, but also how to defend it. The Ukrainian spokesmen in the Sejm had been terrified by the prospect of a Soviet invasion of Eastern Poland since the conclusion of the Russo-German Pact of August 23, 1939, and they offered their full support to the Polish Government. A special law was announced to permit the members of the Sejm and the Senate to fight in the Polish Army. Premier Slawoj-Skladkowski delivered a speech in praise of the memory of Pilsudski. A Polish Army Band was present to play the World War I march of Pilsudski's First Brigade, and the Polish National Anthem, *Jescze Polska nie Zginela!*.

The Polish Army report of September 2nd attempted to conceal the gravity of the Polish military situation on the second day of the war. It was claimed that 37 German airplanes had been shot down as against 12 Polish airplanes, and no mention was made of the fact that virtually the entire Polish Air Force had been destroyed on the first day of the war. The destruction of 100 German tanks was claimed, and special emphasis was placed on the fact that the Polish Westerplatte garrison in Danzig was holding out successfully.[40]

The French Chamber of Deputies and the French Senate met at Paris on September 2nd at 3:00 p.m.. Chamber President Herriot and Senate President Jeannenay read brief speeches. The keynote speech in the Chamber was delivered by Premier Daladier, and in the Senate by Vice-Premier Chautemps. Both men delivered moderate speeches favoring a peaceful solution of the European crisis.

The purpose of the parliamentary sessions was to give the French Government a completely free hand in the conduct of a policy which might lead either to peace or to war. A motion for a secret session and a thorough debate on policy in the Chamber was defeated. Full military credits to sustain the mobilization and possible French participation in war were voted without debate. Pierre Laval spoke in the Senate, and he insisted that it would be unconstitutional for the French Government to participate in hostilities without requesting a declaration of war from the French Parliament. This was an extremely controversial issue among the French politicians. Laval did not hesitate to explain his own attitude toward the crisis. He agreed with Bonnet that the Poles were in default on their obligations to France, and he insisted to Daladier that an unwarranted French declaration of war against Germany would be suicidal for France.[41]

Halifax's Determination to Drive France into War

Halifax was alarmed by the inclination of the French Government to search for new avenues of peace. He wired to British Ambassador Phipps at Paris that the French attitude was causing grave misgivings in London. He added contemptuously, "we shall be grateful for anything you can do to infuse courage and determination into M. Bonnet." Halifax had reached a point where he was prepared to brand any man a coward who did not accept his own tragic plan for war. Halifax explained to Phipps in a subsequent dispatch that he would interpret a vote of credits by the French Parliament as a popular mandate for war against Germany. Bonnet attempted to impress Phipps and Halifax with the fact that the German Air Force in Poland was confining its operations to strictly military objectives. He added that Hitler had offered a demonstration of good will by honoring his earlier pledge in this regard. Phipps was merely able to report to Halifax that the French were prepared to consider a joint note to the Germans in the event that the Italian mediation effort failed, but they were continuing to place their faith in this plan.

The French were "strongly" insisting that at least forty-eight hours be allowed for the expiration of any ultimatum in case the conference plan collapsed. Daladier had told Bonnet that in any case he would not permit hostilities to begin before the night of September 4/5. American Ambassador Bullitt informed President Roosevelt that the French were counting on further German efforts to prevent the outbreak of a general war. Kennard, on the other hand, was bombarding Halifax with demands that both Great Britain and France attack Germany immediately. He was sounding out the Soviet diplomats to discover if the Russians would agree to offer military supplies to the Poles. This chimera appealed to Kennard more than the tangible Italian and French proposals for a conference.[42]

Sir Percy Loraine reported to Halifax on the late afternoon of September 2nd that Hitler had agreed to an armistice and an international conference, and that he was at work on plans to suspend German military operations in Poland. The German leader had declared that he would be able to stop operations on all sectors in Poland by noon on Sunday, September 3rd. Ciano told Loraine that Bonnet was prepared to accept Hitler's request for less than a day on September 2nd and 3rd to arrange the armistice. Ciano told Loraine that he was delighted with this news.

Ciano telephoned Halifax shortly before Cadogan spoke with Bonnet at 5:00 P.M. The Italian Foreign Minister could scarcely believe his ears when Halifax repeated his previous statement to Bonnet that the British Government would not consider the Italian conference plan until Germany had completed the total evacuation of Polish territory. Ciano was amazed that Halifax ignored Hitler's willingness to cooperate in suspending hostilities. Ciano assured Halifax that it had been a great achievement to obtain Hitler's agreement to suspend hostilities on September 3rd, and to enter a conference on the following day. He insisted that a British demand for the withdrawal of German troops was completely unreasonable, and that it would destroy every chance for a peaceful settlement.

The final remark of Ciano revealed the fatal failure of the Italian Foreign Minister to analyze the existing situation in a systematic and thorough fasion. He failed to perceive that British entry into the war was dependent on the consent of France, and that the British would not be able to destroy his peace plan if it was supported by France. Indeed, there is no evidence that Ciano ever stopped to consider this aspect of the situation. He was merely confirming what Halifax hoped would be true when he said that the British were in a position to destroy a peaceful settlement. His remark actually encouraged Halifax. The moment of decision for the Italian mediation effort had arrived, but Ciano was so overwhelmed with indignation at British intransigence that he failed to make the proper comments. He should have taunted Halifax with the fact that the French attitude toward the crisis was entirely different, and that he doubted if Great Britain would challenge Germany without French support. This might have goaded Halifax into making some of the insulting remarks about the French leaders which he had privately conveyed to his diplomats. The situation was complicated by the fact that Ciano continued to fear Halifax at the very moment he was indignant with him. He feared British military power, and he was reluctant to defy Halifax, because of possible British reprisals against Italy. Ciano's climactic conversation with Halifax was actually brief and inconclusive, and the Italian Foreign Minister put down the receiver in a mood of black depression.

The deplorable military and diplomatic weakness of Italy was decisive in frustrating Bonnet's attempt to change French policy in the French Defense Council meeting of August 23, 1939, and it was equally decisive in emasculating the Italian mediation effort on September 2, 1939. Halifax was merely bluffing, but he knew that his bluff might be successful in Italy because of Italian fear of British military power. Ciano received word from Attolico immediately after the conversation with Halifax that Hitler was refraining from replying to the British and French notes of September 1st because he was anxiously awaiting the outcome of the Italian mediation effort. Ciano could not help feeling that he had again let Hitler down in his recent conversation with the British Foreign Secretary. This situation assumes an especially tragic aspect when one anticipates that France, Italy, and Germany, despite their efforts to avert the outbreak of World War II, were destined to suffer crushing military defeats in that approaching war.[43]

Sir Percy Loraine hastened to inform Halifax that Ciano had secured the full support of Germany for a conference before launching his latest diplomatic initiatives at Paris and London. Halifax did not doubt this, but, unlike Ciano, he was fully aware of the crucial importance of the French position. He knew that Bonnet would seek to take the initiative by forcing a change of policy in Great Britain and Poland. Halifax falsely claimed in instructions to Phipps that Hitler was delaying his answer to the French and British notes of the previous day until he had occupied sufficient territory to negotiate on the basis of the Marienwerder sixteen points. It was not likely that this argument would influence Bonnet, because the French Foreign Minister had no objection to a settlement in Poland on the basis of the Marienwerder plan. Bonnet also derived some satisfaction from the fact that Hitler at last had replied to Polish provocations by launching military operations in Poland. He told Anatole de Monzie, the French Minister of Public Works, that he hoped the hoary thesis had been laid to rest that a little firmness would expose the allegedly empty German bluff. Bonnet had realized for a long time that Hitler would fight rather than capitulate in a difficult situation.[44]

The British were disturbed by some of Bonnet's remarks to Cadogan in their 5:00 p.m. telephone conversation.   The French Foreign Minister had refused to agree that the withdrawal of German troops from Poland was an indispensable condition for a conference. Bonnet warned that he would present this question to the French Cabinet. Halifax naturally feared that Bonnet would persuade the French Cabinet to accept the conference plan on the identical terms agreed to by Hitler. Halifax knew that his plans for war would be frustrated if this happened, and that he would have no choice other than to follow the French lead in accepting the plan for a conference. He was determined to do everything possible to destroy the Italian mediation plan before a decision was reached by the French Cabinet.

Halifax was alarmed by Bonnet's statement that Lukasiewicz had thus far failed to present a formal request for French aid to Poland. Halifax concluded from this statement that Bonnet personally continued to oppose a French commitment for war on behalf of Poland. The British Foreign Secretary made several tactical moves to cope with this situation. He decided to maintain pressure on the French Government to complete their deliberations as quickly as possible. He believed that this might deprive Bonnet of sufficient time to win the support of his clleagues for a change in French policy. He professed to be aghast when Bonnet informed him that the French Cabinet would probably not reach a decision before 9:00 p.m. He exerted all possible pressure at Paris, and Bonnet finally conceded that the French Cabinet would endeavor to complete its deliberations by 8:00 p.m.[45]

Phipps warned Halifax that French sentiment was strongly in favor of a negotiated settlement and opposed to war. He cited the moderate statement of Daladier in his Chamber speech that same afternoon: "If reason even now prevailed, France would be willing to work for peace." This statement had produced a round of loud applause from all sections of the French Chamber. Polish Ambassador Lukasiewicz had been observing the proceedings in glum silence, but he became greatly excited when he heard the statement of Daladier and the response which it received.

Loraine warned Halifax that Ciano was loudly proclaiming the vast difference between the response of the British and the French to his mediation effort. The danger existed, from Halifax's standpoint, that the Italian Foreign Minister would suddenly awaken to the fact that France, and not Great Britain, held the key to the situation. Ciano was complimenting Bonnet and declaring that his response was "more forthcoming and willing" than that of Halifax. The British Foreign Secretary was furious when he read this report at 6:00 p.m., and he immediately instructed Phipps to present a strong protest to France. He charged that "the position of the French government was very embarrassing to His Majesty's Government." He complained bitterly that he still did not know where France stood in relation to the British demand for the withdrawal of German troops from Poland. He admitted that he had no reason to believe that the French leaders recognized this as a valid demand. He was resolutely opposed to a forty-eight hour ultimatum in the event that the conference plan failed. The British naval authorities were complaining that this would permit many German merchant ships to escape seizure, and that it would cramp the style of British naval operations.

Phipps replied that it would be impossible to deliver this protest at once. The French Cabinet was now in session. The British Ambassador, who privately favored peace, added philosophically that, in any case, Halifax probably would receive an answer to all the questions which were troubling him sometime between 8:00 and 9:00 p.m Halifax realized at once that he had no further opportunity to exert pressure on the French leaders prior to the outcome of the fateful French Cabinet meeting. He knew that Bonnet would make a supreme attempt at that meeting to commit the French Government to a peaceful settlement. He feared that Bonnet would succeed in this purpose, and that the French Government would come out of the Cabinet session with the avowed purpose of insisting on a conference. The prospect of this final ruin of all his hopes for war against Germany was unbearable to Halifax.[46]

Ciano Deceived by Halifax

Halifax decided to take a desperate gamble. He telephoned Ciano at 6:38 p.m., with the intention of deliberately falsifying the momentary position of the British Government. The French had not yet indicated their definitive response to the Italian mediation plan. The British Government had no intention of opposing Germany without French support. Halifax nevertheless decided to tell Ciano that he was revealing the ultimate British response, and that it was negative. This would be an imprudent lie, but British policy since the Tilea hoax in March 1939 had been based in large part on a tissue of deliberate lies.

Halifax told Ciano that the withdrawal of the German troops from Poland was the essential condition for any conference, and he implied that Great Britain and France were in complete agreement on this important question. Ciano received the false impression that Bonnet had accepted this fatal British maneuver to obstruct a conference prior to attending the French Cabinet, which was still in session. Halifax had received word that Professor Burckhardt was still in Kaunas (Kovno), the Lithuanian capital, some two hundred and fifty miles from Danzig. He insisted to Ciano that Great Britain would demand the restoration of the League High Commissioner and his regime in Danzig before considering the possibility of a conference. Ciano interrupted despairingly again and again to say that Hitler could not possibly fulfill these conditions prior to attending a conference within the next few days. It seemed that the imagaination of Halifax was inexhaustible in providing insuperable obstacles to a successful conference. Ciano finally interrupted to assure Halifax that merely "the withdrawal of troops condition would make the whole scheme impossible for Hitler." The Italian Foreign Minister could not bear this further senseless and sadistic whipping of the dying peace angel. He suspected that Halifax would waste no time in announcing the annihilation of the conference plan to the entire world. It never occurred to him that Halifax would have the audacity to falsify the official French position toward the conference plan. He begged Halifax in vain not to discuss the British attitude toward a conference in Parliament.

There was nothing that Ciano could do to prevent Chamberlain in Parliament at 7:30 p.m. from giving what appeared to be the *coup de grâce* to Italy's peace efforts. The British Prime Minister presented a mendaciously distorted version of the entire delicate scheme which had been arranged to preserve the peace. He asserted that Great Britain could not consent to negotiate at a conference while Polish towns were being bombarded and the Polish countryside was being invaded. Chamberlain knew perfectly well that Hitler had agreed to suspend all hostilities as the necessary condition for any conference, but he was willing at the behest of Halifax to tell any lie to destroy the peace. It was merely a coincidence that this unprincipled mendacity occurred shortly after Winston Churchill had agreed to enter the Government as Parliamentary First Lord of the Admiralty. Churchill had received no advance information of the momentous decisions which the British Government was making. Gilbert and Gott offer a complete inversion of these events in presenting Halifax's telephone conversation with Ciano as an act of appeasement through which the British "Cabinet had been betrayed."[47]

Halifax made a similarly misleading statement in the House of Lords, where he also claimed that the British would not be able to participate in a conference while in Poland "towns are under bombardment." He claimed that "the action taken by the Danzig authorities and the Reichstag yesterday is the final step in the unilateral repudiation of this international instrument (Versailles Treaty) which could only be modified by negotiation." He failed to explain that juridically the Danzig-German Pact of September 1, 1939, was no more illegal than the Anglo-German Naval Pact of 1935, which had been concluded by the British without consulting France, Italy, and the other Versailles signatory Powers. His remark about the "final step" was a Freudian slip which revealed his fear that there would be no new opportunity to attack Germany after the completion of Hitler's program of Versailles Treaty revision.[48]

The Mediation Effort Abandoned by Italy

Unfortunately, the deceitful bluff of Halifax succeeded, and Mussolini concluded that the cause of peace was lost. This was a colossal Italian blunder. There was still no reason to assume that the British would act without France, although Ciano and Mussolini had failed to analyze this aspect of the situation, possibly because of their own great fear of British military power, and their concern about the safety of Italy. There was no excuse for them, despite their muddled thinking on this subject, to believe any statement from Halifax without first checking its accuracy from other sources. Both Ciano and Mussolini knew that the history of British diplomacy was studded with deceit and trickery. The Italian leaders suffered from an uncritical faith that no European leader, including Halifax, could be so ruthless in provoking a new World War after the recent and bitter horrors of World War I. Their judgment was also clouded by vanity. Halifax for several years had cleverly combined flattery and threats in his dealings with the Italian leaders. It was especially tragic that Mussolini, who was a shrewd and capable leader, was not more critical at this time in his evaluation of Ciano. He later realized that Ciano was not sufficiently competent to hold his important post, but by then it was too late.[49]

The situation might have been different had Mussolini been aware of events within the diplomatic corps at Rome. There was ample indication that the French and British were not in accord. Loraine had a furious argument with Francois-Poncet on the evening of September 2nd, and he reported to Halifax in despair, at 7:00 p.m., that all negotiations for a conference should be transferred from Rome to Paris.[50]

Kennard wired Halifax from Warsaw at 8:00 p.m. that Beck was demanding major British air operations on behalf of Poland immediately. The optimistic Polish military announcements could not conceal the fact that the Polish Air Force was no more, and the Polish leaders were sufficiently naive to expect that the British would help them. Kennard was slightly less naive, but he wired the following statement to Halifax: "I trust I may be informed at the earliest possible moment of our declaration of war and that our Air Force will make every effort to show activity on the western front with a view to relieving pressure here." Kennard knew that the British would not send their airplanes to Poland, but he was unaware that they also were not even willing to make a serious military effort in the West to relieve the Poles.

Ciano wired fatal instructions to Attolico in Berlin at 8:20 p.m. on September 2nd. He announced that Mussolini had formally withdrawn his offer to mediate among Great Britain, Germany, Poland, and France. Hitler was advised to abandon his plans for an armistice, and Ciano added that it was useless to proceed with the peace effort when both Great Britain and France were insisting on the withdrawal of German troops as the necessary condition for a conference. The conference proposal was eliminated. Hitler still clung to the hope that one last avenue of escape remained. The British and French had not presented an ultimatum, and they had not declared war. Perhaps the rapidity of the German advance in the local war with Poland, and the senselessness of another World War, would still deter them. The German commanders in Poland were competing with one another to advance more rapidly than required by the schedule of "Operation White," a truly lightning operational plan.[51]

Bonnet Dismayed by Italy's Decision

The French Cabinet failed to reach a final decision on the conditions for a conference in their first session which was adjourned at 8:20 p.m. Bonnet was hopeful that he would persuade his colleagues to accept the conference plan on the terms agreed to by Hitler. He was stunned to learn that the Italians in the meantime had formally abandoned their mediation effort, and that this had automatically terminated the German plans for an armistice. His effort to persuade his colleagues to accept the Italian terms had been rendered pointless at a single stroke, and without his knowledge. He telephoned Ciano at 8:30 p.m. It was his last conversation with the Italian Foreign Minister. Bonnet explained at once that France had not actually accepted the impossible British condition of a German troop withdrawal from Poland. Ciano expressed his amazement at this news, but he did not see how Italy could retrieve her blunder of cancelling her mediation plan. The British were insisting on the withdrawal of the German troops, and Bonnet no longer had the German assurance for an armistice with which to oppose the British lead. Ciano insisted to Bonnet that a new mediation effort would be unpropitious under these circumstances, and the French Foreign Minister reluctantly agreed. This conversation is a striking example of the manner in which resignation and fatalism can paralyze the will under the enormous pressure of a crisis situation.

Unfortunately, despite their good intentions, Bonnet, and especially Ciano, displayed less determination in fighting for peace than did Halifax in promoting war. This distinction made all the difference. Anatole de Monzie, the French Minister of Public Works, would have taken a far more forceful line than Bonnet in insisting that the Italians launch a new mediation effort. He tearfully implored Bonnet, immediately after the latter spoke with Ciano, to renew his attempts for a conference on condition that the German troops agree to stop their advance. He argued that Hitler would very likely agree again to these terms. Bonnet sadly replied that, in his opinion, there was no longer the slightest doubt that such an effort would fail to win the laurels of peace. Halifax was victor, and Germany, Italy, France, and Poland were doomed to desolation and defeat.[52]

Strangely enough, Bonnet, like Hitler, could not suppress the hope that, somehow, peace would still be preserved. At midnight, September 2/3, Bonnet had a long conversation with Guariglia, the Italian Ambassador. The two diplomats agreed that war could easily have been avoided had there been more cooperation from London. Bonnet assured Guariglia that England's refusal to compromise had made the conference impossible. The French Foreign Minister confided that he was still hoping for some "symbolic gesture" from Hitler, which would save the situation. The Italian Ambassador questioned Bonnet closely, but he was unable to receive any concrete suggestion of what Hitler could possibly do. He concluded that Bonnet had merely expressed a feeling of intuition. There was a meeting of minds at that moment between Hitler and Bonnet, but neither of them had much basis for hope.[53]

Halifax waited impatiently for word from Rome following his speech to the House of Lords shortly after 8:00 p.m. At last, Loraine wired Halifax at 9:30 p.m. that the British maneuver had been completely successful. Loraine explained that the Italians "do not feel it possible to press the German Government to proceed with Signor Mussolini's suggestion." The British Foreign Secretary was delighted with this news. His position had been vastly simplified by a single stroke. The French were now on the defensive, and he was determined to drive them into war with single-minded energy.

British Pressure on Daladier and Bonnet

Chamberlain telephoned Daladier at 9:50 p.m.. and claimed with unpardonable distortion that he had faced an "angry scene" in Parliament when he announced that he was still consulting with France on the time limit for an eventual ultimatum. High Dalton, one of the Labour Party leaders, claimed that the two men who were chiefly aroused by Chamberlain's statement were the notorious Tory warmongers, Alfred Duff Cooper and Leopold Amery. Duff Cooper later claimed that the statement of Chamberlain gave him the impression that there would be a "new Munich." Dalton and most of the other Members failed to receive this impression. The actual "angry scene" was staged single-handedly by Leopold Amery. His main grievance was that Chamberlain had not been sufficiently belligerent in his speech. When Arthur Greenwood arose to speak for the Labour Opposition, Amery shouted angrily: "Speak for England!" This was no doubt insulting treatment for the Prime Minister from an irascible Conservative subordinate, but it was a minor incident, and it did not amount to an "angry scene" in the British Parliament. Gilbert and Gott have recently engaged in a new effort to support this myth of the "angry scene" despite all the evidence to the contrary.[54]

Chamberlain told Daladier on the telephone that he wished to inform the British public before midnight that an ultimatum would be delivered in Berlin by Great Britain and France at 8:00 a.m. on September 3rd, and that war would follow at noon if the Germans did not capitulate. Daladier was appalled by the war hysteria revealed by Chamberlain, and by the effrontery of this virtual two hour ultimatum to France. The response of the French Premier was negative. He resented the British assumption that they had won their game. He asserted in desperation that he still had good reason to believe that Ciano was about to renew his mediation effort. He advised against any kind of diplomatic step at Berlin before noon on the following day, and he evaded the British proposition that an ultimatum with a time limit should be delivered.[55]

The Collapse of French Opposition to War

The British diplomats were furious with Daladier for defying their Prime Minister, and for delaying the full enjoyment of their triumph. Halifax decided that the withdrawal of the Italian mediation effort permitted him to take a step which otherwise would have been an enormous gamble. He telephoned Bonnet at 10:30 p.m. that the British ultimatum for 8:00 a.m. the next day would be communicated to the British public before midnight, regardless of the attitude of France. He was unable at this moment, with all the odds in his favor, to disguise his basic dependence upon France. He confided that everything would proceed unilaterally up to the expiration of the British ultimatum at noon the following day. Great Britain at that point would take no action whatever unless the French had previously agreed to follow with their own declaration of war within twenty-four hours.

One can easily imagine the fantastic situation which would have unfolded had the British leaders presented a four-hour ultimatum which the Germans could not possibly accept, and then had done nothing when it expired. The Polish leaders, who in any event did not trust the British, would have concluded that they were the victims of a very subtle conspiracy. The Polish reaction would undoubtedly have been mild compared to that of President Roosevelt. The disappointment of the American President would have known no bounds had the war policy of Halifax disintegrated at the last minute.

Halifax was confident that this situation would not come to pass. Nevertheless, he indicated that he would prefer this to embarking on a war against Germany without French support. It is easy to see from this revelation that it would not have been exceedingly difficult for Ciano and Bonnet to outmaneuver Halifax on the diplomatic stage had they been more skillful in concerting their policies. Bonnet protested that Halifax's proposal for unilateral British action in presenting an ultimatum was very unpalatable. Halifax countered with a typically fantastic claim that, unless war followed immediately, "it seemed very doubtful whether the Government could hold the position here." Churchill later declared that he feared during the final hours of the crisis that the British Government would not intervene in the German-Polish war. He never hinted that the British Ministers in this event would have been driven from office.

Furthermore, this possibility never entered Churchill's mind at the time. Churchill merely observed in a letter to Chamberlain on the night of September 2nd that prospects for the formation of a strong coalition War Cabinet would suffer some injury if Great Britain delayed indefinitely the announcement of her decision.[56]

Halifax was calmly confident by this time, although he was somewhat uncertain about Bonnet's reaction to this long telephone conversation, in which he had not permitted his French colleague to do much of the talking. He drew up a memorandum on the conversation in which he concluded, after some hesitation, that Bonnet had "finally agreed."[57]

Dr. Fritz Hesse of the German Embassy in London discussed the situation with Sir Horace Wilson at the time of the Halifax conversation with Bonnet. Hesse argued for a new effort to arrange a diplomatic conference, but he received no encouragement from Wilson. Hesse was told that Great Britain would have declared war on Germany on September 2nd had it not been for the diplomatic intervention by Mussolini. Hesse guessed from further remarks made by Wilson that Daladier had temporarily applied a brake on British "impetuosity." Hesse hoped that Daladier and Bonnet might succeed at the last moment in preventing an Anglo-French war against Germany.[58]

The British destroyed these hopes by proceeding to announce publicly their forthcoming ultimatum to Germany. Halifax followed up this momentous development with a wire to Henderson at 11:50 p.m., in which he instructed the British Ambassador to "warn" Ribbentrop that he might ask to see him at any hour. This crass discourtesy was a further indication of Halifax's confidence that he had won the game. He knew that the British ultimatum would not be delivered until the following morning, and it was his first impulse to give both Henderson and Ribbentrop a sleepless night. He soon relented as far as Henderson was concerned. He confided to the British Ambassador thirty-five minutes later that there would be no ultimatum until the following morning. The British Ambassador, however, never ceased to be a gentleman, and he promptly passed this reassurance along to Ribbentrop. Shortly afterward, following a new complaint from Kennard about the delay in starting the war, Halifax informed Henderson that the ultimatum would expire at 11:00 a.m. instead of noon (British summer time, German standard time). At this point, Halifax was confident that he had won the game. Gilbert and Gott, in citing Kirkpatrick, contradict their own picture of an imaginary Halifax reluctant to face the prospect of war: "Halifax 'seemed relieved' that the decision had been made. 'He called for beer, which was brought down by a sleepy resident clerk in pyjamas. We laughed and joked . . .' "[59]

French resistance to British impetuosity crumbled rapidly in the face of Halifax's self-assurance and successes. Bonnet concluded fatalistically that, with the Italians now out of the picture, it would be futile to continue to frustrate British designs. The British at 2:00 a.m. on September 3rd announced their final timetable, which was to be a two-hour ultimatum from 9:00 a.m. to 11:00 a.m. Bonnet decided not to test Halifax's twenty-four hour policy in which the British would fail to react to the expiration of their own ultimatum unless the French agreed to follow suit on British terms. Bonnet in the final test did not have sufficient personal courage to assume the primary responsibility in defying the British leaders. He told Phipps that the French ultimatum would expire at 4:00 a.m. on September 4th.

The British and French Declarations of War Against Germany

The British ultimatum note was delivered on schedule by Henderson to Dr. Paul Schmidt, the chief German interpreter at the Foreign Office, at 9:00 a.m. Ribbentrop had explained that he was not in the mood to receive *ultimata* that day. It was a painful moment for Schmidt, who, like other Germans in official circles, was very fond of Henderson.[60]

Schmidt carried the fatal ultimatum to Hitler's office in the Chancellery.

He discovered that the room was silent when he entered. Hitler was sitting at his desk, and Ribbentrop was standing some distance away at one of the windows. Hitler read the ultimatum carefully. He was quite calm, and he displayed no anger when he received the blow. It was the most cruel blow he had ever received. There was a pause after he had finished reading, and he asked pensively of no one in particular: "What now?" This was a momentous question, but no mortal man could answer it. Ribbentrop understood this perfectly. There was another pause, and the German Foreign Minister said quietly: "I assume France will deliver a similar ultimatum within the next few hours."

What more was there to say? Europe was now in the grip of the worst crisis of her entire history. Schmidt was not needed, and he left the office. He announced quietly to a group outside which included most of the principal German dignitaries: "In two hours there will be war between Germany and England." Joseph Goebbels scowled, deep in thought. More formidable tasks faced him now than ever before, because the German people hated the thought of war with England. Goering solemnly spoke for everyone present when he said: "May Heaven have mercy on us if we lose this war!"[61]

Birger Dahlerus had remained in Berlin at the request of Marshal Goering. He made two further telephone calls to the British Foreign Office before the expiration of the British ultimatum. He announced in his first telephone conversation at 10:15 a.m. that he was calling to convey an official German appeal for peace. Dahlerus added that he was personally convinced that discussions would be more successful than war. He emphasized that the Versailles Treaty required further peaceful revision, but Europe did not require a war. He exclaimed that all of his efforts had been inspired by one motive, namely, love of peace.

Dahlerus called again at 10:50 a.m., in great agitation, to announce that the German Government had prepared a reply to the British ultimatum. He hoped that this reply would still reach London before 11:00 a.m. , although he could not guarantee it. He added that Marshal Goering had received formal permission from Hitler to fly to Great Britain on a special peace mission. Dahlerus was about to explain the powers which had been granted to Goering, and the concessions he was prepared to make, but Cadogan cut him short. He announced curtly that the British Government could not delay its decision, and he laid down the receiver.[62]

Dahlerus was unable to inform Cadogan that the German Government had prepared a second note for the eventuality that the British Government would refuse to delay their decision. There was one certain factor in this terrible situation. The German leaders would not cringe before the British once they had been challenged by a British declaration of war.

Ribbentrop received Henderson after the outbreak of the Anglo-German war and gave him a reply addressed to Chamberlain and Halifax. This note was received by Henderson at 11:20 a.m. on September 3rd. It opened with the following spirited declaration: "The German Government and the German people refuse to receive, accept, let alone fulfill demands in the nature of *ultimata* made by the British Government." The German note expounded the thesis that warlike conditions had existed along the German eastern frontier for many months. The note concluded: "The German people and its Government do not, like Great Britain, intend to dominate the world, but they are determined to defend their own liberty, their own independence, and above all their life." The second great struggle between Germany and the British Empire had begun. Halifax in 1939 had repeated the achievement of his kinsman, Sir Edward Grey, in 1914, by involving his people in a tragic and unnecessary conflict deplored in both instances by the leaders of Germany. The first of these struggles weakened the British Empire, and the second produced its irrevocable decline.[63]

French Ambassador Coulondre was received by Weizsaecker at noon. The German State Secretary announced that Ribbentrop was briefly attending a reception for the new Soviet Ambassador to Germany, but that he would return shortly. Coulondre wished to present the French war ultimatum to Weizsaecker, but he was persuaded to wait for Ribbentrop. The German Foreign Minister soon arrived and engaged the French Ambassador in a brief and serious discussion about the tragic *impasse* in Franco-German relations. Less than one year had passed since the promising Franco-German declaration of friendship of December 6, 1938. The French Government had been under further heavy British pressure, and Bonnet had at last agreed to deliver an ultimatum which would expire at 5:00 p.m. the same day. Coulondre complained that he always had feared his mission to Berlin would end in this way.

Attolico reported to Ciano on the latest events in the German capital at 1:15 p.m. Germany was at war with both Great Britain and Poland, and would soon be at war with France. The Italian Ambassador had the satisfaction of noting that Germany was standing alone in this struggle despite the Italo-German alliance of May 1939, but he realized that a European conflict of these dimensions might easily embroil Italy at some later date. This situation might not have resulted had he not persuaded the Italian Government to repudiate the pledge which Ciano had given to Hitler on August 13, 1939.[64]

The Unnecessary War

The Germans, by 5:00 P.M. on September 3rd, were at war with three European Powers, whose total European population was 125,000,000 and whose dominion and colonial populations, from which, of course, Poland was excluded, totaled more than 600,000,000. Germany with her 80,000,000 inhabitants, was capable of defending herself, or of defeating any of her immediate neighbors on land who dared to attack her. The immediate neighbors of Germany did not constitute the major German security problem. Entanglement in war with England led eventually to war with the Soviet Union and the United States. These two colossal Powers had a combined population of nearly 400,000,000, and each of them was capable of producing much more war material than Germany. Hitler had only the doubtful support of much weaker countries, such as Italy and Japan, and of a few of the tiny European nations.

It was an unequal struggle, although the Germans, on numerous occasions, achieved successes which seemed to indicate that they might after all prevent the total destruction of their country. Ultimately German resistance collapsed after nearly six years of savage warfare. There were no longer any Great Powers in Western and Central Europe after the passing of Germany as a Great Power in 1945. As General Albert Wedemeyer admirably put the matter, the Western nations conducted their war against Germany like an Indian scalping party without thought or heed for the future. It was not surprising under these circumstances that the only real victor of World War II was the Soviet Union. The proud British Empire was dwarfed by the Soviet colossus. This would not have been possible without the war policy of Lord Halifax which played directly into the hands of the Communist leaders.

The British leaders failed to learn the lessons of World War I, and there has been no indication that they learned them from World War II. The Conservative Prime Ministers since 1951, Churchill, Eden, and Macmillan, were warmongers in 1938 and 1939. The memoirs of Lord Halifax revealed in 1957 that the former British Foreign Secretary was sanctimoniously complacent and smugly unrepentant. The principal British news weekly, *Time & Tide,* professed to see a far happier world in 1959 than in 1939: "The West does not face today, as did Great Britain and her allies in 1939, an oligarch who lives war for its own sake, backed by a people who largely share his tastes."[65]

This was another way of saying that the British leaders did not dare to "redress the balance of power" by attacking the Soviet Union in 1959 as they attacked Germany in 1939.

The Soviet leaders do not share the earlier admiration of Hitler for the British Empire. The British leaders know that their national security, as they enjoyed it in 1939, is a thing of the past. They see no choice other than to bide their time and to place their trust in the allegedly peaceful intentions of the Soviet Union. These miserable circumstances have failed to increase their wisdom. They still refuse to admit that their aggressions against Germany in 1914 and 1939 were the unnecessary blunders which created their present unenviable situation. *Time & Tide* claimed in 1959 that "to fail in the battle for peace (i.e. appeasement of the Soviet Union) would be to betray the men who fell in the two great wars of this century." The betrayal of the brave British fighting men who died in two unnecessary wars against Germany cannot be redeemed by the present feeble efforts of the British leaders to placate the most formidable enemy which Great Britain has faced throughout her entire history. As Italian diplomatic historian, Mario Toscano, has pointed out, the balance of power has been replaced by the balance of impotence.[66]

CONCLUSION

A marked trend toward a new arrangement of European relations based on the peaceable revision of the old Versailles settlement was rudely interrupted by the unexpected and unnecessary outbreak of World War II in September 1939. Germany had regained her rightful position as the dominant Power in Central Europe during 1938. At that time it seemed only a question of months before she would succeed in establishing relations with all of her immediate neighbors on a solid and dependable basis.

It is necessary to consider briefly in retrospect the European scene immediately after the Munich Conference. Germany was prosperous, and there were numerous indications that France, Great Britain, and Italy were recovering from the effects of the world depression of 1929. There were also hopeful indications that the leaders of France were by this time fully aware of the new realities, and that they were prepared to abandon their old policies of active intervention in Central Europe. This means that the last obstacles to successful Franco-German amity could be removed, because there were no longer any territorial problems or disputes between France and Germany.

Italy had gracefully accepted the reunion of Austria with Germany, and there were no clouds on the horizon of Italo-German relations.

German-Polish relations had shown general improvement for several years prior to 1938, and Hitler's moderate and reasonable attitude toward Poland was highly auspicious for successful cooperation between the two countries in the future.

There were friendly relations between Germany and Hungary, and there was also increasing confidence and friendliness in German relations with such Balkan nations as Rumania and Yugoslavia.

The Soviet Union had been excluded from the deliberations of the Munich Conference, and there was every indication that the Communist Colossus would remain isolated behind the *cordon sanitaire* established shortly after World War I.

Hitler's friendly attitude toward the British Empire was well known. It was evident that Germany had no intention of resuming her earlier rivalry with

Great Britain either in naval or in colonial questions. British world trade was increasing along with German prosperity, and hence there was no reason to expect new economic tensions of a serious nature between the former principal rivals of world trade.

All of this should have meant the beginning of a new era of peaceful development for Europe. Instead, Europe the following year, in 1939, was precipitated into the horrors, decline, and eclipse implicit in World War II.

It has been necessary to take a long and penetrating look behind the curtains of the European scene to discover how the tragedy of 1939 intruded its ugly visage on the world. The major aspects of the situation have been examined, but in the end it has been the march of events in London and Warsaw which has demanded the principal share of the observer's attention.

Halifax in London succeeded in imposing a deliberate war policy on the British Government in 1938-1939 despite the fact that most of the leading official British experts on Germany favored a policy of Anglo-German friendship. Beck in Warsaw adopted a position of full cooperation with the war plans of Halifax despite the numerous warnings he received from Poles aghast at the prospect of witnessing their country hurtle down the road to destruction.

Many efforts were made by German, French, Italian, and other European leaders to avert the catastrophe, but these efforts eventually failed, and the Halifax war policy, with the secret blessings of President Roosevelt and Marshal Stalin, emerged triumphant. These events have been depicted in the course of the previous narrative. The story culminated in the hideous tragedy of an unnecessary war.

World War II had its origins in the British attempt to destroy National Socialist Germany. Lord Halifax later recalled the "wholly irrational pacifist sentiment" in Great Britain when Hitler came to power. Halifax's principal achievement on the British home front, prior to the declaration of war on September 3, 1939, was to persuade the people to "face up to Hitler."[1] He was completely successful in this effort, and the Anglo-American scalping party, as described by General Albert C. Wedemeyer, against Hitler and the German people, and incidentally also against the Italians and Japanese, ended in Europe in the ephemeral triumph of Germany's unconditional surrender. The British Empire since the end of World War II in 1945 has, however, been "facing down" to many nations large and small throughout the world, and the end is not yet.

There was little reason to believe, prior to March 1939, that Great Britain would lead another "crusade" against Germany. The British Government had pursued a strangely inconsistent policy toward Germany throughout the entire 1933-1939 period. It was difficult to say before March 1939 whether more prominent Englishmen approved or disapproved of Hitler.[2]

The British leaders condoned the first important steps in the remilitarization of Germany in 1935 by concluding an Anglo-German naval pact which violated the Treaty of Versailles. France and Italy both indicated that they would have refused to approve of such a measure had the British consulted them. The British, however, evaded their treaty obligation to do so.

British Foreign Secretary Eden later denied, in March 1936, that the military reoccupation of the Rhineland by Hitler was a "flagrant violation" of the principal Locarno treaty. This was regarded in Paris as tantamount to condoning

Hitler's action, but Eden confused the issue by denying that France had previously violated her Locarno engagements in concluding the Franco-Soviet alliance. The German case was built on the contention of such a prior French violation.

This British policy of seemingly supporting both France and Germany in a crucially important Franco-German dispute was mysterious and confusing at that time. The same can readily be said of the ambivalent British role during the Austrian and Czech crises in 1938. It should excite no surprise that the eager acceptance of the Munich agreement in France was based on the assumption that the British intended to abide by this highly realistic new type of approach to the problems of Central Europe.

The secret British shift to a war policy in October 1938, when Halifax took over control of British foreign policy from Chamberlain, was followed by the public proclamation of this new policy by Chamberlain himself at Birmingham on March 17, 1939. This culminated, in turn, in the launching of the new "crusade" against Germany on September 3, 1939.

It is a great temptation to judge the outcome of the events of 1939 by the condition of the British Empire today, but such an approach might easily confuse the major issue. Even an increase in the power and prestige of the British Empire following the War would scarcely have excused the slaughter which produced the ruin and military defeat of such continental European states as France, Italy, Germany, and Poland, not to mention the many neutrals of Europe ultimately devastated in the same maelstrom. Denunciation of the British foreign policy of 1938-1939, by pointing to the vicissitudes now afflicting Great Britain, is like ridiculing a reckless man because he has lost a leg. It does not meet Toynbee's claim that Great Britain had no other choice.

Therefore, a further analytical examination of the record is highly advisable. The Germany of Adolf Hitler had made no move whatever during the 1933-1939 period that threatened the areas of traditional British interest in Western Europe. There was no indication during those years that Germany intended to present selfish or provocative demands on such countries as France, Italy, Holland, Belgium, or Denmark. The problem of the Czechs in Central Europe after the Munich Conference presented a special case. Their homeland was outside the sphere of traditional British interest. The Munich agreement itself had actually been a dead letter since October 1938, when Halifax persuaded the Czechs and Hungarians to ignore Great Britain and France in seeking arbitration of their frontier dispute.

The British Government, after October 1938, repeatedly evaded acceptance of any of the commitments in the Bohemian area which had been suggested at Munich. The British Government, according to both Chamberlain and Halifax, had no right to be consulted about the Hitler-Hacha treaty of March 15, 1939, which represented, as Professor A.J.P. Taylor put it, a conservative solution of the Bohemia-Moravian problem.[3]

The Polish problem and the Danzig dispute followed the latest Czech crisis. The British Government had certain nominal obligations at Danzig as a member of the League of Nations, but similar British commitments to the League regime at Memel had been ignored without difficulty when that traditionally German city was seized by Lithuania. The Germans had presented only friendly suggestions and no belligerent demands involving Danzig by March 31, 1939, when the British Government extended a definite guarantee to Poland which also gave full support to the Polish attitude toward Danzig. German proposals concerning Danzig had previously been rejected by Poland in a manner deliberately calculated to create tension, but official German policy toward Poland before March 31st was exemplary, and was based exclusively on the desire to reach an amicable understanding with the Poles. There was no German action of any kind to justify British intervention in Poland at that time. Indeed, the guarantee of March 31, 1939, revealed that Great Britain was encouraging Poland to adopt a hostile policy toward Germany despite the generous terms which Hitler had offered for a lasting German-Polish settlement. The German offer, it must be repeated, was in no sense accompanied by demands for a settlement within any specific period of time.

Hitler was friendly toward the Poles, whom he liked, and he had also offered innumerable indications that he strongly favored Anglo-German friendship. There had been no German actions against Great Britain or her interests. There was no valid excuse for the British Government to encourage a German-Polish conflict in the hope of involving Germany in a new World War. The warmongering tactics of pro-Soviet intellectuals in Great Britain and the United States, prior to the Soviet-German pact of August 23, 1939, provided no excuse; rather, they should have been a warning. The personal desire of Maxim Litvinov for a war between Germany and the Western Powers was clearly a hint that such a war might be advantageous for Communism and equally injurious to all other parties. There was no justification for a British Conservative Government to engage in war because it was desired by the Communists and their friends. The British Government had ample popular support for a conservative foreign policy.

The actual British foreign policy moves after March 31, 1939, were directed unrelentingly toward war. Everything possible was done to undermine several excellent opportunities for a negotiated settlement of the German-Polish dispute, and for the negotiation of a new Czech settlement based on international guarantees. Instead of working for a satisfactory agreement with Germany—Hitler was willing to be moderate and reasonable in dealing with both the Polish and the Czech questions—Halifax concentrated on intimidating Italy and bullying France because they both favored peace instead of war. The Polish Government was advised by Halifax to reject negotiations with Germany, and Warsaw was constantly assured that British support would be available for any war. The numerous requests of the German Government for mediation between Germany and Poland, or for a direct Anglo-German agreement, were either answered with deceptions or ignored. A maximum effort was made to present the American leaders with a distorted picture of the actual situation in Europe. All of these British moves had their roots in the obsolete, traditional policy of the balance of power.

The unreasonable attitude adopted by the Polish Government in 1939 is no mystery when one considers the grandiose British assurances to Poland after August 1938. The general policy of Jozef Beck against Germany was eminently satisfactory to Lord Halifax, although there was no mutual admiration between the two men and much disagreement arose between them about policy toward the Soviet Union, Rumania, and other countries. The prospect of unlimited

British support for dreams of aggrandizement at the expense of Germany was an irresistable lure to Polish chauvinism. The refusal of the British to guarantee Poland against Soviet aggression was carelessly ignored. The Polish leaders made a German-Polish war inevitable by creating a permanent crisis and refusing to negotiate for its solution. The situation probably would have been entirely different had Poland's former great leader, Jozef Pilsudski, been at the helm.

The policy of Hitler was governed by the fact that the British were goading Poland into war against Germany, and that Germany was again threatened by the prospect of a protracted two-front struggle. The German leader showed restraint in the face of Polish provocations, such as partial mobilization, before the British guarantee of March 31, 1939. He concluded after the guarantee that the key to his problems was in London, and he made many efforts to persuade the British Government to change its course, and to encourage a negotiated settlement. It would have been more profitable for him to concentrate his major diplomatic effort at Paris. The French leaders were genuinely inclined toward peace, and the British would not have waged war against Germany without the support of France.

Hitler eventually launched operations in Poland, following the failure of his numerous negotiation efforts, but this was only after he had decided that war with the Poles had become inevitable in any event. Germany would surely have been ruined very quickly had she become involved in a stalemate in Poland during the October rainy season, and had the French and British on the western front elected such a time to attack with their superior forces. Nevertheless, there was no time before the British declaration of war on September 3, 1939, when Hitler would have opposed a negotiated solution with Poland. An indication of this was shown by his favorable response to the Italian conference plan on September 2, 1939, and his willingness at that time to consider an immediate armistice in Poland. His peace policy foiled because the British Empire decided to challenge Germany before Hitler had completed his program of arriving at amicable understandings with his immediate neighbors.

It is quite likely that a more extensive German armament program after 1936 would have persuaded the British to hold their hand, at least in 1939. Hitler's many appeals to British good-will were quite futile. It is also clearly evident that the situation would have been saved for Hitler had Italy maintained her previous diplomatic solidarity with Germany. The Italian defection from Germany and her neutrality pledge to Great Britain on August 18, 1939, was the decisive factor in frustrating Bonnet's attempt to separate France from Poland at the French Defense Council meeting on August 23, 1939. It gave General Gamelin the excuse to argue that the French military position had improved since the previous Defense Council meeting on March 13, 1939. At that previous meeting, when the attitude of Italy was uncertain, Gamelin had confessed that France was unprepared for a conflict with Germany. The changed position of Italy (neutrality in the event of war) was the only conceivable excuse Gamelin could have used to modify his earlier statement on French military prospects.

Halifax's "success" in promoting World War II resulted primarily from his masterful technique in dealing with prominent Englishmen, and with the Italians and French. His dominant role after the Munich Conference was never challenged in England. and the effectiveness of his diplomacy at Paris and Rome during the last few weeks of peace is beyond dispute. He was far less capable of dealing with the Russians, but the Soviet Union was an alien world which he regarded with indifference, distaste, and contempt. The failure of his negotiations with the Soviet Union made it more difficult to hold France in line, but Halifax ultimately succeeded in even that objective. His main asset in that connection, apart from his successful intimidation of the Italians, was the timidity of French Foreign Minister Georges Bonnet. Bonnet wanted Gamelin, or anyone else, to bear the brunt of British wrath when France refused to go to war. He refused at the last moment to assume that burden himself and to preserve peace.

The indifference of Halifax toward the fate of the Poles made it possible to employ them as an instrument of British policy without compunctions about the inevitably tragic consequences for Poland.

The motives of Halifax in 1939 were clearly derived from the ancient tradition of maintaining British superiority over the nations of Western and Central Europe. He had never questioned the role of his kinsman, Sir Edward Grey, in promoting World War I. Halifax did not propose to tolerate the existence in 1939 of a German Reich more prosperous and more influential than the Hohenzollern Empire which had been destroyed in 1918. It was for the prestige of Great Britain rather than for such mundane considerations as national security or immediate British interests that Halifax became a proponent of war in 1938. The traditional British aim to dominate policy in Continental Europe was the underlying reason why the world experienced the horrors of World War II. It was in pious service to this hoary ideal rather than for personal prestige or profit—he was amply endowed with both prior to 1938—that Halifax conducted his policy. He recognized no restraint of any kind in the pursuit of his objective. He was satisfied that his goal was legitimate and in the closest possible harmony with the ideal expressed in his maiden speech to Parliament so many years earlier: the eternal glory and superiority of the British Empire. That the triumph shared by the British in the subsequent struggle was illusory and temporary, Halifax attributed to the will of Providence.

Others have not so easily achieved even this momentary solace, the solace of the principal perpetrator of World War II. The German people, especially, have been laden with an entirely unjustifiable burden of guilt. It may safely be said that this is the inevitable consequence of English wars, which for centuries have been waged for allegedly moral purposes. It is equally evident that the reconciliation which might follow from the removal of this burden would be in the interest of all nations which continue to reject Communism.

A sober view of the blunders of recent years and their consequences would be the best possible aid in now facing the difficult task of the future. The worst of these blunders was undoubtedly the British decision to encompass the destruction of Germany. Further research within the context of traditional British foreign policy will surely add a great deal to our understanding of this blunder, but it will not justify it.[4] There can be no real justification for the ruin of Europe in this greatest of all wars, waged as a consequence of the antique policy, illusions, and ruthless actions of Lord Halifax, an impressively old-fashioned and pious British aristocrat.

1. Earl of Halifax, *Fullness of Days,* New York, 1957, p. 182.
2. Frederick L. Schuman, *Europe on the Eve: the Crises of Diplomacy 1933-1939,* New York, 1939, pp. 332-346.
3. A.J.P. Taylor, *The Origins of the Second World War,* London, 1961, p. 202.
4. Lord William Strang, *Britain in World Affairs: the Fluctuation in Power and Influence from Henry VIII to Elizabeth II,* New York, 1961, pp. 326ff.; Halifax, in 1939, was in the unique position of being free to choose between two entirely different policies for his country: peace and conciliation, or aggressive war; the greater enthusiasm for peace, despite the presence of vociferous Tory war minority, headed by Churchill, made it far more difficult for Halifax to achieve than to continue with a peaceable policy.

Appendix

Identifications of Persons Mentioned in the Text

Abetz, Otto: friend of Ribbentrop and advocate of Franco-German understanding.

Adams, John: brilliant publicist, politician, and second American president.

Alexander I: Yugoslav sovereign assassinated in 1934.

Alexander I: Russian ruler at the time of the Vienna Congress.

Amery, Leopold: British Conservative politician, born in India, active in colonial affairs, opposed appeasement.

Arciszewski, Miroslaw: Polish career diplomat, friend of Jozef Beck, Minister to Rumania, 1932-1939.

Astakhov, Georgi: Russian Chargé d'Affaires at Berlin.

Astor, Lord Waldorf: British politician and foreign affairs expert.

Attlee, Clement: British Labour Party chief, 1935-1955.

Attolico, Bernardo: Italian Ambassador to Germany.

Baginski, Henryk: popular Polish geopolitician.

Bailly, Léon: leading French newspaperman (*le Jour*).

Baldwin, Stanley: British Conservative Prime Minister, 1924-1929, 1935-1937.

Balfour, Arthur James: British Conservative leader and World War I foreign secretary.

Barnes, Joseph: American journalist in Berlin.

Barthou, Louis: French Foreign Minister, 1933-1934, and friend of Raymond Poincaré.

Baudouin, Paul: French financier and diplomatic trouble-shooter in Italy.

Beaverbrook, Lord Max: British newspaperman and Conservative politician.

Beck, Jozef: Polish Foreign Minister, 1932-1939.

Beck, General Ludwig: German Army staff chief until 1938, underground opponent of Hitler.

Beethoven, Ludwig van: classic German composer.

Benes, Edvard: Czech nationalist and 2nd President of Czechoslovakia.

Benoist-Méchin, Jacques: French historian and expert on military affairs.

Beran, Rudolf: Czech Premier, 1938-1939.

Beraud, Henri: French journalist (*Gringoire*).

Bergery, Gaston: French Radical Socialist politician.

Berl, Emmanuel: leading French newspaperman (*Marianne*).

Beseler, General Hans von: German Governor of Occupied Poland in World War I.

Best, W.K.: Gestapo official in charge of Polish-Jewish deportation action in 1938.

Bethmann-Hollweg, Theobald von: Chancellor of Germany, 1909-1917.

Bevin, Ernest: British Labour Party leader.

Biddle, Anthony: American Ambassador to Poland.

Bismarck, Otto von: Prussian statesman who created the German Second Reich.

Blanqui, Auguste: 19th century French socialist politician and political philosopher.

Blomberg, Werner von: German Defense Minister, 1932-1938.

Bluecher, General Gebhard: Prussian Army commander at Waterloo.

Bluecher, Wuepert von: German Minister to Finland.

Blum, Léon: French Socialist since 1902, leader of French Socialist Party, 1914-1945.

Bobrzynski, Michal: pro-Habsburg Polish statesman and historian.

Bochenskki, Adolf: Krakow historian and expert on Polish foreign policy.

Boening, Robert: Secretary for the Society of German-Polish Friendship.

Boettcher, Viktor: Danzig diplomat and foreign affairs expert.

Bonnet, Georges: French Army officer and politician, repeatedly Cabinet Minister after 1925, Ambassador to United States, 1936-1937, Foreign Minister, 1938-1939.

Botta, André: French Socialist Party leader.

Brauchitsch, Walther von: German Army Commander.

Briand, Aristide: popular French politician and Foreign Minister until 1932.

Brooks, Collin: British publicist and extreme nationalist.

Bruening, Heinrich: German Chancellor, 1930-1932.

Bucard, Marcel: French authoritarian politician, leader of *Francisme*.

Buchanan, George: 1914 British Ambassador to Russia.

Budenny, General Semyon: Bolshevik commander who defeated the Poles in the Ukraine in 1920.

Bullitt, William C.: American Ambassador to USSR, 1933-1936, and to France, 1936-1940

Burckhardt, Carl Jacob: Swiss historian and last League High Commissioner at Danzig.

Burgin, Leslie: British Minister of Transport in the Chamberlain Government.

Bute, Lord John Stewart: British Prime Minister, 1761-1763.

Butler, R.A.B.: British Parliamentary Under-Secretary for Foreign Affairs.

Buxton, Hharles Roden: British Quaker leader and champion of an Anglo-German understanding.

Cadogan, Alexander: British Permanent Under-Secretary for Foreign Affairs after 1937.

Caillaux, Joseph: French reform statesman, ex-Premier, Senator, Radical Socialist leader.

Carol II; Rumanian sovereign, 1930-1940.

Castlereagh, Robert: British Foreign Secretary, 1812-1822.

Catchpool, T.C.P.: British social worker, active in the Sudetenland.

Catherine II: 18th Century Russian sovereign.

Cavour, Camillo: Italian statesman who collaborated with Napoleon III.

Celovsky, Boris: Czech historian, expert on diplomatic history.

Charles II: 17th Century Stuart sovereign of England.

Charles IV (Luxemburg-Premyslid): 14th Century Holy Roman Emperor.

Charles VIII: 15th Century French sovereign.

Chamberlain, Austen: Conservative British Foreign Secretary at the time of the Locarno treaties.

Chamberlain, Joseph: pre-World War I British Conservative Colonial Secretary and champion of protectionism (high tariff).

Chamberlain, Neville: Conservative British Prime Minister, 1937-1940; son of Joseph and brother of Austen.

Chambre, Guy la: French Air Minister.

Champetier de Ribes: French Radical Socialist politician.

Chatfield, Admiral Alfred: First Sea Lord of the British Admiralty, 1933-1938, chairman Indian Defence Comm., 1938-1939.

Chautemps, Camille: French Radical Socialist politician, several times Premier, vice-Premier under Daladier, 1938-1940.

Chéran, Henri: French Minister of Justice in the Doumergue Government.

Chiappe, Jean: Parisian police prefect.

Chodacki, Marjan: Polish career diplomat, Polish High Commissioner at Danzig, 1936-1939.

Chlapowski, Alfred: Polish Ambassador to France, 1924-1936.

Churchill, Winstin: anti-German British Conservative politician.

Chvalkovsky, Frantisek: Czech career diplomat, Foreign Minister after the Munich conference.

Ciano, Galeazzo: Italian Foreign Minister, 1936-1942, son-in-law of Mussolini.

Cincar-Markovic, Aleksander: Yugoslav Foreign Minister.

Clemenceau, Georges: French Premier who favored a harsh peace with Germany in 1919.

Corbin, Charles: French Ambassador to Great Britain.

Cotton, William: British Conservative opponent of Halifax's 1939 policy.

Coulondre, Robert: French Ambassador to Germany, 1938-1939.

Cranborne, Lord Robert: British House of Lords leader; against appeasement in 1938.

Cretzianu, Alexandru: Rumanian diplomatic trouble-shooter in England, 1939.

Cromwell, Oliver: 17th century English revolutionary leader and statesman.

Cromwell, Thomas: English adventurer and politician, adviser to Cardinal Wolsey, later Government Minister, 1534-1540.

Csáky, István: Hungarian Foreign Minister, 1938-1941.

Cvetkovic, Dragisa: Yugoslav Premier, 1939-1941.

Czartoryski, Adam: Polish statesman in close collaboration with Alexander I of Russia since 1795.

Dabski, Jan: Polish National Democratic diplomat; head of Polish delegation at Riga peace negotiations in 1921.

Dahlerus, Birger: Swedish engineer and private diplomatic trouble-shooter.

Daladier, Édouard: French Army officer, history teacher, and Radical Socialist politician; several times Premier, his last and most important term, 1938-1940.

Dalton, Hugh: British Labour Party leader.

Dalimier, Albert: French Radical Socialist politician implicated in the Stavisky affair.

Daszynski, Ignaz: Polish socialist leader and friend of Pilsudski.

Daudet, Alphonse: 19th Century French *revanche* writer and novelist.

Daudet, Léon: novelist, journalist, and conservative politician; son of Alphonse.

Davies, Joseph: American Ambassador to USSR, 1936-1938, Belgium, 1938-9.

Davignon, Jacques: former Belgian foreign minister, envoy to Germany (Minister, 1936-1938; Ambassador, 1938-1940).

Dawson, Geoffrey: friend of Halifax, editor of the London *Times*.

Déat, Marcel: French neo-socialist leader and opponent of Léon Blum.

Delbos, Yvon: French Foreign Minister, 1937-1938.

Denikin, General Anton: Russian nationalist leader who opposed Communism.

Dietrich, Otto: German press chief at Berlin.

Dimitrov, Georgi: Bulgarian Communist; Comintern chief at Moscow.

Dirksen, Herbert von: German Ambassador to Great Britain, 1938-1939.

Dorgerès, Jacques: French farm pressure group leader.

Dmowski, Roman: Polish political philosopher and statesman; advocated collaboration with Russia.

Doriot, Jacques: ex-Communist authoritarian French politician.

Doumenc, Général: chief of the 1939 French military mission to USSR.

Doumergue, Gaston: French President and Premier.

Draganov, Parvan: Bulgarian Minister to Germany in close collaboration with USSR diplomats.

Drax, Admiral Reginald Aylmer Ranfurly Plunkett-Ernle-Erle: chief of 1939 British military mission to USSR.

Dreyfus, Alfred: 19th century French officer condemned for treason and later pardoned.

Druffel, Ernst von: German Consul-General in Bratislava, Slovakia.

Duff Cooper, Alfred: British historian and anti-German Conservative politician.

Duranty, Walter: N.Y. *Times* correspondent in Moscow.

Durcansky, Ferdinand: Slovak nationalist leader.

Eden, Anthony: friend of Churchill and British Foreign Secretary, 1935-1938.

Edward VIII: British sovereign forced to abdicate in 1936.

Eisenlohr, Ernst: German Minister to Czechoslovakia.

Elias, Alois: Czech Premier after March 1939.

Eugene of Savoy, Prince: 18th century Habsburg military hero.

Fabricius, Wilhelm: German Minister to Rumania.

Farley, James: United States Postmaster-General and Democratic Party campaign manager.

Faure, Paul: French Socialist leader.

Fernandez, Ramon: French Communist writer and intellectual leader.

Flandin, Pierre-Étienne: French Foreign Minister during the 1936 Rhineland crisis; opposed the 1939 British war policy.

Fritsch, Werner von: German Army commander demoted in 1938.

Forster, Albert: Danzig National Socialist Party leader.

Franassovici, Richard: Rumanian Minister to Poland.

François-Poncet, André: French Ambassador to Germany, 1931-1938; to Italy, 1938-1940.

Frank, Hans: German Minister of Justice.

Frederick II: 18th Century Hohenzollern ruller of Prussia.

Freysing, Bishop Otto: Hohenstaufen churchman and historian.

Frick, Wilhelm: German Minister of Interior.

Fritzche, Hans: leading official, after Goebbels and Naumann, in the German Propaganda Ministry.

Fudakowski, Senator Kazimierz: Polish politician and banker; advocated a strong policy against Lithuania.

Gaertner, Margarete: German publicist and expert on Danzig.

Gafencu, Grigorie: Rumanian Foreign Minister, friend of Józef Beck.

Gallacher, William: Communist MP from West Fife (Scotland).

Gamelin, General Maurice: French Army Commander.

Gandhi, Mohandas: Indian nationalist and freedom leader.

Garibaldi, Giuseppe: Italian revolutionary leader; captured Sicily and Naples from the Bourbons.

Gauché, Général: chief of French counter-intelligence, 1933-1940.

Gaxotte, Pierre: French conservative journalist (*Je suis partout*).

Geist, Raymond: American diplomat at Berlin, 1929-1939; Chargé d'Affaires, Feb.-May 1939.

George III: British sovereign, 1760-1820.

Gerard, James: American Ambassador to Germany, 1913-1917.

Geddes, Sir Auckland: British Conservative politician and onetime president of the Board of Trade.

Geraud, André: French pro-Communist journalist (Pertinax).

Gide, André: pro-Communist French novelist.

Gluchowski, General Janusz Julian: Polish Vice-Minister of War, 1935-1939.

Goebbels, Joseph: German Minister for Propaganda and Public Enlightenment.

Goerdeler, Carl: Saxon bureaucrat and underground opposition leader against Hitler.

Goering, Hermann: Chief of German Air Force, Reichstag President, Prussian Minister-President, Minister of Economics.

Goga, Octavian: anit-Jewish Rumanian poet and politician; Premier in 1937.

Goluchowski, Agenor: Polish Conservative and Duma representative.

Gorecki, General Roman: chief of Polish World War I veterans.

Gorer, Geoffrey: British sociologist and expert on national character.

Górka, Olgierd: Polish revisionist historian.

Grabski, Wladislaw: Polish National Democratic politician.

Grazynski, Michal: Silesian-Polish insurrectionary: governor of East Upper Silesia since 1926.

Greiser, Artur: Danzig Senate President, 1934-1939.

Greenwood, Arthur: British Labour Party leader.

Grenfell, Russell: British naval officer and military historian, favored reconciliation with Germany.

Grey, Edward: British Foreign Secretary at the outbreak of World War I.

Gruebnau, Walter: Danzig citizen murdered at Kalthof in May 1939.
Gruehn, Erna: German prostitute; married Defense Minister Blomberg.
Grynszpan, Herschel: degenerate murderer of Ernst vom Rath.
Grzybowski, Waclaw: Polish Ambassador to USSR, 1935-1939.
Guariglia, Raffaele: Italian Ambassador to France, 1938-1940.
Gunther, Franklin Mott: American Minister to Rumania, 1937-1940.
Gustav V: Swedish monarch freindly to Germany and Poland.
Hacha, Emil: Czech president, 1938-1939.
Haking, General Richard: early British League High Commissioner at Danzig.
Halecki, Oskar: dean of Polish-American historians.
Halévy, Élie Daniel: French historian; expert on England and on French political tradition.
Halifax, Lord Edward: British Foreign Secretary, 1938-1941.
Hanfstaengl, Ernst: German art expert and press adviser to Hitler until 1937.
Hankey, Maurice: member of British Defence Council and Cabinet Minister until 1938; critical of 1939 Halifax war policy.
Hasbach, Senator Hans: Conservative German politician of Poland.
Hassell, Ulrich von: German Ambassador to Italy, recalled in 1938; German underground leader.
Hearnshaw, F.J.C.: British publicist and supporter of Halifax.
Helfand, Leon: Soviet Chargé d'Affaires at Rome.
Hencke, Andor: German Legation Counsellor at Prague, 1935-1939.
Henderson, Nevile: British Ambassador to Germany, 1937-1939; friend of Chamberlain.
Henlein, Konrad: Sudeten German Party leader in Czechoslovakia.
Henriot, Phillipe: French conservative politician.
Henry VIII: 16th Century British sovereign.
Herbert, Sidney: British Conservative politician and opponent of appeasement in 1938.
Herder, Johann Gottfried: German romanticist and Slavophile.

Herriot, Édouard: French Radical Socialist politician, Premier, President Chamber of Deputies, Mayor of Lyons.
Hertling, Georg von: World War I German Chancellor.
Hesse, Dr. Fritz: German press chief at the London Embassy.
Hindenburg, Paul von: German President, 1925-1934.
Hitler, Adolf: German Chancellor after 1933.
Hlinka, Andreas: Slovakian national hero and independence leader.
Hoare, Reginald: British Minister to Rumania.
Hoare, Samuel (Lord Templewood): British Foreign Secretary in 1935; adviser to Halifax.
Hodza, Milan: Hlasist pro-Czech Slovak politician; Czechoslovak Premier, 1937-1938.
Holsti, Rudolf: Finnish Foreign Minister.
Hoover, Herbert: American President, 1929-1933; critic of Rooseveltian foreign policy.
Horthy, Nicholas: Hungarian admiral; regent of the Hungarian kingdom after 1920.
Hossbach, Friedrich: German Army *liaison* officer.
Hudson, Robert: British trade expert and Government official.
Hull, Cordell: American Senator; Secretary of State, 1933-1945.
Hus, John: Prague University professor after 1398 and religious leader.
Ickes, Harold: American Secretary of the Interior.
Imoni Bela: Hungarian reform politician; Premier, 1937-1938.
Inönü, Ismet: Turkish President and military officer; successor of Kemal.
Inskip, Thomas: British Defence Minister.
Ironside, General Edmund: British Army Inspector-General; after Sept. 1939, British Army Commander.
Janson, Martin von: German Consul-General at Danzig.
Jarman, T.L.: American historian and expert on Germany.
Jaurès, Jean: French Socialist leader assassinated in 1914.
Jaworski, W.L.: pro-Habsburg Polish statesman.
Jebb, Gladwyn: Secretary to Alexander Cadogan.

Jedrzejewicz, Waclaw: Polish Cabinet Minister and historian.

Jefferson, Thomas: brilliant political philosopher and third American President.

Jodl, General Alfred: Bavarian officer and loyal supporter of Hitler.

Johnson, General Hugh: New Deal administrator; critic of Roosevelt's foreign policy.

Jones, Thomas: British Liberal politician and trust executor; friend of Lloyd George and Stanley Baldwin.

Joseph II: 18th Century Holy Roman Emperor and progressive statesman.

Jouvenel, Bertrand de: French writer; advocate of Franco-German understanding.

Jouvenel, Jenry de: French Senator and Ambassador to Italy.

Jules, Henri: French Ambassador to the United States until 1936.

Kaczmarek, Czeslaw: Polish scholar and spokesman of Poles in Germany.

Kaganovich, Lazar: Soviet Politburo member and brother-in-law of Stalin.

Kanya, Kalman: Hungarian Foreign Minister, 1933-1938.

Kasprzycki, Tadeusz: Polish Army staff chief; educated in France.

Kauffmann, Rudolf: National Socialist Party leader in South Tirol.

Kava, Colonel: Polish military attache at Berlin.

Keble, John: Oxford religious leader and poet.

Keitel, General Wilhelm: German Army staff chief executed at Nuremberg, 1946.

Kemal, Mustafa: Turkish general, revolutionary leader; first President of Turkey.

Kennard, William Howard: British career diplomat since 1907; Ambassador to Poland, 1935-1939, and to Polish Government-in-exile, 1939-1941.

Kennedy, Joseph: American Ambassador to Great Britain.

Kerillis, Henri de: leader of the French journalistic crusade against Germany.

Keyes, Roger: British Admiral and Conservative MP from Portsmouth; anti-appeasement in 1938.

Kiderlen-Waechter, Alfred: German Foreign Minister, 1910-1912.

Kirk, Alexander: American Chargé d'Affaires at Berlin in 1939.

Kirov, Sergei: Leningrad administrator murdered in 1934.

Kisielewski, Józef: Polish publicist; expert on Polish minorities abroad.

Knatchbull-Hugessen, Hughe: British diplomat; Ambassador to China, Turkey, and Foreign Office bureau chief.

Koc, Adam: Polish banker and statesman; organizer of the OZON state Party group.

Kordt, Erich: German Foreign Office official and personal assistant to Ribbentrop.

Kordt, Theo: German Charge d'Affaires in London.

Korfanty, Adalbert: Polish National Democrat; organized three insurrections in Upper Silesia.

Kozdon, S.I.: Slonzak mayor of Teschen; deposed by Poles in 1938.

Krofta, Kamil: Czech Foreign Minister and friend of President Benes.

Kucharzewski, Jan: Polish historian fraiendly to Germany; author of *From White to Red Czarism.*

Kundt, Theodor: German minority leader in central Bohemia.

Kunicki, Ryszard Pawel: Polish Foreign Office official critical of Beck's policy.

Kwiatkowski, Eugeniusz: Kraków engineer; Polish Secretary of Commerce from 1926, Vice-Premier from 1935.

Lansbury, George: British Labour Party chief, 1931-1935.

Lauzanne, Stephane: leading French journalist (*le Matin*).

Laval, Pierre: former French Premier and Foreign Minister opposed to the 1939 British war policy.

Lazareff, Pierre: French journalist (*l'Ordre*).

Lebrun, Albert: French President, 1932-1940.

Léger, Alexis: Secretary-General at the French Foreign Office, 1933-1940.

Legrenier, Paul: French journalist and spokesman for a German-Polish understanding (special mission to Berlin, 1939).

Lepecki, Michal: adjutant of Pilsudski; expert on Jewish resettlement.

Lester, Sean: unpopular British League High Commissioner at Danzig, 1933-1936; removed at Danzig's request.

Levy, Louis: French Socialist journalist.

Lebohova, Ekrem Bey: Albanian Foreign Minister.

Lieberman, Herman: Jewish Socialist imprisoned in a Polish concentration camp in 1930.

Lincoln, Abraham: American Civil War President; advocate of negro resettlement.

Lindbergh, Charles: American aviation hero and military expert.

Lindsay, Ronald: British Ambassador to the United States.

Lipski, Józef: Polish Minister and Ambassador to Germany, 1933-1939.

Litvinov, Maxim: Soviet Foreign Affairs Commissar, 1928-1939.

Lloyd George, David: British Prime Minister, 1916-1922.

Lochner, Louis P.: American journalist in Berlin.

Lokolnicki, Jan: Polish Minister to Turkey.

Londonderry, Lord Charles: British Air Minister and advocate of reconciliation with Germany.

Loraine, Sir Percy: British Ambassador to Italy, 1939-1940.

Lord, Robert Howard: Harvard historian and American specialist on Poland and Russia at the Versailles Peace Conference.

Lothian, Philip Kerr, Lord: British foreign Policy expert, Ambassador to the United States, 1939-1941.

Louis XIV: greatest of the Bourbon sovereigns of France; died in 1715.

Lubienski, Michal Tomasz: Polish foreign office official, 1920-1939; Beck's *chef de cabinet.*

Lueck, Kurt: German cultural historian and expert on Poland.

Lukasiewicz, Juliusz: Polish Ambassador to France, 1936-1939; personal friend of Beck.

Lyautey, Général Hubert: French Marshal; member of French Academy.

Mac Donald, Ramsay: British Prime Minister, 1923-1924; 1929-1935.

Mac Donnell, M.S.: early British League High Commissioner at Danzig.

Macmillan, Harold: British publisher and 1938 anti-Appeasement Tory politician.

Mandel, Georges (Jereboam Rothchild): Minister for Colonies in the Daladier Government, 1938-1940.

Mackensen, Field Marshal August von: German World War I hero of Polish and Balkan operations.

Mackensen, Hans Georg: German State Secretary and Ambassador to Italy.

Mackiewicz, Stanislaw: Polish publicist and critic of Beck's policy.

Magistrati, Count Massimo: Italian Chargé d'Affaires at Berlin.

Maisky, Ivan: Soviet Ambassador to Great Britain.

Makins, Roger: British Foreign Office legal expert.

Maria Theresa: 18th Century Queen of Hungary, wife of Holy Roman Emperor Francis I, mother of Joseph II and Leopold II, daughter of Charles VI.

Marx, Karl: political philosopher and father of modern Communism.

Masaryk, Jan: Czech Ambassador to Great Britain; son of President Masaryk.

Masaryk, Thomas: Czech revolutionary leader; first president of Czechoslovakia.

Mastny, Vojtech: Czech Minister to Germany, 1937-1939.

Matteotti, Giacomo: Italian Socialist leader and opponent of Mussolini.

Matuszewski, Ignacy: Polish financier and journalist; friend of Pilsudski.

Maurras, Charles: French royalist journalist and politician.

Mazzarini, Giulio: Italian statesman; first minister of France, 1642-1661.

Meissner, Otto: German State Secretary; assistant to Ebert, Hindenburg, and Hitler.

Merekalov, Alexander: soviet Ambassador to Germany.

Mickiewicz, Adam: Polish romanticist poet and revolutionary.

Mikoyan, Anastas: Soviet official and economic expert.

Moltke, Hans Adolf von: German Minister and Ambassador to Poland, 1931-9.

Moltke, Helmuth von: Prussian General Staff chief and expert on Poland.

Molotov, Vyacheslav: Soviet Foreign Commissar, 1939-1949.

Monnet, Georges: French Socialist leader.

Monzie, Anatole de: Radical Socialist Politician; Minister of Transportation in the Daladier Government.

Moraczewski, Jedrzej: Polish revolutionary and Socialist Premier of Poland.

Morawski, Zygmunt: Polish soldier and chauffeur; perpetrator of the Kalthof murder, May 1939.

Morgenthua, Henry Jr.: Secretary of Treasury in Roosevelt Cabinet.

Morrison, Herbert: British Labour Party leader.

Moscicki, Ignaz: Polish Scientist and President of Poland.

Muensterberg, Willi: Communist agent who organized anti-National Socialist propaganda in Paris.

Mussolini, Benito: Italian Premier, 1922-1945.

Nadolny, Rudolf: former German Ambassador to the USSR.

Naggiar, Paul-Émile: French Ambassador to the USSR, 1938-1940.

Namier, L. Bemstein: British diplomatic historian; notoriously anti-German.

Napoleon I: Emperor of the French; died in British captivity.

Napoleon III: Emperor of the French; captured by Prussia at Sedan in 1870.

Narutowicz, Gabriel: friend of Pilsudski and President of Poland; assassinated in 1922.

Neurath, Konstantin von: German Foreign Minister, 1932-1938; later Protector of Bohemia-Moravia.

Newton, Sir Basil: British Minister to Czechoslovakia until March 1939.

Nicolson, Harold: British diplomatic historian and Conservative politician; anti-appeasement in 1938.

Nietzsche, Friedrich: 19th Century German philosopher admired by Hitler and Mussolini.

Nikita (Nicholas I): sovereign of Montenegro, 1860-1918.

Noël, Léon: French Ambassador to Poland, 1936-1939.

Norman, Montagu: Governor of the Bank of England, 1920-1944; friend of Hjalmar Schacht.

Nye, Gerald: American Senator leading the defense of American neutrality legislation against New Deal attacks, 1939-1941.

Ogilvie-Forbes, George: British Chargé d'Affaires at Berlin and principal assistant of Sir Nevile Henderson; opposed to war in 1939.

Orsenigo, Cesare: Papal Nuncio at Berlin.

Oster, Colonel Hans: German counterintelligence officer and underground opponent of Hitler.

Osusky, Stephan: Czechoslovak Ambassador to France.

Ott, Eugen: German Ambassador to Japan.

Ottokar II (Premyslid): 13th Century Bohemian sovereign.

Paderewski, Ignaz: Polish musician and National Democratic Premier of Poland.

Palacky, Francis: 19th Century Czech nationalist and historian.

Palmerston, Lord Henry: 19th Century British Foreign Secretary.

Papée, Kazimierz: Polish High Commissioner at Danzig; after 1936, Polish Ambassador to the Vatican.

Papen, Franz von: German Chancellor in 1932; later Ambassador to Austria and Turkey.

Paul-Boncour, Joseph: French Radical Socialist politician, several times Foreign Minister.

Paul Karageorgevic: Yugoslav Recent, 1934-1941.

Perkowski, Tadeusz: reailroad executive and assistant to Chodacki at Danzig.

Perth, James Eric Drummond, Lord: Secretary-General of the League of Nations, 1919-1933; British Ambassador to Italy, 1933-1939.

Pétain, Marshal Henri: French World War I hero and defense strategist; Chief of State, 1940-1944.

Petlura, Semyon: Ukrainian Socialist leader; collaborated with Pilsudski after World War I.

Petrescu-Comnen, Nicolae: Rumanian Foreign Minister, 1937-1939; opponent of Józef Beck.

Pfeffer, Karl Heinz: German publicist; expert on Great Britain and the United States.

Phipps, Eric: British Ambassador to France, 1934-1940; former Ambassador to Germany; brother-in-law of Vansittart.

Piasecki, Julian: Polish engineer; Under-Secretary for Transportation, 1933-1939.

Piatkowski, Edmund: Polish soldier killed on the German border in August 1939.

Pichon, Stephen: World War I French Foreign Minister.

Pierce, Franklin: New Hampshire politician; American President after Fillmore.

Pilsudska, Alexandra: widow of Pilsudski; born Suwalki, 1882, studied at Lwów University.

Pilsudski, Józef: Polish revolutionary leader and World War I hero; Dictator of Poland, 1926-1935.

Pitt, William (Lord Chatham): 18th Century British Prime Minister; directed British policy during the decisive phase of the Seven Years' War.

Pitt, William: British Prime Minister, 1783-1801, 1806; led Great Britain in war against France after 1792.

Piux XII: Roman Catholic Pontiff; leader of the European peace campaign, March-September 1939; failed to persuade Beck to negotiate with Germany in August 1939.

Poincaré, Raymond: French lawyer and statesman; served as Premier and President; died in 1934.

Poniatowski, Jan: aristocratic Polish Minister of Agriculture; opposed to major agrarian reforms.

Potemkin, Vladimir: Soviet Assistant Commissar for Freign Affairs.

Potocki, Artur: Polish Conservative leader from Eastern Poland.

Potocki, Jerzy: Polish Ambassador to the United States, 1936-1939.

Potworowski, Gustaw: Polish Minister to Sweden.

Pressard, Georges: French Attorney-General; brother-in-law of Chautemps.

Price, Ward: British journalist and expert on authoritarian systems.

Raczynski, Esward: Polish Ambassador to Great Britain, 1934-1939; top aristocracy; studied at Oxford.

Radziwill, Albrecht: Polish Conservative leader from Western Poland.

Radziwill, Stanislaw: received highest decoration for heroism in the 1920-1921 war with Russia; son of Albrecht.

Raeder, Erich: German Navy Commander-in-Chief.

Rath, Ernst vom: German career diplomat; assassinated at Paris, 1938.

Renaud, Jean: French authoritarian politician; leader of *Solidarité Française*.

Rauschning, Hermann: Danzig National Socialist Senate President, 1933-1934; later anti-German publicist.

Reshetar, John: foremost American historical expert on the Ukraine.

Reynaud, Paul: French conservative politician and financial expert.

Rhodes, Cecil: British imperialist and advocate of Anglo-American-German collaboration.

Ribbentrop, Joachim von: German Foreign Minister, 1938-1945.

Richert, Arvid: Swedish Minister to Germany.

Ritter, Gerhard: German historian; expert on military affairs.

Rocque, François de la: leader of French World War I veterans.

Roosevelt, Franklin: New York politician; American President, 1933-1945.

Ropp, William S. von: British intelligence agent; expert on Germany.

Rosenberg, Alfred: German publicist and National Socialist Party Foreign Affairs Bureau chief.

Rosenfeld, Oriste: French Socialist journalist.

Rosting, Helmer: Danish League High Commissioner at Danzig.

Rothermere, Harold Harmsworth, Viscount: World War I Cabinet Minister; leading Bitish newspaperman.

Rothschild, Maurice de: French financier.

Runciman, Lord Walter: British trade expert and diplomatic trouble-shooter.

Saint-Quentin, René: French Foreign Office offical; Ambassador to United States, 1938-1949.

Salazar, Antonio de Oliviera: Portuguese dictator; ally of Great Britain.

Salisbury, Lord Robert; British Prime Minister, 1885, 1886-1895-1902; advocate of 'splendid isolation'.

Sandys, Duncan: Conservative politician; son-in-law of Churchill; opposed appeasement in 1938.

Sapieha, Eustachy: Polish Conservative leader from Eastern Poland.

Sargent, Porter: American scientist, publicist, and philosopher of education; opponent of Rooseveltian foreign policy.

Sarraut, Albert: French Premier during the 1936 Rhineland crisis.

Sawicki, General Kazimierz; Polish Socialist, 1905-1920; Legion veteran; Polish Army Staff Chief, 1938-1939.

Sayre, F.B.: American Assistant Secretary of State in charge of Anglo-American trade negotiations, 1938.

Schact, Hjalmar: German financial genius; underground opponent of Hitler after September 1939.

Schiller, Friedrich: classic German poet.

Schleicher, Kurt von: German Chancellor, 1932-1933.

Schmidt, Dr. Guido: Austrian Foreign Minister, 1936-1938.

Schmidt, Dr. Paul: famous German interpreter; in German diplomatic service, 1923-1945.

Schmundt, Rudolf: Hitler's military adjutant; murdered by Stauffenberg in 1944.

Schneider, Wilhelm: German politician of Poland; leader of Young German Party dissident faction.

Schulenburg, Friedrich von: German Ambassador to the USSR, 1934-1941.

Schuschnigg, Kurt von: Austrian Dictator, 1934-1938.

Schwerin-Krosigk, Ludwig: Oxford-trained German finance minister, 1932-1945.

Scotland, A.P.: British counter-intelligence chief.

Seeds, William: British Ambassador to the USSR during the futile 1939 Anglo-Soviet negotiations.

Seyss-Inquart, Arthur: Austrian National Socialist leader; opponent of Schuschnigg.

Shepherd, Edward Henry: British Consul-General at Danzig, 1938-1939.

Sidor, Karol: Slovak politician and nationalist leader.

Sienkiewicz, Henryk: Polish romanticist author; advocate of a Polish mission in the East; died in 1916.

Simon, Arlette: mistress of Stavisky; compromised several French political leaders.

Simon, John; Viscount: British Foreign Secretary, 1931-1935; adviser to Halifax, 1935-1941.

Sinclair, Archibald: British Liberal Party leader.

Skoropadski, Pavel: Ukrainian Conservative leader who collaborated with Germany during the last phase of World War I.

Skrzynski, Alexander: Polish Foreign Minister in the 1920's and friend of Pilsudski.

Skulski, Leopold: Polish Premier at the outbreak of the 1920 war with Russia.

Skwarczynski, General Stanislaw: leading Polish staff officer and strategist.

Slawek, Walery: Polish statesman and close personal friend of Pilsudski; chief author of the 1935 Polish constitution.

Slawoj-Skladkowski, General Felician: Polish Premier at the outbreak of war in 1939; also Minister of Interior.

Smigly-Rydz, Edward: Polish Army Commander; Pilsudski's successor as Marshal of Poland.

Smith, Truman: American military attaché at Berlin; friend of Charles Lindbergh.

Smogorzewski, Kazimierz: Polish journalist and expert on Germany.

Sobieski, Jan: 17th Century Polish sovereign and military hero.

Sombart, Werner: German economist and expert on the evolution and structure of capitalism.

Sosnkowski, General Kazimierz; Polish Army Inspector-General; onetime Polish Army Commander and friend of Pilsudski.

Spears, General Edward: British soldier and Conservative politician; opposed appeasement in 1938.

Stalin, Joseph: Soviet *Vozhd* (Supreme leader), 1928-1953.

Stanhope, James: 18th Century Conservative British statesman who promoted a European league of preponderant states.

Stavisky, Alexander: immigrant criminal whose embezzlements produced the 1934 Government crisis in France.

Steinhardt, Lawrence: American Ambassador to the USSR at the outbreak of World War II.

Stephen Bathory: 16th Century sovereign of Poland.

Stojadinovic, Milan: Yugoslav strong man, 1934-1939.

Stolypin, Piotr: Russian Minister-President assassinated in 1911.

Strang, William: Chief of the Central Office of the British Foreign Office after 1936.

Stresemann, Gustav: German Chancellor and Foreign Minister of the Weimar period; advocated German-Soviet collaboration at the expense of Poland.

Stronski, Stanislaw: Polish National Democratic scholar and publicist.

Strzetelski, Stanislaw: Polish Conservative Party leader.

Studnicki, Wladislaw: Polish nationalist scholar and publicist; advocated collaboration with Germany.

Swantopolk; medieval East Pomeranian Slavic chieftain.

Syrovy, General Jan: World War I hero and Czech Premier, 1938-1939.

Szembek, Countess Isabelle: wife of the Polish Under-Secretary for Foreign Affairs.

Szembek, Count Jan: Polish Under-Secretary for Foreign Affairs, 1932-1939; formerly in the Austro-Hungarian diplomatic service.

Sztójay, Doeme: Hungarian Minister to Germany.

Tabouis, Genèvieve: pro-Communist French journalist.

Tardieu, André: French conservative politician and publicist; Tardieu and Caillaux were the leading French elder statesmen after the death of Poincaré in 1934.

Teleki, Paul: Hungarian Prime Minister, 1938-1941.

Tenestu, General: Chief of the Rumanian Army General-Staff.

Thompson, Dorothy: most active of the anti-German American journalists.

Thomsen, Hans: German Chargé d'Affaires in Washington, D.C.

Thorez, Maurice: French Communist Party leader.

Tilea, Virgil: Rumanian Minister and Ambassador to Great Britain, 1939-1940.

Tippelskirch, Werner von: German Chargé d'Affaires at Moscow.

Tiso, Josef: Slovak nationalist leader; Premier after March 1939; hanged by the Czechs, 1947.

Todt, Fritz: German engineer and public works expert.

Tomaszewski, Kazimierz: Polish Army officer and spokesman of a strong policy against Germany.

Toscano, Mario: Italian diplomatic historian.

Tower, Reginald: early British League High Commissioner at Danzig.

Toynbee, Arnold: British historian and foreign affairs expert.

Trott zu Solz, Adam von: German Rhodes scholar and unofficial diplomatic agent.

Trotzky, Leon: exiled Bolshevik leader; assassinated by a Bolshevik agent in 1940.

Truman, Harry: Missouri politician; succeeded Roosevelt as American President in 1945.

Tuka, Adalbert: Slovak national hero and independence leader.

Tukachevsky, Marshal Mikhail: Russian Army Staff Chief executed in 1937.

Umansky, Konstantin: Soviet Ambassador to the United States.

Umiastowski, Roman: Polish historian and expert on Russia.

Urbsys, Juozas: Lithuanian Foreign Minister.

Van Buren, Martin: New York politican; succeeded Andrew Jackson as American President.

Vansittart, Robert Gilbert, Lord: British Permanent Under-Secretary for Foreign Affairs until January 1, 1938; afterward Diplomatic Adviser to His Majesty's Government.

Veesenmeyer, Edmund: diplomatic troubleshooter from Ribbentrop's special foreign policy office.

Victor Emmanuel III: Italian sovereign, 1900-1946.

Viviani, René: French Premier at the outbreak of World War I.

Voroshilov, Kliment: Soviet Politburo member and Defense Minister.

Vuillemin, Général: French Air Force Commander.

Walpole, Robert: 18th Century British politician and statesman; organized the modern English political party system.

Warr, Earl de la: Lord Privy Seal in the Chamberlain Government.

Washington, George: American revolutionary hero; first President of the United States.

Weisskopf, Georges: French journalist (*l'Ordre*).

Weizaecker, Ernst von: State Secretary at the German Foreign Office, 1938-1945.

Welczeck, Johannes von: Silesian aristocrat; German Ambassador to France.

Wellington, General: British commander at Waterloo; later Prime Minister.

620 THE FORCED WAR

Weygand, Général Maxime: chief foreign adviser of Pilsudski during the defense of Warsaw against the Bolsheviks in 1920.

Welles, Sumner: American Under-Secretary of State.

White, W. L.: American Journalist in Berlin.

Wiegand, Karl von: veteran American journalist in Europe.

Wiesner, Rudolf: German politician of Poland; leader of Young German Party.

Wilhelm II: Hohenzollern soveriegn of Germany, 1888-1918.

William III: sovereign of England following the 'glorious revolution' of 1688.

Wilson, Horace: British economic expert and personal adviser of Chamberlain.

Wilson, Hugh: last American Ambassador to united Germany; recalled in 1938.

Wilson, Woodrow: President of the United States and father of the League of Nations.

Witos, Wincenty: Polish agrarian leader and opponent of Pilsudski.

Woermann, Ernst: German Charge d'Affaires at Warsaw.

Wohlthat, Dr. Helmuth: Commissioner of the German Four Year Plan; friend of Hjalmar Schacht.

Wolmer, Lord William: British House of Lords leader; against appeasement in 1938.

Wood, Kingsely: British Air Minister.

Wszelaki, Jan: Polish econimic expert and publicist; adviser of Colonel Koc in England, 1939.

Wysocki, Alfred: Polish Minister to Berlin until 1933 and Foreign Office official.

Wuehlisch, Johann: German Charge d'Affaires at Warsaw.

Zaleski, August: Polish Foreign Minister, 1926-1932.

Zaleski, Mieczlaw: Polish official; advocate of a strong policy against Germany.

Zay, Jean: Minister of Education in the Daadier Government.

Zeligowski, General Lucjan: Polish soldier who defied the League of Nations and seized Wilna for Poland.

Zog: Albanian sovereign, 1928-1939.

Zola, Émile: 19th Century French novelist and liberal agitator.

Zyborski, Waclaw: Polish Ministry of Interior official responsible for German minority problems.

Notes

Chapter 1

1. E.M. House, *The Intimate Papers of Colonel House*, vol. 2, London, 1962, p. 181, notes of February 14, 1916, that Arthur James Balfour, the British Conservative leader, objected that an independent Polish state would be an unwelcome buffer protecting Germany from future Russian hostility. In a memorandum of November, 1916, written immediately after the proclamation of Polish independence, Balfour explained that Poland should remain in the Russian empire, because this "would best suit our interests"; he also favored the enlargement of Russian Poland at the expense of Germany and Austria, *vide* Blanche Dugdale, *Arthur James Balfour*, vol. 2, London, 1932, pp. 435-442; the need to emphasize Poland extensively in an approach to the origins of the European war in 1939 was admirably explained by the Polish diplomat and scholar, Michal Sokolnicki, "A Historian Versus Facts and Documents" (A.J. Toynbee, *The Eve of War, 1939*, London, 1958) in *Pilsudski Institute Research Bulletin*, vol. 16, no. 2, May, 1959. **2.** Concert of Powers developed in the post-1648 period after the myth of the universality of the Holy Roman Empire had been shattered. The Concert was based on the concept of *consensus omnium* or unanimity proceeding from the voluntary recognition of a number of treaties by the principal sovereign states. The major Powers at the time of the Vienna Congress in 1815 were Great Britain, France, Russia, Austria, and Prussia. The Ottoman Empire was not admitted to the Concert until the Paris conference of 1856. For an excellent history of the evolution of the concert system, see David J. Hill, *A History of Diplomacy in the International Development of Europe*, 3 vols., New York, 1921-1925. **3.** C.K. Webster, *The Congress of Vienna, 1814-1815* (Special analysis for the British delegation at Versailles), London, 1919, pp. 98ff., describes the Polish-Saxon problem as the key question of the Vienna Congress: this view was accepted in the widely distributed popular work by H. G. Nicolson, *The Congress of Vienna: a Study in Allied Unity*, London 1946; British Foreign Secretary Castlereagh reported to Prime Minister Liverpool on January 8, 1815, that he had requested Tsar Alexander I to give Prussia extensive Polish territory, C.K. Webster, *British Diplomacy, 1813-1815*, London, 1921, p. 285. See also Comte d'Angeberg, *Le Congrès de Vienne et les Traités de 1815*, vol. 2, Paris 1864, pp. 553ff., and H. Treitschke, *Der Wiener Kongress (Deutsche Geschichte im 19. Jh.* vol. 1), Berlin, 1943, pp. 115ff. **4.** Wladyslaw Konopczynski, *Fryderyk Wielki a Polska*, Poznan, 1947, pp. 105-125, 145-163; Wilhelm Oncken, *Das Zeitalter Friedrichs des Grossen*, vol. 2, Berlin, 1882, pp. 502ff., and *Das Zeitalter der Revolution, des Kaiserreiches und der Befreiungskriege*, vol. 1, Berlin, 1884, pp. 694ff. **5.** Napoléon I forced the new Polish state to join the German Confederation of the Rhine, *vide* Georges Lefebvre, *Napoléon*, Paris 1935, pp. 238-239. Sovereignty over the Duchy was bestowed on the King of Saxony, who received the original copy of the constitution drafted by Napoléon at Dresden in July, 1807; Polish wishes in regard to the constitution were ignored, *vide* Marcel Handlesman, *Napoléon et la Pologne, 1806-1807*, Paris, 1909, pp. 137-153. **6.** Boleslaw Limanowski, *Historia Democracii Polskiej*, vol. 1, 3rd ed., Warsaw, 1946, pp. 284-285. R.F. Leslie, *Polish Politics and the Revolution of November, 1830*, London 1956, pp. viiff., doubts if the common people of Poland would have benefitted had independence been restored in 1831. **7.** Georges Weill, *L'Eveil des Nationalités et la Mouvement Liberal, 1815-1848*, Paris, 1930, pp. 110-116, 123-132, 405-412; on the failure of Russia to appease the stunted autonomous Congress Kingdom which emerged from the 1815 Vienna settlement, see Simon Askenazy, *Rosja-Polska, 1818-1830*, Lwow, 1907. **8.** Josef Pilsudski, *Wpływ Wschodu i Zachodu na Polske w Epoce 1863 R.* in *Pisma Zbiorowe*, vol. 8, New York, 1944, for selected excerpts from Pilsudski's writings; Jozef Feldman, *Bismarck a Polska*, Krakow, 1947, pp. 152ff. **9.** Pilsudski's July 1895 article on Russification policy in *Robotnik* is an example of his brilliant propaganda technique, see *Pisma Zbiorowe*, vol. 1, pp. 97-100. **10.** Wolfgang Windelband, *Bismarck und die europäischen Großmächte 1879-1885*, Berlin, 1940, *passim*.

11. W.L. Langer, *The Franco-Russian Alliance*, Cambridge, Massachusetts, 1931, *passim*. **12.** Wladyslaw Studnicki, *Die polnische Ostmarkenfrage: Denkschrift für deutsche Staatsmänner*, Warsaw, 1917, pp. 4-8; his principle works prior to World War I include *Wspolczesna Syberja*, Krakow, 1897, *Ekonomja Polityczna*, Krakow, 1900, *Rosja w Azji Wschodniej*, Lwow, 1904, *Finlandja i Sprawa finlandzka*, Krakow 1909, *Sprawa Pokska*, Poznan, 1910. **13.** Wladylsaw Studnicki, *System polityczny Europy a Polska*, Warsaw, 1935, pp. 232ff. **14.** Wladyslaw Studnicki, *Irrwege in Polen*, Göttingen, 1951, *passim*. **15.** Stanislaw Mackiewicz, *Historja Polska, 1918-1939*, London, 1941, p. 34. **16.** Kresy actually means a delimited area. **17.** Mackiewicz, *op. cit.*, pp. 34-35. The Polish socialists boycotted the Duma elections, *vide* H. Wereszycki, *Historia Polski, 1864-1918*, vol. 2, Warsaw, 1948, p. 265; for the earlier tradition of Polish collaboration with Russia, *vide* M. Kukiel, *Czartoryski and European Unity*, Princeton, New Jersey, 1955, and especially chapter 3. **18.** Roman Dmowski, *Mysli nowoczesnego Polaka*, 2nd ed., Lwow 1904, pp. 41-61, 141-142 (the 1902 edition was published under the pseudonym R. Skrzycki, *Ibid.*, p. xiii); *La Question Polonaise (Niemoy, Rosya i Kwestya Polska, 1908)* Paris, 1909, pp. 222ff. **19.** Roman Dmowski, *Polytika Polska i Odbudowanie Panstwa*, 2nd ed., Warsaw 1926, pp. 35 ff (this work contains valuable documentary material from the 1914-1919 period). **20.** Roman Dmowski, *Swiat Powojenny i Polska*, Warsaw, 1931, p. 317 (this work offers the most valuable insight into Dmowski's ideas of world politics). **21.** *Ibid.* **22.** Roman Dmowski, *Upadek Mysli Konserwatywney w Polsce*, Warsaw 1914, p. 123 (this work is an elaboration on *Thoughts of a Modern Pole*). Johannes Ahlers, *Polen*, Berlin 1935 pp. 70ff. **23.** Michal Bobrzynski, *Dzieje Polski w Zarysie*, revised ed., 3 vols., Warsaw, 1927-1931, or the earlier edition in Russian, *Ocherki Istoriye Polshe*, 2 vols., St. Petersburg, 1888-1891; see also the excellent biographical introduction by Adam Galos in M. Bobrzynski, *Z Moich Pamietnikow*, Krakow, 1957, pp. iii-lxi; the posthumous memoirs treat the 1908-1913 period; see also W. Feldman, *Stronnictwa i Programy Polityczne w*

Galicia 1846-1906, 2 vols., Krakow, 1907.   **24.** Mackiewicz, *op. cit.*, pp. 29-30.   **25.** Jules Alfred Laroche, *La Pologne de Pilsudski: Souvenirs d' une Ambassade, 1926-1935*, Paris, 1953, p. 225. W. Pobog-Malinowski, *Najnowsza Historia Polityczna Polski, 1864-1945*, vol. 1, Paris, 1953, pp. 193ff.   **26.** W. F. Reddaway, *Marshal Pilsudski*, London, 1938, pp. xiiff.; Leon Wasilewski, *Jozef Pilsudski*, Warsaw, 1935, pp. 5ff.   **27.** Anatole Muhlstein, *Le Maréchal Pilsudski*, vol. 1, *1867-1919*, Paris, 1939, p. 177; Grace Humphrey, *Pilsudski, Builder of Poland*, New York, 1936, p. 123; C. Mettler, *Jozef Pilsudski*, Fribourg, 1938, pp. 99-100; F. W. von Örtzen, *Alles oder Nichts*, Breslau, 1934, p. 203.   **28.** Stanislaw Mackiewicz, *Klucz do Pilsudskiego*, London, 1943, pp 50-53. Pobog-Manilnowski *op. cit.*, vol. 1, pp. 136ff.   **29.** Mackiewica, *Historia Polski*, pp. 97-100.   **30.** *Ibid.*, p. 83.   **31.** Robert Machray, *The Poland of Pilsudski*, London, 1936, pp. 62 ff; W. L. Jaworski, *Listy z Sejmu r. 1910*, Krakow, 1911. Pobog-Malinowski *op. cit.*, vol. 1, pp. 240ff.   **32.** Hans Uebersberger, *Österreich zwischen Russland und Serbien: zur Südslawischen Frage und der Entstehung des Ersten Weltkrieges*, Köln, 1958, pp. 228-229. M. Sokolnicki, *Sprawa Polska na Terenie Miedzynarodowym, 1914-1918* in *Niepodleglosc*, vol. 1, Warsaw, 1930.   **33.** Titus Komarnicki, *Rebirth of the Polish Republic: A Study in the Diplomatic History of Europe, 1914-1920*, London, 1957, pp. 48-50. Werezlycki, *op. cit.*, pp. 288ff.   **34.** Machray, *op. cit.*, pp. 62ff. Marian Kukiel, *Wskrzeszenie Wojska Polskiego in Bellona*, 1959: 1, pp. 14ff.   **35.** Paul Roth, *Die Politische Entwicklung in Kongreßpolen während der deutschen Okkupation*, Leipzig, 1919, pp. 188 ff; for pro-German sentiment in Poland during this period, see Bogdan Hutten-Czapski, *Sechzig Jahre Politik und Gesellschaft*, 2 vols., Berlin, 1936.   **36.** Komarnicki, *op. cit.*, pp. 115-116.   **37.** Roman Dmowski, *Polityka Polska i Odbudowanie Panstwa*, p. 272.   **38.** Komarnicki, *op. cit.*, p. 123.   **39.** James W. Gerard, *My Four Years in Germany*, New York, 1917, p. 268.   **40.** Komarnicki, *op. cit.*, pp. 151-152.   **41.** *Ibid.*, pp. 177-178.   **42.** Mackiewicz, *Historja Polski*, pp. 61-63. Pobog-Malinowski, *op. cit.*, vol. 1, pp. 331ff.; Kukiel, *op. cit.*, *Bellona*, 1959: 2, p. 137.   **43.** Komarnicki, *op. cit.*, pp. 116-117.   **44.** Mackiewicz, *Historja Polski*, pp. 65-66.   **45.** Jozef Pilsudski, *Pisma Zbiorowe*, vol. 5, pp. 24-25. Pobog-Malinowski, *op. cit.*, vol. 1, pp. 367-8; Kukiel, *op. cit.*, *Bellona*, 1959: 4, p. 323.   **46.** *Vide*, Pilsudski's proclamation: *Zolnierze Niemieccy!* in *Pisma Zbiorowe*, vol. 5, pp. 13-14; see also Pilsudski's "Dear Mr. Roman!" letter to Dmowski on December 21, 1918, for L'Union Sacrée Polonaise at the Peace Conference, *Ibid.*, pp. 45-46. Casimir Smorgorzewski, *La Pologne Restaurée*, Paris, 1927, p. 47.   **47.** Komarnicki, *op. cit.*, p. 280.   **48.** *Ibid.*, p. 294.   **49.** *Ibid.*, p. 326.   **50.** *Ibid.*, pp. 333-344.   **51.** Rolf Wingendorf, *Polen: Volk zwischen Ost und West*, Berlin, 1939, pp. 13ff.   **52.** R. Donald, *The Polish Corridor and the Consequences*, London, 1929, pp. 26ff.; Laurence Martin, *Peace without Victory: Woodrow Wilson and the British Liberals*, New Haven, 1958, p. 161.   **53.** Bronislaw Stryzowski, *Zarys Dziejów Narodu i Państwa Polskiego w Latach 1914-1939*, London, 1947, pp. 12-85; H. Läuen, *Polnisches Zwischenspiel: eine Episode der Ostpolitik*, Berlin, 1940, pp. 19-23.   **54.** Machray, *op. cit.*, p. 79.   **55.** Rom Landau, *Pilsudski and Poland*, New York, 1929, pp. 277ff.   **56.** Adam C. Rose, *La Politique Polonaise entre les deux Guerres*, Neuchatel, 1945, pp. 26ff.; Läuen, *op. cit.*, 24ff.   **57.** Mackiewicz, *Historja Polski*, pp. 97-100.   **58.** *Ibid.*, pp. 101-102.   **59.** Läuen, *op, cit.*, pp. 44-52.   **60.** Komarnicki, *op. cit.*, pp. 376-385.   **61.** Tadeusz Kutrzeba, *Wyprawa Kijowska 1920 roku*, Warsaw, 1937, pp. 25ff. see also Tadeusz Teslar, *Propaganda Bolszewicka podczas Wojny polsko-rosyskiej 1920 roku*, Warsaw 1938, pp. 73ff.   **62.** The two coalition groups were the National People's Coalition (Zwiazek Ludowo-Narodowy) and the Union of the People of the Nation (Zjednoczenie Narodowo-Ludowe).
   63. This Party was called officially the Faction of the Polish "Piast" People (Polski Stronnictwo Ludowie "Piast") from the legend that the ancient Piast dynasty was of immediate peasant origin.   **64.** Mackiewicz, *Historja Polski*, p. 114. Pobog-Malinowski, *op. cit.*, Vol. 1, p. 396.   **65.** Komarnicki, *op. cit.*, pp. 328, 356-364.   **66.** A.B. Keith, *The Causes of the War*, London, 1940, p. 69 (no justification for the Upper Silesia partition according to a British international legal expert); Pilsudski did not sympathize with National Democratic insurrection tactics, Läuen *op. cit.*, pp. 34-35.   **67.** Komarnicki, *op cit.*, pp. 466ff.; M Sololnicki, *Jozef Pilsudski a Zagadnienie Rosji*, pp. 51-70, in *Niepodleglosc*, vol. 2, London, 1950.   **68.** Josef Pilsudski, *Rok 1920*, in *Pisma Zbiorowe*, vol. 7, pp. 9ff.; M.K. Dziewanowski, *Pilsudski's Federal Policy, 1919-1921* in *Journal of Central European Affairs*, July, Oct., 1950.   **69.** *Ibid.*, Machray, *op cit.*, pp. 112ff.; Landau, *op cit.*, pp. 175ff.; Mackiewicz, *Historja Polski*, pp. 130-134. Piotr S. Wandycz, *General Weygand and the Battle of Warsaw of 1920* in *Journal of Central European Affairs*, Jan. 1960, deprecates the role of Weygand at Warsaw; in all fairness, it ought to be added that Weygand's own account is extremely modest, *vide* Maxime Weygand, *Mémoires*, vol. 2, Paris, 1957, pp. 83-172.   **70.** Jan Dabski, *Pokoj Ryski: Wspomnienia, Pertraktaoje, Tajne Uklady z Joffem, Listy*, Warsaw, 1931; Peter Jordan, *Poland's Frontiers*, London, 1945, pp. 13ff. *Documents on Polish-Soviet relations, 1939-1945*, vol. 1, London, pp. 3-8, for text of the Riga treaty.   **71.** Komarnicki, *op cit.*, p. 372.   **72.** W. Studnicki, *Kwestja Czechoslowacji a racia stanu Polski*, Warsaw, 1938, pp. 9ff.   **73.** Landau, *op. cit.*, pp. 213ff.; Laroche, *op. cit.*, pp. 19-36; see also Pilsudski's praise of Warutowica in *Pisma Abiorowe*, vol. 6, pp. 36-59, his confidence in Skrzynski, *Ibid.*, vol. 8, pp. 256-259, and his speech at Colosseum Hall, Warsaw, Mar. 21, 1926, *Naczelny Wodz Teorii i Praktyce*, *Ibid.*, pp. 300-311. *Ibid.*, vol. 2, pp. 525ff.   **74.** Jozef Pilsudski, *Ibid.*, vol. 9, pp. 47-48; J. S. Roucek *et al*, *Central-Eastern Europe, Crucible of World Wars*, New York, 1946, pp. 383ff. *Ibid.*, vol. 2, pp. 525ff.   **75.** Henryk Frankel, *Poland: the Struggle for Power*, London, 1946, pp. 71-72, 117ff.   **76.** S.L. Sharp, *Poland: White Eagle on a Red Field*, Cambridge, Massachusetts, 1953, pp. 103-106.   **77.** Mackiewicz, *Historja Polski*, pp. 199-208.   **78.** Raymond Leslie Buell, *Poland: Key to Europe*, New York, 1939, pp. 94ff. Pobog-Malinowski, *op. cit.*, vol. 2, pp. 576ff.   **79.** W. Ipohorski-Lekniewicz, *Minister z Palacu Bruehla*, Buenos Aires, 1943, pp. 73-84.   **80.** *All About Poland: Facts, Figures, Documents*, J. H. Rettinger, ed., London, 1940, pp. 32ff.   **81.** Ipohorski-Lenkiewicz, *op. cit.*, pp. 85-86.   **82.** *Who's Who in Polish America*, Francis Bolek, ed., New York, 1943.   **83.** Ignacy Matuszewski, *Proby Syntez*, Warsaw, 1937, pp. 15-18.   **84.** *Ibid.*, pp. 33-43, 53-122.   **85.** *Ibid.*, pp. 127-139.   **86.** F. Slawoj-Skladkowski, *Strzepy Meldunkow*, 4th. ed., Warsaw, 1938, pp. 67ff.

Chapter 2

1. Annelise Thimme, *Gustav Stresemann: eine politische Biographie zur Geschichte der Weimarer Republik*, Hannover, 1957, pp. 107ff.   2. Zygmunt Gasiorowski, *The German-Polish Nonaggression Pact of 1934* in *Journal of Central European Affairs*, April 1955; on Hitler's policy, see Hermann Mau & Helmut Krausnick, *Deutsche Geschichte der juengsten Vergangenheit, 1933-1945*, Tuebingen, 1956, pp. 75ff.; Hans Grimm, *Warum, Woher-Aber, Wohin?*, Lippoldsberg, 1954, pp. 14ff. Fritz Hesse, *Das Spiel um Deutschland*, Munich, 1953, pp. 7ff.; W. Goerlitz and H. Quint, *Adolf Hitler, eine Biographie*, Stuttgart, 1952, pp. 88ff.; J. Benoist-Mechin, *Éclaircissements sur 'Mein Kampf,' la Doctrine d'Adolf Hitler*, Paris, 1939, pp. 51ff.; J. von Ribbentrop, *Zwischen London und Moskau*, Leoni, Bavaria, 1954, pp. 36ff.; Theodor Heuss, *Hitlers Weg*, Berlin, 1932, pp. 99ff.; P. Georges-Anquetil, *Hitler Conduit le Bal*, Paris, 1939, pp. 132ff.; Hermann Hammer, *Die Deutschen Ausgaben von Hitlers "Mein Kampf"* in *Vierteljahreshefte für Zeitgeschichte*, April 1956, pp. 161ff.; Hermann Lutz, *Foreign Policy in the Third Reich* in *Current History*, April, 1955, pp. 222ff.; Friedrich Stieve, *Ce Que le Monde n'a pas voulu: les Offrres de Paix faites par Hitler entre 1933 et 1939*, Brussels, 1940, *passim;* Francis Neilson, *The Makers of War*, Appleton, Wisconsin, 1950, pp. 66ff. Helmut Heiber, *Adolf Hitler: eine Biographie* is of no value for foreign policy; Hitler's constructive and friendly policy toward Poland received recognition in A.J.P. Taylor, *The Origins of the Second World War*, London, 1961, pp. 68, 80-81, 195-196, 210, 220.   3. Wilhelm Högner, *Die Verratene Republik: Geschichte der deutschen Gegenrevolution*, Munich, 1958, p. 341.   4. H.E. Barnes, "Hiroshima, Assault on a Beaten Foe," in *National Review*, May 10, 1958.   5. Eugenio Coselschi, *II Ministro Beck e la Politica Estera della Polonia*, Rome, 1939; pp. 29ff.; see also Jozef Beck, *Beiträge zur europaischen Politik: Reden, Erklärungen, Interviews, 1932-1939, passim;* for biographies of Beck, see W. Ipohorski-Lenkiewicz, *Minister z Palacu Bruehla*, Buenos Aires, 1943; Konrad Wrzos, *Pulkownik Jozef Beck*, Warsaw, 1939; S. Mackiewicz, *Colonel Beck and his Policy*, London, 1944.   6. Jozef Beck, *Dernier Rapport: Politique Polonaise, 1926-1939*, Neuchatel, 1949, pp. xv-xviii, 19ff.   7. F. Zawdzki and Z. Klimpel, *Z Problemow Wspolczesnej Polityki Zagranicanej*, Warsaw, 1939, pp. 9-112; see also August Zaleski, *Przemowy i Deklaracje*, vol. 2, Warsaw, 1931, pp. 161ff.; J. Lukasiewicz, *Polska jest Mocarstwem*, Warsaw, 1939, pp. 23ff.   8. Hans Roos, *Polen und Europa: Studien zur polnischen Aussenpolitik 1931-1939*, Tuebingen, 1957, pp. 55-56.   9. H. L. Roberts, *The Diplomacy of Colonel Beck in The Diplomats, 1919-1939*, Princeton, 1953, pp. 579ff.   10. Roos, *op. cit..*, pp. 3-4.   11. A. Fabre-Luce, *Locarno: the Reality*, New York, 1928, pp. 78ff. Polish Foreign Minister Skrzynski expressed his disappointment over Locarno in a speech to the Sejm on February 25, 1926.   12. Gerald Freund, *Unholy Alliance: Russian-German Relations from the Treaty of Brest-Litovsk to the Treaty of Berlin*, New York, 1957, pp. 213-244; Zygmunt Gasiorowski, *The Russian Overture to Germany of December 1924* in *Journal of Modern History*, June 1958, p. 117.   13. Jean Matrat, *Histoire des Rélations Franco-Anglaises*, Paris, 1953, pp. 120-121.   14. James W. Christopher, *Conflict in the Far East*, Leyden, 1950, pp. 17ff.   15. Vladimir Potemkin, *et al, Histoire de la Diplomatie*, vol. 3, *1919-1939*, Paris, 1947, pp. 512ff.; Edward Rozek, *Allied Wartime Diplomacy: A Pattern in Poland*, London, 1958, pp. 17-19.   16. S. Mackiewicz, *Historja Polski, 1819-1939*, London, 1941, p. 245.   17. Roos, *op. cit.*, pp. 38-39. On the inability of Stresemann to improve relations with Poland after 1926, *vide* Ludwig Zimmermann, *Deutsche Aussenpolitik in der Ära der Weimarer Republik*, Berlin, 1958, pp. 341ff.   18. *Ibid.*, p. 37.   19. *Ibid.*, pp. 47-48.   20. *Vide*, Henry Roberts, *op. cit.*, pp. 612-614; Boris Celovsky, *Pilsudskis Praeventivkrieg gegen das NS Deutschland: Entstehung, Verbreitung, und Widerlegung einer Legende* in *Die Welt als Geschichte*, 1954:1; Zygmunt Gasiorowski, *Did Pilsudski Attempt to Initiate a Preventive War in 1933?* in *Journal of Modern History*, June 1955; Hans Roos, *Die "Praeventivkriegspläne" Pilsudskis von 1933* in *Vierteljahreshefte für Zeitgeschichte*, Oct. 1955.   21. R. G. Vansittart, *The Mist Procession: The Autobiography of Lord Vansittart*, London, 1958, p. 468.   22. *Ibid.*, p. 469.   23. *Ibid.*, p. 468.   24. H. Meissner and H. Wilde, *Die Machtergreifung: ein Bericht über die Technik des Nationalsozialistischen Staatsreichs*, Stuttgart, 1958, pp. 195-236; Roos, *op. cit.*, pp. 67-68. Hitler from the start was much more moderate about Poland than his first foreign minister, Konstantin von Neurath. Vice-Chancellor Franz von Papen was informed by Neurath on February 9, 1933, that Germany should demand the return of the lost Upper Silesian districts and at least half the corridor, *vide, Documents on German Foreign Policy*, C, vol. 1, no. 18 (hereafter cited as DGFP).   25. *Ibid.*, p. 70.   26. Luigi Villari, *Italian Foreign Policy Under Mussolini*, New York, 1956, pp. 94ff.; Hubert Lagardell, *Mission à Rome: Mussolini*, Paris, 1955, 17ff. *Vide* DGFP, C, vol. 1, no. 95, for discussion of the Four Power Pact at Berlin.   27. Mario Donosti, *Mussolini e l'Europa: la Politica Estera Fascista*, Rome, 1945, pp. 81ff.; Lagardelle, *op. cit.*, pp. 35ff.; Elisabetta Cerruti, *Visti da Vicino: Memorie di un' ambasciatrice*, Milan, 1951, pp. 155ff. German Ambassador Moltke predicted as early as April 19, 1933, that Beck personally would favor an improvement of relations with Germany now that Hitler had come to power, *vide* DGFP, C, vol. 1, no. 167; for Hitler's conversation with Polish Ambassador Wysocki, *ibid.*, no. 201.   28. Alfred Rosenberg, *Die Zukunft einer deutschen Aussenpolitik*, Munich, 1927, pp. 60ff.; Ernst Hanfstaengl, *Unheard Witness*, Philadelphia, 1957, pp. 94ff.   29. L. Wierczynski, J. Modzelewski, *et al, Pologne, 1919-1939*, vol. 1, Neuchatel, 1945, pp. 137ff.; C. Bewley, *Hermann Goering*, Göttingen, 1956, *passim*.   30. Roos, *op. cit.*, pp. 98ff.   31. *Europäische Politik, 1933-1938, im Spiegel der Prager Akten*, F. Berber, ed., Essen, 1942, no. 11. *Vide* DGFP, C, vol. 2, no. 58, for Moltke's November 11, 1933, report on the prospects for an improvement in German-Polish relations.   32. *Ibid.*, nos. 15, 18. *Vide* DGFP, C, vol. 2, no. 90, for Moltke's interesting report of November 28, 1933, on the decline of Pilsudski's health and on the "thousand-year-old anti-German feeling in Poland," as an obstacle to a lasting German-Polish understanding.   33. Gasiorowski, *The German-Polish Nonaggression Pact of 1934*, p. 29; Jules Laroche, *La Pologne de Pilsudski: Souvenirs d'une Ambassade, 1926-1935*, Paris, 1953, pp. 149-150. DGFP, C,

Vol. 2, no. 219, for the text of the German-Polish non-aggression pact of 1934; *ibid.*, no. 221, reveals the extreme irritation at Danzig of Senate President Hermann Rauschning, the later renegade, after the conclusion of the pact; Rauschning was opposed to Hitler's moderate policy toward Poland; see also *Ibid.*, no. 407, for Rauschning's advocacy on April 18, 1934, of the immediate incorporation of Danzig into the German economy in defiance of Poland. **34.** Jan Szembek, *Journal, 1933-1939*, Paris, 1952, p. 197; Roos, *op. cit.*, pp. 127ff. **35.** Gasiorowski, *The German-Polish Nonaggression Pact of 1934*, p. 27. **36.** Wilfred von Oven, *Mit Goebbels bis zum Ende*, vol. 1, Buenos Aires, 1949, pp. 29-33. **37.** Beck, *op. cit.*, pp. 30-31; H. Läuen, *Polnisches Zwischenspiel*, Berlin, 1940, pp. 119-124. **38.** Beck, *op. cit.*, p. 34. **39.** *Ibid.*, pp. 40-41; 57-58. **40.** Roos, *op. cit.*, pp. 172ff. **41.** Beck, *op. cit.*, pp. 61-62. **42.** *Ibid.*, pp. 61-63; Beck's account was confirmed for their writer by Waclaw Jedrezejewicz, who was present at the conference. **43.** Beck, *op. cit.*, pp. 65-66. See also General Fabrycy's account in *Niepodleglosc*, vol. 5, Warsaw, 1935. **44.** *Ibid.* **45.** *Ibid.*, pp. 93-94. **46.** Roos, *op. cit.*, p. 164. vide DGFP, C, vol. 3, no. 532, for Hitler's notes of March 16, 1935, to Italy, Great Britain, France, and Poland. **47.** Beck, *op. cit.*, pp. 96-101. **48.** Ribbentrop, *op. cit.*, pp. 77-80. **49.** Pierre Etienne Flandin, *Politique Francaise, 1919-1940*, Paris, 1947, pp. 193-201. **50.** Roos, *op. cit.*, p. 233. **51.** Beck, *op. cit.*, pp. 113-116. **52.** *Les Événements survenus en France de 1933 à 1945*, vol. 1-2, suppl. vol. 1-9, Parl. Comm. of Inquiry, Paris, 1947-1951; see also Paul Reynaud, *Au Coeur de la Mêlée, 1930-1945*, Paris, 1951, pp. 172ff.; Edouard Herriot, *Jadis*, vol. 2, Paris, pp. 508ff.; J. Paul-Boncour, *Entre Deux Guerres: Souvenirs sur la IIIe Republique*, vol. 3, New York, 1946, pp. 36ff.; Flandin, *op. cit.*, pp. 193ff.; General Gauche, *Le Deuxième Bureau au Travail, 1935-1940*, Paris, 1953, pp. 42ff.; Francois Goguel, *La Politique des Partis sous la IIIe Republique*, Paris, 1946, pp. 425ff. **53.** Geneviève Tabouis, *Ils l'ont appelée Cassandre*, New York, 1942, pp. 259ff. **54.** Gauche, *op. cit.*, pp. 45-47. **55.** *Ibid.* **56.** *Prager Akten*, no. 59. **57.** Beck, *op. cit.*, pp. 113-116; Mackiewicz, *Colonel Beck and his Policy*, pp. 76ff.; Stanislaw Strzetelski, *Where the Storm Broke*, New York, 1942, pp. 38ff. **58.** Roos, *op. cit.*, pp. 238ff. **59.** *Official Documents Concerning Polish-German and Polish-Soviet Relations, 1933-1939*, London, 1940, pp. 12-37, hereafter cited as *Polish White Book*. **60.** See also Olgierd Gorka, *Outline of Polish History, Past and Present*, 2nd. ed., London, 1945, *passim.* **61.** *Miedzy Niemcami a Rosja*, Warsaw, 1937, p. 8. The term *Stanczyki* is also said to be derived from Stanczyk, a famous 16th century jester at the court of Zygmunt I, king of Poland. **62.** *Ibid.*, p11. **63.** *Ibid.*, p. 18. **64.** *Ibid.*, p. 19. **65.** *Ibid.*, p. 22. **66.** *Ibid.*, pp. 25-27. **67.** *Ibid.*, pp. 29-30. **68.** *Ibid.*, p. 30. **69.** *Ibid.* **70.** *Ibid.*, pp. 41-42. **71.** *Ibid.*, pp. 53-59. **73.** *Ibid.*, p. 68. **74.** *Ibid.*, pp. 75-78. **75.** *Ibid.*, pp. 93-110. **76.** *Ibid.*, pp. 124-142. **77.** *Ibid.*, pp. 148-174. **78.** *Ibid.*, p. 175. **79.** *Ibid.*, p. 176. **80.** *Ibid.*, p. 178. **81.** Sisley Huddleston, *Popular Diplomacy and War*, Rindge, N.H. 1954, pp. 159ff. **82.** C. R. Barnett, *Poland, its People, its Society, and its Culture*, New Haven, 1958, pp. 43ff., demonstrates that the impact of World War II on the Polish population was much less than on Russians or Germans.

Chapter 3

1. Titus Komarnicki, *Rebirth of the Polish Republic*, London, 1957, pp. 716-719; Pierre Valmigère, *Und Morgen? Frankreich, Deutschland und Polen*, 2nd. ed., Berlin, 1939, pp. 6, 61ff. **2.** Kurt Lueck, *Der Mythos vom Deutschen in der polnischen Volksüberlieferung und Literatur*, Leipzig, 1943, pp. 477-480, describes the hostile Polish attitude toward Danzig after World War I; the League offered Danzig no real security against Poland. **3.** *Danzig and the Corridor: World Opinion on the Topic of To-day*, Margarete Gaertner, ed , Berlin, 1939, *passim.* **4.** Vide infra, chapters 12-14. **5.** New York *Times*, March 16-21, 1939; *Czas, Gazeta Polska*, March 16-21, 1939. **6.** *Documents on German Foreign Policy*, series D, vol. 5, Washington, D. C., 1953, no. 119. **7.** *Ibid.* **8.** *Documents on the Events Preceding the Outbreak of the War*, New York, 1940, p. 202. **9.** J. von Ribbentrop, *Zwischen London und Moskau*, Leoni, Bavaria, 1954, p. 153. **10.** *Documents on Events*, pp. 214-215. **11.** *Documents on British Foreign Policy, 1919-1939*, series 3, vol. 4, London, 1953, no. 446. **12.** Jan Szembek, *Journal, 1933-1939*, Paris, 1952, pp. 433-434. **13.** Attilio Tamaro, *La Condanna dell 'Italia nel Trattato di Pace*, Bologna, 1952, pp. 194-216. **14.** Hans Roos, *Polen und Europa*, Tübingen, 1957, p. 296. **15.** *Gazeta Polska*, June 20, 1939. **16.** *Gdańsk: Gateway of Poland* (Polish Tourist Society), Warsaw, 1949, p. 8; Henri de Montfort, *Dantzig, Port de Pologne dans le Passé et dans le Présent*, Paris, 1939, pp. 17-24. **17.** Werner Gieve, *Grundfragen der Siedlungsforschung in Nordosteuropa* in *Altpreussische Forschungen*, 1938, Heft 1; see also Paul Simson, *Geschichte der Stadt Danzig*, 3 vol., Danzig, 1913-1918. **18.** H. Lewinsky & R. Wagner, *Danziger Staats — und Völkerrecht*, Danzig, 1927, pp. 181-190. **19.** *Ibid.*; Herbert Matschke, *Die Grundlagen des Internationalen Status von Danzig*, Berlin, 1936, pp. 62ff. **20.** Lewinsky & Wagner, *op. cit.*, pp. 201-211, 651-656. **21.** F. Gross, *Politische Handbuch der Freien Stadt Danzig*, Danzig, 1924, pp. 135ff. **22.** Franz Dettman, *Danzig zwischen Deutschland und Polen*, Berlin, 1939, pp. 24-25; Gross, *op. cit.*, pp. 46-48. **23.** A. Kaetner, *Weisse Fahne über Danzig*, Kiel, 1950, pp. 3ff. **24.** R.&G. Moennig, *Danzig*, Berlin, 1939, pp. 58ff. **25.** Matschke, *op. cit.*, pp. 61-71. **26.** H.L. Leonhardt, *Nazi Conquest of Danzig*, Chicago, 1942, pp. 314ff. **27.** H. Laeuen, *Polnisches Zwischenspiel*, Berlin, 1940, pp. 24ff. **28.** Gieve, *op. cit.* **29.** Ian Morrow, *The Peace Settlement in the German-Polish Borderlands*, London, 1936, p. 17. **30.** Dettmann, *op. cit.*, p. 14. **31.** Grodecki, *et al, Dzieje Polski Sredniowieczney*, vol. 1, Kraków, 1926, pp. 298ff.; C. Smogorzewski, *Poland, Germany, and the Corridor*, London, 1930, pp. 13ff.; J.B. Mason, *The Danzig Dilemma*, Stanford, Calif., 1946, pp. 15ff. **32.** Grodecki, *op. cit.*, vol. 1, pp. 347-348; 362-363; vol. 2, pp. 38-40. **33.** Grodecki, *op. cit.*, vol. 2, pp. 264-266; 268-269; 396-398; the rarity of German-Polish warfare is emphasized by Kurt Lück, *Der Lebenskampf in deutsch-*

polnischen Grenzraum, Berlin, 1943, pp. 9ff.   **34.** Franz Lüdtke, *Ein Jahrtausend Krieg zwischen Deutschland und Polen*, Stuttgart, 1941, pp. 72ff.   **35.** Jerzy Smolenski, *Morze i Pomorze*, Warsaw, 1933, pp. 174ff.; H. Baginski, *Poland and the Baltic*, Edinburgh, 1942, pp. 50-52; Smogorzewski, *op. cit.*, pp. 13ff.   **36.** Grodecki, *op. cit.*, vol. 2, pp. 396-398; W. Konopczynski, *Dzieje Polski Nowozytney*, vol. 1, Warsaw, 1936, pp. 147-150; 158-161; he states that the independence of Danzig was not affected by the Lublin act of union between Poland and Lithuania, pp. 406ff.   **37.** Stanisław Kutrzeba, *Historya Ustroju Polski w Zarysie*, Lwów, 1920, vol. 4, pp. 1ff.   **38.** James W. Gerard, *My Four Years in Germany*, New York, 1917, p. 268.   **39.** Komarnicki, *op. cit.*, pp. 236-237.   **40.** *Ibid.*, pp. 336-337; see also Rudolf Neumann, *Ostpreussen im polnischen Schrifttum*, Danzig, pp. 179-180, on Polish aspirations in East Prussia.   **41.** O. Halecki, *History of Poland*, New York, 1943, p. 281.   **42.** W. Vogel, *Poland as Sea Power and Trading State in Germany and Poland*, A. Brackmann, ed., Munich, 1934, p. 110.   **43.** Morrow, *op. cit.*, pp. 14ff.   **44.** Dettmann, *op. cit.*, pp. 45-47.   **45.** Richard Breyer, *Das Deutsche Reich und Polen*, Würzburg, 1955, pp. 39ff.   **46.** *Polska a Zagranica*, Warsaw, Mar. 21, 1939.   **47.** *Ibid.*, Feb. 1, 1935.   **48.** *Ibid.*, June 22, 1935.   **49.** *Ibid.*, Mar. 5, 1936.   **50.** *Ibid.*, April 27, 1938.   **51.** Roos, *op. cit.*, p. 5.   **52.** *Prager Akten*, F. Berber, ed., Essen, 1942, nos. 25, 34.   **53.** Roos, *op. cit.*, p. 164.   **54.** North Schleswig was held by Denmark, Alsace-Lorraine by France, South Tirol (detached from German Austria in 1919) by Italy, and Posen, most of West Prussia, and part of Upper Silesia by Poland.   **55.** Ribbentrop, *op. cit.*, pp. 124-125.   **56.** Hermann Rauschning, *Die Entdeutschung Posens und Pommerellens*, Berlin, 1931, is the most extreme anti-Polish book written in Germany during this period; Rauschning later made a fortune writing fantastic accounts of German conditions for gullible English-speaking readers; see also H. Rauschning, *Zehn Monate nationalsozialistische Regierung in Danzig*, Danzig 1934.   **57.** *Documents on Events*, p. 180.   **58.** *Ibid.*, pp. 181-183.   **59.** R. Vansittart, *The Mist Procession*, London, 1958, p. 469.   **60.** *Documents on Events*, pp. 185-190.   **61.** Roos, *op. cit.*, pp. 186-189.   **62.** *Documents on Events*, pp. 191-192.   **63.** Marjan Chodacki in conversation with the writer, April 2, 1948; the following statement from Chodacki in 1938 is recorded in Szembek's journal: "Il pense néanmoins que nous devrons régler la question de Dantzig avec les Allemands," Szembek, *op. cit.*, p. 353.   **64.** Leonhardt, *op. cit.*, pp. 308-311; Dettman, *op. cit.*, p. 24.   **65.** *Documents on Events*, p. 193.   **66.** Chodacki in conversation with the writer, Ap. 2, 1948.   **67.** Roos, *op. cit.*, p. 296.   **68.** *Documents on Events*, pp. 194-196.   **69.** Roos, *op. cit.*, p. 296.   **70.** Chodacki in conversation with the writer, Ap. 2, 1948.   **71.** *Akten betreffend: Halifax-Besuch und seine Folgen vom November 1937 bis 30. April 1939*, German Foreign Office Archives, Serial 375:2, pp. 208770-208772; German State Secretary Weizsäcker informed the Polish diplomats in Berlin on December 2, 1937, that Halifax had raised the Danzig question.   **72.** Porter Sargent to the writer, July 20, 1946.

Chapter 4

1. *Foreign Relations of the United States: The Soviet Union, 1933-1939*, Washington D. C., 1952, pp. 291-294; Helmut Sündermann, *Das Erbe des falschen Propheten*, Leoni, Bavaria, 1958, pp. 121-139. For additional information on Hitler's rejection of Marxism prior to his authorship of *Mein Kampf*, *vide* Dietrich Eckart, *Der Bolschewismus von Moses bis Lenin: Zwiegespräch zwischen Adolf Hitler und mir*, Munich, 1925, *passim*.   **2.** *Die Predigt des Bischofs (Dibelius)*, Dec. 7, 1958, in *Die Kirche*, Berlin, 1958/11.   **3.** *Polska a Zagranica*, Warsaw, February 22, 1936.   **4.** *Ibid.*, December 14, 1936. A.J.P. Taylor, *The Origins of the Second World War*, London, 1961, pp. 112ff., emphasizes that the purges beginning in 1936 convinced the West that the USSR was virtually powerless in international affairs; this was at any rate the dominant opinion within the Tory leadership and was the crucial factor in determining the evolution of British foreign policy.   **5.** Burton Klein, *Germany's Preparation for War: a Re-examination* in *American Economic Review*, March 1948, pp. 60ff.; Klaus Knorr, *The War Potential of Nations*, Princeton, N. J., 1956, pp. 59ff.; Hjalmar Schacht, *76 Jahre meines Lebens*, Bad Wörrishofen, 1953, pp. 414ff.; Fritz Hesse, *Das Spiel um Deutschland*, Munich, 1953, pp. 12ff.; Hans Grimm, *Warum-Woher-Aber Wohin?*, Lippoldsberg, 1954, pp. 113ff.; *Nation Europa*, Coburg, May 1959.   **6.** J. von Ribbentrop, *Zwischen London und Moskau*, Leoni, Bavaria, 1954, pp. 44ff.   **7.** *Ibid.*, pp. 73ff.   **8.** *Documents on German Foreign Policy*, D, vol. 1, Washington, D. C., 1949, no. 93; see *Zur Geschichte eines aussenpolitischen Dokuments* in *Deutsche Hochschullehrer-Ztg*, nos. 2, 3/4, Tübingen, 1958, for an excellent intensive analysis of the Ribbentrop memorandum.   **9.** *German Foreign Office Archives*, Serial 1726, pp. 401327-401420, re German mediation efforts in China.   **10.** Hans Roos, *Polen und Europa*, Tübingen, 1957, pp. 209ff.   **11.** Boris Čelovsky, *Das Münchener Abkommen 1938*, Stuttgart, 1958, p. 76.   **12.** Hermann Raschhofer, *Die Sudetenfrage: Ihre Völkerrichtliche Entwicklung vom ersten Weltkrieg bis zur Gegenwart*, Munich, 1953, pp. 13ff.   **13.** Victor S. Mamatey, *The United States and East Central Europe, 1914-1918*, Princeton, 1957, pp. 9ff.; Edvard Beneš, *Le Problem autrichien*, Dijon, 1908, *passim*.   **14.** Arnold Toynbee, *Nationality and the War*, London, 1915, pp. 17ff.   **15.** Oskar Ullrich, *Der Grosse Irrweg der Tschechen*, Berlin, 1943, pp. 251ff.; Edvard Benes, *Der Aufstand der Nationen: der Weltkrieg und die Tschechoslowakische Revolution*, Berlin, 1928, pp. 61ff; the crucial role of Benes is emphasized by T. G. Masaryk, *Die Weltrevolution: Erinnerungen und Betrachtungen*, 1914-1918, Berlin, 1925, pp. 27ff.; Taylor, *op. cit.*, p. 151 states that only the Czechs were genuine Czechoslovaks.   **16.** Mamatay, *op. cit.*, pp. 282-332; Rudolf Urban, *Demokratenpresse im Lichte Prager Geheimakten*, Prague, 1943, *passim*. On the similarity between the Slovak and Sudeten problems, *vide* A. Hrobak, *A New Order for East Central Europe in Sudeten Bulletin* , Munich, 1961, 7/8.   **17.** Compton Mackenzie, *Dr. Benes*, London, 1946, pp. 18ff.   **18.** Umberto Nani, T. G. *Masaryk e l'unità Cecoslovacca*, Milan, 1931, pp. 185-238; Kamil Krofta, *A Short History of Czechoslovakia*, London, 1935, pp. 198ff.   **19.** Erwin Hölzle, *Das Reich und Europa*, Leipzig, 1944, pp. 160ff. In October, 1914, Masaryk claimed to the English historian, R. W. Seton-Watson, that "all Czech parties without exception have the Slav program and Slav sentiments. The nation is Russophile and Serbophile, and this fact cannot be changed. . . ."; Masaryk wanted the Russians to seize East Galicia and Ruthenia and the Czechs to seize Slovakia; this would have produced the common Czech-Russian frontier which has in fact existed since 1945, *vide* Hans Kohn, *The Impact of Pan-Slavism on Central Europe in Review of Politics*, July, 1961.   20. Titus Komarnicki, *Rebirth of the Polish Republic*, London, 1957, pp. 238ff.   21. *Ibid.*, pp. 356ff.   22. *Polska a Zagranica*, Warsaw, May 15, 1936.   23. J. W. Wheeler-Bennet, *Munich: Prologue to Tragedy*, London, 1948, pp. 282-289.   24. R. L. Buell, *Poland: Key to Europe*, New York, 1939, pp. 343-345.   25. W. Grosz, *U Źródel Września 1939*, Warsaw, 1949, pp. 27ff.   26. Winston Churchill, *The Gathering Storm*, Boston, 1948, p. 323; Francis Neilson, *The Churchill Legend*, Appleton, Wisconsin, 1954, pp. 300ff.; Czech Minister Jan Masaryk emphasized the warmongering activities of Churchill in a report to Prague as early as March 15, 1934, see *Prager Akten*, no. 23.   27. Józef Beck, *Dernier Rapport*, Neuchatel, 1949, pp. 159-161.   28. The conversion of the Swedish foreign minister from collective security to neutrality was complete by 1938, see Samuel Abrahamsen, *Sweden's Foreign Policy*, Washington, D. C., 1957, pp. 22-26.   29. Churchill, *op. cit.*, pp. 305-306.   30. Beck, *op. cit.*, pp. 155-156.   31. *Ibid.*, pp. 170-171.   32. Hans Frank, *Im Angesicht des Galgens*, Munich, 1953, pp. 311-320.   33. Alfred Bohmann, *Die Ausweisung der Sudetendeutschen*, Marburg, 1955, pp. 7-15; Raschhofer, *op. cit.*, pp. 133-145.   34. Roos, *op. cit.*, pp. 318-319.   35. *German Foreign Office Archives*, Serial 375:1/2 (*Akten betreffend Halifax-Besuch und seine Folgen vom November 1937 bis 30. April 1939*), pp. 208675-208692.   36. *Documents on German Foreign Policy*, series D, vol. 5. no. 1; hereafter cited as *German Foreign Policy*.   37. Much has been made of Ribbentrop's earlier career as a champagne merchant in various countries, but Maxim Litvinov, the League apostle of collective security, was at one time a corset salesman in London. Suendermann, *op. cit.*, pp. 183ff.; Ribbentrop, *op. cit.*, pp. 16-37; Paul Schwarz, *This Man Ribbentrop: his life and Times*, New York, 1943, pp. 46-62.   38. Erich Kordt, *Nicht aus den Akten*, Stuttgart, 1950, pp. 63-66, 98-111; G. Craig, F. Gilbert, *et al.*, *The Diplomats, 1919-1939*, Princeton, 1953, pp. 408, 420-424; *Der Hochverratsprozess gegen Dr. Guido Schmidt*, Vienna, 1947, pp. 357-371.   39. Kordt, *op. cit.*, pp. 168ff.   40. *German Foreign Policy*, D, vol. 5, no. 3; Komarnicki, *op. cit.*, pp. 225, 334.   41. *German Foreign Policy*, D, vol. 5, nos. 4, 5; *Der Hochverratsprozess gegen Dr. Guido Schmidt*, pp. 352-354; Ulrich Eichstaedt, *Von Dollfuss zu Hitler*, Wiesbaden, 1956, p. 62.   42. Józef Lipski, *Stosunki Polsko-Niemieckie w swietle Aktów Norymberskich* in *Sprawy Miedzynardowe*, London, 1947, no. 2/3.   43. J. W. Wheeler-Bennett, *The Nemesis of Power: the German Army in Politics, 1918-1945*, New York, 1954, pp. 343-344.   44. *German Foreign Policy*, D, vol. 5, nos. 9, 11, 12, 13.   45. *Ibid.*, no. 13.   46. *Ibid.*, no. 14; the German legation at Warsaw was elevated to an embassy in 1934.   47. *German Foreign Policy*, D, vol. 5, nos. 16, 17.   48. *Prager Akten*, nos. 77, 87.   49. Richard Breyer, *Das Deutsche Reich und Polen, 1932-1937*, Wuerzburg, 1955, pp. 39-45.   50. *Ibid.*, pp. 239-251.   51. Maurice Baumont *et al*, *The Third Reich*, New York, pp. 540ff.; see also Louis de Jong, *De Duitse Vijfde Colonne in de Tweede Wereldoorlog*, Amsterdam, 1953, pp. 17ff.   52. *Gazeta Polska*, October 21, 1935.   53. Breyer, *op. cit.*, pp. 274ff.   54. *Ibid.*, pp. 293-294.   55. *Ibid.*, pp. 325-326.   56. W. Foerster, *Generaloberst Ludwig Beck: sein Kampf gegen den Krieg*, Munich, 1953, pp. 154 ff; F. Hossbach, *Zwischen Wehrmacht und Hitler*, Hannover, 1949, pp. 186-194; Wheeler-Bennett, *The Nemesis of Power*, pp. 359-363, 391ff.   57. *Ibid.*   58. *Trial of the Major War Criminals*, vol. 25, Nürnberg, 1947, pp. 402-413; John L. Stipp, *Devil's Diary: the Record of Nazi Conspiracy and Aggression*, Yellow Springs, Ohio, 1955, pp. 3-13; Annelies von Ribbentropp, *"Verschwörung gegen den Frieden,"* Leoni, 1962, pp. 31ff.; Erich Raeder, *Mein Leben*, vol. 2, Tübingen, 1957, pp. 149-150; Hossbach, *op. cit.*, pp. 10, 13; A.J.P. Taylor, *The Origins of the Second World War*, London, 1961, pp. 131-134. Taylor, *op. cit.*, pp. 131-135, does not question the reliability of the Hossbach material; he is content to demonstrate that the material does not contain definite foreign policy decisions of any kind and hence is absolutely worthless as a so-called proof of the allegedly agressive designs of Hitler; Taylor is unsparing in his criticism of the tendentious use of this and similar material by the Allied prosecutors and judges at the Nuremberg trials.   59. *German Foreign Policy*, D, vol. 5, no. 18.   60. *Ibid.*, no. 19.   61. *Ibid.*, no. 20.   62. *German Foreign Office Archives*, Serial 145(*Polen*), pp. 78528-78529.   63. *Prager Akten*, no. 95.

Chapter 5

1. Helmut Suendermann, *Alter Feind — Was Nun? Wiederbegegnung mit England und Engländern*, Leoni, Bavaria, 1956, pp. 73-85; A.J.P. Taylor, The *Origins of the Second World War*, London, 1961, pp. 131ff. The achievements of Hitler in 1938 were summarized as follows by the Oxford historian, A.J.P. Taylor, The *Origins of the Second World War*, London, 1961, p. 187:. "The demonstration had been given that Germany could attain by peaceful negotiation the position in Europe to which her resources entitled her."   2. Hans Grimm, *Warum-Woher-Aber Wohin?*, Lippoldsberg, 1954, pp. 192ff.   3. Hans Roos, *Polen und Europa*, Tübingen, 1957, p. 302; *German Foreign Policy*, D, vol. 5, no. 20.   4. *Ibid.*, no. 25.   5. *Ibid.*, nos. 26, 27, 28.   6. *Ibid.*; Jozef Beck, *Dernier Rapport*, Neuchatel, 1949, pp. 142-143; Edward Carr, *German-Soviet Relations between the Two World Wars, 1919-1939*, Baltimore, 1951, pp. 118ff.   7. *German Foreign Policy*, D, vol. 5, no. 29.   8. *Der Hochverratsprozess gegen Dr. Guido Schmidt*, Vienna, 1947, pp. 357-371. *Vide* DGFP, C, vol. 3, no. 112, for the interesting July 23, 1934, report of German Ambassador Rieth describing Austria as an Italian puppet state; see also *Ibid.*, no. 123, for Hitler's motives in appointing Papen to succeed Rieth.   9. *German Foreign Policy*, D, vol. 5, no. 29; L. B. Namier, *Europe in Decay*, London, 1950, p. 284; Carr, *op. cit.*, pp. 120-121; Gustav Hilger & Alfred G. Meyer, *The Incompatible Allies: a Memoir-History of German-Soviet Relations, 1918-1941*, New York, 1953, pp. 250-287.   10. *German Foreign Policy*, D, vol. 5, no. 29.   11. *Ibid.*, no. 30.   12.

Hermann Rörtsch, *Schuld und Verhängnis: die Fritschkrise im Frühjahr 1938 als Wendepunkt in der Geschichte der nationalsozialistische Zeit*, Stuttgart, 1951, *passim*. 13. Franz von Papen, *Memoirs*, New York, 1953, pp. 376-406; Telford Taylor, *Sword and Swastika: Generals and Nazis in the Third Reich*, New York, 1952, pp. 137ff. 14. Papen, *op. cit.*, pp. 408ff. Taylor, *op. cit.*, p. 142, emphasizes that the initiative for the February 12, 1938, meeting in no sense originated with Hitler. 15. *Der Hochverratzprozess gegen Dr. Guido Schmidt, pp.* 378-380; John L. Stipp, ed., *Diary: the Record of Nazi Conspiracy and Aggression*, Yellow Springs, Ohio, 1955, pp. 23-25. 16. *Schulthess' Europäischer Geschichtskalender*, 1938, vol. 79, Munich, 1939, pp. 24-46. Taylor, *op. cit.*, pp. 143-144, stresses the fact that Hitler praised Schuschnigg in his February 20, 1938, speech, and that he cooperated with the Austrian regime by exercising restraint over the Austrian National Socialists. 17. Stipp, *op. cit.*, pp. 27-39; Galeazzo Ciano, *Diario, 1937-1938*, Rome, 1948, p. 129. Taylor, *op. cit.*, pp. 146-149, notes that Schuschnigg's fraudulent plebiscite scheme was an unexpected challenge and painful suprise to Hitler; Taylor states that the entire Austrian crisis was provoked by Schuschnigg. 18. *Documents on British Foreign Policy, 1919-1939*, III, vol. 1, nos. 2, 8, 15; hereafter cited as *British Foreign Policy:* Ciano, *op. cit.*, pp. 119, 130; Walford Seley, *Diplomatic Twilight, 1930-1940*, London, 1953, pp. 80ff. 19. Stipp, *op. cit.*, p. 56; see also documentary film, *The Rise and Fall of Adolf Hitler*. For the best detailed contemporary account of the exhilarating atmosphere in liberated Austria, *vide* Helmut Suendermann, *Die Grenzen fallen*, 2nd. ed., Munich, 1939, pp. 27ff. 20. Stipp, *op. cit.*, pp. 45-50. 21. Thomas Jones, *A Diary with Letters, 1931-1959*, London, 1954, p. xxxviii. 22. Basil Collier, *The Defence of the United Kingdom*, London, 1957, pp. 63-64; L.V. Pozdeeva, *Anglia i Remilitarisatsia Germanii, 1933-1936*, Moscow, 1956, pp. 158ff; see also Sybil Morrison, *"The Disarmament Myth,"* in *Peace News*, January 6, 1956. 23. Geoffrey Gorer, *Exploring English Character*, New York, 1955, p. 291. 24. Keith Feiling, *The Life of Neville Chamberlain*, London, 1946, pp. 52-185; p. 256. 25. *Ibid.*, p. 265. 26. *Ibid.*, p. 341; Robert Ferrel, *Peace in Their Time*, New Haven, 1952, *passim*. 27. Feiling, *op. cit.*, pp. 367ff.; Viscount Norwich, *Old Men Forget*, London, 1953, p. 229. 28. Alan C. Johnson, *Viscount Halifax*, New York, 1941, pp. 15, 43-73; E.F. Wood, *John Keble*, London, 1907. 29. Johnson, *op. cit.*, p. 85; Francis Neilson, *The Churchill Legend*, Appleton, Wisc., 1954, p. 254. 30. Earl of Halifax, *Fullness of Days*, New York, 1957, pp. 145ff. 31. Johnson, *op. cit.*, pp. 373-374. 32. Johnson, *op. cit.*, pp. 436-437; see also *German Foreign Office Archives*, Serial 375/1, pp. 208675-208861; *German Foreign Policy*, D, vol. 1, no. 31. 33. John Connell, *The "Office": A Study of British Foreign Policy and its Makers, 1919-1951*, London, 1958, pp. 248-255; the German diplomat at London, Dr. Edward Selzam, described Vansittart as a man of "extraordinary ability", "extensive experience", and "magnificent memory," and he suggested that Vansittart in his new position might have even greater influence on British policy than in the past, see *German Foreign Policy*, D, vol. 1, no. 95. 34. *British Foreign Policy*, III, vol. 1, no. 44. For the unpopularity of the Schuschnigg regime, *vide* C.A. Gulick, *Austria from Hapsburg to Hitler*, vol. 2, Berkely, Calif., 1948, *passim*. 35. Halifax, *op. cit.*, pp. 186, 196. Taylor, *op. cit.*, p. 16, is disturbed by the paucity of the Halifax memoirs and dismisses them as a few pages of autobiography; nevertheless, they contain some revealing views. 36. *Ibid.*, p. 200. 37. *Ibid.*, p. 201. 38. Viscount Templewood, *Nine Troubled Years*, London, 1954, pp. 185-258. 39. *Ibid.*, p. 264ff. 40. John Simon, *Retrospect: the Memoirs of the Right Honorable Viscount Simon*, London, 1952, pp. 175ff. 41. William Strang, *Home and Abroad*, London, 1956, p. 14; Strang never learned the German language, *Ibid.*, pp. 30-31. 42. T.L. Jarman, *The Rise and Fall of Nazi Germany*, New York, 1956, p. 187. 43. Strang, *op. cit.*, p. 68. 44. *Foreign Relations of the United States*, 1938, vol. 2, Washington, D. C., 1956, p. 53. 45. *Ibid.*, pp. 270-274. 46. *Ibid.*, pp. 434-436. 47. *Ibid.*, pp. 441-446. 48. *Ibid.*, p. 355. 49. *Ibid.*, p. 392. 50. *Ibid.*, pp. 372-373. 51. *Ibid.*, pp. 360-361. 52. *Ibid.*, pp. 648-649; James Burns, *Roosevelt: The Lion and the Fox*, New York, 1956, p. 387. 53. *Die Entstehung des Krieges von 1939*, Archive Comm. of the German Foreign Office, vol. 1, *Roosevelts Weg in den Krieg*, Berlin, 1943, no. 4. 54. *Ibid.*, pp. 45-48. 55. *Foreign Relations of the United States, 1938*, vol. 1, pp. 1-5; 24-26; 58. 56. J. Benoist-Méchin, *Soixante Jours Qui Ébranlèrent l' Occident, 10 Mai-10 Juillet 1940*, vol. 3, Paris, 1956, pp. 423-424. 57. René d'Argile, *et al, Les Origines Secrètes de la Guerre, 1939-1945*, Paris, 1957, pp. 14ff. 58. *Ibid.*, pp. 22ff.; Georges Bonnet, *Défense de la Paix: de Washington au Quai d' Orsay*, Geneva, 1946, pp. 7-8, 61ff. 59. *Les Événements survenus en France de 1933 à 1945*, suppl. vol. 9, Paris, 1951, pp. 2599ff., for Bonnet testimony, Mar. 15, 21, 22nd & April 5, 1951. Sisley Huddleston, *France: the Tragic Years, 1939-1947*, New York, 1955, pp. 12ff. 60. *Ibid.*, pp. 2613-2617. 61. *Ibid.*, pp. 2613ff. 62. *Ibid.* 63. Bonnet, *op. cit.*, vol. 1, pp. 12-13. 64. *Ibid.*, pp. 22-24. 65. *Ibid.*, pp. 49-50. 66. *Ibid.*, pp. 112-113. 67. *Foreign Relations of the United States, 1938*, vol. 1, p. 15. 68. *Ibid.*, pp. 41-42. 69. *Ibid.*, pp. 5-6. 70. Vladimir Potemkin, *et al, Histoire de la Diplomatie*, vol. 3, Paris, 1945, pp. 646-665; L.N. Ivanov, *Munkenskaya Politika Zapadnik Dershov e Rol SSSR kak destvityelnovo Faktora Mira, 1937-1940*, Moscow, 1947, p. 13; V.A. Matveyev, *Proval Munkenskoi Politiki, 1938-1939*, Moscow, 1955, pp. 3-4. 71. *Prager Akten*, no. 106. 72. Stipp, *op. cit.*, pp. 61-62. 73. *Prager Atken*, no. 113. On the failure of Benés to appease the Sudeten Germans, *vide* J.S. Hajek, *Signal Auf Krieg*, Berlin, 1960, p. 37ff., (Czech edition, Mnichov, Prague, 1958); see also H. Koeniger, *Der Weg nach München*, Berlin, 1958, pp. 16ff; Taylor, *op. cit.*, p. 152, stresses that the Sudeten crisis was automatic and inevitable after developments in Austria. 74. *British Foreign Policy*, III, vol. 1, no. 79. 75. *German Foreign Policy*, D, vol. 2, no. 113. Erwin Wickert, *Dramatische Tage in Hitlers Reich*, Stuttgart, 1952, pp. 119-123. 76. *Ibid.*, nos. 134, 135; Wheeler-Bennett, *Munich*, pp. 45ff. 77. *Prager Akten*, no. 124. 78. *British Foreign Policy*, III, vol. k, no. 250; Celovsky, *op. cit.*, pp. 215ff. Taylor, *op. cit.*, p. 153, recognizes that Benes was impatient to force a crisis with Germany in order to obtain commitments from Great Britain and France. 79. Stipp, *op. cit.*, pp. 63-69. Taylor, *op. cit.*, p. 166, proves that Hitler's revised military directive of May 30, 1938, in no sense constituted a final commitment for action against the Czechs; see also, DGFP, D, vol. 2, no. 282. 80. Gerhard Ritter, *Carl Goerdeler und die deutsche Wiederstandsbewegung*, Stuttgart, 1954, pp. 173-207;

Ian Colvin, *Admiral Canaris: Chef des Geheimdienstes*, Vienna, 1955, pp. 63-70.   **81.** Ullrich, *op. cit.*, pp. 251ff.   **82.** Čelovsky, *op. cit.*, pp. 279-330. The Czechs enforced martial law throughout the Sudetenland, and the Sudeten German Party (SdP) was formally suppressed on September 16, 1938, *vide* Martin Broszat, *Das Sudetendeutsche Freikorps* in *Vierteljahreshefte für Zeitgeschichte*, 1961:1.   **83.** *Ibid.*, pp. 331-332.   **84.** *Schullthess, 1938*, pp. 135-141. Taylor, *op. cit.*, p. 171 emphasizes that Hitler's September 12, 1938, speech contained no definite commitment for action against the Czechs.   **85.** *German Foreign Office Archives, Polen, vom 23 · April 1938 bis 30 · Juni 1939*, Serial 52a, pp. 34465-34467.   **86.** *Schulthess, 1938*, pp. 148-152.   **87.** Arthur Salter, *Personality in Politics: Studies of Contemporary Statesmen*, London, 1947, pp. 73ff.   **88.** Horthy, *op. cit.*, pp. 160-163. See also L. Zsigmond, *Ungarn und sas Münchener Abkommen*, in *Acta Historica*, vol. 4, no. 3/4, Budapest, 1959.   **89.** *German Foreign Policy*, D, vol. 5, no. 52.   **90.** *Dokumenti e Materiale Konuna Vtoroi Mirovoi Voyni*, vol. 1, Moscow, 1948, no. 26; *Prager Akten*, no. 142; *British Foreign Policy*, III, vol. 3, nos. 1, 2, 4.   **91.** Edward Raczynski, *The British-Polish Alliance: its Origin and Meaning*, London, 1948, p. 7. Celovsky, *op. cit.*, p. 223.   **92.** Raczynski, *op. cit.*, pp. 7-8.   **93.** *German Foreign Policy*, D, vol. 15, no. 37.   **94.** *Ibid.*, no. 45. Taylor, *op. cit.*, p. 216, unfortunately misses the evolution of Halifax's Danzig policy; Taylor's statement that "Halifax never wearied of suggesting that Danzig should return to German sovereignty, with safe-guards for Polish trade," was meant by Taylor to apply to 1939 as well as 1938; in reality, the statement is invalid for the period after July, 1938; it is no exaggeration to state that war would have been easy to avert in 1939 had Halifax continued to entertain the attitude toward Danzig attributed to him by Taylor.   **95.** *British Foreign Policy*, III, vol. 3, no. 4.   **96.** Beck, *op. cit.*, pp. 159-160.   **97.** *Ibid.*   **98.** G. Bonnet, *Fin d' une Europe*, Geneva, 1948, p. 21.   **99.** London *Times Literary Supplement*, 1953-1954. The original letter from Bonnet was published in issue no. 2661, Jan. 30, 1953; for the Polish position, see also W. Pobóg-Malinowski, *Najnowsza Historia Polityczna Polski, 1864-1945*, vol. 2, London, 1956, pp. 657ff.   **100.** Wheeler-Bennet, *Munich*, pp. 139ff.   **101.** *British Foreign Policy*, III, vol. 3, no. 11; Beck, *op. cit.*, p. 161.   **102.** *British Foreign Policy*, III, vol. 3, nos. 12, 13.   **103.** *Ibid.*, nos. 15,20.   **104.** *Ibid.*, no. 14.   **105.** *Ibid.*, nos. 22, 23, 32.   **106.** *Ibid.*, no. 34.   **107.** Beck, *op. cit.*, p. 163. The various deceptive Russian offers to aid the Czechs during the crisis are to be found in *New Documents on the History of Munich*, New York, 1958, nos. 7, 39, 55, 57. (Czech edition *Mnichov v Dokumentech*, 2 vol., Prague, 1958); see also Pavel Auersperg, *et al, O Československé Dahraniční Politice, 1918-1939*, Prague, 1956, pp. 362-3.   **108.** Léon Noël, *L'Agression Allemande contre la Pologne*, Paris, 1947, p. 215; Matveyev, *op. cit.*, pp. 67ff.   **109.** Jan Szembek, *Journal*, Paris, 1952, p. 337.   **110.** *British Foreign Policy*, III, vol. 3, no. 38.   **111.** *Ibid.*, no. 48; Beck, *op. cit.*, p. 165.   **112.** *British Foreign Policy*, III, vol. 3, no. 53.   **113.** *Ibid.*, vol. 2, nos. 1033, 1073.   **114.** *Foreign Relations of the United States, 1938*, vol. 1, pp. 650-652.   **115.** *Ibid.*, pp. 653-654.   **116.** *Ibid.*, pp. 664-669.   **117.** *British Foreign Policy*, III, vol. 3, no. 66.   **118.** Szembek, *op. cit.*, pp. 338-339; Luigi Villari, *Italian Foreign Policy under Mussolini*, New York, 1956, pp. 204-218. For Mussolini's telephone conversation with Attolico on September 28, 1938, *vide, Opera Omnia di Benito Mussolini*, vol. 29, Florence, 1959, pp. 165-166.   **119.** *British Foreign Policy*, III, vol. 2, no. 1118. Taylor, *op. cit.*, p. 179, explains that the failure to arrive at an Anglo-German agreement at Bad Godesberg did not modify Hitler's hopes that an agreement would be acheived.   **120.** *Ibid.*, no. 1129.   **121.** *Ibid.*, nos. 1159, 1174.   **122.** Feiling, *op. cit.*, pp. 366-367. For the enthusiastic reception of the Munich agreement in the Sudetenland, *vide*, Emil Franzel, *Sudetendeutsche Geschichte*, Augsburg, 1958, pp. 380-398.   **123.** Čelovsky, *op. cit.*, pp. 452-453; A.J.P. Taylor, *The Origins of the Second World War*, London, 1961, p. 187.   **124.** Pierre Buk, *La Tragédie Tchécoslovaque de Septembre 1938 à Mars 1939*, Paris, 1939, pp. 135-141; Hubert Ripka, *Munich: Before and After*, London, 1939, p. 230.   **125.** Churchill, *op. cit.*, p. 321.   **126.** Bonnet, *Fin d' une Europe*, p. 19.   **127.** *British Foreign Policy*, III, vol. 3, no. 72.   **128.** *Ibid.*, no. 75.   **129.** *Ibid.*   **130.** *Ibid.*, no. 116.   **131.** *German Foreign Policy*, D, vol. 5, no. 55.   **132.** *Ibid.*   **133.** *Ibid.*   **134.** *Nazi Acts of Conspiracy and Aggression*, Washington, D.C., 1946, vol. 4, p. 400, hereafter cited as *Nazi Acts;* A.I. Berndt, *Der Marsch ins Grossdeutsche Reich*, Munich, 1942, vol. 2, pp. 387-388.   **135.** *British Foreign Policy*, III, vol. 3, no. 84.   **136.** *Ibid.*, no. 87.   **137.** *Ibid.*, no. 90.   **138.** *Ibid.*, no. 97.   **139.** *Ibid.*, no. 100.   **140.** *Ibid.*, vol. 2, no. 1228.

Chapter 6

1. *Les Événements survenus en France de 1933 à 1945*, Paris, 1947, vol. 2, pp. 255ff. For analysis of the Post-Munich situation by General Maurice Gamelin.   **2.** Basil Panyeko, *Germany, Poland, and the Ukraine in the 19th Century and After*, January, 1939, pp. 34ff.   **3.** Russel Grenfell, *Unconditional Hatred: German War Guilt and the Future of Europe*, New York, 1954, p. 32.   **4.** Gottfried Zarnow, *Die Geburt der Weltkriege*, Düsseldorf, 1957, p. 205.   **5.** Erich von Manstein, *Aus einem Soldatenleben, 1887-1939*, Bonn, 1958, pp. 341ff.   **6.** Albert Wedemeyer, *Wedemeyer Reports!* New York, 1958, pp. 3-5, C.C. Tansill, *The Back Door to War*, Chicago, 1952, p. 3.   **7.** Hans Grimm, *Warum-Woher-Aber Wohin?*, Lippoldsberg, 1954, p. 219. A.J.P. Taylor, *The Origins of the Second World War*, London, 1961, pp. 176-177, incorrectly claims that the tentative Anglo-French agreement of Sept. 18, 1938, which was extended to include Germany and Italy at Munich, trapped the British by providing for a future gurantee of the Czech state (i.e. allegedly trapped them into an unprecedented guarantee in Eastern Europe); in reality, there were many conditions attached, and Halifax subsequently evaded granting this particular guarantee without any undue difficulty; it is precisely from the Munich conference down to World War II that Taylor's treatment of British policy loses clarity.   **8.** Norman E. Petersen, *Hjalmar Schacht: For and Against Hitler*, Boston, 1954, pp. 296-297; Earl R. Beck, *Verdict on Schacht*, Tallahasee, 1955, pp. 143-144; Burton H. Klein, *Germany's Economic Preparation sfor War;* Cambridge, Mass., 1959, pp. 25, 85-86. **9.** Burton H. Klein, "Germany's Preparation for War: A Re-examination," in *American Economic Review*, March, 1948; see especially Burton Klein, *Germany's Economic Preparation for War*, pp. 187ff. **10.** N.M. Sloutzki, *The World Armaments Race, 1919-1939*, Geneva, 1941, p. 34; *Armaments Year-Book: General and Statistical Information*, Geneva, 1940, pp. 163ff., Klein, *Germany's Economic Preparation for War*, p. 16. **11.** Petersen, *op. cit.*, pp. 70ff.; Hjalmar Schacht, *76 Jahre Meines Lebens*, Bad Wörishofen, 1953, p. 456. **12.** Klein, *op. cit.*, pp. 70ff.; Ulrich Wilk, *Der Deutsche Rüstungsstand im Jahre 1939* in *Nation Europa*, May 1959. Taylor, *op. cit.*, p. 75, takes a realistic position on the scope of German armament. **13.** Basil Collier, *The Defence of the United Kingdom*, London, 1957, pp. 69-73; Grenfell, *op. cit.*, pp. 21ff. **14.** *Ibid.*, pp. 201-243; Grenfell considered the unwillingness of the Roosevelt clique to believe in the safety of the United States to be the strangest phenomenon of the entire period, *Ibid.*, p. 247. **15.** Otto Abetz, *Das Offene Problem*, Cologne, 1951, pp. 160ff.; J Von Ribbentrop, *Zwischen London und Moskau*, Leoni, Bavaria, 1954, p. 43. **16.** Hans Roos, *Polen und Europa*, Tübingen, 1957, pp. 380-390. **17.** J. W. Wheeler-Bennett, *Munich: Prologue to Tragedy*, London, 1948, p. 337. **18.** *The Slovak Question*, Slovak National Council, Geneva, 1940, pp. 17-32; Michael Schwartz, *Die Slowakei: der jüngste Staat Europas*, Leipzig, 1939, pp. 36ff. **19.** Robert Nowak, *Der Künstliche Staat: Ostprobleme der Tschechoslowakei*, Berlin, 1938, pp. 136ff. **20.** The Slovaks were still an unsophisticated people. Veit Harlan's famous anti-Jewish film, *Jud Süss*, was received quietly in Germany, but it produced pandemonium and immediate excesses against the Jews when it was shown in Slovakia. **21.** Jan Szembek, *Journal*, Paris, 1952, pp. 352-353. **22.** Norwid Neugebauer, *The Defense of Poland*, London, 1942, pp. 19ff. **23.** *Foreign Relations of the United States, 1938*, vol.1, pp. 715-719. For the excellent contemporary history of the Spanish Civil War, *vide* Robert Brasillach & Maurice Bardeche, *Histoire de la guerre d'Espagne*, Paris, 1939; for a later diplomatic history, *vide* P. van der Esch, *Prelude to War*, Hague, 1951; for a lengthy recent defense of the Marxist cause in Spain, *vide* Émile Ténine & Pierre Broué, *La Révolution et la Guerre d'Espagne*, Paris, 1961. **24.** Harold Läuen, *Polens Politik der 'integralen Lösung,'* in *Osteuropa*, November, 1938. **25.** John Reshetar in conversation with the writer, Feb. 16, 1947; J. Reshetar, *The Ukrainian Revolution, 1917-1920*, Princeton, 1952, *passim*. **26.** Roman Ilnytzky, *Deutschland und die Ukraine, 1939-1945*, vol. 1/1, Munich, 1955, pp. 60-90; more than half the population of the entire Polish territory annexed by Russia in 1939 was Ukrainian, although the Poles claimed that the total non-Jewish and non-Polish population was only 43.8%, see *Polish Facts and Figures*, no. 2, New York, 1944, pp. 11ff. **27.** Szembek, *op. cit.*, pp. 352ff. **28.** The classic Polish literary account of this catastrophe is Henryk Sienkiewicz, *The Deluge: an Historical Novel of Poland, Sweden, and Russia*, 2 vol., New York, 1891; The Russian side of the same story is Nikolai Gogol, *Taras Bulba: a Tale of the Cossacks*, New York, 1886. **29.** Hans Frank, *Im Angesicht des Galgens*, Munich, 1953, pp. 46ff.; Szembek, *op. cit.*, pp. 352ff. **30.** *German Foreign Policy*, D, vol. 5, no. 64. **31.** *Ibid.* **32.** *British Foreign Policy*, III, vol. 3, no. 114. **33.** Edward Grigg, *British Foreign Policy*, London, 1944, pp. 23ff.; Charles Bewley, *Hermann Goering and the Third Reich*, New York, 1962, pp. 251-271, takes Henderson severely to task for unintentionally deceiving the German leaders about British official thinking. **34.** *British Foreign Policy*, III, vol. 3, no 125. **35.** *Ibid.*, nos. 127, 128. **36.** Hubert Ripka, *Munich: Before and After*, London, 1939, pp. 109-110; Pierre Buk, *La Tragédie Tchécoslovaque de Septembre 1938 à Mars 1939*, Paris, 1939, pp. 66-68. **37.** The Syrový operations in Russia were conducted with the approval of Beneš, see Edvard Beneš, *Der Aufstand der Nationen*, Berlin, 1928, p. 554. **38.** The Petka (five leading Czech political parties) included the National Socialist Party of Beneš, and the National Democrats, Social Democrats, Communists, and Agrarians; the Communists did not participate in the government after Munich, see Hugh Seton-Watson, *Eastern Europe Between the Wars, 1918-1941*, Cambridge, 1945, pp. 172-176. **39.** *British Foreign Policy*, III, vol. 3, nos. 129, 134. **40.** *Ibid.*, nos. 136, 142. **41.** *Foreign Relations of the United States, 1938*, vol., 1, pp. 697-698. **42.** *British Foreign Policy*, III, vol. 3, no. 138. **43.** *Ibid.*, no. 150. **44.** *Ibid.*, no. 179. The Czech Communist leader, Klement Gottwald, delivered a blistering speech denouncing the Munich agreement on Oct. 11, 1938, *vide* K. Gottwald, *Ausgewählte Reden und Aufsätze*, Berlin, 1955, pp. 242-250. **45.** Józef Beck, *Dernier Rapport*, Neuchatel, 1949, p. 169. **46.** *German Foreign Policy*, D, vol. 5, no. 67. **47.** *Ibid.*, no. 58. **48.** *Ibid.*, nos. 59, 60. **49.** *Ibid.*, no. 61. **50.** *Ibid.*, no. 63. **51.** *Ibid.*, nos. 69, 70. **52.** *Ibid.* **53.** Winston Churchill, *The Gathering Storm*, Boston, 1948, pp. 328-329; Emrys Hughes, *Winston Churchill: British Bulldog*, New York, 1955, pp. 173-174; *Schulthess, 1938*, pp. 173-175. **54.** *British Foreign Policy*, III, vol. 3, no. 198. **55.** *Ibid.*, no. 203. **56.** *Ibid.*, no. 204. **57.** Schwartz, *Die Slowakei*, pp. 54-69; H. Raschhofer, *Die Sudetenfrage*, Munich, 1953, pp. 195-197. **58.** Szembek, *op. cit.*, pp. 351-352. **59.** *German Foreign Policy*, D, vol. 5, no. 72. **60.** *Ibid.*, no. 73. **61.** *Ibid.*, no. 74. **62.** *British Foreign Policy*, III, vol. 3, no. 206. **63.** *Ibid.*, no. 208. **64.** *Ibid.*, no. 210. **65.** J. Stipp, *Devil's Diary*, Yellow Springs, 1955, pp. 83-84. Taylor, *op. cit.*, pp. 192-193, explains that Hitler's directive of Oct. 21, 1938, was a precautionary measure and not a plan for any aggressive action. **66.** *British Foreign Policy*, III, vol. 3, no. 210. **67.** *Ibid.*, no. 124. **68.** *Ibid.*, no. 215. **69.** *Ibid.*, no. 216. **70.** *German Foreign Policy*, D, vol. 5, no. 75. **71.** Szembek, *op. cit.*, pp. 356-359. **72.** Robert Nowak, *Die Zukunft der Karpatenukraine* in *Zeitschrift für Geopolitik*, November 1938. **73.** Szembek, *op. cit.*, pp. 358-359. **74.** *German Foreign Policy*, D, vol. 5, no. 76. **75.** Grigorie Gafencu, *Dernier Jours de l'Europe*, Paris, 1946, pp. 31ff. Nicolet Petresco-Comnene, *Preludi del Grande Dramma*, Rome, 1947, pp. 284-293; King Carol said about Beck's plan: "Rumania will not eat this bread," *Ibid.*, p. 284. **76.** Beck, *op. cit.*, pp. 172-174. **77.** *German Foreign Policy*, D, vol. 5, no. 78. **78.** *Ibid.*, no. 79. **79.** Szembek, *op. cit.*, pp. 359-362. **80.** Beck, *op. cit.*, p. 171. **81.** *German Foreign Policy*, D, vol. 5, no. 80. **82.** *Ibid.* **83.** *German Foreign Office Archives*, Serial 52a, p. 34476. **84.** Ribbentrop, *op. cit.*, pp. 154ff. **85.** Erich Kordt, *Nicht aus den Akten*, Stuttgart, 1950, pp. 292ff. **86.** *Polish White Book*, pp. 47-48; *Documents on Events*, p. 200. **87.** *Ibid.*; Beck, *op. cit.*, pp. 182-183. **88.** *German Foreign Policy*, D., vol. 5, no. 81; New York *Times*, Oct. 21, 1938. **89.** *British Foreign Policy*, III, vol. 3, no. 223. **90.**

German Foreign Policy, D, vol. 5, no. 82. **91.** *Ibid.*, no. 83. **92.** *Polish White Book*, pp. 48-50; E. Raczynski, *The British-Polish Alliance*, London, 1948, p. 3. W. Pobóg-Malinowski, *Najnowsza Historia Polityczna Polski, 1864-1945*, vol. 3, London, 1960, p. 3

Chapter 7

1. F. Neilson, *The Makers of War*, Appleton, Wisc., 1950, pp. 180-181. **2.** Adolf Bolcheński, *Miedzy Niemcami a Rosja*, Warsaw, 1937, p. 42. **3.** Edward Rozek, *Allied Wartime Diplomacy: a Pattern in Poland*, London, 1958, p. 445. **4.** William C. Bullitt in conversation with the writer, Feb. 27, 1948. **5.** *Les Événments survenus en France*, suppl. vol. 9, Paris, 1951, p. 2617; René d'Argile *et al, Les Origines Secrètes de la Guerre, 1939-1945*, Paris, 1957, p. 14; Eden later admitted that most British military evaluations of foreign countries during the 1930's were false, *vide*, Anthony Eden, *Facing the Dictators*, Boston, 1962, p. 110. **6.** *Polska a Zagranica, 1938*, Warsaw, 1938, no. 3 **7.** Rolf Wingendorf, *Polen: Volk zwischen Ost und West*, Berlin, 1939, p. 16. **8.** Galeazzo Ciano, *Diario, 1937-1938*, Rome, 1948, pp. 127-128. **9.** Józef Beck, *Dernier Rapport*, Neuchatel, 1949, p. 147. **10.** Hans Roos, *Polen und Europa*, Tübingen, 1957, pp. 308-310. **11.** Beck, *op. cit.*, p. 149. **12.** Roos, *op. cit.*, pp. 311ff. **13.** *German Foreign Office Archives*, Serial 145, pp. 78552-78553. **14.** *German Foreign Policy*, D, vol. 5, no. 32. **15.** Paul Kluke, *et al, Gutachten des Instituts für Zeitgeschichte*, Munich, 1958, pp. 80-82. **16.** *Foreign Relations of the United States, 1938*, vol. 2, p. 650; Joseph Tenenbaum, *Race and Reich*, New York, 1956, pp. 239ff.; see also Michał Lepecki, *Madagaskar*, Warsaw, 1938, for the special mission of Piłsudski's former adjutant to discover the possibilities for Jewish settlement in the sparsely populated French protectorate of Madagascar. **17.** *Foreign Relations of the United States, 1938*, vol. 2, pp. 651-654. Carl J. Burckhardt, *Meine Danziger Mission, 1937-1939*, Munich, 1960, p. 73 **18.** Helmut Heiber, *Der Fall Grünspan* in *Vierteljahreshefte für Zeitgeschichte*, April, 1957, pp. 134ff. **19.** This writer read a carefully documented paper on this theme to a German audience in 1952 under the auspices of the United States Information Service and the Munich *Amerika Haus;* see James G. Randall, *Lincoln, the President: Springfield to Gettysburg*, 2 vol., New York, 1945, for Lincoln's ideas on the Negro question, and August Kubizek, *The Young Hitler I Knew*, Boston, 1955, for the influences which produced Hitler's ideas on the Jewish question. **20.** Kurt Pröller, *Judentum and Kommunismus* in *Volk und Reich*, April, 1939. **21.** This measure of the Polish Government would have been unthinkable outside the context of a fiercely anti-Jewish orientation. Representative Bigelow of Ohio introduced the following resolution in the United States Congress on July 9, 1937: "We cannot but look with dismay upon the fashion in which the present leaders of the Polish Government, with the memory of their own oppression still before them, have returned to the barbarism of the Middle Ages in respect to their Jewish population." See *Congressional Record, House of Representatives*, July 9, 1937; on many occasions after 1933, the number of Jewish petitions received in the United States Congress protesting Polish anti-Jewish measures was larger than those on anti-Jewish measures in Germany; Emanuel Scherer, *Polski i Zydzi*, New York, 1942, is indispensable for the Jewish question in Piłsudski's Poland. **22.** Proeller, *op. cit.* **23.** Jan Szembek, *Journal*, Paris, 1952, pp. 363-364. **24.** *German Foreign Policy*, D, vol. 5, no. 84. **25.** *Ibid.*, nos. 88, 89. **26.** *Ibid.*, no. 91. William L. Shirer, *The Rise and Fall of the Third Reich: a History of Nazi Germany*, New York, 1960, p. 430. **27.** *Ibid.*, no. 92. **28.** *Ibid.* **29.** *Foreign Relations of the United States, 1938*, vol. 2, pp. 380-382, 391-392. **30.** Heiber, *op. cit.;* René d'Argile, *et al, Les Origines Sécrètes de la Guerre, 1939-1945*, Paris, 1957, pp. 217ff. **31.** The assassination of Wilhelm Gustloff, the National Socialist Party leader, by David Frankfurter, occurred in Switzerland in 1936; the National Socialists, like the Marxists, rejected assasination in principle as a legitimate political weapon against a dominant political system; the British Labour MP, George Russel Strauss, raised funds for the assassination of Hitler before the outbreak of World War II, and there were many Communist conspiracies to kill Hitler despite opposing Marxist theory; see *Sunday Pictorial*, London, Dec. 15, 1946; the demand for the assassination of Churchill or Roosevelt was never raised in Germany; Churchill's elaborate precautions against assassination were really quite unnecessary, see W. Churchill, *The Gathering Storm*, Boston, 1948, p. 401 **32.** *German Foreign Policy*, D, Vol. 5, no. 95; See also Milton Meyer, *They Thought They Were Free*, Chicago, 1953, *passim;* Helmut Heiber, *Joseph Goebbels*, Berlin, 1962, pp. 181ff. **33.** *Foreign Relations of the United States, 1938*, vol. 2, pp. 393-402. **34.** *Ibid.*, pp. 405-497; d'Argile, *op. cit.*, p. 233. **35.** *German Foreign Archives (Polen)* Serial 52a, p. 34458. **36.** *German Foreign Policy*, D, vol. 5, no. 34. **37.** *Statistik des Deutschen Reiches*, vol. 552, no. 1, Berlin, 1939; F. Hoffman, *et al, Ost Deutschland*, Kitzingen, 1949, pp. 3ff. **38.** *German Foreign Policy*, D, vol. 5, no. 39. **39.** *Ibid.* **40.** *Ibid.*, no. 42. **41.** *Gazeta Polska*, June 25, 1938. **42.** Richard Breyer, *Das Deutsche Reich und Polen*, Würzburg, 1955, pp. 274ff. **43.** *German Foreign Policy*, D, vol. 5, no. 40. **44.** *Ibid.*, no. 41. **45.** *Ibid.*, no. 43. **46.** *Ibid.*, no. 44. **47.** *Ibid.*, no. 46. **48.** *Ibid.*, no. 47. In connection with the seizure of the German farms, the term confiscation is used deliberately because the compensation was ridiculously small. **49.** *Ibid.*, no. 48. **50.** *Ibid.*, no. 51. **51.** *Ibid.*, no. 53; Colonel Adam Doc in conversation with the writer, march 3, 1948. The Original *Rota (The Oath)* by Maria Konopnicka was directed against the Russians, not the Germans; new versions appeared after her death in 1910; the version sung by Piłsudski's soldiers during World War I described the Germans as a bad brood spawned by the Teutonic Knights; it was the duty of Poles to oppose them; this was at a time when Piłsudski was allied with Germany against Russia, *vide* Kurt Lueck, *Der Mythos vom deutschen in der polnischen Volksüberlieferung und Literatur*, Leipzig, 1938, p. 361. **52.** *German Foreign Office Archives*, Serial 145, pp. 78694-78707, 78644. **53.** *German Foreign Policy*, D, vol. 5, nos. 61, 63, 65, 66. **54.** *Ibid.*, no. 68; *Gazeta Polska*, Oct. 4, 1938. **55.** *German Foreign Office Archives*, Serial 145, pp. 78643-78644. **56.** *Ibid.*, Serial 2842, pp. 549797-549801. **57.** *Ibid.*, Serial

145, p. 78699. **58.** *Documents on Events*, pp. 130-133. **59.** *Ibid.*, pp. 133-137. **60.** *Ibid.*, pp. 141-142. **61,** *Ibid.*, pp. 143-144. **62.** *Ibid.*, pp. 147-150. W. M. Drzewieniecki, *The German-Polish Frontier*, Chicago, 1959, pp. 40-43; Polish excesses against the German minority receive frank recognition in Zoltan Michael Szaz, *Germany's Eastern Frontiers* Chicago, 1960, pp. 61ff. **63.** *German Foreign Policy*, D, vol. 5, no. 86. **64.** *Ibid.*, no. 97. **65.** Szembek, *op. cit.*, pp. 367-379. **66.** *Documents on Events*, p. 202 **67.** *Ibid.* **68.** *Ibid.*, p. 204; *Polish White Book*, p. 52; *German Foreign Office Archives*, Serial 52a, p. 34476. **69.** *German Foreign Policy*, D, vol. 5, no. 102. **70.** *International Military Tribunal*, vol. 10, p. 356. **71.** *German Foreign Policy Archives*, Serial 145, p. 78742. **72.** *German Foreign Policy*, D, vol. 5, no. 102. Burckhardt, *op. cit.*, p. 225. **73.** Szembek, *op. cit.*, pp. 379-381. **74.** *Polish Documents Relative to the Origin of the War*, 1st series, Berlin, 1940. pp. 9-10, hereafter cited as *Polish Documents;* Bullitt and the United States Dept. of State originally denied the authenticity of these documents (see editor's note, Alfred von Wegerer, *The Origins of World War II*, New York, 1941); the authenticity of the documents was confirmed for the present writer by Wacław Jedrzejewicz of the Piłsudski Institute in New York City; J. W. Wheeler-Bennet, *Munich: Prologue to Tragedy*, London, 1948, pp. 309-310, led the way in accepting their authenticity in Great Britain; W.L. Langer & S.E. Gleason, *The Challenge to Isolation, 1937-1940*, New York, 1952, p. 58, seem to question their authenticity; actually, they merely point out that Bullitt and Hull have denied them, and hence Langer and Gleason refused to use them. **75.** *Ibid.* **76.** *German Foreign Policy*, D, vol. 5, no. 103. **77.** Szembek, *op. cit.*, pp. 379-381. **78.** *Ibid.*, pp. 383-384. **79.** *Ibid.*, pp. 384ff.; Beck, *op. cit.*, p. 182. **80.** E. Raczynski, *The British-Polish Alliance*, London, 1948, pp. 9-10. **81.** *British Foreign Policy*, III, vol. 3, no. 298. **82.** *Ibid.*, no. 301. **83.** *Ibid.*, no. 319. T Bierschenk, *Die deutschen Volksgruppen in Polen, 1934-1939*, Goettingen, 1955, pp. 117ff. **84.** *Ibid.*, no. 322. **85.** *German Foreign Policy*, D, vol. 5, no. 102. **86.** *British Foreign Policy*, III, vol. 3, no. 411. **87.** *Ibid.;* no. 430. **88.** *Ibid.* **89.** *Ibid.*, no. 437. **90.** Raczynski, *op. cit.*, pp. 10-11.

Chapter 8

1. G.A. Deborin, *Vtoraya Mirovaya Voyna*, Moscow, 1958, pp. 15-38. **2.** Fritz Hesse, *Das Spiel um Deutschland*, Munich, 1953, pp. 14-15. An excellent reference to Hitler's single-minded desire for friendship and collaboration with Great Britian is Walter Ansel, *Hitler Confronts England*, Durham N.C., 1960, pp. 10-13. **3.** Raymond Postgate, *The Life of George Lansbury*, London, 1951, pp. 313-317. **4.** Thomas Jones, *A Diary with Letters, 1931-1950*, London, 1954, pp. 180-181. **5.** *Ibid.*, pp. 197-200. **6.** Leopold Amery, *My Political Life*, vol. 3, London, 1955, pp. 128-129. **7.** Viscount Rothermere, *My Fight to Rearm Britain*, London, 1939, pp. 30-32, 80-82, 177. **8.** Jones, *Diary*, pp. 240-265; Lloyd George in 1936 insisted that Hitler was arming for defense rather than aggression, see Thomas Jones, *Lloyd George*, Cambridge, Mass., 1951, p. 248. **9.** G. Ward Price, *I Know These Dictators*, London, 1938, *passim;* Lord Londonderry, *Ourselves and Germany*, London, 1938, *passim;* F. L. Schuman, *Europe on the Eve: The Crises of Diplomacy, 1933-1939*, New York, 1939, pp. 341-345. **10.** Jones, *Diary*, p. 330. **11.** K. Feiling, *The Life of Neville Chamberlain*, London, 1946, pp. 366-367. **12.** Emrys Hughes, *Winston Churchill: British Bulldog*, New York, 1955, p. 144; Ernst Hanfstaengel, *Unheard Witness*, Philadelphia, 1957, pp. 193-196; Francis Neilson, *The Churchill Legend*, Appleton, Wisc., 1954, p. 289. Winston Churchill, *Step by Step*, London, 1939, pp. 143-144. **13.** Dennis Bardens, *Portrait of a Statesman: the Personal Life of Sir Anthony Eden*, New York, 1956, pp. 115-126; Anthony Eden, *Facing the Dictators*, Boston, 1962, pp. 69, 148-151. **14.** Jones, *Diary*, pp. 369-370. **15.** John Simon, *Retrospect*, London, 1952, pp. 202-203. **16.** London *Times*, October 3, 1938. **17.** *Ibid.* **18.** Viscount Norwich, *Old Men Forget*, 1953, p. 40. **19.** *Ibid.*, p. 190. **20.** *Ibid.*, pp. 191-208. **21.** *Ibid.*, pp. 229-236. **22.** *Hansard's Parliamentary Debates*, *Commons*, October 3, 1938. **23.** *Ibid.* **24.** Pasquale Villari, *The Life and Times of Niccolo Machiavelli*, vol. 2, London, 1898, pp. 193, 422-423; S.T. Bindoff, *Tudor England*, London, 1950, pp. 96-98; A.F. Pollard, *Wolsey* London, 1929, pp. 219ff. **25.** Maurice Ashley, *England in the 17th Century*, London, 1952, pp. 84ff.; Hilaire Belloc, *Cromwell*, London, 1934, pp. 334ff. **26.** G.N. Clark, *The Later Stuarts, 1660-1714*, Oxford, 1934, pp. 74-78; Ashley, *op. cit.*, pp. 130ff. **27.** Clark, *op. cit.*, pp. 96-97, 131-136, 153-168. **28.** P. Roberts, *The Quest for Security, 1715-1740*, New York, 1947, pp. 255-263; E. Wilson, *Fleury and French Foreign Policy, 1726-1743*, Cambridge, Mass., 1936, *passim.* **29.** Z.E. Rashed, *The Peace of Paris, 1763*, Liverpool, 1951, pp. 17ff.; E. Eyck, *Pitt versus Fox, Father and Son, 1735-1806*, London, 1950, pp. 220ff. **30.** Georges Lefebvre, *Napoléon*, Paris, 1935, pp. 143ff.; L. Madelin, *Talleyrand*, London, 1948, pp. 165ff.; P.R. Rhoden, *Die Klassische Diplomatie*, Berlin, 1939, pp. 13ff.; C.K. Webster, *The Foreign Policy of Castlereagh, 1812-1815*, London, 1931, *passim;* H. Nicolson, *The Congress of Vienna*, London, 1946, pp. 242ff.; and especially the introduction in C.K. Webster, *The Foreign Policy of Palmerston, 1830-1841*, 2 vol., London, 1951. **31.** A.J.P. Taylor, *The Struggle for Mastery in Europe, 1848-1918*, Oxford, 1954, pp. 60-67; W.L. Langer, *European Alliances and Alignments*, 2nd ed., New York, 1950, pp. 292ff. **32.** Taylor, *op. cit.*, pp. xix-xx; 525-526. **33.** *Ibid.*, p.p. 383ff.; A. Malozemoff, *Russian Far Eastern Policy, 1881-1904*, Berkeley, 1958, pp. 173ff. **34.** E. Morand, *L'Angleterre maîtresse des Destinées Françaises*, Paris, 1939, pp. 296ff. **35.** H.H. Cumming, *Franco-British Rivalry in the Post-War Near East*, London, 1938, *passim;* E.A. Adamov, *Evropeyskie Dershal e Grezia v Epokhu Mirovoi Woyni*, Moscow, 1922, and E.A. Adamov, *Razdyel Aziatskoi Turzii*, Moscow, 1924, *passim.* **36.** Morand, *op. cit.*, pp. 302-303; E.H. Carr, *International Relations since the Peace Treaties*, London, 1940, pp. 44-78; W.M. Jordan, *Great Britain, France, and the German Problem, 1918-1939*, London, 1943 pp. 222ff. **37.** C.C. Tansill, *Back Door to War: The Roosevelt Foreign Policy*, Chicago, 1952, pp. 30ff.; L.V. Pozdeeva, *Anglia i Remilitarizatsia Germanii, 1933-1936*, Moscow, 1956, pp. 86ff. **38.** F.P. Walters, *A History of the League of Nations*, vol. 2, London,

1952, ch. 54; Pazdeeva, *op. cit.*, pp. 225-251.   **39.** Hughe Knatchbull-Huggessen, *Diplomat in Peace and War*, London, 1949, p. 128; see also Edward Grigg, *Britain Looks at Germany*, London, 1938, *passim.*   **40.** John E. Wrench, *Geoffrey Dawson and Our Times*, London, 1955, p. 371.   **41.** *Ibid.*, pp. 242, 364; John Connel, *The "Office" : A Study of British Foreign Policy and its Makers, 1919-1951*, London, 1958, p. 274.   **42.** Tom Driberg, *Beaverbrook: A Study in Power and Frustration*, London, 1956, pp. 243-245.   **43.** *Hansard's Parliamentary Debates, Commons*, October 3, 1938. Alan Johnson, *Viscount Halifax*, New York, 1941, pp. 72-73.   **44.** E. Windrich, *British Labour's Foreign Policy*, Stanford, 1952, p. 155.   **45.** Hugh Dalton, *Memoirs*, vol. 2, London, 1957, pp. 26-30, 181-182, 196-197.   **46.** *Hansard's Parliamentary Debates, Commons*, October 3, 1938.   **47.** *Ibid., Lords*, October 3, 1938.   **48.** *Ibid.*, October 4, 1938.   **49.** Edward Rozek, *Allied Wartime Diplomacy: a Pattern in Poland*, London, 1958, p. 9.   **50.** *Hansard's Parliamentary Debates, Commons*, October 4, 1938.   **51.** *Ibid.*, October 5, 1938; Margaret Coit, *Mr. Baruch*, Boston, 1957, pp. 466-467; Francis Neilson, *The Churchill Legend*, Appleton, Wisc., 1954, p. 296.   **52.** Neilson, *op. cit.*, p. 271.   **53.** Winston Churchill, *The Gathering Storm*, Boston, 1948, pp. 343-344; *While England Slept*, New York, 1938, *passim.*   **54.** *Hansard's Parliamentary Debates, Commons*, October 5, 1938.   **55.** *Ibid.*, October 6, 1938.   **56.** Charles Mowat, *Britain between the Wars, 1918-1940*, Chicago, 1955, p. 553.   **57.** *Hansard's Parliamentary Debates, Commons*, October 6, 1938.   **58.** Amery, *op. cit.*, vol. 3, pp. 287-288.   **59.** Jones, *op. cit.*, p. 412; Donald C. Bishop, *The Administration of British Foreign Relations*, Syracuse, New York, 1961, pp. 74-84; Lord Halifax, *Fullness of Days*, New York, 1957, pp. 237-238.   **60.** Johnson, *op. cit.*, p. 412.   **61.** *Foreign Relations of the United States, 1938*, vol. 1, pp. 85-86.   **62.** *Ibid.*, pp. 96-97, 99-100.   **63.** Jones, *op. cit.*, p. 413.   **64.** London *Times*, October 21, 1938.   **65.** *Ibid.*, October 25, 1938.   **66.** *Hansard's Parliamentary Debates, Commons*, November 1-2, 1938.   **67.** London *Times*, December 5, 1938.   **68.** *Hansard's Parliamentary Debates, Commons*, December 7, 1938; London *Times*, December 14, 1938.   **69.** *Ibid.*, January 18, 1939.   **70.** *Ibid.*, January 24, 1939.   **71.** Basil Collier, *The Defence of the United Kingdom*, London, 1957, p. 69   **72.** Jones, *op. cit.*, pp. 410-411; Albert Wedemeyer, *Wedemeyer Reports!* New York, 1958, pp. 40-41, 61.   **73.** Collier, *op. cit.*, p. 26.   **74.** *Ibid.*, pp. 66-68.   **75.** *British Foreign Policy*, III, vol. 3, no. 500.   **76.** *German Foreign Office Archives*, Serial 2130 *(Deutsche Botschaft Rom: 1939 Geheim-Akten)*, pp. 465144-465168.   **77.** Theodor Adamheit, *Sowjetarmee und Weltrevolution*, Berlin, 1942, pp. 260-267.   **78.** *German Foreign Office Archives*, Serial 2130, pp. 465168-465175.   **79.** *Ibid.*, p. 465177.   **80.** *Ibid.*, pp. 465177-465208.

Chapter 9

1. Lord Halifax, *Fullness of Days*, New York, 1957, p. 200; A.J. Toynbee, *et al, The Eve of War, 1939, (Survey of International Affairs, 1939-1946*, vol. 10), London, 1958, pp. 2-14; French acceptance of the British lead in the March 1936 Rhineland crisis was interpreted as an abdication in France, see Alfred Fabre-Luce, *Le Sécrèt de la République*, Paris, 1938, p. 75.   **2.** Basil Collier, *The Defence of the United Kingdom*, London, 1957, p. 25; French counter-intelligence recognized throughout the 1933-1939 period that Hitler was sincere in his desire for friendship with Great Britain, see General Gauché, *Le Deuxième Bureau au Travail*, Paris, 1953, p. 34.   **3.** Jean Matrat, *Histoire des Rélations France-Anglaises*, Paris, 1953, pp. 112-114; Karl Pfeffer, *England: Vormacht der bürgerlichen Welt*, Hamburg, 1940, pp. 8-9. **4.** *Infra*, chapter 22; Raffaele Guarigila, *Riccordi, 1922-1946*, Naples, 1949, pp. 412-416.   **5.** Pierre-Étienne Flandin, *Politique Française, 1919-1940*, Paris, 1947, pp. 13-20; Edward Spears, *Assignment to Catastrophe*, vol. 1, New York, 1954, pp. 3-11.   **6.** *Izvestia*, January 27, 1934; André Tardieu, *Notes de Semaine 1938: L'Année de Munich*, Paris, 1939, pp. 105-130.   **7.** *United States Foreign Relations: The Soviet Union, 1933-1939*, Washington, D.C., 1952, pp. 291-294; Ralph Keeling, *Gruesome Harvest: the Costly Attempt to Exterminate the People of Germany*, Chicago, 1947, pp. 98-110; William Strang, *Home and Abroad*, London, 1956, p. 818.   **8.** Maurice Baumont, *La faillité de la Paix, 1918-1939*, vol. 2, Paris, 1945, p. 818.   **9.** *Annales de la Chambre des Députés: Débats Parlementaires*, Oct. 5, 1938; Joseph Paul-Boncour believed that the French Parliament would have welcomed the resignation of the warmongers (Reynaud, Mandel, Champetier de Ribes), see J. Paul-Boncour, *Entre Deux Guerres: Souvenirs sur la IIIe République*, vol. 3, New York, 1946, pp. 104-105.   **10.** René d'Argile, *et al, Les Origines Sécrètes de la Guerre 1939-1945*, Paris, 1957, pp. 36-43; Maurice Baumont, *Gloires et Tragédies de la IIIe République*, Paris, 1956, p. 377. Albert Lebrun, *Témoignage*, Paris, 1945, pp. 11-13.   **11.** Paul Reynaud, *Au Coeur de la Mêlée, 1930-145*, Paris, 1951, pp. 293ff.   **12.** Lucien Genet, *Cinquante Ans Histoire, 1900-1950*, vol. 3, Paris, 1951, pp. 35ff.; Jacques Bainville, *Journal*, vol. 3, Paris, 1949, pp. 184ff.; Édouard Herriot, *Jadis*, vol. 2, Paris, 1952, pp. 325-328; Francois Goguel, *La Politique des Partis sous la IIIe République*, Paris, 1946, pp. 325-328; Alfred Fabre-Luce, *Caillaux*, Paris, 1933, pp. 253ff.; on the need of public works for unemployment, see *La Vie de la France sous l'Occupation, 1940-1944*, R. Chambrun, ed., Stanford, 1957, pp. 23ff.   **13.** Genet, *op. cit.*, pp. 41-43; André Gide, *Journal*, Paris, 1948, p. 1160.   **14.** *Annales de la Chambre des Députés: Débats Parlementaires*, Jan. 23, 1934, *et seq.*; Henriot announced the fundamental nature of his critique with the following statement: "We are all elected by the people, but the people mock parliamentary regulations and they wish to know the truth," *Ibid.*, vol. 152, p. 283. For the authoritative account on the Stavisky affair by the director of the criminal department of the Sûreté Nationale, *vide* Louis Ducloux, *From Blackmail to Treason: Political Crime and Corruption in France, 1920-1940*, London, 1958, pp. 95-120; an eloquent and detailed contemporary account of the crisis is Georges Suarez, *La Grande Peur de 6 Février au Palais-Bourbon*, Paris, 1934, pp. 3-243; Rudolf Brock, *Stawisky: der Grösse Korruptions-Skandal Europas*, Berlin, 1934, pp. 14ff., is excellent on the background of Stawisky; for a devastating contemporary exposure of the myth that a fascist *coup* had been attempted, *vide* Gaston de Launay & Rene Domange, *La leçon du 6 février* in *La Revue Hébdomadaire*, April 7, 1934; for a brilliant analysis of the impact of the Stavisky crisis on French foreign policy, v *ide* G. Bonnet, *La Quai d' Orsay sous trois Républiques, 1870-1961*, Paris, 1961, pp. 129ff. **15.** Pierre Lazareff, *Deadline: the Behind-the-Scenes Story of the Last Decade in France*, New York, 1942, pp. 74ff.; Herbert Kranz, *Hinter den Kulissen der Kabinette und Generalstäbe, 1933-1940*, Frankfurt, 1941, pp. 32ff.; Phillippe Henriot, *Le 6 février*, Paris, 1934, *passim*. **16.** P. Varfolmeyeva, *Reakzionnaya Vnezhnava Politika Franzuskik Pravik Sozialistov, 1936-1939 Godov*, Moscow, 1949, pp. 14ff.; Leon Trotsky, *Whither France?* New York, 1936, pp. 149-151; Léon Blum, *For All Mankind*, New York, 1946, pp. 54ff.; Léon Blum, *L' Oeuvre de Léon Blum*, vol. 3-4, Paris, 1956-1957; E. M. Earle, *et al, Modern France: Problems of the Third and Fourth Republics*, Princeton, 1951, pp. 136ff.; Jerome Carcopino, *Souvenirs de Sept Ans, 1937-1944*, Paris, 1953, pp. 108-109; Alexandre Zévaès, *Histoire de la Troisième République*, Paris, 1938, pp. 329ff.; Jacques Debu-Bridel, *L' Agonie de la Troisième République, 1929-1939*, Paris, 1948, pp. 385ff.; Maurice Thorez, *Notre Lutte pour la Paix: de la Fausse Paix de Versailles à la Trahison de Munich*, Paris, 1938, pp. 154ff.; André Delmas, *À Gauche de la barricade*, Paris, 1950, pp. 63ff.; J. Danos & M. Gibelin, *Juin 1936*, Paris, 1950, *passim*. Georges Dupeux, *Le Front Populaire et les Élections de 1936*, vol. 1, Paris, 1959, pp. 123ff., notes that the Communists made the really great gains in the elections; see also François Herbette, *L' Expérience Marxiste en France, 1936-1938*, Paris, 1960, pp. 51ff. **17.** Genet, *op. cit.*, vol. 3, pp. 52ff.; André Geraud, *Les Fossoyeurs*, vol. 1, *Gamelin-Daladier-Paul Reynaud*, New York, 1943, pp. 110ff.; Geneviève Tabouis, *Ils l' ont appelée Cassandre*, New York, 1942, pp. 146ff.; Herriot, *op. cit.*, vol. 2, pp. 485-627.; **18.** Varfolomeyeva, *op. cit.*, pp. 14-59; Genet, *op. cit.*, vol. 3, pp. 49-54; D. N. Pritt, *The Fall of the French Republic*, London, 1941, pp. 53ff. Doriot soon became the most formidable critic of the French Communists, *vide* Jacques Doriot, *La France avec nous!* Paris, 1937, pp. 5-139. **19.** *Le Populaire*, October 17, 1934; Herriot, *op. cit.*, vol. 2, pp. 458-461; Genet, *op. cit.*, vol. 3, pp. 92-93; Tabouis, *op. cit.*, pp. 202-205. **20.** Albert Rivaut, *Le Relèvement de l' Allemagne*, Paris, 1938, pp. 76ff.; Henri Lemery, *De la Paix de Briand à la Guerre de Hitler*, Paris, 1949, pp. 123ff. **21.** Alfred Mallet, *Pierre Laval*, vol. 1, Paris, 1955, pp. 11-27, 30-31; for a bitter denunciation of Laval, see Tabouis, *op. cit.*, pp. 258ff. Henry Torrès, *Pierre Laval*, New York, 1941, *passim*, is a lengthy hostile biography by a former close associate; it fails utterly to discredit Laval. **22.** Mallet, *op. cit.*, vol. 1, pp. 29, 31-32, 61ff.; Flandin, *op. cit.*, pp. 194ff. **23.** Hubert Lagerdelle, *Mission à Rome: Mussolini*, Paris, 1955, pp. 3-6; Luigi Villari, *Italian Foreign Policy under Mussolini*, New York, 1956, pp. 75-87. **24.** Lagardelle, *op. cit.*, pp. 10-13, 17-29; Emrys Hughes, *Winston Churchill: British Bulldog*, New York, 1955, pp. 117-123. **25.** Lagardelle, *op. cit.*, pp. 108-118; Mallet, *op. cit.*, vol. 1, pp. 69ff.; Paul Gentizon, *La Conquête de l' Éthiopie*, Paris, 1937, *passim*. **26.** Dennis Bardens, *Portrait of a Statesman*, New York, 1956, pp. 134-141; R. G. Vansittart, *The Mist Procession*, London, 1958, p. 541. **27.** Tabouis, *op. cit.*, pp. 20-21, 108, 113, 147-149, 202-205, 216-253, 258-259. **28.** Mallet, *op. cit.*, pp. 110-116. **29.** Genet, *op. cit.*, vol. 3, pp. 99-100. **30.** *L' Action Française*, January 26, 1936. **31.** Genet, *op. cit.*, vol. 3, pp. 153-161; H. de Montherlant, *Le Solstice de Juin*, Paris, 1941, *passim*. **32.** Joseph Caillaux, *Mes Mémoires*, vol. 3, Paris, 1947, pp. 240-242. Émile Roche, *Caillaux que j' ai connu*, Paris, 1949, pp. 226-238. **33.** Leon Blum, *For All Mankind*, pp. 49, 77-78. **34.** Genet, vol. 3, pp. 163-164. **35.** Tardieu, *op. cit.*, pp. 127-136. **36.** René d' Argile, *op. cit.*, pp. 127-136. **37.** Reynaud, *op. cit.*, pp. 113-114. **38.** *Ibid.*, pp. 234, 253, 272, 287, 290-291. **39.** J. Benoist-Méchin, *Soixante Jours Qui Ébranlèrent l' Occident*, vol. 3, Paris, 1956, p. 14. Paul Reynaud, *Mémoirs: venu de ma Montagne*, vol. 1, Paris, 1960, pp. 462-487. **40.** Henri de Kerillis, *Français! Voici la Guerre*, Paris, 1936, pp. 10, 42, 73-74, 157; J. Benoist-Méchin, *Éclaircissements sur 'Mein Kampf'*, Paris, 1939, pp. 165-186; Georges-Anquetil, *Hitler Conduit le Bal*, Paris, 1939, pp. 25-28; Jean-Louis Aujol, *Le Procès Benoist-Méchin*, Paris, 1948, pp. 562, 605-610; Otto Abetz, *Das Offene Problem*, Wiesbaden, 1951, pp. 36ff.; Friedrich Sieburg, *Blick durchs Fenster: aus zehn Jahren Frankreich und England*, Frankfurt, 1939, p. 241. Kerillis was later bitterly disillusioned about both de Gaulle and the results of World War II, *vide* Henri de Kerillis, *I Accuse de Gaulle*, New York, 1946, *passim*. **41.** Benoist-Méchin, *Soixante Jours*, vol. 3, pp. 424-425. **42.** *For· ign Relations of the United States, 1938*, vol. 1, pp. 711-712. **43.** Anatole de Monzie, *Ci-devant*, Paris, 1941, pp. 14-15. **44.** *Ibid.*, pp. 39-40. **45.** *Ibid.*, pp. 47-53. **46.** Georges Bonnet, *Fin d' une Europe*, Geneva, 1948, pp. 24-26. **47.** *German Foreign Office Archives*, Serial 121, pp. 119449ff. **48.** Zbigniew Kulak, *Spotkanie Ribbentrop-Bonnet, 6 Grudnia 1938 roku in Przeglad Zachodni*, May/June 1957, pp. 4ff.; Bonnet, *op. cit.*, p. 28. **49.** *German Foreign Office Archives*, serial 121, pp. 119462-119463. **50.** *British Foreign Policy*, III, vol. 3, no. 285. **51.** *Ibid.* **52.** *Ibid.*, no. 290. **53.** *Ibid.*, no. 291. **54.** Caillaux, *op. cit.*, vol. 3, pp. 3-25. **55.** *German Foreign Office Archives*, Serial 121, pp. 119464-119466; Kulak, *op. cit.* **56.** Robert Coulondre, *De Staline à Hitler, 1936-1939*, Paris, 1950, pp. 208-211. **57.** *German Foreign Policy*, D, vol. 5, no. 109. **58.** *British Foreign Policy*, III, vol. 3, no. 406. **59.** Bonnet, *op. cit.*, pp. 37-39. **60.** Łukasiewicz in conversation with the writer, Feb. 28, 1948; Léon Noël, *L' Agression Allemande contre la Pologne*, Paris, 1947, pp. 276-280; A. Toynbee, *The Eve of War, 1939*, p. 30. **61.** Bonnet, *op. cit.*, pp. 38-39. **62.** *Ibid.*, p. 36. **63.** Monzie, *op. cit.*, pp. 66-67. **64.** René d' Argile, *op. cit.*, p. 57. **65.** Bonnet, *op. cit.*, pp. 40-41. **66.** Bertrand de Jouvenel, *Le Réveil de l' Europe: Problèmes et Documents*, Paris, 1938, p. 33. **67.** *Ibid.*, p. 36.

Chapter 10

1. René d'Argile, *et al, Les Origines Secrètes de la Guerre 1939-1945*, Paris, 1957, p. 17; F.W. Essler, *Twenty Years of Sudeten-German Losses, 1918-1938*, Vienna, 1938, pp. 58-70. Bertram de Colonna, *Czecho-Slovakia Within*, London, 1938, pp. 54-92; "Diplomaticus," *The Czechs and Their Minorities*, London, 1938, pp. 39-66; Hermann Raschhofer, *Die Sudetenfrage*, Munich, 1953, pp. 105-118; Konrad Heinlein, *Heim ins Reich: Reden, 1937-1938*, Karlsbad, 1939, p. 129. Kurt Glaser, *Czecho-Slovakia: A Critical History*, Caldwell, Idaho, 1961, pp. 41-47. 2. See statement of State Secretary Ernst von Weizsäcker, *Trials of War Criminals before the Nuremburg Military Tribunals, October 1946-April 1949*, vol.12, pp. 914-964, and especially pp. 930ff. 3. Jozef Lettrich, *History of Modern Slovakia*, New York, 1955, pp. 95ff.; Michael Schwartz, *Die Slowakei: der jungste Staat Europas*, Leipzig, 1939, p. 146; Hubert Ripka, *Munich: Before and After*, London, 1939, pp. 359-360. 4. Edvard Beneš, *From Munich to New War and New Victory*, London, 1953, pp. 53-58. 5. *British Foreign Policy*, III, vol. 3, no. 225; Galeazzo Ciano, *Diario, 1937-1938*, Rome, 1948, p. 273. A.J.P. Taylor, *The Origins of the Second World War*, p. 202, recalls that Bohemia-Moravia had been part of the Holy Roman Empire, the German Confederation, and German Austria prior to 1918, and he describes Hitler's policy in March 1938 as one of conservative restoration. 6. *British Foreign Policy*, III, vol. 3, no. 226. 7. *Ibid.*, no. 227. 8. *Ibid.*, vol. 4, no. 248. 9. Jozef Beck, *Dernier Rapport*, Neuchatel, 1949, p. 172. 10. *British Foreign Policy*, III, vol. 3, no. 229. 11. *Ibid.*, nos. 232, 233. 12. *Ibid.*, nos. 236, 237. 13. Galeazzo Ciano, *L'Europa verso la Catastrofe: la Storia d'Europa del 1936 al 1942*, Rome, 1948, pp. 387-389; Luigi Villari, *Italian Foreign Policy Under Mussolini*, NY 1956, pp. 210-211; Mario Donosti, *Mussolini e l' Europa*, Rome, 1945, pp. 105, 129ff. 14. *British Foreign Policy*, III, vol. 3, nos. 240, 242, 246; Ciano, *Diario*, pp. 283-285; Pierre Buk, *La Tragédie Tchécoslovaquie de Septembre 1938 à Mars 1939*, Paris, 1939, pp. 163-165. Petrescu-Comnen wrote to Halifax and Vansittart after World War II asking why Great Britain had done nothing about guaranteeing the Czechs after the Munich conference; Halifax was evasive, and Vansittart replied that "I don't think that any real explanation exists;" Nicolae Petrescu-Comnen, *Preludi del Grande Dramma*, Rome, 1947, pp. 487-489. 15. *German Foreign Policy*, D, vol. 5, no. 90. 16. *British Foreign Policy*, III, vol. 3, nos. 241, 242. 17. *German Foreign Policy*, D, vol. 5, no. 93. 18. *Ibid.*, no. 94. 19. *Ibid.*, no. 104. 20. *Ibid.*, no. 105. 21. *Ibid.*, no. 106; Jan Szembek, *Journal*, Paris, 1952, p. 366. 22. *German Foreign Policy*, D, vol. 5, no. 108. 23. Georges Bonnet, *Fin d'une Europe*, Geneva, 1948, p. 148. 24. *British Foreign Policy*, III, vol. 3, no. 251. 25. *Ibid.*, no. 252. 26. *Ibid.*, no. 255. 27. *Ibid.*, nos. 257, 258, 259. 28. *Ibid.*, nos. 265, 266. 29. *Ibid.*, nos. 267, 270. 30. *Ibid.*, nos. 271, 273. 31. *Ibid.*, nos. 276, 284, 381; *German Foreign Policy*, D, vol. 5, no. 102. 32. *British Foreign Policy*, III, vol. 3, nos. 386, 387, 388, 390. 33. *Ibid.*, no. 390. 34. *Ibid.*, nos. 396, 401; S.H. Thomson, *Czechoslovakia in European History*, Princeton, 1953, pp. 400-402. 35. *British Foreign Policy*, III, vol. 3, no. 408. 36. *Ibid.*; *Les Événements survenus en France*, suppl. vol. 9, Paris, 1951, pp. 2650ff. 37. *British Foreign Policy*, III, vol. 3, no. 413. 38. *Ibid.*, no. 423. 39. Bonnet, *op. cit.*, p. 47. 40. *British Foreign Policy*, III, vol. 3, no. 515. 41. William Strang, *Home and Abroad*, London, 1956, p. 148. 42. Jacques Davignon, *Berlin, 1936-1940*, Paris, 1951, pp. 100-101. 43. *Trials of War Criminals, October 1946-April 1940*, vol. 12, pp. 964ff.; David B. Stenzel, *Nazi Diplomacy from Munich to War*, Berkeley, 1957, ms., pp. 82-85. 44. John L. Stipp, ed., *Devil's Diary*, Yellow Springs, Ohio, 1955, pp. 85-86. Lettrich, *op. cit.*, pp. 104-117. Taylor, *op. cit.*, p. 197, describes British evasion of French wishes in the Czech guarantee question on November 24, 1938, but he fails to analyze the permanent British policy of evasion in this question. 45. Gerhard Ritter, *Carl Gördeler und die deutsche Widerstandsbewegung*, Stuttgart, 1954, pp. 164ff. 46. *British Foreign Policy*, III, vol. 4, no. 5. 47. James Burns, *Roosevelt: the Lion and the Fox*, NY 1956, p. 389; Frederic Sanborn, *Design for War*, 1937-1941, New York, 1951, p. 49. 48. *British Foreign Policy*, III, vol. 4, nos. 26, 28. 49. *Ibid.*; R.E. Sherwood, *Roosevelt and Hopkins, an Intimate History*, New York, 1948, p. 782. 50. *British Foreign Policy*, III, vol. 4, no. 95; R. Coulondre, *De Staline à Hitler, 1936-1939*, Paris 1950, pp. 249-250. 51. *British Foreign Policy*, III, vol. 4, no. 112. 52. W.L. Langer & S. Gleason, *The Challenge to Isolation, 1937-1949*, New York, 1952, p. 166. 53. *British Foreign Policy*, III, vol. 4, nos. 118, 119. Taylor, *op. cit.*, p. 201, points out that Hitler did not actively intervene in the Czech-Slovak dispute prior to the crisis of March 9, 1939, created by Czech action at Bratislava. 54. Thomas Jones, *A Diary with Letters*, 1931-1950, London, 1954, p. 429; *History of the "Times,"* vol. 4, New York, 1952, p. 959. 55. *British Foreign Policy*, III, vol. 4, nos. 123, 124; Raschhofer, *op. cit.*, p. 199. 56. *British Foreign Policy*, III, vol. 4, no. 134. 57. *Ibid.*, no. 138. 58. *Ibid.*, no. 137. 59. *Ibid.*, no. 140. 60. *Ibid.*, no. 146. 61. *Ibid.*, nos. 155, 158. 62. *Ibid.*, no. 163. 63. *Ibid.*, no. 180. 64. *Ibid.*, no. 186. 65. *Ibid.*. 66. *Ibid.*, no. 198; J.W. Wheeler-Bennett, *Munich: Prologue to Tragedy*, London, 1948, p. 341; Lettrich, *op. cit.*, pp. 108-135; Schwartz, *op. cit.*, p. 146; Buk, *op. cit.*, pp. 185ff; Ripka, *op. cit.*, pp. 365ff. 67. *History of the "Times,"* vol. 4, p. 959. 68. John Wrench, *Geoffrey Dawson and Our Times*, London, 1955, p. 389. 69. Stipp, *op. cit.*, pp. 88-90; *British Foreign Policy*, III, vol. 4, nos. 202, 203, 207, 217, 219. 70. *Ibid.*, vol. 7, appendix, pp. 632-633. 71. *Ibid.*, vol. 4, no. 230. 72. *German Foreign Policy*, D, vol. 5, no. 139. 73. Lettrich, *op. cit.*, pp. 129ff.; Wheeler-Bennett, *op. cit.*, p. 345; *British Foreign Policy*, III, vol. 4, nos. 235, 238, 241. 74. *Trials of War Criminals, October 1946-April 1949*, vol. 12, pp. 867-874. 75. *British Foreign Policy*, III, vol. 4, no. 243; Michael Winch, *Republic for a Day*, London, 1939, *passim*. 76. *British Foreign Policy*, III, vol. 4, nos. 246, 248. 77. *Ibid.*; Winston Churchill, *The Gathering Storm*, Boston, 1948, pp. 343-344. 78. Jones, *op. cit.*, pp. 432-433. William L. Shirer, *The Rise and Fall of the Third Reich: a History of Nazi Germany*, New York, 1960, pp. 441-442; J.M. Kirschbaum, *Slovakia: Nation at the Crossroads of Central Europe*, New York, 1960, pp. 128-129. 79. Oskar Ullrich, *Der Grosse Irrweg der Tschechen*, Berlin, 1943, pp. 251ff.; Hans Fritzsche, *The Sword in the Scales*,

London, 1953, pp. 294-295; Schulthess, 1939, Munich, 1940, pp. 63-67. **80.** *Ibid.*, pp. 70-85, 90-91. **81.** *Ibid.*, pp. 126, 138, 144, 148, 153. **82.** *British Foreign Policy*, III, vol. 4, no. 278. **83.** Hans Frank, *Im Angesicht des Galgens*, Munich, 1953, pp. 344-345. **84.** See especially Otakar Odložilik, *Concerning Munich and the Ides of March in Journal for Central European Affairs*, September 1950. **85.** Hans Grimm, *Warum-Woher-Aber-Wohin?*, Lippoldsberg, 1954, pp. 215-216; M. Baumont, *et al.*, *The Third Reich*, New York, 1955, pp. 470-471. **86.** A.J. Toynbee, *et al.*, *The Eve of War, 1939*, London, 1958, p. 48; *British Foreign Policy*, III, vol. 4, no. 279. **87.** *Hansard's Parliamentary Debates, Commons*, March 15, 1939; London *Times*, March 18, 1939; Helmuth Greiner, *Die Oberste Wehrmachtführung, 1939-1943*, Wiesbaden, 1951, p. 273. Shirer, *op. cit.*, pp. 442, 443, 450; Taylor, *op. cit.*, p. 202, correctly describes Hitler's move to Prague as "the unforeseen by-product of developments in Slovakia."

Chapter 11

1. Walter Kolarz, *Myths and Realities in Eastern Europe*, London, 1946, pp. 116ff. **2.** Grigorie Gafencu, *Dernier Jours de l' Europe*, Paris, 1946, pp. 31ff. **3.** Thomas Bailey, *Woodrow Wilson and the Lost Peace*, New York, 1944, pp. 299ff.; Sarah Wambaugh, *Plebiscites since the World War*, vol. 1, 1933, pp. 99ff.; R. Donald, *The Polish Corridor and the Consequences*, London, 1929, pp. 26ff.; for the defense of the status quo, see S.L. Sharp, *Poland: White Eagle on a Red Flag*, Cambridge, Mass., 1953, pp. 134ff. **4.** Harry Rudin, *Armistice 1918*, New Haven, 1944, *passim*. **5.** *German Foreign Policy*, D, vol. 5, no. 86; A.V. Lundstedt, *Superstition or Rationality in Action for Peace?*, London, 1925, pp. 173ff. **6.** Georges Bonnet, *Fin d'une Europe*, Geneva, 1948, pp. 25-26. **7.** Jan Szembek, *Journal*, Paris, 1952, pp. 366ff.; *Dokumenti e Materiali*, vol. 1, no. 44. **8.** Jozef Lipski, *Stosunki Polsko-Niemiecke w swietle Aktow Norymberskich* in *Sprawy Miedzynarodowe*, London, 1947, 2/3, 4; see also T. Cyprian & J. Sawicki, *Sprawy Polskie w Procesie Norymberskim*, Poznan, 1956. **9.** Bonnet, *op. cit.*, p. 125. **10.** Jozef Beck, *Dernier Rapport*, Neuchatel, 1949, pp. 240-275. **11.** J.W. Wheeler-Benett, *Munich: Prologue to Tragedy*, London, 1948, pp. 294ff; Oskar Halecki, *Eugenio Pacelli: Pope of Peace*, New York 1951, p. 103. **12.** Beck, *op. cit.*, p. 172. **13.** *Ibid.*, pp. 160-161, 182. **14.** *Polska a Zagranica*, Warsaw, 1938-1939. **15.** One prominent historian who has failed to see this distinction is Walter Hofer, *Die Entfesselung des zweiten Weltkrieges*, Stuttgart, 1954, pp. 18ff. **16.** W. Goerlitz & H. Quint, *Adolf Hitler: eine Biographie*, Stuttgart, 1952, pp. 514ff.; J.W. Wheeler-Bennett, *The Nemesis of Power: The German Army in Politics, 1918-1945*, New York, 1954, pp. 131-140. **17.** *Foreign Relations of the United States: the Soviet Union, 1933-1939*, Washington, D.C., 1952, pp. 291ff.; Theodor Adamheit, *Sowjetarmee und Weltrevolution*, Berlin, 1942, pp. 257-258. **18.** Richard Breyer, *Das Deutsche Reich und Polen*, Würzburg, 1955, pp. 336-338; Joachim G. Leithäuser, *Diplomatie auf schiefer Bahn*, Berlin, 1953, pp. 46ff. **19.** Beck, *op. cit.*, pp. 62ff. **20.** *Documents on Events*, pp. 152-153. **21.** *Ibid.*, pp. 160ff.; Theodor Oberlander, *Die Landwirtschaft Posen-Pommerellens vor und nach der Abtrennung vom Deutschen Reich*, Berlin, 1937, pp. 62-63; H. Aielmski, *et al.*, *Poland* (ed. B.E. Schmitt), Los Angeles, 1945, pp. 182ff. **22.** *Documents on Events*, pp. 166-176; Leon Noel, *L'Agression Allemande contre la Pologne*, Paris, 1947, pp. 300ff. **23.** *German Foreign Policy*, D, vol. 5, nos. 110, 112. **24.** *British Foreign Policy*, III, vol. 3, no. 385. **25.** *German Foreign Policy*, D, vol. 5, no. 112. **26.** Szembek, *op. cit.*, pp. 390-394. **27.** *German Foreign Policy*, D, vol. 5, no. 113. **28.** Beck, *op. cit.*, pp. 182-183. **29.** *German Foreign Policy*, D, vol. 5, no. 115. **30.** *Ibid.*, no. 116. **31.** *Ibid.*, no. 118; *British Foreign Policy*, III, vol. 3, no. 507. **32.** *Ibid.*, no. 510. **33.** *Ibid.*, no. 511. **34.** Hjalmar Schacht, *76 Jahre meines Lebens*, Bad Wörrishofen, 1953, pp. 456-464; *Schulthess, 1939*, Munich, 1940, pp. 2-7. **35.** Hans Roos, *Polen und Europa*, Tübingen, 1957, pp. 391-393; Noel, *op. cit.*, pp. 285ff. **36.** *German Foreign Policy*, D, vol. 5, no. 119; *Polish White Book*, pp. 54-55; *Documents on Events*, pp. 205-207; *French Yellow Book*, p. 139. **37.** *International Military Tribunal*, 1945-1946, vol. 10, p. 356. **38.** Beck, *op. cit.*, pp. 183-184. **39.** Roos, *op. cit.*, pp. 382-390. **40.** *German Foreign Office Archives*, Serial 52a (Polen), pp. 34538ff. **41.** V. Tanner, *The Winter War: Finland against Russia, 1939-1940*, Stanford, 1957, pp. 3-12. **42.** *German Foreign Policy*, D, vol. 5, no. 120; *Polish White Book*, pp. 54-55; *Documents on Events*, pp. 208-209; A.B. Keith, *The Causes of the War*, London, 1940, pp. 393ff. **43.** *German Foreign Policy*, D, vol. 5, no. 121. **44.** Foreign Relations of the United States, 1939, vol. 1, p. 1. **45.** *German Foreign Office Archives*, Serial 52a, p. 34524. **46.** *German Foreign Policy*, D, vol. 5, no. 122. **47.** Szembek, *op. cit.*, pp. 404-407. **48.** *Ibid.*, p. 408. **49.** *British Foreign Policy*, III, vol. 3, no. 531. **50.** *Ibid.*, no. 542; *French Yellow Book*, p. 52. **51.** *British Foreign Policy*, III, vol. 4, no. 10. **52.** *German Foreign Policy*, D, vol. 5, no. 125. **53.** Beck, *op. cit.*, p. 186; *Polish White Book*, p. 55; A.S. Cardwell, *Poland and Russia*, New York, 1944, p. 24. **54.** *German Foreign Office Archives*, Serial 52a, pp. 34527ff; Annelies von Ribbentrop, "Verschwörung gegen den Prieden," Leoni, Bavaria, 1962, p. 296. **55.** *Ibid.*, p. 34534. **56.** *Ibid.*, Serial 103, p. 111281. **57.** *Polish White Book*, p. 55. **58.** *Documents on Events*, p. 209. **59.** *Polish White Book*, p. 56. **60.** *German Foreign Policy*, D, vol. 5, no. 126. **61.** *British Foreign Policy*, III, vol. 4, no. 31; Noël, *op. cit.*, p. 293. **62.** *Schulthess, 1939*, pp. 14-41. **63.** *Polish White Book*, pp. 56-57. **64.** Szembek, *op. cit.*, pp. 411-414. **65.** *Foreign Relations of the United States, 1939*, vol. 1, p. 8. **66.** *Ibid.*, pp. 9-10. **67.** *British Foreign Policy*, III, vol. 4, no. 32. **68.** *Ibid.*, no. 74; *French Yellow Book*, p. 52; Noël, *op. cit.*, p. 293. **69.** *Polish Documents*, pp. 21-24. **70.** Bonnet, *op. cit.*, pp. 122-125, 142-144. **71.** *Polish Documents*, p. 16. **72.** *Ibid.*, pp. 17-19; F. Berber, *Die Amerikanische Neutralitaet im Kriege, 1939-1941*, Essen, 1943, pp. 42-43. **73.** *British Foreign Policy*, III, vol. 4, no. 84. **74.** *Ibid.*, no. 72; *Documents on Events*, pp. 177-179. **75.** *British Foreign Policy*, III, vol. 4, nos. 108, 139. **76.** *Ibid.*, no. 144. **77.** *Ibid.*, no. 147. **78.** *German Foreign Office Archives*, Serial 52a, pp. 343547, 34555. **79.** *Ibid.*, p. 34538; *Polish Acts of Atrocity against the German Minority in Poland*, New York, 1939, pp. 15ff.; *Documents on*

Events, pp. 196-198; *British Foreign Policy*, III, vol. 4, no. 147; *Czas, Illustrowany Kurjer, Gazeta Polska*, January-March 1939. **80.** *German Foreign Office Archives*, Serial 52a, pp. 34552ff. **81.** *Ibid.*, pp. 34559ff.; *Documents on Events*, p. 154; E. Wiskemann, *Undeclared War*, London, 1939, p. 191. **82.** *German Foreign Office Archives*, Serial 52a, p. 34548; Galeazzo Ciano, *The Ciano Diaries, 1939-1943*, New York, 1946, p. 34. **83.** *German Foreign Office Archives*, Seria 52a, pp. 34558-34561. **8.** *British Foreign Policy*, III, vol. 4, no. 173. **85.** *German Foreign Office Archives*, Serial 52a, p. 34571. **86.** Ciano, *Diaries, 1939-1943*, pp. 33-36. **87.** *Documents on Events*, pp. 155-156. **88.** *German Foreign Policy*, D, vol. 5, no. 130; *Documents on Events*, pp. 158-159. **89.** *German Foreign Policy*, D, vol. 5, no. 131. **90.** *Ibid.*, nos. 133, 135, 138. **91.** *Ibid.*, no. 136. **92.** *British Foreign Policy*, III, vol. 4, nos. 186, 187. **93.** *Ibid.*, no. 189. **94.** *German Foreign Policy*, D, vol. 5, no. 137. **95.** *Ibid.*, no. 140.

Chapter 12

1. *Schulthess, 1939*, Munich, 1940, p. 65. **2.** General Gauché, *Le Deuxième Bureau au Travail*, 1935-40, Paris, 1953, pp. 74-75, 82-83, 91-93. **3.** *German Foreign Office Archives*, Serial 2130, pp. 465760ff. **4.** J. Benoist-Méchin, *Éclaircissements sur Mein Kampf, la Doctrine d'Adolf Hitler*, Paris, 1939, pp. 141-184. **5.** John Wrench, *Geoffrey Dawson and Our Times*, London, 1955, p. 389; Martin Gilbert and Richard Cott, *The Appeasers*, Boston, 1963, p. 234. **6.** Klaus Knorr, *The War Potential of Nations*, Princeton, 1956, p. 59. **7.** Julius Stone, *Aggression and World Order*, Los Angeles, 1958, pp. 32-33; A.J. Toynbee, *et al., The Eve of War, 1939*, London, 1958, p. 48. **8.** *Ibid*, pp. 61-71; Fritz Hesse, *Das Spiel um Deutschland*, Munich, 1953, pp. 163-165. **9.** A.C. Johnson, *Viscount Halifax*, New York, 1941, p. 513; Earl of Halifax, *Fullness of Days*, New York, 1957, pp. 206-208. **10.** John Simon, *Retrospect*, London, 1952, p. 251; C.L. Mowat, *Britain Between the Wars, 1918-1940*, Chicago, 1955, pp. 637-638. **11.** Viscount Templewood, *Nine Troubled Years*, London, 1954, pp. 333-344. **12.** Keith Feiling, *The Life of Neville Chamberlain*, London, 1946, pp. 401, 403. **13.** William Strang, *Rome and Abroad*, London, 1956, pp. 160-161. **14.** Hughe Knatchbull-Hugessen, *Diplomat in Peace and War*, London, 1949, p. 128. **15.** Johnson, *op. cit.*, p. 512; Arthur Salter, *Personality in Politics*, London, 1948, p. 67; L.S. Amery, *My Political Life*, vol. 3, London, 1955, pp. 308-310. **16.** Winston Churchill, *The Gathering Storm*, Boston, 1948, pp. 343-345. A.J.P. Taylor, *The Origins of the Second World War*, London, 1961, p. 203, claims that there was an underground explosion of British public opinion after March 15, 1939, but he fails to indicate any evidence of it prior to Chamberlain's Birmingham speech and the Tilea hoax; the most highly exaggerated presentation of this argument of Taylor's is to be found in A.J. Toynbee, *The Eve of War, 1939*, London, 1958, pp. 2-48. **17.** Thomas Jones, *A Diary with Letters, 1931-1950*, London, 1954, p. 432. **18.** *Les Événements survenu en France de 1933 à 1945*, vol. 2, Paris, 1947, pp. 261-266; *German Foreign Policy*, D, vol. 6, no. 69. **19.** *Les Événements*, vol. 2, pp. 255-256. **20.** *Ibid.*, vol. 2, p. 266; supple. vol. 1, pp. 40-42. **21.** Paul Reynaud, *Au Coeur de la Mêlée*, Paris, 1951, p. 299. **22.** *Les Événements*, suppl. vol. 4, pp. 2037-2058; suppl. vol. 9, pp. 2658ff. **23.** *Foreign Relations of the United States, 1939*, vol. 1, pp. 48-49. **24.** *British Foreign Policy*, III, vol. 4, no. 279. **25.** *Ibid.; German Foreign Policy*, D, vol. 6, no. 35; Hesse, *op. cit.*, p. 161. **26.** Toynbee, *op. cit.*, pp. 85ff. **27.** *Poland in the British Parliament, 1939-1945* (Wacław Jedrzejewicz, ed.), vol. 1, New York, 1946, pp. 61ff. **28.** *German Foreign Policy*, D, vol. 6, no. 34; C.C. Tansill, *Back Door to War*, Chicago, 1952, p. 454; Gilbert and Cott, *op. cit.*, p. 234. **29.** *British Foreign Policy*, III, vol. 4, no. 394. **30.** Norbert Toennies, *Der Krieg vor dem Kriege*, Essen, 1940, pp. 214ff. **31.** Andreas Hillgruber, *Hitler, König Carol und Marschall Antonescu, 1938-1944*, Wiesbaden, 1954, pp. 26, 380. **32.** *British Foreign Policy*, III, vol. 4, nos. 297, 298. **33.** Feiling, *op. cit.*, p. 400; Toennies, *op. cit.*, pp. 211-216; Gilbert and Cott, *op. cit.*, pp. 234-236. Taylor, *op. cit.*, p. 206, admits that Tilea sounded a false alarm on March 17, 1939, but he neglected to explore the role of the British Foreign Office in this situation. **34.** *British Foreign Policy*, III, vol. 4, no. 397. **35.** *Ibid.*, no. 399. **36.** *German Foreign Policy*, D, vol. 6, no. 30. **37.** *Foreign Relations of the United States, 1939*, vol. 1, pp. 74-75. **38.** *International Military Tribunal, 1945-1946*, vol. 10, p. 344; vol. 11, p. 359; *Czas, Gazeta Polska, Völkischer Beobachter* (Munich), March 9-18, 1939; L. Noël, *L'Agression Allemande contre la Pologne*, Paris, 1947, pp. 311-314. **39.** *Czas, Gazeta Polska*, March 15, 1939. **40.** *Ibid.*, March 15-18, 1939. **41.** *British Foreign Policy*, III, vol. 4, no. 291. **42.** *Documents on Events*, pp. 278-279; G. Bonnet, *Fin d'une Europe*, Geneva, 1948, pp. 151-153; R. Coulondre, *De Staline à Hitler, 1936-1939*, Paris, 1950, pp. 254-255. **43.** *British Foreign Policy*, III, vol. 4, no. 390; Józef Beck, *Dernier Rapport*, Neuchatel, 1949, p. 195. **44.** *British Foreign Policy*, III, vol. 4, no. 400. **45.** *Foreign Relations of the United States: The Soviet Union, 1933-1939*, Washington, D.C., 1952, pp. 745ff. **46.** *British Foreign Policy*, III, vol. 4, no. 289. **47.** *Ibid.*, no. 308; Bonnet, *op. cit.*, pp. 151-152. **48.** Herbert von Dirksen, *Moskau, Tokio, London*, 1919-1939, Stuttgart, 1949, pp. 217-236. Taylor, *op. cit.*, p. 205, claims that Chamberlain's Birmingham speech of March 17, 1939, marked a change in emphasis but not in the direction of British foreign policy; this was a feasible view in 1939, but it cannot be sustained today against the evidence from the British archives; Taylor's treatment of Hitler's policy is far superior to his analysis of British policy. **49.** *British Foreign Policy*, III, vol. 4, no. 308; *Documents on Events*, pp. 283-284. **50.** *German Foreign Policy*, D, vol. 6, nos. 8, 15. **51.** *International Military Tribunal, 1945-1946*, vol. 10, pp. 344ff.; Ernst von Weizsäcker, *Memoirs*, London, 1951, pp. 174-176. **52.** *German Foreign Policy*, D, vol. 6, nos. 16, 19, 20. **53.** *Ibid.; Coulondre, op. cit.*, pp. 258-259. **54.** *French Yellow Book*, pp. 89, 97; Beck, *op. cit.*, pp. 188-190. **55.** Coulondre, *op. cit.*, p. 259; Beck, *op. cit.*, pp. 190ff.; Bonnet, *op. cit.*, pp. 41-43. **56.** *British Foreign Policy*, III, vol. 4, no. 417; Dirksen, *op. cit.*, pp. 211-213, 241-243; G. Craig & F. Gilbert, *The Diplomats, 1919-1939*, Princeton, 1953, pp. 481ff. **57.** J. Łukasiewicz, *Rokowania i Wazniejsze Rozmowy za Czas od Marca do Wrzesnia, 1939* (ms.), London, pp. 2-3. **58.** *Ibid..* **59.** *British Foreign Policy,* III, vol. 4, no. 428; Gilbert and Cott, *op. cit.,* p. 238. **60.** *Ibid.,* no. 446; for an analysis of the relative positions of the Powers, see Karl Richter, *Die Politische Stellung der sieben Großmächte als Folge ihrer völkischen Lage im Raum* in *Zeitschrift für Geopolitik,* April 1939. **61.** *British Foreign Policy,* III, vol. 4, no. 448. **62.** *Foreign Relations of the United States: The Soviet Union, 1933-1939,* pp. 746-747.

Chapter 13

1. *German Foreign Office Archives,* Serial 52a, p. 34613. A.J.P. Taylor, *The Origins of the Second World War,* London, 1961, p. 210, summarizes Hitler's attitude toward Poland at the time of his March 25, 1939, Danzig directive as follows: "Hitler's objective was alliance with Poland, not her destruction." **2.** Ernst von Weizsaecker, *Memoirs,* London, 1951, p. 178; *British Foreign Policy,* III, vol. 4, no. 480. **3.** *Ostpreussen,* OP Landsmannschaft, Göttingen, 1947, pp. 39-45. **4.** *British Foreign Policy,* III, vol. 4, no. 459. **5.** *Foreign Relations of the United States, 1939,* vol. 1, pp. 79-80, 84-85. **6.** *Ibid.,* pp. 88-92. **7.** Jan Szembek, *Journal,* Paris, 1952, pp. 433-434. **8.** *Documents on Events,* p. 212. **9.** *Ibid.,* p. 211; F.W. von Örtzen, *Alles oder Nichts,* Breslau, 1934, p. 21. **10.** *Polish White Book,* p. 62; *Documents on Events,* p. 211. **11.** *Ibid.,* pp. 211-214. **12.** Józef Lipski, *Stosunki Polsko-Niemieckie w swietle Aktów Norymberskich* in *Sprawy Miedzynarodowe,* 2/3, London, 1947, pp. 24-25; H. Lehmann, *Englands Spiel mit Polen,* Berlin, 1940, p. 38. **13.** *Documents on Events,* p. 212. **14.** *German Foreign Policy,* D, vol. 6, no. 73; *Polish White Book,* p. 63. **15.** Leon Noël, *L'Agression Allemande contre la Pologne,* Paris, 1947, p. 332. **16.** Szembek, *op. cit.,* p. 433. **17.** *Ibid.,* pp. 433-434. **18.** *Documents on Events,* p. 212; *Campaign in Poland,* 1939, West Point, 1943. **19.** W. Ipohorski-Lenkiewicz, *Minister z Pałacu Bruehla,* Buenos Aires, 1943, pp. 58, 67; Stanislaw Mackiewicz, *Sosnowski,* London, 1944, pp. 9ff. **20.** Norwid Neugebauer, *The Defence of Poland,* London, 1942, pp. 19-81; Martin Gilbert and Richard Cott, *The Appeasers,* Boston, 1963; pp. 240-247; 265-266. See also *Polskie Siły Zbrojne w Drugiej Wojnie Światowey,* vol. 1, part 1, London, 1951, pp. 257ff.; this account also describes earlier Polish military planning against Germany, pp. 109-127; no new German plans against Poland after the advent of Hitler are claimed before April 3, 1939, *Ibid.,* pp. 421ff. **21.** Lipski, *op. cit.,* pp. 25ff. **22.** *Documents on Events,* pp. 213-214. **23.** *Foreign Relations of the United States, 1939,* vol. 1, pp. 96ff. **24.** *Ibid.,* pp. 98-99. **25.** Szembek, *op. cit.,* pp. 435-436, 438-439. **26** *German Foreign Policy,* D, vol. 6, nos. 79, 88. **27.** *Ibid.,* no. 87. **28.** *Ibid.,* no. 99; L.B. Namier, *Diplomatic Prelude, 1938-1939,* London, 1947, p. 91. **29.** *Foreign Relations of the United States, 1939,* vol. 1, p. 101. **30** *German Foreign Policy,* D, vol. 6, no. 101; *Polish White Book,* pp. 65-66. **31.** *International Military Tribunal, 1945-1946,* vol. 10, p. 264; *Documents on Events,* pp. 214-215. **32.** *Polish White Book,* p.66; *Documents on Events,* p.216. **33.** *Ibid.,* p. 217; New York *Times,* March 28, 1939. **34.** *Documents on Events,* p. 219. **35.** *Ibid.,* p. 221. **36** *German Foreign Policy,* D, vol. 6, no. 108; *Documents on Events,* p. 218. **37.** *German Foreign Policy,* D, vol. 6, nos. 112, 115, 118; *Polish White Book,* p. 69; *Foreign Relations of the United States, 1939,* vol. 1, p. 104. **38.** *Ibid.,* p. 102; Noël, *op. cit.,* pp. 319-320. **39.** J. Łukasiewicz, *Przed Gwarancjami Anglii* in *DPDZ (Dziennik Polski i Dziennik Zolnierza),* Feb. 22, 1947; *Polish Documents,* pp. 3, 31. **40.** *Ibid.,* pp. 32-34. **41.** J. Ribbentrop, *Zwischen London un Moskau,* Leoni, Bavaria, 1954, pp. 160-162. **42.** *Festschrift zum Bundestreffen der Schlesier in München, Sept. 13-17, 1951,* and especially Hans Raupach, *Schlesiens unvergaengliche Wirtschaftsleistung,* pp. 61ff., and Hans Schadewaldt, *Die oberschlesische Industrie als einstige deutsche Wirtschaftspotenz,* pp. 65ff. **43.** *British War Blue Book,* London, 1939, p. 130. **44.** *German Foreign Office Archives,* Serial 2842, p. 549564. **45.** Conversations of the writer with members of the *Landsmannschaft Schlesien,* Munich, Sept. 13, 14, 15, 16, 1951. **46.** W. Görlitz & H. Quint, *Adolf Hitler,* Stuttgart, 1952, p. 486; Benno Hubensteiner, *Bayerische Geschichte,* Munich, 1951, pp. 63-68. **47.** Hans Frank, *Im Angesicht des Galgens,* Munich, 1953, pp. 78ff. **48.** *German Foreign Office Archives,* Serial 2130, pp. 465233ff. **49.** *Ibid.,* pp. 465224-465225. **50.** *Ibid.,* pp. 465533-465580. **51.** *German Foreign Office Archives,* Serial 52a, pp. 34586ff.

Chapter 14

1. *German Foreign Office Archives,* Serial 52a, p. 34620; *Foreign Relations of the United States, 1939,* vol. 1, pp. 105-106; Edward Raczynski, *The British-Polish Alliance,* London, 1948, pp. 14-15; F.J.C. Hearnshaw, *The Only Way to Safety in 19th Century and After,* April 1939; for a fuller presentation of Hearnshaw's anti-German views, see *Germany, the Aggressor throughout the Ages,* New York, 1941. **2.** General Gauché, *Le Deuxième Bureau au Travail,* Paris, 1953, pp. 87-88. **3.** Georges Bonnet, *Fin d'une Europe,* Geneva, 1948, pp. 161-162; Juliusz Łukasiewicz, *Rodowania i Wazniejsze Rozmowy,* ms., London, p. 3. **4.** Bonnet, *op. cit.,* pp. 154-155, 164-166. **5.** Łukasiewicz, *op. cit.,* pp. 5-7; see also *Po Zajeciu Pragi* in *DPDZ (Dziennik Polski i Dziennik Zolnierza),* Feb. 20, 1947. **6.** Łukasiewicz, *Rokowania,* pp. 9-11; *Przed Gwarancjami Anglii* in *DPDZ,* Feb. 22, 1947. **7.** Łukasiewicz, *Rokowania,* p. 14. **8.** *British Foreign Policy,* III, vol. 4, no. 518. **9.** *Ibid.,* nos. 518, 523; Martin Gilbert and Richard Cott, *The Appeasers,* Boston, 1963, p. 241. **10.** *New York Times,* Mar. 27, 1939; *French Yellow Book,* pp. 101-102. **11.** L. Noël, *L'Agression Allemande contre la Pologne,* Paris, 1947, pp. 336-342. **12.** *British Foreign Policy,* III, vol. 4, no. 538; W.P. & Z. Coates, *A History of Anglo-Soviet Relations,* London, 1944, pp. 602-603. **13.** *Foreign Relations of the United States, 1939,* vol. 1, pp. 108-110. **14.** *British Foreign Policy,* III, vol. 4, no. 568, 571. **15.** *Ibid.,* nos. 577, 584. **16.** *Polish White Book,* pp. 71-72; Noël, *op. cit.,* p. 323. **17.** W. Jedrzejewicz, *Poland in the British Parliament,*

1939-1945, vol. 1, New York, 1946, p. xi. **18.** Henryk Baginski, *Poland and the Baltic*, Edinburgh, 1942, p. xi; see also H. Baginski in *Czy Wiesz Kto to Jest?*, Warsaw, 1938. **19.** John Wrench, *Geoffrey Dawson and Our Times*, London, 1955, p. 390; Hugh Dalton, *Memoirs*, vol. 2, London, 1957, p. 231. **20.** *Ibid.*, p. 234; L.S. Amery, *My Political Life*, vol. 3, London, 1955, pp. 310-311. **21.** W. Strang, *Home and Abroad*, London, 1956, p. 155. **22.** Thomas Jones, *A Diary with Letters*, London, 1954, p. 431. **23.** *Hansard's Parliamentary Debates*, *Commons*, March 31, 1939; Viscount Templewood, *Nine Troubled Years*, London, 1954, pp. 348-349. **24.** *German Foreign Office Archives*, Serial 52a, p. 34619; J. Davignon, *Berlin, 1936-1940: Souvenirs d'une Mission*, Paris, 1951, p. 102. **25.** *Foreign Relations of the United States, 1939*, vol. 1, pp. 113-114. **26.** *Nazi Acts*, vol. 4, p. 370; J. Beck, *Dernier Rapport*, Neuchatel, 1949, pp. 115-116. **27.** *Nazi Acts*, vol. 6, pp. 916-918. Taylor, *op. cit.*, p. 220, explains that Hitler's military directive of April 3, 1939 in no sense implied that Hitler had decided to go to war against Poland. **28.** N. Baynes, ed., *The Speeches of Adolf Hitler*, vol. 2, London, 1942, pp. 1590ff.; *Schulthess, 1939*, pp. 75-80. **29.** *German Foreign Policy*, D, vol. 6, no. 148; Józef Lipski, *Stosunki Polsko-Niemiecke w swietle Aktów Norymberskich in Sprawy Miedzynarodowe*, 4, London, 1947, p. 24. **30.** *German Foreign Policy*, D, vol. 6, nos. 123, 124. **31.** *Ibid.*, nos. 131, 135. **32.** *Ibid.*, no. 147. **33.** *British Foreign Policy*, III, vol. 5, no. 1. **34.** *Völkischer Beobachter* (Munich), April 5, 1939; Toynbee, *et al., The Eve of War, 1939*, London, 1958, p. 161. **35.** *British Foreign Policy*, III, vol. 5, no. 2. **36.** G.D.H. Cole, *History of the British Labour Party*, London, 1957, p. 368. **37.** *German Foreign Policy*, D, vol. 6, nos. 150, 164, 170, 171; Luigi Villari, *Italian Foreign Policy under Mussolini*, New York, 1956, pp. 219-222. **38.** *British Foreign Policy*, III, vol. 5, no. 10. **39.** *Ibid.*, no. 16. Taylor, *op. cit.*, p. 213, emphasizes that Beck's April 1939 visit to London was confirmation that the British guarantee had placed Poland in a position to dictate events. **40.** Winston Churchill, *The Gathering Storm*, Boston, 1948, p. 401. **41.** *Ibid.*, p. 350; Beck, *op. cit.*, pp. 191-192. **42.** *German Foreign Office Archives*, Serial 52a, pp. 34636-34637; *Foreign Relations of the United States, 1939*, vol. 1, pp. 112-113. **43.** *Ibid.*, pp. 113-114. **44.** *German Foreign Policy*, D, vol. 6, no. 167. **45.** *Ibid.*, no. 169. **46.** *Foreign Relations of the United States, 1939*, vol. 1, p. 115. **47.** *German Foreign Office Archives*, Serial 52a, p. 33652; Łukasiewicz, Rokowania, p. 15. **48.** *Ibid.*, pp. 15-16. **49.** *Ibid.*, pp. 16-17; *Rozbudowa Gwarancji* in *DPDZ*, Feb. 26, 1947. **50.** *Foreign Relations of the United States, 1939*, vol. 1, pp. 117-118. **51.** *Völkischer Beobachter* (Munich), April 25, 1939. **52.** Hans Grimm, *Warum-Woher-Aber Wohin?*, Lippoldsberg, 1954, pp. 229-232.

Chapter 15

1. *Gazeta Polska*, May 6, 1939; see also J.H. Harley, *The Authentic Biography of Colonel Beck*, London, 1939, appendix. A.J.P. Taylor, *The Origins of the Second World War*, London, 1961, p. 216, claims that scarcely anyone believed that Poland was deliberately driving toward war after the British guarantee; nevertheless, a situation had arisen in which there either had to be negotiations or war. **2.** A.J. Toynbee, *et al., The Eve of War, 1939*, London, 1958, pp. 44-47. **3.** *German Foreign Policy*, D, vol. 6, no. 173. **4.** *Ibid.*, nos. 180, 195. **5.** *British Foreign Policy*, III, vol. 5, nos. 18, 26. **6.** These insights are based on the experience of Professor Ralph Lutz of the Hoover Institute on a trip to Germany in 1939. **7.** *British Foreign Policy*, III, vol. 5, no. 26. **8.** F.J.P. Veale, *Advance to Barbarism*, Appleton, Wisc., 1953, pp. 69-72; Stanisław Strzetelski, *Where the Storm Broke*, New York, 1942, p. 68; Burton Klein, *Germany's Preparation for War: a Re-examination* in *American Economic Review*, March 1948, p. 70. **9.** *Nazi Acts*, vol. 6, pp. 919-921. **10.** J. Łukasiewicz, *Rokowania i Wazniejsze Rozmowy*, ms., London, pp. 17-18; see also *Rosbudowa Gwarancji* in *DPDZ*, Feb. 26, 1947. **11.** *Les Événements survenus en France*, suppl. vol. 4 (Noël testimony, April 27, 1948), pp. 843-854; Georges Bonnet, *Fin d'une Europe*, Geneva, 1948, pp. 166-170, 180-181. **12.** Łukasiewicz, *Rokowania*, pp. 20-21. **13.** Jan Szembek, *Journal*, Paris, 1951, pp. 440-441. **14.** *Foreign Relations of the United States, 1939*, vol. 1, pp. 118-119, 120-122. **15.** *Ibid.*, pp. 123-126. **16.** *Ibid.*, p. 118; *Völkischer Beobachter* (Munich), April 13, 1939; Winston Churchill, *The Gathering Storm*, Boston, 1948, pp. 350-351. **17.** C.C. Tansill, *The Back Door to War*, Chicago, 1952, p. 517; F.R. Sanborn, *Design for War, 1937-1941*, New York, 1951, p. 62. **18.** L. Villari, *Italian Foreign Policy Under Mussolini*, New York, 1956, pp. 221-222; *Documents on Events*, p. 311. **19.** *German Foreign Policy*, D, vol. 6, no. 198. **20.** Bonnet, *op. cit.*, pp. 180-181; Łukasiewicz, *Rokowania*, pp. 22-24. **21.** Szembek, *op. cit.*, pp. 443-444. **22.** This meeting was a step toward the secret Bulgar-Serbian treaty of 1912, which led to the Balkan wars, see E.C. Helmreich, *The Diplomacy of the Balkan Wars*, Cambridge, Mass., 1938, *passim*; see also his *Ein Nachtrag zu den serbisch-bulgarischen Abkommen von 1912* in *Berliner Monatshefte*, Dec. 1935; for April 1939, see G. Gafencu, *Derniers Jours de l'Europe*, Paris, 1946, pp. 35ff. **23.** *Ibid.*, p. 36. **24.** *Ibid.*, p. 37. **25.** Józef Beck, *Dernier Rapport*, Neuchatel, 1949, p. 196. **26.** Gafencu, *op. cit.*, pp. 38-47. **27.** *Ibid.*, p. 49. **28.** *Ibid.*; Beck made similar remarks to King Carol of Rumania in June 1937, see J.H. Harley, *The Authentic Biography of Colonel Beck*, pp. 93-94. **29.** Gafencu, *op. cit.*, pp. 49-57. **30.** Bonnet, *op. cit.*, pp. 180-181. **31.** *British Foreign Policy*, III, vol. 5, no. 46. **32.** *Ibid.*, nos. 263, 266. **33.** *Foreign Relations of the United States, 1939*, vol. 1, pp. 130-133. **34.** *Völkischer Beobachter* (Munich), April 25, 1939. **35.** *Foreign Relations of the United States, 1939*, vol. 1, pp. 138-139; *Der Angriff* (Berlin), Apr. 17, 1939; *Völkischer Beobachter* (Munich), April 16-18, 1939. **36.** *German Foreign Policy*, D, vol. 6, no. 178. **37.** Villari, *op. cit.*, pp. 223-224. **38.** *German Foreign Policy*, D, vol. 6, nos. 205, 211; *Nazi Acts*, vol. 4, p. 519. **39.** Mario Toscano, *Le Origini del Patto d'Acciaio*, Florence, 1948, pp. 2-5; *Nazi Acts*, vol. 4, p. 519. **40.** *German Foreign Policy*, D, vol. 6, no. 220; *Foreign Relations of the United States, 1939*, vol. 1, pp. 134-135. **41.** *German Foreign Policy*, D, vol. 6, no. 213; *Polish Documents*, p. 35; *Poland in the British Parliament, 1939-1945*, vol. 1, pp. 36-40. **42.** *German Foreign Policy*, D, vol. 6, no. 227; Gafencu, *op. cit.*, p. 78. **43.** *Ibid.*, pp. 78-

Notes 639

82. **44.** *German Foreign Policy*, D, vol. 6, no. 234; Gafencu, *op. cit.*, pp. 89-90. **45.** *British Foreign Policy*, III, vol. 5, no. 273; Szembek, *op. cit.*, p. 477. **46.** *British Foreign Policy*, III, vol. 5, nos. 274, 275; *Völkischer Beobachter* (Munich), April 21, 1939. **47.** *British Foreign Policy*, III, vol. 5, no. 278. **48.** *Ibid.*, nos. 279, 288. **49.** *German Foreign Policy*, D, vol. 6, no. 261, 262. **50.** *Ibid.*, no. 271. **51.** *Foreign Relations of the United States, 1939*, vol. 1, pp. 158; *German Foreign Policy*, D, vol. 6, no. 272; *Documents on Events*, p. 312. **52.** *German Foreign Policy*, D, vol. 6, nos. 255, 264; J. Davignon, *Berlin, 1936-1940*, Paris, 1951, p. 113. **53.** *German Foreign Policy*, D, vol. 6, nos. 273, 274, 276, 277. **54.** *Ibid.*, no. 290; Szembek, *op. cit.*, pp. 449-450. **55.** R. Coulondre, *De Staline à Hitler, 1936-1939*, Paris, 1950, pp. 261-262, 266. **56.** *Foreign Relations of the United States, 1939*, vol. 1, pp. 159-160. **57.** *Speech delivered by Adolf Hitler before the German Reichstag, April 28, 1938*, German Library of Information, New York, 1939, *passim;* see also *Exchange of Communications between the President of the United States and the Chancellor of the German Reich, April 1939*, New York, 1939, pp. 6-45. **58.** L. Noël, *L'Agression Allemande contre la Pologne*, Paris, 1947, p. 356. **59.** Helmut Schubring, *Deutscher Friedenswille gegen polnischen Nationalhass im Einsatz der deutschen Presse, 1933-1939*, Berlin, 1941, pp. 17ff. **60.** *Nazi Acts*, vol. 6, pp. 187-188; *Der Angriff* (Berlin), May 2, 1939. **61.** *Foreign Relations of the United States, 1939*, vol. 1, pp. 159-160, 176-177; *German Foreign Policy*, D, vol. 6, no. 287, 290, 291. **62.** *Ibid.*, no. 295. **63.** *Ibid.*, nos. 296, 297, 300, 328. **64.** Szembek, *op. cit.*, pp. 451-452. **65.** *Ibid.*, p. 453, A. Upham Pope, *Maxim Litvinoff*, New York, 1943, pp. 445-446. **66.** *French Yellow Book*, pp. 123-125. **67.** *German Foreign Office Archives*, Serial 52a, p. 34706-34707; *Gazeta Polska*, May 6, 1939. **68.** *German Foreign Office Archives*, Serial 52a, p. 34728-34735; *German Foreign Policy*, D, vol. 6, no. 334. **69.** *Gazeta Polska*, May 6, 1939; Harley, *op. cit.*, appendix. **70.** G. Craig & F. Gilbert, *The Diplomats, 1919-1939*, Princeton, 1953, pp. 579ff. **71.** Beck, *op. cit.*, p. 198; Noël, *op. cit.*, pp. 359-361; Chodacki in conversation with the writer, April 2, 1948. **72.** *German Foreign Office Archives*, Serial 52a, p. 34718-34726. **73.** Strzetelski in conversation with the writer, March 3-4, 1948. **74.** *German Foreign Policy*, D, vol. 6, no. 337. **75.** *Ibid.*, no. 335. **76.** *British Foreign Policy*, III, vol. 5, no. 315; *Czas*, May 6, 1939; *Der Angriff*, May 6-8, 1939; Noël, *op. cit.*, p. 362. **77.** *Foreign Relations of the United States, 1939*, vol. 1, pp. 172-175, 180.

Chapter 16

1. Edwin E. Dwinger, *Der Tod in Polen*, Jena, 1940, pp. 8-173. **2.** *German Foreign Policy*, D, vol. 6, nos. 377, 385. **3.** *German Foreign Office Archives*, Serial 2842, p. 549557ff. **4.** *Ibid.*, pp. 549618ff. **5.** *Ibid.*, pp. 549641ff. **6.** *Ibid.*, Serial 52b, pp. 34872-34879. **7.** *Ibid.*, Serial 2842, pp. 549650-549651. **8.** *Dokumente der Deutsche Politik*, vol. 7, Berlin, 1940, pp. 585ff; *Documents on Events*, pp. 397-406. **9.** *German Foreign Office Archives*, Serial 461, p. 225169-225177. **10.** *Documents on Events*, pp. 319-322. **11.** *Ibid.*, pp. 388, 390-395; *German Foreign Office Archives*, Serial 52b, p. 34926ff.; *German Foreign Policy*, D, vol. 6, nos. 367, 387. **12.** *Ibid.*, nos. 403, 409. **13.** *I Documenti Diplomatici Italiani*, VIII, vol. 12, Rome, 1952, no. 37, hereafter cited as *Italian Foreign Policy*; *British Foreign Policy*, III, vol. 5, nos. 575, 577, 579; Chodacki in conversation with the writer, April 2, 1948. **14.** *Poland in the British Parliament, 1939-1945*, vol. 1, London, 1946, p. 92; *British Blue Book*, pp. 19-20; 69-70; *New York Times*, June 13, 1939; see also the interpretation of Polish rights at Danzig in J. Makowski, *Prawno-Panstwowe Polozenie Wolnego Miasta Gdańska*, Warsaw, 1923, pp. 11ff. **15.** *German Foreign Policy*, D, vol. 6, no. 429. **16.** *Ibid.*, nos. 429, 430. **17.** *Ibid.*, no. 464. **18.** G. Bonnet, *Fin d'une Europe*, pp. 218-219; J. Łukasiewicz, *Rokowania i Wazniejsze Rozmowy*, ms., pp. 37-39. **19.** *Ibid.*, p. 40; General M. Gamelin, *Servir*, vol. 2, Paris, 1946, pp. 415-420. *Polskie Siły Zbrojne w Drugiej Wojnie Światowej*, vol. 1, part 1, London, 1951, pp. 96-101. **20.** Bonnet, *op. cit.*, pp. 211, 219-220. **21.** Gamelin, *op. cit.*, vol. 2, pp. 422-427; L. Noël, *L'Agression contre la Pologne*, Paris, 1947, p. 373. **22.** Łukasiewicz, *Rokowania*, pp. 41-49; see also *Rodowania o pozycke francuska in DPDZ*, April 8, 1947. **23.** *British Foreign Policy*, III, vol. 5, nos. 508, 562. **24.** *Polish Documents*, pp. 42-43; Jean Zay, *Souvenirs et Solitude*, Paris, 1945, pp. 177-178. **25.** *British Foreign Policy*, III, vol. 6, no. 250; *Documents on Events*, p. 450; *Poland in the British Parliament*, vol. 1, p. 120; General John Kennedy, *The Business of War*, New York, 1958, pp. 12-18; Peter Esch, *Polen kreuz und quer*, Berlin, 1939, p. 134. A.J.P. Taylor, *The Origins of the Second World War*, London, 1961, p. 221, claims that British refusal to supply the Poles was proof that Halifax was as much concerned about inducing the Poles to be moderate as about restraining Hitler; in reality, this merely indicated that Halifax did not attach much importance to the outcome of military operations on the Polish front in the event of war since the defeat of Poland was considered to be inevitable unless she was supported by the Soviet Union. **26.** *French Yellow Book*, p. 196; W. Churchill, *The Gathering Storm*, Boston, 1948, p. 401. **27.** W. Strang, *Home and Abroad*, London, 1956, pp. 155, 161-162. **28.** *Nazi Acts*, vol. 5, p. 689; W. von Rheinbaben, *Unruhiges Europa*, Berlin, 1939, pp. 47-49. **29.** Galeazzo Ciano, *The Ciano Diaries, 1939-1943*, New York, 1946, pp. 78, 84; Mario Toscano, *Le Origini del Patto d'Acciaio*, Florence, 1948, pp. 99, 148-149, 178-179; Luigi Villari, *Italian Foreign Policy under Mussolini*, New York, 1956, p. 231. **30.** *German Foreign Policy*, D, vol. 6, no. 372, 374, 489. **31.** *Ibid.*, no. 497. **32.** *British Foreign Policy*, III, vol. 6, no. 334. **33.** *German Foreign Policy*, D, vol. 6, nos. 698, 708. **34.** Herbert Dirksen, *Moskau, Tokio, London, 1919-1939*, Stuttgart, 1949, pp. 251ff. **35.** *British Foreign Policy*, III, vol. 6, nos. 354, 370. **36.** *German Foreign Policy*, D, vol. 6, no. 710. **37.** *Ibid.*, no. 746. **38.** *Ibid.*, nos. 748, 752. Taylor, *op. cit.*, pp. 244-245, admits that all British suggestions to Wohlthat were conditional on the solution of the Danzig dispute along lines which would be acceptable to the Poles. **39.** *Ibid.*, nos. 469, 471. **40.** *Ibid.*, nos. 492, 515, 521. **41.** Lev Prchala, *Vers l'Union*, Paris, 1947, pp. 3ff.; *New York Times*, June 14, 18, 19, 1939; *Völkischer Beobachter* (Berlin), June 18, 1939. **42.** *German Foreign Office*

Archives, Serial 461, pp. 22520-22521.   **43.** *Ibid.,* pp. 34845ff.   **44.** *Ibid.,* pp. 34849-34852.   **45.** *Documents on Events,* pp. 433-437.   **46.** *German Foreign Office Archives,* Serial 52a, p. 34853; *Documents on Events,* pp. 437-438.   **47.** *German Foreign Policy,* D, vol. 6, nos. 599, 647.   **48.** *French Yellow Book,* pp. 159, 180-181; Dirksen, *op. cit.,* pp. 217-218.   **49.** Jan Szembek, *Journal,* Paris, 1952, pp. 475-476.   **50.** *German Foreign Office Archives,* Serial 52b, p. 34912.   **51.** *Foreign Relations of the United States, 1939,* vol. 1, pp. 189-90; 194-195, 197-198.   **52.** *German Foreign Policy,* D, vol. 6, nos. 681, 686.   **53.** *Ibid.,* no. 693; *British Blue Book,* pp. 78-81.   **54.** *Ilustrowany Kurjer,* July 13, 14, 26, 27, 1939.   **55.** *Völkischer Beobachter* (Munich), August 1, 8, 1939.   **56.** *Foreign Relations of the United States, 1939,* vol. 1, pp. 202; *German Foreign Policy,* D, vol. 6, no. 721; *British Blue Book,* pp. 81-83.   **57.** *German Foreign Policy,* D, vol. 6, nos. 711, 718; Mario Carofiglio, *Vita di Mussolini e Storia del Fascismo,* Turin, 1953, pp. 361-368.   **58.** *German Foreign Policy,* D, vol. 6, no. 737.   **59.** *German Foreign Office Archives,* Serial 121, pp. 119536-119542; *German Foreign Policy,* D, vol. 6, no. 722.   **60.** *Ibid.,* nos. 755, 767.   **61.** *Poland in the British Parliament,* vol. 1, p. 120; *New York Times,* July 21, 22, 1939; *Ilustrowany Kurjer,* July 22, 1939.   **62.** *Polish White Book,* p. 95; *Documents on Events,* p. 439-440; *French Yellow Book,* pp. 210-214; *New York Times,* August 2-3, 1939. Chodacki in conversation with the writer, April 2, 1948; for Burckhardt's condemnation (twenty years later) of the Polish ultimatum, *vide* C.J. Burckhardt, *Meine Danziger Mission, 1937-1939,* Munich, 1960, pp. 329-330.   **63.** *Polish White Book,* p. 97; *Documents on Events,* pp. 440-441, 453; *French Yellow Book,* p. 217; L.B. Namier, *Diplomatic Prelude, 1938-1939,* London, 1947, p. 256.   **64.** *Ostland-Berichte,* Danzig, 1939, nos. 1-7; *Documents on Events,* pp. 453-455; Noël, *op. cit.,* pp. 397-398.   **65.** *Foreign Relations of the United States, 1939,* vol. 1, pp. 211-214.   **66.** *German Foreign Policy,* D, vol. 6, no. 771; vol. 7, no. 4.   **67.** *Nazi Acts,* vol. 6, p. 937; J.W. Wheeler-Bennett, *The Nemesis of Power,* New York, 1954, pp. 438-439.   **68.** *International Military Tribunal, 1945-1946,* vol. 10, pp. 513-514; W. Görlitz & H. Quint, *Adolf Hitler,* Stuttgart, 1952, p. 526.   **69.** J. Stipp, ed., *Devil's Diary,* Yellow Springs, 1955, pp. 113-120; *International Military Tribunal, 1945-1946,* vol. 9, pp. 116-117; 308ff.; *Nazi Acts,* vol. 7, pp. 848-852.   **70.** *German Foreign Policy,* D, vol. 6, no. 763, 768; Goerlitz & Quint, *op. cit.,* p. 531.   **71.** *German Foreign Policy,* D, vol. 6, no. 784.   **72.** *Ibid.,* no. 781.   **73.** *German Foreign Office Archives,* Serial 52b, p. 34935; Mme. Piłsudska, *Memoirs,* London, 1940, pp. 15-17.   **74.** *Gazeta Polska,* August 7, 1939; London *Times,* Aug. 5, 6, 1939.   **75.** *German Foreign Office Archives,* Serial 52b, p. 34931-34932.   **76.** *Ilustrowany Kurjer,* August 7, 1939; *New York Times,* August 8, 1939.   **77.** *German Foreign Office Archives,* Serial 461, p. 225217-225218.

Chapter 17

1. V.A. Matveyev, *Proval Munkenskoi Politiki, 1938-1939,* Moscow, 1955, pp. 3-4, 258.   **2.** *Les Événements survenus en France,* suppl. vol. 9, pp. 2670, 2680.   **3.** *Ibid.,* suppl. vol. 1, p. 39; William Strang, *Home and Abroad,* London, 1956, p. 198.   **4.** *Krasny Arkhiv: istoricheski Zhurnal,* 1939, 92:1.   **5.** W. Oncken, *Das Zeitalter Friedrichs des Grossen,* vol. 2, Berlin, 1882, p. 346ff.   **6.** Marshal Voroshilov in *Izvestiya (The News),* Moscow, August 26, 1939.   **7.** V. Tanner, *The Winter War: Finland against Russia, 1939-1940,* Stanford, Calif., 1957, pp. 3-18.   **8.** *Foreign Relations of the United States: The Soviet Union, 1933-1939,* Washington, D.C. 1952, pp. 291-294.   **9.** *Ibid.,* pp. 520-527, 544-547, 548-550.   **10.** *Ibid.,* pp. 733-737; *Der Spiegel,* April 23, 1958.   **11.** *Krasny Arkhiv,* 1939, 92:1; *German Foreign Policy,* D, vol. 6, no. 1; *Foreign Relations of the United States: The Soviet Union, 1933-1939,* pp. 739-746; J. von Ribbentrop, *Zwischen London und Moskau,* Leoni, Bavaria, 1954, p. 160.   **12.** *German Foreign Policy,* D, vol. 6, no. 80; *Les Événements survenus en France,* suppl. vol. 9, p. 2670; *Poland in the British Parliament, 1939-1945,* vol. 1, New York, 1946, p. 25.   **13.** Strang, *op. cit.,* pp. 163-164; A.J. Toynbee, *et al., The Eve of War, 1939,* London, 1958, pp. 437ff.   **14.** *German Foreign Office Archives,* Serial 103, p. 111303; *Foreign Relations of the United States: The Soviet Union, 1933-1939,* p. 759; Strang, *op. cit.,* p. 165.   **15.** *German Foreign Policy,* D, vol. 6, no. 215.   **16.** *Ibid.,* no. 325; Strang, *op. cit.,* p. 165.   **17.** *Polish White Book,* p. 183; Grigorie Gafencu, *Derniers Jours de l'Europe,* Paris, 1946, pp. 202-204; L. Noël, *L'Agression Allemande contre la Pologne,* Paris, 1947, p. 377.   **18.** *Falsificators of History,* Soviet FO, Moscow, 1948, pp. 33-34; Noël regarded Grzybowski a poor choice for the Moscow post, Noël, *op. cit.,* pp. 85-86.   **19.** *Poland in the British Parliament,* vol. 1, p. 61; Strang, *op. cit.,* p. 167.   **20.** *Poland in the British Parliament,* vol. 1, pp. 73-74, 86-89; A.U. Pope, *Maxim Litvinoff,* New York, 1943, pp. 431, 445-446; G. Bilaiakin, *Maisky: Ten Years Ambassador,* London, 1944, pp. 242ff.   **21.** *Foreign Relations of the United States: The Soviet Union, 1933-1939,* pp. 764-766; G. Bonnet, *Fin d' une Europe,* Geneva, 1948, pp. 185-186; *New York Times,* June 1, 1939.   **22.** Strang, *op. cit.,* pp. 170-171; A.M. Nekrich, *Politika Angliskovo Imperialisma v Evropa, Okt. 1938-Sept. 1939,* Moscow, 1955, pp. 322f.   **23.** *German Foreign Policy,* D, vol. 6, nos. 389, 424, 446, 451; *Nazi-Soviet Relations, 1939-1941,* pp. 5-9.   **24.** *Ibid.,* pp. 18-21.   **25.** J.W. Wheeler-Bennett, *Brest-Litovsk,* London, 1938, pp. 187ff.; Nekrich, *op. cit.,* pp. 336ff.; Raymond Sontag, in *Foreign Affairs,* April 1957, pp. 517-519.   **26.** *German Foreign Policy,* D, vol. 6, nos. 520, 523, 536.   **27.** *German Foreign Office Archives,* Serial 259, p. 169346; Strang, *op. cit.,* p. 158.   **28.** *Ibid.,* pp. 173, 175-176.   **29.** *Ibid.,* pp. 178-187.   **30.** *Ibid.,* no. 614; *German Foreign Policy,* D, vol. 6, no. 579; *Nazi-Soviet Relations,* pp. 26-32; E. Kordt, *Wahn und Wirklichkeit,* Stuttgart, 1947, p. 158.   **31.** *German Foreign Policy,* D, vol. 6, nos. 582, 726.   **32.** *Nazi-Soviet Relations,* pp. 32-39.   **33.** *Ibid.,* pp. 40-41; *German Foreign Policy,* D, vol. 6, nos. 758, 760; Halifax received full details on current Russo-German negotiations after June 1939 from anti-Hitler German diplomats, see E. Kordt, *Nicht aus den Akten,* Stuttgart, 1950, pp. 313-319.   **34.** *German Foreign Policy,* D, vol. 7, no. 29; *Nazi-Soviet Relations,* pp. 42, 45-46.   **35.** General Doumenc in *Carrefour,* Paris, May 21, 1947; P. Reynaud, *La France a Sauvé l'Europe,* vol. 1, Paris, 1947, p. 586.   **36.** Noël, *op. cit.,* p. 422; L.B. Namier,

Diplomatic Prelude, 1938-1939, London, 1947, p. 205.   **37.** *British Foreign Policy*, III, vol. 7, nos. 2, 19, 30.   **38.** Bonnet, *op. cit.*, pp. 254-257.   **39.** *Ibid.*, pp. 268-271.   **40.** *Les Événements survenus en France*, suppl. vol. 9, p. 2674; Bonnet, *op. cit.*, pp. 276-277; Łukasiewicz, *Rokowania i Wazniejsze Rozmowy*, ms., London, p. 97.   **41.** *Les Événements*, suppl. vol. 9, p. 2675; Bonnet, *op. cit.*, pp. 277-285.   **42.** J. Beck, *Dernier Rapport*, Neuchatel, 1949, pp. 202-204.   **43.** *British Foreign Policy*, III, vol. 7, no. 27.   **44.** *Ibid.*, nos. 30, 34.   **45.** *Ibid.*, no. 34; both letters are in the same document.   **46.** *Ibid.*, no. 38.   **47.** *Ibid.*, nos. 52, 60, 64.   **48.** *Foreign Relations of the United States, 1939*, vol. 1, pp. 225-226.   **49.** *Ibid.*, pp. 248-250, 287-288.   **50.** *Ibid.*, pp. 293-294.   **51.** *Ibid.*, pp. 296-298, 302-303.   **52.** *British Foreign Policy*, III, vol. 7, no. 41; Kordt, *op. cit.*, pp. 336ff.   **53.** Edward Raczynski, *The British-Polish Alliance*, London, 1948, pp. 19-20.   **54.** *Ibid.*, pp. 20-21; *British Foreign Policy*, III, vol. 7, no. 66.   **55.** Bonnet, *op. cit.*, p. 284; Reynaud, *op. cit.*, p. 587; Gafencu, *op. cit.*, pp. 232-233.   **56.** General Gauché, *Le Deuxième Bureau au Travail*, Paris, 1953, pp. 88-94.   **57.** R. Umiastowski, *Russia and the Polish Republic, 1918-1941*, London, 1944, pp. 139-140, italics mine.   **58.** E. Daladier in *Journal Officiel de la République Française: Débats de l'Assemblée Nationale Constituante*, July 19, 1946; J. Łukasiewicz, *Rokowania i Rozmowy* in *DPDZ*, Dec. 6, 1946; *British Foreign Policy*, III, vol. 7, no. 80.   **59.** *Ibid.*, no. 90.   **60.** *Ibid.*, nos. 91, 94, 110.   **61.** *Ibid.*, no. 115; *Les Événements*, suppl. vol. 9, p. 2675.   **62.** Daladier, *op. cit.*; Łukasiewicz, *Rokowania i Rozmowy* in *DPDZ*, Dec. 6, 1946.   **63.** *British Foreign Policy*, III, vol. 7, nos. 103, 123; Doumenc, *op. cit.*; Reynaud, *op. cit.*, p. 588.   **64.** Strang, *op. cit.*, pp. 195-196.   **65.** *British Foreign Policy*, III, vol. 7, no. 158. A.J.P. Taylor, *The Origins of the Second World War*, London, 1961, p. 240, considered the conduct of negotiations with the Soviet Union by Halifax in 1939 incompetent to such a degree that one was compelled to suspect that an agreement was never seriously intended on the British side.

Chapter 18

1. Walther Hofer, *Die Entfesselung des Zweiten Weltkrieges*, Stuttgart, 1954, p. 12.   **2.** *German Foreign Policy*, D, vol. 7, no. 50. A.J.P. Taylor, *The Origins of the Second World War*, London, 1961, p. 255, questions, along with Walther Hofer and others, the sending of a telegram from Berlin to Hitler at Berchtesgaden on August 12, 1939, conveying the contents of the Soviet demarché; no copy of such a telegram has been found, but its existence is confirmed by both the German and Italian archives (Ciano was at Berchtesgaden at the time); Taylor's suggestion that Hitler was merely guessing about Soviet intentions is improbable and unconvincing.   **3.** *Ibid.*, nos. 31, 32, 43.   **4.** *Ibid.*, nos. 44, 59.   **5.** *German Foreign Office Archives*, Serial 2842, pp. 549684-549685; Serial 52b, pp. 34997-35009.   **6.** *German Foreign Policy*, D, vol. 7, no. 63; *Völkischer Beobachter* (Munich) August 18, 1939.   **7.** Galeazzo Ciano, *The Ciano Diaries, 1939-1943*, New York, 1946, pp. 110-116.   **8.** Jan Szembek, *Journal*, Paris, 1952, p. 487; L. Noël, *L'Agression Allemande contre la Pologne*, Paris, 1947, p. 415; *British Blue Book*, p.p. 91-93.   **9.** *Italian Foreign Policy*, VIII, vol. 13, no. 1.   **10.** E. von Weizsäcker, *Memoirs*, London, 1951, p. 198.   **11.** *Italian Foreign Policy*, VIII, vol. 13, no. 4; *Nazi Acts*, vol. 4, pp. 510-511; vol. 8, pp. 517-579.   **12.** *Ibid.*, vol. 8, p. 525; *Nazi-Soviet Relations*, pp. 48-49; E. Kordt, *Wahn und Wirklichkeit*, Stuttgart, 1947, p. 161.   **13.** *Nazi Acts*, vol. 4, pp. 514-515; vol. 8, p. 523.   **14.** *Italian Foreign Policy*, VIII, vol. 13, no. 20.   **15.** *Nazi Acts*, vol. 4, p. 515-516, vol. 8, pp. 523-525.   **16.** *Ibid.*, vol. 8, p. 527.   **17.** *Italian Foreign Policy*, VIII, vol. 13, no. 21, P. Schmidt, *Statist auf diplomatischer Bühne, 1923-1945*, Bonn, 1949, pp. 439-440.   **18.** *Italian Foreign Policy*, VIII, vol. 13, nos. 42, 47, 55.   **19.** *German Foreign Policy*, D, vol. 7, no. 90.   **20.** *Ibid.*, nos. 98, 126.   **21.** *British Foreign Policy*, III, vol. 7, nos. 59, 71.   **22.** *Les Événements survenus en France*, suppl. vol. 9, p. 2680.   **23.** *Italian Foreign Policy*, VIII, vol. 13, no. 102.   **24.** *Ibid.*, nos. 87, 98; *British Foreign Policy*, III, vol. 7, no. 78.   **25.** *Ibid.*, no. 79.   **26.** *Ibid.*, no. 83; *Italian Foreign Policy*, VIII, vol. 13, no. 117.   **27.** *Ibid.*, nos. 123, 127.   **28.** *German Foreign Policy*, D, vol. 7, nos. 72, 104.   **29.** *Ibid.*, nos. 106, 117.   **30.** *Ibid.*, nos. 119, 128, 150, 172.   **31.** *Ibid.*, nos. 176, 182.   **32.** *Ibid.*, no. 197.   **33.** *Ibid.*, no. 56.   **34.** *Ibid.*, nos. 61, 70, 75.   **35.** *Ibid.*, nos. 79, 92; *Nazi-Soviet Relations*, p. 58; W. Görlitz and H. Quint, *Adolf Hitler*, Stuttgart, 1952, p. 530.   **36.** *German Foreign Policy*, D, vol. 7, no. nos. 105, 123; *Nazi-Soviet Relations*, p.p. 61-63; J. von Ribbentrop, *Zwischen London und Moskau*, Leoni, Bavaria, 1954, pp. 180-182.   **37.** *German Foreign Policy*, D, vol. 7, nos. 111, 116.   **38.** *Ibid.*, nos. 120, 125, 131, 133, 140; A. de la Pradelle, *Le Marxisme Tentaculaire*, Issoudun, 1942, pp. 121-122.   **39.** *German Foreign Policy*, D, vol. 7, nos. 142, 152, 157; *Nazi-Soviet Relations*, p. 67.   **40.** *German Foreign Policy*, D, vol. 7, nos. 158, 159, 160, 170.   **41.** *Ibid.*, no. 180; Chodacki in conversation with the writer, Ap. 2, 1948.   **42.** *British Foreign Policy*, III, vol. 7, nos. 123.   **43.** Szembek, *op. cit.*, pp. 490-491.   **44.** *Foreign Relations of the United States, 1939*, vol. 1, pp. 306-307, 342, 355-356.   **45.** *German Foreign Policy*, D, vol. 7, nos. 206, 210, 213; Frank Owen, *The Three Dictators: Mussolini, Stalin, Hitler*, London, 1940, pp. 167ff.   **46.** *German Foreign Policy*, D, vol. 7, nos. 228, 229.   **47.** *Ibid.*, no. 234; *International Military Tribunal, 1945-1946*, vol. 10, pp. 316ff.; A.M. Nekrich, *Politika Angliskovo Imperialisma v Europa*, Moscow, 1955, pp. 402-437; Kordt, *Wahn und Wirklichkeit*, pp. 175ff.; *Falsificators of History*, p. 42; Gafencu aptly noted that the Munich and Moscow pacts were two of a kind (*Derniers Jours*, p. 426); for USSR as *tertius gaudens*, see N. Henderson, *Failure of a Mission*, New York, 1940, pp. 259ff., and Otto Kriegk, *Die Geburt Europas*, Berlin, 1943, pp. 218ff.   **48.** The crucial importance of Stalin's March 1939 speech is emphasized by W.P. & Zelda Coates, *A History of Anglo-Soviet Relations*, London, 1944, p. 601, and A.S. Cardwell, *Poland and Russia: the Last Quarter Century*, New York, 1944, pp. 34ff.   **49.** Helmuth Griener, *Die Oberste Wehrmachtführing, 1939-1943*, Wiesbaden, 1951, pp. 51-52. Walther Hofer, *Die Entfesselung des Zweiten Weltkrieges*, 2nd. ed., Frankfurt a/M, 1960, pp. 68-71.   **50.** J.W. Wheeler-Bennet, *Nemesis of Power*, New York, 1954, pp. 446-449, W.L. Langer & S.E. Gleason, *The Challenge to Isolation, 1937-1940*, New York, 1952, pp. 181-182. **51.** *British Foreign Policy*, III, vol. 7, no. 314; for reliable records, see especially *Raeder Diary*, Washington, D.C., and the account by Admiral Boehm, Washington, D.C. **52.** *British Foreign Policy*, III, vol. 7, nos. 32, 35. **53.** *Ibid.*, no. 37. **54.** *Ibid.*, nos. 49, 141, 145. **55.** *Ibid.*, nos. 150, 152. **56.** General Doumenc in *Carrefour*, Paris, May 21, 1947. **57.** *British Foreign Policy*, III, vol. 7, nos. 164, 165, 198. **58.** *Les Événements survenus en France*, suppl. vol. 9, p. 2680; Georges Bonnet, *Fin d' une Europe*, Paris, 1948, pp. 297-301. **59.** *Ibid.*, pp. 301-302. **60.** *Ibid.*, 303-312. For an account of the previous French Defense Council meeting on March 13, 1939, *vide, Les Événements survenus en France*, vol. 2, pp. 255-256; G. Bonnet, *Le Quai d' Orsay sous trois Républiques, 1870-1961*, Paris, 1961, pp. 287-288, adds another vivid description of Gamelin's blunder. **61.** Général Maurice Gamelin, *Servir*, vol. 1, Paris, 1946, pp. 31,35; P. Reynaud, *La France a Sauvé l' Europe*, vol. 1, Paris, 1947, pp. 133, 589-491. **62.** *British Foreign Policy*, III, vol. 7, nos. 171, 173; London *Times*, Aug. 24, 1939; Bonnet, *op. cit.*, pp. 315-316. **63.** *French Yellow Book*, pp. 259-264. **64.** *Czas*, Aug. 23, 1939; New York *Times*, Aug. 23, 1939; L. Noël, *L'Agression Allemande contre la Pologne*, Paris, 1947, p. 424. **65.** *French Yellow Book*, pp. 259-264; New York *Times*, Aug. 23, 25, 1939. **67.** *German Foreign Policy*, D, vol. 7, nos. 202, 217, 218; *French Yellow Book*, p. 271. **67.** *German Foreign Policy*, D, vol. 7, no. 214; *French Yellow Book*, pp. 259f; *Documents on Events*, pp. 441f. **68.** *Völkischer Beobachter* (Munich), Aug. 21, 1939; *Polish White Book*, p. 103. Jacques Davignon, *Berlin, 1936-1940: Souvenirs d' une Mission*, Paris, 1951, pp. 135-136; *German Foreign Office Archives*, Serial 52b, pp. 35196-35199. **69.** *International Military Tribunal, 1945-1946*, vol.10, pp. 513-515; *Reports on Interrogations of German Prisoners-of-War, September 1945-September 1946*, ms., Hoover Institution, no. 1, pp. 12ff.; H. Schacht, *Abrechnung mit Hitler*, Berlin, 1948, pp. 139-140; *76 Jahre*, Bad Wörrishofen, 1953, pp. 512-513. **70.** A. de la Pradelle, *op. cit.*, pp. 16ff.; Hans Fritzsche, *The Sword in the Scales*, London, 1953, pp. 8-26. Taylor, *op. cit.*, p. 262, correctly emphasizes that the Russo-German pact was not an alliance; he argues less convincingly (Communist sources to the contrary are cited in A. de la Pradelle, *Le Marxisme Tentaculaire*, Issoudon, 1942, pp. 11 ff.) that the Soviet Union, like Hitler, did not expect war.

Chapter 19

1. Hans Grimm, *Warum-Woher-Aber Wohin?*, Lippoldsberg, 1954, pp. 340-344; Fritz Hesse, *Das Spiel um Deutschland*, Munich, 1953, pp. 183-184. Great Britain and France were even further away from Russia in 1914, but Russia, unlike Poland, was a Great Power with some prospect of defending herself. **2.** *British Foreign Policy*, III, vol. 7, no. 178. **3.** *German Foreign Office Archives*, Serial 259, pp. 169766-169769; *Documents on Events*, p. 461. **4.** *Ibid.*, p. 464; *British Blue Book*, p. 99. **5.** *British Foreign Policy*, III, vol. 7, no. 200; *British Blue Book*, p. 99. **6.** *German Foreign Policy*, D, vol. 7, no. 201; *British Foreign Policy*, III, vol. 7, no. 208; *Documents on Events*, p. 466. **7.** *German Foreign Policy*, D, vol. 7, no. 190; *Nazi Acts*, vol. 8, p. 701. **8.** *International Military Tribunal, 1945-1946*, vol. 9, pp. 457-460. **9.** *German Foreign Policy*, D, vol. 7, no. 74; F.J.P. Veale, *Advance to Barbarism*, Appleton, Wisc., 1953, pp. 116ff. **10.** *German Foreign Policy*, D, vol. 7, nos. 84, 85. **11.** *Ibid.*, no. 86. **12.** *ibid.*, no. 87. **13.** H. von Dirksen, *Moskau, Tokio, London*, Stuttgart, 1949, pp. 251ff.; J. Von Ribbentrop, *Zwischen London und Moskau*, Leoni, Bavaria, 1954, pp. 184-185; Hesse, *op. cit.*, pp. 195-202; Grimm, *op. cit.*, p. 317ff. **14.** *German Foreign Policy*, D, vol. 7, nos. 220, 221. **15.** *British Foreign Policy*, III, vol. 7, no. 236. Birger Dahlerus, *Sista Forsoeket*, Stockholm, 1945, pp. 73-76. **16.** *German Foreign Policy*, D, vol. 7, nos. 226, 227. **17.** *International Military Tribunal, 1945-1946*, vol. 9, p. 479; J. Lipski, *Stosunki Polsko-Niemieckie* in *Sprawy Miedzynarodowe*; no. 4, 1947; Anatole de Monzie, *Ci-Devant*, Paris, 1941, pp. 139-140. **18.** *German Foreign Policy*, D, vol. 7, nos. 231, 232, 235, 244, 254, 259. **19.** *Ibid.*, nos. 236, 237, 245; N. Horthy, *Memoirs*, New York, 1957, pp. 176-177. **20.** *German Foreign Policy*, D, vol. 7, nos. 238, 239, 247, 257, 258. **21.** *German Foreign Office Archives*, Serial 259, p. 169780; *Poland in the British Parliament*, vol. 1, New York, 1946, pp. 151-152. **22.** *Ibid.*, p. 157-169; Czeslaw Poznanski, *The Rights of Nations*, London, 1942, pp. 110ff. **23.** M. Sokolnicki, "Dzien 25 Sierpnia 1939" in *Wiadomosai*, London 2/23/47. **24.** *German Foreign Office Archives*, Serial 52b, pp. 35167-35171; *Foreign Relations of the United States, 1939*, vol. 1, pp. 361-362. **25.** *Nazi Acts*, vol. 4, pp. 460-461; *British Foreign Policy*, III, vol. 7, no. 192. **26.** *Ibid., nos.* 202, 317; Georges Bonnet, *Fin d' une Europe*, Geneva, 1948, pp. 291-292. **27.** *British Foreign Policy*, III, vol. 7, no. 212; Queen Victoria in May 1875 suggested to her daughter, the Crown Princess of Prussia, that it might be necessary for the nations of Europe to put down Bismarck as they had once put down Napoleon. **28.** *British Foreign Policy*, III, vol. 7, no. 222; Martin Gilbert and Richard Gatt, *The Appeasers*, Boston, 1963, pp. 271-275. **29.** *Ibid.*, nos. 183, 219, 241, 251. **30.** *Ibid.*, no. 248. **31.** *Ibid.*, nos. 236, 244, 250, 258; Gilbert and Gatt, *op. cit.*, pp. 252ff. **32.** *Italian Foreign Policy*, VIII, vol. 13, nos. 197, 202, 205. **33.** *British Foreign Policy*, III, vol. 7, nos. 261, 263, 268, 269; Bonnet, *op. cit.*, pp. 315-316. **34.** *British Foreign Policy*, III, vol. 7, nos. 270, 272, 280; General de Wiart was utterly disgusted with British policy and with the refusal of the British leaders to permit shipment of military supplies to Poland, see A.C. de Wiart, *Happy Odyssey*, London, 1950, pp. 156-159; he also noted Kennard's reputation for arrogance and for "being a difficult man," *Ibid.*, p. 154. de Wiart's French friends were embittered by British determination to wage a senseless war on behalf of Poland, *ibid.*, p. 160; de Wiart himself was of Walloon origin, and he tended to regard the Polish crisis from a continental viewpoint; he had lived many years in Poland, and he was especially conscious of the Bolshevik danger, *Ibid.*, pp. 99, 126, 153. **35.** *British Foreign Policy*, III, vol. 7, no. 285. **36.** *Italian Foreign Policy*, VIII, vol. 13, nos. 136, 214, 218. **37.** *International Military Tribunal, 1945-1946*, vol. 10, p.270; *Documents on Events*, pp. 468-470; *British Blue Book*, pp. 121-122; L.B. Namier, *Diplomatic Prelude*, London, 1948, pp. 329-331. A.J.P. Taylor, *The*

Origins of the Second World War, London, 1961, p. 264, doubts the seriousness of Hitler's decision to order operations for August 26, 1939. **38.** *British Foreign Policy*, III, vol. 7, no. 283. **39.** *Ibid.*, no. 284. **40.** *Foreign Relations of the United States, 1939*, vol. 1, p. 364; E. Kordt, *Nicht aus den Akten*, Stuttgart, 1950, p. 327. **41.** *German Foreign Office Archives*, Serial 52b, pp. 35178, 35199. **42.** E. Raczynski, *The British-Polish Alliance*, London, 1948, pp. 21-22. *Hansard's Parliamentary Debates, Commons*, Oct. 19, 1939; Taylor, *op. cit.*, pp. 269-270, incorrectly asserts that the British did not know the Italian position when the Anglo-Polish Alliance was signed on August 25, 1939. **43.** *German Foreign Office Archives*, Serial 52b, pp. 35185, 35187. **44.** *Ibid.*, p. 35193; *British Blue Book*, pp. 37-39. **45.** *British Foreign Policy*, III, vol. 7, no. 285. **46.** *French Yellow Book*, p. 267. **47.** *Ibid.*, pp. 267-268. R. Coulondre, *De Staline à Hitler*, Paris, 1950, pp. 287-288; Helmuth Greiner, *Die Oberste Wehrmachtführung, 1939-1943*, Wiesbaden, 1951, pp. 46-47. **48.** H.B. Gisevius, *To the Bitter End*, Boston, 1947, pp. 371-373; Kordt, *op. cit.*, p. 328; *French Yellow Book*, pp. 268-269. **49.** Greiner, *op. cit.*, p.50.

Chapter 20

1. J. Von Ribbentrop, *Zwischen London und Moskau*, Leoni, Bavaria, 1954, pp. 188-189. A.J.P. Taylor, *The Origins of the Second World War*, London, 1961, pp. 272-278, develops an elaborate argument to the effect that peace might have been saved in 1939 had Hitler offered to negotiate on August 28th instead of August 29th; this ignores the fact that Hitler's offer of August 29th was in response to an official British reply, very, very late on August 28th, to the German offer for an Anglo-German alliance made more than three days earlier; the British reply was not delivered to Hitler until 10:30 p.m., on August 28th; this British note contained the deceptive assurance that the Poles were willing to resume negotiations with Germany; in reality, the Poles opposed further negotiations with Germany and British Ambassador Kennard was permitted by Halifax to encourage their intransigent attitude; it would be far more to the point to argue that peace might have been saved had the British demanded that Warsaw resume negotiations at Berlin without further delay. **2.** A.J. Toynbee, *et al, The Eve of War, 1939*, London, 1958, pp. 509ff.; Viscount Chilston in 1958 had the audacity to claim that Germany in 1939 had "approached the apogee of her rearmament effort," *ibid.*, p. 680; actually, German arms production in 1939 was merely 18% of 1944, and German experts were fully aware of the military weakness of Germany, see Earl Beck, *Verdict on Schacht*, Tallahasee, 1955, pp. 143ff.; Norman Peterson, *Hjalmar Schacht*, Boston, 1954, pp. 296-297; C.F. Robinson, *Foreign Logistical Organizations and Methods*, Washington, D.C., 1947, *passim;* Burton Klein, *Germany's Economic Preparations for War*, Cambridge, Mass., 1959, *passim;* "Germany's Preparation for War: A Re-Examination" in *American Economic Review*, March, 1948; Ulrich Wilk, "Der Deutsche Rüstungsstand im Jahre 1939" in *Nation Europa*, May, 1959, pp. 7ff. **3.** Jan Szembek, *Journal*, Paris, 1952, p. 496; Martin Gilbert and Richard Gott, *The Appeasers*, Boston, 1963, pp. 280-281. **4.** *Foreign Relations of the United States, 1939*, vol.1, pp. 368-369. **5.** *Ibid.*, pp. 374-375, 378; *French Yellow Book*, p. 282; L. Noël, *L'Agression Allemande contre la Pologne*, Paris, 1947, p. 439. **6.** *French Yellow Book*, pp. 288-289; *British Blue Book*, pp. 95-96; P. Schmidt, *Statist auf diplomatischer Bühne*, Bonn, 1949, pp. 453-454; New York Times, Aug. 26, 1939. **7.** *German Foreign Policy*, D, vol.7, nos. 266, 271. **8.** *Ibid.*, nos. 277, 280, 282, 301. **9.** *Ibid.*, nos. 307, 317. **10.** *British Foreign Policy*, III, vol. 7, no. 305; G. Bonnet, *Fin d'une Europe*, Geneva, 1948, p. 321. **11.** *British Foreign Policy*, III, vol. 7, nos. 295, 307, 309. **12.** *Ibid.*, nos. 293, 306, 312. **13.** *Ibid.*, nos. 317, 318, 327. **14.** *German Foreign Policy*, D, vol. 7, no. 287. **15.** *British Foreign Policy*, III, vol. 7, no. 335. **16.** *Ibid.*, no. 333; *German Foreign Policy*, D, vol. 7, no.296. **17.** *Foreign Relations of the United States, 1939*, vol. 1, p. 377; *British Foreign Policy*, III, vol. 7, nos. 343, 344, 346. **18.** *Ibid.;* Walter Millis, ed., *The Forrestal Diaries*, New York, 1951, pp. 121-122; Edward Spears, *Assignment to Catastrophe*, vol. 1, New York, 1954, p. 3. **19.** *Ibid.*, pp. 3-4; A.P. Scotland, *The London Cage*, London, 1957, pp. 49-50. **20.** *German Foreign Policy*, D, vol. 7, no. 324; Bonnet, *op. cit.*, pp. 320-321; R. Coulondre, *De Staline à Hitler*, Paris, 1950, pp. 289-291. **21.** *German Foreign Office Archives*, Serial 52b, p. 35203; an Foreign Policy, D, vol. 7, nos. 300, 310. **22.** Coulondre, *op. cit.*, p.291. **23.** *Nazi Acts*, vol. 8, pp. 531-534; *Documents on Events*, pp. 476-477. **24.** *Italian Foreign Policy*, VIII, vol. 13, no. 329; *Nazi Acts*, vol. 4, p. 462; *German Foreign Policy*, D, vol. 7, nos. 358, 370; Coulondre, *op. cit.* p. 291; P.J.P. Veale, *Advance to Barbarism*, Appleton, 1953, pp. 124-138. **25.** *German Foreign Policy*, D, vol. 7, nos. 328, 378. **26.** *German Foreign Office Archives*, Serial 52b, p. 35213; *International Military Tribunal, 1945-1946*, vol. 10, p. 515. **27.** *German Foreign Policy*, D, vol. 7, no. 303; *British Foreign Policy*, III, vol. 7, no. 349; *International Military Tribunal, 1945-1946*, vol. 9, p. 462; Birger Dahlerus, *Sista Forsoeket*, Stockholm, 1945, pp. 80-81. **28.** *German Foreign Policy*, D, vol. 7, no. 312; *British Foreign Policy*, III, vol. 7, no. 349; *Nazi Acts*, vol. 5, p. 42. **29.** *British Foreign Policy*, III, vol. 7, nos. 349, 402. **30.** *Ibid.*, no. 354; *German Foreign Policy*, D, vol. 7, nos. 344, 345, 349, 350, 361. **31.** *British Foreign Policy*, III, vol. 7, nos. 357, 365, 367, 371, 372. **32.** *Ibid.*, nos. 373, 397. **33.** *Ibid.*, no. 397. **34.** *German Foreign Policy*, D, vol. 7, nos. 363, 367. **35.** *Ibid.*, nos. 383, 387, 425. **36.** *British Foreign Policy*, III, vol. 7, no. 409; New York Times, Aug. 26, 1939. **37.** *German Foreign Office Archives*, Serial 52b, p. 35316; *British Foreign Policy*, III, vol. 7, nos. 411, 420; J. Beck, *Dernier Rapport*, Neuchatel, 1949, p. 215. William L. Shirer, *The Rise and Fall of the Third Reich: A History of Nazi Germany*, New York, 1960, p. 575. **38.** *British Foreign Policy*, III, vol. 7, no. 410; Bonnet, *op. cit.*, pp. 323-324. **39.** *British Foreign Policy*, III, vol. 7, nos. 418, 435. **40.** *Ibid.*, nos. 421, 426. **41.** *International Military Tribunal, 1945-1946*, vol. 9, pp. 462-466; *British Blue Book*, pp. 126-128; *French Yellow Book*, p. 296; Dahlerus, *op. cit.*, pp. 89-107. **42.** *Ibid.*, p. 170ff.; *British Foreign Policy*, III, vol. 7, no. 455; *French Yellow Book*, p. 296. **43.**

British Blue Book, p. 128. At the British Foreign Office, the minutes of Kirkpatrick on Henderson's report were the least negative; he stated that a peaceful settlement would be bad for Great Britain, but it might work; Sargent claimed that Hitler's real aim was the disintegration of Poland; Halifax insisted one had to be on guard against the consequences of a peaceful solution; he stressed the advantage that Mussolini had been effectively separated from Hitler, which was not true, he hastened to add, at the time of the Munich conference; he declared that peace might be impossible unless the Nazi regime was overthrown, but that one's attitude "should not be conclusive"; Vansittart insisted that Hitler was seeking to destroy both Poland and the British Empire, v*ide* DBFP, III, vol. 7, no. 455. **44.** *Ibid.*, p. 130; *British Foreign Policy*, III, vol. 7, no. 462. **45.** *Ibid.*, no. 422. **46.** *German Foreign Policy*, D, vol. 7, nos. 395, 398, 411, 415. **47.** *Ibid.*, nos. 417, 418. **48.** *British Foreign Policy*, III, vol. 7, no. 456. **49.** *Ibid.*, nos. 470, 472. **50.** *Ibid.*, nos. 472, 473, 475. **51.** *Ibid.*, nos. 476, 477, 487. **52.** *Ibid.*, no. 478; *German Foreign Policy*, D, vol. 7, nos. 421, 423. **53.** *British Foreign Policy*, III, vol. 7, nos. 482, 489, 492. **54.** *Documents on Events*, pp. 480-482; Franz Halder, *The Halder Diaries*, Washington, D.C., 1950, p. 36. **55.** *German Foreign Policy*, D, vol. 7, no. 431. **56.** *British Foreign Policy*, III, vol. 7, no. 490. Bonnet, *op. cit.*, pp. 327-8. **57.** *British Foreign Policy*, III, vol. 7, no. 493; *French Yellow Book*, p.p. 297-298, 301; Coulondre, *op. cit.*, pp. 297-298; N. Henderson, *Failure of a Mission*, New York, 1940, p. 281; G. Craig & F. Gilbert, *The Diplomats, 1919-1939*, Princeton, 1953, p. 555; L. B. Namier, *Europe in Decay*, London, 1950, pp. 42-43. **57.** *British Foreign Policy*, III, vol. 7, no. 493; **58.** *British Foreign Policy*, III, vol. 7, no. 495. **59.** *Ibid.*, nos. 497, 505, 512; *British Blue Book*, pp. 140-141; *Polish White Book*, pp. 107-108. **60.** *British Blue Book*, p. 141. **61.** *British Foreign Policy*, III, vol. 7, nos. 501, 509. Gordon Craig, *et al, The Diplomats*, Princeton, New Jersey, 1953, pp. 537-554. **62.** *Ibid.*, no. 510.

Chapter 21

1. J. von Ribbentrop, *Zwischen London und Moskau*, Leoni, Bavaria, 1954, pp. 189-191. **2.** *German Foreign Office Archives*, Serial 52b, p. 35342; *German Foreign Policy*, D, vol. 7, no. 451. Helmut Sündermann, *Alter Feind — was nun?* Leoni, 1956, p. 85. **3.** *German Foreign Office Archives*, Serial 52b, pp. 35358-35359. **4.** *Ibid.*, p. 35377. **5.** *Ibid.*, p. 35377. **6.** *Ibid.*, no. 519. **7.** *British Blue Book*, p. 145. **8.** *German Foreign Policy*, D, vol. 7, nos. 445, 450. **9.** *Foreign Relations of the United States, 1939*, vol. 1, p. 392. **10.** *German Foreign Policy*, D, vol. 7, nos. 441, 446, 456. **11.** *British Foreign Policy*, III, vol. 7, nos. 520, 529. **12.** *Ibid.*, nos. 523, 532, 537. **13.** *German Foreign Office Archives*, Serial 52b, pp. 35349-35355. **14.** *French Yellow Book*, p. 300. **15.** *Foreign Relations of the United States, 1939*, vol. 1, pp. 394-395; J. Lipski, *Stosunki Polsko-Niemiecke* in *Sprawy Miedzynarodowe*, 4, London, 1947, p. 47. **16.** *Ibid.*, pp. 47-48; *British Foreign Policy*, III, vol. 7, no. 538. **17.** *Ibid.*, no. 539; *International Military Tribunal, 1945-1946*, vol. 9, p. 468. **18.** *British Foreign Policy*, III, vol. 7, nos. 543, 545, 546, 551; N. Henderson, *Failure of a Mission*, New York, 1940, pp. 282-283. **19.** *British Foreign Policy*, III, vol. 7, nos. 563, 565; W.L. White, *Report on the Germans*, New York, 1947, pp. 24ff. **20.** *British Foreign Policy*, III, vol. 7, no. 568. **21.** *Ibid.*; Frederic R. Sanborn, *Design for War*, New York, 1951, p. 83. **22.** *German Foreign Office Archives*, Serial 2130, pp. 465764-465869. **23.** *Ibid.*, Serial 2131, pp. 466053-466155. **24.** *International Military Tribunal, 1945-1946*, vol. 10, pp. 368, 515; L.B. Namier, *Diplomatic Prelude*, London, 1947, pp. 349-351. **25.** *W Sprawie Przemian etnicznych Pomorza Zachodniego* in *Studia i Materialy do Dziejów Wielkopolski i Pomorza*, vol. 1, Poznan, 1955, pp. 321ff.; see also F. Lorenz, A. Fischer, T. Lehr-Splawinski, *The Cassubian Civilization*, London, 1935, pp. 297ff.; H. Recke, *West Prussia in Germany and Poland*, Munich, 1934; F. Heisz, G. Lohse, W. Wucher, *Deutschland und der Korridor*, Berlin, 1939, pp. 21ff. **26.** *Polish White Book*, pp. 121-123; O. Benson, *Through the Diplomatic Looking-Glass*, Norman, Oklahoma, 1939, p. 188. **27.** *International Military Tribunal, 1945-1946*, vol. 10, pp. 197-199, 367. A.J.P. Taylor, *The Origins of the Second World War*, London, 1946, p. 274, asserts that Ribbentrop was under no obligation to show the copy of the proposals to Henderson because it was a "rough draft" containing emendations by Hitler. **28.** *Ibid.*; *British Foreign Policy*, III, vol. 7, no. 574. **29.** *Ibid.*, no. 575; *International Military Tribunal, 1945-1946*, vol. 9, p. 491. **30.** *British Foreign Policy*, III, vol. 7, nos. 576, 577. **31.** *German Foreign Policy*, D, vol. 7, no. 466. **32.** *International Military Tribunal, 1945-1946*, vol. 9, pp. 469-470; Lipski, *op. cit.*, p. 49. **33.** *German Foreign Policy*, D, vol. 7, nos. 458, 467, 474. **34.** *International Military Tribunal, 1945-1946*, vol. 9, p. 470; *British Blue Book*, pp. 146-147; Bonnet, *Fin d'une Europe*, Geneva, 1948, p. 330. **35.** *International Military Tribunal, 1945-1946*, vol. 9, pp. 470-497. **36.** *Nazi Acts*, vol. 6, pp. 935-936, 978; H.B. Gisevius, *To the Bitter End*, Boston, 1947, p. 376. **37.** O. Halecki, *Eugenio Pacelli: Pope of Peace*, New York, 1951, pp. 92-95. **38.** *Ibid.*, pp. 95-96, 103. **39.** *Ibid.*, pp. 111-117; Jozef Beck, *Dernier Rapport*, Neuchatel, 1949, pp. 212-213. **40.** *Italian Foreign Policy*, VIII, vol. 13, nos. 483, 484, 487. **41.** *Ibid.*, no. 580. **42.** *Ibid.*, no. 515. Bonnet, *op. cit.*, p. 330. **43.** R. Guariglia, *Ricordi, 1922-1946*, Naples, 1949, pp. 361-407. **44.** *British Foreign Policy*, III, vol. 7, no. 581. **45.** *Ibid.*, no. 589. **46.** *Ibid.*, nos. 589, 591, 600. **47.** *German Foreign Office Archives*, Serial 52b, pp. 35381-35382; *German Foreign Policy*, D, vol. 7, no. 475; *International Military Tribunal, 1945-1946*, vol. 9, p. 470; *British Foreign Policy*, III, vol. 7, no. 600; *Foreign Relations of the United States, 1939*, vol. 1, p. 396; L. Nöel, *L'Agression Allemande contra la Pologne*, Paris, 1947, pp. 446-447; Lipski, *op. cit.*, p. 51. **48.** *German Foreign Office Archives*, Serial 52b, p. 35389; *German Foreign Policy*, D, vol. 7, no. 476. Lipski, *op. cit.*, p. 51. **49.** *British Foreign Policy*, III, vol. 7, no. 608. **50.** *Italian Foreign Policy*, VIII, vol. 13, no. 507; *German Foreign Policy*, D, vol. 7, no. 478. **51.** *Ibid.*, no. 480. *Foreign Relations of the United States: The Soviet Union, 1933-1939*, p. 783. **52.** *German Foreign Policy*, D, vol. 7, no. 482. **53.** *Documents on Events*, pp. 490-491. **54.** *German Foreign Policy*, D, vol. 7, no. 485. **55.** *International Military Tribunal, 1945-*

1946, vol. 10, p. 276. **56.** Bonnet, *op. cit.*, p. 284.

Chapter 22

1. Hans Grimm, *Warum-Woher-Aber Wohin?* Lippoldsberg, 1954, p. 374. **2.** *German Foreign Policy*, D, vol. 7, no. 508. **3.** *Ibid.*, nos. 487, 500, 559; *Italian Foreign Policy*, VIII, vol. 13, no. 542; *British Foreign Policy*, III, vol. 7, no. 621. **4.** *Ibid.*, nos. 619, 628. **5.** *Ibid.*, nos. 629, 631. **6.** *Italian Foreign Policy*, VIII, vol. 13, nos. 504, 507. **7.** *Ibid.*, nos. 510, 519. **8.** *Schulthess, 1939*, Munich, 1949, pp. 164-169; *Italian Foreign Policy*, VIII, vol. 13, no. 607. **9.** *Ibid.*, no. 536; *German Foreign Office Archives*, Serial 52c, pp. 35441-35442. **10.** *German Foreign Policy*, D, vol. 7, no. 501. **11.** *British Foreign Policy*, III, vol. 7, nos. 627, 632. **12.** *German Foreign Policy*, D, vol. 7, no. 498. **13.** *British Foreign Policy*, III, vol. 7, no. 639. **14.** Edmund Jan Osmánczyk, *Dowody Prowokacji: Nieznane Archiwum Himmlera*, Kraków, 1951, pp. 19-22, 35ff.; Osmanczyk also stressed the allegedly "barbarous American atrocities in Korea," part II, p. 48ff.; see also *Nazi Acts*, vol. 8, pp. 580-581, and J. Stipp, *Devil's Diary*, Yellow Springs, 1955, pp. 135-136. The preposterous and contradictory Lahousen testimony and the fantastic and pitiful extorted Alfred Naujocks affidavit, both equally unreliable, were part of the unsuccessful efforts at the Nuremberg trials to prove Germany guilty of the Gleiwitz incident; the prosecution also attempted to prove German guilt from the routine procedure of Canaris prior to the outbreak of hostilities in obtaining a quantity of Polish uniforms for use in possible wartime operations. **15.** Eberhard von Zalewski, editor of *Gleiwitzer und Beuthener Heimatblatt*, has received many accounts of this incident from German expellees; the recent effort of Jürgen Runzheimer, *"Der Überfall auf den Sender Gleiwitz im Jahre 1939,"* in *Vierteljahreshefte für Zeitgeschichte*, October, 1962, is notably unsatisfactory; he shows that the Nuremberg witness, Naujocks, was unreliable, but he fails to bring conclusive new evidence. **16.** *British Foreign Policy*, III, vol. 7, no. 644. **17.** *Ibid.*, nos. 651, 652. **18.** *German Foreign Office Archives*, Serial 52c, pp. 35439-35440. **19.** *Ibid.*, pp. 35431-35436; Hans Wendt, *Frankreich Heute und Wir*, Berlin, 1939, pp. 440ff. **20.** *Hansard's Parliamentary Debates, Lords*, September 1, 1939; *German Foreign Office Archives*, Serial 52c, pp. 35440ff. **21.** Georges Bonnet, *Fin d'une Europe*, Geneva, 1948, pp. 327-332, 337. **22.** *Ibid.*, pp. 338-347; *Italian Foreign Policy*, VIII, vol. 13, nos. 530, 542. **23.** *German Foreign Office Archives*, Serial 52c, p. 35406; *British Foreign Policy*, III, vol. 7, nos. 648, 655. **24.** *German Foreign Office Archives*, Serial 52c, p. 35418; *German Foreign Policy*, D, vol. 7, nos. 530, 531. **25.** *British Foreign Policy*, III, vol. 7, nos. 646, 657. **26.** *Ibid.*, no. 663. **27.** *Ibid.*, no. 669; Bonnet, *op. cit.*, pp. 349-350; R. Coulondre, *De Staline à Hitler*, Paris, 1950, p. 312; Martin Gilbert and Richard Gott, *The Appeasers*, Boston, 1963, pp. 309-310. **28.** *British Foreign Policy*, III, vol. 7, nos. 684, 689; *German Foreign Policy*, D, vol. 7, no. 513. **29.** *British Foreign Policy*, III, vol. 7, no. 675. There were actually two such suggestions from Halifax, one at 10 p.m., on August 31st, and a second at 12:50 a.m., on September 1st., *vide*, DBFP, III, vol. 7, nos. 616, 675. **30.** *German Foreign Policy*, D, vol. 7, nos. 515, 519, 520, 522, 533. **31.** *Italian Foreign Policy*, VIII, vol. 13, nos. 541, 559. **32.** *British Foreign Policy*, III, vol. 7, nos. 621, 677, 679. **33.** *Italian Foreign Policy*, VIII, vol. 13, nos. 540, 543. **34.** *Ibid.*, no. 571; Bonnet, *op. cit.*, pp. 353-354. **35.** *Italian Foreign Policy*, VIII, vol. 13, nos. 572, 574; *German Foreign Policy*, D, vol. 7, no. 539. **36.** Bonnet, *op. cit.*, pp. 354-355. **37.** *Italian Foreign Policy*, VIII, vol. 13, nos. 574, 581, 584; *German Foreign Policy*, D, vol. 7, no. 541; Massimo Magistrah, *L'Italia a Beriino, 1937-1939*, Milan, 1956, pp. 447ff.; *British Foreign Policy*, III, vol. 7, no. 710. **38.** Bonnet, *op. cit.*, pp. 356-358. **39.** *Ibid.*, pp. 358-359; *British Foreign Policy*, III, vol. 7, no. 693. **40.** *German Foreign Office Archives*, Serial 52c, pp. 35492-35493. **41.** *Ibid.*, pp. 35498-35505; A. Mallet, *Pierre Laval*, vol. 1, Paris, 1955, pp. 133ff.; J. E. Howard, *Parliament and Foreign Policy in France*, London, 1948, pp. 131-132. **42.** *British Foreign Policy*, III, vol. 7, nos. 694, 699, 700, 704, 705, 708; *Foreign Relations of the United States, 1939*, vol. 1, pp. 408-409; Bonnet, *op. cit.*, p. 356. **43.** *British Foreign Policy*, III, vol. 7, nos. 709, 710. **44.** *Ibid.*, nos. 711, 713; Anatole de Monzie, *Ci-devant*, Paris, 1941, p. 150. **45.** *British Foreign Policy*, III, vol. 7, no. 718. **46.** *Ibid.*, nos. 721, 727. **47.** *Ibid.*, nos. 714, 728, 732; W. Churchill, *The Gathering Storm*, Boston, 1948, pp. 406-407; Gilbert and Gott, *op. cit.*, p. 314. **48.** *German Foreign Office Archives*, Serial 52c, pp. 35481-35483. **49.** Luigi Villari, *Liberation of Italy*, Appleton, Wisc., 1959, p. 2. **50.** *British Foreign Policy*, III, vol. 7, no. 729. **51.** *Ibid.*, no. 734; *Italian Foreign Policy*, VIII, vol. 13, no. 589; E. von Manstein, *Verlorene Siege*, Bonn, 1955, pp. 35-42. **52.** Bonnet, *op. cit.*, pp. 360-362. **53.** *Italian Foreign Policy*, VIII, vol. 13, no. 616. **54.** *British Foreign Policy*, III, vol. 7, no. 739; Viscount Norwich, *Old Men Forget*, London, 1953, p. 259; Hugh Dalton, *Memoirs*, vol. 2, London, 1957, pp. 264-265; L. S. Amery, *My Political Life*, vol. 3, London, 1955, p. 234; Gilbert and Gott, *op. cit.*, pp. 315-317. **55.** *British Foreign Policy*, III, vol. 7, no. 740. **56.** Churchill, *op. cit.*, pp. 384, 407. **57.** *British Foreign Policy*, III, vol. 7, no. 741. **58.** *German Foreign Policy*, D, vol. 7, no. 558.

Bibliography

I. Documents

All About Poland: Facts, Figures, Documents. J. H. Retinger, ed., London, 1940. (Reliable collection of basic material.)

Annales de la Chambre des Députés: Débats Parlementaires. Vol. 152ff., Paris, 1934-1939. (Especially important for French foreign policy debates in Jan. 1936, Oct. 1938, Mar. 1939, Sept. 1939.)

Armaments Year-Book: General and Statistical Information. League of Nations, Geneva, 1940. (Suggestive but inaccurate and unreliable.) *Baedeker's Northern Germany.* 17th revised edition, Leipzig, 1925. (Useful statistics and maps of the German-Polish borderlands.)

Beck, J. *Beiträge zur europäischen Politik: Reden, Erklärungen, Interviews, 1932-1939.* Essen, 1939. (Excellent on speeches of the Polish foreign minister; a small sampling of newspaper interviews.)

Blum, Léon. *L'Exercice du Pouvoir: Discours Prononcés de Mai 1936 à Janvier 1937.* Paris, 1937. (The official public statements of Blum the first time that he was Premier.)

British War Blue Book: Documents Concerning German-Polish Relations and the Outbreak of Hostilities between Great Britain and Germany on September 3, 1939. (Contains some material not available in later British publications.)

Campaign in Poland [classified and restricted]. West Point, New York, 1943. (Expert appraisal of Polish and German plans for war in 1939 with special tribute to the German operational plan.)

Carnets Secrets de Jean Zay, Sept. 1938-Sept. 1939. Philippe Henriot, ed.; Paris, 1942. (Excellent for the secret record of crucial French cabinet meetings with special tribute to the German operational plan.)

Ce Que le Monde n'a pas voulu: les Offres de Paix faites par Hitler entre 1933 et 1939. Brussels, 1940. (Useful compendium of German proposals for agreements with Great Britain and France.)

Chamberlain, N. *In Search of Peace.* New York, 1939. (Collection of speeches by the British Prime Minister, 1937-1939.)

Ciano, Galeazzo. *The Ciano Diaries, 1939-1943.* New York, 1946 (Useful but sketchy account of the Jan.-Sept. 1939 period, possibly altered and deleted.)

Ciano, Galeazzo. *Diario, 1937-1938.* Rome, 1948. (Reliable and extremely interesting source on Italian policy.)

Ciano, Galeazzo. *L'Europa verso la Catastrofe: la Storia d'Europa dal 1936 al 1942.* Rome, 1948. (Useful selected papers; see also English language version: *Ciano's Diplomatic Papers,* M. Muggeridge, ed., London, 1948.

Le Congrès de Vienne et les Traités de 1815, 3 vols. Comte d'Angeberg, ed., Paris, 1864. (Record of 1815 peacemaking from the French archives published by order of Napoleon III after the 1863 Polish uprising.)

Congressional Record, House of Representatives, Senate, 1937-1939. Washington, D.C. (Also selected items from World War II and post World War II periods, i.e. rpt. no. 1841, *81st United States Congress, re* number of Germans in Eastern Europe, etc.; especially useful for petitions concerning European affairs.)

Czy Wiesz Kto to Jest? Warsaw, 1938. (Biographical information on Polish officials and scholars.)

Deutschland-England, 1933-1939: die Dokumente des deutschen Friedens-willens. Essen, 1943, 4th. ed. (Collection of speeches and exchanges between German and British leaders.)

Demokratenpresse im lichte Prager Geheimakten. Rudolf Urban, ed., Prague, 1943. (Reports concerning Czech bribes to the French press, from the Czech diplomatic archives.)

Documents on British Foreign Policy, 1919-1939, 3rd series, vols. 1-7. E. Woodward & R. Butler, eds., London, 1949-1955. (Indispensable for British policy and far more revealing than official British published documents on the pre-1914 period.)

Documents on the Events Preceding the Outbreak of the War. (German White Book). New York, 1940. (Deletes anti-Soviet passages in official dispatches, otherwise accurate; contains much valuable material not included in later publication of German documents.)

Documents on German Foreign Policy, 1918-1945, series D, vols. 1-7. Washington, D.C., 1949-1956; (Indispensable for German Foreign Office, but of limited value in study of Hitler's policy because of failure to include DNB reports which furnished most of his information on events from abroad.)

Documents on Polish-Soviet Relations, 1939-1945, vol. 1, London, 1961. (The early section contains a useful collection of primary sources on Russo-Polish relations after 1918.)

Dokumente der Deutschen Politik, 7 vols. Berlin, 1940. (Contains important official documents on German Policy.)

Dokumente Polnischer Grausamkeit. German Foreign Office, Berlin, 1940. (Record of official Polish terror against the German minority which began before the outbreak of World War II.)

Dokumente über die Alleinschuld Englands am Bombenkrieg gegen die Zivilbevölkerung. Berlin, 1943. (Vital information on British plans in 1938 and 1939 to attack German civilians; all documents are from the French archives.)

Dokumenti e Materiali Konuna Vtroroi Mirovoi Voyni, 2 vols. Moscow, 1948. (Documents from confiscated German archives, and especially the reports of Herbert von Dirksen, German Ambassador in London.)

Dziennik Ustaw Rzeczypospolitej Polskiej. Warsaw, 1937-1939. (Contains laws enacted in Poland; especially useful for agrarian reform decrees involving the German minority.)

The Effects of Strategic Bombing on the German War Economy. U.S. Strategic Bombing Survey, Washington, D.C., 1945. (Useful information on the increase of German war production despite bombing attacks, and revelation of how Germany was slow to utilize her industrial military potential.)

Die Entstehung des Krieges von 1939. Archive Comm., German FO, vol. 1. *Roosevelts Weg in den Krieg: Geheimdokumente zur Kriegspolitik des Präsidenten der Vereinigten Staaten*. Berlin, 1943. (Revelation of Roosevelt's hostile intentions toward Germany after 1933, from French diplomatic archives.)

Europäische Politik, 1933-1938, im Spiegel der Prager Akten. F. Berber, ed., Essen, 1942. (Indispensable collection of excerpts from reports of Czech diplomats abroad.)

Les Événements survenus en France de 1933 à 1945, 11 vols. (series a, 2 vols., series b, 9 vols.) Parl. Comm. of Inquiry, Paris, 1947-1951. (Containing testimony and interrogation of the principal French political and military leaders; indispensable for French policy.)

Exchange of Communications between the President of the United States and the Chancellor of the German Reich, April 1939, New York, 1939. (The Roosevelt telegram of April 15, 1939, and Hitler's reply.)

Foreign Relations of the United States: the Soviet Union, 1933-1939. Washington, D.C., 1952; vol. 1, *1938: General*; vol. 2, *1938: British Empire, Europe, Near East, Africa*, Washington, D.C., 1955; vol. 1, *1939: General; British Empire, Europe*, Washington, D.C., 1956. (Extensive information on American policy in Europe, and the official American interpretation of European events.)

The French Yellow Book. New York, 1939. (The most extensive of the World War II "colored" books; especially useful for the reports of André François-Poncet, French Ambassador to Germany.)

German Foreign Office Archives (Photo Blowups, Hoover Institution):

I. *Akten betreffend: Polen, vom 23. April 1938 bis 30. Juni 1939*. Serial 52a.

II. *Akten betreffend: Polen, vom 1. Juli 1939 bis 31. August 1939* · Serial 52b.

III. *Akten betreffend: den Krieg mit Polen, England, Frankreich, vom 1. September 1939 bis 10. September 1939* · Serial 52c.

IV. *Polen, 1937-1938* · Büro des Staatssekretärs, Serial 145.

V. *Akten betreffend: Russland vom Januar 1939 bis 31. Oktober 1939* · Serial 103.

VI. *Akten betreffend: Deutsch-Französische Beziehungen vom 22. Oktober 1938 bis 18. Juni 1940* · Serial 121.

VII. *Akten betreffend: Deutsch-Englische Beziehungen vom 1. Mai 1939 bis 18. Juni 1940* · Serial 259.

VIII. *Akten betreffend: Halifax-Besuch und seine Folgen von November 1937 bis 30. April 1939*. Serial 375.

IX. *Akten betreffend: Verhältnisse in Polen, 1939*. Serials 908, 909, 910.

X. *Akten betreffend: Verhältnisse in Polen, 1938-1939*. Serial 284.

Deutsche Botschaft Moskau: Akten betreffend Polen, 1938-1939, Serial 461.

Deutsche Botschaft Rom: 1939 Geheim-Akten. (The unpublished documents of the above serials are absolutely crucial for any study of German policy relative to the origins of World War II.)

Gottwald, K. *Ausgewählte Reden und Aufsätze.* Berlin, 1955. (Important source for Czech Communist ideas during the Beneš era.)

Halder, Franz. *The Halder Diaries.* Washington, D.C., 1950. (Contains only a few brief entries on the period prior to World War II.)

Hansard's Parliamentary Debates, Commons, Lords, vols. 323-351, Ap. 26, 1937-Oct. 5, 1939. London, 1937-1939. (Vital for the public debate on British foreign policy and for the official propaganda of the British leaders.)

The History of the Times, vol. 4: *The 150th Anniversary and Beyond, 1912-1948,* Part II, *1921-1948.* New York, 1952. (Important analysis of the close relationship with official British policy.)

Hitler, Adolf. *Der Hitler-Prozess, February 26, 1924–April 1, 1924.* Potsdam, 1934. (Important for Hitler's ideas about German developments since 1918.)

Hitler, Adolf. *Mein Kampf,* 2 vols. Munich, 1925-1927. (Contains Hitler's early basic program; some of it, for instance, relations with France, was later modified.)

Hitler, Adolf. *Die Südtiroler Frage und das deutsche Bündnis-problem,* Munich, 1926. (Hitler's early attempt to explain his Italian policy.)

Der Hochverratprozess gegen Dr. Guido Schmidt vor dem Wiener Volksgericht: die Gerichtlichen Protokolle mit den Zeugenaussagen, unveröffentlichen Dokumenten, sämtlichen Geheimbriefen und Geheimakten. Vienna, 1947. (Indispensable for Austro-German relations, 1934-1938.)

I Documenti Diplomatici Italiani, 8th. series, vols. 12, 13. Rome, 1952. (The documents on Italian relations with Germany, Great Britain, and France are necessary for any study of European diplomatic relations on the eve of World War II.)

The Intimate Papers of Colonel House, 2 vols. London, 1926. (Vital for the American role in shaping the Versailles settlement.)

Journal Officiel de la République Française: Débats de l'Assemblée Nationale Constituante. Paris, 1945-1946. (Especially important for the speeches of Daladier and other French leaders from the 1939 period.)

Krasny-Archiv: istoricheski zhurnal. Moscow, 1938-1939. (Contains official Soviet documents and analyses of foreign policy problems.)

Litvinov, M. *Against Aggression.* London, 1939. (Collection of speeches illustrating clever use of collective security concepts as a means of advancing Soviet interests.)

Mussolini, Benito. *Opera Omnia di Benito Mussolini,* vols. 25-29 (March 1931-June 1940). Florence, 1958-1959. (Contains the principal speeches and newspaper editorials of the Duce.)

Nazi Conspiracy and Aggression, 8 vols. and 2 supplementary vols. Washington, D.C., 1946-1948. (Contains many documents on military and foreign policy not published elsewhere; the documents are not in topical nor chronological sequence.)

Nazi-Soviet Relations, 1939-194, 2 vols. Washington, D.C., 1948. (The first section of these German diplomatic documents concerns the negotiation which produced the Russo-German pact of August 23, 1939.)

New Documents on the History of Munich. New York, 1958. (Especially important for Czecho-Soviet relations.)

Der Nürnberger Prozess, 2 vols. P.A. Steiniger, ed., Berlin, 195?. (Carefully arranged selection of crucial documentary material.)

Official Documents Concerning Polish-German and Polish-Soviet Relations, 1933-1939. London, 1940. (Polish White Book containing reports from envoys and German-Polish conversations.)

Ostland-Berichte. Ostland Institut, Danzig, 1937-1939. (Especially important for an analysis of Polish policy and the Polish press in three years.)

Ostpreussen. O.P. Landsmannschaft, Göttingen, 1947. (Vital statistics on the role and importance of East Prussia in the German economy prior to World War Two.)

Piłsudski, Józef. *Pisma Zbiorowe Józefa Piłsudskiego,* 10 vols. Warsaw, 1937-1938. (Including collected writings and many speeches; indispensable for the study of Piłsudski's ideas and his impact on Poland; see also: *Wybor Pism*, W. Jedrzejewicz, ed., New York, 1942, for one volume of excerpts from the collected works.)

Poland in the British Parliament, 1939-1945, Vol. 1. W. Jedrzejewicz, ed., New York, 1946. (Convenient excerpts concerning Poland from *Hansard's Parliamentary Debates*.)

Polish Documents Relative to the Origin of the War, 1st. series. Berlin 1940. (Documents from the Polish archives illuminating the official American effort to prevent Poland from concluding an agreement with Germany in 1938 or 1939.)

Polish Facts and Figures, nos. 1-8. New York, 1944. (Useful but often misleading statistics concerning Polish minority and economic problems.)

Politik des 20. Jahrhunderts, 3 vols. Adam Buckreis, ed., Nürnberg, 1937-1940. (Useful, detailed outline, especially volume 3: *Weltgeschichte, 1939*.)

Polska a Zagranica, 1934-1939. Ciechanowski collection, Hoover Institution. (Reports from the Polish Foreign Office to foreign missions containing valuable analyses of foreign policy problems; provides an indispensable insight into the official Polish evaluation of foreign countries and their problems.)

Polskie Siły Zbrojne w drugeij wojnie swiatowey, vol. 1: *Kampania wrzesniowa, 1939*. Historical Comm. of the Polish General Staff, London, 1951. (Vital source for Polish military plans in 1939 and criticism of Polish, German, British, and French operations.)

Le Procès Benoist-Méchin: Compte Rendu Intégral des Débats. Jean-Louis Aujol, ed., Paris, 1948. (Valuable source for the attitudes of French intellectuals and scholars toward foreign affairs in the period 1933-1939.)

Le Procès de Riom. Maurice Ribet, ed., Paris, 1945. (Especially important for French military planning prior to World War II.)

Raeder, Erich. *Reflections of the Commander-in-Chief, Navy, on the Outbreak of War, September 3, 1939*, ms. Washington, D.C. (English language version of a vital memorandum; reflects Hitler's surprise at the British declaration of war.)

Report on Danzig. Geneva, 1940. (General statement by C.J. Burckhardt, the last League High Commissioner.)

Reports on Interrogations of German Prisoners-of-War, Made by Members of the Department of State Special Interrogation Mission, Sept. 1945-Sept. 1946, ms. Hoover Institution. (Contains important interviews with German leaders not available in published sources.)

Sammlung der Dokumente zum Reichsstreit Danzig-Gdingen: Ausnutzung des Hafens von Danzig durch Polen. Geneva, 1931. (Vital docunents on Polish economic discrimination against Danzig in favor of Gdynia.)

Sammlung der Gesetz und Verordnungen der Tschecho-Slovakischen Republik und des Protektorates Böhmen und Mähren, 1939. Prague, 1939-1940. (Basic for German policy in Bohemia-Moravia after March 1939.)

Schulthess' Europäischer Geschichtskalender, 1937, 1938, 1939. vols. 78-80. Munich, 1938-1940. (Valuable compendium of speeches, debates, and newspaper reports from the principal countries of Europe prior to World War II.)

Slavonic Encyclopedia, J. Roucek, ed., New York, 1949. (Contains much useful biographical information.)

Soviet Documents on Foreign Policy, 3 vols. Jane Degras, ed., London, 1951-1953. (English language version of official Russian documents from *Krasny Arkhiv* and the Russian newspaper press.)

The Speeches of Adolf Hitler, April 1922-August 1939, 2 vols. Norman H. Baines, ed., London, 1942. (Useful collection of Hitler's speeches; most of the key speeches are condensed and many important passages have been eliminated.)

Sprawy Polskie w Procesie Norymberskim. T. Cyprian & J. Sawicki, eds., Poznań, 1956. (Useful excerpts concerning Poland from the published documents on the Nuremberg trials.)

The Statesman's Year-Book, 1939. London, 1939. (Useful guide to the constitutional systems and national resources of European countries prior to World War II.)

Statistik des Deutschen Reiches, vol. 552. Berlin, 1939. (Contains valuable information from the German census of May 1938.)

Szembek, Jan. *Journal, 1933-1939*. Paris, 1951. (The edited record of the Polish Under-Secretary for Foreign Affairs; contains valuable information on conferences at the Polish Foreign Office.)

Tiso, Jozef. *Die Wahrheit über die Slowakei: Verteidigungsrede vor dem "National"-Gericht in Bratislava, 17 & 18 März 1947*. Munich, 1951. (Slovakian leader's defense of his policy in 1939 and of his country's aspirations to independence.)

Trial of the Major War Criminals before the International Military Tribunal, 42 vols. Nuremberg, 1947-1949. (Includes testimony and interrogation of the surviving German leaders and the documents submitted by the Allied Military Occupation from German archives.)

Trials of War Criminals before the Nürnberg Military Tribunals, Oct. 1946-April 1949, 15. vols. Washington, D.C., 1949. (Especially important for the origins of World War II is vol., 12, *Wilhelmstrassenprozess*, which includes the trial of State Secretary Ernst von Weizsäcker.)

United States Army in World War II, vol. 1: *Prewar Plans and Preparations*. Washington, D.C., 1950. (Useful on the Latin American bogey, other fear of Germany before 1939, and Anglo-American military collaboration after 1937.)

La Vie de la France sous l'Occupation, 1940-1944, vol. 1. Hoover Institution, 1957. (The first volume contains important data on the economic problems confronting France prior to World War II.)

Who's Who in Polish America. Francis Bolek, ed., New York, 1943. (Includes lengthy biographical information on prominant Poles who came to the United States after the outbreak of World War II.)

Zelski, August. *Przemowy i Deklaracje*, 2 vols. Warsaw, 1926-1931. (Contains speeches and statements of Józef Beck's predecessor at the Brühl Palace; the contrasting attitudes of the two Polish foreign ministers toward the role of the League of Nations is especially apparent.)

II. Memoirs and Principal Secondary Sources: British

Amery, L.S. *The German Colonial Claim*. London, 1939. (An alarmist book by a prominant Tory leader.)

Amery, L.S. *My Political Life*, vol. 3: *The Unforgiving Years, 1929-1940*. London, 1955. (Detailed account containing much valuable information on official British policy.)

Ashley, Maurice. *England in the Seventeenth Century*. London, 1952. (Excellent survey and useful reference for the evolution of modern British policy, *vide* ch. 8.)

Attlee, C.R. *As It Happened*. London, 1954. (Important for the change in Labour Party leadership and policy prior to World War II.)

'Audax.' *Men in Our Time*. New York, 1940. (Brilliant and provoking analysis of prominent Tory leaders by an anonymous but well-informed English observer.)

Bannister, Sybil. *I Lived Under Hitler: an Englishwoman's Story*. London, 1957. (Interesting account of Danzig conditions prior to World War II, from a pro-German viewpoint.)

Bardens, Dennis. *Portrait of a Statesman: The Personal Life Story of Sir Anthony Eden*. New York, 1956. (Valuable for Eden's attitude toward European affairs and his relations with Churchill.)

Belgion, Montgomery. *Victor's Justice*. Chicago, 1949. (Excellent criticism of the unfair condemnation of Germany at Nuremberg.)

Belloc, Hilaire. *Cromwell*. London, 1934. (Useful reference for the evolution of modern British policy and Cromwell's rejection of the balance of power, *vide* ch. 8.)

Bennet, George. *The Concept of Empire: Burke to Attlee, 1774-1947*. London, 1953. (Important for London's evaluation of the Empire's attitude toward war with Germany in 1939.)

Bevan, A., Strachey, E., and Strauss, G.R. *What We Saw in Russia*. London, 1931. (An important reference for an understanding of the pro-Soviet orientation of the British Labour Party.)

Bilainkin, George. *Maisky: Ten Years Ambassador*. London, 1944. (Pro-Soviet account of Maisky's mission to London, and an important reference for Anglo-Russian relations in 1938 and 1939.)

Bindoff, S.T. *Tudor England*. London, 1950. (Survey of the English scene at the time of the first adoption of the modern British balance of power theory, *vide* ch. 8.)

Bolloton, Burnett. *The Grand Camouflage: The Communist Conspiracy in the Spanish Civil War*. New York, 1961. (Excellent in explaining just how the Communists seized control of loyalist Spain.)

Brooks, Collin. *Can Chamberlain Save Britain? The Lessons of Munich.* London, 1938. (Frank admission of Great Britain's role as the most warlike nation of modern times; strong support for Chamberlain's military preparations against Germany.)

Brooks, Collin. *Devil's Decade.* London, 1948. (Anti-German and anti-Soviet account of the decline of British power.)

Birnie, Arthur. *An Economic History of Europe, 1760-1939.* London, 1957. (Useful survey of the rise and decline of British industrial proponderance.)

Brogan, D.W. *The Development of Modern France, 1870-1939.* London, 1940. (Lengthy and sympathetic survey with major emphasis on domestic politics.)

Bryans, J. Lonsdale. *Blind Victory: Secret Communications, Halifax-Hassel.* London, 1951. (Mainly on wartime contacts between Halifax and the anti-Hitler Germans, with an interesting insight into the enigmatic attitude toward war or peace with Germany displayed by Halifax on the eve of World War II.)

Bryant, Arthur. *The Turn of the Tide: A History of the War Years Based on the Diaries of Field-Marshal Lord Alanbrooke, Chief of the Imperial General Staff.* New York, 1957. (Useful for British military planning and concern about the attitude of France.)

Buchanan, George. *My Mission to Russia and Other Diplomatic Memories.* London, 1930. (Emphasizes British encouragement of Russian general mobilization in July 1914.)

Bullock, Allan. *Hitler: A Study in Tyranny.* (Primarily a survey of German political history from 1919 to 1945.)

Cardwell, A.S. *Poland and Russia: The Last Quarter Century.* New York, 1944. (A survey of the lasting antagonism in Russo-Polish relations.)

Carr, Edward. *German-Soviet Relations between the Two World Wars, 1919-1939.* Baltimore, 1951. (Excellent general analysis of Russian policy toward Germany and the makeshift nature of the 1939 Pact.)

Carr, Edward. *International Relations Since the Peace Treaties.* London, 1940. (A fair and objective analysis of the failure of the League of Nations and of Anglo-French cooperation.)

Churchill, Winston. *The Gathering Storm.* Boston, 1948. (Valuable for Churchill's attitude; indicates he was not consulted about the formulation of British policy prior to World War II.)

Churchill, Winston. *Great Contemporaries.* London, 2nd ed., 1937. (Contains journalistic sketches revealing Churchill's admiration for power and success.)

Clark, George N. *The Later Stuarts, 1660-1714.* Oxford, 1934. (Useful reference for the evolution of modern British foreign policy, *vide* ch. 8.)

Colonna, Bertram de. *Czecho-Slovakia Within.* London, 1938. (Presents the Sudeten case against the Czechs; contains useful statistics.)

Colonna, Bertram de. *Poland From the Inside.* London, 1939. (States the case against British intervention in Poland.)

Coates, W.P. and **Coates, Z.** *A History of Anglo-Soviet Relations.* London, 1944. (Interesting and strongly pro-Soviet account.)

Cole, G.D.H. *A History of the Labour Party from 1914.* London, 1948. (Valuable for the development of the Pro-Soviet attitude of the British Labour Party.)

Collier, Basil. *The Defence of the United Kingdom.* London, 1957. (Indispensable account of British war production and military planning based on the records of the secret conferences.)

Colvin, Ian. *Admiral Canaris: Chef des Geheimdienstes.* Vienna, 1955. (Valuable account of the secret ties between British-jounalists and agents and the German opposition to Hitler prior to World War II.)

Connell, John (John H. Robertson). *The "Office": A Study of British Foreign Policy and its Makers, 1919-1951.* London, 1958. (Indispensable study on the anti-German prejudice of the permanent staff at the British Foreign Office.)

Dalton, Hugh. *Memoirs,* vol.2, *The Fateful Years, 1931-1945.* London, 1957. (The most useful account of the attitudes of British Labour leaders toward foreign affairs; explains the triumph of the pro-Soviet attitude.)

Dawson, W.H. *Germany Under the Treaty.* London, 1933. (Useful analysis of the impact of the 1919 settlement; sympathetic to Germany.)

Donald, R. *The Polish Corridor and the Consequences.* London, 1929. (An excellent prophetic analysis of the problems created by the Versailles settlement in Eastern Europe.)

Driberg, Tom. *Beaverbrook: A Study in Power and Frustration.* London, 1956. (Excellent analysis of the pressures which prompted the *Daily Express* to abandon its anti-war policy in 1939.)

Driberg, Tom. *Colonnade, 1937-1947.* London, 1949. (Depicts the pressures for a crusade against Fascism in the 1937-1939 period.)

Dugdale, Blanche. *Arthur James Balfour,* 2 vols. London, 1932. (Authoritative biography based on exclusive use of the private papers.)

Eden, Anthony. *Facing the Dictators.* Boston, 1962. (Brings the story down to 1938, with many interesting insights on Eden's sympathy with the Soviet Union in the 1930's.)

Einzig, Paul. *Appeasement Before, During, and After the War.* London, 1947. (Bitterly anti-German account accusing the Tories of a soft policy toward Germany.)

Einzig, Paul. *World Finance, 1938-1939.* London, 1939. (Clever propaganda tract against German economic methods and trade policy.)

Feiling, Keith. *The Life of Neville Chamberlain.* London, 1946. (Valuable and thoughtful analysis based on confidential papers.)

Fraser, Lindley. *Germany Between Two Wars.* London, 1945. (Provocative analysis of German policy for the official British propaganda offensive in occupied Germany after World War II.)

Gorer, Geoffrey. *Exploring English Character.* New York, 1955. (Thoughtful analysis of British habits and public attitudes; excellent insight on susceptibility to the morality theme of war propaganda.)

Grenfell, Russell. *Unconditional Hatred: German War Guilt and the Future of Europe.* New York, 1954. (Outstanding analysis by a leading British military historian; proves there was no German military threat to Great Britain.)

Greenwood, Arthur. *Why We Fight: Labour's Case.* London, 1940. (Attempt to explain Labour's attitude toward the war without emphasizing the confusion produced by the Russo-German pact.)

Grigg, Edward. *British Foreign Policy.* London, 1944. (Defense of British policy in Europe between the World Wars.)

Grigg, Edward. *Britain Looks at Germany.* London, 1938. (Valuable contemporary analysis of the conflicting trends in British opinion.)

Earl of Halifax. *Fullness of Days.* New York, 1957. (Secretive about the major British policy decisions, but valuable for general attitudes; Halifax decided in 1936 that there would be war again with Germany.)

Hancock, W.K., and **Gowing, M.N.** *British War Economy.* London, 1949. (Useful analysis of the British increase in war production prior to World War II.)

Hankey, Maurice. *Politics, Trials, and Errors.* Chicago, 1950. (Frankly critical account of British hostility toward Japan and Germany by a leading policy-maker; the British Government denied Hankey the right to publish his memoirs.)

Harley, J.H. *The Authentic Biography of Colonel Beck.* London, 1939. (Defense of Beck's policy after the 1934 pact with Germany.)

Hearnshaw, F.J.C. *Germany, the Aggressor Throughout the Ages.* New York, 1941. (Most extreme of many smears of German history by a prominant journalist and supporter of Halifax.)

Henderson, Neville. *Failure of a Mission.* New York, 1940. (Contains some interesting information; ignores Henderson's repeated efforts to argue the German case at London.)

Hill, David J. *A History of Diplomacy in the International Development of Europe,* 3 vols. New York, 1921-1925. (Brilliant survey of trends in modern European diplomacy; valuable for the evolution of British policy, *vide* ch. 8.)

Hinsley, F.H. *Hitler's Strategy.* Cambridge [England], 1951. (Interesting survey emphasizing Hitler's wish for peace and friendship with Great Britain.)

Hodgson, Stuart. *Lord Halifax.* London, 1941. (Fairly informative account Halifax's knowledge of the British Empire and European affairs.)

Horler, Sydney. *Now Let Us Hate.* London, 1942. (Ironical treatment emphasizing the seemingly inexplicable shifts of British policy in recent years.)

Howard, John Eldred. *Parliament and Foreign Policy in France: A Study of the Origins, Nature and Methods of the Parliamentary Control of Foreign Policy in France during the Third Republic with Special Reference to the Period from 1919 to 1939.* London, 1948. (Emphasizes the independence from parliamentary control of the French Cabinet in the conduct of foreign policy.)

Huddleston, Sisley. *France: The Tragic Years, 1939-1947.* New York, 1955. (Account by an expert British observer emphasizing the desire for peace in France in 1939.)

Huddleston, Sisley. *Popular Diplomacy and War.* West Ridge, New Hampshire, 1954. (Brilliant analysis of diplomatic blunders after World War I.)

Hughes, Emrys. *Winston Churchill: British Bulldog.* New York, 1955. (Fair and objective account emphasizing the inconsistency of Churchill's opinions during the course of his career.)

Inge, William Ralph. *A Pacifist in Trouble.* London, 1939. (Contains some very shrewd criticism of British foreign policy by a leading Anglican churchman, the Dean of St. Paul's.)

Johnson, Allen Campbell. *Viscount Halifax.* London, 1941. (Most informative of the biographies of Halifax; excellent analysis of his ideas on world affairs.)

Johnson, Hewlett. *Act Now.* London, London, 1939. (Pro-Soviet and anti-German plea for a policy of extensive British intervention in Europe.)

Jones, Thomas. *A Diary with Letters, 1931-1950.* London, 1954. (Indispensable source for the opinions of prominent Englishmen; shows the influence of Abraham Flexner on Jones.)

Jones, Thomas. *Lloyd George.* Cambridge, Mass., 1951. (Sympathetic account which faithfully reflects the many sudden changes of opinion of the veteran Liberal leader.)

Jordan, Peter. *Poland's Frontiers.* London, 1945. (Presents the case for Polish westward expansion and for the annexation of Eastern European territories by Poland after World War I.)

Jordon, W.M. *Great Britain, France, and the German Problem, 1918-1939.* London, 1943. (Useful analysis of British policy decisions prior to World War II; extremely harsh toward Germany.)

Keith, A.B. *The Causes of the War.* London, 1940. (Excellent and dispassionate survey by a leading international jurist.)

Kennedy, General John. *The Business of War.* New York, 1958. (Valuable account of British military planning; critical of Churchill, Ironside, Hore-Belisha.)

King-Hall, Stephen. *Total Victory.* New York, 1942. (Contains full information on the astonishing anti-Hitler newsletter compaign launched by the author in Germany during the spring of 1939.)

Kirkpatrick, Helen. *Under the British Umbrella.* New York, 1939. (Especially interesting on the origins of the myth about the so-called Cliveden Set.)

Knatchbull-Hugessen, Hughe. *Diplomat in Peace and War.* London, 1949. (Especially valuable for the account of Foreign Office decisions in 1938 when the author was in London between assignments to China and Turkey.)

Kochan, Lionel. *Pogrom, 10 November 1938.* London, 1957. (Facile and grotesquely inaccurate account of the demonstrations against the Jews in Germany.)

Kolarz, Walter. *Myths and Realities in Eastern Europe.* London, 1946. (General survey based on extensive information; some brilliant insights.)

Leasor, James. *Rudolf Hess: the Uninvited Envoy.* London, 1962. (Contains interesting background material on the desire shared by Hitler and Hess to arrive at an understanding with Britain.)

Lee, Asher. *The German Air Force.* London, 1946. (Useful analysis revealing the contrast between the modest truth and the propaganda version of the strength of the German air force in 1939 and 1940.)

Leslie, R.F. *Polish Politics and the Revolution of November, 1830.* London, 1956. (Indispensable for the evolution of Polish political thought following the Congress of Vienna.)

Liddell Hart, Basil Henry. *The Defence of Britain.* New York, 1939. (Realistic appraisal of British national security in 1939.)

Liddell Hart, Basil Henry. *Europe in Arms.* New York, 1937. (Useful analysis which exploded the myth that Great Britain *had ever* disarmed.)

Liddell Hart, Basil Henry. *The German Generals Talk.* New York, 1948. (Conveys consternation among German military experts at the prospect of a protracted war in 1938 or 1939.)

Lloyd-George, David. *The Truth about the Peace Treaties,* 2 vols. London, 1938. (Fascinating revelation of Allied diplomacy at Versailles; explains his critical attitude toward some of Poland's territorial aspirations.)

Lord Londonderry. *Ourselves and Germany*. London, 1938. (Cautious statement in favor of an Anglo-German understanding.)

Machrey, Robert. *The Poland of Pilsudski*. London, 1936. (Sympathetic and informative account of the Polish dictatorship after 1926.)

Mackenzie, Compton. *Dr. Beneš*. London, 1946. (Elaborate and detailed defense of the Czech leader from 1914 through World War II.)

Macleod, Ian. *Neville Chamberlain*. London, 1961. (Excellent background for Chamberlain's achievements in British domestic policy; weaker as an attempt to defend his foreign policy.)

Mansergh, Nicholas. *Survey of British Commonwealth Affairs: Problems of External Policy, 1931-1939*. London, 1952. (Defense of British European policy in the context of total world affairs.)

Martienssen, H. *Hitler and his Admirals*. London, 1949. (Unsympathetic account of German naval planning based on special access to confiscated and restricted German sources; stresses German surprise at the outbreak of war with Great Britian in 1939.)

Medlicott, W.N. *British Foreign Policy Since Versailles*. London, 1940. (Stresses British disinterest in the East Europe *status quo* prior to the 1939 guarantee to Poland.)

Morrow, Ian. *The Peace Settlement in the German-Polish Borderlands*. London, 1936. (Excellent, detailed treatment of the problems created by the 1919 peace settlement.)

Lord Mottistone. *Auf der Suche nach der Wahrheit*. Stuttgart, 1937. (Presentation by a 1914 Cabinet Minister of the case for Anglo-German cooperation; emphasizes German social and economic reforms; See also earlier editions: *'Mayflower' Seeks the Truth*. London, 1935.)

Mowat, Charles Loch. *Britain Between the Wars, 1918-1940*. Chicago, 1955. (Especially useful for British financial policy and the British armament policy.)

Muggeridge, Malcolm. *The Sun Never Sets: The Story of England in the Nineteen Thirties*. New York, 1940. (Satirical treatment of British leadership with emphasis on the inconsistencies of foreign policy and the absence of domestic reforms.)

Namier, L.B. *Avenues of History*. London, 1952. (Essays criticizing the concept of objective history etertained by Ranke and his disciples; important in explaining the nature of Namier's anti-German approach to European problems.)

Namier, L.B. *Diplomatic Prelude, 1938-1939*. London, 1947. (His principal study on the origins of World War II; presents the case for the necessity of an Anglo-German war.)

Namier, L.B. *Europe in Decay*. London, 1950. (Sequel to the above, with special emphasis on recent French memoirs; attacks the French attempt to arrive at an understanding with Germany.)

Namier, L.B. *In the Nazi Era*. London, 1952. (Second sequel to the above, with principal emphasis on Germany and attacking the German opposition to Hitler for failure to be more aggressive.)

Nicoll, Peter H. *Britain's Blunder*. London, 1953. (Vigorous case against the British policy in 1939 and the guarantee to Poland; the greatly-enlarged German edition is entitled *Englands Krieg gegen Deutschland*.)

Nicolson, Harold. *The Congress of Vienna: A Study in Allied Unity*. London, 1946. (Useful in explaining the British role in the anti-Polish settlement of 1815.)

Viscount Norwich. *Old Men Forget*. London, 1953. (Vital in explaining Duff Cooper's hostility toward Germany, and his attitude toward the other British leaders.)

Owen, Frank. *The Three Dictators: Mussolini, Stalin, Hitler*. London, 1940. (Considerably less hostile toward Stalin than the others; illustrates British propaganda techniques from the 1939 period.)

Patterson, Eric J. *Pilsudski, Marshal of Poland*. Bristol, 1935. (Accurate and readable general biography.)

Petrie, Charles. *The Chamberlain Tradition*. London, 1952. (Excellent sympathetic analysis of the Chamberlains in British policy from 1895 to 1940.)

Pickles, Dorothy. *French Politics*. London, 1953. (Valuable for the Radical Socialist regime in France in 1939.)

Pitt-Rivers, George Lane-Fox. *The Czech Conspiracy: A Phase in the World-War Plot*. London, 1938.

(Pro-German view of the 1938 Sudeten crisis.)

Price, G. Ward. *I Know These Dictators.* London, 1938. (Sympathetic account of Hitler and Mussolini based on personal interviews.)

Price, G. Ward. *Year of Reckoning.* London, 3rd. ed., 1939. (An alarmist account reflecting the change of position by Price after the Munich conference.)

Pollard, A.F. *Wolsey.* London, 1929. (Detailed study useful in explaining the influence of Thomas Cromwell on Wolsey and Henry VIII; with the adoption of the balance of power doctrine from Italy began the evolution of modern British policy, *vide* ch. 8.)

Pope, Arthur Upham. *Maxim Litvinoff.* New York, 1943. (Pro-Soviet account of the father of collective security in the 1930's; emphasizes the Russian case against the Munich conference.)

Postgate, Rayomond. *The Life of George Lansbury.* London, 1951. (Useful information on the efforts of the deposed British Labour Leader to promote an Anglo-German understanding, 1937-1939.)

Pritt, D.N. *The Fall of the French Republic.* London, 1941. (Provocative pro-Soviet analysis of French politics.)

Reddaway, W.F. *Marshal Piłsudski.* London, 1938. (Useful and stimulating account based on careful use of Polish sources.)

Reitlinger, Gerald. *Die Endlösung: Hitlers Versuch der Ausrottung der Juden Europas, 1939-1945.* Berlin, 1956. (Contains some material on the Jewish question prior to World War II by a leading British expert; see also: *The Final Solution,* London, 1955; *The SS: Alibi of a Nation,* London, 1954.)

Reynolds, P.A. *British Foreign Policy in the Inter-War Years.* London, 1954. (Useful survey based on extensive sources; anti-appeasement.)

Rogerson, Sidney B. *Propaganda and the Next War.* London, 1938. (Remarkable prediction of the World War II program and the propaganda and diplomatic methods required to achieve official British aims.)

Viscount Rothermere. *My Fight to Rearm Britain.* London, 1939. (Expresses an apology for earlier efforts to promote an Anglo-German understanding.)

Rothstein, Andrew. *The Munich Conspiracy.* London, 1958. (Fascinating pro-Soviet account of the 1938 Czech crisis; claims the Sudeten Germans were largely Czech rather than German.)

Salter, Arthur. *The Dual Policy.* Oxford, 1939. (Expresses the hope that Britain will continue to search for peace while preparing for war.)

Salter, Arthur. *Personality in Politics.* London, 1947. (Especially useful for the defense of Chamberlain and his leadership abilities.)

Salter, Arthur. *Security: Can We Retrieve It?* London, 1939. (Presents argument that British interests did not require war after Munich.)

Scaevola. *A Study in Forgery.* London, 1945. (Brief survey of the international Communist subversive movement.)

Scanlon, John. *Very Foreign Affairs.* London, 1939. (Delightful satire on the hopeless inconsistencies of British foreign policy.)

Scotland, A.P. *The London Cage.* London, 1957. (Contains analysis by British intelligence expert on pro-German sentiment in England early in 1939.)

Selby, Walford. *Diplomatic Twilight, 1930-1940.* London, 1953. (Especially useful for analysis of the anti-German diplomacy conducted from the British embassy in Vienna prior to March 1938.)

Seton-Watson, Hugh. *Eastern Europe between the Wars, 1918-1941.* Cambridge [England], 1945. (Brief survey with much useful information on politics in Czechoslovakia.)

Seton-Watson, R.W. *A History of the Czechs and Slovaks.* London, 1940. (Emphasizes the Czech case against Germay.)

Shaw, D.K. *Prime Minister Neville Chamberlain.* London, 1939. (Early biography emphasizing Chamberlain's achievements before he became Prime Minister in 1937.)

Simon, John. *Retrospect: The Memoirs of the Right Honorable Viscount Simon.* London, 1952. (Contains largely familiar material, but also occasional opinions which are extremely revealing.)

Sloan, P. *Russia — Friend or Foe?.* London, 1939. (Defense of Russian policy.)

Spears, General Edward. *Assignment to Catastrophe*, vol. 1: *Prelude to Dunkirk, July 1939-May 1940*. New York, 1954. (Reveals Churchill's desire for war in August 1939 and French hostility to Halifax's policy.)

Strang, William. *Britain in World Affairs: The Fluctuation in Power and Influence from Henry VIII to Elizabeth II*. New York, 1961. (Vital for the traditional British balance of power policy.)

Strang, William. *Home and Abroad*. London, 1956. (Indispensable source for the study of British policy in 1939; contains much useful information on British objectives.)

Taylor, A.J.P. *The Origins of the Second World War*. London, 1961. (An excellent British historical performance; Hitler is completely exonerated from the old propaganda charge of having plotted war in 1939.)

Taylor, A.J.P. *The Struggle for Mastery in Europe, 1848-1918*. Oxford, 1954. (Erudite and interesting anti-German account explaining much in the evolution of recent British policy.)

Viscount Templewood. *Nine Troubled Years*. London, 1954. (Extremely informative record revealing the identity of views between Hoare and Halifax.)

Viscount Templewood. *The Unbroken Thread*. New York, 1950. Private memoirs of Hoare which reveal his world of values and ideas.)

Toynbee, A.J. et al. *Survey of International Affairs, 1939-1946*, 10 vols. London, 1951-1958, and especially vol. 1: *The World in March 1939*, London, 1951; vol. 10: *The Eve of War, 1939*, London, 1958. (Contains useful information on 1939.)

Vansittart, Robert Gilbert. *Lessons of My Life*. New York, 1943. (Contains wartime propaganda against Germany; see also *Black Record*, London, 1941.)

Vansittart, Robert Gilbert. *The Mist Procession: The Autobiography of Lord Vansittart*. London, 1958. (Contains much new information; especially useful for the 1933-1937 period.)

Veale, F.J.P. *Advance to Barbarism*. Appleton, Wisconsin, 1953. (Especially useful for early British plans to bomb the civilian population of Germany.)

Webster, C.K. *British Diplomacy, 1813-1815*. London, 1921. (Contains vital documents revealing the anti-Polish policy of Great Britain at the Vienna Congress.)

Webster, C.K. *The Congress of Vienna*. London, 1919. (Brilliant analysis prepared for the British delegation at Versailles.)

Webster, C.K. *The Foreign Policy of Castlereagh, 1812-1815*. London, 1931. (Excellent on British fears of both France and Russia.)

Webster, C.K. *The Foreign Policy of Castlereagh, 1815-1822*. London, 1925. (Describes the struggle for control of British policy after the Congress of Vienna.)

Webster, C.K. *The Foreign Policy of Palmerston, 1830-1841*, 2 vols. London, 1951. (An excellent introduction explains British balance of power policy.)

Walters, F.P. *A History of the League of Nations*, 2 vols. London, 1952. (Contains useful information on the principal diplomatic crises of the 1930's.)

Webster, Nesta. *Surrender of an Empire*. London, 1933. (Fascinating and prophetic analysis of British decline.)

Wheeler-Bennett, J.W. *Brest-Litovsk: The Forgotten Peace, March 1918*. London, 1938. (Useful but misleading record of the negotiations; virtually no information on the actual terms of the treaty.)

Wheeler-Bennett, J.W. *Munich: Prologue to Tragedy*. London, 1948. (Informative analysis based on extensive research; weak on British policy.)

Wheeler-Bennett, J.W. *The Nemesis of Power: The German Army in Politics, 1918-1945*. New York, 1954. (Valuable record of the opposition to Hitler of many German military leaders.)

Wiart, Adrian Carto de. *Happy Odyssey*. London, 1950. (Military memoirs vital for British relations with Poland in 1939.)

Winch, Michael. *Republic for a Day*. London, 1939. (Useful chronicle of the Carpatho-Ruthenian independence movement in 1938 and 1939.)

Wiskemann, Elizabeth. *Germany's Eastern Neighbors: Problems Relating to the Oder-Neisse Line and the Czech Frontier Regions*. London, 1956. (Anti-German defense of the Soviet *status quo* in Eastern Europe: contains useful background information on the pre-1939 period.)

Wiskemann, Elizabeth. *The Rome-Berlin Axis.* London, 1949. (Claims, based on extensive research, that the Axis was a mistake for Italy.)

Wiskemann, Elizabeth. *Undeclared War.* London, 1939. (Anti-German analysis of Hitler's program of territorial revision.)

Wrench, John E. *Geoffrey Dawson and Our Times.* London, 1955.

Zeman, Z.A.B. *Germany and the Revolution in Russia, 1915-1918.* Oxford, 1958. (Extremely useful background for German policy in Eastern Europe under Hitler.)

III. Memoirs and Principal Secondary Sources: French

Albert, C. *L'Angleterre contre l'Europe.* Paris, 1941. (The British criticized for paralyzing France prior to attacking Germany.)

René d'Argile, J. Ploncard d'Assac, Michel de Mauny, Jacques Béarn, Henry Coston, Pierre Cousteau, Henri Lebre. *Les Origines Secrètes de la Guerre 1939-1945.* Paris, 1957. (Vitally important revisionist work analyzing the Munich conferences, war propaganda, the French press, official British and French policy.)

Aron, Raymond. *The Opium of the Intellectuals.* New York, 1957. (Analysis of the debilitating effect of Communist propaganda on the Western countries.)

Aron, Robert. *Les Grands Dossiers de l'Histoire Contemporaine.* Paris, 1962. (Excellent on Laval, Pétain, Brasillach, and Degrelle before and during World War II.)

Bardeche, Maurice. *Der Weg nach Vorn.* Göttingen, 1952. (Stimulating critique of pro-Soviet policies in the Western countries.)

Bartel, P. *Le Maréchal Piłsudski.* Paris, 1955. (Sympathetic treatment of Piłsudski's career and the Polish dictatorship.)

Baumont, Maurice. *La Faillite de la Paix,* 2 vols. Paris, 1951. (Interesting general survey of diplomatic relations between the World Wars; critical of Allied treatment of Germany after World War II.)

Baumont, Maurice. *Gloires et Tragédies de la IIIe République.* Paris, 1956. (Contains brilliant analyses of leading French political personalities.)

Baumont, Maurice, et al. *The Third Reich* (Unesco publ.) New York, 1955. (Individual studies on aspects of German policy; the sections on foreign affairs are of special interest.)

Bauvier, J. & Gacon, J. *La Vérité sur 1939.* Paris, 1953. (Especially useful for the criticism of British policy toward Poland.)

Benoist-Méchin, Jacques. *Éclaircissements sur Mein Kampf, la Doctrine d'Adolf Hitler.* Paris, 1939. (The only lengthy competent analysis of Hitler's volumes printed in Western countries prior to World War II.)

Benoist-Méchin, Jacques. *Geschichte des Deutschen Heeres seit dem Waffenstillstand, 1918-1938,* vol. 1. Berlin, 1938. (Contains a brilliant analysis of the moral impact on Germany of Versailles.)

Benoist-Méchin, Jacques. *Soixante Jours Qui Ébranlèrent l'Occident, 10 Mai - 10 Juillet 1940,* vol. 3: *La Fin du Régime, 26 Juin - 10 Juillet 1940.* Paris, 1956. (Third volume contains valuable analyses of the leading personalities of the French regime in 1939.)

Blum, Léon. *For All Mankind.* New York, 1946. (An attempt to blame French Communism for the failure of the Popular Front; also the thesis of the inevitability of World War II; written during World War II internment.)

Blum, Léon. *L'Oeuvre de Léon Blum,* 4 vols. Paris, 1954-1957. (Vital for the Popular Front and Blum's attitude toward Germany and Italy.)

Bonnet, Georges. "Les Accords Berard–Jordana," in *Écrits de Paris,* Feb. 1948. (Vital in explaining how Bonnet put an end to French support of the Communists.)

Bonnet, Georges. *Défense de la Paix: de Washington au Quai d'Orsay.* Geneva, 1948. (Essential for Bonnet's career and attitudes.)

Bonnet, Georges. *Fin d'une Europe: de Munich à la Guerre.* Geneva, 1948. (Brilliant analysis of 1938-1939 diplomatic events based on personal experience and French archive material.)

Brassilach, R., and Bardeche, M. *Histoire de la guerre d'Espagne.* Paris, 1939. (Important source for

French Popular Front aid to the Spanish Reds during the Civil War in Spain.)

Brinton, Fernand de. *Mémoirs.* Paris, 1949. (Useful for understanding of efforts to promote a Franco-German *rapprochment.*)

Buk, Pierre. *La Tragédie Tchécoslovaque de Septembre 1938 à Mars 1939.* Paris, 1939. (Stimulating but sometimes inaccurate version of the collapse of the Czech state; contains important material.)

Caillaux, Joseph. *Mes Mémoires,* 3 vols. Paris, 1942-1947. (Especially the third volume on efforts for peace and on the overthrow of Blum.)

Carcopino, Jerome. *Souvenirs de Sept Ans, 1937-1944.* Paris, 1953. (Representative of French intellectuals intensely hostile to Mussolini and to Fascism.)

Champeaux, Georges. *La Croisade des Démocraties,* 2 vols. Paris, 1941. (Stimulating critique of British and American pressures to involve France in war with Germany.)

Chauvineau, Général. *Une Invasion est-elle encore possible?.* Paris, 1939. (Argument against extensive French military commitments in Eastern Europe because of defensive strategy; claims France as secure against foreign attack.)

Paul Coblentz. *Georges Mandel.* Paris, 1947. (Especially useful on Mandel's hostility toward Germany.)

Coulondre, Robert. *De Staline à Hitler: Souvenirs de deux ambassades, 1936-1939.* Paris, 1950. (Indispensable for Franco-German relations after the Munich conferance.)

Dacier, Michel. "Le Leçon du Hradschin," in *Écrits de Paris,* Ap. 1948. (How Beneš ruined the Czechs.)

Danos, J. and **Gibelin, M.** *Juin 1936.* Paris, 1950. (Detailed analysis of the Popular Front triumph and program.)

Daudet, Léon. *Le Drame franco-allemand.* Paris, 1940. (Classic account by a conservative Frenchman seeking a workable Franco-German understanding.)

Debu-Bridel, Jacques. *L'Agonie de la Troisième République.* Paris, 1948. (Especially useful for impact of the world economic depression and British policy on France.)

Doriot, Jacques. *La France avec nous!* Paris, 1937. (Vital for the case against the Communists in France.)

Doumenc, Général. "Moscow, Aug. 1939," in *Carrefour* [Paris], May 21, 1947. (Important for Doumenc instructions to grant Russian requests in Poland.)

Duclos, Paul. *Le Vatican et la Seconde Guerre Mondiale.* Paris, 1958. (Useful for papal diplomacy in the Spring and Summer of 1939.)

Ducloux, Louis. *From Blackmail to Treason: Political Crime and Corruption in France, 1920-1940.* London, 1958. (Excellent account of the corrupt political obstruction of justice.)

Dupeux, Georges. *Le Front Populaire et Les Élections de 1936,* 2 vols. Paris, 1959. (The best account of the Popular Front victory in 1936.)

Fabre-Luce, Alfred. *Caillaux.* Paris, 1933. (Excellent background on the former Premier and Senate leader of the 1930's.)

Fabre-Luce, Alfred. *La Fumée d'un Cigare.* Paris, 1949. (Biographical study of Churchill and his impact on French policy.)

Fabre-Luce, Alfred. *Journal de la France,* vol. 1: *Mars 1939-Juillet 1940.* Trevoux, 1940. (Moving account of the difficulties which beset France after the launching of Halifax's war policy.)

Fabre-Luce, Alfred. *Locarno: the Reality.* New York, 1928. (Indispensable for an understanding of the attitudes of intelligent Frenchmen toward the supposedly permanent terms of this *provisorium.)*

Fabre-Luce, Alfred. *Le Secret de la République.* Paris, 1938. (Emphasizes the need to recognize the change in France's position in Europe.)

Fabry, Jean. "Le 'Tournant' des sanctions contre l'Italie, Juin 1935-Mai 1936," in *Ecrits de Paris,* Feb. 1948. (Vital for the failure of Laval's policy.)

Feinberg, N. *La Question des minorités à la Conference de la Paix de 1919-1920.* Paris, 1929. (Account of the struggle for the imposition of minority pacts on the countries of Eastern Europe.)

Flandin, Pierre-Étienne. *Politique Française, 1919-1940.* Paris, 1947. (Useful in explaining Flandin's changed attitude towad Germany after 1936.)

François-Poncet, André. *Souvenirs d'une Ambassade à Berlin, Sept. 1931-Oct. 1938.* Paris, 1946. (Explains the manner in which the former French ambassador won the confidence of Hitler without revealing his own hostility toward Germany.)

François-Poncet, André. *De Versailles à Potsdam. 1919-1945.* Paris, 1948. (Interesting survey of German developments.)

Gamelin, Général. *Servir: Les Armées Françaises de 1940,* 2 vols. Paris, 1946. (Especially useful for doubts and misgivings of French military men about war with Germany in 1939.)

Gauché, Général. *Le Deuxième Bureau au Travail, 1935-1940.* Paris, 1953. (Indespensable record of French intelligence estimates of the European situation; especially useful for England, Germany, Poland, and Russia.)

Général de Gaulle. *The Call to Honour, 1940-1942: War Memoirs.* New York, 1955. (Useful for pre-World War II conflict about French military strategy and defense plans.)

Genet, Lucien. *Cinquante Ans d'Histoire, 1900-1950,* 3 vols. Paris, 1950. (Excellent account based largely on newspaper sources.)

Gentizon, Paul. *La Conquête de l'Éthiopie.* Paris, 1937. (Useful analysis explaining the disastrous effect of the Ethiopian War on Franco-Italian relations.)

Georges-Anquetil. *Hitler Conduit le Bal.* Paris, 1939. (Journalistic treatment of Hitler's aspirations and conflicting French views toward Germany.)

Gide, André. *Journal, 1889-1939.* Paris, 1948. (Contains several interesting observations on Hitler's tactics and strategy.)

Goguel, François. *La Politique des Partis sous la IIIe République.* Paris, 1946. (Extremely useful analysis of French political parties and their aims; indispensable for French politics prior to World War II.)

Handelsman, Marcel. *Napoléon et la Pologne, 1806-1807.* Paris, 1909. (Excellent account of the imperious manner with which Napoleon treated the Poles following the Prussian defeats of Jena and Auerstädt.)

Henriot, Philippe. *Comment mourut la Paix: le Procès des Responsables.* Paris, 1941. (Stimulating criticism of the Popular Front and of English influence on French policy.)

Herbette, Françoise. *L'Expérience Marxiste en France, 1936-1938.* Paris, 1960. (Detailed account of the Blum experiment from the Marxist viewpoint.)

Herriot, Édouard. *La France dans le Monde.* Paris, 1933. (Last important statement of the influential behavior of the left wing of French Radical Socialism in favor of collaboration with Germany.)

Herriot, Édouard. *Jadis.* vol. 2: *D'une Guerre à l'autre, 1914-1936.* Paris, 1952. (Describes conversion to an anti-German and anti-Italian policy; vital for his opposition to Daladier and Bonnet in 1938 1939.)

Jouvenel, Bertrand de. *Le Réveil de l'Europe: Problèmes et Documents.* Paris, 1938. (Brilliant statement for a new French policy in Europe based on understanding with Germany.)

Jouvenel, Bertrand de. *D'une guerre à l'autre,* 2 vols. Paris, 1940-1941. (Analysis of the failure of French post-World War I policy and the pressures which produced French involvement in World War II.)

Kerillis, Henri de. *Français! Voici la Guerre.* Paris, 1936. (Militant statement of an important French journalist explaining his decision to substitute an anti-German campaign for anti-Soviet tactics.)

Kerillis, Henri de. *I Accuse de Gaulle.* New York, 1946. (Contains many personal revelations vital for understanding the author as the leading *belliciste*.)

Lacour-Gayet, Robert. *La France au XXe Siècle.* Paris, 1954. (Especially useful for shifts in French Foreign policy.)

Lagardelle, Hubert. *Mission à Rome: Mussolini.* Paris, 1955. (Indispensable for Franco-Italian relations prior to World War II; describes the excellent opportunities for lasting Franco-Italian understanding.)

Laroche, Jules Alfred. *La Pologne de Piłsudski: Souvenirs d'une Ambassade, 1926-1935.* Paris, 1953. (Penetrating and informative account of the Polish system after 1926 and of Franco-Polish relations.)

Laval, Pierre. *The Diary of Pierre Laval.* New York, 1948. (Brilliant exposition of thought by the former French Premier.)

Lazareff, Pierre. *De Munich à Vichy.* New York, 1944. (Contains much interesting private information about the French leaders.)

Lazareff, Pierre. *Deadline: The Behind-the-Scenes Story of the Last Decade in France.* New York, 1942. (Interesting and frank analysis by a prominent journalist.)

Lebrun, Albert. *Témoignage.* Paris, 1945. (Especially useful for the close collaboration between the French President and Édouard Herriot).

Lefebvre, Georges. *Napoléon.* Paris, 1935. (Contains an excellent survey of French policy in Poland prior to the Congress of Vienna.)

Lemery, Henri. *De la Paix de Briand à la Guerre de Hitler.* Paris, 1949. (Provocative analysis of French policy favorable to Herriot and Reynaud and hostile to Laval and Bonnet.)

Levée, Madeleine. *Les Précourseurs de la indépendence tcheque et slovaque à Paris.* Paris, 1936. (Valuable account of World War I activities of Masaryk and Beneš and their influence on French policy.)

Madelin, Louis. *Talleyrand.* London, 1948. (Useful brief account of Anglo-French conflict in the age of Napoleon I.)

Mallet, Alfred. *Pierre Laval,* 2 vols. Paris, 1955. (Indispensable for French foreign policy prior to World War II; sympathetic toward Laval.)

Marion, Paul. *Leur Combat: Lénine, Mussolini, Hitler, Franco.* Paris, 1939. (Balanced and informative account of key European trends.)

Massenon, Léo. "Edouard Bénès et le Slavisme," in *Écrits de Paris,* Oct. 1948. (Excellent on the evolution of the political ideas of Benes.)

Matrat, Jean. *Histoire des Relations Franco-Anglaises.* Paris, 1953. (Useful survey of the English factor in French history and policy.)

Maurois, André. *A History of England.* New York, 3rd ed., 1958. (Emphasizes the importance of the balance of power concept in British policy.)

Milhaud, Édgard. *La France avait Raison.* Neuchâtel, 1945. (Useful for French foreign policy in the years immediately after World War I.)

Miquel, Pierre. *Poincaré.* Paris, 1961. (The authoritative biography of the *belliciste* from Lorraine.)

Montfort, Henri de. *Dantzig, Port de Pologne dans le Passé et dans le Présent.* Paris, 1939. (Presents the Polish case at Danzig.)

Monzie, Antatole de. *Ci-devant.* Paris, 1941. (Indispensable for the inside story of French foreign policy from the Munich conference to the outbreak of World War II.)

Morand, E. *L'Angleterre Maîtresse des Destinées Françaises.* Paris, 1939. (Useful account of injuries suffered by France from British diplomacy and war.)

Noël, Léon. *L'Agression Allemande contre la Pologne.* Paris, 1939. (Vital for Franco-Polish relations after 1936 and the animosity between Beck and Noël.)

Paul-Boncour, J. *Entre Deux Guerres: Souvenirs sur la IIIe République,* vol. 3: *Sur les chemins de la défaite, 1935-1940.* New York, 1946. (Useful for the case in favor of the militant policy of Blum and against the conciliatory efforts of Daladier and Bonnet.)

Paul-Boncour, J. *Recollections of the Third Republic,* vol. 1. New York, 1957. (Especially useful for introductory statement on issues confronting French foreign policy.)

'Pertinax' (André Geraud). *Les Fossoyeurs,* vol. 1: *Gamelin-Daladier -Paul Reynaud.* New York, 1943. (Especially useful for biographical information on Daladier; bitter, pro-Communist attack against Reynaud for voting for Pétain in 1940.)

Pietri, Françoise. *Mes Années d'Espagne, 1940-1948.* Paris, 1954. (Contains excellent background information on Bonnet and his policies.)

Pradelle, A. de la. *Le Marxisme Tentaculaire.* Issoudon, 1942. (Brilliant exposure of Communist aims in Europe based on Communist Party records in France and Switzerland.)

Rebatet, Lucien. *Les Décombres.* Paris, 1942. (Useful criticism of French circles working for war in cooperation with Halifax in 1939.)

Recouly, Raymond. *Les Causes de notre Effondrement.* Paris, 1941. (Dispassionate analysis of policy moves which produced French involvement in war in 1939 and French military defeat in 1940.)

Reynaud, Paul. *Au Cœur de la Mêlée, 1930-1945.* Paris, 1951. (Detailed and useful account in defense of the thesis that Reynaud had the answers for French economic and foreign policy problems; see also the earlier edition, *La France a Sauvé l'Europe.*)

Reynaud, Paul. *Mémoires: venu de ma Montagne,* vol. 1. Paris, 1960. (Covers Reynaud's background and his personal life until 1936.)

Rivault, Albert. *Le Relèvement de l'Allemagne.* Paris, 1938. (Useful account of the recovery of Germany.)

Roche, Emile. *Caillaux que j'ai connu.* Paris, 1949. (The best firsthand account of Callaux on the eve of World War II.)

Rossier, Edmund. *Du Traité de Westphalie à l'Europe de Versailles.* Paris, 1938. (Useful survey on the evolution of modern French policy.)

Rougier, Louis. *Créance Morale de la France.* Montreal, 1945. (Excellent for Franco-Russian relations and the alliance of 1933.)

Simon, Yves. *La Grande Crise de la République Française.* Montreal, 1941. (Defense of Popular Front policies and of extensive military commitment in Eastern Europe: advocates a permanent post-World War II Franco-Polish alliance against Germany.)

Sloves, C.H. *La France et l'Union Soviétique.* Paris, 1935. (Excellent for Franco-Soviet relations on the eve of the 1935 pact.)

Suarez, Georges. *La Grande Peur de 6 Février au Palais-Bourbon.* Paris, 1934. (Contains excellent sketches of prominent French political leaders.)

Suarez, Georges, and **Laborde, Guy.** *Agonie de la Paix, 1935-1939.* Paris, 1942. (Contains an excellent early revisionist criticism of the Halifax war policy.)

Tabouis, Geneviève. *Ils l'ont appelée Cassandre.* New York, 1942. (Vital for the collaboration of French journalists favoring war with the British press and Foreign Office.)

Tardieu, André. *La Note de Semaine, 1936.* Paris, 1937. (Criticism of French defense planning and French policy toward Germany and Italy; rejects the German case on Locarno.)

Tardieu, André. *Notes de Semaine 1938: l'Année de Munich.* Paris, 1939. (Adoption of a more friendly approach to Germany; hostile toward official American policy in Europe; penetrating criticism of French domestic politics.)

Thorez, Maurice. *Notre Lutte pour la Paix: de la Fausse Paix de Versailles à la Trahison de Munich.* Paris, 1938. (Useful for Soviet arguments against the Munich conference and reconciliation between France and Germany.)

Torres, Henry. *Pierre Laval.* New York, 1941. (A formidable effort to discredit Laval.)

Valmigère, Pierre. *Und Morgen? Frankreich, Deutschland, und Polen.* Berlin, 2nd ed., 1939. (French revisionist argument against the Versailles settlement in Eastern Europe.)

Valois, Georges. *Guerre ou blocus économique.* Paris, 1939. (Brilliant argument in favor of political understanding and economic cooperation between France and Germany.)

Verax, S. "Exc. L'Honorable William C. Bullitt," in *Revue des Deux Mondes,* July 1, 1939 (Useful officially-inspired criticism of Bullitt's incendiary role on the European diplomatic scene.)

Weill, Georges. *L'Éveil des Nationalités et le Mouvement Libéral, 1815-1848.* Paris, 1930. (Useful survey, especially important for Polish revolutionary efforts against Russia after the Congress of Vienna.)

Weygand, Général Maxime. *En lisant les Mémoires de Guerre du Général de Gaulle.* Paris, 1955. (Devastating criticism of tendentious comments by the French resistance hero, de Gaulle; defense of Weygand's policy of encouraging public confidence in the French military defense.)

Weygand, Général Maxime. *Mémoires,* vol. 2: *Mirages et Réalité.* Paris, 1957. (A moderate, modest and factual account.)

Zay, Jean. *Souvenirs et Solitude.* Paris, 1945. (Especially useful for official American policy encouraging a Franco-German war.)

Zevaes, Alexandre. *Histoire de la Troisième République.* Paris, 1938. (Important for the role of the

French Senate in the overthrow of the Blum Popular Front.)

IV. Memoirs and Principal Secondary Sources: German

Abetz, Otto Friedrich. *Das offene Problem: ein Rückblick auf zwei Jahrzehnte deutscher Frankreich politik.* Köln, 1951. (Indispensable for the Hitler-Ribbentrop policy of reconciliation with France.)

Abshagen, Karl Heinz. *Canaris: Patriot und Weltbürger.* Stuttgart, 1949. (Useful for the German opposition to Hitler and British access to secret German policy decisions.)

Abshagen, Karl Heinz. *King, Lords and Gentlemen: Influence and Power of the English Upper Classes.* London, 1939. (Brilliant study of the contemporary English scene by a German Rhodes scholar.)

Adamheit, Theodor. *Sowietarmee und Weltrevolution: Moskaus Angriff gegen Europe und die Welt.* Berlin, 1942. (Vitally important survey of Russian military and foreign policy based on official Soviet pronouncements and statistics.)

Ahlers, Johannes. *Polen.* Berlin, 1935. (Excellent account of developments in Poland after World War I.)

Krüger, F.P. (Peter Alding). *Juden in England,* 2 vols. Berlin, 1940-1942. (Contains important biographical information on several British leaders.)

Anrich, Ernst. *Deutsche Geschichte, 1918-1939.* Leipzig, 1941. (Basic survey of German history between the two world wars.)

Assman, Kurt. *Deutsche Schicksalsjahre.* Wiesbaden, 1950. (Important pro-British account of major policy decisions based on extensive use of unpublished British and German sources.)

Aubin, H., et al. *Deutschland und der Osten: deutsche Ostforschung: Ergebnisse und Aufgaben seit dem ersten Weltkrieg,* 2 vols. Leipzig, 1942-1943. (Contains carefully documented research on the Czechs, Poles, and German policy in Eastern Europe.)

Bail, O. *Die völkerrechtliche Lage der Freien Stadt Danzig.* Berlin, 1939. (One of several useful systematic studies on the confusing international status of Danzig prior to World War II.)

Bargatzky, W. *Der Sinn der englischen Festlandspolitik.* Munich, 1939. (Useful analysis of the application of the traditional British balance of power policy.)

Beck, F.A. *Der Aufgang des Germanischen Weltalters.* Bochum, 1944. (Interesting analysis of European prospects predicated on the assumption of ultimate reconcilation between Britain and Germany.)

Beckmann, Ewald. *Der Dolchstoss-Prozess in München.* Munich, 1925. (Vital for Hitler's thought about Germany's role in European affairs.)

Benton, W., and Grimm, G. *Nuremberg: German Views of the War Trials.* Dallas, 1955. (Contains mild criticism of the methods employed and the decisions reached in the prosecution of the German leaders.)

Berber, F. *Die Amerikanische Neutralität im Kriege, 1939-1941.* Essen, 1943. (Useful criticism of official American policy in Europe; contains a section on the period immediately prior to World War II.)

Berndt, A.I. *Der Marsch ins Grossdeutsche Reich,* 2 vols. Munich, 1942. (Useful official German documentation of policy in Austria and Czechoslovakia.)

Beumelberg, Werner. *Deutschland in Ketten.* Munich, 1931. (Indispensable for the for the full realization of German impotence under the Versailles system.)

Beyer, H. and Lehr, O. *Grosse Deutsche im Ausland: eine volksdeutsche Geschichte in Lebensbilder.* Stuttgart, 1939. (Useful for the role of German pioneers in the economic and cultural development of Eastern Europe.)

Bierschenk, Theodor. *Die deutschen Volksgruppen in Polen, 1934-1939.* Göttingen, 1955. (Useful description of the political and economic organizations of the German minority.)

Bohmann, Alfred. *Die Ausweisung der Sudetendeutschen.* Marburg, 1955. (Especially important for economic conditions under Czech rule prior to 1938.)

Borresholm, Boris von. *Dr. Goebbels nach Aufzeichnungen aus seiner Umgebung.* Berlin, 1949. (Contains much trivial matter and occasional penetrating insights into German propaganda methods.)

Brackmann, Albert. *Germany and Poland.* Munich, 1934. (Contains several brilliant studies of German-Polish relations; see especially W. Vogel, "Poland as Sea Power and Trading State," and H.Recke, "West Prussia.")

Breyer, Richard. *Das Deutsche Reich und Polen, 1932-1937: Aussenpolitik und Volksgruppenfragen.* Würzburg, 1955. (Indispensable on the conflicts among minority groups in Poland.)

Brock, Rudolf. *Stawisky: der größte Korruptionsskandal Europas.* Berlin, 1934. (Excellent detailed account of the depredations of Stavisky.)

Broda, Ernst. *Benötigt die tschechoslowakische Republik den Anschluss fremdnationaler Gebiete?.* Vienna, 1919. (Trenchant criticism by a leading expert of the aggrandizement of the new Czech state.)

Bross, Werner. *Gespräche mit Hermann Göring während des Nürnberger Prozesses.* Flensburg, 1950. (Useful for Göring's ideas, but unreliable for the larger European scene.)

Broszat, Martin. "Das Sudetendeutsche Freikorps" in *Vierteljahrshefte für Zeitgeschichte,* 1961:1. (Important source on Sudeten efforts against the Czechs after the Runciman mission.)

Brönner-Höpfner, Elizabeth. *Die Leiden des Memelgebietes.* Berlin, 1934. (Indispensable for the Lituanian seizure of Memel and the disadvantages of foreign rule for the local German population.)

Brügel, J.W. "Eine Zerstürte Legende um Hitlers Aussenpolitik" in *Vierteljahrshefte für Zeitgeschichte,* Oct. 1957. (Criticism of German policy in 1939 in the context of post-World War II memoirs.)

Buchheit, Gert. *Mussolini und das Neue Italien.* Berlin, 4th ed., 1941. (Excellent for German-Italian relations and Mussolini's plans for conciliation in Europe.)

Conze, Werner. *Polnische Nation und Deutsche Politik im Ersten Weltkrieg.* Cologne, 1958. (Excellent on Polish political movements prior to 1914 and wartime policy of General Hans von Beseler.)

Dahms, Hellmuth Günther. *Der Spanische Bürgerkrieg, 1936-1939.* Tübingen, 1962. (Takes account of the most recent sources and offers an excellent synthesis.)

David, H. *Englands Europäische Politik.* Bern, 1924. (Especially valuable for English policy at the Congress of Vienna.)

Dehio, Ludwig. *Deutschland und die Weltpolitik im 20. Jahrhundert.* Stuttgart, 1955. (Useful for problems of German foreign policy; especially critical of Wilhelm II and Hitler.)

Dehio, Ludwig. *Gleichgewicht oder Hegemonie.* Stuttgart, 1948. (Suggestive essays concerning the British role in Europe and the impact on France and Germany.)

Dettmann, Franz. *Danzig zwischen Deutschland und Polen.* Berlin, 1939. (Valuable on problems created by the Versailles settlement.)

Dieckhoff, Hans H. *Zur Vorgeschichte des Roosevelt-Krieges.* Berlin, 1943. (Analysis of Roosevelt's war policy after 1937 by the last German Ambassador to the United States.)

"Diplomaticus." *The Czechs and Their Minorities.* London, 1938. (Detailed German propaganda treatment of the Czech case.)

Dirksen, Herbert von. *Moskau, Tokio, London: Erinnerungen und Betrachtungen zu zwanzig Jahren deutscher Aussenpolitik, 1919-1939.* Stuttgart, 1949. (Vital for Anglo-German relations; reveals the impact of British propaganda on the German Ambassador.)

Dönitz, Karl. *Zehn Jahre und Zwanzig Tage.* Bonn, 1958. (Brilliant account of German naval matters, with useful information on German foreign policy prior to World War II.)

Dornberger, Walther. *Der Schuss ins Weltall.* Esslingen, 1952. (Reveals that Hitler did not expect the development of decisive new military weapons in 1939.)

Dwinger, E.E. *Der Tod in Polen: die Volksdeutsche Passion.* Jena, 1940. (Describes the massacres of Germans in Poland and the helplessness of German minority groups.)

Eckart, Dietrich. *Der Bolschewismus von Moses bis Lenin: Zwiegespräch zwischen Adolf Hitler und mir.* Munich, 1925. (Important for Hitler's early ideas about Communism.)

Eichstädt, Ulrich. *Von Dollfuss zu Hitler: Geschichte des Anschlusses Österreichs, 1933-1938.* Wiesbaden, 1956. (Carefully documented analysis; indispensable for the 1938 Austrian crisis.)

Esch, Peter. *Polen kreuz und quer.* Berlin, 1939. (Fascinating personal observations by an expert on Poland.)

Essler, F.W. *Twenty Years of Sudeten-German Losses, 1918-1938.* Vienna, 1938. (Useful analysis of Czech policy in the Sudetenland.)

Fabry, Philipp W. *Der Hitler-Stalin Pakt, 1939-1941: ein Beitrag zur Methode sowjetischer Aussenpolitik.* Darmstadt, 1962. (Best study of the reasons for the Hitler-Stalin pact and its failure.)

Flicke, W. *Die Rote Kapelle.* Hilden, 1949. (Account of intrigues and plots in the German espionage service.)

Federau, Fritz. *Der Zweite Weltkrieg: seine Finanzierung in Deutschland.* Tübingen, 1962. (Confirms the conclusions of Burton Klein on the conservative approach of leading German economists to defense expenditures.)

Förster, W. *Generaloberst Ludwig Beck: sein Kampf gegen den Krieg.* Munich, 1953. (Vital for the German military opposition to Hitler in 1938 and 1939.)

Foertsch, Hermann. *Schuld und Verhängnis: die Fritschkrise im Frühjahr 1938 als Wendepunkt in der Geschichte der nationalsozialistischen Zeit.* Stuttgart, 1951. (Carefully documented account deploring the failure of a German army revolt against Hitler in 1938; contains much useful information.)

Frank, Hans. *Im Angesicht des Galgens: Deutung Hitler und seiner Zeit auf Grund eigener Erlebnisse und Erkenntnisse.* Munich, 1953. (Indispensable for the evolution of Hitler's ideas and policies and for conditions in Germany prior to World War II.)

Franzel, Emil. *Die Politik der Sudetendeutsche in der Tschechoslovakei, 1918-1938.* Gräfelfing, 1952. (Valuable study of the programs of the major Sudeten political groups.)

Franzel, Emil. *Sudetendeutsche Geschichte.* Augsburg, 1958. (Excellent scholarly narrative; especially good on the 1938 period.)

Fritzsche, Hans. *The Sword in the Scales.* London, 1953. (The most important description of the principal Nuremberg trial by a defendant; contains important suggestions concerning German policy in the 1938-1939 period.)

Guartner, Margarete. *Danzig and the Corridor: World Opinion on the Topic of Today.* Berlin, 1939. (Contains useful introductory material and comments from nearly one hundred prominent spokesmen of the Western countries criticizing the Versailles terms at Danzig.)

Gieve, Werner. "Grundfragen der Siedlungsforschung in Nordosteuropa," in *Altpreussische Forschungen, 1938,* Heft 1. (Clear detailed analysis of the complex problems in research on German and non-German settlements along the Baltic Sea.)

Gisevius, H.B. *To the Bitter End.* Boston, 1947. (Useful source on the German opposition to Hitler; sometimes unreliable on important issues and details.)

Görlitz, W., and Quint, H. *Adolf Hitler: eine Biographie.* Stuttgart, 1952. (Avoids Hitler's personal life and thought and concentrates on his policies; contains much useful information.)

Graml, Hermann. *Der 9 November 1938.* Bonn, 1953. (Interesting account of the 1938 anti-Jewish demonstrations.)

Greiner, Helmuth. *Die Oberste Wehrmachtführung, 1939-1943.* Wiesbaden, 1951. (Authoritative and indispensable record of German military planning and aims.)

Grimm, Friedrich. *Frankreich und der Korridor.* Hamburg, 1939. (Useful compendium of critical comments by Frenchmen on the 1919 settlement in Eastern Europe.)

Grimm, Hans. *Warum-Woher-Aber Wohin?* Lippoldsberg, 1954. (Brilliant study of Hitler and his time; indispensable for the analysis of German policy.)

Gross, F. *Politisches Handbuch der Freien Stadt Danzig.* Danzig, 1924. (Vital for the organization of political life and for the constitutional system of the Free City regime.)

Halder, Franz. *Hitler als Feldherr.* Munich, 1949. (Useful for the German opposition to Hitler and conflicts over military policy.)

Hammer, Hermann. "Die Deutschen Ausgaben von Hitlers *Mein Kampf*," in *Vierteljahrshefte für Zeitgeschichte,* April 1956. (Important for Hitler's later attitude toward his own writing and his refusal to make changes despite regret for some early statements.)

Hanfstängl, Ernst. *Unheard Witness.* Philadelphia, 1957. (Important source for the evolution of Hitler's ideas, although somewhat distorted by excessive editing.)

Haussherr, Hans. "Hardenberg und der Friede von Basel," in *Historische Zeitschrift,* Oct. 1957. (Important for the political isolation of Prussia at the time of the 3rd Polish partition in 1795.)

Heiber, Helmut. *Adolf Hitler: eine Biographie.* Berlin, 1960. (Brief biography written from a jaundiced Nuremberg trial perspective.)

Heiber, Helmut. "Der Fall Grünspan," in *Vierteljahrshefte für Zeitgeschichte,* April 1957. (Indispensable for the Polish passport crisis and anti-Jewish demonstrations in Germany of 1938.)

Heike, Otto. *Das Deutschtum in Polen.* Bonn, 1955. (Useful survey on economic and emigration trends of the German minority in Poland.)

Heiss, F. Lohse, G., and **Wücher, W.** *Deutschland und der Korridor,* Berlin, 1939. (The German case against the Versailles Corridor settlement and subsequent Polish policy.)

Hemmerle, Eduard. *Der Weg in die Katastrophe: von Bismarcks Sturz bis zum Ende Hitlers.* Munich, 1948. (An able and detailed criticism of German policy on the eve of the two World Wars.)

Henlein, Konrad. *Heim ins Reich: Reden aus den Jahren 1937 und 1938.* Karlsbad, 1939. (Important for the evolution of Henlein's policy toward the Czechs.)

Hesse, Fritz. *Deutsche Politik von Brüning bis Adenauer.* Munich, 1953. (Useful for Hitler's attempted solutions of problems; strength of Hitler's system in 1939 receives emphasis.)

Hesse, Fritz. *Das Spiel um Deutschland.* Munich, 1953. (Indispensable for Ribbentrop's role in German policy.)

Heuss, Theodor. *Hitlers Weg: eine historisch-politische Studie über den Nationalsozialismus.* Berlin, 1932. (Dispassionate and valuable analysis of Hitler's program shortly before his appointment in 1933.)

Hilger, G. and **Meyer, A.G.** *The Incompatible Allies: A Memoir-History of German-Soviet Relations, 1918-1941.* New York, 1953. (Vital for the Russian and German motives which produced the 1939 pact.)

Hilger, G. *Wir und der Kreml.* Frankfurt, 1956. (Contains personal experiences and ideas from the 1939 period.)

Hillgruber, Andreas. *Hitler, König Carol und Marschall Antonescu: die deutsch-rumänischen Beziehungen, 1938-1944.* Wiesbaden, 1954. (Contains useful information on the Tilea hoax and the actual relations of friendship between Germany and Rumania in 1939.)

Hoegner, Wilhelm. *Die Verratene Republik: Geschichte der deutschen Gegenrevolution.* Munich, 1958. (Contains some useful information about Hitler's political tactics.)

Hölzle, Erwin. *Der Osten im ersten Weltkrieg.* Leipzig, 1944. (Indispensable for the history of the Slavic communities behind the German front in World War I.)

Hoffman, F., *et al. Ostdeutschland.* Kitzingen, 1949. (Contains useful statistical information on conditions prior to World War II.)

Hoffman, Heinrich. *Hitler Was My Friend.* London, 1955. (Vital for the personal life and personality of Hitler.)

Hossbach, F. *Zwischen Wehrmacht und Hitler.* Hannover, 1949. (Vital for the German opposition to Hitler and the role played by Hossbach and other officers.)

Hubensteiner, Benno. *Bayerische Geschichte.* Munich, 1951. (Useful for the settlement and development of Austria by Bavarian pioneers.)

Jaksch, Wenzel. *Benesch war Gewarnt.* Munich, 1949. (Brilliant criticism of the pro-Communist course of President Beneš.)

Jaksch, Wenzel. *Europas Weg nach Potsdam.* Stuttgart, 1958. (Indispensable on the failure of Czech minority policy prior to 1938 and on German policy after the Munich conference.)

Johanssen, Theodor. *Gdingen.* Danzig, 1928. (Pioneer study of the implications for Danzig of a major Polish port on the Baltic Sea.)

Jost, W. *Was wir vom Weltkrieg nicht wissen.* Leipzig, 1938. (Graphic work stressing the futility of World War I.)

Kähler, S.A. *Zwei deutsche Bündnisangebote, 1889 und 1939.* Göttingen, 1948. (Interesting comparison between the efforts of Bismarck and Hitler to achieve alliances with England.)

Kätner, Alfred. *Weiße Fahne über Danzig.* Kiel, 1950. (Graphic description of the annihilation of German Danzig by the Soviet Union in 1945.)

Kern, Erich. *Von Versailles zu Adolf Hitler: der schreckliche Friede.* Göttingen, 1961. (The best analysis of the problems which arose for Germany from the 1919 peace settlement.)

Kluke, Paul, *et. al. Gutachten des Institute für Zeitgeschichte.* Munich, 1958. (Contains important analyses of German policy from documentary sources.)

Knierem, August von. *The Nuremberg Trials.* Chicago, 1959. (Legal analysis of the 12 American trials at Nuremberg, 1946-1949, with occcasional items of unusual historical interest, *i.e.,* the annexation of East Galicia by Tsarist Russia during World War I.)

Koch, Erwin. *Das Feuer der Sterne: die Geschichte des Roten Mondes und der schmutzigen Bombe.* Berlin, 1958. (Reveals how emigrants from Europe attempted to exploit German scientific discoveries prior to World War II for the development of atomic weapons against Germany.)

Kohl, Louis von. *Der Wortbruch von Versailles.* Berlin, 1935. (Exhaustive analysis of the Allied betrayal of the 1918 armistice agreement.)

Koitz, H. *Männer um Pilsudski.* Breslau, 1934. (Interesting biographical sketches of Polish leaders.)

Kordt, Erich. *Nicht aus den Akten...: Die Wilhelmstraße in Frieden und Krieg: Erlebnisse, Begegnungen und Eindrücke, 1928-1945.* Stuttgart, 1950. (Vital source on German policy from a German diplomat at Berlin secretly in contact with the British.)

Kordt, Erich. *Wahn und Wirklichkeit.* Stuttgart, 1947. (Primarily useful for material on Russo-German relations.)

Kramer, Hans. *Die Großmächte und die Weltpolitik, 1789-1945.* Innsbruck, 1952. (Especially useful for the interpretation of German policy after 1871.)

Kranz, Herbert. *Hinter den Kulissen der Kabinette und Generalstäbe: eine französische Zeit- und Sittengeschichte, 1933-1940.* Frankfurt, 1941. (Important for British influence on French military and foreign policy.)

Kraus, H., *et al. Deutschlands Ostproblem: eine Untersuchung der Beziehungen des deutschen Volkes zu seinen östlichen Nachbarn.* Würzburg, 1957. (Defense of the traditional German role in Eastern Europe and German claims in the East.)

Krausnick, Helmut. *Vorgeschichte und Beginn des militärischen Widerstandes gegen Hitler.* Munich, 1956. (Defense of the military conspiracies in Germany prior to World War II.)

Krausnick, Helmut. "Legenden um Hitlers Aussenpolitik" in *Vierteljahrshefte für Zeitgeschichte,* July 1954. (Use of the Nuremberg trial documents to challenge Fritz Hesse's interpretation of Ribbentrop's policy, *vide: Das Spiel um Deutschland.*)

Kriegk, Otto. *Die Geburt Europas.* Berlin, 1943. (Condemnation of the balance of power and defense of an integrated Europe.)

Kriegk, Otto. *Wer Treibt England in den Krieg?* Berlin, 1939. (Criticism of the war agitation of Churchill and his circle.)

Kubizek, August. *The Young Hitler I Knew.* Boston, 1955. (Indispensable and reliable account of the early development of Hitler's ideas.)

Kuhn, Walter. *Siedlungsgeschichte Oberschlesiens.* Würzburg, 1954. (Excellent source for the historical development and preponderant German character of Upper Silesia.)

Landgraf, Hugo. *Kampf um Danzig.* Dresden, 1940. (Interesting historical survey of power struggles in the Danzig area.)

Läuen, Harald. "Polens Politik der 'integralen Lösung,'" in *Osteuropa,* November 1938. (Useful analysis of Polish elections and official domestic policy in 1938.)

Läuen, Harald. *Polnische Tragödie.* Stuttgart, 1955. (Outstanding analysis of recent trends in Polish thought by a leading expert.)

Läuen, Harald. *Polnisches Zwischenspiel: eine Episode der Ostpolitik.* Berlin, 1940. (Brilliant analysis of official Polish policies.)

Laubert, Manfred. *Die Preußische Polenpolitik von 1772-1914.* Kraków, 1944. (Excellent study of the contradictory trends in Prussian policy toward the Poles.)

Laurie, A.P. *Great Britain's Policy after Munich.* Berlin, 1940. (The British accused of responding to the Munich conference by planning the destruction of Germany.)

Lehmann, H. *Englands Spiel mit Polen.* Berlin, 1940. (British intervention blamed for the German-Polish conflict.)

Leithäuser, Joachim G. *Diplomatie auf schiefer Bahn.* Berlin, 1953. (Blunders of German diplomats prior to two World Wars.)

Lemberg, Eugen. *Geschichte des Nationalismus in Europa.* Munich, 1950. (Vital analysis of the traditional German role in Eastern Europe under the impact of modern nationalism.)

Lemberg, Eugen. "Zur Geschichte der deutschen Volksgruppen in Ost-Mitteleuropa," in *Zeitschrift für Ostforschung,* no. 3, Marburg, 1952. (Brilliant analysis of the German role in the East.)

Lewinsky, H., and **Wagner, R.** *Danziger Staats – und Völkerrecht.* Danzig, 1927. (Excellent for the constitutional and international status of Danzig.)

Loessner, A. *Josef Piłsudski, eine Lebensbeschreibung auf Grund seiner eigenen Schriften.* Leipzig, 1935. (Useful and sympathetic biography of Poland's dictator.)

Lorentz, F., Fischer, A., and **Lehr-Splawinski, T.** *The Cassubian Civilization.* London, 1935. (Systematic study of a unique Slavic minority group living among the Poles and Germans of West Prussia.)

Ludat, Herbert. "Polens Stellung in Ostmitteleuropa," in *Geschichte und Gegenwart,* Berlin, 1939. (Poland criticized for seeking a larger European role not warranted by her size and strength..)

Lück, Kurt. *Deutsche Aufbaukräfte in der Entwicklung Polens.* Plauen, 1934. (Useful survey on the contribution of the German element to the growth of Poland.)

Lück, Kurt, *et al. Deutsche Gestalter und Ordner im Osten.* Leipzig, 1942. (The role of German pioneers in the development of Eastern Europe.)

Lück, Kurt. *Der Lebenskampf im deutsch-polnischen Grenzraum.* Berlin, 1943. (Stresses the competition of individuals and the rarity of German-Polish wars.)

Lück, Kurt. *Der Mythos vom deutschen in der polnischen Volksüberlieferung und Literatur: Forschungen zur deutsch-polnischen Nachbarschaft im Ostmitteleuropäischen Raum.* Leipzig, 1938. (Indispensable classic work on Polish attitudes toward Germany; highly praised in Polish reviews.)

Lück, Kurt. *Volksdeutsche Soldaten unter Polens Fahnen.* Berlin, 1940. (Stresses loyal service of minority Germans in the Polish Army of 1939.)

Lüdtke, Franz. *Ein Jahrtausend Krieg zwischen Deutschland und Polen.* Stuttgart, 1941. (Pessimistic survey of the legacy of German-Polish relations.)

Lufft, H.A.L. *Der britische Imperialismus.* Berlin, 1940. (Critical survey of British imperialism after World War I by an expert on American and British Empire history.)

Lutz, Hermann. "Foreign Policy in the Third Reich," in *Current History,* April 1955. (Critical survey of German policy objectives.)

Lutz, Hermann. *Franco-German Unity: Basis for European Peace.* Chicago, 1957. (Stimulating critical analysis devoted largely to German policy.)

Lutz, Hermann. *Lord Grey and the World War.* New York, 1928. (Basic revisionist work on the consequences of Grey's secret diplomacy in 1914.)

Manstein, Erich von. *Aus einem Soldatenleben., 1887-1939.* Bonn, 1958. (Vital for German military planning and soldiers' attitudes.)

Manstein, Erich von. *Verlorene Siege.* Bonn, 1955. (Contains expert evaluation of the 1939 German operational plans.)

Marcks, Erich. *Englands Machtpolitik.* Stuttgart, 1940. (Vital on the balance of power in the 18th and 19th century English policy.)

Matschke, Herbert. *Die Grundlagen des Internationalen Status von Danzig.* Berlin, 1936. (Best survey of the juridical complexities of the Danzig situation.)

Mau, Hermann, and **Krausnick, Helmut.** *Deutsche Geschichte der jüngsten Vergangenheit, 1933-1945.* Tübingen, 1956. (Expert survey with principal emphasis on foreign affairs.)

Maurer, Emil. *Frankreichs politischer Weg.* Leipzig, 1940. (Sympathetic account of developments which produced the French defeat; hopeful on future Franco-German relations.)

Meissner, Hans Otto, and **Wilde, Harry.** *Die Machtergreifung: ein Bericht über die Technik des nationalsozialistischen Staatsstreichs.* Stuttgart, 1958. (Important critical account on the launching of Hitler's system in Germany.)

Meissner, Hans Otto. *The Man with Three Faces.* New York, 1955. (Anti-Hitler book based on personal experiences and contacts of the author.)

Meissner, Hans Otto. *Staatssekretär unter Ebert, Hindenburg, Hitler.* Hamburg, 1950. (Indispensable for many important German policy conferences; highly reliable source.)

Möning, Richard, and **Gisela.** *Danzig.* Berlin, 1939. (Able presentation of the situation at Danzig immediately prior to World War II.)

Moltke, Helmuth. *Darstellung der inneren Verhältnisse und der gesellschaftlichen Zustandes in Polen.* Berlin, 1832. (Fascinating pro-Polish classic on the situation after the Congress of Vienna; see also *Gesammelte Schriften und Denkwürdigkeiten des General-Feldmarschalls Grafen Helmuth von Moltke,* vol. 2, Berlin, 1891.)

Müller, H. *Die polnische Volksgruppe im Deutschen Reich.* Warsaw, 1941. (Important source for the efficient organization of the minority Poles in Germany prior to World War II.)

Moravec, Emanuel. *Das Ende der Benesch-Republik: die tschechoslowakische Krise 1938.* Prague, 3rd ed., 1941. (Important source for the 1938 crisis within Czechoslovakia.)

Neumann, Rudolf. *Ostpreußen im polnischen Schrifttum.* Danzig, 1931. (Useful source for widespread Polish aspirations to annex German East Prussia.)

Norden, Albert. *So Werden Kriege Gemacht.* Berlin, 1950. (Communist criticism of German policy prior to World War II.)

Nowak, Robert. *Der Künstliche Staat: Ostprobleme der Tschechoslowakei.* Berlin, 1938. (Important for Slovak and Ruthenian resentment toward Czech rule.)

Nowak, Robert. "Die Zukunft der Karpatenukraine," in *Zeitschrifte für Geopolitik.* November 1938. (Important source for Ruthenian conditions after the Munich conference.)

Oberländer, Theodor. *Die Landwirtschaft Posen-Pommerellens vor und nach der Abtrennung vom Deutschen Reich.* Berlin, 1937. (Excellent study of the decline of agriculture in the former German provinces under Polish rule.)

Oertzen, F.W. von. *Alles oder Nichts.* Breslau, 1934. (Important book by an influential writer sceptical of the prospects for German-Polish cooperation.)

Oncken, Wilhelm. *Das Zeitalter Friedrichs des Großen,* 2 vols. Berlin, 1882. (Classic study of European relations based on archive materials; especially useful for the situation in Poland.)

Oncken, Wilhelm. *Das Zeitalter der Revolution: des Kaiserreiches und der Befreiungskriege,* 2 vols. Berlin, 1884. (Especially useful for English policy in Europe.)

Oven, Wilfred von. *Mit Goebbels bis zum Ende,* 2 vols. Buenos Aires, 1949. (Sympathetic and revealing account of German propaganda aims.)

Papen, Franz von. *Memoirs.* New York, 1953. (Indispensable for German diplomacy in Austria.)

Pfeffer, Karl Heinz. *England: Vormacht der bürgerlichen Welt.* Hamburg, 1940. (Vital for British aims and propaganda in Germany.)

Pritzkoleit, Kurt. *Wem Gehört Deutschland: eine Chronik von Besitz und Macht.* Vienna, 1957. (Contains useful statistics on pre-German economic assets.)

Proeller, Kurt. "Judentum und Kommunismus," in *Volk und Reich,* April 1939. (Interesting analysis of Communist objectives in Europe.)

Puttkamer, E. von. *Die polnische Nationaldemokratie.* Krakow, 1943. (Vital for the anti-German program of the National Democrats.)

Rahn, Rudolf. *Ruheloses Leben.* Düsseldorf, 1949. (Contains interesting observations on German policy in 1939 by the last German Ambassador to Italy.)

Raschhofer, Hermann. *Die Sudetenfrage: ihre Völkerrechtliche Entwicklung vom ersten Weltkrieg bis zur Gegenwart.* Munich, 1953. (Contains much useful information on Sudeten grievances and aims.)

Raupach, Hans, et al. *Festschrift zum Bundestreffen der Schlesier in München, 1951.* Munich, 1951. (Useful essays on the importance of Upper Silesia to Germany prior to World War II.)

Rauschning, Hermann. *Die Entdeutschung Posens und Pomerellens.* Berlin, 1931. (Violently anti-Polish denunciations of conditions in the former German provinces.)

Rauschning, Hermann. *Zehn Monate nationalsozialistische Regierung in Danzig.* Danzig, 1934. (Survey of changes and improvements by the National Socialist Senate President.)

Rheinhaben, W. von. *Unruhiges Europa: Tatsachen und Probleme.* Berlin, 1939. (Presents the case for a strong Germany in Central Europe.)

Ribbentrop, Annelies von. *Verschwörung gegen den Frieden.* Leoni, 1962. (Contains excellent exposures of many familiar items of the Nuremberg Trial propaganda arsenal.)

Ribbentrop, Joachim von. *Zwischen London und Moskau: Erinnerungen und letzte Aufzeichnungen, aus dem Nachlass herausgeben von Annelies von Ribbentrop.* Leoni, 1954. (Indispensable for German policy; emphasizes German desire for friendship with England.)

Richter, Karl. "Die politische Stellung der sieben Großmächte als Folge ihrer völkischen Lage im Raum," in *Zeitschrift für Geopolitik,* April 1939. (Emphasizes the gigantic material superiority of the Soviet Union, the United States, and the British Empire.)

Rintelen, Enno von. *Mussolini als Bundesgenosse: Erinnerungen des deutschen Militärattaches in Rom, 1936-1943.* Tübingen, 1951. (Stresses Italy's military weakness.)

Ritter, Gerhard. *Carl Goerdeler und die deutsche Widerstandsbewegung.* Stuttgart, 1954. (Indispensable for the contacts of the German opposition to Hitler with British leaders prior to World War II.)

Rohden, P.R. *Die klassische Diplomatie.* Berlin, 1939. (Brilliant study of the limited aims and conservative methods of traditional diplomacy; illustrates the departures of the Wilsonian era.)

Rönnefarth, Helmuth. *Die Sudetenkrise in der internationalen Politik: Entstehung, Verlauf, Auswirkung.* 2 vol. Wiesbaden, 1961. (The most informative German account of the 1938 Czech crisis.)

Roos, Hans. *Polen und Europa: Studien zur polnischen Aussenpolitik, 1931-1939.* Tübingen, 1957. (Important pro-Polish and anti-German account of the difficulties between Germany and Poland.)

Roos, Hans. "Die 'Präventivkriegspläne' Piłsudskis von 1933," in *Vierteljahrshefte für Zeitgeschichte,* Oct. 1955. (Attempt to question the authenticity of Piłsudski's preventive war plans prior to their definitive confirmation by Lord Vansittart.)

Rosenberg, Alfred. *Ideological Struggles and International Enmity.* Berlin, 1939. (States the case against solving ideological rivalries by military action.)

Rosenberg, Alfred. *Die Zukunft einer deutschen Aussenpolitik.* Munich, 1927. (Basic for Hitler–Rosenberg disagreements on policy.)

Roth, Paul. *Die politische Entwicklung in Kongresspolen während der deutschen Okkupation.* Leipzig, 1919. (Vital for Germany policy in favor of Polish independence during World War I.)

Rothfels, Hans, *et al. Das Dritte Reich und Europa.* Tutzing, 1956. (Contains interesting brief insights on varied aspects of German policy.)

Ruge, F. *Der Seekrieg.* Annapolis, 1957. (Emphasizes German unpreparedness for a major war in 1939.)

Sandberger, D. *Die englische Politik bei den Pariser Friedensverhandlungen 1919.* Stuttgart, 1938. (Excellent for secret British diplomacy in the 1914-1919 period, and on the evolution of policy.)

Sasse, Heinz Günther. *England/Deutschlands Widerpart: die deutsch-englischen Beziehungen von 1815-1940.* Berlin, 1941. (Stresses British opposition to the German customs union, German unification, German colonial policy, and German territorial revision after World War I.)

Schacht, H. *Abrechnung mit Hitler.* Berlin, 1948. (Valuable for German economic policy under the first and second Four Year Plans.)

Schacht, H. *76 Jahres meines Lebens.* Bad Wörrishofen, 1953. (Valuable for German defense expenditures and German opposition to Hitler.)

Scharp, Heinrich. *Abschied von Europa?* Frankfurt a/M, 1953. (Useful survey of chaotic European situations since 1914.)

Schildiener, A. *Der russisch-Deutsche Flirt vor Kriegsbeginn,* ms. (Report on the Moscow situation of 1939 by a member of the German Embassy; stresses contrasts between Russia and the West.)

Schmidt, Paul. *Statist auf diplomatischer Bühne, 1923-1945.* Bonn, 1949. (Indispensable first-hand account of German policy in the making.)

Schramm, Wilhelm von. *Conspiracy among Generals.* New York, 1956. (Explains the irresolute tactics of the German military opposition to Hitler.)

Schubring, Helmut. *Deutscher Friedenswille gegen polnischen Nationalhass im Einsatz der deutschen Presse, 1933-1939.* Berlin, 1941. (Excellent survey of the anti-German line of most of the Polish press.)

Schwartz, Michael. *Die Slowakei: der jüngste Staat Europas.* Leipzig, 1939. (Valuable source for Slovakian conditions, 1938-1939, and the Slovakian independence movement.)

Schweppenburg, H. *Erinnerungen eines Militärattachés in London, 1933-1936.* Stuttgart, 1949. (Important for British armament plans.)

Seraphim, P.H. *Polen und seine Wirtschaft.* Königsberg, 1937. (Stimulating criticism of Polish economic policy by a leading expert.)

Sieburg, Friedrich. *Blick durchs Fenster: aus zehn Jahren Frankreich und England.* Frankfurt a/M, 1939. (Contains several important insights on French attitudes toward Germany; pro-French and pro-British in tone.)

Six, F.A. *Die Presse in Polen.* Berlin, 1938. (Analytical survey of contrasts in the Polish press despite the Polish dictatorship.)

Sonnemann, T. *Die zweimalige Einkreisung.* Berlin, 2nd ed., 1943. (Thoughtful comparison of British tactics in seeking to strangle Germany in two World Wars.)

Stoye, Johannes. *Frankreich zwischen Furcht und Hoffnung.* Berlin, 1938. (Brilliant analysis of conflicting trends in France by a leading German expert on comparative government.)

Styra, Robert. *Das polnische Parteiwesen und seine Presse.* Posen, 1936. (Useful on the organization of political journalism in Poland.)

Sünderman, Helmut. *Alter Feind — Was Nun? Wiederbegegnung mit England und Engländern.* Leoni, 1956. (Excellent analysis of the anti-German tactics of Churchill and Vansittart..)

Sünderman, Helmut. *Das Dritte Reich.* Leoni, 1959. (Contains a brilliant analysis of crisis conditions which brought Hitler to power in 1933.)

Sünderman, Helmut. *Das Erbe des falschen Propheten.* Leoni, 1958. (Valuable in explaining German fear and dislike of Soviet Marxism prior to World War II.)

Sünderman, Helmut. *Die Grenzen fallen.* Munich, 2nd ed., 1939. (Indispensable primary source on conditions in Austria and Sudetenland after their liberation in 1938.)

Thimme, Annelise. *Gustav Stresemann: eine politische Biographie zur Geschichte der Weimarer Republik.* Hannover, 1957. (Critical of the annexationist aspirations of Weimar foreign policy.)

Thorwald, Jürgen. *Die ungeklärten Fälle.* Stuttgart, 1950. (Reveals the limitations of German air armament in 1939.)

Thorwald, Jürgen. *Wen Sie verderben wollen.* Stuttgart, 1952. (Contains useful information on Alfred Rosenberg.)

Thost, H.W. *England wollte keinen Frieden!* Berlin, 1941. (Excellent on 1939 British policy in Poland.)

Tönnies, Norbert. *Der Krieg vor dem Kriege: Englands Propaganda bis zum 3. September 1939.* Essen, 1940. (Contains the first important analysis of the Tilea hoax.)

Treitschke, H. *Der Wiener Kongress.* Berlin, 1943. (Classic attack on a peace settlement at the expense of the Central European peoples, and especially the Germans, Italians, and Poles.)

Turnwald, W.K. *Renascence or Decline of Central Europe: The Sudeten German-Czech Problem.* Munich, 1954. (Useful criticism of the 1919 Czech settlement.)

Übersberger, Hans. *Österreich zwischen Russland und Serbien.* Vienna, 1958. (Contains vital new information on Serbian and Russian plots against Austria-Hungary prior to World War I.)

Ulrich, Oskar. *Der große Irrweg der Tschechen.* Berlin, 1943. (Vital on Czech policies and the counter-movements of the minorities.)

Wegerer, Alfred von. *The Origins of World War II.* New York, 1941. (Brief presentation of the German case by the world's leading expert on World War I origins, i.e., *Ausbruch des Weltkrieges*, 2 vols., Hamburg, 1939.)

Weizsäcker, Ernst von. *Memoirs.* London, 1951. (Indispensable for German policy in the Czech and Memel questions.)

Weizsäcker, Wilhelm. *Geschichte der Deutschen in Böhmen und Mähren.* Hamburg, 1950. (Vital in depicting the role of Bohemia-Moravia as a part of Germany for one thousand years.)

Welkisch, K. "Die Wahlen in Polen," in *Osteuropa,* Dec. 1938. (Vital in explaining the electoral reverses suffered by the Government bloc.)

Wendt, Hans. *Frankreich heute und wir.* Berlin, 1939. (Excellent account of French political developments after the Popular Front.)

Wenger, Paul W. *Wer gewinnt Deutschland?* Stuttgart, 1959. (Fascinating pro-Polish and anti-German account of German policy in Eastern Europe.)

Werner, Bruno E. *Die Galeere.* Frankfurt a/M, 1949. (Excellent for German intellectual life prior to World War II.)

Windelband, Wolfgang. *Bismarck und die europäischen Großmächte, 1879-1885.* Essen, 1940. (Exhaustive study of European diplomacy, especially useful for Bismarck's policy of preventing conflicts in Eastern Europe.)

Wingendorf, Rolf. *Polen: Volk zwischen Ost und West.* Berlin, 1939. (Contains fascinating personal experiences in Poland and analyses of Polish attitudes.)

Wittram, Reinhard. *Baltische Geschichte, 1180-1918.* Munich, 1954. (Valuable for German Baltic settlement and Polish Baltic policy.)

Zarnow, Gottfried. *Die Geburt der Weltkriege.* Düsseldorf, 1957. (Useful criticism of German policy prior to two World Wars.)

Ziehen, Ernst. "Der Streit um die Westerplatte in Danzig im März 1933," in *Westpreussen-Jahrbücher,* vol. 2, Leer, East Friesland, 1952. (Excellent analysis of Polish threats at Danzig.)

Ziesel, Ernst. *Das Leben Vaerläßt uns nicht.* Stuttgart, 1954. (Excellent for popular German desire for peace in 1939.)

Zimmermann, Ludwig. *Deutsche Aussenpolitik in der Ära der Weimarer Republik.* Berlin, 1958. (Especially important for the efforts of Streseman to improve relations with Poland.

Zischka, Anton. *Englands Bündnisse.* Leipzig, 1940. (Excellent presentation of England's sensational record as an unreliable alliance partner.)

V. Memoirs and Principal Secondary Sources: Polish

Askenazy, Simon. *Danzig and Poland.* London, 1921. (Emphasizes the traditional importance to Danzig of the Polish hinterland.

Askenazy, Simon. *Rosja–Polska, 1815-1830.* Lwów, 1907. (Brilliant analysis of the situation in Poland after the Vienna Congress and the reasons for Polish discontent.)

Baginski, Henryk. *Poland and the Baltic.* Edinburgh, 1942. (The case for Polish expansion presented by a leading Polish geopolitician.)

Beck, Józef. *Dernier Rapport: Politique Polonaise, 1926-1939.* Neuchâtel, 1949. (Indispensable for Polish policy prior to World War II.)

Bierowski, Thaddee. *La Ville Libre de Dantzig et la guerre polono-bolchévique de 1920.* Danzig, 1932. (Stresses the failure of the League authorities to permit the maximum military use of Danzig by Poland.)

Bobrzyński, Michał. *Dzieje Polski w Zarysie,* 3 vols. Warsaw, 2nd ed. 1927-1931. (Classic defense of the tradition of decentralized government in Poland.)

Bobrzyński, Michał. *Z Moich Pamietników.* Kraków, 1957. (Posthumous publication of memoirs from the period before 1914 with a valuable biographical introduction.)

Bocheński, Adolf. *Miedzy Niemcamy a Rosja.* Warsaw, 1937. (Indispensable for Polish foreign policy prior to World War II; defends a policy of hostility toward both Germany and the Soviet Union.)

Borowik, Józef. *Gdynia, Poland's Gateway to the Sea.* Torun, 5th ed., 1934. (Valuable survey of the growth and importance of Poland's major new port.)

Cepnik, H. *Edward Smigły-Rydz, generalny inspektor sil zbrojnych.* Warsaw, 1936. (Especially useful for traditions and organizations of the Polish Army.)

Coselschi, E. *Il Ministro Beck e la politica estera della Polonia.* Rome, 1939. (Especially useful for German-Polish relations and traditional Polish friendship for Italy.)

Czerwinski, Witold. *Le Problème de l'Indépendence Économique de la Pologne.* Paris, 1932. (Stresses Polish dependence on foreign capital and German trade.)

Dabski, Jan. *Pokoj Ryski: Wspomnieniea, Pertraktacje, Tajne Uklady z Joffem, Listy.* Warsaw, 1931. (Contains valuable documents and reveals how the Polish National Democrats dominated the peace negotiations with Russia at Riga.)

Deresiewicz, Janusz, *et al. Studia i Materialy do Dziejów Wielkopolski i Pomorza,* 2 vols. Poznań, 1955-1956. (Valuable for the Polish national struggle against German rule in Posen and West Prussia.)

Dmowski, Roman. *Pisma,* 9 vols. Czestachowa, 1938-1939. (Vital for the thought of the most influential of all Polish political philosophers: see also *Myśli nowoczesnego Polaka,* Lwów, 2nd ed., 1904; *Polityka Polska i Odbudowanie Państwa,* Warsaw, 1925; *La Question Polonaise,* Paris, 1909; *Świat powojenny i Polska,* Warsaw, 1931; *Upadek Myśli Konserwatywney w Polsce,* Warsaw, 1914.)

Dombrowski, Roman. *Mussolini: Twilight and Fall.* London, 1956. (Contains useful information on Ciano.)

Drzewieniecki, W.M. *The German-Polish Frontier.* Chicago, 1959. (Desperate effort to convert the American public to the Oder-Neisse line; tendentious and biased.)

Dziewanowski, M.K. "Piłsudski's Federal Policy, 1919-1921," in *Journal of Central European Affairs,* July-Oct. 1950. (Valuable on Polish aspirations in Eastern Europe after World War II.)

Feldman, J. *Bismarck a Polska.* Kraków, 1947. (Important revisionist work on Bismarck's attitude toward the Poles.)

Feldman, W. *Stronnictwa i programy polityczne w Galicji, 1846-1906,* 2 vols. Kraków, 1947. (Important revisionist work on Bismarck's attitude toward the Poles.)

Frankel, Henryk. *Poland: The Struggle for Power.* London, 1946. (Especially useful for economic conditions in Poland between the Wars.)

Gasiorowski, Zygmunt. "The German-Polish Non-Aggression Pact of 1934," in *Journal of Central European Affairs,* April, 1955. (Excellent study of the implications of the German-Polish *rapprochement* of 1934; for further important contributions see: "Did Piłsudski Attempt to Initiate a Preventive War in 1933?" in *Journal of Modern History,* June 1955; "The Russian Overture to Germany of December 1924," *Ibid.,* June 1958; "A Note on Louis L. Gerson's 'Woodrow Wilson and the Rebirth of Poland,'" in *Polish Review,* 2/4, 1957.)

Gdańsk: Gateway of Poland. Polish Tourist Society, Warsaw, 1949. (Pro-Communist survey, with much information, of the Danzig situation from the Middle Ages to 1945.)

Giertych, Jedrzej. *Polityka Polksa w dziejach Europy.* London, 1947. Vital in stressing Poland's role as a bulwark against Russia.)

Gorecki, R. *Poland and her Economic Development.* London, 1935. (Presents the case for the industrialization of Poland.)

Górka, Olgierd. *Narod a Państwa.* Warsaw, 1937. (Useful survey of Polish political traditions.)

Górka, Olgierd. *Optymizm i Pesymizm w Histojografij Polskiej: Odwrocenie Pojec.* Lwów, 1936. (Stresses the transformation of Poland's historical position from major to minor European Power.)

Górka, Olgierd. *Outline of Polish History, Past and Present.* London, 2nd ed., 1945. (Excellent for Polish foreign relations.)

Grabski, Stanisław. *The Polish-Soviet Frontier.* London, 1943. (Presents the Polish case for the 1921 Riga line.)

Grodecki, S., *et al. Dzieje Polski Sredniowieczeny,* 2 vols, Kraków, 1926. (Excellent detailed survey of modern Polish history.)

Grosz, Wiktor. *U Zrodel Wrzesnia 1939.* Warsaw, 1949. (Bitter attack on Józef Beck and his policies.)

Halecki, O. *Borderlands of Western Civilization: A History of East Central Europe.* New York, 1952. (Especially useful for the case against Soviet control of White Russia and the entire Ukraine.)

Halecki, O. *Eugenio Pacelli: Pope of Peace.* New York, 1951. (Important on papal diplomacy prior to World War II.)

Halecki, O. *History of Poland.* New York, 1943. (Especially useful on Polish independence aspirations after 1815.)

Halecki, O. *The Limits and Divisions of European History.* New York, 1950. (Presents the case for an anti-German, anti-Russian, and pro-Western Central Eastern Europe.)

Halecki, O. *et al. Poland.* New York, 1957. (Vital for economic and political conditions in Poland between the Wars.)

Hutten-Czapski, Bogdan. *Sechzig Jahre Politik und Gesellschaft,* 2 vols. Berlin, 1936. (Vital source for the ideas of pro-German Polish nationalism.)

Ipohorski-Lenkiewicz, W. *Minister z Pałacu Bruehla.* Buenos Aires, 1943. (Excellent for Beck's personal opinions.)

Jaworski, W.L. *Listy z Sejmu r. 1910.* Kraków, 1911. (Useful on Polish-Ukrainian rivalry in Galicia prior to World War I.)

Kasprzak, S. *Stosunek Czech do Polski, 1914-1921.* Warsaw, 1936. (Vital on the conflict of interests which culminated in the Czech seizure of Teschen.)

Kasprzycki, Tadeusz. *Third Europe.* Warsaw, 1939. (Presents the case for a Polish dominated Central Europe.)

Katelbach, T. "Co poprzedziło polskie ultimatum do Litwy," in *Kultura,* no. 4. Paris, 1956. (Vital for the Polish-Lithuanian crisis of March 1938.)

Kirkien, L. *Miedzy Wisła a ujściem Dunaju: Problem baltyckoczarnomorski.* Warsaw, 1932. (Presents the case for an anti-German, anti-Soviet Central Eastern European federation.)

Knoll, R. *Uwagi o polskiej polityce 1939.* Warsaw, 1939. (Defense of Polish foreign policy toward Germany and Russia.)

Komarnicki, Titus. *Rebirth of the Polish Republic: A Study in the Diplomatic History of Europe, 1914-1920.* London, 1957. (Indispensable for the Polish question in World War II.)

Konopczynski, Władisław. *Dzieje Polski Nowozytney,* vol. 1. Warsaw, 1936. (Brilliant survey of Poland at her peak as a major European power.)

Konopczynski, Władisław. *Fryderyk Wielki a Polska.* Poznań, 1947. (Useful on 18th. century Prussian policy in Poland.)

Konopczynski, Władisław. *Konfederacja Barska.* Warsaw, 1936. (Vital for the Russian infiltration of Poland in the 18th. century.)

Korusiewicz, Leon. *Polish-German Relations, 1934-1939.* PhD thesis, University of California at Berkely, 1955. (Defense of all major aspects of Polish policy prior to World War II.)

Kot, Stanisław. *Listy z Rosji do Gen. Sikorskiego.* London, 1956. (Contains important introductory analysis of Russo-Polish relations.)

Kowalski, J., *et al. The War in Poland.* New York, 1942. (Useful on Polish military planning.)

Kukiel, M. *Czartoryski and European Unity.* Princeton, New Jersey, 1955.

Kukiel, M. "Wskrzeszenie Wojska Polskiego," in *Bellona,* 1-4, London, 1959.

Kulak, Zbiegniew. "Spotkanie Ribbentrop-Bonnet, 6 Grudnia 1938 roku," in *Przeglad Zachodni,* May/June 1957. (Supports the thesis of a free German hand in Eastern Europe after Munich.)

Kuronski, E. *Polozenie Prawne ludnosci polskiej w Trzeciej Rzeszy.* Kattowice, 1938. (Presentation of grievances on the treatment of the Polish minority in Germany.)

Kutrzeba, Stanislaw. *Historja Ustroju Polski w Zarysie,* 4 vols., Lwów, 1920. (Especially useful for the earlier phases of Polish history.)

Kutrzeba, Tadeusz. *Wyprawa Kijowska 1920 roku.* Warsaw, 1937. (Vital for Polish-Ukrainian relations and the 1920 Russo-Polish war.)

Kwasieborski, W. *Nad Odra i nad Dniepren: przeszlosc i przyszlosc polskiej myśli imperialnej.* Warsaw, 1939. (Critical analysis of Polish imperialist apirations after World War I.)

Landau, Rom. *Piłsudski and Poland.* New York, 1929. (Sympathetic account of the rise of Piłsudski's dictatorship.)

Lepecki, Michał. *Madagaskar.* Warsaw, 1938. (Plea for the creation of a special haven for Polish Jews by Piłsudksi's former military adjutant.)

Limanowski, Bolesław. *Historia Demokracii Polskiej,* 2 vols., Warsaw, 3rd ed., 1946. (Classic account of the revolutionary tradition in Poland.)

Lipski, Józef. "Nowe przyczynki dotyczace wybuchu wojny polsko-niemieckiej w 1939 r.," in *Bellona,* no. 1, London, 1950. (Vital for German-Polish relations prior to World War II.)

Lipski, Józef. "Prczyczynki do polsko-niemieckiej deklaracji o nieagresji," in *Bellona,* London, Jan./Feb. 1951. (Vital for German assurances which produced the German-Polish *rapprochement* of 1934.)

Lipski, Józef. "Stosunki Polsko-Niemieckji w swietle Aktów Norymberskich," in *Sprawy Miedzynardowe,*nos. 2, 3/4, London, 1947. (Vital for German efforts to arrive at an understanding with

Poland in 1938 and 1939.)

Lowczowski, Gustaw. "Polska Doktryna Wojenna, 1919-1939," in *Bellona*, 1960/1. (Important for Polish military theory.)

Lubowski, K.H. *Der Auswärtige Dienst der Republik Polen.* Göttingen, 1933. (Useful analysis of the Polish foreign service organization.)

Łukasiewicz, Juliusz. *Polska jest Mocarstwem.* Warsaw, 1939. (Demands that Poland be recognized as one of the Great Powers.)

Łukasiewicz, Juliusz. *Rokowania i Wazniejsze Rozmowy za Czas od Marca do Wrzesnia, 1939.* London (unpublished). (Indispensable for Polish policy in 1939; see also "Rokowania i Rozmowy;" "Po Zajeciu Pragi;" "Przed Gwarancjami Anglii;" "Rozbudowa Gwarancji;" "Rokowania o pozycke francuska;" in *Dziennik Polski i Dziennik Zolnierza*,Dec. 6, 1946, Feb. 20,22,26 and April 8, 1947.)

Maciejewski, K. *Jak Możemy Podnieść Potege Państwa Naszego?.* Warsaw, 1939. (Appeal for patriotic sacrifices to increase the power of the Polish state.)

Mackiewicz, Stanisław. *Colonel Beck and his Policy.* London, 1944. (Criticism of the inconsistencies of Polish policy.)

Mackiewicz, Stanisław. *Historja Polski, 1918-1939.* London, 1941. (Vital for Polish political thought between the two World Wars.)

Mackiewicz, Stanisław. *Klucz do Piłsudskiego.* London, 1943. (Brilliant brief analysis of Piłsudski's national program.)

Mackiewicz, Stanisław. *Sosnkowski.* London, 1944. (Reveals the unpopularity after 1935 of Piłsudski's principal military collaborator.

Makowski, J. *Prawno-Państwowe Polozenie Wolnego Miasta Gdanska.* Warsaw, 1923. (Vital for Polish rights at Danzig after 1918.)

Matuszewski, Ignacy. *Granice Zachodnie.* New York, 1943. (Explains Polish aspirations for the annexation of German territory.)

Matuszewski, Ignacy. *Próby Syntez.* Warsaw, 1937. (Indispensable for the political program of the Polish leaders after 1935.)

Mettler, C. *Józef Piłsudksi.* Fribourg, 1938. (Sympathetic study of Piłsudski's career.)

Michalowski, Roman, et al. *Niemcy i Polska: Dyskusja z powodu Ksiazki "D.u.P.".* Lwów., 1934. (Contains replies by Polish scholars to recent German interpretations of German-Polish relations; see also *Poland and Europe: A German Appraisal,* Warsaw, 1934.)

Muhlstein, Anatole. *Le Maréchal Piłsudski,* vol. 1: *1867-1919.* Paris, 1939. (Excellent for the early career of Piłsudski.)

Neugebauer, Norwid. *The Defense of Poland.* London, 1942. (Vital for the fatally deficient Polish military strategy of 1939.)

Osmańczyk, Edmund Jan. *Dowody Prowokacji: Nieznane Archiwum Himmlera.* Kraków, 1951. (Pro-Communist charges of German provocations in 1939 and American atrocities in Korea in 1950.)

Paderewski, I.J. *The Paderewski Memoirs.* London, 1939. Vital for the Polish position at the Versailles conference in 1919.)

Piatkowski, H. "Bitwa nad Wkra w Ramach Operacji Warszawskiej 1920 R.," in *Bellona*, 1960/3. (Interesting detailed account of the 1920 battle for Warsaw.)

Plutynski, Antoni. *The German Paradox: A Study of German Political and Economic Life, with Special Consideration of the Problem of East Prussia.* London, 1933. (Presents the case for Polish territorial aspirations in Eastern Germany.)

Plutynski, Antoni. *We Are 115 Millions.* London, 1944. (Plea for a Polish dominated anti-Soviet bloc in Eastern Europe.)

Pobog-Malinowski, W. *Józef Piłsudski,* 2 vols. Warsaw, 1935. (Contains much useful documentation.)

Pobog-Malinowski, W. *Najnowsza Historia Polityczna Polski, 1864-1945,* 3 vols. Paris, 1953, 1956; London, 1960. (The leading narrative account by a Piłsudski disciple; unfortunately, the section on the origins of World War II is very brief.)

Potocki, Alfred. *Master of Lancut.* London, 1959. (Excellent reference on the Polish aristocracy between the wars.)

Poznanski, Czeslaw. *The Rights of Nations.* London, 1942. (Presents the Polish case against Germany.)

Raczynski, Count Edward. *The British-Polish Alliance: Its Origin and Meaning.* London, 1948. (Vital for Anglo-Polish relations; contains a confirmatory introduction from Lord Halifax.)

Rose, Adam C. *La Politique Polonaise entre les deux Guerres.* Neuchâtel, 1945. (Excellent for Polish foreign policy.)

Rozek, Edward J. *Allied Wartime Diplomacy: A Pattern in Poland.* London, 1958. (Questions the Polish policy of accepting British support against Germany.)

Rutkowski, J. *Historia Gospodarcza Polski,* 2 vols. Poznań, 1950. (Pro-Russian treatment of Polish history.)

Scherer, Emanuel. *Polska i Zydzi.* New York, 1942. (Indispensable for the Jewish question and Jewish organizations in Poland.)

Sienkiewiecz, Henryk. *The Deluge: an historical novel of Poland, Sweden, and Russia,* 2 vols. New York, 1891. (Classic romanticist view of the decline of Poland as a modern Great Power.)

Sieroszewski, Wacław. *Marszalek Józef Piłsudski.* Warsaw, 1934. (Useful for Piłsudski's thoughts on diplomacy and military matters.)

Sławoj-Składkowski, F. *Strzepy Meldunków.* Warsaw, 4th. ed., 1938. (Intimate reflections on contacts with Piłsudski and with cabinet colleagues by the last Polish premier prior to World War II.)

Smorgorzewski, C. *Poland, Germany, and the Corridor.* London, 1930. (Stiff review opposing German revisionist aspirations in the Danzig area.)

Smorgorzewski, Casimir. *La Pologne Restaurée.* Paris, 1927. (Vital for the role of Dmowski at the Paris Peace Conference in 1919.)

Smolenski, Jerzy. *Morze i Pomorze.* Warsaw, 1933. (Interesting cultural and geographical description of West Prussia.)

Sobieski, Wacław. *Der Kampf um die Ostsee.* Leipzig, 1933. (Defense of Polish aspirations for a major maritime role.)

Sokolnicki, Michał. "Dzien 25 Sierpnia 1939." in *Wiadamosci* Feb. 23., 1947. (Emphasizes the effect of the Anglo-Polish alliance on Hitler's military planning.)

Sokolnicki, M. "Sprawa Polska na Terenie Miedzynarodowym, 1914-1918," in *Niepodleglosc,* vol. 1, Warsaw, 1930. (Important for the Polish question in international relations during World War I.)

Strasburger, Henryk. *Sprawa Gdanska.* Warsaw, 1937. (Presents the case for additional special Polish rights at Danzig.)

Stryzowski, Bronisław. *Zarys Dziejow Narodu i Państwa Polskiego w Latach 1914-1939.* London, 1947. (Excellent brief survey of Polish history prior to World War II.)

Strzetelski, Stanisław. *Where the Storm Broke.* New York, 1942. (Interesting account revealing the impact of war propaganda in Poland after March 1939.)

Studnicki, Władysław. *System Polityczyny Europy a Polska.* Warsaw, 1935. (Brilliant presentation of the case for a German-Polish understanding; German edition, *Polen im Politischen System Europas,* Berlin, 1936; other vitally important books by the same author include *Kwestja Czechoslowacji a racja stanu Polski,* Warsaw 1938; *Irrwege in Polen,* Göttingen, 1951; *Die Polnische Ostmarkenfrage: Denkschrift für deutsche Staatsmänner,* Warsaw, 1917; *Die Umgestaltung Mittel-Europas durch den gegenwärtigen Krieg,* Berlin, 1915; *Finlandja i Sprawa finlandzka,* Kraków, 1909; *Sprawa Polska,* Poznań, 1910; *Rosja w Azji wschodniej,* Lwów, 1904; *Wspolczesna Syberja,* Kraków, 1897.)

Sworakowski, Witold. *Stosunki Polsko-Czeskie.* Warsaw, 1936. (Presents the Polish case on Teschen.)

Teslar, J.A. *Edward Smigły-Rydz, Marszalek Polski, Życiorys.* Warsaw, 1937. (Sympathetic account; especially useful for political changes in 1935 and 1936.)

Teslar, Tadeusz. *Propaganda Bolszewicka podczas Wojny polsko-rosyjskiej 1920 roku.* Warsaw, 1938. (Vital for the Russian attempt to create a Communist Poland in 1920.)

Umiastowski, Roman. *Russia and the Polish Republic, 1918-1941.* London, 1942. (Explains Polish fears of Russian expansion prior to World War II.)

Wasilewski, Leon. *Józef Piłsudski.* Warsaw, 1935. (Valuable study based on personal contacts and expert military knowledge.)

Wasiutńyski, W. *Miedzy III Rzesza i III Rusia.* Warsaw, 1939. (Emphasizes the threat to Poland from the Soviet Union during any German-Polish conflict.)

Wawrzkowicza, Eugeniusz. *Anglia a Sprawa Polska, 1813-1815.* Krakow, 1919. (Excellent on English obstruction of Polish aspirations at the Vienna Congress.)

Wegierski, Dominik. *September, 1939.* London, 1940. (Moving account of the outbreak of war in Poland; critical of the Polish Jews.)

Wellisz, Leopold. *Foreign Capital in Poland.* London, 1938. (Competent analysis by a leading financial expert of the extensive foreign ownership in Poland.)

Wereszycki, H. *Historia Polski, 1864-1918,* 2 vols., Warsaw, 1948. (The principal Polish Marxist account of the period following the unsuccessful rising against Tsarist Russia in 1863.)

Wielhorski, W. *Polska a Litwa: Stosunki wzajemne w biegu dziejów.* London, 1947. (Vital for the Polish-Lithuanian conflict after World War I.)

Wierczynski, L., Modzelewski, J., et al. *Pologne, 1919-1939,* vol. 1. Neuchâtel, 1945. (Contains important insights on Piłsudski.)

Wonschowa, Maria. *Oda do Gdańska.* Warsaw, 1925. (Literary expression of Polish aspirations at Danzig after World War I.)

Wrzos, Konrad. *Pułkownik Józef Beck.* Warsaw, 1939. (Emphasizes Beck's collaboration with Piłsudski.)

Zawadski, F., Klimpel, Z. *Z Problemow wspolczesnej polityki zagranicznei.* Warsaw, 1939. (Survey of Polish minority groups abroad.)

VI. Memoirs and Principal Secondary Sources: Other

Abrahamsen, Samuel. *Sweden's Foreign Policy.* Washington, D.C., 1957. (Useful for Swedish abandonment of collective security after 1936.)

Adamov, E.A. *Evropeyskiye Dershal e Grezia v Epokhu Mirovoi Voyni.* Moscow, 1922. (Useful on Anglo-French intervention and rivalry in Greece.)

Adamov, E.A. *Razdyel Aziattskoi Turzii.* Moscow, 1924. (Describes conflicting imperial interests in the Near East.)

Albrecht-Carrie, Rene. *Italy from Napoleon to Mussolini.* New York, 1950. (Contains some interesting insights on Italian foreign policy.)

Albrecht-Carrie, Rene. *A Diplomatic History of Europe Since the Congress of Vienna.* New York, 1958. (Especially useful for survey of British policy.)

Alekseyev, A.M. *Voennye Financi Kapitalisticheskik Gosudarstvi.* Moscow, 1949. (Vital for deficit financing of Western armament campaigns.)

Alfieri, Dino. *Dictators Face to Face.* New York, 1955. (Reveal's Mussolini's admiration for Hitler.)

Allen, H.C. *Great Britain and the United States, 1783-1952.* New York, 1952. (Presents the case for Anglo-American collaboration in world affairs.)

Ansel, Walter. *Hitler Confronts England.* Durham, N.C., 1960. (Excellent for Hitler's many efforts to arrive at an understanding with England after he became Chamcellor of Germany.)

Armstrong, H.F. *Chronology of Failure: The Last Days of the French Republic.* New York, 1940. (Condemns French reluctance to go to war with Germany in 1939.)

Auersperg, Pavel, et al. *O Československé Zahraničnì Politica, 1918-1939.* Prague, 1956. (Excellent source for the increasing anxiety of the Czech leaders from the assassination of Barthou in 1934 to the Munich conference in 1938.)

Bailey, T.A. *The Man in the Street: The Impact of American Public Opinion on Foreign Policy.* New York, 1948. (Useful in measuring the limited effect of the alarmist campaign against Germany prior to World War II.)

Bailey, T.A. *Woodrow Wilson and the Great Betrayal.* New York, 1945. (Analyzes Wilson's failure to adhere to the 14 points and the rejection of his leadership.)

Bailey, T.A. *Woodrow Wilson and the Lost Peace.* New York, 1944. (Explains the defeat of the League and Versailles Treaty in the United States.)

Barnes, H.E. *The Genesis of the World War.* New York, 2nd ed., 1927. (Brilliant and thorough analysis of World War I origins; especially crucial for World War I policies of Great Britain and the United States, and for the British impact on French and Russian policies.

Barnes, H.E., *et al*: *Perpetual War for Perpetual Peace: A Critical Examination of the Foreign Policy of Franklin Delano Roosevelt and its aftermath.* Caldwell, Idaho, 1953. (Indispensable for American policy in relation to World War II.)

Barnes, H.E. *The Struggle Against the Historical Blackout.* 9th ed. ca. 1954. (Important for historiography concerning World War II.)

Barnett, Clifford. *Poland, its People, its Society, its Culture.* New Haven, 1958. (Excellent on changes produced in Poland by World War II.)

Basseches, N. *Stalin.* London, 1952. (Useful on Stalin's hostility toward the Western countries.)

Beard, Charles. *The Devil Theory of War: An Inquiry into the Nature of History and the Possibility of Keeping Out of War.* New York, 1936. (Stimulating analysis of the insidious war propaganda ar gument; for Roosevelt's skill in deceiving the American people about his aims prior to 1940, see Beard's *American Foreign Policy in the Making, 1932-1940.* New Haven, 1946.)

Beck, Earl R. *Verdict on Schacht: A Study in the Problem of Political "Guilt".* Tallahassee, 1955. (Vital for German armament production prior to World War II.)

Beloff, Max. *The Foreign Policy of Soviet Russia, 1929-1941,* 2 vols. New York, 1949. (Useful survey of Russian policy based largely on newspaper sources.)

Beneš, Edvard. *Der Aufstand der Nationen: der Weltkrieg und die tschechoslowakische Revolution.* Berlin, 1928. (Vital for the understanding of Czech aspirations at Paris in 1919.)

Beneš, Edvard. *Memoirs of Dr. Edvard Beneš: From Munich to New War and New Victory.* London, 1953. (Vital for the changing attitude of the former Czech president toward his successor, Dr. Hacha.)

Benson, O. *Through the Diplomatic Looking-Glass.* Norman, Okla., 1939. (Stimulating early attempt to depict the final diplomatic crisis prior to World War II.)

Bess, Demaree. "Why Stalin Wants War in Europe," in *Saturday Evening Post,* Oct. 14, 1939. (Brilliant contemporary analysis of Soviet policy.)

Bewley, Charles. *Hermann Göring.* Göttingen, 1956. (Valuable study of Göring's life and ideas by the former Irish minister to Berlin.)

Bonsal, S. *Suitors and Suppliants: The Little Nations at Versailles.* New York, 1946. (Stimulating analysis of the 1919 treaties from the perspective of the smaller nations.)

Bourret, M.L. *The German-Polish Frontier of 1919.* Stanford, Calif., 1945. (Basic for the Versailles settlement between Germany and Poland.)

Browder, Earl. *The Second Imperialist War.* New York, 1940. (Contains Communist criticisms of the policies of the Western countries prior to World War II.)

Buell, Raymond Leslie. *Poland: Key to Europe.* New York, 1939. (Useful survey on Poland; criticizes the Polish leaders for failing to accept the German negotiation offer in August 1939.)

Burckhardt, Carl J. *Meine Danziger Mission, 1937-1939.* Munich, 1960. (Interesting memoirs of the former League High Commissioner at Danzig; as Goering said of the Dahlerus memoirs at Nurember g: "The emphasis would have been quite different had Germany not lost the war.")

Burns, James MacGregor. *Roosevelt: The Lion and the Fox.* New York, 1956. (Especially useful on Rooseveltian foreign policy.)

Cameron, Elizabeth. *Prologue to Appeasement.* Washington, D.C., 1942. (Vital for the evolution of French foreign policy from the first Daladier Government through the Rhineland crisis of 1936.)

Capek, Karel. *President Masaryk Tells His Story.* London, 1934. (Useful on Czech policies during the first fifteen years of independence.)

Carofiglio, Mario Fusti. *Vita di Mussolini e Storia del Fascismo.* Turin, 1953. (Emphasizes Mussolini's concern at the drift toward war in 1939.)

Čelovsky, Boris. *Das Münchener Abkommen 1938.* Stuttgart, 1958. (Indispensable detailed analysis of the 1938 Sudeten crisis by a leading Czech historian.)

Čelovsky, Boris. "Piłsudskis Präventivkrieg gegen das NS Deutschland: Entstehung, Verbreitung und Widerlegung einer Legende," in *Die Welt als Geschichte,* 14. Jahrgang. (Attempt to question the preventive war plans of 1933 prior to the confirmation by Vansittart in 1958.)

Cerruti, Elisabetta. *Visti da Vicino: Memorie di un'ambasciatrice.* Milan, 1951. (Fascinating personal impressions of Hitler and Mussolini by the Hungarian wife of an Italian diplomat.)

Christopher, James W. *Conflict in the Far East.* Leiden, 1950. (Indispensable for the role of the Soviet Union in fomenting trouble in the Far East after 1929.)

Coit, Margaret L. *Mr. Baruch.* Boston, 1957. (Useful on the collaboration between Baruch and Churchill.)

Cumming, H.H. *Franco-British Rivalry in the Post-War Near East.* London, 1938. (Explains how the British leaders attempted to eliminate France as a colonial Power in the Near East.)

Czebe, Jeno, and **Petho, Tibor.** *La Hongrie dans la deuxième Guerre Mondiale.* Budapest, 1946. (Emphasizes the pro-Polish attitude of Hungary and Hungary's independent policy toward Germany.)

Dahlerus, Birger. *Sista Forsoeket.* Stockholm, 1945. (Vital for German efforts to arrive at an understanding with Britain in August and September 1939.)

Davignon, Vicomte Jacques. *Berlin, 1936-1940: Souvenirs d'une Mission.* Paris, 1951. (The former Belgian foreign minister and Minister [later Ambassador] to Germany criticizes British policy and explains important aspects of German policy.)

Deborin, G.A. *Vtoraya Mirovaya Voyna.* Moscow, 1958. (Concise history of World War II with a section on the Communist view of the 1939 crisis.)

Degrelle, Leon. *Ich War Gefangener.* Nuremberg, 1944. (Excellent on first-hand impressions of the Rexist leader in 1938 and 1939.)

Dell, Robert. *The Geneva Racket, 1920-1939.* New York, 1939. (Criticizes the League of Nations brand of collective security.)

Deutscher, I. *Stalin: A Political Biography.* London, 1949. (Useful on Stalin's control over Soviet foreign policy.)

Donosti, Mario. *Mussolini e l'Europa: la Politica Estera Fascista.* Rome, 1945. (Critical of Mussolini but emphasizes the peaceful program of Italy's foreign policy in 1939.)

Draskovich, Slobodan. *Tito: Moscow's Trojan Horse.* Chicago, 1957. (Contains useful information on the Communist revolutionary program in Eastern Europe prior to World War II.)

Drummond, Donald. *The Passing of American Neutrality, 1937-1941.* Ann Arbor, 1955. (Defends Roosevelt's efforts to overcome the American neutrality policy prior to World War II.)

Dulles, John Foster. *War, Peace, and Change.* New York, 1939. (Criticizes collective security and the attempts to preserve the *status quo* in Eastern Europe.)

Dumke, Glen, Cave, Floyd, *et al.* *The Origins and Consequences of World War II.* New York, 1948. (Emphasizes American responsibility for the 1919 peace settlement in Europe and the subsequent drift toward war.)

Earle, E.M., *et al.* *Modern France: Problems of the Third and Fourth Republics.* Princeton, 1951. (Contains useful sections on French foreign policy.)

Esch, P. van de. *Prelude to War.* Hague, 1951. (Vital analysis of the Spanish Civil War and the pro-Franco policy of Great Britain.)

Estrada, José. *Cuando Inglaterra quedó sola.* Madrid, 1940. (Critical analysis of British intervention in Eastern Europe and the second crusade against Germany.)

Eyck, Erich. *Pitt versus Fox, Father and Son, 1735-1806.* London, 1948. (Vital for the evolution of modern British policy, *vide* ch. 8.)

Falsificators of History. Soviet Foreign Office, Moscow, 1948. (Contains official Soviet criticism of British policy in 1939 to accompany the separate publication of confiscated German documents.)

Freund, Gerald. *Unholy Alliance: Russian-German Relations from the Treaty of Brest-Litovsk to the Treaty of Berlin.* New York, 1957. (Useful for the Stresemann policy of seeking the collaboration of the Soviet Union against Poland.)

Friedman, Phillip. *Their Brothers' Keepers.* New York, 1957. (Survey of the widespread sympathy for the Jews among the non-Jewish populations of Europe in the period of World War II.)

Furnia, Arthur H. *The Diplomacy of Appeasement: Anglo-French Relations and the Prelude to World War II, 1931-1938.* Washington, D.C., 1960. (Important for the role of Bonnet in French foreign policy.)

Gafencu, Grigorie. *Derniers Jours de l'Europe.* Paris, 1946. (Indispensable for German and Polish policies after the Polish partial mobilization of March 1939.)

Gafencu, Grigorie. *Les Préliminaires de la Guerre à l'Est.* Geneva, 1944. (Vital for the pro-Soviet attitude of German Ambassador von Schulenburg at Moscow.)

Gerard, James W. *My Four Years in Germany.* New York, 1917. (Vital for German-American discussions on peace terms during World War II.)

Glaser, Kurt. *Czecho-Slovakia: A Critical History.* Caldwell, Idaho, 1961. (Excellent exposure of the Czechoslovak myth.)

Gogol, Nikolai. *Taras Bulba: A Tale of the Cossacks.* New York, 1886. (Classic Russian literary version of the beginning of Poland's decline as a major European Power.)

Guariglia, Raffaele. *Ricordi, 1922-1946.* Naples, 1949. (Indispensable for Franco-Italian relations immediately prior to World War II.)

Gulick, C.A. *Austria from Habsburg to Hitler,* 2 vols. Berkely, California, 1948. (Indispensable source on the unpopularity of the Dollfuss and Schuschnigg dictatorships in Austria.)

Hájek, J.S. *Signal auf Krieg.* Berlin, 1960. (Czech edition, Mnichov, Prague, 1958; the principal Czech Marxist account of the events leading to Munich.)

Hale, Richard Walden. *Democratic France: The Third Republic from Sedan to Vichy.* New York, 1941. (Defense of Blum's Popular Front and foreign policy.)

Helmreich, E.C. *The Diplomacy of the Balkan Wars.* Cambridge, Massachusetts, 1938. (Classic study of Russian intervention in the Balkans prior to World War I; for secret diplomacy of the period, see also "Ein Nachtrag zu den serbisch-bulgarischen Abkommen von 1912," in *Berliner Monatshefte,* Dec., 1935.)

Hitchcock, B.B. *I Built a Temple for Peace.* London, 1940. (Sympathetic biography of President Benes, emphasizing his reliance on the League of Nations to protect Czech interests.)

Hodža, Milan. *Die neue Situation Europas und die Tschechoslowakei.* Prague, 1938. (Defense of Czech diplomacy and minority policies.)

Hoejer, Torvald. "Die Genesis der schwedischen Neutralität: die Aussenpolitik Schwedens im 19. Jahrhundert," in *Historische Zeitschrift,* August 1958. (Emphasizes the difficulties encountered by Sweden in breaking from her traditional policy of alliances; eloquent testimony to the value of a genuine policy of neutrality.)

Hofer, Walther. *Die Entfesselung das zweiten Weltkrieges: eine Studie über die Internationalen Beziehungen im Sommer 1939.* Stuttgart, 1954. (Superficial attempt to blame Germany and the Soviet Union for the outbreak of World War II. 2nd ed., Frankfurt, a.M., 1960, contains additional documentary records.)

Hooker, James R. "Lord Curzon and the 'Curzon Line'" in *Journal of Modern History,* June 1958. (Disposes of the legend that the British Government proposed a Russo-Polish frontier in 1920.)

Horthy, Nicholas. *Memoirs.* New York, 1957. (Indispensable for the Hungarian peace policy prior to World War II.)

Humphrey, Grace. *Piłsudski, Builder of Poland.* New York, 1936.) Sympathetic study based on extensive use of documentary sources.)

Ilnytskyj, Roman. *Deutschland und die Ukraine, 1934-1945,* vol. 1, parts 1 & 2. Munich, 1955-1956. (Contains useful information on the struggle between the Poles and Ukrainians in the Western Ukraine prior to World War II; deplores the absence of a German Ukrainian policy.)

Ivanov, L.N. *Munkenskaya Politika Zapadnik Dershov e Rol SSSR. Kak destvityelnovo Faktora Mira, 1937-1940.* Moscow, 1947. (Brief analysis condemning the Munich policy of the Western Powers.)

Jarman, T.L. *The Rise and Fall of Nazi Germany.* New York, 1955. (Contains useful information on German internal conditions and foreign policy.)

Jones, Francis Clifford. *Japan's New Order in East Asia: Its Rise and Fall, 1937-1945.* London, 1954. (Useful for Japanese relations with Britain, Germany, and Russia in the 1939 period.)

Jong, Louis de. *De Duitse Vijfde Colonne in de Tweede Wereldoorlog.* Amsterdam, 1953. (Especially useful for Poland and the absence of underground activities by the German minority.)

Keeling, Ralph. *Gruesome Harvest: The Costly Attempt to Exterminate the People of Germany.*

Chicago, 1947. (Stimulating criticism of British and American intervention policies in Europe.)

Kelly, D.M. *22 Cells in Nuremberg.* New York, 1947. (Especially useful for information on the character and opinions of Goering.)

Kerner, R.J. *Bohemia in the 18th. Century.* New York, 1932. (Classic study of a placid period of Austrian rule in the Czech ethnic area.)

Kirschbaum, J.M. *Slovakia: Nation at the Crossroads of Central Europe.* New York, 1960. (Indispensable for the truth about the Slovak crisis of 1939.)

Klein, Burton. *Germany's Economic Preparations for War.* Cambridge, Massachusetts, 1959. (The definitive study of German military policy.)

Klein, Burton. "Germany's Preparation for War: A Reexamination," in *American Economic Review,* March 1948. (Pioneer study exposing the fallacious assumption of an all-out German armament effort prior to World War II.)

Koehl, R.L. *RKFDV: German Resettlement and Population Policy, 1939-1945.* Cambridge, Massachusetts, 1958.(Contains useful information on Polish persecution of the German minority prior to World War II.)

Knorr, Klaus. *The War Potential of Nations.* Princeton, 1956. (Contains information on the moderate dimensions of German armament preparation prior to World War II.)

Krieger, L. *The German Idea of Freedom.* Boston, 1957. (Explains the National Socialist concept of emphasizing the importance of the people and minimizing the importance of the state.)

Krofta, Kamil. *A Short History of Czechoslovakia.* London, 1935. (Defense of Little Entente and Pro-Soviet Czech policies.)

Kybal, Vlastimil. *Les Origines diplomatiques de l'État tchécoslovaque.* Prague, 1929. (Emphasizes the importance of Czech propaganda efforts in France and the United States.)

Langer, W.L., and **Gleason, S.** *The Challenge to Isolation, 1937-1940.* New York, 1952. (Contains much useful information on European diplomacy and American policy; defends Roosevelt's program to destroy Germany.)

Langer, W.L. *European Alliances and Alignments.* New York. 2nd ed., 1950. (Vital for British policy after the unification of Germany; reveals British unwillingness to protect Belgium from invasion in 1887.)

Leeds, Stanton B. *These Rule France: The Story of Édouard Daladier and the men around Daladier.* New York, 1940. (Extensive and interesting background information on leading French politicians.)

Lengyel, Émil. *The Cauldron Boils.* New York, 1932. (Useful for chronic tension between Germany and Poland in the Danzig area.)

Leonhardt, H.L. *Nazi Conquest of Danzig.* Chicago, 1942. (Contains useful information on Danzig National Socialism prior to World War II.)

Lettrich, Jozef. *History of Modern Slovakia.* New York, 1955. (Pro-Czech account of Slovakian nationalism.)

Lewis, F. *Case History of Hope.* New York, 1958. (Optimistic analysis of current conditions in Poland; defense of the Polish decision to challenge Germany in 1939.)

Litvinov, Maxim. *Notes for a Journal.* New York, 1955. (Reflection of Soviet views on foreign policy prior to World War II; probably a forgery.)

Lundstedt, A.V. *Superstition or Rationality in Action for Peace?.* London, 1925. (Denunciation of the League of Nations system by a leading Swedish expert on international law.)

Machray, Robert. *East Prussia: Menace to Poland and Peace.* Chicago, 1944. (Summary of Polish arguments since World War I for the annexation of German East Prussia.)

Magistrati, Massimo. *L'Italia a Berlino, 1937-1939.* Milan, 1956. (Excellent for inside attitudes at the Italian Embassy in Berlin.)

Malozemoff, Andrew. *Russian Far Eastern Policy, 1881-1904.* Berkely, 1958. (Contains useful information on the launching of the 20th. Century British alliance policy and the use of Japan as an instrument against Russia in Asia.)

Mamatey, Victor S. *The United States and East Central Europe, 1914-1918: A Study in Wilsonian Diplomacy and Propaganda.* Princeton, 1957. (Indispensable for Czech aspirations and American policy in Europe.)

Manly, Chesly. *The Twenty Year Revolution: From Roosevelt to Eisenhower.* Chicago, 1954. (Useful for Rooseveltian tactics in promoting American intervention in Europe.)

Martin, Laurence. *Peace Without Victory: Woodrow Wilson and the British Liberals.* New Haven, 1958. (Especially useful for the adoption and the betrayal of the 14 points.)

Masaryk, T.G. *Die Weltrevolution: Erinnerungen und Betrachtungen, 1914-1918.* Berlin, 1925. (Indispensable source for the ideas of the Czech revolutionary leaders.)

Mason, J.B. *The Danzig Dilemma.* Stanford, California, 1946. (Useful study of Danzig-Polish disputes prior to World War II.)

Matveyev, V.A. *Proval Munkenskoi Politiki, 1938-1939.* Moscow, 1955. (Major Communist study of British and French policy in Central Europe immediately prior to World War II.)

Mayer, Milton. *They Thought They Were Free: The Germans, 1935-1945.* (Primary emphasis on the anti-Jewish demonstrations of November 1938.)

Micaud, C.A. *The French Right and Nazi Germany, 1933-1939.* Durham, North Carolina, 1943. (Emphasizes the shift of the French conservatives from hostility to conciliation toward Germany.)

Mikhailov, P.M. *SZA i Anglia poslye Vtoroi Mirovoi Voynia.* Moscow, 1956. (Critical analysis of Anglo-American collaboration during World War II; condemns British policy toward the Soviet Union in 1939.)

Millis, Walter, ed. *The Forrestal Diaries.* New York, 1951. (Contains useful information on American Ambassador Kennedy and Prime Minister Chamberlain.)

Nani, Umberto. *T.G. Masaryk e l'unità Cecoslovacca.* Milan, 1931. (Sympathetic account of Czech problems in the world economic depression.)

Neilson, Francis. *The Churchill Legend.* Appleton, Wisconsin, 1954. (Brilliant study of Churchill's opportunistic search for power and glory.)

Neilson, Francis. *The Makers of War.* Appleton, Wisconsin, 1950. (Contains valuable insights into the European diplomatic problems of 1938 and 1939.)

Neilson, Francis. *The Tragedy of Europe,* 5 vols. Appleton, Wisconsin, 1940-1946. (A day-by-day commentary on the course of the war, containing valuable political insights and predictions.)

Nekrich, A.M. *Politika Angliskovo Imperialisma v Evropa, Okt. 1938-Sept. 1939.* Moscow, 1955. (The most extensively documented and useful Soviet monograph on British European policy Munich.)

Perla, Leo. *What is 'National Honor'?.* New York, 1918. (Contains valuable insights on the employment of the national honor concept; especially useful in analyzing the Beck speech of May 5, 1939.)

Peterson, Norman E. *Hjalmar Schacht: For and against Hitler.* Boston, 1954. (Especially useful on German armament production prior to World War II.)

Petresco-Comnene, Nicolae. *Preludi del Grande Dramma.* Rome, 1947. (Important first-hand account by Gafencu's predecessor at the Rumanian Foreign Office.)

Pirow, Oswald. "War der zweite Weltkrieg unvermeidbar?," in *Nation Europa,* No. 4, 1952. (Account by the former South African minister for war of a futile mediation mission to England and Germany in the autumn of 1938; special stress on British hostility toward Germany.)

Potemkin, Vladimir, et al. *Histoire de la Diplomatie,* vol. 3: 1919-1939. Paris, 1948. (Detailed analysis often based on timely documentation.)

Pozdeeva, L.V. *Anglia i Remilitarizatsia Germanii, 1933-1936.* Moscow, 1956. (Contains scathing denunciations of the Anglo-German naval pact of 1935 and British acceptance of Hitler's military reoccupation of the Rhineland in 1936.)

Prchala, Lev. *Vers L'Union.* Paris, 1947. (Pro-Polish Czech general's account favoring a federation of Central-Eastern Europe; contains useful information on Polish-Czech relations after Munich.)

Presseisen, Ernst C. *Germany and Japan: A Study in Totalitarian Diplomacy.* Hague, 1958. (Especially useful for the failure of German-Japanese alliance negotiations during the 1938-1939 period.)

Ramos Oliveira, Antonio. *Historia social y politica de Alemania, 1800-1950.* Mexico City, 1952. (Useful and sympathetic survey of German problems and achievements.)

Randall, James G. *Lincoln the President: Springfield to Gettysburg,* 2 vols. New York, 1945. (Contains information useful for a comparison between Lincoln's concern about the Negroes and Hitler's attitude toward the Jews.)

Rashed, Z.E. *The Peace of Paris, 1763.* Liverpool, 1951. (Useful for evolution of modern British policy, *vide* ch. 8.)

Reshetar, John. *The Ukrainian Revolution, 1917-1920.* Princeton, 1952. (Vital background for the problem of minorities in Poland and the Soviet Union.)

Rich, Norman, ed. *Holstein Papers: Memoirs, Diaries, and Correspondence of Friedrich von Holstein, 1837-1909,* 2 vols. Cambridge, England, 1955. (Contains useful information on German attempts to cope with British hostility prior to World War II.)

Riess, Curt. *Joseph Goebbels: A Biography.* London, 1949. (Especially useful for early ideas and conversion to National Socialism.)

Ripka, Hubert. *Munich: Before And After.* London, 1939. (Indispensable for Czech policy after the loss of Sudetenland.)

Roberts, H.L., *et al. The Diplomats, 1919-1939.* Princeton, 1953. (Contains numerous useful studies of principal European diplomats; the Western crusade against Germany is defended, and W.C. Bullitt is accused of being insufficiently anti-German [!].)

Robinson, C.F. *Foreign Logistical Organizations and Methods.* Washington, D.C., 1947. (Contains useful information on the German armament program prior to World War II.)

Rossi, A. *Deux Ans d'Alliance Germano-Soviétique.* Paris, 1949. (Emphasizes the Italian role in promoting a *rapprochement* between Russia and Germany.)

Rossi, Vittorio. *Soviet.* Milan, 1951. (Contains useful information on Stalin's attitudes toward European affairs.)

Roucek, J.S., *et al. Central-Eastern Europe: Crucible of World Wars.* New York, 1946. (Valuable survey of the policies of Poland and her neighbors prior to World War II.)

Rudin, Harry. *Armistice 1918.* New Haven, 1944. (Emphasizes the unreliability of Wilson's armistice assurances to the Germans in the Autumn of 1918.)

Salvatorelli, Luigi, and **Mira, Giovanni.** *Storia del Fascismo: l'Italia dal 1919 al 1945.* Rome, 1952. (Contains useful information on Italian foreign policy in 1939.)

Salvemini, G. *Prelude to World War II.* New York, 1954. (Lengthy analysis denouncing Italian policy after 1934 as a major cause for the outbreak of World War II.)

Sanborn, Frederic R. *Design for War: A Study of Secret Power Politics, 1937-1941.* New York, 1951. (Vital for the provocations of Roosevelt in Europe prior to World War II and the evolution of the official but secret American interventionist policy.)

Schmitt, B.E., ed. *Poland.* Los Angeles, 1945. (Contains useful essays by American and Polish scholars on political and economic problems.)

Schuman, Frederick L. *Europe on the Eve: The Crises of Diplomacy, 1933-1939.* (Stimulating criticism of Fascism, National Socialism, and British policy in Europe.)

Schwarz, Paul. *This Man Ribbentrop: His Life and Times.* New York, 1943. (Contains useful essays by American and Polish scholars on political and economic problems.)

Seabury, Paul. *The Wilhelmstrasse: A Study of German Diplomats Under the Nazi Regime.* Berkeley, California, 1954. (Contains useful background information on Ribbentrop, Weizsäcker, and Neurath.)

Shafer, Boyd C. *Nationalism: Myth and Reality.* New York, 1955. (Provocative anti-nationalist approach to modern European history; condemns European nationalisms without criticizing American nationalism.)

Sharp, S.L. *Poland: White Eagle on a Red Flag.* Cambridge, Massachusetts, 1953. (Weak on Polish foreign policy, but extremely useful on domestic affairs.)

Sherwood, R.E. *Roosevelt and Hopkins: An Intimate History.* New York, 1948. (Vital source for Roosevelt's plans to involve the United States in foreign wars.)

Shirer, William L. *The Rise and Fall of the Third Reich: A History of Nazi Germany.* New York, 1960. (This so-called definitive history actually consists of a maze of errors, obsolete information, and distortions.)

Sloutzki, N.M. *The World Armaments Race, 1919-1939.* Geneva, 1941. (Contains useful information, but unreliable on Germany and Russia.)

The Slovak Question. Slovak National Council, Geneva, 1940. (Documented criticism of the 1919 treaties and Czech policy in Slovakia.)

Snyder, Louis. *German Nationalism: The Tragedy of a People.* Harrisburg, Pennsylvania, 1952. (Contains useful information on the life and ideas of Alfred Rosenberg.)

Souvarine, Boris. *Stalin: A Critical Survey of Bolshevism.* New York, 1936. (Vital for Stalin's methods of rule.)

Stenzel, David B. *Nazi Diplomacy from Munich to War.* Ph.D. Thesis, University of California, Berkely, 1957. (Especially useful for Hitler's Czech policy after Munich and German Relations with Japan.)

Stipp, John L. *Devil's Diary: The Record of Nazi Conspiracy and Aggression.* Yellow Springs, Ohio, 1955. (Contains commentaries on German policy and a convenient arrangement of documentary materials.)

Stone, Julius. *Aggression and World Order: A Critique of United Nations Theories of Aggression.* Los Angeles, 1958. (Contains valuable analysis of the limitations of the 1928 Kellogg-Briand Pact.)

Summers, H.B. *Anglo-American Agreement.* New York, 1938. (Plea for Anglo-Saxon political collaboration in the wake of economic cooperation.)

Suñer, Ramon Serrano. *Entre Hendaya y Gibralter.* Madrid, 1947. (Excellent on the foreign policy of Nationalist Spain.)

Sweezy, Maxime. *The Structure of the Nazi Economy.* Cambridge, Massachusetts, 1941. (Contains some useful information on German economic policy.)

Tamaro, Attilio. *La Condanna dell'Italia nel Trattato di Pace.* Bologna, 1952. (Contains useful comparisons between the Trieste and Danzig problems.)

Tanner, Vaeinoe. *The Winter War: Finland Against Russia, 1939-1940.* Stanford, 1957. (Traces Russian demands for Finnish territory after 1938.)

Tansill, C.C. *Back Door to War: The Roosevelt Foreign Policy.* Chicago, 1952. (Brilliant analysis of Roosevelt's policies in Europe and Asia, with extensive European background materials.)

Taylor, Telford. *Sword and Swastika: Generals and Nazis in the Third Reich.* New York, 1952. (Extensively documented analysis; contains much useful information.)

Tenenbaum, Joseph. *Race and Reich.* New York, 1956. (Contains useful information on German and Polish attempts to promote Jewish emigration.)

Thomson, S.H. *Czechoslovakia in European History.* Princeton, 1953. (Extensively documented pro-Czech survey; valuable for Czech policy prior to Munich.)

Tommasini, Francesco. *La Risurrezione della Polonia.* Milan, 1925. (Vital for Polish diplomacy at the Paris Peace Conference.)

Toscano, M. *L'Italia e gli Accordi Tedesco-Sovietica dell Agosto 1939.* Florence, 1952. (Mussolini's attempt to exploit the German-Soviet agreement in the interest of a peaceful European settlement.)

Toscano, M. *Le Origini del Patto d'Acciaio.* Florence, 1948. (Indispensable for Italian reservations at the time of the alliance with Germany.)

Treadgold, Donald W. *Twentieth Century Russia.* Chicago, 1959. (Ch. 21 is especially useful for Soviet diplomacy in the 1936-1939 period.)

Tucker, Robert W. *The Just War: A Study of Contemporary American Doctrine.* Baltimore, 1960. (Excellent source on American illusions in world affairs.)

Varfolomeyeva, P. *Reakzionnaya Vnezhnaya Politika Franzuskik Pravik Sozialistov, 1936-1939 Godov.* Moscow, 1949. (Criticism of the failure of the French Popular Front.)

Viereck, G.S. *The Strangest Friendship in History.* London, 1933. (Basic for the role of E.M. House in Wilson's abandonment of the 14 points at Versailles.)

Villari, Luigi. *Italian Foreign Policy Under Mussolini.* New York, 1956. (Indispensable for Italian policy prior to World War II; especially useful for Italian attempts to preserve European peace in 1938 and 1939.)

Villari, Luigi. *The Liberation of Italy, 1943-1947.* Appleton, Wisconsin. 1959. (Contains useful information on Ciano.)

Villari, Pasquale. *The Life and Times of Niccolo Machiavelli,* 2 vols. London, 1898. (Contains useful information on Italian theory concerning the balance of power, *vide* ch. 8.)

Wambaugh, Sarah. *Plebiscites Since the World War,* 2 vols. Washington, D.C., 1933. (Vital for European plebiscites after World War I.)

Wandycz, Piotr S. *France and Her Eastern Allies, 1919-1925.* Minneapolis, 1962. (Excellent for the background of the Czech-Polish disputes of the 1930's.)

Wathen, M.A. *The Policy of England and France Toward the Anschluss.* Washington, D.C., 1954. (Especially useful for the British effort to improve relations with Italy as a means of frustrating German policy on Austria.)

Werth, Alexander. *France and Munich: Before and After the Surrender.* New York, 1939. (Contains some useful information; violently hostile toward a Franco-German *rapprochement.)*

Werth, Alexander. *Which Way France?* New York, 1937. (Defense of the Blum leadership in France.)

Wilson, E. *Fleury and French Foreign Policy, 1726-1743.* Cambridge, Massachusetts. 1936. (Useful for British balance of power policy, *vide* ch. 8.)

Windrich, Elaine. *British Labour's Foreign Policy.* Stanford, 1952. (Especially useful for the pro-Soviet orientation of the British Labour Party.)

Wolfers, Arnold. *Britain and France Between Two Wars.* New York, 1940. (Excellent pioneer study of British checks on French policy after World War I.)

Wormser, René. *The Myth of the Good and Bad Nations.* Chicago, 1954. (Excellent exposure of Rooseveltian pro-Soviet propaganda before World War II.)

Yakhontoff, V.A. *U.S.S.R. Foreign Policy.* New York, 1954. (Useful survey of Russian policy, based on official Soviet sources.)

Yalman, Ahmed Emin. *Turkey in My Time.* Norman, Oklahoma, 1956. (Illustrates the internal instability of Turkey after the death of Mustafa Kemal.)

Zsigmond, L. "Ungarn und das Münchener Abkommen," in *Acta Historica,* vol. 4, no. 3/4, Budapest, 1959. (Important for Hungarian foreign policy in 1938.)

Zuev, F. *Mezhdunarodny Imperializm-Organizator Napadeniya Panskoi Polshi na Sovietskuyu Rossiyu, 1919-1920 Godov.* Moscow, 1954. (Excellent for policies of foreign states toward Poland during the 1920 war with the USSR.)

Note: References in the text to British, French, German, Polish, Russian, and American newspapers and periodicals are cited in the footnotes.

Index

I

Ickes, Harold, 278
Illustrowany Kurjer (Poland), 478
  Soviet agreement, 275
  Polish oppression in Silesia, 390
  German bluff, 408
  Polish military incursions, 419
  Roosevelt message to Soviets, 440
Imredy, Bela, 110
  resignation rumors, 374
India
  Halifax arrives, 97
  German trade decline, 555
Inskip, Thomas, 189
Ireland, 524
Ironside, Edmund
  visit to Warsaw, July 1939, 396
  Polish army maneuvers, 397
  September 1 mediation, 577
Isolationism, in U.S.
  Americans hostile to war, 241
  neutrality legislation, 338
  Soviet pact strengthens, 495
Isvolski, Alexander, 17
Italy, 42
  Chamberlain policy, 95
  Austria and Hungary influence, 150
  prestige loss post-Anschluss, 151
  15th c. balance-of-power politics, 184
  Laval in France, 211
  French rapprochement with Germany, 224
  British hopes for dependence, 255
  Hitler speech, April 1939, 280
  Ciano visits Warsaw, 286
  Baudouin mission, Feb. 1939, 296
  Hitler fears extremism, 322
  Hitler and Tirol, 1920s, 329
  anti-Germanization measures, Tirol 330
  Albanian protectorate talks, 348
  Polish relations, 379
  Halifax seeks support, 397
  worry about Polish-German tension 409
  hope for German-Soviet pact, 430
  Ciano-Hitler talks, 455
  Ciano promises solidarity, 457
  Henderson's peace hopes, 473
  French military conference, August 23, 476
  Attolico misleads, 491
  determined to avoid war, 493
  Mussolini qualifies alliance, 505
  Hitler-Ribbentrop conference, August 25, 510
  Hitler seeks support again, 516
  some French propose attacking, 517
  neutrality disclosure to British, 526

  German opinion of, 528
  reduction in German imports, 555
  German trade, 1939, 556
  mediation effort, August 31, 564
  France proposes compromise settlement, 572
  Ciano fears British offensive, 584
  mediation effort, 585
  Chamberlain distorts peace scheme 592
  abandons mediation effort, 593
  content in 1939, 601
Ivanov, Grigorie, 540
Izvestia, 529

J

Jablonka Pass, 515
Janson, Martin von, 576
Japan, 533
  Roosevelt's public notes, April 1939 360
  Soviet victories, 424
  Anti-Comintern pact, 433
  Ciano-Hitler talks, August 1939, 455
  Beck anger at Rumania, 235
  Slovaks to Warsaw, 245
  Halifax contacts re Tilea, 303
  no Polish-Soviet alliance, 312
  750,000 Poles under arms, 336
  Halifax announces guarantee, 338
  Moltke distressed, 356
  Danzig inquiries, 366
  Beck on Ribbentrop's Danzig plan 370
  guarantee stiffens Poles, 375
  reacts to Beck speech, 386
  Danzig militia, 409
  Danzig ultimatum, August 1939, 413
  Polish-Russian collaboration, 437
  doubts Halifax Soviet policy, 439
  Beck's rejection of Soviet pact, 444
  Burckhardt meeting, August 1939 453
  Beck complacent about German pact, 468
  reprimand from Halifax, 501
  fears new Hitler Poland proposal 503
  ignores German mistreatment in Poland, 503
  German-Polish negotiations unlikely, 527
  Polish intransigence, 530
  Poles mobilize, 537
  Beck: no negotiations, 538
  Beck wants Danzig renounced, 539
  Poles think unbalanced, 543
  negotiation instructions vague, 552
  reports on Ribbentrop-Lipski

Z